CC5K6 Strategies for crisis prevention and intervention.
CC5K7 Strategies for preparing individuals to live harmoniously and productively in a cult...
CC5K8 Ways to create learning environments that allow individuals to retain and appreciate their ...
language and cultural heritage.
CC5K9 Ways specific cultures are negatively stereotyped.
CC5K10 Strategies used by diverse populations to cope with a legacy of former and continuing racism

**Skills:**
CC5S1 Create a safe, equitable, positive, and supportive learning environment in which diversities are valued.
CC5S2 Identify realistic expectations for personal and social behavior in various settings.
CC5S3 Identify supports needed for integration into various program placements.
CC5S4 Design learning environments that encourage active participation in individual and group activities.
CC5S5 Modify the learning environment to manage behaviors.
CC5S6 Use performance data and information from all stakeholders to make or suggest modifications in learning environments.
CC5S7 Establish and maintain rapport with individuals with and without exceptional learning needs.
CC5S8 Teach self-advocacy.
CC5S9 Create an environment that encourages self-advocacy and increased independence.
CC5S10 Use effective and varied behavior management strategies.
CC5S11 Use the least intensive behavior management strategy consistent with the needs of the individual with exceptional learning needs.
CC5S12 Design and manage daily routines.
CC5S13 Organize, develop, and sustain learning environments that support positive intracultural and intercultural experiences.
CC5S14 Mediate controversial intercultural issues among students within the learning environment in ways that enhance any culture, group, or person.
CC5S15 Structure, direct, and support the activities of paraeducators, volunteers, and tutors.
CC5S16 Use universal precautions.

Special Education Content Standard #6: Communication
**Knowledge:**
CC6K1 Effects of cultural and linguistic differences on growth and development.
CC6K2 Characteristics of one's own culture and use of language and the ways in which these can differ from other cultures and uses of languages.
CC6K3 Ways of behaving and communicating among cultures that can lead to misinterpretation and misunderstanding.
CC6K4 Augmentative and assistive communication strategies.
**Skills:**
CC6S1 Use strategies to support and enhance communication skills of individuals with exceptional learning needs.
CC6S2 Use communication strategies and resources to facilitate understanding of subject matter for students whose primary language is not the dominant language.

Special Education Content Standard #7: Instructional Planning
**Knowledge:**
CC7K1 Theories and research that form the basis of curriculum development and instructional practice.
CC7K2 Scope and sequences of general and special curricula.
CC7K3 National, state or provincial, and local curricula standards.
CC7K4 Technology for planning and managing the teaching and learning environment.
CC7K5 Roles and responsibilities of the paraeducator related to instruction, intervention, and direct service.
**Skills:**
CC7S1 Identify and prioritize areas of the general curriculum and accommodations for individuals with exceptional learning needs.
CC7S2 Develop and implement comprehensive, longitudinal individualized programs in collaboration with team members.
CC7S3 Involve the individual and family in setting instructional goals and monitoring progress.
CC7S4 Use functional assessments to develop intervention plans.
CC7S5 Use task analysis.
CC7S6 Sequence, implement, and evaluate individualized learning objectives.
CC7S7 Integrate affective, social, and life skills with academic curricula.
CC7S8 Develop and select instructional content, resources, and strategies that respond to cultural, linguistic, and gender differences.
CC7S9 Incorporate and implement instructional and assistive technology into the educational program.
CC7S10 Prepare lesson plans.
CC7S11 Prepare and organize materials to implement daily lesson plans.
CC7S12 Use instructional time effectively.
CC7S13 Make responsive adjustments to instruction based on continual observations.
CC7S14 Prepare individuals to exhibit self-enhancing behavior in response to societal attitudes and actions.

Special Education Content Standard #8: Assessment
**Knowledge:**
CC8K1 Basic terminology used in assessment.
CC8K2 Legal provisions and ethical principles regarding assessment of individuals.
CC8K3 Screening, pre-referral, referral, and classification procedures.
CC8K4 Use and limitations of assessment instruments.
CC8K5 National, state or provincial, and local accommodations and modifications.

**Skills:**

CC8S1   Gather relevant background information.
CC8S2   Administer nonbiased formal and informal assessments.
CC8S3   Use technology to conduct assessments.
CC8S4   Develop or modify individualized assessment strategies.
CC8S5   Interpret information from formal and informal assessments.
CC8S6   Use assessment information in making eligibility, program, and placement decisions for individuals with exceptional learning needs, including those from culturally and/or linguistically diverse backgrounds.
CC8S7   Report assessment results to all stakeholders using effective communication skills.
CC8S8   Evaluate instruction and monitor progress of individuals with exceptional learning needs.
CC8S9   Create and maintain records.

Special Education Content Standard #9: Professional and Ethical Practice

**Knowledge:**

CC9K1   Personal cultural biases and differences that affect one's teaching.
CC9K2   Importance of the teacher serving as a model for individuals with exceptional learning needs.
CC9K3   Continuum of lifelong professional development.
CC9K4   Methods to remain current regarding research-validated practice.

**Skills:**

CC9S1   Practice within the CEC Code of Ethics and other standards of the profession.
CC9S2   Uphold high standards of competence and integrity and exercise sound judgment in the practice of the professional.
CC9S3   Act ethically in advocating for appropriate services.
CC9S4   Conduct professional activities in compliance with applicable laws and policies.
CC9S5   Demonstrate commitment to developing the highest education and quality-of-life potential of individuals with exceptional learning needs.
CC9S6   Demonstrate sensitivity for the culture, language, religion, gender, disability, socio-economic status, and sexual orientation of individuals.
CC9S7   Practice within one's skill limit and obtain assistance as needed.
CC9S8   Use verbal, nonverbal, and written language effectively.
CC9S9   Conduct self-evaluation of instruction.
CC9S10   Access information on exceptionalities.
CC9S11   Reflect on one's practice to improve instruction and guide professional growth.
CC9S12   Engage in professional activities that benefit individuals with exceptional learning needs, their families, and one's colleagues.

Special Education Content Standard #10: Collaboration

**Knowledge:**

CC10K1   Models and strategies of consultation and collaboration.
CC10K2   Roles of individuals with exceptional learning needs, families, and school and community personnel in planning of an individualized program.
CC10K3   Concerns of families of individuals with exceptional learning needs and strategies to help address these concerns.
CC10K4   Culturally responsive factors that promote effective communication and collaboration with individuals with exceptional learning needs, families, school personnel, and community members.

**Skills:**

CC10S1   Maintain confidential communication about individuals with exceptional learning needs.
CC10S2   Collaborate with families and others in assessment of individuals with exceptional learning needs.
CC10S3   Foster respectful and beneficial relationships between families and professionals.
CC10S4   Assist individuals with exceptional learning needs and their families in becoming active participants in the educational team.
CC10S5   Plan and conduct collaborative conferences with individuals with exceptional learning needs and their families.
CC10S6   Collaborate with school personnel and community members in integrating individuals with exceptional learning needs into various settings.
CC10S7   Use group problem-solving skills to develop, implement, and evaluate collaborative activities.
CC10S8   Model techniques and coach others in the use of instructional methods and accommodations.
CC10S9   Communicate with school personnel about the characteristics and needs of individuals with exceptional learning needs.
CC10S10   Communicate effectively with families of individuals with exceptional learning needs from diverse backgrounds.
CC10S11   Observe, evaluate, and provide feedback to paraeducators.

*continues on back inside cover*

EIGHTH EDITION

# Exceptional Children

## An Introduction to Special Education

### William L. Heward
*The Ohio State University*

PEARSON

Merrill
Prentice Hall

Upper Saddle River, New Jersey
Columbus, Ohio

Library of Congress Cataloging-in-Publication Data

Heward, William L.
      Exceptional children : an introduction to special education / William L. Heward.—8th ed.
        p. cm.
      Includes bibliographical references and index.
      ISBN 0-13-119170-5
        1. Special education—United States. 2. Exceptional children—United States. I. Title.
  LC3981.H49 2006
  371.9'0973—dc22

                                                                        2004061624

**Vice President and Executive Publisher:** Jeffery W. Johnston
**Editor:** Allyson P. Sharp
**Editorial Assistant:** Kathleen S. Burk
**Development Editor:** Heather Doyle Fraser
**Production Editor:** Mary M. Irvin
**Design Coordinator:** Diane C. Lorenzo
**Text Designer:** Kristina D. Holmes
**Photo Coordinator:** Valerie Schultz
**Cover Designer:** Terry Rohrbach
**Cover Image:** Getty One
**Production Manager:** Pamela D. Bennett
**Director of Marketing:** Ann Castel Davis
**Marketing Manager:** Autumn Purdy
**Marketing Coordinator:** Tyra Poole

This book was set in Berkeley by Carlisle Communications, Ltd. It was printed and bound by Courier Kendallville, Inc. The cover was printed by The Lehigh Press, Inc.

**Photo Credits:** See the page following the index.

Pearson Education Ltd.                    Pearson Education Australia Pty. Limited
Pearson Education Singapore Pte. Ltd.     Pearson Education North Asia Ltd.
Pearson Education Canada, Ltd.            Pearson Educación de Mexico, S.A. de C.V.
Pearson Education—Japan                   Pearson Education Malaysia Pte. Ltd.

10 9 8 7 6 5 4 3 2 1
ISBN: 0-13-119170-5

*For Jill*

# About the Author

**William Lee Heward** grew up in Three Oaks, Michigan, rooting for the Chicago Cubs. He majored in psychology and sociology as an undergraduate at Western Michigan University, earned his doctorate in special education at the University of Massachusetts, and joined the special education faculty at The Ohio State University in 1975. Bill has had several opportunities to teach and lecture abroad, including serving as a Senior Fulbright Lecturer in Special Education in Portugal and Visiting Professor of Psychology at Keio University in Tokyo. In 1985, he received Ohio State University's highest honor for teaching excellence, the Alumni Association's Distinguished Teaching Award.

Bill's current research interests focus on methods classroom teachers can use to increase the frequency with which each student actively responds and participates during group instruction and on methods for helping students with disabilities generalize and maintain newly learned knowledge and skills. His research has appeared in the field's leading peer-reviewed journals, including *Behavioral Disorders, Education and Training in Developmental Disabilities, Exceptional Children, Learning Disabilities Research & Practice, Research in Developmental Disabilities, Teacher Education and Special Education, Teaching Exceptional Children*, and *The Journal of Special Education*.

Bill has coauthored or edited seven other textbooks, and he has written for the popular market. His book *Some Are Called Clowns* (Crowell, 1974) chronicled his five summers as a pitcher for the Indianapolis Clowns, the last of the barnstorming baseball teams.

# Preface

Special education is an ongoing story of people. It is the story of a preschool child with multiple disabilities who benefits from early intervention services. It is the story of a child with mental retardation whose parents and teachers work together to ensure she participates in classroom and extracurricular activities with her peers. It is the story of a middle school student with learning disabilities who helps his parents and teachers plan an instructional program that builds upon his strengths and addresses his weaknesses. It is the story of the gifted and talented child who brings new insights to old problems, the high school student with cerebral palsy who is learning English as his second language, and the young woman with visual impairments who has recently moved into her own apartment and rides a city bus to work. Special education is also the story of the parents and families of exceptional children and of the teachers and other professionals who work with them.

I hope you will find the eighth edition of *Exceptional Children* an informative, accessible, and interesting introduction to the ongoing story of special education. Whether you are an undergraduate in a preservice teacher training program or a general education teacher with years of experience, I encourage you to continue your study and involvement with children and adults with special needs.

## TEXT ORGANIZATION AND STRUCTURE

My primary goals for the eighth edition remain the same as for previous editions: to present an informative and responsible introduction to the professional practices, trends, and research that define contemporary special education while also conveying the diversity and excitement of this changing field. The book begins with "A Personal View of Special Education"—ten perspectives on the purpose and responsibilities of special education—followed by fifteen chapters organized into three parts.

Part 1, Foundations for Understanding Special Education, includes three chapters. Chapter 1 presents an overview of terminology, laws, policies, and practices that are consistent with the Individuals with Disabilities Education Act (IDEA) and the exceptional child's right to receive a free, appropriate education in the least restrictive environment. Information on the IDEA Improvement Act of 2004 is included in this and other chapters. Chapter 2 describes the referral, assessment, program planning, and placement of students with special education needs. Chapter 3 discusses the important role parents and families play in the decision-making process for addressing the individual educational needs of their children and how special educators can form effective partnerships with parents from culturally and linguistically diverse backgrounds.

Part 2, Educational Needs of Exceptional Students, contains ten categorical chapters of exceptionality. Chapters 4 through 13 introduce the definitions, characteristics, prevalence, causes, historical background, assessment techniques, instructional strategies, placement alternatives, and current issues and future trends for specific categories of special education needs, including giftedness and talent.

Part 3, Special Education Across the Life Span, describes the role of special education during two critical developmental periods in the lives of exceptional children. Chapter 14 examines early childhood special education and the important role early intervention plays in nurturing the development of young children with special needs and those who are at risk for acquiring disabilities. Chapter 15 discusses transition from secondary school and the responsibility educators and parents share in preparing students with disabilities for adulthood.

## KEY THEMES AND FEATURES

As I said earlier, the story of special education is an ongoing one that is written every day by teachers across the country serving the needs of all children in a variety of settings. The stories of some of these exceptional teachers are included in these pages. The work of these educators is reflected in the narrative and the features of this text and shows how special educators can engage students in classroom instruction by using effective strategies in a culturally responsive manner.

### Exceptional Teachers Engage Students in Classroom Instruction

*Featured Teacher Essays*   Each chapter begins with a first-person essay by master teachers that reflects the joys, challenges, and realities of teaching exceptional children.

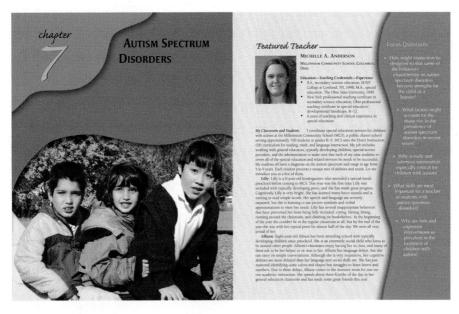

Drawn from urban, suburban, and rural school districts across the country, the 17 featured teachers share personal experiences and wisdom gathered from years of instructing children in a variety of school settings. After reading each essay, you can learn more about the teacher's classroom and students by visiting the Featured Teacher module on the Companion Website (**www. prenhall. com/heward**). Six of these teachers are also featured on the Exceptional Teachers CD-ROM that accompanies this text.

*Exceptional Teachers Multimedia CD-ROM*   This multimedia interactive CD-ROM includes 54 video clips with supporting commentary, artifacts, and discussion questions developed in collaboration with dozens of general education and special education teachers at six schools. The content of the CD-ROM is integrated throughout the text through a

CD-ROM icon at specific points in the chapter narrative, and in some of the Featured Teacher essays and Teaching & Learning boxes. (See "Supplements and Resources for the Student" on p. viii for more in-depth information on the CD-ROM.)

## Exceptional Teachers Use Research-Based Strategies in the Classroom

*Teaching & Learning Boxes*   The foundation of special education, without which everything would fall apart, is good instruction provided by teachers, day in and day out. To inform you of the critical elements of good instruction and provide numerous examples of application, each chapter includes one or more Teaching & Learning feature box(es) that describe a wide range of effective teaching interventions. From classroom management and peer support strategies for inclusion to curriculum modifications and suggestions for creating multimedia activity schedules for children, these boxes provide clear and practical guidelines for designing, implementing, and evaluating instruction for students with disabilities. All of the strategies described in the Teaching & Learning features are classroom-tested and supported by research documenting their effectiveness. Furthermore, each Teaching & Learning feature includes a step-by-step "How to Get Started" section for implementing the strategy in the classroom.

*Tips for Beginning Teachers*   Each chapter culminates with practical, quick tips for beginning teachers on how to avoid common pitfalls in the classroom. These suggestions, offered by the master teacher(s) featured in the chapter, range from tips for successful co-teaching and collaboration with families, to finding a mentor, learning about students' cultures, becoming student advocates, and celebrating each student's accomplishments, no matter how small.

## Exceptional Teachers Are Culturally Responsive

*Diversity & Exceptionality Boxes*   Diversity and multicultural issues and perspectives are inherent throughout this book. However, in certain chapters, there is more information that deserves to be highlighted. This feature describes strategies teachers can use in the classroom for working with students from culturally and linguistically diverse backgrounds.

*Profiles & Perspectives Boxes*   Each chapter contains one or more Profiles & Perspectives essay(s) that highlight the personal struggles, triumphs, and stories of students with exceptionalities or those involved in special education. For example, in "Mental Retardation: Is It Time to

Abandon the Myth?" (Chapter 4), J. David Smith argues that the term *mental retardation* is inappropriate, misleading, and should be abandoned. In "The Autism Wars" (Chapter 7), Catherine Maurice, author of the powerful best-seller *Let Me Hear Your Voice*, describes the enormous difficulties faced by parents of children with autism in choosing scientifically tested interventions from the many myths, fads, and miracle cures that surround autism.

# OTHER KEY FEATURES OF THE EIGHTH EDITION

## Focus Questions

Each chapter begins with five questions that provide a framework for studying the chapter and its implications. These Focus Questions serve as discussion starters for introducing, overviewing, concluding, or reviewing chapter content.

## CEC Performance-Based Standards

Although special education teacher certification and licensure requirements vary from state to state, all special educators are expected to demonstrate a common set of competencies. The Council for Exceptional Children's (CEC) Performance-Based Standards for Beginning Special Education Teachers is a comprehensive set of knowledge and skill standards organized within 10 domain areas (e.g., Foundations, Individual Learning Differences, Instructional Strategies, Assessment). The CEC Standards were developed in collaboration with the Interstate New Teacher Assessment and Support Consortium (INTASC) and serve as the basis for curriculum content of teacher preparation programs approved by the National Council for the Accreditation of Teacher Education (NCATE). Individual teachers can use the standards as a guide/template for assessing their own progress as professionals (Crutchfield, 2003).

*Due process safeguards*

**Council for Exceptional Children** Content Standards for Beginning Teachers—Common Core: Issues, assurances, and due process rights related to assessment, eligibility, and placement within a continuum of services (CC1K6).

The Common Core standards are printed on the inside front cover of the text. Margin notes throughout the text link critical content to specific knowledge and skill statements from CEC's Performance-Based Standards for Beginning Teachers. Look for margin notes such as the one shown here with the CEC icon.

## Coverage of PRAXIS II Tests

The PRAXIS II™ tests—the Subject Assessment/Specialty Area Tests of the PRAXIS Series of Professional Assessments for Beginning Teachers™—assess students' knowledge of content standards. Many states require a passing score on one or more PRAXIS II tests for licensure or certification as a special education teacher. A PRAXIS Study Grid in the Appendix shows where content areas of the PRAXIS II Test, Special Education Core Principles, are discussed in the text. A listing of the PRAXIS Special Education Core Principles is on the inside back cover of this text.

# SUPPLEMENTS AND RESOURCES FOR THE STUDENT

## Exceptional Teachers Multimedia CD-ROM

As you use the CD-ROM packaged with this text, you will see some of the master teachers featured in the text in action. These teachers (from six different schools) work in a variety of classroom settings to engage students in learning using the research-based strategies discussed in the text. Any time content is connected to a video clip on the CD-ROM, readers will see a CD-ROM margin note that directs them to the appropriate clip on the CD.

Each of the six schools on the CD has nine video clips, with a total of 54 clips on the CD. Examples of the type of footage you will see include: a kindergarten teacher using choral responding to conduct a classwide morning warm-up activity, collaborative learning activities in an inclusive middle school science classroom, a teacher using puppets to help preschoolers with disabilities learn language and social skills, a parent-teacher conference, and an IEP meeting.

To see an inclusive classroom for children with autism and their typically developing peers, go to "Oakstone Academy" on the *Exceptional Teachers* CD-ROM and click on "Circle Time" and "Puppet Stories."

Each of the video clips on the CD-ROM also includes two audio commentaries by the teachers or the authors of the CD-ROM (Bill Heward and Charles Wood). These commentaries help users to synthesize and connect video footage to chapter content and the current trends in the field.

## Student Study/Media Guide

The Student Study/Media Guide provides you with a useful resource for learning about exceptional children, their families, and the field of special education. Chapter objectives, chapter overviews, chapter-at-a-glance tables, guided reviews, homework assignments, "What Do You Think?" activities covering current and controversial issues, and self-check quizzes allow you to review course content, apply new knowledge and skills, and prepare for tests and exams.

This guide also connects content from the text to the Companion Website and the Exceptional Teachers Multimedia CD-ROM with activities and questions for further reflection.

## Companion Website

A user-friendly Companion Website (**www.prenhall.com/heward**), designed to complement this text, is integrated into the textbook via margin notes. Identified by the Companion Website logo, these notes direct you to online materials that will assist in reviewing chapter content, doing research online, and accessing related materials and professional resources. The Companion Website enhances learning by giving students access to:

 To review the necessary parts of an IEP, go to the "What Components Make Up IEPs?" in Part 1 of "Developing Quality IEPs: A Case-Based Tutorial" in Chapter 2 on the Companion Website, **www.prenhall.com/heward**.

- **Study Aids**—*Essential Concepts, Chapters-at-a-Glance, Guided Reviews, Focus Questions, SAFMEDS for Key*

*Terms,* and interactive *Chapter Quizzes* help you gauge your understanding of chapter content.

- **Bonus Video Clips**—Extended and in-depth looks at classroom teaching practices from the schools featured on the Exceptional Teachers Multimedia CD-ROM.
- **Templates and Resources for Completing Activities/Assignments.**
- **Reflective Questions and Activities**—Each chapter contains reflective questions related to the Teaching & Learning, Profiles & Perspectives, and Diversity & Exceptionality features in the text. The *In-Class Activities* module offers different types of activities for each chapter, including *Group Activities* and *Response Card Activities.*
- **More Information about the Teachers Featured in the Text**—The *Featured Teacher* module provides real artifacts from in-service teachers who teach students with the disabilities covered in the text.
- **Resources Related to Chapter Topics**—*Web Links* in each chapter help students access additional information on chapter topics and areas of study.
- **Specialized Assignments**— The assignments module houses different types of assignments to help you through the topics studied in the text. These assignments include *Position Papers, What Do You Think?,* and *Make It, Use It* activities.
- **An Open Forum for Communication**—You can collaborate and communicate with other students enrolled in classes like yours all across the country using the *Message Board* feature.
- **Developing Quality IEPs: A Case-Based Interactive Tutorial**—walks you through the development of Individualized Education Programs (IEPs) and familiarizes you with criteria for assessing their quality. The tutorial includes six case studies with related exercises and a variety of additional resources, web links, journal articles, and forms for developing and evaluating IEPs. Margin notes in Chapter 2 direct you to relevant information and activities in the IEP tutorial.

## SUPPLEMENTS AND RESOURCES FOR THE INSTRUCTOR

### Video Library

Course instructors receive a complimentary set of four compelling videos that can be used to supplement and extend information and issues introduced in the text. *Exceptional Teachers in Action* includes all 54 video clips from the *Exceptional Teachers Multimedia CD-ROM. Guidelines for Making Decisions About IEP Services,* produced by the Vermont Department of Education, helps IEP team members, including families, make informed decisions about what special education and related services are necessary and appropriate for children with disabilities. *Together We Can!,* produced by the Juniper Gardens Children's Project in Kansas City, describes a classwide peer tutoring program in which every student in a general education classroom participates as both tutor and tutee. *LifeLink* highlights a program that provides opportunities for secondary students with disabilities to learn independent living skills and prepare for life in the adult community.

### Companion Website

Located at **www.prenhall.com/heward,** the user-friendly website that accompanies this text provides online resources for professors as well as students. Professors can access online materials by going to the Instructor's Resources section of the Companion Website. Here you will find supplemental lectures corresponding to PRAXIS and CEC standards and competencies; suggested discussion questions, class activities, and homework assignments; answers to activities printed in the Student Study Media Guide; and additional resources for effective instruction. Instructors also have access to the Syllabus Manager™ tool which allows them to create and customize syllabi online. See Instructor Resource Center section below for information on downloading PowerPoint slides and online versions of the Instructor's Manual and Test Bank.

## Instructor's Manual

An expanded and improved Instructor's Manual includes numerous recommendations for presenting and extending text content. The manual consists of chapter objectives and overviews of essential concepts; connections to CEC and PRAXIS standards; class discussion and essay/position paper topics; in-class activities such as cooperative group activities, SAFMEDS, response card activities, and ideas for debates; guest speakers; application exercises; and homework assignments. Additional video and Internet resources are also provided for each chapter.

## Overhead Transparencies/PowerPoint Slides

The transparencies—available in PowerPoint slide format on the Instructor Resource Center at **www.prenhall.com**—highlight key concepts, summarize content, and illustrate figures and charts from the text. Acetate transparencies are available for use with the text for qualified adopters (contact your local sales representative for more information).

## Test Bank and TestGen Software

A completely revised test bank of more than 750 questions also accompanies the text. These multiple-choice, short answer, and essay questions can be used to assess students' recognition, recall, and synthesis of factual content and conceptual issues from each chapter. The computerized version of the test bank (TestGen) is available in a Windows and Macintosh format, along with assessment software allowing professors to create and customize exams and track student progress.

## Instructor Resource Center

The Instructor Resource Center opens the door to a variety of print and media resources in downloadable, digital format. As a registered faculty member, you can log in directly to premium online products, download resource files directly to your computer, and receive immediate access and instructions for installing Course Management content to your campus server.

Digital resources available for *Exceptional Children,* 8e include:

- Text-specific PowerPoints
- An online version of the Instrcutor's Manual
- OneKey Course Management options including Blackboard and WebCT
- Access and instructions for downloading a Blackboard cartridge or WebCT e-Pack

To access these items online, go to **www.prenhall.com** and click on the Instructor Support button and then go to the Download Supplements section. Here you will be able to login or complete a one-time registration for a user name and password.

## OneKey Course Management

OneKey is Prentice Hall's exclusive new online resource for students and instructors. OneKey is an integrated online course management resource featuring everything students and instructors need for work in or outside of the classroom, available in the nationally hosted CourseCompass platform, as well as WebCT and Blackboard. For more information about OneKey, please contact your local Merrill representative prior to placing your textbook order.

# Acknowledgments

Many people contributed ideas, insights, and suggestions that greatly enhanced the substance and quality of the eighth edition of *Exceptional Children*. A supremely talented and hard-working team of professionals at Merrill/Prentice Hall provided assistance and support throughout the planning, manuscript development, and production stages of this edition. Acquisitions Editor Allyson Sharp provided much appreciated support and encouragement for the eighth edition and was instrumental in convincing me of the importance of the *Exceptional Teachers* CD-ROM project. Development Editor Heather Doyle Fraser was a source of numerous suggestions and valued constructive criticism while I worked on the manuscript. And I appreciated Heather's gentle but effective way of reminding me when (yet another) chapter was past due and what would happen to me if I did not complete it post-haste. Heather was particularly helpful in organizing the video shoots for the *Exceptional Teachers* CD-ROM that accompanies the text.

Dawn Potter copyedited the manuscript with the same balance of technical skill and respect for an author's writing style as she did with the previous two editions. Thanks to proofreader Rebecca Bobb's careful reeding, there is knot a single typo in the entyre book. I owe a special note of gratitude to Penny Burleson, who obtained permissions to reprint published material. She was a savior. To be most useful as a resource to students, a comprehensive textbook must have a complete and accurate reference list and functional indexes. With scissors, tape, and a great deal of patience, Bret Workman put together the "mother of all reference lists," and Do Mi Stauber created the name and subject indexes. The effective and meaningful portrayal of special education requires excellent photographs, and I appreciated the keen eye and thoughtful work of Photo Editor Valerie Schultz, who accompanied me on photo shoots at local schools and finding several photos for this edition. I think you'll agree that Kristina Holmes's talents as a text and cover designer are apparent in the book's attractive appearance and appealing, accessible layout.

In the end, it was Production Editor Mary Irvin who made sure that all the words, tables, figures, charts, photos, special features boxes, and margin notes got between covers. That the book was published at all, let alone on time and with all of its many parts in the right places, is due to Mary's diligent attention to detail and ability to keep countless elements of the production process, including a sometimes confused author, on schedule.

Director of Marketing Ann Castel Davis, who served as Acquisitions Editor for three previous editions of *Exceptional Children*, Marketing Manager Autumn Purdy, Marketing Coordinator Tyra Poole, and Editorial Assistant Kathy Burk all contributed encouraging words.

No one author can capture the many perspectives and areas of expertise that make up a field as diverse and dynamic as special education. Many special education teachers and researchers have contributed to the currency and quality of this

## Acknowledgments

text. I am grateful to the 17 special and general education teachers who graciously shared their knowledge and personal experience through the Featured Teacher Essays and the Tips for Beginning Teachers in each chapter: Mary Allaire-Gifford, Michelle Anderson, Gail Gantt Bettis, Carolyn Crangle, Jeanna Mora Dowse, Diane Ellis, Steven Everling, Douglas Jackson, Patricia Lambert, Kimberly Lundy, Bethany Maheady, Jean Michielli-Pendl, Carol Richards-Yarnell, Mary Kate Ryan-Griffith, Judith A. Resnik, Ronni H. Spratt, Sandra Trask-Tyler, and Michael Wang. The individual and collective talents, wisdom, and accomplishments of these teachers provide great optimism for the future of special education.

The currency and quality of this text have been enhanced tremendously by original Teaching & Learning and Profiles & Perspectives essays authored exclusively for this text by the following educators: Sheila Alber (University of Southern Mississippi); Patty Barbetta (Florida International University); Anne Bauer (University of Cincinnati) and Mary Ulrich (Miami University); Judy Carta (Juniper Gardens Children's Project, University of Kansas); Jill Dardig, (Ohio Dominican University); Gail Fitzgerald (University of Missouri) and Kevin Koury (California University of Pennsylvania); Marsha Forest and Jack Pearpoint (Centre for Integrated Education and Community, Toronto); Bonnie Grossen (University of Oregon); Barbara Horvath (Monroe County Community School Corporation, Blooming-ton, IN); Jonathan Kimball (Woodfords Family Services, Portland, ME) and Robert Stromer (University of Massachusetts Medical School); Moira Konrad and David Test (University of North Carolina at Charlotte); Nancy Marchand-Martella and Ronald Martella (Eastern Washington University); Mary Salmon (Ohio State University), Stacie McConnell (Oakstone Academy), Diane Sainato (Ohio State University), and Rebecca Morrison (Oakstone Academy); Barbara Schirmer (Detroit Mercy University) and Albert Ingram (Kent State University); Elaine Silliman and Jill Beasman (University of South Florida); J. David Smith (The University of Virginia's College at Wise); Marti Snell (University of Virginia) and Rachel Janney (Radford University); and Jo Webber and Brenda Scheuermann (Southwest Texas State University).

The following professors—all of whom teach the introduction to special education course—reviewed the previous edition and provided comments and suggestions that contributed to this edition: Gerlinde G. Beckers, Southeastern Louisiana University; Susan L. Gibbs, University of North Carolina at Charlotte; Linda H. Parrish, Texas A&M University; Kathleen McCoy, Arizona State University; Donna M. Murphy, Edinboro University of Pennsylvania; and Crystal Ladwig, University of Florida.

The *Exceptional Teachers* CD-ROM was nearly another book in itself. I could not have accomplished it without the contributions, both logistic and substantive, of my doctoral student and co-author Charles Wood. Chuck could not have been a better collaborator. His knowledge of what it means to be an effective special education teacher, his commitment to research-based practices, and his sensitivity to and compassion for people made him the ideal colleague to work with. Chuck was a true co-author and collaborator. He contributed many excellent ideas for video clips and audio commentaries; his insight, diligence, and reliability were invaluable. Video ethnographer Carl Harris, a former professor of education, filmed all of the video clips with great skill and sensitivity. Thanks also to the many teachers, administrators, parents, and students whose time, effort, and ideas made the *Exceptional Teachers* video project a reality. I wish to give a special note of thanks to Larry Meheady (SUNY Fredonia), Rebecca Morrison (Director, Oakstone Academy), Chris Brady (Principal, Como Elementary School), and Jim Cowardin (CEO, Millennium Community School) for their assistance with the video.

I am indebted to Professor Jane Piirto (Ashland University) for co-authoring Chapter 14—Giftedness and Talent. Sheila Alber (University of Southern Mississippi), David Bicard (Hawthorne Country Day School, NY), and Charles Wood (Ohio State) co-authored the Student Study/Media Guide and the Instructor's Manual. The Test Bank was prepared by Theresa Hessler (Ohio State) and Charles Wood. This group of special educators—each of whom has taught the introduction to special education course numerous times—has produced a very strong set of ancillary materials, and I am confident that students and instructors will appreciate and benefit from their hard work and creativity. Special thanks to Chuck for taking the lead in organizing materials for the Companion Website.

Finally, I will always be grateful to Mike Orlansky, a former colleague, friend, and co-author of the first four editions of *Exceptional Children*.

Most of all, I continue to benefit from the support and love of my family—wife Jill, son Lee, and daughter Lynn.

# Contents

# Chapter 9

# Chapter 10

# Chapter 11

# Chapter 12

# Chapter 13

# Part 3

# Chapter 14

## Chapter 15

## Transitioning to Adulthood  592

## *Postscript*

*Note: Every effort has been made to provide accurate and current Internet information in this book. However, the Internet and information posted on it are constantly changing, so it is inevitable that some of the Internet addresses in this textbook will change.*

# Special Features

## • Teaching & Learning

## • *Diversity & Exceptionality*

# • Profiles & Perspectives

# Exceptional Children

# Prologue

# A Personal View of Special Education

My primary goal in writing this book is to describe the history, practices, advances, problems, and challenges that make up the complex and dynamic field called special education in as complete, clear, up to date, and accurate a manner as possible. This, of course, is much easier said than done: an author's personal views are surely implicit in those descriptions—between the lines, as they say. Because my personal beliefs and assumptions about special education—which are by no means unique, but neither are they held by everyone in the field—affect both the substance and the tone of the book, I believe I owe you, the reader, an explicit summary of those views. So, here are 10 assumptions that underlie and guide my efforts to understand, contribute to, and convey the field of special education.

*People with disabilities have a fundamental right to live and participate in the same settings and programs—in school, at home, in the workplace, and in the community— as do people without disabilities.*　That is, the settings and programs in which children and adults with disabilities learn, live, work, and play should, to the greatest extent possible, be the same settings and programs in which people without disabilities participate. People with disabilities and those without have a great deal to contribute to and learn from one another. We cannot do that without regular, meaningful interaction.

*Individuals with disabilities have the right to as much self-determination as we can help them achieve.*　Special educators have no more important teaching task than that of helping children and young adults with disabilities learn how to increase their level of decision making and control over their own lives. Thus, self-determination and self-advocacy skills should be featured curriculum components for all students with disabilities.

*Special education must expand and improve the effectiveness of its early identification and prevention efforts.*　When a disability or a condition that places a child at risk for a disability is detected early, the chance of lessening its impact (or preventing it altogether) is greater. We have made great strides in the early detection of physical disabilities, sensory impairments, and developmental delays in infants and preschoolers; but we have a long way to go in making a commitment to identifying young children who are at risk for less visible disabilities, such as learning disabilities and emotional and behavioral disorders.

*Special education must do a better job of helping students with disabilities transition from school to adult life.*　Although increasing numbers of special education students are leaving high school for college or a job, a place to live on their own, and friends with whom to share recreational and leisure activities in the community, such positive outcomes elude far too many young adults with disabilities. Special education cannot be satisfied with improving students' achievement on classroom-based measures only. We must work equally hard to ensure that the education students receive during their school years prepares them to deal successfully with and enjoy the multifaceted demands and opportunities of adulthood.

*Special education must improve its cultural competence.*   When a student with disabilities has the additional challenge of learning in a new or different culture or language, it is critically important that her teachers provide culturally responsive curriculum and instruction. Teachers who are most effective in helping these children combine fundamentally sound instructional methods with sensitivity to and respect for their students' heritage and values.

*School and family partnerships enhance both the meaningfulness and the effectiveness of special education.*   Professionals have too long ignored the needs of parents and families of exceptional children, often treating them as patients, clients, or even adversaries instead of realizing that they are partners with the same goals. Some special educators have given the impression (and, worse, believed it to be true) that parents are there to serve professionals, when in fact the opposite is more correct. We must recognize parents as a child's first—and, in many ways, best—teachers. Learning to work effectively with parents is one of the most important skills the special educator can acquire.

*The efforts of special educators are most effective when they incorporate the input and services of all of the disciplines in the helping professions.*   It is foolish to argue over territorial rights when we can accomplish more by working together within an interdisciplinary team that includes our colleagues in psychology, medical and health services, counseling, social services, and vocational rehabilitation.

*All students have the right to an effective education.*   As educators, our primary responsibility is to design and implement effective instruction for academic, social, vocational, and personal skills. These skills are the same ones that influence the quality of our own lives: working effectively and efficiently at our jobs, being productive members of our communities, maintaining a comfortable lifestyle in our homes, communicating with our friends and family, and using our leisure time meaningfully and enjoyably. Instruction is ultimately effective when it helps the students we serve acquire and maintain positive lifestyle changes. To put it another way, the proof of the process is in the product. Therefore, …

*Teachers must demand effectiveness from the curriculum materials and instructional tools they use.*   For many years conventional wisdom has fostered the belief that it takes unending patience to teach children with disabilities. I believe this view does a great disservice to students with special needs and to the educators—both special and general education teachers—who teach them. Teachers should not wait patiently for exceptional students to learn, attributing lack of progress to some inherent attribute or faulty process within the child, such as mental retardation, learning disability, attention-deficit disorder, or emotional disturbance. Instead, the teacher should use direct and frequent measures of the student's performance as the primary guide for modifying instruction to improve its effectiveness. This, I believe, is the real work of the special educator. Numerous examples of instructional strategies and tactics demonstrated to be effective through rigorous scientific research are described and illustrated throughout this text. Although you will not know how to teach exceptional children after reading this or any other introductory text, you will gain an appreciation for the importance of explicit, systematic instruction and an understanding of the kinds of teaching skills a competent special educator must have. And finally, I believe that …

*The future for individuals with disabilities holds great promise.*   We have only begun to discover the myriad ways in which to improve teaching, increase learning, prevent and minimize the conditions that cause disabilities, encourage acceptance, and use technology to compensate for disabilities. Although I make no specific predictions for the future, I am certain that we have not come as far as we can in learning how to help exceptional individuals build and enjoy fuller, more independent lives in the school, home, workplace, and community.

# FOUNDATIONS FOR UNDERSTANDING SPECIAL EDUCATION

# THE PURPOSE AND PROMISE OF SPECIAL EDUCATION

# Featured Teacher

## CAROL RICHARDS

SWANTON ELEMENTARY SCHOOL DISTRICT
SWANTON, VERMONT

*Education—Teaching Credentials—Experience*
- B.S., special education, Bloomsburg State University, Pennsylvania, 1975
- M.A., special education, Johnson State College, Vermont, 1985
- Vermont professional level II certification in special education, K–12
- 30 years of teaching experience, 28 years as a special educator

The students I work with have a wide range of mild to severe disabilities and are served under various IDEA categories such as learning disabilities, mental retardation, behavioral disorders, physical and health impairments (including ADHD), and students with multiple disabilities. I team with second- and third-grade general education teachers to develop individualized goals, behavior plans, and accommodations for their students' programs. I provide direct instruction to students, design accommodations to help students be successful in the general education classroom, and help teachers plan how to incorporate students' IEP goals into regular class activities. I also coordinate and conduct comprehensive evaluations to determine special education eligibility. Other important components of my work include data collection to measure students' progress on IEP goals, coordinating support from related services specialists, training paraeducators, and scheduling IEP team meetings.

***Collaboration and Teaming*** Our school uses a collaborative team model to plan and provide special education services by setting up core and extended teams around kids. A core team may be the general education classroom teacher and parents, the special educator and paraeducator, and the speech-language pathologist. The extended team might also include a physical therapist (PT), an occupational therapist (OT), a school psychologist, an administrator, the school nurse, a family worker in the home, or a consultant from the Vermont interdisciplinary team. There are many variations in team makeup, depending on the child's needs. I interact weekly with teachers, parents, paraeducators, the school psychologist and guidance counselors, the Title I teacher, the administrators, and other special educators. We delegate and share tasks to keep everything running smoothly: overall program development at the school level, IEP development, delivery of instruction, and problem solving. The staff members of the Swanton schools believe it takes a community to raise a child, and our collaborative teaming helps us put our beliefs into practice.

***IEP Goals*** All of our IEP goals are written to address Vermont state curriculum standards. We often write short-term instructional objectives using a rubric of increasing levels of performance—*Getting There*, *Good*, and *Great*—as shown in the following rubric.

## Focus Questions

- When is special education needed? How do we know?

- If categorical labels do not tell us what and how to teach, why are they used in special education?

- Why have court cases and federal legislation been required to ensure that children with disabilities receive an appropriate education?

- How can a special educator provide all three kinds of intervention— preventive, remedial, and compensatory— on behalf of an individual child?

- What do you think are the three most important challenges facing special education today? Why? Read your answer again after finishing this book.

*Annual goal.* By 6/10/06, Sam will organize his ideas and communicate them in writing to the "Great" level (see rubric). (Vermont curriculum standards addressed: 1.5—Students draft, revise, edit, and critique written products so that final drafts are appropriate in terms of purpose, organization, details, and voice, or tone. 1.6—Students' independent writing demonstrates command of appropriate English conventions, including grammar, usage, and mechanics.)

| Writing Skill Development Sequence | Objective 1: Getting There (11/06) | Objective 2: Good (2/06) | Objective 3: Great (6/06) |
|---|---|---|---|
| Organizes his ideas and communicates them in writing | Organizes ideas verbally with assistance, then dictates one or more detail sentences that support a provided idea or a paragraph topic | Organizes ideas verbally for two or more detailed sentences or in response to a question with assistance, then dictates his thoughts | Organizes ideas verbally for a complete paragraph within a writing piece or a response to a question with adult assistance, then dictates his thoughts |
| Communicates responses in a way that shows he takes some responsibility for his writing | Shares responsibility for his written responses by writing the controlled spelling patterned words he has practiced/learned (refer to spelling rubric,) with an adult writing the more difficult words for him | Shares responsibility for his written responses by writing the controlled spelling patterned words he has practiced/learned (refer to spelling rubric,) with an adult writing the more difficult words for him | Shares responsibility for his written responses by writing the controlled spelling patterned words he has practiced/learned (refer to spelling rubric) with an adult writing the more difficult words for him |
| Adds detail to his responses | After reviewing his writing (with adult support), adds descriptive words/phrases/clauses to his sentences to provide clarification or more detail | After reviewing his writing (with adult support), adds descriptive words/phrases/clauses to his sentences to provide clarification or more detail | After reviewing his writing (with adult support), adds descriptive words/phrases/clauses to his sentences, and adds at least one more full sentence to provide clarification or more detail |
| Writes a summary sentence that includes a labeled answer for a word problem | Uses a template to finish a sentence that labels his answer to a word problem | With assistance, labels his answer, then writes a sentence that includes his answer and its label and uses words from the question of the problem | Independently writes a sentence for the answer to a word problem that includes his answer and its label and words from the question of the problem |

*Teaching Strategies* I use the following teaching strategies frequently:

- **Think-alouds.** Having students talk as they try to solve a problem or perform a task allows me to evaluate their understanding of skill sequences and where their understanding breaks down or is inconsistent. It also helps students become aware of what they are thinking. The think-aloud strategy helps students generalize skills from one situation and task to the next.
- **Checklists and scripts.** All students in our school are encouraged to use checklists to help them get their materials ready for an activity or to guide them through revising and editing their written work. Most special education students need direct instruction and lots of modeling and practice to learn to use checklists effectively. I use the same checklists that the students do, so my modeling reinforces and teaches their use. When needed, I help develop individualized checklists for special situations, with input from the general education teachers. Some students do better in a step-by-step skill, such as regrouping in subtraction, with a checklist or a script for each problem: e.g., "Is the bottom number bigger? If yes, then…. " In addition, I have created behavioral checklists to remind students to use proper body behavior while attending to learning in class. A small card on the desk or somewhere in the student's

materials can have stick-figure drawings and a few key words to remind a student to keep feet on the floor and hands on his desk, face his body toward the speaker, and look at the speaker. The checklists are gradually withdrawn and replaced with self-talk in which a student begins to internally monitor his behavior. This strategy is paired with feedback from the teacher during and/or after the practice sessions.

- **In-school homework.** After I have observed a student be fairly fluent with a skill in a controlled setting, she and I will discuss a plan about where she will use the skill independently throughout the day. The student then reports back to me on her use of and success with the skill. This process strengthens the student's awareness of what she is thinking and improves her ability to recall information or apply a skill across settings and situations. This takes lots of practice, and it helps when the classroom teacher or paraeducator reminds the student or praises her for appropriately using her new knowledge or skill.

- **Peer tutoring.** Peer tutoring can be very effective for teaching curriculum content such as math facts, science or social studies facts, vocabulary, or sight words. A peer presents five or six flash cards that include three or four known and two unknown items. As the unknown cards are learned, they become known cards; and older flash cards are gradually replaced with new ones when the student is ready. Charts can be used to record results, and the cards with known information can be recirculated into the drills so the knowledge is not forgotten.

- **Reading-fluency drills.** When teaching reading skills to students, I incorporate speed drills at all levels on materials that can already be decoded: letters, words, phrases/sentences, and passages. I also provide speed drills on sight-word lists. Students like to graph their progress. This graphing provides visual evidence of improvement for students who are often frustrated with their struggles in reading.

To learn more about teaching strategies used by Ms. Richards, to to the Teacher Feature page on the Companion Website at **www.prenhall.com/heward**.

*What I Like Most about Being a Special Educator*     I enjoy helping students figure out how to learn. It is so exciting when a student sees how a strategy works or suddenly understands a concept after putting in a lot of time and effort. It makes all of our hard work more than worth it!

It is also important to help students understand the importance of becoming an active participant in their learning. I have found that helping students visualize *how* they are learning helps them be *active and motivated* in their learning. For instance, some students get frustrated with the number of repetitions and amount of effort they have to expend on developing phonemic awareness and phonics skills for reading and writing. When this happens, I find it helpful to have a discussion about the science behind learning differences.

This year I showed a few dyslexic students some of the recent research on the differences between brain activity of "good" readers and that of struggling readers like themselves. I showed them research on how interventions (translated as "lots of hard work by both teachers and students") could help develop clear pathways in their brains similar to those of "good" readers. We visualized shoveling the snow to create pathways and having to reshovel when storms blocked what had seemed easier on days before.

One severely dyslexic student started with one vowel and a few consonants and has watched his skills and use of strategies grow. By the third trimester, he had worked so hard every day at school and at home that he was seeing his efforts translate into reading success! He was gaining confidence in his word-attack skills; and on one of our final days of the year together, I talked about how well he was able to persist and drill skills until he had shoveled clean the pathways in his brain. He proudly replied that he did not shovel; instead he "plowed" the paths so they would stay open. Helping this student become an active participant in his learning will help him continue the process in years to come. This is the type of success story that makes me proud and passionate about being a special educator.

To better understand the topics that will be covered in this chapter, go to the Essential Concepts and Chapter-at-a-Glance modules in Chapter 1 of the Companion Website, **www.prenhall.com/heward**.

Definition of exceptional children

Council for Exceptional Children    Content Standards for Beginning Teachers—Common Core: Similarities and differences of individuals with and without exceptional learning needs (CC2K5).

Definition of impairment, disability, handicap, and at risk

Council for Exceptional Children    Content Standards for Beginning Teachers—Common Core: Similarities and differences of individuals with and without exceptional learning needs (CC2K5).

Educating children with special needs or abilities is a difficult challenge. Teachers and related professionals who have accepted that challenge—special educators—work in a dynamic and exciting field. To begin to appreciate some of the action and excitement, as well as the persistent and emerging challenges, that characterize this important and frequently controversial field, it is necessary to examine some concepts and perspectives that are basic to understanding exceptional children and special education.

# WHO ARE EXCEPTIONAL CHILDREN?

All children exhibit differences from one another in terms of their physical attributes (e.g., some are shorter, some are stronger) and learning abilities (e.g., some learn quickly and are able to remember and use what they have learned in new situations; others need repeated practice and have difficulty maintaining and generalizing new knowledge and skills). The differences among most children are relatively small, enabling these children to benefit from the general education program. The physical attributes and/or learning abilities of some children, however—those called **exceptional children**—differ from the norm (either below or above) to such an extent that they require an individualized program of special education and related services to fully benefit from education. The term *exceptional children* includes children who experience difficulties in learning as well as those whose performance is so superior that modifications in curriculum and instruction are necessary to help them fulfill their potential. Thus, *exceptional children* is an inclusive term that refers to children with learning and/or behavior problems, children with physical disabilities or sensory impairments, and children who are intellectually gifted or have a special talent. The term *students with disabilities* is more restrictive than *exceptional children* because it does not include gifted and talented children. Learning the definitions of several related terms will help you better understand the concept of exceptionality.

Although the terms *impairment, disability,* and *handicap* are sometimes used interchangeably, they are not synonymous (see Table 1.1). **Impairment** refers to the loss or reduced function of a particular body part or organ (e.g., a missing limb). A **disability** exists when an impairment limits a person's ability to perform certain tasks (e.g., walk, see, add a row of numbers) in the same way that most persons do. A person with a disability is not *handicapped,* however, unless the disability leads to educational, personal, social, vocational, or other problems. For example, if a child who has lost a leg learns to use a prosthetic limb and thus functions in and out of school without problems, she is not handicapped, at least in terms of her functioning in the physical environment.

**Handicap** refers to a problem or a disadvantage that a person with a disability or an impairment encounters when interacting with the environment. A disability may pose a hand-

**TABLE 1.1**    **Definitions of impairment, disability, and handicap**

| Term | Definition |
|------|------------|
| Impairment | Any loss or abnormality of psychological, physiological, or anatomical structure or function. |
| Disability | Any restriction or lack (resulting from an impairment) of ability to perform an activity in the manner or within the range considered normal for a human being. |
| Handicap | A disadvantage for a given individual, resulting from an impairment or a disability, that limits or prevents the fulfillment of a role that is normal (depending on age, sex, and social or cultural factors) for that individual. |

Source: World Health Organization. (1993). *International classification of impairments, disabilities, and handicaps* (pp. 27–29). Geneva, Switzerland: Author.

icap in one environment but not in another. The child with a prosthetic limb may be hand-icapped (i.e., disadvantaged) when competing against nondisabled peers on the basketball court but may experience no handicap in the classroom. Individuals with disabilities also experience handicaps that have nothing to do with their disabilities but are the result of negative attitudes and the inappropriate behavior of others who needlessly restrict their access and ability to participate fully in school, work, or community activities.

The word *handicapped* is thought to come from a game that involved a "cap in the hand," and it has the contemporary meaning of assigning extra weight (a handicap) to better performers to "level" a playing field and enhance wagering (Treanor, 1993). Unfortunately, the word conjures up the negative image of a person with disabilities begging in the street. In most instances today, the person-first *with disabilities* is preferred over the term *handicapped.*

**At risk** refers to children who, although not currently identified as having a disability, are considered to have a greater-than-usual chance of developing one. The term is often applied to infants and preschoolers who, because of conditions surrounding their births or home environments, may be expected to experience developmental problems at a later time. The term is also used to refer to students who are experiencing learning problems in the regular classroom and are therefore at risk of school failure or of being identified for special education services.

Some exceptional children share certain physical characteristics and/or patterns of learning and behavior. These characteristics fall into the following categories of exceptionality:

- Mental retardation (developmental disabilities)
- Learning disabilities
- Emotional and behavioral disorders
- Autism
- Communication (speech and language) disorders
- Hearing impairments
- Visual impairments
- Physical and health impairments
- Traumatic brain injury
- Multiple disabilities
- Giftedness and special talents

As stated previously, all children differ from one another in individual characteristics along a continuum; exceptional children differ markedly from the norm so that an individually designed program of instruction—in other words, special education—is required if they are to benefit fully from education. It is a mistake to think that there are two distinct kinds of children—those who are exceptional and those who are regular. Exceptional children are more like other children than they are different. Nevertheless, an exceptional child does differ in important ways from his peers without disabilities. And whether and how we recognize and respond to those differences will have a major impact on the child's success in school and beyond. Keep these critical points in mind as you read and learn about the exceptional children described in this text and the special education programs designed to help them.

# HOW MANY EXCEPTIONAL CHILDREN ARE THERE?

It is impossible to state precisely the number of exceptional children for many reasons, among them (1) the different criteria used by states and local school systems to identify exceptional children, (2) the relative resources and abilities of different school systems to provide preventive services so that an at-risk student does not become a special education student, (3) the imprecise nature of assessment and the large part that subjective judgment plays in the interpretation of assessment data, and (4) the fact that a child may

Although children with disabilities have special instructional needs, they are, above all, children.

be identified as eligible for special education at one time in his school career and not eligible (or included in a different disability category) at another time.

The most complete and accurate information on how many children with disabilities live in the United States is derived from the child count data collected each year by the U.S. Department of Education. More than 6.3 million children and youth with disabilities, ages 3 to 21, received special education services during the 2003–2004 school year (U.S. Department of Education, 2004). Table 1.2 shows the number of school-age students who received special education under each of the disability categories used by the federal government.

**TABLE 1.2** **Number of students ages 6–21 who received special education services under the federal government's disability categories (2003–2004 school year)**

| Disability Category | Number | Percent of Total |
|---|---|---|
| Specific learning disabilities | 2,816,361 | 47.2 |
| Speech or language impairments | 1,118,543 | 18.8 |
| Mental retardation | 570,643 | 9.6 |
| Emotional disturbance | 482,597 | 8.1 |
| Other health impairments | 449,093 | 7.5 |
| Autism | 140,473 | 2.3 |
| Multiple disabilities | 131,225 | 2.2 |
| Hearing impairments | 71,188 | 1.2 |
| Orthopedic impairments | 67,772 | 1.1 |
| Developmental delay | 65,878 | 1.1 |
| Visual impairments | 25,294 | 0.4 |
| Traumatic brain injury | 22,459 | 0.4 |
| Deaf-blindness | 1,603 | <0.1 |
| All disabilities | 5,963,129 | 100.0 |

*Source:* From U.S. Department of Education. (2004). *Individuals with Disabilities Education Act (IDEA) data* (Table AA3). Washington, DC: Author. Available at *http://www.ideadata.org/PartBdata.asp*.

Let's take a quick look at some other numerical facts about special education in the United States.

- The number of children and youth who receive special education has grown every year since a national count was begun in the 1976–1977 school year.
- New early intervention programs have been major contributors to the increases since 1986. During the 2003–2004 school year, 679,212 preschoolers (ages 3 to 5) and 272,082 infants and toddlers (birth through age 2) were among those receiving special education.
- Children with disabilities in special education represent approximately 11% of the school-age population ages 6 to 17.
- The number of children who receive special education increases from age 3 through age 9. The number served decreases gradually with each successive age year after age 9 until age 17. Thereafter, the number of students receiving special education decreases sharply.
- Eighty-four percent of all children and youth ages 6 to 21 receiving special education are reported under four disability categories: (1) learning disabilities (47.2%), (2) speech and language impairment (18.8%), (3) mental retardation (9.6%), and (4) emotional disturbance (8.1%).
- The percentage of students receiving special education under the learning disabilities category has grown dramatically (from 23.8% to 47.2%), whereas the percentage of students with mental retardation has decreased by more than half (from 24.9% to 9.6%) since the federal government began collecting and reporting child count data in 1976–1977.
- About twice as many males as females receive special education.
- The vast majority—approximately 85%—of school-age children receiving special education have mild to moderate disabilities.
- The "typical" child receiving special education in the United States is an elementary-age boy with learning disabilities who spends part of each school day in the regular classroom and part in a resource room.
- Although federal law does not mandate special education for children who are gifted and talented as it does for children with disabilities, during the 2001–2002 school year, 43 states reported serving more than 2.3 million students in K–12 gifted programs (Council of State Directors of Programs for the Gifted, 2003).

# WHY DO WE LABEL AND CLASSIFY EXCEPTIONAL CHILDREN?

Centuries ago, labeling and classifying people were of little consequence; survival was the main concern. Those whose disabilities prevented their full participation in the activities necessary for survival were left on their own to perish and, in some instances, were even killed (Berkson, 2004). In later years, derogatory labels such as "dunce," "imbecile," and "fool" were applied to people with mental retardation or behavior problems, and other demeaning words were used for persons with other disabilities or physical deformities. Regardless of the terms used, their function was the same: to exclude the person with disabilities from the facilities, activities, and privileges of everyday life.

## LABELING AND ELIGIBILITY FOR SPECIAL EDUCATION

Labeling is required to be included for special education. Under current law, to receive special education services, a child must be identified as having a disability (i.e., labeled) and, in most cases, must be further classified into one of that state's categories, such as mental retardation or learning disabilities. In practice, therefore, a student becomes eligible for special education and related services because of membership in a given category. (IDEA allows children ages 3 to 9 to be identified as *developmentally delayed* and receive special education services without the use of a specific disability label.)

Some educators believe that the labels used to identify and classify exceptional children today stigmatize them and serve to deny them opportunities in the mainstream (e.g., Danforth & Rhodes, 1997; Kliewer & Biklen, 1996; Reschly, 1996). Others argue that a workable system of classifying exceptional children (or their exceptional learning needs) is a prerequisite to providing needed special educational services (e.g., Kauffman, 1999; MacMillan, Gresham, Bocian, & Lambros, 1998) and that reducing the stigma associated with disability requires honest and open recognition of the condition and that using more "pleasant" terms minimizes and devalues the individual's situation and need for supports.

> The stigma of cancer has not abated because people tried to cloak it with euphemisms, new terms considered more upbeat and less offensive. Image our reaction if someone were to say, "We no longer use the word *cancer;* now we use less unpleasant terms, such as *prolific cells* or *challenging tissue.*" The stigma of cancer has abated because people were encouraged to confront it for what it is, treat it, and prevent it. Cancer of any type is not nice, not desirable, not anything we would wish for someone we love, but something to be acknowledged and treated. We want people who don't have it to avoid it if they can, even as we want our society to be accepting and supportive of those who have it. We should work for a similar understanding and response to disability—a realistic, no-nonsense depiction of what it is and a loving, supportive attitude toward those who have disabilities. (Kauffman, 2003, p. 196)

*Pros and cons of labeling*

Council for Exceptional Children — Content Standards for Beginning Teachers—Common Core: Issues in definition and identification of individuals with exceptional learning needs (CC1K5).

Classification is a complex issue involving emotional, political, and ethical considerations in addition to scientific, fiscal, and educational interests (Luckasson & Reeve, 2001). As with most complex issues, there are valid perspectives on both sides of the labeling question. The reasons most often cited for and against the classification and labeling of exceptional children are the following:

### Possible Benefits of Labeling

- Labeling recognizes meaningful differences in learning or behavior and is a first and necessary step in responding responsibly to those differences. As Kauffman (1999) points out, "Although universal interventions that apply equally to all,... can be implemented without labels and risk of stigma, no other interventions are possible without labels. Either all students are treated the same or some are treated differently. Any student who is treated differently is inevitably labeled.... When we are unwilling for whatever reason to say that a person has a problem, we are helpless to prevent it.... Labeling a problem clearly is the first step in dealing with it productively" (p. 452).
- Labeling may lead to a protective response in which children are more accepting of the atypical behavior of a peer with disabilities than they would be of a child without disabilities who emitted that same behavior. (A protective response—whether by peers, parents, or teachers—toward a child with a disability can be a disadvantage if it creates learned helplessness and diminishes the child's chances to develop independence [Weisz, Bromfield, Vines, & Weiss, 1985].)
- Labeling helps professionals communicate with one another and classify and evaluate research findings.
- Funding and resources for research and other programs are often based on specific categories of exceptionality.
- Labels enable disability-specific advocacy groups (e.g., parents of children with autism) to promote specific programs and spur legislative action.
- Labeling helps make exceptional children's special needs more visible to policymakers and the public.

### Possible Disadvantages of Labeling

- Because labels usually focus on disability, impairment, and performance deficits, some people may think only in terms of what the individual cannot do instead of what she can or might be able to learn to do.

- Labels may stigmatize the child and lead peers to reject or ridicule the labeled child. (Not all labels used to classify children with disabilities are considered equally negative or stigmatizing. One factor possibly contributing to the large number of children identified as learning disabled is that many professionals and parents view "learning disabilities" as a socially acceptable classification [MacMillan, Gresham, Siperstein, & Bocian, 1996].)
- Labels may negatively affect the child's self-esteem.
- Labels may cause others to hold low expectations for a child and differentially treat her on the basis of the label, which may result in a self-fulfilling prophecy. For example, in one study, student teachers gave a child labeled "autistic" more praise and rewards and fewer verbal corrections for incorrect responses than they gave a child labeled "normal" (Eikeseth & Lovaas, 1992). Such differential treatment could impede the rate at which a child learns new skills and contribute to the development and maintenance of a level of performance consistent with the label's prediction.
- Labels that describe a child's performance deficit often acquire the role of explanatory constructs (e.g., "Sherry acts that way *because* she is emotionally disturbed").
- Even though membership in a given category is based on a particular characteristic (e.g., deafness), there is a tendency to assume that all children in a category share other traits as well, thereby diminishing the detection and appreciation of each child's uniqueness (Gelb, 1997; Smith & Mitchell, 2001).
- Labels suggest that learning problems are primarily the result of something wrong within the child, thereby reducing the systematic examination of and accountability for instructional variables as the cause of performance deficits. This is an especially damaging outcome when the label provides a built-in excuse for ineffective instruction (e.g., "Jalen hasn't learned to read because he's learning disabled").
- A disproportionate number of children from some minority and diverse cultural groups are included in special education programs and thus have been assigned disability labels.
- Special education labels have a certain permanence; once labeled, it is difficult for a child to ever again achieve the status of simply being just another kid.
- Classifying exceptional children requires the expenditure of a great amount of money and professional and student time that might be better spent in planning and delivering instruction (Chaikind, Danielson, & Brauen, 1993).

Clearly, there are strong arguments both for and against the classification and labeling of exceptional children. On the one hand, most of the possible benefits are experienced not by individual children but by groups of children, parents, and professionals who are associated with a certain disability category. On the other hand, all of the potential negative aspects of labeling affect the individual child who has been labeled. Of the possible advantages of labeling listed previously, only the first two could be said to benefit an individual child directly. However, the argument that disability labels associate diagnosis with proper intervention is tenuous at best, particularly when the kinds of labels used in special education are considered. What Becker, Engelmann, and Thomas (1971) wrote more than three decades ago is still true today: "[The labels] rarely tell the teacher who can be taught in what way. One could put five or six labels on the same child and still not know what to teach him or how" (p. 436).

*Effects of labels on behavior of others*

 Council for Exceptional Children — Content Standards for Beginning Teachers—Common Core: Teacher attitudes and behaviors that influence behavior of individuals with exceptional learning needs (CC5K4).

Changing the label used to identify or classify Jeffrey's disability won't lessen the impact of his disability. But referring to him as "Jeffrey, a third grader," instead of "a mentally retarded boy," helps us recognize his strengths and abilities—what he can do—instead of focusing on the disability as if it were his sole defining characteristic.

Although the pros and cons of using disability category labels have been widely debated for several decades, neither conceptual arguments nor research has produced a conclusive case for the total acceptance or absolute rejection of labeling practices. Most of the studies conducted to assess the effects of labeling have produced inconclusive, often contradictory, evidence and have generally been marked by methodological weakness.

## Alternatives to Labeling

A number of alternative approaches to classifying exceptional children that focus on educationally relevant variables have been proposed over the years (e.g., Adelman, 1996; Hardman, McDonnell, & Welch, 1997; Iscoe & Payne, 1972; Sontag, Sailor, & Smith, 1977). For example, Reynolds, Zetlin, and Heistad (1996) proposed a system they call "20/20 analysis" as an alternative, nonlabeling approach to the traditional, categorically driven model of special education. The lowest-achieving 20% and the highest-achieving 20% of students would be identified and eligible for broad (noncategorical) approaches to improvement of learning opportunities.

> In 20/20 Analysis, we begin with measuring progress of students in important areas of learning and identifying those at the margins—those who are not learning well and those showing top rates of learning.... At all times the focus is on outcome variables.... The idea is to look to the margins in learning progress and to identify those who most urgently require adapted instruction. (Reynolds & Heistad, 1997, p. 441)

Some noted special educators have suggested that exceptional children be classified according to the curriculum and skill areas they need to learn.

> But if we shouldn't refer to these special children by using those old labels, then how should we refer to them? For openers, call them Rob, Amy, and Jose. Beyond that, refer to them on the basis of what you're trying to teach them. For example, if a teacher wants to teach Brandon to compute, read, and comprehend, he might call him a student of computation, reading, and comprehension. We do this all the time with older students. Sam, who attends Juilliard, is referred to as "the trumpet student"; Jane, who attends Harvard, is called "the law student." (T. C. Lovitt, personal communication, January 14, 2002)

In a system similar to this, called **curriculum-based measurement**, students are assessed and classified relative to the degree to which they are learning specific curriculum content (Deno, 1997; Howell & Nolet, 2000; Jones, 2001). Educators who employ curriculum-based measurement believe that it is more important to assess (and thereby classify) students in terms of acquisition of the knowledge and skills that make up the school's curriculum than to determine the degree to which they differ from the normative score of all children in some general physical attribute or learning characteristic.

Even though curriculum-based assessment is being used more frequently, use of the traditional labels and categories of exceptional children is likely to continue. The continued development and use of educationally relevant classification systems, however, make it more likely that identification and assessment will lead to effective instructional programs for children, promote more educationally meaningful communication and research among professionals, and perhaps decrease some of the negative aspects of current practices.

# WHY ARE LAWS GOVERNING THE EDUCATION OF EXCEPTIONAL CHILDREN NECESSARY?

## An Exclusionary Past

It is said that a society can be judged by the way it treats those who are different. By this criterion, our educational system has a less than distinguished history. Children who are different because of race, culture, language, gender, socioeconomic status, or exceptional-

*Curriculum-based assessment*

Council for Exceptional Children Content Standards for Beginning Teachers—Common Core: Basic terminology used in assessment (CC8K1).

For continued discussion of labeling and how we should talk about disabilities, including the perspectives of several people with disabilities, see "What's in a Name? The Labels and Language of Special Education" in the profiles & perspectives module in Chapter 1 of the Companion Website, **www.prenhall.com/heward**.

ity have often been denied full and fair access to educational opportunities (Banks & Banks, 2004; Smith, 2004). (It's important, however, to note that past practices were not entirely negative. Long before there was any legal requirement to do so, many children with special needs were educated by devoted teachers and parents [cf. Safford & Safford, 1996].)

Although exceptional children have always been with us, attention has not always been paid to their special needs. In the past, many children with disabilities were entirely excluded from any publicly supported program of education. Before the 1970s, many states had laws permitting public schools to deny enrollment to children with disabilities (Murdick, Gartin, & Crabtree, 2006). Local school officials had no legal obligation to grant students with disabilities the same educational access that nondisabled students enjoyed. One state law, for example, allowed schools to refuse to serve "children physically or mentally incapacitated for school work"; another state had a law stipulating that children with "bodily or mental conditions rendering attendance inadvisable" could be turned away. When these laws were contested, the nation's courts generally supported exclusion. In a 1919 case, for example, a 13-year-old student with physical disabilities (but normal intellectual ability) was excluded from his local school because he "produces a depressing and nauseating effect upon the teachers and school children" (Smith, 2004, p. 4).

When local public schools began to accept a measure of responsibility for educating certain exceptional students, a philosophy of segregation prevailed—a philosophy that continued unchanged until recently. Including children with disabilities in regular schools and classes is a relatively recent phenomenon. Children received labels—such as *mentally retarded, crippled,* or *emotionally disturbed*—and were confined to isolated and segregated classrooms, kept apart from the other children and teachers in the regular education program. One special education teacher describes the crude facilities in which her special class operated and the sense of isolation she felt in the 1960s:

> I accepted my first teaching position, a special education class in a basement room next door to the furnace. Of the 15 "educable mentally retarded" children assigned to work with me, most were simply nonreaders from poor families. One child had been banished to my room because she posed a behavior problem to her fourth-grade teacher.
>
> My class and I were assigned a recess spot on the opposite side of the play yard, far away from the "normal" children. I was the only teacher who did not have a lunch break. I was required to eat with my "retarded" children while other teachers were permitted to leave their students.... Isolated from my colleagues, I closed my door and did my thing, oblivious to the larger educational circles in which I was immersed. Although it was the basement room, with all the negative perceptions that arrangement implies, I was secure in the knowledge that despite the ignominy of it all I did good things for children who were previously unloved and untaught. (Aiello, 1976, p. 14)

Children with mild learning and behavioral problems usually remained in the regular classroom but received no special help. If they did not make satisfactory academic progress, they were termed "slow learners" or simply "failures." If their deportment in class exceeded the teacher's tolerance for misbehavior, they were labeled "disciplinary problems" and suspended from school. Children with more severe disabilities—including many with visual, hearing, and physical or health impairments—were usually placed in segregated schools or institutions or kept at home. Gifted and talented children seldom received special attention in schools. It was assumed they could make it on their own without help.

Society's response to exceptional children has come a long way. As our concepts of equality, freedom, and justice have expanded, children with disabilities and their families have moved from exclusion and isolation to inclusion and participation. Society no longer regards children with disabilities as beyond the responsibility of the local public schools. No longer may a child who is different from the norm be turned away from school because someone believes that he is unable to benefit from typical instruction. Recent legislation and court decisions confirm that all children with disabilities have the right to a *free, appropriate program of public education in the least restrictive environment.*

The provision of equitable educational opportunities to exceptional children has not come about by chance. Many laws and court cases have had important effects on public education in general and on the education of children with special needs in particular. And the process of change is never finished; legal influences on special education are not fixed or static but fluid and dynamic (Yell, 2006).

## Separate Is Not Equal

The history of special education, especially in regard to the education of children with disabilities in regular public schools, is related to the civil rights movement. Special education was strongly influenced by social developments and court decisions in the 1950s and 1960s, especially the landmark case *Brown v. Board of Education of Topeka* (1954). This case challenged the practice of segregating students according to race. In its ruling in the *Brown* case, the U.S. Supreme Court declared that education must be made available to all children on equal terms:

> Today, education is perhaps the most important function of state and local governments. Compulsory school attendance laws and the great expenditure for education both demonstrate our recognition of the importance of education to our democratic society. It is required in the performance of our most basic responsibilities.... In these days, it is doubtful that any child may reasonably be expected to succeed in life if he is denied the opportunity of an education. (*Brown v. Board of Education*, 1954)

The *Brown* decision began a period of intense concern and questioning among parents of children with disabilities, who asked why the same principles of equal access to education should not apply to their children. Numerous court cases were initiated in the 1960s and early 1970s by parents and other advocates dissatisfied with an educational system that denied equal access to children with disabilities. Generally, the parents based their arguments on the 14th Amendment to the Constitution, which provides that no state shall deny any person within its jurisdiction the equal protection of the law and that no state shall deprive any person of life, liberty, or property without due process of law.

## Equal Protection

In the past, children with disabilities usually received differential treatment; that is, they were excluded from certain educational programs or were given special education only in segregated settings. Basically, when the courts have been asked to rule on the practice of denial and segregation, judges have examined whether such treatment is rational and whether it is necessary. One of the most historically significant cases to examine these questions was the class-action suit *Pennsylvania Association for Retarded Children (PARC) v. Commonwealth of Pennsylvania* (1972). The association challenged a state law that denied public school education to certain children considered "unable to profit from public school attendance."

The lawyers and parents supporting PARC argued that even though the children had intellectual disabilities, it was neither rational nor necessary to assume they were ineducable and untrainable. Because the state was unable to prove that the children were, in fact, ineducable or to demonstrate a rational need for excluding them from public school programs, the court decided that the children were entitled to receive a free, public education. In addition, the court maintained that parents had the right to be notified before any change was made in their children's educational program.

The wording of the PARC decision proved particularly important because of its influence on subsequent federal legislation. Not only did the court rule that all children with mental retardation were entitled to a free, appropriate public education, but the ruling also stipulated that placements in regular classrooms and regular public schools were preferable to segregated settings.

It is the Commonwealth's obligation to place each mentally retarded child in a free, public program of education and training appropriate to the child's capacity.... placement in a regular public school class is preferable to placement in a special public school class and placement in a special public school is preferable to placement in any other type of program of education and training. (*PARC v. Commonwealth of Pennsylvania*, 1972)

In addition to the *Brown* and *PARC* cases, several other judicial decisions have had far-reaching effects on special education. The rulings of some of these cases were incorporated into subsequent federal legislation, notably the Individuals with Disabilities Education Act.

# THE INDIVIDUALS WITH DISABILITIES EDUCATION ACT

In 1975 Congress passed Public Law 94–142, a landmark piece of legislation that has completely changed the face of education in this country. P.L. 94–142 was originally called the Education for All Handicapped Children Act. Since it became law in 1975, Congress has reauthorized and amended P.L. 94–142 five times. The 1990 amendments renamed the law the Individuals with Disabilities Education Act—often referred to by its acronym, IDEA. The most recent reauthorization of IDEA is titled The Individuals with Disabilities Education Improvement Act of 2004.

IDEA has affected every school in the country and has changed the roles of regular and special educators, school administrators, parents, and students with disabilities in the educational process. Its passage marked the culmination of the efforts of a great many educators, parents, and legislators to bring together in one comprehensive bill this country's laws regarding the education of children with disabilities. The law reflects society's concern about treating people with disabilities as full citizens with the same rights and privileges that all other citizens enjoy.

The Individuals with Disabilities Education Improvement Act of 2004 states that the purpose of IDEA is

1. (A) to ensure that all children with disabilities have available to them a free, appropriate public education that emphasizes special education and related services designed to meet their unique needs and prepare them for further education, employment, and independent living; (B) to ensure that the rights of children with disabilities and parents of such children are protected; and (C) to assist States, localities, educational service agencies, and Federal agencies to provide for the education of all children with disabilities;
2. to assist States in the implementation of a statewide, comprehensive, coordinated, multidisciplinary, interagency system of early intervention services for infants and toddlers with disabilities and their families;
3. to ensure that educators and parents have the necessary tools to improve educational results for children with disabilities by supporting system improvement activities; coordinated research and personnel preparation; coordinated technical assistance, dissemination, and support; and technology development and media services; and
4. to assess, and ensure the effectiveness of, efforts to educate children with disabilities. (H.R. 1350, Sec 601 (d)).

## Six Major Principles of IDEA

IDEA is directed primarily at the states, which are responsible for providing education to their citizens. The majority of the many rules and regulations defining how IDEA operates fall under six major principles that have remained basically unchanged since 1975 (Turnbull & Cilley, 1999; Turnbull & Turnbull, 2000):

*Zero Reject.* Schools must educate *all* children with disabilities. This principle applies regardless of the nature or severity of the disability; no child with disabilities may be excluded from a public education. The requirement to provide special education to all students with disabilities is absolute between the ages of 6 and 17. If a state provides educational services to children without disabilities between the ages of 3 to 5 and 18 to 21, it must also

✎ *Helpful Hint*

Federal legislation is designated by a numerical system. Public Law 94-142, for example, was the 142nd bill passed by the 94th Congress. Federal statues and regulations are published in the *United States Code.* The IDEA citation 20 U.S.C. §1400[c] refers to *United States Code,* Title 20, Section 1400, Subsection c. The regulations for IDEA, which spell out the details for meeting the law's provisions, are contained in the *Code of Federal Regulations,* or C.F.R.

*Major principles of IDEA*

Council for Exceptional Children  Content Standards for Beginning Teachers—Common Core: Rights and responsibilities of students, parents, teachers and other professionals, and schools related to exceptional learning needs (CC1K4).

In the past, many children like Rachel and Brandon were denied access to education in public schools.

educate all children with disabilities in those age groups. Each state education agency is responsible for locating, identifying, and evaluating all children, from birth to age 21, residing in the state with disabilities or who are suspected of having disabilities. This requirement is called the *child find system.*

*Nondiscriminatory Identification and Evaluation.*   Schools must use nonbiased, multifactored methods of evaluation to determine whether a child has a disability and, if so, whether special education is needed. Testing and evaluation procedures must not discriminate on the basis of race, culture, or native language. All tests must be administered in the child's native language, and identification and placement decisions cannot be made on the basis of a single test score. These provisions of IDEA are known as *protection in evaluation procedures.*

*Free, Appropriate Public Education (FAPE).*   All children with disabilities, regardless of the type or severity of their disability, shall receive a free, appropriate public education. This education must be provided at public expense—that is, without cost to the child's parents. An **individualized education program (IEP)** must be developed and implemented to meet the unique needs of each student with a disability. The IEP specifies the child's unique educational needs, states present levels of performance, identifies measurable annual goals and short-term objectives, and describes the specific special education and related services that will be provided to help the child attain those goals and benefit from education. (IEPs will be discussed in detail in Chapter 2.)

*Least Restrictive Environment (LRE).*   IDEA mandates that students with disabilities be educated with children without disabilities to the maximum extent appropriate and that students with disabilities be removed to separate classes or schools only when the nature or severity of their disabilities is such that they cannot receive an appropriate education in a general education classroom with supplementary aids and services. IDEA creates a presumption in favor of inclusion in the regular classroom by requiring that a student's IEP contain a justification and explanation of the extent, if any, to which a child will not participate with nondisabled peers in the general academic curriculum, extracurricular activities, and other nonacademic activities (e.g., lunch, recess, transportation, dances). To ensure that each student with disabilities is educated in the least restrictive environment appropriate for her needs, school districts must provide a continuum of placement and service alternatives. (The LRE and the continuum of services are discussed in detail in Chapter 2.)

*Due process safeguards*

Council for Exceptional Children   Content Standards for Beginning Teachers—Common Core: Issues, assurances, and due process rights related to assessment, eligibility, and placement within a continuum of services (CC1K6).

*Due Process Safeguards.*   Schools must provide due process safeguards to protect the rights of children with disabilities and their parents. Parental consent must be obtained for initial and all subsequent evaluations and placement decisions regarding special education. Schools must maintain the confidentiality of all records pertaining to a child with disabilities and make those records available to the parents. When parents of a child with disabilities disagree with the results of an evaluation performed by the school, they can obtain an independent evaluation at public expense. When the school and parents disagree on the identification, evaluation, placement, or provision of a free, appropriate public education and related services for the child, the parents may request a due process hearing. States are also required to offer parents an opportunity to resolve the matter through mediation by a third party before holding a due process hearing. Parents have the right to attorney's fees if they prevail in due process or judicial proceedings under IDEA. The law also includes provisions that allow the court to award reasonable attorney's fees to the prevailing school district against the attorney of a parent, or the parent who files a complaint that is frivolous, unreasonable, without foundation, or filed for any improper purpose, such as to harass.

Although "due process hearings are a last resort to resolve conflicts or problems between school districts and parents" (Getty & Summey, 2004, p. 40), they occur with increasing frequency. The majority of due process hearings are over placement or program issues (Newcomer & Zirkel, 1999). In cases contesting placement issues, parents were seeking a more restrictive educational setting 67% of the time (Havey, 1999).

*Parent and Student Participation and Shared Decision Making.* Schools must collaborate with parents and students with disabilities in the design and implementation of special education services. The parents' (and, whenever appropriate, the student's) input and wishes must be considered in IEP goals and objectives, related-service needs, and placement decisions.

## Other Provisions of IDEA

*Extending Special Education Services to Infants, Toddlers, and Preschoolers.* Noting that states were serving at most about 70% of preschool children with disabilities and that early intervention services for infants and toddlers with disabilities from birth through age 2 were scarce or nonexistent in many states, Congress included provisions in the Education of the Handicapped Act Amendments in 1986 (P.L. 99–457) to expand services for these segments of the population. Beginning with the 1990–1991 school year, each state was required to fully serve all preschool children with disabilities ages 3 to 5—that is, with the same services and protections available to school-age children—or lose all future federal funds for preschoolers with disabilities.

P.L. 99–457 included an incentive grant program to encourage states to provide early intervention services to infants and toddlers with disabilities and their families—that is, children from birth through age 2 who need early intervention services because they are experiencing developmental delays or have a diagnosed physical or mental impairment likely to result in developmental delays. With the reauthorizations of IDEA in 1997 (P.L. 105–17) and again in 2004 (H.R. 1350), Congress reaffirmed the nation's commitment to a system of early intervention services. Rather than mandate special services for this age group, IDEA encourages each state to develop and implement a statewide, comprehensive, coordinated, multidisciplinary, inter-agency program of early intervention services for infants and

School districts must provide related services to students with disabilities—such as transportation in specially equipped vans or buses—so they may have access to and benefit from a public education.

**TABLE 1.3** **Types and definitions of related services that students with disabilities may need to benefit from education**

| Related Service | Definition |
|---|---|
| Audiology | (1) Identifying children with hearing loss. (2) Determining the range, nature, and degree of hearing loss. (3) Providing habilitative activities, such as auditory training, speech reading, hearing evaluation, and speech conservation. (4) Creating and administering programs for prevention of hearing loss. (5) Counseling and guidance of pupils, parents, and teachers, regarding hearing loss. (6) Determining the child's need for group and individual amplification, selecting and fitting an appropriate hearing aid, and evaluating the effectiveness of amplification. |
| Counseling services | Services provided by qualified social workers, psychologists, guidance counselors, or other qualified personnel. |
| Early identification and assessment | Implementing a formal plan for identifying a disability as early as possible in a child's life. |
| Medical services | Services provided by a licensed physician to determine a child's medically related disability that results in the child's need for special education and related services. |
| Occupational therapy | (1) Improving, developing, or restoring functions impaired or lost through illness, injury, or deprivation. (2) Improving ability to perform tasks for independent functioning when functions are impaired or lost. (3) Preventing, through early intervention, initial or further impairment or loss of function. |
| Orientation and mobility services | Services provided to children who are blind or have visual impairments to assist them in traveling around their school or environment. |
| Parent counseling and training | Assisting parents in understanding the special needs of their child and providing parents with information about child development. |
| Physical therapy | Services provided by a qualified physical therapist. |
| Psychological services | (1) Administering psychological and educational tests, and other assessment procedures. (2) Interpreting assessment results. (3) Obtaining, integrating, and interpreting information about child behavior and conditions relating to learning. (4) Consulting with other staff members in planning school programs to meet the special needs of children as indicated by psychological tests, interviews, and behavioral evaluations. (5) Planning and managing a program of psychological services, including psychological counseling for children and parents. |

toddlers with disabilities and their families. The encouragement is in the form of a gradually increasing amount of federal money to be awarded to states that identify and serve all infants and toddlers with disabilities. Various education and human services agencies within each state work together to provide services such as medical and educational assessment, physical therapy, speech and language intervention, and parent counseling and training. These early intervention services are prescribed and implemented according to an **individualized family services plan (IFSP)** written by a multidisciplinary team that includes the child's parents. (IFSPs are discussed in Chapter 14.)

*Related Services and Assistive Technology.*    Children with disabilities have sometimes been prevented from attending regular schools or benefiting from educational activities by circumstances that impede their access or participation. A child who uses a wheelchair, for example, may require a specially equipped school bus. A child with special health needs may require medication several times a day. A child with an orthopedic impairment may

| Related Service | Definition |
|---|---|
| Recreation | (1) Assessment of leisure function. (2) Therapeutic recreation services. (3) Recreation programs in schools and community agencies. (4) Leisure education. |
| Rehabilitative counseling services | Services provided by qualified personnel in individual or group sessions that focus specifically on career development, employment preparation, achieving independence, and integration in the workplace and community. |
| School health services | Services provided by a qualified school nurse or other qualified person. |
| Social work services in the schools | (1) Preparing a social or developmental history on a child with a disability. (2) Group and individual counseling with the child and family. (3) Working with those problems in a child's living situation (home, school, and community) that affect the child's adjustment in school. (4) Mobilizing school and community resources to enable the child to learn as effectively as possible. |
| Speech pathology | (1) Identification of children with speech or language impairments. (2) Diagnosis and appraisal. (3) Referral for medical or other professional attention. (4) Provision of speech and language services for the habilitation and prevention of communicative problems. (5) Counseling and guidance of parents, children, and teachers regarding speech and language impairments. |
| Transportation | (1) Travel to and from school and between schools. (2) Travel in and around school buildings. (3) Specialized equipment if required to provide special transportation for a child with a disability (e.g., special or adapted buses, lifts, and ramps). |
| Assistive technology devices and services | Devices and related services that increase, maintain, or improve the functional capabilities of children with disabilities. |

*Source:* IDEA Regulations, 34 C.F.R. §300.24; Authority: 20 U.S.C. §1401 (22).

need physical therapy to maintain flexibility and use of her arms and legs. IDEA requires that schools provide any **related services** (e.g., special transportation, counseling, physical therapy) and **assistive technology**—devices and services such as visual aids, augmentative communication devices, specialized equipment for computer access—that a child with disabilities may need to access and benefit from special education. Table 1.3 provides definitions of the types of related services included in the IDEA regulations. As Downing (2004) notes, however, this list should not be considered exhaustive; other services may be provided if the IEP team deems they are necessary for the student to benefit from special education.

 Sometimes an off-the-shelf consumer product may be the assistive technology needed to help a student with disabilities achieve success in the classroom. See Teaching & Learning, "Organization Is at Hand," later in this chapter.

*Federal Funding of Special Education.* Laws and regulations calling for special education would have limited value if the schools lacked the necessary financial resources. Congress backed up its mandate for free, appropriate public education by providing federal funds to help school districts meet the additional costs of educating children with disabilities. However, educating students with disabilities is very expensive. Chaikind et al. (1993) reported a per-pupil annual cost of approximately $7,800 in 1989–1990 dollars, or about 2.3 times the cost of educating each pupil in regular education. They found that costs of special education services varied considerably by disability category, ranging from under $1,000 per student with speech and language impairments to more than $30,000 per student with deaf-blindness.

State and local educational administrators contend that federal financial assistance for the education of students with disabilities has not been sufficient and that schools are hard pressed to meet the requirements in IDEA. When Congress passed IDEA in 1975, its intent was to provide federal funds for 40% of the total costs of educating children with disabilities. However, during the 1998–1999 school year the federal government provided only 8% of the average dollar amount needed to educate a student with disabilities over and above per-pupil expenditures to provide general education service (Parrish, 2001). While federal funding has increased in recent years, it has never reached more than about 12 percent of the national average (Chambers, Parrish, & Harr, 2002).

States cannot use federal funds to serve more than 12% of their school-age students in special education. IDEA requires that the vast majority of the federal funds received by the states be passed on to local school districts. States can elect to use up to 10% of their federal allocation for state-level activities such as direct and supportive services for students with disabilities (e.g., support to state residential schools for students with sensory impairments), supervision, and compliance monitoring. In addition, each state is required to develop a *comprehensive system for personnel development*, including in-service training programs for regular education teachers, special education teachers, school administrators, and other support personnel.

According to the Council for Exceptional Children (2004), the Individuals with Disabilities Education Improvement Act of 2004 failed to provide full funding necessary for states to meet the law's many mandates.

> CEC has long advocated for the mandatory full funding of IDEA, and the funding levels authorized in this bill fall in line with our recommended approach to reaching full funding. However, in the 1975 special education legislation, Congress promised to reach full funding by 1981. But, instead of providing funds to pay for 40 percent of the additional cost of educating a student with disabilities, the federal government is only providing 18.6 percent of that additional cost in fiscal year 2004. At the rate Congress is funding IDEA, full funding will never be reached.
>
> The implications of a "glide path" to full funding are much the same as they have been in the past: an unfunded mandate. While H.R. 1350 authorizes Congress to appropriate money to achieve full funding, it still does not make IDEA an entitlement program, thereby guaranteeing mandatory full funding. Instead, IDEA funding is still at the whim of Congressional appropriators and will continue to financially burden State and local education agencies in educating students with disabilities. (p. 7)

*Tuition Reimbursement.* Parents and school officials sometimes disagree about whether placement in a private school is the most appropriate way to meet the needs of a student with disabilities. IDEA stipulates that, in cases in which an appropriate education cannot be provided in the public schools, children with disabilities may be placed in private school programs at no cost to their parents. This has proven to be a particularly controversial aspect of the law (Yell, 2006).

## Key Features Introduced by the Individuals with Disabilities Education Improvement Act of 2004

Although it retained all of the major principles and components of IDEA, the Individuals with Disabilities Education Improvement Act of 2004 entailed numerous changes, several of which may have significant impact on the field in the coming years.

*Paperwork Reduction.* The purpose of this part of the reauthorization "is to provide an opportunity for States to identify ways to reduce paperwork burdens and other administrative duties that are directly associated with the requirements of this title, in order to increase the time and resources available for instruction and other activities aimed at improving educational and functional results for children with disabilities" (Sec 609 (a)(1)). The law authorized the Secretary of Education to grant waivers of statutory requirements of, or regulatory requirements relating to, Part B of IDEA to up to 15 states for a period of time not to exceed 4 years. States wishing to participate in this pilot project will submit proposals

This text went to press a few weeks after the IDEA Improvement Act was signed into law. The implications of the changes in the new law will be clarified when the final federal regulations that detail how the law is to be implemented are issued. For further discussion of the new law and links to the published regulations when they are released, go to the "IDEA Improvement Act of 2004" in Chapter 1 of the Companion Website, **www.prenhall.com/heward**.

# Organization Is at Hand:
# PDAs in the Inclusive Classroom

*by Anne M. Bauer  and Mary E. Ulrich*

Marco is sitting in his ninth-grade government class. His teacher is using an overhead projector, reviewing for the upcoming quiz. Marco is listening intently but is only making an occasional note. At the end of the class Marco approaches the teacher, who picks up her handheld digital assistant. Marco passes his PDA and she "beams" him the overheads. Marco thanks the teacher and pockets his PDA.

Getting and staying organized is a persistent challenge for students with disabilities in inclusive settings. The traditional learning strategies we try to teach students often involve pencil-and-paper skills, which may not be a strength or an interest. Students, however, are interested in and have grown up with handheld video games, remote controls, computers, and cellular phones. This familiarity can play a role in motivating and helping students apply the strategies we teach them as they use PDAs or other technology applications.

There are many possible applications for PDAs in inclusive settings. For students who need support in organization, PDAs can be used for the following:

- *Self-management.*   Alarms on PDAs serve as reminders to begin a new task, to self-check if the student is working on the appropriate task, or to take medication.
- *To-do lists.*   Lists allow students to record activities that must be completed by a designated time.
- *Long-term project planning.*   Longer assignments can be broken into manageable segments.
- *Tracking progress.*   Students can use the PDA to monitor their grades.
- *Generating a master schedule.*   Students can record assignments, activities, and events so that they begin to see the "big picture" of their schoolwork, extracurricular activities, and home activities.

PDAs may also support a student's academic and vocational goals. The multiple programs on PDAs eliminate the need for the student to carry a spell checker, a dictionary, a calculator, and a plan book, so there are fewer items to forget or misplace. In addition, PDAs may provide specific accommodations:

- Teachers may beam the contents of their overhead transparencies, lecture notes, or homework to students.
- Software and keyboards allow teachers and students to use word-processing programs compatible with desktop computer programs.
- Students may receive beamed notes or assignments that they then synchronize on their home computers, printing out copies to review.
- Written assignments may be completed and edited.

Handheld digital assistants also support collaboration in these ways:

- *Behavior management plans.*   Students may self-record their behavioral data on the PDA or use it to self-cue. Student or teacher may enter reminders into the PDA, with alarms set throughout the day for tutoring sessions and other activities or for taking medication. During transition times and when students finish their assigned tasks, PDAs can provide quiet alternative activities as well.
- *Parent-teacher communication.*   Teachers are able to write notes to parents, identify school events, develop the classroom schedule or calendar, or provide the class phone list and beam the information to students. Parents then check the PDA for this essential information without worrying that something has been forgotten at school.
- *Homework communication.*   Teachers and peers may enter homework and long-term assignments

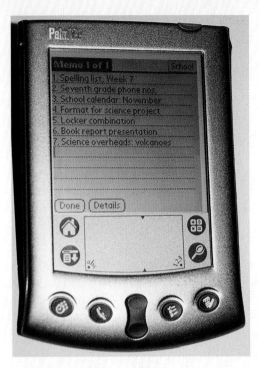

Students learn to use PDAs quickly for a variety of classroom applications.

A PDA can function as a portable homework hotline for parents.

on their own handhelds and beam them to students with disabilities for whom recording assignments is difficult. The parent may send a message back to the teacher regarding the amount of time the assignment took or any challenges the student encountered in completing it.

- *Vocational and life-skills accommodations.* PDAs not only help students monitor their work schedules and supplies but can provide checklists for job completion. Job coaches may add the task analysis for a job assignment, allowing students to make sure the job is completed thoroughly and accurately.

## HOW TO GET STARTED

Students are ready and able to use handheld technology. Because of universal design, students have many alternative ways of recording assignments and other activities. With new programs becoming available as shareware almost daily, the potential for PDAs in supporting students with disabilities seems endless. Here are some suggestions for effective use of PDAs in the classroom and how they can support students with disabilities in inclusive settings:

- *Provide alternatives for inputting information if necessary.* Limited fine-motor skills make entering data on a PDA difficult for some students. Though we introduced keyboards to help the students who

were struggling with learning to write in the way recognized by the PDA, fine-motor skills remained a challenge for some students. However, in these circumstances a peer may enter the information for the student, or the teacher may enter information on his or her PDA and beam it to the students who require that level of support.

- *Check and test programs used by students.* The Internet is a wonderful source for free software programs, but there are many poorly designed programs for PDAs. It is very important to check and test new programs to make sure they do not use up too much memory or include graphic and/or text content inappropriate for school.
- *Set rules for PDA use.* Management is an issue with PDAs as students quickly learn how to beam notes or answers to each other. Teachers should not be naïve about these issues. Create a clear set of rules for PDAs and monitor their use.
- *Provide suggestions for equipment that will keep PDAs safe.* PDAs don't bounce. Inexpensive cases are essential, and passport wallets worn around the neck or a belt pack may be needed for younger students.
- *Synchronize frequently.* Teach students to synchronize their PDAs with a desktop computer frequently. Keep in mind that synchronization may need to occur at school and plan accordingly.
- *Keep spare batteries on hand.* Suggest that students keep an extra set of batteries in their book bags at all times. In addition, teachers should keep a small supply of extra batteries in their classrooms.
- *Don't be afraid to push the buttons and see what happens.* We teachers are often behind our students on the technology learning curve. While students

find it fun to experiment with and learn or try new programs, their teachers may find it a hassle or even a bit intimidating.

Additional information on using handheld computers in inclusive classrooms can be found in Bauer and Ulrich (2002).

---

Anne M. Bauer is a member of the teacher education faculty at the University of Cincinnati, where she teaches in the early childhood/early childhood special education program and conducts research related to supporting young children in general education. Her son and daughter, who both have learning disabilities, use PDAs to support their inclusion. Mary E. Ulrich is the parent of a young adult with disabilities and is a member of the special education faculty at Miami University in Oxford, Ohio, where she studies issues of inclusion.

 To learn more about these strategies and answer questions about what you have learned, go to the Teaching & Learning module in Chapter 1 of the Companion Website, **www.prenhall.com/heward**.

specifying how they plan to reduce paperwork without negatively affecting civil rights requirements, or the right of a child with disabilities to receive a free appropriate education as described in IDEA.

*Benchmarks and Short-Term Objectives Deleted from Most IEPs.* Benchmarks and short-term objectives, statements specifying a progressive series of smaller achievements in route to an annual learning goal, are now required only in IEPs for students who take the school district's alternative assessments related to alternative achievement standards. Although this is expected to reduce the overall amount of paperwork for special education teachers, it is unknown what effects, if any, this will have on individual program planning and the effectiveness of the instruction that ensues.

*Multi-Year IEPs.* The new law authorizes pilot projects in up to 15 states in which local school districts, with consent and participation of parents, will be allowed to develop comprehensive, multi-year IEPs, which can be in effect for up to 3 years. A multi-year IEPs is intended to enable long-term planning that coincides with "natural transition points" in a child's life, such as transitioning from preschool to elementary grades or from secondary grades to post-secondary activities.

*Highly Qualified Teachers.* One of the key goals of the federal No Child Left Behind (NCLB) legislation, which will be discussed later in this chapter, is that all children will be taught by "highly qualified" teachers. In an attempt to align IDEA with NCLB, the 2004 reauthorization of IDEA includes for the first time definitions of "highly qualified" special educators. The basic requirements to be a "highly qualified" special educator as stipulated in the law are: (1) hold full state certification as a special education teacher (including certification obtained through alternative routes to certification), or (2) pass the state special education teacher licensing examination, and as a result hold a license to teach in the state as a special education teacher. Additional licenses are required to be "highly qualified." Special educators teaching two or more core subjects or teaching students working toward "alternate achievement standards" must meet additional requirements.

*Identifying Students with Learning Disabilities.* Identifying a severe discrepancy between a child's academic achievement and intellectual ability has been the most commonly used method for diagnosing learning disabilities. However, as we will see in Chapter 5, the validity and reliability of the discrepancy approach are highly suspect. The new law states that "when determining whether a child has a specific learning disability... a local educational agency shall not be required to take into consideration whether a child has a severe discrepancy between achievement and intellectual ability" (Sec 614 (b)(6)(A)). In addition, the IDEA Improvement Act states that, "In determining whether a child has a specific learning disability, a local educational agency may use a process that determines if the child responds to scientific, research-based intervention as a part of the evaluation procedures (Sec 614 (b)(6)(B)). "Response-to-instruction," a promising approach to identifying learning disabilities that combines early identification and prevention, will be discussed in Chapter 5.

## Legal Challenges Based on IDEA

Although IDEA has resulted in dramatic increases in the number of students receiving special education services and in greater recognition of the legal rights of children with disabilities and their families, it has also brought about an ever-increasing number of disputes concerning the education of students with disabilities. Parents and other advocates have brought about thousands of due process hearings and hundreds of court cases. Due process hearings and court cases often place parents and schools in confrontation and are expensive and time-consuming (Getty & Summey, 2004; Lanigan, Audette, Dreier, & Kobersy, 2001).

It is difficult to generalize how judges and courts have resolved the various legal challenges based on IDEA. There have been many different interpretations of *free, appropriate education* and *least restrictive environment*. The federal statute uses these terms repeatedly; but in the view of many parents, educators, judges, and attorneys, the law does not define them with sufficient clarity. Thus, the questions of what is appropriate and least restrictive for a particular child and whether a public school district should be compelled to provide a certain service must often be decided by judges and courts on consideration of the evidence presented to them. Some of the key issues ruled on by the courts are the extended school year, related services, disciplinary procedures, and the fundamental right to an education for students with the most severe disabilities. Table 1.4 on pages 30–31 summarizes key judicial decisions that have had significant impact on special education and the lives of individuals with disabilities and their families.

*Extended School Year.*  Most public school programs operate for approximately 180 days per year. Parents and educators have argued that, for some children with disabilities, particularly those with severe and multiple disabilities, a 180-day school year is not sufficient to meet their needs. In *Armstrong v. Kline* (1979), the parents of five students with severe disabilities claimed that their children tended to regress during the usual breaks in the school year and called on the schools to provide a period of instruction longer than 180 days. The court agreed and ordered the schools to extend the school year for these students. Several states and local districts now provide year-round educational programs for some students with disabilities, but there are no clear and universally accepted guidelines as to which students are entitled to free public education for a longer-than-usual school year.

*Related Services.*  The related-services provision of IDEA has been highly controversial, creating much disagreement about what kinds of related services are necessary and reasonable for the schools to provide and what services should be the responsibility of the child's parents. The first case based on IDEA to reach the U.S. Supreme Court was *Board of Education of the Hendrick Hudson Central School District v. Rowley* (1982). Amy Rowley was a fourth grader who, because of her hearing loss, needed special education and related services. The school district had originally provided Amy with a hearing aid, speech therapy, a tutor, and a sign-language interpreter to accompany her in the regular classroom. The school withdrew the sign-language services after the interpreter reported that Amy did not make use of her services: Amy reportedly looked at the teacher to read her lips and asked the teacher to repeat instructions rather than get the information from the interpreter. Amy's parents contended that she was missing up to 50% of the ongoing instruction (her hearing loss was estimated to have left her with 50% residual hearing) and was therefore being denied an appropriate public school education. The school district's position was that Amy, with the help of the other special services she was still receiving, was passing from grade to grade without an interpreter. School personnel thought, in fact, that an interpreter might hinder Amy's interactions with her teacher and peers. It was also noted that this service would cost the school district as much as $25,000 per year. The Supreme Court ruled that Amy, who was making satisfactory progress in school without an interpreter, was receiving an adequate education and that the school district could not be compelled to hire a full-time interpreter.

The second P.L. 94–142 case to reach the Supreme Court was *Irving Independent School District v. Tatro* (1984). In this case, the Court decided that a school district was obligated to provide catheterization and other related medical services to enable a young child with physical impairments to attend school. In the 1999 *Cedar Rapids v. Garret F.* case, the Supreme Court reaffirmed and extended its ruling in the *Tatro* case. (See Chapter 11 for further discussion of the *Tatro* and *Garret* cases.)

*Disciplining Students with Disabilities.*    Some cases have resulted from parents' protesting the suspension or expulsion of children with disabilities. The case of *Stuart v. Nappi* (1978), for example, concerned a high school student who spent much of her time wandering in the halls even though she was assigned to special classes. The school sought to have the student expelled on disciplinary grounds because her conduct was considered detrimental to order in the school. The court agreed with the student's mother that expulsion would deny the student a free, appropriate public education as called for in IDEA. In other cases, expulsion or suspension of students with disabilities has been upheld if the school could show that the grounds for expulsion did not relate to the student's disability. In 1988, however, the Supreme Court ruled in *Honig v. Doe* that a student with disabilities could not be expelled from school for disciplinary reasons, which meant that, for all practical purposes, schools could not recommend expulsion or suspend a student with disabilities for more than 10 days.

The IDEA amendments of 1997 (P.L. 105–17) contained provisions that enable school districts to discipline students with disabilities in the same manner as students without disabilities, with a few notable exceptions. If the school seeks a change of placement, suspension, or expulsion in excess of 10 days, the IEP team and other qualified personnel must review the relationship between the student's misconduct and her disability. This review is called a **manifestation determination** (Katsiyannis & Maag, 2001). If it is determined that the student's behavior is not related to the disability, the same disciplinary procedures used with other students may be imposed. However, the school must continue to provide educational services in the alternative placement.

The Individuals with Disabilities Education Improvement Act of 2004 revised the discipline provisions of the law such that under special circumstances (e.g., student brings or possesses a weapon to or at school; possesses, uses, or sells illegal drugs at school; inflicts serious injury upon someone at school or a school function), school personnel have the authority to remove a student with disabilities to an interim alternative educational setting for up to 45 school days, whether or not the misconduct was related to the child's disability.

*Right to Education.*    The case of *Timothy W. v. Rochester School District* (1989) threatened the zero-reject philosophy of IDEA. In July 1988, Judge Loughlin of the district court in New Hampshire ruled that a 13-year-old boy with severe disabilities and quadriplegia was ineligible for education services because he could not benefit from special education. The judge ruled in favor of the Rochester School Board, which claimed that IDEA was not intended to provide educational services to "*all* handicapped students." In his decision, the judge determined that the federal law was not explicit regarding a "rare child" with severe disabilities and declared that special evaluations and examinations should be used to determine "qualifications for education under PL 94–142."

In May 1989, a court of appeals overturned the lower court's decision, ruling that public schools must educate all children with disabilities regardless of how little they might benefit or the nature or severity of their disabilities. The three-judge panel concluded that

*Manifestation determination*

Council for Exceptional Children    Content Standards for Beginning Teachers—Common Core: Laws, policies, and ethical principles regarding behavior management planning and implementation (CC1K2).

## TABLE 1.4 Major court cases that have influenced special education and the lives of individuals with disabilities

| Date | Court Case | Educational Implications |
|------|-----------|--------------------------|
| 1954 | *Brown v. Board of Education of Topeka* (Kansas) | The case established the right of all children to an equal opportunity for an education. |
| 1967 | *Hobson v. Hansen* (Washington, DC) | The court declared the tracking system, in which children were placed into either regular or special classes according to their scores on intelligence tests, unconstitutional because it discriminated against African American and poor children. |
| 1970 | *Diana v. State Board of Education* (California) | A Spanish-speaking student in California had been placed in a special class for children with mental retardation based on the results of intelligence tests given in English. The court ruled that children cannot be placed in special education on the basis of culturally biased tests or tests given in other than the child's native language. |
| 1972 | *Mills v. Board of Education of the District of Columbia* | Seven children had been excluded from the public schools in Washington, DC, because of learning and behavior problems. The school district contended that it did not have enough money to provide special education programs for them. The court ruled that financial problems cannot be allowed to have a greater impact on children with disabilities than on students without disabilities and ordered the schools to readmit the children and serve them appropriately. |
| 1972 | *Pennsylvania Association for Retarded Citizens v. the Commonwealth of Pennsylvania* | This class action suit established the right to free public education for all children with mental retardation. |
| 1972 | *Wyatt v. Stickney* (Alabama) | The decision declared that individuals in state institutions have the right to appropriate treatment within those institutions. |
| 1979 | *Larry P. v. Riles* (California) | The court ruled that IQ tests used to place African American children in special classes were inappropriate because they failed to recognize the children's cultural background and the learning that took place in their homes and communities. The court ordered that IQ tests could not be used as the sole basis for placing children into special classes. |
| 1979 | *Armstrong v. Kline* (Pennsylvania) | The case established the right of some children with severe disabilities to an extension of the 180-day public school year. |
| 1982 | *Board of Education of the Hendrik Hudson Central School District v. Rowley* (New York) | This was the first case based on P.L. 94–142 to reach the U.S. Supreme Court; while denying the plaintiff's specific request, the Court upheld for each child with disabilities the right to a personalized program of instruction and necessary supportive services. |
| 1983 | *Abrahamson v. Hershman* (Massachusetts) | The court ruled that residential placement in a private school was necessary for a child with multiple disabilities who needed around-the-clock training and required the school district to pay for the private placement. |
| 1984 | *Department of Education v. Katherine D.* (Hawaii) | The court ruled that a homebound instructional program for a child with multiple health impairments did not meet the least restrictive environment standard and called for the child to be placed in a class with children without disabilities and provided with related medical services. |

TABLE 1.4 *continued*

| Date | Court Case | Educational Implications |
|------|-----------|--------------------------|
| 1984 | *Irving Independent School District v. Tatro* (Texas) | The court ruled that catheterization was necessary for a child with physical disabilities to remain in school and that it could be performed by a nonphysician, thus obligating the school district to provide that service. |
| 1984 | *Smith v. Robinson* (Rhode Island) | The court ordered the state to pay for the placement of a child with severe disabilities in a residential program and ordered the school district to reimburse the parents' attorney fees. The U.S. Supreme Court later ruled that P.L. 94–142 did not entitle parents to recover such fees, but Congress subsequently passed an "Attorney's Fees" bill, leading to enactment of P.L. 99–372. |
| 1985 | *Cleburne v. Cleburne Living Center* (Texas) | The Supreme Court ruled unanimously that communities cannot use a discriminatory zoning ordinance to prevent establishment of group homes for persons with mental retardation. |
| 1988 | *Honig v. Doe* (California) | The court ruled that children with disabilities cannot be excluded from school for any misbehavior that is disability-related (in this case, "aggressive behavior against other students" on the part of two "emotionally handicapped" students) but that educational services could cease if the misbehavior is not related to the disability. |
| 1989 | *Timothy W. v. Rochester School District* (New Hampshire) | The U.S. Appeals Court upheld the literal interpretation that P.L. 94–142 requires that all children with disabilities be provided with a free, appropriate, public education, unconditionally and without exception. The three-judge appeals court overturned the decision of a district court judge, who had ruled that the local school district was not obligated to educate a 13-year-old boy with multiple and severe disabilities because he could not benefit from special education. |
| 1999 | *Cedar Rapids v. Garret F.* | U.S. Supreme Court rules that a local school district must pay for the one-on-one nursing care for a medically fragile student who required continuous monitoring of his ventilator and other health-maintenance routines. The case reaffirmed and extended the Court's ruling in the 1984 Tatro case that schools must provide any and all health services needed for students with disabilities to attend school as long as performance of those services does not require a licensed physician. |

"schools cannot avoid the provisions of EHA [Education of the Handicapped Amendments] by returning to the practices that were widespread prior to the Act's passage … unilaterally excluding certain handicapped children from a public education on the ground that they are uneducable."

Challenges to existing services and differing views on whether a particular program is appropriate or least restrictive are certain to continue. Although the courts will probably grant some requests in the future and deny others, it is now a well-established principle that each student with disabilities is entitled to an individualized program of special instruction and related services that will enable him to benefit from an education in as least restrictive a setting as possible.

# Related Legislation

*Gifted and Talented Children.*   IDEA does not apply to gifted and talented children. However, other federal legislation has addressed the specialized needs of these students. P.L. 95–561, the Gifted and Talented Children's Education Act of 1978, provides financial incentives for state and local education agencies to develop programs for students who are gifted and talented. The law provides for the identification of gifted and talented children and includes special procedures for identifying and educating those from disadvantaged backgrounds. The law makes funding available for in-service training programs, research, and other projects aimed at meeting the needs of gifted and talented students.

In 1982 the Education Consolidation Act phased out the federal Office of Gifted and Talented and merged gifted education with 29 other programs. Federal dollars to support these 30 wide-ranging education programs (K–12) are sent to the states in the form of block grants. Each state has the responsibility to determine what portion, if any, of the block grant funds will be used to support programs and services for students who are gifted and talented.

Congress passed the Jacob K. Javits Gifted and Talented Student Education Act (P.L. 100–297) in 1988 as part of the Elementary and Secondary Education Bill. This moderately funded act (approximately $10 million in 1996) provided federal money for demonstration grants, a national research center, and a position within the U.S. Department of Education with responsibility for gifted education. The Javits Act specified that the federal funds be directed primarily to economically disadvantaged children, limited-English-proficient students, and students with disabilities who are gifted and talented.

*Section 504 of the Rehabilitation Act of 1973.*   Another important law that extends civil rights to people with disabilities is Section 504 of the Rehabilitation Act of 1973. This regulation states, in part, that "no otherwise qualified handicapped individual shall, solely by reason of his handicap, be excluded from the participation in, be denied the benefits of, or be subjected to discrimination in any program or activity receiving federal financial assistance." This law, worded almost identically to the Civil Rights Act of 1964 (which prohibited discrimination based on race, color, or national origin), has expanded opportunities to children and adults with disabilities in education, employment, and various other settings. It requires provision of "auxiliary aids for students with impaired sensory, manual, or speaking skills"—for example, readers for students who are blind and people to assist students with physical disabilities in moving from place to place. This requirement does not mean that schools, colleges, and employers must have all such aids available at all times; it simply means that no person with disabilities may be excluded from a program because of the lack of an appropriate aid.

Section 504 is not a federal grant program; unlike IDEA, it does not provide any federal money to assist people with disabilities. Rather, it "imposes a duty on every recipient of federal funds not to discriminate against handicapped persons" (Johnson, 1986, p. 8). "Recipient," of course, includes public school districts, virtually all of which receive federal support. Most colleges and universities have also been affected; even many students in private institutions receive federal financial aid. The Office of Civil Rights conducts periodic compliance reviews and acts on complaints when parents, disabled individuals, or others contend that a school district is violating Section 504.

Architectural accessibility for students, teachers, and others with physical and sensory impairments is an important feature of Section 504; however, the law does not call for a completely barrier-free environment. Emphasis is on accessibility to programs, not on physical modification of all existing structures. If a chemistry class is required for a premedical program of study, for example, a college might make this program accessible to a student with physical disabilities by reassigning the class to an accessible location or providing assistance to the student in traveling to an otherwise inaccessible location. All sections of all courses need not be made accessible, but a college should not segregate students with disabilities by assigning them all to a particular section regardless of disability. Like IDEA, Section 504 calls for nondiscriminatory placement in the "most integrated setting appropriate" and has served as the basis for many court cases over alleged discrimination against individuals with disabilities, particularly in their right to employment. For a discussion of what teachers need to know about Section 504, see T. E. C. Smith (2002). Table 1.5 summarizes federal legislation regarding the education and rights of individuals with disabilities.

*Americans with Disabilities Act.*   The Americans with Disabilities Act (P.L. 101–336) was signed into law in 1990. Patterned after Section 504 of the Rehabilitation Act of 1973, the Americans with Disabilities Act (ADA) extends civil rights protection of persons with disabilities to private-sector employment, all public services, public accommodation, transportation, and telecommunications. A person with a disability is defined in ADA as a person (1) with a mental or physical impairment that substantially limits her in a major life activity (e.g., walking, talking, working, self-care); (2) with a record of such an impairment (e.g., a person who no longer has heart disease but who is discriminated against because of that history); or (3) who is regarded as having such an impairment (e.g., a person with significant facial disfiguration due to a burn who is not limited in any major life activity but is discriminated against). The major provisions of ADA are as follows:

The Americans with Disabilities Act requires employers to make reasonable accommodations to allow a person with disabilities to perform essential job functions.

- Employers with 15 or more employees may not refuse to hire or promote a person because of a disability if that person is qualified to perform the job. Also, the employer must make reasonable accommodations that will allow a person with a disability to perform essential functions of the job. Such modifications in job requirements or situation must be made if they will not impose undue hardship on the employer.
- All new vehicles purchased by public transit authorities must be accessible to people with disabilities. All rail stations must be made accessible, and at least one car per train in existing rail systems must be made accessible.
- It is illegal for public accommodations to exclude or refuse persons with disabilities. Public accommodations are everyday businesses and services, such as hotels, restaurants, grocery stores, and parks. All new buildings must be made accessible, and existing facilities must remove barriers if the removal can be accomplished without much difficulty or expense.
- Companies offering telephone service to the general public must offer relay services to individuals who use telecommunications devices for the deaf (e.g., text telephones) 24 hours per day, 7 days per week.

## No Child Left Behind Act

The most recent and far-reaching federal legislation on education was enacted when Congress reauthorized the Elementary and Secondary Education Act in 2001 and renamed it the No Child Left Behind Act (NCLB). A U.S. Department of Education (2002) publication that introduced NCLB to educators described the legislation as

> a landmark in education reform designed to improve student achievement and change the culture of America's schools. This new law, which President George W. Bush described as "the cornerstone of my administration," represents a sweeping overhaul of federal efforts to support elementary and secondary education in the United States. (p. ix)

The ultimate goal of NCLB is that all children will be proficient in all subject matter by the year 2014 and will be taught by qualified teachers highly trained in their subjects. States are expected to make annual progress toward the 100% goal by 2014, with initial emphasis

## TABLE 1.5 Federal legislation concerning the education and rights of exceptional children

| Date | Legislation | Educational Implications |
|------|-------------|--------------------------|
| 1958 | National Defense Education Act (P.L. 85–926) | Provided funds for training professionals to train teachers of children with mental retardation |
| 1961 | Special Education Act (P.L. 87–276) | Provided funds for training professionals to train teachers of deaf children |
| 1963 | Mental Retardation Facility and Community Center Construction Act (P.L. 88–164) | Extended support given in P.L. 85–926 to training teachers of children with other disabilities |
| 1965 | Elementary and Secondary Education Act (P.L. 89–10) | Provided money to states and local districts for developing programs for economically disadvantaged and disabled children |
| 1966 | Amendment to Title I of the Elementary and Secondary Education Act (P.L. 89–313) | Provided funding for state-supported programs in institutions and other settings for children with disabilities |
| 1966 | Amendments to the Elementary and Secondary Education Act (P.L. 89–750) | Created the federal Bureau of Education for the Handicapped (today's Office of Special Education) |
| 1968 | Handicapped Children's Early Assistance Act (P.L. 90–538) | Established the "first chance network" of experimental programs for preschool children with disabilities |
| 1969 | Elementary, Secondary, and Other Educational Amendments (P.L. 91–230) | Defined learning disabilities and provided funds for state-level programs for children with learning disabilities |
| 1970 | Education Amendments of 1970 (P.L. 91–230) | Mandated a study of the gifted that resulted in the *Marland Report* (1972), which many states used as a basis for building programs for gifted and talented students |
| 1973 | Section 504 of the Rehabilitation Act (P.L. 93–112) | Declared that a person cannot be excluded on the basis of disability alone from any program or activity receiving federal funds |
| 1974 | Education Amendments (P.L. 93–380) | Extended previous legislation; provided money to state and local districts for programs for gifted and talented students for the first time; protected the rights of children with disabilities and their parents in placement decisions |
| 1975 | Developmental Disabilities Assistance and Bill of Rights Act (P.L. 94–103) | Affirmed the rights of citizens with mental retardation (MR) and cited areas in which services must be provided for people with MR and other developmental disabilities |
| 1975 | Education for All Handicapped Children Act (EAHCA) (P.L. 94–142) | Mandated free, appropriate public education for all children with disabilities ages 6 to 21; protected the rights of children with disabilities and their parents in educational decision making; required the development of an IEP for each child with a disability; stated that students with disabilities must receive educational services in the least restrictive environment. |
| 1978 | Gifted and Talented Children's Education Act of 1978 (P.L. 95–561) | Provided funds for in-service training programs, research, and other projects aimed at meeting the needs of gifted and talented students |
| 1983 | Amendments to the Education of the Handicapped Act (P.L. 98–199) | Required states to collect data on the number of youth with disabilities exiting their systems and to address the needs of secondary students making the transition to adulthood; gave incentives to states to provide services to infants and preschool children with disabilities |
| 1984 | Developmental Disabilities Assistance and Bill of Rights Acts (P.L. 98–527) | Mandated the development of employment-related training activities for adults with disabilities |
| 1986 | Handicapped Children's Protection Act (P.L. 99–372) | Provided authority for the reimbursement of attorney's fees to parents who prevail in a hearing or court case to secure an appropriate education for their child |

TABLE 1.5 *continued*

| Date | Legislation | Educational Implications |
| --- | --- | --- |
| 1986 | Education for the Handicapped Act Amendments of 1986 (P.L. 99–457) | Required states to provide free, appropriate education to all 3- to 5-year-olds with disabilities who were eligible to apply for federal preschool funding; included incentive grants to encourage states to develop comprehensive interdisciplinary services for infants and toddlers (birth through age 2) and their families |
| 1986 | Rehabilitation Act Amendments (P.L. 99–506) | Set forth regulations for the development of supported employment programs for adults with disabilities |
| 1988 | Jacob K. Javits Gifted and Talented Students Education Act (P.L. 100–297) | Provided federal funds in support of research, teacher training, and program development for the education of gifted and talented students |
| 1988 | Technology-Related Assistance for Individuals with Disabilities Act of 1988 (P.L. 100–407) | Created statewide programs of technology assistance for persons of all ages with disabilities |
| 1990 | Americans with Disabilities Act (P.L. 101–336) | Provided civil rights protection against discrimination to citizens with disabilities in private sector employment; provided access to all public services, public accommodations, transportation, and telecommunications |
| 1990 | Individuals with Disabilities Education Act Amendments (IDEA) of 1990 (P.L. 101–476) | Renamed the EAHCA; added autism and traumatic brain injury as new categories of disability; required all IEPs to include a statement of needed transition services no later than age 16; expanded the definition of related services to include rehabilitation counseling and social work services |
| 1994 | Goals 2000: Educate America Act (P.L. 103–227) | Provided federal funds for the development and implementation of educational reforms to help achieve eight national education goals by the year 2000. |
| 1997 | Individuals with Disabilities Education Act (IDEA) of 1997 (P.L. 105–17) | Added several major provisions including: a regular education teacher must be a member of the IEP team; students with disabilities must have access to the general education curriculum; the IEP must address positive behavior support plans where appropriate; students with disabilities must be included in state- or district-wide testing programs; if a school seeks to discipline a student with disabilities resulting in change of placement, suspension, or expulsion for more than 10 days, a "manifestation determination" by the IEP team must find that the student's misconduct was not related to the disability |
| 2001 | No Child Left Behind Act of 2001 (Reauthorization of the Elementary and Secondary Education Act (P.L. 105-17) | NCLB's ultimate goal is that all children will be proficient in all subject matter by the year 2014. School districts are expected to make annual progress toward the 100% goal, ensure that all children are taught by "highly qualified" teachers, and use curriculum and instructional methods validated by rigorous scientific research. Schools that do not make sufficient yearly progress are initially targeted for assistance and then subject to corrective action and ultimately restructuring. |
| 2004 | Individuals with Disabilities Education Improvement Act of 2004 (H.R. 1350) | Retained major components and principles of IDEA; key changes include: pilot program for reducing paperwork, benchmarks and short-term objectives required only in IEPs for students who take alternative assessments related to alternative achievement standards; pilot program for multi-year IEPs; "response-to-instruction" may be used to identify learning disabilities; "highly qualified" special education teacher defined; under special circumstances (e.g., brings a weapon to school) a student with disabilities may be removed from school to an interim setting for up to 45 days whether or not the misconduct was related to the child's disability. |

on assuring that every child can read at or above grade level by the end of third grade and that all teachers teaching in core academic subjects are "highly qualified" by the end of the 2005–2006 school year. NCLB has four key principles—stronger accountability for results, greater flexibility for schools' use of federal funds, more options for parents, and an emphasis on curriculum and instructional methods that have been demonstrated to work.

*Accountability.*　Although IDEA already required students with disabilities to participate in state- and district-wide assessments, NCLB requires annual tests in reading and math in grades 3 through 8 for all students (Ziegler, 2002). Test results must be disaggregated for students by poverty levels, race, ethnicities, disabilities, and limited English proficiency. Each school and children from each category must achieve state-determined pass rates, which will gradually rise. Annual school "report cards" will provide comparative information on the performance of each school. By doing so, they will empower parents to make more informed choices about their children's educations. These report cards are intended to show not only how well students are doing on meeting standards but also the progress that disaggregated groups are making in closing achievement gaps. Districts and schools that do not make sufficient yearly progress toward state proficiency goals for their students are initially targeted for assistance and then are subject to corrective action and ultimately restructuring. Schools that meet or exceed objectives will be eligible for "academic achievement awards." Thus, the term *high-stakes testing* refers to the system of sanctions for schools that do not meet and incentives for the schools that do.

*Flexibility and Local Control.*　NCLB gives states and school districts increased flexibility in how they can use federal education funds. Most districts may transfer up to 50% of the federal formula grant funds they receive under the Improving Teacher Quality State Grants, Educational Technology, Innovative Programs, and Safe and Drug-Free Schools programs to any one of these programs or to their Title I program without separate approval.

*Enhanced Parental Choice.*　NCLB gives parents of children in low-performing schools several options. Parents with children in schools that fail to meet state standards for two consecutive years may transfer their children to a better-performing public school, including a public charter school, within their district. If they do so, the district must provide transportation, using Title I funds if necessary. Students from low-income families in schools that fail to meet state standards for 3 years are eligible to receive supplemental educational services—including tutoring, after-school services, and summer school. In addition, NCLB provides increased support to parents, educators, and communities to create new charter schools. Parents can also choose to have their students attend a safe school within their district if they attend persistently dangerous schools or are the victim of a violent crime while in their school.

*Focus on What Works.*　NCLB puts a special emphasis on determining what educational programs and practices have been clearly demonstrated to be effective through rigorous scientific research. The NCLB-funded Reading First programs are a prime example. NCLB provides support for scientifically based reading instruction in the early grades under the new Reading First program and in preschool under the new Early Reading First program. Reading First is designed to help states, school districts, and schools ensure that every child can read at grade level or above by the end of third grade through the implementation of instructional programs and materials, assessments, and professional development grounded in scientifically based reading research. Evidence-based instructional programs focus on the five key areas that research has identified as essential components of reading instruction—phonemic awareness, alphabetic principle (i.e., phonics), fluency with text, vocabulary, and comprehension (National Reading Panel, 2000; National Research Council, 1998).

*Implications for Students with Disabilities.*　It is too early to know how NCLB will affect students with disabilities and the quality of education they receive. The inclusion of all students' scores on high-stakes tests in a school district's report card has resulted in higher expectations for achievement by students receiving special education and increased accountability of schools to help them attain it. Some students with mild to moderate disabilities are provided with accommodations (e.g., additional time, large print) when taking district- and statewide tests. Students with severe disabilities for whom standard academic achievement tests would be inappropriate can take alternative assessments (e.g., a video portfolio demonstrating improvements in language or adaptive behavior) if their IEP team recommends them (Bolt & Thurlow, 2004). NCLB expects all students to make adequate progress, but it is not yet clear how states will define adequate progress for students with severe intellectual disabilities (Browder & Cooper-Duffy, 2003).

Noting that NCLB is a complex and controversial law, Yell and Drasgow (2005) state, "For the first time, education is accountable for making improvement in students' academic performance. NCLB points educators toward the tool that will allow schools to make meaningful changes in the academic achievement of their students: scientifically-based research" (p. 118). Indeed, the emphasis on scientifically proven curriculum and instruction, especially with the Reading First grants, offers the promise of effective reading instruction in the early grades, which could reduce the number of children who require special education because of reading problems.

While acknowledging some of positive aspects of NCLB, Moores compared it to the overly optimistic, and subsequently scrapped Goals 2000: Educate America Act of 1994.

> Despite its failure to meet unrealistic targets, the Goals 2000 effort had some positive impact. It drew attention to the need for improved instruction and accountability, especially in terms of measurable outcomes. It also provided the background for the much more ambitious No Child Left Behind legislation, which may be thought of as a sort of Goals 2014, but with more teeth and more financial backing than Goals 2000.... There is a clear commitment to improving American education. As with Goals 2000, NCLB has some very positive elements to it.
>
> Having said that, NCLB could also be an unmitigated disaster. There are political and financial considerations. Bipartisan support seems to be eroding, with increasing criticism of the legislation and its implementation. Originally 32 billion dollars was authorized for NCLB for fiscal year 2004, but Congress only appropriated 22 billion dollars, with the states, many of which are facing budget deficits, expected to pick up the slack and still meet the federal requirements. This raises the specter of one more underfunded federal mandate.
>
> The main problem, of course, is that the goals are impossible; 100% success will never be attained and we all know it. In Garrison Keillor's mythical Norwegian-American town of Lake Woebegone in Minnesota all of the men were handsome, all of the women were beautiful, and all of the children were above average. Perhaps all of those children would meet the proficiency standards, but in real life it will never happen.
>
> ...I went on the web to check results for six of the largest school districts for my home state, Maryland, for 2002–2003. The goal for reading was that only 43.4%—not 100%—of students had to score at the proficient level. The results were disappointing, but expected, with children from low income or limited English environments struggling. The biggest gap, however, occurred with children in the special education category. Special education children did not meet the 43.4% goal in any school district, meaning that all the districts technically could be labeled as failing. This is patently foolish. We all know that when NCLB was passed little or no consideration was given to children receiving special services. (Moores, 2004, p. 348)

## WHAT IS SPECIAL EDUCATION?

Special education is a complex enterprise that can be defined and evaluated from many perspectives. One may, for example, view special education as a legislatively governed enterprise whose practitioners are concerned about issues such as due process procedures for informing parents about their right to participate in decisions about their children's education programs and the extent to which all of the school district's IEPs include each component as required by IDEA. From a purely administrative point of view, special education can be seen as the part of a school system's operation that requires certain teacher-pupil ratios in the classroom and uses special formulas to determine levels of funding for related-services personnel. And from a sociopolitical perspective, special education can be seen as an outgrowth of the civil rights movement, a demonstration of society's changing attitudes about people with disabilities. Each of these perspectives has some validity, and each has and continues to play an important role in defining what special education is and how it is practiced. None of these views, however, reveals the fundamental purpose or essence of special education as *instructionally based intervention*.

## Special Education As Intervention

Special education is, first of all, purposeful intervention designed to prevent, eliminate, and/or overcome the obstacles that might keep an individual with disabilities from learning and from full and active participation in school and society. There are three basic types of intervention: preventive, remedial, and compensatory.

*Preventive Intervention.*   Preventive intervention is designed to keep potential or minor problems from becoming a disability. Preventive intervention includes actions that stop an event from happening and those that reduce a problem or condition that has already been identified. Prevention can occur at three levels (Simeonsson, 1994):

- **Primary prevention** is designed to reduce the number of new cases (**incidence**) of a problem; it consists of efforts to eliminate or counteract risk factors so that a disability is never acquired. Primary prevention efforts are aimed at all relevant persons. For example, in a schoolwide program to prevent behavior disorders, school- and classroom-wide systems of positive behavior support would be provided for all students, staff, and settings (Sugai & Horner, 2005).
- **Secondary prevention** is aimed at reducing the number existing cases (**prevalence**) of an already identified problem or condition or eliminating the effects of existing risk factors; it is aimed at individuals exposed to or displaying specific risk factors. To continue the example of a schoolwide program to prevent behavior disorders, specialized interventions would be aimed only at those students exhibiting early signs of troubled behavior.
- **Tertiary prevention** is intended to minimize the impact of a specific condition, to prevent the effects of a disability from worsening; it is aimed at individuals with a disability. For example, intensive interventions would be aimed at students identified with emotional and behavioral disorders.

Preventive efforts are most promising when they begin as early as possible—even before birth, in many cases. In later chapters, we explore some of the promising new methods for preventing and minimizing the effects of disabilities. Unfortunately, primary and secondary prevention programs have only just begun to affect the incidence, prevalence, and severity of disabilities in this country. And it is likely that we will be well into the 21st century before we achieve a significant reduction in the incidence of disabilities. In the meantime, we must rely on remedial and compensatory efforts to help individuals with disabilities achieve fuller and more independent lives.

*Preventive, remedial, and compensatory interventions*

Council for Exceptional Children   Content Standards for Beginning Teachers—Common Core: Models, theories, and philosophies that form the basis for special education practice (CC1K1).

*Remedial Intervention.*   Remediation attempts to eliminate specific effects of a disability. In fact, the word *remediation* is primarily an educational term; the word *rehabilitation* is used more often by social service agencies. Both have a common purpose: to teach the person with disabilities skills for independent and successful functioning. In school, those skills may be academic (reading, writing, computing), social (getting along with others; following instructions, schedules, and other daily routines), personal (eating, dressing, using the toilet without assistance), and/or vocational (career and job skills to prepare secondary students for the world of work). The underlying assumption of remedial intervention is that a person with disabilities needs special instruction to succeed in typical settings.

*Compensatory Intervention.* Compensatory interventions involve teaching special skills or the use of devices that enable successful functioning. This third type of intervention involves teaching a substitute (i.e., compensatory) skill that enables a person to perform a task in spite of the disability. For example, although remedial instruction might help a child with cerebral palsy learn to use her hands in the same way that others do for some tasks, a headstick and a template placed over a computer keyboard may compensate for her limited fine-motor control and enable her to type instead of write lessons by hand. Compensatory interventions are designed to give the person with a disability an asset that nondisabled individuals do not need—whether it be a device such as a headstick or special training such as mobility instruction for a child without vision.

## Special Education As Instruction

Ultimately, *teaching* is what special education is most about. But the same can be said of all of education. What, then, is *special* about special education? One way to answer that question is to examine special education in terms of the *who*, *what*, *how*, and *where* of its teaching.

*Who.* We have already identified the most important *who* in special education: the exceptional children whose educational needs necessitate an individually planned program of instruction. Teachers, both general education classroom teachers and special educators (those who have completed specialized training programs to prepare them to work with students with special needs), provide the instruction that is the heart of each child's individualized program of education. Working with special educators and regular classroom teachers are many other professionals (e.g., school psychologists, speech-language pathologists, physical therapists, counselors) and paraprofessionals (e.g., classroom aides) who help provide the educational and related services that exceptional children need. This interdisciplinary team of professionals, working together with parents and families, bears the primary responsibility for helping exceptional children learn despite their special needs.

*What.* Special education can sometimes be differentiated from general education by its curriculum—that is, by *what* is taught. Although every student with disabilities needs access to and support in learning as much of the general education curriculum as possible, the IEP goals and objectives for some special education students will not be found in state standards or the school district's curriculum guide. Some children with disabilities need intensive, systematic instruction to learn skills that typically developing children acquire without instruction. The term *functional curriculum* is often used to describe the knowledge and skills needed by students with disabilities to achieve as much success and independence as they can in daily living, personal-social, school, community, and work settings. For example, self-help skills such as dressing, eating, and toileting are a critically important component of the school curriculum for many students with severe disabilities. Also, as discussed previously, some children are taught certain skills to compensate for or reduce the handicapping effects of a disability. A child who is blind may be taught how to read and write in braille, whereas a sighted child does not need these skills.

*How.* Special education can also be differentiated from general education by its use of specialized, or adapted, materials and methods. This difference is obvious when you observe a special educator use sign language with students who are deaf or witness another teach a child how to communicate his wishes by pointing to pictures in a special booklet he carries with him. When watching a special educator gradually and systematically withdraw verbal and physical prompts while helping a student learn to perform the steps of a task, you may find the differentiated nature of special education instruction less obvious; but it is no less specialized.

Special education is individually planned, specially designed, intensive instruction.

*Where.*    Special education can sometimes be identified by *where* it takes place. Although the majority of children with disabilities receive most of their education in regular classrooms, the others are someplace else—mostly in separate classrooms and separate residential and day schools. And many of those in regular classrooms spend a portion of each day in a resource room, where they receive individualized instruction. Table 1.6 lists the definitions of six educational placements used by the U.S. Department of Education. (To learn how students in one resource room obtain teacher assistance, see Teaching & Learning, "Signaling for Help," later in this chapter.)

Special educators also teach in many environments not usually thought of as school. An early childhood special educator may spend much of his time teaching parents how to work with their infant or toddler at home. Special education teachers, particularly those who work with students with severe disabilities, often conduct *community-based instruction,* helping their students learn and practice functional daily living and job skills in the actual settings where they must be used (Owens-Johnson & Hamill, 2002).

Three out of four school-age children with disabilities received at least part of their education in regular classrooms during the 2003–2004 school year (see Figure 1.1). This includes 49.9% who were served in the regular classroom and 27.7% who were served for part of each school day in a resource room, a special setting in which a special educator provides individualized instruction. About one-fifth of all children with disabilities are educated in separate classrooms within a regular school. About 3% of school-age students with disabilities—usually those with severe disabilities—are educated in special schools. Residential schools serve less than 1% of all children with disabilities, as do nonschool environments such as homebound or hospital programs.

The vast majority of children in the two largest groups of students with disabilities spend at least part of the school day in regular classrooms: 86% of children with learning disabilities and 95% of children with speech or language impairments (see Table 1.7 on p. 43). In contrast, only 42% of children with mental retardation, 44% of children with

**TABLE 1.6** **Federal government's definitions of educational placements for students with disabilities**

| Educational Setting | Definition |
| --- | --- |
| Regular classroom | Students receive a majority of their education program in a regular classroom and receive special education and related services outside the regular classroom for less than 21% of the school day. |
| Resource room | Students receive special education and related services outside the regular classroom for at least 21% but no more than 60% of the school day. |
| Separate classroom | Students receive special education and related services outside the regular classroom for 61% to 100% of the school day. |
| Separate school | Students receive special education and related services in a public or private separate day school for students with disabilities, at public expense, for more than 50% of the school day. |
| Residential facility | Students receive special education and related services in a public or privately operated residential facility in which children receive care or services 24 hours a day. |
| Homebound/hospital | Students receive special education and related services in a hospital or homebound program. |

*Source:* Adapted from U.S. Department of Education. (2000). Twenty-second annual report to Congress on the implementation of the Individuals with Disabilities Education Act (p. II-14). Washington, DC: Author.

**FIGURE 1.1**
**Percentage of all students with disabilities ages 6 through 21 served in six educational placements (2003–2004 school year)**
*Source:* From U.S. Department of Education. (2004). *Individuals with Disabilities Education Act* (IDEA) data (Table AB2). Washington, DC: Author. Available at **http://www.ideadata.org/ PartBdata.asp**.

Notes: Separate school includes both public and private separate school facilities.  Residential facility includes both public and private residential facilities.

autism, 29% of children with multiple disabilities, and 36% of children with deaf-blindness were educated in regular classrooms for part of each day during the 2003–2004 school year, although these figures represent increases over those of previous years.

## Defining Features of Special Education

What, then, is special education? At one level, it is an important part of society's response to the needs of exceptional children and the rights of individuals with disabilities—a response brought about by parental advocacy, litigation, legislation, and, increasingly, self-advocacy by disabled persons themselves. At another level, special education is a profession

# Signaling for Help

Resource rooms are busy places. Students come and go throughout the school day, each according to an individualized schedule. Each student who comes to the resource room does so because of a need for intensive individualized instruction. The IEP objectives for any given group of students in a resource room at any one time often cover a wide range of academic and social skills. Because of the varied skill levels and the ever-changing student groupings in the resource room, the special education teacher must often manage several types and levels of instruction at once. To accomplish this, students are often assigned individualized learning activities. Resource room teachers face a difficult challenge: the need to be in several places at once. While students work at their desks, learning centers, or computers, the teacher moves about the room, providing prompts, encouragement, praise, and corrective feedback to individual students as needed.

Students in a resource room are usually working on the skills for which they need the most help—that is, difficult material they have not yet mastered. Therefore, an effective and efficient system with which students can signal the resource room teacher for assistance is needed. Hand raising, the typical attention-getting signal in the classroom, poses several problems. It is difficult to continue to work while holding one's hand in the air, a situation that results in a great deal of down time while students wait for the teacher to get to them. In addition, if several students are waving their hands in competition for the teacher's attention, it is distracting to other students and to the teacher. If unsuccessful in getting the teacher's help, students may give up trying whenever they run into difficulty. Even worse, students who are unsuccessful in obtaining the teacher's assistance may stop discriminating their need for help and simply continue to practice errors.

Students need an effective, quiet means of signaling for help that allows them to keep working with the assurance

Signal flags are a simple and effective way for students to obtain teacher assistance and feedback.

that their teacher will recognize their need for help. In Ronni Hochman Spratt's resource room for middle school students with disabilities, each student has a small flag made of colored felt, a dowel rod, and a 1 1/4-inch cube of wood. (You'll read more about Ms. Spratt and her students in Chapter 5.) When one of Ronni's students needs assistance or wants her to check completed work, the student simply stands the flag up on his desk. While waiting for the teacher, the student can either go on to another item or work on materials in a special folder. With this simple and inexpensive system, down time is greatly reduced; and neither Ronni nor her students are distracted by hand waving or calling out. (An effective signaling device can also be made from an empty can wrapped with red and green construction paper [Kerr & Nelson, 2002]. Students turn the can on one end or the other to signal "I'm working" or "I need help.")

Ronni asked her students to write down what they thought of the signal flag system after using it for about 3 months.

> This is one of the best way to work in sted of raising your hand you raise your flag and keep on working but if you raise you hand you can't keep working. That is special because I get more work done. If she is working with some one els you raise it and she will get to you as fast as she can. (Brent)

The flags in Miss Hochman's room are used for assistance from the teacher. When Miss Hochman is working you raise your flag and she will help you as soon as she has time. But you keep on working, like going on to the next problem. (Pam)

 To learn more about these strategies and answer questions about what you have learned, go to the Teaching & Learning module in Chapter 1 of the Companion Website, **www.prenhall.com/heward**.

**TABLE 1.7** **Percentage of students ages 6 through 21 served in six educational environments (2003–2004 school year)**

| Disability Category | Regular Classroom | Resource Room | Separate Classroom | Separate School | Residential School | Homebound or Hospital |
|---|---|---|---|---|---|---|
| Specific learning disabilities | 48.7 | 37.3 | 13.0 | 0.6 | 0.2 | 0.2 |
| Speech or language impairments | 88.2 | 6.8 | 4.6 | 0.3 | <0.1 | <0.1 |
| Mental retardation | 11.6 | 30.2 | 51.8 | 5.3 | 0.5 | 0.5 |
| Emotional disturbance | 30.3 | 22.5 | 30.2 | 12.0 | 3.7 | 1.2 |
| Other health impairments | 51.1 | 30.5 | 15.0 | 1.5 | 0.3 | 1.6 |
| Multiple disabilities | 12.1 | 17.2 | 45.8 | 20.3 | 2.4 | 2.2 |
| Autism | 26.8 | 17.7 | 43.9 | 10.2 | 1.1 | 0.4 |
| Orthopedic impairments | 46.7 | 20.9 | 26.2 | 3.6 | 0.8 | 1.8 |
| Hearing impairments | 44.9 | 19.1 | 22.2 | 6.9 | 6.6 | 0.2 |
| Developmental delay | 51.2 | 28.1 | 18.7 | 1.7 | 0.1 | 0.2 |
| Visual impairments | 54.6 | 16.9 | 15.7 | 5.9 | 6.3 | 0.6 |
| Traumatic brain injury | 34.6 | 29.9 | 27.1 | 5.9 | 0.9 | 1.5 |
| Deaf-blindness | 22.2 | 13.9 | 33.6 | 16.6 | 12.3 | 1.4 |
| All disabilities | 49.9 | 27.7 | 18.5 | 2.8 | 0.7 | 0.4 |

*Source:* From U.S. Department of Education. (2004). *Individuals with Disabilities Education Act* (IDEA) data (Table AB2). Washington, DC: Author. Available at *http://www.ideadata.org/PartBdata.asp*

with its own history, cultural practices, tools, and research base focused on the learning needs of exceptional children and adults. But at the level where exceptional children most meaningfully and frequently contact it, *special education is individually planned, specialized, intensive, goal-directed instruction.* When practiced most effectively and ethically, special education is also characterized by the use of research-based teaching methods, the application of which is guided by direct and frequent measures of student performance (Bushell & Baer, 1994; Greenwood & Maheady, 1997). Table 1.8 shows the dimensions and defining features of special education.

*Defining features of special education*

Council for Exceptional Children
Content Standards for Beginning Teachers—Common Core: Models, theories, and philosophies that form the basis for special education practice (CC1K1).

## CURRENT AND FUTURE CHALLENGES

Special education has accomplished a great deal in recent years, and there is legitimate reason for those in the field to feel good about its progress. Much has been accomplished in terms of making a free, appropriate education available to many children with disabilities who were previously denied access to one. Much has been learned about how to effectively teach children with severe disabilities—those whom many previously had assumed were incapable of learning. Special educators and families are learning to work as partners on behalf of exceptional children. Technological advances have helped many students overcome

**TABLE 1.8  Dimensions and defining features of special education instruction**

| Dimension | Defining Features |
| --- | --- |
| Individually planned | • Learning goals and objectives selected for each student based on assessment results and input from parents and student<br>• Teaching methods and instructional materials selected and/or adapted for each student<br>• Setting(s) where instruction will occur determined relative to opportunities for student to learn and use targeted skills |
| Specialized | • Sometimes involves unique or adapted teaching procedures seldom used in general education (e.g., constant time delay, token reinforcement, self-monitoring)<br>• Incorporates a variety of instructional materials and supports—both natural and contrived—to help student acquire and use targeted learning objectives<br>• Related services (e.g., audiology, physical therapy) provided as needed<br>• Assistive technology (e.g., adapted cup holder, head-operated switch to select communication symbols) provided as needed |
| Intensive | • Instruction presented with attention to detail, precision, structure, clarity, and repeated practice<br>• "Relentless, urgent" instruction (Zigmond & Baker, 1995)<br>• Efforts made to provide incidental, naturalistic opportunities for student to use targeted knowledge and skills |
| Goal-directed | • Purposeful instruction intended to help student achieve the greatest possible personal self-sufficiency and success in present and future environments<br>• Value/goodness of instruction determined by student's attainment of outcomes |
| Research-based methods | • Recognition that all teaching approaches are not equally effective<br>• Instructional programs and teaching procedures selected on basis of research support |
| Guided by student performance | • Careful, ongoing monitoring of student progress<br>• Frequent and direct measures/assessment of student learning used to inform modifications in instruction |

physical or communication disabilities. Throughout the remaining chapters, many of these advances will be examined; but it is difficult to describe the state of the art of a large and ever-changing discipline such as special education. It is even more difficult to predict what special education will look like and be able to accomplish in the future.

Although the beginnings of the field can be traced back several centuries (Safford & Safford, 1996), in many respects special education is still in its formative years. There is a great deal that must be done to make it more useful to those who need it most. Here are four areas that many in the field consider critical.

## Close the Research-to-Practice Gap

Special education can be nothing more, or less, than the quality of instruction provided by teachers (Heward & Dardig, 2001). Contrary to the contentions of some authors, special education research has produced a significant and reliable knowledge base about effective teaching practices (Lovitt, 2000; Spear-Swerling & Sternberg, 2001; Vaughn, Gersten, & Chard, 2000). No knowledgeable person will argue that research has discovered everything that is important to know about teaching exceptional students. There are many questions to be answered, the pursuit of which will no doubt lead to other questions yet to be asked.

While there is a significant gap between what is relatively well understood and what is poorly understood or not understood at all, the more distressing gap may be between what research has discovered about teaching and learning and what is practiced in many classrooms (Heward, 2005). For example, scientific research has helped us discover a great deal of knowledge about areas such as what features of early reading instruction will reduce the number of children who later develop reading problems (Kame' enui, Good, & Harn, 2005; National Reading Panel, 2000), how to enhance the success of students with learning disabilities in content-area classes (Deshler et al., 2001), how to teach students the skills they need to more effectively self-determine and self-manage their lives (Algozzine, Browder, Karvonen, Test, & Wood, 2001), and what components of secondary special education programs increase students' success in making the transition from school to work (Kohler & Field, 2003). Unfortunately, numerous studies report that the education received by many students with disabilities does not take advantage of that knowledge (e.g., Moody, Vaughn, Hughes, & Fischer, 2000; Wagner, Blackorby, Cameto, & Newman, 1994; Wehby, Symons, Canale, & Go, 1998).

It is critically important for special education to close the gap between the field's knowledge of evidence-based practices and the curriculum and instruction provided to students (Carnine, 1997; Gersten, 2001; Heward, 2003; Vaughn, Klingner, & Hughes, 2000). Instructional practices supported by scientific research are featured in the Teaching & Learning boxes and described throughout this text.

*Using research-based practices*

**Council for Exceptional Children** Content Standards for Beginning Teachers—Common Core: Methods to remain current regarding research-validated practice (CC9K4).

## Increase the Availability and Intensity of Early Intervention and Prevention Programs

It is better to intervene earlier than later. The recent increase in special education and family-focused services for infants, toddlers, and preschoolers who have disabilities or are at risk for developmental delay is a positive sign. More efforts must be made, however, to ensure that high-quality early intervention and special education preschool programs become more widely available.

## Improve Students' Transition from School to Adult Life

When special education is judged by its ultimate product—the youth who leave secondary school programs—it becomes clear how much further the field must progress. Too many young adults with disabilities are unsuccessful and unhappy in their postschool adjustment. Special education must improve the transition of youth with disabilities from school to life in their communities.

## Improve the Special Education–General Education Partnership

As stated previously, most of the more than 6 million school-age students with disabilities spend the majority of the school day in the regular classroom. This is borne out by a national survey that found that 96% of general education teachers reported that they were currently teaching students with disabilities or had done so in the past (U.S. Department of Education, 2001). However, fewer than a third of those teachers felt they were well prepared to teach students with special needs.

In addition to the 10% to 12% of the school-age population receiving special education services, another 10% to 20% experience difficulties with learning or behavior problems that interfere with their ability to succeed in school. Special and general educators must develop strategies for working together and sharing their knowledge and resources to prevent these millions of at-risk and struggling students from becoming failures of our educational system.

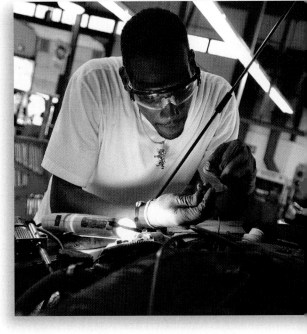

The ultimate effectiveness of special education must be measured by its ability to help secondary students with disabilities make a successful transition to adult life.

These four areas are by no means the only important issues facing special education to-day. We can easily identify numerous other challenges that many in the field argue are equally important:

- Increase the availability and quality of special education programs for gifted and talented students.
- Apply advances in assistive technology to greatly reduce or eliminate the disabling effects of physical and sensory impairments.
- Combat the pervasive effects of childhood poverty on development and success in school. (One in five American children under the age of 5 is living in poverty, and nearly 4 in 10 African American and Hispanic children live in poverty [Fujira & Yakima, 2000].)
- Eliminate cultural and racial bias from the special education referral and indentification process.
- Ensure that students with disabilities from diverse groups receive an education that respects and is responsive to their cultural and linguistic backgrounds.
- Meet the critical shortage of certified special education teachers.
  - There is a severe and chronic shortage of certified special education teachers in the U.S. (McLeskey, Tyler, & Flippin, 2004). In the 2000–2001 school year, 47,532 special education teaching positions were held by personnel who did not hold certification for the primary teaching assignment (U.S. Department of Education, 2003). The demand for certified teachers of students with emotional and behavioral disorders is especially critical.
  - Because of this shortage, only 63% of first-year special educators held the appropriate certification for their primary assignment.
  - The Bureau of Labor Statistics (1999) predicts that the demand for new teachers will continue to grow at a rapid pace, requiring an additional 135,000 to 200,000 special education teachers by 2010.
- Develop appropriate accommodations and alternative assessments so that the participation of students with disabilities in district- and statewide tests provides fair and valid measures of their learning.
- Increase access to technologies that can enhance the educational performance and personal independence of individuals with disabilities.
- Help students with disabilities acquire self-determination and self-advocacy skills.
- Improve the quality of pre- and in-service training programs to ensure that all special educators meet professional standards (CEC, 2003).
- Provide mentoring programs for beginning special education teachers and ongoing professional support for teachers to increase the effectiveness and retention of the teaching force.
- Improve the behavior and attitudes of people without disabilities toward those with disabilities.
- Open more opportunities for individuals with disabilities to participate in the full range of residential, employment, and recreational options available to persons without disabilities.

We do not know how successful special education will be in meeting these challenges. Only time will tell. And, of course, special educators do not face these challenges alone. General education; adult service agencies such as vocational rehabilitation, social work, and the science and practice of medicine; legislators; and society as a whole must all help find solutions. But we do know that a large and growing group of people is working hard to respond to these challenges—people with and without disabilities, people within and outside special education. Whatever professional and personal goals you follow, I hope your introductory study of special education will encourage you to become part of that group.

# Tips for Beginning Teachers

## Some Fundamentals for Success and Survival
*by Carol Richards*

### SEEK OUT A MENTOR

It is good to have a connection with an experienced teacher in your school when you are first starting out. A mentor will meet with you regularly to help you develop and refine your teaching skills and introduce you to school routines and expectations. She may be able to observe you and provide feedback on your performance in teaching and behavior management when you feel you need some help in problem solving or refining your techniques. Mentors can also help new teachers manage their time more effectively so they can stay on top of daily, weekly, and monthly duties.

### LEARN THE GENERAL EXPECTATIONS OF YOUR SCHOOL

Get to know the daily routines, staff meeting schedules, and record keeping requirements for all teachers so you can focus more of your energies on the education of your students.

### INCREASE POSITIVE FAMILY CONTACTS

Create a log sheet as a reminder to call parents when good things happen (and as documentation you have done so). These little things can brighten the day of a student and her family and help you develop a positive rapport with families.

### PROVIDE SUPPORT STAFF TRAINING

Much of the training for paraeducators and teacher assistants takes place through unplanned, everyday modeling, weekly meetings, and consultation on a one-to-one level or with the classroom teacher and parents in group meetings for students. However, planned group trainings are also important. For example, a September training might include instruction on how to read an IEP and accompanying reports. Monthly group sessions can work on teaching and reviewing skills (e.g., phonemic awareness—what it is and how it can be taught), how to teach students to self-monitor behaviors, or how to provide accommodations and collect data in the classroom. Try to meet once a month with the paraeducators who work with your students. Sometimes it is also helpful to ask other support staff to attend, such as a speech-language pathologist, to add a different perspective to the training.

### PLAN FOR DATA COLLECTION

Set up templates or structures for recording data collected on a regular basis—e.g., time-on-task observation sheets, discrete trial grids, a cover sheet for meeting notes, rubric templates for developing goals and objectives during a meeting, and a graph for recording fluency counts.

### POST THE DELEGATION OF TASKS IN A MEETING

After any meeting it is helpful to provide minutes that include the date, agenda, those in attendance, and a section that documents what tasks were delegated and to whom. When keeping notes by hand, use multiple-copy paper so you can give a copy to the teacher and the parent and still have one for yourself. This way, everyone has a record of the tasks they need to complete before the next meeting. For example, the parent may have the task of scheduling an eye exam for her child or sending in some photos of her child for an upcoming "student of the week" poster. The teacher may have responsibility for completing a running record of a classroom text for an informal assessment of reading. The special educator may have the task of observing the student in a specific school environment to collect data on a behavior or a skill discussed at the meeting. Listing the jobs on the cover sheet provides all participants with a reminder of their shared responsibility for the student's program.

### BE AN EFFICIENT CONSUMER OF TIME

Special educators are always being pulled in many directions. They are constantly trying to problem-solve, observe, provide instruction, and offer constructive and positive feedback. To do all of these jobs effectively, you need to use your time wisely. For instance, whenever a short block of time is available, work on IEP progress reports on the computer, even if you only have 10–15 minutes. Or eat lunch with a different teacher each day so you can have scheduled time to address student programs.

# KEY TERMS AND CONCEPTS

 To print your own set of SAFMED flash cards for studying and mastering these terms, go to the Companion Website, **www.prenhall.com/heward**.

assistive technology, p. 23
at risk, p. 11
disability, p. 10
exceptional children, p. 10
handicap, p. 10
impairment, p. 10
incidence, p. 38

individualized education program
(IEP), p. 20
prevalence, p. 38
primary prevention, p. 38
related services, p. 23
secondary prevention, p. 38
tertiary prevention, p. 38

# SUMMARY

## Who Are Exceptional Children?

- Exceptional children are those whose physical attributes and/or learning abilities differ from the norm, either above or below, to such an extent that an individualized program of special education is necessary.
- *Impairment* refers to the reduced function or loss of a particular body part or organ.
- A *disability* exists when an impairment limits a person's ability to perform certain tasks in the same way that most persons do.
- *Handicap* refers to the problems a person with a disability encounters when interacting with the environment.
- A child who is at risk is not currently identified as having a disability but is considered to have a greater-than-usual chance of developing one if intervention is not provided.

## How Many Exceptional Children Are There?

- Children in special education represent approximately 11% of the school-age population.
- The four largest categories of children with disabilities receiving special education are learning disabilities, speech and language impairments, mental retardation, and emotional disturbance.
- The vast majority of children receiving special education have mild disabilities.
- Three out of four students with disabilities receive at least part of their education in regular classrooms.

## Why Do We Label and Classify Exceptional Children?

- Some believe that disability labels have negative effects on the child and on others' perceptions of her and can lead to exclusion; others believe that labeling is a necessary first step to providing needed intervention and is important for comparing and communicating about research findings.
- Alternative approaches to classifying exceptional children that do not rely on disability labels have been proposed, e.g., classifying students by the curriculum and skill areas they are learning.
- In curriculum-based assessment, students are assessed and classified relative to the degree to which they are learning specific curriculum content.

## Why Are Laws Governing the Education of Exceptional Children Necessary?

- Before the 1970s, many states had laws permitting public schools to deny enrollment to children with disabilities. When local public schools began to accept a measure of responsibility for educating certain exceptional students, a philosophy of segregation prevailed.

- Special education was strongly influenced by the case of *Brown v. Board of Education* in 1954, in which the U.S. Supreme Court declared that education must be made available to all children on equal terms.
- In the class-action lawsuit *PARC* (1972), the Court ruled that all children with mental retardation were entitled to a free, appropriate public education and that placements in regular classrooms and regular public schools were preferable to segregated settings.
- All children with disabilities are now recognized to have the right to equal protection under the law, which has been interpreted to mean the right to a free public education in the least restrictive environment.
- All children with disabilities and their parents have the right to due process under the law, which includes the rights to be notified of any decision affecting the child's educational placement, to have a hearing and present a defense, to see a written decision, and to appeal any decision.
- Court decisions have also established the rights of children with disabilities to fair assessment in their native language and to education at public expense, regardless of the school district's financial constraints.

## The Individuals with Disabilities Education Act

- The passage of IDEA by Congress in 1975 marked the culmination of the efforts of many educators, parents, and legislators to bring together in one comprehensive bill this country's laws regarding the education of children with disabilities. The law encompasses six major principles:
  - *Zero reject.* Schools must educate all children with disabilities. This principle applies regardless of the nature or severity of the disability.
  - *Nondiscriminatory identification and evaluation.* Schools must use nonbiased, multifactored methods of evaluation to determine whether a child has a disability and, if so, whether special education is needed.
  - *Free, appropriate public education.* All children with disabilities shall receive a free, appropriate public education at public expense. An individualized education program (IEP) must be developed and implemented for each student with a disability.
  - *Least restrictive environment.* Students with disabilities must be educated with children without disabilities to the maximum extent appropriate, and they should be removed to separate classes or schools only when the nature or severity of their disabilities is such that they cannot receive an appropriate education in a general education classroom.
  - *Due process safeguards.* Schools must provide due process safeguards to protect the rights of children with disabilities and their parents.
  - *Parent and student participation and shared decision making.* Schools must collaborate with parents and with students with disabilities in the design and implementation of special education services.
- IDEA requires states to provide special education services to all preschoolers with disabilities ages 3 to 5. This law also makes federal money available to encourage states to develop early intervention programs for disabled and at-risk infants and toddlers from birth to age 2. Early intervention services must be coordinated by an individualized family services plan (IFSP).
- The Individuals with Disabilities Education Improvement Act of 2004 includes several provisions likely to impact the field: paperwork reduction, benchmarks and short-term objectives required only in IEPs for students who take alternative assessments; multi-year IEPs; definitions of "highly qualified" special education teachers; and "response-to-instruction" method for identifying learning disabilities as an alternative to the achievement-ability discrepancy model.

- Court cases have challenged the way in which particular school districts implement specific provisions of IDEA. Rulings from the various cases have established the principle that each student with disabilities is entitled to a personalized program of instruction and related services that will enable him to benefit from an education in as integrated a setting as possible.
- The Gifted and Talented Children's Education Act (P.L. 95–561) provides financial incentives to states for developing programs for gifted and talented students.
- Section 504 of the Rehabilitation Act forbids discrimination in all federally funded programs, including educational and vocational programs, on the basis of disability.
- The Americans with Disabilities Act (P.L. 101–336) extends the civil rights protections for persons with disabilities to private-sector employment, all public services, public accommodations, transportation, and telecommunications.
- The No Child Left Behind Act requires schools to make annual progress toward the ultimate goal of all children being proficient in all subject matter by 2014, every child reading at or above grade level by the end of third grade at the end of 2005–2006, and a "highly qualified" teacher in every classroom. The law emphasizes use of evidence-based teaching methods.

## What Is Special Education?

- Special education consists of purposeful intervention efforts at three levels: preventive, remedial, and compensatory.
- Special education is individually planned, specialized, intensive, goal-directed instruction. When practiced most effectively and ethically, special education uses research-based teaching methods and is guided by direct and frequent measures of student performance.

## Current and Future Challenges

- Among the many challenges faced by special education today are the following:
  - Bridging the research-to-practice gap
  - Making early intervention programs more widely available to infants, toddlers, and preschoolers who have disabilities or are at risk for developing them
  - Improving the ability of young adults with disabilities to make a successful transition from school to community life
  - Working more effectively with general education to better serve the many students who have not been identified as disabled but who are not progressing in the general education program

To check your comprehension of chapter contents, go to the Guided Review and Quiz modules in Chapter 1 of the Companion Website, **www.prenhall.com/heward**.

# PLANNING AND PROVIDING SPECIAL EDUCATION SERVICES

# Featured Teachers ———————————

## MARY ALLAIRE-GIFFORD AND JEAN MICHIELLI-PENDL

DUNKIRK MIDDLE SCHOOL
DUNKIRK, NEW YORK

Mary Allaire-Gifford

*Mary Allaire-Gifford: Education—Teaching Credentials—Experience*
- B.A., elementary education, Grove City College, Grove City, Pennsylvania, 1984
- M.S., special education, State University of New York, College at Buffalo, Buffalo, New York, 2003
- New York State certification in special education and elementary education
- 20 years of teaching experience: 13 years in regular education, grades 4–6; 7 years as a special educator

Jean Michielli-Pendl

*Jean Michielli-Pendl: Education—Teaching Credentials—Experience*
- B.A., elementary education, State University of New York, College at Fredonia, Fredonia, New York, 1972
- M.S., curriculum and instruction, State University of New York, College at Fredonia, Fredonia, New York, 1998
- New York State certification in elementary education
- 32 years of teaching experience: 4 years as an ESL teacher; 15 years in regular education, grades 2–5; 13 years as a sixth-grade science teacher

*Two Teachers Making Inclusion Work: Our Classroom, Our Students*
**Jean:** I have taught for 32 years in a variety of settings. I began in an ESL classroom where the students all spoke Spanish. The skills I taught were intended to enable the students to function in the regular classroom. The following years I taught second, fifth, and sixth grades as a general education teacher.

The greatest challenge the past three decades occurred when our entire school district adopted a full inclusion model to meet the needs of our special education students. I felt quite unprepared, even after many years in the classroom. I had honed my skills in classroom techniques to better serve my diversified population. However, I never was responsible for meeting the needs of special education students and their IEPs. This new responsibility came with a new challenge … a co-teacher!

Co-teaching is very different from teaching in a room with the support of Title I teachers, aides, or student teachers. Co-teaching is sharing the teaching responsibilities with another teacher to best meet the needs of students in *our* classroom.

## Focus Questions

- Why must the planning and provision of special education be so carefully sequenced and evaluated?

- Why does the effectiveness of special education depend on collaboration and teaming?

- How should the quality of a student's individualized education program be judged?

- Is the least restrictive environment always the regular classroom? Why?

- What elements must be in place for special education to be appropriate in inclusive classrooms?

**Mary:** Our school is organized by teams, two at each grade level. I am one of the two special education teachers assigned to my team, the Shining Stars. Generally, there are 12–16 students with disabilities on each team. Students on my team this year are receiving special education services under the IDEA categories of learning disabilities, speech-language impairments, other health impairment, hearing impairment, and autism. In years past, we have had students with mild mental retardation and emotional and behavioral disorders. Students with disabilities, for the most part, attend all general education classes with their nondisabled peers. However, there is one 40-minute self-contained math class and one 40-minute self-contained reading class at each grade level, both taught by a special education teacher.

Each year my assignment has changed slightly. Some years I work in social studies classes, some years in language arts classes, but the one constant has been working in the science classes with Jean. Our science classes have had anywhere from 18 to 27 students, and generally including four or five have disabilities. My role as an inclusion teacher is varied. I am responsible for ensuring implementation of the IEPs for all students with disabilities on my team and for writing the following year's IEPs of students for whom I am case manager. I provide notes, study guides, guided notes, organizational strategies, and other accommodations. Planning, making instructional materials, and teaching lessons with Jean are part of my day. Jean and I develop tests and quizzes together; then during them, I make sure test accommodations are being followed. I keep records of when and how we have worked toward the successful completion of goals and objectives for the students' IEPs.

To see and hear Jean and Mary discuss the importance of collaboration and making co teaching work for the benefit of all students, go to "Dunkirk Middle School" in Chapter 2 of the Companion Website (**www.prenhall.com/heward**) and click on "Team Teaching 1 and 2."

***Creating a Successful Classroom Environment Together***      **Jean:** Mary brings much to the co-teaching team. She was a regular education teacher initially in her career and then studied to be a special educator. Mary is an expert in designing specialized instruction to meet IEP goals, and I am the content specialist. She is a strict taskmaster; I am a humanist. Our different qualities create a learning atmosphere in which students can grow and develop. Our co-teaching and classroom is much like a family unit. A co-teaching team is really a work in progress. It evolves each day as the students we serve and their needs change over time.

**Mary:** The success of our co-teaching is a result of many factors. We both take pride in what we do and strive to do our best. Jean and I make time to co-plan. That is the backbone of co-teaching. We use 40 minutes once a week for co-planning our weekly lessons. Jean and I decide on which strategies we will use to convey the lessons. We plan which goals and objectives from the IEPs will be targeted. Each morning the agenda is posted for the day. Careful, consistent planning, sequencing, and constant evaluation make our co-teaching seamless. It allows us to adjust lesson pacing and reteach as needed. When entering our science class, it is difficult to tell which teacher is the general education teacher and which is the special education teacher.

**Jean:** Mary and I challenge anyone who enters our class to identify those students who are special education students. We feel very strongly that our job is to assist *all* students. I don't teach just the regular students while Mary assists the students with special needs. Both of us teach all the students. We work hard at making sure that the students see us as equal teachers in the room. It is common in many inclusion models to have the special education teacher assigned as a consultant teacher to the regular teacher's classroom. This was not the model we adopted. We each teach every day, sometimes the whole class and sometimes small groups. The groups are always mixed by ability and needs. This allows all the students an equal education, which is required by IDEA.

***Teaching Strategies***      Good teaching strategies are important for all students, and we've learned that the instructional strategies we initially incorporated to assist students with special education needs—such as guided lecture notes, colored markers, and Post-It notes to hold their place when working on vocabulary—also help the regular education students.

Most class periods include a cooperative learning activity. We realized the talents and strengths that each child could bring to a group. The students learn to respect one another as fellow classmates and contributors. Two collaborative learning strategies we use often are *numbered heads together* and *think-pair-share*.

**Numbered Heads Together**   When using this strategy, students are seated in heterogeneous groups of three or four, and each student is given a number. We have found that students with disabilities who are working with their nondisabled peers put forth more effort and create fewer disruptions in class than they do when they are grouped homogeneously. The teacher asks the class a question. Each group discusses the question and then comes up with an answer. It is important that every person in the group knows the answer to the question.

Numbered heads together is beneficial in several ways. First, students enjoy it. They participate actively and enthusiastically. Second, this strategy promotes cooperation within the group rather than competition. All students must know the answer, so group members help each other understand not only the answer but also the *how* and *why* behind it. Finally, the strategy encourages individual responsibility. When a group member's number is called, that person alone has to give the final answer. As a review strategy, numbered heads together is highly effective.

**Think-Pair-Share**   Many times we give one response card to a pair of students. The students are asked a question and then engage in a practice called think-pair-share. They think quietly for 5–10 seconds, then pair-up with their partners to discuss the answer to the question. Finally, they write their collective response on the card and flip it over. When all or most of the students are done, we ask the class to show their response cards to us. We can assess their answers and respond by reteaching or continuing with the lesson. This technique keeps all students on task and offers them time to discuss and check their understandings with a classmate. For fun and an element of competition, the students usually keep a tally of the number of questions they answer correctly.

**What We Like Most about Being Co-Teachers**   **Mary:** I love seeing students with disabilities being successful academically and socially in general education classes. I enjoy working with people who push me to be my best, who care about all students, and who do not consider students with disabilities as only *my* students.

**Jean:** I like being able to work with another professional adult in the room. It enhances my teaching. We have fun in our classroom.

**Reflections on Teaching**   **Jean:** My biggest "ah-hah!" moment came when I first taught in an inclusion classroom. Peter, a child with Down syndrome, was placed in my last-period science class. He was functioning at a first-grade level in reading and writing. Despite 30 years of teaching experience, I thought I would never be able to teach Peter properly. It was unreasonable, I thought, to expect this young man to learn sixth-grade science. This was unjust to both Peter and myself!

Contrary to my fears, Peter made great progress. He not only grew in science, but in reading and writing too. He surpassed his IEP goals and impressed all who were involved in his progress. However, Peter was not the only person in the classroom who made progress that year. I finally came to realize the full potential and positive impact of including special children in a regular education setting. All my students grew that year. We learned much more than science concepts. We learned life's lessons of persistence, patience, tolerance, and true understanding. I owe a lot of my professional growth to Peter.

**Mary:** In our first year of co-teaching, many colleagues told Jean and me that inclusion just could not work. And we feared in our hearts that they were right. But we were committed to making inclusion work, and we did. Eighty-five percent of the students with disabilities passed all their general education classes. Having taught in

To watch Jean and Mary use these teaching strategies and others in their classroom, go to "Dunkirk Middle School" on the CD-ROM and click on "Heads Together," "Pair-Share 1 and 2," "Response Cards," and "Response System."

self-contained classes with no textbooks in a school kitchen, I knew that separate was not equal, but I did not know the right answer or how or where to find it. After 3 years of co-teaching inclusion classes, I know the answer now and how inclusion can work successfully in the classroom.

**Jean and Mary:** Although we feel that the general education classroom works for most students with disabilities, it is not the most appropriate setting for all of them. Some students need a more specialized setting. But it is better to start in a least restrictive environment and move toward a more restrictive environment as needed rather than the other way around.

 To check your comprehension of chapter content, go to the Guided Review and Quiz modules in Chapter 2 of the Companion Website, **www.prenhall.com/heward**.

In Chapter 1, *special education* was defined as individually planned, specialized, intensive, goal-directed instruction. But how do teachers know what kinds of modifications to curriculum and instruction an individual child needs? And toward what goals should instruction be directed? In this chapter, we examine the basic process by which special education is planned, devoting particular attention to four critical aspects of educating students with disabilities: (1) the importance of teaming and collaboration among professionals, (2) the individualized education plan (IEP), (3) the least restrictive environment (LRE), and (4) inclusive education.

# THE PROCESS OF SPECIAL EDUCATION

IDEA mandates a particular sequence of events that schools must follow in identifying and educating children with disabilities. Although the rules and regulations that state and local school districts must follow are formal and sometimes redundant for legal purposes, the process is designed to answer a sequence of questions that makes both educational and common sense:

- Which students might need special education?
- Does this particular child have a disability that adversely affects his educational performance? In other words, is this student eligible for special education? If the answer is yes, then....
- What are the specific educational needs that result from the child's disability?
- What specialized methods of instruction, accommodations, curricular modifications, related services, and/or supplementary supports are necessary to meet those needs so the student can be involved and progress in the general curriculum and life of the school?
- Who is best suited to provide the special education and related services the student needs?
- What placement is the least restrictive environment in which the student can be provided with an appropriate education?
- Is special education helping the student make progress? Is it working?

Figure 2.1 identifies the major steps in the sequence of planning, implementing, and evaluating special education and highlights some of the key procedures, elements, or requirements of each step. With the exception of the first step, prereferral intervention, each step in the process is required by IDEA. (Although not required to do so, some states follow a process similar to the one shown in Figure 2.1 on pp. 58–59 for planning individualized education programs for gifted and talented students.)

## Prereferral Intervention

A child who may need special education usually comes to the attention of the schools because (1) a teacher or parent reports concern about differences in learning, behavior, or development or (2) the results of a screening test suggest a possible disability. (Screening tests are relatively quick, inexpensive, and easy-to-administer assessments given to large groups of children to find out who might have a disability and need further testing. For example, most schools administer vision screening tests to all elementary children.) Before referring the child for more formal testing and evaluation for special education, however, most schools initiate a process known as *prereferral intervention*.

Prereferral intervention is an informal, problem-solving process with two primary purposes: (1) to provide immediate instructional and/or behavior management assistance to the child and teacher and (2) to reduce the chances of identifying a child for special education who may not be disabled (McNamara & Hollinger, 2003; Salvia & Ysseldyke, 2001). Many schools use *intervention assistance teams* (also called *student support teams, teacher assistance teams,* or *instructional support teams*) to help classroom teachers devise and implement interventions for students who are experiencing either academic or behavioral difficulties so that they can remain in the regular classroom (Logan, Hansen, Nieminen, & Wright, 2001). Prereferral intervention has the potential to prevent or reduce the frequency of future student problems by strengthening the teacher's capacity to effectively intervene with a greater diversity of children (Fuchs, Fuchs, Bahr, Fernstrom, & Stecker, 1990).

Intervention assistance teams are not required by IDEA, so each state is free to determine whether to include the prereferral intervention process in its special education regulations. A survey of directors of special education in all 50 states plus the District of Columbia found that 43% of states mandated a prereferral process for students suspected of having a disability and an additional 29% of the states recommend it (Buck, Polloway, Smith-Thomas, & Cook, 2003). This study also found that general education teachers and counselors most often led the intervention assistance teams.

When prereferral intervention is successful in ameliorating the problems that originally caused teachers or parents to be concerned about the child, it also prevents the costly and time-consuming process of assessment for special education eligibility. A school district may not, however, use prereferral intervention to delay formal evaluation and assessment of a student who is eligible for special education (Yell, 2006).

## Evaluation and Identification

Teachers seldom refer children for minor or frivolous learning or behavior problems. In practice, about 90% of children who are referred are formally evaluated for special education, and about 73% of those who are tested are found eligible for special education (Ysseldyke, 2001). IDEA requires that all children suspected of having a disability receive a nondiscriminatory **multifactored evaluation (MFE).** Either the school or the parents can request that a child be evaluated for special education. Regardless of the source of the referral, the parents must be notified of the school's intent to test their child, and they must give their consent to the evaluation. The Individuals with Disabilities Education Improvement Act of 2004 requires that within 60 days of receiving parental consent for evaluation, the school district must complete the evaluation to determine the child's eligibility for special education and identify the educational needs of the child.

IDEA is explicit in describing some do's and don'ts that school districts must follow when evaluating a child for special education:

Conduct of Evaluation—In conducting the evaluation, the local educational agency shall—

(A) use a variety of assessment tools and strategies to gather relevant functional, developmental, and academic information, including information provided by the parent, that may assist in determining—

(i) whether the child is a child with a disability; and

(ii) the content of the child's individualized education program, including information related to enabling the child to be involved in and progress in the general education curriculum, or, for preschool children, to participate in appropriate activities;

*Prereferral intervention*

Council for Exceptional Children — Content Standards for Beginning Teachers—Common Core: Screening, prereferral, referral, and classification procedures (CC8K3).

To see an intervention assistance team share ideas for helping a student who is experiencing difficulties in the regular classroom, go to "Dunkirk Middle School" on the CD-ROM and click on "Team Meeting."

*Multifactored evaluation*

Council for Exceptional Children — Content Standards for Beginning Teachers—Common Core: Legal provisions and ethical principles regarding assessment of individuals (CC8K2).

# FIGURE 2.1 The basic steps in planning, providing, and evaluating special education

**PREREFERRAL INTERVENTION**
- Teacher or parent reports concern with child's learning, behavior, or development, or results of a screening test indicate a possible disability.
- Parents are notified.
- Intervention assistance team works with classroom teacher to plan and help implement modifications in curriculum and instruction in an attempt to solve the problem.
- Prereferral intervention is not required by IDEA; it may not be used to delay referral and evaluation of an eligible student.

**Successful: Process stops**

**Not successful: Child referred for evelation**

**MULTIFACTORED EVALUATION (MFE)**
- Parent consent for testing and evaluation must be obtained.
- Evaluation must not discriminate on basis of race, culture, language, or gender.
- MFE considers all areas related to the suspected disability (e.g., academic performance, general intelligence, social behavior, vision, health).
- MFE uses a variety of assessment tools and strategies (e.g., formal tests, direct observations in classroom, parental input).
- MFE should provide information to help determine if the child has a disability, what kinds of related services may be needed, and how the child can participate in the general education curriculum.

**IDENTIFICATION**
- A team of qualified professionals and the parents review MFE results and all relevant information to determine if the child has a disability and is therefore eligible for special education.
- Parents participate in interpretation of assessment results and the eligibility decision.

**No disability: Special education not needed**

**Disability: Eligible for special education**

**PROGRAM PLANNING: INDIVIDUAL EDUCATION PLAN (IEP)**
- An IEP team is created to plan child's IEP.
- Parents participate as equal partners; the student participates when appropriate.
- The IEP is an individually tailored program of special instruction, related services, assistive technology, and supplemental aids and services to meet the child's needs that result from the disability. It must include
  - Measurable annual goals, including benchmarks or short-term objectives
  - A statement of services to enable the student to be involved in and progress in the general academic curriculum and extracurricular and other nonacademic activities
  - A statement on the extent to which the student will participate in state- and district-wide testing programs
  - A positive behavior intervention plan if necessary
  - Transition needs and services beginning at age 14
- Instruction and related services needed by the child must be identified without regard to cost to or availability in the district.

**PLACEMENT IN LEAST RESTRICTIVE ENVIRONMENT (LRE)**
- Placement is determined by the IEP team after the child's educational needs and the services needed to meet them have been identified.
- IDEA presupposes the general education classroom as the starting point for the LRE.
- The IEP must contain an explanation of the extent, if any, to which the child is to be removed from the general education classroom.
- Parents participate in and must consent to the placement decision.

**(continues)**

## FIGURE 2.1 continued

**IMPLEMENT SPECIAL EDUCATION (FAPE)**

- The IEP is implemented in the LRE.
- The child participates in the general curriculum and extracurricular activities of the school.
- The child participates in state- and district-wide assessments. (The IEP specifies accommodations or alternative assessments if necessary.)
- Parents can request a change of program and placement.

**REVIEW AND EVALUATION**

- Parents must be provided with periodic reports on the child's progress toward meeting annual goals (e.g., quarterly reports concurrent with the issuance of report cards).
- The IEP must be reviewed periodically, but not less frequently than annually, to determine whether the annual goals for the child are being met.
- The IEP team revises the IEP as appropriate to address any lack of expected progress in annual goals and in the general education curriculum.
- The IEP team may decide that the disability is no longer present or that the child's education is no longer adversely affected by the disability and that special education services are no longer needed.

Special Education Terminated

Special Education Continued

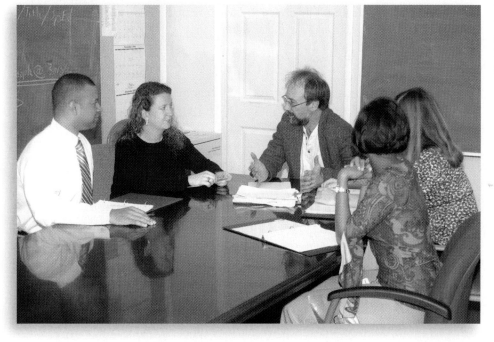

"Here's another idea we could try." Intervention assistance teams plan strategies to help children with learning or behavioral problems remain in the regular classroom.

(B) not use any single measure or assessment as the sole criterion for determining whether a child is a child with a disability or determining an appropriate educational program for the child; and

(C) use technically sound instruments that may assess the relative contribution of cognitive and behavioral factors, in addition to physical or developmental factors.

Additional Requirements—Each local educational agency shall ensure that

(A) assessments and other evaluation materials used to assess a child—
   (i) are selected and administered so as not to be discriminatory on a racial or cultural basis;
   (ii) are provided and administered in the language and form most likely to yield accurate information on what the child knows and can do academically, developmentally, and functionally, unless it is not feasible to so provide or administer;

(iii) are used for purposes for which the assessments or measures are valid and reliable;

(iv) are administered by trained and knowledgeable personnel; and

(v) are administered in accordance with any instructions provided by the producer of such assessments;

(B) the child is assessed in all areas of suspected disability;

(C) assessment tools and strategies that provide relevant information that directly assists persons in determining the educational needs of the child are provided; and

(D) assessments of children with disabilities who transfer from one school district to another school district in the same academic year are coordinated with such children's prior and subsequent schools, as necessary and as expeditiously as possible, to ensure prompt completion of full evaluations. (Individuals with Disabilities Education Improvement Act of 2004, H.R. 1350, Sec. 614(b)(2))

The multifactored evaluation is conducted by a school-based *multidisciplinary evaluation team,* sometimes called a *student study team,* which includes the child's parents. The team examines the test results and all other relevant information to determine if the child has a disability and needs special education. An MFE must do more than just provide information on the existence of a disability for determining eligibility for special education. IDEA requires evaluation reports to also provide information about the child's educational needs and how to meet them.

*Disproportional Representation of Students from Culturally Diverse Groups in Special Education.* Culturally and linguistically diverse students are both underrepresented and overrepresented in special education (Artiles, Aguirre-Munoz, & Abedi, 1998; Artiles & Zamora-Durán, 1997; Correa, Blanes-Reyes, & Rapport, 1995; Daugherty, 2001; Ford, 1998; MacMillan & Reschly, 1998; Oswald & Coutinho, 2001; Oswald, Coutinho, Best, & Singhy, 1999; Patton, 1998).

Table 2.1 shows the percentage, by disability category, of students from race/ethnicity groups who received special education in the 2003–2004 school year. Black and Native

**TABLE 2.1** **Racial/ethnic composition (percentage) of students ages 6 through 21 served by disability in the 2003–2004 school year**

| Disability | American Indian/ Alaskan | Asian/ Pacific Islander | Black (Not Hispanic) | Hispanic | White (Not Hispanic) |
|---|---|---|---|---|---|
| Specific learning disabilities | 1.5 | 1.6 | 19.4 | 20.1 | 57.3 |
| Speech or language impairments | 1.2 | 2.8 | 15.6 | 16.3 | 64.0 |
| Mental retardation | 1.1 | 1.9 | 34.2 | 13.9 | 48.9 |
| Emotional disturbance | 1.4 | 1.2 | 28.6 | 10.2 | 58.6 |
| Other health impairments | 1.1 | 1.4 | 16.1 | 9.2 | 72.2 |
| Autism | 0.7 | 5.0 | 15.7 | 10.4 | 68.2 |
| Multiple disabilities | 1.3 | 2.4 | 20.3 | 14.1 | 61.9 |
| Hearing impairments | 1.2 | 4.8 | 16.3 | 21.0 | 56.6 |
| Orthopedic impairments | 0.9 | 3.1 | 14.5 | 18.0 | 63.5 |
| Developmental delay | 3.1 | 2.7 | 22.1 | 8.8 | 63.3 |
| Visual impairments | 1.1 | 3.8 | 17.7 | 17.8 | 59.5 |
| Traumatic brain injury | 1.3 | 2.4 | 17.6 | 11.9 | 67.1 |
| Deaf-blindness | 2.3 | 4.5 | 13.8 | 20.8 | 58.7 |
| All disabilities | 1.4 | 2.0 | 20.5 | 16.7 | 59.5 |
| Resident population (2002–2003) | 1.0 | 4.0 | 15.1 | 16.9 | 63.0 |

*Source:* Data on students served from U. S. Office of Special Education. (2004). *Individuals with Disabilities Education Act (IDEA) data* (Table AA15). Washington, DC: Author. Available at *http://www.ideadata.org/tables27th\ar_aa15.htm.* Data on resident population from U. S. Office of Special Education. (2003). *Individuals with Disabilities Education Act (IDEA) data* (Table AA3). Washington, DC: Author. Available at *http://www.ideadata.org/tables26th\ar_af8.htm.*

American students were overrepresented in special education programs, while Asian and white students were underrepresented in the special education population. Hispanic students were generally represented among the special education population at a rate comparable to their proportion of the resident school-age population. Although data aggregated nationally can obscure significant differences at the state and local level, some disparities are evident, especially for black students in the disability categories of mental retardation and emotional disturbance. For example, while African Americans account for 15.1% of the school-age population, they represent 28.6% of all students receiving special education for emotional and behavioral disorders (U. S. Office of Special Education, 2004).

Is this overrepresentation fair? As a group, are culturally and linguistically diverse students more likely to have a disability than white children are—because, for example, a much greater proportion of them are born to mothers without access to maternal health care, live in poverty, and reside in single-parent households with limited exposure to language? Or are there inherent problems in the referral and placement process that bias the placement of minority children (Knotek, 2003)? The answer to these controversial and complex questions is that probably both explanations are partly true (Serna, Forness, & Nielson, 1998).

Hosp and Reschly (2003) studied referral rates for intervention or assessment. Their meta-analysis of 10 studies of referral rates found significant racial differences in referral rates between African American and Caucasian students but no significant differences between Hispanic students and Caucasian students.

Although somewhat controversial, the meaning of disproportionate representation has been difficult to pinpoint. MacMillan and Reschly (1998) believe that all of the indices and data must be considered for an accurate representation of the enrollment patterns among culturally and linguistically diverse students, including (1) percentage of total student enrollment by group, (2) percentage of special program enrollment by group, and (3) percentage of the group in the special program. For example, they point out that according to a U. S. Department of Education Office of Civil Rights (1990) compliance report, nearly 35% of students classified with mild mental retardation (MMR) were African American, but only 2% of African American students were classified as MMR.

Harry (1994) has emphasized that disproportionality is relative, not absolute. She believes there is great variability in over- and underrepresentation in special education by states and local school districts. She argues that there is a problem when the percentage of minority students in the special education program is larger than the percentage of that group in the general educational system. The lack of consistent criteria and the collection of disaggregated enrollment data continue to hinder the examination of this problem. Nonetheless, invalid assessments and placement of diverse students in special education are problematic because they can stigmatize students and deny them appropriate educational interventions that match their full learning capacities.

The fact that culturally diverse students are identified as having mental retardation, emotional disturbance, or learning disabilities is not, in itself, a problem. All students with a disability that adversely affects their educational performance have the right to special education services, whatever their racial or ethnic background. Disproportionate representation is problematic if it means that children have been wrongly placed in special education or results in segregation and stigmatization. In other instances students' disabilities may be overlooked because of their membership in a racial or ethnic minority group, meaning they are denied access to needed special education as a result. In either case, the process of referral and identification has not been applied equally across different groups of students.

*Recognizing and Combating Cultural and Racial Bias in Referral and Identification Procedures.* The presence of large numbers of culturally diverse students, however, raises several important concerns about our education practices. Understanding the reasons for the disproportionality phenomenon in special education is not simple. Several factors must be considered, including the sociopolitical context of U. S. schools and communities (Nieto, 2000a). However, three areas have been identified as integral to this problem: (1) incongruity between teachers and culturally diverse students and families, which may lead to biased referrals; (2) inaccurate assessment of culturally diverse students, leading to false special education; and (3) ineffective curriculum and instructional practices for culturally diverse students (Correa & Heward, 2003).

Today's teachers are mostly white (90%) and female (66%) (U. S. Department of Education, 1998), and these predominately middle-class educators are teaching a growing number of culturally and linguistically diverse students (Fox & Gay, 1995; Pavri, 2001). For example, with respect to the overrepresentation of African American students in the emotional and behavior disorders category, some researchers contend that there is an African American behavioral style that conflicts with white teachers' expectations for classroom behavior (Hale, 2001; Hilliard, 1992; Townsend, 2000). "When African American students 'behave' in modes affirmed and sanctioned by dimensions of African American culture (Boykin, 1983) and those modes are unfamiliar to or misinterpreted by teachers, most of whom are white, their behavior is often perceived as inappropriate" (Webb-Johnson, 2003, p. 5).

Bias in the assessment process is another contributing factor in the disproportionate numbers of culturally diverse students in special education. The testing methods used to identify students for services are an inexact science at best; and the likelihood of obtaining valid, accurate, and unbiased assessment results is lower when the student in question is from a culturally or linguistically different background (Correa et al., 1995; Langdon, Novak, & Quintanar, 2000; Ortiz, 1997; Utley & Obiakor, 2001). Figueroa (1989) calls the current practice of psychological testing of children from culturally and linguistically diverse groups "random chaos" because it is so fraught with problems.

A major challenge for special educators is to disentangle English-language skills and/or culturally linked behaviors from academic or learning skills. Barrera (1995) notes that there are three potential sources of learning problems in children who come from culturally and linguistically diverse backgrounds: (1) unrecognized cultural/linguistic diversity, (2) deficits stemming from chronic poverty or trauma, and (3) disabilities. Inappropriate referral to special education can occur if educators and school psychologists are unable to correctly separate the presence of unrecognized diversity or deficits from disability.

Learning deficits do not result from diversity of sociocultural beliefs, values, world views, and preferences. "Rather, they result from the constraints that chronic poverty or unaddressed trauma can place on a child's access to the experiences and knowledge deemed normative for all children by the cultural group(s) with which their families affiliate" (p. 58). Barrera (1995) contends that special education services are neither appropriate nor most efficient for learning difficulties that are not the result of inherent disabilities.

> If, for example, a child has experienced trauma that remains unaddressed, simply reducing task complexity will not be a sufficient response. Or if, on the other hand, the child has intact learning abilities and an age appropriate repertoire of skills, but can not understand the language of instruction, it is equally inappropriate and wasteful of both financial and human resources to generate a complete interdisciplinary assessment and special education program instead of simply providing needed linguistic support. It is important, therefore, to understand the specific difficulties that may stem from unrecognized diversity or deficits. Once understood, pre-referral intervention can be directed toward eliminating their impact and assessing whether any difficulties remain. It is these difficulties, that remain after diversity and deficit have been addressed, that are the appropriate target for special education. (p. 64)

Understanding the complex issues related to the disproportionate numbers of culturally diverse students in special education requires that educators understand the problems with incongruity between a teacher's interactions with students and families from diverse cultures, the assessment and referral process in special education, and ineffective instructional and discipline practices (Craig, Hall, Haggart, & Perez-Selles, 2000; Ford, 2000; Townsend, 2000). To better meet the needs of students with disabilities from culturally diverse backgrounds, schools should address three issues. First, staff must become culturally responsive to students and families. Second, staff must implement appropriate assessment strategies for determining the educational needs of culturally diverse students. Third, educators should implement culturally responsive practices that support a multicultural approach to curriculum and instruction (Banks & Banks, 2004; Gollnick & Chinn, 2002).

Self-awareness is the first step on the journey toward becoming a culturally proficient teacher. To understand and fully appreciate the diversity that exists among the students and families that special educators

Teachers are most effective when curriculum content and instructional methods are responsive to the cultural, ethnic, and linguistic diversity among their students.

serve, we must first understand and appreciate our own cultures. All cultures have built-in biases, and there are no right or wrong cultural beliefs. Cultural self-awareness is the bridge to learning about other cultures. "It is not possible to be truly sensitive to someone else's culture until one is sensitive to one's own and the impact that cultural customs, values, beliefs, and behaviors have on practice" (Lynch & Hanson, 1998, p. 39). (See Diversity & Exceptionality, "A Cultural Journey," later in this chapter.)

## Program Planning

If the evaluation team determines that a child has a disability that is adversely affecting his educational performance, an IEP team is formed and charged with planning an individualized education program (IEP). The IEP team determines the *what* (learning goals and objectives), *how* (specialized instruction and related services), *who* (teachers and related-service providers), and *when* (frequency of specialized instruction and related services) of a child's special education program. A critically important element of special education practice, the IEP process will be described in detail later in this chapter.

## Placement

After the child's educational needs and the special education and related services necessary to meet those needs are determined, the IEP team determines the least restrictive environment (LRE) in which an appropriate education can be provided to the child. The placement of children with disabilities is one of the most debated and often misunderstood aspects of special education and IDEA and will be discussed in depth later in this chapter and throughout the text.

## Review and Evaluation

In addition to being specialized, intensive, and goal-directed instruction—when it is properly practiced—special education is also continuously evaluated education. All aspects of a child's IEP—progress on goals and outcomes, delivery of specialized instruction and related services, appropriateness of placement—are reviewed and open for change. The IEP must be thoroughly and formally reviewed on an annual basis. However, schools must notify parents of their child's progress in the general curriculum and toward IEP goals and objectives at least as often as parents of nondisabled students receive information about their children's school performance.

# A Cultural Journey

*by Eleanor W. Lynch and Marci J. Hanson*

Culture is unique to individuals, but the concept is universal. All of us have a cultural, ethnic, racial, linguistic, and religious (or nonreligious) heritage that influences our current beliefs, values, and behaviors. To learn more about your own heritage, take this cultural journey.

*Origins*
1. When you think about your roots, what place(s) of origin do you identify for your family?
2. Have you ever heard any stories about how your family or your ancestors came to the place where you grew up or how they came to the United States? Briefly, what were the stories?
3. Are there any foods that you or someone else prepares that are traditional for your place of origin or some other aspect of your heritage? What are they? What is their significance?
4. Are there celebrations, ceremonies, rituals, or holidays that your family celebrates that reflect your place of origin or some other aspect of your heritage? What are they? How are they celebrated?
5. Do you or does anyone else in your family speak a language other than English because of your origins? If so, what language(s)?
6. Do you recall sociocultural factors in your family that made you different from your friends, classmates, neighbors, or others in your community? Consider your family's socioeconomic status, educational level, constellation, or worldview.
7. Can you think of one piece of advice handed down through your family that reflects the values held by your ancestors? What is it? Does it reflect a cultural, religious, or individual value?

*Beliefs, Biases, and Behaviors*
1. Have you ever heard anyone make a negative comment about people from your place(s) of origin or about another aspect of your heritage? How did you handle it?
2. As you were growing up, do you remember discovering that your family did anything differently from other families because of your culture, religion, or ethnicity? What was it?
3. Have you ever been with someone in a work situation who did something because of his or her culture, religion, or ethnicity that seemed unusual to you? What was it? Why did it seem unusual?
4. Have you ever felt uncomfortable, upset, or surprised by something that you saw when you were traveling in another part of the United States or the world? If so, what was it?
5. How did what you saw in question 4 make you feel? Pick some descriptive words to explain your feelings. How did you react? In retrospect, how do you wish you would have reacted?
6. Have you ever done anything that you think was culturally inappropriate when you have been in another country or with someone from a different culture? In other words, have you ever done something that you think might have been upsetting or embarrassing to another person? What was it?

*Imagine*  Imagine that for one month out of this year you will become a member of another cultural or ethnic group.

1. Of which group would you choose to be a part? Why?
2. What is one value from that group that attracts you?
3. Is there anything about that culture or ethnic group that concerns or frightens you?
4. Name one concrete way in which you think your life would be different if you were from that culture or ethnic group.

*Source:* Reprinted from Lynch, E., & Hanson, M. (2004). *Developing cross-cultural competence: A guide for working with children and their families* (3rd ed., pp. 76-77). Published by Paul H. Brookes Publishing, P.O. Box 10624, Baltimore, MD 21285-0624. Used by permission of the publisher and the authors.

To further your understanding of and answer questions about what you have learned, go to the Diversity & Exceptionality module in Chapter 2 of the Companion Website, **www.prenhall.com/heward**.

No matter how appropriate the goals and benchmarks or short-term objectives on a student's IEP, the document's usefulness is limited without direct and ongoing monitoring of student progress (Greenwood & Maheady, 1997; McDonough et al., 2005). Unfortunately, many teachers do not collect and use student performance data to evaluate the effectiveness of their instruction. Although three-fourths of the 510 special education teachers in one survey indicated that frequently collected student performance data are "important," many indicated they most often relied on anecdotal observations and subjective measures (e.g., checklists, letter grades) for determining whether or not IEP objectives were met; and 85% said they "never" or "seldom" collected and charted student performance data to make instructional decisions (Cooke, Heward, Test, Spooner, & Courson, 1991). Frequent and systematic measurement and charting of student learning does not have to be difficult or too time-consuming. Farlow and Snell (1994); Giek (1992); and Gunter, Miller, Venn, Thomas, and House (2002) describe a variety of practical and efficient procedures for obtaining and using student performance data to monitor student progress toward IEP objectives.

# COLLABORATION AND TEAMING

Special education is a team game. The third-grade teacher who works with Sharelle in the regular classroom, the speech-language pathologist who meets with Sharelle's teacher each week to co-plan language activities, the special education teacher who provides Sharelle with intensive reading instruction each day in the resource room and collaborates with her general education teacher on instructional modifications for Sharelle in math and science, and the adapted physical education teacher who works with Sharelle in the gymnasium are all members of a team that plans, delivers, and evaluates a program of special education and related services designed to meet the unique set of individual needs that arise from Sharelle's disability. Without open, honest, and frequent communication and collaboration between and among the members of Sharelle's team, the quality of her education is likely to suffer.

## Collaboration

Collaboration has become a common and necessary practice in special education (Dettmer, Thurston, & Dyck, 2005; Shapiro & Sayers, 2003; Walther-Thomas, Korinek, McLaughlin, & Williams, 2000). Teachers who work with students with disabilities and other students who are difficult to teach have discovered they are better able to diagnose and solve learning and behavior problems in the classroom when they work together (Giangreco, Cloninger, Dennis, & Edelman, 2000; Snell & Janney, 2005). Three ways in which team members can work collaboratively are through coordination, consultation, and teaming (Bigge, Stump, Spagna, & Silberman, 1999).

*Monitoring student progress*

**Council for Exceptional Children** Content Standards for Beginning Teachers—Common Core: Evaluate instruction and monitor progress of individuals with exceptional learning needs (CC8S8).

*Paraeducators*—also known as *paraprofessionals, teacher aides,* and *instructional assistants*—play an important role in delivering special education services to students with disabilities (Giangreco & Doyle, 2002; Riggs, 2001). To watch three well-trained paraeducators in action at Blendon Middle School, go to the CD-ROM and click on "Paraprofessional support."

Working together, these teachers are better able to diagnose and solve learning problems.

*Coordination* is the simplest form of collaboration, requiring only ongoing communication and cooperation to ensure that services are provided in a timely and systematic fashion. Although an important and necessary element of special education, coordination does not require service providers to share information or specifics of their efforts with one another. Fortunately for Sharelle, the four educators on her IEP team do much more than simply coordinate who is going to work with her when.

In *consultation,* team members provide information and expertise to one another. Consultation is traditionally considered unidirectional, with the expert providing assistance and advice to the novice. However, team members can, and often do, switch roles from consultant to consultee and back again. Sharelle's third-grade teacher, for example, receives expert advice from the speech-language pathologist on strategies for evoking extended language from Sharelle during cooperative learning groups but takes the consultant's role when explaining details of the science curriculum to Sharelle's resource room teacher.

## Teaming

Intervention assistance team, child study team, IEP team: each step of the special education process involves a group of people who must work together for the benefit of a child with special needs. For special education to be most effective, these groups must become functioning and effective teams (Clark, 2000; Hunt, Soto, Maier, & Doering, 2003; Thomas, Correa, & Morsink, 2001). *Teaming* is the most difficult level of collaboration to achieve; it also pays the most dividends. Teaming "bridges the two previous modes of working together and builds on their strengths while adding the component of reciprocity and sharing of information among all team members through a more equal exchange" (Bigge et al., 1999, p. 13). There are several levels or ways in which this can happen. Table 2.2 shows examples of coordination, consultation, and teaming activities by special educators.

Although there are many variations of the team approach in terms of size and structure, each member of a team generally assumes certain clearly assigned responsibilities and recognizes the importance of learning from, contributing to, and interacting with the other members of the team. Many believe that the consensus and group decisions arising from a team's involvement provide a form of insurance against erroneous or arbitrary conclusions in the complex issues that face educators of students with disabilities. In practice, three team models have emerged (McGonigel, Woodruff, & Roszmann-Millican, 1994).

*Multidisciplinary Teams.* **Multidisciplinary teams** are composed of professionals from different disciplines who work independently of one another. Each team member conducts assessments, plans interventions, and delivers services. Teams that operate according to a multidisciplinary structure risk the danger of not providing services that recognize the child as an integrated whole; they must be careful not to "splinter" the child into segments along disciplinary lines. (An old saying described the child with disabilities as giving "his hands to the occupational therapist, his legs to the physical therapist, and his brain to the teacher" [Williamson, 1978].) Another concern is the lack of communication among team members.

*Interdisciplinary Teams.* **Interdisciplinary teams** are characterized by formal channels of communication between members. Although each professional usually conducts discipline-specific assessments, the interdisciplinary team meets to share information and develop intervention plans. Each team member is generally responsible for implementing a portion of the service plan related to his discipline.

*Transdisciplinary Teams.* The highest level of team involvement, but also the most difficult to accomplish, is the *transdisciplinary team*. Members of transdisciplinary teams seek to provide services in a uniform and integrated fashion by conducting joint assessments, sharing information and expertise across discipline boundaries, and selecting goals and interventions that are discipline-free (Gallivan-Fenlon, 1994; Giangreco, Edelman, & Dennis, 1991). Members of transdisciplinary teams also share roles (often referred to as *role release*);

**TABLE 2.2** **Examples of coordination, consultation, and teaming activities in special education**

| Activity | Examples |
|---|---|
| Coordination | • special and general education teachers working out class schedules and support schedules for students<br>• therapists and general and special education teachers working out schedules for therapy interventions<br>• general and special education teachers coordinating grading procedures and policies<br>• special education teachers working with job coaches and transition teachers to set community-based experience schedules for students |
| Consultation | • special education teachers assisting general education teachers<br>• vocational education teachers working with community employers<br>• related service personnel providing support to special education and general education teachers |
| Teaming | • special and general education teachers, administrators, counselors, support staff, and school psychologists working together on prereferral teams to design and implement interventions in general education classrooms<br>• special and general education teachers co-teaching in the classroom<br>• paraprofessionals working with general education teachers<br>• special and general education teachers serving together on curriculum-planning teams<br>• team of professionals working together to determine whether a child is eligible for special education services<br>• IEP teams working together to assess the current performance of a student to determine continued eligibility for special education services |

*Source*: Reprinted from Bigge, J. L., Stump, C. S., Spagna, M. E., & Silberman, R. K. (1999). *Curriculum, assessment, and instruction for students with disabilities* (p. 14). Belmont, CA: Wadsworth. Used by permission.

in contrast, members of multidisciplinary and interdisciplinary teams generally operate in isolation and may not coordinate their services to achieve the integrated delivery of related services. Regardless of the team model, team members must learn to put aside professional rivalries and work collaboratively for the benefit of the student.

## Co-Teaching

*Co-teaching*—two or more teachers planning and delivering instruction together, usually in an inclusive classroom—has become increasingly important in special education. Co-teaching takes many different forms depending on the purpose of the lesson, the individualized objectives and needed supports for students with disabilities, and the teachers' relative levels of expertise with the content (Dettmer et al., 2005; Vaughn, Schumm, & Arguelles, 1997). Salend (2005) described five different co-teaching arrangements (see Figure 2.2):

- *One teaching/one helping.* One teacher instructs the whole class while the other circulates to collect information on student performance and offers help. This arrangement takes advantage of the expertise of one teacher in a specific subject area.
- *Parallel teaching.* When it is necessary to lower the student-teacher ratio, both teachers teach the same materials to two equal-sized groups of students.
- *Station teaching.* When covering difficult curriculum content that does not require sequential presentation, both teachers present different content at the same time to two equal groups of students and then switch groups and repeat the lesson.
- *Alternative teaching.* When teachers need to work with certain students to individualize instruction, remediate skills, promote mastery, or offer enrichment, one teacher works with a smaller group or individual students while the other works with the rest of the class.

## FIGURE 2.2
### Examples of co-teaching arrangements

*Source:* From Salend, S. J. (2005). *Creating inclusive classrooms: Effective and reflective practices for all students* (5th ed.), (p. 169). Upper Saddle River, NJ: Merrill/Prentice Hall.

One Teaching/One Helping

Parallel Teaching

Station Teaching

Alternative Teaching

Team Teaching

To watch expert teachers use several of these co-teaching arrangements in inclusive classrooms, go to "Dunkirk Middle School" on the CD-ROM and click on "Dunkirk School Number 3."

- *Team teaching.* Teachers plan and teach a lesson together; this method is used when it is desirable to blend talents and expertise. (adapted from p. 168)

As Mary Allaire-Gifford and Jean Michielli-Pendl emphasized at the beginning of this chapter, meticulous planning, open communication, and flexibility are keys to successful co-teaching. Suggestions for making co-teaching effective can be found in Dieker (2002); Vaughn et al. (1997); and Villa, Thousand, and Nevin (2004).

## INDIVIDUALIZED EDUCATION PROGRAM

The individualized education program (IEP) is the centerpiece of the special education process. IDEA requires that an IEP be developed and implemented for every student with disabilities between the ages of 3 and 21. (*Individualized family service plans [IFSPs]* are developed for infants and toddlers [from birth until age 3] with disabilities. IFSPs are described in Chapter 14.) The law is specific about who is to take part in developing the IEP and what it must include.

## IEP Team

Each IEP must be the product of the collaborative efforts of the members of an **IEP team**, the membership of which is specified in IDEA:

The term "individualized education program team" or "IEP Team" means a group of individuals composed of—

1. the parents of a child with a disability;
2. not less than one regular education teacher of the child (if the child is, or may be, participating in the regular education environment);
3. not less than one special education teacher, or if appropriate, at least one special education provider of such child;
4. a representative of the local education agency who—
   i. is qualified to provide, or supervise the provision of, specially designed instruction to meet the unique needs of children with disabilities;
   ii. is knowledgeable about the general curriculum; and
   iii. is knowledgeable about the availability of resources of the local education agency;
5. an individual who can interpret the instructional implications of evaluation results, who may be a member of the team described in clauses (1) through (6);
6. at the discretion of the parent or the school, other individuals who have knowledge or special expertise regarding the child, including related service personnel as appropriate; and
7. whenever appropriate, the child with a disability. (Individuals with Disabilities Education Improvement Act of 2004, H.R. 1350, Sec 614 (d)(B))

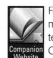 For additional information on the IEP team, go to "Who Creates an IEP?" in Part 1 of "Developing Quality IEPs: A Case-Based Tutorial" in Chapter 2 of the Companion Website, **www.prenhall.com/heward**

## IEP Components

All IEPs must include the following seven components:

1. A statement of the child's present levels of academic achievement and functional performance, including—
   (a) how the child's disability affects the child's involvement and progress in the general education curriculum;
   (b) for preschool children, as appropriate, how the disability affects the child's participation in appropriate activities; and
   (c) for children with disabilities who take alternate assessments aligned to alternate achievement standards, a description of benchmarks or short-term objectives;
2. A statement of measurable annual goals, including academic and functional goals, designed to—
   (a) meet the child's needs that result from the child's disability to enable the child to be involved in and make progress in the general education curriculum; and
   (b) meet each of the child's other educational needs that result from the child's disability;
3. A description of how the child's progress toward meeting the annual goals described in subclause (2) will be measured and when periodic reports on the progress the child is making toward meeting the annual goals (such as through the use of quarterly or other periodic reports, concurrent with the issuance of report cards) will be provided;
4. A statement of the special education and related services and supplementary aids and services, based on peer-reviewed research to the extent practicable, to be provided to the child, or on behalf of the child, and a statement of the program modifications or supports for school personnel that will be provided for the child—
   (a) to advance appropriately toward attaining the annual goals;
   (b) to be involved in and make progress in the general education curriculum in accordance with subclause (I) and to participate in extracurricular and other nonacademic activities; and
   (c) to be educated and participate with other children with disabilities and nondisabled children in the activities described in this subparagraph;

*Participation and progress in the general curriculum*

Council for Exceptional Children   Content Standards for Beginning Teachers—Common Core: Identify and prioritize areas of the general curriculum and needed accommodations (CC7S1).

5. An explanation of the extent, if any, to which the child will not participate with nondisabled children in the regular class and in the activities described in subclause (IV)(cc);
6. (a) a statement of any individual appropriate accommodations that are necessary to measure the academic achievement and functional performance of the child on State and districtwide assessments consistent with section 612(a)(16)(A); and (b) if the IEP Team determines that the child shall take an alternate assessment on a particular State or districtwide assessment of student achievement, a statement of why—
   (aa)   the child cannot participate in the regular assessment; and
   (bb)   the particular alternate assessment selected is appropriate for the child;
7. The projected date for the beginning of the services and modifications described in subclause (4), and the anticipated frequency, location, and duration of those services and modifications (Individuals with Disabilities Education Improvement Act of 2004, H.R. 1350, Sec 614 (d)(1)(A)(i))

IEPs for older students must also include information on how the child's transition from school to adult life will be supported:

8. Beginning not later than the first IEP to be in effect when the child is 16, and updated annually thereafter—
   a. appropriate measurable postsecondary goals based upon age appropriate transition assessments related to training, education, employment, and, where appropriate, independent living skills;
   b. the transition services (including courses of study) needed to assist the child in reaching those goals; and
   c. beginning not later than 1 year before the child reaches the age of majority under State law, a statement that the child has been informed of the child's rights under this title, if any, that will transfer to the child on reaching the age of majority under section 615(m). (Individuals with Disabilities Education Improvement Act of 2004, H.R. 1350, Sec 614 (d)(1)(A)(i))

To review the necessary parts of an IEP, go to the "What Components Make Up IEPs?" in Part 1 of "Developing Quality IEPs: A Case-Based Tutorial" in Chapter 2 on the Companion Website, **www.prenhall.com/heward**.

## IEP Functions and Formats

The IEP is a system for spelling out where the child is, where she should be going, how she will get there, how long it will take, and how to tell if and when she has arrived. Thus, a good IEP serves as both a road map and a guidebook for meeting the challenges posed by a student's disability. The annual goals and benchmarks identify the destinations for the journey and provide signposts along the way.

The IEP provides teachers and parents with the opportunity (and, we might add, the responsibility) to first be *realistic* about the child's needs and goals and then to be *creative* about how to meet them. Being realistic does not mean taking a pessimistic or limited view of the child's capabilities or potential. It means analyzing how specially designed instruction and related services can help the student get from her present levels of performance to future goals.

To better understand how a student's present level of performance is the foundation of the IEP, complete the "Present Level of Performance" tutorial in Part 2 of "Developing Quality IEPs: A Case-Based Tutorial" in Chapter 2 of the Companion Website, **www.prenhall.com/heward**.

The IEP is also a measure of accountability for teachers and schools. Whether a particular school or educational program is effective will be judged, to some extent, by how well it is able to help children meet the goals and objectives set forth in their IEPs. Like other professionals, teachers are being called on to demonstrate effectiveness; and the IEP provides one way for them to do so. A child's teacher and school cannot be prosecuted in the courts if the child does not achieve the goals set forth in the IEP. Nevertheless, the school must be able to document that a conscientious and systematic effort was made to achieve those goals (Huefner, 2000). The IEP is, however, much more than an accountability device. Its potential benefits are improved planning (including planning for the student's needs after he leaves school); consistency; regular evaluation; and clearer communication among parents, teachers, and others involved in providing services to the student (Lytle & Bordin, 2001; Menlove, Hudson, & Suter, 2001; Test et al., 2004).

IEP formats vary widely across school districts, and schools may go beyond the requirements of the law and include additional information. Bateman and Linden (1998) caution against overreliance on standardized forms and computers for creating IEPs. "Forms by their very nature tend to interfere with true individualization.... a proper form will contain all the required elements in the simplest way possible, allowing for the most flexibility and creativity" (p. 57). Figure 2.3 shows the "non-form" for IEPs recommended by Bateman and Linden. The first page identifies the student, IEP team members, and special factors to consider as required by the 1997 IDEA amendments. The "heart of the IEP" (p. 72) begins on the second page in the form of a three-column sequence from needs and present levels of performance, to services that will be provided, to goals and objectives. The IEP form concludes with additional IDEA requirements and, for older students, transition components.

Figure 2.4 (p. 74) shows portions of the IEP for Curt, a ninth grader and low achiever seen by the school district as a poorly motivated student with a disciplinary problem and a bad attitude. Curt's parents see their son as a discouraged and frustrated student with learning disabilities, especially in written language.

One of the most difficult tasks for the child study team is determining how inclusive the IEP document should be. Strickland and Turnbull (1993) state that the definition of special education as "specially designed instruction" should be a key element in determining what should go into a student's IEP.

*Each area of functioning that is adversely affected by the student's disability must be represented by an annual goal on the IEP.*

> The determination of whether instruction is "specially designed" must be made by comparing the nature of the instruction for the student with a disability to instructional practices used with typical students at the same age and grade level. If the instructional adaptations that a student with a disability requires are (1) significantly different from adaptations normally expected or made for typical students in that setting, and if (2) the adaptations are necessary to offset or reduce the adverse effect of the disability on learning and educational performance, then these adaptations should be considered "specially designed instruction" and should be included as part of the student's IEP, regardless of the instructional setting. (p. 13)

It is important for educators and parents to recognize that an IEP is not the same as a curriculum. "IEP objectives are not comprehensive enough to cover the entire scope and sequence of what a student is to learn. The content taught by most special educators goes far beyond what is written in the IEP. Sometimes special educators try to incorporate an entire curriculum into the IEP, resulting in an overly long, detailed IEP" (Browder, 2001, p. 35).

Each area of functioning that is adversely affected by the student's disability must be represented by an annual goal on the IEP. Goals are measurable statements of what the IEP team believes the student can accomplish in one year if the special services provided are effective. Figure 2.5 (p. 75) includes some do's and don'ts concerning IEP annual goals.

*Role of IEP team*

Council for Exceptional Children Content Standards for Beginning Teachers—Common Core: Develop and implement a comprehensive, longitudinal, individualized program in collaboration with team members (CC7S2).

## Problems and Potential Solutions

Since its inception, the IEP process has been problematic (Huefner, 2000; Yell & Drasgow, 2000). More than 20 years ago, Gallagher (1984) wrote that the IEP is "probably the single most unpopular aspect of the law, not only because it requires a great deal of work, but also because the essence of the plan itself seems to have been lost in the mountains of paperwork" (p. 228). Studies of actual IEPs seem to support Gallagher's contention (Smith, 1990a, 1990b; Smith & Brownell, 1995). Smith and Simpson (1989), for example, evaluated the IEPs of 214 students with behavioral disorders and found that one-third of the IEPs lacked necessary mandated components. A study that examined IEPs for high school students found that transition-related goals included vague outcomes (e.g., "will think about best place to live," "will explore jobs"), no evaluation procedures, and very few adaptations in activities or materials (Grigal, Test, Beattie, & Wood, 1997).

**FIGURE 2.3** **Example of an IEP form**

*Source:* Reprinted from Bateman, B. D., & Linden, M. L. (1998). *Better IEPs: How to develop legally correct and educationally useful programs* (3rd ed.), (pp. 97, 98, 99). Longmont, CO: Sopris West. Used by permission.

# Individualized Education Program

Student's Name _____ Date of IEP Meeting _____

Date of Birth _____ Grade _____ Primary Contact Person/Case Manager _____

**Copies of this IEP will circulate among staff members who are working with this student.**
**Please observe the Federal and state laws that protect the student's right**
**to confidentiality of education records.**
**Do NOT share with unauthorized persons,**
**and do NOT include sensitive information such as disability category or IQ.**

## Participants

| Signature | Position |
|-----------|----------|
|           |          |
|           |          |
|           |          |
|           |          |
|           |          |
|           |          |
|           |          |
|           |          |
|           |          |
|           |          |
|           |          |
|           |          |
|           |          |

## Special Factors to Consider

For all students, consider:
- ❏ Strengths of the student
- ❏ Concerns of the parent(s)
- ❏ Need for assistive technology

If behavior impedes learning of the student or others, consider:
- ❏ Strategies, including positive behavioral interventions
- ❏ Supports to address behavior

If the student has limited English proficiency, consider:
- ❏ Language needs as they relate to the student's IEP

If the student is blind or visually impaired, consider:
- ❏ Instruction in the use of Braille (unless the IEP team decides instruction in Braille is inappropriate)

Consider communication needs (language & communication needs for students with hearing impairments), including:
- ❏ Opportunities for direct communication with peers and professionals in the student's language and communication mode
- ❏ Opportunities for direct instruction in the student's language and communication mode

| Unique Educational Needs, Characteristics, and Present Levels of Performance (PLOPs) | Special Education, Related Services, Supplemental Aids & Services, Assistive Technology, Program Modifications, Support for Personnel | Measurable Annual Goals & Short-Term Objectives or Benchmarks • To enable the student to participate in the general curriculum • To meet other needs resulting from the disability |
|---|---|---|
| *(include how the disability affects the student's ability to progress in the general curriculum)* | *(include frequency, duration, & location)* | *(include how progress toward goals will be measured)* |
| | *[This is the most important part of the IEP. See Figure 2.4 for sample entries.]* | |

**FIGURE 2.3** *continued*

**Progress Reports**

The parents will receive regular reports about (the student's)
(a) progress toward achieving annual goals
(b) and the extent to which that progress is sufficient to enable achievement of goals by the end of the year
Progress reports will take the form of _____

_____

and the parents will receive them _____ times/year (which is at least as often as parents of children who are not on IEPs receive progress reports). Reports will include **specific** information about progress on each IEP goal.

**Participants With Nondisabled Students**

Explanation of the extent to which (the student) will **not** participate with nondisabled children in (a) regular classes _____

_____
_____
_____
_____

(b) special education services _____
_____
_____
_____
_____

**Participation in State- and District-Wide Assessments**

(The student) needs the following modifications in the administration of state- or district-wide assessments _____
_____
_____

The IEP team has decided that (the student) will **not** participate in any state- or district-wide assessments
(a) because _____
_____
_____

(b) (The student) will instead be assessed by _____
_____
_____

**Transition Planning**

(The student) has reached age 14, and (his or her):
(a) goals for life after high school include _____
_____
_____

(b) course of study is linked to student transition goals by
_____
_____

(The student) has reached age 16, and:
(a) the following activities are needed to promote transition to post-high school life
• Instruction _____
_____
_____

• Related services _____
_____
_____

• Community experiences _____
_____
_____

• Development of employment and other adult living objectives _____
_____
_____

• Acquisition of daily living skills and functional vocational evaluation _____
_____
_____

(b) (The student) does not need one or more of the activities listed above because _____
_____

(The student) will reach the age of majority under state law on (date). (He or she) has received notice (at least a year in advance) of all rights under the IDEA that will transfer to (him or her) at that time.

_____
Student's Signature

But properly including all of the mandated components in an IEP is no guarantee that the document will guide the student's learning and teachers' teaching in the classroom, as intended by IDEA. Although most educators support the idealized concept of the IEP, inspection and evaluation of IEPs often reveal inconsistencies between what is written on the document and the instruction that students experience in the classroom (Smith & Brownell, 1995). Bateman and Linden (1998) contend:

> Sadly, most IEPs are horrendously burdensome to teachers and nearly useless to parents and children. Far from being a creative, flexible, databased, and individualized application of the best of educational interventions to a child with unique needs, the typical IEP is "empty," devoid of specific services to be provided. It says what the IEP team hopes the student will be able to accomplish, but little if anything about the special education interventions and the related services or the classroom modifications that will enable him or her to reach those goals. (p. 63)

**FIGURE 2.4** Portions of an IEP for Curt, a ninth grader with learning disabilities and a history of disciplinary problems

Source: Reprinted from Bateman, B. D., & Linden, M. L. (1998). *Better IEPs: How to develop legally correct and educationally useful programs* (3rd ed.), (pp. 97, 98, 99). Longmont, CO: Sopris West. Used by permission.

| Unique Educational Needs, Characteristics, and Present Levels of Performance (PLOPs) | Special Education, Related Services, Supplemental Aids & Services, Assistive Technology, Program Modifications, Support for Personnel | Measurable Annual Goals & Short-Term Objectives or Benchmarks |
|---|---|---|
| | | • To enable student to participate in the general curriculum<br>• To meet other needs resulting from the disability |
| *(include how the disability affects the student's ability to progress in the general curriculum)* | *(include frequency, duration, & location)* | *(include how progress toward goals will be measured)* |
| Study Skills/Organizational Needs:<br>    How to read text<br>    Note taking<br>    How to study notes<br>    Memory work<br>    Be prepared for class, with materials<br>    Lengthen and improve attention span and on-task behavior<br><br>Present Level:<br>Curt currently lacks skill in all these areas. | 1. Speech/lang: therapist, resource room teacher, and content area teachers will provide Curt with direct and specific teaching of study skills, i.e. Note taking from lectures; Note taking while reading text; How to study notes for a test; Memorization hints; Strategies for reading text to retain information.<br>2. Assign a "study buddy" for Curt in each content area class.<br>3. Prepare a motivation system for Curt to be prepared for class with all necessary materials.<br>4. Develop a motivational plan to encourage Curt to lengthen his attention span and time on task.<br>5. Provide aide to monitor on-task behaviors in first month or so of plan and teach Curt self-monitoring techniques.<br>6. Provide motivational system and self-recording form for completion of academic tasks in each class. | Goal: At the end of academic year, Curt will have better grades and, by his own report, will have learned new study skills.<br>Obj. 1: Given a 20-30 min. lecture/oral lesson, Curt will take appropriate notes as judged by that teacher.<br>Obj. 2: Given 10-15 pgs. of text to read, Curt will employ an appropriate strategy for retaining info.—i.e., mapping, webbing, outlining, notes, etc.—as judged by the teacher.<br>Obj. 3: Given notes to study for a test, Curt will do so successfully as evidenced by his test score.<br><br>Goal: Curt will improve his on-task behavior from 37% to 80% as measured by a qualified observer at year's end.<br>Obj. 1: By 1 month, Curt's on-task behavior will increase to 45%.<br>Obj. 2: By 3 months, Curt's on-task behavior will increase to 60%.<br>Obj. 3: By 6 months, Curt's on-task behavior will increase to 80% and maintain or improve until end of the year. |
| Academic Needs/Written Language:<br>Curt needs strong remedial help in spelling, punctuation, capitalization, and usage.<br><br>Present Level:<br>Curt is approximately 2 grade levels behind his peers in these skills.<br><br>Adaptations to Regular Program:<br>• In all classes, Curt should sit near the front of the class.<br>• All teachers should help Curt with study skills as trained by spelling/language specialist and resource room teacher.<br>• Curt should be called on often to keep him involved and on task.<br>• Teachers should monitor Curt's work closely in the beginning weeks/months of his program. | 1. Provide direct instruction in written language skills (punctuation, capitalization, usage, spelling) by using a highly structured, well-sequenced program. Services provided in small group of no more than four students in the resource room, 50 minutes/day.<br>2. Build in continuous and cumulative review to help with short-term rote memory difficulty.<br>3. Develop a list of commonly used words in student writing (or use one of many published lists) for Curt's spelling program. | Goal: Within one academic year, Curt will improve his written language skills by 1.5 or 2 full grade levels.<br>Obj. 1: Given 10 sentences of dictation at his current level of instruction, Curt will punctuate and capitalize with 90% accuracy (checked at the end of each unit taught).<br>Obj. 2: Given 30 sentences with choices of usage, at his current instructional level, Curt will perform with 90% accuracy.<br>Obj. 3: Given a list of 150 commonly used words in writing, Curt will spell with 90% accuracy. |

FIGURE 2.5  Some do's and don'ts for IEP annual goals

| Do | Don't |
| --- | --- |
| • Include at least one goal for every area of functioning (e.g., academic, social, vocational) adversely affected by the disability. | • Include goals for areas of the general education curriculum and functioning that are not adversely affected by the disability (e.g., the IEP for a student with a physical disability who has no special needs in academics does not need to address goals in math or science). |
| • Ask how a potential goal will increase the student's access to and benefit from the general education curriculum and other school activities. | • Write goals and objectives in unmeasurable terms (e.g., "Geoff will improve his math skills" or "Suzie will be successful in the regular classroom"). |
| • Ask to what extent achieving a potential goal will improve the child's present and future life. | • Select goals from a preprinted or computerized list (though in some curriculum areas, such as math, a hierarchy of sequenced short-term objectives can be used once the goal has been determined). |
| • Prioritize the goals within each area of functioning. | • Select goals based on the availability of services. |
| • Make sure each goal includes objective criteria by which the student's progress can be measured (e.g., "By June, Martin will read grade-level text at 100 wpm with 5 or fewer errors"). | • Select goals because other students in the school with the same disability have those goals on their IEPs. |
| • Write two or three measurable, short-term objectives or benchmarks that will enable families, students, and educators to monitor progress during the year and, if appropriate, revise the IEP. | • Choose goals based on the present or presumed future placement of the student. IEP goals and the specially designed instruction needed to meet those goals must be determined before the IEP team discusses placement. |
| • Ask the parents and, when appropriate, the student if the goals and objectives "look right." | |

Although IDEA requires parent participation and encourages students to participate, research on parent and student involvement in the IEP process has produced mixed results. A study of 393 middle school and high school IEP meetings found that when students attended their own IEP meetings, both general educators and parents reported that they felt more comfortable saying what they thought, understood more of what was said, and knew better what to do next (Martin, Huber Marshall, & Sale, 2004). However, students rated themselves lower than all other IEP meeting participants in terms of knowing the reason for the meetings, what they should do there, feeling comfortable saying what they thought, understanding what was said, and feeling good about the meeting.

Students are often unfamiliar with the IEP process and too seldom are active participants (Lovitt & Cushing, 1994). Although 95% of 523 respondents to an on-line survey of CEC members reported student involvement in IEP meetings was important, only 34% said they were satisfied with the level of student involvement in IEP meetings (Mason, Field, & Sawilosky, 2004).

Nevertheless, after reviewing 16 studies investigating curricula or strategies to increase students' involvement in their IEP process, Test and colleagues (2004) concluded that "research to date has verified that students with widely varying disabilities can be actively

For strategies to encourage and facilitate the effective participation of students in their own IEPs, see "Someone's Missing" in the Teaching & Learning Module in Chapter 2 of the Companion Website, **www.prenhall.com/heward**.

For help writing meaningful annual goals and objectives, complete Part III of "Developing Quality IEPs: A Case-Based Tutorial" in Chapter 2 of the Companion Website, **www.prenhall.com/heward**.

*Least restrictive environment*

Council for Exceptional Children Content Standards for Beginning Teachers—General Curriculum and Independence Curriculum Referenced Standards: Principles of normalization and concept of least restrictive environment (GC1K8, IC1K7).

involved in the IEP process" (p. 405). Mason, McGahee-Kovac, and Johnson (2004) describe a six-session program to prepare students to lead their IEP meetings. Students progress through three levels:

*Level 1*—Student presents information about or reads from his or her transition plan for the future.

*Level 2*—Student explains his or her disability, shares information on individual strengths and weaknesses (present levels of performance), and explains the accommodations needed.

*Level 3*—Student leads the IEP conference, including Level 1 and Level 2 responsibilities, introductions, and closing. (p. 19)

Just as students need instruction in the IEP process, so do general education teachers. In the study by Martin et al. (2004), general education teachers rated themselves lower than all other IEP meeting participants, including students, on the extent to which they helped make decisions and knew what to do next. General education teachers ranked second lowest (only to students) in knowing the reason for the meetings, talking at the meetings, feeling comfortable saying what they thought, understanding what was said, and feeling good about the meeting.

Special and regular educators are working together to create procedures for developing IEPs that go beyond compliance with the law and actually serve as a meaningful guide for the specially designed instruction a student with disabilities needs. Several tools have been developed to assist IEP teams in the critical process of designing a truly appropriate education, including a variety of strategies for involving all IEP team members and writing good goals and objectives (Gibb & Dyches, 2000; Hammer, 2004; Lignugaris/Kraft, Marchand-Martella, & Martella, 2001; Keyes & Owens-Johnson, 2003; Lytle & Bordin, 2001; Menlove et al., 2001; Rock, 2000; Walsh, 2001; Wood, Karvonen, Test, Browder, & Algozzine, 2004). For example, Choosing Outcomes and Accommodations for Children (COACH) is a field-tested IEP process that guides child study teams through the assessment and planning stages of IEP development in a way that results in goals and short-term objectives directly related to functional skills in integrated settings (Giangreco, Cloninger, & Iverson, 1998).

# LEAST RESTRICTIVE ENVIRONMENT

IDEA requires that every student with disabilities be educated in the **least restrictive environment (LRE).** Specifically, the law stipulates that

> to the maximum extent appropriate, children with disabilities, including children in public or private institutions or other care facilities, [will be] educated with children who are not disabled, and that special classes, separate schooling or other removal of children with disabilities from the regular educational environment [may occur] only when the nature or severity of the disability is such that education in regular classes with the use of supplementary aids and services cannot be achieved satisfactorily. (20 U.S.C., Sec. 1412 [a] [5])

Thus, the LRE is the setting that is closest to a regular school program and also meets the child's special educational needs. Least restrictive environment is a relative and wholly individualized concept; the LRE for one 10-year-old student who is blind might be inappropriate for another 10-year-old with a similar visual impairment. And the LRE for both students may change over time. Since the passage of IDEA, there have been many differences of opinion over which type of setting is least restrictive and most appropriate for students with disabilities. Some educators and parents consider any decision to place a student with disabilities outside the regular classroom to be overly restrictive; most, however, recognize that full-time placement in a regular classroom is restrictive and inappropriate if the child's educational needs cannot be adequately met in that environment.

## A Continuum of Services

Children with disabilities and their families need a wide range of special education and related services. Today, most schools provide a **continuum of services**—that is, a range of

The least restrictive environment is a relative concept; the LRE for one child may be inappropriate for another.

placement and service options to meet the individual needs of students with disabilities. The continuum can be symbolically depicted as a pyramid, with placements ranging from the regular classroom at the bottom to special schools, residential facilities, and hospital or homebound placements at the top (see Figure 2.6). The fact that the pyramid is widest at the bottom indicates that most children with disabilities are served in *regular classrooms* and that the number of children who require more intensive and specialized placements gets smaller as we move up the continuum. As noted in Chapter 1, the majority of children receiving special education services have mild disabilities. As the severity of a disability increases, typically the need for more specialized services also increases, while the number of students involved decreases. However, the fact that a larger proportion of children with severe disabilities are educated in placements outside of the regular classroom does not mean that the LRE for a student with severe disabilities is necessarily a special class or a separate school.

Five of the eight placement options depicted in Figure 2.6 are available in regular public school buildings. Children at the first three levels on the continuum have full-time placements in general education classrooms and receive various degrees and types of support by special teachers who consult or co-teach with the general education teachers. In a *resource room,* a special educator provides instruction to students with disabilities for part of the school day, either individually or in small groups. Children who require full-time placement in a *separate classroom* (also called a *self-contained classroom*) are with other children with disabilities for most of the school day and interact with children without disabilities only at certain times, such as during lunch, recess, or perhaps art and music. Although the separate classroom provides significantly fewer opportunities for interaction with nondisabled children than the regular classroom does, it provides more integration than does placement in *separate schools* or *residential schools,* which are attended only by children with disabilities. A student in a *homebound or hospital setting* receives special education and related services on an individual basis and has few opportunities to interact with other students.

## Determining the LRE

The IEP team determines the proper placement for a child after the child's needs that result from the disability and the special education and related services necessary to meet those

*Continuum of services*

Council for Exceptional Children — Content Standards for Beginning Teachers—General Curriculum and Independence Curriculum Referenced Standards: Continuum of placement and services available for individuals with disabilities (GC1K5, IC1K4).

**FIGURE 2.6** **Continuum of educational services for students with disabilities**

needs have been determined. For many years special education operated like this: (1) a student found eligible for special education was labeled with a disability category; (2) the student was placed into a program for students with that particular disability; and (3) a not-so-individualized version of the already-in-place program was written down and presented as the student's IEP, even though the program continued as usual whether or not the "new" student was in it. This is the wrong way.

The legally mandated and educationally sound process goes like this: (1) the school must determine whether the child has a disability and is therefore eligible for special education; (2) the child's needs must be determined and an IEP developed that specifies the special education and related services that are needed to meet those needs; and (3) the child is then placed in the least restrictive environment in which an appropriate program can be provided and the child can make satisfactory educational progress.

Bateman and Linden (1998) describe the difference between the wrong way and the IDEA way:

> For many, the old way is deeply ingrained and it seems practical.... for example, "Joe is learning disabled, so we'll put him in the resource room for learning disabled students and then have the resource teacher write up one more copy of the ongoing program in that room and call it the IEP." Instead, one should have said, "Joe is eligible, Joe's individual needs are X, Y, Z, and can be met by services A, B, C (his IEP) which we can implement in placement P." Districts have tried to fit children into programs,... rather than flexibly and creatively designing new programs one child at a time. (p. 67)

The general education classroom is the starting point for the IEP team's discussion of placement. Before considering that special instruction and related services will be delivered in any setting other than the regular classroom, the IEP team must discuss if the IEP goals can be achieved in the regular classroom. Removal of a child with disabilities from the general education classroom should take place only when the nature and severity of the child's disabilities are such that an appropriate education in that setting cannot be achieved. Placement decisions should be made by "determining whether a particular placement option will support the effective instructional practices that are required for a particular child to achieve his or her individual objectives and goals" (Zigmond, 2003, p. 198).

Placement of a student with disabilities should not be viewed as all or nothing at any one level on the continuum. The IEP team should consider the extent to which the student can effectively be integrated into each of three dimensions of school life: the general academic curriculum, extracurricular activities (e.g., clubs), and other school activities (e.g., recess, mealtimes). The LRE "provision allows for a 'mix and match' where total integration is appropriate under one dimension and partial integration is appropriate under another dimension" (Turnbull & Cilley, 1999, p. 41).

In addition, placement must not be regarded as permanent. The continuum concept is intended to be flexible, with students moving from one placement to another as dictated by their individual educational needs. The IEP team should periodically review the specific goals and objectives for each child—they are required to do so at least annually—and make new placement decisions if warranted. The child's parents must be informed whenever any change in placement is being considered so that they can either consent or object to the change and present additional information if they wish.

Because neither IDEA nor the regulations that accompany it specify exactly how a school district is to determine LRE, numerous conflicts have arisen; some have led to court cases. After reviewing the rulings of four LRE disputes that reached U.S. courts of appeals, Yell (1995) concluded that "for some students with disabilities, the appropriate and least restrictive setting will not be the regular education classroom.... The IEP team, as the courts have indicated, needs to employ a balancing test, weighing the desirability of integration against the obligation to furnish an appropriate education" (p. 402).

*Determining LRE*

Council for Exceptional Children — Content Standards for Beginning Teachers—Common Core: Issues, assurances, and due process rights related to assessment, eligibility, and placement within a continuum of services (CC1K6).

# INCLUSIVE EDUCATION

Although often confused, the terms *inclusion* and *least restrictive environment* are not synonymous. **Inclusion** means educating students with disabilities in regular classrooms; the LRE principle requires that students with disabilities be educated in settings as close to the regular class as possible in which an appropriate program can be provided and the child can make satisfactory educational progress. For many students with disabilities, an inclusive classroom and the least restrictive environment are one and the same; but that is not always so. Much discussion and controversy and many misconceptions have arisen regarding the inclusion of students with disabilities in regular classrooms (Kauffman & Hallahan, 1994; Kavale & Forness, 2000; Mitchell, 2004a, 2004b; Sasso, 2001; Schwartz, 2005).

Although many parents of children with disabilities strongly support inclusion, others have resisted it just as strongly, thinking that the regular classroom does not offer the intense, individualized education their children need. For example, a study of parents of children with severe disabilities found some parents in favor of and some against inclusion (Palmer, Fuller, Arora, & Nelson, 2001). Another study found that most parents of elementary students with learning disabilities who received reading instruction in resource rooms had strong positive attitudes toward the resource room program and were reluctant to have their children reintegrated into general education classes for reading instruction (Green & Shinn, 1995).

As we have seen, what the law does call for is the education of each child with disabilities in the least restrictive environment, removed no farther than necessary from the regular public school program. IDEA does not require placement of all children with disabilities in regular classes, call for children with disabilities to remain in regular classes without necessary support services, or suggest that general education teachers should educate students with disabilities without help from special educators and other specialists. Although not all children with disabilities attend regular classes, it is true that regular classroom teachers are expected to deal with a much wider range of learning, behavioral, sensory, and physical differences among their students than was the case just a few years ago. Thus, provision of in-service training for general educators is an important (and sometimes overlooked) requirement of IDEA. General education teachers are understandably wary of having children with disabilities placed in their classes if little or no training or support is provided. The role of regular classroom teachers is already a demanding one; they do not want their classes to become any larger, especially if they perceive exceptional children as unmanageable. Regular classroom teachers are entitled to be involved in decisions about children who are placed in their classes and to be offered continuous consultation and other support services from administrators and their special education colleagues (Kennedy & Fisher, 2001; Kochar, West, & Taymans, 2000).

We know that simply placing a child with disabilities in a regular classroom does not mean that she will learn and behave appropriately or be socially accepted by children without disabilities (Cook & Semmel, 1999; Division for Learning Disabilities, 2001; Freeman & Alkin, 2000).

Although some educators have expressed concern that the presence of students with disabilities impairs the academic achievement of students without disabilities, there is no evidence of this. McDonnell and colleagues (2003) found no significant differences in the reading and math achievement of 324 students without disabilities who were enrolled in inclusive classes compared to the achievement of 221 students without disabilities. Cole, Waldron, and Majd (2004) reported that 334 students without disabilities in inclusive classrooms actually made greater gains in reading and math than did than a comparison group of 272 students without disabilities who were educated in "traditional" classrooms. When considering the results of studies such as these, it is important to consider that the most critical factor impacting student achievement may be quality of instruction and not the presence or absence of students with disabilities.

Nor, it should be pointed out, does placement in a special education setting guarantee that a child will receive the specialized instruction he or she needs (e.g., Moody, Vaughn, Hughes, & Fischer, 2000). It is important for special educators to teach appropriate social skills and behavior to the child with disabilities and to educate nondisabled children about their classmates. Examples of effective inclusion programs can be found at age levels ranging from preschool (Sandall, Schwartz, & Joseph, 2000) to high school (Bauer & Brown, 2001), and they include children whose disabilities range from mild (Hock, Schumaker, & Deshler, 1999) to severe (Fisher & Ryndak, 2001). Numerous strategies for successfully including students with disabilities in the general education program can be found in Beninghof (1998), Friend & Bursuck (1999), Kochar et al. (2000), Lewis and Doorlag (2006), Mastropieri & Scruggs (2004), Salend (2005), and Wood (2006).

Cooperative learning activities provide a strategic approach for integrating students with disabilities into both the academic curriculum and the social fabric of the classroom. *Cooperative learning* can take many forms, but in most models all students in the class are assigned to small heterogeneous groups and help one another learn to achieve a shared academic goal (Johnson & Johnson, 1987; Slavin, 1986). According to Slavin (1990), two elements should be present: hold all students in the group accountable, and promote positive interdependence—i.e., students are accountable for both their own achievement and the group's performance.

1. *Group goals (positive interdependence).* All members of the group work together to earn grades, rewards, or other recognition of success for the group.
2. *Individual accountability.* Each student within the group must demonstrate his or her learning and contribute in a specific way for the group to obtain success.

*Facilitating inclusion*

Council for Exceptional Children Content Standards for Beginning Teachers—General Curriculum and Independence Curriculum Referenced Standards: Barriers to accessibility and acceptance of individuals with disabilities (GC5K1, IC5K2).

However, the manner in which group members contribute may differ to meet individualized needs and learning objectives.

Well-designed cooperative learning activities keep students actively engaged and motivated to succeed. In addition to improved academic outcomes, cooperative learning can also promote positive social relationships, friendships, and mutual supports among students with and without disabilities in the classroom, which are vital to successful inclusion (Blake, Wang, Cartledge, & Gardner, 2000; Maheady, Mallette, Harper, & Sacca, 1991; Wolford, Alber, & Heward, 2001).

Classwide peer tutoring is a form of cooperative learning with more than two decades of research demonstrating its effectiveness as an instructional approach for teaching reading, math, social studies, and a wide range of specialized subject areas to (and by) students with and without disabilities in inclusive classrooms (Heron, Welsch, & Goddard, 2003; Maheady, Mallette, & Harper, in press). (See Teaching & Learning, "Classwide Peer Tutoring," on the following pages.)

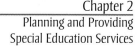

To see cooperative learning strategies in the inclusive classroom, go to the CD-ROM and click to "Heads Together" and "Pair-Share" at "Dunkirk Elementary School" and "Dunkirk Middle School."

## Arguments For and Against Full Inclusion

Some special educators believe that the continuum of services should be dismantled and all students with disabilities placed in regular classrooms. For example, in a paper widely cited by advocates of full inclusion, Taylor (1988) contends that the LRE model

1. *Legitimates restrictive environments.* To conceptualize services in terms of restrictiveness is to legitimize more restrictive settings. As long as services are conceptualized in this manner, some people will end up in restrictive environments.

2. *Confuses segregation and integration with intensity of services.* As represented by the continuum, LRE equates segregation with the most intensive services and integration with the least intensive services. The principle assumes that the least restrictive, most integrated settings are incapable of providing the intensive services needed by people with severe disabilities. However, segregation and integration on the one hand and intensity of services on the other are separate dimensions.

3. *Is based on a readiness model.*" Implicit in LRE is the assumption that people with developmental disabilities must earn the right to move to the least restrictive environment. In other words, the person must "get ready" or "be prepared" to live, work, or go to school in integrated settings.

Shared activities with individualized outcomes and a sense of belonging and group membership for all students are two defining features of inclusive education.

4. *Supports the primacy of professional decision making.* LRE invariably is framed in terms of professional judgments regarding "individual needs." The phrase "least restrictive environment" is almost always qualified with words such as "appropriate," "necessary," "feasible," and "possible" (and never with "desired" or "wanted").

5. *Sanctions infringements on people rights.* The question imposed by LRE is not whether people with disabilities should be restricted, but to what extent.

6. *Implies that people must move as they develop and change.* As LRE is commonly conceptualized, people with disabilities are expected to move toward increasingly less restrictive environments. Even if people move smoothly through a continuum, their lives would be a series of stops between transitional placements.

7. *Directs attention to physical settings rather than to the services and supports people need.* By its name, the principle of the LRE emphasizes facilities and environments designed specifically for people with disabilities. The field has defined the mission in terms of creating "facilities," first large ones and now smaller ones, and "programs," rather than providing the services and supports to enable people with disabilities to participate in the same settings used by other people. (from pp. 45–48)

# Classwide Peer Tutoring: Collaborative Learning for Students with Disabilities in Inclusive Classrooms

Meaningful inclusion of students with disabilities into the academic and social life of the regular classroom presents a difficult challenge. The regular classroom teacher is not only accountable for delivering individualized instruction to these and other students whose learning is at risk but is also expected to ensure all other learners' academic success and integrate the whole class socially. In-class tutoring is one method that has been used to individualize instruction without requiring students to leave the classroom. Often untapped but always available, the students themselves can be sources of tutoring help in every classroom.

Although the idea of peer tutoring (same-age classmates teaching one another) is not new (Lancaster, 1806), it has become the focus of much interest and research in special education. Traditional peer tutoring involves singling out students who have not mastered a particular skill for special help from a few high-achieving students who are assigned as tutors. In contrast, classwide peer tutoring (CWPT) includes low achievers and students with disabilities as full participants in an ongoing, whole-class activity.

## FOUR EVIDENCE-BASED MODELS

Four models for designing and implementing systematic peer tutoring have emerged from more than 20 years of solid empirical research as peer tutoring models have been successfully implemented, evaluated, and refined to varying degrees across a range of age and grade levels in both general and special education settings. (For a review of these models, see Maheady, Mallette, and Harper, in press)

*Peer Assisted Learning Strategies (PALS)*, developed at George Peabody College, was developed over 15 years by researchers working collaboratively with local school districts (Fuchs & Fuchs, 1998). Three versions of PALS are currently available. The original program was designed for use in reading and math for students in grades 2–6 (Fuchs, Fuchs, Mathes, & Simmons, 1996). More recently, researchers have added K-PALS for kindergarten (Mathes, Clancy-Menchetti, & Torgesen, 2003), First Grade PALS for beginning reading instruction (Mathes, Torgesen, Allen, & Howard-Allor, 2003), and High School PALS for content-area instruction (L. Fuchs, Fuchs, & Kazdan, 1999).

The *Juniper Gardens Children's Project CWPT Model* was the brainchild of Greenwood, Delquadri, and Carta (1997). Perhaps its most compelling support, however, came from a 12-year experimental longitudinal study (Greenwood & Delquadri, 1995; Greenwood, Delquadri, & Hall, 1989). Here researchers compared groups of at-risk and non-risk students who had or had not received CWPT instruction. They found that CWPT increased students' active engagement during instruction in grades 1 to 3; improved pupil achievement at grades 2, 3, 4, and 6; reduced the number of CWPT students in need of special education services by seventh grade, and decreased the number of students who dropped out of school by the end of 11th grade (Greenwood et al., 1997; Greenwood, Meheady, & Delquadri, 2002).

*SUNY Fredonia Classwide Student Tutoring Teams (CSTT)* represent a hybrid peer tutoring program combining elements of Slavin's (1986) Student Team Learning model with components from the Juniper Gardens CWPT model. Pupils work in four-member, heterogeneous learning teams and take turns reading and responding to items on teacher-developed study guides and/or concept cards. Tutor roles rotate clockwise on each item, and the process continues until a predetermined time limit (e.g., 20–30 minutes) has elapsed (Maheady, Harper, Sacca, & Mallette, 1991; Maheady, Sacca, & Harper, 1987).

 To download the *CSTT Instructor's Manual*, go to "Peer-Tutoring Resources" in the Teaching & Learning Module in Chapter 2 of the Companion Website, **www.prenhall.com/heward**.

Research on the *Ohio State University CWPT Model* began in the late 1970s and early 1980s in an effort to find a low-cost, relatively easy approach for individualizing instruction of basic reading and math skills with diverse groups of learners in the primary grades (e.g., Cooke, Heron, & Heward, 1983; Heron, Heward, Cooke, & Hill, 1983; Heward, Heron, & Cooke, 1982; Parson & Heward, 1979). The OSU model has been replicated and extended by hundreds of classroom teachers in elementary, middle, and secondary schools across a wide range of curriculum areas such as spelling, science facts and vocabulary, algebra, geometry, reading fluency, foreign language vocabulary, and social studies (e.g., Gardner et al., 2001; Miller, Barbetta, & Heron, 1994; Wright, Cavanaugh, Sainato, & Heward, 1995). Daily sessions last about 20 minutes, and each student serves as both tutor and tutee during the session. In the role of tutee, each child responds to questions posed by his or her partner (tutor) over an individualized set of unknown facts, problems, or items determined by a teacher-given pretest. The basic elements of this model are described later in this box.

To see students using the peer tutoring system described here, go to "Oakstone Academy" on the CD-ROM and click on "Peer Tutoring."

**Tutoring Folders.**    Each student in the class has a tutoring folder (see Figure A) containing a set of 10 task cards on specific curriculum content. Each card identifies one word, problem, concept, or fact to be taught to the child's tutoring partner. The task cards are placed in a GO pocket on one side of the folder. Also in the folder is a track to record the tutee's progress, markers to use for recording, and a STOP pocket to collect learned cards.

**Tutor Huddle.**    When the questions or answers on the task cards are unknown to the tutors and cannot be depicted on the back of the card (e.g., abstract words that the tutor is also learning), the daily peer tutoring session begins with children getting their folders and participating in a 5-minute "tutor huddle" with two or three other tutors. In the huddle, the tutors take turns orally presenting the words or problems they will shortly be responsible for teaching to their partners. (Meanwhile, their partners are in other tutor huddles working on the content that they, too, will soon be teaching.) Fellow tutors confirm correct responses by saying yes and help identify words a tutor doesn't know. The teacher circulates around the room, helping tutor huddles that cannot identify or agree on a given word. Careful construction of the tutor huddles usually ensures that at least one student in each group will know or be able to recognize each task card. A tutor huddle is unnecessary for curriculum content with standard questions and answers provided on the backs of cards for the tutor to see (e.g., math facts, geometric shapes, equations).

**Practice.**    After the tutor huddle, partners pair up to practice their words. One child begins in the role of tutor, presenting the task cards as many times as possible during as 5-minutes practice period, shuffling the set of cards after each round. Tutors are trained to praise their partners' correct responses from time to time. When a student makes an error, the tutor says, "Try again." If the student still does not respond correctly, the tutor says, for example,

**FIGURE A**    Peer tutoring folder.

*Source:* Adapted from "Total Tutoring for Special and General Educators [Instructor's Manual] by T. E. Heron & W. L. Heward, 2000. Columbus, OH: The Ohio State University Special Education Program. Used by permission.

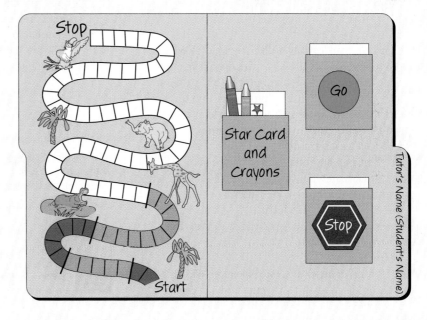

"This word is *tree;* say *tree*." A timer signals the end of the first practice period, and the partners switch roles. While students are tutoring, the teacher walks around the room, prompting and rewarding good tutoring behaviors, answering questions, and generally supervising the activity.

**Testing.** After the second practice period, the students reverse roles again; and the first tutor tests her partner by presenting each task card once with no prompts or cues. The teacher gives tutors about 5 minutes each to test and record their tutees' progress. Cards that a tutee reads or answers correctly are placed in one pile and missed cards in another. Roles are then switched again, and the first tutor is now tested on the words she practiced. The tutors then mark the back of each card to identify if it was "correct" or "incorrect" during the test. Each tutor records his tutee's daily progress on the chart. When a child correctly responds to a task card on the test for three consecutive sessions, that item is considered learned and is moved to the folder's STOP pocket. When all 10 cards have been learned, a new set of words is placed in the GO pocket. The session ends with tutors praising and complimenting each other for their good work.

## CHARACTERISTICS COMMON TO ALL FOUR MODELS

These four CWPT models have several characteristics in common. Each can be used to actively engage *all* pupils in the classroom simultaneously, an aspect that should make them particularly appealing to general education teachers. Each model employs a reciprocal peer tutoring system so that every student has the opportunity to tutor and be tutored. Moreover, each program contains highly structured and evidence-based instructional components that are delivered by well-trained peers and monitored by diligent teachers.

- *Clearly defined learning tasks/responses.* CWPT programs are based on clearly defined learning tasks and explicitly defined peer tutoring roles and teaching responsibilities. Tutoring procedures are often scripted, and each tutor is expected to use standard procedures with little variation.
- *Individualized instruction.* In CWPT, teachers give frequent pre- and post-tests to determine learning tasks that match the current needs of each student. Additionally, because CWPT uses a one-on-one tutor/pupil ratio, each learner's performance can be observed, checked, and redirected in ways not otherwise possible in traditional teacher-led instruction.
- *High rates of active student responding (ASR).* Well-designed CWPT programs provide each

student with many opportunities to respond. Depending on the learning task, students may make 100 or more responses during a 10-minute peer tutoring session. Total ASR is increased further in reciprocal CWPT programs because each student responds to the academic task in the role of tutee (initial responses to tutor's prompts, repeating missed items) and tutor (prompting responding, discriminating between correct and incorrect responses, and providing instructional feedback).

- *Immediate feedback and praise for correct responses.* Peer tutors provide feedback and praise to their tutees, and the teacher provides feedback to the tutors as a means of promoting high-quality peer teaching and learning during CWPT sessions. Formal point/reward systems are used in many CWPT programs to motivate participation and make learning fun.
- *Systematic error correction.* Tutors immediately and systematically correct mistakes by their tutees. Accurate error correction by tutors who themselves are learning the material can be achieved by using materials that show the correct response to the tutor or by the "tutor huddle" procedure.
- *Measurement of student progress.* All research-backed CWPT programs incorporate direct and frequent measurement of each student's progress. These data are obtained in a variety of ways, such as daily end-of-session assessments given by tutors, regularly scheduled teacher-administered "check outs" of students' performance, and weekly pre- and post-tests and curriculum-based measurements. In some programs, items missed on follow-up assessments are put back into the student's folder for additional practice.
- *Motivation for students.* Students have fun doing CWPT programs that have some sort of game-like format, team goals, and charted progress.

### HOW TO GET STARTED

To see examples of peer tutoring folders; task cards for various curriculum areas; and how-to manuals for designing, implementing, and evaluating research-based CWPT programs, go to "Peer Tutoring Resources" in Chapter 2 of the Companion Website, **www.prenhall.com/heward**.

 To learn more about classwide peer tutoring and test what you have learned, go to the Teaching & Learning module in Chapter 2 of the Companion Website, **www.prenhall.com/heward**.

There is no clear consensus in the field about the meaning of inclusion. To some, inclusion means full-time placement of all students with disabilities in regular classrooms; to others, the term refers to any degree of integration into the mainstream. Stainback and Stainback (1996), strong advocates and leaders of the inclusion movement, define an inclusive school as "a place where everyone belongs, is accepted, supports, and is supported by his or her peers and other members of the school community in the course of having his or her educational needs met" (p. 3). Giangreco et al. (2000) contend that "inclusive education is in place only when all five features [shown in Figure 2.7] occur on an ongoing, daily basis" (p. 294).

Virtually all special educators support the responsible inclusion of students with disabilities in regular classrooms and the development and evaluation of new models for working more cooperatively with general educators to serve all students (e.g., Kochar et al., 2000; Schwartz, 2005; Smith & Hilton, 1997; Vaughn, Schumm, & Brick, 1998). Descriptions of many research-based model programs and strategies for successfully and meaningfully including students with disabilities as full members in the academic and social life of regular classrooms are provided throughout this text. (To learn about some common mistakes made in well-intended efforts to include students with disabilities and how to avoid them, see Profiles & Perspectives, "Inclusion Missteps," later in this chapter.)

*Components of inclusive education*

 Council for Exceptional Children — Content Standards for Beginning Teachers—Common Core: Use strategies to facilitate integration into various settings (CC4S1).

---

Inclusive education is in place when each of these five features occurs on an ongoing, daily basis.

1. *Heterogeneous Grouping*   All students are educated *together* in groups where the number of those with and without disabilities approximates the *natural proportion*. The premise is that "students develop most when in the physical, social, emotional, and intellectual presence of nonhandicapped persons in reasonable approximations to the natural proportions" (Brown, Ford, Nisbet, Sweet, Donnellan, & Gruenewald, 1983, p. 17). Thus, in a class of 25 students, perhaps there is one student with significant disabilities, a couple of others with less significant disabilities, and many students without identified disabilities working at various levels.

2. *A Sense of Belonging to a Group*   All students are considered members of the class rather than visitors, guests, or outsiders. Within these groups, students who have disabilities are welcomed, as are students without disabilities.

3. *Shared Activities with Individualized Outcomes*   Students share educational experiences (e.g., lessons, labs, field studies, group learning) at the same time (Schnorr, 1990). Even though students are involved in the same activities, their learning objectives are individualized and, therefore, may be different. Students may have different objectives in the same curriculum area (e.g., language arts) during a shared activity. This is referred to as *multi-level instruction* (Campbell, Campbell, Collicott, Perner, & Stone, 1988; Collicott, 1991; Giangreco & Meyer, 1988; Giangreco & Putnam, 1991). Within a shared activity, a student also may have individualized objectives from a curriculum area (e.g., social skills) other than that on which other students are focused (e.g., science). This practice is referred to as *curriculum overlapping* (Giangreco & Meyer, 1988; Giangreco & Putnam, 1991).

4. *Use of Environments Frequented by Persons without Disabilities*   Shared educational experiences take place in environments predominantly frequented by people without disabilities (e.g., general education classrooms, community worksites).

5. *A Balanced Educational Experience*   Inclusive education seeks an individualized balance between the academic/functional and social/personal aspects of schooling (Giangreco, 1992). For example, teachers in inclusion-oriented schools would be as concerned about students' self-image and social network as they would be about developing literacy competencies or learning vocational skills.

## FIGURE 2.7
### Components of inclusive education

*Source:* Reprinted from Giangreco, M. F., Cloninger, C. J., Dennis, R. E., & Edelman, S. W. (2000). Problem-solving methods to facilitate inclusive education. In R. A. Villa & J. S. Thousand (Eds.), *Restructuring for caring and effective education: Piecing the puzzle together* (2nd ed.), (p. 294). Baltimore: Brookes. Used by permission.

**FIGURE 2.8** CEC's policy on inclusive schools

*Source:* Reprinted from the supplement to *Teaching Exceptional Children, 25*(4), May 1993. Used by permission.

The Council for Exceptional Children (CEC) believes all children, youth, and young adults with disabilities are entitled to a free and appropriate education and/or services that lead to an adult life characterized by satisfying relations with others, independent living, productive engagement in the community, and participation in society at large. To achieve such outcomes, there must exist for all children, youth, and young adults with disabilities a rich variety of early intervention, educational, and vocational program options and experiences. Access to these programs and experiences should be based on individual educational needs and desired outcomes. Furthermore, students and their families or guardians, as members of the planning team, may recommend the placement, curriculum option, and the exit document to be pursued.

CEC believes that a continuum of services must be available for all children, youth, and young adults. CEC also believes that the concept of inclusion is a meaningful goal to be pursued in our schools and communities. In addition, CEC believes children, youth, and young adults with disabilities should be served whenever possible in general education classrooms in inclusive neighborhood schools and community settings. Such settings should be strengthened and supported by an infusion of specially trained personnel and other appropriate supportive practices according to the individual needs of the child.

Most special educators, however, are not in favor of eliminating the LRE concept and dismantling the continuum of alternative placements. The Council for Exceptional Children, the major professional organization in special education, supports inclusion as a "meaningful goal" to be pursued by schools but believes that the continuum of services and program options must be maintained and that IEP planning teams must make placement decisions based on the student's individual educational needs (see Figure 2.8). Position statements on inclusion by the Council for Learning Disabilities, the Learning Disabilities Association of America, and The Association for Persons with Severe Handicaps (TASH) can be found in Chapters 5 and 12. The discussion of inclusion continues throughout the text.

Zigmond (2003) reminds us what special education is and that asking what is the "best place" to educate students with disabilities misses the point.

> The bedrock of special education is instruction focused on *individual* needs. The very concept of "one best place" contradicts this commitment to individualization. Furthermore, results of research on how groups of students respond to treatment settings do not help the researcher or practitioner make an individualized decision for an individual student's plan.
>
> Special educators understand about individual differences. Special educators understand that no matter how hard they try or how well they are taught, there are some students who will never be able to learn on the same schedule as most others, who will take so long to learn some things that they will have to forego learning other things, or who will need to be taught curricular content that is not ordinarily taught. Special educators understood this when they fought hard for the legal requirement of the Individualized Education Program for children with disabilities, to permit formulation of unique programs of instruction to meet unique individual needs. By continuing to ask, "What is the best place?" we are ignoring what we know....
>
> I can say with some certainty that place is not what makes special education "special" or effective. Effective teaching strategies and an individualized approach are the more critical ingredients in special education, and neither of these is associated solely with one particular environment. (pp. 196, 198).

For two differing perspectives on full inclusion, see "Moving toward Inclusive Education" and "Inclusion versus Full Inclusion" in the Profiles & Perspectives module in Chapter 2 of the Companion Website, **www.prenhall.com/heward**.

# Inclusion Missteps

*by Ilene S. Schwartz*

Some program practices being implemented in the name of inclusion are neither inclusive nor good practice under any circumstances. High-quality inclusive programming requires more than a belief that inclusion is the right thing to do. It requires all the instructional expertise that a high-quality segregated special education program requires. In addition, it requires that teachers be able to work collaboratively with other adults, understand and appreciate the general education curriculum and the school's culture, and be flexible. Following are some common missteps that so-called inclusive programs can make.

## ASSUMING THAT "BEING THERE" IS ENOUGH

One of the axioms of inclusive education is that children with disabilities will learn appropriate skills and behaviors by spending time with typically developing peers. Although being a member of a group and participating in a normalized setting is important, being there is just not enough.

One of the most robust findings of about 40 years of research on mainstreaming and inclusion is that if you put a child with disabilities and a child without disabilities in a room together without any special programming, you will most likely get a child with disabilities and a child without disabilities who are in the same room but are not interacting (Odom & Brown, 1993). To achieve social interactions and integration, we need to plan for them (Sandall & Schwartz, 2002). We need to figure out what supports are needed by the child with disabilities, the child(ren) without disabilities, and the adults who work in the classroom and how to provide those supports. Inclusion is an active process; "being there" implies that it is a passive process.

## "DUMPING" RATHER THAN PLANNING

Here's a conversation I experience more often than I like to admit. I meet a general education teacher at a social gathering,

Teaching children to work in group activities is a key to successful inclusion.

and she asks me what I do. When I say that I teach special education and do research in inclusion, she shakes her head in disgust and says, "Inclusion does not work." She goes on to explain that her one experience with inclusion consisted of having a student with a disability placed in her classroom with no advanced planning and no ongoing support. At this point I explain that she did not experience inclusion. Rather, she experienced dumping, and I agree: dumping does not work.

Inclusion requires that all participants, including the general education teacher, be involved in program planning, implementation, and evaluation. Inclusion requires that if training for the adults in the setting is required (e.g., for the general education teacher and paraprofessionals), it must be done before the child is placed in the setting. Inclusion requires ongoing consultation and support as needed for all members of the team. Inclusion means that if a child with learning disabilities is in a general education classroom, she receives the type of explicit instruction needed to ensure meaningful academic progress.

## NOT INDIVIDUALIZING TO MEET STUDENTS' NEEDS

Individualization is one of the basic tenets of special education. Our discipline and federal law both declare individualization to be a core principle. We often forget this, however, when we plan for inclusion. Time and again, parents come to IEP meetings requesting that their child be educated in an inclusive setting and are told, "Our district does not do that, " "Your child does not have the right set of skills, " or "We can do inclusion, but your child can't attend your neighborhood school because it is not our inclusive school."

Decisions made by IEP teams, including placement, should be based on students' needs, not existing district programs or what has happened in the past. High-quality inclusive practices must be student-centered; that is, they must address the priorities identified by the student and the family and provide adequate support and instruction so that the student makes meaningful progress toward those priorities.

## OVERUSING INSTRUCTIONAL ASSISTANTS

Parents of children with disabilities in inclusive schools often advocate for one-on-one instructional assistants for their children. They believe that more adult attention is better. As a result, the adults who interact most often with students with disabilities are instructional assistants. As a result, the majority of instruction for our most challenging students is provided by the staff members with the least amount of training. Many instructional assistants have received little or no training and may have had no previous experience in working with children with disabilities. These assistants, who are most often kind-hearted and nice to the students, unwittingly reinforce inappropriate behaviors, interfere with potential interactions with peers, systematically teach students to depend on adults, allow them to escape from demands, and often complete assignments for the students. At the same time, the teacher observes that the student is happy, sometimes engaged, and docile (cf. Winett & Winkler, 1972) and turns her attention to the 20-something other students in her class.

## FOCUSING ON ACTIVITIES RATHER THAN OBJECTIVES

Many inclusive classrooms emphasize fitting in with the ongoing activity rather than focus on addressing specific objectives. This often results from incohesive planning by the IEP team, including the instructional assistant. For example, if the activity is journal writing and no planning has been done, the instructional assistant may hand-over-hand prompt the child to write a sentence rather than al-low him to work independently on his objectives of tracing shapes, appropriately grasping the pencil, and beginning at the top of the paper and working to the bottom. Outlining the objectives for each student in an activity matrix (Sandall & Schwartz, 2002) is one good way to ensure that objectives will not be lost in the flurry of changing classroom activities.

## UNDERESTIMATING THE EFFECTIVENESS OF EXPLICIT INSTRUCTION

Teaching works. Luckily, the special education literature is full of instructional strategies with evidence of effectiveness. Although our discipline has validated many strategies to teach students many different skills, these strategies are used too infrequently and sometimes are not even acknowledged in inclusive classrooms. Instead of focusing on how to teach a specific skill or behavior, the focus of the team is how to feign normality during every part of the day. Some teachers resist adding extra supports for children with disabilities because they think it is not fair to the typically developing children. It is important to remember that being fair does not mean treating everyone the same. It means striving for equally meaningful outcomes. Providing different types or amounts of instruction does not interfere with inclusion. It is the essence of inclusive education.

## ASSUMING THAT SITTING QUIETLY IS AN APPROPRIATE ALTERNATIVE TO PARTICIPATION

Children learn by doing. Participation—taking part in the activity—is an essential component of learning what the activity is teaching. Although ensuring the full participation of all the students in the class on the same activity is not the goal of inclusive classrooms; participation (with support as necessary) in a meaningful activity is. One key to facilitating a meaningful level of participation is to use appropriate curriculum modifications and adaptations. For example, if the children in the class are reading silently, the child with disabilities could be listening to the book (or a similar book) on tape. If the children are working on creative writing, the child with disabilities could either be answering questions about a story, drawing, or dictating a story.

Another key to facilitating participation is to have thorough knowledge, both conceptual and practical, of instructional strategies to teach children to work independently, to participate in group activities, and to be active members of the classroom. By using the appropriate level of prompting and reinforcement, teachers can facilitate high levels of engagement in classroom activities or in adapted but similar activities.

Although IDEA and court rulings have consistently declared that inclusion is a right, not a privilege, in reality, it is the children whose parents advocate voraciously or show up to the IEP meetings with an attorney who are included most often. Other children, who may present the same educational and behavioral challenges but whose parents do not know that they have the right to question the school's decision, are placed in segregated classes. For inclusive education to achieve its full potential, educators must work with all children and families to provide equal access to all opportunities.

Ilene Schwartz is professor of special education at the University of Washington, where she directs a project to develop school-based services for young children with autism and prepares early childhood teachers to work with young children with severe disabilities in inclusive settings.

*Source:* Adapted from Schwartz, I. S. (2005). Inclusion and applied behavior analysis: Mending fences and building bridges. In W. L. Heward, T. E. Heron, N. A. Neef, S. M. Peterson, D. M. Sainato, G. Cartledge, R. Gardner, III, L. D. Peterson, S. B. Hersh, & J. C. Dardig (Eds.), *Focus on behavior analysis in education: Achievements, challenges, and opportunities* (pp. 241–244). Upper Saddle River, NJ: Merrill/Prentice Hall. Used by permission.

 To further your understanding of and answer reflective questions about the concepts and issues presented here, go to the Profiles & Perspectives module in Chapter 2 of the Companion Website, **www.prenhall.com/heward**.

# WHERE DOES SPECIAL EDUCATION GO FROM HERE?

The promise of a free, appropriate public education for all children with disabilities is an ambitious one. The process of bringing about this goal has been described in such lofty terms as a "new Bill of Rights" and a "Magna Carta" for children with disabilities (Goodman, 1976). Weintraub and Abeson (1974) wrote in support of IDEA before the bill's passage: "At the minimum, it will make educational opportunities a reality for all handicapped children. At the maximum, it will make our schools healthier learning environments for all our children" (p. 529). Today, most observers acknowledge that substantial progress has been made toward fulfillment of that promise.

IDEA has had far-reaching effects. As Turnbull and Turnbull (2001) observe, the student is no longer required to meet the requirements of the school, but the school is required to fit the needs of the student. Schools today provide far more than academic instruction. In effect, they have become diversified agencies offering services such as medical support, physical therapy, vocational training, parent counseling, recreation, special transportation, and in-service education for staff members. In place of the once-prevalent practice of excluding children with disabilities, schools now seek the most appropriate ways of including them. Schools are committed to providing wide-ranging services to children from diverse backgrounds and with different learning needs.

Most citizens—both within and outside the field of education—have welcomed the inclusion and participation of children with disabilities in their schools and communities. Additionally, the greater involvement of parents and families in the educational process and the emphasis on team planning to meet individual needs throughout the life span are widely regarded as positive developments. Reports from teachers and students, as well as a growing number of research studies, indicate that many children with disabilities are being successfully educated in regular schools and that, for the most part, they are well accepted by their schoolmates without disabilities.

Despite this ample evidence of progress toward providing equal educational opportunity, it is equally true that many people—again, inside and outside the field of education—have detected significant problems in the implementation of IDEA (e.g., Finn, Rotherham, & Hokanson, 2001). Most states and local school administrators maintain that the federal government has never granted sufficient financial resources to help with the high costs of educating students with disabilities. Special education teachers express dissatisfaction about excessive paperwork, unclear guidelines, and inappropriate grouping of students with disabilities. Many are concerned that too many students from culturally diverse groups are identified for special education. General education teachers contend that they receive little or no training or support when students with disabilities are placed in their classes. Some parents of children with disabilities have voiced opposition to full inclusion. There are many other problems, real and perceived, and no quick fix or easy solution can be offered.

The Individuals with Disabilities Education Improvement Act of 2004 includes revised language and new clauses addressing a range of special education concerns. One of most significant issues addressed by the reauthorization of IDEA is that many teachers of children with disabilities are not fully certified as special education teachers. The critical shortage of properly trained and certified special education teachers, a problem that has plagued special education for many years, was underscored by the requirement in the No Child Left Behind (NCLB) legislation that all children will be taught by qualified teachers highly trained in their subject matter. The challenge before Congress was how to reconcile the requirement that all teachers be "highly qualified" with the reality: there is simply not enough capacity in our nation's teacher training programs to produce the number of special educators needed by the field.

Part of Congress's solution to this dilemma was to include language in the reauthorization that specified basic requirements to be considered a "highly qualified" special education teacher. Such a teacher must possess full state certification as a special education teacher (including certification obtained through alternative routes to certification) or pass the state special education teacher licensing examination. The Council for Exceptional Children (CEC) (2004) is particularly critical of the fact that the new legislation automatically recognizes an individual who has passed a state exam or enrolled in an alternative certification program as a "highly qualified" special educator.

> [This] is disturbing in two ways. First it will pressure State policymakers with shortages of qualified special educators to permit individuals to become "highly qualified" by simply passing a State license test. This … flies in the face of literally every professional society's standards. The *sine qua non* of special education is the focus on expertise to alter instruction for individuals so as to facilitate their successful learning. These special education skills must be assessed through multiple performance evaluations, not a single paper and pencil test. If individuals are permitted to become "highly qualified" based simply on a test score, it will trivialize the term "highly qualified."
>
> Second, this IDEA reiterates the NCLB requirements that allow individuals to be considered "highly qualified" as of the first day they enroll in an "alternative preparation program" even if these individuals have never taught a single lesson in a classroom. Special educators diligently develop trust relations with the parents, families, and communities with whom they collaborate, and this sort of "government speak" is significantly detrimental to the trust relationship necessary between professionals and the people for whom they are working. (p. 5)

At the same time that it lowered the basic requirements for consideration as a "highly qualified" special education teacher, the 2004 reauthorization of IDEA added requirements for special educators who teach students working on "alternate achievement standards" and for those who teach multiple subjects to students with disabilities. For example, a special education teacher who is not new to the profession and who teaches two or more core academic subjects exclusively to children with disabilities must "demonstrate competence in all the core academic subjects in which the teacher teaches in the same manner as is required for an elementary, middle, or secondary school teacher who is not new to the profession" (H.R. 1350, Sec 602 [10] [D] [ii]). New teachers to the profession will have 2 years after their date of employment to meet the additional licensure requirements. The new IDEA "highly qualified" requirements do not address early childhood special educators.

CEC (2004) summarized its serious concerns with the new law's description of what constitutes a "highly qualified" special education teacher as follows:

[T]he language in IDEA attempts to directly tie special educators "highly qualified" requirements to the subject matter requirements for general educators in NCLB with little recognition for the integrity of special educators, special education licensure, the multiple settings in which special educators deliver services, the diverse roles within which special educators function, and the very diversity of the individuals for whom they work. This insensitivity will make implementation practically impossible. . . .

The result is an extraordinary federal intrusion into what has been the domain of States and the profession. It is an overly simplified attempt by the federal government to force States into uniform general education requirements for subject matter knowledge for special educators.

The implications of these requirements for CEC members and all practicing special educators in far too many cases will result in requirements that are bureaucratic and intrusive. However impractical or unsound the myriad of consequences, they are becoming law at least for now, and CEC members will need to assess their individual situations in light of these requirements. CEC members in leadership positions will need to be vigilant to the pressures to lower licensing requirements in order to meet requirements for what the law describes as "highly qualified" special educators. In addition, members must advocate for rigorous alternative preparation programs. (p. 4, 6)

Special education is at a crossroads. Once, access to educational opportunity was the primary issue for children with disabilities. Would they receive an education at all? Could they be served in their local community and neighborhood schools? While some access

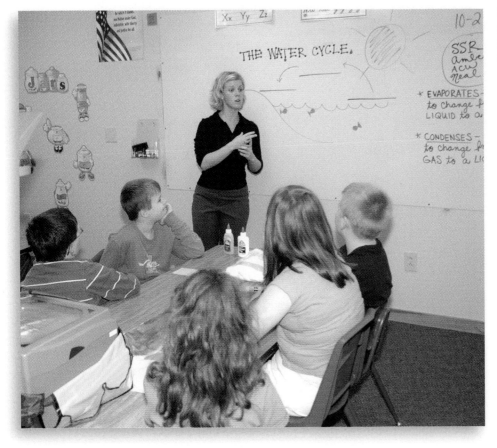

Regardless of where services are delivered, the most crucial variable is the quality of instruction that each child receives.

problems continue to persist (e.g., particularly for children who live in poverty or in extremely isolated areas and for children of migrant and homeless families), the primary concern today is about the appropriateness and effectiveness of special education.

> Today, all children with disabilities receive special education and related services. Some children benefit from a special education that includes curricular elements and instructional technologies that were unavailable just a few years ago.... While special education can rightfully be proud of its accomplishments, the educational outcomes for many students with disabilities are disappointing. As a group, students with disabilities fare poorly on virtually every measure of academic achievement and social adaptation....
>
> We believe that these poor outcomes for students with disabilities reflect not so much the field's lack of knowledge about how to teach these students, as they are testament to education's collective failure to systematically implement available knowledge.... As a result, many children with disabilities are receiving a special education that is not nearly as effective as it could be. In essence, the potential effectiveness of the special education received by many of the more than 6 million children who participate in special education today is neutralized by the presence of weak approaches that are selected on the basis of ideology instead of research results. (Heward & Silvestri, 2004, p. 193)

Can we fulfill the promise of a free, appropriate public education for all students with disabilities? The answer depends in part on the ability of professionals to work together; assume new roles; communicate with each other; and involve parents, families, and students with disabilities themselves. But above all, educators must realize that the most crucial variable in the effectiveness of special education is the quality of instruction that children receive.

Special education is serious business. The learning and adjustment problems faced by students with disabilities are real; and their prevention, remediation, and compensation require intensive, systematic intervention. Regardless of who does it or where it takes place, good teaching must occur. Exceptional children deserve no less.

# Tips for Beginning Teachers

## Making Co-Teaching Work
### by Mary Allaire-Gifford and Jean Michielli-Pendl

Cooperative teaching is an integral part of the inclusion process. But for co-teaching to be a successful experience, certain issues must be addressed before, during, and after working together. Co-teaching is always a work in progress, and communication and commitment must be nurtured continually.

### OPEN THE LINES OF COMMUNICATION

Communication wasn't easy for us in the beginning. It took effort, time, and consideration. We were strangers when we were told that we were going to co-teach. Even though we taught in the same district, we knew nothing about each other. Make an effort to get to know your partner and keep your lines of communication open from the beginning, and your transition to co-teaching will be easier.

### MAKE CO-PLANNING TIME SACRED

Establish a set co-planning time at least once a week. Shut the door to minimize distractions and interruptions. Have texts, lesson-plan books, and supplementary materials ready. Plan instruction for the week. Mondays and Fridays tend to have more interruptions and holidays. Thursday seems to be the best day. Write the agenda for the lesson on the board daily. Each day, take 5 minutes to review the lesson plan and assign roles.

### ESTABLISH CLEAR ROLES AND RESPONSIBILITIES

It is important to establish roles and responsibilities at the onset of the co-teaching experience. You are looking for equity, not equality. Co-teaching is a lot like a marriage. You never give 50/50. Sometimes you give 90% and your co-teacher gives 10%. Sometimes you are both giving 60%. Following is a list of roles and responsibilities that must be addressed before walking into the classroom:

- Who creates and presents the rules and procedures?
- Who is responsible for discipline?
- Who corrects the papers?
- Who computes students' grades and enters them into the grade book?
- Who maintains the classroom, supplies, etc., and orders more when necessary?
- Who teaches what, when, how, and whom during each lesson?
- How is personal space handled?

### BE FLEXIBLE ABOUT EVERYTHING

Even though you've agreed upon a basic plan for who is responsible for various tasks, you must be flexible. You can never say, "Oh, that's not my job," or "He's not a special education student, so I can't help." If you react in this way, the partnership will not last long. Additionally, once you have established an idea of your co-teaching roles and responsibilities, it is important to continually reevaluate how things are working in the classroom. Some ideas look good on paper, but don't work in practice. Give yourself the freedom to change as necessary.

### COMMIT TO BE COMPATIBLE

Co-teaching does not mean each teacher must follow the same teaching style; rather, it is having respect for the other person's judgment, values, and knowledge. You have to be confident in the other person as a professional. Different styles meld to make the classroom experience more diverse. Be willing to try new ideas, change, listen to your partner, attend professional development events, and laugh and cry together.

# KEY TERMS AND CONCEPTS

continuum of services, p. 76

IEP team, p. 69

inclusion, p. 79

least restrictive environment (LRE), p. 76

multifactored evaluation (MFE), p. 57

# SUMMARY

*The Process of Special Education*

- IDEA mandates a particular sequence of events that schools must follow in identifying and educating children with disabilities.
- Prereferral intervention is an informal, problem-solving process used by many schools to (1) provide immediate instructional and/or behavior management assistance to the child and teacher and (2) reduce the chances of identifying a child for special education who may not be disabled.
- All children suspected of having a disability must receive a nondiscriminatory multifactored evaluation (MFE) for determining eligibility for special education and to provide information about the child's educational needs and how to meet them.
- An individualized education program (IEP) must be planned and provided for each child with a disability that is adversely affecting her educational performance.

*Collaboration and Teaming*

- Coordination, consultation, and teaming are three modes of collaboration that team members can use.
- Three models for teaming are multidisciplinary, interdisciplinary, and transdisciplinary. Transdisciplinary teams conduct joint assessments, share information and expertise across discipline boundaries, and select discipline-free goals and interventions.
- Co-teaching means that two or more teachers plan and deliver instruction together, usually in an inclusive classroom. It has become an increasingly common practice. Co-teaching arrangements include: one teaching/one helping, parallel teaching, alternative teaching, and team teaching.

*Individualized Education Program*

- An IEP planning team must include at least (1) the parents of the child; (2) one regular education teacher of the child; (3) one special education teacher; (4) a representative of the local education agency; (5) an individual who can interpret the instructional implications of evaluation results; (6) other individuals who have knowledge or special expertise regarding the child, including related-service personnel as appropriate; and (7) whenever appropriate, the student.
- Although the formats vary widely from district to district, each IEP must include these seven components:
  a. The child's present levels of educational performance
  b. Measurable annual goals, including benchmarks or short-term objectives for students who take altrnative assessments aligned to alternative standards.
  c. The special education and related services and supplementary aids and services to be provided to the child
  d. An explanation of the extent, if any, to which the child will not participate with nondisabled children in the regular class
  e. Any individual modifications in the administration of state- or district-wide assessments of student achievement that are needed for the child to participate in such assessments (or alternative assessments)

f. The projected date for the beginning of the services and modifications described in number 3 and the anticipated frequency, location, and duration of those services and modifications

g. How the child's progress toward the annual goals will be measured and how the child's parents will be regularly informed of their child's progress

- Beginning when the student reaches age 16, IEPs must also include information on how the child's transition from school to adult life will be supported.
- Without direct and ongoing monitoring of student progress toward IEP goals and objectives, the document's usefulness is limited.
- The IEP is a measure of accountability for teachers and schools; however, a teacher and a school cannot be prosecuted if the child does not achieve all of the goals set forth in the IEP.

*Least Restrictive Environment*

- The LRE is the setting closest to the regular classroom that also meets the child's special educational needs.
- The LRE is a relative concept; the LRE for one child might be inappropriate for another.
- The continuum of services is a range of placement and service options to meet the individual needs of students with disabilities.
- The IEP team must determine the LRE after it has designed a program of special education and related services to meet the child's unique needs.

*Inclusive Education*

- Inclusion describes the process of integrating children with disabilities into regular schools and classes.
- Studies have shown that well-planned, carefully conducted inclusion can be generally effective with students of all ages, types, and degrees of disability.
- A few special educators believe that the LRE principle should give way to full inclusion, in which all students with disabilities are placed full time in regular classrooms.
- Cooperative learning activities in which students work in small heterogeneous groups to help one another achieve a common academic goal or product can be an effective strategy for integrating students with disabilities into the academic and social fabric of the classroom.
- Most special educators and professional organizations, such as CEC, support inclusion as a goal but believe that the continuum of services and program options must be maintained and that placement decisions must be based on the student's individual educational needs.

*Where Does Special Education Go from Here?*

- The promise of a free, appropriate public education for all children with disabilities is an ambitious one, but substantial progress has been made toward fulfillment of that promise.
- Implementation of IDEA has brought problems of funding, inadequate teacher training, and opposition by some to the inclusion of children with disabilities into regular classes.
- Regardless of where services are delivered, the most crucial variable is the quality of instruction that each child receives.

Companion Website — To check your comprehension of chapter contents, go to the Guided Review and Quiz modules in Chapter 2 of the Companion Website, **www.prenhall.com/heward**.

# Collaborating with Parents and Families in a Culturally and Linguistically Diverse Society

# Featured Teachers

Carolyn Crangle

## CAROLYN CRANGLE AND BETHANY MAHEADY

**DUNKIRK CITY SCHOOL DISTRICT**
**DUNKIRK, NEW YORK**

### Ms. Crangle's Education—Teaching Credentials—Experience

- B. S., special studies, SUNY Fredonia, Fredonia, New York, 1988; M.Ed., special education, State University College at Buffalo, Buffalo, New York, 1992
- New York State permanent certification in special education, K–12
- 16 years of experience as an elementary-level special educator

Bethany Maheady

### Ms. Maheady's Education—Teaching Credentials—Experience

- B.A., Spanish, SUNY Fredonia, Fredonia, New York, 1975; M.S., education/developmental reading, SUNY Fredonia, Fredonia, New York, 1977
- New York State permanent certification in education, K–6; Spanish certification, 7–12
- 30 years of teaching experience as a general educator working with bilingual, limited-English-proficient (LEP), and special-needs students in regular classroom settings

**Current Teaching Positions and Duties**    We have taught together at Dunkirk Elementary School Number 3 for the past 13 years. School Number 3 is a small urban school (300 pupils) with a high proportion of culturally and linguistically diverse students, most of whom come from home environments with very limited resources. Historically, our school has had a reputation as a tough setting because so many of our children have significant learning and behavioral challenges. Initially, we worked together to mainstream children with special needs into general education classes, primarily in their areas of strength. We subsequently created a blended classroom—what we now call inclusion—that involved the full-time placement of our general and special education students in a common, age-appropriate setting.

In the beginning, we shared responsibility for instructional planning, implementation, and evaluation and routinely used small heterogeneous learning groups and a proactive and positive classroom-management approach to create a safe and productive learning environment. All support services were "pushed in," and we established a comprehensive parent-involvement program that emphasized frequent and ongoing communication, building upon students' strengths, and parental empowerment. Currently, we work in a full-inclusion

## Focus Questions

- What can a teacher learn from the family of a child with disabilities?

- In what ways can a child's disability affect the family system and roles of parents?

- How can a teacher who is not the parent of a child with a disability communicate effectively and meaningfully with parents of exceptional children?

- How can a teacher communicate effectively and meaningfully with families from diverse cultures?

- How much parent and family involvement is enough?

To see the positive classroom environment that Ms. Crangle and Ms. Maheady have created, go to "Dunkirk Elementary School" on the *Exceptional Teachers* CD-ROM.

program in which instructional services are planned and provided collaboratively by general, special, and support personnel.

### Collaborating with Parents and Families: Respecting Difference and Diversity

Given the extensive needs of our students, it is critical that we work collaboratively with their parents and caregivers. At times, this is easier said than done. Many of our parents face extreme challenges in their daily lives. Moreover, cultural and linguistic factors (e.g., non-native-English-speaking ability, different cultural expectations related to the roles of teachers and parents/caregivers) occasionally impede effective collaboration. However, we try to look on the positive side of our circumstances. We are quite privileged to work in such a culturally and linguistically enriched environment. At School Number 3 we celebrate diversity regularly and publicly. For example, we often enlist parent volunteers to prepare ethnic foods and participate in multicultural programs. Occasionally, this will bring the uninvolved parent into the classroom in a nonthreatening manner. We also never forget to provide thank-you notes as well as reminders about upcoming parent-teacher conferences. After eating rice and beans and dancing merengue together, parents and caregivers often feel more comfortable and welcome at school and are more inclined to participate again in the future.

At School Number 3, we teach respect for and acceptance of difference and diversity. We have created an inviting classroom environment with an open-door policy. We encourage parents to observe or volunteer in the classroom, attend IEP meetings and annual reviews, and participate in our ongoing school-home communication systems. We're quite fortunate at School Number 3 because many teachers and staff members are bilingual in Spanish and English. This allows us to communicate orally and in writing in parents' native language. We also model good working relationships by collaborating with all related-services personnel and including parents as significant members of our instructional team.

To see Nicole's IEP meeting and parent-teacher conference, go to "Dunkirk Elementary School" on the *Exceptional Teachers* CD-ROM.

### Strategies for Specific Students and Families

Some parents are well informed and highly involved in their children's educational programs. For instance, we met Nicole's parents at the beginning of the school year. They were initially concerned about her transition from a local private school to School Number 3. Nicole is a shy and sensitive girl with special needs. By communicating frequently and openly, we developed a partnership with her parents; and Nicole had a positive and productive school year. She developed self-confidence, new friendships, and a wide range of knowledge and skills. At her annual review meeting, Nicole's mom stated that this was the most rewarding meeting about her daughter she had ever experienced. She thanked everyone on the team for caring so much and working so hard to ensure her daughter's success in school. She is a concerned and supportive parent, and we recognized this often in our ongoing interactions.

It is also critical to recognize that parents can play a powerful advocacy role in their children's educational program. Johnny, a bilingual student with special needs, for example, had a long history of academic failure in literacy despite intensive, ongoing remedial instruction. For quite a while, we had sought a laptop computer and keyboard training to enhance Johnny's literacy and content-area skills. However, it was not until his mother became actively involved by specifically requesting such adaptive equipment that he actually gained access to the technology. Ongoing collaboration among Johnny's personal aide, mother, and teachers allowed us to provide the much-needed instructional assistance both within and out of school.

Finally, we have refined our Instructional Support Team concept by inviting parents to participate more actively in their children's educational programs. We ask for their input, for example, in instructional and behavioral goal setting and offer suggestions for intervention strategies that can be used at home. We also continually monitor parents' satisfaction with the educational services being provided. Ultimately, our success as educators depends on the extent to which we can engage parents and families in their children's life-long learning.

The family is the most powerful and pervasive influence in a young child's life. Long before a professional with the job title "teacher" arrives, parents and family members help the child learn literally hundreds of skills. A parent is a child's first teacher, the person who gives encouragement, prompts, praise, and feedback. With rare exceptions, no one ever knows or cares about a child as much as a parent does. Yet only recently have special educators begun to understand these fundamental truths.

For years, many educators viewed parents as either troublesome (if they asked too many questions or, worse, offered suggestions about their child's education) or uncaring (if they did not jump to attention whenever the professional determined the parent needed something—usually advice from the professional). Parents, too, have often seen professionals as adversaries. But today, parent involvement and family support are understood as essential elements of special education. Special educators have given up the old notion that parents should not be too involved in their children's educational programs and now realize that parents and families are powerful and necessary allies.

To better understand the topics that will be covered in this chapter, go to the Essential Concepts and Chapter-at-a-Glance modules in Chapter 3 of the Companion Website, **www.prenhall.com/heward**.

## SUPPORT FOR FAMILY INVOLVEMENT

A number of forces have combined to focus attention on the importance of a strong parent/family–teacher partnership based on mutual respect and participation. Although many factors have contributed to the increased emphasis on collaboration between parents and teachers in the education of exceptional children, three issues are clear: (1) parents want to be involved, (2) research and practice have shown that educational effectiveness is enhanced when parents and families are involved, and (3) federal law requires collaboration between schools and families.

### Parents: Advocating for Needed Change

For decades, parents of exceptional children have advocated for equal access to educational opportunities for their children, and they have done so with impressive effectiveness. As we learned in Chapters 1 and 2, parents played the primary role in bringing about litigation and legislation establishing the right to a free and appropriate public education for all children with disabilities.

The first parent group organized for children with disabilities was the National Society for Crippled Children, formed in 1921. The United Cerebral Palsy Association, organized in 1948, and the National Association for Retarded Citizens (now called The Arc), organized in 1950, are two national parent organizations largely responsible for making the public aware of the special needs of children with disabilities. The Learning Disabilities Association of America (LDA), formed in 1963, also organized by and consisting mostly of parents, has been instrumental in bringing about educational reform. Parent members of The Association for Persons with Severe Handicaps (TASH), founded in 1975, have been forceful and effective advocates for family-focused educational services and the inclusion of students with severe and multiple disabilities in neighborhood schools and general education classrooms. Many parent organizations continue today to advocate for effective education, community acceptance, needed services, and the rights of individuals with disabilities.

Families have the greatest vested interest in their children and are usually the most knowledgeable about their children's needs. The developers of a highly regarded program for planning and implementing inclusive educational programs for students with disabilities agree. They present four powerful arguments for viewing active family involvement as the cornerstone of relevant and longitudinal educational planning:

*Family involvement as cornerstone for planning*

Council for Exceptional Children — Content Standards for Beginning Teachers—Common Core: Family systems and the role of families in supporting development (CC2K4).

- *Families know certain aspects of their children better than anyone else does.* As educators, we must remind ourselves that we spend only about half the days of the year with our students, seeing them less than a third of each of those days. Nonschool time may provide key information that has educational implications, such as the nature of a student's interests, motivations, habits, fears, routines, pressures, needs, and health.

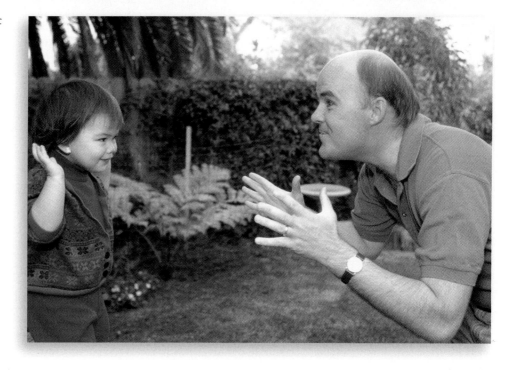

- *Families have the greatest vested interest in seeing their children learn.* In our professional eagerness to help children learn, we sometimes convey the message to parents that teachers care more about children than parents do. Of course, this is rarely the case.
- *The family is likely to be the only group of adults involved with a child's educational program throughout her entire school career.* Over the course of a school career, a student with special educational needs will encounter so many professionals that it will be difficult for the family to remember all of their names. Some of these professionals will work with the child for a number of years, others for a year or less. Professionals are encouraged to build upon an ever-evolving, family-centered vision for the child rather than reinventing a student's educational program each year as team membership changes.
- *Families must live with the outcomes of decisions made by education teams all day, every day.* People rarely appreciate having someone else make decisions that will affect their lives without being included in the decision-making. As professionals making decisions, we must constantly remind ourselves that these decisions are likely to affect other people besides the child and have an effect outside of school. (Giangreco, Cloninger, & Iverson, 1998, pp. 19–22)

## Educators: Striving for Greater Effectiveness

To meet the special needs of children with disabilities, educators must expand the traditional role of the classroom teacher. This expanded role demands that we view teaching as more than instructing academic skills in the classroom. Today's special educator attaches high priority to designing and implementing instructional programs that enable students with disabilities to use and maintain academic, language, social, self-help, recreation, and other skills in school, at home, and in the community. As part of their home and community life, children may participate in some 150 different kinds of social and physical settings (Dunst, 2001). The large number of nonschool settings in which children live, play, and learn illustrates two important points. First, the many different settings and situations illustrate the extent of the challenge teachers face in helping children use newly learned skills throughout their daily lives. Second, the many different settings and social situations children experience in home and community provide extended opportunities for learning and practicing important skills. It is clear that to be maximally effective, teachers must look beyond the classroom for assistance and support, and parents and families are natural and necessary allies.

Extensive evidence shows that the effectiveness of educational programs for children with disabilities is increased when parents and families are actively involved (e.g., Cronin, Slade, Bechtel, & Anderson, 1992; Guralnick, 1997; Hardin & Littlejohn, 1995; Keith et al., 1998). At the very least, teachers and students benefit when parents provide information about their children's use of specific skills outside the classroom. But parents can do much more than just report on behavior change. They can provide extra skill practice and teach their children new skills in the home and community. When parents are involved in identifying what skills their children need to learn (and, just as important, what they do *not* need to learn), the hard work expended by teachers is more likely to produce outcomes with real significance in the lives of children and their families.

## Legislators: Mandating Parent and Family Involvement

Parent involvement was a key element in the Education of All Handicapped Children Act (P. L. 94–142), the original federal special education law. Each reauthorization of the law has strengthened and extended parent and family participation in the education of children with disabilities. For example, Congress reaffirmed and made clear its belief in the importance of parent and family involvement in the introduction to IDEA 1997: "Over 20 years of research and experience has demonstrated that the education of children with disabilities can be made more effective by . . . strengthening the role of parents and ensuring that families of such children have meaningful opportunities to participate in the education of their children at school and at home" (U.S.C 601[c][5][B]).

Parent participation in the form of shared decision making is one of six basic rules, or principles, of IDEA that form the general framework for carrying out national policies for the education of children with disabilities. IDEA provides statutory guidelines that schools must follow with parents of children with disabilities with regard to referral, testing, placement, and program planning and evaluation. In addition, the law provides due process procedures if parents believe that their child's needs are not being met.

We have identified three factors responsible for increased parent and family involvement in the education of children with disabilities: parents want it, educators know it's a good idea, and the law requires it. But the most important reasons why families and educators should strive to develop collaborative partnerships are the benefits to the child with disabilities:

- Increased likelihood of targeting meaningful IEP goals
- Greater consistency and support in the child's two most important environments: home and school
- Increased opportunities for learning and development
- Access to expanded resources and services

# Understanding Families of Children with Disabilities

When parents and teachers work together for the mutual benefit of a child with disabilities, they make a powerful team. To work together, they must communicate with one another. Effective communication is more likely when each party understands and respects the responsibilities and challenges faced by the other. For educators, an important initial step in developing a partnership with families is to strive for an understanding of how a child with disabilities might influence the family system and the many interrelated roles of parenthood.

*IDEA and parent participation*

Council for Exceptional Children — Content Standards for Beginning Teachers—Common Core: Rights and responsibilities of students, parents, teachers, other professionals, and schools related to exceptional learning needs (CC1K4).

To learn how a parent-teacher partnership built on communication and mutual respect benefited a student, his family, and his teacher, see "In Support of Jay," in Chapter 3's Profiles & Perspectives module on the Companion Website, **www.prenhall.com/heward**.

# The Impact of a Child with Disabilities on the Family

The birth of a baby with disabilities or the discovery that a child has a disability is an intense and traumatic event. Many studies have been conducted on the emotional responses and adjustments of parents of children with disabilities (e.g., Blacher, 2001; Eden-Piercy, Blacher, & Eyman, 1986; Ferguson, 2003; Frey, Fewell, & Vadasy, 1989; Johnson, 1993). This research has shown that most parents go through an adjustment process, trying to work through their feelings. For example, widely cited research by Blacher (1984) found three consistent stages of adjustment. First, parents experience a period of emotional crisis characterized by shock, denial, and disbelief. This initial reaction is followed by a period of alternating feelings of anger, guilt, depression, shame, lowered self-esteem, rejection of the child, and overprotectiveness. Eventually, parents reach a third stage in which they accept their child. Based on their observations of 130 participants in two parent support groups over a period of several years, Anderegg, Vergason, and Smith (1992) have developed a revised model of Blacher's work they call the grief cycle, which consists of three stages: confronting, adjusting, and adapting.

Poyadue (1993) suggests a stage beyond acceptance or adapting that involves appreciation of the positive aspects of family life with a child with a disability. There is growing evidence supporting this concept. For example, Patterson and Leonard (1994) interviewed couples whose children required intensive home care routines because of chronic and complex health care needs and found roughly equal numbers of positive and negative responses. Among the positive responses was that caregiving brought the couple closer together and created a stronger bond among family members. In another study, the majority of 1,262 parents of children with disabilities agreed with the following statements about being the parent of a child with a disability: "The presence of my child is very uplifting. Because of my child, I have many unexpected pleasures. My child is the reason I am a more responsible person" (Behr, Murphy, & Summers, 1992, p. 26). Skinner, Bailey, Correa, and Rodriguez (1998) found many of the 150 Latina mothers in their study believed that having a child with disabilities made them better mothers. And parents in several studies reported not only coping successfully with the challenges posed by a child with disabilities but said that their families experienced benefits because of the child (Bradley, Knoll, & Agosta, 1992; Meyer, 1995; Naseef, 2001; Stainton & Besser, 1998).

Educators should refrain from expecting parents of children with disabilities to exhibit typical reactions. Relying on any stages-of-adjustment theory as the basis for planning or delivering family services poses three potential problems. First, it is easy to assume that all parents must pass through a similar sequence of stages and that time is the most important variable in adjustment. In fact, parents react to the arrival of a child with disabilities in many ways (Lin, 2000; Turnbull & Turnbull, 2006; Ulrich & Bauer, 2003). For some parents, years may pass, but they still are not comfortable with their child. Yet other parents, as we have just discussed, report that having a child with disabilities has strengthened their life or marriage (Scorgie & Sobsey, 2000). The sequence and time needed for adjustment are different for every parent. The one common thread is that almost all parents and families can be helped during their adjustment by sensitive and supportive friends and professionals (Fox, Vaughn, Wyatte, & Dunlap, 2002).

A second concern is that many parents view stages of mourning and adjustment as patronizing and condescending, which hinders meaningful communication (Snow, 2001). And third, some stages-of-adjustment theories have a distinct psychiatric flavor, which may lead professionals to mistakenly assume that parents must be maladjusted in some way and in need of counseling.

## The Many Roles of the Exceptional Parent

Parenthood is an awesome responsibility, and parenting any child requires tremendous physical and emotional energy. All parents share a great deal in common. Hart and Risley (1995), who conducted a longitudinal study of 42 families with young typically developing children, noted: "Raising children made all the families look alike. All the babies had to be fed, changed, and amused. As we went from one home to another we saw the same activities and lives centered on caregiving.... Most impressive of all that the parents had in common was the continual and incredible challenge a growing child presents" (pp. 53, 55).

Parents of children with disabilities, however, sometimes experience added stress caused by their child's physical, emotional, and financial demands. Educators who are not parents of a child with disabilities, chronic illness, or severe problem behavior cannot possibly know the 24-hour, 7-day reality of being the parent of such a child (Fox et al., 2002). Nonetheless, they should strive to understand how a child with special needs affects (and is affected by) the family system.

In addition to providing love and affection, parents of children with disabilities must fulfill at least nine other varied and demanding roles.

*Caregiver.*    Taking care of any young child is a demanding task. But the additional caregiving requirements of children with disabilities can be tremendous and cause added stress (Smith, Oliver, & Innocenti, 2001). And the level of care needed by some children with severe disabilities or chronic health conditions can be nonstop:

> Mike sleeps when he wants to, mostly during the day. He sleeps with a heart monitor on which alarms several times per night, because he stops breathing frequently. Usually I'm up by 8:00 and often cannot go to bed until 12:00 or 1:00 because of Mike's feedings, medication. It's hard to fit all of this into a day and still have time for sleep.

> Douglas's tube caught on the door handle and his trach came out. I panicked, but Douglas's father was home and he "simply" reinserted the trach and reattached the tube to the ventilator machine. Douglas meanwhile had turned gray, then blue for just a minute or less. I was crying as he began breathing again and his color came back. (Bradley et al., 1992)

Although many parents receive help from extended family members and friends in caring for a child with disabilities, the amount and level of help is often insufficient. Respite care can reduce the mental and physical stress on parents and families created by the day-to-day responsibilities of caring for a child with disabilities (see Figure 3.1).

*Provider.*    Food, clothing, shelter, activities (e.g., music lessons, sports, hobbies): parents pay a lot of money to raise a typically developing child from birth to adulthood. Providing for a child with disabilities, however, usually means additional expenses, sometimes in the tens of thousands of dollars. For example, consider the economic impact on this family of a child with physical disabilities and chronic health problems:

> We had to find another place to live with first floor bedroom, widened doorways, enlarged front porch, central air, ramp, van. House renovation: $10,000. Van: $18,500. Air: $1,450. Porch: $1,400. Ramp: $1,000. Furnishings to accommodate supplies: $800. We've got the following equipment: Suction machine, portable suction machine, generator for emergency power, hospital bed, air pressure mattress, wheelchair, room monitor, humidifier, bath chair, oxygen, air cleaner, gastronomy tube pump, breathing treatment machine. And all the following expenses have gone up: formula, diapers, appliances, utility bills, medications. (Bradley et al., 1992)

It is not just families of children with physical disabilities or health conditions who face financial burdens. Many parents of children with learning and behavioral problems pay thousands of dollars for specific treatments, behavioral intervention programs, and in-home therapy. While some families receive federal, state, and/or private assistance for such extra expenses, most families have to pay their own way. On top of the additional expenses, families of children with disabilities often have reduced income because one parent works part time instead of full time or must withdraw from the workforce altogether to care for the child (Barnett & Boyce, 1994).

*Teacher.*    Most children learn many skills without anyone teaching them. Children with disabilities, however, often do not acquire new skills as naturally or independently as their

*Roles of exceptional parents*

 Content Standards for Beginning Teachers—Common Core: Concerns of families of individuals with exceptional learning needs and strategies to help address these concerns (CC10K3) (also CC2K4).

*Respite care*

 Content Standards for Beginning Teachers—Common Core: Concerns of families of individuals with exceptional learning needs and strategies to help address these concerns (CC10K3).

## FIGURE 3.1 Respite care: Support for families

Parents of nondisabled children frequently hire others to care temporarily for their children. The range of day care options available to families of children with disabilities, however, is severely limited. Many parents of children with severe disabilities identify the availability of reliable, high-quality child care as their single most pressing need (Grant & McGrath, 1990; Warfield & Hauser-Cram, 1996). One study found that 56% of parents of children with disabilities reported having difficulty finding child care, compared to only 3% of parents of children without disabilities reporting the same problem (Emlen, 1998). In response to this need, many communities have developed respite care programs. **Respite care** is the short-term care of a family member with disabilities to provide relief for parents from caretaking duties.

Quality respite care can reduce the mental and physical stress on parents and families created by the day-to-day—in some cases, moment-to-moment—responsibilities of caring for a child with disabilities. Respite care has also been correlated with reduced requests for long-term residential placement of children with disabilities and improved family functioning (Neef, Parrish, Egel, & Sloan, 1986). The mother of a son born with a neurological condition that produces frequent seizures and extreme hyperactivity describes her family's experience with respite care:

> During the first four years of Ben's life, we averaged four hours of sleep a night. We were wearing ourselves out; I have no doubt we would have completely fallen apart. My husband, Roger, used his vacations for sleeping in. The respite program came along just in time for us. It was hard at first. There's an overwhelming guilt that you shouldn't leave your child. We didn't feel like anyone else could understand Ben's problems. But we had to get away. Our church gave us some money, with orders to take a vacation. It was the first time Roger and I and our 12-year-old daughter, Stacy, had really been together since Ben was born.

Another parent expressed what respite care has meant to her family:

> Our son Tom's autism has meant a lot of restrictions in our family life for the past 25 years, bringing with it many problems and much resentment. At last we have been given a no-strings-attached, low-cost way to loosen some of those restrictions. Funny thing is, our Tom is such a nice guy—it's sure good to be able to get far enough away every so often to be able to see that.

Families and their advocates can locate respite service providers in their communities by visiting the National Respite Locator Service website, *www.respitelocator.org.*

typically developing peers do. In addition to learning systematic teaching techniques, some parents must learn to use and/or teach their children to use special equipment and assistive devices such as hearing aids, braces, wheelchairs, and adapted eating utensils (Parette & Brotherson, 1996).

*Counselor.* All parents are counselors in the sense that they deal with their children's changing emotions, feelings, and attitudes. But in addition to all of the normal joys and pains of raising a child, parents of a child with disabilities must deal with their child's feelings that result from his particular disability: "Will I still be deaf when I grow up?" "I'm not playing outside anymore; they always tease me." "Why can't I go swimming like the other kids?" Parents play an important role in how the child with disabilities comes to feel about himself. Their interactions can help develop an active, outgoing child who confidently tries new experiences or a withdrawn child with negative attitudes toward himself and others.

*Behavior Support Specialist.*    All children act out occasionally, and all parents are challenged and frustrated from time to time by their children's noncompliance and misbehavior. But the frequency and severity of challenging behaviors exhibited by some children with disabilities can make it nearly impossible for some families to experience and enjoy normal routines of daily life (Fox et al., 2002). Turnbull and Ruef (1996) interviewed 14 families with children with mental retardation who frequently exhibited problem behavior. The parents reported that their children frequently engaged in at least one of four categories of problem behavior: aggression toward others, property destruction, self-injurious behavior, or pica (eating inedible objects). The children's problem behavior fell into one of two domains, according to the behavior's impact on the child and the family: dangerous behavior (e.g., "He punches his face a lot on the jaw line—his cheek bone, his mouth, occasionally his forehead.... He will eventually bleed from his mouth") and difficult behavior (e.g., "When I am around him it is constant noise. He talks or squawks. By afternoon I am frazzled") (p. 283). Such behavior demands specialized and consistent treatment, and some parents of exceptional children must become skilled in behavior-support techniques to achieve a semblance of normal family life (e.g., see Boulware, Schwartz, & McBride, 2001; Delaney & Kaiser, 2001; Luchshyn, Dunlap, & Albin, 2002; Vaughn, Clarke, & Dunlap, 1997).

*Parent of Siblings without Disabilities.*    As with studies investigating parental reactions to a child with disabilities, the results of research on the effects of such children on their siblings have varied. Some studies have found negative effects, such as a higher incidence of emotional or behavioral problems (Orsillo, McCaffrey, & Fisher, 1993) or lower self-esteem (McHale & Gamble, 1989) in siblings of children with disabilities. But other studies have found that siblings had fewer behavioral problems (Carr, 1988) or were more likely to display prosocial behavior (Stoneman, Brody, Davis, & Crapps, 1989), nurturing, and affection toward their brother or sister with disabilities (Stoneman, 1998) than were siblings of children without disabilities. The positive relationships between a sibling and his or her brother or sister with disabilities often last well into adulthood (Orsmond & Seltzer, 2000).

It is clear, however, that children are deeply affected by having a brother or a sister with special needs (Caro & Derevensky, 1997; McHugh, 2003). Brothers and sisters of a child with disabilities often have concerns about their sibling's disability: uncertainty regarding the cause of the disability and its effect on them, uneasiness about the reactions of friends, a feeling of being left out or being required to do too much for the child with disabilities (Dyson, Edgar, & Crnic, 1989). Parents play key roles in determining the nature of the relationship between their children and the extent to which their children without disabilities develop into happy, well-adjusted adolescents and adults.

*Marriage Partner.*    Having a child with disabilities can put stress on a marriage. Specific stressors can be as diverse as arguing over who is to blame for the child's disability; disagreeing about expectations for the child's behavior; and spending so much time, money, and energy on the child with disabilities that little is left for each other (Cohen, Agosta, Cohen, & Warren, 1989). It is a mistake, however, to assume that the presence of a child with disabilities has a negative effect on marital relations. Some studies have found that a child with disabilities strengthens a marriage in part because of a couple's shared commitment to the child (Sandler & Mistretta, 1998; Scorgie & Sobsey, 2000).

Chapter 3
Collaborating with Parents and
Families in a Culturally and
Linguistically Diverse Society

To learn how educators and one family worked together to provide positive behavioral support for a young boy with challenging behavior, see the Teaching & Learning Module "A Parent-Professional Partnership in Positive Behavioral Support," in Chapter 3 of the Companion Website, **www.prenhall.com/heward**.

Nondisabled brothers and sisters often have special needs and concerns because of their sibling's disability.

**TABLE 3.1** The four life-cycle stages of a person with disabilities: Issues and strategies for family members

| | LIFE-CYCLE STAGES | |
|---|---|---|
| | **Early Childhood, ages 0–5** | **Childhood, ages 6–12** |
| **Issues for Parents** | • Obtaining an accurate diagnosis<br>• Informing siblings and relatives<br>• Locating early intervention services<br>• Participating in IFSP meetings<br>• Seeking to find meaning in the exceptionality<br>• Clarifying a personal ideology to guide decisions<br>• Addressing issues of stigma<br>• Identifying positive contributions of exceptionality<br>• Setting great expectations | • Establishing routines to carry out family functions<br>• Adjusting emotionally to educational implications<br>• Clarifying issues of mainstreaming versus special class placement<br>• Advocating for inclusive experiences<br>• Participating in IEP conferences<br>• Locating community resources<br>• Arranging for extracurricular activities<br>• Developing a vision for the future |
| **Issues for Siblings** | • Less parental time and energy for sibling needs<br>• Feelings of jealousy because of less attention<br>• Fears associated with misunderstandings about exceptionality | • Division of responsibility for any physical care needs<br>• Oldest female sibling may be at risk<br>• Limited family resources for recreation and leisure<br>• Informing friends and teachers<br>• Possible concern about younger sibling surpassing older<br>• Issues of mainstreaming into same school<br>• Need for basic information on exceptionality |
| **Enhancing Successful Transitions** | • Begin preparing for the separation of preschool children by periodically leaving the child with others.<br>• Gather information and visit preschools in the community.<br>• Encourage participation in Parent to Parent programs. (Veteran parents are matched in one-to-one relationships with parents who are just beginning the transition process.)<br>• Familiarize parents with possible school (elementary and secondary) programs, career options, or adult programs so they have an idea of future opportunities. | • Provide parents with an overview of curricular options.<br>• Ensure that IEP meetings provide an empowering context for family collaboration.<br>• Encourage participation in Parent to Parent matches, workshops, or family support groups to discuss transitions with others. |

*Information Specialist/Trainer for Significant Others.* Grandparents, aunts and uncles, neighbors, the school bus driver: all of these people can be important influences on a child's development. While parents of a child without disabilities can reasonably expect her to receive certain kinds of treatment from significant others, parents of children with disabilities know they cannot necessarily depend on appropriate actions and reactions from others. These parents must try to ensure that other people interact with their child in ways that support their child's dignity, acceptance, opportunities for learning, and maintenance of adaptive behaviors. One mother describes her response to anyone who stares at her son with Down syndrome: she looks the person squarely in the eye and says, "You seem interested in my son. Would you like to meet him?" (Schulz, 1985, p. 6). This usually ends the staring and often creates an opportunity to provide information or begin a friendship.

*Advocate.* IDEA not only defines the rights of parents of children with disabilities but also requires specific efforts and responsibilities. Although some involvement in the educational

**TABLE 3.1** *continued*

| | LIFE-CYCLE STAGES | |
| --- | --- | --- |
| | **Adolescence, ages 12–21** | **Adulthood, ages 21–** |
| **Issues for Parents** | • Adjusting emotionally to possible chronicity of exceptionality<br>• Identifying issues of emerging sexuality<br>• Dealing with physical and emotional changes of puberty<br>• Addressing possible peer isolation and rejection<br>• Planning for career/vocational development<br>• Arranging for leisure activities<br>• Expanding child's self-determination skills<br>• Planning for postsecondary education | • Addressing supported employment and living options<br>• Adjusting emotionally to any adult implications of dependency<br>• Addressing the need for socialization opportunities outside the family<br>• Initiating career choice or vocational program<br>• Planning for possible need for guardianship |
| **Issues for Siblings** | • Overidentification with sibling<br>• Greater understanding of differences in people<br>• Influence of exceptionality on career choice<br>• Dealing with possible stigma and embarrassment<br>• Participation in sibling training programs<br>• Opportunity for sibling support groups | • Possible issues of responsibility for financial support<br>• Addressing concerns regarding genetic implications<br>• Introducing new in-laws to exceptionality<br>• Need for information on career/living options<br>• Clarify role of sibling advocacy<br>• Possible issues of guardianship |
| **Enhancing Successful Transitions** | • Assist families and adolescents to identify community leisure activities.<br>• Incorporate into the IEP skills that will be needed in future career and vocational programs.<br>• Visit or become familiar with a variety of career and living options.<br>• Develop a mentor relationship with an adult with a similar exceptionality and an individual who has a career that matches the student's strengths and preferences. | • Provide preferred information to families about guardianship, estate planning, wills, and trusts.<br>• Assist family members in transferring responsibilities to the individual with an exceptionality, other family members, or service providers as appropriate.<br>• Assist the young adult or family members with career or vocational choices.<br>• Address the issues and responsibilities of marriage and family for the young adult. |

*Source:* Adapted from Turnbull, A. P., & Turnbull, H. R. (1990, 1997, 2001). *Families, professionals, and exceptionality: Collaborating for empowerment* (2nd ed., pp. 134–135; 3rd ed., p. 149; 4th ed., p. 173). Upper Saddle River, NJ: Merrill/Prentice Hall. Used by permission.

process is expected and desirable for all parents, participation is a must for parents of exceptional children. They must acquire special knowledge (e.g., different kinds of related services), learn special skills (e.g., how to participate effectively in IFSP/IEP meetings), and be consistent and firm in presenting their wishes regarding learning goals and placement options for their child (Hanson et al., 2001). In addition, many parents of children with disabilities have concerns over and above those of most parents; they must often advocate for effective educational services and opportunities for their children in a society that devalues persons with disabilities (Kozloff & Rice, 2000; Yell & Drasgow, 2000). For example, while all parents may be concerned about having adequate community playgrounds, the parents of a child who uses a wheelchair may find themselves having to fight long and hard for an accessible playground.

## Changing Needs As Children Grow

Another way to increase our understanding of how a child with disabilities might affect his or her family and vice versa is to examine the likely impact of the child's and family's changing needs at various ages (Blacher, 2001). Table 3.1 identifies possible issues and concerns

*Family life-cycle stages*

Council for Exceptional Children
Content Standards for Beginning Teachers—Common Core: Concerns of families of individuals with exceptional learning needs and strategies to help address these concerns (CC10K3).

that parents and siblings face during four life-cycle stages and suggests strategies for supporting families as they pass through the stages. And the demands of parenting a child with disabilities often do not end when the child reaches adulthood. Many parents in their 70s and 80s continue to care for their adult children with disabilities (Llewellyn, Gething, Kendig, & Cant, 2004).

# DEVELOPING AND MAINTAINING FAMILY-PROFESSIONAL PARTNERSHIPS

In an effort to better understand the characteristics of effective family-professional partnerships, Blue-Banning, Summers, Frankland, Nelson, & Beegle (2004) conducted in-depth focus groups and interviews with 137 adult family members of children with and without disabilities and 53 professionals. The participants represented a wide range of ethnic groups and socioeconomic levels and resided in Kansas, North Carolina, and Louisiana. The results suggested that collaborative partnerships are facilitated by professional behaviors clustered around these six dimensions: communication, commitment, equality, trust, skill, and respect (see Table 3.2).

The study by Blue-Banning and her colleagues gives empirical support to something that we have known for a long time but practice too seldom. Effective school-home partnerships are characterized by family members and professionals jointly pursuing shared goals in a climate of mutual respect and trust. Families receive supports in the form of the knowledge and resources that empower them to participate as full partners, and professionals receive input from families that helps them be more effective teachers.

Regular two-way communication with parents is the key operational element of the partnership. Without open, honest communication between teacher and parent, many of the positive outcomes we have examined cannot be achieved. The family members in the study by Blue-Banning et al. (2004) said they needed frequent communication, but they also highlighted the importance of the quality of communication. "Family members stressed that communication should be honest and open, with no hidden information and no 'candy-coating' of bad news" (p. 173). Family members and professionals emphasized the need for two-way communication, stating that both professionals and parents should listen carefully and nonjudgmentally to what each other has to say. One father stated it like this:

> The first thing is to listen to us ... because we know our kids better than anybody.... I think some of these people have preconceived notions about everything.... So if I tried to say to them [professionals] something, it'd be LISTEN TO ME. (p. 175)

## Principles of Effective Communication

"A good conversation is neither a fight nor a contest. Circular in form, cooperative in manner, and constructivist in intent, it is an interchange of ideas by those who see themselves not as adversaries but as human beings come together to talk and to listen and to learn from one another" (Martin, 1985, p. 10). Wilson (1995) recommends five principles for effective communication between educators and parents.

*Accept Parents' Statements.*   Accepting parents' statements means conveying through verbal and nonverbal means that what parents say is valued. Parents are more likely to speak freely and openly when they believe that what they say is respected. Acceptance means conveying, "I understand and appreciate your point of view." It does not mean the teacher must agree with everything that a parent says.

*Principles of effective communication*

Council for Exceptional Children   Content Standards for Beginning Teachers—Common Core: Foster respectful and beneficial relationships between families and professionals (CC10S3).

**TABLE 3.2  Six dimensions of high-quality family-professional partnerships and professional behaviors that facilitate them**

| Collaborative Partnership Theme | Indicators |
|---|---|
| *Communication:* The quality of communication is positive, understandable, and respectful among all members at all levels of the partnership. The quantity of communication is also at a level to enable efficient and effective coordination and understanding among all members. | Sharing resources<br>Being clear<br>Being honest<br>Communicating positively<br>Being tactful<br>Being open<br>Listening<br>Communicating frequently<br>Coordinating information |
| *Commitment:* The members of the partnership share a sense of assurance about (a) each other's devotion and loyalty to the child and family, and (b) each other's belief in the importance of the goals being pursued on behalf of the child and family. | Demonstrating commitment<br>Being flexible<br>Regarding work as "more than a job"<br>Regarding child and family as "more than a case"<br>Encouraging the child and family<br>Being accessible to the child and family<br>Being consistent<br>Being sensitive to emotions |
| *Equality:* The members of the partnership feel a sense of equity in decision making and service implementation, and actively work to ensure that all other members of the partnership feel equally powerful in their ability to influence outcomes for children and families. | Avoiding use of "clout"<br>Empowering partners<br>Validating others<br>Advocating for child or family with other professionals<br>Allowing reciprocity among members<br>Being willing to explore all options<br>Fostering harmony among all partners<br>Coming to the table/avoiding "turfism"<br>Acting "equal" |
| *Skills:* Members of the partnership perceive that others on the team demonstrate competence, including service providers' ability to fulfill their roles and to demonstrate "recommended practice" approaches to working with children and families. | Taking action<br>Having expectations for child's progress<br>Meeting individual special needs<br>Considering the whole child or family<br>Being willing to learn |
| *Trust:* The members of the partnership share a sense of assurance about the reliability or dependability of the character, ability, strength, or truth of the other members of the partnership. | Being reliable<br>Keeping the child safe<br>Being discreet |
| *Respect:* The members of the partnership regard each other with esteem and demonstrate that esteem through actions and communications. | Valuing the child<br>Being nonjudgmental<br>Being courteous<br>Exercising nondiscrimination<br>Avoiding intrusion |

*Source:* From Blue-Banning, M., Summers, J. A., Frankland, H. C., Nelson, L. L., & Beegle, G. (2004). Dimensions of family and professional partnerships: Constructive guidelines for collaboration. *Exceptional Children, 70,* p. 174. Copyright 2004 by the Council for Exceptional Children. Reprinted with permission.

## FIGURE 3.2 Active listening

The following excerpts contrast the communication styles of two early childhood teachers, a passive listener and an active listener, while discussing IEP goals with a parent.

**Passive Listening**

*Parent:* I would very much like to have my child use his communication board on a more regular basis. Currently, he becomes very frustrated because he can't tell us what he needs. [The parent frowns and looks sad.]

*Passively listening teacher:* All the students in my class are able to speak. We will have the speech language pathologist work with Andy so that he can speak as well. [The teacher is fiddling with papers she needs for her next parent conference.]

*Parent:* Perhaps you didn't read Andy's file carefully. His cerebral palsy is so involved that he isn't able to make any understandable speech sounds. We have already had him evaluated by a speech therapist, and he created the communication board for Andy so he could develop his language skills.

*Passively listening teacher:* [Still looking at her other papers.] We have an excellent speech language pathologist. She will have Andy talking in no time. Andy can work with her during circle time since that is oral and Andy wouldn't be able to participate.

*Parent:* We don't want Andy to miss out on circle time. He loves to be a part of the group. We can choose appropriate pictures to put on his communication board so he can respond with the rest of the children. He gets very frustrated when he is not allowed to be with the rest of the students.

*Passively listening teacher:* Oh, we don't let the children bring toys to the circle. He has to be able to speak up like everyone else. Also, I've been meaning to talk to you about his behavior. He has been refusing to cooperate with our group activities. I'd like to send him to time out when this happened.

*Parent:* [She gives a big sigh.] As I've said, Andy gets very frustrated when he isn't able to communicate and when he isn't a part of the group. I don't think time out would be the right answer for this problem.

*Passively listening teacher:* Well, if you don't allow us to control his behavior, I don't know how Andy is ever going to be able to be a part of this class. [She looks at her watch, ready to end the meeting.]

Source: Adapted from Howard, V. F., Williams, B. F., & Lepper, C. (2005). *Very young children with special needs: A formative approach for today's children* (3rd ed.), (pp. 121–122). Upper Saddle River, NJ: Merrill/Prentice Hall. Used by permission.

---

*Active listening*

Council for Exceptional Children Content Standards for Beginning Teachers—Common Core: Foster respectful and beneficial relationships between families and professionals (CC10S3).

*Listen Actively.* Good listeners attend and respond to a conversation partner in a sincere and genuine manner. A good listener pays attention to the content of what is being said, noting who said it and how. For example, in an IFSP/IEP conference attended by extended family members, an educator should notice if a grandparent seems to be speaking for the child's parents or if the mother and father express different opinions about an issue through tones of voice or body language. An active listener not only interprets, sorts, and analyzes what the speaker says but also responds to the speaker's message with animation and interest (Howard, Williams, & Lepper, 2005). Figure 3.2 illustrates the skill of active listening.

*Question Effectively.* To the extent possible, educators should use open-ended questions when communicating with parents, especially during conferences. For example, an open-ended question such as "What did Sharena do with her homework project last week?" is more likely to evoke a descriptive and informative reply from parents than is the closed-ended question "Is Sharena having trouble with her homework?" which might result in a yes or no response. Questions to parents should not focus solely on problems or deficits, and teachers must respect families' desire to keep some things private and "in the family" (Turnbull & Turnbull, 2006).

**FIGURE 3.2** *continued*

**Active Listening**

*Actively listening teacher:*  We didn't address this in our last IEP meeting, but I think Cherise has matured in her language and self-help skills enough that she is ready to start toilet training. What do you think about this? [Teacher leans forward and looks parent in the eye.]

*Parent:*  Do you really think she could learn to go by herself? If would be such a relief not to have her in diapers, now that we are expecting another child. [The parent smiles.]

*Actively listening teacher:*  [Nods enthusiastically.] I just want to explain what this would involve and make sure we can work on this at both home and school. I'd like to check her every 15 minutes to see if there is a pattern to when she is wet and then start putting her on the potty at those most likely times each day. Can you do the same thing when she is at home with you in the afternoon and evening? [The teacher watches the parent's face and notices that her mouth falls a little.]

*Parent:*  I don't think I could check every 15 minutes. We have the two older ones, so I'm always driving them to activities; and Cherise's therapy sessions usually run at least 45 minutes and I don't like to disturb her once she's started a session. [The parent sits back in her chair, pushing away from the table.]

*Actively listening teacher:*  Of course, you are probably on the go so much there isn't a lot of down-time when you could stop and do this every 15 minutes. Is there any period of time, like maybe the hour just before bed that you could work on this? I find kids learn toilet-training so much faster when we work on it at school and at home. [The teacher raises her eyebrows in a hopeful gesture.]

*Parent:*  Maybe I could ask my husband to watch Cherise when I take her older sister to her dance lessons. That way she'd be home for the two hours before bed. Would that be enough to make a difference?

*Actively listening teacher:*  I appreciate you rearranging your hectic schedule. I think that could make a big difference, and once Cherise is out of diapers, you'll have a little more free time with the new baby.

*Parent:*  I'm so glad you think we can do this. It would make a big difference not to have two in diapers, and Cherise will be happier if she can be like the big girls. [She hesitates.] But what if I can't carry through at home? What if she doesn't learn?

*Actively listening teacher:*  I know it's hard to do these things at home when your hands are full. We'll keep working on it at school. Cherise might not learn right away, but I've got some ways to motivate her. You just let me know if you don't think it's going well at home and we'll go back to the drawing board.

*Parent:*  Thank you for being so understanding. I'll give it my best shot. I'm so glad you thought to work on this. It's like you read my mind.

*Encourage.*  It is important for parents to hear good news about their son or daughter. Describing or showing parents specific instances of their child's good behavior or improved performance encourages parental involvement.

*Stay Focused.*  Although greetings and some small talk are desirable before getting down to business, conversations between parents and teachers should focus on the child's educational program and progress. Educators must be sensitive to cultural differences and the idiosyncratic conversational styles of individual families (Dennis & Giangreco, 1996; Wilson & Hughes, 1994). But they must also learn to distinguish when extended small talk is drifting too far from the purpose at hand so that they can refocus the conversation.

## Identifying and Breaking Down Barriers to Parent-Teacher Partnerships

Let's face it: parents and teachers do not always communicate effectively and cooperate with one another. They may sometimes even seem to be on opposite sides, battling over what each thinks is best for the child. The child, unfortunately, never wins that battle. She needs to have the people responsible for the two places where she spends most of her life—home and school—work together to make those environments consistent with and supportive of her job of learning. Teachers should work to increase the likelihood that their interactions with parents and families are characterized by cooperation. They must be responsive to the practices and beliefs of families from diverse cultural backgrounds and identify and eliminate attitudes and behaviors that block family involvement.

*Professional Roadblocks to Communication.* Sometimes parents and teachers make assumptions about and hold attitudes toward one another that are counterproductive. Teachers sometimes complain that parents are uninterested, uncooperative, or hostile. Parents may complain that educators are negative, unavailable, or patronizing. We should examine factors that cause friction between parents and teachers, not to determine fault but to identify what we can change and improve. Professionals who recognize that some of their own behaviors may diminish the potential for productive partnerships with parents are in a better position to change their actions and obtain the benefits that such relationships can provide.

While educators cannot directly change the attitudes of parents, they can—and, as professionals, must—identify and eliminate personal behaviors that may serve as barriers to communication with families. Some professionals hold stereotypes and false assumptions about what parents of children with disabilities must be like and what they need (Adelman, 1994; Dyson, 1996; Voltz, 1994). These attitudes often lead to poor relationships between families and professionals. We should not be surprised if parents feel intimidated, confused, angry, hostile—or just terminate their involvement altogether—when educators interact with them in any of the following ways:

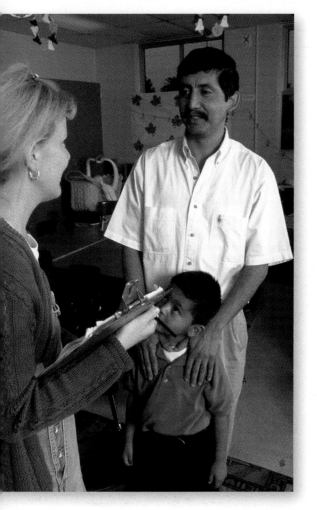

Parent-teacher communication is enhanced when teachers actively listen to what parents say.

Roadblocks to communication

Council for Exceptional Children Content Standards for Beginning Teachers—Common Core: Foster respectful and beneficial relationships between families and professionals (CC10S3).

- *Treating parents as vulnerable clients instead of equal partners.* Professionals who see parents only as helpless souls in need of assistance make a grave mistake. Teachers need parents and what they have to offer as much as parents need teachers (Sonnenschein, 1981).
- *Keeping professional distance.* Most professionals in human services develop some degree of distance to avoid getting too involved with a client—supposedly to maintain objectivity and credibility. But aloofness or coldness in the name of professionalism has hindered or terminated many parent-teacher relationships. Parents must believe that the educators working with their children really care about them (Nelson, Summers, & Turnbull, 2004).
- *Treating parents as if they need counseling.* Some professionals make the faulty assumption that having a child with disabilities causes a parent to need therapy or parent education. A mother of a child who attended a preschool for students with developmental delays described her frustration: "Everybody who came here was aimed at me. Everybody is telling me 'You need parent counseling.' I mean I have lived for 30 years. I never needed help and all of a sudden I need help on how to do this and help on how to do that. I feel like they are saying John is not the problem, I am the problem" (Rao, 2000, p. 481).
- *Blaming parents for their child's condition.* Some parents do feel responsible for their child's disability and, with a little encouragement from a professional, can be made to feel completely guilty. A productive parent-professional relationship focuses on collaborative problem solving, not blame (Singer, Powers, & Olson, 1996).

Chapter 3
Collaborating with Parents and
Families in a Culturally and
Linguistically Diverse Society

- *Disrespecting parents as less intelligent.* Teachers sometimes give too little recognition to parents' information and suggestions. Parents are considered too biased, too involved, or too unskilled to make useful observations (Lake & Billingsley, 2000). Some professionals concede that parents have access to needed information but contend that parents are not able to, or should not, make any decisions based on what they know. "They treat me like I'm uneducated. They break down things into real small pieces and then ask me to repeat things. I have gone to nursing school. I can read. Maybe they met other people who cannot read but they can ask me 'Rose, can you read?' They treat you like you are a child" (Rao, 2000, p. 481).
- *Treating parents as adversaries.* Some teachers expect the worst whenever they interact with parents. Even when that attitude can be partially explained by previous unpleasant encounters with unreasonable parents, it usually becomes a self-fulfilling prophecy and is at best a negative influence on new relationships.
- *Labeling parents.* Some educators seem eager to label parents (Sonnenschein, 1981). If parents disagree with a diagnosis or seek another opinion, they are *denying;* if parents refuse a suggested treatment, they are *resistant;* and if parents insist that something is wrong with their child despite test evidence to the contrary, they are *anxious.*

*Conflict Resolution through Dialoguing.* Not all ineffective parent-teacher relationships are caused by professional mishandling. Some parents are genuinely difficult to work with or unreasonable. There are situations in which parents fight long and hard for services for their child. But after services are found and the child is receiving an appropriate education, the parents continue their intense advocacy until minor issues with professionals become major confrontations. One mother stated, "For years I have scrapped and fought for services. Now I come on like gangbusters over issues that are really not that important. I don't like what has happened to me. I've ended up to be an aggressive, angry person" (Bronicki & Turnbull, 1987, p. 10).

Although some teachers voice concern that parents of children with disabilities are unrealistic and make too many demands of schools (e.g., Chesley & Calaluce, 1997), most recognize that these parents, like all parents, are simply advocating for the best possible educational services and outcomes for their children. When someone sees things differently from us and we both have vested interests in the outcome, we often resort to argument in an attempt to resolve our differences. Although a teacher may "win" an argument with parents—if one defines winning as forcing the parents to agree verbally or simply give up their perspective—arguing is rarely a useful tool in a partnership. *Dialoguing* is an approach to conflict resolution in which both parties try to see each other's point of view. Gonzalez-Mena (2002) points out differences between a dialogue and an argument:

*Dialoguing to resolve conflicts*

Council for Exceptional Children — Content Standards for Beginning Teachers—Common Core: Foster respectful and beneficial relationships between families and professionals (CC10S3).

- The object of an argument is to win; the object of a dialogue is to gather information.
- The arguer tells; the dialoguer asks.
- The arguer tries to persuade; the dialoguer seeks to learn.
- The arguer see two opposing views and considers hers the valid or best one; the dialoguer is willing to understand multiple viewpoints. (p. 110)

Most of us are better at arguing than we are at dialoguing. That's probably because we have had much more practice with the former. We tend to argue first and think rationally (if we do at all) later. But later might be too late if in "winning" the argument, we have damaged the parent-teacher relationship.

So how does one switch from an argument to a dialogue in the heat of the moment? Start by noticing your body language. Sometimes you can just change your body language, and an energy switch will follow. Then it's a matter of doing one simple thing: listening to the other person. To truly listen, one must suspend judgments and focus on what's being said rather than just gathering ammunition for the next attack. Really hearing someone is extremely simple, but it's not easy. (Gonzalez-Mena, 2002, p. 111)

After adopting open body language and beginning to listen, Gonzalez-Mena (2002) recommends using the RERUN approach: reflect, explain, reason, understand, and negotiate.

- *Reflect.*   Acknowledge what you perceive the other person is thinking or feeling. If you understand what the person is feeling, you might say, "I think you're looking at it this way." If you perceive that the other person is very emotional, acknowledge that perception: "You sound really upset." Such responses invite the person to talk more. People who know that their feelings and thoughts are received and accepted are more likely to listen and be open to your thoughts.
- *Explain.*   Remember, we have two ears and one mouth—a reminder that we should listen twice as much as we talk.
- *Reason.*   The explanation of your perspective should include the reason you believe or feel the way that you do.
- *Understand.*   Next comes the hardest part. Tune in to both thoughts and feelings and try to understand the situation from both points of view. You don't have to say anything out loud at this point; just be sure you have clarity. You may have to talk inwardly to yourself to get it. Self-reflection is an important part of the process. When you think you understand, you're ready for the next step.
- *Negotiate.*   Try brainstorming together until you can find a mutually satisfying solution. Don't give up. Refuse to take an either-or attitude. If you don't get stuck in a dualistic frame of mind, you can probably find a third or fourth solution that is different from or combines both of your stances on the matter. Creative negotiators can open up new avenues of action that no one has ever thought of before. (adapted from Gonzalez-Mena, 2002, p. 111)

For additional suggestions on resolving conflicts and disagreements with parents, see Heron and Harris (2001), Lambie (2000), Margolis and Brannigan (1990), and Simpson (1996).

# WORKING WITH CULTURALLY AND LINGUISTICALLY DIVERSE FAMILIES

Differences in the cultural and linguistic beliefs and practices of professionals and families often serve as barriers to parent involvement (Greenen, Powers, & Lopez-Vasquez, 2001; Harry, Kalyanpur, & Day, 1999). Teachers who fail to recognize and respect differences between their own cultural perspectives and the culturally based values and beliefs of families are prone to make biased and faulty judgments about parents that weaken the parent-teacher relationship.

## Understanding and Respecting Cultural Differences

Involving families who come from diverse backgrounds in school activities is often challenging. Antunez (2000) outlines several barriers that might exist in working with parents and families from culturally diverse backgrounds.

- *Language skills.*   Inability to understand the language of the school is a major deterrent to the parents who have not achieved full English proficiency. In these cases, interactions with the schools are difficult, and, therefore, practically nonexistent.
- *Home/school partnerships.*   In some cultures, such as many Hispanic ones, teaming with the school is not a tradition. Education has been historically perceived as the responsibility of the schools, and parent intervention is viewed as interference with what trained professionals are supposed to do.
- *Work interference.*   Work is a major reason stated by parents for noninvolvement in school activities. Conflicts between parent and school schedules may mean parents cannot attend school events, help their children with homework, or in other ways become active participants in their children's education.

Chapter 3

Collaborating with Parents and
Families in a Culturally and
Linguistically Diverse Society

- *Knowledge of the school system.* A great number of low-income parents view schools as an incomprehensible and purposefully exclusionary system. Lack of trust is often the result of misunderstanding the perceived intentions of each party. Sending home communications in English only and scheduling meetings at times when parents cannot attend serve to reinforce parent apprehension. Schools often misperceive the lack of involvement that results from mistrust and apprehension as a lack of concern for the children's education.
- *Self-confidence.* Many parents of English language learner students believe that their participation does not help schools perform their jobs as educational institutions; as a result, they separate themselves from the process. Parents who feel uncomfortable in the school setting are less likely to be involved than those who have developed a sense of equal partnership are.
- *Past experiences.* Many non-English speaking parents have had negative education experiences of their own, and these memories linger through adulthood. In some cases, these parents have fallen victim to racial and linguistic discrimination by the schools. Negative feelings toward home-school interaction are often reinforced when schools communicate with parents only to share bad news about their children. (pp. 4–5)

The demands and challenges faced by families who may less educated, poor, or isolated from the dominant American culture may prevent them from becoming actively involved in school partnerships. The literature on culturally diverse families supports the following six notions about these families (Cartledge, Kea, & Ida, 2000; Correa & Jones, 2000; Gollnick & Chinn, 2002; Harry, 1992b; Hernandez, 2001; Kalyanpur & Harry, 1999; Lian & Fontánez-Phelan, 2001; Lynch & Hanson, 1998; Park, Turnbull, & Park, 2001; Thomas, Correa, & Morsink, 2000):

1. *Many families may be English-language learners, be less well educated, have low socioeconomic status, or be undocumented immigrants.* Thus, practitioners should provide materials in both the native and English language and preferably communicate with the family directly through home visits or by telephone. Some parents are not able to read their native language and may depend on older children who are English-dominant to translate materials for them.

2. *Practitioners must understand that, although the parents may not have finished school or are unable to read, they are "life educated" and know their child better than anyone else does.* In Spanish, the term *educado* (educated) does not mean "formal schooling" but means that a child is skilled in human relations, well mannered, respectful of adults, and well behaved.

3. *If families are undocumented immigrants, they are naturally fearful of interaction with anyone representing authority.* Our role as special educators is not to engage in the activities of the Office of Immigration and Naturalization Services. Our focus is on educating children, who by law are not a suspect class (Correa, Gollery, & Fradd, 1988). Building families' trust and cooperation, even if they are undocumented immigrants, is important.

4. *Families from culturally diverse backgrounds tend to be family-oriented.* Extended family members—*compadres* or *padrinos* (godparents) in the Hispanic culture— may play important roles in child rearing and family decisions. A child's disability or even a mild language problem may be an extremely personal subject for discussion with outsiders, and solutions for problems may lie within the family structure. It is important for educators to respect this informal kinship system of support and to understand that we may represent a much more formal and impersonal support service for these families. The close, insular aspect of a family is a strength that helps the family function and cope with the stresses sometimes associated with raising a child with a disability (Bailey, Skinner, Correa, Arcia, et al., 1999; Dunst, Trivette, & Deal, 1988).

5. *It is important to know that culturally diverse families may have different experiences with and views about disability, and some may hold idiosyncratic ideologies and practices about the cause and treatment of disability.* For example, in some Hispanic cultures,

parents may believe that God sent the child with disabilities to them as a gift or blessing, while others may believe the child was sent as a test or a punishment for previous sins. In recent studies on Latino families, parents acknowledged transforming their lives since the birth of their child by becoming better parents (Bailey, Skinner, Correa, Arcia, et al., 1999; Bailey, Skinner, Correa, Blanes, et al., 1999). Most families were positive in describing the child with disabilities, and very few reported the presence of the child with disabilities as a negative sign or punishment from God for sins. The role of faith in God was extremely important for families coping with the child, more so than formal religious activities such as church attendance or Bible studies (Bailey, Skinner, Correa, Blanes, et al., 1999; Skinner, Correa, Skinner, & Bailey, 2001). Interestingly, among many Native American groups, it is not considered negative or tragic to have a child born with a disability. "It is assumed the child has the prenatal choice of how he wishes to be born and, if [disabled], is so by choice" (Stewart, 1977, p. 439).

Although previous literature has reported the existence of folk beliefs and alternative treatments for disabilities in some cultural groups, more recent research finds that for Puerto Rican and Mexican families such beliefs are not prevalent (Bailey, Skinner, Correa, Blanes, et al., 1999; Skinner et al., 2001). Families did report knowing about *el mal ojo* (the evil eye) or *el susto* (a scare or fright experienced by the pregnant mother) as explanations given for disabilities but did not believe them to be true of their own children with disabilities. They reported that some family members (usually the elders) might believe that, to cure the child, the family must make *mandas* (offerings to God or a Catholic saint) or seek the help of a *curandero* (a local healer). However, almost all families interviewed used traditional western medicine to treat the child with disabilities.

Content Standards for Beginning Teachers—General Curriculum and Independence Curriculum Referenced Standards: Potential impact of differences in values, languages, and customs that can exist between the home and school (CC1K10) (also CC3K4, CC6K3, CC10K4).

6. *The educational system—in particular, the special education system—may be intimidating to the family.* Although this may be true for many white families as well, for the family from a non-English-language background or one that is less well educated and poor, professionals' use of educational language and jargon, their nonverbal communication, and their possible insensitivity may be especially intimidating. Furthermore, parents with disabilities may also find themselves disenfranchised from their child's special education program, often not wanting to engage in any school-home interaction. Some families may even put the professional on a pedestal and, believing the professional is the expert, not question or comment on their own wishes for their child's education.

## Providing Culturally Responsive Services to Families

Educators can increase parent involvement by using culturally responsive and respectful strategies such as the following (Al-Hassan & Gardner, 2002; Parette & Petch-Hogan, 2000):

- Have native-speaking individuals make initial contacts.
- Use trained interpreters during conferences.
- Conduct meetings in family-friendly settings.
- Identify and defer to key decision makers in the family.
- Recognize that families from diverse cultures may view time differently from the way professionals do and schedule meetings accordingly.
- Provide transportation and child care to make it easier for families to attend school-based activities.

*Family Interviews.* Dennis and Giangreco (1996) advise that teachers should understand a broad range of families' cultural aspects. A good way to gain knowledge and understanding of family values and priorities for a child with disabilities is to conduct family interviews. Dennis and Giangreco suggest that professionals seek help from cultural interpreters before the interview and carefully ascertain the literacy and language status of family members. In conducting the interview, professionals should be prepared to adapt the time frame to meet the needs of the family and be flexible and responsive to the family's interaction style.

Gabel (2004) suggests using a **cultural interpreter**—a person "who can create bridges of understanding between school and home culture. These individuals do not necessarily have to speak the home language of an immigrant family, but they must have enough of a basic understanding of the home culture to help the school understand that home culture and to help the family understand school culture, policies, and practices" (p. 23).

*Cultural Reciprocity.* Educators should also work toward understanding how differing values and belief systems may influence families' perspectives, wishes, and decisions. For example, a special educator who views disability as a physical phenomenon that can be measured and treated in an objective way may have difficulty developing an effective partnership with parents from a culture that views disability as a blessing or a punishment that is to be treated with spiritual perspective (Harry, Rueda, & Kalyanpur, 1999; Bailey, Skinner, Correa et al., 1999).

*A culturally responsive educator strives to develop awareness of and respect for the beliefs and values held by parents and family members from diverse cultural groups.*

Understanding differences between our own perspectives and those of people from other cultures and ethnic groups requires careful examination of our own cultural background and belief system. The questions and issues posed in "A Cultural Journey" (see Chapter 2) suggest one way to begin such a personal assessment, the initial step in working toward cultural reciprocity. "Understanding that our own beliefs and practices are but one cultural variation should make it easier to respect, and therefore to serve, the wide diversity of families whose children are served by special education programs" (Harry, 2003, p. 138). See Diversity & Exceptionality, "Building Cultural Reciprocity," later in this chapter.

*Cultural reciprocity*

 Council for Exceptional Children — Content Standards for Beginning Teachers—General Curriculum and Independence Curriculum Referenced Standards: Culturally responsive factors that promote effective communication and collaboration with individuals with exceptional learning needs, families, school personnel, and community members (CC10K4) (also CC3K4, CC6K3).

# METHODS OF HOME-SCHOOL COMMUNICATION

Although no single method of communication will be effective or even appropriate with every parent and family, teachers can increase the number of families they reach and the frequency of communications with those families by making several methods of home-school communication available to parents. Some parents and families prefer face-to-face meetings; others appreciate receiving written messages or phone calls; still others communicate more frequently and efficiently via e-mail or fax machine. Teachers should ask parents which methods of communication they prefer.

## Parent-Teacher Conferences

Although parent-teacher conferences are as common to school as recess and homework, they are not always an effective vehicle for communication. Too often, parent-teacher conferences are stiff, formal affairs with anxious teachers and worried parents who wonder what bad news they will hear this time. Fortunately, parents and teachers are learning to talk with one another in more productive ways. In a face-to-face meeting, they can exchange information and coordinate their efforts to assist the child with disabilities in school and at home. Parent-teacher conferences should not be limited to the beginning and end of the school year but scheduled regularly.

*Preparing for the Conference.* Preparation is the key to effective parent-teacher conferences. It entails establishing specific objectives for the conference, obtaining and reviewing

# Building Cultural Reciprocity

A service provider and a family member meet for the first time. If the parent's perspective of the world is similar to the service provider's, then a positive connection generally occurs. However, if the parent holds a belief system different from the service provider's, difficulties typically arise. According to Beth Harry, a faculty member at the University of Miami, the source of the difficulty is often a point of view that is defined and limited by cultural orientation.

According to Harry, stumbling blocks often arise when service providers and families do not recognize and accept the other's culture.

> For example, I found that individuals from Puerto Rican backgrounds tended to view disabilities as more severe conditions than do people from the mainstream United States—in fact, many of our high-incidence disabilities were not seen by them as disabilities, but simply as individual characteristics within the normal range. We observed that when parents from Puerto Rico realized their views were not valued by Anglo service providers, they stopped participating in their children's educational process.
>
> The process of acculturation takes time, and professionals who are hoping to make a difference for children must be willing to take the initiative in building a bridge between the cultures of diverse families and the culture of schools.

To build this bridge, Harry advocates that professionals initiate a two-way process of information sharing and understanding called *cultural reciprocity*. The process is recursive, meaning that each step informs the others.

- **Step 1.** Identify the cultural values that are embedded in your interpretation of a student's difficulties or in a recommendation for service. Ask yourself which values underlie your recommendation. Next, analyze experiences that have contributed to your holding of these values. Consider the roles of nationality, culture, socioeconomic status, and professional education in shaping your values.

- **Step 2.** Find out whether the family being served recognizes and values your assumptions and, if not, how family members' views differ from yours.

- **Step 3.** Acknowledge and give explicit respect to any cultural differences identified, and fully explain the cultural basis of your assumptions.

- **Step 4.** Through discussion and collaboration, determine the most effective way of adapting your professional interpretations or recommendations to the value system of this family.

Harry points out that "by developing your own cultural self-awareness, you are able to recognize the cultural underpinnings of your professional practice. This, in turn, enables you to facilitate conversations with the families." Through the process, families also acquire knowledge about the special education system, which supports them in making informed decisions about services. "With cultural reciprocity, we find not only better relationships, but more reasonable goals that are implemented."

**One Teacher's Personal Account** "Before learning the reciprocity process, I was somewhat closed-minded," shares Yamile Llano, a Miami, Florida, high school teacher who is Hispanic of Cuban origin. As a graduate student in one of Professor Beth Harry's special education courses, Llano was required to participate in a number of activities with families based on Harry's cultural reciprocity research. One activity involved attending a social event with one of her students and his family. Llano selected Jack, an African American youngster, and arranged to attend church with him and his family. Following is an excerpt from Ms. Llano's journal entry:

> I was very nervous. I was on my way to a Baptist church in a predominantly black neighborhood. My stomach was in knots. . . . I am of Catholic faith and I was not sure what to expect. As I waited for the family, many people looked at me as if were lost. I really did not fit in; I stood

out like a sore thumb. . . . I felt as if I were intruding. As people stared at me, I simply smiled and said, "Hello." I just wanted to disappear. When I saw Jack's family, I felt more comfortable. They welcomed me very warmly, and Jack shook my hand for the first time. It was then I felt I was in a very warm atmosphere. The church felt like one big family—very different from the church I regularly attend. At my church, when people walk in, they are very quiet and very careful not to make the slightest noise. At Jack's church, everyone was happy and no one whispered. This made me feel good. Jack's family interacted with everyone. I noticed that everyone greeted Jack—just like everyone else. No one treated him differently. Jack was accepted as he is. I tried to see if anyone treated Jack differently, but I saw no evidence of that. Instead, what I saw was a close-knit community that was accepting of Jack's disability.

Many times we make assumptions about people based on race, religion, and other factors that hinder us from mixing and mingling with other people. I thought people in the church would not be accepting of me because of my race and my religion—but I was wrong!

According to Llano, that experience taught her a lot about herself. She encourages other teachers to move outside their circles and experiences and into the lives of their students and families. "You will feel richer for the experience."

*Source*: Adapted from ERIC/OSEP Special Project. (2001). *Family involvement in special education*. (Research Connections in Special Education, no. 9), (pp. 4–5). Arlington, VA: ERIC Clearinghouse on Disabilities and Gifted Education.

 To further your understanding of and answer reflective questions about the issues and strategies presented here, go to Chapter 3's Diversity & Exceptionality module on the Companion Website, **www.prenhall.com/heward**

---

a computer printout or list of the student's grades, selecting examples of the student's work and perhaps a graph or chart showing his cumulative progress, and preparing an agenda for the meeting (Courson & Hay, 1996; Dodd, 1996; Stephens & Wolf, 1989). Figure 3.3 shows a parent-teacher conference outline that can be used for preparing an agenda and recording notes of the meeting.

*Conducting the Conference.*   Most parent-teacher conferences for school-age children are held in the child's classroom because (1) the teacher feels comfortable in familiar surroundings; (2) the teacher has ready access to student files and instructional materials; (3) the classroom itself serves as a reminder to the teacher of things the child has done; and (4) the classroom, with its desks, chairs, and teaching materials, reminds both teacher and parents that the purpose of the conference is their mutual concern for improving the child's education. Wherever parent conferences are held, the area should be arranged so that it is conducive to partnership interactions (Courson & Hay, 1996). Teachers should not make the mistake of hiding behind their desks, creating a barrier between themselves and the parents, or of seating parents in undersized chairs meant for students.

Stephens and Wolf (1989) suggest a 4-step sequence for parent-teacher conferences:

1. *Build rapport.*   Establishing mutual trust and the belief that the teacher really cares about the student is important to a good parent-teacher conference (Perl, 1995). A minute or two should be devoted to relevant small talk. The teacher might begin with something positive about the child or family instead of a superficial statement about the weather or traffic.
2. *Obtain information.*   Parents can provide teachers with important information for improving instruction. As suggested earlier, teachers should use open-ended questions that cannot be answered with a simple yes or no. For example, "Which activities in school has Felix mentioned lately?" is better than "Has Felix told you what we are doing now in school?" The first question encourages the parent to provide more information; the teacher is trying to build a conversation, not preside over a question-and-answer session. Throughout the conference, the teacher should show genuine interest in listening to parents' concerns, avoid dominating the conversation, and stay focused on the purpose of the meeting. Above all, teachers should refrain from making comments that lecture ("Do you realize. . . . "),

*Planning and conducting parent-teacher conferences*

Council for Exceptional Children   Content Standards for Beginning Teachers—Common Core: Plan and conduct collaborative conferences with individuals with exceptional learning needs and their families (CC10S5) (also CC7S3).

**FIGURE 3.3   Outline for a parent-teacher conference**

### Conference Outline

Date _____ 2-8-06 _____                    Time _____ 4:30 - 5:00 _____

Student's Name _____ Jeremy Wright _____
Parents' Name(s) _____ Barbara and Tom Wright _____
Teacher's Name _____ Tim G. _____
Other Staff Present _____ None _____

Objectives for Conference:   (1) Show graph of J's reading progress, (2) find out about spelling program,
  (3) get parents' ideas: intervention for difficulties on playground/in gym, (4) share list of books for leisure reading

Student's Strengths   • good worker academically, wants to learn
  • excited about progress in reading fluency

Area(s) Where Improvement Is Needed:   • continue w/spelling @ home
  • arguments & fighting w/other kids

Questions to Ask Parents:   • Interactions w/friends while playing in neighborhood?
  • How would they feel about f'dback from classmate re: playground/gym behavior?
  • Consequences?

Parent's Responses/Comments:   • very pleased w/reading - want to build on it.
  • wondering how long w/in-home spelling?
  • willing to give rewards @ home: playground/gym

Examples of Student's Work/Interactions:   • graph of corrects/errors per min.: reading
  • weekly pre- & post-test scores: spelling.

Current Programs and Strategies Used by Teacher:   • reading: silent read, two 1-min. time trials, self-charting
  comprehension practice
  • spelling: practice w/tape recorder, self-checking

Suggestions for Parents:   • continue spelling games (invite friends)
  • Show interest in/play fantasy games (Dung. & Dragons) w/J

Suggestions from Parents:   • Try using some high-interest spelling words (e.g., joust, castle)
  • Matt & Amin could help with playground/gym program

Follow-up Activities:   (Agreed to in conf)
  Parents:   • Continue to play spelling game 2 nights per week
  • Take J to library for adventure books
  Teacher:   • Ask J for high-interest words & use 3-4 in his weekly list.
  • Develop peer intervention strategy w/Matt, Amin & J (group contingency?)

Date to Call for Follow-up:
  Feb. 22 (Wednesday) _____ (check when called)

criticize or judge ("That was a mistake.... "), or threaten ("Unless you take my advice.... "), all of which block communication (Simpson, 1996; Turnbull & Turnbull, 2006; Wilson, 1995).

3. *Provide information.*   The teacher should give parents concrete information about their child in jargon-free language. The teacher should share examples of school-work and data on student performance—what has already been learned and what needs to be learned next. If the student has not made much progress, parents and teacher should look together for ways to improve it.

4. *Summarize and follow up.* The conference should end with a summary of what was said. The teacher should review strategies agreed on during the conference and indicate the follow-up activities that either party will do to help carry out those strategies. Some teachers record notes on a laptop computer during the conference, printing out a copy at the conclusion of the meeting so that parents will also have a record of what was said or agreed to.

These strategies are relevant to all types of parent-teacher meetings. However, IEP and IFSP planning and evaluation meetings, which are discussed in Chapters 2 and 14 respectively, entail additional procedural requirements. Detailed suggestions for planning and conducting parent-teacher conferences can be found in Jordan, Reyes-Blane, Peel, Peel, and Lane (1998); Kroth and Edge (1997); Simpson (1996); and Turnbull and Turnbull (2006). For some families, holding a conference in the home might be appropriate and appreciated (Edens, 1997).

To see Ms. Crangle and Ms. Maheady conduct a parent-teacher conference, go to "Parent-Teacher Conference" at "Dunkirk Elementary School" on the *Exceptional Teachers* CD-ROM.

## Written Messages

Although much can be accomplished in face-to-face meetings, they require considerable time to plan and conduct, so they cannot take place frequently. But parent-teacher conferences should not be the sole means of home-school communication. Written messages, especially when part of a systematic program of ongoing information exchange, can be an excellent way of maintaining home-school communication.

Teachers should never rely on written messages, regardless of their form, as the sole method of communicating with parents. Teachers must also be sensitive to the cultural and linguistic backgrounds and educational levels of parents (Al-Hassan & Gardner, 2002). For example, Harry (1992a) reports that because one group of Hispanic parents had to spend a great deal of time translating and trying to understand a school's written messages, they viewed those messages as a nuisance that further alienated them from their children's school.

Showing parents examples of their children's progress sets the occasion for parental praise and approval of student effort.

*Happy Grams.* The easiest and quickest types of home-school written messages are short notes informing parents of something positive their child has accomplished at school. Many teachers regularly send happy grams home with their students, giving parents an opportunity to praise the child at home and stay abreast of activities in the classroom. A book by Kelly (1990) includes tear-out masters of school-home notes that can be duplicated and used for a variety of communication purposes.

*Two-Way, Home-School Note Systems.* A two-way, parent-teacher communication system can be built around a reporting form or a notebook that the child carries between home and school. Teachers can develop and use a standard form or checklist, such as the one shown in Figure 3.4, to inform parents about their child's homework assignments and behavior in the classroom (Cronin et al., 1992; Olympia, Andrews, Valum, & Jensen, 1993; Sicley, 1993). Parents sign the form to indicate they have received it and can use the form themselves to provide information or request assistance from the teacher(s). To be most effective, home-school communication forms should be simple to use, with spaces for teachers and parents to circle or check responses and to write short notes to one another.

*Home-school written communications*

Council for Exceptional Children Content Standards for Beginning Teachers—Common Core: Involve the individual and family in setting instructional goals and monitoring progress (CC7S3).

**Assignment Monitoring Sheet**

Name _____ Date: _____

| PERIOD | ASSIGNMENT | FEEDBACK | COMMENT | SIGNATURE |
|--------|-----------|----------|---------|-----------|

| PERIOD | ASSIGNMENT | FEEDBACK | | | COMMENT | SIGNATURE |
|--------|-----------|----------|------|-----|---------|-----------|
| 1 | | HWC<br>HWNC | CWC<br>CWNC | AB<br>UB | | |
| 2 | | HWC<br>HWNC | CWC<br>CWNC | AB<br>UB | | |
| 3 | | HWC<br>HWNC | CWC<br>CWNC | AB<br>UB | | |
| 4 | | HWC<br>HWNC | CWC<br>CWNC | AB<br>UB | | |
| 5 | | HWC<br>HWNC | CWC<br>CWNC | AB<br>UB | | |
| 6 | | HWC<br>HWNC | CWC<br>CWNC | AB<br>UB | | |
| 7 | | HWC<br>HWNC | CWC<br>CWNC | AB<br>UB | | |

KEY:
HWC = HomeWork Completed          HWNC = HomeWork Not Completed
CWC = ClassWork Completed          CWNC = ClassWork Not Completed
AB  = Acceptable Behavior          UB   = Unacceptable Behavior
*********************************************************************************************************

**Parent Feedback/Assistance Request**

Feedback or Issue of Concern:
_____
_____
_____

Action Requested:     phone conference          _____
                      conference at school       _____
                      none                       _____

Best day/time to contact:        day: _____
                                 time: _____

Parent Signature: _____ Phone: _____

*Source:* From "Home-School Partnerships" by M. E. Cronin, D. L. Slade, C. Bechtel, and P. Anderson, 1992, *Intervention in School and Clinic,* 27(5), 286–292. © 1992 by PRO-ED, Inc. Reprinted with permission.

Home-school dialogue notebooks offer another form of written communication between parents and teachers (Hall, Wolfe, & Bollig, 2003). Williams and Cartledge (1997) describe a notebook system that Williams used to communicate regularly with the parents of children with emotional and behavioral disorders. The children attended an urban school, and all came from low socioeconomic backgrounds. Williams and Cartledge emphasize the importance of being organized, persistent, and flexible in expectations for parent participation. Figure 3.5 shows some sample parent-teacher notebook exchanges.

Parent responses are needed to make the notebook system work. How did we get parents to respond regularly and meaningfully? The secret is the teacher's consistency, persistence, and

---

**FIGURE 3.5   Sample parent-teacher notebook exchanges**

**The teacher said:**
William had a great first day at school. He did as much as he could with his hand. Please go through the papers that he brought home and explain them to him. He had a great start, and I am sure that he is just going to do fine.

**Then the parent said:**
William had a great evening. He was very anxious about school. His goal for this semester is to have straight As. Thanks so much for being so kind with him.

**The teacher said:**
Mrs. R, thank you very much for attending our class feast yesterday. That was very nice of you, and I want you to know that it was greatly appreciated. I am pleased that Jason is making progress both academically and socially—which could not have happened without your support and cooperation.

**Then the parent said:**
Mrs. W., thank you very much for the lunch. It was very good. I am glad that Jason is making progress especially with his behavior. I hope this will continue. Jason misplaced his homework and could not find it. Would you please send another homework home today so that he will be able to get the credit?

**The parent said:**
I checked some of Jermain's papers. Please don't accept sloppy work. He is making some mistakes, and I think he is not paying attention to his work. He loves to come to school, and he is making some new friends. He said you have been very helpful. He had a great weekend.

**Then the teacher said:**
Jermain had a pleasant day at school today. He did his assignments and followed directions. I talked with him about his writing and taking time with his work. He promised to do better. Let me know when you want to come in for the conference so that I can make time to be available for you before Thursday.

**The parent said:**
Matt practiced his spelling words. He finally gave me his spelling book this morning. When is the science project due? Matt could not remember when. He read a cookbook for a half-hour and made out a grocery list for supper from the recipes.

**Then the teacher said:**
Matt's day at school was fine. He did his assignments and followed directions on the playground. The science project is due in tomorrow morning. He is concerned that he might not be able to put it together before tomorrow. I told him that he should do his best and bring whatever he has in. We will be doing our cooking on Friday, and you are welcome to attend if it is convenient for you.

---

*Source:* Reprinted from Williams, V. L., & Cartledge, G. (1997). Passing notes to parents. *Teaching Exceptional Children, 30*(1), 32. Used by permission of the Council for Exceptional Children, Reston, VA.

caring.... I found that to make the system work, I had to be well organized and disciplined. I had to read 10 notebook entries every day and make my own entries. In my classroom, I placed a basket near the door.... As soon as the students entered the classroom, they were to put their notebook in the basket before going to breakfast. I would read the parent notes while the students were eating breakfast, and I also used lunch or periods when students attended art, music, and physical education classes as times to review parent messages. I usually wrote to the parents during the afternoon recess period.

Needless to say, not all parents immediately embraced this communication system. This is where persistence became important; I refused to give up. I always tried to respond positively to every parent, and I worked to help them gradually increase their levels of participation. Some parents were comfortable with just signing their names on the notebook to let me know that they had read my message; some were comfortable writing about their child's activities during the previous night; and some would go further to share special or personal events that they felt would be of significance to their child's schooling. (Williams & Cartledge, 1997, p. 32)

*Home-School Contracts.* A home-school contract specifies parent-delivered rewards for the child contingent on her behavior or academic performance in the classroom (Smith, 1994). For example, Kerr and Nelson (2002) describe a home-school contract developed by the teacher and parents of a child who interrupted the teacher and disrupted other students during math and social studies classes. The student received a checkmark for each class period that he participated in class discussions instead of disrupting others; when he earned 50 checkmarks, his parents agreed to buy him a gerbil. Home-school contracts use parent-controlled rewards, build in parent recognition and praise of the child's accomplishments, and involve the teacher and parents together in a positive program to support the child's learning.

*Class Newsletters and Websites.* Class newsletters or websites are additional methods of fostering home-school communication. Even though putting together a class newsletter or designing a website requires a lot of work, in many cases it is worth the effort. Most teachers today have access to a computer and word-processing software. A one- to three-page monthly newsletter can give parents—especially those who do not attend meetings or open houses—information that is too long or detailed to give over the telephone. A newsletter is also an excellent way to recognize parents who participate in various activities. By making the newsletter or website a class project, the teacher can include student-written stories and news items and can create an enjoyable learning activity for the entire class.

*Telephone Calls.* Regular telephone calls can be an effective and efficient way to maintain home-school communication and parent involvement (Gartland, 1993). A brief conversation that focuses on a child's positive accomplishments lets parents and teachers share the child's success and recognize each other's contributions. Short, positive calls from the teacher also reduce parents' fear that calls from school always indicate a problem. Teachers should set aside time on a regular basis so that each child's parent receives a call at least once every two or three weeks. Teachers should ask parents what times they prefer to receive calls. Keeping a log helps to maintain the schedule and reminds teachers of any necessary follow-up.

Telephone answering machines are a convenient, low-cost technology for home-school communication. By recording daily messages on an answering machine, teachers can give parents a great deal of information for relatively little cost. Parents can call and listen at their convenience, literally 24 hours a day. Recorded telephone messages can provide schoolwide and classroom-by-classroom information, good news (e.g., citizen of the month), and suggestions for working with children at home (Heward, Heron, Gardner, & Prayzer, 1991; Minner, Beane, & Prater, 1986; Test, Cooke, Weiss, Heward, & Heron, 1986). Parent callers can also leave messages on the machine, pose a question, offer an idea or suggestion for the teacher, and so on.

Whatever modes or forms of parent-teacher communication are used, educators should follow the suggestions in Teaching & Learning, "Ten Guidelines for Communicating with Parents and Families" on the next page.

*Guidelines for communicating with parents*

Council for Exceptional Children Content Standards for Beginning Teachers—Common Core: Foster respectful and beneficial relationships between families and professionals (CC10S3) (also CC1K7 & CC9S7).

# Ten Guidelines for Communicating with Parents and Families

Regardless of the mode of parent-teacher communication or differences in cultural experiences and language backgrounds of the participants, the following suggestions are valuable guidelines for educators in their interactions with parents and families. Contrast these 10 guidelines with the professional roadblocks to communication described earlier.

**1.** *Don't assume that you know more about the child, his needs, and how those needs should be met than his parents do.* If you make this assumption, you will usually be wrong and, worse, will miss opportunities to obtain and provide meaningful information.

**2.** *Junk the jargon.* Educators who use technical terminology will have difficulty communicating effectively with parents (or with anyone else, for that matter). Speak in clear, everyday language and avoid the alphabet soup of special education (e.g., FAPE, IFSP, MFE).

**3.** *Don't let assumptions and generalizations about parents and families guide your efforts.* If you are genuinely interested in what a father or mother feels or wants, ask. Do not assume a parent is in the *x, y,* or *z* stage and therefore needs *a, b,* or *c.*

**4.** *Be sensitive and responsive to the cultural and linguistic backgrounds of parents and families.* The information and support services desired by families from different cultural and ethnic groups vary, and majority educators must work to be sensitive to those differences (Harry et al., 1999; Lynch & Hanson, 2004).

**5.** *Don't be defensive or intimidated.* Unless you are one, you cannot ever really know what being the parent of a child with disabilities is like. But as a trained teacher, you do know something about helping children with disabilities learn. That's your job; it's what you do every day with lots of children. Offer the knowledge and skills you have without apology, and welcome parents' input.

**6.** *Refer families to other professionals when needed.* As a teacher, you interact with parents and families in an effort to improve the child's educational program. You are not a marriage counselor or a therapist. If a parent or a family member indicates the need for non-special education services, offer to refer him to professionals and agencies qualified to provide them.

**7.** *Help parents strive for a realistic optimism.* Children with disabilities and their families benefit little from professionals who are doom-and-gloom types or who minimize the significance of a disability. Help parents analyze, plan, and prepare for their child's future (Giangreco et al., 1998; Turnbull & Turnbull, 2006).

**8.** *Start with something parents can be successful with.* For many parents, involvement in their child's educational program is a new experience. When parents show an interest in helping their child at home, don't set them up to fail by giving them complicated materials, complex instructions, and a heavy schedule of nightly tutoring. Begin with something simple that is likely to be rewarding to the parent and the child.

**9.** *Respect a parent's right to say no.* Most educators are eager to share what they know and to help families plan and carry out shared teaching goals. But professionals sometimes "fail to recognize the more basic needs of families, one of which is to not need a professional support person! . . . there comes a time when parents and other members of the family wish to be left alone" (Howard et al., 2005, p. 124).

**10.** *Don't be afraid to say, "I don't know."* Sometimes parents will ask questions that you cannot answer or request services you cannot provide. The mark of a real professional is knowing the limits of your expertise and when you need help. It is okay to say, "I don't know." Parents will think more highly of you.

 To learn more about these strategies and answer questions about what you have learned, go to the Teaching & Learning module in Chapter 3 of the Companion Website, **www.prenhall.com.heward**.

# OTHER FORMS OF PARENT INVOLVEMENT

## Parents As Teachers

Typically developing children learn many skills that children with disabilities do not learn without systematic instruction. For children with disabilities, the casual routines of everyday life at home and in the community may not provide enough practice and feedback to teach them important skills. Many parents of exceptional children have responded to this challenge by systematically teaching their children self-help and daily living skills or by providing home-based academic tutoring to supplement classroom instruction.

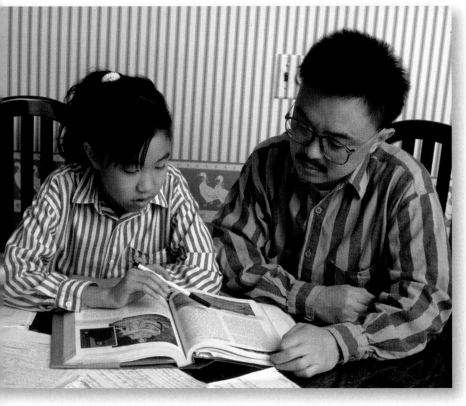

Properly conducted, home-based parent tutoring sessions strengthen the child's educational programs and are enjoyable for the child and the parent.

Parents can serve as effective teachers for their children, a conclusion supported by numerous research studies and parent involvement projects in which parents have successfully taught their children at home (e.g., Barbetta & Heron, 1991; Leach & Siddall, 1992; Thurston & Dasta, 1990). Research shows that parents can enhance the development of children with disabilities by teaching them at home (e.g., Baker, 1989; Delaney & Kaiser, 2001; Snell & Beckman-Brindley, 1984; Wedel & Fowler, 1984). And the majority of parents who participate in systematic home tutoring programs organized by their child's school describe it as a positive experience for them and their children. A mother and father wrote: "We really enjoyed teaching M. to tell time, and he enjoyed working with us. He learned so quickly and we were so happy and proud to see the progress he was making. We have two other children. Doing this program allowed us to spend time alone with M." (Donley & Williams, 1997, p. 50).

Usually, if parents wish to tutor their children at home, they can and should be helped to do so. Properly conducted, home-based parent tutoring strengthens a child's educational program and gives enjoyment to both child and parent. Guidelines for home-based parent tutoring include the following (Bowen, Olympia, & Jensen, 1996; Hudson & Miller, 1993):

*Parents as tutors*

Council for Exceptional Children Content Standards for Beginning Teachers—Common Core: Assist individuals with exceptional learning needs and their families in becoming active participants in the educational team (CC10S4) (also CC1K7).

- *Keep sessions short.*   Aim for 15- to 20-minute sessions 3 or 4 days per week.
- *Make the experience positive.*   Parents should praise the child's attempts.
- *Keep responses to the child consistent.*   By praising the child's successful responses (materials and activities at the child's appropriate instructional level are a must) and providing a consistent, unemotional response to errors (e.g., "Let's read that word again, together"), parents can avoid the frustration and negative results that can occur when home tutoring is mishandled.
- *Use tutoring to practice and extend skills already learned in school.*   For example, use spelling or vocabulary words from school as the questions or items for an adapted board game (Wesson, Wilson, & Higbee Mandelbaum, 1988).
- *Keep a record.*   Parents, like classroom teachers, can never know the exact effects of their teaching unless they keep records. A daily record enables both parents and child

to see gradual progress that might be missed if subjective opinion is the only basis for evaluation. Most children do make progress under guided instruction, and a record documents that progress, perhaps providing the parent with an opportunity to see the child in a new and positive light.

It is important for professionals to consider carefully to what extent parent tutoring is appropriate. Not all parents want to teach their children at home or have the time to learn and use the necessary teaching skills—and professionals must not interpret that situation as an indication that parents do not care enough about their children. Teachers must not assume that parents who choose not to participate in home teaching programs are uninterested in their children. Some parents may choose not to do home tutoring because they feel it may compete with other activities in the home and negatively affect their family's overall quality of life (Parette & Petch-Hogan, 2000).

For specific programs and techniques teachers can use to help parents who do wish to tutor their children at home, see Bowen et al. (1996) and Miller, Barbetta, and Heron (1994). For suggestions for supporting parents who want to help their children with homework and study skills, see Patton, Jayanthi, and Polloway (2001); Jensen, Sheridan, Olympia, and Andrews (1994); and Luckner (1994).

## Parent Education and Support Groups

Education for parenting is not new; programs date back to the early 1800s. But as a result of greater parent involvement in the education of children with disabilities, many more programs are offered for and by parents. Parent groups can serve a variety of purposes: from one-time-only dissemination of information on a new school policy, to make-it-and-take-it workshops in which parents make instructional materials to use at home (e.g., a math facts practice game), to multiple-session programs on IEP/IFSP planning or behavior support strategies.

*Parent education and parent support groups*

Council for Exceptional Children   Content Standards for Beginning Teachers—Common Core: Concerns of families of individuals with exceptional learning needs and strategies to help address these concerns (CC10K3).

There is consistent agreement in the parent education literature on the importance of involving parents in planning and, whenever possible, actually conducting parent groups (Kroth & Edge, 1997; Turnbull & Turnbull, 2006). To determine what parents want from a parent program, educators should use both open and closed needs-assessment procedures. An *open needs assessment* consists of questions like these:

The best family time for my child is when we _____.

I will never forget the time that my child and I _____.

When I take my child to the store, I am concerned that she will _____.

The hardest thing about having a special child is _____.

I wish I knew more about _____.

A *closed needs assessment* asks parents to choose, from a list of possibilities, topics they would like to learn more about. For example, educators can give parents a list of topics (e.g., bedtime behavior, interactions with siblings, homework, making friends, planning for the future) and ask them to check any item that is something of a problem and circle any topics that are of major concern or interest.

Bailey and Simeonsson (1988) have developed a family-needs survey consisting of 35 items organized into six categories (e.g., information, support, finances, family functioning). Because they have obtained different profiles of responses for mothers and fathers, they recommend that both mothers and fathers complete the survey. They also recommend combining open-ended questions with an overall assessment of family needs. They simply ask parents to list on a piece of paper their five greatest needs as a family. By examining the results of needs-assessment questionnaires, parents and professionals together can plan parent education groups that respond to families' real needs.

✎ *Helpful Hint*

The Beach Center on Disability
at the University of Kansas
provides technical assistance for
a national network of Parent to
Parent support programs. Visit
the Beach Center website at
**www.beachcenter.org.**

## Parent to Parent Groups

Parent to Parent programs help parents of children with special needs become reliable allies for one another (Santelli, Poyadue, & Young, 2001). The programs give parents of children with disabilities the opportunity to receive support from a veteran parent who has experienced or still is experiencing similar circumstances and challenges. It carefully matches trained and experienced parents in a one-to-one relationship with parents who have been newly referred to the program. "Because the two parents share so many common disability and family experiences, an immediacy of understanding is typically present in the match. This makes the informational and emotional support from the veteran parents all the more meaningful" (Santelli et al., 1997, p. 74). The first Parent to Parent program, called Pilot Parents, was formed in 1971 by the parent of a young child with Down syndrome in Omaha, Nebraska. Today, there are more than 550 active local Parent to Parent groups and 29 statewide programs.

When helping families assess their strengths and needs, professionals should not overlook the importance of leisure time.

## Parents As Research Partners

Researchers in special education are concerned about the social validity of their studies (Schwartz & Baer, 1991). Are they investigating socially significant variables? Are the methods used to change student performance acceptable? Did the changes observed make any real difference in the child's life? Who better than parents can identify meaningful outcomes, observe and measure performance in the home and community, and let researchers know if their ideas and findings have any real validity?

A model research-partnership program conducted at the Fred S. Keller School in New York embraces parents as full partners in conducting action research with their children. "The parents are the scientists, and they conduct empirical studies under the supervision of the schools' parent educators" (Donley & Williams, 1997, p. 46). Parents are assisted in the development of their research projects by their child's teachers, other parents, and a paid parent educator. The experience culminates with a poster session presentation at the end of the school year during which the parent-scientists display the academic, social, and affective gains achieved by their children. Donley and Williams recognize that some school programs do not have the resources to hire a parent educator. They provide several suggestions for schools with more limited resources to approximate their model.

Kay and Fitzgerald (1997) believe that collaborative action research projects foster closer bonds between teachers and parents and provide parents with the satisfaction of knowing what works with their child and why. They recommend that parents participate in action research by helping brainstorm research questions, collect performance data on their children, and share the outcomes with other parents and teachers. Kay and Fitzgerald recognize that involving parents in home-based research experiences can, at times, be overwhelming; but they view the benefits as far outweighing the disadvantages. Whether the parents participate as paid or volunteer members of a research team, they are involved in collecting performance data on their children, talking about these data on a regular basis with other parents, and displaying them in an informal and supportive environment at the end of the year (Donley & Williams, 1997).

## How Much Parent Involvement?

It is easy to get carried away with a good concept, especially one like parent and family involvement, which has so much promise for positive outcomes. But teachers and everyone else involved in providing special education services to children with disabilities must not take a one-sided, unidirectional view of parent involvement. Sometimes the time and energy required for parents to participate in home-based tutoring programs or parent education groups cause stress among family members or guilt if the parents cannot fulfill teachers' expectations (Callahan, Rademacher, & Hildreth, 1998; Turnbull & Turnbull, 2006). The time required to provide additional help to a child with disabilities may take too much time and attention away from other family members (Parette & Petch-Hogan, 2000).

Kroth and Edge (1997) describe the mirror model for parent involvement (see Figure 3.6), which recognizes that parents have a great deal to offer as well as a need to receive services from special educators. The model attempts to give parents an equal part in deciding what services they need and what services they might provide to professionals or other parents. The top half of the model assumes that professionals have certain information, knowledge, and skills that should be shared with parents to help them with their children. The

*Mirror model for parent involvement*

Council for Exceptional Children    Content Standards for Beginning Teachers—Common Core: Models and strategies of consultation and collaboration (CC10K1).

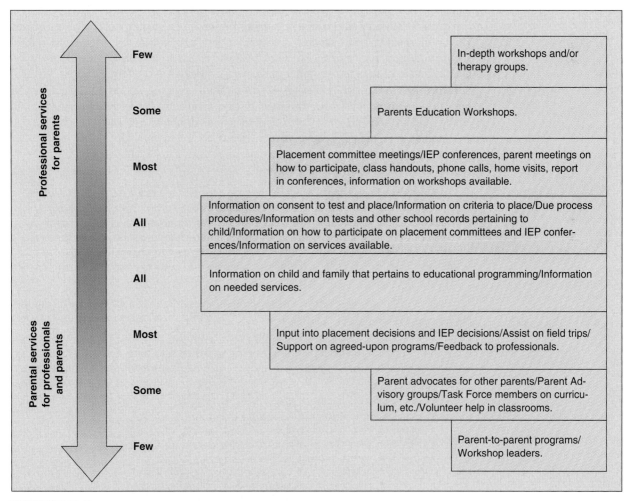

**FIGURE 3.6  Mirror model for parent involvement**

*Source*: From Kroth, R. L., & Edge, D. (1997). *Strategies for communicating with parents of exceptional children* (3rd ed.). Denver: Love. Reprinted by permission.

bottom half of the model assumes that parents have information, knowledge, and skills that can help professionals be more effective in assisting children. The model assumes that not all parents need everything that professionals have to offer and that no parent should be expected to provide everything. All parents should be expected to provide and obtain information, most will be active participants in IEP planning, and fewer will participate in or contribute to workshops and extended parent education groups.

## CURRENT ISSUES AND FUTURE TRENDS

Special educators and families of children with disabilities will continue to develop more effective ways of working together. These efforts will be increasingly driven by the complementary values of family-centered services and family empowerment. Family-centered services are predicated on the belief that the child is part of a family system and that effective change for the child (who is one part of the system) cannot be achieved without helping the entire family (the whole system) (Turnbull & Turnbull, 2006).

The rationale for family empowerment is based on the belief that families are the primary and most effective social institution, that families cannot be replaced, that parents are and should remain in charge of their families, and that the role of professionals is to help parents in their capacity as family leaders (Callister, Mitchell, & Talley, 1986). Empowerment can be viewed as a process of enabling families to take control of their lives by providing information and resources and helping families learn to use them. The specific actions and supports that result in meaningful and effective empowerment will vary across families and even change across time and within a specific family (Jones, Garlow, Turnbull, & Barber, 1996). Dunlap and Fox (1997) define family supports as "any and all actions that serve to strengthen and sustain the family system, especially as these actions pertain to the family's assimilation and understanding of the child's disability" (p. 4).

Another emerging perspective, particularly with families involved in early intervention programs for infants and toddlers, is the movement toward a *strength-based approach* to conceptualizing and providing family supports:

> A strength-based philosophy is a critical belief, an all-pervasive attitude that informs all of the professional's interactions with families. It assumes that all families have strengths they can build on and use to meet their own needs, to accomplish their own goals, and to promote the well-being of family members. The family-professional relationship starts not from an assessment of problems related to the child with a disability but from an attempt to fully understand the way in which the family successfully accomplishes its goals and manages its problems. (Powell, Batsche, Ferro, Fox, & Dunlap, 1997, p. 4)

Professionals and parents are working to develop and provide a wide range of supportive services for families of children with disabilities. Programs are being implemented to help parents plan effectively for their family's future; develop problem-solving skills; and acquire competence in financial planning, coping with stress, locating and using community services, and finding time to relax and enjoy life—to name just a few areas of emphasis.

Parents and family are the most important people in a child's life. Effective and caring teachers should be next in importance. Working together, teachers, parents, and families can and do make a difference in the lives of exceptional children.

# Tips for Beginning Teachers

*by Carolyn Crangle and Bethany Maheady*

## BE AWARE OF AND APPRECIATE YOUR OWN CULTURE

- Educate yourself about your own ethnic perceptions, attitudes, and behaviors.
- Awareness and appreciation of diversity can be acquired by reading, attending classes and/or professional development activities, community involvement and seeking out direct instructional opportunities with students from diverse backgrounds.

## LEARN ABOUT YOUR STUDENTS' CULTURE, LANGUAGE, AND THEIR CURRENT HOME CHARACTERISTICS AND LIVING ARRANGEMENTS

- Try to create a mutual feeling of trust, open-mindedness, and concern.
- Learn about your students' lives by making home visits, familiarizing yourself with the neighborhood, and participating in community events.
- If your pupils have special learning needs, then you must also learn about the nature of their disability.

## LISTEN TO THE PARENTS AND CAREGIVERS OF YOUR STUDENTS—THEY KNOW THEIR CHILDREN WELL AND WANT WHAT IS BEST FOR THEM

- Let parents/caregivers know that you share a common goal—to do what's best for their children—and that if everyone works together, the goal is more likely to be reached.
- Validate the information, feelings, and concerns parents share with you by letting their ideas influence your instructional decision making.

## EMPOWER YOUR STUDENTS' PARENTS AND CAREGIVERS TO BECOME LIFE-LONG ADVOCATES AND EDUCATIONAL SUPPORTERS FOR THEIR CHILDREN

- Make parents and caregivers aware of their legal rights and responsibilities, share effective instructional strategies, and provide them with the instructional tools to help their children succeed in school.
- Foster awareness of relevant support services such as translators, school social workers, and relevant advocacy groups.

## COMMUNICATE EFFECTIVELY, FREQUENTLY, AND POSITIVELY WITH THE PARENTS

- Verbal and written interactions should be clear, concise, and informative.
- Whenever possible, communicate in the family's native language.
- Use parent-friendly language to communicate early and often: Parent-teacher and/or IEP conferences, home-school journals, home notes, happy grams, student progress reports, daily/weekly assignment sheets and report card conferences are all useful tools for effective communication.

## COLLABORATION AMONG PARENTS/CAREGIVERS AND PROFESSIONAL EDUCATORS IS ESSENTIAL

- Instructional roles and responsibilities must be clearly defined.
- All participants must be open-minded and flexible to change.
- Discussions must remain focused on the improvement of pupil outcomes.

# KEY TERMS

cultural interpreter, p. 117

respite care, p. 104

# SUMMARY

## Support for Family Involvement

- Three factors are responsible for the increased emphasis on parent and family involvement in the education of children with disabilities: parent advocacy, educators' desire to increase their effectiveness, and legislative mandates.
- A successful parent-teacher partnership provides benefits for the professional, the parents, and—most important—the child.

## Understanding Families of Children with Disabilities

- All parents and family members must adjust to the birth of a child with disabilities or the discovery that a child has a disability. This adjustment process is different for each parent, and educators should not make assumptions about an individual parent's stage of adjustment.
- Parents of children with disabilities fulfill nine roles and responsibilities: caregiver, provider, teacher, counselor, behavior support specialist, parent of siblings without disabilities, marriage partner, information specialist/trainer for significant others, and advocate for school and community services.
- A family member's disability affects parents and siblings without disabilities in different ways during the different life-cycle stages.
- Respite care—the temporary care of an individual with disabilities by nonfamily members—is a critical support for many families of children with severe disabilities.

## Developing and Maintaining Family-Professional Partnerships

- Five principles for effective communication between educators and parents are accepting what is being said, active listening, questioning appropriately, encouraging, and staying focused.
- Differences in the cultural and linguistic beliefs and practices of professionals and families often serve as barriers to parent involvement.
- Attitudes of and behaviors by professionals that serve as barriers to communication with parents and families include making assumptions about the services and information that parents need, treating parents as clients or adversaries instead of partners, keeping professional distance, blaming parents for their child's disability or performance, acting as if parents need counseling, disrespecting parents' suggestions, and labeling parents who don't act the way the professional believes they should.
- Dialoguing is an approach to conflict resolution in which both parties try to see each other's point of view.

## Working with Culturally and Linguistically Diverse Families

- Differences in the cultural and linguistic beliefs and practices of professionals and families often serve as barriers to parent involvement.
- Cultural interpreters help the school understand the home culture and help the family understand school culture, policies, and practices.
- Understanding differences between our own perspectives and those of people from other cultures and ethnic groups requires careful examination of our own cultural background and belief system.

## Methods of Home-School Communication

- The three most common modes of home-school communication are parent-teacher conferences, written messages, and telephone calls.
- Following are ten guidelines for working with parents and families of children with disabilities:
  - Don't assume you know more about a child than the parents do.
  - Junk the jargon and speak in plain, everyday language.
  - Don't let assumptions or generalizations guide your efforts.
  - Be sensitive and responsive to cultural and linguistic differences.
  - Don't be defensive toward or intimidated by parents.
  - Refer families to other professionals when needed.
  - Help parents strive for realistic optimism.
  - Start with something that parents can be successful with.
  - Allow and respect parents' right to say no.
  - Don't be afraid to say, "I don't know."

## Other Types of Parent Involvement

- Many parents can and should learn to help teach their child with disabilities.
- Parents and professionals should work together in planning and conducting parent education groups.
- Parent to Parent groups give parents of children with disabilities support from veteran parents who are experiencing similar circumstances and challenges.
- Parents who serve as action research partners help brainstorm research questions, collect performance data on their children, and share those data with other parents and teachers.
- The mirror model of parent involvement assumes that not all parents need everything that professionals have to offer and that no parent should be expected to participate in everything.

## Current Issues and Future Trends

- Professionals who work with parents should value family needs and support families in maintaining control over the services and supports they receive.
- The rationale for family empowerment is based on the belief that families are the primary and most effective social institution, that families cannot be replaced, that parents are and should remain in charge of their families, and that the role of professionals is to help parents in their capacity as family leaders.
- Family-centered services are predicated on the belief that the child is part of a family system and that effective change for the child cannot be achieved without helping the entire family.
- A strength-based approach to family supports assumes that all families have strengths they can build on and use to meet their own needs, accomplish their own goals, and promote the well-being of family members.

To check your comprehension of chapter contents, go to the Guided Review and Quiz modules in Chapter 3 of the Companion Website, **www.prenhall.com/heward**.

# EDUCATIONAL NEEDS OF EXCEPTIONAL STUDENTS

*part*

# 2

# MENTAL RETARDATION

# Featured Teacher

### SANDIE TRASK-TYLER

BLENDON MIDDLE SCHOOL
WESTERVILLE, OHIO

*Education—Teaching Credentials—Experience*
- B.S., special education, Ohio Dominican University, 1983
- M.A., special education and applied behavior analysis, The Ohio State University, 1989
- Ohio developmental handicaps, K–12; multiple handicaps, K–12
- 20 years of teaching: first 6 years at the Ohio State School for the Blind teaching secondary students with visual impairments and mental retardation

*Current Teaching Position and Students*    The eight sixth, seventh, and eighth graders in my self-contained classroom have a wide range of abilities and educational needs associated with mild to severe mental retardation. Most have additional disabilities, such as communication disorders or physical and motor problems, and usually remain with me in my classroom throughout their middle school years. Each student needs individualized instruction and supports in self-help and daily-living skills, social and communication skills, and functional academics.

*Classroom Support*    The students spend most of the day in my classroom working on both individualized lessons and group activities. Two aides help me with instructional activities and accompany students when they attend general education classes such as art, physical education, and music. They are responsible for implementing behavior interventions, providing student instruction, and collecting data. Related-service staff, including a speech therapist, an occupational therapist, and a physical therapist, team up with me on classroom activities and offer their expertise to promote student success and independence. This past year I collaborated with seventh-grade science and social studies teachers to include my students in hands-on activities in their classrooms and complete a service-learning project together. I also modified course material to cover topic areas that my students would be able to work on independently. I have been fortunate to work with many student teachers. I welcome their fresh perspectives on activities and find it motivating to have someone to team-teach with and share ideas. Each student spends about 15 minutes a day with a reading buddy, an eighth grader without disabilities who shares activities such as reading flash cards or curriculum and/or completing reading worksheets. This is a wonderful social and learning opportunity for all participants.

*Functional Curriculum*    My job is to prepare students for life in their community and eventual transition into the real world. All of my students have individualized daily schedule checklists on their desks that lists various activities to be completed. The foundation of my class instruction is based on my students' IEP goals. To track lesson implementation and student performance, I keep a notebook for each student indexed by subject areas. I create a data collection sheet

## Focus Questions

- What is most important in determining a person's level of adaptive functioning: intellectual capability or a supportive environment?

- What is to be gained by classifying a child with mental retardation by the intensities of supports she needs to access and benefit from education?

- What should curriculum goals for students with mental retardation emphasize?

- What are the most important features of effective instruction for students with mental retardation?

- What is necessary to make education for a student with mental retardation appropriate in an inclusive classroom?

for each IEP goal and objective and put it into the corresponding section. I also use class attendance books to check off the dates we work on each student objective. This helps me quickly identify what has and has not been worked on each day.

Within each curricular area, I identify functional activities students should work on and focus on teaching these targeted skills that will facilitate student independence. Math skills include coin recognition and values, coin combinations, price recognition, calculator skills, time telling, chart and calendar interpretation, counting items, and measurement skills, which include rulers, yardsticks, and measuring cups and spoons. Students work on various reading and writing activities in language arts. For reading, I usually select the Edmark Functional Sight Word Series, which includes four 100-word sets of fast food/restaurant words, grocery words, signs around the community, and job/work words. In addition to that program, I may also have the student work in the Edmark Reading Milestones Series, which allows them to read stories at their own reading level and complete workbook pages. Writing activities include completing a note to go home, creating a shopping list, writing their address, filling out a form, and completing modified book reports.

Science lessons focus on what we interpret and use in our everyday life. I do lessons on weather and temperature, plant identification and growth, equipment use and safety, and animal care. We conduct experiments that can be applied to everyday life such as ingredient substitution in recipes. Skills in social studies include reading maps and understanding directions; recognizing different cultures; and identifying government figures, facts, and symbols. To work on vocational skills, all of the students have at least one classroom job. Each student gets work-related experience with tasks such as delivering mail, filling the pop machine, recycling paper and pop cans, watering plants, answering the telephone, collating and stapling papers, sorting and wrapping coins, and shredding paper. I emphasize the importance of starting and completing real-work activities independently. These jobs integrate a variety of skills such as counting, traveling around the school building, getting and putting away supplies, using appropriate social greetings, and interpersonal skills.

During group lessons, I make sure that each student has his own materials so everyone can respond and practice together. My primary teaching strategy is repetition with feedback. We practice skills over and over and work on generalizing across settings, staff, materials, and situations. I plan classroom activities that integrate many curricular areas so students can practice their skills in a more natural context. One of their favorite activities is food preparation. I create recipes that use various sight words, kitchen vocabulary, equipment, and measurements. Students must use their safety skills and their social skills to communicate with one another when sharing ingredients. Food preparation is a wonderful way to work on fine-motor skills, the use of both hands, and/or midline crossing in a functional activity. Before the cooking activity, students write out their shopping list, look through a grocery circular to find needed items, and shop for the items. At the store, students work on reading their shopping lists, writing down prices, unloading carts, and paying for their groceries. Another very rewarding activity that integrates various skills is our classroom auction. I videotaped an actual auction and had the auctioneer come to our classroom to talk about his job. We then practiced bidding as we would at an auction. I developed a classroom reinforcement program using the auction concept. Students earn classroom money for completing homework, completing jobs, and getting "caught being good." At the end of each week, we have a class auction, and students are able to bid on items of interest. The skills that students work on during this activity include withdrawing and depositing money into their savings accounts. I have an enlarged copy of an actual checkbook that works well. Students who have difficulty writing can use deposit, withdrawal, date, and number stamps. Students also work on calculator skills, writing skills, money-management skills (do I have enough money to bid?), and group-interaction skills. It has been very exciting to watch the students learn about handling money.

This year our service-learning project included working with other seventh-grade students to learn about plants and sharing them with a community nursing home. We learned about different types of flowers and vegetables and conducted a science experiment growing seeds in different types of soil. Students compared the various seed appearances and labeled each seed with a different letter. They picked a seed they wanted to follow as it sprouted and grew. Each student was responsible for watering, measuring, and collecting data on her plant growth. Students entered their results into the computer and graphed growth. We grew flowers, vegetables, and herbs. As the plants were growing, students created and decorated clay pots. They also designed gift tags using their writing and word-processing skills. When the plants were mature, we walked to a nearby nursing home and gave the residents plants in our handmade pots. We also planted the vegetable and herb plants in a separate garden area so the residents could enjoy fresh tomatoes and cucumbers. This was an awesome activity to integrate community service, student cooperation and teamwork, science activities, language arts skills, student creativity, and math skills.

*Motivating My Students and Me*     I love the opportunity to create new experiences that make learning effective and fun and build on some of my interests. For example, I've incorporated my passion for auctions into a successful reinforcement program. I also enjoy creative art activities, especially refinishing furniture with paint and découpage. My students have learned the safety skills and techniques involved in sanding, priming, painting, stamping, and découpaging furniture. We have decorated plant stands, stools, a desk unit, a record-player stand, bookshelves, and a bench.

*Communicating with Parents*     Parents know they can call or e-mail me anytime at school or home. We are fortunate to have a phone in our classroom so students can work on telephone skills. They get excited when they answer the phone and a parent is on the other end. We have a weekly class newsletter, and every student contributes at least one article per week. I use a digital camera to insert pictures of the students involved in the classroom activities, and I also include a description of the highlights for the upcoming week. All students take home and receive an e-mail copy of the newsletter, and I e-mail it to other teachers and related-service specialists. I also organize a monthly family-out-to-eat night at various local restaurants so students and families can socialize with one another.

 To see an example of the class newsletter with stories by Ms. Trask-Tyler's students, go to the Feature Teacher module on the Companion Website, **www.prenhall.com/heward**

*What I Like Best about Being a Special Education Teacher*     The best part of my job is having the ability to create fun activities that reinforce and possibly teach other skills. The necklace business has been a wonderful activity to incorporate many student objectives into a functional outcome. We live in "Buckeye Country," and a lot of people here are avid fans of The Ohio State University Buckeyes. A few years ago, as a class activity, we made buckeye necklaces for my students to wear during the football season. When other teachers started asking us to make necklaces for them and their friends, a class business was born! This project allows students at all ability levels to participate. It is exciting to watch the students build skills and self-esteem through making and selling their product. The students take turns performing different jobs such as production manager, marketing manager, and quality-control manager. As a result, they learn about the process of buying the materials needed, producing the product, and selling the product. The students have to manage the money for expenses and then decide how to use the profit.

A consultant colleague says he never knows what he'll see next in my classroom. He mentions the "campsite," a tent one student uses as a quiet retreat from the busy classroom; the "vending machine," where students can use classroom money to buy a treat; the claw-foot "bathtub" where students can relax and read books or complete independent work; and the "Barnes and Noble area," a student-created nook where they can sit in soft chairs with a drink and read and/or listen to books on tape, CDs, or vintage records. His praise challenges me to think of other ways to enhance my classroom environment to better meet the needs and interests of my students.

To better understand the topics that will be covered in this chapter, go to the Essential Concepts and Chapter-at-a-Glance modules in Chapter 4 of the Companion Website, **www.prenhall.com/heward**.

When they hear the words "special education," the first thing many people think of is mental retardation. Indeed, the first public school special education classes in 1896 were for children with mental retardation. Of course, things have changed a great deal since then. Recent years have witnessed significant improvements in the education and treatment of children and adults with mental retardation. Persons with mental retardation have enjoyed increased opportunities to experience the benefits and responsibilities of participating in the educational and community mainstream.

Most people have some notion of what mental retardation is and what people with mental retardation are like. Unfortunately, although there is considerable and growing public awareness of mental retardation, much of that awareness consists of misconceptions, oversimplifications, and fear. For example, undergraduate special education majors recorded these statements from people outside the university who were making everyday references to mental retardation:

> After telling a fellow waitress about her career plans to teach children labeled as having mental retardation,... her co-worker's response was, "Why would you want to teach children who cannot learn?" ...
>
> A hairdresser burned herself on a hot curling iron. "I must be retarded," she remarked. "I always burn myself on this thing." ...
>
> Two co-workers discussed the location of a bar in another part of the city.... The listener ... had some idea of where the bar was located. He asked a question to confirm his idea, "Is it across the street from the funny farm?" The co-worker confirmed that the bar was, in fact, across from the "funny farm," a residential facility for persons with mental retardation....
>
> She expressed many things to me as I explained special education including being scared of those people.... She told me over and over how she felt sorry for them. (Danforth & Navarro, 1998, pp. 36–40)

This chapter presents some key factors in understanding the complex concept called mental retardation. It also looks at some contemporary instructional practices that have improved educational outcomes for students with mental retardation.

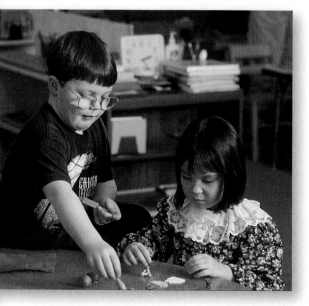

Which student has mental retardation? The term mental retardation identifies substantial limitations in functioning; it is not something inherent within the individual.

## DEFINITIONS

Some children are so clearly and consistently behind their peers in academic, social, language, and self-care skills that it is obvious to anyone who interacts with them that they require special education and related services. How mental retardation is defined is not much of an issue for these children; they experience pervasive and substantial limitations in all or most areas of development and functioning. But this group is only a small portion of the total population of persons with mental retardation. The largest segment consists of school-age children with mild retardation. How mental retardation is defined determines what special educational services many thousands of children are eligible (or ineligible) to receive. Thus, disagreements among professionals over what constitutes mental retardation are much more than academic exercises or philosophical debates. A subtle difference between two definitions can determine whether the label *mental retardation* is associated with a particular child and whether or not appropriate educational supports are provided (Luckasson et al., 2002).

Many definitions of mental retardation have been proposed, adopted, and debated over the years. First, we will look at the most frequently used approach to defining and classifying mental retardation, one based primarily on the assessment of intellectual functioning. Then we will examine the most recent definition of mental retardation, which is based on the levels of supports needed for the individual to function effectively.

# Definition in IDEA

The American Association on Mental Retardation (AAMR), the leading professional organization concerned with the study, treatment, and prevention of mental retardation, has played a leadership role in defining mental retardation. In 1973, AAMR published a definition that was incorporated into IDEA and continues to serve today as the basis by which most states identify children for special education services under the disability category of mental retardation. That definition, with minor rewording, was published in the organization's 1983 manual on terminology and classification of mental retardation: "Mental retardation refers to significantly subaverage general intellectual functioning resulting in or associated with deficits in adaptive behavior and manifested during the developmental period" (Grossman, 1983, p. 11).

In IDEA, **mental retardation** is defined as "significantly subaverage general intellectual functioning existing concurrently with deficits in adaptive behavior and manifested during the developmental period that adversely affects a child's educational performance" (34 C.F.R., Sec. 3000. 7[b][5]).

The definition includes three criteria. First, "significant subaverage intellectual functioning" must be demonstrated before mental retardation is diagnosed. The word *significant* refers to a score of two or more standard deviations below the mean on a standardized intelligence test (a score of approximately 70 or less; IQ testing will be discussed later in the chapter). Second, an individual must be well below average in both intellectual functioning and adaptive behavior; that is, intellectual functioning is not the sole defining criterion. Third, the definition specifies that the deficits in intellectual functioning and adaptive behavior must occur during the developmental period to help distinguish mental retardation from other disabilities (e.g., impaired performance by an adult due to head injury). The criterion "that adversely affects a child's educational performance" in the IDEA definition is automatically met when a child exhibits substantial limitations in intellectual functioning and adaptive behavior.

Persons with mental retardation have traditionally been classified by the degree or level of intellectual impairment as measured by an IQ test. The most widely used classification method cited in the professional literature consists of four levels of mental retardation according to the range of IQ scores shown in Table 4.1. The range of scores representing the high and low ends of each level indicates an awareness of the inexactness of intelligence testing and the importance of clinical judgment in determining level of severity.

Educators have often used different terms for the various degrees of mental retardation. For many years, students with mental retardation in the public schools were classified as either *educable mentally retarded (EMR)* or *trainable mentally retarded (TMR)*. These terms referred to mild and moderate levels of retardation, respectively. Children with severe and profound mental retardation were not included in this two-level classification system because they were often denied a public education and were likely to reside in a state-operated institution. Although one still encounters the terms EMR and TMR today, most special educators consider them to be archaic and inappropriate because they suggest predetermined achievement limits (Beirne-Smith, Patton, & Kim, 2006).

*Definitions of MR*

Council for Exceptional Children Content Standards for Beginning Teachers of Students with MR/DD: Definitions and issues related to the identification of individuals with MR/DD (MR1K1).

| Level | Intelligence Test Score |
|---|---|
| Mild retardation | 50–55 to approximately 70 |
| Moderate retardation | 35–40 to 50–55 |
| Severe retardation | 20–25 to 35–40 |
| Profound retardation | Below 20–25 |

**TABLE 4.1**

**Classification of mental retardation by measured IQ score**

*Source:* Based on the *AAMR's Classification of Mental Retardation* (Grossman, 1983) and the *Diagnostic and Statistical Manual of Mental Disorders (DSM-IV)* (American Psychiatric Association, 1994).

*ILEP classification system*

Content Standards for Beginning Teachers of Students with MR/DD: Relate levels of support to the needs of the individual (MR3S1) (also CC2K2).

Although Emily needs extensive supports in some areas of life functioning, she needs only limited supports in other areas.

# AAMR's Definition Based on Needed Supports

In 1992, the AAMR published a definition and approach for diagnosing and classifying mental retardation that represented a conceptual shift from viewing mental retardation as an inherent trait or permanent condition to a description of the individual's present functioning and the environmental supports needed to improve it. That definition was revised in 2002 and reads as follows:

> Mental retardation is a disability characterized by significant limitations in both intellectual functioning and in adaptive behavior as expressed in conceptual, social, and practical adaptive skills. This disability originates before age 18.

The following five assumptions are essential to the application of the definition:

1. Limitations in present functioning must be considered within the context of community environments typical of the individual's age peers and culture.
2. Valid assessment considers cultural and linguistic diversity as well as differences in communication, sensory, motor, and behavioral factors.
3. Within the individual, limitations often coexist with strengths.
4. The purpose of describing limitations is to develop a profile of needed supports.
5. With appropriate personalized supports over a sustained period, the life functioning of the person with mental retardation generally will improve. (Luckasson et al., 2002, p. 13)

AAMR's "2002 System" provides conceptual and procedural recommendations for functionally classifying mental retardation according to a profile of needed supports. This approach represents a change from classifying mental retardation on the basis of estimates of an individual's intellectual deficiencies to estimating the intensities of supports needed to improve functioning in her school, home, community, and work environments. Needed supports are identified and classified by an interdisciplinary team according to four levels of intensities: intermittent, limited, extensive, and pervasive (ILEP) (see Table 4.2). The ILEP system combines two prevailing theories about mental retardation:

> The system acknowledged the existence of genuine impairments in the individual but also reflected the idea that expression of the impairments is strongly affected by the life arrangements of the individual: Biology in a social context. The 1992 system changed the focus of evaluation from determining what place an individual held on the IQ continuum to what can the person do and what supports does the person need in order to function better. (Luckasson & Reeve, 2001, p. 50)

An interdisciplinary team develops a profile of the types and intensity of needed supports within each of five dimensions: intellectual abilities; adaptive behavior (conceptual, practical, social skills); participation, interactions, and social roles; health (physical health, mental health, etiological factors); and context (environments, culture, and opportunities).

# IDENTIFICATION AND ASSESSMENT

## Assessing Intellectual Functioning

When assessing intellectual functioning as part of an evaluation for mental retardation, an intelligence (IQ) test is given by a school psychologist or other professional trained to administer and interpret such tests. An IQ test consists of a series of questions (e.g., vocabu-

## TABLE 4.2 Definitions of intensities of supports for individuals with mental retardation

| | |
|---|---|
| *Intermittent* | Supports on an "as needed basis." Characterized by episodic nature, person not always needing the support(s), or short-term supports needed during life-span transitions (e.g., job loss or an acute medical crisis). Intermittent supports may be high or low intensity when provided. |
| *Limited* | An intensity of supports characterized by consistency over time, time-limited but not of an intermittent nature, may require fewer staff members and less cost than more intense levels of support (e.g., time-limited employment training or transitional supports provided during the school to adult period). |
| *Extensive* | Supports characterized by regular involvement (e.g., daily) in at least some environments (such as work or home) and not time-limited (e.g., long-term support and long-term home living support). |
| *Pervasive* | Supports characterized by their constancy and high intensity; provided across environments; potential life-sustaining nature. Pervasive supports typically involve more staff members and intrusiveness than do extensive or time-limited supports. |

*Source:* Reprinted from the American Association on Mental Retardation (AAMR). (2002). *Mental retardation: Definition, classification, and systems of supports* (10th ed.), (p. 152). Washington, DC: Author. Used by permission.

lary, similarities), problem solving (e.g., mazes, block designs), memory, and other tasks assumed to require certain degrees of intelligence to answer or solve correctly (Venn, 2004). The child's performance on those items is used to derive a score representing her intelligence.

In addition to being *standardized tests*—the same questions and tasks are always presented in a certain, specified way with the same scoring procedures used each time the test is administered—IQ tests are norm-referenced tests. When it is being developed, a **norm-referenced test** is administered to a large sample of people selected at random from the population for whom the test is intended. Test scores of persons in the norming sample are then used to represent how scores on the test are generally distributed throughout the population.

IQ scores seem to be distributed throughout the population according to a phenomenon called the **normal curve**, shown in Figure 4.1. To describe how a particular score varies from the mean, or average score, of all the scores in the norm sample, a mathematical concept called the **standard deviation** is used. An algebraic formula is applied to the scores achieved by the norm sample on a test to determine what value equals one standard deviation for that test. A child's IQ test score can then be described in terms of how many standard deviations above or below the mean it is. Theoretically, an equal number of people score above and below the mean and about 2.3% of the population falls two or more standard deviations below the mean, which the AAMR calls "significantly subaverage."

According to the AAMR, a diagnosis of mental retardation requires an IQ score approximately two standard deviations below the mean, which is approximately 70 or below on the two most widely used intelligence tests, the Wechsler Intelligence Scale for Children—Third Edition (WISC-III) (Wechsler, 1991) and the Stanford-Binet IV (Thorndike, Hagen, & Sattler, 1986). The AAMR emphasizes that the IQ cutoff score of 70 is intended only as a guideline and should not be interpreted as a hard-and-fast requirement (Luckasson et al., 2002). A higher IQ score of 75 or more may also be associated with mental retardation if, according to a clinician's judgment, the child exhibits deficits in adaptive behavior thought to be caused by impaired intellectual functioning.

Although IQ tests have been widely criticized, they can provide useful information. IQ scores are particularly useful for objectively identifying an overall performance deficit and have proven to be the best single predictor of school achievement. Because IQ tests are

*Standardized tests, norm-referenced tests, the normal curve, and standard deviation*

Council for Exceptional Children Content Standards for Beginning Teachers of Students with MR/DD: Specialized terminology used in the assessment of individuals with MR/DD (MR8K1) (also CC8K1).

*IQ scores and diagnosis of MR*

Council for Exceptional Children Content Standards for Beginning Teachers of Students with MR/DD: Definitions and issues related to the identification of individuals with MR/DD (MR1K1).

**FIGURE 4.1** **Theoretical distribution of IQ scores on the normal curve**

| | | | | | | | | | |
|---|---|---|---|---|---|---|---|---|---|
| Standard deviations | -4 | -3 | -2 | -1 | 0<br>"average" | +1 | +2 | +3 | +4 |
| Stanford-Binet score | 36 | 52 | 68 | 84 | 100 | 116 | 132 | 148 | 164 |
| WISC-R score | 40 | 55 | 70 | 85 | 100 | 115 | 130 | 145 | 160 |

*Issues to consider with IQ tests/scores*

Council for Exceptional Children Content Standards for Beginning Teachers—Common Core: Uses and limitations of assessment instruments (CC8K4).

composed largely of verbal and academic tasks—the same things a child must master to succeed in school—they correlate highly with school achievement.

Even though the major intelligence tests are among the most carefully constructed and researched psychological assessment instruments available, they are still far from perfect and have both advantages and disadvantages. Here are several more important considerations:

- *The concept of intelligence is a hypothetical construct.* No one has ever seen a thing called intelligence; it is not a precise entity but something we infer from observed performance. We assume it takes more intelligence to perform some tasks than it does to perform others.
- *An IQ test measures only how a child performs at one point in time on the items included on the test.* An IQ test samples only a small portion of an individual's skills and abilities; we infer from that performance how a child might perform in other situations (Overton, 2003).
- *Intelligence tests can be culturally biased.* The Binet and Wechsler IQ tests tend to favor children from the population on which they were normed—primarily white, middle-class children. Some of the questions may tap learning that only a middle-class child is likely to have experienced. Both the Binet and Wechsler, which are highly verbal, are especially inappropriate for children for whom English is a second language (Venn, 2004).
- *IQ scores can change significantly.* IQ scores can change, particularly in the 70–85 range that formerly constituted borderline retardation (Venn, 2004). Hence, observers are hesitant to use the label *mental retardation* on the basis of an IQ score that might increase after a period of intensive, systematic intervention.
- *Intelligence testing is not an exact science.* Among the many variables that can affect an individual's IQ score are motivation, the time and location of the test, and inconsistency or bias on the test giver's part in scoring responses that are not precisely covered by the test manual.
- *Results of an IQ test should never be used as the sole basis for making a decision on the provision or denial of special education services.* An IQ score is just one component of a multifactored, nondiscriminatory assessment.

- *Results from an IQ test should not be used to target educational objectives or design instruction.* Results of teacher-administered, criterion-referenced assessments of a student's performance of curriculum-specific skills are generally more useful for planning what to teach. Results of direct and frequent measurement of a student's performance during instruction provide needed information for evaluating and modifying teaching practices.

## Assessing Adaptive Behavior

**Adaptive behavior** is "the collection of conceptual, social, and practical skills that have been learned by people in order to function in their everyday lives" (Luckasson et al., 2002, p. 73). Systematic assessment of adaptive behavior is important for reasons other than the diagnosis of mental retardation. The adaptive skills exhibited by a person with mental retardation—as well as the nature and severity of maladaptive behaviors—are critical factors in determining the supports he requires for success in school, work, community, and home environments (Rush & Francis, 2000; Schalock, 1999). A number of instruments for assessing adaptive behavior have been developed. Most consist of a series of questions that someone familiar with the individual, such as a teacher or a parent, answers.

*AAMR Adaptive Behavior Scale.* A frequently used instrument for assessing adaptive behavior by school-age children is the AAMR Adaptive Behavior Scale—School (ABS-S) (Lambert, Nihira, & Leland, 1993). The ABS-S consists of two parts. Part 1 contains 10 domains related to independent functioning and daily living skills (e.g., eating, toilet use, money handling, numbers, time); Part 2 assesses the individual's level of maladaptive (inappropriate) behavior in seven areas (e.g., trustworthiness, self-abusive behavior, social engagement). Another form, the ABS-RC, assesses adaptive behavior in residential and community settings (Nihira, Leland, & Lambert, 1993).

*Vineland Adaptive Behavior Scales.* The Vineland Adaptive Behavior Scales are available in three versions. The Interview Editions in Survey Form or Expanded Form are administered by an individual, such as a teacher or a direct caregiver, who is very familiar with the person being assessed (Sparrow, Balla, & Cicchetti, 1984a, 1984b). The Classroom Edition is designed to be completed by a teacher (Sparrow, Balla, & Cicchetti, 1985).

*Scales of Independent Behavior—Revised.* The Scales of Independent Behavior—Revised (SIB-R) (Bruninks, Woodcock, Weatherman, & Hill, 1996) can be used to measure adaptive behavior of individuals ranging in age from infancy to 80+ years. The SIB-R's 14 subscales (e.g., social interaction, eating and meal preparation, money and value) take 45 to 60 minutes to administer in a structured interview or checklist format. The SIB-R also includes eight optional problem behavior subscales.

Measurement of adaptive behavior has proven difficult, in large part because of the relative nature of social adjustment and competence: what is considered appropriate in one situation or by one group may not be in or by another (Schalock, 1999). Nowhere is there a list that everyone would agree describes exactly those adaptive behaviors all of us should exhibit. As with IQ tests, cultural bias can be a problem in adaptive behavior scales; for instance, one item on some scales requires a child to tie a laced shoe, but some children have never had a shoe with laces. Ongoing research on the measurement of adaptive behavior may help resolve these problems.

## CHARACTERISTICS

Mental retardation means substantial limitations in age-appropriate intellectual and adaptive behavior. It is seldom a time-limited condition. Although many individuals with

*Assessing adaptive behavior*

Content Standards for Beginning Teachers of Students with MR/DD: Adaptive behavior assessment (MR8K3).

mental retardation make tremendous advancements in adaptive skills (some to the point of functioning independently and no longer being considered under any disability category), most are affected throughout their life span (Hawkins, Eklund, James & Foose, 2003).

Many children with mild retardation are not identified until they enter school and sometimes not until the second or third grade, when more difficult academic work is required. Most students with mild mental retardation master academic skills up to about the sixth-grade level and are able to learn job skills well enough to support themselves independently or semi-independently. Some adults who have been identified with mild mental retardation develop excellent social and communication skills and once they leave school are no longer recognized as having a disability.

Children with moderate retardation show significant delays in development during their preschool years. As they grow older, discrepancies in overall intellectual development and adaptive functioning generally grow wider between these children and age mates without disabilities. People with moderate mental retardation are more likely to have health and behavior problems than are individuals with mild retardation.

Individuals with severe and profound mental retardation are almost always identified at birth or shortly afterward. Most of these infants have significant central nervous system damage, and many have additional disabilities and/or health conditions. Although IQ scores can serve as the basis for differentiating severe and profound retardation from one another, the difference is primarily one of functional impairment. Chapter 12 is devoted to the characteristics and education of students with severe disabilities.

## Cognitive Functioning

Deficits in cognitive functioning and learning styles characteristic of individuals with mental retardation include poor memory, slow learning rates, attention problems, difficulty generalizing what they have learned, and lack of motivation.

*Cognitive functioning of students with MR*

Council for Exceptional Children

Content Standards for Beginning Teachers of Students with MR/DD: Psychological, social/emotional, and motor characteristics of individuals with MR/DD (MR2K3) (also CC2K2, CC3K5).

*Memory.* Students with mental retardation have difficulty remembering information. As would be expected, the more severe the cognitive impairment, the greater the deficits in memory. In particular, research has found that students with mental retardation have trouble retaining information in short-term memory (Bray, Fletcher, & Turner, 1997). *Short-term memory*, or working memory, is the ability to recall and use information that was encountered just a few seconds to a couple of hours earlier—for example, remembering a specific sequence of job tasks an employer stated just a few minutes earlier. Merrill (1990) reports that students with mental retardation require more time than their nondisabled peers to automatically recall information and therefore have more difficulty handling larger amounts of cognitive information at one time. Early researchers suggested that once persons with mental retardation learned a specific item of information sufficiently to commit it to *long-term memory*—information recalled after a period of days or weeks—they retained that information about as well as persons without retardation (Belmont, 1966; Ellis, 1963).

More recent research on memory abilities of persons with mental retardation has focused on teaching metacognitive or executive control strategies, such as rehearsing and organizing information into related sets, which many children without disabilities learn to do naturally (Bebko & Luhaorg, 1998). Students with mental retardation do not tend to use such strategies spontaneously but can be taught to do so with improved performance on memory-related and problem-solving tasks as an outcome of such strategy instruction (Hughes & Rusch, 1989; Merrill, 1990).

*Learning Rate.* The rate at which individuals with mental retardation acquire new knowledge and skills is well below that of typically developing children. A frequently used measure of learning rate is *trials to criterion*—the number of practice or instructional trials needed before a student can respond correctly without prompts or assistance. For example, while just 2 or 3 trials with feedback may be required for a typically developing child to learn to discriminate between two geometric forms, a child with mental retardation may need 20 to 30 or more trials to learn the same discrimination.

Because students with mental retardation learn more slowly, some educators have assumed that instruction should be slowed down to match their lower rate of learning. Research has shown, however, that students with mental retardation benefit from opportunities to learn to "go fast" (Miller, Hall, & Heward, 1995).

*Attention.* The ability to attend to critical features of a task (e.g., to the outline of geometric shapes instead of dimensions such as their color or position on the page) is a characteristic of efficient learners. Students with mental retardation often have trouble attending to relevant features of a learning task and instead may focus on distracting irrelevant stimuli. In addition, individuals with mental retardation often have difficulty sustaining attention to learning tasks (Zeaman & House, 1979). These attention problems compound and contribute to a student's difficulties in acquiring, remembering, and generalizing new knowledge and skills.

Effective instructional design for students with mental retardation must systematically control for the presence and saliency of critical stimulus dimensions as well as the presence and effects of distracting stimuli. After initially directing a student's attention to the most relevant feature of a simplified task and reinforcing correct responses, the complexity and difficulty of the task can gradually be increased. A student's selective and sustained attention to relevant stimuli will improve as he experiences success for doing so.

*Generalization of Learning.* Students with disabilities, especially those with mental retardation, often have trouble using their new knowledge and skills in settings or situations that differ from the context in which they first learned those skills. Such transfer or generalization of learning occurs without explicit programming for many children without disabilities but may not be evident in students with mental retardation without specific programming to facilitate it. Researchers and educators are no longer satisfied by demonstrations that individuals with mental retardation can initially acquire new knowledge or skills. One of the most important and challenging areas of contemporary research in special education is the search for strategies and tactics for promoting the generalization and maintenance of learning by individuals with mental retardation. Some of the findings of that research are described later in this chapter and throughout this text.

*Motivation.* Some students with mental retardation exhibit an apparent lack of interest in learning or problem-solving tasks (Switzky, 1997). Some individuals with mental retardation develop *learned helplessness,* a condition in which a person who has experienced repeated failure comes to expect failure regardless of his or her efforts. In an attempt to minimize or offset failure, the person may set extremely low expectations for himself and not appear to try very hard. When faced with a difficult task or problem, some individuals with mental retardation may quickly give up and turn to or wait for others to help them. Some acquire a problem-solving approach called *outer-directedness,* in which they seem to distrust their own responses to situations and rely on others for assistance and solutions.

Rather than an inherent characteristic of mental retardation, the apparent lack of motivation may be the product of frequent failure and prompt dependency acquired as the result of other people's doing things for them. After successful experiences, individuals

To learn about one strategy for building students' fluency, see "How Many Can You Do in 1 Minute?" in Chapter 4's Teaching & Learning module of the Companion Website, **www.prenhall.com/heward**.

*Learned helplessness and outer-directedness*

Council for Exceptional Children Content Standards for Beginning Teachers of Students with MR/DD: Psychological, social/emotional, and motor characteristics of individuals with MR/DD (MR2K3) (also CC2K2).

with mental retardation do not differ from persons without mental retardation on measures of outer-directedness (Bybee & Zigler, 1998). The current emphasis on teaching self-determination skills to students with mental retardation is critical in helping them to become self-reliant problem solvers who act upon their world rather than passively wait to be acted upon (Wehmeyer, Martin, & Sands, 1998).

## Adaptive Behavior

*Adaptive behavior of individuals with MR/DD*

Council for Exceptional Children — Content Standards for Beginning Teachers of Students with MR/DD: Psychological, social/emotional, and motor characteristics of individuals with MR/DD (MR2K3) (also CC2K2).

By definition children with mental retardation have substantial deficits in adaptive behavior. These limitations can take many forms and tend to occur across domains of functioning. Limitations in self-care skills and social relationships as well as behavioral excesses are common characteristics of individuals with mental retardation.

*Self-Care and Daily Living Skills.*   Individuals with mental retardation who require extensive supports must often be taught basic self-care skills such as dressing, eating, and hygiene. Direct instruction and environmental supports such as added prompts and simplified routines are necessary to ensure that deficits in these adaptive areas do not come to seriously limit one's quality of life. Most children with milder forms of mental retardation learn how to take care of their basic needs, but they often require training in self-management skills to achieve the levels of performance necessary for eventual independent living.

*Social Development.*   Making and sustaining friendships and personal relationships present significant challenges for many persons with mental retardation. Limited cognitive processing skills, poor language development, and unusual or inappropriate behaviors can seriously impede interacting with others. It is difficult at best for someone who is not a professional educator or staff person to want to spend the time necessary to get to know a person who stands too close, interrupts frequently, does not maintain eye contact, and strays from the conversational topic. Teaching students with mental retardation appropriate social and interpersonal skills is one of the most important functions of special education.

*Behavioral Excesses and Challenging Behavior.*   Students with mental retardation are more likely to exhibit behavior problems than are children without disabilities. Difficulties accepting criticism, limited self-control, and bizarre and inappropriate behaviors such as aggression or self-injury are often observed in children with mental retardation. Some of the genetic syndromes associated with mental retardation tend to include abnormal behavior (e.g., children with Prader-Willi syndrome often engage in self-injurious or obsessive-compulsive behavior). In general, the more severe the retardation, the higher the incidence of behavior problems. Individuals with mental retardation and psychiatric conditions requiring mental health supports are known as "dual diagnosis" cases. Data from one report showed that approximately 10% of all persons with mental retardation served by the state of California were dually diagnosed (Borthwick-Duffy & Eyman, 1990). Although there are comprehensive guidelines available for treating psychiatric and behavioral problems of persons with mental retardation (Rush & Francis, 2000), much more research is needed on how best to support this population.

## Positive Attributes

Descriptions of the intellectual functioning and adaptive behavior of individuals with mental retardation focus on limitations and deficits and paint a picture of a monolithic group of people whose most important characteristics revolve around the absence of desirable traits. But individuals with mental retardation are a huge and disparate group composed of people with highly individual personalities (Smith & Mitchell, 2001b). Many children and adults with mental retardation display tenacity and curiosity in learning, get along well with others, and are positive influences on those around them (Reiss & Reiss, 2004; Smith, 2000).

Changing definitions of mental retardation, the schools' reluctance to apply the label to children with mild mental retardation, and the changing status of schoolchildren with mild mental retardation (many are no longer identified after leaving school) contribute to the difficulty of estimating the number of people with mental retardation (Larson et al., 2001). Historically, the federal government estimated the prevalence at 3% of the general population, although recent analyses find little objective support for this figure. If prevalence figures were based on IQ scores alone, theoretically 2.3% of the population would have mental retardation (see Figure 4.1).

Basing prevalence estimates on IQ scores only, however, ignores the other necessary criterion for mental retardation—deficits in adaptive functioning and the need for supports. Some professionals believe that if adaptive behavior is included with intellectual ability when estimating prevalence, the figure would drop to about 1%. In fact, two recent national studies estimated the prevalence of mental retardation at 0.78% (Larson et al., 2001) and 1.27% of the U.S. population (Fujiura, 2003).

The 1% estimate is consistent with data reported by the U.S. Office of Special Education Programs (2004) on the number of children receiving special education. During the 2003–2004 school year, 570,643 students ages 6 through 21 received special education under the disability category of mental retardation. These students represented 9.6% of all school-age children in special education, or about 1% of the total school-age population. Mental retardation is the third-largest disability category after learning disabilities and speech or language impairments.

Prevalence rates vary greatly from state to state. For example, the prevalence of mental retardation as a percentage of total school enrollment in 2002–2003 ranged from a low of 0.33% (New Hampshire) to a high of 2.47% (West Virginia) (U.S. Office of Special Education Programs, 2004). Such differences in prevalence are in large part a function of the widely differing criteria for identifying students with mental retardation (Denning, Chamberlain, & Polloway, 2000). Prevalence figures also vary considerably among districts within a given state (McDermott, 1994).

Although they are challenged by significant limitations in learning and adaptive behavior, these two young people with mental retardation also possess many positive attributes.

# CAUSES AND PREVENTION

## Causes

More than 750 causes of mental retardation have been identified (Dykens, Hodapp, & Finucane, 2000). Figure 4.2 lists etiological factors associated with mental retardation that are categorized by the AAMR as **prenatal** (occurring before birth), **perinatal** (occurring during or shortly after birth), or **postnatal** (occurring after birth) causes. All of these etiologic factors associated with mental retardation can be classified as either biomedical or environmental (social, behavioral, educational). However, both biological

*Causes of MR*

Council for Exceptional Children    Content Standards for Beginning Teachers of Students with MR/DD: Causes and theories of intellectual disabilities and implications for prevention (MR2K1).

## FIGURE 4.2  Etiological risk factors for mental retardation

| Timing | Biomedical | Social | Behavioral | Educational |
|--------|-----------|--------|-----------|-------------|
| Prenatal | 1. Chromosomal disorders<br>2. Single-gene disorders<br>3. Syndromes<br>4. Metabolic disorders<br>5. Cerebral dysgenesis<br>6. Maternal illnesses<br>7. Parental age | 1. Poverty<br>2. Maternal malnutrition<br>3. Domestic violence<br>4. Lack of access to prenatal care | 1. Parental drug use<br>2. Parental alcohol use<br>3. Parental smoking<br>4. Parental immaturity | 1. Parental cognitive disability without supports<br>2. Lack of preparation for parenthood |
| Perinatal | 1. Prematurity<br>2. Birth injury<br>3. Neonatal disorders | 1. Lack of access to birth care | 1. Parental rejection of caretaking<br>2. Parental abandonment of child | 1. Lack of medical referral for intervention services at discharge |
| Postnatal | 1. Traumatic brain injury<br>2. Malnutrition<br>3. Meningoencephalitis<br>4. Seizure disorders<br>5. Degenerative disorders | 1. Impaired child caregiver<br>2. Lack of adequate stimulation<br>3. Family poverty<br>4. Chronic illness in the family<br>5. Institutionalization | 1. Child abuse and neglect<br>2. Domestic violence<br>3. Inadequate safety measures<br>4. Social deprivation<br>5. Difficult child behaviors | 1. Impaired parenting<br>2. Delayed diagnosis<br>3. Inadequate early intervention services<br>4. Inadequate special-educational services<br>5. Inadequate family support |

*Source:* From the American Association on Mental Retardation (AAMR). (2002). *Mental retardation: Definition, classification, and systems of supports* (10th ed.), (p. 127). Washington, DC: Author. Used by permission.

and environmental factors are often relevant in individual cases of mental retardation (Beirne-Smith et al., 2006).

Authors of a review of 13 epidemiological studies concluded that, for approximately 50% of cases of mild mental retardation and 30% of cases of severe mental retardation, the cause is unknown (McLaren & Bryson, 1987). Nevertheless, knowledge of etiology is critical to efforts designed to lower the incidence of mental retardation (Moser, 2000) and may have implications for some educational interventions (Hodapp & Dykens, 2001; Powell, Houghton, & Douglas, 1997).

*Biomedical Causes.* Specific biomedical causes are identified for about two-thirds of individuals with more severe forms of mental retardation (Batshaw, 2002). It is important to understand that none of the etiologic factors shown in Figure 4.2 is mental retardation. These conditions, diseases, and syndromes are commonly associated with mental retardation; but they may or may not result in the deficits of intellectual and adaptive functioning that define mental retardation. "The cause of mental retardation is whatever causes this impairment in functioning. A biomedical risk factor may be present, but by itself it does not cause mental retardation" (Luckasson et al., 2002, p. 126). Any risk factor, such as low birth weight or Trisomy 21 (Down syndrome), only causes mental retardation when it results in impaired intellectual and adaptive functioning sufficient to meet the criteria for diagnosis.

Some of the health conditions and disorders shown in Figure 4.2 require special education and related services as disabilities in their own right and/or are causes of other disabilities whether or not mental retardation is also involved. A number of these conditions are discussed in Chapter 9 (cytomegalovirus [CMV], meningitis, rubella) and Chapter 11 (diabetes, epilepsy, head injuries, hydrocephalus, muscular dystrophy, spina bifida).

Table 4.3 describes some of the more common prenatal conditions that often result in mental retardation. The term *syndrome* refers to a number of symptoms or characteristics that occur together and provide the defining features of a given disease or condition. **Down syndrome** and **fragile-X syndrome** are the two most common causes of inherited mental retardation.

*Environmental Causes.*    Individuals with mild mental retardation, those who require less intensive supports, make up about 85% of all persons with mental retardation. In the vast majority of those cases there is no demonstrable evidence of organic pathology—no brain damage or other biological problem. When no biological factor is evident in an individual with mental retardation, the cause is presumed to be *psychosocial disadvantage,* the combination of a poor social and cultural environment early in the child's life. The term *developmental retardation* is also used as a synonym for psychosocial disadvantage to refer to mental retardation thought to be caused primarily by environmental influences such as minimal opportunities to develop early language, child abuse and neglect, and/or chronic social or sensory deprivation. Although there is no direct proof that social and environmental deprivation causes mental retardation, it is generally believed that these influences are responsible for most cases of mild retardation.

Research conducted at the Juniper Gardens Children's Project has led to a hypothesis of developmental retardation as an intergenerational progression in which the cumulative experiential deficits in social and academic stimulation are transmitted to children from low socioeconomic status (SES) environments (Greenwood et al., 1992; Greenwood, Hart, Walker, & Risley, 1994). Figure 4.3 illustrates the progression of developmental retardation in terms of low academic achievement and early school failure. There are several key contributors to this cycle of environmentally caused retardation (Greenwood et al., 1994):

1.  Limited parenting practices that produce low rates of vocabulary growth in early childhood
2.  Instructional practices in middle childhood and adolescence that produce low rates of academic engagement during the school years
3.  Lower rates of academic achievement and early school failure and early school dropout
4.  Parenthood and continuance of the progression into the next generation (p. 216)

Additional support for the hypothesis of developmental retardation is provided by McDermott (1994), who has found that much of the variability in prevalence rates of mental retardation reported by different school districts is explained by SES status. Her findings are "consistent with the notion that a large percentage of mental retardation is based on environmental causes, most notably, deprivation in the early years of life" (p. 182). Children who live in poverty have a higher than normal chance of being identified as mentally retarded (Fujiura & Yamaki, 2000).

# Prevention

Probably the biggest single preventive strike against mental retardation (and many other disabling conditions, including blindness and deafness) was the development of an effective rubella vaccine in 1962. When **rubella** (German measles) is contracted by mothers during the first 3 months of pregnancy, it causes severe damage in 10% to 40% of unborn children. Fortunately, this cause of mental retardation can be eliminated if women are vaccinated for rubella before becoming pregnant.

Advances in medical science have enabled doctors to identify certain genetic influences strongly associated with mental retardation. Genetic disorders are detected during pregnancy by two types of tests: screening procedures and diagnostic tests. Obstetricians

*Psychosocial disadvantage and developmental retardation*

Council for Exceptional Children    Content Standards for Beginning Teachers of Students with MR/DD: Causes and theories of intellectual disabilities and implications for prevention (MR2K1) (also CC2K3).

*Prevention of MR*

Council for Exceptional Children    Content Standards for Beginning Teachers of Students with MR/DD: Causes and theories of intellectual disabilities and implications for prevention (MR2K1).

**TABLE 4.3  Some prenatal conditions associated with mental retardation**

| Syndrome | Definition/Cause | Remarks/Characteristics |
|---|---|---|
| Down syndrome | Caused by chromosomal abnormality; most common of three major types is trisomy 21, in which 21st set of chromosomes is a triplet rather than a pair. Most often results in moderate level of mental retardation, although some individuals function in mild or severe range. Affects about 1 in 1,000 live births; probability of having a baby with Down syndrome increases to approximately 1 in 30 for women at age 45. | Best-known and well-researched biological condition associated with mental retardation; estimated to account for 5–6% of all cases. Characteristic physical features: short stature; flat, broad face with small ears and nose; upward slanting eyes; small mouth with short roof, protruding tongue may cause articulation problems; hypertonia (floppy muscles); heart defects common; susceptibility to ear and respiratory infections. Older persons at high risk for Alzheimer's disease. |
| Fetal alcohol syndrome (FAS) | Mother's excessive alcohol use during pregnancy has toxic effects on fetus, including physical defects and developmental delays. Diagnosed when the child has two or more craniofacial malformations and growth is below the 10th percentile for height and weight. Children who have some but not all of the diagnostic criteria for FAS and a history of prenatal alcohol exposure are diagnosed with fetal alcohol effect (FAE), a condition associated with hyperactivity and learning problems. | One of the leading known causes of mental retardation, FAS has an incidence higher than Down syndrome and cerebral palsy. In addition to cognitive impairments, some children experience sleep disturbances, motor dysfunctions, hyperirritability, aggression, and conduct problems. Although risk of FAS is highest during first trimester of pregnancy, pregnant women should avoid drinking alcohol in any amount. |
| Fragile X syndrome | A triplet, repeat mutation on the X chromosome interferes with production of FMR-1 protein, which is essential for normal brain functioning; majority of males experience mild to moderate mental retardation in childhood and moderate to severe deficits in adulthood; females may carry and transmit the mutation to their children but tend to have fewer disabilities than affected males. | Affects approximately 1 in 4,000 males; the most common inherited cause of mental retardation and the most common clinical type of mental retardation after Down syndrome. Characterized by social anxiety and avoidance (avoiding eye contact, tactile defensiveness, turning the body away during face-to-face interactions, and stylized, ritualistic forms of greeting); preservative speech often includes repetition of words and phrases. |

routinely provide noninvasive screening procedures, such as ultrasound and *maternal serum alphafetoprotein* (AFP), to women whose pregnancy is considered at risk for a congenital disability. Maternal serum screening measures the amount of AFP and other biochemical markers in the mother's bloodstream and can identify pregnancies at risk for disabilities such as Down syndrome and spina bifida.

Invasive diagnostic tests, such as amniocentesis and chorion villus sampling, can confirm the presence of various disorders. **Amniocentesis** requires withdrawing a sample of fluid from the amniotic sac surrounding the fetus during the second trimester of pregnancy (usually the 14th to 17th week). Fetal cells are removed from the amniotic fluid and grown in a cell culture for about 2 weeks. At that time, a chromosome and enzyme analysis is performed to identify the presence of about 80 specific genetic disorders before birth. Many of these disorders, such as Down syndrome, are associated with mental retardation.

A prenatal diagnostic test that may eventually replace amniocentesis is **chorion villus sampling (CVS).** A small amount of chorionic tissue (a fetal component of the developing placenta) is removed and tested. A significant advantage of CVS is that it can be performed earlier than amniocentesis (during the 8th to 10th week of pregnancy). Because fetal cells exist in relatively large numbers in the chorion, they can be analyzed immediately without waiting 2 to 3 weeks for them to grow. Although CVS is being used more often, it has been associated with a miscarriage rate of about 10 in 1,000 (compared with 2.5 in 1,000 for amniocentesis) and is still considered experimental.

**TABLE 4.3** *continued*

| Syndrome | Definition/Cause | Remarks/Characteristics |
|---|---|---|
| Klinefelter syndrome (XXY males) | Males receive an extra X chromosome. Sterility, underdevelopment of male sex organs, acquisition of female secondary sex characteristics are common; sometimes includes mild levels of cognitive retardation. | XXY males often have problems with social skills, auditory perception, language, sometimes mild levels of cognitive retardation; more often associated with learning disabilities than with mental retardation. |
| Phenylketonuria (PKU) | Genetically inherited condition in which a child is born without an important enzyme needed to break down an amino acid, phenylalanine, found in many common foods; failure to break down this amino acid causes brain damage that often results in aggressiveness, hyperactivity, and severe mental retardation. | Mental retardation resulting from PKU has been virtually eliminated in the United States through widespread screening. By analyzing the concentration of phenylalanine in a newborn's blood plasma, doctors can diagnose PKU and treat it with a special diet. Most children with PKU who receive a phenylalanine-restricted diet early enough have normal intellectual development. |
| Prader-Willi syndrome | Caused by deletion of a portion of chromosome 15. Initially, infants have hypertonia (floppy muscles) and may have to be tube fed. Initial phase is followed by development of insatiable appetite; constant preoccupation with food can lead to life-threatening obesity if food seeking is not monitored. Affects 1 in 10,000 to 25,000 live births. | Associated with mild retardation and learning disabilities; behavior problems common: impulsivity, aggressiveness, temper tantrums, obsessive-compulsive behavior; some forms of self-injurious behavior, such as skin picking; delayed motor skills, short stature, small hands and feet, underdeveloped genitalia. |
| Williams syndrome | Caused by deletion of material on the seventh chromosome; range of cognitive functioning ranges from normal to mild and moderate levels of mental retardation. | Characteristic elfin-like facial features; physical features and manner of expression exudes cheerfulness and happiness; described as "overly friendly," lack of reserve toward strangers; often have uneven profiles of skills, with strengths in vocabulary and story-telling skills and weaknesses in visual-spatial skills; often hyperactive, may have difficulty staying on task and low tolerance for frustration or teasing. |

*Source:* Beirne-Smith, Patton, & Kim (2006); Belser & Sudhalter (2001); Dimitropoulos, Feurer, Butler, & Thompson (2001); Dykens (2000); Dykens & Rosner (1999); Hagerman & Cronsiter (1996); Levine & Wharton (2000); Luckasson et al. (2002); Mervis, Klein-Tasman, & Mastin (2001); Sudhalter & Belser (2001); Symons, Butler, Sanders, Feurer, & Thompson (1999); Symons, Clark, Roberts, & Bailey (2001); Thomas (2001).

In the United States, women who are at risk for giving birth to a baby with a disabilities on the basis of the parents' genetic backgrounds are commonly referred to **genetic counseling** (Roberts, Stough, & Parrish, 2002). Genetic counseling consists of a discussion between a specially trained medical counselor and the prospective parents about the possibility that they may give birth to a child with disabilities. For discussions of ethical considerations of genetic testing for disabilities, see Beirne-Smith et al. (2006), Kuna (2001), and Smith and Mitchell (2001a).

Newborn screening tests for inherited conditions and biomedical risk factors are now mandatory in every state. A procedure called *tandem mass spectrometry* developed in the late 1980s measures various components of blood, urine, or plasma in about 2 minutes for 20 to 30 different metabolic disorders (Nehring, 2003). A simple blood test administered to virtually every baby born in the United State has drastically reduced the incidence of mental retardation caused by **phenylketonuria (PKU).** By analyzing the concentration of phenylalanine in a newborn's blood plasma, doctors can diagnose PKU and treat it with a phenylalanine-restricted diet. Most children with PKU who receive treatment have normal intellectual development (Beirne-Smith et al., 2006).

Toxic exposure through maternal substance abuse and environmental pollutants (e.g., lead poisoning) are two major causes of preventable mental retardation that can be combated

**FIGURE 4.3** Schematic illustration of the intergenerational progression of developmental retardation

*Source:* Reprinted from Greenwood, C. R., Hart, B., Walker, D., & Risley, T. (1994). The opportunity to respond and academic performance revisited: A behavioral theory of developmental retardation and its prevention. In R. Gardner, III, D. M. Sainato, J. O. Cooper, T. E. Heron, W. L. Heward, J. W. Eshleman, & T. A. Grossi (Eds.), *Behavior analysis in education: Focus on measurably superior instruction* (p. 216). Pacific Grove, CA: Brookes/Cole. Used by permission.

with education and training (Howard, Williams, & McLaughlin, 1994; Schroeder, 1987). These medical advances have noticeably reduced the incidence of mental retardation caused by some of the known biological factors, but huge advancements in research are needed to reach the goal of lowering the incidence of biomedical mental retardation by 50%, as stated by the President's Committee on Mental Retardation in 1976.

As we have noted, most children with mental retardation are in the mild range, and their developmental delays have no clear-cut etiology. These are the children whose mental retardation is thought to be primarily the result of an impoverished environment during their early years. The poor environment may be a result of parental neglect, poverty, disease, bad diet, and other factors—many of which are completely out of the hands of the child's parents. In Chapter 14 we will discuss several early intervention programs aimed at reducing the incidence of developmental retardation. Although measuring the effects of programs that aim to prevent psychosocial retardation is much more difficult than measuring the decreased number of children affected by a disease such as PKU, the preliminary results of these projects are encouraging; and some models of effective early intervention have been identified (Guralnick, 1997).

## EDUCATIONAL APPROACHES

The search for effective methods for educating students with mental retardation began more than 200 years ago, when Jean Marc Gaspard Itard kept a detailed diary of his efforts to teach a young boy who was found in the woods and thought to be a feral child. Itard, whom many consider to be the father of special education, showed that intensive, systematic intervention could produce significant gains with a child thought to be incapable of learning (Itard, 1806/1962).

Since Itard's time, researchers working in mental retardation have developed numerous methods of specialized instruction, some of which have contributed to improved practice in all areas of education. Similarly, efforts by early advocates on behalf of children and adults with mental retardation blazed trails for advocacy groups representing individuals with other disabilities. Table 4.4 highlights some key historical events and their implications for the education and treatment of children and adults with mental retardation.

*History of MR*

Council for Exceptional Children    Content Standards for Beginning Teachers of Students with MR/DD: Historical foundations and classic studies of MR/DD (MR1K4).

## TABLE 4.4    A history of the education of children with mental retardation: Key events and implications

| Date | Historical Event | Educational Implication |
|------|------------------|-------------------------|
| 1799 | Jean Marc Gaspard Itard published an account of his work with Victor, the Wild Boy of Aveyron. | Itard showed that intensive treatment could produce significant learning. Many consider Itard to be the father of special education. |
| 1848 | Edouard Seguin helped establish the Pennsylvania Training School. | This was the first educational facility for persons with mental retardation in the United States. |
| 1850 | Samuel Gridley Howe began the School for Idiotic and Feeble Minded Youth. | This was the first publicly funded residential school in the United States. |
| 1896 | The first public school class for children with mental retardation began in Providence, RI. | This began the special class movement, which grew to 1.3 million children in 1974, the year before IDEA. |
| 1905 | Alfred Binet and Theodore Simon developed a test in France to screen those students not benefiting from the regular curriculum. | The test enabled empirical identification of students with mental retardation and contributed to the growth of the special class movement. |
| 1916 | Lewis Terman of Stanford University published the Stanford-Binet Intelligence Scale in the United States. | Many schools adopted IQ testing as a means of identifying children with below-average general intelligence. |
| 1935 | Edgar Doll published the Vineland Social Maturity Scale. | It provided a standardized method for assessing a person's adaptive behavior, which later became part of the definition of mental retardation. |
| 1950 | Parents formed the National Association for Retarded Children (known today as The Arc). | The Arc remains a powerful and important advocacy organization for persons of all ages with mental retardation. |
| 1959 | AAMR published its first manual on the definition and classification of mental retardation, with diagnosis based on an IQ score of one standard deviation below the mean (approximately 85) (Heber, 1959). | Many students were identified in the borderline category of mental retardation and served in special classes for "slow learners" or EMR students. |
| 1961 | John F. Kennedy established the first President's Panel on Mental Retardation. | The panel's first report (Mayo, 1962) made recommendations that helped guide national policy with respect to mental retardation (e.g., citizenship, education, prevention). |
| 1969 | Bengt Nirje published a key paper defining normalization. Wolf Wolfensberger championed normalization in the United States. | Normalization became a leading philosophy guiding the development and delivery of educational, community, vocational, and residential services for persons with mental retardation. |
| 1973 | AAMR published a revised definition that required a score on IQ tests of two standard deviations below the mean (approximately 70 or less) and concurrent deficits in adaptive behavior. | This effectively eliminated mild mental retardation. |
| 1992 | AAMR published "System '92," a radically different definition of mental retardation with a classification system based on intensities of supports. | New definition and classification system generated cautious support by some and concern by others; few states used the '92 system for identifying and planning services for students with mental retardation. |
| 2002 | AAMR published a revision of the 1992 definition; retains classification by intensities of supports; returns to IQ of approximately two standard deviations below mean; adds social participation and interactions as fifth dimension of functioning. | Impact of AAMR's newest definitional system will be determined in coming years. |

# Curriculum Goals

What do students with mental retardation need to learn? Not too many years ago, children with mild mental retardation were presented with a slowed- and/or watered-down version of the general education curriculum that focused largely on traditional academic subjects. For example, a group of children with mild mental retardation might spend several weeks on a geography unit learning the 50 states and their capitals. Students with more severe forms of mental retardation spent many hours putting pegs into pegboards and sorting plastic sticks by color because it was believed that these isolated skills were developmental prerequisites for more meaningful activities. Unfortunately, knowing that Boise is the capital of Idaho or being able to sort by color did not help these students become more independent.

*Functional curriculum goals*

Council for Exceptional Children Content Standards for Beginning Teachers of Students with MR/DD: Plan instruction for independent functional life skills relevant to the community, personal living, sexuality, and employment (MR7S3).

*Functional Curriculum.*   In recent years, identifying functional curriculum goals for students with mental retardation has become a major priority for special educators. Learning activities in a functional curriculum are chosen because they will maximize a student's independence, self-direction, and enjoyment in everyday school, home, community, and work environments.

Browder and Snell (2000) define functional academics as "the most useful parts of the 'three R's'—reading, writing, and arithmetic" (p. 497). Choosing functional academic targets is not as simple as it might seem. The most useful part of writing for one student (e.g., making a grocery list) may not be a functional writing skill for another student (e.g., writing the number of items packaged on the job). Careful assessment of each student's current routines must be conducted to find those skills that are required and/or could be used often. Skills that are likely to be required by future environments should also be considered.

Teachers must be on guard against the faulty assumption that a traditional academic skill cannot be functional because it is not a typical activity or learning outcome for students with mental retardation. For example, while *crystal* and *limestone* might not seem to be functional sight words, such words might be extremely functional for a student with a rock collection (Browder, 2000).

Clark (1994) suggests that teachers determine functional knowledge or skills by seeking answers to these questions:

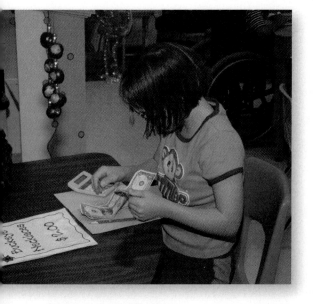

Serving as sales clerk for the project that she and her classmates created helps Sarah learn functional skills.

- Does the content focus on necessary knowledge and skills … [so that the student can] function as independently as possible in the home, school, or community?
- Does the content provide a scope and sequence for meeting future needs?
- Do the student's parents think the content is important for both current and future needs?
- Does the student think the content is important for both current and future needs?
- Is the content appropriate for the student's chronological age and current intellectual, academic, or behavioral performance level(s)?
- What are the consequences to the student of not learning the concepts and skills? (p. 37)

An even simpler approach to determining whether any given skill represents functional curriculum is to contemplate this question from the student's perspective: "Will I need it when I'm 21?" (Beck, Broers, Hogue, Shipstead, & Knowlton, 1994). The answer to this question is critical because when educators fail to relate curriculum for a student with mental retardation to outcomes with direct relevance to that student's eventual independence and quality of life, "years of valuable opportunities for meaningful learning can be wasted" (Knowlton, 1998, p. 96).

*Life Skills.*    As students with mental retardation reach middle and secondary school, the emphasis on learning functional skills that will help them transition to adult life in the community becomes especially critical. Several models and taxonomies of adult functioning are available that can be used as the framework from which to build functional curriculum activities (e.g., Brolin, 1997; Dever, 1988). For example, *Life Skills Instruction* includes 147 major life demands that are associated with a variety of specific life skills and organized around six domains of adult functioning (Cronin, Patton, & Wood, 2005). Table 4.5 shows examples of how academic and social-skills instruction can be related to some of these life skills.

*Integrating life skills into curriculum*

Council for Exceptional Children — Content Standards for Beginning Teachers—Common Core: Integrate affective, social, and life skills with academic curricula (CC7S7).

*Self-Determination.*    Self-determined learners set goals, plan and implement a course of action, evaluate their performance, and make adjustments in what they are doing to reach their goals. **Self-determination** has been defined as

> a combination of skills, knowledge, and beliefs that enable a person to engage in goal directed, self-regulated, autonomous behavior. An understanding of one's strengths and limitations together with a belief in oneself as capable and effective are essential to self-determination. When acting on the basis of these skills and attitudes, individuals have greater ability to take control of their lives and assume the role of successful adults. (Field, Martin, Miller, Ward, & Wehmeyer, 1998b, p. 2)

Realizing the concept of self-determination in the classroom means teaching skills and attitudes to enable skills such as choice/decision making, goal setting, problem solving, self-evaluation, self-management, self-advocacy, and self-awareness. Learning self-determination skills can serve as both a curriculum goal in its own right as well as a means to help students achieve other learning outcomes (Wehmeyer, Palmer, Agran, Mithaug, & Martin, 2000). For example, Agran, Blanchard, Wehmeyer, and Hughes (2002) taught four middle school students with mental retardation a 4-step problem-solving sequence to achieve self-set goals related to their participation and success in the general education classroom.

*Self-determination*

Council for Exceptional Children — Content Standards for Beginning Teachers—Common Core: Use procedures to increase the individual's self-awareness, self-management, self-control, self-reliance, and self-esteem (CC4S5) (also CC7S14).

> First, the student was taught to verbalize, "What is the problem?" and to say out loud what it was. Second, the student was taught to ask, "What can I do about it?" and to verbalize the proposed solution, Third, the student was taught to implement the proposed solution. Last, the student was taught to ask, "Did that fix the problem?" For example, Natalie was taught to ask herself, "What is the problem?" and to respond by saying, "I need to say at least one sentence during class." After responding to teacher or student questions, she would ask, "Did that fix the problem?" Following class she would count the number of verbal comments she had made. Next, she would ask, "Did I meet my goal?" (p. 283)

Self-determination requires a complex set of skills and is a lofty goal for any student. However, students with mental retardation can learn self-determination skills, and those who do are more likely to achieve IEP goals and make a successful transition from school to adult life (Agran, Snow, & Swaner, 1999; German, Martin, Huber Marshall, & Sale, 2000). Several research-validated curriculum models and instructional materials have been developed for teaching self-determination to students with disabilities (e.g., Algozzine, Browder, Karvonen, Test, & Wood, 2001; Test, Karvonen, Wood, Browder, & Algozzine 2000; Wehmeyer et al., 2000). Recommendations for teaching self-determination and lesson-plan templates are provided by Test, Browder, Karvonen, Wood, and Algozzine (2002).

An important and initial component of self-determination is teaching students to take responsibility for their learning. Students should be taught to take an active role in their learning at an early age. Teaching students with disabilities to recruit assistance from the classroom teacher is one strategy for helping them succeed in general education classrooms and to take an active role in their education. For example, Craft, Alber, and Heward (1998) taught four fourth graders with mental retardation to recruit teacher attention while they worked on spelling assignments in a general education classroom. They were taught to

**TABLE 4.5**  **Relationship of scholastic/social skills to adult life skills**

| | Employment Education | Home and Family | Leisure Pursuits | Community Involvement | Emotional–Physical Health | Personal Responsibility Relationships |
|---|---|---|---|---|---|---|
| Reading | Reading classified ads for jobs | Interpreting bills | Locating and understanding movie information in a newspaper | Following directions on tax forms | Comprehending directions on medication | Reading letters from friends |
| Writing | Writing a letter of application for a job | Writing checks | Writing for information on a city to visit | Filling in a voter registration form | Filling in your medical history on forms | Sending thank you notes |
| Listening | Understanding oral directions of a procedure change | Comprehending directions | Listening to a weather forecast to plan an outdoor activity | Understanding campaign ads | Attending lectures on stress | Taking turns in a conversation |
| Speaking | Asking your boss for a raise | Discussing morning routines with family | Inquiring about tickets for a concert | Stating your opinion at the school board meeting | Describing symptoms to a doctor | Giving feedback to a friend |
| Math applications | Understanding difference between net and gross pay | Computing the cost of doing laundry in a laundromat versus home | Calculating the cost of a dinner out versus eating at home | Obtaining information for a building permit | Using a thermometer | Planning the costs of a date |
| Problem-solving | Settling a dispute with a co-worker | Deciding how much to budget for rent | Role-playing appropriate behaviors for various places | Knowing what to do if you are the victim of fraud | Selecting a doctor | Deciding how to ask someone for a date |
| Survival skills | Using a prepared career-planning packet | Listing emergency phone numbers | Using a shopping-center directory | Marking a calendar for important dates (e.g., recycling, garbage collection) | Using a system to remember to take vitamins | Developing a system to remember birthdays |
| Personal-social | Applying appropriate interview skills | Helping a child with homework | Knowing the rules of a neighborhood pool | Locating self-improvement classes | Getting a yearly physical exam | Discussing how to negotiate a price at the flea market |

*Source:* From *Life Skills Instruction: A Practical Guide for Integrating Real Life Content into the Curriculum at the Elementary and Secondary Levels for Students with Special Needs or Who Are Placed at Risk* by M. E. Cronin and J. R. Patton, & S. J. Wood, 2005, Austin, TX: PRO-ED. Copyright 2005 by PRO-ED. Reprinted by permission.

show their work to the teacher two to three times per session and to make statements such as "How am I doing?" or "Look, I'm all finished!" Recruitment training, which was conducted in the special education classroom, increased the frequency of each student's recruiting, the frequency of teacher praise, the percentage of worksheet items completed, and the accuracy with which the students completed the assignments. After the study the general education teacher stated, "They fit in better, they were more a part of the group, and they weren't being disruptive because they were working." (To learn more about this strategy for teaching students to take an active role in their learning, see Teaching & Learning, "'Look, I'm All Finished!'" later in this chapter.)

## Instructional Methods

Students with mental retardation learn best when instruction is explicit and systematic and instructional methods are derived from empirical research, such as the following practices (Heward, 2003):

- Assess each student's present levels of performance to help identify and prioritize the most important instructional targets.
- Define and task-analyze the new knowledge or skills to be learned.
- Design instructional materials and activities so the student has frequent opportunities for active student response in the form of guided and independent practice.
- Use **mediated scaffolding** (i.e., provide and then fade prompts and cues so student can respond to naturally occurring stimuli).
- Provide systematic consequences for student performance in the form of contingent reinforcement, instructional feedback, and error correction.
- Incorporate fluency-building activities into lessons.
- Incorporate strategies for promoting the generalization and maintenance of newly learned skills.
- Conduct direct and frequent measurements of student performance and use those data to inform instructional decisions. (p. 197)

Some of these components of effective instruction are described here; others will be discussed in subsequent chapters.

*Task Analysis.*   **Task analysis** means breaking down complex or multistep skills into smaller, easier-to-learn subtasks. The subskills or subtasks are then sequenced, either in the natural order in which they are typically performed or from easiest to most difficult. Assessing a student's performance on a sequence of task-analyzed subskills helps pinpoint where instruction should begin.

*Task analysis*

Council for Exceptional Children   Content Standards for Beginning Teachers—Common Core: Use task analysis (CC7S5).

During the task-analysis stage of instructional planning, it is important to consider the extent to which the natural environment requires performance of the target skill for a given duration or at a minimum rate. For example, Test, Spooner, Keul, and Grossi (1990) included specific time limits for each of the 17 steps in a task analysis used to teach two secondary students with severe mental retardation to use the public telephone to call home. The specific sequence of steps and the time limit for each step were determined by having two adults without disabilities use the telephone.

*Active Student Response.*   Contemporary educational research is unequivocal in its support of the positive relationship between students' active engagement with academic tasks and their achievement. Providing instruction with high levels of active student participation is important for all learners, but it is particularly important for students with disabilities: "For children who are behind to catch up, they simply must be taught more in less time. If the teacher doesn't attempt to teach more in less time ... the gap in general knowledge between a normal and handicapped student becomes even greater" (Kame' enui & Simmons, 1990, p. 11).

# "Look, I'm All Finished!" Recruiting Teacher Attention

### by Sheila R. Alber and William L. Heward

Preparation of students with disabilities for inclusion in general education classrooms should include instruction in classroom survival skills. Attending to instruction, following directions, and completing assigned seatwork are skills likely to enhance a student's acceptance and success in the regular classroom. Because teachers value such "good student" behaviors, students are also likely to receive teacher praise and attention for exhibiting them.

But classrooms are busy places, so teachers can easily overlook students' important academic and social behaviors. Research shows that teachers are more likely to pay attention to a disruptive student than to one who is working quietly and productively (Walker, 1997). It is hard for teachers to be aware of students who need help, especially low-achieving ones who are less likely to ask (Newman & Golding, 1990).

Although teachers in general education classrooms are expected to adapt instruction to serve students with disabilities, this is not always the case. Most secondary teachers interviewed by Schumm et al. (1995) believed that students with disabilities should take responsibility for obtaining the help they need. Thus, politely recruiting teacher attention and assistance can help students with disabilities function more independently and actively influence the quality of instruction they receive.

## RECRUITING CAN WORK

Students of various ages and abilities have learned to recruit teacher and peer attention for performing a wide range of tasks in classroom and community settings: preschoolers with developmental delays for completing pre-academic tasks and staying on task during transitions (Connell, Carta, & Baer, 1993; Stokes, Fowler, & Baer, 1978) as well as students with learning disabilities (Alber, Heward, & Hippler, 1999; Wolford, Alber, & Heward, 2001), behavioral disorders (Morgan, Young, & Goldstein, 1983), and

mental retardation while performing academic tasks in regular classrooms (Craft et al., 1998) and secondary students with mental retardation for improved work performance in vocational training settings (Mank & Horner, 1987).

## WHO SHOULD BE TAUGHT TO RECRUIT?

**Withdrawn Willamena.** Willamena seldom asks a teacher anything. Because she is so quiet and well behaved, her teachers sometimes forget she's in the room. Withdrawn Willamenas are prime candidates for recruitment training.

**In-a-Hurry Harry.** Harry is usually half-done with a task before his teacher finishes explaining it. Racing through his work allows him to be the first to turn it in. But his work is often incomplete and error-filled, so he doesn't hear much praise from his teacher. Harry would benefit from recruitment training that includes self-checking and self-correction.

**Shouting Shelly.** Shelly has just finished her work, and she wants her teacher to look at it—right now! But Shelly doesn't raise her hand. She gets her teacher's attention—and disrupts most of her classmates—by shouting across the room. Students like Shelly should be taught appropriate ways to solicit teacher attention.

**Pestering Pete.** Pete always raises his hand, waits quietly for his teacher to come to his desk, and then politely asks, "Have I done this right?" But sometimes he repeats this routine a dozen times in a 20-minute period, and his teachers find it annoying. Positive teacher attention often turns into reprimands. Recruitment training for Pete, and for all students, will teach him to limit the number of times he cues his teachers for attention.

## HOW TO GET STARTED

1. *Identify target skills.* Students should recruit teacher attention for target skills that are valued and therefore likely to be reinforced—e.g., writing neatly and legibly, working accurately, completing assigned work, clean-

Politely recruiting teacher attention and assistance is one way students can influence the quality of instruction they receive.

ing up at transitions, and making contributions when working in a cooperative group.

2. *Teach self-assessment.* Students should self-assess their work before recruiting teacher attention (e.g., Sue asks herself, "Is my work complete?"). After the student can reliably distinguish between complete and incomplete work samples, she can learn how to check the accuracy of her work with answer keys or checklists of the steps or components of the academic skill. Or she can spot-check two or three items before asking the teacher to look at it.

3. *Teach appropriate recruiting.* Teach students when, how, and how often to recruit and how to respond to the teacher after receiving attention.

- *When?* Students should signal for teacher attention after they have completed and self-checked a substantial part of their work. Students should also be taught when not to try to get their teacher's attention (e.g., when the teacher is working with another student, talking to another adult, taking the lunch count).

- *How?* The traditional hand raise should be part of every student's recruiting repertoire. Other methods of gaining attention should be taught depending upon teacher preferences and routines in the general education classroom (e.g., have students signal they need help by standing up a small flag on their desks; expect students to bring their work to the teacher's desk for help and feedback).

- *How often?* While helping Withdrawn Willamena learn to seek teacher attention, don't turn her into a Pestering Pete. How often a student should recruit varies across teachers and activities (e.g., independent seatwork, cooperative learning groups, whole-class instruction). Direct observation in the classroom is the best way to establish an optimal

rate of recruiting; it is also a good idea to ask the regular classroom teacher when, how, and with what frequency she prefers students to ask for help.

- *What to say?* Students should be taught several statements that are likely to evoke positive feedback from the teacher (e.g., "Please look at my work." "Did I do a good job?" "How am I doing?"). Keep it simple, but teach the student to vary her verbal cues so she will not sound like a parrot.

- *How to respond?* Students should respond to their teacher's feedback by establishing eye contact, smiling, and saying, "Thank you." Polite appreciation is very reinforcing to teachers and will increase the likelihood of more positive attention the next time.

4. *Model and role-play the complete sequence.* Begin by providing students with a rationale for recruiting (e.g., the teacher will be happy you did a good job, you will get more work done, your grades might improve). Thinking aloud while modeling is good way to show the recruiting sequence. While performing each step, say, "Okay, I've finished my work. Now I'm going to check it. Did I put my name on my paper? Yes. Did I do all the problems? Yes. Did I follow all the steps? Yes. Okay, my teacher doesn't look busy right now. I'll raise my hand and wait quietly until she comes to my desk." Have another student pretend to be the regular classroom teacher and come over to you when you have your hand up. Say, "Mr. Patterson, please look at my work." The helper says, "Oh, you did a very nice job." Then smile and say, "Thank you, teacher." Role-play with praise and offer corrective feedback until the student correctly performs the entire sequence on several consecutive trials.

5. *Prepare students for alternate responses.* Of course, not every student cue will result in teacher praise; some efforts to recruit may even be followed by criticism (e.g., "This is all wrong. Pay better attention the next time."). Use role-playing to prepare students for these possibilities and have them practice polite responses (e.g., "Thank you for helping me with this.").

Politely recruiting teacher attention and assistance is one way students can actively influence the quality of instruction they receive. For more information on teaching students to recruit teacher attention, see Alber and Heward (2000).

Sheila R. Alber is a faculty member in the Department of Special Education at the University of Southern Mississippi.

*Source:* Adapted from Alber, S. R., & Heward, W. L. (1997). Recruit it or lose it! Training students to recruit contingent teacher attention. *Intervention in School and Clinic, 5,* 275–282. Used with permission.

To learn more about these strategies and answer questions about what you have learned, go to the Teaching & Learning module in Chapter 4 of the Companion Website, **www.prenhall.com/heward**.

Effective instruction for all students, with or without disabilities, is characterized by frequent opportunities for active student response and systematic feedback.

Various terms such as *active student response, opportunity to respond,* and *academic learning time* are used to refer to this important variable.

**Active student response (ASR)** can be defined as an observable response made to an instructional antecedent. To say it less technically, ASR occurs when a student emits a detectable response to ongoing instruction. The kinds of responses that qualify as ASR are as varied as the kinds of lessons that are taught. Depending upon the instructional objective, examples of ASR include words read, problems answered, boards cut, test tubes measured, praise and supportive comments spoken, notes or scales played, stitches sewn, sentences written, workbook questions answered, and fastballs pitched. The basic measure of how much ASR a student receives is a frequency count of the number of academic responses emitted within a given period of instruction. (Heward, 1994, p. 286)

When all variables are held constant (e.g., quality of curriculum materials, students' prerequisite skills, motivational variables), an ASR-rich lesson will generally result in more learning than does a lesson in which students make few or no responses.

*Systematic Feedback.* Instructional feedback—information provided to students about their performance—falls into two broad categories: praise and/or other forms of confirmation or **positive reinforcement** for correct responses, and error correction for incorrect responses. Feedback is generally most effective when it is specific, immediate, positive, frequent, and differential (comparing the student's present performance with past performance; e.g., "You read 110 words today, Jermon. That's five more than yesterday.") (Van Houten, 1984).

Several studies have found that providing a type of feedback that Werts and colleagues call *instructive feedback* can increase the efficiency of instruction for students with mental retardation and other disabilities (Werts, Caldwell, & Wolery, 2003; Werts, Wolery, Gast, & Holcombe, 1996). When giving feedback to students on their responses to targeted items, the teacher intentionally and methodically presents "extra information." For example, when praising a student's correct response when reading the word *corn,* the teacher might say,

"Right, this word is *corn*; it is a vegetable." The instructive feedback is the statement "it is a vegetable."

Using feedback effectively is one of the most important skills for teachers (Konold, Miller, & Konold, 2004). Effective teachers change the focus and timing of the feedback they provide as a student progresses from initial attempts at learning a new skill through practicing a newly acquired skill. When a student is first learning a new skill or content knowledge, feedback ideally follows each response (see Figure 4.4). Feedback during this initial **acquisition stage of learning** should focus on the accuracy and form of the student's response. By providing feedback after each response, the teacher reduces the likelihood that the student will practice errors.

During the **practice stage of learning,** when the student can perform the new skill with accuracy, she should be allowed to make a series of responses before feedback is provided. Feedback during the practice stage should emphasize the correct rate at which the student performs the target skill. Providing feedback after each response during the practice stage of learning may have a detrimental effect by blocking the student's opportunity to develop fluency by "going fast."

*Transfer of Stimulus Control.*   Trial-and-error learning is inefficient and frustrating for students without disabilities. For students with mental retardation and other learning problems, it is likely to be a complete waste of time. Instead of waiting to see whether the student will make a correct response, the effective teacher provides a prompt (e.g., physical guidance, verbal directions, picture cues, prerecorded auditory prompts) that makes a correct response very probable. For example, Wood, Frank, and Hamre-Nietupski (1996) provided picture prompts for students to help them correctly perform each step in a task analysis for opening a combination lock found on student lockers. The correct response is reinforced,

For suggestions on using corrective feedback, see "What to Do When Students Make Mistakes" in Chapter 4's Teaching & Learning module of the Companion website, **www.prenhall.com/heward**.

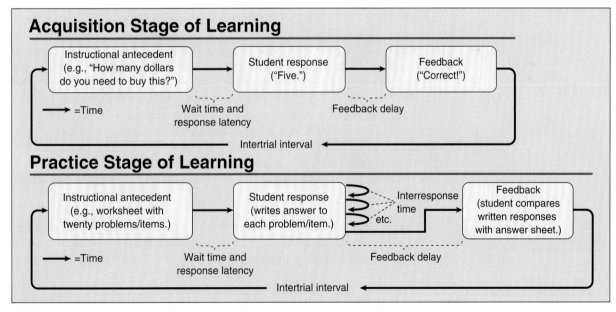

**FIGURE 4.4   Feedback within a series of instructional trials during the acquisition and practice stages of learning**

*Source:* Reprinted from Heward, W. L. (1994). Three "low-tech" strategies for increasing the frequency of active student response during group instruction. In R. Gardner, III, D. M. Sainato, J. O. Cooper, T. E. Heron, W. L. Heward, J. W. Eshleman, & T. A. Grossi (Eds.), *Behavior analysis in education: Focus on measurably superior instruction* (p. 284). Pacific Grove, CA: Brooks/Cole. Used with permission.

the prompt is repeated, and another correct student response is reinforced. The response prompts are then gradually and systematically withdrawn so that the student's behavior comes under the stimulus control of the curriculum content or things in the natural environment that typically serve as cues for that skill (Wolery, Ault, & Doyle, 1992).

*Generalization and Maintenance.* **Generalization** and **maintenance** refer to the extent to which students use what they have learned across settings and over time. Although there is still much to be learned about helping students with mental retardation and other disabilities get the most out of what they learn, the promising beginnings of a reliable "technology of generalization" have been developed (Baer, 1999; Horner, Dunlap, & Koegel, 1988). Here are three examples of many strategies for promoting generalization and maintenance:

*Promoting generalization and maintenance*

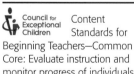

Council for Exceptional Children Content Standards for Beginning Teachers—Common Core: Use strategies to facilitate maintenance and generalization of skills across learning environments (CC4S4).

- *Aim for naturally occurring reinforcement contingencies.* The most basic strategy for promoting generalization and maintenance is to increase the probability that a student's new skill will be reinforced in the natural environment (e.g., the regular classroom, the playground, the community, recreational and work settings). This can be accomplished by (1) teaching only functional skills that are needed and likely to be valued by people in the student's natural environment and (2) teaching students to perform new skills with the accuracy and fluency necessary to produce reinforcement in the natural environment.
- *Program common stimuli.* If the generalization setting differs greatly from the setting where teaching takes place, the student may not perform the new behavior. There are two basic ways to program common stimuli: (1) incorporate into the teaching situation as many typical features of the generalization setting as possible and (2) create a new common stimulus that the student learns to use in the teaching setting and can transport to the generalization setting, where it prompts or assists performance of the target skill. Sandie Trask-Tyler applied this technique in her master's thesis when she taught secondary students with mental retardation and visual impairments to use tape-recorded recipes to prepare snack foods. (See Teaching & Learning, "I Made It Myself and It's Good!" in Chapter 10.)
- *Community-based instruction.* Teaching in the actual setting where students are ultimately to use their new skills increases the probability of generalization and maintenance. Community-based instruction is a widely used practice in special education with a good research base to support it (Owens-Johnson & Hamill, 2002). However, simply conducting instruction in the community does not guarantee generalization and maintenance. A poorly designed lesson will be ineffective regardless of where it is conducted. And community-based instruction can be expensive and is typically not available on a daily basis. Morse and Schuster (2000) found that 2 days per week of community-based instruction supplemented by simulation training in the classroom was effective in teaching students with mental retardation to shop for groceries.

*Direct and Frequent Measurement.* Teachers should verify the effects of their instruction by directly and frequently measuring student performance. Measurement is *direct* when it objectively records the learner's performance of the behavior of interest in the natural environment for that skill. Measurement is *frequent* when it occurs on a regular basis; ideally, measurement should take place as often as instruction occurs.

*Direct and frequent measurement*

Council for Exceptional Children Content Standards for Beginning Teachers—Common Core: Evaluate instruction and monitor progress of individuals with exceptional educational needs (CC8S8) (also CC7S13).

When teachers do not collect direct and frequent measurements of students' performance to verify the effects of instruction, they are prone to two mistakes: (1) continuing ineffective instruction when no real learning has occurred (e.g., perhaps a teacher believes a certain type of instruction is effective) and (2) discontinuing an effective program of instruction because subjective judgment finds no improvement (e.g., without object measures it is difficult to discern that a student's reading rate has increased from 70 words per minute to 80 words per minute. (Heward, 2005, p. 321)

Community-based instruction provides these students an opportunity to acquire vocational skills in a real work setting.

# EDUCATIONAL PLACEMENT ALTERNATIVES

Children with mild retardation were traditionally educated in self-contained classrooms in the public schools. Today many children with mild and moderate mental retardation are being educated in regular classrooms, with a special educator helping the classroom teacher with individualized instruction for the child and providing extra tutoring in a resource room as needed.

During the 2003–2004 school year, 11.6% of students with mental retardation were educated in the regular classroom, with 30.2% being served in resource room programs and 51.8% in separate classes (U.S. Office of Special Education Programs, 2004). About 6% of students with mental retardation attend special schools or residential facilities. Sometimes a number of small neighboring school districts pool their resources to offer a special school program for students with moderate, severe, and profound mental retardation. However, many special educators today believe that separate schools prohibit students from obtaining an education in the least restrictive environment and that all children should attend their local neighborhood schools regardless of the type or severity of their disability (e.g., Baumgart & Giangreco, 1996; Brown et al., 1989a).

As we saw in Chapter 2, simply putting a child with disabilities into a regular classroom does not mean that he will be accepted socially or receive the most appropriate and needed instructional programming. This may be especially true for students with mental retardation, whose presence in the regular classroom represents a novel challenge for many teachers. For example, although 97% of general education teachers who responded to a national survey about grading practices reported that they had taught students with learning

*Placement alternatives for students with MR*

**Council for Exceptional Children** Content Standards for Beginning Teachers of Students with MR/DD: Continuum of placement services available for individuals with MR/DD (MR1K3).

disabilities and 73% had taught students with behavior disorders, only 23% indicated they had taught students with mental retardation (Bursuck et al., 1996).

Many special and regular educators, however, are developing programs and methods for integrating the instruction of students with mental retardation into that of their nondisabled classmates. Systematically planning for the focus student's inclusion in the classroom through team games and collaborative learning and group investigation projects and directly training all students in specific skills for interacting with one another are just some of the methods for increasing the chances of a successful regular class placement (Bauer & Brown, 2001; Dugan et al., 1995; Giangreco, 1997; Grenot-Scheyer, Fisher, & Staub, 2001; Janney & Snell, 1996, 1997; Kennedy & Fisher, 2001; Krajewski & Flaherty, 2000; Putnam, 1998). Peer tutoring and peer buddy programs have also proven effective in promoting the instructional and social inclusion of students with mental retardation into regular classrooms (Campbell Miller, Cooke, Test, & White, 2003; Copeland et al., 2002; Mortweet et al., 1999; Staub, Spaulding, Peck, Gallucci, & Schwartz, 1996). (See Teaching & Learning, "Some Things We've Learned about Inclusion" on the next page.)

Students with mental retardation often benefit from similar programs for students who are not disabled. During the early elementary grades, students with mental retardation as well as their chronological-age peers need instruction in basic academic skills. Reading, mathematical calculations, and writing are core curricular areas that should be included in programs for all students (Al Otaiba & Hosp, 2004; Horstmeier, 2004; Joseph & Seery, 2004). During this period, many students with mental retardation benefit from full or partial inclusion in regular classroom settings.

*Facilitating inclusion for students with MR*

Council for Exceptional Children Content Standards for Beginning Teachers of Students with MR/DD: Approaches to creating positive learning environments for individuals with MR/DD (MR5K1) (also CC4S1).

As students get older, their needs begin to differ and thus curricular differentiation becomes an important consideration.... Rather than being integrated into a world history class, many students with mental retardation may be better served by learning the necessary functional skills for independent living. Skills such as job readiness, how to use leisure time, how to budget and shop, how to cook and how to maintain a household are important. While all individuals must learn these skills in order to be independent, most students learn them on their own, without specific instructional activities that focus on these areas. Students with mental retardation, on the other hand, often need structured learning experiences in order to learn these skills. (Smith & Hilton, 1994, pp. 6–7)

The relative appropriateness of inclusion in the regular classroom may change for some students as they move from the elementary grades to the secondary level, when opportunities for community-based instruction in vocational and life skills are

Many students with mental retardation benefit from instruction in basic academic and social skills in inclusive classrooms.

critical. The extent to which a student with mental retardation, like all students with disabilities, is educated in a general education classroom should be determined by the student's individual needs. "School inclusion can then be seen as a means (as opposed to just a goal unto itself) toward the ultimate objective of community inclusion and empowerment" (Polloway, Smith, Patton, & Smith, 1996, p. 11).

# Some Things We've Learned about Inclusion

*by Martha E. Snell and Rachel E. Janney*

Inclusion involves creating a mainstream where everyone fits and learns. Inclusion affects the location of students, the supports provided, the roles school staff fill, and the ways in which teachers interact with each other. In inclusive schools:

- All students attend their neighborhood school.
- Students with disabilities are members of general education classrooms with their age peers; their numbers reflect the natural proportion of students with disabilities.
- Special education supports follow students into the mainstream.
- Inclusion is planned individually to enable active and meaningful participation in learning and social activities. Planning addresses classes and schedule, amount and kinds of support, accommodations and modifications, and any related services.

## BENEFITS OF INCLUSION

Most educators agree that inclusion involves complex change, but knowing what inclusion is still may not convince people to make the change. Why include students with disabilities, especially those with extensive support needs? Because inclusion provides benefits to students with disabilities, typical students, and teachers.

For students with disabilities, we know that inclusion can lead to social benefits and skill improvements (Dugan et al., 1995; Fryxell & Kennedy, 1995; Hunt, Staub, Alwell, & Goetz, 1994; Kennedy, Shukla, & Fryxell, 1997; Shukla, Kennedy, & Cushing, 1998). These benefits mean not being separated from typical peers but sharing class membership; having increased social interactions; gaining positive social relationships; expanding one's peer network and making friends; and having peers who

can be models for communication, social skills, dress, style, increased alertness, and improved academic learning and motivation for learning.

For typical students, benefits cluster in the personal growth domain (Cushing & Kennedy, 1997; Kishi & Meyer, 1994; Shukla et al., 1998). Students demonstrate improvements in attitudes toward people different from themselves, increased social responsibility, and self-confidence. They have an opportunity to expand peer networks and form meaningful relationships with students in the mainstream.

General education teachers describe unanticipated rewards from their own interactions with focus students; these teachers are positively motivated by discovering that students with disabilities have personalities, can learn, and can contribute in class.

Most benefits of inclusion depend on how schools plan for, implement, and support change and then sustain outcomes. Searching the literature for supportive evidence produces a mixed bag of findings. It seems that the challenges of including students with extensive cognitive and/or physical disabilities may be fewer than those of including students prone to emotional outburst or aggression. But categorizing students as "easier to include" or "harder to include" is an error-prone strategy. Only by planning needed supports on an individual basis can educators help inclusion yield benefits.

## UNWRITTEN AGREEMENTS BETWEEN TEACHERS

Observations and interviews with teachers and students from 10 classrooms in elementary schools practicing inclusion have taught us a great deal (Janney & Snell, 1996, 1997). For example, classroom teachers and special education teachers have unwritten contracts about the roles they play to support the students with moderate and severe disabilities included in their classrooms:

- Classroom teachers continued to have primary authority for the class and the included child when

Inclusion is about students having membership in classrooms with nondisabled peers.

scissors) or response modalities (listening to a taped story rather than looking at a book because of visual impairments). Sometimes instructional activities were modified to enable the focus child to participate socially, not academically: just sitting with a group doing math activities or holding a book that others were reading. Finally, special education teachers used parallel activities that differed from classmates' activities, were carried out separately but in the classroom, and in which only the focus child participated (e.g., working on money skills while classmates did addition and subtraction). Inclusion was successful when students fit in both socially and instructionally.

## LESSONS ABOUT HELPING AND SOCIALIZATION

Observations also taught us about how teachers use peer interactions to include students with disabilities in their elementary general education classrooms. We learned that classroom teachers developed rules for peers to help the included child:

- *Who could help the focus student with class work.* Typical students could not help each other, but they could help the focus student.
- *When to help the focus student.* Typical students could help if they were "helper of the day" or asked by the teacher, but not when the teacher was teaching or if the focus student rejected assistance.
- *How to help.* Typical students could help in ways that let the focus student participate as much as he or she could. "Don't do it for her" was a guideline teachers taught peers (but did not always follow themselves).

We have repeatedly observed general and special education teachers teach three important lessons that facilitate socialization between students and their classmate with disabilities. The main teaching approach was to model lessons through their own behavior toward the focus student—to "practice what they preached."

he was treated like classmates—for example, during class activities, recess, P.E., circle time, reading and math, and field trips.

- Special education teachers or classroom aides assumed primary responsibility when the focus child was treated differently from classmates: for example, during individualized tutoring or related services for health or physical needs.
- When including students with more extensive support needs, the teachers would, as much as possible, (1) keep focus students near their peers, (2) treat them like their classmates, and (3) provide them with the same or similar activities and materials.

After all, as these teachers told us, inclusion is about students having membership in classrooms with nondisabled peers. So why separate them or treat them differently?

## TEACHERS' MODIFICATIONS

To implement these assumptions, teachers made three kinds of changes. First, they modified their typical roles because the focus student was shared between two teachers and the classroom teacher now had at least one new staff member in and out of the classroom. Second, they modified class routines and the classroom itself. For example, peers were allowed to walk with focus students and help them stay with the class on the way to lunch, P.E., and other activities; schedules allowed time for students with physical disabilities to make transitions; reading circles were moved so positioning equipment would fit. Third, teachers modified instructional activities to enable focus students to participate academically and socially. Sometimes changes were simplifications (fewer spelling words); sometimes they involved different materials (specialized

| Lessons | Examples |
| --- | --- |
| *Just another student.* Treat focus students like other students as much as possible. | Use greetings, joking styles as with other students; include them in all class activities; and apply the same rules for everyone's behavior. |
| *Age appropriate.* Encourage focus students to look and act in ways that reflect their actual age, not "like babies." Use the same rule to guide peer interactions. | Use age-appropriate greetings, tone of voice, teaching and leisure materials, and clothes. |

*Back off.* Adults should draw peers into academic or social activities with focus children and then back off to avoid hampering their interactions.

Pull peers into the activity and make it fun; then leave. Or help a focus student into the sandbox among peers; then move away and monitor from a distance.

## TEACHERS WORKING TOGETHER

We observed kindergarten and first-grade teachers over a school year as they practiced inclusion in an elementary school and found that they naturally used problem-solving strategies with their teammates to address problems that arose with the children who had high support needs (Snell & Janney, 2005). Teachers' concerns clustered into several areas: disagreement about students' goals and problems, challenges with coordination and communication, and difficulties putting solutions into place and evaluating them. Their approach for addressing these concerns, while not articulated as steps, consisted of steps similar to traditional models: identify the problem, gather information, generate potential solutions, evaluate potential solutions, implement, and evaluate. Under pressure for solutions, however, they often discussed and generated ideas too quickly, which curtailed brainstorming as a team and meant that ideas were tried out before being well formed and improved through repeated application of these steps. These findings lend support for team problem solving as an essential element of the meaningful inclusion of children with disabilities; but given the logistical constraints of teaching, it is critical that school administrators lend strong support to regular team collaboration (e.g., preserving time for teaming and valuing its outcomes).

Martha E. Snell is a professor at the University of Virginia, where she directs the graduate programs in severe disabilities and early childhood special education. She is past president of The Association for Persons with Severe Disabilities and a co-author of the AAMR's *Mental Retardation: Definition, Classification and Systems of Supports* (Luckasson et al., 2002). Rachel Janney is professor of special education at Radford University, where she trains teachers to work with students with mental retardation.

 To learn more about these strategies and answer questions about what you have learned, go to the Teaching & Learning module in Chapter 4 of the Companion Website, **www.prenhall.com/heward**.

# CURRENT ISSUES AND FUTURE TRENDS

Two issues confronting the field of mental retardation today are the continued evolution of the definition of mental retardation and increasing the acceptance and membership of persons with mental retardation in society.

## The Evolving Definition of Mental Retardation

During the past 4 decades, the conception of mental retardation has undergone numerous changes in terminology, IQ score cutoff, and the relative role of adaptive functioning. In each case, those changes have reflected an ongoing attempt to better understand mental retardation in order to achieve more effective and reliable systems of identification, classification, research, and habilitation.

Some professionals in the field of mental retardation have criticized the AAMR's 1992/2002 definition (e.g., Borthwick-Duffy, 1994; Greenspan, 1997; Jacobson & Mulick, 1996; MacMillan, Gresham, & Siperstein, 1993; Vig & Jedrysek, 1996). Concerns include the following:

*Continuing debate and evolution of definition of MR*

Council for Exceptional Children Content Standards for Beginning Teachers of Students with MR/DD: Trends and practices within the field of MR/DD (MR1K5) (also CC1K5).

- IQ testing will remain a primary (and in practice perhaps the only) means of diagnosis.
- Adaptive skills cannot be reliably measured with current assessment methods.
- The levels of needed supports are too subjective.
- Classification will remain essentially unchanged in practice because the four intensities of supports—intermittent, limited, extensive, and pervasive—will simply replace the four levels of retardation based on IQ scores—mild, moderate, severe, and profound.

Recognizing these criticisms and the difficulty of describing the implications of the new definition for the field of mental retardation, the AAMR's Ad Hoc Committee on Terminology and Classification concluded its presentation and discussion of its most recent definition with this observation:

> The field of mental retardation is currently in a state of flux regarding not just a fuller under-standing of the condition of mental retardation, but also in the language and processes we use in naming, defining and classifying.... This state of flux is both frustrating and challenging. It is frustrating because it prohibits one from relying on past language, definitions, and models of mental retardation that can be a source of stability and permanence to some. However, the state is also challenging for it provides the opportunity to incorporate the current and evolv-ing understanding of the condition of mental retardation and the factors that influence the lives of people in their societies. Whether perceived from a scientific or social perspective, the condition of mental retardation is being thought of differently today throughout the world. (Ad Hoc Committee on Terminology and Classification, 2001, p. 12)

It is not yet known how AAMR's new conceptualization of mental retardation will in-fluence special education practice. A national survey of state departments of education found that the new definition had had minimal impact on changing state guidelines for identifying students with mental retardation (Denning, Chamberlain, & Polloway, 2000). In an official position statement adopted by its board of directors (Smith, 1994), CEC's Di-vision on Developmental Disabilities praised the new definition for focusing greater atten-tion on the needs of individuals instead of on degrees of deficiency residing within the person with mental retardation and for providing the field with a positive stimulus for de-bate on issues critical to persons with mental retardation. The statement notes, however, that the changes required by and the implications of the new definition are so profound that they "require the most careful consideration before they are implemented in special educa-tion practices" (p. 179).

The debate over the definition of mental retardation will surely continue. The late Burton Blatt, one of the field's most prolific, influential, and controversial figures, argued that when all is said and done mental retardation is best viewed as an administrative cate-gory. In his book, *Conquest of Mental Retardation* (1987), Blatt wrote, "Simply stated, some-one is mentally retarded when he or she is 'officially' identified as such" (p. 72).

There is discussion in the field about changing the name from *mental retardation* to an-other term. In 2002 the CEC's Division on Mental Retardation/Developmental Disabilities officially changed its name to the Division on Developmental Disabilities. Some authors have even suggested that the entire concept of mental retardation should be eliminated be-cause of the stigma and negative expectations attached to people who receive the label (cf. Smith & Mitchell, 2001b; Taylor & Blatt, 1999). (See Profiles & Perspectives, "Mental Re-tardation: Is It Time To Abandon The Myth?" on the next page.)

But regardless of the term used to identify the combination of intellectual and adaptive behavior limitations currently known as mental retardation—or even if society decides not to identify and name it—substantial challenges in learning and independence constitute a real disability for the children and adults who experience them. And helping individuals with disabilities achieve to their fullest potential is what special education is all about.

## Acceptance and Membership

Since the early 1970s, the principle of **normalization** has provided a conceptual founda-tion and touchstone for improving the life experiences of persons with mental retardation. The concept, which originated in Scandinavia, was first described in an American publica-tion by Bengt Nirje (1969) in a book published by the President's Committee on Mental Retardation. Recently, Perske (2004) reexamined Nirje's original "eight planks of normal-ization" such as a normal rhythm of the day, a normal routine of life (e.g., live in one place and work in another), a normal rhythm of the year (e.g., holidays, personal religious days,

*AAMR and CEC's Division on DD*

Council for Exceptional Children Content Standards for Beginning Teachers of Students with MR/DD: Organizations and publications in the field of MR/DD (MR9K1).

# Mental Retardation: Is It Time to Abandon The Myth?

*by J. David Smith*

Mental retardation is an inappropriate, misleading, and often harmful term that has been used to refer to a very heterogeneous group of people who have greater differences among them than similarities. I argue that it is time to abandon the term *mental retardation* and believe that the term *developmental disabilities* is a better way to describe the needs of this diverse group of people.

## THE INVENTION OF MENTAL RETARDATION

Burton Blatt (1999) once described mental retardation as an "invented disease" (p. 86). In remarks published after his death, he further described retardation as a story about a large group of people that is both unnecessary and untrue. He compared it to the invention of old age as a disease. We recognize today that the physical health of an individual cannot be described or assumed by the number of years that person has lived. According to Blatt, people have made similar assumptions about children and adults who have been aggregated under the term *mental retardation*. As usual, Blatt was ahead of his time. He went on to acknowledge that there are people with problems for whom a compassionate society must provide care and treatment. He included people who may not "read well ... or think well" in this category. "But in each instance the 'disease' is not mental retardation, but something else.... The best way to cure an invented disease is to forget it. The best way to reduce abuses of people unlucky enough to have 'caught' invented diseases is to offer no treatment, because abuse is the only treatment for an invented disease" (p. 95). While we must recognize that much compassionate care and many valiant teaching efforts have been provided to persons identified as having mental retardation, the term has also resulted in much misunderstanding of their needs and potentials.

## THE MYTH OF MENTAL RETARDATION

Trent (1994) defined *mental retardation* as a "construction whose changing meaning is shaped both by individuals who initiate and administer policies, programs and practices, and the social context to which these individuals are responding" (p. 2). He argued that the term has sometimes been used in the name of science, sometimes in the name of protecting people, and sometimes in the name of economic necessity. Even though special educators and other human-service professionals have used the term in their efforts to serve these people, mental retardation as a category has too often been used for the purpose of controlling individuals perceived to be a threat, an inconvenience, or a societal drain.

In 1961, Thomas Ssasz rocked the psychiatric world by proclaiming that a "myth of mental illness" existed which had led to misunderstanding and mistreatment of the people who were described as being mentally ill. He asserted that the medical terminology associated with the vast array of emotional and social difficulties that people may encounter in life was inaccurate and misleading. According to Ssasz, although the term *mental illness* "made good historical sense—stemming as it does from the historical identity of medicine and psychiatry—it makes no rational sense. Although mental illness might have been a useful concept in the nineteenth century, today it is scientifically worthless and socially harmful" (p. ix). Similarly, mental retardation has made historical sense as an effort to identify and serve a group of people with disabilities. Unfortunately, those disabilities have been so diverse that the term has fallen short of the intended goal of serving these people as well as they deserve.

## DISAGGREGATING MENTAL RETARDATION

In 1992, and again in 2002, the American Association on Mental Retardation delineated more than 350 causes of mental retardation (Luckasson et al., 1992, 2002). This list does not, however, take into account the varying degrees and specific types of disabilities associated with those etiologies. If these variables are added, the multiple and complex meanings of what is called mental retardation are staggering. Mental retardation is held together as a category by the notion that there is some fundamental essence to the universe of characteristics and the vastly differing needs of the people identified by the term. Clearly, however, the term has been used to describe a vast aggregation of diverse human circumstances. The only rationale for this aggregation appears to be the reasoning that the category contains people with intellectual, social, and developmental traits that make them more alike than different. This is simply not the case. Many persons called mentally retarded are more different than they are alike. A person who is described as having a need for *intermittent* support will almost certainly be more similar to a person without mental retardation than to a person who is described as having mental retardation and a *pervasive* need for support.

The authors of the 1992 AAMR manual characterized their revisions to the definition and classification of mental retardation as a paradigm shift. The shift consisted of two facets. First was a change in the conception of mental retardation from a trait existing in an individual to an expression of the interaction between a person and his environment. Second was an emphasis on the pattern of the person's needs rather than her deficits (Schalock et al., 1994). This shift was repeated and made more emphatic in the 2002 revision of the AAMR manual. These revisions have been positive changes in the conceptualization of mental retardation. In my opinion, however, another step is needed.

Paradigm shifts may be critical to the advancement and improvement of any field of endeavor. Thomas Kuhn (1962), in his classic book *The Structure of Scientific Revolutions*, defined paradigms as shared world views. He argued that shared views eventually become so strong and institutionalized that only a sudden and dramatic break from these conventional perspectives can bring on a positive revolution in thinking.

The effort to define mental retardation in a scientifically accurate manner has gone on for centuries. The effort to define it in a way that promotes greater sensitivity to the needs of people described by the term has also been continuous. A scientifically sound and socially helpful definition of the term *mental retardation* may not, however, be achievable. Perhaps the paradigm shift that is now needed is an even more dramatic one than that presented in the recent AAMR manuals. The best definition of mental retardation may well be no definition at all.

I believe it is time to admit that the term is, to use Ssasz's (1961) words, "scientifically worthless and socially harmful." It is time to face the reality that it is a manifestation of typological reasoning. The idea that the term accurately describes a *type* of person has created a false and unhelpful categorization of these people. Perhaps the plurality of the term *developmental disabilities* would more effectively describe the heterogeneity of the people who have previously been labeled as mentally retarded. It would be a more accurate term and would likely be less stigmatizing because of its generality.

Although the implications of abandoning the term for resource allocations and the provision of services must be carefully addressed, the term *mental retardation* should become an artifact of the evolution of our thinking about children and adults with developmental disabilities. The millions of people within the spectrum of developmental disabilities who have been described as mentally retarded deserve this change in the manner in which they are regarded and treated. A new term may provide an opportunity to enhance our vision of who these people are as individuals and our understanding of their rightful place in our communities.

J. David Smith is a professor of education and psychology at the University of Virginia's College at Wise. His interests include the history of mental retardation, the eugenics era, and the impact of social policy on people with disabilities. His books include *Minds Made Feeble: The Myth and Legacy of the Kallikaks, The Sterilization of Carrie Buck,* and *In Search of Better Angels: Stories of Disability in the Human Family.*

 To further your understanding of and answer reflective questions about the concepts and issues presented here, go to the Profiles & Perspectives module in Chapter 4 of the Companion Website, **www.prenhall.com/heward**.

and relaxation days are respected), a normal developmental experience of the life cycle (e.g., adults experiencing the settings and atmospheres enjoyed by typical adults), valuing individual choices (e.g., allowing the dignity and freedom to fail), and so forth.

Wolf Wolfensberger (1972), one of the first and best-known champions of normalization in the United States, wrote that the principle refers to the use of progressively more normal settings and procedures "to establish and/or maintain personal behaviors which are as culturally normal as possible" (p. 28). Normalization is not a single technique or set of procedures but an overriding philosophy. It says that persons with mental retardation should, to the greatest extent possible, be both physically and socially integrated into everyday society regardless of their degree or type of disability.

While the principle of normalization has helped individuals with mental retardation who are physically present in many school, community, and work settings today, it has not gained them acceptance and true membership. Wolfensberger (1983) has proposed the concept of *social role valorization (SRV)* as a necessary and natural extension of the normalization principle. He writes, "The most explicit and highest goal of normalization must be the creation, support, and defense of valued social roles for people who are at risk of social devaluation" (p. 234).

*Normalization and social role valorization*

Council for Exceptional Children — Content Standards for Beginning Teachers of Students with MR/DD: Trends and practices within the field of MR/DD (MR1K5) (also CC4S5).

> The key premise of SRV is that people's welfare depends extensively on the social roles they occupy: People who fill roles that are positively valued by others will generally be afforded by the latter the good things of life, but people who fill roles that are devalued by others will typically be badly treated by them. This implies that in the case of people whose life situations are very bad, and whose bad situations are bound up with occupancy of devalued roles, then if the social roles they are seen as occupying can somehow be upgraded in the eyes of perceivers, their life conditions will usually improve, and often dramatically so. (Wolfensberger, 2000, p. 105)

Perhaps the greatest current expression and extension of the normalization/SRV concept in special education can be found in the growing movement toward teaching self-determination skills to individuals with mental retardation. Self-determination involves acting as the primary agent in one's life and "making choices and decisions regarding one's quality of life free from undue influence or interference" (Wehmeyer, Kelchner, & Richards, 1996, p. 632). In his presidential address to the AAMR, Wagner (2000) offered this example of the relationship between self-determination and social role valorization:

> How do we really start to implement this dream of highly valued roles in society? One thing we need to do is begin to celebrate the people who, in fact, currently have highly valued roles. Let me tell you about some of my heroes.... there is Christina. She has big dreams. What makes Christina unique is that her dreams are really good. About 6 years ago, she was mainstreamed into a large high school. In central Louisiana. She no sooner got there than she decided that she was going to become a cheerleader. Much to our amazement, she went out for the cheerleading squad and became a cheerleader. Then, a few years later when she was a senior, Christina decided that she wanted to be Homecoming Queen. She saw no problem at all with the fact that she has Down syndrome. She was going to be the Homecoming Queen. Well, lo and behold, she ran for Homecoming Queen and won. Christina is my heroine of big dreams. She did not let her handicaps stand in the way of realizing her dreams. I think it is also a testament to that high school that they did not let her handicaps stand in the way either. (p. 442)

Among the most important things that special educators can do are helping students like Christina identify their goals and providing the instruction and supports that will enable them to pursue those goals. As support for self-determination and social role valorization grows among both educators and the public, the time draws nearer when all persons with mental retardation will experience the benefits of valued membership in integrated school, community, and employment settings.

# Tips for Beginning Teachers

## Organization Is Key
### *by Sandie Trask-Tyler*

### GET TO KNOW YOUR STUDENTS BEFORE THE SCHOOL YEAR STARTS

1. Send a welcome note to all of your students in the middle of the summer and include a picture of yourself. Highlight something they can look forward to when school starts.
2. Organize a class get-together for your students and their families before the start of school. This is a great opportunity for everyone to meet each other and a wonderful way for parents to network.

### BE PREPARED TO BUY EXTRA CLASSROOM SUPPLIES

1. Stock up on classroom supplies during the back-to-school sales in the summer.
2. Save your personal spending receipts for classroom purchases. You may be able to use these expenditures on your taxes.
3. Shop at yard sales and auctions for all types of items you can use in your classroom at a great price.

### CREATE A SYSTEM OF ORGANIZATION THAT WORKS FOR YOU

1. Label boxes, shelves, and cabinets with words and/or pictures of what belongs there to assist staff and students in locating and replacing items.
2. Create a spreadsheet of student and staff information such as phone numbers, addresses, parents' names, etc., and keep a copy at home and school for easy access.
3. Create a spreadsheet with students' school information, including date of birth, MFE due date, IEP due date, related services, etc.
4. Set up a notebook or clipboard for each student with his corresponding IEP data sheets. You can group them into the different curricular areas and even insert student work samples so all of their learning information is in one location.
5. Set up a teacher binder that includes general substitute teacher information, overall class schedule, student transportation information, copies of emergency information, drill procedures, each student's IEP and other classroom information (such as the previously mentioned spreadsheets).

## KEY TERMS AND CONCEPTS

 To print your own set of SAFMED flash cards for studying and mastering these terms, go to the Companion Website, **www.prenhall.com/heward**.

# SUMMARY

## Definition

- The definition incorporated into IDEA states that mental retardation involves both significantly subaverage general intellectual functioning and deficits in adaptive behavior manifested between birth and age 18. Intellectual functioning is usually measured with a standardized intelligence test and adaptive behavior with an observation checklist or scale.
- There are four degrees of mental retardation as classified by IQ score: mild, moderate, severe, and profound.
- AAMR's 2002 definition of mental retardation represents a shift away from conceptualizations of mental retardation as an inherent trait or permanent state of being to a description of the individual's present functioning and the environmental supports needed to improve it.
- Classification of mental retardation according to AAMR's 2002 definition is based on four levels and intensities of supports needed to improve functioning in the environments in which the individual lives: intermittent, limited, extensive, and pervasive.

## Identification and Assessment

- An intelligence (IQ) test consists of a series of questions (e.g., vocabulary, similarities), problem solving (e.g., mazes, blocks design), memory, and other tasks assumed to require certain amounts of intelligence to answer or solve correctly.
- IQ scores seem to be distributed throughout the population according to a phenomenon called the normal curve. Theoretically, about 2.3% of the population falls two or more standard deviations below the mean, which the AAMR calls "significantly subaverage."
- The IQ cutoff score of 70 is intended only as a guideline and should not be interpreted as a hard-and-fast requirement. A higher IQ score of 75 or more may be associated with mental retardation if, according to a clinician's judgment, the child exhibits deficits in adaptive behavior thought to be caused by impaired intellectual functioning.
- Because IQ tests are composed largely of verbal and academic tasks—the same things a child must master to succeed in school—they correlate highly with school achievement.
- Adaptive behavior consists of the conceptual, social, and practical skills that people need to function in their everyday lives.
- Systematic assessment of adaptive behavior is important because the adaptive skills exhibited by a person with mental retardation—as well as the nature and severity of maladaptive behaviors—are critical factors in determining the nature and degree of supports she requires for success in school, work, community, and home environments.
- Most instruments for assessing adaptive behavior consist of a series of questions answered by someone familiar with the individual.
- Measurement of adaptive behavior has proven difficult, in large part because of the relative nature of social adjustment and competence: what is considered appropriate in one situation or by one group may not be in or by another.

## Characteristics

- Children with mild mental retardation may experience substantial performance deficits only in school. Their social and communication skills may be normal or nearly so. They are likely to become independent or semi-independent adults.
- Most children with moderate mental retardation show significant developmental delays during their preschool years.

- Research has found that students with mental retardation have trouble retaining information in short-term memory.
- Students with mental retardation do not tend to use metacognitive or executive control strategies such as rehearsing and organizing information. When taught to use such strategies, their performance on memory-related and problem-solving tasks is likely to improve.
- Students with mental retardation learn at a significantly slower rate than that of typically developing children.
- Students with mental retardation often have trouble attending to relevant features of a learning task and instead may focus on distracting irrelevant stimuli. In addition, individuals with mental retardation often have difficulty sustaining attention.
- Students with mental retardation often have trouble using their new knowledge and skills in settings or situations that differ from the context in which they first learned those skills.
- Some individuals with mental retardation develop learned helplessness, a condition in which a person expects failure regardless of his efforts.
- Some students with mental retardation exhibit outer-directedness; they seem to distrust their own responses to situations and rely on others for assistance and solutions.
- Children with mental retardation have substantial deficits in adaptive behavior that take many forms and tend to occur across domains of functioning. Limitations in self-care skills and social relationships as well as behavioral excesses are common characteristics of individuals with mental retardation.

## Prevalence

- Theoretically, 2.3% of the population would score two standard deviations below the norm on IQ tests; but this does not account for adaptive behavior, the other criterion for diagnosis of mental retardation. Many experts now cite an incidence figure of approximately 1% of the total population.
- During the 2003–2004 school year, approximately 1% of the total school enrollment received special education services under the disability category of mental retardation.

## Causes and Prevention

- More than 750 causes of mental retardation have been identified.
- Etiology is unknown for most individuals with mild mental retardation. Increasing evidence, however, suggests that psychosocial disadvantage in early childhood is a major cause of mild mental retardation.
- Recent scientific advances—including genetic counseling, amniocentesis, CVS, virus vaccines, and early screening tests—are helping reduce the incidence of clinical or biologically caused retardation.
- Although early identification and intensive educational services to high-risk infants show promise, there is still no widely used technique to decrease the incidence of mental retardation caused by psychosocial disadvantage.

## Educational Approaches

- Curriculum should focus on functional skills that will help the student be successful in self-care, vocational, domestic, community, and leisure domains.
- Major components of explicit systematic instruction are task analysis, active student response, systematic feedback, transfer of stimulus control from teacher-provided cues and prompts to natural stimuli, programming for generalization and maintenance, and direct and frequent measurement.

## Educational Placement Alternatives

- Approximately 50% of students with mental retardation are educated in separate classrooms, 30% in resource rooms, and 12% in regular classrooms.
- During the early elementary grades, many students with mental retardation benefit from full or partial inclusion in regular classroom settings.
- Strategies for facilitating successful regular class placement include planning for the focus student's inclusion in the classroom through team games, collaborative learning, and group investigation projects and by directly training all students in specific skills for interacting with one another.
- The relative appropriateness of inclusion in the regular classroom may change for some students with mental retardation as they move from the elementary grades to the secondary level, when opportunities for community-based instruction in vocational and life skills are critical.
- The extent to which a student with mental retardation, like all students with disabilities, is educated in a general education classroom should be determined by the student's individual needs.

## Current Issues and Future Trends

- Changes and debate over the definition of mental retardation are likely to continue and reflect the ongoing need to better understand mental retardation in order to achieve more effective and reliable systems of identification, classification, research, and habilitation.
- The principles of normalization, social role valorization, and self-determination are important in helping individuals with mental retardation achieve acceptance and membership in society.

To check your comprehension of chapter contents, go to the Guided Review and Quiz modules in Chapter 4 of the Companion Website, **www.prenhall.com/heward**.

# LEARNING
# DISABILITIES

# Featured Teacher

### RONNI HOCHMAN SPRATT

HASTINGS MIDDLE SCHOOL
UPPER ARLINGTON, OHIO

*Education—Teaching Credentials—Experience*
- B. S., special education, State University College at Buffalo, New York, 1971
- M. A., special education, The Ohio State University, 1974
- Ohio certification in learning disabilities, K–12; emotional disturbance, K–12; developmental handicaps, K–12; reading
- 32 years of experience as special educator

Some students with learning disabilities treat their school lives like their bedrooms: they leave stuff all over the place. It might be cute and okay for a little while, but it's no way to achieve in school or live your whole life. Organizational and self-management skills are keys to a student's success in the regular curriculum. Whether or not those skills are on a student's IEP, I always show students how to get organized, help them set and focus on reachable short-term goals, and teach them some self-monitoring and self-evaluation skills.

For example, Eduardo, a new student from Venezuela, is an adorable and very friendly boy in my class. Eduardo wasn't turning in his homework in a couple of his general education classes, and his parents were covering for him. We discussed the reasons that this could not continue. He'd have to show me his work every day; and if it wasn't completed appropriately, he'd redo it during lunch in my room. He complained, which I ignored; but he complied, which I praised. In the last grading period of the year he earned his best grades ever and showed an achievement jump of at least two grade levels this year. All of his hard work is paying off; and he is taking responsibility for himself, his actions, and his education. He's started to take off.

***My Students and Classroom***    Sixteen seventh and eighth graders spend time in my cross-categorical resource room every day, Eduardo among them. Eight students have learning disabilities, and the others have a variety of impairments and conditions: Tourette's syndrome, attention-deficit/hyperactivity disorder (ADHD), Asperger syndrome, and traumatic brain injury. Our school day consists of nine 42-minute periods. Students come and go throughout the day and are in the resource room for as few as one or as many as five periods. Most students are in the room for two or three periods each day, where they receive individual and small-group instruction in reading, writing, math, and organizational and self-control skills.

I believe it's important to create a physical and social environment where students like Eduardo feel safe and willing to take risks with learning. This is a place where there is mutual respect and the uniqueness of each individual is valued. The first thing my students learn is that there are high academic and behavioral standards in my classroom, for them and for me. These standards

## Focus Questions

- Why has the concept of learning disabilities proven so difficult to define?

- Do most students who are identified as learning disabled have a true disability? Or are they just low achievers or victims of poor instruction?

- What are the most important skills for an elementary-age student with learning disabilities to master? A secondary student?

- How do basic academic skills and learning strategies relate to each other?

- Should all students with learning disabilities be educated in the regular classroom?

are clearly defined, and the students know exactly what's expected each day. And although these high standards are ever-present, the students also know it's okay to make mistakes in my classroom.

I emphasize organizational skills, self-advocacy, and personal responsibility. A typical day in my classroom begins when students first enter the room, show me their plan books, and turn in any work that is due. Every day we write down the assignments for my class, and I advise the students to do the same for their other classes as well. Then students get started on their work. Some do peer tutoring for vocabulary building, others begin writing on the computers, and several work with me on a lesson from the SRA Corrective Reading program. The students self-evaluate their work as much as possible.

Each student sets a weekly accuracy or fluency goal for every subject or skill area. There are graphs all over the room, and the students chart their performance every day. Each student has a graph for the number of words written in his journal, another graph for vocabulary words learned in peer tutoring, a graph for scores on corrective reading worksheets, and a homework graph. Students who turn in all of their homework and in-class assignments Monday through Thursday are not assigned homework over the weekend. This is a practice that the students and I enjoy equally!

***Connecting with General Education***     I tell my students it's their job to find out what each of their general education teachers expects. I say, think of your teacher as an employer or boss that you want to please. If that teacher sees you trying, she'll help you. But if she sees you unprepared, slouching, and talking in class, she's much less likely to go out of her way in an already busy and hectic class.

At the beginning of the year, every student writes a letter to each of her general education teachers. This really helps the special education students get off to a good start in the general education classroom. Students use the letters to introduce themselves and their families, describe their interests and hobbies, and state what they hope to accomplish in each class during the year. The students must also articulate their special educational needs and describe how they think the teacher can help them learn and be successful. The general education teachers tell me that these letters ease their concerns and give them some information with which to begin a relationship with the students. During the first week of school we work on writing, editing, and revising these letters in my classroom. When we are all satisfied with our work, the students print their letters, sign them, and then deliver them to the appropriate teachers.

***Advice for Someone Considering a Career in Special Education***     To be a successful special educator, you have to be excited, enthusiastic, and passionate about the profession of teaching and your students. Being a special education teacher is too important and too difficult to do well if you're not committed. (And I'd say the same thing to anyone considering a career as a general education teacher.) Spend as much time in schools and classrooms as you can, and look for every opportunity to work with students with special needs. If you find out that teaching isn't what you thought or wanted it to be, that's fine. If you can't wait to get back in the classroom each time you leave—well, most days anyway—then pursue it with passion.

After you become a licensed teacher, stay interested and active in your profession. Find a good mentor who will talk with you about curriculum and instruction and who you can come to with problems or concerns. Attend in-service workshops and, later, help plan and present them. One of the best ways to stay current and active and to learn from others is to attend and present at conferences and teacher development programs.

Being multi-task-oriented is key—you have to be able to do many things at the same time. I'm sure every special educator knows this to be true; but if you're not organized and can't time-share on multiple tasks, you will not stay in the field for very long.

You hear a lot about teachers getting burned out. I believe that some of the teachers who state burnout as the reason they're leaving the classroom were never really that happy to be there in the first place. If you've never been lit, you can't be burned out!

To see some of the "Dear Teacher" letters by Ms. Spratt's students, visit the Teacher Feature module in Chapter 5 of the Companion Website, **www.prenhall.com/heward**

**What I Like Most about Being a Special Educator**    I recently trained my 50th student teacher, Nikia Bryant. The photo on pages 1 and 209 shows Nikia working with some of my students. There's nothing more rewarding for me than helping a new teacher get started on his or her career. The fact that there is almost always a student teacher or field-experience student in my classroom means I have to be able to explain and defend everything I do. So I'm always thinking about what I'm doing and why I'm doing it, which makes me a better teacher.

For the past 6 years, I've served as a clinical educator for The Ohio State University's special education program, spending one day every other week observing student teachers. Not only does this give me the opportunity to work with a larger number of preservice teachers, but I get to observe and pick up ideas from the cooperating teachers in all those different classrooms. The day I stop learning in this job is the day I'll give it up. I can honestly say that I am as excited about what I do now as when I began more than 30 years ago.

B y the late 1950s most public schools had established special education programs (or at least offered some type of special service) for children with mental retardation, students with physical disabilities, children with sensory impairments, and those with emotional and behavioral disorders. But there remained a group of children who were having serious learning problems at school yet did not fit into the existing categories of exceptionality. They did not appear to be handicapped. The children seemed physically intact, yet they were unable to learn certain basic skills and subjects at school. In searching for help for their children, parents turned to physicians and psychologists. (Remember, the schools had no programs for these children.) Understandably, these professionals viewed the children from the vantage points of their respective disciplines. As a result, terms such as *brain damage, minimal brain dysfunction, neurological impairment, perceptual handicap, dyslexia,* and *aphasia* were often used to describe or account for the children's learning problems. Many of these terms are still used today because a variety of disciplines continue to influence the field of learning disabilities.

The term *learning disabilities* was coined by Samuel Kirk in a 1963 address to a group of parents whose children were experiencing serious difficulties in learning to read, were hyperactive, or could not solve math problems. The parents liked the term and that very evening voted to form the Association for Children with Learning Disabilities. Today, the organization's name is the Association for Children and Adults with Learning Disabilities (ACALD), and it is a powerful advocacy group for persons with learning disabilities. In 1975 *learning disabilities* was included as a special education category in IDEA.

No area of special education has experienced as much rapid growth, extreme interest, and continuing controversy as learning disabilities. The number of children identified as learning disabled has nearly tripled since the passage of IDEA, making this category the largest in special education and fueling an ongoing debate on the nature of the learning disability concept. Some believe the increase in the number of children identified as learning disabled indicates the true extent of the disability. Others contend that too many low achievers—children without a disability who are simply doing poorly in school—have been improperly identified as learning disabled, placing a severe strain on the limited resources available to serve those students challenged by a true disability.

There is considerable confusion and disagreement among professionals and parents on even the most basic question: what is a learning disability? In some ways, learning disabilities bring out both the worst and the best that special education has to offer. Learning disabilities has served as a breeding ground for fads and miracle treatments ("New Vitamin and Diet Regimen Cures Learning Disabilities!"). At the same time, some of the most innovative

To better understand the topics that will be covered in this chapter, go to the Essential Concepts and Chapter at a Glance modules in Chapter 5 of the Companion Website, **www.prenhall.com/heward**

*ACALD*

 Council for Exceptional Children    Content Standards for Beginning Teachers of Students with LD: Professional organizations and sources of information relevant to the field of LD (LD9K2).

teachers and scholars in special education have devoted their careers to learning disabilities. And many instructional strategies first developed for students with learning disabilities have influenced and benefited the entire field of education.

# DEFINITIONS

Numerous definitions for learning disabilities have been proposed, but none has been universally accepted. The two definitions that have had the most influence are the federal definition in IDEA and a definition proposed by the National Joint Committee on Learning Disabilities.

## The IDEA Definition

*IDEA definition of LD*

Council for
Exceptional
Children     Content
Standards for
Beginning Teachers—Common
Core: Issues in definition and
identification of individuals with
exceptional learning needs
(CC1K5).

In IDEA, **learning disabilities** is defined as follows:

*In General*—The term "specific learning disability" means a disorder in 1 or more of the basic psychological processes involved in understanding or in using language, spoken or written, which disorder may manifest itself in an imperfect ability to listen, think, speak, read, write, spell, or to do mathematical calculations.

*Disorders Included*—Such term includes such conditions as perceptual disabilities, brain injury, minimal brain dysfunction, dyslexia, and developmental aphasia.

*Disorders Not Included*—Such term does not include a learning problem that is primarily the result of visual, hearing, or motor disabilities, of mental retardation, of emotional disturbance, or of environmental, cultural, or economic disadvantage. (Individuals with Disabilities Education Improvement Act of 2004, H.R. 1350, Sec. 602[30])

## The NJCLD Definition

The National Joint Committee on Learning Disabilities (NJCLD), a group composed of official representatives from 10 professional organizations involved with students with learning disabilities, believes that the federal definition of learning disabilities contains several inherent weaknesses (Myers & Hammill, 1990):

1. *Exclusion of adults.* Learning disabilities can occur at all ages, and the IDEA definition refers only to school-age children.
2. *Reference to basic psychological processes.* Use of the phrase "basic psychological processes" has generated extensive and perhaps unnecessary debate on how to teach students with learning disabilities; and how to teach is a curricular issue, not a definitional one.
3. *Inclusion of spelling as a learning disability.* Because spelling can be subsumed under "written expression," it is redundant and should be eliminated from the definition.
4. *Inclusion of obsolete terms.* Inclusion of terms such as *dyslexia, minimal brain dysfunction, perceptual impairments,* and *developmental aphasia,* which historically have proven difficult to define, only adds confusion to the definition.
5. *Wording of the exclusion clause.* The final clause in the IDEA definition suggests that learning disabilities cannot occur along with other disabilities. A more accurate statement, according to the NJCLD, is that a person may have a learning disability along with another disability but not *because of* another disability.

In response to these problems with the federal definition, the NJCLD proposed the following definition:

Learning disabilities is a general term that refers to a heterogeneous group of disorders manifested by significant difficulties in the acquisition and use of listening, speaking, reading, writing, reasoning, or mathematical abilities.

These disorders are intrinsic to the individual and presumed to be due to central nervous system dysfunction, and may appear across the life span. Problems in self-regulatory behaviors, social perception, and social interaction may exist with learning disabilities but do not themselves constitute a learning disability.

Although learning disabilities may occur concomitantly with other handicapping conditions (for example, sensory impairment, mental retardation, serious emotional disturbance) or with extrinsic influences (such as cultural differences, insufficient or inappropriate instruction), they are not the result of those conditions or influences. (NJCLD, 1989, p. 1)

## Operationalizing the Federal Definition

A survey of all 50 states found that most of them use the IDEA definition of learning disabilities or some variation of it (Mercer, Jordan, Allsopp, & Mercer, 1995). When operationalizing the definition for the purpose of identifying students with learning disabilities, most states and school districts require that three criteria be met:

1. A severe discrepancy between the student's intellectual ability and academic achievement
2. An exclusion criterion: the student's difficulties are not the result of another known condition that can cause learning problems
3. A need for special education services

*IQ-Achievement Discrepancy.* Children with learning disabilities exhibit an unexpected difference between general ability and achievement—a discrepancy that would not be predicted by the student's general intellectual ability (Kavale & Forness, 2000). Children who are having minor or temporary difficulties in learning should not be identified as learning disabled. According to federal guidelines that accompanied the original IDEA, only children with a true disability, as evidenced by a "severe discrepancy between achievement and intellectual ability," were to be identified as learning disabled (U.S. Office of Education, 1977b, p. 65083).

The federal government proposed several mathematical formulas for determining a severe discrepancy. All of the proposed formulas were eventually rejected, and the final rules and regulations for IDEA did not contain a specific definition of and formula for determining a severe discrepancy. This left states to find their own criteria for implementing the definition of learning disabilities. Although the federal definition no longer mentions "discrepancy," the most common practice for identifying children with learning disabilities is to determine if a severe discrepancy exists between their expected and actual achievement. This involves comparing a student's score on an IQ test with his score on a standardized achievement test. While such a comparison seems simple on the surface, in practice it is fraught with problems (Fletcher et al., 2002; Fuchs, Fuchs, Mathes, Lipsey, & Roberts, 2002; Gresham, 2002; Kavale, 2002).

Many students underachieve academically. How is unexpected underachievement caused by a "hidden disability" to be distinguished from underachievement that might result from factors such as poor motivation or faulty instruction? Confusion and disagreement about exactly how a severe discrepancy should be determined have led to widely differing procedures for identifying and classifying students as learning disabled (Kavale, 2002; Ysseldyke, 2001). There is great disparity among states and local school districts in how they operationalize the definition (MacMillan & Siperstein, 2002). As a result, the percentage of children identified

*Ability-achievement discrepancy*

Council for Exceptional Children — Content Standards for Beginning Teachers of Students with LD: Philosophies, theories, models, and issues related to individuals with LD (LD1K2).

Students with learning disabilities have significant learning problems that cannot be explained as primarily the result of another recognized disability or lack of opportunity to learn due to environmental, cultural, or economic conditions.

as learning disabled ranges across states from a low of 2.0% of the total school-age population in Kentucky to 6.2% in Rhode Island (U.S. Department of Education, 2004).

*Exclusion.* The IDEA definition of learning disabilities is meant to identify students with significant learning problems that are not "primarily the result" of other conditions that can impede learning, such as another recognized disability or lack of opportunity to learn due to environmental, cultural, or economic conditions. The word *primarily* in the definition recognizes that learning disabilities can coexist with other disabilities; but when that is considered the case, the student typically receives services under the other disability category.

*Need for Special Education.* Students with learning disabilities show specific and severe learning problems despite normal educational efforts and therefore need specially designed instruction that is tailored (i.e., specially designed) to meet their unique needs (Simmons, Kame'enui, & Chard, 1998). This criterion is meant to avoid the overidentification of children who have not had the opportunity to learn. Such children should progress normally as soon as they receive typically effective instruction at a curricular level appropriate to their current skills.

# CHARACTERISTICS

To describe the various categories of exceptionality, observers typically list the physical and psychological characteristics often exhibited by the individuals who make up that group. For example, early in the field's history a task force commissioned to identify the characteristics of children with learning disabilities (the term *minimal brain dysfunction* was used to describe these children at that time) found that 99 separate characteristics were reported in the literature (Clements, 1966). The inherent danger in such lists is the tendency to assume, or to look for, each of those characteristics in all children considered in the category. This danger is especially troublesome with learning disabilities because the category includes children who exhibit a wide range of learning, social, and emotional problems. In fact, Mercer and Pullen (2005) suggest that it is theoretically possible for an individual with learning disabilities to exhibit one of more than 500,000 combinations of cognitive or socioemotional problems.

Learning disabilities are associated with problems in listening, reasoning, memory, attention, selecting and focusing on relevant stimuli, and the perception and processing of visual and/or auditory information. These perceptual and cognitive processing difficulties are assumed to be the underlying reason why students with learning disabilities experience one or more of the following characteristics: reading problems, deficits in written language, underachievement in math, poor social skills, attention deficits and hyperactivity, and behavioral problems.

## Reading Problems

Difficulty with reading is by far the most common characteristic of students with learning disabilities. It is estimated that 90% of all children identified as learning disabled are referred for special education services because of reading problems (Kavale & Forness, 2000). Some professionals now believe the term *learning disabilities,* which encompasses so many different types of learning problems, hinders our understanding of the causes, developmental courses, and outcomes of the reading problems experienced by many children (Fletcher et al., 2002). They recommend developing specific definitions and research bases for each type of learning disability (e.g., reading disabilities, math disabilities).

Evidence suggests that specific reading disability, also called dyslexia, is a persistent deficit, not simply a developmental lag in linguistic or basic reading skills (Lyon, 1995). The International Dyslexia Association defines **dyslexia** as

> a specific learning disability that is neurobiological in origin. It is characterized by difficulties with accurate and/or fluent word recognition and by poor spelling and decoding abilities. These difficulties typically result from a deficit in the phonological component of language that is often unexpected in relation to other cognitive abilities and the provision of effective classroom instruction. (Lyon, Shaywitz, & Shaywitz, 2003, p. 2)

Children who fail to learn to read by the first grade tend to fall farther and farther behind their peers, not only in reading but in general academic achievement as well. For example, longitudinal studies have found that 74% of children who are diagnosed as learning disabled because of reading problems remain disabled in the ninth grade (Fletcher et al., 1994; Stanovich & Siegel, 1994).

Recent research has revealed a great deal about the fundamental nature of children's reading disabilities and the type of instruction most likely to prevent and remediate reading problems (Jenkins & O'Conner, 2002; Kame'enui, Good, & Harn, 2005; National Reading Panel, 2000; Smith, Baker, & Oudeans, 2001). In summarizing this research, Torgesen and Wagner (1998) state that (1) the "most severe reading problems of children with learning disabilities lie at the word, rather than the text, level of processing" (i.e., inability to accurately and fluently decode single words), and (2) the most common cognitive limitation of these children involves a dysfunction in the awareness of the phonological structure of words in oral language (p. 226). (To learn what research tells us about how to prevent reading disabilities in young children, see Profiles & Perspectives, "Six Principles for Early Reading Instruction," later in this chapter.)

Recent research suggests that children with severe reading disabilities, particularly those who are resistant to interventions effective for the majority of struggling readers, may share a second processing problem in addition to deficits in phonological awareness. Many children and adults with dyslexia show a significant deficit in visual naming speed (the ability to rapidly name visually presented stimuli) compared to a typical reader (Lovett, Steinbach, & Frijters, 2000; Wolf, Bowers, & Biddle, 2000). When asked to state the names of visually presented material such as letters, many individuals with reading disabilities have difficulty rapidly retrieving and stating the names of the letters, even though they know the letter names. The term *double deficit hypothesis* is used to describe children who exhibit underlying deficits in phonological awareness and rapid naming speed (Wolf & Bowers, 2000).

Of course, comprehension is the goal of reading. And comprehension lies at the phrase, sentence, paragraph, and story level, not in identifying single words. But the inability to rapidly identify words impairs comprehension in at least two ways. First, faster readers encounter more words and idea units, thereby having the opportunity to comprehend more. Second, assuming that both word recognition and comprehension consume finite cognitive processing resources, a struggling reader who devotes more processing resources to identify words has "fewer cognitive processing resources ... available for comprehension. The less efficient word reading of students with reading disabilities overloads working memory and undermines reading comprehension" (Jenkins & O'Conner, 2001, pp. 1–2).

*Dyslexia/reading disabilities*

Council for Exceptional Children — Content Standards for Beginning Teachers—Common Core: Educational implications of characteristics of various exceptionalities (CC2K2).

*Phonological awareness*

Council for Exceptional Children — Content Standards for Beginning Teachers of Students with LD: Effects of phonological awareness on the reading abilities of individuals with LD (LD3K2).

*Comprehension and beginning reading instruction*

Council for Exceptional Children — Content Standards for Beginning Teachers of Students with LD: Relationships among reading instruction methods and LD (LD7K1) (also LD3K3).

Difficulty with reading is by far the most common characteristic of students with learning disabilities.

# Six Principles for Early Reading Instruction

### by Bonnie Grossen

Extensive research by the National Institute of Child Health and Human Development (NICHD) over the past 30 years has produced more than 2,000 peer-reviewed journal articles about early reading acquisition and reading difficulties. (See Lyon [1995] and National Reading Panel [2000] for a review.) Six key principles of effective beginning reading instruction can be derived from this growing body of highly replicable scientific findings.

1. *Begin teaching phonemic awareness directly in kindergarten.* Phonemes are the individual sounds in words that make a difference in meaning if changed. Many children and adults who cannot read are not aware of phonemes. Children and adults who can read are aware of phonemes. A child is phonemically aware if she can do some of these things (Simmons, Kame'enui, Coyne, & Chard, 2002):

   - *Phoneme deletion.* What word would be left if the /k/ sound were taken away from "cat"?
   - *Word-to-word matching.* Do "pen" and "pipe" begin with the same sound?
   - *Blending.* What word would we have if you put these sounds together: /s/, /a/, /t/?
   - *Sound isolation.* What is the first sound in "rose"?
   - *Phoneme segmentation.* What sounds do you hear in the word "hot"?
   - *Phoneme counting.* How many sounds do you hear in the word "cake"?
   - *Odd word out.* What word starts with a different sound: "bag," "nine," "beach," "bike"?
   - *Sound-to-word matching.* Is there a /k/ sound in "bike"?

   If phonemic awareness does not develop by age 5 or 6, it is unlikely to develop later without instruc-

Explicit instruction of letter–phoneme relationships prevents reading problems better than encouraging children to figure out the sounds for the letters by giving clues.

tion. In other words, don't wait for this crucial reading readiness skill to develop. Phonemic awareness activities such as rhyming games have a positive effect on reading acquisition and spelling for nonreaders. Teachers should start teaching phonemic awareness before beginning instruction in letter-phoneme relationships and continue phonemic awareness activities while teaching the letter-phoneme relationships.

2. *Teach each letter-phoneme relationship explicitly.* Only about 40 to 50 letter-sound relationships are necessary to read. Figure A shows the 48 most regular letter-phoneme relationships. Telling children explicitly what single sound a given letter or letter combination makes prevents reading problems better than encouraging children to figure

| | | | |
|---|---|---|---|
| **a** as in "fat" | **i** as in "sit" | **r** | **er** as in "fern" |
| **g** as in "goat" | **c** as in "cat" | **o-e** as in "pole" | **qu** as in "quick" |
| **v** | **w** as in "well" | **z** | **ai** as in "maid" |
| **m** | **f** | **ch** as in "chip" | **ay** as in "hay" |
| **l** | **b** | **ou** as in "cloud" | **sh** as in "shop" |
| **e** | **j** | **kn** as in "know" | **ar** as in "car" |
| **t** | **a-e** as in "cake" | **ea** as in "beat" | **igh** as in "high" |
| **h** | **n** | **oy** as in "toy" | **th** as in "thank" |
| **u-e** as in "use" | **i-e** as in "pipe" | **oa** as in "boat" | **au** as in "haul" |
| **s** | **d** | **ee** as in "need" | **ew** as in "shrewd" |
| **u** | **k** | **ph** as in "phone" | **ir** as in "first" |
| **p** | **y** as in "yuck" | **oi** as in "boil" | **aw** as in "lawn" |

out the sounds for the letters by giving clues. Many children have difficulty figuring out the individual letter-phoneme correspondences if they hear them only in the context of words and word parts. Therefore, phonemes should be separated from words for instruction. For example, the teacher shows the children the letter "m" and says, "This letter says /mmm/."

A new phoneme and other phonemes the children have learned should be practiced for about 5 minutes each day in isolation. The rest of the lesson should use these phonemes in words and stories composed of only the letter-phoneme relationships the children have learned in isolation up to that point.

3. *Teach frequent, highly regular letter-sound relationships systematically.* To teach systematically means coordinating the introduction of the letter-phoneme relationships with the material the children are asked to read. The words and stories should be composed of only the letter-phoneme relationships the children have learned. The order of the introduction of letter-phoneme relationships should be planned to allow reading material composed of meaningful words and stories as soon as possible. For example, if the first three letter-phoneme relationships the children learn are /a/, /b/, /c/, the only real word the children can read is "cab." But if the first three letter-phoneme relationships are /m/, /a/, /s/, the children can read "am," "Sam," "mass," "ma' am."

4. *Show children exactly how to sound out words.* After children have learned two or three letter-phoneme relationships, teach them how to blend the sounds into words. Show them how to move sequentially from left to right through spellings as they sound out each word. Every day practice blending words composed of only the letter-phoneme relationships the children have learned.

5. *Give children connected, decodable text to practice the letter-phoneme relationships.* Children need extensive practice in applying their knowledge of letter-sound relationships to reading. The most effective integration of phonics and reading occurs with *decodable text*—text composed of words that use the letter-phoneme relationships the children have learned to that point and a limited number of sight words that have been systematically taught. As the children learn more letter-phoneme relationships, the texts become more sophisticated.

Texts that are less decodable do not integrate phonological knowledge with actual reading. For example, the first sentence children read in one meaning-based program with an unintegrated phonics component was "The dog is up." The sound-letter relationships the children had learned up to this point were /d/, /m/, /s/, /r/, /t/. By applying their phonics knowledge, the children could only read "_____ d_____ _____ _____." But if children have learned /a/, /s/, /m/, /b/, /t/, /h/, /f/, /g/, /i/, they can read "Sam has a big fist." The sentence is 100% decodable because the phonics component has been integrated properly into the child's real reading.

Text that is less decodable requires children to use prediction or context to figure out words. Although prediction is valuable in comprehension for predicting the next event or predicting an outcome, research indicates that it is not useful in word recognition. Consider the following sample of authentic text by Jack London. One child was able to decode approximately 80% of the text; the parts he was unable to decode accurately are omitted.

He had never seen dogs fight as these w_____ish c_____ f_____t, and his first ex_____ t_____t him an unf_____able l_____n. It is

true, it was a vi_____ ex_____, else he would
not have lived to pr_____it by it. Curly was the
v_____. They were camped near the log store,
where she, in her friend_____ way, made
ad_____ to a husky dog the size of a full-_____
wolf, th_____ not half so large as _____he.
_____ere was no w_____ing, only a leap in like
a flash, a met_____ clip of teeth, a leap out
equal_____ swift, and Curly's face was ripped
open from eye to jaw.

The use of predictable text rather than decodable text might allow children to use prediction to figure out a passage. However, the strategy
would not transfer to real reading, as the London
passage demonstrates. Predictable text gives children false success. While such success may motivate many children, ultimately they will not be
successful readers if they rely on text predictabil-
ity to read.

6. *Use interesting stories to develop language comprehension.*   Research does not rule out the use of interesting, authentic stories to develop language
comprehension. But it does recommend not using
these stories as reading material for nonreaders.
Teacher-read stories play an important role in
building children's oral language comprehension,
which ultimately affects their reading comprehension. Story-based activities should be structured to
build comprehension skills, not decoding skills.

Using real stories to develop comprehension
should be balanced with the decoding instruction
described in the first five principles. While children are learning to decode, instruction for comprehension and instruction for decoding should
be conducted separately; but both types of instruction should occur. In other words, balance
but don't mix. A common misconception is that
the teacher should embed instruction of letter-

phoneme relationships in the context of real
stories. This mixture of decoding and comprehension instruction in the same instructional activity is clearly less effective, even when the
decoding instruction is fairly structured (Foorman, Francis, Fletcher, Schatschneider, & Mehta,
1998; Torgesen, Wagner, & Rashotte, 1997).

During the early stages of reading acquisition, children's oral language comprehension level
is much higher than their reading comprehension
level. The stories teachers read to children to build
their comprehension should be geared to their oral
language comprehension level. The material used
to build children's decoding should be geared to
their decoding skills, with attention to meaning.
Although decodable text can be meaningful and
engaging, it will not build children's comprehension skills or teach them new vocabulary to the
extent that might be needed. Comprehension
strategies and new vocabulary should be taught
using orally presented stories and texts that are
more sophisticated than the early decodable text
the children read. The teacher should read these
stories to the children and discuss the meaning
with them. After the children become fluent
decoders, they can apply these comprehension
strategies to their own reading.

Bonnie Grossen is director of the Center for Applied Research in Education at the University of Oregon. Her interests include identifying the
best interventions for solving educational problems, especially in the
areas of reading and science instruction, critical thinking, and problem
solving for diverse learners.

To further your understanding of and answer reflective
questions about the concepts and strategies presented
here, go to the Profiles & Perspectives module in Chapter 5
of the Companion Website, **www.prenhall.com/heward**.

## Written Language Deficits

*Written language deficits*

Council for
Exceptional
Children   Content
Standards for
Beginning Teachers—Common
Core: Educational implications of
characteristics of various
exceptionalities (CC2K2) (also
LD3K3).

Many students with learning disabilities have problems with writing and spelling. When
compared to their peers without disabilities, students with learning disabilities perform significantly lower across most written expression tasks, especially vocabulary, grammar,
punctuation, and spelling (Newcomer & Barenbaum, 1991). Some students have a specific
disability with written language. For example, Figure 5.1 shows the story written by a 10-
year-old student when shown an illustration of prehistoric cavemen. Sean's oral reading of
his story reveals a huge disparity between his written and oral language abilities.

Compounding the weak language base that many students with learning disabilities
bring to the writing task is an approach to the writing process that involves minimal planning, effort, and metacognitive control (Englert et al., 1991; Graham & Harris, 1993). Many
of these students use a "retrieve-and-write" approach in which they retrieve from immediate memory "whatever seems appropriate and write it down" (De La Paz & Graham, 1997,

**FIGURE 5.1** Written language sample from a 10-year-old student with learning disabilities

| Sean's Written Story | Sean's Oral Reading of His Story |
| --- | --- |
| A loge tine ago they atene a cosnen they head to geatthere on fesee o One day tere were sane evesedbeats all gaseraned tesene in cladesn they hard a fest for 2 meanes. | A long time ago there were ancient cave men. They had to get their own food. One day there were some wildebeests. They all gathered them and killed them. They had a feast for two months. |

*Source:* Courtesy of Timothy E. Heron, The Ohio State University.

p. 295). They seldom use the self-regulation and self-assessment strategies of competent writers: setting a goal or plan to guide their writing, organizing their ideas, drafting, self-assessing, and rewriting. As a result, they produce poorly organized compositions containing a few poorly developed ideas (Sexton, Harris, & Graham, 1998).

Fortunately, the writing and spelling skills of most students with learning disabilities can be improved through strategy instruction, frequent opportunities to practice writing, and systematic feedback (Alber & Walshe, 2004; Goddard & Heron, 1998; Graham & Harris, 2003; Marchisan & Alber, 2001; Scott & Vitale, 2003; Williams, 2002). For example, Figure 5.2 shows the improvements in the writing of a seventh grader with learning disabilities after instruction and practice with software programs with speech feedback and word prediction components (Johnston, 1994a, 1994b).

## Math Underachievement

Numerical reasoning and calculation pose major problems for many students with learning disabilities. Students with learning disabilities perform lower than normally achieving children with every type of arithmetic problem at every grade level (Cawley, Parmar, Foley, Salmon, & Roy, 2001). Deficits in retrieving number facts and solving story problems are

**FIGURE 5.2** Journal entries written by a seventh-grade student with learning disabilities, before and after instruction and practice with software programs with speech feedback and word prediction components

**November 21**
Prompt: Describe your idea of the "ideal" thanksgiving dinner

MY FAVORITE FOOD IS A GRILL HOG IN A PUMPKIN IN A ROAST HAM IN A MAYBE A TURKEY my favorite DESSERT food strawberry pie THE END

**February 27**
Prompt: Describe your favorite clock

The clock that I have it is very old it was the first clock that my grandpa had it run off of current and it might go to the time it will go off in a little bird will comes at of the box. The box look like a house in it has a to pendulums on the bottom of the house inside of the house it has people in it. On the otside it has to door on it in it has to windows the color is color is brown on the top of the clock it is black.

*Source:* From Williams, S. C. (2002). How speech-feedback and word-prediction software can help students write. *Teaching Exceptional Children, 34*(3), 76. Used by permission.

Caitlin's daily session in the "writing room" is spent practicing, self-evaluating, and self-editing the specific writing skills identified on her IEP.

*Social, attention, and behavioral problems*

Council for Exceptional Children    Content Standards for Beginning Teachers of Students with LD: Psychological, social, and emotional characteristics of individuals with LD (LD2K3) (also CC2K2).

particularly evident (Jordan & Hanich, 2000; Ostad, 1998). The math competence of students with learning disabilities progresses about 1 year for every 2 years in school, and the skills of many children plateau by age 10 or 12 (Cawley, Parmar, Yan, & Miller, 1998).

Given these difficulties, it is not surprising that more than 50% of students with learning disabilities have IEP goals in math (Kavale & Reese, 1992). As with reading and writing, explicit, systematic instruction that provides guided, meaningful practice with feedback usually improves the math performance of students with learning disabilities (e.g., Fuchs & Fuchs, 2003; Gagnon & Maccini, 2001; Owen & Fuchs, 2002; Marsh & Cooke, 1996; Witzel, Mercer, & Miller, 2003).

## Social Skills Deficits

After reviewing 152 different studies, Kavale and Forness (1996) concluded that about 75% of students with learning disabilities exhibit deficits in social skills. Poor social skills often lead to rejection, low social status, fewer positive interactions with teachers, difficulty making friends, and loneliness—all of which are experienced by many students with learning disabilities regardless of classroom placement (Haager & Vaughn, 1995; Ochoa & Palmer, 1995; Pavri & Monda-Amaya, 2000). The poor social skills of students with learning disabilities may be due to inability to perceive emotions of others, specifically nonverbal affective expressions (Most & Greenbank, 2000).

Some students with learning disabilities, however, experience no problems getting along with their peers and teachers. For example, Sabornie and Kauffman (1986) reported no significant difference in the sociometric standing of 46 learning disabled high school students and 46 peers without disabilities. Moreover, they discovered that some of the students with learning disabilities enjoyed socially rewarding experiences in inclusive classrooms.

One interpretation of these contradictory findings is that social competence and peer acceptance are not characteristics of learning disabilities but outcomes of the different social climates created by teachers, peers, parents, and others with whom students with learning disabilities interact (Vaughn, McIntosh, Schumm, Haager, & Callwood, 1993). Researchers have begun to identify the types of problems experienced by children with learning disabilities who are ranked low in social acceptance and to discover instructional arrangements that promote the social status of students with learning disabilities in the regular classroom (Bryan, 1997; Court & Givon, 2003; Vaughn, Elbaum, & Schumm, 1996).

## Attention Problems and Hyperactivity

Some students with learning disabilities have difficulty attending to a task and/or display high rates of purposeless movement (hyperactivity). Children who consistently exhibit this combination of behavioral traits may be diagnosed as having attention-deficit/hyperactivity disorder (ADHD). ADHD is described in some detail in Chapter 11.

## Behavioral Problems

Some students with learning disabilities display behavioral problems in the classroom. Research has consistently found a higher-than-normal rate of behavioral problems among students with learning disabilities (Cullinan, 2002). In a study of 790 students enrolled in K–12 learning disabilities programs in Indiana, the percentage of students with behavioral problems (15%) remained consistent across grade levels (McLeskey, 1992). Although these data definitely show increased behavioral problems among children with learning disabilities, the relationships between the students' behavior problems and academic difficulties are not known. In other words, we do not know whether the academic deficits or the behavioral problems cause the other difficulty. And it is important to note that many children with learning disabilities exhibit no behavioral problems at all.

Regardless of the interrelationships of these characteristics, teachers and other caregivers responsible for planning educational programs for students with learning disabilities need skills in dealing with social and behavioral difficulties as well as academic deficits. Some of these important teaching skills are described in Chapter 6.

## The Defining Characteristic

Although students who receive special education under the learning disabilities category are an extremely heterogeneous group, it is important to remember that the fundamental, defining characteristic of students with learning disabilities is specific and significant achievement deficits in the presence of adequate overall intelligence.

The difference between what students with learning disabilities "are expected to do and what they can do ... grows larger and larger" over time (Deshler, Schumaker, & Lenz, 2001, p. 97). The performance gap becomes especially noticeable and handicapping in the middle and secondary grades, when the academic growth of many students with disabilities plateaus. By the time they reach high school, students with learning disabilities are the lowest of the low achievers, performing below the 10th percentile in reading, written language, and math (Hock, Schumaker, & Deshler, 1999).

The difficulties experienced by children with learning disabilities—especially for those who cannot read at grade level—are substantial and pervasive and usually last across the life span (Price, Field, & Patton, 2003). The tendency to think of learning disabilities as a "mild" disability erroneously supports "the notion that a learning disability is little more than a minor inconvenience rather than the serious, life-long condition it often is [and] detracts from the real needs of these students" (Hallahan, 1998, p. 4).

*Academic achievement of students with LD*

Council for Exceptional Children — Content Standards for Beginning Teachers—Common Core: Educational implications of characteristics of various exceptionalities (CC2K2) (also LD3K3).

## PREVALENCE

Learning disabilities is by far the largest of all special education categories. During the 2003–2004 school year, 2.8 million students ages 6 to 21 received special education under the specific learning disabilities category (U.S. office of Special Education, 2004). This figure represents 47% of all school-age children with disabilities and means that about 5 of every 100 students in the United States have a learning disability. Males with learning disabilities outnumber females by a 3-to-1 ratio across grade levels.

The number of students identified with learning disabilities has grown tremendously since the passage of IDEA. The current number is triple the number of students with learning disabilities who received special education in 1976–1977, the first year the federal government reported such data. Swanson (2000) notes that the rising incidence of children with learning disabilities might be considered an epidemic. Each year, approximately 120,000 additional students are identified with learning disabilities, a number equal to all Americans who contracted AIDS, hepatitis, and tuberculosis in 1995 (Rousch, 1995).

Many educators are alarmed by the rising prevalence figures for learning disabilities. They believe the ever-increasing numbers of students classified as learning disabled are the result of overidentification and misdiagnosis of low-achieving students, which reduces the resources available to serve the students who are truly learning disabled. Some authorities have expressed concern that the concept of learning disabilities is poorly defined and functions as a catch-all category for any student who is experiencing learning problems and does not meet eligibility requirements for other disability categories. For example, Reid Lyon (1999) of the National Institute of Child and Human Development suggests that learning disabilities have become "a sociological sponge to wipe up the spills of general education" (p. A1).

Some authorities, however, believe the current number of students being served as learning disabled may not be a gross overestimate and may be closer to the truth than most people have previously thought. Hallahan (1992) points to the newness of the field of learning disabilities and to societal/cultural changes (e.g., poverty, substance abuse by pregnant women) as two possible reasons for the increase in prevalence figures.

> Exactly what proportion of the increase represents bogus cases of learning disabilities is open for speculation and future research. In the meantime, we should be open to the idea that at least some of the increase represents students who are in very real need of learning disabilities services. (p. 528)

## CAUSES

In most cases, the cause (etiology) of a child's learning disability is unknown. Many causes have been proposed, a situation that probably reflects the highly diverse nature of students with learning disabilities. Just as there are different types of learning disabilities (e.g., dyslexia, language disabilities, math disabilities), there are likely to be different causes. Four suspected causal factors are brain damage, heredity, biochemical imbalance, and environmental causes.

### Brain Damage or Dysfunction

Some professionals believe that all children with learning disabilities suffer from some type of brain injury or dysfunction of the central nervous system. Indeed, this belief is inherent in the NJCLD definition of learning disabilities, which states that learning disorders are "presumed to be due to central nervous system dysfunction." In cases in which actual evidence of brain damage cannot be shown (and this is the situation with the majority of children with learning disabilities), the term *minimal brain dysfunction* is sometimes used, especially by physicians. This wording implies brain damage by asserting that the child's brain does not function properly.

Recent advances in magnetic resonance imaging (MRI) technology have enabled researchers to discover that specific regions of the brains of some individuals with reading and language disabilities show activation patterns during phonological processing tasks that are different from the patterns found in the brains of nondisabled individuals (Miller, Sanchez, & Hynd, 2003; Richards, 2001; Simos, Breier, Fletcher, Bergman, & Papanicolaou, 2000). The actual structure of the brain of some children with reading disabilities is slightly different from that of children without disabilities (Leonard, 2001).

This research holds great promise for understanding the biological bases of dyslexia and other specific learning disabilities. However, as Leonard (2001) points out, we do not yet know how and to what extent the brain's neural networks are affected by the child's experiences (i.e., learning) and vice versa. Thus, we do not know whether neurobiological factors associated with learning disabilities contribute to the learning problems of children, are the product of an unstimulating environment, or a combination. However, there is growing evidence that differences in the ways in which reading-disabled and normal children's brains are activated weakens with intensive remedial reading instruction (Richards, 2001). Shaywitz et al. (2004) reported that an average of 105 hours of individual tutoring that focused on teaching the *alphabetic principle* (how letters and combinations of letters represent the small segments of speech called phonemes) and oral reading fluency practice not only improved children's reading fluency but "facilitated the development of the neural systems that underline skilled reading" (p. 933).

Special educators must beware of placing too much emphasis on theories linking learning disabilities to brain damage or brain dysfunction, for three major reasons. First, not all children with learning disabilities display clinical (medical) evidence of brain damage, and not all children with brain damage have learning disabilities. The second problem is that assuming a child's learning problems are caused by a dysfunctioning brain can serve as a built-in excuse for ineffective instruction. When a student with suspected brain damage fails to learn, his teachers may be quick to presume that the brain injury prevents him from learning and be slow to analyze and change instructional variables. Third, whether "learning disabilities in an individual case are symptoms that result from brain injury or developmental delay will not essentially alter the methods of teaching the student" (Myers & Hammill, 1990, p. 22).

> Current interpretations of the role of constitutional factors show reciprocal relations with the environment, such that environmental factors (e.g., instruction) must be in place to develop the neural networks that support academic skills. Even genetic studies of reading disability show that only about 50 percent of the variability in reading skills can be explained by genetic factors—the remainder is environmental. Learning disabilities represent interplays of constitutional and environmental factors that are not yet well understood. (Fletcher et al., 2001, p. 7)

## Heredity

Siblings and children of persons with reading disabilities have a slightly greater than normal likelihood of having reading problems. There is growing evidence that genetics may account for at least some family links with dyslexia (Pennington, 1995; Raskind, 2001). Research has located possible chromosomal loci for the genetic transmission of phonological deficits that may predispose a child for reading problems later (Cardon et al., 1994; Kaplan et al., 2002).

## Biochemical Imbalance

It was once theorized that biochemical disturbances within a child's body caused learning disabilities. For example, Feingold (1975, 1976) claimed that artificial colorings and flavorings in many of the foods children eat can cause learning disabilities and hyperactivity. He recommended a treatment for learning disabilities that consisted of a diet with no foods containing synthetic colors or flavors. In a comprehensive review of research studies that tested the special diet, Spring and Sandoval (1976) concluded that there was very little scientific evidence to support Feingold's theory. In response to the controversy over diet treatments, the American Council on Science and Health (1979) issued the following statement:

> Hyperactivity will continue to be a frustrating problem until research resolves the questions of its cause, or causes, and develops an effective treatment. The reality is that we still have a great deal to learn about this condition. We do know now, however, that diet is not the answer. It is clear that the symptoms of the vast majority of the children labeled "hyperactive" are not related to salicylates, artificial food colors, or artificial flavors. The Feingold diet creates extra work for homemakers and changes the family lifestyle … but it doesn't cure hyperactivity. (p. 5)

It was also suggested that learning disabilities can be caused by the inability of a child's bloodstream to synthesize a normal amount of vitamins (Cott, 1972). Some physicians began megavitamin therapy with children with learning disabilities, which consisted of massive daily doses of vitamins in an effort to overcome the suspected vitamin deficiencies. Two studies designed to test the effects of megavitamin treatment with learning disabled and hyperkinetic children found that huge doses of vitamins did not improve the children's performance (Arnold, Christopher, Huestis, & Smeltzer, 1978; Kershner, Hawks, & Grekin, 1977). Today, most professionals in learning disabilities give little credence to biochemical imbalance as a significant cause of children's learning problems.

## Environmental Factors

Although very difficult to document as primary causes of learning disabilities, environmental factors—particularly impoverished living conditions early in a child's life and poor instruction—probably contribute to the achievement deficits experienced by many children in this special education category. The tendency for learning disabilities to run in families suggests a correlation between environmental influences on children's early development and subsequent achievement in school. Evidence for this relationship can be found in longitudinal research such as that conducted by Hart and Risley (1995), who found that infants and toddlers who received infrequent communication exchanges with their parents were more likely to show deficits in vocabulary, language use, and intellectual development before entering school.

Another environmental variable that is likely to contribute to children's learning problems is the quality of instruction they receive. Many special educators today believe that Engelmann (1977) was correct when he claimed more than 25 years ago that the vast majority of "children who are labeled 'learning disabled' exhibit a disability not because of anything wrong with their perception, synapses, or memory, but because they have been seriously mistaught" (pp. 46–47).

Although the relationship between poor instruction and learning disabilities is not clear, there is a great deal of evidence showing that many students' learning problems can be remediated by direct, intensive, and systematic instruction. It would be naive to think, however, that the achievement problems of all children with learning disabilities are caused entirely by inadequate instruction. Nevertheless, from an educational perspective, intensive, systematic instruction should be the treatment of first choice for all students with learning disabilities.

# ASSESSMENT

Five forms of assessment are frequently used with students with learning disabilities: standardized achievement tests, criterion-referenced tests, informal reading inventories, curriculum-based measurement, and direct daily measurement.

## Standardized Tests

*Standardized achievement tests*

Council for Exceptional Children   Content Standards for Beginning Teachers of Students with LD: Terminology and procedures used in the assessment of individuals with LD (LD8K1).

Standardized intelligence and achievement tests are widely used with children with learning disabilities because a discrepancy between intellectual ability and achievement is the primary factor in determining eligibility for special education services. Standardized tests are norm-referenced, which means they have been constructed so that one student's score can be compared with the scores of other students of the same age who have taken the test. (Intelligence tests were discussed in Chapter 4.) Some standardized achievement tests are designed to measure a student's overall academic achievement—e.g., the Iowa Tests of Basic Skills (Hoover, Hieronymus, Frisbie, & Dunbar, 1996), the Peabody Individual Achievement Test (Markwardt, 1998), the Woodcock-Johnson III Tests of Achievement (Woodcock, McGrew, & Mather, 2001), and the Wide Range Achievement Test—3 (WRAT) (Wilkinson, 1994). Scores on these tests are reported by grade level; a score of 3.5, for example, means that the student's score equaled the average score by those students in the norm group who were halfway through the third grade.

Some norm-referenced tests are designed to measure achievement in certain academic areas. Frequently administered reading achievement tests include the Gates-MacGinitie Reading Tests (MacGinitie, MacGinitie, Maria, & Dreyer, 2000), the Gray Oral Reading Tests (Wiederholt & Bryant, 2001), the Test of Reading Comprehension (Brown, Hammill, & Wiederholt, 1995), and the Woodcock Reading Mastery Test (Woodcock, 1998). Norm-referenced tests used to assess mathematics achievement include KeyMath—Revised: A Diagnostic Inventory of Essential Skills (Connolly, 1998), the Stanford Diagnostic Mathematics Test (Beatty, Madden, Gardner, & Karlsen, 1995), and the Test of Mathematical Abilities (Brown, Cronin, & McEntire, 1994).

## Criterion-Referenced Tests

**Criterion-referenced tests** differ from norm-referenced tests in that a child's score on a criterion-referenced test is compared with a predetermined criterion, or mastery level, rather than with normed scores of other students. The value of criterion-referenced tests is that they identify the specific skills the child has already learned and the skills that require instruction. One criterion-referenced test widely used by special educators is the Brigance Diagnostic Comprehensive Inventory of Basic Skills (Brigance, 1999), which includes 140 skill sequences in four subscales: readiness, reading, language arts, and math. Some commercially distributed curricula now include criterion-referenced test items for use as both a pretest and a posttest. The pretest assesses the student's entry level to determine which aspects of the program he is ready to learn; the posttest evaluates the effectiveness of the program. Criterion-referenced tests can be, and often are, informally developed by classroom teachers.

## Informal Reading Inventories

Teachers' growing awareness of the inability of formal achievement tests to provide useful information for planning instruction has led to greater use of teacher-developed and -administered tests, particularly in the area of reading. An informal reading inventory usually consists of a series of progressively more difficult sentences and paragraphs that a student is asked to read aloud. By directly observing and recording aspects of the student's reading skills—such as mispronounced vowels or consonants, omissions, reversals, substitutions, and comprehension—the teacher can determine the level of reading material that is most suitable for the child and the specific reading skills that require remediation (Carnine, Silbert, Kame'enui, & Tarver, 2004).

## Curriculum-Based Measurement

Any measurement system must be valid and reliable. Repeatedly putting a ruler in a pot of water might yield a reliable measure of 3 inches, but it would not produce a valid measure of the water's temperature. As silly as that example might seem, too often measures used in education fail to provide a meaningful index of children's progress in the curriculum. **Curriculum-based measurement (CBM)** involves frequent assessment of a student's progress in learning the objectives that make up the curriculum in which the student is participating (Deno, 1985; Fuchs & Fuchs, 1996; Howell & Nolet, 2000). CBM is a *formative evaluation* method in that it provides information on student learning as instruction takes place over time. By contrast, the result of a *summative evaluation* cannot be used to inform instruction because it is conducted after instruction has been completed (e.g., at the end of a grading period or school year). One study found that teachers who used CBM made an average of 2.5 changes in students' instructional plans over the course of 20 weeks, compared to an average of just 0.27 changes by teachers who were not using CBM (Fuchs, Fuchs, Hamlett, & Steeker, 1991). Other studies have reported that students whose teachers tailor instruction plans on CBM data perform and achieve better academically than do students whose teachers do not use CBM (Steeker & Fuchs, 2000; Wesson, 1991).

In addition to being valid and reliable, curriculum-based measures should be easy to administer; cost- and time-efficient; and, perhaps most important, sensitive to small, incremental changes in student performance over time (Kame'enui et al., 2005). A relatively new kind of CBM is the Dynamic Indicators of Basic Early Literacy Skills (DIBELS) (Good & Kaminski, 2003). DIBELS was developed to be an efficient indicator of key reading skills for early identification of children at risk for reading difficulties and to assess the effects of interventions designed to prevent such failure. DIBELS consists of four 1-minute fluency measures used to regularly monitor the development of prereading and early reading skills. Research has demonstrated that children who meet the benchmark goal for each measure are likely (odds greater than 80%) to become proficient readers (Good, Simmons, & Kame'enui, 2001). The four DIBELS measures and their respective benchmarks are as follows:

- *Initial sounds fluency.* This assesses a child's skill to identify and produce the initial sound of a given word. The examiner shows four pictures to the child, names each picture, and then asks the child to identify the picture that begins with the sound the examiner produced orally (e.g., "This is *cup, bat, rake,* and *fan.* Which picture begins with /b/?"). Benchmark: 25 or more initial sounds per minute by the middle of kindergarten.

*Criterion-referenced tests*

Council for Exceptional Children — Content Standards for Beginning Teachers of Students with LD: Terminology and procedures used in the assessment of individuals with LD (LD8K1) (also CC8K4).

*Informal reading inventories, CBM, and direct daily measurement*

Council for Exceptional Children — Content Standards for Beginning Teachers of Students with LD: Terminology and procedures used in the assessment of individuals with LD (LD8K1) (also CC8K4).

- *Phonemic segmentation fluency.* This assesses a child's skill to produce the individual sounds within a given word. For example, the examiner says, "Mat," and the student says, "/m/–/a/–/t/" and receives a point for each correct phoneme produced. Benchmark: 35 or more phonemes per minute by the end of kindergarten.
- *Nonsense word fluency.* This assesses a child's knowledge of letter-sound correspondences as well her ability to blend letters together to form unfamiliar "words." For example, if the stimulus word is "vaj," the student could say, "/v/–/a/–/j/" or say the word /vaj/ to obtain a total of three letter-sounds correct. Benchmark: 50 or more letter sounds per minute by the middle of first grade.
- *Oral reading fluency.* This assesses a child's skill in reading connected text. Students read an unfamiliar passage of grade-level material for 1 minute. The final score is the number of words read correctly in that minute. Benchmark: 40, 90, and 110 or more words read correctly per minute by the end of first, second, and third grade respectively. (adapted from the official DIBELS home page, http://dibels.uoregon.edu, retrieved September 2, 2004)

In the 2003–2004 school year, 4,725 schools in the United States and Canada were using the DIBELS measurement system to assess the early literacy development of more than 1 million students in grades K–3. Kame'enui and colleagues (2005) provide a detailed account of how DIBELS measures can provide an index of early identification and assessment of children at risk for reading failure.

## Direct Daily Measurement

Direct daily measurement means observing and recording a child's performance on the specific skill being taught each day that it is taught. In a program teaching multiplication facts, for example, the student's performance of multiplication facts would be assessed each day that multiplication was taught. Measures such as correct rate (number of facts stated or written correctly per minute), error rate, and percent correct are often recorded.

Two advantages of direct daily measurement are clear. First, it gives information about the child's performance on the skill under instruction. Second, this information is available on a continuous basis so that the teacher can modify instruction in accordance with changing (or unchanging) performance, not because of intuition, guesswork, or the results of a test that measures something else (Bushell & Baer, 1994). Direct and frequent measurement is the cornerstone of the behavioral approach to education introduced in Chapter 4 and is becoming an increasingly popular assessment and evaluation technique in all areas of special education.

*Precision Teaching.* Some teachers of students with learning disabilities use a special system for direct daily measurement called **precision teaching** (Lindsley, 1996). Precision teachers make instructional decisions based on changes in the frequency of a student's performance (e.g., number of words read correctly per minute) as plotted on a standard graphic display called the *standard celeration chart*. Precision teaching is neither a specific method of teaching nor a curriculum; it is a way of evaluating the effects of instruction and making instructional decisions. Additional information about precision teaching and the standard celeration chart can be found in Beck, Conrad, and Anderson (1995); Cooper, Kubina, and Malanga (1998); Graf and Lindsley (2002); and Kubina and Cooper (2001).

Not long ago, instruction of students with learning disabilities emphasized the remediation of basic skill deficits, often at the expense of providing opportunities for students to express themselves, learn problem-solving skills, or contact the general education curriculum in a meaningful way. "The overemphasis on the 'basics' with the exclusion of any creative or cognitively complex activities provides many students with LD an unappealing intellectual diet" (Gersten, 1998, p. 163). (Table 5.1 [pp. 198–199] describes some key historical events and their implications for the education of students with learning disabilities. More detailed accounts of the history of the learning disabilities field can be found in Hallahan and Mock [2003] and Mercer and Pullen [2005].)

In recent years, however, the field has begun to shift its instructional focus from a remediation-only mode to an approach designed to give students with learning disabilities meaningful access to and success with the core curriculum. By incorporating the six principles of effective instructional design shown in Figure 5.3, educators can make curriculum and instruction more effective for students with and without disabilities (Kame'enui, Carnine, Dixon, Simmons, & Coyne, 2002; Klingner & Vaughn, 1999).

Research has also shown that students with learning disabilities (1) have difficulty organizing information on their own, (2) bring limited stores of background knowledge to many academic activities, and (3) often do not approach learning tasks in effective and efficient ways. Thus, contemporary best practice in educating students with learning disabilities is characterized by explicit instruction, content enhancements, and learning strategies (Gersten, 1998; Hock et al., 1999; Swanson, 2001).

*History of LD*

Council for Exceptional Children — Content Standards for Beginning Teachers of Students with LD: Historical foundations, classical studies, and major contributors in the field of LD (LD1K1).

---

## FIGURE 5.3  Six major principles of effective instructional design

**Big Ideas**
 Highly selected concepts, principles, rules, strategies, or heuristics that facilitate the most efficient and broadest acquisition of knowledge.

**Conspicuous Strategies**
 Sequence of teaching events and teacher actions that make explicit the steps in learning. They are made conspicuous by the use of visual maps or models, verbal directions, full and clear explanations, etc.

**Mediated Scaffolding**
 Temporary support for students to learn new material. Scaffolding is faded over time.

**Strategic Integration**
 Planful consideration and sequencing of instruction in ways that show the commonalities and differences between old and new knowledge.

**Primed Background Knowledge**
 Related knowledge, placed effectively in sequence, that students must already possess in order to learn new knowledge.

**Judicious Review**
 Sequence and schedule of opportunities learners have to apply and develop facility with new knowledge. The review must be adequate, distributed, cumulative, and varied.

*Source:* From Kame'enui, E. J., Carnine, D. W., & Dixon, R. C. (2002). Introduction. In E. J. Kame'enui, D. W. Carnine, R. C. Dixon, D. C. Simmons, & M. D. Coyne (Eds.), *Effective teaching strategies that accommodate diverse learners* (2nd ed.), (p. 9). Upper Saddle River, NJ: Merrill/Prentice Hall. Reprinted by permission.

| TABLE 5.1 | A history of the education of children with learning disabilities: Key events and implications | |
|---|---|---|
| **Date** | **Historical Event** | **Educational Implication** |
| late 1930s–early 1940s | Research by Alfred Strauss and colleagues with children with mental retardation and brain injury at the Wayne County Training School in Michigan found relationships between brain injury and disorders that interfered with learning: perceptual disorders, perseveration, disorders of conceptual thinking, and behavioral problems such as hyperactivity and impulsivity. | In the book, *Psychopathology and Education of the Brain-Injured Child,* Strauss and Lara Lehtinen (1947) recommended strategies for relieving perceptual and conceptual disturbances of children with brain injury and thus reducing their symptomatic learning problems. |
| 1950s–1960s | By the early 1950s, most public schools had established special education programs for children with mental retardation, sensory impairments, physical disabilities, and behavioral disorders. But there remained a group of children who were having serious learning problems at school, yet did not fit into any of the existing categories of exceptionality. They did not "look" disabled; the children seemed physically intact, yet they were unable to learn certain basic skills and subjects at school. | In searching for help with their children's problems, parents turned to other professionals—notably doctors, psychologists, and speech and language specialists. Understandably, these professionals viewed the children from the perspectives of their respective disciplines. As a result, terms such as *brain damage, minimal brain dysfunction, neurological impairment, perceptual handicap, dyslexia,* and *aphasia* were often used to describe and to account for the children's learning and behavior problems. |
| 1963 | The term *learning disabilities* was coined by Samuel Kirk in an address to a group of parents whose children were experiencing serious difficulties in learning to read, were hyperactive, or could not solve math problems. | The parents liked the term and, that very evening, voted to form the Association for Children with Learning Disabilities (ACLD). |
| 1966 | A national task force identified 99 different characteristics of children with *minimal brain dysfunction* (the term used at the time) reported in the literature (Clements, 1966). | The inherent danger in such lists is a tendency to assume that each of those characteristics is exhibited by *all* of the children considered to be in the category. This danger is especially troublesome with learning disabilities, because the children who make up the category are an extremely heterogeneous group. |
| mid 1960s–1970s | The concept of process, or ability, testing grew out of the belief that learning disabilities are caused by a basic underlying difficulty of the child to process, or use, environmental stimuli in the same way that children without disabilities do. Two of the most widely used process tests used for diagnosing and assessing learning disabilities were developed during this time: the Illinois Test of Psycholinguistic Abilities (ITPA) (Kirk, McCarthy, & Kirk, 1968) and the Marianne Frostig Developmental Test of Visual Perception (Frostig, Lefever, & Whittlesey, 1964). | The ability training approach dominated special education for children with learning disabilities, from the field's inception through the 1970s. The three most widely known ability training approaches were psycholinguistic training, based on the ITPA; the visual-perceptual approach (Frostig & Horne, 1973); and the perceptual-motor approach (Kephart, 1971). |

# EXPLICIT INSTRUCTION

Explicit instruction involves carefully designed materials and activities that provide structures and supports that enable all students to make sense of new information and concepts. According to Cazden (1992), teachers should be "explicit about what needs to be done, or said, or written—rather than leaving it to learners to make inferences from experiences that are unmediated by help" (p. 111). In other words, explicit instruction is anything but learning by trial and error. Teachers use explicit instruction when they do the following (Carnine, Jones, & Dixon, 1994; Gersten, 1998):

| Date | Historical Event | Educational Implication |
|---|---|---|
| **TABLE 5.1** *continued* | | |
| **1968** | The National Advisory Committee on Handicapped Children drafted and presented to Congress a definition of learning disabilities. | This definition was later incorporated into IDEA and used to govern the dispersal of federal funds for support of services to children with learning disabilities. |
| **1968** | The Division for Children with Learning Disabilities (DCLD) was established within the Council for Exceptional Children (CEC). | DCLD has become the largest division of CEC. |
| **1969** | The Children with Learning Disabilities Act (part of P.L. 91–230) was passed by Congress. | This legislation authorized a five-year program of federal funds for teacher training and the establishment of model demonstration programs for students with learning disabilities. |
| **late 1970s– early 1980s** | Reviews of research showing the ineffectiveness of psycholinguistic training (Hammill & Larsen, 1978), the visual-perceptual approach (Myers & Hammill, 1976), and perceptual-motor approaches (Kavale & Mattison, 1983) are published. | Process testing and ability training gradually gave way to increased use of a skill training approach. If a student has not learned a complex skill and has had sufficient opportunity and wants to succeed, a skill trainer would conclude that the student has not learned the necessary prerequisite skills and provides direct instruction and practice on those prerequisite skills. |
| **1975** | Congress passed the Individuals with Disabilities Education Act (P.L. 94-142) | Learning disabilities was included as one of the disability categories in IDEA. |
| **1980s and 1990s** | Research on instructional design, content enhancements, and learning strategies provides additional knowledge on effective teaching methods for students with learning disabilities. | Skill training approach supplemented with increased emphasis on helping students with learning disabilities have meaningful contact with the general curriculum. |
| **2001** | In response to concerns about the large number of children identified as learning disabled, the U.S. Office of Special Education sponsored a Learning Disabilities Summit in Washington, DC. | Nine white papers were developed on topics such as diagnostic decision making, classification models, early identification, and the nature and legitimacy of learning disabilities as a disability (available at http://www.air.org/LDsummit/paper.htm). |
| **2004** | Individuals with Disabilities Education Improvement Act of 2004 changes requirements for determining whether a child has a specific learning disability. | Schools are no longer required to consider whether a child has a severe discrepancy between achievement and intellectual ability and may use a process that determines if the child responds to scientific, research-based intervention as part of the evaluation procedures. |

1. Provide students with a sufficient range of examples to illustrate a concept or problem-solving strategy.
2. Provide models of proficient performance, including step-by-step strategies (at times) or broad, generic questions and guidelines that focus attention and prompt deep processing.
3. Have students explain how and why they make decisions.
4. Provide frequent, positive feedback for student performance so students persist in activities.
5. Provide adequate practice opportunities that entail interesting and engaging activities.

See Teaching & Learning, "Explicit Instruction," later in this chapter.

 The highly effective **Direct Instruction** curricula authored by Engelmann and colleagues are based on a thoroughly developed model of explicit instruction (Adams & Carnine, 2003; Engelmann, 1997; Marchand-Martella, Slocum, & Martella, 2004). See "What Is Direct Instruction?" in Chapter 5 of the Companion Website, **www.prenhall.com/heward**.

# Explicit Instruction

*by Nancy E. Marchand-Martella and Ronald C. Martella*

Although most teachers have read or heard about the importance of explicit instruction, many are unsure about how to include the fundamental principles and practices of explicit instruction into their daily lessons.

**Explicit Instruction Defined**   Explicit, or *direct* instruction (little "d," little "i"), is "a systematic method of teaching with emphasis on proceeding in small steps, checking for student understanding, and achieving active and successful participation by all students" (Rosenshine, 1987, p. 34). This type of instruction is also referred to as "demonstration-prompt-practice" (Stevens & Rosenshine, 1981). Rosenshine (1986) provides highlights of research on explicit instruction of well-defined knowledge and skills such as math procedures, grammatical rules, and vocabulary. These highlights include the following:

- Start every lesson by correcting the previous day's homework and reviewing what students have recently been taught.
- Describe the goals of today's lesson.
- Present new material in small steps, giving clear and detailed explanations of the skill(s) to be learned (modeling), checking often for student understanding through strategic questioning.
- Provide repeated opportunities for students to practice in an active manner and to obtain feedback on their performance (guided practice).
- Monitor student learning through varied exercises (e.g., seatwork).
- Continue providing practice opportunities until students are performing skills independently and with ease (independent practice).
- Review previous week's lesson at the beginning of each week; review what students have learned over the past 4 weeks at the end of each month.

Thus, explicit instruction can be summarized as unambiguous, clear, and *direct* teaching (Arrasmith, 2003)—teachers show students what to do, give them opportunities to practice with teacher feedback, and then provide opportunities for students to apply these skills on their own over time. It is not "trial-and-error learning," "discovery," "exploration," "facilitated learning," or some other approach where teachers *assist* performance rather than *directly provide* knowledge/information to students (Harris & Graham, 1996).

**Why Explicit Instruction Is Important**   Students qualify for special education because they are significantly behind their peers in one or more academic areas. These students must be accelerated in their learning to catch up, so teachers must do *more* in *less* time. The most effective way of shortening the learning time for these students is through the direct teaching of skills.

"Instructional approaches that have yielded significant outcomes for students with LD are characterized as being well specified, explicit, carefully designed, and closely related to the area of instructional need (reading, spelling, math)" (Vaughn & Linan-Thompson, 2003, p. 140). For example, instruction found to be most effective in teaching students to read involves systematic and explicit techniques (i.e., instruction includes a carefully selected set of skills organized into a logical sequence) (Armbruster, Lehr, & Osborn, 2003; NICHD, 2000). Additionally, explicit instructional techniques are fundamental for students who are acquiring math skills—"the teacher reveals or makes transparent the connections between knowledge acquisition and knowledge application, rather than leaving the student to discover those connections more incidentally" (Fuchs & Fuchs, 2001, p. 93). Therefore, in explicit instruction, teachers initially take full responsibility for student learning but gradually relinquish responsibility to students as they become successful—"this progression can be seen as a continuum that moves from teacher modeling, through guided practice using prompts and cues, to independent and fluent performance by the learner" (Rosenshine, 1986, p. 69).

## EXAMPLES OF EXPLICIT INSTRUCTION IN PUBLISHED CURRICULA

Several curriculum programs feature explicit instruction. Perhaps the most well-known is Direct Instruction in reading, math, and language published by Science Research Associates. Figure A shows Exercise 5 from Lesson 104 of *Reading Mastery Plus, Level K* (Englemann, Osborn, Bruner, Englemann, & Davis, 2002). In this lesson, the sound for the letter *m* (/m/) is introduced by the teacher (modeling) and practiced by the students (guided practice). The /m/ is reviewed in the same lesson and over subsequent lessons during independent practice activities.

Figure B shows a phonemic awareness activity from *Scott Foresman Reading*, Grade 1, Unit 1, Week 2, Day 5 (Pearson Education, 2000). As can be seen, the sound /k/ is introduced by the teacher (modeling) and practiced by the students (guided practice). The /k/ is reviewed in the same lesson and over subsequent lessons during independent practice activities.

## HOW TO GET STARTED

Following are guidelines and suggestions for teachers who want to incorporate principles of explicit instruction into nonexplicit lessons:

1. *Determine whether or not a lesson is explicit.* Teachers can recognize if a lesson is explicit or not

---

### LETTER SOUNDS
### EXERCISE 5

Introducing the new sound mmm as in mat

a. (Touch the first ball of the arrow.) "You're going to learn a new sound. My turn to say it. When I move under the letter, I'll say the sound. I'll keep on saying it as long as I touch under it. Get ready." (Move quickly to the second ball of the arrow. Hold for two seconds.) "mmm."

b. (Touch the first ball of the arrow.) "My turn again. Get ready." (Move quickly to the second ball of the arrow. Hold for two seconds.) "mmm."

c. (Touch the first ball of the arrow.) "My turn again. Get ready." (Move quickly to the second ball of the arrow. Hold for two seconds.) "mmm."

d. (Touch the first ball of the arrow.) "Your turn. When I move under the letter, you say the sound. Keep on saying it as long as I touch under it. Get ready." (Move quickly to the second ball of the arrow. Hold for two seconds.) *"mmm."* "Yes, mmm."

e. (Touch the first ball of the arrow.) "Again. Get ready." (Move quickly to the second ball of the arrow. Hold for two seconds.) *"mmm."* "Yes, mmm."

f. (Repeat e until firm.)

g. (Call on different children to do d.)

h. "Good saying mmm."

**To correct**
(If the children do not say *mmm*:)

1. "mmm."

2. (Touch the first ball of the arrow.) "Say it with me. Get ready." (Move quickly to the second ball of the arrow. Hold for two seconds. Say *mmm* with the children.) *"mmm."*

3. (Touch the first ball of the arrow. "Your turn. Get ready." (Move quickly to the second ball of the arrow. Hold for two seconds.) *"mmm."*

---

**FIGURE A**  Script from a Direct Instruction lesson using explicit instruction to introduce a new letter-sound correspondence.

*Source:* From *Reading Mastery Plus, Level K* (Exercise 5 from Lesson 104). Copyright 2002 by SRA/McGraw-Hill. Used by permission.

| Day 5 |
| :--: |
| **Phonemic Awareness** |

| | | |
| --- | --- | --- |
| Review c/k/, /n/, /p/, /a/ | Materials: Picture Cards: *cat, net, pail, apple* | Display *cat* and say: "This is cat. What is this: The first sound in *cat* is /k/. What is the first sound in *cat*?" Continue modeling with *net, pail, and apple*. |
| Ongoing Assessment Assess Initial c/k/, /n/, /p/, /a/ | | Say: "I am going to say three words. They all begin with the same sound. I want you to tell me what the first sound is. Listen carefully. What is the first sound in these words: *cake, cap, can*? The first sound in *cake, cap,* and *can* is /k/. Say it with me: /k/, /k/, /k/. Your turn. What is the first sound in *nest, nail, and nine*?" Continue the assessment with *pail, peach, pig; at, apple, astronaut; carrot, cookie, cow*. |
| Assess Medial /a/ | Materials: Picture Cards: *bat, cap, hat, jam, fan* | Display *bat*. Say: "This is *bat*, /b/ /a/ /t/. What is this? The middle sound in *bat* is /a/. What is the middle sound in *bat*?" Say: "I am going to show you a picture. I want you to tell me the name of the picture and the middle sound." Display *cap* and say: "This is *cap*, /k/ /a/ /p/. What is this? What is the middle sound?" Continue the assessment routine with *hat, jam, fan,* and *bat*. |

**FIGURE B**  Example of lesson using explicit instruction for phonemic awareness skills
*Source:* From *Scott Foresman Reading*, Grade 1, Unit 1, Week 2, Day 5. Copyright 2000 by Pearson Education. Used by permission.

by considering the directedness of the information provided to the students. For example, if students are expected to find answers on their own without previous instruction, the lesson is not likely to be explicit. Phrases such as "encourage children to identify," "challenge children to say," "help children focus," "work with children to build," "help them discover," and "facilitate learning by" are used in nonexplicit programs.

Explicit programs are more likely to use phrases such as "My turn to say it," "I'm going to show you," "Watch me," "This is _____," and "Let's say it together." In explicit programs and instruction, teachers model or show students how to do something, provide students with practice and teacher feedback, and include independent activities for students to practice on their own.

2. *Once you identify nonexplicit instructional formats, make them more explicit.* For example, the following sample illustrates nonexplicit instruction from *Rigby Literacy*, Grade 1, Level 4, Day 1, "The animal walk" (Rigby, 2004).

   **Initial and final consonant sounds** Find the words *like* and *little* in the book. What is the same

about these words? Let's say the words aloud. What sound do you hear at the beginning of each word? Find the words *slug* and *bug*. What is the same about these words? Let's say the words aloud. What sound do you hear at the end of each word? (p. 94).

Teachers can make this lesson more explicit by

a. *Modeling* what is the same about these words (e.g., "Find the words *like* and *little* in the book. Both of these words begin with the sound /l/.)
b. Providing *guided practice* (e.g., "What sound is the same in both of these words?" "Yes, /l/.")
c. Including *independent practice* activities (e.g., students complete independent assignments focused on /l/)

Nancy E. Marchand-Martella and Ronald C. Martella are professors of special education at Eastern Washington University.

 To learn more about these strategies and answer questions about what you have learned, go to the Teaching & Learning module in Chapter 5 of the Companion Website, **www.prenhall.com/heward**

# Content Enhancements

Educating students with learning disabilities at the middle and secondary levels is particularly difficult. Most are "ill-prepared for high school" and have reading and language skills at the 4th- to 5th-grade level (Deshler, Schumaker, Lenz, et al., 2001). Lectures and assigned readings in textbooks are widely used in middle and high school classrooms to present academic content to students. The teacher talks and assigns a portion of a high-vocabulary, content-dense text; and students are held responsible for obtaining, remembering, and using the information later (usually on a quiz or a test). A combination of poor reading, listening, note taking, and study skills, compounded by a limited store of background knowledge, makes obtaining needed information from reading, lectures, and homework assignments a daunting task for students with learning disabilities.

*Content enhancement* is the general name given to a wide range of techniques teachers use to enhance the organization and delivery of curriculum content so that students are better able to organize, comprehend, and retain that information (Hock et al., 1999; Hudson, Lignugaris/Kraft, & Miller, 1993; Lenz & Bulgren, 1995). To most effectively use a content enhancement approach, teachers must

> think critically about the content they cover, determine what approaches to learning need to be in operation for students to be successful,... The teacher, in effect, teaches content and learning processes simultaneously...stressing what the students should learn as well as how. (Baker, Gersten, & Scanlon, 2002, p. 67)

Let's take a brief look at several types of content enhancements helpful to students with learning disabilities.

*Guided Notes.* Students who take good notes and study them later consistently receive higher test scores than do students who only listen to the lecture and read the text (Kiewra, 2002; Norton & Hartley, 1986). The listening, language, and, in some cases, motor-skill deficits of many students with learning disabilities, however, make it difficult for them to identify what is important and write it down correctly and quickly enough during a lecture (Boyle, 2001). While trying to choose and write one concept in a notebook, the student with learning disabilities might miss the next two points. Although various strategies and formats for effective note taking have been identified, they are seldom taught to students (Mercer & Mercer, 2005).

Guided notes are a method for organizing and enhancing curriculum content and providing students with disabilities and their regular classroom peers with a means of actively participating during a lecture (Heward, 2001; Lazarus, 1996). **Guided notes** are teacher-prepared handouts that provide an outline of the lecture, which students complete during class by writing in key facts, concepts, and/or relationships. Experimental studies have found that students at all achievement levels in elementary through postsecondary classrooms consistently earn higher quiz and test scores when using guided notes than they earn when taking their own notes (e.g., Austin, Lee, Thibeault, Carr, & Bailey, 2002; Beckley, Al-Attrash, Heward, & Morrison, 1999; Hamilton, Seibert, Gardner, & Talbert-Johnson, 2000; Lazarus, 1993; Sweeney et al., 1999). In addition to improved retention of course content, other advantages of guided notes include the following (Heward, 2001):

- Students must actively respond to and interact with the lesson's content.
- Because the location and number of key concepts, facts, and relationships are highlighted, students are better able to determine if they're "getting it." As a result, students are more likely to ask the teacher for clarification of key points.
- Students produce a standard set of accurate notes for subsequent study.
- Teachers must prepare the lesson carefully.
- Guided notes help teachers stay on task with the lesson.

*Content enhancements: Guided notes, graphic organizers, and mnemonic strategies*

Council for Exceptional Children Content Standards for Beginning Teachers of Students with LD: Methods for guiding individuals in identifying and organizing critical content (LD4K5).

For suggestions on creating and using guided notes, see "Guided Notes" in Chapter 5's Teaching & Learning Module of the Companion Website, **www.prenhall.com/heward**

A variation of guided lecture notes, *structured reading worksheets* are teacher-prepared supplements that help students study and comprehend assigned reading from content-rich textbooks by prompting to find points and write key points (Alber, Nelson, & Brennan, 2002).

*Graphic Organizers.* **Graphic organizers**—visual-spatial arrangements of information containing words or concepts connected graphically—can help students see meaningful hierarchical, comparative, and sequential relationships (Dye, 2000; Horton, Lovitt, & Bergerud, 1990; Ives & Hoy, 2003). Bulgren, Deshler, Schumaker, and Lenz (2000) have developed a graphic device and teaching routine called the *concept anchoring table/routine* that helps students relate a new concept to a concept and information with which they are already familiar (see Figure 5.4). Students complete the anchoring table as part of a 7-step, teacher-guided instructional routine that enables students to use their background experiences and knowledge to understand the new concept. Research has shown that the concept anchoring routine helps students learn abstract or complex information such as "federalism" or "commensalism" (Bulgren et al., 2000; Deshler, Schumaker, Bulgren, et al., 2001).

*Mnemonics.* Research has demonstrated that mnemonics (memory-enhancing strategies) can help students with learning disabilities recall specific academic content (Brigham & Brigham, 2001; Swanson, 1999). **Mnemonic strategies**—which combine special presen-

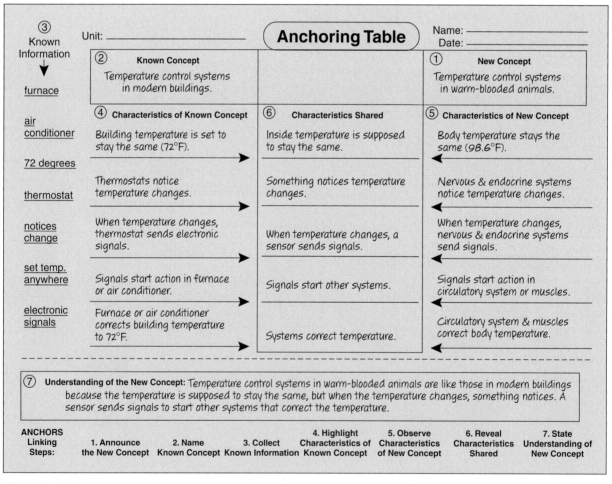

**FIGURE 5.4** **Example of a concept anchoring table for the concept "temperature control systems in warm-blooded animals"**

*Source:* Deshler, D. D., Schumaker, J. B., Bulgren, J. A., Lenz, B. K., Jantzen, J., Adams, G., Carnine, D., Grossen, B., Davis, B., & Marquis, J. (2001). Making things easier: Connecting new knowledge to things students already know. *Teaching Exceptional Children, 33*(4), 84. Used by permission.

tation of information with explicit strategies for recall—are most often used to help students remember large amounts of unfamiliar information or make connections between two or more facts or concepts. Three of the most commonly used mnemonic strategies by special education teachers are letter strategies, keyword method, and pegword method.

*Letter strategies* are acronyms and acrostics. Common examples of acronym mnemonics are HOMES to remember the names of the Great Lakes (Huron, Ontario, Michigan, Erie, and Superior) and FACE to remember the four notes in the spaces between the lines on a music staff. Acrostics are sentences in which the first letter of each word stands for a different word. For example, "Kids playing croquet on freeways get smashed" can help students remember the life sciences classification system: kingdom, phylum, class, order, family, genus, and species (Kleinheksel & Summy, 2003); and "Every good boy deserves fudge" reminds them of the notes on the five lines of the music staff.

The *keyword method* is useful when linking a new, unfamiliar word with familiar information. Mastropieri and Scruggs (2004) give the following example of how a teacher could use a keyword mnemonic for helping a student remember that the Italian word *strada* means "road." First, identify a keyword for *strada* that sounds like the new word but is familiar and easy to picture. In this case, "straw" would be a good keyword because it sounds like *strada* and is easy to picture. Next, draw (or ask students to imagine) a picture of the keyword and its referent doing something together. In this case, the interactive picture could show straw lying on a road (see Figure 5.5). Finally, the teacher instructs the student to look at the picture and begins the following dialogue to help the student acquire the keyword strategy:

> The Italian word *strada* means road. The keyword for *strada* is *straw*. Remember this picture of straw lying on a road? Remember this picture of what? Good, straw lying on a road. Now, when I ask you for the meaning of *strada*, think first of the keyword, *straw*. Then think back to the picture with the straw in it, remember that the straw was on a road, and then retrieve the answer, *strada* means road. Now what does *strada* mean? Good, *strada* means road. And how did you remember that? Good, you thought of the key word, *straw*, and remembered the picture of *straw* on the road. (Mastropieri & Scruggs, 2004, p. 293)

The *pegword method* employs rhyming words for numbers (1 is "bun," 2 is "shoe," 3 is "tree," etc.) when information to be remembered is numbered or ordered. For example, to remember that Newton's first (or number 1) law of motion is that objects at rest tend to stay

To learn more about teaching mnemonics to students, see "Mnemonic Strategies" in Chapter 5 of the Companion Website, **www.prenhall.com/heward**.

**FIGURE 5.5** **Mnemonic picture for remembering that the Italian word *strada* means "road"**

*Source:* Mastropieri, M. A., & Scruggs, T. E. (2004). *The inclusive classroom: Strategies for effective instruction* (2nd ed.), (p. 293). Upper Saddle River, NJ: Merrill/Prentice Hall. Used by permission.

Strada (Straw)          Road

Straw

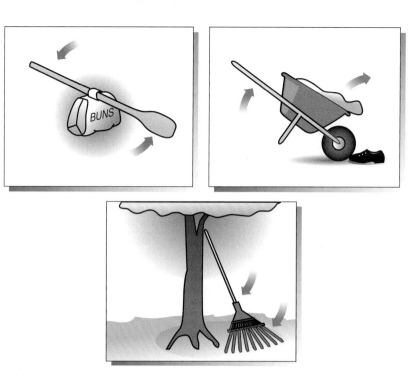

at rest, show a picture of a *bun* (1) resting. To remember that insects have six legs, create a picture of insects on *sticks* (6). Figure 5.6 shows pictorial representations of pegwords to remember three classes of levers.

*Learning Strategies.*    Proficient learners approach tasks and problems systematically. They identify what needs to be done, make a plan, and evaluate their progress. An accomplished writer knows how to identify and organize the content of a paper to enhance its persuasiveness. When adding a series of unlike fractions, a skilled math student immediately looks to see if all of the denominators are even numbers. Unless they are explicitly taught, however, many students with learning disabilities are unaware of the strategies, or "tricks of the trade," that proficient learners use (Deshler & Schumaker, 1993).

A learning strategy can be defined as "an individual's approach to a learning task. A strategy includes how a person thinks and acts when planning, executing, and evaluating performance on a task and its outcomes" (Deshler & Lenz, 1989, p. 205). Donald Deshler and Jean Schumaker and their colleagues at the University of Kansas (Schumaker & Deshler, 1992) have conducted extensive research on how to help students with learning disabilities acquire and use effective learning strategies. They have developed, field-tested, and validated a learning strategies curriculum for adolescents with learning disabilities (Ellis, Deshler, Lenz, Schumaker, & Clark, 1991).

Students use task-specific strategies to guide themselves successfully through a learning task or problem. A mnemonic device might be used to help students remember the steps of the strategy. For example, Maccini and Hughes (2000) taught secondary students with learning disabilities to recite the letters in S.T.A.R. as cues for the steps in systematically solving algebra word problems: search the problem, translate the words into an equation, answer the problem, and review the solution.

## EDUCATIONAL PLACEMENT ALTERNATIVES

### Regular Classroom

IDEA requires that students with disabilities be educated with their nondisabled peers and have access to the core curriculum to the maximum extent possible and that they be re-

---

*Learning strategies*

Council for Exceptional Children    Content Standards for Beginning Teachers of Students with LD: Methods for teaching individuals to independently use cognitive processing to solve problems (LD4K4).

*Placement alternatives*

Council for Exceptional Children    Content Standards for Beginning Teachers—Common Core: Demands of learning environments (CC5K1).

206

moved from the regular classroom only to the extent that their disability necessitates. During the 2003–2004 school year, 48.7% of students with learning disabilities were educated in regular classrooms (U.S. Office of Special Education, 2004).

All of the methods described in the previous section for enhancing the general education curriculum help promote the success of students with learning disabilities in the regular classroom. Special educators can facilitate the success of these students in regular classrooms by teaching them behaviors that are valued by regular class teachers. For example, when asked to rate which of 30 different social skills were critical for success in the classroom, the majority of 366 teachers in grades K–12 rated self-control (controlling temper in conflict situations) and cooperation (complying with teacher's directions) as the most essential (Lane, Pierson, & Givner, 2003). Table 5.2 lists the 10 things that 89 regular education high school teachers identified as most important for success in the regular education classroom. Another strategy for increasing the likelihood of successful inclusion is to interview successful students to find out their secrets for success in a particular teacher's classroom (Monda-Amaya, Dieker, & Reed, 1998).

Research on the academic achievement of students with learning disabilities in inclusive classrooms is mixed. Some studies have reported better learning outcomes for students with learning disabilities in inclusive general education classrooms than in pull-out programs (e.g., Baker, Wang, & Walberg, 1995; Rea, McLaughlin, & Walther-Thomas, 2002).

Other studies of students with learning disabilities in the regular classroom have reported disappointing achievement results (e.g., Schumm, Moody, & Vaughn, 2000), concerns about inadequate instruction (e.g., Chard & Kame'enui, 2000), and poor acceptance by teachers and/or peers (e.g., Cook, 2001; Cook, Tankersley, Cook, & Landrum, 2000).

Many studies have compared the social functioning and self-concepts of students with learning disabilities in different educational placements. The contention of advocates of full inclusion for students with learning disabilities is that pull-out services such as resource room and special class placement stigmatize students, thus damaging self-concept and limiting opportunities to develop relationships with typical peers. For example, Wiener and Tardif (2004) studied 117 children with learning disabilities in different educational placements and found a "slight superiority of the more inclusive programs" (p. 30) with respect to peer acceptance, number of friends, self-perceptions of mathematics competence, and behavior problems. However, the authors noted that the differences between groups were not large and were "especially small when compared to the differences between children with and without learning disabilities. Wiener and Tardif warned that "it would be inappropriate to conclude that the major variable influencing the social and emotional adjustment of children with LD is the special education placement" (p. 30).

**TABLE 5.2** **The 10 most important things a student with learning disabilities should do to achieve success in a regular education classroom**

| Student Skill/Behavior | Mean Rating* |
|---|---|
| Follows directions in class | 3.72 |
| Comes to class prepared with materials | 3.48 |
| Uses class time wisely | 3.48 |
| Makes up assignments and tests | 3.43 |
| Treats teachers and peers with courtesy | 3.40 |
| Completes and turns in homework on time | 3.37 |
| Works cooperatively in student groups | 3.19 |
| Completes tests with a passing grade | 3.19 |
| Appears interested in subject | 2.90 |
| Takes notes in class | 2.88 |
| *Skills are ordered from most to least important as ranked by teachers; 4 is the highest possible score. | |

Source: Reprinted from "Instructional Practices in Mainstreamed Secondary Classrooms" by L. Ellet, 1993, *Journal of Learning Disabilities, 26,* 59. © 1993 by PRO-ED, Inc. Used by permission.

However, Elbaum (2002) conducted a meta-analysis of 36 studies examining the self-concept of students with learning disabilities in different placements and concluded that, "contrary to the stigmatization perspective, students with LD placed in regular classrooms did not, overall, have higher self-concepts than students placed in either part-time or full-time special education classrooms" (p. 222). But Elbaum properly noted that, while no one placement is preferable in terms of self-concept for all students with LD, individual students may be "profoundly affected by a placement that jeopardized their self-esteem" and that, when making placement decisions for a child, IEP teams "should guard against a priori assumptions about the benefit or detriment of specific placements to students' self-concept. Each student's social and emotional needs, as well as the student's own preference with regard to placement options, ought to be taken into account" (pp. 222, 223).

Some school districts employ a collaborative teaching model to support the full inclusion of students with learning disabilities. Collaborative teaching involves in-class support by a special education teacher who provides instructional assistance to students with disabilities and perhaps some co-teaching with the general education teacher (Zigmond & Magiera, 2001). Data from two studies, however, question the effectiveness of this model. Boudah, Schumaker, and Deshler (1997) found that both the general education teachers and the special education teachers devoted more than half of their time to noninstructional tasks and spent less than 10% of their time presenting curriculum content. Not surprisingly, Boudah et al. also reported disappointing outcome measures for the students with learning disabilities who were included in those classrooms. The authors of another study that examined the experiences of 25 elementary students with learning disabilities who participated in a full-inclusion program concluded that "full-time placement in the general education classroom with in-class support from special education teachers is not sufficient to meet the needs of these students. They require combined services that include in-class support and daily, intensive, one-on-one instruction from highly trained personnel" (Klingner, Vaughn, Hughes, Schumm, & Elbaum, 1998, p. 159).

## Consultant Teacher

A consultant teacher provides support to regular classroom teachers and other staff members who work directly with students with learning disabilities. The consultant teacher helps the regular teacher select assessment devices, curriculum materials, and instructional activities. The consultant may even demonstrate teaching methods or behavior management strategies. A major advantage of this model is that the consultant teacher can work with several teachers and thus indirectly provide special education services to many children. A major drawback is that the consultant has little or no direct contact with the children. Heron and Harris (2001) describe procedures that consultant teachers can use to increase their effectiveness in supporting children in the regular classroom.

## Resource Room

A resource room is a specially staffed and equipped classroom where students with learning disabilities come for one or several periods during the school day to receive individualized instruction. A resource room teacher serves an average of 20 students with disabilities. During the 2003–2004 school year, 37% of students with learning disabilities were served in resource rooms (U.S. Office of Special Education, 2004).

The resource teacher is a certified special educator whose primary role is to teach needed academic skills, social skills, and learning strategies to the students who are referred to the resource room. Students typically attend their general education classrooms for most of the school day and come to the resource room only for one or more periods of specialized instruction in the academic and/or social skill areas in which they need the most help. In addition to teaching students with learning disabilities, the resource teacher also works closely with each student's regular teacher(s) to suggest and help plan each student's program in the regular classroom.

Some advantages of the resource room model are that (1) students do not lose their identity with their regular class peer group; (2) students can receive the intense, individualized instruction they need every day, which might not be possible for the regular class teacher to provide; and (3) flexible scheduling allows the resource room to serve a fairly large number of students. Some disadvantages of resource rooms are that they (1) require students to spend time traveling between classrooms, (2) may result in inconsistent instructional approaches between settings, and (3) make it difficult to determine whether students should be held accountable for what they missed while out of the regular classroom.

## Separate Classroom

During the 2003–2004 school year, 13% of students with learning disabilities were served in separate classrooms (U.S. Office of Special Education, 2004). In a separate classroom, the learning disabilities teacher is responsible for all educational programming for a group of 8 to 12 students with learning disabilities. The academic achievement deficiencies of some children with learning disabilities are so severe that they need full-time placement in a setting with a specially trained teacher. In addition, poor work habits and inappropriate social behaviors make some students with learning disabilities candidates for the separate classroom, where distractions can be minimized and individual attention stressed. As was noted in Chapter 2, it is important that IEP teams do not consider placement in a separate classroom (or any other educational setting) as permanent. A student should be placed in a separate classroom only after legitimate and supported attempts to serve her effectively in less restrictive environments have proven unsuccessful.

*In a resource room, students with learning disabilities can receive intense, specialized instruction on the academic and social skills in which they need the most help.*

# CURRENT ISSUES AND FUTURE TRENDS

The field of learning disabilities is so large, dynamic, and controversial that an entire volume could easily be devoted to a discussion of current issues. In response to concern about the large and increasing number of children who have been identified as learning disabled, the U.S. Office of Special Education sponsored a national Learning Disabilities Summit in Washington, DC, in 2001. Nationally recognized experts were invited to review the most current research and prepare papers discussing implications of and recommendations for policy, research, and practice on a variety of pressing issues, including discrepancy models and alternative approaches for diagnosing learning disabilities (Gresham, 2002; Kavale, 2002), classification of learning disabilities (Fletcher et al., 2002), the difficulty of differentiating students with learning disabilities from other underachieving students (Fuchs et al., 2002), and early identification and prevention of learning disabilities (Jenkins & O'Conner, 2002). All of the LD Summit papers have been published in a book edited by Bradley, Danielson, and Hallahan (2002) and are important reading for anyone who wishes to seriously explore current issues and likely trends in learning disabilities.

We will briefly discuss three current issues: movement to redefine learning disabilities as inadequate response to instruction, the continuing debates about the true nature of learning disabilities, and full inclusion. We close with an observation on the importance of maintaining a positive approach in our work with children with learning disabilities.

*LD Summit papers*

Council for Exceptional Children   Content Standards for Beginning Teachers—Common Core: Models, theories, and philosophies that form the basis for special education practice (CC1K1) (also CC1K3).

## Redefining Learning Disabilities As Inadequate Response to Instruction

Perhaps the most significant development from the LD Summit has been increased interest in and research on an approach to identifying learning disabilities called **response to instruction** or *response to treatment*. The ability-achievement discrepancy approach focuses on within-child factors, excluding factors such as the quality of instruction the child has received. The ability-achievement discrepancy requires a student to fall far behind and precludes early identification and prevention. A response-to-instruction approach shifts the identification of learning disabilities from a "wait to fail" model to one of early identification and prevention (Vaughn & Fuchs, 2003b).

Researchers who have implemented intensive programs of remedial instruction for struggling readers in the early grades report that a small percentage of students (5%–7%) fail to make adequate progress (e.g., O'Conner, 2000; Torgesen, 2001). "It is reasonable to think that these students, whose response to treatment is significantly lower than expected, could be identified with reading/learning disabilities (Vaughn et al., 2003, p. 393).

Curriculum-based measurement, as already discussed, is the primary assessment device for the response-to-treatment model. Students are considered at risk if both their level of performance and rate of growth on the CBM are well below those of their classmates. These students then receive an intensive fixed-duration trial (e.g., 10–15 weeks) of individual or small-group supplemental tutoring using a research-validated program.

> Responsiveness to this intensive prevention trial is the operative concept within this "response-to" model. That is, if the student responds to the intensive prevention trials, then the student is deemed disability-free (and remediated); he or she then is returned to the original classroom environment. Failure to respond confirms the presence of a LD. …
>
> If the child fails to respond to a program with which the vast majority of children learn, then the inference is that the child's deficits render learning uniquely challenging and require a special education. The failure to respond verifies that the deficit resides in the individual, not the instructional program. (Vaughn & Fuchs, 2003b, pp. 139, 142)

Recognizing the problems inherent in the discrepancy approach to determining eligibility for special education and with concern for the large and growing number of children being identified under the learning disabilities category, Congress made two significant changes to the requirements for determining whether a child has a specific learning disability in the Individuals with Disabilities Education Improvement Act of 2004. The new law states that "when determining whether a child has a specific learning disability . . . a local educational agency shall not be required to take into consideration whether a child has a severe discrepancy between achievement and intellectual ability . . . . [and] a local educational agency may use a process that determines if the child responds to scientific, research-based intervention as a part of the evaluation procedures" (Sec 614 [b] [6] [A] [B]).

Although a response to instruction model holds promise—especially in terms of early identification and prevention, reducing bias in identification from subjective teacher screenings, linking identification measures to important student outcomes—there are many conceptual, methodological, and policy-related issues and pitfalls that must be addressed (e.g., what CBM measures to use, what form and intensity of remedial instruction should be implemented when identifying nonresponders, and training personnel to implement the model). The Council for Exceptional Children (CEC) (2004) published this initial assessment of the new directions for identifying children with learning disabilities:

> CEC recognizes that the use of the aptitude-achievement discrepancy model continues to be a controversial component in the identification of LD and shares those concerns. However, since there are no research-based alternatives that have been sufficiently validated at this time, CEC recommends that the Secretary [of Education] establish a research priority and sufficient funds be allocated to validate psychometric, nonpsychometric and "response-to-treatment" methods of identification. Particular attention should be given to the fidelity of the response-to-treatment method on a large scale and its impact on disproportional representation of children from culturally and linguistically diverse backgrounds. (p. 14)

To learn more about the response to instruction see Fuchs, Fuchs, McMaster, and Al Otaiba (2003); Kame'enui et al. (2005); and Vaughn and Fuchs (2003a).

## Will the Student with Real Learning Disabilities Please Stand Up?

The field of learning disabilities continues to struggle with defining the nature of the unexpected learning problems it was created to study and treat. Although virtually everyone in education recognizes that present definitions of learning disabilities are inadequate, finding a definition that provides clear-cut criteria for identification and serves as a standard by which to interpret and assess research findings has "proven easier said than done" (Conte & Andrews, 1993, p. 149).

*To Tell the Truth* was a popular TV game show in the 1960s. A panel of celebrities asked questions of three contestants, only one of whom was actually the person all were pretending to be. In some respects, the search to find the truly learning disabled among the many students who do poorly in school is like that TV game show. Many questions (in the form of achievement tests, intelligence tests, and still more tests) are given to the contestants (students), whose answers are judged by a panel of experts (school psychologists, teachers, and administrators) charged with picking out the students with real learning disabilities from the pretenders. The differences, of course, are also significant. On the game show, the consequences for a wrong answer were no more serious than a loud buzzer and a consolation prize; but in the game of identifying students with learning disabilities, mistakes are costly. An answer of "no, he's not learning disabled" can be devastating for the student who truly needs specially designed instruction to meet his individual learning needs. If the team of selection experts concludes "yes, there is one" when the student's underachievement is primarily a result of insufficient contact with appropriate general education curriculum and instruction, then the limited resources available to help students with learning disabilities are stretched further.

Fuchs, Fuchs, Mathes, et al. (2001) concluded the executive summary of their LD Summit paper, "Is 'Learning Disabilities' Just a Fancy Term for Low Achievement?," with these observations:

> Given that learning disabled (LD) students' reading achievement is worse than that of low-achieving students [who are not identified as LD], and assuming that many LD students' instructional needs can be addressed only by special education, why not simply use very low achievement as the primary criterion to identify LD and dispense with technically inadequate discrepancy formulas and controversial and divisive IQ tests?... Whether LD qualifies as a distinct diagnostic entity or occurs in varying degrees of severity, as hypertension and obesity do, findings indicate that researchers and practitioners tend to identify children with more severe reading problems as LD. Given this, it seems reasonable that special education, with its capacity to provide intensive reading instruction, be directed at this group of children. (p. 8).

The discussion of what constitutes a true learning disability will no doubt go on for some time. We close this discussion of the difficulties in defining learning disabilities by recognizing a central truth: labeling does not cause disabilities, nor will the removal of a label cure them. From an educator's standpoint, the most important issue should not revolve around whether to consider the academic deficiencies exhibited by a student as evidence of a disability (Macht, 1998). Instead, we should focus our resources and energies on determining how to go about assessing and effectively remediating the specific academic and social-skill deficits in each student's repertoire. What a child's learning problem is called is not so important; what *is* important is that schools provide an educational program responsive to the individual needs of all children who have difficulty learning.

*Difficulty defining and identifying LD*

Council for Exceptional Children — Content Standards for Beginning Teachers of Students with LD: Philosophies, theories, models, and issues related to individuals with LD (LD1K2).

## Should All Students with Learning Disabilities Be Educated in the Regular Classroom?

For the majority of students with learning disabilities, the least restrictive environment for all or most of the school day is the regular education classroom attended by their same-age peers. The movement toward full inclusion of all students with disabilities in regular classrooms, however, has many professionals and advocates for students with learning disabilities worried. They think that although the full-inclusion movement is based on strong beliefs and has the best intentions at heart, little research supports it ("Award-Winning Researchers Raise Questions about 'Inclusion,'" 2001; Fuchs & Fuchs, 1994; Kauffman & Hallahan, 1994; Swanson, 2000). They fear that the special education services for students with learning disabilities guaranteed by IDEA—particularly the meaningful development and implementation of IEPs and the identification of the least restrictive environment for each student along a continuum of placement options—will be lost if full inclusion becomes reality. They wonder how, for example, a high school student with learning disabilities who spends the entire school day in regular education subject-matter classes will receive the individualized reading instruction at the fourth-grade level that she needs.

All of the major professional and advocacy associations concerned with the education of children with learning disabilities have published position papers against full inclusion (CLD, 1993; DLD, 1993; LDA, 1993; NJCLD, 1993 [see Figure 5.7]). Each group recognizes and supports the placement of students with learning disabilities in regular classrooms to the maximum extent possible, given that the instructional and related services required to meet each student's individualized educational needs are provided; but they strongly oppose policies that mandate the same placement and instruction for all students with learning disabilities. Each group believes that special education for students with learning disabilities requires a continuum of placement options that includes the possibility of some or even all instruction taking place outside the regular classroom.

For some students with learning disabilities, the regular education classroom may actually be more restrictive than a resource room or special class placement when the instructional needs of the student are considered—and remember that academic deficit is the primary characteristic and remedial need of students with learning disabilities (Baker & Zigmond, 1995). Note, however, that placing a student with learning disabilities in a pull-out program or special class does not guarantee that he will receive the intensive, specialized instruction he needs. For example, Moody, Vaughn, Hughes, and Fischer (2000) found that only three of the six resource room teachers they observed provided differentiated reading materials and instruction to match the individualized needs of their students.

The collective message of research on outcomes for students with learning disabilities in inclusive classrooms and other settings is consistent with the findings for students with other disabilities: the location in which a student is taught is not as important as the quality of instruction that student receives.

## Maintaining a Positive Focus

With its unending stream of claims, counterclaims, and controversy, the area of learning disabilities at times seems to lose sight of its fundamental goals and some commonsense truths. Tom Lovitt (1977), who has contributed classroom-based research on virtually every aspect of the education of children with learning disabilities for more than 35 years, once wrote that, all things being equal, a teacher who imparts many skills to many children is good, and one who does not is not. After all, teaching is helping children learn new things. Although Lovitt believes that the development of children's academic and social skills is the primary purpose for teachers and students to come together, he also warns us to not become so concerned with fixing everything we believe is wrong with the student that we forget about recognizing and building upon all that is positive.

*Perspectives on full inclusion*

Council for Exceptional Children — Content Standards for Beginning Teachers of Students with LD: Philosophies, theories, models, and issues related to individuals with LD (LD1K2) (also CC5K1).

*CLD, DLD, LDA, & NJCLD*

Council for Exceptional Children — Content Standards for Beginning Teachers of Students with LD: Professional organizations and sources of information relevant to the field of LD (LD9K2).

**FIGURE 5.7** **A Reaction to Full Inclusion: A Reaffirmation of the Right of Students with Learning Disabilities to a Continuum of Services**

The National Joint Committee on Learning Disabilities (NJCLD) supports many aspects of school reform. However, one aspect of school reform that the NJCLD cannot support is the idea that all students with learning disabilities must be served only in regular education classrooms, frequently referred to as fault inclusion. The Committee believes that full inclusion, when defined this way, violates the rights of parents and students with disabilities as mandated by the Individuals with Disabilities Education Act (IDEA).

Because each student with learning disabilities has unique needs, an individualized program must be tailored to meet those needs. For one student, the program may be provided in the regular classroom; yet for another student, the regular classroom may be an inappropriate placement. Therefore, the NJCLD supports the use of a continuum of services and rejects the arbitrary placement of all students in any one setting.

In Issues in the Delivery of Educational Services to Individuals with Learning Disabilities the NJCLD stated its support and commitment to "a continuum of education placements, including the regular education classroom that must be available to all students with learning disabilities and must be flexible enough to meet their changing needs." This was reaffirmed in 1991 in Providing Appropriate Education for Students with Learning Disabilities in Regular Education Classrooms, which recommended that public and private education agencies should "establish system-wide and state-based plans for educating students with learning disabilities in the regular education classroom when such placement is appropriate. The responsibility for developing plans must be shared by regular and special educators, parents, and student consumers of the services. Once developed, a plan must be supported at all levels of the educational system."

In summary, the NJCLD supports educational reform and efforts to restructure schools. As stated in School Reform: Opportunities for Excellence and Equity for Individuals with Learning Disabilities, "NJCLD demonstrates a deep concern and desire that parents, professionals, and policy makers work cooperatively in planning and implementing reforms. We strongly urge that strategies be developed within the reform movement to improve education for students with learning disabilities." As these strategies are developed, it is necessary to ensure that each student with a learning disability is provided a continuum of service options that will guarantee a free, appropriate public education based on the student's individual needs.

*Source:* Reprinted from National Joint Committee on Learning Disabilities (NJCLD). Available online: http://www.ldonline.org/njcld/react_inclu.html (retrieved January 17, 2005). Used by permission.

Although we don't know how to really define LD youngsters (and heaven knows we've tried), we do know that often they don't do as well as their non-LD mates in oral and silent reading, reading comprehension, spelling, mathematics, history, science, geography, industrial arts, music, or family living. Because of these many deficits and deviations, we teachers, in all good faith, set out to remediate as many of the "shortfalls" as possible so that youth with learning disabilities will be as normal and wonderful as we are. We should reconsider this total remedial approach to learning disabilities. One reason for considering an alternative should be obvious if we thought of a day in the life of a student with learning disabilities. First, the teacher sets out to remediate his reading, then his math, and then his language, social skills, and soccer playing. Toward the end of the day, she attempts to remediate his metacognitive deficits. That lad is in a remediation mode throughout the day. Is it any wonder that some of these youngsters have self-concepts, self-images, self-esteems, and attributions that are out of whack?

We should spend some time concentrating on these youngsters' positive qualities. If a girl is inclined toward mechanics, or a boy to being a chef, we should nurture those skills. And if a child doesn't have a negotiable behavior, we should locate one and promote it. I can't help but think that if every youngster, LD or otherwise, had at least one trade, skill, or technique about which he or she was fairly competent, that would do more for that youngster's adjustment than would the many hours of remediation to which the child is subjected. Perhaps that accent on the positive would go a long way toward actually helping the remediation process. If children knew they could excel in something, that might help them become competent in other areas as well. (T. C. Lovitt, September 2, 2004, personal communication)

# Tips for Beginning Teachers

## Nothing Succeeds Like Success
### by Ronni Hochman Spratt

*Get to know your students personally.* Each student is different, but they all respond to genuine, personal attention. Every day I try to have a brief, personal conversation with each student. I can tell you about what each one likes to eat, her favorite and least favorite bands, what TV shows she watches, what she's excited about, what she's worried about, and her hopes for the future. Once students trust you and know that you're not going anywhere—that you're consistent—they are very open and responsive. They know I truly care about them. So when I don't let up on them academically and demand their best efforts and signs of improvement, they're okay with it. When I have to discipline students, they understand. They know I'm doing it because I care about them and their success. Of all the notes and letters I've received from parents and students, one of my favorites was from an eighth-grade boy, who wrote, "Even though I have been bad at times, she's still there for me the whole way."

*Discover and build upon each student's strengths.* I believe a key to helping students access the general education curriculum is identifying the student's strengths and then putting him back into the regular classroom only in the areas in which he can experience a great amount of success. I use the student's time in the resource room to build those skills he needs to be completely integrated into the general education classroom—whether it's learning to read faster or learning to stay on task long enough to complete independent seatwork.

*Expect your students to learn and then provide the supports that enable them to do so.* Nothing succeeds like success. Provide supports that enable students to have some success and then gradually withdraw them. Today's hot word for this approach is "scaffolding"—a strategy that effective special educators have always used.

*Hold high expectations and stick to them.* Students need to know that we consistently expect them to succeed and do their best. The first time a student hands me a beautiful piece of writing, I smile and say, "Whoa, Charlotte, you just made a big mistake! You showed me how well you can do. I will never accept anything less from you." Once a student has shown me she can do quality work, I won't accept shoddy work.

*Enjoy the students—they're so much fun!* If you just take the time to get to know them, they'll be willing to do anything for you. And they'll teach you some things and provide lots of laughs along the way. Sure, there are some difficult days—some are downright disastrous. Have a sense of humor and use it! It will help you through those difficult days and allow you to enjoy your students' successes all the more.

# KEY TERMS AND CONCEPTS

criterion-referenced tests, p. 194
curriculum-based measurement
(CBM), p. 195
dyslexia, p. 185
graphic organizers, p. 204

guided notes, p. 203
learning disabilities, p. 182
mnemonic strategies, p. 204
precision teaching, p. 196
response to instruction, p. 209

 To print your own set of SAFMED flash cards for studying and mastering these terms, go to Chapter 5 of the Companion Website, **www.prenhall.com/heward**.

## SUMMARY

### Definitions

- There is no universally agreed-on definition of learning disabilities. Most states require that three criteria be met: (1) a severe discrepancy between potential or ability and actual achievement, (2) learning problems that cannot be attributed to other disabilities, and (3) special educational services needed to succeed in school.
- No matter which definition is used, educators should focus on each student's specific skill deficiencies for assessment and instruction.

### Characteristics

- Most students with learning disabilities show one or more of the following characteristics: reading problems, deficits in written language, underachievement in math, social-skills deficits, problems with attention and hyperactivity, and behavioral problems.
- The fundamental, defining characteristic of students with learning disabilities is specific and significant achievement deficiency in the presence of adequate overall intelligence.

### Prevalence

- Learning disabilities form the largest category in special education. Students with learning disabilities represent one-half of all students receiving special education.
- About three times as many boys as girls are identified as learning disabled.

### Causes

- Although the actual cause of a specific learning disability is seldom known, four types of suspected causal factors are brain damage, heredity, biochemical imbalance, and environmental factors.
- Specific regions of the brains of some individuals with reading and language disabilities show abnormal activation patterns during phonological processing tasks.
- Genetics may account for at least some family links with dyslexia. Research has located possible chromosomal loci for the genetic transmission of phonological deficits that may predispose a child for reading problems later.
- Most professionals today give little credence to biochemical imbalance as a significant cause of learning disabilities.
- Environmental factors—particularly impoverished living conditions early in a child's life and poor instruction—contribute to the achievement deficits of many children with learning disabilities.

### Assessment

- Norm-referenced tests compare a child's score with the scores of age mates who have taken the same test.
- Criterion-referenced tests, which compare a child's score with a predetermined mastery level, are useful in identifying specific skills the child has learned as well as skills that require instruction.

- Teachers use informal reading inventories to observe directly and record a child's reading skills.
- Curriculum-based measurement is a formative evaluation method that measures a student's progress in the actual curriculum in which she is participating.
- Direct and daily measurement involves assessing a student's performance on a specific skill each time it is taught.
- Precision teaching is a special type of direct and daily measurement in which the standard celeration chart is used to guide instructional decisions based on changes in a student's frequency of performance.

## Educational Approaches

- Contemporary best practice in educating students with learning disabilities includes approaches such as explicit instruction, content enhancements, and learning strategies.
- Content enhancements, such as graphic organizers, visual displays, guided notes, and mnemonic strategies, make curriculum content more accessible to students with learning disabilities.
- Learning strategies help students guide themselves successfully through specific tasks or general problems.

## Educational Placement Alternatives

- Most students with learning disabilities spend at least part of each school day in the regular classroom.
- In some schools, a consultant teacher helps regular classroom teachers work with children with learning disabilities.
- In the resource room, a specially trained teacher works with children on particular skill deficits for one or more periods per day.
- A few children with learning disabilities attend separate classrooms. This placement option, however, should be used only after legitimate attempts to serve the child in a less restrictive setting have failed; and it should not be considered permanent.

## Current Issues and Future Trends

- Response to instruction, a promising approach to the early identification and prevention of learning disabilities, uses CBM of at-risk children's progress during 10–15 weeks of intensive individual or small-group tutoring. Failure to respond to this treatment confirms a learning disability.
- Discussion and debate about what constitutes a true learning disability are likely to continue. It is important for schools to respond to the individual needs of all children who have difficulty learning.
- Most professionals and advocates for students with learning disabilities do not support full inclusion, which would eliminate the continuum of service-delivery options.
- In addition to their academic and social-skills deficits, students with learning disabilities possess positive attributes and interests that teachers should identify and try to strengthen.

To check your comprehension of chapter contents, go to the Guided Review and Quiz modules in Chapter 5 of the Companion Website, **www.prenhall.com/heward**.

# EMOTIONAL AND BEHAVIORAL DISORDERS

# Featured Teacher

## MICHAEL WANG

BUCKEYE RANCH SCHOOL
SOUTHWESTERN CITY SCHOOLS DISTRICT,
GROVE CITY, OHIO

### Education—Teaching Credentials—Experience
- B.A., general education, East China Normal University, Shanghai, 1987
- M.A., special education/students with emotional handicap, The Ohio State University, 1998
- Ohio certification in emotional handicaps, K–12; elementary and middle school principal
- 6 years of teaching students with emotional and behavioral disorders

**Current Position and Students**     I have been working at the Buckeye Ranch School, a residential school for children with severe emotional and behavioral disorders (EBD), for 6 years. My first 4 years were spent teaching language arts, reading, math, science, and social studies to students with emotional disturbances in a self-contained classroom. For the past 2 years, I have served as principal at the school. Our school has 11 classrooms for students with EBD, who range in age from 10 to 18. Some of our students also receive special education and related services because of learning disabilities, deafness and hearing loss, and communication disorders.

Our student population is about 60% white and 40% African American. Most of our students come from low socioeconomic backgrounds. Some do not have an adult role model in their life at all. Because the majority live on campus, staff members get to know the students very well and not only serve as teachers and advisors but also as those missing adult role models.

**IEP Goals**     IEPs at our school—as they should in any school—focus on the unique emotional, behavioral, and academic needs of each student. Although challenging and often hard-to-understand behavior problems are what bring students to our school, people are often surprised to learn that academic goals feature so prominently on our students' IEPs. If special education does not address the academic learning needs of students with emotional and behavioral disorders, it does them a great disservice. Following are examples of IEP goals and objectives for two of our students.

*Tim.* Tim is 14 years old and a very poor reader. Although he can pronounce unfamiliar words, his comprehension is poor. Tim's IEP team, of which he is an active participant, determined that much of his special education should focus on improving his reading skills to help him in the classroom and in daily life. Here are some of the short-term objectives on Tim's IEP:

- Volunteering to read aloud in his classes at least once per day
- Reading passages of increasing length and complexity each school day while maintaining at least 80% accuracy in responding to factual comprehension questions
- Orally summarizing the basic plot and events of a story with 80% accuracy

## Focus Questions

- Why should a child who behaves badly be considered disabled?

- Who is more severely disabled: the acting-out, antisocial child or the withdrawn child?

- How are behavior problems and academic performance interrelated?

- How can a teacher's efforts to defuse a classroom disturbance contribute to an escalation of misbehavior?

- What are the most important skills for teachers of students with emotional and behavioral disorders?

*Rich.* Rich is a 17-year-old young man whose frequent emotional and physical outbursts toward others have left him with few friends and hindered his educational performance in the classroom. A major IEP goal for Rich is learning to maintain self-control and resolve confrontations peacefully. Here are some of the short-term objectives on Rick's IEP:

- Initiating at least four positive conversations each day with peers, teachers, and other school staff members
- Using his understanding of "offense cycles" identified with his counselor as a means to self-monitor behavior
- Resolving problems without the use of verbal or physical aggression at least 80% of the time

***Curriculum Materials and Teaching Strategies***     Many students with emotional and behavioral disorders do not recognize and comply with authority. But because many also love to listen to good stories, I incorporate social skills instruction into reading by using a program called *Working Together: Building Children's Social Skills through Folk Literature* (Cartledge & Kleefeld, 1994). The strategies offered in this program enable students to improve their reading and social skills while doing something they enjoy. First, we listen to the recorded story, and then we discuss the content. Then I turn the folk literature into role plays incorporating the students' needs and interests. When I teach reading, I consistently use this folk literature as a reading textbook. The students love the stories and the fact that I incorporate their interests into the lessons. In this way, I not only gain students' respect but also enable them to learn from what I am teaching.

Another strategy is to empower the students to become student leaders. The beneficial effects of using peers as group leaders to increase social and academic achievements have been well documented in the research literature. I have found that students are generally receptive to the information delivered by members of their own age group, who reflect similar backgrounds and problems they share.

***Collaboration and Teaming***     The Buckeye Ranch School serves students from all over the country. We have a team approach that provides students with educational instruction and a variety of counseling, therapy, and other support services. Every day we interact with different professional team members to exchange information with each other in order to better serve our students. For example, the clinicians and other social workers from the Buckeye Ranch conduct daily therapy and one-on-one counseling with the students. During these sessions, students express their feelings; and clinicians work with the students on issues such as anger management, problem solving without the use of physical or verbal aggression, substance abuse, sexual abuse, and how to get along with adults and peers.

If a student has a bad day, I let my clinician know right away. We have team meetings once a week so we can discuss treatment plans for each student. I also listen to the clinician for tips on how to serve the students better. On different occasions and depending on the issues at hand, I interact with language and vocational therapists and school psychologists.

***What I Like Most about Being a Special Educator***     Each new school year, I encounter a group of students with many needs—socially, emotionally, and academically. It is a huge challenge to help these students develop and achieve to their potential, but I love this challenge; and it is especially rewarding to see their remarkable growth by the end of the year. An experience with one of my former students is a great example. When Rick came to us, he was the king of noncompliance. Giving him directions produced a torrent of abusive verbal and sometimes physical aggression as well. By observing and listening to him, I began to realize that he was sending a very important message through his behavior—he wanted me to reach out to him. I found out that Rick loved to play table tennis, so we signed a behavioral contract. We agreed through this contract that if he could stay in the classroom the whole day without being removed more than twice for disruptive outbursts, I would play table tennis with him for 30 minutes after school. He made tremendous progress as the school year progressed. Before he was discharged from the program, Rick was functioning as a student leader and a great teacher helper.

I received a call from Rick the day after he left Buckeye Ranch to return to his home school. He said he missed me and his friends from the Buckeye Ranch School but that he was doing fine in the new foster home. He also told me that he wanted to go to college because I expected him to do so. I was very touched by this conversation. Sometimes as teachers, we underestimate our impact on students' futures; yet students like Rick constantly reinforce the notion that educators make a huge impact on their lives. I am one of those lucky few who can help shape students' futures, and their social and academic growth gives meaning to my work as a special educator.

Childhood should be a happy time: a time for playing, making friends, and learning—and for most children it is. But some children's lives are in constant turmoil. Some children strike out at others, sometimes with disastrous consequences. Others are so shy and withdrawn that they seem to be in their own worlds. In either case, playing with others, making friends, and learning all the things a child must learn are extremely difficult for them. These are children with emotional and behavioral disorders. They are referred to by a variety of terms: emotionally disturbed, socially maladjusted, psychologically disordered, emotionally handicapped, or even psychotic if their behavior is extremely abnormal or bizarre.

Many children with emotional and behavioral disorders are seldom really liked by anyone—their peers, teachers, siblings, even parents. Sadder still, they often do not even like themselves. The child with behavioral disorders is difficult to be around, and attempts to befriend him (most are boys) may lead to rejection, verbal abuse, or even physical attack. Although most children with emotional and behavioral disorders are of sound mind and body, their noxious or withdrawn behavior is as serious an impediment to their functioning and learning as are the physical and developmental disabilities that challenge other children. Children with emotional and behavioral disorders make up a significant portion of students who need special education.

To better understand the topics that will be covered in this chapter, go to the Essential Concepts and Chapter at a Glance modules in Chapter 6 of the Companion Website, **www.prenhall.com/heward**

## DEFINITIONS

Like their colleagues in mental retardation and learning disabilities, special educators who work with students with emotional and behavioral disorders have been struggling to reach consensus on a definition. A clear definition of emotional and behavioral disorders is lacking for numerous reasons. First, disordered behavior is a social construct; there is no clear agreement about what constitutes good mental health. All children behave inappropriately at times. How often, with how much intensity, and for how long must a student engage in a particular behavior before he is considered disabled because of the behavior? Second, different theories of emotional disturbance use concepts and terminology that do little to promote meaning from one definition to another. Third, expectations and norms for appropriate behavior are often quite different across ethnic and cultural groups. Finally, sometimes emotional and behavioral disorders occur in conjunction with other disabilities (notably mental retardation and learning disabilities), making it difficult to tell whether one condition may be the result or the cause of the other.

Although many definitions of behavioral disorders have been proposed, the two that have had the most influence are the definition in IDEA and one proposed by a coalition of professional associations concerned with children with behavior problems.

Council for Exceptional Children    Content Standards for Beginning Teachers of Students with E/BD: Educational terminology and definitions of individuals with E/BD (BD1K1).

# IDEA Definition of Emotional Disturbance

Emotional disturbance is one of the disability categories in IDEA under which children may receive special education services. IDEA defines serious emotional disturbance as follows:

(I) The term means a condition exhibiting one or more of the following characteristics over a long period of time and to a marked degree that adversely affects educational performance:

   (a) An inability to learn which cannot be explained by intellectual, sensory, and health factors;

   (b) An inability to build or maintain satisfactory interpersonal relationships with peers and teachers;

   (c) Inappropriate types of behavior or feelings under normal circumstances;

   (d) A general pervasive mood of unhappiness or depression; or

   (e) A tendency to develop physical symptoms or fears associated with personal or school problems.

(II) The term includes schizophrenia. The term does not apply to children who are socially maladjusted, unless it is determined that they have an emotional disturbance. (U.S. Department of Education, 1999, p. 12422)

At first glance, this definition may seem straightforward enough. It identifies three conditions that must be met: *chronicity* ("over a long period of time"), *severity* ("to a marked degree"), and *difficulty in school* ("adversely affects educational performance"); and it lists five types of problems that qualify. But in fact, this definition is extremely vague and leaves much to the subjective opinion of the authorities who surround the child. What do terms such as *satisfactory* and *inappropriate* really mean? Differing degrees of teacher tolerance for student behavior (Schwartz, Wolfe, & Cassar, 1997; Shinn, Tindal, & Spira, 1987), differences between teachers' and parents' expectations for student behavior (Aaroe & Nelson, 2000), and the fact that expectations for behavior vary across ethnic and cultural groups (Taylor, Gunter, & Slate, 2001) make the referral and identification of students with emotional and behavioral disorders a difficult and subjective process.

And how does one determine that some behavior problems represent "social maladjustment" whereas others indicate true "emotional disturbance"? Many children experiencing significant difficulties in school because of their behavior are ineligible for special education under IDEA because their problems are considered to be "merely" conduct disorders or discipline problems (Forness & Kavale, 2000).

The federal definition was derived from a single study conducted by Eli Bower (1960) in the Los Angeles county schools more than 40 years ago (Forness & Kavale, 2000). Bower himself never intended to make a distinction between emotional disturbance and social maladjustment. Indeed, he has stated that the five components of the definition were, in fact, meant to be indicators of social maladjustment (Bower, 1982).

It is difficult to conceive of a child who is sufficiently socially maladjusted to have received that label but who does not display one or more of the five characteristics (especially b) included in the federal definition. As written, the definition seemingly excludes children on the very basis for which they are included. This illogical criterion for ineligibility, the dated and arbitrary list of the five characteristics that are not supported by recent research, and the subjective wording that enables school districts to not serve many children with behavioral problems have produced strongly voiced criticism of the federal definition (e.g., Cline, 1990; Forness & Knitzer, 1992; Kauffman, 2005; Wood et al., 1997).

## CCBD Definition of Emotional or Behavioral Disorders

In response to the problems many saw with the federal definition, the Council for Children with Behavioral Disorders (CCBD, 1989) drafted a new definition using the term *emotional*

**FIGURE 6.1** *"Behaviorally disordered" or "emotionally disturbed"?*
*Does it make a difference?*

The Council for Children with Behavioral Disorders (CCBD) has officially adopted the position that the term *behaviorally disordered* is more appropriate than the term *emotionally disturbed.* The CCBD endorses use of *behaviorally disordered* because (1) it does not suggest any particular theory of causation or set of intervention techniques, (2) it is more representative of the students who are disabled by their behavior and are being served under IDEA, and (3) it is less stigmatizing (Huntze, 1985). The concern about stigmatization may have some merit, at least in terms of how teachers perceive children. Two studies found that the label *behaviorally disordered* implies less-negative dimensions to teachers than does *emotionally disturbed* (Feldman, Kinnison, Jay, & Harth, 1983; Lloyd, Kauffman, & Gansneder, 1987). Both pre- and in-service teachers indicated they thought children labeled as behaviorally disordered were more teachable and likely to be successful in a regular classroom than were children identified as emotionally disturbed.

*or behavioral disorder* (Figure 6.1). The CCBD definition was later adopted by the National Mental Health and Special Education Coalition (a group of 30 education, mental health, and child advocacy organizations) and subsequently submitted to the U.S. Congress as a proposed replacement for the IDEA definition of serious emotional disturbance. The CCBD definition reads as follows:

1. The term "emotional or behavioral disorder" means a disability that is characterized by emotional or behavioral responses in school programs so different from appropriate age, cultural, or ethnic norms that the responses adversely affect educational performance, including academic, social, vocational or personal skills; more than a temporary, expected response to stressful events in the environment; consistently exhibited in two different settings, at least one of which is school-related; and unresponsive to direct intervention in general education, or the condition of the child is such that general education interventions would be insufficient.
2. The term includes such a disability that co-exists with other disabilities.
3. The term includes a schizophrenic disorder, affective disorder, anxiety disorder, or other sustained disorder of conduct or adjustment, affecting a child if the disorder affects educational performance as described in paragraph (1). (Federal Register, February 10, 1993, p. 7938)

The CCBD definition clarifies the educational dimensions of the disability; focuses directly on the child's behavior in school settings; places behavior in the context of appropriate age, ethnic, and cultural norms; and increases the possibility of early identification and intervention (McIntyre & Forness, 1996). Perhaps most important, it does not require "meaningless distinctions between social and emotional maladjustment, distinctions that often waste diagnostic resources when it is already clear that serious problems exist" (Forness & Kavale, 2000, p. 267).

## CHARACTERISTICS

Children with emotional or behavioral disorders are characterized primarily by behavior that falls significantly beyond the norms of their cultural and age group on two dimensions: externalizing and internalizing. Both patterns of abnormal behavior have adverse effects on children's academic achievement and social relationships.

*Council for Children with Behavior Disorders (CCBD)*

Council for Exceptional Children — Content Standards for Beginning Teachers of Students with E/BD: Professional and ethical practice, organizations and publications relevant to the field of E/BD (BD9K1).

*Externalizing behaviors and noncompliance*

Council for
Exceptional
Children   Content
Standards for
Beginning Teachers of Students
with E/BD: Social characteristics
of individuals with E/BD
(BD2K3).

# Externalizing Behaviors

The most common behavior pattern of children with emotional and behavioral disorders consists of antisocial, or externalizing behaviors. In the classroom, children with *externalizing behaviors* frequently do the following (adapted from Walker, 1997, p. 13):

- Get out of their seats
- Yell, talk out, and curse
- Disturb peers
- Hit or fight
- Ignore the teacher
- Complain
- Argue excessively
- Steal
- Lie
- Destroy property
- Do not comply with directions
- Have temper tantrums
- Are excluded from peer-controlled activities
- Do not respond to teacher corrections
- Do not complete assignments

Rhode, Jensen, and Reavis (1998) describe noncompliance as the "king-pin behavior" around which other behavioral excesses revolve. "Noncompliance is simply defined as not following a direction within a reasonable amount of time. Most of the arguing, tantrums, fighting, or rule breaking is secondary to avoiding requests or required tasks" (p. 4). Clearly, an ongoing pattern of such behavior presents a major challenge for teachers of antisocial children. "They can make our teaching lives miserable and single-handedly disrupt a classroom" (Rhode et al., 1998, p. 3).

All children sometimes cry, hit others, and refuse to comply with requests of parents and teachers; but children with emotional and behavioral disorders do so frequently. Also, the antisocial behavior of children with emotional and behavioral disorders often occurs with little or no provocation. Aggression takes many forms—verbal abuse toward adults and other children, destructiveness and vandalism, and physical attacks on others. These children seem to be in continuous conflict with those around them. Their own aggressive outbursts often cause others to strike back. It is no wonder that children with emotional and behavioral disorders are seldom liked by others and find it difficult to establish friendships.

Many believe that most children who exhibit deviant behavioral patterns will grow out of them with time and become normally functioning adults. Although this optimistic outcome holds true for many children who exhibit problems such as withdrawal, fears, and speech impairments (Rutter, 1976), research indicates that it is not so for children who display consistent patterns of aggressive, coercive, antisocial, and/or delinquent behavior (Patterson, Cipaldi, & Bank, 1991; Trembley, 2000; Wahler & Dumas, 1986). The stability of aggressive behavior over a decade is equal to the stability of intelligence (Kazdin, 1987).

A pattern of antisocial behavior early in a child's development is the best single predictor of delinquency in adolescence.

*Early pattern of antisocial behavior*

Council for
Exceptional
Children   Content
Standards for
Beginning Teachers—Common
Core: Effects an exceptional
condition can have on an
individual's life (CC3K1) (also
BD2K3).

> Preschoolers who show the early signs of antisocial behavior patterns do not grow out of them. Rather, as they move throughout their school careers, they grow into these unfortunate patterns with disastrous results to themselves and others. This myth that preschoolers will outgrow antisocial behavior is pervasive among many teachers and early educators and is very dangerous because it leads professionals to do nothing early on when the problem can be effectively addressed. (Walker, Colvin, & Ramsey, 1995, p. 47)

Children who enter adolescence with a history of aggressive behavior stand a very good chance of dropping out of school, being arrested, abusing drugs and alcohol, having marginalized adult lives, and dying young (Lipsey & Derzon, 1998; Walker et al., 1995). Students with emotional and behavioral disorders are 13.3 times more likely to be arrested during their school careers than nondisabled students are (Doren, Bullis, & Benz, 1996a), and 58% are arrested within five years of leaving high school (Chesapeake Institute, 1994).

## Internalizing Behaviors

Some children with emotional and behavioral disorders are anything but aggressive. Their problem is the opposite—too little social interaction with others. They are said to have *internalizing behavioral disorders*. Although children who consistently act immaturely and withdrawn do not present the threat to others that antisocial children do, their behavior creates a serious impediment to their development. These children seldom play with others their own age. They usually do not have the social skills needed to make friends and have fun, and they often retreat into daydreams and fantasies. Some are fearful of things without reason, frequently complain of being sick or hurt, and go into deep bouts of depression. Obviously, such behavior limits a child's chances to take part in and learn from the school and leisure activities in which normal children participate. (Table 6.1 describes the most common types of anxiety disorders and mood disorders seen in school-age children.)

Children who exhibit the internalizing behaviors characteristic of some types of anxiety and mood disorders may be less disturbing to classroom teachers than are antisocial children. Because of this, they are in danger of not being identified. Happily, the outlook is fairly good for the child with mild or moderate degrees of withdrawn and immature behavior who is fortunate enough to have competent teachers and other school professionals responsible for his development. Carefully targeting the social and self-determination skills the child should learn and systematically arranging opportunities for and reinforcing those behaviors often prove successful.

It is a grave mistake, however, to believe that children with emotional disorders that result primarily in internalizing behaviors have only mild and transient problems. The severe anxiety and mood disorders experienced by some children not only cause pervasive impairments in their educational performance—they also threaten their very existence. Indeed, without identification and effective treatment, the extreme emotional disorders of some children can lead to self-inflicted injury or even death from substance abuse, starvation, or suicidal behavior.

Internalizing behavioral disorders limit a child's chances to take part in and learn from the school and leisure activities in which normal children participate.

*Internalizing behaviors*

 Council for Exceptional Children    Content Standards for Beginning Teachers of Students with E/BD: Social characteristics of individuals with E/BD (BD2K3).

## Academic Achievement

Most students with emotional and behavioral disorders perform one or more years below grade level academically (Cullinan, 2002). Many of these students exhibit significant deficiencies in reading (Coleman & Vaughn, 2000; Maughan, Pickles, Hagell, Rutter, & Yule, 1996) and in math achievement (Greenbaum et al., 1996). In addition to the challenges to learning caused by their behavioral excesses and deficits, many students with emotional or behavioral disorders also have learning disabilities and/or language delays, which compound their difficulties in mastering academic skills and content (Glassberg, Hooper, & Mattison, 1999; Kaiser, Hancock, Cai, Foster, & Hester, 2000).

The following dismal academic outcomes for students with emotional and behavioral disorders are derived from several nationwide studies (Chesapeake Institute, 1994; U.S. Department of Education, 1998, 1999; Valdes, Williamson, & Wagner, 1990):

- Two-thirds cannot pass competency exams for their grade level.
- They have the lowest grade-point average of any group of students with disabilities.
- They have the highest absenteeism rate of any group of students.

*Academic achievement of students with E/BD*

Council for Exceptional Children    Content Standards for Beginning Teachers—Common Core: Educational implications of characteristics of various exceptionalities (CC2K2).

**TABLE 6.1  Types of anxiety, mood, and other emotional disorders in children**

| Condition | Characteristics/Symptoms | Remarks |
|---|---|---|
| *ANXIETY DISORDERS* | Maladaptive emotional state or behaviors caused by excessive and often irrational fears and worries. | |
| **Generalized anxiety disorder** | Excessive, unrealistic worries, fears, tension that lasts six months or more; in addition to chronic anxiety, symptoms include restlessness, fatigue, difficulty concentrating, muscular aches, insomnia, nausea, excessive heart rate, dizziness, and irritability. | Excessive worrying interferes with normal activities. Children tend to be very hard on themselves, striving for perfection, sometimes redoing tasks repeatedly; they may also seek constant approval or reassurance from others. Usually affects children between the ages of 6 and 11. |
| **Phobias** | Intense fear reaction to a specific object or situation (such as snakes, dogs, or heights); level of fear is inappropriate to the situation and is recognized by the person as being irrational; can lead to the avoidance of common, everyday situations. | Most phobias can be treated successfully with behavior therapy techniques such as systematic desensitization (gradual and repeated exposure to feared object or situation while relaxing) and self-monitoring. |
| **Obsessive/compulsive disorder (OCD)** | Persistent, recurring thoughts (obsessions) that reflect exaggerated anxiety or fears; typical obsessions include worry about being contaminated, behaving improperly, or acting violently. The obsessions may lead an individual to perform a ritual or routine (compulsions)—such as washing hands, repeating phrases, or hoarding—to relieve the anxiety caused by the obsession. | OCD most often begins in adolescence or early adulthood. Most individuals recognize their obsessions are irrational and that the compulsions are excessive or unreasonable. Behavioral therapy is effective in treating most cases of OCD; medications are often effective. |
| **Anorexia nervosa** | Refusal to maintain body weight at or above a minimally normal weight for age and height. Obsessive concern with body weight or shape. Intense anxiety about gaining weight or becoming fat, even though severely underweight. Two subtypes: restricting food intake by starving oneself down to an abnormal weight and binge-eating/purging. | Anorexia and bulimia (see below) are primarily disorders of females, particularly adolescent girls. Early in the course of anorexia, the person often denies the disorder. Depression, anxiety, compulsive exercise, social withdrawal, and substance abuse are often associated with eating disorders. |
| **Bulimia nervosa** | Recurrent episodes of (a) binge eating (eating in a discrete period of time an amount of food much larger than most people would eat under similar circumstances while feeling that one cannot stop eating) and (b) inappropriate compensatory behavior in order to prevent weight gain (e.g., self-induced vomiting, misuse of laxatives or other medications, fasting, excessive exercise). | Preoccupation with weight and shape and excessive self-evaluation are primary symptoms of both anorexia and bulimia. Many patients demonstrate a mixture of both anorexic and bulimic behaviors. |
| **Post-traumatic stress disorder** | Prolonged and recurrent emotional reactions after exposure to a traumatic event (e.g., sexual or physical assault, unexpected death of a loved one, natural disaster, witnessing or being a victim of acts of war or terrorism). Symptoms: flashbacks and nightmares of the traumatic event; avoiding places or things related to the trauma; emotional detachment from others; and difficulty sleeping, irritability, or poor concentration. | Increased recognition of PTSD in children has occurred in the U.S. since the terrorist attacks of September 11, 2001. Individual and group counseling and support activities can be helpful. Teachers can help by providing an environment in which the child with PTSD feels safe and positive social attention for the child's involvement with normal activities. |
| **Selective mutism (also called elective mutism, speech phobia)** | Child speaks normally to specific person or group (e.g., family members) but refuses to talk to others. May be a response to trauma, more often caused by anxiety or fear of speaking in certain settings or to certain individuals or groups. | Treatment uses positive approach, no attention or punishment for not speaking, reinforcement for approximations of speaking (e.g., participation in class activities, non-speech vocalizations). |

| | | |
|---|---|---|
| **MOOD DISORDERS** | Characterized by impaired functioning due to episodes of abnormally depressed or elevated emotional state. | |
| **Depression** | Marked by pervasive sad mood and sense of hopelessness. Symptoms include social withdrawal; irritability; feelings of guilt or worthlessness; inability to concentrate; loss of interest in normal activities; drastic change in weight, appetite, or sleeping pattern; prolonged crying bouts; recurring thoughts of suicide. Several symptoms must be exhibited over a period of time and not be temporary, reasonable responses to life circumstances (e.g., grief over death of a family member). | It is estimated that 15% to 20% of adolescents experience depression at one time or another; adolescent girls are twice as likely as are boys to be depressed. Depression is often overlooked in children, especially when symptoms are overshadowed by externalizing behavioral disorders. Teachers should be attentive for signs of possible depression and refer students for evaluation. |
| **Bipolar disorder (formerly called manic-depressive disorder)** | Alternative episodes of depressive and manic states. During manic episodes, person is in an elevated mood of euphoria—a feeling of extraordinary elation, excitement—and exhibits three or more of the following symptoms: excessive egotism; very little sleep needed; incessant talkativeness; rapidly changing thoughts and ideas in uncontrolled order; easily distracted; agitated, "driven" activities; and participation in personally risky activities. The peak age at onset of first symptoms falls between the ages of 15–19. Five years or more may elapse between the first and second episodes, but the time periods between subsequent episodes usually narrow. | Some patients are reluctant to participate in treatment because they find the experience of mania very enjoyable. Patients often recall this experience and minimize or deny entirely the devastating features of full-blown mania or the demoralization of a depressive episode. Regular patterns of daily activities, including sleeping, eating, physical activity, and social and/or emotional stimulation may help. Medications are often effective in treating acute episodes, preventing future episodes, and in providing stabilizing moods between episodes. |
| **OTHER DISORDERS** | | |
| **Schizophrenia** | A severe psychotic disorder characterized by delusions, hallucinations (hearing voices), unfounded fears of persecution, disorganized speech, catatonic behavior (stupor and muscular rigidity), restricted range and intensity of emotional expression (affective flattening), reduced thought and speech productivity, and decreased initiation of goal-directed behavior. Onset typically occurs during adolescence or early adulthood. Most persons with schizophrenia alternate between acute psychotic episodes and stable phases with few or no symptoms. Affects males and females with equal frequency. | Although there is no cure at present, most children with schizophrenia benefit from a variety of treatments, including antipsychotic medication, behavioral therapy, and educational interventions such as social skills training. The general goals of treatment are to decrease the frequency, severity, and psychosocial consequences of psychotic episodes and to maximize functioning between episodes. |
| **Tourette syndrome** | An inherited neurological disorder characterized by motor and vocal tics (repeated and involuntary movements) such as eye blinking, facial grimacing, throat clearing or sniffing, arm thrusting, kicking, or jumping. About 15% of cases include *coprolalia* (repeated cursing, obscene language, and ethnic slurs). Symptoms typically appear before age 18; males affected 3 to 4 times more often than females. Many students with TS also have attentional problems, impulsiveness, compulsions, ritualistic behaviors, and learning disabilities. | Tics are experienced as irresistible; student may seek a secluded spot to release symptoms after delaying them. Tics are more likely during periods of tension or stress, and decrease with relaxation or when focusing on an absorbing task. Tolerance and understanding of symptoms are of paramount importance to students with TS; untimed exams (in a private room if vocal tics are a problem), and permission to leave the classroom when tics become overwhelming are often helpful. |

*Sources:* American Psychiatric Association (1999, 2000a, 2000b, 2000c); Anxiety Disorders Association of America (2001). Brigham and Cole (1999); Cullinan (2002); Kauffman (2005); Maag (2003); Morris and Kratochwill (1998); Stark, Bronik, Wong, Wells, and Ostrander (2000); Tourette Syndrome Association (2000); von Hahn (2004).

- Only 20%–25% leave high school with a diploma or certificate of completion, compared to 50% of all students with disabilities and 76% of all youth in the general population.
- More than 50% drop out of high school.

The strong correlation between low academic achievement and behavioral problems is not a one-way relationship. The disruptive and defiant behavior of students with emotional and behavioral disorders "almost always leads to academic failure. This failure, in turn, predisposes them to further antisocial conduct" (Hallenbeck & Kauffman, 1995, p. 64).

## Intelligence

Many more children with emotional and behavioral disorders score in the slow learner or mildly retarded range on IQ tests than do children without disabilities. Valdes et al. (1990) reported a mean IQ of 86 for students with emotional and behavioral disorders, with about half of their sample scoring between 71 and 90. The students in a study by Cullinan, Epstein, and Sabornie (1992) had an average IQ score of 92.6. On the basis of his review of research related to the intelligence of children with emotional and behavioral disorders, Kauffman (2005) concluded that "although the majority fall only slightly below average in IQ, a disproportionate number, compared to the normal distribution, score in the dull normal and mildly retarded range, and relatively few fall in the upper ranges" (p. 207).

Whether children with emotional and behavioral disorders actually have any less real intelligence than do children without disabilities is difficult to say. An IQ test measures how well a child performs certain tasks at the time and place the test is administered. It is almost certain that the disturbed child's inappropriate behavior has interfered with past opportunities to learn many of the tasks included on the test. Rhode et al. (1998) estimate that the average student actively attends to the teacher and to assigned work approximately 85% of the time, but that students with behavior disorders are on task only about 60% or less of the time. This difference in on-task behavior can have a dramatic impact on academic learning. (To learn about one strategy for keeping students actively engaged with instruction, see Teaching & Learning, "Using Response Cards to Increase Participation and Achievement," later in this chapter.)

## Social Skills and Interpersonal Relationships

The ability to develop and maintain interpersonal relationships during childhood and adolescence is an important predictor of present and future adjustment. As might be expected, many students with emotional and behavioral disorders experience great difficulty in making and keeping friends (Cartledge & Milburn, 1995; Gresham, Lane, MacMillan, & Bocian, 1999). The results of a study by Schonert-Reichl (1993) comparing the social relationships of secondary students with behavioral disorders with those of same-age peers without disabilities is typical of much of the published literature on social skills of students with emotional and behavioral disorders. The students with behavioral disorders reported lower levels of empathy toward others, participation in fewer curricular activities, less frequent contacts with friends, and lower-quality relationships than were reported by their peers without disabilities.

## PREVALENCE

Estimates of how many children have emotional and behavioral disorders vary widely. Cullinan and Epstein (1995) suggest that a "rule of one-third" describes the prevalence of behavior disorders: that approximately 33% of children will experience behavior problems that concern their teachers at some time during any given year, that the behavior of about one-third of those children (or 10% of the school-age population) will require intervention

*Response cards*

Council for
Exceptional
Children   Content
Standards for
Beginning Teachers—Common
Core: Select, adapt, and use
instructional strategies and
materials according to
characteristics of the individual
with exceptional learning needs
(CC4S3).

or assistance of school personnel outside the regular classroom, and one-third of that group (about 3%) will have behavioral problems significant enough to warrant special education. After reviewing studies on prevalence, Koyanagi and Gaines (1993) concluded that between 3% and 5% of children have emotional and behavioral problems sufficient to warrant intervention. A national consortium of special educators and researchers who are developing schoolwide discipline and positive behavioral support programs estimates that between 1% and 7% of students have chronic problems with behavior that require intensive, individualized intervention and supports (Sugai, Sprague, Horner, & Walker, 2000).

Such varying estimates suggest that different criteria are being used to decide what constitutes emotional or behavioral disorders. Differences in prevalence figures, however, stem as much from how the data are collected as they do from the use of different definitions (Cullinan, 2002). Most surveys ask teachers to identify students in their classes who display behavior problems at that point in time. Many children exhibit inappropriate behavior for short periods, and such one-shot screening procedures will identify them.

Annual reports from the federal government, however, show that far fewer children are being served than the most conservative prevalence estimates. The 482,597 children ages 6 to 21 who received special education under the IDEA category of emotional disturbance during the 2002–2003 school year represented only about 0.7% of the school-age population (U.S. Department of Education, 2004). Although this figure marked the greatest number of children with emotional and behavioral disorders ever served and ranked emotional disturbance as the fourth-largest disability category in special education (8.1% of all students ages 6 through 21 served under IDEA), it means that most children with emotional and behavioral disorders are not receiving special education.

The number of children being served represents less than half of the 2% estimate the federal government used previously in its estimates of funding and personnel needs for students with emotional and behavioral disorders. Kauffman (2005) believes that social policy and economic factors caused the government to first reduce its estimate of the prevalence of behavioral disorders (from 2% to 1.2%) and then to stop publishing an estimate altogether. "The government obviously prefers not to allow wide discrepancies between prevalence estimates and the actual number of children served. It is easier to cut prevalence estimates than to serve more students" (p. 50).

Regardless of what prevalence study one turns to, it is evident there are many thousands of schoolchildren whose emotional and behavior problems are adversely affecting their educational progress but who are not presently receiving the special education they need. Although IDEA clearly mandates that all children with disabilities receive individualized special education services, the uncertain meaning of many aspects of the definition allows determination of whether a child is behaviorally disordered to be more a function of a school district's available resources to provide the needed services than a function of the child's actual needs for such services.

*Gender.* The vast majority of children identified for special education because of emotional or behavioral disorders are boys (Cullinan, 2002). Boys identified as emotionally or behaviorally disordered are likely to have externalizing disorders and to exhibit antisocial, aggressive behavior. Although girls with emotional and behavioral disorders are more likely to show internalizing disorders such as anxiety and social withdrawal, research shows that girls have problems with aggression and antisocial behavior as well (Talbott & Thiede, 1999).

*Juvenile Delinquency.* The word *delinquent* is a legal term; however, many of the offenses that an adolescent commits to be labeled delinquent constitute a behavioral disorder. In 1999, law enforcement agencies made about 2.5 million arrests of persons under the age of 18 (Snyder, 2000). Juveniles, who comprise about 20% of the total population, were involved in 16% of all violent crime arrests and 32% of all property crime arrests in 1999.

# Using Response Cards to Increase Participation and Achievement

Rashawn raised his hand for the last time. He wanted to answer several of his teacher's questions, especially when she asked whether anyone could name the clouds that look like wispy cotton. But it wasn't his day to get called on. He tried to follow along but lost interest and laid his head on his desk.

Dean did get called on once, but he didn't raise his hand too often. It was easier just to sit there. If he were quiet and still like Rashawn, then he wouldn't have to think about learning all this weather stuff. But it got too hard for Dean to just sit, so he started acting out. This got his teacher's attention.

"Dean, please pay attention!"

"Stop that, Dean!"

"Dean, how do you expect to learn this material for tomorrow's test if you're not part of the group?"

The next day, Rashawn and Dean did poorly on the test of meteorology concepts. Each boy had a history of poor school achievement; and teachers sometimes used slow learner, attention deficit disorder, learning disabilities, emotional disturbance, and behavioral disorders as explanations for their lack of success. But perhaps their poor scores, as well as their chronic underachievement, were directly influenced by the quality of instruction they received.

Neither boy had actively participated during the previous day's lesson. Instead of being active learners who responded frequently to the lesson's content, both boys were at best passive observers. Educational research has shown that students who respond actively and often usually learn more than do students who passively attend to instruction (Fisher & Berliner, 1985; Greenwood, Delquadri, & Hall, 1984; Heward, 1994). Although most teachers recognize the importance of active student participation, it is difficult to implement during group instruction. Teachers commonly pose a question to the entire class and then call on one student. This technique often results in frequent responses by high-achieving students and few or no responses by low-achieving students such as Rashawn and Dean (Maheady, Mallete, Harper, & Saca, 1991). Response cards (RCs) are one alternative to the traditional hand-raising (HR) and one-student-participating-at-a-time method of group instruction (Heward et al., 1996).

## WHAT ARE RESPONSE CARDS?

Response cards are cards, signs, or items simultaneously held up by all students to display their responses to a question or problem presented by the teacher. There are two basic types: preprinted and write-on. When using preprinted RCs, each student selects from a personal set of cards the one with the answer he wishes to display. Examples include yes/true and no/false cards, numbers, colors, traffic signs, molecular structures, and parts of speech. Instead of a set of different cards, a single preprinted RC with multiple answers can be given to each student (e.g., a card with clearly marked sections identified as proteins, fat, carbohydrates, vitamins, and minerals for use in a lesson on healthful eating habits). In its humblest version, the preprinted RC with multiple responses is a "pinch card": the student responds by holding up the card with her fingers pinching the part displaying her answer. Colored clothespins also make good pinching tools. Preprinted RCs may also have built-in devices for displaying answers, such as a cardboard clock with movable hour and minute hands.

When using write-on RCs, students mark their answers on blank cards that are erased between learning trials. A set of 40 durable write-on RCs can be made from a 4-by-8-foot sheet of white laminated bathroom board (available from builders' supply stores). The cost is generally less than $20, including the charge for cutting the sheet into 9-by-12-inch RCs. Dry-erase markers are available at most office supply stores, and paper towels or tissues will easily wipe the RCs clean.

Response cards, which are easily created for any curriculum area, enable each student in the class to answer every question or problem presented by the teacher.

Students can also use small chalkboards as write-on RCs, but responses may be difficult for the teacher to see in a full-size classroom. Write-on RCs can be custom-made to provide background or organizing structure for responses. For example, music students might mark notes on an RC that has permanent treble and bass clef scales; students in a driver's education class could draw where their car should go on RCs with permanent street intersections.

**Research** The effects of RCs on student participation and learning have been evaluated through a series of studies in regular and special education classrooms at the elementary, middle, and secondary levels (e.g., Armendariz & Umbreit, 1999; Cavanaugh, Heward, & Donelson, 1996; Christle & Schuster, 2003; Davis & O' Neill, 2004; Godfrey, Grisham-Brown, Schuster, & Hemmeter, 2003; Narayan, Heward, Gardner, Courson, & Omness, 1990). A study by Gardner, Heward, and Grossi (1994) compared the use of write-on RCs with HR during whole-class science lessons in an inner-city fifth-grade classroom. The study produced three major findings.

First, when RCs were used, each student responded to teacher-posed questions an average of 21.8 times per 30-minute lesson, compared to a mean of 1.5 academic responses when the teacher called on individuals. The higher participation rate takes on additional significance when its cumulative effect is calculated over the course of an 180-day school year. If RCs were used instead of HR for just 30 minutes per day, each student in the class would make an additional 3,700 academic responses during the school year. Second, all 22 students scored higher on next-day quizzes and two-week review tests that followed lessons with RCs than they did on quizzes and tests that followed lessons with HR. Third, all but one student preferred RCs over raising their hands to be called on.

In addition to increased academic participation and learning outcomes for students, several studies have found improved on-task behavior and/or decreases in the frequency of disruptions and inappropriate behavior when response cards were used (e.g., Armendariz & Umbreit, 1999; Christle & Schuster, 2003; Davis & O' Neill, 2004; Godfrey et al., 2003; Lambert, Cartledge, Lo, & Heward, 2004).

## HOW TO GET STARTED

### Suggestions for All Types of RCs

- Model several question-and-answer trials and give students practice on how to use RCs.
- Maintain a lively pace throughout the lesson; keep intervals between trials short.
- Give clear cues when students are to hold up and put down their cards.
- Students can learn from watching others; do not let them think it is cheating to look at classmates' RCs.

### Suggestions for Using Preprinted RCs

- Design the cards to be as easy to see as possible (e.g., consider size, print type, color codes).
- Make the cards easy for students to manipulate and display (e.g., put answers on both sides of the cards; attach a group of related cards to a ring).
- Begin instruction on new content with a small set of fact/concept cards (perhaps only two), gradually adding additional cards as students' skills improve.

### Suggestions for Using Write-On RCs

- Limit language-based responses to 1–3 words.
- Keep a few extra markers on hand.
- Be sure students do not hesitate to respond because they are concerned about making spelling mistakes:

(1) provide several practice trials with new terms before the lesson begins; (2) write new terms on the chalkboard and tell students to refer to them during the lesson; and/or (3) use the "don't worry" technique, telling students to try their best but that misspellings will not count against them.

• Students enjoy doodling on their response cards. After a good lesson, let students draw on the cards for a few minutes.

To see teachers using response cards in inclusive classrooms, go to "Dunkirk Elementary School" and "Dunkirk Middle School" on the *Exceptional Teachers* CD-ROM.

To learn more about these strategies and answer questions about what you have learned, go to the Teaching & Learning module in Chapter 6 of the Companion Website, **www.prenhall.com/heward**

Arrest rates for juveniles increase sharply during the junior high years. This pattern probably reflects both the greater harm adolescents can cause to society as a result of their inappropriate behavior and the fact that younger children are often not arrested (and therefore do not show up on the records) for committing the same acts that lead to the arrest of an older child. Younger children, however, are being arrested, and they are committing more crimes than in the past. Children under 15, for example, accounted for 67% of all juvenile arrests for arson in 1999. Although boys are generally arrested for crimes involving aggression (e.g., assault, burglary) and girls have been associated with sex-related offenses (e.g., prostitution), more and more violent offenses are being committed by girls (Siegel & Senna, 1994; Snyder, 2000). In 1999, girls accounted for 27% of all juvenile arrests.

About half of all juvenile delinquents are *recidivists* (repeat offenders). Recidivists are more likely to begin their criminal careers at an early age (usually by age 12), commit more serious crimes, and continue a pattern of repeated antisocial behavior as adults (Farrington, 1995; Tolan & Thomas, 1995). One study in Oregon found that 20% of juvenile offenders committed 87% of all crimes by juveniles (Wagner & Lane, 1998). Because only a fraction of the total number of criminal acts committed by juveniles are reported (i.e., around 12% to 15% [Henggler, 1989]), it is impossible to know the extent of the problem.

# CAUSES

*Causes of E/BD*

Council for Exceptional Children    Content Standards for Beginning Teachers of Students with E/BD: Etiology and diagnosis related to various theoretical approaches in the field of E/BD (BD2K1).

The behavior of some children with emotional or behavioral disorders is so self-destructive and apparently illogical that it is difficult to imagine how they got that way. We shake our heads in bewilderment and ask, "Where did that behavior come from?"

Numerous theories and conceptual models have been proposed to explain abnormal behavior (see Kauffman, 2005). Regardless of the conceptual model from which emotional or behavioral disorders are viewed, the suspected causes can be grouped into two major categories: biological and environmental.

## Biological Factors

*Brain Disorders.*   Many individuals who have brain disorders experience problems with emotion and behavior. Brain disorders are the result of either *brain dysgenesis* (abnormal brain development) or *brain injury* (caused by influences such as disease or trauma that alter the structure or function of a brain that had been developing normally up to that point). (Traumatic brain injury is discussed in Chapter 12.) For the vast majority of children with emotional and behavioral disorders, however, there is no evidence of brain disorder or injury.

*Genetics.*   There is evidence of a genetic link to some forms of emotional and behavioral disorders (Weiner, 1999). The disorder with the strongest research support for a genetic risk factor is *schizophrenia*, a severe and debilitating form of mental illness characterized by auditory hallucinations (hearing voices), delusions, unfounded fears of persecution, and disordered speech. Relatives of schizophrenics have an increased risk of acquiring schizophrenia that cannot be explained by environmental factors alone; and the closer the relation, the higher the probability of acquiring the condition (Gottesman, 1991). However, genetics alone has not been found to cause schizophrenia. A person in either of the two highest risk groups (a child of two parents with schizophrenia or an identical twin of a sibling with the condition) still has a less than 50% chance of developing schizophrenia (Plomin, 1995).

*Temperament.* Some researchers believe that all children are born with a biologically determined temperament. There is no agreed-upon definition of temperament, but it is generally conceived to be a person's behavioral style or typical way of responding to situations. An infant who seldom cries but smiles and coos when passed from one person to another might be said to have an easygoing temperament. In contrast, an infant who is distractable, frequently fusses, and withdraws from new situations might show signs of a difficult temperament. There is some research evidence showing that an easy or positive temperament is correlated with resilience to stress (Smith & Prior, 1995) and that a difficult temperament at an early age increases the likelihood of behavior problems in adolescence (Caspi, Henry, McGee, Moffitt, & Silva, 1995).

Although a child's inborn temperament may not in itself cause a behavior problem, it may predispose the child to problems (Carey, 1998). Thus, certain events that might not produce abnormal behavior in a child with an easygoing temperament might result in disordered behavior by the child with a difficult temperament.

## Environmental Factors

Dodge (1993) has identified three primary environmental factors that contribute to the development of conduct disorder and antisocial behavior: (1) an adverse early rearing environment, (2) an aggressive pattern of behavior displayed when entering school, and (3) social rejection by peers. Considerable research evidence supports Dodge's contention that these causal factors occur in sequence (Patterson, Reid, & Dishion, 1992; Sprague & Walker, 2000). The settings in which these events occur are the home, the community, and the school.

*Home.* The relationship children have with their parents, particularly during the early years, is critical to the way they learn to behave. Observation and analysis of parent-child interaction patterns show that parents who treat their children with love, are sensitive to their children's needs, and provide praise and attention for desired behaviors tend to have children with positive behavioral characteristics. More than two decades of research have shown that antisocial children are more likely to come from homes in which parents are inconsistent disciplinarians, use harsh and excessive punishment to manage behavior problems, spend little time engaged in prosocial activities with their children, do not monitor the whereabouts and activities of their children, and show little love and affection for good behavior (Biglan, 1995; McEvoy & Welker, 2000; Patterson et al., 1992; Walker et al., 1995). When such conditions are present in the home, a young child may be "literally trained to be aggressive during episodes of conflict with family members" (Forgatch & Paterson, 1998, p. 86).

Because of the research on the relationship between parental child-rearing practices and behavior problems, some mental health professionals have been quick to pin the blame for children's behavior problems on parents. But the relationship between parent and child is dynamic and reciprocal; in other words, the behavior of the child affects the behavior of the parents just as much as the parents' actions affect the child's actions (Sameroff, 2001). Therefore, at best it is not practical and at worst it is wrong to blame parents for the behavior problems of their children. Instead, professionals must work with parents to help them systematically change certain aspects of the parent-child relationship in an effort to prevent and modify those problems (Landy, 2002; Zionts, Simpson, & Zionts, 2001).

*Influence of home and community*

Council for Exceptional Children — Content Standards for Beginning Teachers—Common Core: Characteristics and effects of the environmental milieu of the individual with exceptional learning needs and the family (CC2K3) (also CC2K4).

*Community.*    When students associate with peers who exhibit antisocial behavior, they are more likely to experience additional trouble in the community and at school. Gang membership, drug and alcohol abuse, and deviant sexual behavior are community factors that contribute to the development and maintenance of an antisocial lifestyle (Biglan, 1995; Harland, 1997; Walker et al., 1995).

*School.*    School is where children spend the largest portion of their time outside the home. Therefore, it makes sense to observe carefully what takes place in schools in an effort to identify factors that may contribute to problem behavior. Also, because most children with emotional and behavioral disorders are not identified until they are in school, it seems reasonable to question whether school actually contributes to the incidence of behavioral disorders. Schooling practices that contribute to the development of emotional and behavioral problems in children include ineffective instruction that results in academic failure, unclear rules and expectations for appropriate behavior, inconsistent and punitive discipline practices, infrequent teacher praise and approval for academic and social behavior, and failure to individualize instruction to accommodate diverse learners (Colvin, Kameénui, & Sugai, 1993; Gunter, Denny, Jack, Shores, & Nelson, 1993; Lago-Delello, 1998; Mayer, 1995).

There is no question that what takes place in the classroom can maintain and actually strengthen deviant behavioral patterns even though the teacher is trying to help the child. Consider the all too common interaction between teacher and student illustrated in Figure 6.2 (Rhode et al., 1998). It begins with a teacher request that the student ignores and follows a predictable and escalating sequence of teacher pleas and threats that the student counters with excuses, arguments, and eventually a full-blown tantrum. The aggression and tantruming is so aversive to the teacher that she withdraws the task demand (thereby reinforcing and strengthening the student's disruptive behavior) so the student will stop

*Teacher's reaction to noncompliance*

Council for Exceptional Children    Content Standards for Beginning Teachers—Common Core: Teacher attitudes and behaviors that influence behavior of individuals with exceptional learning needs (CC5K4).

**FIGURE 6.2**  **Coercive pain control**

*Source:* Reprinted from Rhode, G., Jensen, W. R., & Reavis, H. K. (1998). *The tough kid book: Practical classroom management strategies* (p. 5). Longmont, CO: Sopris West. Used with permission.

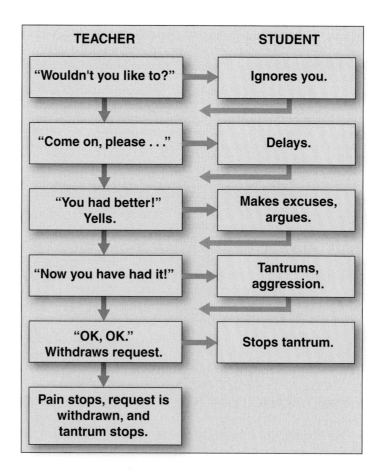

tantruming (thereby reinforcing the teacher's withdrawing the request) (Gunter et al., 1993; Maag, 2001). This process has been called *coercive pain control* because the child learns to use painful behavior (e.g., arguing, making excuses, tantruming, property destruction, even physical aggression) to get what he wants (Patterson, 1982).

## A Complex Pathway of Risks

It is impossible to identify a single factor or isolated event as the definite cause of a child's emotional or behavioral disorders. Most behavioral problems are the accumulated effect of exposure to a variety of family, neighborhood, school, and societal risk factors. And research into genetics and brain-related factors has not advanced to the point where the presence and contribution of a genetic predisposition for greater susceptibility or resilience to a given risk factor can be identified. The greater the number of risk factors and the longer a child's exposure to them, the greater the probability that the child will experience negative outcomes (Sprague & Walker, 2000). Figure 6.3 illustrates this pattern of antisocial behavior

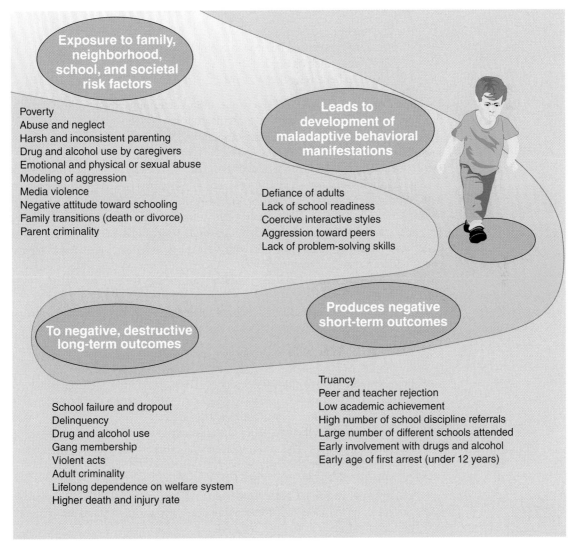

**FIGURE 6.3** **The path to long-term negative outcomes for children and youth who are at risk for school failure, delinquency, and violence**

*Source:* Reprinted from Walker, H. M., & Sprague, J. R. (1999). The path to school failure, delinquency, and violence: Causal factors and some potential solutions. *Intervention in School and Clinic, 35,* 67.

development as originally conceived by Patterson and his colleagues (Patterson, 1982; Patterson, Reid, & Dishion, 1992). Although the interplay of these risk factors is complex, and the specific contribution of any given risk factor cannot be determined, the outcome is highly predictable.

Although knowledge of these risk factors provides information necessary for planning and implementing prevention programs (Dwyer, Osher, & Hoffman, 2000; Sprague & Walker, 2000; Vance, Fernandez, & Biber, 1998), teachers should know that effective intervention and treatment of children's existing behavior problems do not require precise knowledge of etiology. Attempting to determine the extent to which various factors in a child's past are responsible for his current behavior problems is "an impossible and quite unnecessary task. Disruptive child behavior can be changed very effectively without knowing the specific, original causes for its acquisition and development" (Walker, 1997, p. 20).

## IDENTIFICATION AND ASSESSMENT

Assessment of emotional and behavioral disorders, as with all disabilities, should answer four basic questions concerning special education services:

1. Who might need help?
2. Who really does need help (who is eligible)?
3. What kind of help is needed?
4. Is the help benefiting the student?

The primary purpose of initial assessment is not to determine whether the child has something called an emotional and behavioral disorder but to see whether the child's behavior is different enough to warrant special services and, if so, to indicate what those services should be.

In practice, however, many school districts do not use any systematic method for identifying children with emotional and behavioral disorders. This is because most children with emotional and behavioral disorders identify themselves. Antisocial children seldom go unnoticed: "To have one in your classroom is to recognize one" (Rhode et al., 1998, p. 3). This does not mean, however, that identification is a sure thing. Identification of emotional disturbance is always more difficult with younger children because the behavior of all young children changes quickly and often. Also, there is danger that some children with internalizing behaviors go undetected because their problems do not draw the attention of parents and teachers.

Walker (1997) recommends that school-related assessment of children with behavior problems include the following:

- Whenever possible, address the specific reason(s) underlying problematic or deficient student behavior.
- Provide a road map to guide the design and implementation of effective interventions.
- Always give high priority to the vast reservoir of information teachers have about student performance and behavioral characteristics.
- Use more than one method (e.g., rankings, checklists, direct observations) in more than one setting (e.g., classroom, playground, home), and involve more than one social agent (e.g., parents, teachers, peers).
- Consider teacher judgment as one of the most valid and valuable sources of decision-making information available for developing alternative solutions to the problem.
- Collect only the essential information necessary to understand the school-related problems (adapted from pp. 72–73).

*Screening tools for E/BD*

Council for Exceptional Children Content Standards for Beginning Teachers of Students with E/BD: Characteristics of behavioral rating scales (BD8K1) (also CC8K3).

## Screening Tests

Children who display patterns of antisocial behavior upon entering school run the risk of developing more serious and long-standing behavior problems as they progress through school and life. Sprague and Walker (2000) stress the importance of systematically screening and identifying as early as possible those children who are at risk for developing serious patterns of antisocial behavior. Screening is the process of differentiating between children who are not likely to be disabled and those who either show signs of behavioral disturbance or seem to be at risk for developing behavior problems. Children identified through a screening process then undergo more thorough assessment to determine their eligibility for special education and their specific educational needs.

Most screening devices consist of behavior rating scales or checklists that are completed by teachers, parents, peers, and/or children themselves. Brief descriptions of four screening tests for emotional and behavioral disorders follow.

*Behavior Rating Profile (BRP-2).* This test includes six subtests that can be used independently or in any combination (Brown & Hammill, 1990). The Teacher Rating Scale includes 30 items that teachers rate on a 4-point scale from "very much like the student" to "not at all like the student" (e.g., "Doesn't follow class rules."). Parents complete the 30-item Parent Rating Scale in a similar manner (e.g., "Is shy, clings to parents."). Students answer true/false questions on the three Student Rating Scales (Home, School, and Peer) (e.g., "Other kids don't seem to like me very much."). The Sociogram is a peer-nomination activity in which each student in the class identifies three classmates in response to questions such as "Which of the girls and boys in your class would you most (or least) like to work with on a class project?"

*Child Behavior Checklist (CBCL).* This test comes in teacher report, parent report, and child report forms and can be used with children ages 5 through 18 (Achenbach & Edelbrock, 1991). The teacher's form includes 112 behaviors (e.g., "cries a lot," "not liked by other pupils") that are rated on a 3-point scale: "not true," "somewhat or sometimes true," or "very true or often true." The CBCL also includes items representing social competencies and adaptive functioning such as getting along with others and acting happy.

*Systematic Screening for Behavioral Disorders (SSBD).* This test is the most systematic, fully developed instrument presently available for screening children for possible emotional and behavioral disorders. The SSBD employs a 3-step **multiple gating screening** process for progressively narrowing down the number of children suspected of having serious behavior problems (Walker & Severson, 1990). In Gate I, classroom teachers rank-order every student in their classrooms according to behavioral profiles on two dimensions: externalizing problems and internalizing problems. The top three students on each teacher's list progress to Gate II, the Critical Events Index.

Even though the teacher is trying to help, a child's deviant behavioral patterns can be maintained and actually strengthened by what takes place in the classroom.

> Critical events are behavioral pinpoints of high salience and intensity that do not depend on frequency to define their severity. Any occurrence of these target behaviors is viewed as an indicator of major disruption of social-behavioral adjustment processes in school. Critical events have been characterized as analogous to "behavioral earthquakes" in terms of their ecological disruptiveness and severity (Todis, Severson, & Walker, 1990, pp. 75–76).

The 33 items that make up the Critical Events Index include externalizing behaviors such as "is physically aggressive with other students" and "makes lewd or obscene gestures" and internalizing behaviors such as "vomits after eating" and "has auditory or visual hallucinations." Students who exceed normative criteria on the Critical Events Index advance to Gate III of the SSBD, which consists of direct and repeated observations during independent seatwork periods in the classroom and on the playground during recess. Children who meet or exceed cutoff criteria for either or both observational measures are referred to child study teams for further evaluation to determine their eligibility for special education.

*Behavioral and Emotional Rating Scale (BERS).* This test assesses a student's strengths in 52 items across 5 areas of functioning: interpersonal strengths (e.g., reacts to disappointment in a calm manner); family involvement (e.g., participates in family activities); intrapersonal strengths (e.g., demonstrates a sense of humor), school functioning (e.g., pays attention in class), and affective strengths (e.g., acknowledges painful feelings of others) (Epstein & Sharma, 1998). Data from a strength-based assessment such as the BERS may be used to present positive attributes of students in IEP meetings, as an aid in writing IEP goals and objectives, and as an outcome measure to document a student's progress on strength-related IEP goals and objectives (Epstein, Hertzog, & Reid, 2001).

## Projective Tests

A **projective test** consists of ambiguous stimuli (e.g., "What does this inkblot look like to you?") or open-ended tasks (e.g., "Complete this sentence for me: 'Most girls like to.... '"). It is assumed that responses to items that have no right or wrong answer will reveal a person's true personality characteristics. The most famous projective test is the Rorschach Test (Rorschach, 1942), which consists of a set of 10 cards, each containing an inkblot, the left and right halves being mirror images of each other. The subject is shown one card at a time and told, "Tell me what you see, what it might be for you. There are no right or wrong answers."

Another well-known projective test is the Thematic Apperception Test (TAT) (Morgan & Murray, 1935). A person taking the TAT is shown a series of pictures and asked to make up a story about each picture, telling who the people are; what they are doing, thinking, and feeling; and how the situation will turn out.

Although sometimes interesting, the results of projective tests are of minimal value in planning or evaluating special education. Projective tests assess an indirect and extremely limited sample of a child's behavioral repertoire and, just as important, they do not assess how the child typically acts over a period of time. One-time measures—whether direct or indirect—are not a sufficient basis for identifying the presence of an emotional or behavioral disorder or planning education and treatment.

## Direct Observation and Measurement of Behavior

*Measurable dimensions of behavior*

 Content Standards for Beginning Teachers—Common Core: Basic terminology used in assessment (CC8K1).

In assessment by direct observation and measurement, the actual behaviors that cause concern about a child are clearly specified and observed in the settings in which they normally occur (e.g., in the classroom, on the playground). Behavior can be measured objectively along several dimensions: frequency, duration, latency, magnitude, and topography (see Figure 6.4).

The advantage of assessing and describing emotional and behavioral disorders in terms of these dimensions is that identification, design of instructional strategies, and evaluation of the effects of treatment can all revolve around objective measurement. This approach leads to a direct focus on the child's problem—the behavior that is adversely affecting his life—and ways of dealing with it such as strengthening a desired alternative behavior as opposed to concentrating on some presumed (and unreachable) problem within the child.

## Functional Behavioral Assessment

*Functional behavioral assessment*

Content Standards for Beginning Teachers—Common Core: Use functional assessments to develop intervention plans (CC7S4).

**Functional behavioral assessment** (FBA) is a systematic process of gathering information to help IEP teams understand why a student may be engaging in challenging behavior. Interviews and direct observation are used to obtain information about the setting events and environmental factors that predict and trigger the problem behavior and the consequences for the behavior that may be maintaining it (Chandler & Dahlquist, 2006; Heckaman, Conroy, Fox, & Chait, 2000; O' Neill et al., 1997; Peterson & Neef, 2006). This information is used to generate hypotheses about what the behavior's function, or purpose, is for the student. Two major types of behavioral function are (1) to get something the student wants (positive reinforcement) (e.g., hitting other students produces one-on-one attention from

## FIGURE 6.4  Five measurable dimensions of behavior

**FREQUENCY:**  how often a particular behavior occurs per standard unit of time (e.g., six talkouts per minute). All children cry, get into fights with other children, and sulk from time to time; yet we are not apt to think of them as emotionally disturbed. The primary difference between children with behavioral disorders and other children is the frequency, or rate, with which these behaviors occur. Although disturbed children may not do anything their nondisabled peers do not do, they do certain undesirable things too often (e.g., crying, hitting others) and/or engage in adaptive behaviors too infrequently (e.g., playing with others).

**DURATION:**  how long a child engages in a given activity (e.g., worked on math problems for 12 minutes). The amount of time children with behavioral disorders engage in certain activities is often markedly different—either longer or shorter—from that of other children. For example, most young children have temper tantrums, but the tantrums generally last no more than a few minutes. A child with emotional and behavioral disorders may tantrum for more than an hour at a time. The problem may also be one of too short a duration. For example, some children with emotional and behavioral disorders cannot stick to an academic task for more than a few seconds at a time.

**LATENCY:**  the time that elapses between the opportunity to respond and the beginning of the behavior. The latency of a child's behavior may be too long (e.g., several minutes elapse before he begins to comply with the teacher's request) or too short (e.g., the child immediately begins screaming and tantruming at the slightest provocation or frustration, thus having no time to consider more appropriate alternative behaviors).

**MAGNITUDE:**  the strength or intensity of behavior. The magnitude of a child's responses may be too little (e.g., talking in a volume so low that she cannot be heard) or too much (e.g., slamming the door).

**TOPOGRAPHY:**  the physical shape or form of behavior. Printing your name in block letters and signing your name in cursive have different topographies. Some children with emotional and behavioral disorders emit behaviors that are seldom, if ever, seen in typical children (setting fires, self-abuse). These behaviors may be maladaptive, bizarre, or dangerous to the child or others.

the teacher), and (2) to avoid or escape something the student doesn't want (negative reinforcement) (e.g., disruptive behavior when the teacher presents academic tasks results in removal of the task). The hypotheses are then used to guide the development of an intervention plan to identify and teach more appropriate replacement behaviors and to reduce the frequency or severity of the problem behavior.

This information can be used to improve the effectiveness and efficiency of behavioral intervention (Lalli, Browder, Mace, & Brown, 1993; Umbreit, 1995). For example, knowing that a student's tantrums are maintained by teacher attention suggests a different intervention than one indicated for misbehavior that is maintained by escape from challenging academic tasks.

Functional behavioral assessment might also include a **functional analysis,** the systematic manipulation of several antecedent or consequent events surrounding the target behavior in an attempt to verify the function of the behavior for the child (e.g., systematically varying the difficulty of academic tasks to test if the child's oppositional behavior is triggered by difficult tasks) (Iwata, Dorsey, Slifer, Bauman, & Richman, 1994). Because functional analysis purposely results in occurrences of the problem behavior, only highly trained personnel who have attained appropriate consents from parents/guardians and ensured that adequate safeguards are in place to protect the student and others from any harm should conduct it. (Functional analysis is discussed further in Chapter 12.)

# EDUCATIONAL APPROACHES

## Curriculum Goals

What should students with emotional and behavioral disorders be taught? An obvious but only partially correct answer is they should learn to control their antisocial behavior. For many years, programs serving students with behavioral disorders focused on treating mal-adaptive behavior at the expense of academic instruction. As a result, students who already possessed deficient academic skills fell even further behind their peers. Special education for students with emotional and behavioral disorders must also include instruction in the social and academic skills required for success in school, community, and vocational settings.

*Social skills curricula and
instruction*

Council for Exceptional Children    Content Standards for Beginning Teachers of Students with E/BD: Sources of specialized materials for individuals with E/BD (BD4K1).

*Social Skills.*    Social skills instruction is an important curriculum component for students with emotional and behavioral disorders. Many of these students have difficulty holding a conversation, expressing their feelings, participating in group activities, and responding to failure or criticism in positive and constructive ways. They often get into fights and alter-cations because they lack the social skills needed to handle or defuse provocative incidents. The slightest snub, bump, or misunderstood request—which would be laughed off or ig-nored by most children—can precipitate an aggressive attack by some students.

Numerous social skills curricula and training programs have been published; several rec-ommended ones are described in Figure 6.5. Television programs (Bryan & Ryan, 2001) and children's books have also been used to teach social skills to students with emotional and behavioral disorders (Brame, 2000; Sridhar & Vaughn, 2000). (To find out how teachers used a TV program to help a student become more likable to his classmates, see Figure 6.6.)

*Academic Skills.*    Although students with emotional and behavioral disorders require spe-cial education to work on their specific behavior problems and social skills deficits, acade-mic instruction cannot be neglected (Lane, Gresham, & O'Shaughnessy, 2002). Most children with emotional and behavioral disorders are already achieving below their nondis-abled peers; reading, writing, and arithmetic are as important to children with emotional and behavioral disorders as they are to any child who hopes to function successfully in society.

Fortunately, most students with emotional and behavioral disorders make excellent progress when provided with explicit, systematic instruction (see Mooney, Epstein, Reid, &

---

## FIGURE 6.5    Recommended social skills curricula

*Getting Along with Others* (Jackson, Jackson, & Monroe, 1983): includes 32 lessons across 17 social skills areas such as following directions, handling name calling and teasing, and offering to help. Available from Research Press, Department 95, P.O. Box 9177, Champaign, IL 61826.

*Skillstreaming the Adolescent: A Structured Learning Approach to Teaching Prosocial Skills* (Goldstein et al., 1997): activities designed to increase self-esteem and develop competence in dealing with peers, family, and authority figures. Skillstreaming programs for elementary and preschool children are also available. Published by Research Press (see above).

*Taking Part: Introducing Social Skills to Children* (Cartledge & Kleefeld, 1991): helps students in preschool classrooms through third grade learn social skills in six units: making conversation, communicating feelings, expressing oneself, cooperating with peers, playing with peers, and responding to aggression and conflict. Published by American Guidance Service, 4201 Woodland Road, Circle Pines, MN 55014.

*The Prepare Curriculum: Teaching Prosocial Competencies* (Goldstein, 1999): designed for students who are aggressive, withdrawn, or otherwise deficient in social competencies. Activities and materials for middle and high school students in 10 areas, such as problem solving, anger control, stress management, and cooperation. Published by Research Press (see above).

*The Walker Social Skills Curriculum:* includes *ACCEPTS: A Curriculum for Children's Effective Peer and Teacher Skills* (Walker et al., 1983), for children grades K–6, and *ACCESS: Adolescent Curriculum for Communication and Effective Social Skills* (Walker, Todis, Holmes, & Horton, 1988) for students at the middle and high school levels. Available from PRO-ED, 8700 Shoal Creek Boulevard, Austin, TX 78757.

*Working Together* (Cartledge & Kleefeld, 1994): incorporates stories and activities based on folk literature to teach social skills to students in grades 3–6 and older students with special needs. Published by American Guidance Service (see above).

## FIGURE 6.6  Jacob's story

Jacob was a slight young man who had a wry sense of humor and often played the role of class clown. He sometimes made sarcastic, personal attacks on his teachers and other students. This behavior often disrupted class and frequently resulted in disciplinary referrals. For this reason, Jacob had trouble making and keeping friends in school, a problem which exacerbated the feelings of loneliness and upheaval he experienced living in foster care.

During an Amazing Discoveries lesson titled, "Does Everyone See the Same Thing?" Jacob and the other students were asked to watch a short segment of the television show, *Home Improvement*. As they watched, students kept track of the number of put-downs they heard. At the end of the segment, the students reported the number of put-downs they had counted for the characters. As is often the case, there were wide variations in what the youth perceived as insulting. The social lesson was that conflict often arises when people have different ideas about what kinds of comments are put-downs. This helped Jacob understand that sometimes he was hurting those around him without meaning to.

After this lesson, his teacher noticed that Jacob started apologizing when his funny comments seemed to hurt others' feelings. She also noticed that the other students would recall the lesson when letting Jacob know that his jokes were hurtful. After a while, Jacob began using his great sense of humor in less hurtful ways and seemed to become a more engaged member of the class.

*To learn more about the Amazing Discoveries program and other projects designed to provide social, academic, and behavioral supports for secondary students with emotional and behavior disorders, go to http://www.air.org/cecp/safetynet.htm/*

*Source:* Bryan, T., & Ryan, A. K. (2001). Jacob's story: Amazing discoveries. In A. K. Ryan (Ed.), *Strengthening the safety net: How school can help youth with emotional and behavioral needs complete their high school education and prepare for life after school* (p. 10). Burlington: University of Vermont, School Research Office.

Nelson [2003] and strategies described in Chapters 4 and 5). And effective instruction is the foundation for effective classroom management. Teachers must guard against the tendency to provide students with behavior problems limited academic instruction in the form of easier tasks, fewer opportunities to respond, and lowered expectations because they wish to avoid students' noncompliance and outbursts (Gunter et al., 1993; Sutherland, Alder, & Gunter, 2003; Wehby, Symons, Canale, & Go, 1998).

## Behavior Management

*Discipline and Schoolwide Systems of Behavior Support.*  Traditionally, discipline in the schools has focused on the use of punishment in an effort to control the misbehavior of specific students. Not only is punishment generally ineffective in achieving long-term suppression of problem behavior, particularly for students with chronic histories of behavior problems, it does not help students learn desired, prosocial behaviors. Among the most important advances in student discipline procedures over the past decade is the development of schoolwide behavior support systems that promote and support positive behaviors by all students. The goals of schoolwide systems are to define, teach, and support appropriate behaviors in a way that enhances the academic and social behavior success of all students (Lewis & Sugai, 1999).

Schools that implement schoolwide systems of positive behavior support use a team-based approach to teach appropriate behavior to all students in the school. All teachers and school staff participate in teaching and rewarding desired student behavior, there are clearly defined and consistently applied consequences for rule violations, and objective data are

*Schoolwide positive behavior support*

Council for Exceptional Children  Content Standards for Beginning Teachers of Students with E/BD: Prevention and intervention strategies for individuals at risk of E/BD (BD4K4).

used to evaluate and continually improve the system (Algozzine, Audette, Ellis, Marr, & White, 2000; Peterson & Lacy-Rismiller, 2005; Sugai & Horner, 2005). Successful school-wide systems of behavior support are characterized by the following (Center for Positive Behavioral Interventions & Supports, 2001):

1. *Behavioral expectations are stated.* A small number of behavioral expectations are clearly defined. These often are simple, positively framed rules such as "Be respectful, be responsible, and be safe" or "Respect yourself, respect others, and respect property."

2. *Behavioral expectations are defined and taught.* The behavioral expectations are taught to all students in the building. Specific examples are provided for behavioral expectations (e.g., "Being respectful in class means raising your hand when you want to speak or get help. During lunch or in the hall, being respectful means using a person's name when you talk to him or her."). Behavioral expectations are taught directly with a systematic format: the general rule is presented, the rationale for the rule is discussed, positive examples ("right way") are described and rehearsed, negative examples ("wrong way") are described and modeled, and students practice the "right way" until they demonstrate fluent performance.

3. *Appropriate behaviors are acknowledged.* Appropriate behaviors are acknowledged on a regular basis. Some schools do this through formal systems (tickets, rewards); others do it through social events. Schools strive to establish a ratio of four positive adult interactions with students for every one that is negative.

4. *Behavioral errors are corrected proactively.* When students violate behavioral expectations, clear procedures are needed for showing them that their behavior was unacceptable and preventing unacceptable behavior from resulting in inadvertent rewards.

5. *Program evaluations and adaptations are data-driven and made by a team.* Successful schools establish a simple, efficient strategy for continually assessing if they are being successful and a decision-making process that allows adaptation to behavioral challenges. At the schoolwide level, general measures of the school climate include behavior incident reports, attendance rates, tardies, detention and suspension rates, etc.

6. *Individual student support systems are integrated with schoolwide discipline systems.* Schoolwide behavior support does not replace the need for a comprehensive set of more intensive interventions for the 1% to 7% of students in most schools who require more individualized and ongoing behavioral support (see Figure 6.7).

*Proactive classroom management*

Council for Exceptional Children Content Standards for Beginning Teachers—Common Core: Basic classroom management strategies for individuals with exceptional learning needs (CC5K2) (also BD4S2, BD5S1).

*Contingent teacher praise and positive reinforcement*

Council for Exceptional Children Content Standards for Beginning Teachers of Students with E/BD: Theory of reinforcement techniques in serving individuals with E/BD (BD1K5).

*Classroom Management.* Teachers of students with emotional and behavior disorders must design and manage classroom environments that are effective in not only decreasing antisocial behavior but also increasing the frequency of positive teacher-student interactions as a basis for building positive behavior and academic success (Gunter et al., 1993; Shores, Gunter, & Jack, 1993). This is a very tall order. Fortunately, teachers can turn to a strong base of clearly defined, research-validated practices for guidance on effective classroom management (e.g., Algozzine & Kay, 2002; Cipani, 2004; Kerr & Nelson, 2006; Rhode, Jensen, & Morgan, 2003).

The majority of classroom behavior problems can be prevented by the use of proactive behavior management. *Proactive strategies* are preplanned interventions that anticipate behavior problems and stop them before they occur. "It is much more difficult to remediate the problems caused by a Tough Kid than to prevent them. Once a teacher has lost the management tempo in a classroom and things are out of control, it is far more difficult to reestablish control" (Rhode et al., 1998, p. 19).

Proactive strategies include structuring the physical environment of the classroom (e.g., have the most difficult students sit nearest the teacher), establishing clear rules and expectations for appropriate behavior (Bicard, 2000), scheduling and sequencing lesson activities to minimize down time, presenting instructions to students in ways that increase the

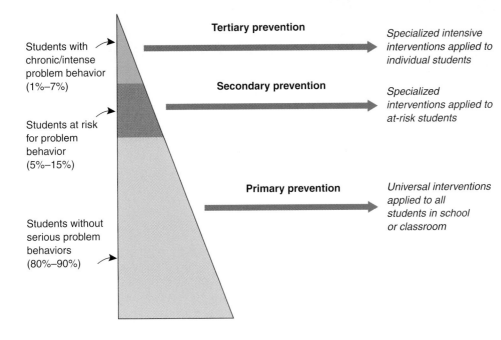

**FIGURE 6.7**
**Continuum of effective behavior support**
*Source:* Adapted from U.S. Department of Education (2000). *Twenty-second annual report to Congress on the implementation of the Individuals with Disabilities Education Act* (p. III-16). Washington, DC: Author.

Students with chronic/intense problem behavior (1%–7%)

Students at risk for problem behavior (5%–15%)

Students without serious problem behaviors (80%–90%)

**Tertiary prevention**

*Specialized intensive interventions applied to individual students*

**Secondary prevention**

*Specialized interventions applied to at-risk students*

**Primary prevention**

*Universal interventions applied to all students in school or classroom*

probability of compliance (Walker & Sylvester, 1998), keeping students actively engaged during instruction (Christle & Schuster, 2003; Godfrey et al., 2003; Gunter, Hummel, & Conroy, 1998; Sutherland & Wehby, 2001), and using praise and positive reinforcement to motivate desired behavior (Maag, 2001; Sutherland, Wehby, & Yoder, 2002; Webber & Scheuermann, 1991; Witzer & Mercer, 2003). (See Teaching & Learning, "The Power of Teacher Praise," later in this chapter.)

Managing the classroom environment for students with emotional and behavior disorders requires a great deal of knowledge and skill. In addition to the strategies already mentioned, teachers must know when and how to use a large set of behavioral teaching tools such as **shaping, contingency contracting, extinction** (ignoring disruptive behavior), **differential reinforcement of other behavior** (reinforcing any behavior except the undesirable response), **response cost, time out** (restricting a student's access to reinforcement for a brief time following an inappropriate behavior), and **overcorrection** (requiring restitution beyond the damaging effects of the antisocial behavior, as when a child who takes another child's cookie must return it plus one of her own). These techniques should not be implemented as isolated events but incorporated into an overall instructional and classroom management plan that includes the previously mentioned proactive strategies and perhaps a **level system** in which students access greater independence and more privileges as they demonstrate increased behavioral control (Anderson & Katsiyannis, 1997; Barbetta, 1990a; Cruz & Cullinan, 2001).

When designing and implementing classroom management strategies, teachers of students with emotional and behavioral disorders must be careful not to create an environment in which coercion is the primary means by which students are motivated to participate and follow rules. In addition to promoting escape and avoidance behavior by those being coerced, coercive environments do not teach what to do as much as they focus on what not to do (Sidman, 1989). Two other methods of proactive and positive classroom management are teaching self-management skills to students and using peer mediation and support.

*Proactive classroom management includes keeping students actively engaged during instruction.*

 To see teachers using a variety of proactive, positive classroom management and motivational systems, go to the "Classroom Management" and "Class Reward" clips at Como Elementary School, "Classroom Climate" at Dunkirk Elementary School, "The Clocklight" at Millennium Community School, and "Class Auction" at Blendon Middle School.

# The Power of Teacher Praise

Social approval, often conveyed through verbal praise, is a powerful reinforcer for most people. The positive effects of teacher praise on student performance have been known for a long time (Hall, Lund, & Jackson, 1968; Madsen, Becker, & Thomas, 1968; Zimmerman & Zimmerman, 1962)—a very long time, in fact (Gilchrist, 1916). Research has shown repeatedly the positive effects of contingent praise on the behavior of infants (e.g., Poulson & Kymissis, 1988), preschoolers (e.g., Connell, Randall, Wilson, Lutz, & Lamb, 1993; Fox, Shores, Lindeman, & Strain, 1986; Wolery, 2000), school-age students (e.g., Kratochwill & Stoiber, 2000; Martella, Marchand-Martella, Young, & MacFarlane, 1995; Martens, Lochner, & Kelly, 1992; Staub, 1990; Sutherland, Wehby, & Copeland, 2000), and adults (e.g., Haseltine & Mittenburger, 1990).

Yet many educators do not appreciate that the systematic use of contingent praise and attention may be the most powerful motivational and classroom management tool they have (Flora, 2004). Teacher praise and attention is especially important for students with learning and behavior problems.

## MISGUIDED ADVICE

Some argue against the use of praise and rewards for student performance (Deci, Koestner, & Ryan, 1999; Hintz & Driscoll, 1988; Lepper, Keavney, & Drake, 1996; Ryan & Deci, 1996). Alfie Kohn (1993a, 1993b, 2001), in particular, has achieved considerable popularity, claiming that extrinsic motivators such as incentive plans, grades, and verbal praise damage the intrinsic motivation of students and employees to perform and learn. Using faulty interpretations of research of questionable validity, Kohn argues that praise is not only ineffective but actually harmful in an article titled, "Five Reasons to Stop Saying 'Good Job!'" Kohn (2001) warned early childhood teachers that praising and rewarding students for their accomplishments manipulates children, creates praise junkies, steals their pleasure, causes children to lose interest, and reduces achievement. Not only does this stand in stark contrast to an extensive research literature showing the positive benefits of such practices, the "planned use of positive reinforcement is antithetical to [Kohn's pejorative description of the practice as] blurted-out judgments, slathered-on praise, knee-jerk tendencies, and evaluative eruptions" (Strain & Joseph, 2002, p. 58).

Research conducted in classrooms and laboratories does not support Kohn's contention that students are "punished by rewards" (Cameron, 2005). Cameron, Banko, and Pierce (2001) conducted a meta-analysis of 145 experimental studies and concluded there was no scientific evidence for detrimental effects of reward on intrinsic motivation.

> These findings are given more importance in light of the fact that the group-design experiments on rewards and intrinsic motivation were primarily designed to detect detrimental effects. The reward contingencies examined in this literature can be viewed as a subset of the many possible arrangements of the use of reward in everyday life.... What is clear at this time is that rewards do not inevitably have pervasive negative effects on intrinsic motivation. Nonetheless, the myth continues. (pp. 21, 27)

## LOW RATES OF TEACHER PRAISE

Kohn and others concerned that teachers are praising their students too frequently need not worry. In spite of its documented effectiveness in increasing academic performance and desired student behaviors, studies over the past three decades have consistently found very low rates of teacher praise. In a study of 104 teachers in grades 1 through 12, White (1975) found that rates of teacher praise dropped with each grade level; and in every grade after second, the rate at which teachers delivered statements of disapproval to students exceeded the rate of teacher approval. Numerous studies have reported similar low rates of teacher praise in regular classrooms and special education classrooms (e.g., Baker & Zigmond, 1990; Deno, Maruyama, Espin, & Cohen, 1990; Harrop & Swinson, 2000; Nowacek, McKinney, & Hallahan, 1990). Especially discouraging are several studies in classrooms for students with emotional and behavioral disorders that found teachers' rates of praise as low as 1 per hour or less (Shores et al., 1993; Van Acker, Grant, & Henry, 1996; Wehby, Symons, & Shores, 1995).

## FOUR POSSIBLE REASONS FOR INFREQUENT TEACHER PRAISE

*Some teachers worry that students will come to expect to be praised or rewarded.* They believe students should want to learn for intrinsic reasons. It would be wonderful if all students came to school prepared to work hard and to learn for "intrinsic" reasons. The ultimate intrinsic motivator is success itself (Skinner, 1989)—using new knowledge and skills effectively enough to enjoy control over one's environment, be it solving a new algebra problem or reading a mystery with sufficient fluency and endurance to find out who did it. But it is naïve and irresponsible for educators to expect students with few skills and a history of failure to work hard without positive consequences. Contingent teacher praise and other extrinsic motivators such as points toward a grade or slips of paper as entries in the classroom lottery are proven to help students attain the performance levels necessary to meet the naturally existing reinforcement contingencies of success.

*Some teachers believe that praising takes too much time away from teaching.* Detecting and praising performance improvements, particularly by low-achieving students who have experienced little academic success, is one of the most effective forms of teaching. It is unfortunate that some educators believe they are not teaching when they are praising student accomplishments.

*Some teachers feel it is unnatural to praise.* Teachers who think it is unnatural to praise students' good behavior are, in some respects, correct. The natural contingencies of the classroom undermine the use of praise and strengthen reprimanding behavior. Teacher reprimands typically produce an immediate change in student behavior (e.g., the child stops disrupting class), which negatively reinforces reprimanding (Maag, 2001). By contrast, when a teacher praises a student for behavior, such as working quietly in class, there is usually no immediate consequence that reinforces the teacher's praising behavior (e.g., the student just continues working as before). Although praising a student who is working quietly may increase the future frequency of that behavior, no immediate consequences occur to reinforce the teacher's praising behavior. The pervasiveness of these naturally occurring contingencies is supported by the fact that while few teachers must be taught to identify misbehavior and issue reprimands, many teachers need help learning to catch students being good.

*Classrooms are busy, and many student behaviors worthy of praise and attention go unnoticed.* Teachers may not notice many desirable behaviors if students do not call attention to themselves. Teachers are more likely to notice and pay attention to a disruptive student than to a student who is working quietly and productively.

## HOW TO GET STARTED

- *Always be on the lookout for student behavior worthy of praise.* Even the most unskilled and unruly student is correct or obedient sometimes. Don't miss these critical teaching moments.
- *Arrange opportunities for students to do something well just so you can give approval.* For example, an easy way to provide a low-achieving student with an opportunity to succeed in front of his classmates is to ask a question he is likely to know and then call on him to answer.
- *Don't worry about sounding wooden and unnatural at first.* Teachers are often concerned their students will think they are not being genuine. Practice four or five praise statements you can say when you observe specific behaviors or performance improvements by your students. Providing specific praise and approval is like any other skill; you'll get better with practice.
- *Use self-management to increase your praise rate.* Set a goal to give a certain number of praise statements in a class period. Prompt yourself to praise desired student behavior by marking reminders in your lesson plan or by playing a cassette tape with randomly spaced beeps. Self-record your praising behavior by marking a card or moving pennies from one pocket to another. Reward yourself with a treat after school for meeting your goal. Start small and gradually increase your daily goal as your praising skills improve. (To see the self-management strategies a first-year teacher used to increase his use of contingent praise, visit Chapters 6's Teaching & Learning module on the Companion Website.)
- *Don't worry about over praising.* Of all the mistakes a teacher might make, providing too much praise and approval for students' good academic and social behaviors is not likely to be one of them.

All of the teachers on the *Exceptional Teachers* CD-ROM are experts in using praise and attention to promote student learning. To see an especially effective use of teacher praise in a fast-paced math lesson, go to the "Teacher Praise" clip at Oakstone Academy.

To learn more about these strategies and answer questions about what you have learned, go to the Teaching & Learning module in Chapter 6 of the Companion Website, **www.prenhall.com/heward**

*Self-Management.*   Many children with emotional and behavioral disorders believe they have little control over their lives. Things just seem to happen to them, and being disruptive is their means of reacting to an inconsistent and frustrating world. Self-management can help them learn responsibility and achieve self-determination (Wehmeyer & Schalock, 2001). Self-management is also an important tool for promoting the generalization and maintenance of treatment gains from one setting to another.

Of the many forms of self-management, self-monitoring and self-evaluation are the most widely used and most researched. **Self-monitoring** is a relatively simple procedure in which the student observes and records the occurrence (and sometimes the nonoccurrence) of his own behavior; **self-evaluation** involves comparing one's behavior against a standard or goal.

An impressive demonstration of the effectiveness of self-management techniques for the generalization of improved behavior across classroom settings was reported more than 20 years ago by Rhode, Morgan, and Young (1983). Six students with emotional and behavioral disorders learned to bring their highly disruptive and off-task behaviors under control in a resource room with a combination of techniques that featured self-monitoring and self-evaluation. Initially, the teacher rated each student and awarded points at 15-minute intervals on a scale from 5 (great) to 0 (poor) for classroom behavior and academic work. Then the students began to evaluate their own behavior with the same rating system. The teacher continued to rate each student.

Teacher and students compared their ratings. If the student's rating was within one point of the teacher's, he received the number of points he had given himself. If teacher and student matched exactly, the student earned an additional bonus point. The teacher then began to fade the number of times she also rated the students. After the students were behaving at acceptable levels and accurately self-evaluating their behavior, they began to self-evaluate once every 30 minutes in the regular classroom. Eventually, the self-evaluation cards and point system were withdrawn, and students were encouraged to continue to self-evaluate themselves privately. During the study's final phase, the students' level of appropriate behavior in the regular classroom was as high as their nondisabled peers.

Numerous studies have demonstrated that students with behavior problems can effectively use self-monitoring and self-evaluation to help regulate their behavior (e.g., Carr & Punzo, 1993; Dunlap et al., 1995; Gumpel & Shlomit, 2000; Levendoski & Cartledge, 2000; Moxley, 1998; Peterson, Young, West, & Hill Peterson, 1999; Webber, Scheuermann, McCall, & Coleman, 1993; Wood, Murdock, Cronin, Dawson, & Kirby, 1998). For detailed procedures and materials for teaching self-monitoring and other self-management skills to students, see Daly and Ranalli (2003), McConnell (1999), and Young, West, Smith, and Morgan (1991). To learn about a software program children can use to create self-management tools, see Teaching & Learning, "KidTools and KidSkills," later in this chapter.

*Peer Mediation and Support.*   The power of the peer group can be an effective means of producing positive changes in students with behavioral disorders (Barbetta, 1990a; Coleman & Webber, 1988). Strategies for teaching peers to help one another decrease inappropriate behavior include the following:

- *Peer monitoring.*   A student is taught to observe and record a peer's behavior and provide the peer with feedback (Fowler, Dougherty, Kirby, & Kohler, 1986; Smith & Fowler, 1984).
- *Positive peer reporting.*   Students are taught, encouraged and reinforced for reporting each other's positive behaviors (Bowers, MicGinnis, Ervin, & Friman, 1999).
- *Peer tutoring.*   In serving as academic or social skills tutors for one another, students with emotional and behavioral disorders may also learn better social skills (Blake, Wang, Cartledge, & Gardner, 2000; Cochran, Feng, Cartledge, & Hamilton, 1993).

---

*Self-monitoring and self-evaluation*

 Council for Exceptional Children  Content Standards for Beginning Teachers—Common Core: Use procedures to promote individual's self-awareness, self-management, self-control, self-reliance, and self-esteem (CC4S5) (also CC4S2, CC4S4).

To see the self-management strategies a first-year special education teacher used to increase his use of contingent praise, go to the Teaching & Learning module on the Companion Website, **www.prenhall.com/heward**

*Peer-mediated support and interventions*

Council for Exceptional Children  Content Standards for Beginning Teachers of Students with E/BD: Functional classroom designs for individuals with E/BD (BD5K2).

- *Peer confrontation.* Peers are trained to confront one another when inappropriate behavior occurs or is about to occur, explaining why the behavior is a problem and suggesting or modeling an appropriate alternative response (Salend, Jantzen, & Giek, 1992; Sandler, Arnold, Gable, & Strain, 1987).

Implementing a peer support, or group process, model is much more complicated than bringing together a group of children and hoping they will benefit from positive peer influence. Most children with serious emotional and behavioral disorders have not been members of successfully functioning peer groups in which appropriate behavior is modeled and valued (Hallenbeck & Kauffman, 1995), nor have many such children learned to accept responsibility for their actions (Rockwell & Guetzloe, 1996). The teacher's first and most formidable challenge is helping promote group cohesiveness.

Although group process treatment programs take many forms, most incorporate group meetings and group-oriented contingencies. Two types of group meetings are usually held daily. A planning meeting is held each morning in which the group reviews the daily schedule, each group member states a behavioral goal for the day, peers provide support and suggestions to one another for meeting their goals, and a group goal for the day is agreed on. An evaluation meeting is held at the end of each day to discuss how well the individual and group goals were met, and each group member must give and receive positive peer comments. Problem-solving meetings are held whenever any group member, including the teacher, feels the need to discuss a problem. The group identifies the problem, generates several solutions, discusses the likely consequences of each solution, develops a plan for the best solution, and makes verbal commitments to carry out the plan. **Group contingencies** specify certain rewards and privileges that are enjoyed by the group if their behavior meets certain criteria. The criteria for earning the rewards, as well as the rewards themselves, are determined by the group. The teacher functions as a member of the group but has veto power when necessary.

(For one teacher's personal reflections on teaching students with emotional and behavioral disorders with a group process approach, see "My Return Voyage," in Chapter 6's Profiles & Perspectives module on the Companion Website, **www.prenhall.com/heward.**

## Fostering Strong Teacher-Student Relationships

In addition to academic and behavior management skills, the teacher of children with emotional and behavioral disorders must be able to establish healthy and positive child-teacher relationships. William Morse (1976, 1985), one of the pioneers in the education of children with emotional and behavioral disorders, identified two important affective characteristics necessary for teachers to relate effectively and positively to students with behavior problems. Morse called these traits differential acceptance and empathetic relationship.

*Differential acceptance* means the teacher can receive and witness frequent and often extreme acts of anger, hate, and aggression from children without responding similarly. Of course, this is much easier said than done. But the teacher of students with emotional and behavioral disorders must view disruptive behavior for what it is—behavior that reflects the student's past frustrations and conflicts with himself and those around him—and try to help the child learn better ways of behaving. Acceptance should not be confused with approving or condoning antisocial behavior; the child must learn that he is responding inappropriately. Instead, this concept calls for understanding without condemning.

Having an *empathetic relationship* with a child refers to a teacher's ability to recognize and understand the many nonverbal cues that often are the keys to understanding the individual needs of emotionally disturbed children. Teachers should communicate directly and honestly with behaviorally troubled children. Many of these children have already had experience with supposedly helpful adults who have not been completely honest with them. Children with emotional and behavioral disorders can quickly detect someone who is not genuinely interested in their welfare.

The teacher of children with emotional and behavioral disorders must also realize that his actions serve as a powerful model. Therefore, it is critical that the teacher's actions and attitudes be mature and demonstrate self-control. At the same time, teachers who take

*Differential acceptance and empathetic relationship*

Council for Exceptional Children — Content Standards for Beginning Teachers—Common Core: Teacher attitudes and behaviors that influence behavior of individuals with exceptional learning needs (CC5K4).

# KidTools and KidSkills: Self-Management and Learning Tools for Children

*by Gail Fitzgerald and Kevin Koury*

KidTools and KidSkills are computer-based programs that help children create and use a variety of self-management, organizational, and learning strategy materials. Both programs encourage children to take responsibility for changing and managing their own social and academic behaviors. The programs consist of easy-to-complete templates that let children be as independent as possible in identifying personal behaviors or academic learning needs, selecting the tool to support the task, developing a personalized plan, and printing the tool for immediate classroom or home use.

First Step KidTools and First Step KidSkills are designed for children ages 7–10; Second Step KidTools and Second Step KidSkills are designed for children ages 11–14. There is overlap between the two programs, with the Second Step versions including some higher-level thinking and problem-solving procedures.

## KIDTOOLS

KidTools supports children's self-management skills to identify behaviors, make plans, and monitor implementation of the plans. KidTools includes cognitive-behavioral intervention procedures for three types, or levels, of control. All three levels emphasize what children say and think to themselves as they execute their behavior plans.

1. *External control* procedures may be necessary to establish control over problem behaviors before the child moves to shared- or self-control interventions. In these procedures, the adult provides direction and structure for appropriate behaviors. KidTools available for this level of intervention are point cards.
2. *Shared control* techniques provide a transition step for encouraging the child to develop self-control. Problem solving and making plans to change or learn a behavior is emphasized. The child and adult jointly participate in these procedures. KidTools for this level of intervention

are contracts, make-a-plan cards, and problem-solving planning tools.
3. *Internal control* techniques assist children through cues and structure provided by a variety of self-monitoring procedures.

## KIDSKILLS

KidSkills helps children be successful in school by getting organized, completing tasks, and using learning strategies. The programs provide computer-generated templates in the areas of getting physically organized, learning new stuff, organizing new information, preparing for tests, and doing homework projects. KidSkills programs complement the KidTools programs and operate the same in terms of selecting tools, entering content, record keeping, and adult supports.

## TOOL RESOURCES AND SKILL RESOURCES

In addition to the programs for children, information data bases about the tools and strategies are provided for parents and teachers who assist children with self-management and learning strategies. Each data base includes guidelines for each procedure, steps for implementation, age-appropriate examples, troubleshooting tips, and references to related resources. The user can navigate through the information, return to a menu to select new strategies, or search the entire data base using the Find function.

## RATIONALE FOR KIDTOOLS AND KIDSKILLS

KidTools and KidSkills were developed around the concept of positive, cognitive-behavioral interventions. Children are encouraged to express their social and academic behaviors in positive terms. They focus on positive behaviors and being successful rather than stopping negative behaviors and failure. For example, they decide, "I will use my inside voice," rather than be reminded, "Don't talk loudly in class." Children learn organizational and learning strategies they can use in general and special settings. The computerized tools serve as bridges to support students in behaving and learning. This assistive technology works because it provides direct instruction as well as scaffolds to support learning at the "right time, right form, and right place."

For these materials to be successful, teachers or parents must first provide instruction in behavior-change techniques and self-monitoring. Children need to understand the concept of a behavior as something they do or think, be able to name behaviors, understand how to monitor whether behaviors occur or not, and assume some level of responsibility for their own behaviors. Children need to learn how and when to use organizational and learning strategies and use self-monitoring techniques in applying the strategies across settings.

## HOW TO GET STARTED

Children will need to be taught to use self-talk cues and inner speech to give themselves directions. Each self-management procedure in KidTools has variations that will need to be taught, demonstrated, and practiced with

children before they can be used independently. The organizational and learning strategies in KidSkills are generic but require teaching, practice, and teacher help in applying the tools before independent use. Once children know the prerequisite skills, the program can be used with minimal teacher help. Ongoing support by the teacher or parent will ensure that the process remains effective and positive for children.

Effective introduction to the use of KidTools and KidSkills follows the steps of direct instruction:

- **Discuss behavioral and task expectations.** The teacher can use setting or task demands to initiate discussion about expectations. Students can verbalize what they must do to be successful and identify challenges in meeting the expectations. Students should be able to demonstrate the behaviors and do the tasks before using the tools.
- **Introduce the software tools.** The tool programs can be introduced to the whole class using a computer and projection device. The teacher can demonstrate the menu of available tools and highlight a variety, including how to navigate the program, how to enter content into the tools, and how to save and print out completed tools.
- **Model and demonstrate use of the tools.** Using pre-selected tools for specific purposes, the teacher can solicit student input while demonstrating the software. The finished tools can be printed out for students to have copies. A discussion of their actual use follows.
- **Provide guided practice.** Using available computer equipment, in a lab for group practice or in the classroom for independent or small-group practice, the teacher can guide and oversee student development of tools. It helps to have students verbalize their content before filling in the tool. The guided practice step assures correct software use.
- **Provide independent practice.** The teacher can help students identify authentic uses for the tools and provide opportunities for creating and using tools. During independent use, teachers should provide encouragement and reinforcement for student tool use and successful outcomes in supervised situations.
- **Facilitate generalization.** The teacher can help students identify authentic needs and uses of tools across school and home environments. The teacher can assist by prompting tool use, problem solving, and communicating with other teachers and parents about the procedures.

## STRATEGY TOOLS

A secondary version, called Strategy Tools, is currently under development for the Windows platform with a 2006 release date; it will include enhanced self-management and learning strategy tools, transition planning tools, and self-training modules for secondary students.

## PROGRAM AVAILABILITY

The programs can be freely downloaded from the KTSS website (**http://kidtools.missouri.edu**) in both Windows and Macintosh versions. Additional materials on the website include downloadable training modules for teachers with video demonstrations and practice materials. The programs are also available on CD-ROM at cost from Instructional Materials Laboratory (**http://www.iml.coe.missouri.edu**). The KTSS programs have been developed with partial funding by the U.S. Department of Education, Office of Special Education Programs.

Gail Fitzgerald is associate professor of information systems and learning technologies at the University of Missouri–Columbia. Kevin Koury is professor and chair of special education at California University of Pennsylvania. Gail and Kevin are co-developers of the KidTool Support System materials funded by a U.S. Department of Education SteppingStones project.

To learn more about these strategies and answer questions about what you have learned, go to the Teaching & Learning module in Chapter 6 of the Companion Website, **www.prenhall.com/heward**

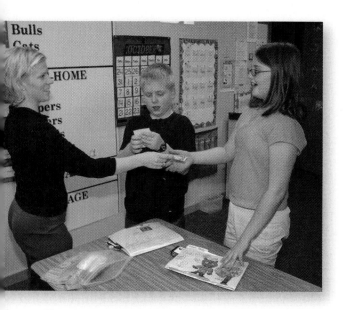

Teachers who focus on alterable variables, such as the systematic use of praise and attention for desired behavior, are those most likely to make a difference in the lives of children with emotional and behavioral disorders.

*Alterable variables*

Council for Exceptional Children    Content Standards for Beginning Teachers—Common Core: Effective management of teaching and learning (CC5K3).

themselves too seriously risk overreacting to emotionally charged situations with students and burnout. Richardson and Shupe (2003) note that teachers can use an appropriate sense of humor to build relationships with students, diffuse conflict, engage learners, and help manage their own stress levels.

# A FOCUS ON ALTERABLE VARIABLES

The twofold task of the teacher of children with emotional and behavioral disorders is helping students (1) replace antisocial and maladaptive behaviors with more socially appropriate behaviors and (2) acquire academic knowledge and skills. The frequent displays of antisocial behavior, the absence of appropriate social skills, and the academic deficits exhibited by many students with emotional and behavioral disorders make this a staggering challenge. The challenge is all the more difficult because the teacher seldom, if ever, can control (or even know) all of the factors affecting a student's behavior. There is typically a host of contributing factors over which the teacher can exert little or no influence (e.g., the delinquent friends with whom the student associates before and after school). But it does little good to bemoan the student's past (which no one can alter) or to use all of the things in the student's current life that cannot be changed as an excuse for failing to help the student in the classroom.

Special educators should focus their attention and efforts on those aspects of a student's life that they can effectively control. Bloom (1980) uses the term *alterable variables* to refer to things that both make a difference in student learning and can be affected by teaching practices. Alterable variables include key dimensions of curriculum and instruction such as the amount of time allocated for instruction; the sequence of activities within the overall lesson; the pacing of instruction; the frequency with which students actively respond during instruction; how and when students receive praise or other forms of reinforcement for their efforts; and the manner in which errors are corrected. The teachers who focus on the identification and systematic management of alterable variables are those most likely to make a difference in the lives of children with emotional and behavioral disorders.

# EDUCATIONAL PLACEMENT ALTERNATIVES

Students with emotional and behavioral disorders are served across the continuum of educational placements. During the 2003–2004 school year, approximately 30% of school-age children with emotional and behavioral disorders were educated in separate classrooms, 23% in resource rooms, 30% in regular classrooms with consultation, 12% in special schools, and 5% in residential or homebound placements (U.S. Department of Education, 2004). Although the trend in recent years has been for increased placement of students with emotional and behavior disorders in regular classrooms, slightly more than half of all students in this disability category receive their education in separate classrooms, special schools, and residential facilities.

*Placement alternatives*

Council for Exceptional Children    Content Standards for Beginning Teachers of Students with E/BD: Advantages and disadvantages of placement options and the continuum of service for individuals with E/BD (BD5K1).

The relatively high proportion of students with emotional or behavior disorders who are served in more restrictive settings compared to students in most other disability categories probably reflects the fact that only students with the most severe behavioral problems are identified and served. As a result, most students receiving special education because of emotional or behavioral disorders have serious, long-standing problems that require intensive interventions in highly structured environments. Consistent implementation of the specialized supports and programming needed by these students can be very difficult in the regular classroom (Brigham & Kauffman, 1998).

A major challenge of educating students with emotional and behavioral disorders is arranging an environment in which academic as well as social skills can be learned at acceptable rates and the safety of all students is protected. Supporters of full inclusion believe that the regular classroom can be made into such an environment for all students with disabilities. Some positive outcomes have been reported for students with emotional and behavioral disorders in regular classrooms. For example, a study comparing middle school students who spent the entire school day in separate classrooms with students who participated in various classes in regular classrooms for at least one hour per day found that the students who spent part of the day in regular classrooms had better academic records and better work habits than did the students who spent the entire day in special classes (Meadows, Neel, Scott, & Parker, 1994). Although these results seem to support the contention that students with emotional and behavioral disorders should be educated in regular classrooms, the authors point out that the students included in the regular classrooms did not exhibit the extreme aggression, lack of self-control, or degree of withdrawal that the students who stayed in the special classrooms did. They also noted that placement in general education classrooms typically represents "a major reduction,… if not a complete cessation, of differential programming" (p. 178). That is, the general education teachers did not make instructional or management accommodations to meet the needs of the students with behavior problems. Without specialized instruction or accommodations, it is hard to imagine how students with severe emotional and behavioral disorders would receive an appropriate education in the regular classroom.

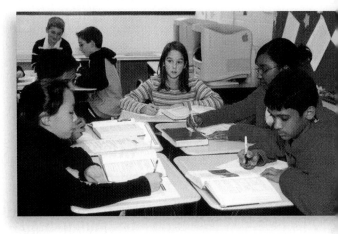

A major challenge of educating students with emotional and behavioral disorders is arranging an environment in which academic and social skills can be learned at acceptable rates.

After reviewing 25 studies comparing the progress of students with emotional and behavioral disorders in different educational placements, Schneider and Leroux (1994) concluded that special programs (which included resource rooms, self-contained classrooms, special schools, and treatment centers) appear to be more effective in promoting academic achievement than is the regular classroom, but better gains in children's self-concept are noted for less restrictive settings. Another review found that students in self-contained classrooms showed more decreases in disruptive behavior than did students placed in general education classrooms (Stage & Quiroz, 1997).

While supporting the education of students with emotional and behavioral disorders in the regular classroom when their individual needs can be met, the Council for Children with Behavioral Disorders (CCBD, 1993) does not believe that the regular classroom is the most appropriate placement for all students with emotional and behavioral disorders.

> CCBD supports a full continuum of mental health and special education services for children and youth with emotional or behavioral disorders. We believe that educational decisions depend on individual student needs. Consequently,… CCBD does not support the notion that all … students with emotional or behavioral disorders are always best served in general education classrooms. (p. 1)

When an IEP team makes the decision to place a student with emotional or behavioral disorders in a regular classroom or to transition a student from a more restrictive setting to the regular classroom, it is imperative that the student and the general education teacher be prepared before and supported after the placement. Preparation includes identifying the behavioral and academic expectations of the regular classroom, assessing the student's current skills against those expectations, teaching the student additional skills needed to meet those expectations, and in-service training for the teacher on special techniques of behavior management (Nelson, 2000; Rhode et al., 1998). Support following the regular class placement should include a crisis intervention support plan and ongoing consultation and in-class modeling and intervention by a special educator trained to work with students with behavioral disorders (Fuchs, Fuchs, Fernstrom, & Hohn, 1991; Shapiro, Miller, Swaka, Gardill, & Handler, 1999; Walker et al., 1995).

# CURRENT ISSUES AND FUTURE TRENDS

Special education for students with emotional and behavioral disorders faces a number of critical and ongoing issues. We discuss five of the most pressing of these issues here.

## Serving All Students with Emotional and Behavioral Disorders

A continuing concern of many advocates for children with emotional and behavioral disorders is revising the federal definition of this disability so that all children with emotional and behavioral problems that adversely affect their educational performance are eligible for special education. As we have discussed, the current federal definition of "seriously emotionally disturbed" distinguishes between students who exhibit a "true" emotional disturbance (considered a disability covered under IDEA) and those whose antisocial behaviors are thought to be the result of social maladjustment (and thus are not eligible for special education under IDEA). Attempts to sort and label students as socially maladjusted or conduct disordered from those with emotional disturbances in order to deny them needed special education services is both unethical and a waste of time (Nelson, 2000). All students with behavioral problems need and deserve effective special education.

## Preventing Emotional and Behavioral Disorders

In addition to serving all children who already exhibit emotional or behavioral disorders, we must greatly increase efforts to identify children who are at risk for developing behavior problems and to prevent the development of antisocial behavior. Despite public concern over school safety and youth violence and widespread recognition that antisocial behavior is a chronic disabling condition that exacts tremendous social and financial costs for society, we do little to prevent it. Instead of intervening early when problems are small and more likely to respond to intervention, we wait until children are older and their antisocial behavior is well established and much more difficult to change.

Why don't we make a concerted effort to prevent behavior problems in children? Kauffman (1999) has suggested several factors that obstruct the prevention of emotional and behaviorial disorders in children: a misguided optimism that children who exhibit antisocial behavior at a young age will grow out of it; worry that identifying and labeling a child as at risk might cause stigma for the child and his family; concern that because no system of screening is perfect, some children will be misidentified; and an unwillingness to spend the money needed to pay for a comprehensive program of screening, identification, and early intervention.

The knowledge and tools for early detection and prevention are available (e.g., Sprague & Walker, 2000; Strain & Timm, 2001). What is needed is the national resolve and commitment of resources sufficient for a large-scale program of early detection and prevention.

## Disciplining Students with Disabilities

Disciplining students with disabilities for serious school offenses is a controversial and sometimes contentious issue. The 1997 amendments to IDEA added a number of rules and regulations pertaining to the discipline of students with disabilities. These provisions of the law are intended to help school administrators maintain a safe school environment while protecting the rights of students with disabilities to an appropriate education. These discipline rules in IDEA are especially relevant to students with behavioral disorders, who by definition are receiving special education because of their problem behavior.

*Disciplining students with disabilities*

Council for Exceptional Children — Content Standards for Beginning Teachers—Common Core: Laws, policies, and ethical principles regarding behavior management planning and implementation (CC1K2).

School districts are able to discipline students with disabilities in the same manner as they do students without disabilities, with a few notable exceptions (Yell, Rozalski, & Drasgow, 2001). A student with disabilities can be suspended from school for disciplinary reasons for a total of 10 days per school year. A suspension in excess of 10 days is considered a change of placement, which can be done only by the IEP team.

If a student with a disability commits an act that would result in suspension of more than 10 days or expulsion of a student without disabilities (e.g., bringing a gun or drugs to school), the IEP team and other qualified personnel must review the relationship between the student's misconduct and his disability. This review is called a **manifestation determination.** The IEP team may conclude that the behavior that resulted in disciplinary action was not a manifestation of the student's disability only when all of the following criteria are met (Katsiyannis & Maag, 2001):

1. The special education services, supplementary aids and services, and behavior intervention strategies provided to the student before the incident were consistent with the student's IEP and placement.
2. The student's disability did not impair his ability to understand the impact and consequences of the behavior subject to the disciplinary action.
3. The disability did not impair the student's ability to control the behavior that caused the disciplinary action.

If the IEP team determines that the student's behavior is not a manifestation of his disability, the same disciplinary procedures used with other students may be imposed and the student removed to an interim alternative education setting school or home instruction. However, the school must continue to provide educational services in the alternative educational setting.

Several authors have noted the extreme difficulty and apparent paradox of trying to determine whether or not the misbehavior of a student who is receiving special education because of a chronic history of such behavior is related to his disability (Katsiyannis & Maag, 2001; Smith, 1997, 2000; Yell et al., 2000). Nevertheless, schools are required by law to make exactly that decision. Currently, no empirically validated methods exist for determining whether misbehavior that warrants disciplinary action is related to a student's disability. Development of valid and reliable methods for conducting a manifestation determination and providing continued support and treatment of students whose placement is changed as the result of suspension are immediate challenges for the field.

When Congress reauthorized IDEA in 2004, it added language to the discipline provisions of the law giving school personnel the authority to "consider any unique circumstances on a case-by-case basis" when deciding whether to change the placement of a child with a disability who violates a code of student conduct. The new law identifies three "special circumstances" under which a student's placement may be changed whether or not the misconduct was related to the child's disability:

> School personnel may remove a student to an interim alternative educational setting for not more than 45 school days without regard to whether the behavior is determined to be a manifestation of the child's disability, in cases where a child—
>
> (i) carries or possesses a weapon to or at school, on school premises, or to or at a school function under the jurisdiction of a State or local educational agency;
>
> (ii) knowingly possesses or uses illegal drugs, or sells or solicits the sale of a controlled substance, while at school, on school premises, or at a school function under the jurisdiction of a State or local educational agency; or
>
> (iii) has inflicted serious bodily injury upon another person while at school, on school premises, or at a school function under the jurisdiction of a State or local educational agency. (The Individuals with Disabilities Education Improvement Act of 2004, Sec 615 [k] [1] [G])

## Improving Services for Youth in the Juvenile Corrections System

Improving special education services for school-age youths with disabilities in correctional institutions is another important challenge. About 450,000 school-age youths are placed in detention centers or training schools each year in the United States, with another 300,000 sent to adult jails (Leone, Rutherford, & Nelson, 1991). Students with emotional and behavioral disorders are 13.3 times more likely to be arrested during their school careers than nondisabled students are (Doren, Bullis, & Benz, 1996a); and 20% of students with emotional and behavioral disorders are arrested at least once before they leave school, compared with 9% for all students with disabilities and 6% of all students (Chesapeake Institute, 1994). The educational outlook is bleak for juveniles with disabilities who find themselves in jails and detention centers. Although it can be argued that adjudicated delinquents are, by virtue of the behaviors that precipitated their arrest, behaviorally disordered, most juvenile offenders receive few or no special education services (McIntyre, 1993a). Those incarcerated youths who do receive special education services typically receive substandard services (Leone & Meisel, 1997).

## Developing Wraparound Systems of Comprehensive Care

Many children with emotional and behavioral disorders and their families need and receive an array of mental health and social services such as foster care, child welfare, and community recreation programs. Traditionally, each of those services is provided by a separate agency, each with its own location, procedures, intake forms, and record-keeping system. Just accessing the services requires families to make a series of visits, and the services often overlap one another and leave significant areas of need unserved. An increasing trend in recent years has been the development of community-based systems of care in which mental health and social service agencies collaborate in an effort to wrap a coordinated, interwoven set of comprehensive services around the child. The most effective wraparound programs are characterized by child- and family-centered interventions and supports, interagency cooperation with shared goals, and individualized care that fits programs around a child's needs rather than fitting the child into already determined programs (Stroul & Friedman, 1996).

Increasingly, schools are participating in and, in some cases, serving as the coordinating agency for wraparound service programs (e.g., Anderson & Matthews, 2001; Duckworth et al., 2001; Eber, Nelson, & Miles, 1997). Woodruff et al. (1999) identified several features of successful school-based *wraparound programs:* (1) they emphasize

*Wraparound services*

Council for Exceptional Children — Content Standards for Beginning Teachers of Students with E/BD: Services, networks and organizations for individuals with E/BD (BD10K1).

schoolwide prevention; (2) school personnel advocate for and empower families to be partners in the services designed to help their children; (3) professionals from child and family welfare, mental health, juvenile justice, and other community agencies serve the child in the school as well as in the community; and (4) a school-based case manager co-ordinates the services to ensure that they support the student's learning at school, at home, and in the community.

## Challenges, Achievements, and Advocacy

The issues presented here are not new. Most have been recognized, discussed, and debated for decades. And each will likely remain problems well into the future. Many other issues and problems could be added to the list (Katsiyannis & Yell, 2004; Polsgrove & Ochoa, 2004). Although the challenges faced by those who work with and advocate for students with emotional and behavioral disorders appear daunting and unrelenting, the field has experienced significant advancements and successes to help guide the future (Walker, Sprague, Close, & Starlin, 1999–2000; Webber & Scheuermann, 1997). For example, the field has identified specific program components and instructional practices that, when used in combination, are likely to result in successful outcomes for students with emotional and behavioral disorders (Epstein, Kutash, & Duchnowski, 1998; Peacock Hill Working Group, 1991). Many of those achievements and best practices have been described in this chapter. We must now work diligently to close the gap between what is known about effective special education for students with emotional and behavioral disorders and what those students experience each day in the classroom.

# Tips for Beginning Teachers

## Working with Students with Emotional and Behavioral Disorders
### by Michael Wang

Trying to meet the many social, emotional, and academic needs of students with emotional and behavioral disorders can be overwhelming at times. Here are a few things that I recommend for any educator who works with these children.

*Commit yourself to the social and academic achievement of students.* Devote your professional time and energy to planning, implementing, and evaluating special instruction designed to make a difference in your students' lives.

- Don't let the students' needs for effective academic instruction get lost in your efforts to teach them more appropriate social skills.
- Extend learning activities beyond the typical classroom settings whenever possible.
- Surround yourself with other teaching professionals who enjoy their students and the profession of teaching and avoid those who have a negative attitude toward teaching students with disabilities.

*Set high expectations for students and create a learning environment that supports and makes possible student success.* Make it clear to students that you expect them to progress behaviorally and academically and that you are prepared to help them achieve.

- Review the expectations for behavior and learning with your students at the beginning of each school day. Provide explicit examples.
- Evaluate the students' success with these expectations at the end of each school day. Use explicit examples and encourage a group discussion on the value of what they learned that day.

*Establish a healthy working relationship with each student.* Learning how to relate to each student is a key to success as a teacher of children with emotional and behavior disorders. You need to be an astute observer and an active listener and to communicate directly and openly with the students.

- Tell students often, and show them by your actions, that you care about their success. Meet individually with students to discuss their progress and answer their questions.
- Try to ask each student something about his personal interests, concerns, or goals each day. Asking something as simple as, "What did you think of the game last night?" can lead to a positive interaction.
- Find something each day to laugh or joke about with your students.

*Be consistent.* Students with emotional and behavioral disorders need consistency, especially from the adults in their lives.

- Set up and abide by a consistent classroom structure and routines.
- When possible, prepare students for significant changes that will take place.

*Keep your cool.* Try to keep your cool with students at all times. You can't have a thin skin or take it personally when students act out.

- Apply predetermined consequences for rule violations in a calm, unemotional manner.
- Whenever you feel yourself starting to get upset or angry, take a deep breath, count to 10, and then come back to the student.
- When you make a mistake with your students (and you will), apologize. Students will respect you for it.

*Lighten up and have a life.* Teaching students with emotional and behavior disorders is a serious job that demands and deserves serious attention. But getting too wrapped up in our work is a surefire path to burnout and stubborn ineffectiveness.

- Don't take yourself too seriously. Laugh at yourself from time to time and encourage your students to join in the fun.
- Develop and pursue outside hobbies and interests.

# KEY TERMS AND CONCEPTS

duration (of behavior), p. 239
externalizing behaviors, p. 224
frequency (or rate) (of behavior), p. 239
functional analysis, p. 239
functional behavior assessment, p. 238
group contingencies, p. 247
internalizing behaviors, p. 225
latency (of behavior), p. 239

level system, p. 243
magnitude (of behavior), p. 239
manifestation determination, p. 253
multiple gating screening, p. 237
projective test, p. 238
self-evaluation, p. 246
self-monitoring, p. 246
topography (of behavior), p. 239

To print your own set of SAFMED flash cards for studying and mastering these terms, go to the Companion Website,
**www.prenhall.com/heward**

# SUMMARY

## Definitions

- There is no single, widely used definition of emotional and behavioral disorders. Most definitions require a child's behavior to differ markedly (extremely) and chronically (over time) from current social or cultural norms.
- Many leaders in the field do not like the definition of "seriously emotionally disturbed" in IDEA because students who are socially maladjusted are not eligible for special education services.
- The CCBD and the NMHSEC have proposed a definition of emotional and behavioral disorders as a disability characterized by "behavioral or emotional responses in school programs so different from appropriate age, cultural, or ethnic norms that they adversely affect educational performance."

## Characteristics

- Children with externalizing problems frequently exhibit antisocial behavior; many become delinquents as adolescents.
- Children with internalizing problems are overly withdrawn and lack social skills needed to interact effectively with others.
- As a group, students with emotional and behavioral disorders perform academically at least 1 or more years below grade level; many have difficulty in reading and math.
- A large number of students with emotional or behavioral disorders also have learning disabilities and/or language delays.
- On the average, students with emotional and behavioral disorders score somewhat below normal on IQ tests.
- Many students with emotional and behavioral disorders have difficulty developing and maintaining interpersonal relationships.

## Causes

- Biological factors related to development of behavioral disorders include brain disorders, genetics, and temperament.
- Environmental etiological factors occur in home, community, and school.
- Although knowledge of causes is necessary for planning and implementing prevention programs, effective intervention and treatment of children's existing behavior problems does not require precise knowledge of etiology.

## Prevalence

- Estimates of the prevalence of behavioral disorders vary widely. Several research studies suggest that 3% to 5% have emotional and behavioral problems that warrant special treatment.
- Far fewer children with emotional and behavioral disorders are receiving special education than the most conservative prevalence estimates.

## Identification and Assessment

- Systematic screening should be conducted as early as possible to identify children who are at risk for developing serious patterns of antisocial behavior.
- Most screening devices consist of behavior rating scales or checklists that are completed by teachers, parents, peers, and/or children themselves.
- Projective tests often yield interesting results, but they are rarely useful in planning and implementing interventions.
- Direct and continuous observation and measurement of specific problem behaviors within the classroom can indicate whether and for which behaviors intervention is needed. Five measurable dimensions of behavior are rate, duration, latency, magnitude, and topography.
- Functional behavioral assessment employs interviews, direct observation, and sometimes functional analysis to identify the setting events and environmental factors that predict and trigger problem behavior and the consequences that may be maintaining it.

## Educational Approaches

- Students with emotional and behavioral disorders require systematic training in social skills and academics.
- Schoolwide systems of positive behavior support and discipline focus on teaching appropriate behavior to all students in the school.
- A good classroom management system uses proactive strategies to create a positive, supportive, and noncoercive environment that promotes prosocial behavior and academic achievement.
- Self-management skills can help students develop control over their environment, responsibility for their actions, and self-direction.
- Group process approaches use the influence of the peer group to help students with emotional and behavioral disorders learn to behave appropriately.
- Teachers should concentrate their resources and energies on alterable variables—those things in a student's environment that the teacher can influence that make a difference in student learning and behavior.
- Two important affective traits for teachers of students with emotional and behavioral disorders are differential acceptance and empathetic relationship.

## Educational Placement Alternatives

- Most students with emotional and behavioral disorders are served in self-contained or resource classrooms.
- Nearly half of students with emotional and behavioral disorders spend at least part of the school day in regular classrooms.
- Comparing the behavioral and academic progress of students with emotional and behavioral disorders in different educational placements in an effort to determine which

setting is the best is difficult because students with milder disabilities are included first and more often, whereas those students who exhibit more severe behavioral disturbances tend to remain in special classes.

- When a student with emotional or behavioral disorders is placed in a regular classroom, it is imperative that the student and the general education teacher be prepared before and supported after the placement.

## Current Issues and Future Trends

- There are five pressing challenges for the field of emotional and behavioral disorders:
  - Making all students with emotional and behavioral disorders eligible for special education services
  - Preventing emotional and behavioral disorders through screening, identification, and early intervention
  - Developing valid and reliable methods for conducting manifestation determinations required by IDEA disciplinary provisions
  - Improving services for youths in the juvenile corrections system
  - Developing wraparound systems of comprehensive care

 To check your comprehension of chapter contents, go to the Guided Review and Quiz modules in Chapter 6 of the Companion Website, **www.prenhall.com/heward**

# AUTISM SPECTRUM DISORDERS

# Featured Teacher ————————

## MICHELLE A. ANDERSON

MILLENNIUM COMMUNITY SCHOOL COLUMBUS, OHIO

*Education—Teaching Credentials—Experience*
- B.S., secondary science education, SUNY College at Cortland, NY, 1998; M.A., special education, The Ohio State University, 1999
- New York professional teaching certificate in secondary science education; Ohio professional teaching certificate in special education: developmental handicaps, K–12
- 6 years of teaching and clinical experience in special education

**My Classroom and Students**     I coordinate special education services for children with autism at the Millennium Community School (MCS), a public charter school serving approximately 700 students in grades K–5. MCS uses the Direct Instruction (DI) curriculum for reading, math, and language instruction. My job includes working with general educators, typically developing children, special-service providers, and the administration to make sure that each of my nine students receives all of the special education and related services he needs to be successful. My students all have a diagnosis on the autism spectrum and range in age from 5 to 9 years. Each student presents a unique mix of abilities and needs. Let me introduce you to a few of them.

**Lilly**: Lilly is a 6-year-old kindergartner who attended a special-needs preschool before coming to MCS. This year was the first time Lilly was included with typically developing peers, and she has made great progress. Cognitively, Lilly is very bright. She has learned many letter sounds and is starting to read simple words. Her speech and language are severely impaired, but she is learning to use picture symbols and verbal approximations to meet her needs. Lilly has several inappropriate behaviors that have prevented her from being fully included: crying, hitting, biting, running around the classroom, and climbing on bookshelves. At the beginning of the year she couldn't be in the regular classroom at all, but by the end of the year she was with her typical peers for almost half of the day. We were all very proud of her.

**Allison**: Eight-year-old Allison has been attending school with typically developing children since preschool. She is an extremely social child who loves to be around other people. Allison's classmates enjoy having her in class, and many of them ask to be her helper or sit next to her. Allison has language delays, but she can carry on simple conversations. Although she is very inquisitive, her cognitive abilities are more delayed than her language and social skills are. She has just mastered identifying some colors and shapes but struggles to learn letters and numbers. Due to these delays, Allison comes to the resource room for one-on-one academic instruction. She spends about three-fourths of the day in her general education classroom and has made some great friends this year.

## Focus Questions

- How might instruction be designed so that some of the behaviors characteristic of autism spectrum disorders become strengths for the child as a learner?

- What factors might account for the sharp rise in the prevalence of autism spectrum disorders in recent years?

- Why is early and intensive intervention especially critical for children with autism?

- What skills are most important for a teacher of students with autism spectrum disorders?

- Why are fads and unproven interventions so prevalent in the treatment of children with autism?

**Mustafa**: A 7-year-old first grader, Mustafa spends half of each school day in the regular classroom with his typically developing peers and receives pull-out services in my room. Although Mustafa can speak in sentences, he doesn't often use his speech in communicative ways. He frequently exhibits delayed echolalia—repeating phrases, sentences, and stories that he has heard before. For example, he might repeat part of the dialogue from a movie or the day's weather and school lunch menu from the morning announcements. When prompted, Mustafa will use speech to express his wants and needs, and he'll often greet his peers and teachers and attempt to engage them in play or song. We have expanded on this interest by having some peers come to the resource room and teach Mustafa how to interact after the initial greeting or invitation. The other students really enjoy playing with Mustafa, and they are eager to help him when he is in the regular classroom. Mustafa is very motivated by letters, words, and stories. He enjoys participating in the *DI Reading Mastery* groups in the regular classroom as well as using an online computer program called *Headsprout*.

**Aurora**: Aurora is a 5-year-old kindergartner. When the school year began, she had severe tantrums whenever encountering new experiences. She seemed to be very intelligent, but it was difficult to get her to respond to most questions. Socially, Aurora had a difficult time interacting with peers and teachers; and as a result, she spent most of her time in my classroom for the first half of the school year. However, Aurora has really started to flourish in the structured instructional environment at MCS. Clear and consistent expectations helped her to learn the routine and feel more comfortable with those around her. By the end of the year we realized just how bright Aurora is. She was spending most of her day in the regular classroom, was learning to read, and could carry on some complex conversations. Aurora is still a little shy around other children, but we have high hopes—and some good plans—to help her develop some friendships over the next school year.

*IEP Goals*     IEPs for the students you've just met include goals such as the following:

### Lilly
1. Lilly will vocally identify objects using 1- to 3-word phrases when presented with a picture and the question, "What is this?"
2. Lilly will place pictures of desired items on a sentence strip and present them to her teacher, aide, or parents to express her wants and needs at least 10 times during the day.

### Allison
1. Allison will answer simple social questions asked by a peer (e.g., "What are you doing Allison?" "Playing with this toy.")
2. Allison will walk independently between classrooms with and without peers.

### Mustafa
The medication Mustafa takes for a seizure disorder causes lethargy and weight gain. To help him increase his energy, physical fitness, and overall health, his IEP team developed several goals like these:

1. Mustafa will independently choose healthy snacks during 80% of snack periods.
2. Mustafa will engage in physical activity for 30 minutes per day.

### Aurora
1. Aurora will engage in turn-taking play with a peer for 5 minutes.
2. Aurora will follow arrival and departure routines in her general education classroom.

***Teaching Strategies***     Four of the most important components of the teaching programs for all of the students involve task analysis (breaking down tasks into smaller, teachable units), involving typically developing peers in the teaching of social skills, providing copious amounts of positive reinforcement for students' correct responses, and using the data we collect on each student's performance during every lesson to guide what the next lesson on that skill will look like. Two additional strategies have been exceptionally useful for including some of my students in the regular classroom: picture schedules and token boards.

*Picture Schedules.*   The picture schedule we've used with several of my students includes small pictures (taken with an I-Zone Polaroid camera) mounted on a clipboard that serves as the student's schedule. A duplicate of each picture is placed in corresponding locations (e.g., a picture of the student participating in small-group instruction is Velcroed to the back of the student's chair in the small-group area). The student is taught to check her schedule, go to the area shown in the next picture, complete the activity, and attach that picture to her schedule. When a student has completed all of the activities shown on her schedule and the corresponding pictures are attached to the clipboard, she brings it to my classroom for a reward (each student has a morning and an afternoon schedule). These schedules have increased the students' independence by allowing them to transition between activities and classrooms without assistance.

*Token Boards.*   A second teaching tool we use frequently is a token board. A small token board is made for each student. Tokens are attached to the back of the board, and the front contains spaces for the tokens. The tokens are individualized for each student. One student likes Sponge Bob Square Pants stickers. The token board for an older student uses bingo chips that are less conspicuous. The students are taught how the token boards work while they are in my classroom. They choose what they want to earn (rewards include things such as video time, small snacks, preferred toys, playing a game with a friend, a certificate to take home). Each time a teacher "catches" a student doing something good, the student receives a token. When a student's token board is filled, he can turn it in for his reward. These token boards are used by all of the teachers that the student interacts with throughout the day.

***What I Like Most about Being a Special Educator***     People get involved in special education for many reasons. Some have family members with special needs; others worked at camps or schools for exceptional children when they were younger. For me, a career in special education didn't occur to me until I was about to graduate from college. I had taken a couple of classes in special education and decided to take a summer job working with children with autism. I had no idea what I was in for: the only time I had heard of autism was in the movie *Rain Man*. Was I in for a surprise! The three little boys I met that summer changed my life forever.

Every experience I have had since that summer has confirmed that special education is the field for me. It's a demanding job, with a lot of paperwork and some exhausting days. But there are so many powerful rewards. The parents I work with often come to my class with a variety of emotions ranging from fear, to depression, to an overwhelming desire to do everything and anything for their child. The parents of my students are the most amazing people in the world. The gratitude I receive and the joy I get to share with them when their child has success is worth all the work. Too often, we don't take the time to appreciate the small things in life; but in this field you realize how much work goes into some of those "small" accomplishments. This is why I love going to work every day. And because I work with a team of teachers and administrators who believe in using scientifically validated approaches to teaching, I get to share in a lot of these success stories.

To access a guided tour of Ms. Anderson's classroom and several additional video clips of her students engaged in some of the curriculum activities described in this essay, open the *Exceptional Teachers* CD-ROM, and click on "Millennium Community School."

Autism is one of the most intriguing, fascinating, and "baffling" of childhood disorders (Simpson, 2001, p. 68). It can also be one of the most frightening, exhausting, and heartbreaking experiences for the parents and families of children with the condition. Until recently, the prognosis for children with autism was extremely poor, with problems of daily living persisting into adulthood and requiring intensive supervision and supports for more than 90% of individuals (Bristol et al., 1996; Matson, 1994). On the brighter side, however, a great deal of exciting and promising research is producing better futures for many children and young adults with autism and their families

The field of autism has undergone enormous changes in recent years; and the condition has moved from being a relatively unrecognized disability, even with the field of special education, to one of widespread interest in education and society in general. Still, much remains unknown about the disability. Richard Simpson (2004), who like most people, was "both fascinated and spellbound" (p. 137) by children with autism when he first began working with them more than 30 years ago, has written:

To better understand the topics that will be covered in this chapter, go to the Essential Concepts and Chapter at a Glance modules in Chapter 7 of the Companion Website, **www.prenhall.com/heward**.

> In spite of the extraordinary recent media coverage and other attention that autism has received, it continues to have the same mystique that it had when I first entered the field. That is, in spite of significant advancements in treating and understanding individuals with autism spectrum disorders, the disability remains a mystery. Even when viewed through a disability lens, individuals with ASD are a particularly challenging and enigmatic group. (p. 138)

## DEFINITIONS

Autism is a neurobehavioral syndrome marked by qualitative impairments of social interaction; communication; and restricted, repetitive, and stereotyped patterns of behavior. Leo Kanner, a psychiatrist at Johns Hopkins Hospital in Baltimore, was the first to describe and name the condition when he published case reports on a group of 11 children in 1943. He wrote that the children displayed behaviors that differed "so markedly and uniquely from anything reported so far, that each case merits...a detailed consideration of its fascinating peculiarities" (Kanner, 1943/1985, p. 11). The children he described shared the following characteristics:

- Difficulty relating to others in a typical manner
- Extreme aloneness that seemed to isolate the child from the outside world
- Resistance to being picked up or held by parents
- Significant speech deficits, including mutism and echolalia
- In some cases, very good rote memory
- Early specific food preferences
- Obsessive desire for repetition and sameness
- Bizarre, repetitive behavior such as rocking back and forth
- Lack of imagination, few spontaneous behaviors such as typical play
- Normal physical appearance

Kanner called this condition *early infantile autism*.

### Definition of Autism Spectrum Disorders in DSM-IV

Today, autism is one of five disorders of childhood subsumed under the umbrella term *pervasive developmental disorder (PDD)* (American Psychiatric Association, 2000a). Most professionals now use the term **autism spectrum disorders (ASD)** instead of PDD (Volkmar & Pauls, 2003). The five subtypes of ASD are autistic disorder, Asperger syndrome, Rett's syndrome, childhood disintegrative disorder, and pervasive developmental disorder—not otherwise specified (PDD-NOS). These related disorders are differentiated from one another primarily by the age of onset and severity of various symptoms.

*Autistic Disorder.* **Autistic disorder** is marked by three defining features with onset before age 3: (1) qualitative impairment of social interaction (e.g., lack of social or emotional reciprocity); (2) qualitative impairment of communication (e.g., delay or total absence of spoken language); and (3) restricted, repetitive, and stereotyped patterns of behavior, interests, and activities (e.g., persistent preoccupation with parts of objects). The combination of behavioral deficits (e.g., inability to relate to others, lack of functional language) and behavioral excesses (e.g., self-stimulation, bizarre and challenging behaviors) makes children with "classic autism" stand out as strikingly different from most children. Figure 7.1 shows the DSM-IV diagnostic criteria for autistic disorder.

*Asperger Syndrome.* At the mild end of the autism spectrum is **Asperger syndrome.** Although recognized descriptions of Asperger syndrome vary somewhat, the most distinctive feature is impairments in all social areas, particularly an inability to understand how to interact socially (Safran, 2002). Children with Asperger syndrome do not have general language

A child with autism spectrum disorders might focus his attention on one object or activity for hours.

delay, and most have average or above-average intelligence. Individuals with high-functioning autism are distinguished from those with Asperger syndrome because autism is associated with marked early language delay. Figure 7.2 shows the DSM-IV diagnostic criteria for Asperger syndrome.

Following are other characteristics exhibited by many individuals with Asperger syndrome (Barnhill et al., 2000; Marks et al., 2003; Myles & Simpson, 2001; Safran, 2001):

- Repetitive and stereotyped behaviors, perseveration
- Intense interest in a particular subject, often atypical things or parts of things (e.g., tractors or washing-machine motors), to the exclusion of everything else
- Preoccupation with one's own interests
- Clumsiness, difficulty with fine- and/or gross-motor activities
- Impaired use of nonverbal behaviors related to social interaction such as eye gaze, facial expression, body posture, and gestures
- Inflexible adherence to routines
- Fascination with maps, globes, and routes
- Superior rote memory, tendency to amass many related facts
- Difficulty judging personal space
- Speech and language skills impaired in the area of semantics, pragmatics, and prosody (volume, intonation, inflection, and rhythm)
- Difficulty understanding others' feelings
- Pedantic, odd speech patterns; formal style of speaking
- Extensive vocabulary, reading commences at an early age (hyperlexia)
- Perfectionist, frustrated when asked to submit work one feels is below standard

Their peculiarities and lack of social skills make it very hard for children with Asperger syndrome to develop and maintain friendships. Because they have normal or above-normal intelligence and often are highly verbal, students with Asperger syndrome are sometimes misdiagnosed or considered slackers by teachers and peers.

*Rett Syndrome.* **Rett syndrome** is a distinct neurological condition that begins between 5 and 30 months of age following an apparently normal early infancy. The baby's head growth slows, purposeful use of the hands is replaced with stereotypic hand movements (e.g., wringing and mouthing), there is a gradual onset of unsteadiness and awkward gait, and severe impairments in language and cognitive abilities ensue. Seizures are common. Rett

**FIGURE 7.1** DSM-IV diagnostic criteria for autistic disorder

A. A total of six (or more) items from (1), (2), and (3), with at least two from (1), and one each from (2) and (3):

1. Qualitative impairment in social interaction, as manifested by at least two of the following:
   a. Marked impairment in the use of multiple nonverbal behaviors such as eye-to-eye gaze, facial expression, body postures, and gestures to regulate social interaction.
   b. Failure to develop peer relationships appropriate to developmental level.
   c. A lack of spontaneous seeking to share enjoyment, interests, or achievements with other people (e.g., by a lack of showing, bringing, or pointing out objects of interest).
   d. Lack of social or emotional reciprocity.

2. Qualitative impairments in communication as manifested by at least one of the following:
   a. Delay in, or total lack of, the development of spoken language (not accompanied by an attempt to compensate through alternative modes of communication such as gestures or mime).
   b. In individuals with adequate speech, marked impairments in the ability to initiate or sustain a conversation with others.
   c. Stereotyped and repetitive use of language or idiosyncratic language.
   d. Lack of varied, spontaneous make-believe play or social imitative play appropriate to developmental level.

3. Restricted repetitive and stereotyped patterns of behavior, interests, and activities, as manifested by at least one of the following:
   a. Encompassing preoccupation with one or more stereotypic and restricted patterns of interest that is abnormal either in intensity or focus.
   b. Apparently inflexible adherence to specific, nonfunctional routines or rituals.
   c. Stereotypic and repetitive motor mannerisms (e.g., hand or finger flapping or twisting, or complex whole-body movements).
   d. Persistent preoccupation with parts of objects.

B. Delays or abnormal functioning in at least one of the following areas, with onset prior to age 3 years: (1) social interaction, (2) language as used in social communication, or (3) symbolic or imaginative play.

C. The disturbance is not better accounted for by Rett's Disorder or Childhood Disintegrative Disorder.

Reprinted from American Psychiatric Association. (2000). *Diagnostic and statistical manual of mental disorders* (4th ed., text rev.), (p. 75). Washington, DC: Author.

syndrome primarily affects girls. Although it is on the ASD continuum, Rett's syndrome is considered to be a distinct neurological condition.

*Childhood Disintegrative Disorder.* **Childhood disintegrative disorder** shares behavioral characteristics with autistic disorder, but the condition does not begin until after age 2 and sometimes not until the child has reached age 10. Medical complications are common, and the prognosis for significant improvement is usually very poor.

*Pervasive Developmental Disorder—Not Otherwise Specified (PDD-NOS).* Children who meet some, but not all, of the qualitative or quantitative criteria for autistic disorder are often diagnosed as having **pervasive developmental disorder—not otherwise specified**

**FIGURE 7.2**  **DSM-IV diagnostic criteria for Asperger syndrome**

A.  Qualitative impairment in social interaction, as manifested by at least two of the following:
   (1)  Marked impairments in the use of multiple nonverbal behaviors such as eye-to-eye gaze, facial expression, body postures, and gestures to regulate social interaction
   (2)  Failure to develop peer relationships appropriate to developmental level
   (3)  A lack of spontaneous seeking to share enjoyment, interests, or achievements with other people (e.g., by a lack of showing, bringing, or pointing out objects of interest to other people)
   (4)  Lack of social or emotional reciprocity

B.  Restricted repetitive and stereotyped patterns of behavior, interests, and activities, as manifested by at least one of the following:
   (1)  Encompassing preoccupation with one or more stereotyped and restricted patterns of interest that is abnormal either in intensity or focus
   (2)  Apparently inflexible adherence to specific, nonfunctional routines or rituals
   (3)  Stereotyped and repetitive motor mannerisms (e.g., hand or finger flapping or twisting, or complex whole-body movements)
   (4)  Persistent preoccupation with parts of objects

C.  The disturbance causes clinically significant impairment in social, occupational, or other important areas of functioning.

D.  There is no clinically significant general delay in language (e.g., single words used by age 2 years, communicative phrases used by age 3 years).

E.  There is no clinically significant delay in cognitive development or in the development of age-appropriate self-help skills, adaptive behavior (other than social interaction), and curiosity about the environment in childhood.

F.  Criteria are not met for another specific pervasive developmental disorder or schizophrenia.

Reprinted from American Psychiatric Association. (2000). *Diagnostic and statistical manual of mental disorders* (4th ed., text rev.), (p. 84). Washington, DC: Author.

**(PDD-NOS).** All children with PDD-NOS have significant impairments in socialization with difficulties in either communication or restricted interests. The boundaries for PDD-NOS are not well defined, and children with socialization problems as the result of other conditions may be misdiagnosed.

## Educational Definition of Autism in IDEA

When Congress reauthorized IDEA in 1990 (P.L. 101–476), autism was added as a disability category under which children were entitled to special education. IDEA defines the disability as follows:

   (i)  *Autism* means a developmental disability affecting verbal and nonverbal communication and social interaction, generally evident before age 3, that adversely affects a child's performance. Other characteristics often associated with autism are engagement in repetitive activities and stereotyped movements, resistance to environmental change or change in daily routines, and unusual responses to sensory experiences. The term does not apply if a child's educational performance is adversely affected primarily because the child has a serious emotional disturbance as defined in paragraph (c)(4) of this section.

   (ii)  A child who manifests the characteristics of "autism" after age 3 could be diagnosed as having "autism" if the criteria in paragraph (c)(1)(i) of this section are satisfied. (34 C.F.R., Sec. 300.7 (c) (1) [1999])

# CHARACTERISTICS

As we look at some of the most commonly observed characteristics of children with autism spectrum disorders, remember these important points. Some children on the spectrum are very severely affected in most or all domains of functioning, while others are only mildly affected. There is considerable overlap of the conditions along the spectrum, meaning that children with different diagnoses may share many characteristics. On the other hand, two children with the same diagnosis may be affected in markedly different ways. "There is no single behavior that is always typical of autism and no behavior that would automatically exclude an individual child from a diagnosis of autism" (National Research Council, 2001, p. 11).

## Impaired Social Relationships

Many children with ASD have difficulty perceiving the emotional state of others, expressing emotions, and forming attachments and relationships. Parents often report that their attempts to cuddle and show affection to the child are met with a profound lack of interest on the child's part. The child seems not to know or care whether he is alone or in the company of others.

Many children with ASD fail to exhibit social gestures such as showing and pointing things out to others or waving and nodding their head at others. Although some children with ASD "demonstrate basic gestures such as pulling, pushing, or leading others by the hand to get things they want, the use of these gestures typically lacks any social component; the child seems to be using the adult just as a means to an end" (Professional Development in Autism Center, 2004, n.p.).

Deficits in *joint attention* are very common in children with ASD (Stahl & Pry, 2002). Joint attention refers to such behaviors as looking where someone else is looking, as when a baby notices that his mother has turned her head to look at something and does the same, or when the baby turns its head or eyes in the direction that someone is pointing. Joint attention allows the young child and another person to interact with the same frame of reference, an important factor in the development of language and social skills.

## Communication and Language Deficits

About half of children with autistic disorder are mute; they do not speak, but they may hum or occasionally utter simple sounds. The speech of those who do talk may consist largely of **echolalia**—verbatim repetitions of what people around them have said—and non-contextual speech phrases without any apparent communicative purpose. For example, Murphy (2003) reported that throughout the day a 7-year-old boy with autism repeated phrases he had heard from movies, cartoons, television shows, announcers of sporting events, and teachers during math instruction such as the following:

> "Hermione, we need to go find Harry!"
> "Hi Squidward!"
> "Angelica, help me!"
> "Today's Noggin show was brought to you by your good friends at McDonald's."
> "Jeff Gordon rounds the far outside turn!"
> "Add five carry the one." (p. 22)

Some children with ASD have acquired an impressive vocabulary but do not use it in appropriate or useful ways.

A common characteristic of children with autism is the concrete or literal processing of verbal information. Straightforward cause-and-effect relationships and questions that have a definite answer are more easily understood than abstract concepts or idiomatic expressions. For example, "the concept of using an umbrella to stay dry in the rain is very concrete and easy for a child with autism to understand, whereas an idiomatic figure of speech such as 'it's raining cats and dogs,' may prove incomprehensible to a child with autism" (Professional Development in Autism Center, 2004, n.p.).

One of the most common deficits of children with autism is their lack of understanding of the social meanings of language. Michelle Anderson provides the following example:

> Many children with ASD can learn to request and label items, but understanding the subtleties of humor is often something that remains confusing into adulthood. That's why we were so excited one day when Sammy came up with a new response to an old question. Sammy had been taught to answer the question "What is your mommy's name?" Then one day in December he surprised us all when instead of answering "Chris Hall," he looked right at us with a serious face and responded, "Chris—mis." Three seconds later he started cracking up and saying, "Mommy is Christmas!" "Mommy is Christmas!" We all laughed along with him; and since then, he has come up with many more jokes to delight everyone around him. (personal communication, 2004)

## Intellectual Functioning

Children with autism spectrum disorders span the entire range of IQ. A diagnosis of autism can be made in a child with severe or profound mental retardation as well as in a child who is intellectually gifted. Although autism spectrum disorders occur across the full range of intellectual abilities, between 70% and 80% of individuals with autistic disorder also have mental retardation (Romanczyk, Weinter, Lockshin, & Ekdahl, 1999). The terms *low-functioning autism* and *high-functioning autism* are sometimes used to differentiate individuals with and without mental retardation.

Uneven skill development is a common characteristic of autism, and about 10% to 15% of children exhibit "splinter skills"—areas of relatively superior performance that are unexpected compared to other domains of functioning. For example, a child may draw very well or remember things that were said a week before but have no functional language and will not make eye contact with others.

A very few persons are **autistic savants,** people with extraordinary ability in an area such as memorization, mathematical calculations, or musical ability while functioning at the mental retardation level in all other areas (Kelly, Macaruso, & Sokol, 1997; Treffert, 1989). The betting calculations by Raymond in the movie *Rain Man* are illustrative of savant syndrome.

Many children with autism exhibit *overselectivity*, the tendency to focus on a minute feature of an object or a person rather than the whole. For example, if shown a guitar for the first time, a child might focus on the sound hole and not consider anything else about the instrument, such as its size, shape, other parts, or even the sound that it makes. This overselectivity interferes with the child's understanding of what a guitar is—the totality of its parts and function. The tendency to overselect hinders his learning of new concepts and interferes with his ability to interpret relevant meaning from the environment.

Another tendency often seen in individuals with autism spectrum disorder is obsessive attention on a specific object or activity. This focused attention may last for a long time if uninterrupted and is often very difficult to break. For instance, if a child with autism has

Mustafa's token board reminds him to use his developing speech and social skills when interacting with others.

focused his attention on trains, he may continually choose to play with trains and resist playing with other toys. Focused attention may impede his ability to shift attention to other people or activities, such as a parent who is entering the room or another child who is attempting to join his play.

Some children with autism possess a strong aptitude for rote memory for certain things. For example, a child with autism may be able to name all of the Cy Young Award winners in the major leagues and repeat the script of an entire video verbatim. Yet the same child may have difficulty recalling what he did during recess or remembering the sound that the letter *k* makes.

## Unusual Responsiveness to Sensory Stimuli

Many children with autism react to sensory stimulation in atypical ways. This takes the form of over- and underresponsiveness to sensory stimulation. An *overresponsive* (hypersensitive) individual may not be able to stand certain sounds, dislike being touched or the feel of certain textures, and refuse to eat foods with certain smells or tastes. In her autobiography, *Thinking in Pictures and Other Reports of My Life with Autism*, Temple Grandin (1995) describes how overly sensitive skin and certain sounds bothered her as a child.

> Washing my hair and dressing to go to church were two things I hated as a child.... Scratchy petticoats were like sandpaper scraping away at raw nerve endings.... loud noises were also a problem, often feeling like a dentist's drill hitting a nerve. They actually caused pain. I was scared to death of balloons popping because the sound was like an explosion in my ear. Minor noises that most people can tune out drove me to distraction.... My ears are like microphones picking up all sounds with equal intensity. (pp. 66–68)

An *underresponsive* (hyposensitive) child appears oblivious to sensory stimulation to which most people react. Some children with autism do not seem to feel pain in a normal way. Some underresponsive children will spin round and round, rock back and forth, or rub and push things hard into their skin to create additional forms or higher intensities of stimulation. It is not uncommon for an individual with autism to display a combination of both over- and underresponsiveness—for example, being hypersensitive to tactile stimulation but unresponsive to many sounds.

> We may move directly in front of the child, smile, and talk to him, yet he will act as if no one is there. We may not feel that the child is avoiding or ignoring us, but rather that he simply does not seem to see or hear.... As we get to know the child better, we become aware of the great variability in this obliviousness to stimulation. For example, although the child may give no visible reaction to a loud noise, such as a clapping of hands directly behind his ears, he may orient to the crinkle of a candy wrapper or respond fearfully to a distant and barely audible siren. (Lovaas & Newsom, 1976, p. 308)

## Insistence on Sameness and Perseveration

Children with autism often have issues about routines or repetitive behaviors. Many demonstrate an obsessive need for sameness. They may have great difficulty when home or classroom routines are changed, possibly throwing huge tantrums. They may insist upon having everything in the same place all the time and get very upset if anything is moved. Sometimes a verbal child with autism may show this desire for sameness in a preoccupation with a certain subject or area of interest to the exclusion of all others. This child may talk incessantly about one topic, regardless of how bored his listeners are with it, and show no interest in anything else. He may ask the same question over and over, regardless of the reply.

## Ritualistic and Unusual Behavior Patterns

Some children with autism engage in ritualistic routines and repetitive behaviors. They may exhibit **stereotypic behavior**, very repetitive acts such as rocking their bodies when in a sitting position, twirling around, flapping their hands at the wrists, or humming a set of three or four notes over and over again. A child may spend hours at a time gazing at his cupped hands, staring at lights, spinning objects, clicking a ballpoint pen, and so on.

## Problem Behavior

Students with autism are more likely to exhibit behavior problems that might take the form of aggression toward others and/or themselves.

> Often the parents report that the child sometimes bites himself so severely that he bleeds, or that he beats his head against walls or sharp pieces of furniture so forcefully that large lumps rise and his skin turns black and blue. He may beat his face with his fists.... Sometimes the child's aggression will be directed outward against his parents or teachers in the most primitive form of biting, scratching, and kicking. Some of these children absolutely tyrannize their parents by staying awake and making noises all night, tearing curtains off the window, spilling flour in the kitchen, etc. (Lovaas & Newsom, 1976, p. 309)

## Positive Attributes and Strengths of Students with ASD

Reading descriptions of communication impairments, skill deficits, and behavioral excesses experienced by individuals with ASD, you may find it easy to overlook their strengths and positive attributes. Not all individuals with ASD are always unattached to those around them or behave in a stilted manner. As Greenspan and Weider (1997) remind us, many children with autism are "quite loving and caring, thoughtful and creative" (p. 88).

As we might expect, there is a noticeable difference between descriptions of autism and Asperger syndrome by people with and without the conditions (Kluth, 2004). While people without the disabilities tend to focus on the impairments to normal functioning, a number of people with autism and Asperger syndrome have described positive features associated with their disability. For example, Temple Grandin (1995), an adult with autism who has a Ph.D. in animal science and designs environments and equipment to improve the humane and healthful handling of livestock, describes positive features associated with her disability:

It is important not to overlook the many positive attributes and strengths of children with autism.

> I think in pictures. Words are like a second language to me. I translate both spoken and written words into full-color movies, complete with sound, which run like a VCR tape in my head. When somebody speaks to me, his words are instantly translated into pictures. Language-based thinkers often find this phenomenon difficult to understand, but in my job as an equipment designer for the livestock industry, visual thinking is a tremendous advantage. (p. 19)

Liane Willy (2001), a woman with Asperger syndrome, writes:

> We can describe a situation like no one else. We can tell you what intangibles feel like and secret flavors taste like. We can describe for you, in unbelievable depth, the intricate details of our favorite obsessions. (p. 29)

# SCREENING AND DIAGNOSIS

Because the specific neurobiological mechanisms that cause autism are not known, the primary method for determining if a child has an autism spectrum disorder is observation of behavioral characteristics. There is no medical test for autism spectrum disorders; diagnosis is most often made according to criteria described in the DSM-IV (see Figures 7.1 and 7.2 for autistic disorder and Asperger syndrome) (American Psychiatric Association, 2000a).

# Screening

Early diagnosis is highly correlated with dramatically better outcomes. Autism can reliably be diagnosed at 18 months, and researchers are actively pursuing reliable methods for detecting warning signs in children as young as 12 months.

Many parents of children with autism report that their baby developed in typical fashion for the first year or more, acquiring some meaningful communication skills and enjoying cuddling and hugging. But then between 12 and 15 months of age, the child began showing an oversensitivity to certain sounds or touch; no longer seemed to understand even simple words or gestures; and became increasingly withdrawn, aimless, and perseverative (Greenspan, 1992). Sometimes the early warning signs appear well before the baby's first birthday. When they do appear during the first year of life, they usually are not in the form of delays in major motor milestones (Landa, 2003). Many babies who are later diagnosed with autism often sit, crawl, and start to walk on time but show delayed or unusual development in social and communication domains.

Signs that warrant concern during the first year and a half of life include lack of pointing or gestures, infrequent or poor-quality imitation of the caregiver's facial expression, no single words by 16 months, lack of smiling, not responding to name being called, lack of joint attention (e.g., not looking at what parent points to), and loss of previously acquired language or social skills at any age (Filipek et al., 2000; Landa, 2004; Professional Development in Autism Center, 2004). In addition to these early markers, very young children with ASD may engage in repetitive and stereotyped patterns of specific behaviors, repeating certain behaviors over and over; saying scripted verses from familiar videos or TV shows over and over; or showing obsessive interest in certain objects, activities, or parts of objects.

*Checklist for Autism in Toddlers (CHAT).* The Checklist for Autism in Toddlers (CHAT) identifies children at age 18 months who are at risk for social-communication disorders (Baron-Cohen, Allen, & Gillberg, 1992). It is a short questionnaire with nine items filled out by the parents and five items by a primary health care worker. The CHAT looks at (1) joint attention, including pointing to show and gaze monitoring (e.g., looking to where a parent is pointing); and (2) pretend play (e.g., pretending to pour tea from a toy teapot). Any child who fails the CHAT should be rescreened approximately 1 month later. If he fails the CHAT for a second time, the child should be referred to a specialist for a diagnostic evaluation.

If a child passes the CHAT on the first administration, no further action needs to be taken. However, passing the CHAT does not guarantee that a child will not go on to develop a social-communication problem of some form. If parents are worried, they should seek referral.

*Modified Checklist for Autism in Toddlers (M–CHAT).* The M-CHAT (Robins, Fein, Barton, & Green, 2001) is an expanded American version of the original CHAT, which was developed in the U.K. Its goal is to improve the sensitivity of the CHAT for an American audience. Of the M-CHAT's 23 questions, those found to best discriminate between children diagnosed with and without autism spectrum disorders were 9 items pertaining to social relatedness and communication, such as the following:

- Does your child ever use his/her index finger to point, to indicate interest in something?
- Does your child ever bring objects over to you (parent) to show you something?
- Does your child imitate you? (e.g., if you make a face, will your child imitate it?)
- If you point at a toy across the room, does your child look at it?

A child fails the M-CHAT when two or more of the critical items are failed or when any three items are failed. Not all children who fail the checklist will meet criteria for a diagnosis on the autism spectrum. However, children who fail the checklist should be evaluated in more depth by the physician or referred for a developmental evaluation with a specialist.

✎ *Helpful Hint*

First Signs, Inc., is a national nonprofit organization dedicated to educating parents and physicians about the early warning signs of autism and other developmental disorders (http://www.firstsigns.org).

# Diagnosis

Children who fail screening tests or whose parents or professionals have reason for concern undergo a complete dianostic evaluation. A diagnosis of autism should be given by a professional with expertise in autism. That professional could be a psychologist, a psychiatrist, a developmental pediatrician, or a neurologist. It is important for the clinician to directly observe the child in addition to using an autism diagnostic tool with proven validity and reliability.

Following are brief descriptions of several of the growing number of rating scales, observation checklists, and diagnostic interviews that have been developed to aid the examiner's evaluation of the child suspected of having autism spectrum disorders. However, professionals and parents should remember that no single test or assessment device is failproof, especially when diagnosing a disability with such a wide range of expression. Gupta (2003) notes that although the idea that autism disorders fall on a spectrum is popular, "it is vague with no clearcut endpoints that state clearly when normal variation ends and disorder begins, and it does not address the issue of discordance among the three key domains of autistic symptoms in which a vast range of permutations and combinations are possible" (p. 62). Gupta suggests that including different shades of the disorder under one rubric increases the likelihood of both false positives (incorrect diagnosis of a person who does not have the disability) and false negatives (failing to diagnose a disability in an individual who has it), which in turn leads to disagreements and conflicts over obtaining and paying for needed services.

*Childhood Autism Rating Scale (CARS).* One of the most widely used instruments for diagnosing autism, the Childhood Autism Rating Scale (CARS) consists of 15 items that are rated on a 1 to 4 scale based on information from a parent report, records, and direct observation of the child (Schopler, Reichler, & Renner, 1988).

*Autism Diagnostic Interview—Revised.* The Autism Diagnostic Interview—Revised is semistructured interview of the primary caregivers of a child or adult suspected of having autism (Lord, 1997; Lord, Rutter, & Le Couteur, 1994). Questions cover communication, social development and play, repetitive and restrictive behaviors, behavior problems, and family characteristics.

*Gilliam Autism Rating Scale (GARS).* Based on the DSM-IV definitions of autism spectrum disorders, the Gilliam Autism Rating Scale (GARS) has four subtests: stereotyped behavior, communication, social interactions, and developmental disturbance (Gilliam, 1995). The GARS is good for identification and diagnosis of individuals over age 3.

*Asperger Syndrome Diagnostic Scale (ASDS).* The Asperger Syndrome Diagnostic Scale (ASDS) is designed to identify Asperger syndrome in children ages 5 through 18 (Myles, Bock, & Simpson, 2001). It consists of 50 yes-no items that can be answered by parents, family members, teachers, speech and language pathologists, psychologists, and other professionals familiar with the child. The ASDS yields a quotient that predicts the likelihood that the individual assessed has Asperger syndrome.

# PREVALENCE

Students with autism spectrum disorders constitute the fastest-growing category in special education. Not long ago, autism was considered a rare disorder, with an estimated incidence of about 6.5 in 10,000 children (Gillberg, 1995). More recent population studies have reported much higher incidence rates. The Autism Society of America (2000) has estimated that autism occurs in as many as 20 in 10,000 people, a figure consistent with data reported by one state (California Department of Developmental Services, 1999). Some researchers estimate that autism affects as many as 60 per 10,000 children (Kadesjo, Gillberg, & Hagberg, 1999). This would make autism more common than childhood cancer, Down syndrome, or diabetes. If we include adults with ASD, recent estimates range from 34 per 10,000 people (Yergin-Allsopp et al., 2003) to as many as 121 per 10,000 (Kadesjo et al., 1999). The incidence of autism is so high that some states have reported it to be an epidemic (Feinberg & Vacca, 2000). Boys are affected about 4 times more often than girls are (Fombonne, 1999).

In the 2003–2004 school year, 140,473 students ages 6 to 21 received special education services under the IDEA category of autism (U.S. Department of Education, 2004). This figure represents a remarkable increase of more than 4 times the 34,101 students with autism served just 7 years before. It is not clear what factors are responsible for the huge increase in the number of students being served under this disability category. The huge increase may be due to more awareness of autism spectrum disorder, more widespread screening and better assessment procedures, greater availability of services for the diagnostic category, and/or an actual increase in the true incidence of autism spectrum disorders (Fombonne, 2003; Gillberg & Wing, 1999). But clearly the increased number of children being identified with ASD is presenting a "daunting challenge" for the schools and communities that must develop the infrastructure and expertise needed to serve them (Simpson, 2004, p. 138).

## CAUSES

Numerous causes of autism have been proposed over the years. For a long time it was thought that parents who were indifferent to the emotional needs of their children caused autism. This notion may have had its beginnings in Kanner's (1943/1985) observations that many of the parents of his original "autistic" group were preoccupied and that "there were very few really warmhearted fathers and mothers" (p. 50).

During the 1950s and 1960s Bruno Bettelheim perpetuated the notion that autism could be attributed to the psychopathology of parents. Bettelheim's (1967) theory of *psychogenesis* claimed that autism was an outcome of disinterested, cold parents who were unable to develop an emotional bond with their children. Sadly, mothers of children with autism were called "refrigerator mothers" and led to believe they were the cause of their children's disability.

For parents, the idea that they are to blame creates a great deal of guilt on top of the grief already experienced when they find their toddler exhibiting the disturbing behaviors characteristic of autism. No causal link between parental personality and autism has ever been discovered; and in 1977, the National Society for Autistic Children (today the Autism Society of America) stated, "No known factors in the psychological environment of a child have been shown to cause autism." Nevertheless, many parents "are still trying to overcome the guilt and the professional bullying associated with that initial blame" (Scheuermann & Weber, 2002, p. 2).

Although the precise neurobiological mechanisms that cause autism have not yet been discovered, "it is clear that autism reflects the operation of factors in the developing brain (National Research Council, 2001, p. 11). (The cause of Rett's syndrome has been identified as an abnormality in the MECP2 gene on the X chromosome.) Recent research shows a clear biological origin for autism in the form of abnormal brain development, structure, and/or neurochemistry (Akshoomoff, 2000; Mauk, Reber, & Batshaw, 1997). Numerous genetic links to autism have been established, but we still do not completely understand their causal relationships (Autism Research Institute, 1998; Mueller & Courchesne, 2000). Autism might best be viewed as a behavioral syndrome that may be produced by multiple biological causes (Berney, 2000; Mueller & Courchesne, 2000). Experts now suspect that genes may make a child more susceptible to autism but that environmental factors may trigger it. What these environmental factors are is still unknown.

✎ *Helpful Hint*

An excellent source of reliable, science-based information about causes and proposed biological treatments for autism is the website sponsored by the National Alliance for Autism Research, "Exploring Autism: A Look at the Genetics of Autism," **www.exploringautism.org**.

It is not known what causes autism, although research continues to get us closer to answering that question. There is clearly a genetic component to the disorder: having one child with autism greatly increases the chances of having another child with autism. However, genetics is not the only factor involved because if one identical twin has autism, the other twin may not. Since identical twins share the same genes, some other factor must be contributing to the presence of autism. The current theory among autism genetics researchers supports the idea of complex inheritance. This means that multiple genetic factors are likely to be involved, which in combination may predispose an individual to developing autism. In addition to having the right combination of autism-related genes, exposure to certain environmental factors might lead to the development of autism in some individuals (National Alliance for Autism Research, 2002).

Although questions have been raised about whether vaccinations (specifically, the measles-mumps-rubella [MMR] vaccine and vaccines containing thimerosal and used for protection against diphtheria, tetanus, pertussis, and hepatitis B) could be a factor involved in autism, no evidence of this relationship has been found (Immunization Safety Review Committee, 2004).

# EDUCATIONAL APPROACHES

Children with autism are among the most difficult students to teach. They require carefully planned, meticulously delivered, and continually evaluated and analyzed instruction. Seldom does a child with autism make progress without education that is truly special.

This reality, combined with the "uniqueness of autism and the myriad ways in which persons with autism spectrum disorders manifest their disability," has made the area "fertile ground" for the advancement of countless strategies (Simpson, 2001, p. 68). Table 7.1 summarizes some key events in the history of understanding and treating autism and their educational implications. More detailed treatments of the history of autism can be found in Gupta (2003) and Rimland (1994).

In recent years, a great deal of exciting and promising research is contributing to better futures for children with autism and their families (e.g., Dawson & Osterling, 1997; Green, 2001; Maurice & Taylor, 2005; Panerai, Ferrante, Caputo, & Impellizzeri, 1998; Schwartz, Sandall, Garfinkle, & Bauer; 1998; Simpson, 2001). In this section, we will look at the importance of early intervention, introduce applied behavior analysis as treatment approach, and identify several specific tactics for teaching children with autism spectrum disorders.

## Critical Importance of Early Intensive Behavioral Intervention

Intensive, behaviorally based early intervention has helped some children with autism learn communication, language, and social skills so that they have been able to succeed in general education classrooms (Jacobson, Mulick, & Green, 1998). One of the earliest and most powerful examples of the potential of systematic early intervention on the lives of children with autism is the work of Ivar Lovaas and his colleagues at the University of California at Los Angeles (Lovaas, 1987; Smith, Eikeseth, Klevstrand, & Lovaas, 1997; Smith & Lovaas, 1998). In 1987 Lovaas reported the results of a study that provided a group of 19 children with autism with an intensive early intervention program of one-to-one behavioral treatment for more than 40 hours per week for 2 years or more before they reached age 4. Intervention also included parent training and mainstreaming into a regular preschool environment. When compared with a group of 19 similar children at age 7, the children in the early intervention group had gained 20 IQ points and had made major advances in

Aurora's academic and social skills have begun to flourish in a structured and consistent learning environment.

## TABLE 7.1    A history of the education of children with autism: Key events and implications

| Date | Historical Event | Educational Implications |
|---|---|---|
| 1911 | Eugen Bluer, a Swiss psychiatrist, coins the term *autism*—from the Greek word, *autos*(self)—to describe patients with schizophrenia who actively withdrew from social contact. | When used later to name a condition in children who displayed behaviors similar to Bluer's patients, the term *autism* implied that children purposively withdrew from those around them. |
| 1943 | Leo Kanner, a child psychiatrist at Johns Hopkins University, describes the characteristics of a childhood disorder he calls *early infantile autism*. | Kanner's observation that "there were very few really warmhearted fathers and mothers" caused some to speculate that indifferent, nonresponsive parents were responsible for the disorder. |
| 1944 | Hans Asperger, an Austrian pediatrician with a special interest in "psychically abnormal" children, publishes a paper describing a pattern of behavior based on his work with more than 400 children with "autistic psychopathy." | The combination of behaviors and abilities he described later came to be known as Asperger syndrome. |
| 1965 | Autism Society of America (ASA) is founded (originally National Society for Autistic Children). | ASA's mission is to promote lifelong access and opportunity for all individuals within the autism spectrum and their families to be fully participating, included members of their community. |
| 1967 | Bruno Bettleheim's book, *An Empty Fortress*, advanced the notion that children actively or purposively withdrew into their own worlds because of cold and uncaring parents. | Bettleheim's theory that autism was caused by "refrigerator mothers" led to much professional blaming and mistreatment of parents and devastating guilt. |
| 1981 | Lorna Wing publishes an article in Great Britain in which the term *Asperger syndrome* is used for the first time. | Wing's seminal paper generated renewed interest in Asperger syndrome, especially in Europe. |
| 1987 | Ivar Lovaas published results of the Young Autism Project, in which children with autism participated in an intensive early intervention program of one-to-one behavioral treatment for more than 40 hours per week for 2 years or more before age 4. | This was the first study to show that early, intensive, behavioral intervention could enable some children with autism to achieve normal functioning. It gave hope to parents and provided other researchers and practitioners with principles on which to build. |
| 1990 | Individuals with Disabilities Education Act (IDEA) Amendments of 1990 (P.L. 101–476) are made law. | Autism was added as a new disability category under which children were entitled to special education. |
| 1993 | Catherine Maurice's *Let Me Hear Your Voice: A Family's Triumph over Autism* is published. | This powerful account of a mother's efforts to find help for her two children brought attention to the importance of science-based treatment for autism. |
| 1994 | Asperger syndrome is officially recognized in the *Diagnostic and Statistical Manual of Mental Disorders (DSM-IV)* as a pervasive developmental disability within the autism spectrum. | This created increased awareness of AS among clinicians, researchers, and educators. |
| 1994 | The National Alliance for Autism Research (NAAR) is founded, the first organization in the United States dedicated to promoting research seeking to identify causes and potential biomedical cures for autism. | NAAR-funded research has been leveraged into more than $48 million in autism research awards by the National Institute of Health and other funding sources and has led to advances in the neurosciences and other scientific fields. |
| 1998 | The Association for Science in Autism Treatment (ASAT) is founded with the twin goals of disseminating accurate, science-based information about autism and promoting access to effective, science-based evaluation and treatment for all people with autism. | ASAT's newsletter, *Science in Autism Treatment*, and its website (**www.asatonline.org**) provide valuable information to families, professionals, and policymakers. |
| 2002 | CEC's Division on Developmental Disabilities (DDD) includes ASD within its purview. | Special educators with interests in ASD have a centralized source of information and a voice within CEC. |

educational achievement. Nine of the children were able to move from first to second grade in a regular classroom and were considered by their teachers to be well adjusted.

Follow-up evaluations of the same group of 19 children several years later at the average age of 11.5 years showed that the children had maintained their gains (McEachin, Smith, & Lovaas, 1993). In particular, 8 of the 9 "best outcome" children were considered to be "indistinguishable from average children on tests of intelligence and adaptive behavior" (p. 359). In discussing the outcomes of this research, Lovaas (1994) states:

> After 1 year of intensive intervention, fifty percent of the children can be integrated into regular kindergarten classrooms. Then, we have them repeat kindergarten to get a head start on first grade. Successful passing of first grade is the key. Those that pass first grade are likely to obtain normal IQ scores and normal functioning. The children who don't make it into first grade are likely to need intensive supports for their entire life. (n.p.)

Although some have questioned the validity and generality of this research (e.g., Gresham & MacMillan, 1997a, 1997b), the work of Lovaas and his colleagues was a landmark accomplishment in the education of children with autism (Baer, 2005). First, they discovered and validated at least some of the factors that can be controlled to help children with autism achieve normal functioning in a regular classroom. Second, the successful results offer real hope and encouragement for the many teachers and parents who are desperate to learn how to help children with autism.

## Applied Behavior Analysis

The teaching methods used in the Lovaas early intervention project were derived from **applied behavior analysis (ABA).** ABA is a systematic approach for designing, conducting, and evaluating instruction based upon scientifically verified principles describing how the environment affects learning (Alberto & Troutman, 2006; Cooper, Heron, & Heward, 2006). Teaching methods derived from applied behavior analysis are used effectively not only with learners who experience autism and other disabilities but also with students in general education (Crandall, Jacobson, & Sloane, 1997; Heward et al., 2005).

From the perspective of ABA, "autism is a syndrome of behavioral deficits and excesses that have a biological basis but are nonetheless amenable to change through carefully orchestrated, constructive interactions with the physical and social environment" (Green, 2001, p. 73). As a treatment, ABA shows great evidence of its effectiveness (*Clinical Practice Guideline*, 1999; Professional Development in Autism Center, 2004). ABA uses behavioral principles such as positive reinforcement to teach children skills in a planned, systematic manner. Children receive repeated opportunities across the day, settings, people, and materials to practice their new skills.

> In many respects, it is a misnomer to refer to "the ABA approach." Although ABA offers educators a collection of teaching techniques whose effectiveness has been empirically validated, it does not prescribe any particular instructional method. ABA includes a philosophy, a set of principles from which situation-specific educational interventions with a high probability of success can be derived, and—most important—a data-driven method for continuously evaluating the effectiveness of those interventions. (Heward, 2005, p. 321)

Because of the documented accomplishments of some children with autism after receiving intensive ABA therapy, many parents and practitioners have been advocating for ABA programs and services for children with autism. However, misunderstandings about ABA are widespread, and many teachers and parents have a very narrow view of what ABA is and is not. (See Figure 7.3, "What Is ABA").

One of the most common misconceptions is the belief that ABA consists only of **discrete trial training (DTT),** one-on-one sessions during which a routinized sequence of contrived learning trials is presented as teacher and child sit at a table. For example, an item

**FIGURE 7.3** **What Is ABA?**

ABA stands for *applied behavior analysis,* a scientific discipline devoted to improving and understanding human behavior. ABA focuses on objectively defined, observable behaviors that are important to the daily lives of the participants, and it seeks to improve those behaviors while demonstrating reliable relationships between the procedures employed and the improvements in behavior.

## What ABA Is

**ABA is individualized.** (This is the *applied* of ABA.) Teaching goals are determined by a careful assessment of the current skills and behavioral deficits of the individual in the context of his environment. Skills to be taught are not selected from a predetermined list, but are selected on an individual basis. Behaviors that are most likely to produce beneficial outcomes for the child and his family are the primary focus of ABA-based teaching.

**ABA is data-based evaluation and decision making.** (This is the *behavior* of ABA.) Direct and frequent measurement is the foundation of ABA. Measurement is direct when a learner's performance of the target behavior is observed and recorded as it occurs in the natural environment for that skill. Frequent measurement is better than infrequent measurement. Ideally, measurement should occur as often as instruction occurs.

**ABA is designed to be effective.** (This is the *analysis* of ABA.) Because data are collected directly and frequently during instruction, assessment of learning is continuous. By examining the data, teachers, therapists, and parents can determine whether or not the instruction is working. If the child is not making reasonable progress, instruction is modified.

**ABA is doable.** Although ABA requires far more than learning to administer a few simple procedures, it is not so complicated as to be prohibitive. Parents can learn the basic principles of ABA and can incorporate teaching strategies based on those principles into daily interactions with their children. For example, a parent can work on her child's greeting behavior throughout the day. Whenever the child encounters a new person or a parent or sibling greets the child, they can prompt the child to wave and make eye contact and then praise and reinforce that behavior.

**ABA is, in the words of one mother of a young child with autism, "Good old-fashioned hard work."** ABA is not a magic bullet or a miracle cure. It requires diligent, continuous analysis of the relationship between behavior and the environment in which behavior occurs. Because behavior is always happening, teaching is always happening. ABA is certainly intensive; but when used correctly as the basis for designing and evaluating treatment for young children with autism, ABA can produce meaningful, life-changing results.

## What ABA Is Not

**ABA does not prescribe instructional settings, teaching formats, or materials.** ABA can be used to guide discrete trial instruction for reading skills delivered by a teacher while sitting at a table with a child. ABA can also guide a parent's provision of incidental learning trials for language acquisition while giving her child a bath. ABA does not require that certain items be used as rewards or consequences for behavior. The items and activities to be used as rewards (technically called *reinforcers*) are determined by the child's preferences and by the effects those items and activities have when provided as consequences for the child's behavior.

Because ABA does not dictate any specific type of instructional method or format, the phrase "ABA method" is a misnomer. ABA is broader than any "brand name" method of behaviorally based instruction or therapy (e.g., Lovaas method, PECS, the verbal behavior method). Many service providers and parents mistakenly believe that ABA is one of these ABA-based brand names. However, training in a brand name is no substitute for in-depth training in the science of applied behavior analysis.

**ABA is not bribery.** Every effort is made to increase children's motivation and make learning fun. Naturally occurring consequences are used as reinforcers whenever possible. For example, instead of using just teacher praise or edible items when teaching play and social skills to children, naturally occurring consequences, such as access to favorite toys and interacting with other children, are provided as reinforcers for appropriate use of play and socialization behaviors.

**ABA is not punitive.** Positive strategies are used until they are exhausted, and reinforcers are delivered systematically to increase appropriate behavior. The goal of ABA is not to decrease maladaptive behavior but to increase the strength and frequency of appropriate behavior. An important element of ABA is to determine the function of behavior. For example, does a child tantrum and hit himself or others because he wants attention? Does he throw things because he needs help? Knowing why a child exhibits challenging behaviors allows parents and teachers to teach appropriate replacement behaviors, such as tapping a person on the shoulder to get attention or using spoken words or a communication device to say, "I need help."

Adapted from Silvestri, S. M., Wood, C. L., Allen, N. J., Anderson, M. A., Murphy, C. M., & Heward, W. L. (in press). What is ABA? In E. A. Boutot & M. Tincani (Eds.), *Autism articles: What parents need to know.* Austin, TX: PRO-ED.

or instruction is presented (e.g., "Clap your hands."), the child responds, and reinforcement is provided for a correct response. Each sequence of antecedent stimulus, child response, and consequence is a trial.

As Baer (2005) points out,

The discrete trial method of teaching, or DTT, is as old as teaching and much older than education. It can be described as follows:

1. The teacher prepares a set of problems to present to a student one at a time.
2. This sequence is usually in an optimum order for teaching and learning, to the best of the teacher's ability.
3. The student responds or fails to respond to each problem.
4. The teacher responds to each of the student's responses or nonresponses, rewarding or acknowledging correct responses; ignoring, correcting, or reproving incorrect responses; and either ignoring or prompting responses after nonresponses.
5. The cumulative effect of this teaching is to impart a new set of integrated facts, a concept, or a skill.

The discrete trial method is the method whereby children learn games and parents teach children language. It is commonly used in school classrooms for teaching any subject matter. DTT is the method of Socratic dialogue, it is often how law students are taught their most useful skills, and it is often how medical interns are taught clinical and diagnostic skills. (p. 10)

[DTT] is used in countless variations. Whether DTT is drudgery or sublimely informative depends not on its format, but on how skillfully the teacher has prepared what the student will encounter and how skillfully the teacher can answer whatever response to the encounters the student may make. (p. 24)

DTT is not ABA, and ABA can be done without DTT. However, DTT plays an important role in ABA-based programming for children with autism, and it is a teaching method that special educators should know how to use with a high degree of skill. It is also important to know that using discrete trials is just one type of teaching arrangement, and ABA programming uses a variety of procedures to help individuals with autism acquire and generalize new skills (Anderson & Romanczyk, 1999; Green, 2001; Sundberg & Partington, 1998). Following is a partial list of systematic strategies based on ABA for teaching students with autism:

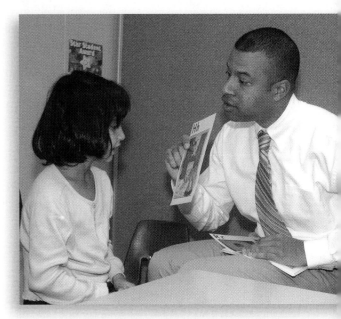

Instructional sessions featuring discrete trial training are an important part of Ayah's school day.

- Strategies for shifting control over a student's responses from contrived stimuli to naturally occurring stimuli and events he encounters in his environment (Green, 2001)
- Alternative forms of communication such as the Picture Exchange Communication System (Bondy & Frost, 2002; Schwartz, Garfinkle, & Bauer, 1998; Sundberg & Partington, 1998)
- Peer-mediated interventions for social relationships (McConnell, 2002; Strain & Schwartz, 2001)
- Methods of errorless discrimination learning (Sidman, 1994)
- Development of stimulus equivalence classes in which students learn relationships that are not taught directly, thereby expanding the power of instruction (Sidman, 1994)
- Functional assessment of challenging behavior (Horner, Carr, Strain, Todd, & Reed 2002)
- Pivotal response intervention (Koegel, Koegel, Harrower, & Carter, 1999)
- Naturalistic language strategies (Goldstein, 2002; McGee, Morrier, & Daly, 1999). (See Teaching & Learning, "Using Naturalistic Teaching Strategies to Build Communication Skills for Students with Severe Disabilities," in Chapter 12.)

ABA is not a panacea; it is the most effective intervention we have at the current time. ABA does not offer answers as to why autism happens; if offers a practical means of helping children who are autistic. ABA is not a biological intervention, although it may have concrete impact on a developing nervous system. ABA will not recover all kids from autism, but it will recover some. ABA does not solve all of our problems, and I hope that something easier to administer and cheaper will come along sometime soon—but for the moment, ABA offers all children with autism, every one of them, a real opportunity to learn. (Maurice & Taylor, 2005, p. 35)

Excellent descriptions of a variety of teaching methods based on ABA for children with autism can be found in Harris and Handleman (2000); Koegel and Koegel (1995); Maurice, Green, and Foxx (2001); and Scheuermann and Webber (2002).

## Strategies to Help Children with Autism Cope with Social Situations and Increase their Independence in the Classroom

Social stories and picture activity schedules are two relatively new and promising interventions for students with autism.

*Social Stories.* A major challenge for many individuals with autism is learning to tolerate change and how and when to use communication and social interaction skills within the typical rules and conventions that govern social situations (Wetherby & Rydell, 2000). Social stories explain social situations and concepts, including expected behaviors of the persons involved, in a format understandable to an individual with ASD. Social stories can answer a child's questions about concepts and provide information about social behavior that she is not likely to ask for or obtain in other ways (Gray, 1994, 2000). According to Gray and Garand (1993), social stories can be used to describe a situation and expected behaviors, explain simple steps for achieving certain goals or outcomes, and teach new routines and anticipated actions. Although the purpose of social stories is to describe the situation, not direct the child's behavior (Gray, 1994), a number of studies have reported improvements in children's behavior after systematic exposure to social stories (e.g., Hagiwara & Myles, 1999).

Providing social stories before an event or activity can decrease a child's anxiety, improve his behavior, and help him understand the event from the perspective of others (Gray & Garand, 1993; Hagiwara & Myles, 1999; Ivey, Heflin, & Alberto, 2004; Kuoch & Mirenda, 2003).

Ivey and colleagues (2004) found that three 5- to 7-year-old boys with autism increased their independent and appropriate participation in novel activities when parents introduced stories to the children and read them once a day for 5 days before the events. In addition to story text (see Figure 7.4), photographs and line drawings depicting key information and important aspects of the events were attached to each page.

*Picture Activity Schedules.* Some level of independent performance is needed for success in inclusive classroom settings (Massey & Wheeler, 2000). For preschoolers with autism, a lack of play skills "might prevent opportunities for learning and successful participation in inclusive classrooms. The impending isolation might serve to perpetuate the children's deficits in socialization and communication" (Morrison, Sainato, BenChaaban, & Endo, 2002, p. 58). Several studies have found that children with autism can be taught to use *picture activity schedules* to increase their independence in selecting and carrying out a sequence of activities in the classroom (e.g., Bevill, Gast, MaGuire, & Vail, 2001; Bryan & Gast, 2000; Massey & Wheeler, 2001; McClannahan & Krantz, 1999; Morrison et al., 2002). For examples of activity schedules and information on creating and using them in the classroom, (see Teaching & Learning, "Promoting Independence among Children with Autism," on pp. 282–283.)

 To watch young children with autism use picture schedules to plan their classroom activities, go to "Oakstone Academy" on the *Exceptional Teachers* CD-ROM and click on "Picture Schedules."

**FIGURE 7.4** **Full text of the birthday party social story used with young children with ASD. Page separations are indicated by line spaces. Each page of the story included photographs or a line drawing depicting key concepts and activities.**

The next time I go see Michelle, it will be a very special day. It will be Michelle's birthday. Everyone has a birthday one time a year. Usually people like to have a party to celebrate. We will have a party for Michelle's birthday.

To get ready for the party, we will decorate the room. We will tape streamers on the table. Streamers are long papers that have pretty colors and hang down toward the floor. We might have a balloon at Michelle's party. We can tape the balloon to the table by the long streamers.

Next we will decorate Michelle's cake. The cake will already be made. We'll decorate it using frosting and sprinkles. We can use the frosting to write her name, initials, or just "happy birthday" on the cake. We can use sprinkles to put pretty colors on the cake.

Next we need to set the table for eating the cake and drinking juice. We will need a plate, cup, and napkin for each person at the party. There will be only two people at Michelle's party, Michelle and me. I can put a plate, cup, and napkin on the table for each of us.

After the table is set, it will be time for the party. We will sing "Happy Birthday" to Michelle. Then Michelle will cut the cake, and we can eat and drink. We can talk about the party while we're eating and drinking.

We will have fun until the party is over. I will take the long streamers off of the table and put them in a bag. Then we will clean up everything else. It will be time to do something else.

From Ivey, M. L., Heflin, L. J., & Alberto, P. (2004). The use of social stories to promote independent behaviors in novel events for children with PDD-NOS. *Focus on Autism and Other Developmental Disabilities, 19,* p. 170. Used by permission.

# EDUCATIONAL PLACEMENT ALTERNATIVES

During the 2003–2004 school year, approximately 27% of students with autism were educated in the regular classroom, with 18% being served in resource room programs and 44% in separate classes (U.S. Department of Education, 2004). About 11% of students with autism attended special schools or residential facilities.

## Regular Classroom

A strong argument for educating children with autism in inclusive settings is that socially competent children are an essential ingredient for peer-mediated interventions, one of the best-researched and most effective types of interventions for young children with autism. As McConnell (2002) notes, however, "the data suggest strongly that inclusion is a necessary, but not likely sufficient, condition for social interaction interventions for young children with autism" (p. 367). For examples of how teachers can arrange an environment that motivates and enables children to use and extend their developing social skills in various activities across the day, see Teaching & Learning, "Including Preschool Children with Autism," on pp. 286–288.

To see an inclusive classroom for children with autism and their typically developing peers, go to "Oakstone Academy" on the *Exceptional Teachers* CD-ROM and click on "Circle Time" and "Puppet Stories."

# Promoting Independence among Children with Autism: Multimedia Activity Schedules

*by Jonathan W. Kimball and Robert Stromer*

Devon and two friends are playing with the train set in their preschool classroom. Suddenly a timer beeps from across the room, and Devon scurries from the play center toward the sound. The beeping comes from a computer, and the monitor displays a photograph of Devon playing with a locomotive. Devon uses the mouse to click a large button in the corner of the screen and watches as a new photo appears, depicting the classroom's sand table. This photo also has a button. When he clicks it, Devon sees a 10-second video clip of one inviting another to play at the sand table. A new photo appears that shows Devon at the sand table with other children. Devon leaves the computer, approaches a friend, and says, "Come play," as he leads the other child toward the sand table.

In this vignette, Devon, a 4-year-old with autism, is following an activity schedule presented on a computer. Before learning to follow such a schedule, Devon had received intensive teacher instruction in a number of play skills: playing with trains and sand, building with blocks, playing a picture-matching memory game, and "cooking" on the toy stove.

Unfortunately, before learning to use an activity schedule, Devon, like many children with autism, would not spontaneously demonstrate even the skills he had mastered during guided practice. Instead, during free time he remained alone and engaged in repetitive or nonfunctional rituals known as stereotypy—for instance, rapidly flapping his hands or stacking Legos in a particular pattern—until an adult asked him to participate in one of the centers. In the vignette, however, adults are conspicuously absent.

## ACTIVITY SCHEDULES AND ACTIVE KIDS

Part of a larger group of assistive technology known as visual supports, an activity schedule traditionally is a series of separate images—photos, icons, or words depicting activities a child can perform—presented in sequence in a notebook or on cards. Once a child such as Devon can complete three or four activities in isolation, he may be ready to learn how to follow an activity schedule to perform these activities in a sequence. Activity schedules (not unlike low-tech pocket calendars or high-tech PDAs used by adults) have an excellent track record in helping children with autism remain engaged in a sequence of activities, for extended periods of time, without adult prompting. Students have successfully employed activity schedules:

- for work tasks and leisure
- at school or at home
- for finite (a worksheet or a puzzle) or open-ended (reading or ball play) skills
- in a group or alone

Once children become competent with a schedule, they are often able to follow it when the images are rearranged or when new ones are substituted or added.

An activity schedule essentially exchanges one form of prompting for another. This is a distinction with a real difference: the child who has learned to employ a portable visual schedule no longer requires a teacher or a parent to tell her when to initiate one activity and when to move on to the next. Thus, a child who previously relied on adults for direction may become a child who is self-directed, at least for the given activities and over what can be a significant period of time. Beyond being a mere mechanism for prompting, then, an activity schedule can be a major tool for promoting independence.

**Multimedia Activity Schedules**   Children with autism have difficulty understanding or responding appropriately to complex stimuli such as spoken words or the human face. Research has shown, however, that these children attend very well to two-dimensional images such as what appears on television or computer monitors—in fact, Devon, like many children with autism often watches videos

| 1. Click on Activity Photo | 2. Look at Video |
|---|---|
|  |  |

| 3. Look at Cue to Play | 4. Initiate Activity |
|---|---|
|  |  |

| 5. Do Activity | 6. Put Materials Away |
|---|---|
|  |  |

**Devon's independence and social interactions with classmates have increased dramatically since he learned to use multimedia activity schedules.**

and plays on computers to the exclusion of most other activities. If visual prompts like those in activity schedules must be attended to in order to be effective, and if children with autism are naturally motivated to attend to computers, then it is sensible to conclude that children with autism may readily learn to follow activity schedules presented via computer. Once having brought activity schedules to the computer, it is a short step to bringing the audiovisual capabilities of computers to activity schedules.

The marriage of these two technologies is greater than the sum of their parts. More than an expensive toy, the computer becomes a means of delivering instruction; more than a prompting system, the activity schedule becomes a context for embedding auditory and visual instructional material. In other words, once a child has acquired the skill of schedule-following, she may then learn additional skills while following a multimedia schedule. The computer integrates two forms of instructional and assistive technology (in this case, activity schedules and video modeling) that have usually been researched and developed separately. Children with autism have not only learned to independently follow computer schedules but in doing so have also learned skills such as the following:

- Sight-word reading
- Spelling
- Daily living skills
- Functional play routines
- Social-communication skills such as asking for help or, like Devon, seeking a playmate

Because lack of social skills is a defining feature of autism, Devon's accomplishment is truly significant. Importantly, once children have learned new skills while following computer activity schedules, they have retained those skills when the same pictures are presented in portable notebooks.

## HOW TO GET STARTED

**Notebook schedules.** Lynn McClannahan and Patricia Krantz (1999) provide an excellent guide for developing and using notebook activity schedules. The closest thing to a manual for this type of technology, the book discusses prerequisite skills, preparing a first schedule, proceeding from teaching a child to follow a schedule to using them to foster social skills, and troubleshooting.

**Multimedia schedules.** Teaching with multimedia schedules requires a few more steps for teachers. Teachers should be comfortable with Microsoft PowerPoint and with handling digital cameras and images. In fact, developing schedules in PowerPoint that include sounds, videos, and even built-in beeping timers like Devon's entails only a few basic steps, which are detailed in Rehfeldt, Kinney, Root, and Stromer (2004). While multimedia schedules have the potential to capitalize on the naturally motivating properties of computers and video, children with autism should also be able to imitate actions from videos and use a computer mouse or touchscreen. Devon's teacher, using the steps outlined by McClannahan and Krantz, taught him his first activity schedule on a computer before he then learned to complete the same activities following a notebook schedule. Now when Devon moves from one activity to the next in his schedule, a stranger might have difficulty distinguishing him from his typically developing playmates.

Jonathan W. Kimball is a senior behavior analyst at Woodfords Family Services in Portland, Maine. Robert Stromer is an associate professor and a senior scientist at the University of Massachusetts Medical School, Shriver Center, in Waltham, Massachusetts. They gratefully acknowledge the contributions of Elizabeth M. Kinney and Bridget A. Taylor to the development of multimedia activity schedules.

 To learn more about this strategy and answer questions about what you have learned, go to the Teaching & Learning module in Chapter 7 of the Companion Website, **www.prenhall.com/heward**.

Aurora's improving ability to participate in group activities is helping her benefit from the increasing amount of time she spends in the regular classroom.

## Resource Room

It is important to recognize that the regular classroom will not be the least restrictive environment for all students with autism spectrum disorder.

> Most children with severe and pervasive disabilities need a classroom that will start at their unique skill levels. The children need to learn numerous and diverse behavior changes, probably different in each of their cases, that, cumulatively, would enable each child to enter and benefit from the general curriculum. To assign children with autism who do not possess those skills to the usual public school classroom is to assign them to regression. (Baer, 2005, p. 9)

Because instructional time is such a precious commodity for students with disabilities, it must be used wisely. For no group of children is this more true than it is for students with autism. Because the potential is high for significant improvements in functioning by children with autism who receive early and intensive behaviorally based education and treatment, the phrase "make every minute count" is more than just a slogan. In addition to using words such as *intensive, specialized*, and *focused*, we do not exaggerate by invoking the term *urgent* when describing the special education these children receive.

All of the students with autism enrolled at the Millennium Community School spend a portion of each school day in the regular classroom with same-age peers. They also spend part of the day in the resource room. Each student comes to the resource room for intensive, specialized instruction focused on her IEP goals and objectives.

Instruction in the resource room typically features a high frequency of instructional trials per minute; careful specification of and planning for transferring the control of student's responses from teacher-contrived antecedent and consequent stimuli to naturally occurring events; specific strategies for promoting the generalization of newly learned skills to the regular classroom, the community, and the home; continuous recording of data on each child's performance of targeted skills; and the daily review of those data as the basis for making curricular and instructional decisions.

Michelle Anderson points out several basic strategies for increasing the likelihood that students will use their new skills in other settings. Providing supplemental or booster lessons in the resource room using the same curriculum materials the students encounter in the general education classroom can enhance students' success with those materials in the regular classroom. A resource room can provide an effective setting in which to conduct small-group learning activities with nondisabled peers from the regular classroom. The presence of regular classroom peers while practicing and learning new skills, especially social and language skills, can make generalization to the regular classroom more natural and likely.

## CURRENT ISSUES AND FUTURE TRENDS

An entire book could easily be devoted to current issues in autism. The highly unique characteristics of individuals with autism spectrum disorder "have fueled debates over the cause of the disorder as well as preferred educational programming and intervention choices" (Simpson, 2004, p. 138). For example, parents have filed numerous due process hearings and court cases contending that a free appropriate public education (FAPE) for children with autism requires the "Lovaas method" and that school districts should pay the high costs of this particular form of early intensive behavioral intervention (Nelson & Huefner, 2003; Yell & Drasgow, 2000). The terms *applied behavior analysis* (ABA) and *discrete trial training* (DTT) are also used in these cases, causing confusion and acrimony among parents, schools, and autism professionals who should be working together for the children's benefit.

A hotly debated current issue revolves around the question of whether or not children with autism can, as the result of effective education and treatment, improve so significantly, thoroughly, and permanently as to be considered "recovered" from autism. The opinions of researchers, practitioners, and other experts in autism differ greatly on the possibility of full recovery. The National Research Council (2001) has concluded that

> The core deficits in autism have generally been found to persist in some degree in most persons with autistic spectrum diagnoses. There is no research base explaining how "recovery" might come about or which behaviors might mediate general change in diagnosis or cognitive level. Although there is evidence that interventions lead to improvements and that some children shift specific diagnoses with the spectrum and change in severity of cognitive delay in the preschool years there is not a simple, direct relationship between any particular current intervention and "recovery" from autism. Because there is always room for hope, recovery will often be a goal for many children, but in terms of planning services and programs, educational objectives must describe specific behaviors to be acquired or changed. (pp. 43–44)

Instructional activities with nondisabled peers in the resource room helps Mustafa generalize his newly learned skills to the regular classroom.

A longstanding problem in the field of autism is the popularity of unproven educational interventions and other forms of treatment and therapy for children with autism. Swimming with dolphins, megadoses of vitamins, strange diets, weighted vests, hormone injections, and holding therapy are just some of the treatments for which fantastic claims have been made. Because educators need to understand this issue, we will look at two examples of unproven treatments that promised great outcomes and were used widely, identify several factors that contribute to the continued appearance and popularity of dubious interventions, and then suggest several resources that special educators and parents can consult for objective information.

## Distinguishing Unproven Interventions from Evidence-Based Treatments

Although special education has always been fertile ground for fads and exaggerated claims (Jacobson, Mulick, & Foxx, 2005), the field of autism "is particularly well known for its willingness to embrace and/or maintain a liberal tolerance toward unproven and controversial interventions and treatments. A number of these purportedly effective methods appear to have neither empirical nor logical foundation" (Simpson, 2004, p. 139).

Many controversial treatments and cures for autism have been promoted, most without scientific evidence of their effects and benefits (Heflin & Simpson, 2002; Jacobson et al., 2005; Romanczyk et al., 1999). Two examples are facilitated communication and secretin therapy.

*Facilitated Communication.* **Facilitated communication (FC)** is a process by which a communication partner, called a facilitator (most often a teacher, sometimes a friend or parent), provides physical support to assist an individual who cannot speak or whose speech is limited to typing on a keyboard or pointing at pictures, words, or other symbols on a communication board. Facilitated communication was first developed in Australia for use with persons with cerebral palsy (Crossley, 1988; Crossley & Remington-Guerney, 1992). It was brought to the United States and used primarily with persons with autism and mental retardation by Biklen, who claimed that individuals with autism and other severe disabilities can carry on typed conversations on complex topics such as current events and economics after training with FC. Advocates reported that FC has produced dramatically more sophisticated language than the user is able to produce by speech, signing, or gestures (Biklen, 1990, 1992; Crossley, 1988), which led to speculations of an "undisclosed literacy"

# Including Preschool Children with Autism: Five Strategies that Work

### by Ilene S. Schwartz, Felix F. Billingsley, and Bonnie M. McBride

Children with autism and other developmental disabilities are included in the Alice H. Hayden Preschool at the University of Washington, a comprehensive program for approximately 150 children from birth through age 6 and their families. Each classroom has 15 children: 9 qualifying for special education services, 6 typically developing. The classrooms serve children with a wide range of abilities—from severe disabilities, to mild language delay, to giftedness. About 30% of the children with disabilities have autism. Each class has a head teacher, an assistant teacher, and at least one aide.

We consider five strategies central to providing educational services for young children with disabilities in inclusive settings. They are tricks of the trade for helping children with autism and other developmental disabilities acquire skills, develop relationships, and participate as full class members.

## TEACH COMMUNICATION AND SOCIAL COMPETENCE

Without communication and social interactions among children, an inclusive program may provide little more than parallel instruction.

- *Use the Picture Exchange Communication System (PECS) to help children without functional verbal skills communicate effectively.* PECS teaches children to communicate with pictures and symbols (Bondy & Frost, 1994; Schwartz, Garfinkle, & Bauer, 1998). Most children with autism quickly learn to use PECS to communicate in understandable and acceptable ways about the things that are important to them.
- *Provide systematic instruction in imitation skills.* Imitation is critical to learning from and relating to others. Embed imitation training throughout the day—in small groups, opening circle, gym, and outdoor play.
- *Plan opportunities for students with disabilities to interact directly with typically developing peers.* At opening circle, begin with a desirable toy such as a jar of bubbles and then help all children share the toy directly with other children instead of passing the toy from child to teacher to child.

Here's an example:

Mark, who has autism, sits at the art center with several classmates. He sees that his favorite painting utensil, Dot Art paints, is next to Mary, who is typically developing and new to the class. Mark uses his symbols to build the sentence "I want Dot Art paint" and extends it toward Mary. Ben, who has been in Mark's class for a year, sees that he is trying to communicate with Mary, who is painting and doesn't notice. Ben turns to Mary and says, "Mary, Mark is talking to you. Take the sentence from him and see what he wants." Mary takes Mark's sentence strip, looks at the picture, and gives him the Dot Art paint. Ben says, "If you want it back, you can just ask Mark for it. We have to share in our class."

## USE INSTRUCTIONAL STRATEGIES THAT MAINTAIN THE CLASS'S NATURAL FLOW

Rather than isolating children with disabilities to provide individualized instruction, teach within the context of developmentally appropriate activities and routines.

- *Draw peers into the instructional situation.*
- *Use naturalistic teaching procedures.* Instruction should involve activities that are interesting to students, take advantage of child-initiated interactions, and use naturally occurring consequences.
- *Use different cues and prompts to ensure that each child receives adequate support.* Provide only what help is required so the children do not become dependent on teacher assistance.

Here's an example:

One of Jacob's IEP objectives is to learn to match similar objects. During small-group time his class made collages using various art supplies. Before the activity, his teacher placed five shapes of different colors on his collage. As the activity began, the teacher gave him five corresponding color shapes to match. The teacher provided sufficient prompts for him to complete the matching task as independently as possible. He continued to work on his collage alongside his classmates.

## TEACH AND PROVIDE OPPORTUNITIES FOR INDEPENDENCE

While interdependence is appropriate and normal in human relationships, we also expect children to become increasingly independent as they grow.

- *Give children choices whenever possible and teach choice making when necessary.*
- *Picture schedules can help some children learn to follow the sequence and duration of daily activities.* Visual cues can ease transitions between activities, increase engagement, and provide structure for trying new activities and play materials. Over time, the schedules can be faded.
- *Because it is easy to overlook nonverbal children, give them frequent chances to respond to teacher initiations.*
- *Maintain high expectations for all children.* Celebrate small victories and immediately "up the ante," all the while believing that the child has the ability to reach the next objective.

Here's an example:

It is free-choice time in Jon's classroom, and he has been having a difficult day. Transitions are always challenging for him, but today there has been more crying and mild self-injury than we have seen in 6 weeks. When the teacher announces that everyone can make his first choice, Jon walks to the wall and looks at his schedule. It has his name and six picture/symbols on it representing activity centers that are open during free choice. The first two pictures show centers in which Jon is developing play skills; the third is his favorite—the computer center. The next two are less preferred areas, and the last picture shows "Jon's choice," which means he can pick any activity he wants. Although he is still whimpering, he looks at the schedule, touches the first picture, sets a kitchen timer next to the schedule, and walks to a center. As he engages in this routine, he calms down. He plays in the center with other children until the timer goes off. Then he walks back to the schedule, takes off the first picture and puts it in the "finished pocket" at the bottom, and repeats the routine.

## BUILD A CLASSROOM COMMUNITY THAT INCLUDES ALL CHILDREN

Classrooms are learning communities where everyone can make a valuable contribution and has something to learn.

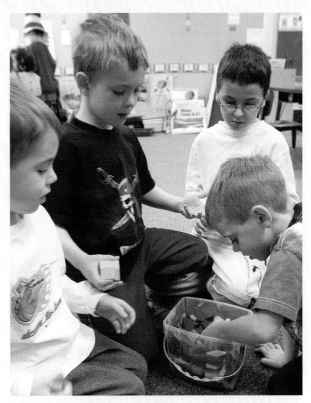

Inclusive classrooms are learning communities where everyone can make a valuable contribution and has something to learn.

Both large-group activities (e.g., opening circle, songs, stories, plays) and small-group activities (e.g., cooperative games, art projects, pre-academic activities) help create a classroom community.

- *Use activities that will engage children with a large range of abilities.* Plan open-ended activities that use preferred materials, support many responses, and address strengths of children with disabilities.
- *Allow every child to have a turn and play a role.* For example, every child, including children with autism, takes a turn being in charge of handing out materials. This puts the children with disabilities on an equal footing with others in the group and requires them to be communicative partners with peers as they request materials.

Here's an example:

It is "show and share" day, and Sophie, a 5-year-old with autism, is ready. In her lap she has a special toy from her grandmother and a cue card with words and symbols her teacher has prepared. When it's her turn, she walks to the front of the circle, holds up her toy, looks at the notecard, and follows the routine of telling her classmates two things about her toy. Then she asks, "Any questions?" After calling on classmates and answering two questions, she returns to her seat, puts her toy and cue card behind her, and picks up the notecard at her place. The teacher prepared this card with cues to support Sophie's participation as an audience member.

## PROMOTE GENERALIZATION AND MAINTENANCE OF SKILLS

Unless skills are demonstrated across a variety of situations and maintained over time, children will have limited ability to participate meaningfully in inclusive environments.

- *Target skills that will be useful in each child's life.* Skills a child needs in many situations and those typically enjoyed by same-age children are likely to be generalized and maintained because they are frequently practiced and produce naturally reinforcing outcomes.
- *Use instructional prompts judiciously and fade them rapidly.* To keep children from depending on adult assistance and direction, use the least directive and intrusive prompt that ensures successful skill performance. Fade the prompt as quickly as possible without disrupting performance.
- *Distribute learning trials naturally.* Capitalize on teaching opportunities that occur within natural school routines and activities. This increases the likelihood of generalization and maintenance because it "duplicates the occasions in which the skill should occur after instruction ceases" (Billingsley, Liberty, & White, 1994, p. 90).
- *Use common materials for instruction.* Teach with materials frequently found in preschools, child-care settings, and the homes of young children. Arrange for children to practice with these materials across many settings in the classroom.

Here's an example:

Joey has difficulty in the dramatic play area. To promote skill development, his teacher provides systematic instruction of a pretend play sequence during small-group time, using a simple play script with pictures and words and the same materials available in the dramatic play center this week. The teacher models the sequence, following the pictures in the script book and reciting corresponding words. Then Joey takes a turn while the teacher helps. Later, during free play, he enters the dramatic play area and sees the familiar pretend play props and his picture script book. He begins following the sequence without adult assistance.

*Source*: Adapted from Schwartz, I. S., Billingsley, F. F., & McBride, B. M. (1998). Including children with autism in inclusive preschools: Strategies that work. *Young Exceptional Children, 1*(2), 19–26. Used by permission.

 To learn more about these strategies and answer questions about what you have learned, go to the Teaching & Learning module in Chapter 7 of the Companion Website, **www.prenhall.com/heward**.

consistent with "normal intellectual functioning" by individuals previously thought to have severe or profound intellectual disabilities.

FC produced tremendous interest and controversy, both in the professional literature and in the popular media. Claims of meaningful and extensive communication and vocabulary use by individuals with autism or mental retardation whose use of language had previously been nonexistent or extremely limited generated understandable excitement that a powerful and widely effective new treatment might have been discovered. Even though little or no scientific evidence was available to support these claims, FC was soon being widely implemented in special education and adult human services programs serving individuals with disabilities. During the 1990s, many state education and mental retardation agencies and school districts hired FC experts and sent their teachers to be trained in the new technique. Many children and adults with disabilities were "facilitated" on a daily basis. All of this was done in the absence of any rigorous, scientific evaluation of FC.

Although some educators and many parents raised questions from the beginning about the efficacy and appropriateness of FC, asking for data supporting its use, many more were too excited about the promises of this new wonder therapy to ask many questions. But as the uniformly negative results of carefully controlled empirical studies on FC accumulated (e.g., Oswald, 1994; Simpson & Myles, 1995; Wheeler, Jacobson, Paglieri, & Schwartz, 1993), more began to question its use. Research designed to validate FC has repeatedly demonstrated either facilitator influence (correct or meaningful language is produced only when the facilitator "knows" what should be communicated) or no unexpected language competence compared with the participants' measured IQ or a standard language assessment. Green (1992), who reviewed 15 studies in which FC was experimentally evaluated with 138 individuals, concluded that "none of the 138 participants was shown to be the source of the assisted communications. In fact, there is strong evidence in several [studies] that the communications were controlled *entirely* by the assistants" (p. 9).

In the light of the overwhelming scientific evidence showing that the communication attributed to individuals with severe disabilities during FC was influenced by the facilitator (Rimland, 1993), several prominent professional organizations passed resolutions or position statements cautioning that FC is unproven and that no important decisions should be made regarding a student's or client's life that are based on the process unless authorship can be confirmed (e.g., AAMR, 1994; APA, 1994).

*Secretin Therapy.* This is a good example of how a systematic line of carefully controlled experiments can help separate fact from fiction and hype from legitimate hope. Secretin is an amino acid hormone released within the proximal duodenum in response to gastric acid secretion. Horvath et al. (1998) reported improvements in function in three children with autism who were experiencing gastrointestinal problems and had received intravenous infusions of purified porcine secretin to assess their pancreatic functioning. This report was followed by an explosion of interest in secretin as a treatment for autism, with multiple Internet sites devoted to its use and availability. However, numerous highly-controlled studies employing **double-blind, placebo-controlled** studies have found no significant differences on any measure of language, behavior, or autism symptom severity after treatment with secretin compared to treatment with a placebo (Coniglio et al., 2001; Dunn-Geier et al., 2000; Molloy et al., 2002; Owley et al., 1999; Sandler et al., 1999).

Another study reported that children with autism/PDD with chronic, active diarrhea exhibited a reduction in aberrant behavior when treated with secretin but that problem behaviors of children with autism/PDD who did not have gastrointestinal problems were unaffected by the treatment (Kern, Miller, Evans, & Trivedi, 2002). If discomfort from gastrointestinal problems is a causal factor for some of a child's problem behaviors and secretin relieves that discomfort, it is possible that secretin therapy is correlated with problem behavior in such children—but not because it is related to autism.

## Why Do Fads Thrive?

Parents and teachers of children with a devastating disability such as autism are easy targets for interventions that promise cures. As many authors and families have noted, who among us, parent or teacher, wouldn't look for anything that might help (Maurice & Taylor, 2005).

Children with autism need and deserve an education derived from scientific research, not unproven treatments and fads.

> On the Internet, and in huge conferences, parents are encouraged to mix up chemical cocktails for their children, to put them on radical diets, to subject them to hours of brushing and stroking, even to inject them with unproven substances. Often, the promoters of these fads encourage parents to submit testimonials, and these testimonials are then published as "research." One colleague estimates that there are now over 100 proposed treatments—each one has its web site, its passionate advocates, its claim to copious research. (Maurice, 2004, n.p.)

Unproven treatment fads for children with autism thrive

- When the available treatments are not producing cures for the majority of those treated.
- When the underlying cause of a disorder is mysterious.
- Because hope and need are far stronger motivators than reason or skepticism.
- When we lean too much on the authority, fame, or niceness of those promoting the fads.
- Because often, neither parents nor the professionals they consult understand what constitutes credible evidence (adapted from Maurice, 2004).

But in fact, programs for children with autism spectrum disorders that have adopted unproven methods have slowed students' progress and fostered the creation of unrealistic expectations. Such "overreliance on undocumented interventions and treatments has complicated the process of discriminating innovative interventions that have promise for effective professional application from those whose primary strength is hyperbole and exaggeration" (Simpson, 2004, p. 140).

Fortunately, there are systematic evaluations of autism treatments and objective reports that parents and professionals can turn to, such as the National Research Council's (2001) report *Educating Children with Autism*, the State of Maine's *Report of the Autism Task Force* (1999) and *Clinical Practice Guidelines: Report of the Recommendations* (1999), published by the New York State Department of Health.

(To read one parent's perspectives on the anguish of trying to separate unsubstantiated claims from scientifically validated treatments for her two children, see Profiles & Perspectives, "The Autism Wars," which follows.)

# The Autism Wars

*by Catherine Maurice*

Many parents I know, as well as many researchers and clinicians, routinely use the phrase "the autism wars." We know what we're talking about, but people unfamiliar with the politics of autism diagnosis and treatment might not. Briefly, "the autism wars" refers to the fierce infighting and conflicting claims of individuals or groups, each of whom claims to know how best to treat children with autism and derides the theories and methods of the other camps. In an environment where funding is scarce, fear and passion run high, and children's futures are at stake, the autism wars can generate much rancor, to say nothing of confusion.

On Monday, for example, a parent may consult one doctor and be told to place her child in a therapeutic nursery. The doctor will tell the parent to avoid at all costs any program based on behavior analysis because such programs are manipulative, damaging, and tantamount to dog training. On Tuesday, the parent might be told that therapeutic nurseries have little impact on autistic behaviors and often reinforce such behaviors in spite of their warm and fuzzy talk about "nurturing the whole child" and "finding the hidden child within the autistic shell." On Wednesday, the parent is informed (say, by another parent writing on the Internet) that massive doses of vitamin B6 can produce meaningful language in the child or that an injection of secretin can have a positive effect on the symptoms of autism. In the course of hearing or reading these recommendations, the parent learns that professionals are "not to be trusted" and that parents should always "trust their own instincts" and "follow their hearts" when it comes to selecting autism treatments. On Thursday, the same parent is advised to try "an eclectic approach: a little of this and a little of that." (Soon, because of fear and longing, "a little of this and a little of that" becomes an astonishing array of "treatments" levied onto 3- and 4-year-old children.) Finally, on Friday, the parent is told that there is not a whole lot that anyone can do for autism anyway, so why not come to a weekly support group to discuss "coping" and "feelings" with a coping facilitator?

For a parent of a newly diagnosed child or for a young person intending to teach students with autism, the barrage of conflicting messages can produce frustration, fear, and even despair. It is nothing short of outrageous that the organizations and individuals to whom parents and caregivers have turned for help have by and large failed to produce a set of clear, strong, discriminatory guidelines based on sound scientific principles as well as humanitarian concerns to lead people through the morass of so-called options for autism treatments.

Instead, many experts have tolerated, even encouraged, this time-consuming and expensive experimentation on our children—perhaps to remain popular with parents, who love anyone who gives them hope. But if my child is diagnosed with cancer, I need hope laced with truth. Otherwise, I will chase every apricot pit and bottle of shark cartilage I can afford as long as there is someone, anyone, who tells me that these things might help. If my child had cancer, I could presumably go to a reputable cancer center and find out which treatments have solid empirical research behind them, which treatments are still experimental, which ones are "alternative" (an unfortunate euphemism for "there are no scientific data supporting this treatment"), and which are known to cause harm. A reputable cancer treatment center, in other words, would give me the objective information I needed to make a truly informed choice about my child's well-being. But with autism, bogus therapies have been allowed free rein. The situation may be beginning to change now; but for far too long, too much money, time, and energy have been wasted on fad after fad, "breakthrough" after "breakthrough." Colleagues have estimated that there are now more than 100 such miracle cures and "exciting new interventions" currently being marketed to an extremely vulnerable population (Lockshin, Gillis, & Romanczyk, in press).

I have had two children diagnosed with autism. The sudden loss of language, the increasingly odd and stereotypical behaviors, the avoidance of eye contact, the tantrums, the toe-walking, the crying, the withdrawal into absence and staring—only a parent who has been through this can understand what it means to watch your child slip away into some foreign world, where she herself seems increasingly frustrated and frightened by her inability to communicate her most basic needs. When my daughter and then later my son received this terrifying diagnosis, many people, both professionals and parents, told me how "expert" they were in autism. I was told about their degrees, their far-flung reputations, and their personal experience. But few people had ever bothered to read, much less refer me to, published data in peer-reviewed, science-based journals. All was opinion; all was anecdote; all was theory.

Through the grace of God, I managed to stumble my way through many deviations, mistakes, and wrong turns until I found the program and the people who could truly help my children. Although I was told that applied behavior analysis was cold and harmful, that autism was lifelong, severe, and incurable, I managed somehow to hold onto a little flame of reason in the face of opinion and ideology. The research was there. The data were there. None of the other saviors and experts had anywhere close to the 30-year history of empirical evidence that the field of behavior analysis has accrued. For decades, men and women in the behavioral sciences have researched how human beings learn; and their work has led to monumental gains in understanding how children with autism can learn, sometimes to the point where they can make very significant progress or even recover.

In 1995, both my daughter and my son were reevaluated (by the same people who first diagnosed them) and were found to have "no significant residua of autism." Throughout their school years, they have been enrolled in regular education, without the need for any special services. My daughter, 18 years old, has just graduated from high school and will be attending a 4-year, selective liberal arts college. My son, age 16, has completed his sophomore year in high school, earning high honors for the year. And yes, they have friends; they have their own personalities and opinions about everything; and they know what it means to empathize with another, to feel another's joy or pain or fear. (Speaking of picking up on someone else's fear, my daughter had to fire me as her driving instructor. It appears that I am not very good at hiding hysteria and dread. She got her license, but only because her father is somehow able to remain calm as his children get behind the wheel of a car.)

No, recovery does not happen to all families who choose intensive behavioral intervention, and that truth cannot be stated often enough. There is still so much work

to do in order to understand clearly what causes autism and how to prevent it, cure it, or help children recover from it. So far, only a minority of children who receive intensive early intervention are reaching a level of functioning where they are no longer considered autistic. I am glad that the National Alliance for Autism Research (NAAR) was founded to advance the search for a biological understanding of autism. I am glad that other groups, organizations, and research centers around the country are focusing more money and time on the biomedical side of autism. We need serious scholarship and research if we are ever to alleviate the symptoms of autism in every child who receives this diagnosis. One day, I know, such efforts will lead to treatments that may be more effective, less costly, and less labor-intensive than applied behavior analysis (ABA).

However, as such research is going forward, let us not abandon the children who are alive today or leave them floundering in a sea of controversial alternative therapies. At the moment, it appears that ABA offers the best hope for progress. No, not all children will recover under intensive ABA, but virtually all children seem to make appreciable progress. Most develop some level of meaningful language, even if problems remain. Today, I know many families who delight in their children's ever-growing capacity to communicate verbally, to learn, and to love; and even as their children grow older, the learning never ceases.

Does that mean that I believe that applied behavior analysis is the only current worthwhile treatment for autism? It is not a question of what I or anyone else believes. It is a question of what objective data exist to back up any treatment claim. The education and treatment of children with autism should be based on scientific research, on logic, on common sense, on ethics—not on belief. "Belief" is what has produced those scores of *exciting new breakthrough treatments* that you can find on the Internet. Today, more than ever, it is incumbent upon all of us to turn to science—the hard science, not the pseudoscience that abounds in popular books, newsletters, and Internet chat rooms—for guidance on how to help children with autism. And for the sake of all our children, we should never just accept at face value what anyone tells us about research. We need to ask for that research, read it, and find out where it was published. Find out about relevant peer review, control groups, intake evaluations, outcome data, and independent confirmation of findings. Beware of self-published research or research that relies heavily on parent surveys. One of the hallmarks of good research is finding every possible way to eliminate observer bias. A survey that parents fill out and submit over the Internet about what they think works or not, when so many families are combining three or more treatments at once, is not considered an objective piece of data; and it is irresponsible for anyone to publish the results of such surveys as research. And frankly, as parents are checking out this treatment or that treatment, they need to take a hard look at who is making what kind of money from their need and desire and tears. In the history of autism, many bogus treatments have been rushed to market before demonstrating anywhere near enough evidence of their safety and effectiveness. The profiteers are not going to voluntarily curb their behavior. As long as parents are willing to pay thousands of dollars for snake oil, people will sell them snake oil. Only consumers can decide whether or not to keep the purveyors of such marginal treatments in business. It is up to all of us to bring the same kind critical thinking to autism treatments as we would, at the very least, to the purchase of a used car.

Reason and tenderness can walk hand in hand. Judgment, intelligence, compassion, and mercy all have their place in autism treatment. We parents love our children. That's a given. We owe it to them to separate profiteering from progress, sense from nonsense, hope from hype.

### Recommended Readings about Science, Pseudoscience, and Discriminatory Thinking

Quackwatch: Your guide to health fraud, quackery, and intelligent decisions. **www.quackwatch.org**.

Sagan, C. (1995). *The demon-haunted world: Science as a candle in the dark.* New York: Random House.

Singer, M. T., & Lalich, J. (1996). *Crazy therapies: What are they? Do they work?* San Francisco: Jossey-Bass.

### Recommended Organizations, Websites, and Publications

Autism Biomedical Information Network. **www. autism-biomed.org**.

Maurice, C., Green, G., & Luce, S. C. (Eds.). (1996). *Behavioral intervention for young children with autism: A manual for parents and professionals.* Austin, TX: PRO-ED.

National Alliance for Autism Research. **www. NAAR.org**.

*Report of the autism task force.* (1999). Augusta: Maine Administrators of Services for Children with Disabilities. **www.madsec.org**.

*Science in autism treatment: The newsletter of the Association for Science in Autism Treatment.* 175 Great Neck Road, Suite 406; Great Neck, NY 11021; (516) 466–4400; **http://www.asatonline.org**.

---

Catherine Maurice holds a Ph.D. in French literature and literary criticism from New York University. She is the author of *Let Me Hear Your Voice; A Family's Triumph over Autism* (Knopf, 1993), published in multiple languages throughout the world, and the principal editor of two books on research-based interventions for autism: *Behavioral Intervention for Young Children with Autism: A Manual for Parents and Professionals* (Maurice, Green, & Luce, 1996) and *Making a Difference: Behavioral Intervention for Autism* (Maurice, Green, & Foxx, 2001). She was a founding member of the Association for Science in Autism Treatment (ASAT) and continues to serve on its advisory board. In 2001, *Psychology Today* named her the recipient of its Mental Health Award. She lectures widely about the importance of bringing more accountability and scientific rigor into the education and treatment of children with autism.

 To further your understanding of and answer reflective questions about the concepts and issues presented here, go to the Profiles & Perspectives module in Chapter 7 of the Companion Website, **www.prenhall.com/heward**.

# Tips for Beginning Teachers

## Working with Students with Autism
### by Michelle A. Anderson

### AIM HIGH, START SMALL, AND CELEBRATE

What should you expect a student with autism to learn in a school year? How can you possibly get from here to there, while keeping yourself and your students motivated? Here are three tips:

- *Create and maintain high expectations.* Children with autism cannot reach their full potential without having teachers who hold high expectations for them.

- Break learning goals into a set of small steps. Set significant learning goals for your students, but divide them into smaller subgoals and objectives. If an important goal for one of your students is making friends with other children in the regular classroom, break this goal into smaller, teachable units: maintaining eye contact, responding to peers' questions, initiating interactions, and taking turns. This will increase your opportunities to provide focused instruction and your student's chances of achieving the larger goal.
- *Celebrate accomplishments.* Each time a student moves another step toward reaching your high expectations for success, celebrate that achievement with him and his family.

## TEACH IMMEDIATELY USEFUL SKILLS FIRST

Your students will have many learning needs. Most will exhibit communication, self-help, academic, and social skills that are far behind those of typical children. You will not be able to teach everything at once, so start with skills that will be immediately useful to your students and have a great impact on their daily lives. Specific skills for each child will vary. However, answering questions such as the following will help reveal them:

- What are your student's needs? Can he make his needs known?
- Does the student have the basic skills necessary to be included in the regular education classroom?
- Can the student take care of her own personal needs?
- Does the student know how to respond when other children ask him to play?

## FOCUS ON TEACHING SKILLS, NOT DECREASING BEHAVIORS

Some students with autism have frequent tantrums, are aggressive toward others, make stereotypic movements, or engage in self-injurious behaviors. Children with autism, like all children, may engage in challenging and harmful behaviors because they have not learned appropriate ways in which to meet their needs.

- *Create and use interventions that offer children alternative behaviors.* Interventions that focus solely on reducing the frequency of negative behaviors are often ineffective and shortsighted because they do not teach the children alternative, appropriate ways to control their world.
- *Try to determine what function a negative behavior has for a student.* For example, when James throws a tantrum, is he usually involved in a diffi-

cult task or an undesirable activity? After you have discovered this function, then teach an appropriate replacement behavior (e.g., teach James how to signal or ask for a break from a task).

## MAKE YOUR PRAISE MORE EFFECTIVE

Praise is an effective and easy-to-use tool for increasing positive behaviors. However, some students with autism do not naturally respond to praise. To make your praise more effective for students, do the following:

- Pair your praise and approval with the presentation of preferred items and activities that your students like (e.g., small edible treats, tickles, hugs, access to a preferred toy). Do this often.
- Provide praise and attention when the student is engaged in any appropriate activity that he loves to do. This is another way to pair your praise statements with existing reinforcers for the student.

## INCREASE LANGUAGE USE THROUGHOUT THE DAY

Many students with autism have severe speech and language deficits. Regardless of a student's current language ability or form of communication (e.g., speech, sign language, picture symbols), repetition and practice in meaningful contexts are critical ingredients.

- Embed frequent opportunities for students to use language skills within teacher-directed and peer-assisted lessons and in less-structured learning activities and transitions.
- Take advantage of naturally occurring situations throughout the day when students can practice their growing language skills.
- Remember that even students with limited verbal ability benefit from being required to respond with verbal approximations.

## DON'T FORGET TO HAVE FUN

Teaching is demanding work; it requires focus, diligence, structure, and planning. But hard work should not be confused with drudgery. When teachers act bored, unhappy, and frustrated, their students often respond in kind. Students with autism—like all students, young and old—are more likely to work hard for and learn more from teachers who clearly enjoy being in the classroom than they will from teachers who just go through the motions. So smile, laugh, and have fun with your students. They will be happier and more motivated to learn, and you'll enjoy going to school each day, too.

# KEY TERMS AND CONCEPTS

applied behavior analysis (ABA), p. 277
Asperger syndrome, p. 265
autism spectrum disorders, p. 264
autism, p. 267
autistic savant, p. 269
childhood disintegrative disorder, p. 266
discrete trial training, p. 277

double-blind, placebo-controlled study, p. 289
echolalia, p. 268
facilitated communication, p. 285
pervasive developmental disorders-not otherwise specified (PDD-NOS), p. 266
Rett syndrome, p. 265

 To print your own set of SAFMED flash cards for studying and mastering these terms, go to the Companion Website, **www.prenhall.com/heward**.

# SUMMARY

## Definition

- Autism spectrum disorders (ASD) include five developmental disabilities of childhood: autistic disorder, Asperger syndrome, childhood disintegrative disorder, pervasive developmental disorder not otherwise specified (PDD-NOS), and Rett's syndrome.
- Autistic disorder is marked by three defining features, with onset before age 3: (1) qualitative impairment of social interaction; (2) qualitative impairment of communication; and (3) restricted, repetitive, and stereotyped patterns of behavior, interests, and activities.
- Asperger syndrome is marked by impairments in all social areas, particularly an inability to understand how to interact socially. Other defining characteristics include repetitive and stereotyped behaviors, preoccupation with atypical things, pedantic speech patterns, and difficulties with motor activities. Children with Asperger syndrome do not have general language delay, and most have average or above-average intelligence.
- Childhood disintegrative disorder shares characteristics with autistic disorder, but the condition does not begin until after age 2 and sometimes not until age 10.
- Pervasive developmental disorder not otherwise specified (PDD-NOS) is the diagnosis given to children who meet some, but not all, of the criteria for autistic disorder. PDD-NOS is marked by significant impairments in socialization with difficulties in either communication or restricted interests.
- Rett's syndrome, a distinct neurological condition that begins between 5 and 30 months of age, is marked by a slowing of head growth, stereotypic hand movements, a gradual onset of unsteadiness and gait, and severe impairments in language and cognitive abilities.

## Characteristics

- Some children with ASD are severely affected in most or all domains of functioning, while others are only mildly affected. Children with different diagnoses along the spectrum may share many characteristics.
- Impaired social relationships include difficulty in perceiving the emotional state of others, expressing emotions, and forming attachments and relationships, and deficits in joint attention (e.g., not looking at what a parent points to).
- Many children with ASD do not speak. Echolalia is common among those who do talk.
- Children with ASD tend to exhibit concrete or literal processing of verbal information and have difficulty understanding the social meanings of language.
- A diagnosis of ASD can be made for a child with severe or profound mental retardation as well as for one who is intellectually gifted. Many children with ASD exhibit the following cognitive and learning characteristics:
  - Overselectivity—the tendency to focus on a minute feature of an object or a person rather than the whole
  - Obsessive attention on a specific object or activity for long periods of time

- Strong aptitude for rote memory for certain things but difficulty recalling recent events
- Uneven skill development—areas of relatively superior performance that are unexpected compared to other domains of functioning
- Very rarely, autism savant syndrome—an extraordinary ability in a specific area or skill while functioning at the mental retardation level in all other areas
- Children with ASD may show unusual responsiveness to sensory stimuli: overresponsiveness (hypersensitivity)—e.g., intense dislike of certain sounds, being touched, or the feel of certain textures—and/or underresponsiveness (hyposensitivity)—e.g., no reaction to stimuli that are painful to most people.
- Children may obsess about having everything in their environment stay the same and become very upset when items are moved or routines change
- Children may exhibit stereotypic and self-stimulatory behaviors, such as rocking their bodies when in a sitting position, twirling around, flapping hands, flicking fingers; or spinning things.
- Children may exhibit aggressive and self-injurious behavior.

## Screening and Diagnosis

- Autism can reliably be diagnosed at 18 months of age.
- Screening of babies showing early warning signs is critical because early diagnosis is correlated with dramatically better outcomes.
- Signs that warrant concern during the first 18 months of life include lack of pointing or gestures, infrequent or poor imitation, no single words by 16 months, lack of smiling, not responding to name, lack of joint attention, and loss of previously acquired language or social skills.
- There is no medical test for autism spectrum disorders; a diagnosis is most often made according to criteria in the DSM-IV.

## Prevalence

- Historically considered a rare disorder, recent estimates show autism occurs in as many as 1 in 500 people.
- Boys are affected about 4 times more often than are girls.
- Students with ASD constitute the fastest-growing category in special education.
- Reasons for the huge increase in the number of children with ASD receiving special education are not clear, but may include more awareness of the disability, more widespread screening and better assessment procedures, greater availability of services via the disability category, and an actual increase in the true incidence of the disability.

## Causes

- For many years, it was widely thought that parents who were indifferent to the emotional needs of their children caused autism. However, no causal link between parental personality and autism was ever discovered.
- Recent research shows a clear biological origin for autism in the form of abnormal brain development, structure, and/or neurochemistry.
- Some experts believe that certain genes may make a child more susceptible to autism but that exposure to certain environmental factors may lead to the development of the disorder in some individuals.

## Educational Approaches

- Children with autism are among the most difficult to teach of all students; they require carefully planned, meticulously delivered, and continually evaluated and analyzed instruction.
- Although the prognosis for children with autistic disorder has traditionally been extremely poor, early and intensive behaviorally based education and treatment have helped some children achieve communication, language, and social skills so they can succeed in general education classrooms.

- Among the many treatments and therapies available for helping children with autism, applied behavior analysis (ABA)—a systematic approach for designing, conducting, and evaluating instruction using scientifically verified principles describing how the environment affects learning—has the clearest and most consistent research evidence supporting its effectiveness.
- Discrete trial training (DTT) is an important part of ABA programming for children with autism. However, doing DTT does not constitute ABA, and ABA can be done without DTT.
- ABA programming uses a variety of procedures to help individuals with autism acquire and generalize new skills, such as strategies for shifting stimulus control, the Picture Exchange Communication System (PECS), peer-mediated interventions, functional assessment, pivotal response intervention, and naturalistic teaching strategies.
- Social stories, which explain social situations and expected behaviors of the persons involved in a format understandable to a student with ASD, can decrease a child's anxiety about an event, improve his behavior, and help him understand events from the perspective of others.
- Picture activity schedules—a series of images, photos, icons or video clips depicting activities a child can perform, presented in sequence—can help children with autism independently select and carry out a sequence of activities in the classroom.

## Educational Placement Alternatives

- Approximately 1 in 4 students with ASD are served in regular classrooms.
- Numerous research-based strategies for helping students with ASD acquire skills, develop relationships, and participate as full class members in inclusive settings have been developed.
- About 18% of students with ASD are served in resource rooms, 44% in separate classrooms, and 11% in separate schools.
- Instruction in the resource room or other specialized setting should feature a high frequency of instructional trials, procedures for transferring control of student responses from teacher-contrived events to naturally occurring events, strategies for promoting the generalization of newly learned skills, and daily review of data on each child's performance for making curricular and instructional decisions.
- Regardless of the setting in which a child with autism is served, the presence of socially competent children is essential because peer-mediated interventions are among the most effective types of interventions for teaching communication and social skills to children with ASD.

## Current Issues and Future Trends

- Early, intensive, behaviorally based intervention for children with autism is expensive; and parents and advocacy groups have filed numerous due process hearings and court cases contending that a free appropriate public education (FAPE) for children with autism requires this particular form of treatment and that school districts should pay for it.
- Although some children with autism have progressed so significantly that they no longer carry the diagnostic label, the opinions of experts differ greatly on the issue of recovery from autism.
- A serious problem in the field of autism is the popularity of unproven interventions and therapies.
- Parents and professionals should select autism treatments on the basis of careful and systematic evaluations of the scientific evidence of their effects and benefits.

To check your comprehension of chapter contents, go to the Guided Review and Quiz modules in Chapter 7 of the Companion Website, **www.prenhall.com/heward**.

*chapter*

# 8

# COMMUNICATION DISORDERS

# Featured Teacher

## STEVEN EVERLING

NORTHWEST ELEMENTARY SCHOOL
PINELLAS COUNTY SCHOOL DISTRICT,
LARGO, FLORIDA

*Education—Teaching Credentials—Experience*
- B. A., communication sciences and disorders, University of South Florida, 1995
- M. S., speech-language pathology, University of South Florida, 2000
- Florida, speech and language impaired, K–12; Florida, licensure as a speech-language pathologist; certificate of clinical competence in speech-language pathology from the American Speech-Language-Hearing Association
- 8 years of experience as a speech-language pathologist

***Current Teaching Position and Students***    I've been a speech-language pathologist in the Pinellas County Schools for 8 years. My first 4 years were in a middle school. For 3 years I taught the entire academic curriculum—language arts, reading, math, science, and social studies—in a self-contained classroom for students with severe language impairments. The emphasis was on promoting language development across the curriculum. The next year, I taught language arts to students who were in the language-impaired resource program and provided pull-out speech therapy services to students with impairments of articulation, voice, and fluency. For the past 4 years, I have delivered speech and language services in both a resource room and an inclusion setting at Northwest Elementary, a K–5 building with about 700 students.

The 50 students I'm serving this year are between the ages of 5 and 12 and are classified as speech and/or language impaired. Students range among grades K–5. Some of my students also receive services because of mental retardation, learning disabilities, or emotional disturbance.

***IEP Goals***    Here are examples of IEP goals and objectives for some of my students this year:

*Annual goal.*    Brian will complete story-related activities on four out of five opportunities over five consecutive sessions.

> *Short-term objective 1.*    Brian will sequence story events.
>
> *Short-term objective 2.*    Brian will identify and discuss the conflict and resolution of a story, with or without prompts.

*Annual goal.*    Sarena will increase speech intelligibility by decreasing the use of a consonant deletion pattern at the appropriate developmental level on 8 of 10 opportunities over five consecutive sessions.

> *Short-term objective 1.*    Sarena will be able to decrease her rate of speech.
>
> *Short-term objective 2.*    Sarena will more closely approximate consonant sounds within utterances in the speech therapy room.

## Focus Questions

- How are speech and language interrelated?

- How should a teacher respond to a child who says, "The dogs runned home"? To a child who says, "That foop is dood"?

- What are common elements of effective interventions for speech and language impairments?

- What are the most important functions of an alternative and augmentative communication system?

- Why are naturalistic interventions more likely to result in maintenance and generalization of a child's new speech and language skills?

*Annual goal.*   Lee will increase fluent speech on four out of five opportunities over five consecutive sessions.

> *Short-term objective 1.*   Lee will identify fluent and nonfluent speech in himself.
>
> *Short-term objective 2.*   Lee will identify struggle behaviors in himself.
>
> *Short-term objective 3.*   Lee will produce sentences fluently using an easy onset strategy.

**Curriculum Materials and Teaching Strategies**   I try to create functional communication situations that best support my students' individual speech and language needs. For students with language-related impairments, this includes making connections to reading and spelling wherever appropriate. I help students develop meaningful strategies they can implement as active learners to construct their own meanings through both interpersonal interactions and interactions with print. Examples of thematic materials that I have found useful include *Literature-Based Reading Activities* (Yopp & Yopp, 2001) and *The Magic of Stories: Literature-Based Language Intervention* (Strong & North, 1996), among others.

For children with language needs, strategies have to be specific to the individual child. In general, I have found that many children with language disabilities have significant problems making inferences in both the oral and print domains. For example, Brian, an 11-year-old with specific learning disabilities and language impairments, could not organize the structure of a storybook. He couldn't get the gist of a story. Brian's special education teacher and I collaborated on teaching him several ways to organize text-based information. These strategies included story search procedures to find important information and story maps and other graphic organizers to arrange key information so that reasonable inferences could be made. I help students with articulation, voice, or fluency problems develop techniques and strategies that enable them to be more effective communicators in their everyday school and home environments.

To see some of the strategies Mr. Everling uses to promote his students' language skills, go to Chapter 8's Teacher Feature module on the Companion Website, **www.prenhall.com/heward**.

**Collaboration and Teaming**   Every school day I work and interact with several different professionals. I collaborate with general education and special education teachers to help them become aware of the unique communication needs of students with speech and/or language impairments. I also explain and demonstrate techniques they can use to facilitate language learning and assist in the generalization of skills and strategies the students have learned in speech and language therapy. I talk frequently with the school psychologist because the speech and language assessments I administer are often a component of the multifactored evaluations conducted whenever a student is referred for special education. On occasion, I interact with the occupational and physical therapists on ways we can assist each other with skill carryover for students.

**What I Like Most about Being a Special Educator**   There are two things I like most about being a special educator. First, I enjoy working with a variety of students, each of whom presents a unique set of speech and/or language needs. From the student who stutters, to the student who exhibits speech sound errors, to the student who has difficulties with language-based concepts, finding effective strategies for communicative success is always rewarding. Second, I appreciate collaborating with other educators and school personnel who share a similar desire to help students achieve their potential.

**Advice to Someone Considering a Career in Special Education**   My main advice for anyone considering a career in special education is to be flexible because each day in the classroom you'll be confronted with new situations and challenges. Additionally, it is important to have an open and honest line of communication with your students' parents. Frequent communication with parents not only encourages appropriate student behavior but also increases the likelihood that the skills you are teaching in the classroom will be practiced and reinforced in the home environment—and this is so important for students receiving special education services.

*The Most Difficult Thing about Being a Special Educator*    The most difficult thing about this job is finding enough time in the day to get everything accomplished: student instruction, lesson planning, IEPs and related paperwork, parent contacts, schoolwide faculty duties and responsibilities, just to name a few. However, I have found that the longer I work in the school system, the more efficiently and effectively I am able to manage the multiple responsibilities of a special educator's typical school day.

*Most Meaningful Accomplishments As a Special Educator*    My most meaningful accomplishments occur when my students demonstrate improvement in their ability to be effective communicators. For example, a first-grade student, John, who was receiving services for both specific learning disabilities and speech impairments, presented with such a severe phonological impairment that his speech was nearly impossible to understand. John produced most speech sounds in the front of his mouth while omitting sounds at the end of words, which made his speech unintelligible to most listeners. For example, toward the end of our first therapy session, when John said, "Ti to toe." I had to ask him to repeat himself a couple of times before I realized he was trying to say, "Time to go." All of John's utterances exhibited similar speech patterns. Over the course of his first- and second-grade years, I saw John 2 hours per week for speech therapy. At the beginning of his first-grade year, his reluctance to speak was a clear effect of his not being understood by his parents, teachers, and friends. One can imagine John's frustration: always being asked to repeat himself and then still not being understood. By the end of his second-grade year, John's speech, while still noticeably in error, was for the vast majority of utterances intelligible to those with whom he most commonly interacted. By that time, John had become a much more verbal and assertive child, a result, at least partially, of his now being able to more effectively communicate with others. Students like John make my responsibilities as a speech-language pathologist real and meaningful.

 To learn how Mr. Everling helped John overcome his speech problems, go to Chapter 8's Teacher Feature module on the Companion Website, **www.prenhall.com/heward**.

Communication—the sending and receiving of information—is such a fundamental part of the human experience that we cannot stop communicating even when we want to. You may decide to say nothing, but sometimes saying nothing communicates a great deal. Still, imagine trying to go through an entire day without speaking. How would you make contact with other people? You would be frustrated when others did not understand your needs and feelings. By the end of the day, besides feeling exhausted from trying to make yourself understood, you might even start to question your ability to function adequately in the world.

Although relatively few people with communication disorders are completely unable to express themselves, an exercise such as the one just described would increase your awareness of some of the problems and frustrations faced every day by children and adults who cannot communicate effectively. Children who cannot absorb information through listening and reading and/or cannot express their desires, thoughts, and feelings in spoken words are virtually certain to encounter difficulties in their schools and communities. When communication disorders persist, it may be hard for children to learn and develop and to form satisfying relationships with other people.

To better understand the topics that will be covered in this chapter, go to the Essential Concepts and Chapter at a Glance modules in Chapter 8 of the Companion Website, **www.prenhall.com/heward**.

## DEFINITIONS

Before we define communication disorders, a discussion of some basic terms is necessary.

## Communication

**Communication** is the interactive exchange of information, ideas, feelings, needs, and desires. It involves encoding, transmitting, and decoding messages. Each communication interaction includes three elements: (1) a message, (2) a sender who expresses the message, and (3) a receiver who responds to the message. Although intra-individual communication occurs when the same person is both sender and receiver of the same message (e.g., when we talk to ourselves or write a note to remind ourselves to do something when we read it later), communication most often involves at least two participants, each playing the dual roles of sender and receiver.

In addition to enabling some degree of control in a social environment, communication serves several important functions, particularly between teachers and children (Lindfoors, 1987; Owens, 2005).

*Narrating.*   Children need to be able to tell (and follow the telling of) a story—that is, a sequence of related events connected in an orderly, clear, and interesting manner. Five-year-old Cindy tells her teacher, "I had a birthday party. I wore a funny hat. Daddy made a cake, and Mommy took pictures." Fourteen-year-old Ian tells the class about the events leading up to Christopher Columbus's first voyage to America.

*Explaining/Informing.*   Teachers expect children to interpret the explanations of others in speech and writing and to put what they understand into words so that their listeners or readers will be able to understand it too. In a typical classroom, children must respond frequently to teachers' questions: "Which number is larger?" "How do you suppose the story will end?" "Why do you think George Washington was a great president?"

*Requesting.*   Children are expected to communicate their wishes and desires to others in socially appropriate ways. A child who has learned to state requests clearly and politely is more likely to get what she wants and less likely to engage in inappropriate behavior as a way to communicate her needs.

*Expressing.*   It is important for children to express their personal feelings and opinions and to respond to the feelings of others. Speech and language can convey joy, fear, frustration, humor, sympathy, anger. A child writes, "I have just moved. And it is hard to find a friend because I am shy." Another tells her classmates, "Guess what? I have a new baby brother!" Through such communicative interactions, children gradually develop a sense of self and an awareness of other people.

Although speech and language form the message system most often used in human communication, spoken or written words are not necessary for communication to occur. In fact, it has been estimated that between 50% and 90% of the information in some face-to-face interactions may be communicated by nonspeech means (Lue, 2001; Owens, 2005). Both paralinguistic behaviors and nonlinguistic cues play major roles in human communication. *Paralinguistic behaviors* include speech modifications (e.g., variations in pitch, intonation, rate of delivery, pauses) and nonlanguage sounds (e.g., "oohh," laughter) that change the form and meaning of the message. *Nonlinguistic cues* include body posture, facial expressions, gestures, eye contact, head and body movement, and physical proximity.

## Language

**Language** is a formalized code used by a group of people to communicate with one another. All languages consist of a set of abstract symbols—sounds, letters, numbers, elements of sign language—and a system of rules for combining those symbols into larger units (Hulit & Howard, 2002; Owens, 2005). There are more than 6,000 languages spoken in the world (McLaughlin, 1998). Languages are not static; they grow and develop as tools for communication as the cultures and communities of which they are part change (Ovando, 2004).

The symbols and rules governing language are essentially arbitrary no matter what language is spoken. The arbitrariness of language means there is usually no logical, natural, or required relationship between a set of sounds and the object, concept, or action it represents.

The word "whale," for example, brings to mind a large mammal that lives in the sea; but the sound of the word has no apparent connection with the creature. "Whale" is merely a symbol we use for this particular mammal. A small number of *onomatopoeic* words—such as "tinkle,", "buzz, " and "hiss"—are considered to sound like what they represent, but most words have no such relationship. Likewise, some hand positions or movements in sign language, called *iconic signs,* look like the object or event they represent (e.g., tipping an imaginary cup to one's lips is the manual sign for "drink"). Remember, language is used to express descriptions of and relations between objects and events; it does not reproduce those objects and events.

Good communicators use nonlinguistic cues such as body posture and gestures and pragmatic conversational skills such as turn taking.

*Five Dimensions of Language.* Language is often described along five dimensions that define its *form* (phonology, morphology, syntax), *content* (semantics), and *use* (pragmatics). **Phonology** refers to the linguistic rules governing a language's sound system. Phonological rules describe how sounds can be sequenced and combined. The English language uses approximately 45 different sound elements, called **phonemes.** Only the initial phoneme prevents the words "pear" and "bear" from being identical, for example; yet in one case we think of a fruit, in the other a large animal.

The **morphology** of a language is concerned with the basic units of meaning and how those units are combined into words. **Morphemes,** the smallest elements of language that carry meaning, can be sounds, syllables, or whole words. *Free morphemes* can stand alone (e.g., "fit," "slow"). *Bound morphemes* do not carry meaning by themselves; they are grammatical markers that change the meaning of words when attached to free morphemes (e.g., "unfit," "slowly"). The word "baseballs" consists of two free morphemes ("base" and "ball") and one bound morpheme ("s").

**Syntax** is the system of rules governing the meaningful arrangement of words into sentences. If morphemes could be strung together in any order, language would be an unintelligible tangle of words. Syntactical rules are language-specific (e.g., Japanese and English have different rules); and they specify the acceptable (i.e., grammatical) relationships among the subject, verb, object, and other sentence elements. The meaning of a sentence cannot be derived from the congregate meanings of the individual words; it is found in the interactive meanings of those words as the result of their grammatical and sequential relationships with one another. For example, "Help my chicken eat," conveys a meaning much different from "Help eat my chicken."

**Semantics** has to do with the meaning of words and combinations of words. A competent language user possesses semantic knowledge that includes vocabulary and concept development, connotative meanings by context ("hot" refers to air temperature when discussing the weather but means something else when talking about an athlete's recent performance), categories ("collies" and "beagles" are "dogs"), and relationships between words such as antonyms and synonyms.

**Pragmatics** is a set of rules governing how spoken language is used to communicate. There are three kinds of pragmatic skills (ASHA, 2004a): (1) using language to achieve various communicative functions and goals (e.g., greeting, informing, demanding, promising, requesting); (2) adapting or changing language to the conversational context (e.g., talking differently to a baby than to an adult, providing background information for an unfamiliar listener); and (3) following rules for conversations or narrative (e.g., beginning and ending a conversation, taking turns, staying on the topic, rephrasing when misunderstood, keeping proper distance, facial expressions, gestures). Rules vary across languages and cultures.

## Speech

**Speech** is the oral production of language. Although it is not the only vehicle for expressing language (e.g., gestures, manual signing, pictures, and written symbols are also used), speech is the fastest, most efficient method of communication by language. Speech sounds are the product of four separate but related processes (Hulit & Howard, 2002): *respiration* (breathing provides the power supply for speech); *phonation* (the production of sound when the vocal folds of the larynx are drawn together by the contraction of specific muscles, causing the air to vibrate); *resonation* (the sound quality of the vibrating air, shaped as it passes through the throat, mouth, and sometimes nasal cavities); and *articulation* (the formation of specific, recognizable speech sounds by the tongue, lips, teeth, and mouth). Figure 8.1 shows the normal speech organs.

Speech is one of the most complex and difficult human endeavors. Hulit and Howard (2002) describe just some of what happens in speaking a single word, "statistics."

> The tip of the tongue is lifted from a resting position to an area on the roof of the mouth just behind the upper teeth called the alveolar ridge to produce the "s" sound. The tongue is pressed against the alveolar ridge hard enough to produce constriction, but not so hard as to stop the airflow altogether. As the speaker slowly contracts the muscles of exhalation under precise control, air is formed between the tip of the tongue and the alveolar ridge. Leaving the tongue in the same area, the speaker now presses a little harder to stop the airflow and then quickly releases the contact for the production of the "t" sound. The tongue drops to a neutral position and the vocal folds in the larynx vibrate to produce the vowel "a." The speaker turns off the larynx and lifts the tongue to the alveolar ridge for the next "t," then vibrates the vocal folds for the vowel "i" while the tongue stays in a forward but slightly lowered position. The speaker turns the larynx off again and moves the tongue to the alveolar ridge yet again to produce the controlled constriction for the next "s," followed by increased pressure to stop the air

**FIGURE 8.1    Normal speech organs**

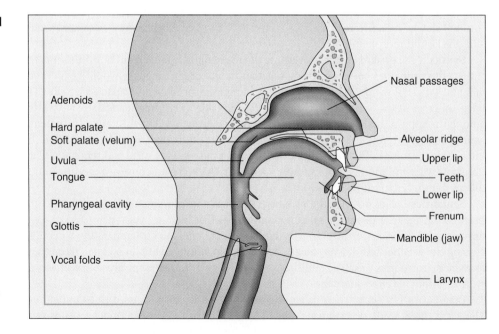

flow and release it for the "t." The larynx is turned on one more time and the tongue lowered to a neutral position for the "i," and then turned off as the tongue arches to the back of the mouth where it contacts the velum, or fleshy part of the roof of the mouth, for the "k." Finally, the tongue tip darts to the alveolar ridge for the production of the final "s" sound. All of this occurs in the production of *one* word! (pp. 4–5)

Most languages begin in oral form, developed by people speaking with each other. Reading and writing are secondary language forms that use graphic symbols to represent the oral form. There is no one-to-one correspondence, however, between **graphemes** (print symbols or letters) and phonemes.

## Normal Development of Speech and Language

Despite the complexity of speech and language, most children, without any formal instruction, learn to talk during the first few years of life. The process of learning language is a remarkable one that is not fully understood. For centuries parents, teachers, and scholars have been fascinated by the phenomenon of language acquisition in children.

Understanding how young, typically developing children acquire language is helpful to the teacher or specialist working with children who have delayed or disordered communication. Knowledge of normal language development can help the specialist determine whether a particular child is simply developing language at a slower-than-normal rate or whether the child shows an abnormal pattern of language development. Figure 8.2 identifies some of the key features of speech and language development of a typically developing child. As we consider normal language development, remember that the ages at which children acquire certain speech and language skills are not rigid and inflexible. Children's abilities and early environments vary widely, and all of these factors affect language development. Nevertheless, most children follow a relatively predictable sequence in their acquisition of speech and language.

As the descriptions in Figure 8.2 indicate, children's words and sentences often differ from adult forms while the children are learning language. Children who use structures such as "All gone sticky" and "Where he is going?"; pronunciations such as "cwackers" and "twuck"; or word forms such as "comed," "goed," or "sheeps" gradually learn to replace them with acceptable adult forms. These early developmental forms drop out as the child matures, usually without any special drilling or direct instruction (Hulit & Howard, 2002; Owens, 2005). It is also worth noting that children often produce speech sounds inconsistently. The clarity of a sound may vary according to factors such as where the sound occurs in a word and how familiar the word is to the child. Children whose expressive vocabularies consist of fewer than 50 words and/or produce limited word combinations at 24 months of age are considered late talkers. Kelly (1998) reviews the late talker literature and makes recommendations for serving this population of children.

A major longitudinal study has provided a great deal of information about the social and linguistic environment in which typical children learn to talk. Hart and Risley (1995, 1999) conducted monthly hour-long observations over a period of 2½ years of children from 42 diverse families. The researchers recorded everything said by, to, and around each of the children during unstructured activities in their daily lives at home. Of the many interesting results of this landmark study, two findings are especially notable. First, children between the ages of 11 and 36 months of age are exposed to a tremendous amount of spoken language. "Perhaps most striking of all our findings … was the sheer amount of children's exposure to talk and interaction among the people around them. Over the years of observation, we regularly recorded an average of 700–800 utterances per hour within the children's hearing" (Hart & Risley, 1999, p. 34).

Second, children who are learning to talk practice their new skill relentlessly, actively participating in literally thousands of learning trials every day. They say words again and again, they repeat what they hear, they describe things, they talk to themselves while playing, they say what they want, they ask questions, and they respond to questions. After the

*Normal language development*

Council for Exceptional Children — Content Standards for Beginning Teachers—Common Core: Educational implications of characteristics of exceptionalities (CC2K1).

## FIGURE 8.2 Overview of normal language development

**Birth to 6 months**

- Infant first communicates by crying, which produces a reliable consequence in the form of parental attention.

- Different types of crying develop—a parent can often tell from the baby's cry whether she is wet, tired, or hungry.

- Comfort sounds—coos, gurgles, and sighs—contain some vowels and consonants.

- Comfort sounds develop into babbling, sounds that in the beginning are apparently made for the enjoyment of feeling and hearing them.

- Vowel sounds, such as /i/ (pronounced "ee") and /e/ (pronounced "uh"), are produced earlier than consonants, such as /m/, /b/, and /p/.

- Infant does not attach meaning to words she hears from others but may react differently to loud and soft voices.

- Infant turns eyes and head in the direction of a sound.

**7 to 12 months**

- Babbling becomes differentiated before the end of the first year and contains some of the same phonetic elements as the meaningful speech of 2-year-olds.

- Baby develops **inflection**—her voice rises and falls.

- She may respond appropriately to "no," "bye-bye," or her own name and may perform an action, such as clapping her hands, when told to.

- She will repeat simple sounds and words, such as "mama."

**12 to 18 months**

- By 18 months, most children have learned to say several words with appropriate meaning.

- Pronunciation is far from perfect; baby may say "tup" when you point to a cup or "goggie" when she sees a dog.

- She communicates by pointing and perhaps saying a word or two.

- She responds to simple commands such as "Give me the cup" and "Open your mouth."

**18 to 24 months**

- Most children go through a stage of **echolalia,** in which they repeat, or echo, the speech they hear. Echolalia is a normal phase of language development, and most children outgrow it by about the age of 2½.

- There is a great spurt in acquisition and use of speech; baby begins to combine words into short sentences, such as "Daddy bye-bye" and "Want cookie."

- Receptive vocabulary grows even more rapidly; at 2 years of age she may understand more than 1,000 words.

- Understands such concepts as "soon" and "later" and makes more subtle distinctions between objects such as cats and dogs and knives, forks, and spoons.

children in the Hart and Risley study said their first word at an average age of 11 months, their number of utterances per hour increased steadily. On average, at 19 months of age the children became talkers: their frequency of utterances containing recognizable words had grown to exceed the frequency of nonword utterances (see Figure 8.3). At 28 months, the children became speakers: their frequency of talking matched their parents'. At age 3, the children said an average of 1,400 words per hour, using an average of 232 different words per hour and almost 20,000 total words in a 14-hour waking day.

**FIGURE 8.2** *continued*

Chapter 8
Communication Disorders

**2 to 3 years**
- The 2-year-old child talks, saying sentences such as "I won't tell you" and asking questions such as "Where my daddy go?"
- She participates in conversations.
- She identifies colors, uses plurals, and tells simple stories about her experiences.
- She can follow compound commands such as "Pick up the doll and bring it to me."
- She uses most vowel sounds and some consonant sounds correctly.

**3 to 4 years**
- The normal 3-year-old has lots to say, speaks rapidly, and asks many questions.
- She may have an expressive vocabulary of 900–1,000 different words, using sentences of three to four words.
- Sentences are longer and more varied: "Cindy's playing in water"; "Mommy went to work"; "The cat is hungry."
- She uses speech to request, protest, agree, and make jokes.
- She understands children's stories; grasps such concepts as funny, bigger, and secret; and can complete simple analogies such as "In the daytime it is light; at night it is. . . . "
- She substitutes certain sounds, perhaps saying "baf" for "bath" or "yike" for "like."
- Many 3-year-olds repeat sounds or words ("b-b-ball," "l-l-little"). These repetitions and hesitations are normal and do not indicate that the child will develop a habit of stuttering.

**4 to 5 years**
- The child has a vocabulary of more than 1,500–2,000 words and uses sentences averaging five words in length.
- She begins to modify her speech for the listener; for example, she uses longer and more complex sentences when talking to her mother than when addressing a baby or a doll.
- She can define words such as "hat," "stove," and "policeman" and can ask questions such as "How did you do that?" or "Who made this?"
- She uses conjunctions such as "if," "when," and "because."
- She recites poems and sings songs from memory.
- She may still have difficulty with consonant sounds such as /r/, /s/, /z/ and /j/ and with blends such as "tr," "gl," "sk," and "str."

**After 5 years**
- Language continues to develop steadily, although less dramatically, after age 5.
- A typical 6-year-old uses most of the complex forms of adult English and has an expressive vocabulary of 2,600 words and a receptive understanding of more than 20,000 words.
- Most children achieve adult speech sound production by age 7.
- Grammar and speech patterns of a child in first grade usually match those of her family, neighborhood, and region.

*Sources*: Adapted from ASHA (2001d); Hart & Risley (1999); Hodson (1994); Hulit & Howard (2002); Owens (2005); Porter & Hodson (2001); Shames & Anderson (2002).

**FIGURE 8.3** **Normal pattern of growth in talking**

*Source*: Hart, B., & Risley, T. R. (1999). *The social world of children learning to talk* (p. 280). Baltimore: Brookes. Used with permission.

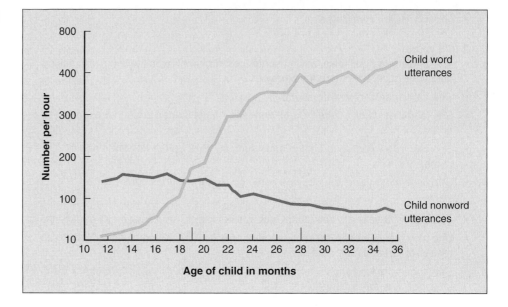

## Communication Disorders Defined

The American Speech-Language-Hearing Association (ASHA, 1993) defines a **communication disorder** as "an impairment in the ability to receive, send, process, and comprehend concepts or verbal, nonverbal and graphic symbols systems. A communication disorder may be evident in the processes of hearing, language, and/or speech" (p. 40).

By how much must a child's communication abilities differ from those of others for the difference to be considered an impairment? As previously noted, the development of speech and language is a highly individual process. No child conforms exactly to precise developmental norms; some advanced, some are delayed, and some acquire language in an unusual sequence. The range of normalcy of any dimension of speech or language is tremendous. Hulit and Howard (2002) observe:

> We have no exact standards for how much language a normal speaker has or even for how well he uses the language he has. We have vague ideas about acceptable male and female voices, but most of us have a tolerance for voices that go beyond even our own standards. We may notice that well-known television journalists such as Tom Brokaw and Barbara Walters have some problems with "r" and "l," but few of us would consider these individuals speech-defective. So how do we determine what a communication defect is? (pp. 362–363)

When does a communication difference become a communication disorder? In making such judgments, Haynes and Pindzola (2004) emphasize the impact that a communication pattern has on one's life. A communication difference would be considered a disability, they note, when any one of these criteria is met:

- The transmission and/or perception of messages are faulty.
- The person is placed at an economic disadvantage.
- The person is placed at a learning disadvantage.
- The person is placed at a social disadvantage.
- The person's self-esteem or emotional growth is negatively affected.
- The problem causes physical damage or endangers the health of the person.

To be eligible for special education services, a child's communication disorders must have an adverse effect on learning. The definition of *speech or language impairments* in IDEA reads: "a communication disorder, such as stuttering, impaired articulation, a language impairment, or a voice impairment that adversely affects a child's educational performance" (20 U.S.C. 1401 [3], Section 300. 7[c] [11]).

Like all disabilities, communication disorders vary widely by degree of severity. The speech and language of some children deviate from the normal to such an extent that they have serious difficulties in learning and interpersonal relations. Children who are not able to make themselves understood or who cannot comprehend ideas that are spoken to them by others are likely to be severely handicapped in virtually all aspects of education and personal adjustment. A severe communication disorder may lead others—teachers, classmates, people in the community—to erroneously believe the child does not care about the world around him or simply has nothing to say (Downing, 1999).

Specialists in the field of communication disorders make a distinction between speech impairments and language impairments. A child may have a speech impairment, a language impairment, or both.

*Speech Impairments.* A widely used definition considers speech to be impaired "when it deviates so far from the speech of other people that it (1) calls attention to itself, (2) interferes with communication, or (3) provokes distress in the speaker or the listener" (Van Riper & Erickson, 1996, p. 110). The three basic types of **speech impairments** are articulation disorders (errors in the production of speech sounds), fluency disorders (difficulties with the flow or rhythm of speech), and voice disorders (problems with the quality or use of one's voice). Each will be discussed later in the chapter.

It is always important to keep the speaker's age, education, and cultural background in mind when determining whether speech is impaired. A 4-year-old girl who says, "Pwease weave the woom" would not be considered to have a speech impairment, but a 40-year-old woman would surely draw attention to herself with that pronunciation because it differs markedly from the speech of most adults. A traveler unable to articulate the /l/ sound would not be clearly understood when he tries to buy a bus ticket to Lake Charles, Louisiana. A male high school student with an extremely high-pitched voice might be reluctant to speak in class for fear of being mimicked and ridiculed by his classmates.

Many children have mild to moderate speech disorders. Usually their speech can be understood, but they may mispronounce certain sounds or use immature speech, like that of younger children. These problems often disappear as a child matures. If a mild or moderate articulation problem does not improve over an extended period or if it appears to have an adverse effect on the child's interaction with others, referral to a speech-language pathologist is indicated (Owens, 1999).

*Language Impairments.* ASHA (1993) defines a **language disorder** as "impaired comprehension and/or use of spoken, written, and/or other symbol systems. The disorder may involve (1) the form of language (phonology, morphology, and syntax), (2) the content of language (semantics), and/or (3) the function of language in communication (pragmatics) in any combination" (p. 40).

Some children have serious difficulties in understanding language or expressing themselves through language. A child with a *receptive language disorder* may be unable to learn the days of the week in proper order or may find it impossible to follow a sequence of commands such as "Pick up the paint brushes, wash them in the sink, and then put them on a paper towel to dry." A child with an *expressive language disorder* may have a limited vocabulary for her age, be confused about the order of sounds or words (e.g., "hostipal," "aminal," "wipe shield winders"), and use tenses and plurals incorrectly (e.g., "Them throwed

*Definition of speech and
language impairments*

Council for Exceptional Children — Content Standards for Beginning Teachers—Common Core: Issues in definition and identification of individuals with exceptional learning needs (CC1K5).

Most children learn patterns of speech and language appropriate to their families and neighborhoods before they enter school.

a balls"). Children with difficulty in expressive language may or may not also have difficulty in receptive language. For instance, a child may be able to count out six pennies when asked and shown the symbol 6, but she may not be able to say the word "six" when shown the symbol. In that case, the child has an expressive difficulty, but her receptive language is adequate. She may or may not have other disorders of speech or hearing.

## Communication Differences Are Not Disorders

*Dialects and communication differences*

Council for Exceptional Children — Content Standards for Beginning Teachers—Common Core: Issues in definition and identification of individuals with exceptional learning needs (CC1K5) (also CC2K5 and CC6K1).

Before entering school, most children have learned patterns of speech and language appropriate to their families and communities. The way each of us speaks is the result of a complex mix of influences, including race and ethnicity, socioeconomic class, education, occupation, geographical region, and peer group identification (Salend & Salinas, 2003). Every language contains a variety of forms, called **dialects**, that result from historic, linguistic, geographical, and sociocultural factors. Each dialect shares a common set of rules with the standard language. Standard American English (as used by most teachers, in textbooks, and on newscasts) is an idealized form seldom used in everyday conversation. As it is spoken in North America, English includes at least 10 regional dialects (e.g., Appalachian English, Southern English, New York dialect, Central Midland) and several sociocultural dialects (e.g., Black English, Latino English) (Ovando, 2004; Owens, 2005).

The dialect of any group of people is neither inferior nor superior to the dialect spoken by another group. "There are dialects of English spoken by many people and dialects spoken by fewer people, but number of speakers does not indicate superiority or correctness. Every dialect of English is linguistically correct within the rules that govern it, and every dialect of English is as valid as any other" (Hulit & Howard, 2002, p. 324). A child who uses a dialect different from the dominant culture of the school should not be treated as having a communication disorder (Battle, 1998; Seymour, Bland-Stewart, & Green, 1998; Van Keulen, Weddington, & DeBose, 1998).

If the teacher does not accept natural communication differences among children and mistakenly assumes that a speech or language impairment is present, problems may arise in the classroom and in parent-teacher communication (Reed, 2005). On the other hand, some children with communication differences have communication disorders within their dialects, and such impairments must not be overlooked (Payne & Taylor, 2002; Van Keulen et al., 1998).

# CHARACTERISTICS

## Speech Sound Errors

There are four basic kinds of speech sound errors:

- *Distortions.* A speech sound is distorted when it sounds more like the intended phoneme than another speech sound but is conspicuously wrong. The /s/ sound, for example, is relatively difficult to produce; children may produce the word "sleep" as "schleep," "zleep," or "thleep." Some speakers have a lisp; others a whistling /s/. Distortions can cause misunderstanding, although parents and teachers often become accustomed to them.
- *Substitutions.* Children sometimes substitute one sound for another, as in saying "train" for "crane" or "doze" for "those." Children with this problem are often certain they have said the correct word and may resist correction. Substitution of sounds can cause considerable confusion for the listener.
- *Omissions.* Children may omit certain sounds, as in saying "cool" for "school." They may drop consonants from the ends of words, as in "pos" for "post." Most of us leave out sounds at times, but an extensive omission problem can make speech unintelligible.
- *Additions.* The addition of extra sounds makes comprehension difficult. For example, a child might say "buhrown" for "brown" or "hamber" for "hammer."

Traditionally, all speech sound errors by children were identified as articulation problems and thought to be relatively simple to treat (McReynolds, 1990). Articulation refers to the movement of muscles and speech organs necessary to produce various speech sounds. Research during the past two decades, however, has revealed that many speech sound errors are not simply a function of faulty mechanical operation of the speech apparatus but are directly related to problems in recognizing or processing the sound components of language (phonology).

*Articulation Disorders.* An **articulation disorder** means that a child is at present not able to produce a given sound physically; the sound is not in his repertoire of sounds. A severe articulation disorder is present when a child pronounces many sounds so poorly that his speech is unintelligible most of the time; even the child's parents, teachers, and peers cannot easily understand him. The child with a severe articulation disorder may say, "Yeh me yuh a da wido," instead of "Let me look out the window," or perhaps, "Do foop is dood" for "That soup is good." The fact that articulation disorders are prevalent does not mean that teachers, parents, and specialists should regard them as simple or unimportant. On the contrary, as Haynes and Pindzola (2004) observe, an articulation disorder severe enough to interfere significantly with intelligibility is a debilitating communication problem; and articulation disorders are not necessarily easy to diagnose and treat effectively.

*Phonological Disorders.* A child is said to have a **phonological disorder** if she has the ability to produce a given sound and does so correctly in some instances but does not produce the sound correctly at other times. Children with expressive phonological disorders are apt to experience problems in academic areas, and they are especially at risk for difficulties in spelling (Clarke-Klein & Hodson, 1995) and reading (Larrivee & Catts, 1999).

Determining whether a speech sound error is primarily an articulation or a phonological disorder is important because the treatment goals and procedures differ. General indicators used by clinicians for differentiating between articulation disorders and phonological disorders are shown in Figure 8.4.

## Fluency Disorders

Normal speech makes use of rhythm and timing. Words and phrases flow easily, with certain variations in speed, stress, and appropriate pauses. ASHA (1993) defines a **fluency disorder** as an "interruption in the flow of speaking characterized by atypical rate, rhythm, and repetitions in sounds, syllables, words, and phrases. This may be accompanied by excessive tension, struggle behavior, and secondary mannerisms" (p. 40).

*Stuttering.* The best-known (and probably least understood) fluency disorder is **stuttering,** a condition marked by rapid-fire repetitions of consonant or vowel sounds, especially at the beginnings of words, prolongations, hesitations, interjections, and complete verbal blocks (Ramig & Shames, 2002). It is believed that approximately 3 million people in the United States stutter (Lue, 2001). Developmental stuttering is considered a disorder of childhood. It usually begins between the ages of 2 and 6, and 98% of cases begin before the age of 10 (Mahr & Leith, 1992). It is believed that 4% of children stutter for 6 months or more and that 70% to 80% of children 2 to 5 years old who stutter recover spontaneously, some taking until age 8 to do so (Yairi & Ambrose, 1999). Stuttering is far more common among males than females, and it occurs more frequently among twins. The

Although Joshua's physical disabilities make it difficult for him to articulate speech sounds well enough to be understood, his communication board has opened up social interaction for him.

*Articulation and phonological disorders*

Council for Exceptional Children — Content Standards for Beginning Teachers—Common Core: Educational implications of characteristics of various exceptionalities (CC2K2).

*Fluency disorders*

Council for Exceptional Children — Content Standards for Beginning Teachers—Common Core: Educational implications of characteristics of various exceptionalities (CC2K2).

**FIGURE 8.4  Distinguishing articulation and phonological disorders**

| Articulation Disorder | Phonological Disorder |
| --- | --- |
| • Difficulty with only a few sounds, with limited effect on intelligibility<br><br>• Consistent misarticulation of specific sounds<br><br>• Sounds errors are motoric<br><br>• Co-existing communication disorders possible but not as likely as with phonological disorders | • Multiple sound errors with obvious impairment of intelligibility<br><br>• Inconsistent misarticulation of sounds<br><br>• Can motorically produce sound but not in appropriate places<br><br>• Errors consistent with a phonological process (e.g., final consonant deletion, making an error on a sound in one position but producing that sound correctly in another position, as in omitting "t" in "post" but producing "t" in "time")<br><br>• Other language delays likely (because phonology is a component of language) |

*Source:* Hall, Oyer, and Haas (2001); Sunderland (2004).

prevalence of stuttering is about the same in all western countries: regardless of what language is spoken, about 1% of the general population has a stuttering problem at any given time. The causes of stuttering remain unknown, although the condition has been studied extensively with some interesting results (Bloodstein, 1995). Stuttering tends to run in families; but it is not known whether this is the result of a genetic connection (Yairi, 1998), an environment conducive to the development of the disorder, or a combination of hereditary and environmental factors.

Stuttering is situational; that is, it appears to be related to the setting or circumstances of speech. A child may be likely to stutter when talking with people whose opinions matter most to him, such as parents and teachers, and in situations such as being called on to speak in front of the class. Most people who stutter are fluent about 95% of the time; a child with a fluency disorder may not stutter at all when singing, talking to a pet dog, or reciting a poem in unison with others. Reactions and expectations of parents, teachers, and peers clearly have an important effect on any child's personal and communicative development.

*Cluttering.*   One type of fluency disorder is known as **cluttering**, a condition in which speech is very rapid, with extra sounds or mispronounced sounds. The clutterer's speech is garbled to the point of unintelligibility. Hulit and Howard (2002) point out two differences between stuttering and cluttering: (1) the stutterer is usually acutely aware of his fluency problems, while the clutterer may be oblivious to his disorder; (2) when a stutterer is asked to pay more attention to his speech, he is likely to stutter more; but the clutterer can often improve his fluency by monitoring his speech.

## Voice Disorders

*Voice disorders*

Council for Exceptional Children   Content Standards for Beginning Teachers—Common Core: Educational implications of characteristics of various exceptionalities (CC2K2).

Voice is the sound produced by the larynx. A **voice disorder** is characterized by "the abnormal production and/or absences of vocal quality, pitch, loudness, resonance, and/or duration, which is inappropriate for an individual's age and/or sex" (ASHA, 1993, p. 40). A voice is considered normal when its pitch, loudness, and quality are adequate for communication and it suits a particular person. A voice—whether good, poor, or in between—is closely identified with the person who uses it.

Voice disorders are more common in adults than in children. Considering how often some children shout and yell without any apparent harm to their voices, it is evident that the vocal cords can withstand heavy use. In some cases, however, a child's voice may be difficult to understand or may be considered unpleasant (Sapienza & Hicks, 2002). *Dysphonia* describes any condition of poor or unpleasant voice quality.

The two basic types of voice disorders involve phonation and resonance. A *phonation disorder* causes the voice to sound breathy, hoarse, husky, or strained most of the time. In severe cases, there is no voice at all. Phonation disorders can have organic causes, such as growths or irritations on the vocal cords; but hoarseness most frequently comes from chronic vocal abuse, such as yelling, imitating noises, or habitually talking while under tension. Misuse of the voice causes swelling of the vocal folds, which in turn can lead to growths known as vocal nodules, nodes, or polyps. A breathy voice is unpleasant because it is low in volume and fails to make adequate use of the vocal cords.

A voice with a *resonance disorder* suffers from either too many sounds coming out through the air passages of the nose (*hypernasality*) or, conversely, not enough resonance of the nasal passages (*hyponasality*). The hypernasal speaker may be perceived as talking through her nose or having an unpleasant twang. A child with hypernasality has speech that is excessively nasal, neutral, or central-sounding rather than oral, clear, and forward-sounding (Hall et al., 2001). A child with hyponasality (sometimes called *denasality*) may sound as though he constantly has a cold or a stuffed nose, even when he does not. As with other voice disorders, the causes of nasality may be either organic (e.g., cleft palate, swollen nasal tissues, hearing impairment) or functional (perhaps resulting from learned speech patterns or behavior problems).

## Language Impairments

Language impairments can involve problems in one or more of the five dimensions of language: phonology, morphology, syntax, semantics, and pragmatics. Language impairments are usually classified as either receptive or expressive. As described previously, *receptive* language impairment interferes with the understanding of language. A child may, for example, be unable to comprehend spoken sentences or follow a sequence of directions. An *expressive* language impairment interferes with the production of language. The child may have a very limited vocabulary, may use incorrect words and phrases, or may not even speak at all, communicating only through gestures. A child may have good receptive language when an expressive disorder is present or may have both expressive and receptive disorders in combination. The term *language-learning disabilities (LLD)* is sometimes used to refer to children with significant receptive and/or expressive language disorders.

To say that a child has a language delay does not necessarily mean that the child has a language disorder. As Reed (2005) explains, a language delay implies that a child is slow to develop linguistic skills but acquires them in the same sequence as normal children do. Generally, all features of language are delayed at about the same rate. A language disorder, however, suggests a disruption in the usual rate and sequence of specific emerging language skills. For example, a child who consistently has difficulty in responding to who, what, and where questions but who otherwise displays language skills appropriate for her age would likely be considered to have language impairment.

Children with serious language disorders are almost certain to have problems in school and with social development. They frequently play a passive role in communication. Children with impaired language are less likely to initiate conversations than are their peers. When language-disordered children are asked questions, their replies rarely provide new information related to the topic. It is often difficult to detect children with language disorders; their performance may lead people to mistakenly classify them with disability labels such as mental retardation, hearing impairment, or emotional disturbance, when in fact these descriptions are neither accurate nor appropriate.

Children with oral language problems are likely to have difficulties in both reading and writing. Catts (1993) reported that 83% of kindergarteners with speech-language delays

*Receptive and expressive language impairments*

Council for Exceptional Children

Content Standards for Beginning Teachers—Common Core: Educational implications of characteristics of various exceptionalities (CC2K2).

*Language delays*

Council for Exceptional Children

Content Standards for Beginning Teachers—Common Core: Educational implications of characteristics of exceptionalities (CC2K1).

eventually qualified for remedial reading services. The problem is compounded because children with speech-language delays are more likely than their typically developing peers to be "treatment-resistors" to generally effective early literacy interventions (Al Otaiba, 2001).

## PREVALENCE

Estimates of the prevalence of communication disorders in children vary widely. Reliable figures are hard to come by because investigators often employ different definitions of speech and language disorders and sample different populations. In the 2003–2004 school year, 1,118,543 children ages 6 to 21 received special education services under the IDEA category of "speech or language impairments" (U.S. Department of Education, 2004). This number represents about 1.7% of the resident population and 18.8% of all students receiving special education services, which makes speech or language impairments the second-largest category after learning disabilities.

However, the actual number of children with speech and language impairments is much higher. It is estimated that approximately 50% of children who receive special education services because of another primary disability (e.g., mental retardation, learning disabilities, hearing impairments) also have communication disorders (Hall et al., 2001).

According to a national survey by ASHA (2001e), school-based speech-language pathologists (SLPs) work with an average of 53 students each month. Approximately half of all elementary students who are served by SLPs have speech and language production problems (see Table 8.1). Fewer than 1 in 10 children with speech and language impairments have fluency disorders.

Speech and language impairments are more prevalent among males than females and are about the same in each of the major geographical regions of the United States. Approximately two-thirds of school-age children served by speech-language pathologists are boys (Hall et al., 2001). The percentage of children with speech and language disorders decreases significantly from the earlier to the later school grades.

## CAUSES

Many types of communication disorders and numerous possible causes are recognized. A speech or language impairment may be *organic*—that is, attributable to damage, dysfunction, or malformation of a specific organ or part of the body. However, most communication disorders are not considered organic but are classified as functional. A *functional communication disorder* cannot be ascribed to a specific physical condition, and its origin is

**TABLE 8.1** **Percentage of elementary children served by speech-language pathologists, by type of communication disorder**

| Disorder | Grades K-3* | Grades 4-6* |
|---|---|---|
| Speech sound production | 58.2 | 48.7 |
| Spoken language production | 47.5 | 48.2 |
| Spoken language comprehension | 38.4 | 41.9 |
| Intelligibility | 16.9 | 3.6 |
| Fluency | 3.4 | 8.8 |
| Pragmatics | 1.7 | 1.6 |
| Voice | 0.6 | 0.5 |

*Percentage totals exceed 100% because many students are treated for multiple disorders.
*Source:* American Speech-Language-Hearing Association (2001e).

not clearly known. McReynolds (1990) points out that decades of research on the causes of many speech and language impairments have produced few answers. A child's surroundings provide many opportunities to learn appropriate and inappropriate communication skills, and some specialists believe that functional communication disorders derive mainly from environmental influences.

## Causes of Speech Impairments

Examples of physical factors that frequently result in speech impairments are **cleft palate**, paralysis of the speech muscles, absence of teeth, craniofacial abnormalities, enlarged adenoids, and traumatic brain injury. **Dysarthria** refers to a group of speech disorders caused by neuromuscular impairments in respiration, phonation, resonation, and articulation. Lack of precise motor control needed to produce and sequence sounds causes distorted and repeated sounds. An organic speech impairment may be a child's primary disability, or it may be secondary to other disabilities, such as mental retardation or cerebral palsy.

## Causes of Language Disorders

Factors that can contribute to language disorders in children include cognitive limitations or mental retardation, hearing impairments, behavioral disorders, structural abnormalities of the speech mechanism, and environmental deprivation (Hall et al., 2001). Language is so important to academic performance that it can be impossible to differentiate a learning disability from a language disorder (Silliman & Diehl, 2002).

Some severe disorders in expressive and receptive language result from injury to the brain. **Aphasia** describes a loss of the ability to process and use language. Aphasia is one of the most prevalent causes of language disorders in adults, most often occurring suddenly after a cardiovascular event (stroke). Head injury is a significant cause of aphasia in children. Aphasia may be either expressive or, less commonly, receptive. Children with mild aphasia have language patterns that are close to normal but may have difficulty retrieving certain words and tend to need more time than usual to communicate. Children with severe aphasia, however, are likely to have a markedly reduced storehouse of words and language forms.

Research indicates that genetics may contribute to communication disorders. Scientists in Britain have discovered a gene area that affects speech (Porterfield, 1998), and other researchers have reported genetic links to phonological disorders (Uffen, 1997) and stuttering (Yairi, 1998).

Environmental influences also play an important part in delayed, disordered, or absent language. The communication efforts of some children are reinforced; other children, unfortunately, are punished for talking, gesturing, or otherwise attempting to communicate. A child who has little stimulation at home and few chances to speak, listen, explore, and interact with others will probably have little motivation for communication and may well experience delays in language development (Ratner, 2004).

# IDENTIFICATION AND ASSESSMENT

"Don't worry; she'll grow out of it."

"Speech therapists can't help a child who doesn't talk."

"He'll be all right once he starts school."

These are common examples of misguided, inaccurate, yet widely held attitudes toward communication disorders. Although some children who experience temporary, mild speech impairments or language delays do get better, many do not improve and deteriorate without intervention. To avoid the consequences of unrecognized or untreated speech and language impairments, it is especially important for children to receive professional assessment and evaluation services (Hall et al., 2001).

## Screening and Teacher Observations

In some school districts, speech-language pathologists screen the spoken language abilities of all kindergarten children. These screenings might involve norm-referenced tests, informal assessments developed by the SLP, and questionnaires or checklists for parents and teachers (McCauley, 2001). Classroom teachers also play an important role in identifying children who may have speech and language impairments. A checklist such as the one in Figure 8.5 can be used to identify children with whom the speech-language pathologist can conduct individualized screening for possible communication disorders. Children who fail a speech and language screening test are candidates for a systematic, in-depth evaluation.

*Screening for communication disorders*

Council for Exceptional Children — Content Standards for Beginning Teachers—Common Core: Screening, pre-referral, referral, and classification procedures (CC8K3).

## Evaluation Components

Testing procedures vary according to the suspected type of disorder. Often the specialist conducts broad screenings to detect areas of concern and then moves to more detailed testing in those areas. There is no perfect test or method of assessing children's speech

---

**FIGURE 8.5  A checklist for identifying speech and language problems in the classroom**

Directions: The following behaviors may indicate that a child in your classroom has a language impairment that is in need of language intervention. Please check the appropriate items.

_____ Child mispronounces sounds and words.

_____ Child omits words, endings, such as plural -s and past tense -ed.

_____ Child omits small, unemphasized words, such as auxiliary verbs or prepositions.

_____ Child uses an immature vocabulary, overuses empty words, such as "one" and "thing," or seems to have difficulty recalling or finding the right word.

_____ Child has difficulty comprehending new words and concerns.

_____ Child's sentence structure seems immature or over-reliant on forms, such as subject-verb-object. It's unoriginal, dull.

_____ Child has difficulty with one of the following:

    _____ Verb tensing    _____ Articles    _____ Auxiliary verbs

    _____ Pronouns    _____ Irreg. verbs    _____ Prepositions

    _____ Word order    _____ Irreg. plurals

_____ Child has difficulty relating sequential events.

_____ Child has difficulty following directions.

_____ Child's questions often poorly formed.

_____ Child has difficulty answering questions.

_____ Child's comments often off topic or inappropriate for the conversation.

_____ There are long pauses between a remark and the child's reply or between successive remarks by the child. It's as if the child is searching for a response or is confused.

_____ Child appears to be attending to communication but remembers little of what is said.

*Source:* Robert E. Owens, Jr. *Language Disorders: A Functional Approach to Assessment and Intervention,* 3/e. Published by Allyn and Bacon, Boston, MA. Copyright © 1999 by Pearson Education. Reprinted by permission of the publisher.

and language (Silliman & Diehl, 2002). Most examiners will use a variety of assessment devices and approaches in an effort to obtain as much relevant information as possible to inform diagnostic decisions and treatment plans. A comprehensive evaluation to detect the presence and extent of a communication disorder would likely include the following components:

- *Case history and physical examination.* Most professional speech and language assessments begin with the creation of a case history about the child. This typically involves completing a biographical form that includes information such as the child's birth and developmental history, health record, scores on achievement and intelligence tests, and adjustment to school. The parents may be asked when the child first crawled, walked, and uttered words. Social skills, such as playing readily with other children, may also be considered. The specialist carefully examines the child's mouth, noting any irregularities in the tongue, lips, teeth, palate, or other structures that may affect speech production. If the child has an organic speech problem, the child is referred for possible medical intervention.

- *Articulation test.* Speech errors by the child are assessed. A record is kept of the sounds that are defective, how they are being mispronounced, and the number of errors. Examples of articulation tests include the Photo Articulation Test (Lippke, Dickey, Selmar, & Soder, 1997) and the Goldman-Fristoe Test of Articulation (Goldman & Fristoe, 2000).

- *Hearing test.* Hearing is usually tested to determine whether a hearing problem is causing the suspected communication disorder. Audiometry, a formal procedure for testing hearing, is discussed in Chapter 9.

- *Auditory discrimination test.* This test is given to determine whether the child is hearing sounds correctly. If unable to recognize the specific characteristics of a given sound, the child will not have a good model to imitate. The Test of Auditory Discrimination (Goldman, Fristoe, & Woodcock, 1990) is frequently used.

- *Phonological awareness and processing.* Included in the many phonological skills of children who are competent speakers and users of language is the ability to distinguish the presence and absence of speech sounds, differences between and among sounds, and when individual sounds begin and end. They can remember language sounds and reproduce them at a later time. Children without phonological awareness and processing skills not only have problems with receptive and expressive oral language but also have great difficulties in learning to read. Phonological processing measures include the Test of Phonological Awareness (Torgeson & Bryant, 1994) and the Comprehensive Test of Phonological Processing (Wagner, Torgeson, & Rahsotte, 1999).

- *Vocabulary and overall language development test.* The amount of vocabulary a child has acquired is generally a good indicator of language competence. Frequently used tests of vocabulary include the Peabody Picture Vocabulary Test—III (Dunn &

*Assessment and diagnosis of communication disorders*

**Council for Exceptional Children** Content Standards for Beginning Teachers—Common Core: Screening, pre-referral, referral, and classification procedures (CC8K3) (also CC8K1).

A comprehensive assessment of communication disorders includes articulation, auditory discrimination, vocabulary tests, and a language sample.

Dunn, 1997) and the Comprehensive Receptive and Expressive Vocabulary Test (Wallace & Hammill, 2002). An overall language test, such as the Test of Language Development (Hammill & Newcomer, 1997) and the Clinical Evaluation of Language Fundamentals (Semel, Wiig, & Secord, 1995), assesses the child's understanding and production of language structures (e.g., important syntactical elements such as the concept that conjunctions show relations between the sentence elements they connect).

- *Language samples.* An important part of any evaluation for communication disorders is obtaining accurate samples of the child's expressive speech and language. The examiner considers factors such as intelligibility and fluency of speech, voice quality, and use of vocabulary and grammar. Some speech-language pathologists use structured tasks to evoke language samples. They may, for example, ask a child to describe a picture, tell a story, or answer a list of questions. Most specialists, however, use informal conversation to obtain language samples, believing that the child's language sample will be more representative if the examiner uses natural conversation rather than highly structured tasks (Hadley, 1998). Open-ended questions such as "Tell me about your family" are suggested rather than yes-no questions or questions that can be answered with one word, such as "What color is your car?" To ensure a complete and accurate record of the talk and reduce distractions for the child caused by note taking, examiners usually tape-record the child's language samples.

- *Observation in natural settings.* Objective observation and measurement of children's language use in social contexts is an important element of assessment for communication disorders. It is imperative that the observer samples the child's communication behavior across various settings rather than limit it to a clinic or an examining room. A parent-child observation is frequently arranged for young children. The specialist provides appropriate toys and activities and requests the parent to interact normally with the child.

After all the data from the multifactored evaluation have been gathered, the speech-language pathologist reviews the results of the case. Because there is often so much assessment information, some SLPs use computer programs to help organize and analyze the results (Hall et al., 2001). A treatment plan is then developed in cooperation with the child's parents and teachers to set up realistic communication objectives and determine the methods that will be used.

*Assessment of Communication Disorders in Language Minority Children.* IDEA requires that assessment for the purpose of identifying children with disabilities be conducted in the child's native language. Although there are a few standardized language-proficiency tests available in languages other than English (see McLaughlin & Lewis [2005] for a review), translation or adaptation of tests into other languages poses certain problems (Díaz-Rico & Weed, 2002; National Research Council, 2000). For example, DeAvila (1976) pointed out the great variety in language within Hispanic populations and notes that when Mexican American children were given a test in Spanish that was developed with a population of Puerto Rican children, they performed even more poorly than on an admittedly unfair English test. To illustrate the confusion that may result from inappropriate translations, DeAvila observed that a Spanish-speaking child may use any one of five distinct words to describe a kite, depending on the family's country of origin: *cometa, huila, volantin, papalote,* or *chiringa.* Thus, although translation of tests and other materials into a child's native language may be helpful in many instances, care must be taken to avoid an improper translation that may actually do a disservice to the culturally and linguistically different child.

See Diversity and Exceptionality, "Assessing the Communicative Competence of Culturally Diverse Students."

Various approaches are employed in the treatment of children with communication disorders. *Speech-language pathologist (SLP)* is the preferred term for the school-based professional with primary responsibility for identifying, evaluating, and providing therapeutic services to children with communication disorders (ASHA, 2001e). But terms such as *speech therapist, speech clinician*, and *speech teacher* are still used in some schools. As a key member of a child's IEP team, the SLP's goal is to correct the child's speech and/or language problems or to help the child achieve the maximum communicative potential, which may involve compensatory techniques and/or augmentative and alternative means of communication (Hall et al., 2001). Speech-language pathology addresses both organic and functional causes and encompasses practitioners with numerous points of view who use a wide range of accepted intervention techniques.

Some SLPs employ structured exercises and drills to correct speech sounds; others emphasize speech production in natural language contexts. Some prefer to work with children in individual therapy sessions; others believe that group sessions are advantageous for language modeling and peer support. Some encourage children to imitate the therapist's speech; others have the child listen to tapes of his own speech. Some specialists follow a structured, teacher-directed approach in which targeted speech and language behaviors are precisely prompted, recorded, and reinforced; others use less structured methods. Some SLPs focus on a child's expressive and receptive communication; others devote attention to other aspects of the child's behavior and environment, such as developing self-confidence and improving interactions with parents and classmates. Clearly, many possible options can be explored in devising effective, individualized treatment plans for students with communication disorders.

## Treating Speech Sound Errors

A general goal of specialists in communication disorders is to help the child speak as clearly and pleasantly as possible so that a listener's attention will focus on the child's message rather than how he says it.

*Articulation Errors.* The goals of therapy for articulation problems are acquisition of the correct speech sound(s), generalization of the sound(s) to all speaking settings and contexts (especially the classroom), and maintenance of the correct sound(s) after therapy has ended. Traditional articulation therapy involves discrimination and production activities.

*Discrimination activities* are designed to improve the child's ability to listen carefully and detect the differences between similar sounds (e.g., the /t/ in "take," the /c/ in "cake") and to differentiate between correct and distorted speech sounds. The child learns to match his speech to that of a standard model by using auditory, visual, and tactual feedback. A generally consistent relationship exists between children's ability to recognize sounds and their ability to articulate them correctly.

*Production* is the ability to produce a given speech sound alone and in various contexts. Therapy emphasizes the repetitive production of sounds in various contexts, with special attention to the motor skills involved in articulation. Exercises are employed to produce sounds with differing stress patterns. The SLP may have the child carefully watch how sounds are produced and then use a mirror to monitor his own speech production. Children are expected to accurately produce problematic sounds in syllables, words, sentences, and stories. They may tape-record their own speech and listen carefully for errors. Therapy progresses from having the child articulate simple sounds in isolation; then in syllables, words, phrases, sentences, and structured conversation; and finally in unstructured conversation. As in all communication training, it is important for the teacher, parent, and specialist to provide a good language model, reinforce the child's improving performance, and encourage the child to talk.

## DIVERSITY & EXCEPTIONALITY

# Assessing the Communicative Competence of Culturally and Linguistically Diverse Students

It is not always easy to distinguish between a student whose learning and communication problems result from a disability and a student whose primary need is systematic, culturally responsive instruction that values and builds upon the skills he already possesses in his native language to enable him to improve his English communicative and literacy skills (Jimenez, 2002; Ovando, 2004). While all educators must be careful not to confuse communication differences with delayed or disordered speech and language, proper assessment of the speech-language skills of children from diverse cultural, linguistic, and socioeconomic backgrounds can pose a difficult challenge for language-majority educators (Salend & Salinas, 2003).

It should not be surprising that students who are English-language learners and students whose first language is English but who speak a nonstandard dialect often perform poorly on formal tests of English speech and language skills. It is important that the results of formal language tests not be the sole basis for diagnosing a speech or language impairment. Results of formal speech and language tests administered by a competent SLP should be supplemented with direct obser-

vations of a student's communicative behaviors in natural settings where he can use whichever language he is most comfortable with.

Carefully selected language-proficiency tests coupled with an analysis of authentic conversational behavior provide the opportunity to better evaluate a student's true communicative competence. One method for gathering information from such natural observations is to look for the occurrence of specific communicative skills. Zamora-Durán and Reyes (1997) developed the checklist shown here to assess the communicative competence of culturally and linguistically diverse children in four skill areas: grammatical, sociolinguistic, discourse, and strategic. Students who consistently demonstrate the skills on this checklist when talking and interacting with peers and teachers in the classroom are not likely to have a serious communication disorder.

 To further your understanding of and answer questions about the issues and strategies presented here, go to the Diversity & Exceptionality module in Chapter 8 of the Companion Website, **www.prenhall.com/heward**.

*Phonological Errors.* When a child's spoken language problem includes one or more phonological errors, the goal of therapy is to help the child identify the error pattern(s) and gradually produce more linguistically appropriate sound patterns (Barlow, 2001). For example, a child who frequently omits final consonants might be taught to recognize the difference between minimally contrastive words—perhaps using a set of cards with the words "sea," "seed," "seal," "seam," and "seat" (Hall et al., 2001). Therapeutic tasks are constructed so that the child is rewarded for following directions (e.g., "Pick up the 'seal' card") and speaking clearly enough for the therapist to follow his or her directions (e.g., the child directs the SLP to give him the "seat" card). To respond correctly, the child must attend to and use the information in the final consonant sound.

Sounds are not taught in isolation. Children with phonological problems can often articulate specific sounds but are not using those sounds in proper linguistic context.

Although the distinction between articulation errors and phonological errors is important, many children with communication disorders have problems with both. The thera-

| Grammatical | Sociolinguistic | Discourse | Strategic |
|---|---|---|---|
| ☐ Uses noun/verb agreement | ☐ Demonstrates various styles of social register in speech, for example, when interacting with peers or adults | ☐ Retells an event with attention to sequence | ☐ Joins groups and acts as if understands activities |
| ☐ Uses pronouns correctly | | ☐ Explains activity in present or near future | ☐ Demonstrates expressive ability |
| ☐ Uses proper syntax | | ☐ Shares experiences spontaneously | ☐ Counts on friends for help |
| ☐ Uses verb tenses appropriately | ☐ Uses diminutives | ☐ Tells stories with personal emphases | ☐ Switches language to resolve ambiguities |
| ☐ Uses dialectical variations | ☐ Uses terms of endearment | ☐ Switches languages for elaboration | ☐ Observed and imitates language patterns |
| ☐ Uses complex sentence structure | ☐ Uses courtesy, etiquette terms, and titles of respect | ☐ Switches language to clarify statements | ☐ Asks for information |
| | ☐ Uses appropriate variations in intonation | ☐ Switches language to experiment with new language | ☐ Reads to gain information |
| | | | ☐ Uses a dictionary |
| | | | ☐ Asks for repetition |
| | | | ☐ Takes risks and guesses at language meaning |
| | | | ☐ Attempts difficult words and constructions |

*Source:* From "From Tests to Talking in the Classroom: Assessing Communicative Competence" by G. Zamora-Durán & E. Reyes. In A. Artiles & G. Zamora-Durán (Eds.), *Reducing Disproportionate Representation of Culturally Diverse Students in Special and Gifted Education* (1997, p. 51). Reston, VA: Council for Exceptional Children. © 1997 by the Council for Exceptional Children. Reprinted with permission.

peutic approaches for articulation and phonological disorders are not incompatible and can be used in conjunction for some children.

## Treating Fluency Disorders

Throughout history, people who stutter have been subjected to countless treatments—some of them unusual, to say the least. Past treatments included holding pebbles in the mouth, sticking fingers into a light socket, talking out of one side of the mouth, eating raw oysters, speaking with the teeth clenched, taking alternating hot and cold baths, and speaking on inhaled rather than exhaled air (Ham, 1986; Hulit & Howard, 2002). For many years, it was widely thought that a tongue that was unable to function properly in the mouth caused stuttering. As a result, it was common for early physicians to prescribe ointments to blister or numb the tongue or even to remove portions of the tongue through surgery!

Application of behavioral principles has strongly influenced recent practices in the treatment of fluency disorders (Inghram, 2003). A therapist using this methodology regards stuttering as learned behavior and seeks to eliminate it by establishing and encouraging fluent speech. For example, one stuttering treatment program called the Lidcombe Program trains parents to positively reinforce their child's fluent utterances in the home. Onslow, Packman, and Harrison (2003) report that studies evaluating the effectiveness of the Lidcombe Program with over 750 children worldwide have reported a 95% success rate.

Children may learn to manage their stuttering by deliberately prolonging certain sounds or by speaking slowly to get through a "block." They may increase their confidence and fluency by speaking in groups, where pressure is minimized and successful speech is positively reinforced. They may learn to monitor their own speech and to reward themselves for periods of fluency (Ryan, 2004). They may learn to speak to a rhythmic beat or with the aid of devices that mask or delay their ability to hear their own speech. Tape recorders are often used for drills, simulating conversations, and documenting progress.

Children often learn to control their stuttering and produce increasingly fluent speech as they mature. No single method of treatment has been recognized as most effective. Stuttering frequently decreases when children enter adolescence, regardless of which treatment method was used. Often, the problem disappears with no treatment at all. Results from studies of the phenomenon of spontaneous recovery from stuttering have reported that 65% to 80% of children diagnosed as stutterers apparently outgrow or get over their dysfluencies without formal intervention (Yairi & Ambrose, 1999). Nevertheless, a speech-language pathologist should be contacted when a child exhibits signs of stuttering or when the parents are concerned about speech fluency. Although some children who stutter get better without help, many do not. Early intervention may prevent the child from developing a severe stutter. In its initial stages, stuttering can almost always be treated successfully by teachers, parents, and a speech-language pathologist working together. When interacting with a child who stutters, a teacher should pay primary attention to what the child is saying rather than to his difficulties in saying it. When the child experiences a verbal block, the teacher should be patient and calm, say nothing, and maintain eye contact with the child until he finishes speaking. Figure 8.6 offers additional suggestions for how classroom teachers can help children with speech dysfluencies.

Teachers can help a child who stutters by providing a good speech model, improving the child's self-esteem, and creating a good speech environment.

*Interacting with a child who stutters*

Council for Exceptional Children — Content Standards for Beginning Teachers—Common Core: Teacher attitudes and behaviors that influence behavior of individuals with exceptional learning needs (CC5K4).

## Treating Voice Disorders

A thorough medical examination should always be sought for a child with a voice disorder. Surgery or other medical interventions can often treat organic causes. In addition, SLPs sometimes recommend environmental modifications; a person who is consistently required to speak in a noisy setting, for example, may benefit from the use of a small microphone to reduce vocal straining and shouting (Sapienza & Hicks, 2002). Most remedial techniques, however, offer direct vocal rehabilitation, which helps the child with a voice disorder gradually learn to produce more acceptable and efficient speech. Voice therapy often begins with teaching the child to listen to his own voice and learn to identify those aspects that need to be changed. Depending on the type of voice disorder and the child's overall circumstances, vocal rehabilitation may include activities such as exercises to increase breathing capacity, relaxation techniques to reduce tension, or procedures to increase or decrease the loudness of speech (Harris & Harris, 1997; Johnston & Umberger, 1996).

Because many voice problems are directly attributable to vocal abuse, behavioral principles can be used to help children and adults break habitual patterns of vocal misuse. For example, a child might self-monitor the number of abuses he commits in the classroom or at home, receiving reinforcement for gradually lowering the number of abuses over time. Computer technology has also been successfully applied in the treatment of voice disorders. Some instruments enable speakers to see visual representations of their voice patterns on a screen or a printout; speakers are thus able to monitor their own vocalizations visually as well as auditorily and to develop new patterns of using their voices more naturally and efficiently (Bull & Rushakoff, 1987).

## Treating Language Disorders

Treatments for language disorders are also extremely varied. Some programs focus on pre-communication activities that encourage the child to explore and that make the environment conducive to the development of receptive and expressive language. Clearly, children must have something they want to communicate. And because children learn through im-

**FIGURE 8.6** Helping the child who stutters in the classroom

There is no single treatment for stuttering because the causation, type, and severity of nonfluencies vary from child to child. Despite this variability, teachers can significantly help a child who stutters by providing a good speech model, improving the child's self-esteem, and creating a good speech environment.

*Provide a Good Speech Model*
- *Reduce your rate of speech.* Young children often imitate the speech rate of their parents and other significant adults. This rate may be inappropriately fast for the child's motoric and linguistic competencies. Slower speech provides the child with time needed to organize thoughts, choose vocabulary and grammatical form, and plan the speech act motorically.

- *Create silences in your interactions.* Pauses placed at appropriate places in conversation help create a relaxed communication environment, slower rate of speech, and a more natural speech cadence. Pause for 2 to 3 seconds before responding to a child's questions and statements.

- *Model simple vocabulary and grammatical forms.* Stuttering is more likely to occur in longer words, words that are used less frequently, and more grammatically complex sentences.

- *Model normal nonfluencies.* You may need to make a conscious effort to use normal nonfluencies, such as interjections ("um" or "ah") or an occasional whole-word repetition, phrase repetition, or pause. Knowing that even fluent speech contains nonfluencies will help children accept nonfluencies and reduce the fear of speaking.

*Improve the Child's Self-Esteem*
- *Disregard moments of nonfluency.* Reinforce occurrences of fluency and ignore nonfluencies. Do not give instructions such as "Slow down," "Take a deep breath," or "Stop and start over," which imply that the child is not doing enough. This might increase guilt and diminish self-confidence.

- *Show acceptance of what the child expresses rather than how it is said.* Ask the child to repeat only the parts of the utterance that were not understood rather than those that were nonfluent. This request indicates that you did listen and that the message is important.

- *Treat the child who stutters like any other child in the class.* Do not reduce your expectations because of the nonfluencies.

- *Acknowledge nonfluencies without labeling them.* Do not refer to the problem of stuttering. Instead, use words that the child uses to describe her speech, such as "bumpy" or "hard." Assure the child that it is okay to have dysfluencies; everyone does.

- *Have the child feel in control of speech.* Follow the child's lead in conversation. Speech will more likely be fluent if the child can talk about areas of interest.

- *Accept nonfluencies.* Try not to be overly concerned about normal nonfluencies because you see the child as a stutterer. Maintain eye contact and remain patient.

*Create a Good Speech Environment*
- *Establish good conversational rules.* Interruptions may distract the child and increase nonfluencies. Ensure that no one interrupts and that everyone gets a chance to talk.

- *Listen attentively.* Active listening lets the child know that content is important. Use naturalistic comments (e.g., "Yes, Johnny, that is a large blue truck.") in place of absent-minded "uh-huhs" and generic statements (e.g., "Good talking!").

- *Suggest that the child cease other activities while speaking.* It is sometimes difficult to perform two different motoric acts, such as coloring and talking, simultaneously. Asking the child to stop other activities while speaking may improve fluency.

- *Prepare the child for upcoming events.* The emotionality of birthdays, holidays, field trips, and changes in the daily schedule may cause apprehension and increase stuttering. Discussing upcoming events can reduce fear associated with the unknown and should enhance the child's fluency.

*Source:* From LaBlance, G. R., Steckol, K. F., & Smith, V. L. (1994). Stuttering: The role of the classroom teacher. *Teaching Exceptional Children, 26*(2), 10–12. Adapted by permission.

itation, it is important for the teacher or specialist to talk clearly, use correct inflections, and provide a rich variety of words and sentences.

The changing and expanding role of school-based SLPs today includes connecting children's oral language to literacy components of the curriculum as much as possible (ASHA,

*Naturalistic interventions/milieu teaching strategies*

Council for Exceptional Children    Content Standards for Beginning Teachers—Common Core: Design learning environments that encourage active participation in individual and group activities (CC5S4) (also CC4S3).

2001d; Merritt & Culatta, 1998). This is done in a variety of ways. For example, children with very limited oral language might be taught how to orally "read" pictures as a language enhancement activity (Alberto & Fredrick, 2000). Children with language impairments might develop written language skills by exchanging e-mail letters to pen pals (Harmston, Strong, & Evans, 2001).

Speech-language pathologists are increasingly employing naturalistic interventions to help children develop and use language skills. Naturalistic approaches were developed as an alternative to didactic language interventions because children often experienced difficulties in generalizing new skills from structured teaching settings to everyday contexts. In contrast to didactic teaching approaches, which use contrived materials and activities (e.g., pictures, puppets) and massed trials to teach specific skills, naturalistic interventions are characterized by dispersed learning trials carried out in the natural environment as opportunities occur for teaching functional communication. Naturalistic approaches occur in the context of normal conversational interchanges that follow the child's "attentional lead" (Goldstein, Kaczmarek, & Hepting, 1994).

Kaiser and Grim (2006) make the following recommendations about naturalistic interventions, which are also known as *milieu teaching strategies*:

- Teach when the child is interested.
- Teach what is functional for the student at the moment.
- Stop while both the student and the teacher are still enjoying the interaction.

Naturalistic interventions involve structuring the environment to create numerous opportunities for desired child responses (e.g., holding up a toy and asking, "What do you want?") and structuring adult responses to a child's communication (e.g., the child points outside and says, "Go wifth me," and the teacher says, "Okay, I'll go with you."). Effective milieu teaching more closely resembles a conversation than a structured instructional episode (Kaiser & Grim, 2006). However, good naturalistic teaching does not mean the teacher should wait patiently to see whether and when opportunities for meaningful and interesting language use by children occur. Environments in which language teaching takes place should be designed to catch students' interest and increase the likelihood of communicative interactions that can be used for teaching purposes. Six strategies for arranging environments that create naturally occurring language teaching opportunities are described in Figure 8.7.

No matter what the approach to treatment, children with language disorders need to be around children and adults with something interesting to talk about. As Reed (2005) points out, it was assumed for many years that a one-to-one setting was the most effective format for language intervention. Emphasis was on eliminating distracting stimuli and focusing a child's attention on the desired communication task. Today, however, it is generally recognized that language is an interactive, interpersonal process and that naturally occurring intervention formats should be used to expose children with language disorders to a wide range of stimuli, experiences, contexts, and people that cannot be replicated in one-to-one therapy.

Whatever intervention methods they use, effective speech-language pathologists establish specific goals and objectives, keep precise records of their students' performance, and arrange the learning environment so that each child's efforts at communication will be rewarded and enjoyable.

## Augmentative and Alternative Communication

**Augmentative and alternative communication (AAC)** refers to a diverse set of strategies and methods to assist individuals who are unable to meet their communication needs through speech or writing. AAC has three components (Kangas & Lloyd, 2002):

1. A representational symbol set or vocabulary
2. A means for selecting the symbols
3. A means for transmitting the symbols

**FIGURE 8.7** Six strategies for increasing naturalistic opportunities for language teaching

1. **Interesting materials.** Students are likely to communicate when things or activities in the environment interest them. *Example:* James lay quietly on the rug, with his head resting on his arms. Ms. Davis sat at one end of the rug and rolled a big yellow ball right past James. James lifted his head and looked around for the ball.

2. **Out of reach.** Students are likely to communicate when they want something that they cannot reach. *Example:* Mr. Norris lifted a drum off the shelf and placed it on the floor between Judy and Annette, who were both in wheelchairs. Mr. Norris hit the drum three times and then waited, looking at his two students. Judy watched and clapped her hands together. Then, she reached for the drum with both arms outstretched.

3. **Inadequate portions.** Students are likely to communicate when they do not have the necessary materials to carry out an instruction. *Example:* Mr. Robinson gave every student except Mary a ticket to get into the auditorium for the high school play. He told his students to give their tickets to the attendant. Mr. Robinson walked beside Mary toward the entrance. When Mary reached the attendant, Mr. Robinson paused and looked at Mary. She pointed to the tickets in his hand and signed "give me." Mr. Robinson gave her a ticket and she handed it to the attendant who said "Thank you. Enjoy the play."

4. **Choice-making.** Students are likely to communicate when they are given a choice. *Example:* Peggy's favorite pastime is listening to tapes on her tape recorder. On Saturday morning, Peggy's father said to her, "We could listen to your tapes" (pointing to the picture of the tape recorder on Peggy's communication board) "or we could go for a ride in the car" (pointing to the picture of the car). "What would you like to do?" Peggy pointed to the picture of the tape recorder. "OK, let's listen to this new tape you like," her father said as he put the tape in and turned on the machine.

5. **Assistance.** Students are likely to communicate when they need assistance in operating or manipulating materials. *Example:* Tammy's mother always places three clear plastic containers with snacks (cookies, crackers, popcorn) on the kitchen table before Tammy returns from school. When Tammy arrives home and is ready for a snack, she goes to the table and chooses what she wants. The containers are hard to open, so Tammy usually brings the container with her chosen snack to her mother. Her mother responds to this nonverbal request by modeling a request form that specifies Tammy's choice (e.g., "Open popcorn.")

6. **Unexpected situations.** Students are likely to communicate when something happens that they do not expect. *Example:* Ms. Esser was helping Kathy put on her socks and shoes after rest time. After assisting with the socks, Ms. Esser put one of the shoes on her own foot. Kathy stared at the shoe for a moment and then looked up at her teacher, who was smiling. "No," laughed Kathy, "my shoe."

*Source:* From Kaiser, A. P., & Grim, J. C. (2006). Teaching functional communication skills. In M. E. Snell & F. Brown (Eds.), *Instruction of students with severe disabilities* (6th ed.). Upper Saddle River, NJ: Merrill/Prentice Hall. Reprinted by permission.

Each of the three components of AAC may be unaided or aided. *Unaided techniques* do not require a physical aid or device. They include oral speech, gestures, facial expressions, general body posture, and manual signs. Of course, individuals without disabilities use a wide range of unaided augmentative communication techniques. *Aided techniques* of communication involve an external device or piece of equipment. AAC devices can be simple, low-tech affairs or sophisticated electronic equipment (Lahm & Everington, 2002).

*Augmentative and alternative communication*

 Council for Exceptional Children — Content Standards for Beginning Teachers—Common Core: Augmentative and assistive communication strategies (CC6K4).

Individuals who do not speak so that others can understand must have access to vocabulary that matches as nearly as possible the language they would use in various situations if they could speak. Beukelman and Miranda (1998) suggest that decisions about what items to include in a student's augmentative vocabulary should take into account the following:

- Vocabulary that peers in similar situations and settings use
- What communication partners (e.g., teachers, parents) think will be needed
- Vocabulary the student is already using in all modalities
- Contextual demands of specific situations

*Symbol Sets and Symbol Systems.* After selecting the vocabulary for an AAC system, a collection of symbols must be chosen or developed to represent the vocabulary. There are numerous commercially available *symbol sets,* a collection of pictures or drawings in which each symbol has one or more specified meanings, from which a person's AAC vocabulary might be constructed. Symbol sets—such as the Oakland Picture Dictionary (Kirsten, 1981), Picture Communication Symbols (Mayer-Johnson, 1986), and the Pictogram Ideogram Communication symbols (Johnson, 1985)—are graphic, which means that the symbols look like the object or concept they represent as much as possible. Mayer-Johnson has an electronic version of its symbols that can be incorporated into picture overlays. Symbol sets may also be homemade, consisting of photos, pictures, and perhaps words and the alphabet.

In contrast to symbol sets, *symbol systems* are structured around an internal set of rules that govern how new symbols are added to the system. One of the best-known symbol systems is Blissymbolics, which represents concepts through a combination of geometric shapes. The user of Blissymbolics combines multiple symbols to create new meanings (e.g., "school" is communicated by selecting the symbols "house-gives-knowledge"). Because many of the Blissymbolics are abstract, however, and do not look like the concept they represent, some individuals have difficulty learning the system. Figure 8.8 shows how common concrete and abstract vocabulary are represented by Bliss symbols and six other symbol sets.

*Selecting the Symbols.* Symbols are selected in augmentative communication by direct selection, scanning, or encoding responses (Kangas & Lloyd, 2002). *Direct selection* involves pointing to the symbol one wishes to express with a finger or fist or sometimes with a wand attached to the head or chin. With a limited number of selections widely spaced from one another, the user can select symbols by "eye pointing." *Scanning* techniques present choices to the user one at a time, and the user makes a response at the proper time to indicate which item or group of selections she wants to communicate. Scanning can be machine- or listener-assisted (e.g., the listener may point to symbols one at a time while watching for the user's eye blink, which signals selection). *Encoding* involves giving multiple signals to indicate the location of the symbol or the item to be selected. Usually, the user makes a pair of responses that directs the listener to a specific printed message on a reference list. In a display in which symbols are organized by color and number, for example, a student can first touch one card (to select the red group of messages) and then make a second pointing response to indicate which number message in the red group is intended. (Figure 8.9 gives suggestions on how to communicate with a person who uses AAC.)

*Transmitting the Symbols.* Once vocabulary and a symbol set have been selected, a method of transmitting the symbols must be determined. The most common tool for augmentative communication display and transmission is the *communication board,* a flat area (often a tray or a table attached to a wheelchair) on which the symbols are

This communication device enables the user to select and transmit synthesized speech via a wand attached to the head.

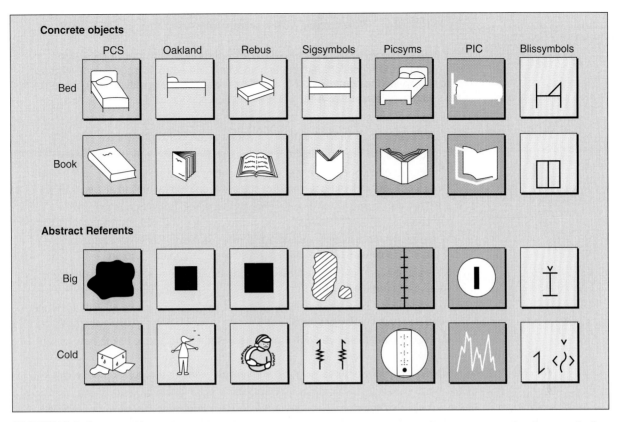

**FIGURE 8.8** **Examples from widely used graphic symbol sets (PCS = Picture Communication Symbols; PIC = Pictogram Ideogram Communication)**

*Source:* From Vanderheiden, G. C., & Lloyd, L. L. (1986). Non-speech modes and systems. In S. W. Blackstone (Ed.), *Augmentative communication* (ff. 49–161). Rockville, MD: American Speech-Language-Hearing Association. Reprinted by permission.

arranged for the user to select. A student may have a basic communication board of common words, phrases, numbers, and so forth for use across many situations. He may also have various situational boards, or miniboards, with specific vocabulary for certain situations (e.g., at a restaurant, in science class). Symbols can also be transported and displayed in a wallet or a photo album.

A variety of electronic devices offers a wide range of alternatives for transmitting communication symbols. Dedicated communication aids—such as the Prentke Romich Intro Talker, the Prentke Romich Liberator, DECtalk by Digital Equipment Company, and Sentinent System's Dynavok—offer computerized speech selection and transmission. To learn how the Dynavok and other assistive technology were used to help an 11-year-old boy who was unable to speak and participate in the regular classroom, see Erickson and Koppenhaver (1998). (Physicist Stephen W. Hawking describes his AAC device in Profiles & Perspectives, "My Communication System," later in this chapter.)

> A student might need more than one ACC device. Anna, a second grader with severe disabilities, uses her BIGmack, with its voice output to respond "I'm here" when her teacher takes the attendance every morning. She also uses another voice-output communication aid with 8 messages (Message Mate) to request specific things she wants or needs throughout the day (e.g., water, a break, time on the computer). Although she makes good use of facial expressions and vocalizations, Anna also relies on an adapted photo album that contains pictures from magazines, postcards, and photographs with different comments written underneath them to serve as a conversation book during social times with her classmates. (Downing, 2000, p. 35)

**FIGURE 8.9   How to talk with a person who uses AAC**

Communicating with someone who does not speak can be a challenging, even unnerving, experience for many natural speakers. Here are 10 suggestions for those who use speech to communicate that will help improve the quality of their conversations with people who use AAC:

- Introduce yourself.
- Ask the person to show you how the communication system works.
- Pause to let the person construct a message. Be patient; it might take a while.
- Relax and give yourself a chance to get used to a slower rhythm of communication. Don't feel like you have to fill all the silent spaces by talking all the time.
- Be sure to give your new friend a chance to ask you questions or to make comments.
- Even though you might guess what's coming next from context, don't finish the person's sentences unless given permission or prompted to do so.
- Interact at eye-to-eye level if you can. If the person's in a wheelchair, you might grab a chair and sit across from her.
- Pay attention to facial expressions and gestures, just as you would with someone who communicates by speech.
- Don't be afraid to say you don't understand something and to ask to have it repeated.
- Talk directly to the person; don't communicate with her through someone else.

*Source:* Adapted from Blackstone, S. W. (1991). Beyond public awareness: The road to involvement! *Augmentative Communication News, 4*(2), 6. Used by permission of Augmentative Communication, Inc., Monterey, CA.

# EDUCATIONAL PLACEMENT ALTERNATIVES

*Placement alternatives*

Council for
Exceptional
Children       Content
Standards for
Beginning Teachers—Common
Core: Issues, assurances, and
due process right related to
assessment, eligibility, and
placement with a continuum of
services (CC1K6).

During the 2003–2004 school year, approximately 88.2% of children with speech or language impairments were served in the regular classroom—6.8% in resource rooms and 4.6% in separate classes (U.S. Department of Education, 2004). A wide variety of service delivery models for students with communication disorders are used within these three educational placement options. ASHA recognizes the following seven service delivery models (ASHA Ad Hoc Committee on the Roles and Responsibilities of the School-Based Speech-Language Pathologist, 1999).

## Monitoring

The SLP monitors or checks on the student's speech and language performance in the regular classroom. This option is often used just before a student is dismissed from therapy.

## Pull-out

The traditional and still most prevalent model of service delivery is the pull-out approach, sometimes called *intermittent direct service*. The child may be seen individually or in small groups of up to three children. Depending upon the needs of the individual child, pull-out may involve sessions of up to 1 hour 5 days per week.

According to ASHA (2001e), most of the students receiving services from school-based speech-language pathologists during the 1999–2000 school year met with the SLP at least two times a week, most often for 21–30 minute sessions. The classroom teacher and the SLP collaborate so that curriculum materials used in the classroom can be incorporated into the child's speech and language therapy sessions.

# My Communication System

*by Stephen W. Hawking*

*Stephen W. Hawking is Lucasian Professor of Mathematics and Theoretical Physics at the University of Cambridge. He has amyotrophic lateral sclerosis (ALS). Sometimes called Lou Gehrig's disease, ALS is a motor neuron disease of middle or late life that involves progressive degeneration of nerve cells that control voluntary motor functions. Initial symptoms usually entail difficulty in walking, clumsiness of the hands, slurred speech, and an inability to swallow normally. The muscles of the arms and legs waste away; eventually, walking is impossible and control of the hands is lost, although sensation remains normal. There is no known cause or cure for ALS. Professor Hawking responded to our request to describe the augmentative communication system he uses by writing the following story.*

In my third year at Oxford, I noticed that I seemed to be getting clumsier, and I fell over once or twice for no apparent reason. Shortly after my 21st birthday, I went into the hospital for tests. I was in for two weeks, during which time I had a wide variety of tests. After all that, they didn't tell me what I had, except that it was not multiple sclerosis and that I was an atypical case. I didn't feel like asking for more details because they were obviously bad.

The realization that I had an incurable disease that was likely to kill me in a few years was a bit of a shock. But I didn't die. In fact, although there was a cloud hanging over my future, I found, to my surprise, that I was enjoying life in the present more than before. I began to make progress with my research.

Up to 1974, I was able to feed myself and get in and out of bed. However, things were getting more difficult, so in 1980 we changed to a system of community and private nurses, who came in for an hour or two in the morning and evening. This lasted until I caught pneumonia in 1985 and had to have a tracheotomy operation. After this, I had to have 24-hour nursing care.

Before the operation, my speech had been getting more slurred, so only a few people who knew me well could understand me. But at least I could communicate. I wrote scientific papers by dictating to a secretary, and I gave seminars through an interpreter, who repeated my words more clearly. However, the tracheotomy removed my ability to speak altogether. For a time, the only way I could communicate was to spell out words letter by letter, by raising my eyebrows when someone pointed to the right letter on a spelling card. It is pretty difficult to carry on a conversation like that, let alone write a scientific paper.

Today, I communicate with a computer system. A computer expert in California, Walter Woltosz, sent me a program he had written called Equalizer. This program allowed me to select words from a series of menus on the screen by pressing a switch in my hand. A switch operated by head or eye movement could also control the program. When I have built up what I want to say, I can send it to a speech synthesizer. At first, I just ran the Equalizer program through a desktop computer. However, David Mason, of Cambridge Adaptive Communications, who is also the husband of one of my nurses, put together the system I now use. I have a Datavue 25 computer mounted to the back of my wheelchair that runs from a battery under the chair's seat. The

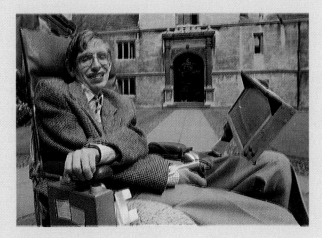

Physicist Stephen W. Hawking

screen is mounted where I can see it, though you have to view it from the right angle. I run a program called Living Center, written by a company called Words Plus of Sunnyvale, California. A cursor moves across the upper part of the screen. I can stop it by pressing a switch in my hand. In this way, I can select words that are printed on the lower part of the screen. This system allows me to communicate much better than I could before; I can manage up to 15 words a minute. I can either speak what I have written or save it on a disk. I can then print it out or call it back and speak it sentence by sentence, like I'm doing now. Using this system, I have written a book and a dozen scientific papers. I have also given a number of scientific and popular talks. They have been well received. I think that is in large part due to the quality of my speech synthesizer, made by Speech Plus, also of Sunnyvale, California.

One's voice is very important. If you have a slurred voice, people are likely to treat you as mentally deficient: "Does he take sugar?" This synthesizer is by far the best I have heard because it varies the intonation and doesn't speak like a Dalek. The only trouble is that it gives me an American accent; however, the company is working on a British version.

I have had motor neuron disease for practically all my adult life, and I am often asked, "How do you feel about having ALS?" The answer is, "Not a lot." I try to lead as normal a life as possible and not think about my condition or regret the things it prevents me from doing, which are not that many. It has not prevented me from having a very attractive family and being successful in my work. This is thanks to the help I have received from my wife, my children, and a large number of other people and organizations. I have been lucky, in that my condition has progressed more slowly than is often the case. But it shows that one need not lose hope.

 To further your understanding of and answer questions about the issues raised by Professor Hawking, go to the Profiles & Perspectives Module in Chapter 8 of the Companion Website, **www.prenhall.com/heward**.

Many speech-language professionals believe it is impossible to adequately serve a child with speech or language impairments with an isolated, pull-out approach (two or three 30-minute sessions each week with a specialist) (Harn, Bradshaw, & Ogletree, 1999). Because communication is seen as occurring most appropriately in the natural environment, remedial procedures are increasingly carried out in the regular classroom during ongoing routines rather than in a special speech room.

## Collaborative Consultation

There is an increasing tendency for communication disorders specialists to serve as consultants for regular and special education teachers (and parents) rather than spend most of their time providing direct services to individual children (Dohan & Schulz, 1998). Speech-language pathologists who work in school settings more often function as team members concerned with children's overall education and development. The speech-language pathologist often provides training and consultation for the regular classroom teacher, who may do much of the direct work with a child with communication disorders. The specialist concentrates on assessing communication disorders, evaluating progress, and providing materials and techniques. Teachers and parents are encouraged to follow the specialist's guidelines.

## Classroom-Based

Increasingly, SLPs are working as educational partners in the classroom, mediating between students' communication needs and the communication demands of the curriculum. Other terms used for speech and language services provided directly in the regular classroom include curriculum-based, transdisciplinary, interdisciplinary, and inclusive programming. Language and speech goals can be integrated into daily curriculum activities when SLPs become classroom collaborators. The advantage is that services are brought to the child and the teacher, and communication connections with the curriculum are made more directly. Hall et al. (2001) and Lue (2001) offer numerous suggestions for how teachers can help children with communication disorders in the classroom. (On the next page, the Teaching & Learning essay, "Active Learning Dialogues for Students with Language Learning Disabilities," describes how SLPs can use instructional discourse in the classroom to increase children's language competence.)

# Active Learning Dialogues for Students with Language Learning Disabilities

### by Elaine R. Silliman and Jill L. Beasman,
### University of South Florida

Dramatic changes continue in how speech-language pathologists work in schools. Traditionally, the SLP was seen as an outside expert who intervened with children who had language and communication disabilities. Children's needs were typically addressed by pulling them out of the classroom; they were brought to the services. Although pull-out services still continue as the primary model of service delivery, studies show that this model is not an effective or efficient way to facilitate real language learning in relation to the curriculum (ASHA, 1996). Because SLPs have knowledge about the oral language basis of reading, writing, and spelling, they are assuming new roles and responsibilities in the classroom (ASHA, 2001d; Silliman, Ford, Beasman, & Evans, 1999). Thus, more SLPs are working as educational partners in the classroom because language and speech goals can be more fully integrated into daily curriculum activities when SLPs become classroom collaborators (Ehren, 2000; Hadley, Simmerman, Long, & Luna, 2000). The advantage is that services are brought to children and teachers, and communication connections with the curriculum are made more directly.

The major purpose of verbal communication is to create understanding between people. This understanding is made possible through dialogue, the active exchange of messages between speakers and listeners or writers and readers. All classroom teaching and learning consists of dialogue between teachers (or SLPs) and students (Stone, 2002). But not all dialogue is good teaching and learning.

## PASSIVE LEARNING DIALOGUES

The dialogue in Figure A is an excerpt from a lesson on community workers taught by an SLP. The SLP was the classroom teacher for this kindergarten–grade 1 special education group of eight children with language learning disabilities (LLD). This lesson characterizes traditional

| | |
|---|---|
| *SLP:* | Boys and girls, remember this morning when we went to go visit this worker? (Points to picture on board of cafeteria worker.) |
| *Lily:* | The chef. |
| *SLP:* | The chef—the chef, and who can tell me what the chef's job is to do? |
| *Group:* | To cook food. |
| *SLP:* | To make food. What else? Remember when we went to the cafeteria and we saw the chefs in our cafeteria? They did a couple of jobs. |
| *Mary:* | Made food. |
| *SLP:* | They made food, and after they've made the food and you eat your food and you put your trays up, what else do they do? |

**FIGURE A** Sample of instructional dialogue from "The Chef Lesson"

language learning activities: the dialogue creates the illusion that real learning is taking place (Silliman, Bahr, Beasman, & Wilkinson, 2000; Stone, 2002).

- *Learning through language is presented in fragmented, discrete skills.* Students are involved in "language experience time," which treats language and communication as a subject area rather than a learning tool that can be applied across the curriculum.

- *Learning is a one-way activity in which the SLP is a knowledge transmitter.* Students are expected to pay attention and respond to the adult's frame of reference. The purpose of adult communication is to assess continually what students know by asking known-answer questions such as "Who can tell me what the chef's job is?" and "What else does a chef

331

do?" Students' contributions are limited to short responses such as "To cook food," and "Make food."

- *The SLP assumes a power role.* The SLP controls who can talk, when talking can take place, and what will be talked about. Language learning tends to be reduced to students' recalling what they know; it does not relate to any real communication purposes.

Passive learning dialogues teach students that learning means giving the right answer, creating the illusion that meaningful learning occurs. For example, the major reason for students to participate in the dialogue is to provide accurate answers to the knowledge-testing questions. In contrast, active learning dialogues teach students that learning through language and communication is a process of discovering possible answers to questions.

## ACTIVE LEARNING DIALOGUES

Active learning dialogues are guided by theme-based learning in which the communication goals for a student with an LLD are integrated across the curriculum and into all classroom activities. Active learning dialogues are linked to students' real-world experience through problem solving. Outcomes are functional. Children learn that listening, speaking, reading, and writing always have real purposes, such as understanding what others have to say and communicating to others what they want to say. "Lesson talk should sound like conversation,… not recitation" (Englert, Tarrant, Mariage, & Oxer, 1994, p. 167).

In the active learning dialogue in Figure B, students have just read a science book on spiders. They are developing a semantic web to organize their reading comprehension. Tom, who has a severe LLD, is attempting to write about what he has learned and becomes orally engaged in persuading Jerry, another student with an LLD, about the importance of having specific knowledge about spiders. The SLP facilitates. This dialogue demonstrates some of the shared interactional features that build active learning contexts (Brookes & Brookes, 1993; Silliman, Mills, & Murphy, 1997).

## HOW TO GET STARTED

- *Integrate primary sources of information and good literature into curriculum/intervention activities.* Students draw on a variety of information sources from the Internet to scientific literature.

- *View students as critical thinkers.* The SLP mediates the many ways that students can think, analyze, and communicate about what they are learning (e.g., through discussion, cooperative writing, drawing). Responsibility for learning is shared between the SLP and the students. This division of power communicates to students that, first, they must take responsibility for

| | |
|---|---|
| SLP: | Okay, Tom, since Amanda thought of that sentence, do you want to make one of your own? |
| Tom: | Spiders. Ooooh, you know on swing sets where—where all that stuff is hanging in the little tubes? Inside those. You know what I'm talking about (to SLP). |
| SLP: | So how are you going to write that, Tom? |
| Tom: | Spiders live in |
| Jerry: | in little houses. (overlaps Tom's speaking turn in trying to help him) |
| Tom: | No, Jerry, no. Spiders live in tubes. |
| Amanda: | Tubes, huh? |
| SLP: | What might these tubes be? |
| Jerry: | How can spiders live in dinky little tubes? They're too large. |
| Tom: | No, those like play set thingies. |
| Jerry: | Yeah, but they're too stinky. Dinky. |
| Tom: | You know on the swing set, the little tunnels. There in the swing set? |
| Jerry: | How can they get in there? How can they get in there when they're already too high? |
| Tom: | They climb in them. They have claws. |
| Jerry: | Then how are they going to get back out? |
| Amanda: | They don't, Jerry. They live there forever. |
| Tom: | Jerry, you are the weirdest. Man. |
| Beatrice: | Forever, forever, and forever. |
| Tom: | They don't come out. They wait for the food to come in, OK? |

**FIGURE B** Sample of instructional conversations from "The Spider Dialogue" (Participants are the SLP; Tom, age 9 years, 5 months; and Jerry, age 9 years, 6 months (both of whom have an LLD); and Beatrice, age 8 years, 1 month; and Amanda, age 8 years, 3 months (both of whom are typical language learners.)

what is learned and how, and, second, they are viewed as competent to do so.

- *Use dialogue that promotes instructional conversations.* Students' reasons for decisions are sought, relative to their individual comprehension levels, to advance cognitive, linguistic, and communicative abilities. Jerry challenged Tom to explain how spiders can "live in dinky little tubes" and "how they [the spiders] can get in there."

- *Support student collaboration.* Students often work in cooperative groups to (1) develop ownership of their own learning, (2) explore ideas through talking together, (3) discover similarities that relate concepts, and (4) make new applications (Palincsar, Collins, Marano, & Magnusson, 2000). Tom demonstrated these four outcomes of cooperative learning. He clearly views himself as knowledgeable about the attributes of spiders and their habitats. He attempted to explain his reasoning to Jerry, a process that Amanda and Beatrice reaffirmed throughout the interactions

with their questions and comments. He drew on his real-world knowledge to offer an analogy for Jerry (although the analogy lacks some linguistic clearness—"those play set thingies"). Finally, he applied what he had learned from reading (and, to a lesser extent, writing) to inform others.

 To further your understanding of and answer questions about active learning dialogues, go to the Teaching & Learning module in Chapter 8 of the Companion Website, **www.prenhall.com/heward**.

## Self-Contained Classroom

Students with the most severe communication disorders are served in self-contained special classrooms for children with speech or language impairments. During the 2003–2004 school year, approximately 1 in 20 children with speech or language impairments were served in separate classes (U.S. Department of Education, 2004).

## Community-Based

In community-based models, speech and language therapy is provided outside of the school, usually in the home. This model is most often used with preschoolers and sometimes for students with severe disabilities, with an emphasis on teaching functional communication skills in the community.

## Combination

There are variations of all these models, and many schools and SLPs serve children using combinations of two or more models (Borsch & Oaks, 1993; Blosser & Kratcoski, 1997).

## CURRENT ISSUES AND FUTURE TRENDS

In the future, specialists in communication disorders may function even more indirectly than they do today. They will continue to work as professional team members, assisting teachers, parents, physicians, and other specialists in recognizing potential communication disorders and in facilitating communication skills. Training classroom teachers and parents in how to promote children's speech and language development will become an ever-more-important aspect of the SLP's responsibilities (Al Otaiba & Smartt, 2003).

### Speech-Language Therapist or Language-Related Education Consultant?

A growing controversy among some members of the SLP profession is the extent to which services for students with speech and language impairments provided in inclusive classrooms should take "a therapeutic focus" versus an "educational focus" (Prelock, 2000a, 2000b). Although speech-language pathologists in the schools are being encouraged to provide services within inclusive models, they often express concern that they are becoming more like classroom teachers and that the therapy they should be providing to

333

students on their caseloads is getting watered down as a result. Ehren (2000) discusses these concerns and offers solutions to the role confusion and dissatisfaction of many SLPs who provide in-classroom speech-language services. Ehren suggests that SLPs can preserve their role identity and the integrity of services provided by maintaining a therapeutic focus and sharing the responsibility for student success with classroom teachers.

## Changing Populations

Speech-language pathologists who work in schools are likely to find themselves working with increasing numbers of children with severe and multiple disabilities who previously did not receive specialized services from speech-language pathologists. Caseloads have grown in many school districts, and financial restrictions make it virtually impossible for all students with speech or language impairments to receive adequate services from the relatively few specialists who are employed. Even though all students with disabilities are entitled to receive all of the special education and related services they need, the schools' limited resources necessitate difficult decisions at the local level. Some programs may choose to provide special services only to those students with the most severe speech and language impairments. Others may concentrate their professional resources on higher-functioning students who are considered to have the best potential for developing communication skills. Parents, advocates, and professional organizations will play an instrumental role in determining which children will receive specialized speech and language services.

Paraprofessional personnel may, in the future, be more widely trained to work directly with children who have speech and language disorders, while professionals will concentrate on diagnosis, prescriptive programming, evaluation, and the use of technology. Peer tutoring or therapy approaches using students without disabilities as language models are likely to become more prevalent. These approaches may allow more students to receive specialized help.

Currently, speech and language intervention programs are heavily oriented toward the preschool and school-age population. Although early detection and intervention will clearly remain a high priority among communication disorders specialists, there is a need for long-term studies to document the effectiveness of early intervention on later speech and language development. Professionals are also becoming increasingly aware of the special speech and language needs of adolescents and adults, many of whom have untreated communication problems. The future will likely see greater attention to the assessment and treatment of speech and language disorders caused by the aging process.

## Across-the-Day Interventions

The traditional role of the speech-language pathologist will probably continue to change, from that of offering direct therapy to students to "facilitating the implementation of communication interventions in the classroom environment" (Goldstein et al., 1994, p. 106). As we have discussed, naturalistic interventions that take place in the actual environments in which children use language are increasingly becoming the norm.

But naturalness is no guarantee of effectiveness. As Goldstein et al. (1994) point out, the real challenge lies in designing and implementing across-the-day interventions that can be used effectively by teachers and other significant persons in the child's life. The most effective communication disorders specialist of the future will be expert not only in designing interventions that can be implemented in the classroom and home but also in training and supporting teachers and parents in carrying out those interventions.

# Tips for Beginning Teachers

*by Steve Everling*

## LANGUAGE IMPAIRMENTS

Although each student with a language impairment presents a unique profile, there are some general strategies that teachers can implement when working with these students.

- *Thoroughly explain new vocabulary.* Students with language impairments often have problems learning and retaining new words, so explaining new vocabulary is essential. To create an environment for success for these students, present the new vocabulary orally and in writing with a definition, and then provide visual cues (pictures) and examples. After presenting and explaining these words, post the visual cues in the classroom so that students can refer to them as needed.
- *Embed new vocabulary across the curriculum.* Students will need a lot of practice and repetition with new vocabulary. The best way to provide this practice is to create opportunities for the students to use the vocabulary across content areas and in different contexts. For example, if you are teaching farm animal vocabulary, have students read books about farm animals during reading, design a farm animal habitat during science, and graph animal characteristics (e.g., which animals eat hay, which animals are big, etc.) as part of their math lesson.
- *Provide longer wait time.* Students with language impairments sometimes need a little longer to formulate and express responses to questions. Wait 3 or 4 seconds longer than you normally would to give the student a chance to answer and don't interrupt or hurry the student with her answer.
- *Break multistep directions into smaller components.* Complying with a teacher's complex, multistep direction, "Put your paper in your desk and push in your chair before you go to the bathroom," may be overwhelming for a student with a language impairment. To lessen frustration and create more opportunities for compliance, break up your directions into smaller tasks, such as:
  *Step 1:* "Put your paper in your desk."
  *Step 2:* "Stand up and push in your chair."
  *Step 3:* "Now you may go to the bathroom."
  Do not move onto a new direction until the student completes each task successfully. Once the student consistently follows shorter directions, you can start to give longer directions.

## ARTICULATION ERRORS

Although students in the primary grades exhibit variability in speech sound development, most typically developing children consistently make most speech sounds by the time they begin kindergarten.

- *Do not confuse typical speech sound development with serious articulation errors.* Even typically developing children sometimes have difficulty with the /r/ and /l/ sounds and complex consonant blends, like the /str/ in *street*, which may not fully develop until first or second grade. However, a kindergarten child who is difficult to understand may be at risk for communication and literacy learning problems, so be sure to monitor his progress.
- *Consult with your school's SLP if you have a hard time understanding a child's speech.* Anytime you are uncertain whether a student's speech sound development is where it should be, consult with your school's speech-language pathologist. The SLP will be able to answer your questions and, if need be, begin a formal evaluation and intervention process with the student.

## STUTTERING

Many teachers are unsure of what to do with a student who stutters. Here are a few general guidelines:

- *Don't anticipate what the student wants to say and finish the utterance for her.* Instead, try to listen attentively, letting the student work through the stuttering moment on her own.
- *Consistently model a relaxed and unhurried speaking style.* Your calm and steady speech will have a more positive effect on the student than telling him to "slow down" or "relax."
- *Ask the student what strategies she uses to speak more fluently.* It is okay to speak openly and individually with the student about her stuttering. Implementing these strategies in the classroom can make the educational process more effective and enjoyable for the student and give her a sense of empowerment.

# KEY TERMS AND CONCEPTS

To print your own set of SAFMED flash cards for studying and mastering these terms, go to the Companion Website, **www.prenhall.com/heward**.

aphasia, p. 315
articulation disorder, p. 311
augmentative and alternative communication (AAC), p. 324
expressive disorder, p. 309
fluency disorder, p. 311
language disorder, p. 309
language, p. 302
morpheme, p. 303
morphology, p. 303

phoneme, p. 303
phonological disorder, p. 311
phonology, p. 303
pragmatics, p. 303
receptive disorder, p. 309
semantics, p. 303
speech, p. 304
stuttering, p. 311
syntax, p. 303
voice disorder, p. 312

# SUMMARY

## Definitions

- Communication is any interaction that transmits information. Narrating, explaining, informing, requesting, and expressing are major communicative functions.
- A language is an arbitrary symbol system that enables a group of people to communicate. Each language has rules of phonology, morphology, syntax, semantics, and pragmatics that describe how users put sounds and ideas together to convey meaning.
- Speech is the oral production of language; it is the fastest and most efficient method of communication by language.
- Normal language development follows a relatively predictable sequence. Most children learn to talk and use language without any formal instruction; by the time they enter first grade, their grammar and speech patterns match those of the adults around them.
- A communication disorder is "an impairment in the ability to receive, send, process, and comprehend concepts or verbal, nonverbal and graphic symbol systems" (ASHA, 1993, p. 40).
- A child has a speech impairment if his speech draws unfavorable attention to itself, interferes with the ability to communicate, or causes social or interpersonal problems.
- The three basic types of speech impairments are articulation disorders (errors in the production of speech sounds), fluency disorders (difficulties with the flow or rhythm of speech), and voice disorders (problems with the quality or use of one's voice).
- Some children have trouble understanding language (receptive language disorders); others have trouble using language to communicate (expressive language disorders); still others have language delays.
- Speech or language differences based on cultural or regional dialects are not communication disorders. However, children who use a different dialect may also have speech or language disorders.

## Characteristics

- There are four basic kinds of sound speech errors: distortions, omissions, substitutions, and additions.
- A child with an articulation disorder is not able to produce a given sound physically.
- A child with a phonological disorder has the ability to produce a given sound and does so correctly in some instances but not at other times.
- Stuttering, the most common fluency disorder, is marked by rapid-fire repetitions of consonant or vowel sounds, especially at the beginnings of words, prolongations, hesitations, interjections, and complete verbal blocks.
- A voice disorder is characterized by abnormal vocal quality, pitch, loudness, resonance, and/or duration for the speaker's age and sex.
- Language impairments involve problems in phonology, morphology, syntax, semantics, and/or pragmatics; they are usually classified as either receptive or expressive.

## Prevalence

- Slightly less than 2% of school-age children receive special education for speech and language impairments, the second-largest disability category under IDEA.
- Nearly twice as many boys as girls have speech impairments.
- Children with articulation and spoken language problems represent the largest category of speech-language impairments.

## Causes

- Although some speech and language impairments have physical (organic) causes, most are functional disorders that cannot be directly attributed to physical conditions.

## Identification and Assessment

- Assessment of a suspected communication disorder may include some or all of the following components: (1) case history and physical examination, (2) articulation test, (3) hearing test, (4) auditory test, (5) phonological awareness and processing, (6) vocabulary and overall language development test, (7) language samples, and (8) observation in natural settings.

## Educational Approaches

- Speech language pathologists (SLP) employ a wide range of techniques for identifying, evaluating, and providing therapeutic services to children. These include structured exercises and drills as well as individual and group therapy sessions.
- A general goal of treating speech and sound errors is to help the child speak as clearly as possible. Addressing articulation and phonological errors involves discrimination and production activities. Fluency disorders can be treated with the application of behavioral principles and self-monitoring, although many children recover spontaneously.
- Voice disorders can be treated surgically or medically if the cause is organic. Most remedial techniques offer direct vocal rehabilitation. Behavioral principles help break habitual patterns of misuse.
- Language disorder treatments vary widely. Precommunication activities encourage exploration of expressive language. SLPs connect oral language to literacy components of the curriculum. Naturalistic interventions disperse learning trials throughout the natural environment and normal conversation.
- Augmentative and alternative communication may be aided or unaided and consists of three components: a representational symbol set or vocabulary, a means for selecting the symbols, and a means for transmitting the symbols.

## Educational Placement Alternatives

- Most children with speech and language problems attend regular classes.
- ASHA recognizes seven service delivery models: monitoring, pull-out, collaborative consultation, classroom-based, self-contained classroom, community-based, and combination.

## Current Issues and Future Trends

- Specialists will probably function even more indirectly in the future. In-service training will become even more important.
- SLP professionals will deal with the controversy as to whether services should take a therapeutic versus educational focus.
- Changing populations mean growing caseloads and more children with severe and multiple disabilities receiving therapy for communication disorders.
- Across-the-day interventions mean that interventions must be applicable not only in the classroom but also by teachers and parents.

To check your comprehension of chapter contents, go to the Guided Review and Quiz modules in Chapter 8 of the Companion Website, **www.prenhall.com/heward**.

# DEAFNESS AND HEARING LOSS

# Featured Teacher

## DOUGLAS JACKSON

EL PASO REGIONAL DAY SCHOOL PROGRAM
FOR THE DEAF
HILLSIDE ELEMENTARY SCHOOL,
EL PASO, TEXAS

### Education—Teaching Credentials—Experience

- B.A., social studies education, University of Northern Colorado, 1978
- M.S., education of the deaf, University of Rochester/National Technical Institute for the Deaf, New York, 1982
- Texas and Florida certifications in hearing impaired, K–12; social studies (secondary); and gifted, K–12
- 20 years of experience teaching students with special needs

***Current Teaching Position***     For the past 10 years, I have taught science, social studies, math, and art to elementary-age deaf students at Hillside Elementary. Texas is divided into regional day school programs as far as deaf education is concerned. The El Paso Regional Program is housed in the El Paso Independent School District. At Hillside Elementary, a regular neighborhood school of about 700 students, nine deaf-ed. teachers, two speech therapists, and interpreters serve 70 deaf students. We serve the students of 13 school districts in our region. Some students travel as much as an hour each way to come to school. This is not unusual. Hearing impairment is a low-incidence disability and a very cost-intensive one.

***Students***     I have five students in my fifth-grade homeroom, all of whom receive special education and related services under the IDEA categories of hearing and speech or language impairments. Almost all of our students are Hispanic, and some come from homes in which Spanish is the primary or only language. A couple of our students have deaf parents who were born in Mexico.

Socioeconomically, we run the gamut. Some of our students come from middle-class families, and some come from poor families. Sometimes desperately so. We get to know our students very well, and our students get to know each other better than their own siblings sometimes.

***Curriculum Materials and Teaching Strategies***     We try to parallel the materials and the units that are covered in the general education curriculum, adapting a lot of the language in the texts. I often turn textbook content into plays that incorporate the students' personalities and interests and take advantage of the great resources provided by local culture. Sometimes students draw backgrounds and create props, and we videotape these plays. I use participatory theater as a teaching tool for several reasons: (1) plays help the students understand the material better, (2) active learning is always better than passive attending, (3) plays personalize the material—helping the students understand that the events and concepts they're learning about are central to the history and current life of their world,

## Focus Questions

- In what ways do the child who is deaf and the child who is hard of hearing differ?

- How do students who identify culturally with the Deaf community view hearing impairment?

- Why can't reading simply replace speech as a means of learning and understanding English?

- How do oral/aural, total communication, and bilingual-bicultural approaches differ in their philosophies and teaching methods?

- Why has American Sign Language (ASL) not been fully accepted as the language of instruction in educational programs for deaf children?

(4) plays bring out the students' natural creativity, and (5) the plays help the students feel less daunted by the textbook. We also use technology—video letters with deaf students in other places, distance-learning sessions with the Texas School for the Deaf, and structured Internet research assignments.

I incorporate activities that help our students teach each other. This year we're incorporating the Pillars of Character across the curriculum. Our upper-elementary students are working in small groups to create puppet plays involving situations that require responsibility. To get them started, last Friday we wrote and performed a prototypical video puppet play. It involved an old lady who was too sick to walk her dogs every day. One of the students played a kid who promises to walk her dogs every day. Later that week some of his friends try to talk him into a mall trip that will cause him to shirk his responsibility. The students seemed to respond pretty well. They have completed making their puppets and will start writing their scripts on Monday.

You may be wondering how kids sign and manipulate puppets at the same time. Obviously they can't sign and hold the puppets simultaneously, so we cheat. We tape the puppets to the set we have created, orient the audience to the characters and the set before the play begins, and then the students read the parts. It seems to work. I do the same thing every year for a series of Puppet Economics plays I use before my fifth graders play the Stock Market Game Worldwide.

In the past three years I have been doing much more inclusion with regular fifth- and fourth-grade classes, with a great deal of success both educationally and socially. My students have also done many PowerPoint presentations for classmates, faculty members, and outside groups, including a presentation on effective mainstreaming that was presented at the beginning of the school year to faculty members at our elementary, middle, and high school campuses, and a presentation on our mock trials and the rights of deaf people in our system of justice (especially the right to have an interpreter), which we presented to the local bar association and to our sheriff and the deputy police chief. It is amazing to see how much more powerful these messages are when they are delivered by smart, funny, charming, and dynamic young people than when they are offered by a middle-aged bald man such as myself. It is rewarding watching students master the tools that can help them overcome their own problems.

To learn more about how Mr. Jackson uses plays, mock trials, and the Internet as teaching tools, go to Chapter 9's Teacher Feature module on the Companion Website, **www.prenhall.com/heward**.

***Personal Qualities Important for Special Educators***     Being a great teacher is like being a great lawyer, doctor, chef, or artist. You are always that profession. I mean, look at Van Gogh or Picasso or Renoir. They were always themselves—every brushstroke a fingerprint of the artist. You can't tell where the self ends and the profession begins. Great teachers do that. They don't just look at the state standards and try to decide how they will cover them. They're always seeing the world through the eyes of a teacher; and when something new and interesting happens to them, they think how they can share that experience with their students. I would be lying if I said that I had this skill from day 1. Many of my early efforts as a teacher were 10 steps forward and 9 steps back, sometimes 9 steps forward and 10 steps back. It is something that I am still working on now—I am very much a work in progress.

Lately I have been thinking a lot about the past and future of my field. So much has happened within the past few years in this field, particularly from a technological standpoint, and much of it may have a tremendous impact on the young minds whose educations have been entrusted to me. A great teacher acquires new information, and makes it his or her own so that the students can make it their own. Having this enormous array of tools at my disposal has made me aware of the great strides made by pioneers in my field who didn't have all of these cool toys. My fellow teachers and I are walking in the footsteps of giants—in truth, giants who frequently and sometimes heatedly disagreed with each other, but giants who paved the way for generations of teachers and students to come. A great teacher honors those giant footsteps and makes the best effort he or she can when the footsteps end, and he or she must expand the trail in his or her size 10½ Nikes.

*A Memorable Moment*    There have been many, so I'll share the first one that pops to mind. Our students love school. Many come from hearing families that can't communicate with them, and all are frequently in social situations with people who can't communicate with them. Consequently, school is an oasis of communication for them. Once, while gathering for a field trip, we passed the marquee in front of school. One of my students looked at the sign and read, "Saturday School," which referred, of course, to a mandatory program for students who had misbehaved during the week. Several other students gasped, "Saturday school! Can we come?" It's always great to hear that the customers want more, not less, of your service. And the only thing more meaningful than the knowledge that you have provided an oasis of communication for a child is the realization that it is your mission to broaden the boundaries of that communication oasis to include the outside world.

A s Lou Ann Walker, the child of deaf parents, observes in her autobiography, people who have normal hearing usually find it difficult to fully appreciate the enormous importance of the auditory sense in human development and learning: "Nature attaches an overwhelming importance to hearing. As unborns we hear before we can see. Even in deep comas, people often hear what is going on around them. For most of us, when we die, the sense of hearing is the last to leave the body" (Walker, 1986, p. 165).

A sighted person can simulate blindness by closing her eyes or donning a blindfold, but it is virtually impossible for a hearing person to turn off his ears. The basic structure of the inner ear is present in the fetus at 6 months, and hearing begins before birth (Brownell, 1999). Throughout life, all hearing animals obtain information about the world around them, from all directions, 24 hours a day. When a twig snaps behind us, we don't have to be looking to know that we are not alone.

In addition to its tremendous survival advantage, hearing plays the lead role in the natural, almost effortless manner by which most children acquire speech and language. Newborns respond to sounds by startling or blinking. At a few weeks of age, infants with normal hearing can listen to quiet sounds, recognize their parents' voices, and pay attention to their own gurgling and cooing sounds. At 1 month, hearing infants prefer natural speech sounds over nonlanguage sounds (Mehler et al., 1988). By 6 months, hearing infants can discriminate the speech sounds of the language to which they have been exposed from the sounds of other languages (Werker & Lalonde, 1988). By the time they are 1 year old, hearing children can produce many of the sounds of their language and are speaking their first words. Children develop language by constantly hearing people talk and associating these sounds with innumerable activities and events. Sound acquires meaning, and children quickly learn that people convey information and communicate their thoughts and feelings by speaking and hearing.

In contrast, for children who cannot hear speech sounds, learning a spoken language is anything but natural or effortless. Children who are deaf simply do not have access to an auditorally based language. As we will see, however, when children who are deaf are exposed to a visual, sign-based language as their first language, they acquire language and

To better understand the topics that will be covered in this chapter, go to the Essential Concepts and Chapter at a Glance modules in Chapter 9 of the Companion Website, **www.prenhall.com/heward**.

It may be impossible for a person with normal hearing to fully comprehend the immense difficulties a prelingually deaf child faces trying to learn language.

communication skills in a manner quite similar to the acquisition of speech by hearing children. Some children with hearing loss can hear speech with hearing aids or other technologies, and techniques such as speech training and speechreading enable many children with hearing loss to communicate effectively. Whether a child's hearing loss is mild or profound, early identification and assessment are keys to providing needed special education services.

# DEFINITIONS

*Definitions: hearing impairment, deaf, residual hearing, hard of hearing*

Council for
Exceptional
Children    Content
Standards for
Beginning Teachers—D/HH:
Educational definitions and
identification criteria for
individuals who are D/HH
(DH1K1).

Like other disabilities, hearing loss can be defined and classified from different perspectives and for different purposes. A medical definition describes the degree of hearing loss on a continuum from mild to profound. Educational definitions of hearing loss focus on the child's ability to use his hearing to understand speech and learn language and the effects of educational performance. For example, IDEA uses the category label **hearing impairment** to indicate a hearing loss that adversely affects educational performance and thereby makes the child eligible for special education. Most special educators distinguish between children who are deaf and those who are hard of hearing.

Normal hearing generally means that a person has sufficient hearing to understand speech. Under adequate listening conditions, a person with normal hearing can interpret speech in everyday situations without using any special device or technique. A child who is **deaf** is not able to use hearing to understand speech. Even with a hearing aid, the hearing loss is too great to allow a deaf child to understand speech through the ears alone. Although a deaf person may perceive some sounds through **residual hearing**, she uses vision as the primary modality for learning and communication.

A child who is **hard of hearing** has a significant hearing loss that makes some special adaptations necessary. Children who are hard of hearing are able to use their hearing to understand speech, generally with the help of a hearing aid. Though they may be delayed or deficient, the speech and language skills of a hard of hearing child are developed mainly through the auditory channel.

Many persons who are deaf do not view their hearing loss as a disability and consider the term *hearing impairment* inappropriate and demeaning because it suggests a deficiency or pathology. Like other cultural groups, members of the Deaf community share a common language and social practices. When the cultural definition of hearing loss is used, *Deaf* is spelled with a capital *D*, just as an uppercase letter is used to refer to a person who is French, Japanese, or Jewish. While person-first language is considered the appropriate way to refer to individuals with disabilities, persons who identify with the *Deaf culture* prefer terms such as teacher of the Deaf, school for the Deaf, and Deaf person. (To learn more about Deaf culture see Diversity & Exceptionality, "Defiantly Deaf," later in this chapter, and "Deaf President Now!" on the Companion Website, **www.prenhall.com/heward**.

*Deaf culture and community*

Council for
Exceptional
Children    Content
Standards for
Beginning Teachers—D/HH:
Cultural dimensions of hearing
loss that may affect the
individual (DH3K2) (also
DH1K2).

## How We Hear

**Audition,** the sense of hearing, is a complex and not completely understood process. The function of the ear is to gather sounds (acoustical energy) from the environment and to transform that energy into a form (neural energy) that can be interpreted by the brain. Figure 9.1 (p. 345) shows the major parts of the human ear. The *outer ear* consists of the external ear and the auditory canal. The part of the ear we see, the **auricle,** funnels sound waves into the **auditory canal (external acoustic meatus)** and helps distinguish the direction of sound.

When sound waves enter the external ear, they are slightly amplified as they move toward the **tympanic membrane** (eardrum). Variations in sound pressure cause the eardrum to move in and out. These movements of the eardrum change the acoustical energy into mechanical energy, which is transferred to the three tiny bones of the *middle ear* (the *hammer, anvil,* and *stirrup*). The base (called the *footplate*) of the third bone in the sequence, the

# Defiantly Deaf: Deaf People Live, Proudly, in Another Culture, but Not a Lesser One

*by Andrew Solomon*

The protest at the Lexington Center, which includes New York's oldest Deaf school, is an important stage in the Deaf struggle for civil rights, and on April 25, the first day of student demonstrations, I ask an African-American from the 11th grade whether she has also demonstrated for race rights. "I'm too busy being Deaf right now," she signs. "My two older brothers aren't Deaf, so they're taking care of being black. Maybe if I have time I'll get to that later."

Another student intercedes. "I am black and Deaf and proud and I don't want to be white or hearing or different in any way from who I am." Her signs are pretty big and clear. The first student repeats the sign "proud"—her thumb, pointing in, rises up her chest—and then suddenly they are overcome with giggles and go back to join the picket line.

This principle is still new to me, but it has been brewing in the Deaf community for some time: while some deaf people feel cut off from the hearing world, or disabled, for others, being Deaf is a culture and a source of pride. ("Deaf" denotes culture, as distinct from "deaf," which is used to describe pathology.) A steadily increasing number of deaf people have said that they would not choose to be hearing. To them, the word "cure"—indeed the whole notion of deafness as pathology—is anathema.

The Deaf debates are all language debates. "When I communicate in A.S.L., my native language," M. J. Bienvenu, a political activist, said to me, "I am living my culture. I don't define myself in terms of 'not hearing' or of 'not' anything else." A founder of the Bicultural Center (a sort of Deaf think tank), M. J. is gracious, but also famously terrifying: brilliant, striking-looking and self-possessed, with signing so swift, crisp and perfectly controlled that she seems to be rearranging the air in front of her into a more acceptable shape. Deaf of Deaf, with Deaf sisters, she manifests, like many other activists, a pleasure in American Sign Language that only poets feel for English. "When our language was acknowledged," she says, "we gained our freedom." In her hands "freedom"—clenched hands are crossed before the body, then swing apart and face out—is like an explosion.

## A "FAMILY" GATHERING

I attended the National Association of the Deaf convention in Knoxville, Tennessee, with almost 2,000 Deaf participants. At Lexington, I saw Deaf people stand up to the hearing world. I learned how a TTY works, met pet dogs who understood sign, talked about mainstreaming and oralism and the integrity of visual language. I became accustomed to doorbells that flashed lights instead of ringing. But none of this could have prepared me for the immersion that is the NAD convention, where the brightest, most politicized, most committed Deaf gather for political focus and social exchange. There, it is not a question of whether the hearing will accept the existence of Deaf culture, but of whether Deaf culture will accept the hearing.

In 1988, students at Gallaudet University, the world's only university dedicated exclusively to the education of deaf students, successfully demonstrated for a deaf person to be appointed president after a hearing person who was unable to use sign language had been selected for the position.

I arrive the night of the president's reception. There are 1,000 people in the grand ballroom of the Hyatt Regency, the lights turned up because these people are unable to communicate in darkness. The crowd is nearly soundless; you hear the claps that are part of the articulation of A.S.L., the clicks and puffing noises the deaf make when they sign, and occasionally their big uncontrolled laughter. People greet each other as if they have been waiting forever for these encounters—the Deaf community is close, closed and affectionate.

Deaf people touch each other far more than the hearing, and everyone here hugs friends. I, too, find myself hugging people as if I have known them forever. Yet I must be careful of the difference between a friendly and a forward embrace; how you touch communicates a world of meaning in Deaf circles. I must be careful of looking abstractedly at people signing; they will think I am eavesdropping. I do not know any of the etiquette of these new circumstances. "Good luck with the culture shock," more than one person says to me, and I get many helpful hints.

As I look across the room it seems as if some strange human sea is breaking into waves and glinting in the light, as thousands of hands move at stunning speed, describing a spatial grammar with sharply individual voices and accents. The association is host to the Miss Deaf America pageant, and the young beauties, dressed to the nines and sporting their state sashes, are objects of considerable attention. "Look how beautifully she expresses herself," says someone, pointing to one contestant, and then, of another: "Can you believe that blurry Southern signing? I didn't think anyone really signed like that!" (Regional variations of sign can be dangerous: the sign that in New York slang means "cake" in some Southern states means "sanitary napkin.")

The luminaries of the Deaf world—activists, actors, professors—mix comfortably with the beauty queens. I am one of perhaps a dozen hearing people at this party. I have heard Deaf people talk about how their "family" is the Deaf community. Rejected in so many instances by parents with whom they cannot communicate, united by their struggle with a world that is seldom understanding of them, they have formed inviolable bonds of love of a kind that are rare in hearing culture. At the National Association of the Deaf, they are unmistakable. Disconcerting though it may sound, it is impossible, here, not to wish you were Deaf. I had known that Deaf culture existed, but I had not guessed how heady it is.

The Association members are a tiny minority, less than 10 percent of the nation's Deaf; most deaf people are what the Deaf call "grass roots." The week after the convention, the national Deaf bowling championships in Baltimore will attract a much larger crowd, people who go to Deaf clubs, play cards and work in blue-collar jobs. Below them in the Deaf status structure are the peddlers (the Deaf word for the mendicants who "sell" cards with the manual alphabet on subways—the established Deaf community tried as early as the 40's to get them off the streets).

At the V.I.P. party after the radiant Miss Deaf Maryland has won, I am talking to Alec Naiman, a world traveler who was one of the pilots at this year's Deaf fly-in at the Knoxville airport. We are discussing a trip he made to China. "I met some Deaf Chinese people my first day, and went to stay with them. Deaf people never need hotels; you can always stay with other Deaf people. We spoke different signed languages, but we could make ourselves understood. Though we came from different countries, Deaf culture held us together. By the end of the evening we'd talked about Deaf life in China, and about Chinese politics, and we'd understood each other linguistically and culturally. No hearing American could do that in China," he says. "So who's disabled then?"

## MAKING THE IRREGULAR REGULAR

How to reconcile this Deaf experience with the rest of the world? Should it be reconciled at all? M. J. Bienvenu has been one of the most vocal and articulate opponents of the language of disability. "I am Deaf," she says to me in Knoxville, drawing out the sign for "Deaf," the index finger moving from chin to ear, as though she is tracing a broad smile. Considerably gentler now than in her extremist heyday in the early 80's, she acknowledges that "for some deaf people, being deaf is a disability. Those who learn forced English while being denied sign emerge semi-lingual rather than bilingual, and they are disabled people. But for the rest of us, it is no more a disability than being Japanese would be."

I have heard of a couple who opted for an abortion when they heard that their child was hearing, so strong a view did they hold on the superiority of Deaf ways. But I also met many Deaf individuals who objected to the way that the Deaf leadership (focused around the National Association of the Deaf) have presumed to speak for all the deaf people of America. There were plenty who said that being deaf is of course a disability, and that anything you could do about it would be welcome. They were righteously indignant at the thought of a politically correct group suggesting that their problems weren't problems.

It is tempting in the end, to say that there is no such thing as a disability. Equally, one might admit that almost everything is a disability. There are as many arguments for correcting everything as there are for correcting nothing. Perhaps it would be most accurate to say that "disability" and "culture" are really matters of degree. Being Deaf is a disability and a culture in modern America; so is being gay, so is being black; so is being female; so even, increasingly, is being a straight white male. So is being paraplegic, or having Down syndrome. What is at issue is which things are so "cultural" that you wouldn't think of "curing" them, and which things so "disabling" that you must "cure" them—and the reality is that for some people each of these experiences is primarily a disability experience while for others it is primarily a cultural one.

*Source:* Excerpt from Solomon, A. (1994, August 28). Defiantly deaf. *New York Times.* © 1994 by Andrew Solomon, reprinted with the permission of The Wylie Agency.

To further your understanding of and answer reflective questions about the perspectives and issues presented here, go to Chapter 9's Diversity & Exceptionality module on the Companion Website, **www.prenhall.com/heward**.

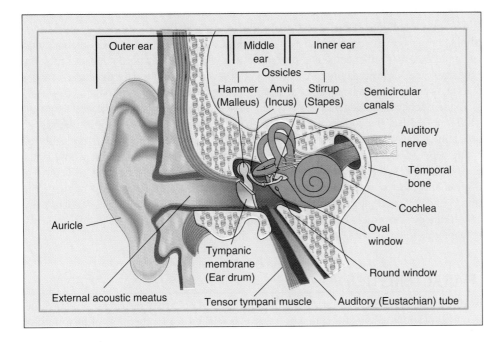

**FIGURE 9.1**
**Basic anatomy of the human ear**

stirrup, rests in an opening called the *oval window*, the path through which sound energy enters the inner ear. The vibrations of the three bones (together called the **ossicles**) transmit energy from the middle ear to the inner ear with little loss.

The most critical and complex part of the entire hearing apparatus is the *inner ear*, which is covered by the *temporal bone*, the hardest bone in the entire body. The inner ear contains the **cochlea**, the main receptor organ for hearing, and the *semicircular canals*, which control the sense of balance. The cochlea, named for its resemblance to a coiled snail shell, consists of two fluid-filled cavities that contain 30,000 tiny hair cells arranged in four rows. Energy transmitted by the ossicles moves the fluid in the cochlea, which in turn stimulates the hair cells. Each hair cell has approximately a hundred tiny spines, called *cilia*, at the top. When the hair cells are stimulated, they displace the fluid around them, which produces minute electrochemical signals that are transmitted along the auditory nerve to the brain. High tones are picked up by the hair cells at the basal, or lowest turn of the cochlea, and low tones stimulate hair cells at the apex, or top, of the cochlea.

## The Nature of Sound

Sound is measured in units that describe its intensity and frequency. Both dimensions of sound are important in considering the needs of a child with a hearing loss. The intensity or loudness of sound is measured in **decibels (dB)**. Zero dB represents the smallest sound a person with normal hearing can perceive, which is called the *zero hearing-threshold level* (HTL), or **audiometric zero.**

Larger dB numbers represent increasingly louder sounds on a ratio scale in which each increment of 10 dB is a tenfold increase in intensity. A low whisper 5 feet away registers about 10 dB, a running automobile about 65 dB, and Niagara Falls about 90 dB. Conversational speech 10 to 20 feet away ranges from approximately 20 to 55 dB. A sound of about 125 dB or louder will cause pain to the average person.

The frequency, or pitch, of sound is measured in cycles per second, or **hertz (Hz);** 1 hertz equals 1 cycle per second. Pure tones consist of one frequency only. Speech and most environmental sounds are complex tones made up of a variety of frequencies. The lowest note on a piano has a frequency of about 30 Hz, middle C about 250 Hz, and the highest note about 4,000 Hz. Human hearing is limited to a range of about 20 to 20,000 Hz, but many audible sounds are outside the speech range, the frequency range of ordinary conversation. Although a person who cannot hear very low sounds (e.g, a foghorn) or very high sounds (e.g., a piccolo) may suffer some inconvenience, she will encounter no significant problems in the classroom or everyday life. A person with a severe hearing loss in the speech range, however, is at a great disadvantage in acquiring and communicating in a spoken language.

The frequency range generally considered most important for hearing spoken language is 500 to 2,000 Hz, but some speech sounds have frequencies below or above that range. For example, the /s/ phoneme (as in the word "sat") is a high-frequency sound, typically occurring between 4,000 and 8,000 Hz (Northern & Downs, 1991). A student whose hearing loss is more severe at the higher frequencies will thus have particular difficulty in discriminating the /s/ sound. Conversely, phonemes such as /dj/ (the sound of the "j" in "jump") and /m/ occur at low frequencies and will be more problematic for a student with a low-frequency hearing loss. As you might expect, a student with a high-frequency hearing loss tends to hear men's voices more easily than women's voices.

*Degree and frequency range of hearing loss*

Council for Exceptional Children    Content Standards for Beginning Teachers—D/HH: Effects of sensory input on the development of language and cognition (DH6K3) (also, CC2K2).

## CHARACTERISTICS

Any discussion of characteristics of students who are deaf or hard of hearing should include three qualifications. First, students who receive special education because of hearing loss comprise an extremely heterogeneous group (Easterbrooks, 1999). It is a mistake to assume that a commonly observed behavioral characteristic or average level of academic achievement is representative of all children with hearing loss.

Second, the effects of hearing loss on a child's communication and language skills, academic achievement, and social and emotional functioning are influenced by many factors, including the type and degree of hearing loss, the age at onset, the attitudes of the child's parents and siblings, opportunities to acquire a first language (whether through speech or sign), and the presence or absence of other disabilities (Moores, 2001; Schirmer, 2004).

Third, generalizations about how deaf people are supposed to act and feel must be viewed with extreme caution (Andrews, Leigh, & Weiner, 2004). Lane (1988), for example, makes a strong case against the existence of the so-called psychology of the deaf. He shows the similarity of the traits attributed to deaf people in the professional literature to traits attributed to African people in the literature of colonialism and suggests that those traits do not "reflect the characteristics of deaf people but the paternalistic posture of the hearing experts making these attributions" (p. 8). In addition, he argues that the scientific literature on the psychology of the deaf is flawed in terms of test administration, test language, test scoring, test content and norms, and its description of subject populations, arguments that have been noted by other researchers as well (Moores, 2001; Paul & Quigley, 1990).

### English Literacy

A child with a hearing loss—especially a prelingual loss of 90 dB or greater—is at a great disadvantage in acquiring English language skills. Hearing children typically acquire a large vocabulary and a knowledge of grammar, word order, idiomatic expressions, fine shades of meaning, and many other aspects of verbal expression by listening to others and to themselves from early infancy. A child who, from birth or soon after, is unable to hear the speech of other people will not learn speech and language spontaneously, as do children with normal hearing. Since reading and writing involve graphic representations of a phonologically based language, the deaf child must strive to decode and produce text based on a language for which she may have little or no understanding.

Students with hearing loss have smaller vocabularies when compared to peers with normal hearing, and the gap widens with age (ASHA, 2001a). Children with hearing loss learn concrete words like "tree," "run," "book," and "red" more easily than abstract words like "tired," "funny," "equal to," and "freedom." They also have difficulty with function words and verb phrases like "the," "an," "are," and "have been."

They may omit endings of words, such as the plural "-s," "-ed," or "-ing." Because the grammar and structure of English often do not follow logical rules, a person with prelingual hearing loss must exert a great deal of effort to read and write with acceptable form and meaning. For example, if the past tense of "talk" is "talked," then why doesn't "go" become "goed"? If the plural of "man" is "men," then shouldn't the plural of "pan" be "pen"? Learning words with multiple meanings is difficult. It is not easy to explain the difference between the expressions "He's beat" (tired) and "He was beaten" to a person who has never had normal hearing.

Deaf students often have difficulty differentiating questions from statements. Most have difficulty understanding and writing sentences with passive voice (*The assignment was given yesterday.*) and relative clauses (*The gloves I left at home are made of leather*). Many students who are deaf write sentences that are short, incomplete, or improperly arranged. The following sentences taken from stories written by elementary deaf students illustrate some of the English literacy problems attributable to not hearing spoken language:

Bobby is walked.

The boy sees a brown football on the hold hand.

The trees is falling a leaves.

The happy children is friending.

To learn how the Internet can be used to help deaf students become better writers, see Teaching & Learning, "Internet Chat Environment," later in this chapter.

## Speaking

Atypical speech is common in many children who are deaf or hard of hearing. All of the challenges that hearing loss poses to learning the vocabulary, grammar, and syntax of English aside, not being able to hear one's own speech makes it difficult to assess and monitor it. As a result children with hearing loss may speak too loudly or not loudly enough. They may speak in an abnormally high pitch or sound like they are mumbling because of poor stress, poor inflection, or poor rate of speaking. The speech of children with hearing loss may be difficult to understand because they omit quiet speech sounds such as /s/, /sh/, /f/, /t/, and /k/, which they cannot hear.

## Academic Achievement

Most children with hearing loss have difficulty with all areas of academic achievement, especially reading and math. Studies assessing the academic achievement of students with hearing loss have routinely found them to lag far behind their hearing peers, and the gap in achievement between children with normal hearing and those with hearing loss usually widens as they get older (ASHA, 2001a). The average deaf student who leaves high school at age 18 or 19 is reading at about the fourth-grade level (Allen 1994; Holt, 1993; Kuntze, 1998), and their mathematics performance is in the range of fifth to seventh grade (Allen,

*English literacy skills*

 Content Standards for Beginning Teachers—D/HH: Effects of sensory input on the development of language and cognition (DH6K3) (also, CC2K1, CC2K2, DH3K4).

 For more ideas on teaching writing to students who are deaf, see "Writer's Workshop," in Chapter 9 of the Companion Website, **www.prenhall.com/heward**.

*Speech skills*

 Content Standards for Beginning Teachers—D/HH: Effects of sensory input on the development of language and cognition (DH6K3) (also, CC2K2, DH3K4).

# Internet Chat Environment
# Online Conversations between Deaf and Hearing Students

*by Barbara R. Schirmer and Albert L. Inghram*

Conversation is the milieu of language acquisition for all children. For children to learn language, they need a considerable amount of experience in conversation with adults. Through many conversations about mutually interesting topics, children discern the underlying rules of the language. For deaf children, face-to-face spoken conversations are typically fraught with inconsistent and incomplete language models because they miss the elements they cannot hear or speechread. If they are conversing in American Sign Language, the structure is unlike English, so they learn the structure of ASL but not that of English.

Written English can offer consistent and complete models of English but not the give and take of conversation. The qualities of conversation that promote language development in young hearing and deaf children are well-formed and short sentences, redundancy, and focus on shared perceptions (Garton & Pratt, 1998; Masataka, 1996; Reilly & Bellugi, 1996; Schirmer, 2000). Although books and stories can offer the first two, sharing perceptions is unique to conversations. Written conversations in the form of dialogue journals and e-mail have been used by teachers, but there is little evidence in the literature that these strategies result in improved written language of deaf students (Johnson, 1997; Lieberth, 1991; Weiserbs, 2000).

Online chats can provide a closer match to face-to-face conversation because the dialogue can take place in real time. A teacher can monitor instructional conversations and incorporate linguistic features that are targeted language goals for the child. Online chat environments have the added advantage of being highly motivating to students. Educators are increasingly using them to provide interactive learning experience and to extend the educational experience beyond the classroom (Ingram, Hathorn, & Evans, 2000; Kearsley, 2000).

We set up online chats between deaf and hearing students separated by distance, and even by time zone. We used The Palace software, which was free to upload from the Internet. When the students logged on to our Palace server, they could see a visual depiction of White Hall at Kent State University. Each student's name appeared below an avatar, which the student could dress up with props. Typed comments appeared for a few seconds in dialogue balloons above the avatar's head and also in a log window on the right of the screen, which maintained a record of the entire conversation. Each day, teams of one deaf student and one hearing student met with the online teacher for 10–20 minutes apiece. The teacher assigned each team a science project. They discussed the project online and looked up information on the Internet when their team was not interacting on The Palace. The online teacher used an intervention strategy that encouraged the deaf students to use language features such as descriptors and conjunctions, which were identified as linguistic goals for these students. We found that the targeted language features appeared with greater frequency and the students highly enjoyed conversing with peers in real time. Figure A is an interview with one of the deaf students that was conducted at the conclusion of the study.

## HOW TO GET STARTED

The following guidelines will facilitate successful online chats between students:

- *Age or grade level.* Students should be beyond the emergent or beginning stages of reading and writing development.
- *Technology skills.* Students must have relatively good keyboarding skills to keep up with the online conversation. They also should have some knowledge of how to search the Internet.
- *Cooperative learning.* It is helpful if the students have participated in cooperative learning activities

**FIGURE A** Interview with one of the deaf students at the conclusion of the study

in their classrooms so that they understand how to work with a partner in carrying out a project.

- *Online teacher.* An adult should monitor the online conversation. The online teacher can provide instruction and direction as well as focus on the deaf child's linguistic skills. The online teacher can be a parent volunteer, an aide, or an older student.

- *Learning unit.* The learning unit should be a topic that is relevant and motivational to all of the students. We found that middle and high school students liked the topic of astronomy, began with many conceptions (and misconceptions) about the stars and planets, and could find much information on the Internet.

- *Scheduling.* The schedule needs to be planned carefully, and everyone needs to be flexible about unforeseen problems. Student absences, school-wide activities, and unreliable Internet connections occurred frequently during our research study.

- *Software.* We chose The Palace software because it is easy to use, visually appealing, relatively secure from others joining our conversations, and cost-free. Other Internet chat software is available, enabling text-only rooms or adding two-dimensional or three-dimensional visual environments. It is crucial to make sure that the school does not have a firewall in place that prevents access or that a request to remove the firewall is made before beginning the project. We found that having a laptop available that could gain access through a modem and telephone line was helpful.

- *Writing goals and growth.* The online chat environment can provide substantial opportunity for the deaf student to actively participate during instruction. The more that the student responds in writing and receives feedback from a skilled peer or the online teacher during the instructional conversation, the more likely it is that the student's language will develop and writing will improve.

Barbara R. Schirmer is vice president of academic affairs and professor of special education at University of Detroit Mercy. She is the author of *Language and Literacy Development in Children Who Are Deaf* (Allyn & Bacon, 2000). Albert L. Inghram is assistant professor of educational technology at Kent State University.

To further your understanding of the strategy presented here and answer questions about what you have learned, go to Chapter 9's Teaching & Learning module on the Companion Website, **www.prenhall.com/heward**.

1986, 1994). Approximately 30% of deaf students are functionally illiterate when they leave school, compared to less than 1% of hearing students (Paul & Jackson, 1993).

Paul and Quigley (1990) summarize this dismal state of affairs:

> No general improvement in achievement in most students who are severely to profoundly hearing-impaired has been observed since the … early years of the 20th century. The average student completing a secondary education program is still reading and writing at a level commensurate with the average 9- to 10-year-old hearing student. Achievement in mathematics is about one or two grades higher. (p. 227)

It is important not to equate academic performance with intelligence. Deafness itself imposes no limitations on the cognitive capabilities of individuals (Moores, 2001), and some deaf students read very well and excel academically (Lichtenstein, 1998; Williams & Finnegan, 2003). The problems that students who are deaf often experience in education and adjustment are largely attributable to the mismatch between their perceptual abilities and the demands of spoken and written English.

## Social Functioning

Hearing loss can influence a child's behavior and socioemotional development. Children with severe to profound hearing losses often report feeling isolated, without friends, and unhappy in school, particularly when their socialization with other children with hearing loss is limited. These social problems appear to be more frequent in children with mild or moderate hearing losses than in those with severe to profound losses (ASHA, 2001a). Concerns about lack of friendship and acceptance were reported by 50% of the 40 deaf and hard of hearing children in one study (Davis, Elfenbein, Schum, & Bentler, 1986). Data obtained from parents in the same study suggested that children with hearing loss were more likely to have behavioral difficulties in school and social situations than were children with normal hearning. Even a slight hearing loss can cause a child to miss important auditory information, such as the tone of a teacher's voice while telling the class to get out their spelling workbooks, which can lead to the child's being considered inattentive, distractible, or immature (Easterbrooks, 1999).

Children with hearing loss frequently express feelings of depression, withdrawal, and isolation, particularly those who experience adventitious loss of hearing (Meadow-Orlans, 1985; Sheetz, 2004). A study of more than 1,000 deaf adolescents who were considered disruptive in the classroom (Kluwin, 1985) found that the most frequently related factor was reading ability; that is, students who were poorer readers were more likely to exhibit problem behaviors in school.

Research has not provided clear insights into the effects of hearing loss on behavior; however, it appears that the extent to which a child with hearing loss successfully interacts with family members, friends, and people in the community depends largely on others' attitudes and the child's ability to communicate in some mutually acceptable way (Ita & Friedman, 1999; Marschark & Clark, 1998). Children who are deaf with deaf parents are thought to have higher levels of social maturity and behavioral self-control than do deaf children of hearing parents, largely because of the early use of manual communication between parent and child that is typical in homes with deaf parents.

Many individuals who are deaf choose to work, live, and socialize primarily with other deaf people; members of hearing society may mistakenly view this as clannishness. Certainly, communication plays a major role in anyone's adjustment. Most individuals with hearing loss are fully capable of developing positive relationships with their hearing peers when a satisfactory method of communication can be used.

## PREVALENCE

According to the American Speech-Language-Hearing Association (ASHA, 2001a), 95 of every 1,000 people have a chronic hearing loss, and about 28 million Americans experi-

### Sidebar (left column)

*Academic achievement*

Council for Exceptional Children    Content Standards for Beginning Teachers—D/HH: Effects of sensory input on the development of language and cognition (DH3K4) (also, CC2K2, DH2K2).

*Social functioning*

Council for Exceptional Children    Content Standards for Beginning Teachers—D/HH: Impact of educational placement options with regard to cultural identity and linguistic, academic, and social-emotional development (DH3K1) (also DH3K2, CC2K5, CC2K6).

ence some difficulty in receiving and processing aural communication. The large majority of persons with hearing loss are adults; it is estimated that 54% of persons over age 65 experience some limitations in hearing (Benson & Marano, 1998).

The U.S. Public Health Service (1990) estimates that 83 out of every 1,000 children in the United States have an educationally significant hearing loss, and that severe to profound hearing loss occurs in about 9 of every 1,000 school-age children.

During the 2003–2004 school year, 71,188 students ages 6 to 21 received special education services under the disability category of hearing impairments (U.S. Department of Education, 2004). This represents 1.2% of all school-age students who received special education services and about 0.1% of the resident student population. The actual number of school-age children with hearing loss in special education programs is somewhat higher because some children with hearing impairments are counted under another primary disability category (e.g., mental retardation, cerebral palsy, deaf-blind). It is not known precisely the percentage of these students who are deaf or hard of hearing. A national survey of early intervention programs serving children with hearing loss reported that 46% of the children were deaf and 54% hard of hearing (Meadow-Orlans, Mertens, Sass-Lehrer, & Scott-Olson, 1997).

About 25% of students who are deaf or hard of hearing have another disabling condition, most notably learning disabilities (9%), mental retardation (8%), vision problems (4%), and emotional or behavioral disorders (4%) (Holden-Pitt & Diaz, 1998). It is estimated that 9% of students with hearing loss have two or more additional disabilities (Shildroth & Hotto, 1994).

# Types and Causes of Hearing Loss

## Types and Age of Onset

The two main types of hearing loss are conductive and sensorineural. **Conductive hearing loss** results from abnormalities or complications of the outer or middle ear. A buildup of excessive wax in the auditory canal can cause a conductive hearing loss, as can a disease that leaves fluid or debris. Some children are born with incomplete or malformed auditory canals. A hearing loss can also be caused if the eardrum or ossicles do not move properly. As its name implies, a conductive hearing loss involves a problem with conducting, or transmitting, sound vibrations to the inner ear. If the rest of the auditory system is intact, conductive hearing losses can often be corrected through surgical or medical treatment. Hearing aids are usually beneficial to persons with conductive impairments.

**Sensorineural hearing loss** refers to damage to the auditory nerve fibers or other sensitive mechanisms in the inner ear. The cochlea converts the physical characteristics of sound into corresponding neural information that the brain can process and interpret; impairment of the cochlea may mean that sound is delivered to the brain in a distorted fashion or not delivered at all. Amplification (making the source of sound louder) may not help the person with a sensorineural hearing loss. Surgery or medication cannot correct most sensorineural hearing loss. The combination of both conductive and sensorineural impairments is called a *mixed hearing loss*.

Hearing loss is also described in terms of being *unilateral* (present in one ear only) or *bilateral* (present in both ears). Most students who receive special education for hearing loss have bilateral losses, although the degree of impairment may not be the same in both ears. Children with unilateral hearing loss generally learn speech and language without major difficulties, although they tend to have problems localizing sounds and listening in noisy or distracting settings.

It is important to consider the age of onset—whether a hearing loss is **congenital** (present at birth) or **acquired** (appears after birth). The terms **prelingual hearing loss** and **postlingual hearing loss** identify whether a hearing loss occurred before or after the development of spoken language. A child who, from birth or soon after, is unable to hear the

*Types of hearing loss*

Council for Exceptional Children — Content Standards for Beginning Teachers—D/HH: Effects of sensory input on the development of language and cognition (DH1K3).

*Age of onset*

Council for
Exceptional    Content
Children    Standards for
Beginning Teachers—D/HH:
Impact of the onset of hearing
loss, age of identification, and
provisions of services on the
development of the individual
who is D/HH (DH2K2).

speech of other people will not learn speech and language spontaneously, as do children with normal hearing. To approximate the experience of a child who is deaf from birth or early childhood, watch a television program in which a foreign language is being spoken— with the sound on the TV set turned off (Furth, 1973). You would face the double problem of being unable to read lips and understand an unfamiliar language. Of the deaf and hard of hearing children served in special education programs, 95% have a prelingual hearing loss (Commission on Education of the Deaf, 1988).

A child who acquires a hearing loss after speech and language are well established, usually after age 2, has educational needs very different from the prelingually deaf child. The educational program for a child who is prelingually deaf usually focuses on acquisition of language and communication, whereas the program for a child who is postlingually deaf usually emphasizes the maintenance of intelligible speech and appropriate language patterns.

## Causes of Congenital Hearing Loss

*Causes of hearing loss*

Council for
Exceptional    Content
Children    Standards for
Beginning Teachers—D/HH:
Etiologies of hearing loss that
can result in additional sensory,
motor, and/or learning
differences (DH1K3).

Although more than 400 causes of hearing loss have been identified, the exact cause is listed as "unknown" for up to 50% of children with hearing loss in some studies (Gallaudet University, 1998; Moores, 2001).

*Genetic Factors.* About one-half of all congenital deafness is caused by genetic abnormalities (Tran & Grunfast, 1999). Genetic hearing loss may be autosomal dominant, autosomal recessive, or X-linked (related to the sex chromosome). *Autosomal dominant hearing loss* exists when one parent, who carries the dominant gene for hearing loss and typically has a hearing loss, passes the gene on to the child. In this case there is at least a 50% probability that the child will also have a hearing loss. The probability is higher if both parents have the dominant gene or if both grandparents on one side of the family have hearing loss due to genetic causes.

Approximately 80%–90% of inherited hearing loss is caused by *autosomal recessive hearing loss* in which both parents typically have normal hearing and carry a recessive gene (Tran & Grunfast, 1999). In this case there is a 25% probability that the child will have a hearing loss. Because both parents usually have normal hearing, and because no other family members have hearing loss, there is no prior expectation that the child may have a hearing loss.

In *X-linked hearing loss*, the mother carries the recessive trait for hearing loss on the sex chromosome and passes it on to male offspring but not to females. This kind of hearing loss is rare, accounting for only about 1%–2% of hereditary hearing loss.

Even though 90% of children who are deaf are born to hearing parents, about 30% of the school-age population of students who are deaf have relatives with hearing loss (Moores, 2001). Because most hereditary deafness is the result of recessive genetic traits, the marriage of two deaf persons results in only a "slightly increased risk of deafness in their children because there is a small chance that both parents would be affected by the same exact genetic deafness" (Northern & Downs, 1991, p. 90).

Hearing loss is one of the known characteristics of more than 200 genetic syndromes, such as Down syndrome, Usher syndrome, Treacher Collins syndrome, and fetal alcohol syndrome.

*Maternal Rubella.* Although rubella (also known as German measles) has relatively mild symptoms, it can cause deafness, visual impairment, heart disorders, and a variety of other serious disabilities in the developing child when it affects a pregnant woman, particularly during the first trimester. A major epidemic of rubella in the United States and Canada between 1963 and 1965 accounted for more than 50% of the students with hearing loss in special education programs in the 1970s and 1980s. Since an effective vaccine was introduced in 1969, the incidence of hearing loss caused by rubella has decreased significantly.

*Congenital Cytomegalovirus (CMV).* Both rubella and **cytomegalovirus (CMV)** are members of a group of infectious agents known as TORCHES (toxophasmosis, rubella, cytomegalovirus, herpes simplex, and syphilis). CMV is a common viral infection, and most people who are infected with it experience minor symptoms such as respiratory infections that soon disappear. Approximately 1% of infants have CMV on their saliva; and 10% of those may later develop various conditions including mental retardation, visual impairment, and, most often, hearing impairment. It is estimated that 4,000 children are born in the United States each year with significant hearing impairments caused by CMV infection (Strauss, 1999). At present, there is no known prevention or treatment for CMV. However, a blood test can determine if a woman of childbearing age is at risk for developing an initial CMV infection during pregnancy.

*Prematurity.* It is difficult to precisely evaluate the effects of prematurity on hearing loss, but early delivery and low birth weight are more common among children who are deaf than among the general population.

## Causes of Acquired Hearing Loss

*Otitis Media.* A temporary, recurrent infection of the middle ear, **otitis media** is the most common medical diagnosis for children. Nearly 90% of all children will experience otitis media at least once, and about one-third of children under age 5 have recurrent episodes (Bluestone & Klein, 2001). Antibiotics usually are an effective treatment; but if untreated, otitis media can result in a buildup of fluid and a ruptured eardrum, which causes permanent conductive hearing loss.

*Meningitis.* The leading cause of postlingual hearing loss is meningitis, a bacterial or viral infection of the central nervous system that can, among its other effects, destroy the sensitive acoustic apparatus of the inner ear. Children whose deafness is caused by meningitis generally have profound hearing losses. Difficulties in balance and other disabilities may also be present.

*Ménière's Disease.* A fairly rare disorder of the inner ear, Ménière's disease is characterized by sudden and unpredictable attacks of vertigo (dizziness), fluctuations in hearing, and *tinnitus* (a ringing in the ears without external stimulation). In its severest form, Ménière's disease can be incapacitating. Little is understood about the mechanisms underlying the condition, and at present there is no reliable treatment or known cure (Schessel, 1999). Ménière's disease most often appears in people between the ages of 40 and 60, but it can affect children under the age of 10.

*Noise-Induced Hearing Loss.* Noise pollution—repeated exposure to loud sounds, such as industrial noise, jet aircraft, guns, and amplified music—is increasingly recognized as a cause of hearing loss. Exposure to "toxic noise is the main culprit" for approximately one-third of the 28 million Americans with permanent hearing loss (Kulman, 1999, p. 2). Noise-induced hearing loss is the most common occupational disease and the second most frequently self-reported occupational injury (ASHA, 2000).

Hearing loss caused by chronic exposure to recreational and occupational noise often occurs gradually, and the person may not realize his hearing is being damaged until it is too late (Haller & Montgomery, 2004). Prolonged exposure to noise above 90 dB can cause gradual hearing loss. Regular exposure of more than 1 minute to noise at 110 dB risks permanent hearing loss.

Herer, Knightly, and Steinberg (2002) identified the following warning signs for excessive noise: being within 3 feet of someone and having to shout to be understood, experiencing ringing in the ears (tinnitus) after leaving the area, and hearing only muffled or soft sounds 1 to 2 hours later.

✎ *Helpful Hint*

For more information about noise-induced hearing loss and how to prevent it, visit the Wise Ears website, **www.nidcd.nih.gov/health/wise**.

# IDENTIFICATION AND ASSESSMENT

*Early identification of hearing loss*

Council for Exceptional Children   Content Standards for Beginning Teachers—D/HH: Specialized terminology used in assessing individuals who are D/HH (DH8K1) (also DH2K2).

## Assessment of Infants

The earlier a hearing loss is identified, the better a child's chances are for receiving early intervention and treatment and for developing good language and communication skills (Calderon & Naidu, 2000). Unfortunately, hearing loss goes undetected in many children, and detection does not always lead quickly to intervention. A national survey of parents of preschool children with hearing loss found that parents suspected their baby had a hearing loss at an average age of 17 months and had the diagnosis confirmed at a mean age of 22 months (Meadow-Orlans et al., 1997). Half of the hard of hearing children in this study did not have their hearing loss diagnosed until they were 2.5 years old. More discouraging are the data on the lag time between diagnosis and intervention: children waited an average of 8 months for a hearing aid, 10 months for speech and auditory services, and 11 months to begin sign language.

*Typical development of behaviors related to sound*

Council for Exceptional Children   Content Standards for Beginning Teachers—D/HH: Effects of sensory input on the development of language and cognition (DH3K4) (also CC2K5).

All infants, hearing and deaf alike, babble, coo, and smile. Later on, children who are deaf tend to stop babbling and vocalizing because they cannot hear themselves or their parents, but the baby's increasing silence may go unnoticed for a while and then be mistakenly attributed to other causes. Figure 9.2 lists some common auditory behaviors emitted by infants with normal hearing. Failure to demonstrate these responses may mean that an infant has a hearing loss, and an audiological exam is recommended.

As of 1999, the legislatures of 29 states had mandated the screening of all newborn infants (Diefendorf, 1999). The two most widely used methods of screening for hearing loss in infants measure physiological reactions to sound. With *auditory brain stem response,* sensors placed on the scalp measure electrical activity as the infant responds to auditory stimuli. In *otoacoustic emission* screening, a tiny microphone placed in the baby's ear detects the "echoes" of hair cells in the cochlea as they vibrate to sound (Ross & Levitt, 2000).

*Audiometry and audiograms*

Council for Exceptional Children   Content Standards for Beginning Teachers—D/HH: Specialized terminology used in assessing individuals who are D/HH (DH8K1) (also DH8K2).

## Pure-Tone Audiometry

A procedure called *pure-tone audiometry* is used to assess the hearing of older children and adults. The examiner uses an **audiometer,** an electronic device that generates sounds at different levels of intensity and frequency. The child, who receives the sound either through earphones (air conduction) or through a bone vibrator (bone conduction), is instructed to hold up a finger when he hears a sound and to lower it when he hears no sound. The test seeks to determine how loud sounds at various frequencies must be before the child is able to hear them. Most audiometers deliver tones in 5 dB increments from 0 to 120 dB, with each dB level presented in various frequencies, usually starting at 125 Hz and increasing in octave intervals (doubling in frequency) to 8,000 Hz. The results of the test are plotted on a chart called an **audiogram** (see Figure 9.3 on pp. 358–359).

To obtain a hearing level on an audiogram, the child must be able to detect a sound at that level at least 50% of the time. For example, a child

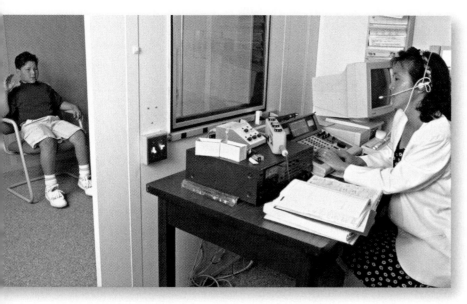

An audiometer generates tones of precise intensity and frequency.

## FIGURE 9.2  Expected auditory behaviors

**1 Month**
- Jumps or startles in response to loud noises
- Begins making gurgling sounds
- Responds to voice

**3 Months**
- Coos, babbles
- Turns to voices
- May quiet down to familiar voices close to ear
- Stirs or awakens from sleep when there is a loud sound relatively close by

**6 Months**
- Makes vocal sounds when alone; engages in vocal play
- Turns head toward sounds or when name is called and speaker is not visible
- Vocalizes when spoken to directly
- Imitates sounds

**9 Months**
- Responds differently to a cheerful versus angry voice
- Tries to copy the speech sounds of others
- Babbling acquires inflection

**12 Months**
- Locates a sound source by turning head (whether the sound is at the side, above, or below level)
- Ceases activity when parent's voice is heard
- Responds to own name
- Uses single words such as *mama* or *dada* correctly
- Vocalizes emotions
- Laughs spontaneously
- Disturbed by nearby noise when sleeping
- Imitates sounds and words
- Understands some familiar phrases or words
- Responds to music or singing
- Increases type and amount of babbling

**18 Months**
- Comes when called
- Responds to *no*
- Follows simple commands
- Uses 4–10 words in addition to *mama* or *dada*

**24 Months**
- Has vocabulary of more than 50 words
- Uses two words together
- Follows simple directions
- Responds to rhythm of music
- Uses voice for a specific purpose
- Shows understanding of many phrases used daily in life
- Plays with sound-making objects
- Uses well-inflected vocalization
- Refers to himself/herself by name
- Names a picture or object

*Source:* Adapted from Cleeland (1984); Gleason (1999); Northern and Downs (1991).

who has a 60 dB hearing loss cannot detect a sound until it is at least 60 dB loud, in contrast to a child with normal hearing, who would detect that same sound at a level between 0 and 10 dB.

## Speech Audiometry

**Speech audiometry** tests a person's detection and understanding of speech. A list of one- and two-syllable words is presented at different dB levels. The **speech reception threshold (SRT),** the dB level at which the individual can understand half of the words, is measured and recorded for each ear. It is important to recognize that while a child might identify single words 50% of the time when spoken at a given volume and frequency, that does not always translate into ability to follow conversational speech (Woolsey, 1999).

## Alternative Audiometric Techniques

Several alternative techniques have been developed for testing the hearing of children and individuals with severe disabilities who are not able to understand and follow conventional audiometry procedures (Roeser & Yellin, 1987). In **play audiometry,** the child is taught to perform simple but distinct activities, such as picking up a toy or putting a ball into a cup, whenever she hears the signal, either pure tones or speech. A similar procedure is **operant conditioning audiometry,** in which the child receives a token or a small candy when he pushes a lever in the presence of a light paired with a sound. No reinforcer is given for pushing the lever when the light and sound are off. Next, the sound is presented without the light. If the child pushes the lever in response to the sound alone, the examiner knows the child can hear that sound. **Behavior observation audiometry** is a passive assessment procedure in which the child's reactions to sounds are observed. A sound is presented at an increasing level of intensity until a response, such as head turning, eye blinking, or cessation of play, is reliably observed.

## Degrees of Hearing Loss

*Degree and frequency range of hearing loss*

Council for Exceptional Children
Content Standards for Beginning Teachers—D/HH: Effects of sensory input on the development of language and cognition (DH6K3) (also CC2K2).

Hearing loss is usually described by the terms *slight, mild, moderate, severe,* and *profound,* depending on the average hearing level, in decibels, throughout the frequencies most important for understanding speech (500 to 2,000 Hz). It is important to recognize, however, that no two children have exactly the same pattern of hearing, even if their responses on a hearing test are similar. Just as a single intelligence test cannot provide sufficient information to plan a child's educational program, the special education needs of a child with hearing loss cannot be determined from an audiometric test alone. Children hear sounds with differing degrees of clarity, and the same child's hearing ability may vary from day to day. Some children with very low levels of measurable hearing are able to benefit from hearing aids and can learn to speak. On the other hand, some children with less apparent hearing loss are not able to function well through the auditory channel and must rely on vision as their primary means of communication.

Figure 9.3 shows the audiograms of four children with mild, moderate, severe, and profound hearing loss and describes some of the effects. Although no audiogram depicting a slight hearing loss is shown, children who are unable to hear or discriminate speech sounds at less than 25 dB may experience major obstacles to learning (Bess, 1999; Schirmer, 2004). Even a minimal hearing loss of 15 dB that "may not be problematic for a linguistically sophisticated person who has disciplined attending skills … can sabotage the overall development of an infant or child who is in the process of learning language and acquiring knowledge" (Pakulski & Kaderavek, 2002, p. 97).

In years past, it was assumed that individuals who were deaf simply did not hear at all. But hearing loss occurs in many degrees and patterns, and nearly all deaf children have some amount of residual hearing. Modern methods of testing hearing and improved technology for the amplification of sound enable many children with even severe and profound hearing loss to use their residual hearing productively.

## Technologies that Amplify or Provide Sound

*Hearing Aids.*   A *hearing aid* is an amplification device; it makes sounds louder. Early versions indiscriminately amplified all sounds, which made them ineffective for most children with sensorineural hearing loss. Modern hearing aids can differentially amplify selected frequencies, and therefore can be tailored to each child's individual pattern of hearing loss (House, 1999).

There are dozens of kinds of hearing aids; they can be worn behind the ear, in the ear, on the body, or incorporated into eyeglass frames. Children can wear hearing aids in one or both ears (monaural or binaural aids). Whatever its shape, power, or size, a hearing aid picks up sound, magnifies its energy, and delivers this louder sound to the user's middle ear. In many ways, the hearing aid is like a miniature public address system, with a microphone, an amplifier, and controls to adjust volume and tone.

Although hearing aids help many children increase their awareness of sound, it is important to understand that hearing aids make sounds louder but not necessarily clearer. Thus, children who hear sounds with distortion will still experience distortion with hearing aids. The effect is similar to turning up the volume on an old transistor radio: you can make the music louder, but you cannot make it clearer. Even the most powerful hearing aids generally cannot enable children with severe and profound hearing losses to hear speech sounds beyond a distance of a few feet. A hearing aid cannot correct a hearing loss in the same way that eyeglasses or contact lenses correct vision or by itself enable a deaf child to function without additional special education services or supports. In all cases, it is the wearer of the hearing aid, not the aid itself, who does most of the work in interpreting conversation.

The earlier in life a child can be fitted with an appropriate hearing aid, the more effectively he will learn to use hearing for communication and awareness. Today, it is not at all unusual to see infants and preschool children wearing hearing aids; the improved listening conditions become an important part of the young child's speech and language development. To derive the maximum benefit from a hearing aid, a child should wear it throughout the day. Residual hearing cannot be effectively developed if the aid is removed or turned off outside the classroom.

It is difficult for any child to learn in a noisy classroom, but children who are deaf or hard of hearing are especially reliant on good classroom acoustics in order to hear and comprehend spoken language. Hearing aids offer minimal benefit in noisy and reverberant classrooms (Nelson, 2001). A signal-to-noise ratio (SNR) of at least +15 dB is considered necessary for students to achieve maximum benefit of a personal amplification device and their residual hearing (ASHA, 1995). An

*Hearing aids*

Council for Exceptional Children  Content Standards for Beginning Teachers—D/HH: Strategies for stimulating and using residual hearing (DH6K8).

To derive maximum benefit from a hearing aid, a child should wear it throughout the day.

**Mild Loss (41 to 55 dB)**

Vicki:

- Is able to understand face-to-face conversation with little difficulty
- Misses much of the discussion that goes on in her classroom–particularly if several children are speaking at once or if she cannot see the speaker clearly
- Has some classmates who are unaware she has a hearing loss
- Benefits from wearing a hearing aid
- Receives occasional speech and language assistance from a speech-language pathologist

**Audiogram for Vicki, who has a mild hearing loss**

**Moderate Loss (56 to 70 dB)**

Antoine:

- Without a hearing aid can only hear conversation if it is loud and clear
- Can hear male voices more easily than female voices (loss is less pronounced in the lower frequencies)
- Finds it impossible to follow most class discussions, even though his teacher arranges favorable seating for him
- Has impaired but intelligible speech
- Attends a part-time special class for children with hearing loss and is in a regular classroom for part of the day

**Audiogram for Antoine, who has a moderate hearing loss**

**FIGURE 9.3** Audiograms for students with mild, moderate, severe, and profound degrees of hearing loss and the effects of different degrees of hearing loss on speech and language and probable educational needs

## Severe Loss (71 to 90 dB)

Brante:

- Can hear voices only if they are very loud and 1 foot or less from her ear
- Wears a hearing aid, but it is unclear how much she gains from it
- Can distinguish most vowel sounds but hears only a few consonants
- Can hear a door slamming, a vacuum cleaner, and an airplane flying overhead
- Communicates by speech and signs
- Must always pay close visual attention to a person speaking with her
- Splits her school day between a special class and a regular classroom with an educational interpreter

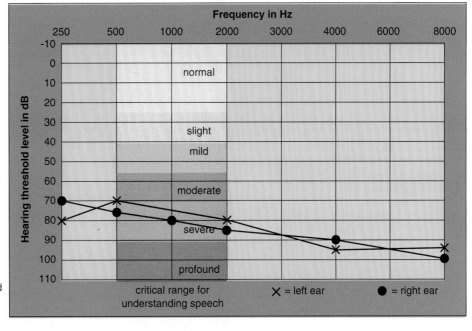

Audiogram for Brante, who has a severe hearing loss

---

## Profound Loss (91 dB or more)

Steve:

- Cannot hear conversational speech at all
- Has a hearing aid that helps him be aware of certain loud sounds, such as a fire alarm or a bass drum
- Uses vision as his primary modality for learning
- Uses American Sign Language as his first language and principal means of communication
- Has not developed intelligible speech
- Attends a residential school for the deaf

Audiogram for Steve, who has a profound hearing loss

ambient noise level of 35 dB or less will generally allow all speakers' voices to reach all students at the desired +15 dB SNR. However, classrooms today are more active and nosier than ever. When Knecht, Whitelaw, and Nelson (2000) recorded noise levels in 32 unoccupied elementary classrooms, they found only four with background noise levels within the recommended limit. The average ambient noise in most of the other classrooms was 10 dB to 15 dB above the ASHA guideline.

*Assistive Listening Devices.*    Group assistive listening devices can solve the problems caused by distance, noise, and reverberation in the classroom. In most systems, a radio link is established between the teacher and the children with hearing loss, with the teacher wearing a small microphone transmitter (often on the lapel, near the lips) and each child wearing a receiver that doubles as a personal hearing aid (Crandell & Smaldino, 2001a). An FM radio frequency is usually employed, and wires are not required, so teacher and students can move freely around the classroom. The FM device creates a listening situation comparable to the teacher's "being only 6 inches away from the child's ear at all times" (Ireland, Wray, & Flexer, 1988, p. 17).

*Cochlear Implants.*    Unlike hearing aids, which deliver amplified sound to the ear, a **cochlear implant** bypasses damaged hair cells and stimulates the auditory nerve directly. The implant is surgically placed under the skin behind the ear. An implant has four basic parts: an external *microphone,* which picks up sound from the environment; an external *speech processor,* which selects and arranges sounds picked up by the microphone; a *transmitter;* and a *receiver/stimulator,* which receives signals from the speech processor and converts them into electric impulses. *Electrodes* collect the impulses from the stimulator and send them directly to the brain via the auditory nerve (see Figure 9.4).

*Group listening devices*

Council for Exceptional Children    Content Standards for Beginning Teachers—D/HH: Strategies for stimulating and using residual hearing (DH6K8).

*Cochlear implants*

Council for Exceptional Children    Content Standards for Beginning Teachers—D/HH: Issues and trends in the field of education of individuals who are D/HH (DH1K4) (also DH3K2).

**FIGURE 9.4**    **Internal and external components of the cochlear implant**

Cochlear implant surgery usually takes 2 to 3 hours, and the child stays overnight in the hospital. About 4 weeks later, the child returns to the implant center for initial stimulation of the device and tune-up sessions over 2–3 days. An implant does not restore or create normal hearing. It can, however, give a deaf person a useful auditory understanding of the environment and help him or her to understand speech. Approximately 25,000 people worldwide have received cochlear implants since their approval by the Food and Drug Administration in 1989 (NIDCD, 2001). In the United States, some 14,000 people have implants; about half of these are children, most between the age of 2 and 6.

When coupled with intensive post-implantation therapy, cochlear implants can help young children acquire speech, language, developmental, and social skills. While there are still many questions to be answered about cochlear implants, initial research reports have described significant improvements in speech perceptions, speech production, and language skills compared to peers without cochlear implants (McKinley & Warren, 2000; Spencer, 2001). It is not yet known if there is an optimal age for implantation, but earlier implantation seems to yield better outcomes.

Tremendous controversy surrounds cochlear implants. Many members of the Deaf community are vehemently opposed to cochlear implants and consider the procedure to be a form of genocide of the Deaf culture (e.g., Laborit, 1998; Lane & Bahan, 1998). Luterman (1999) offers the following explanation of a position that is difficult for most hearing people to understand:

> People who have never heard do not experience hearing impairment as a loss. This is why they can believe, much to the consternation of the normally hearing population, that deafness is a cultural difference rather than a deficit. It would be analogous, for example, to those who had ESP thinking that the rest of us were terribly handicapped in our communication abilities, while we who do not possess ESP and have never had it do not feel the least handicapped. The only way we would is if those with ESP constantly reminded us of our deficiency and tried to "fix" us. (p. 75)

To read more about the contrasting views of deafness as a cultural difference or as a sensory impairment to be remedied, see Diversity & Exceptionality, "Defiantly Deaf," previously in this chapter, and Profiles & Perspectives, "Deafness: The Dilemma," which follows later in this chapter.

## Supports and Technologies That Supplement or Replace Sound

*Interpreters.*  Interpreting—signing the speech of a teacher or other speaker for a person who is deaf—began as a profession in 1964 with the establishment of a professional organization called the Registry of Interpreters for the Deaf (RID). Many states have programs for training interpreters, who must meet certain standards of competence to be certified by the RID. The organization was initially comprised primarily of freelance interpreters, who interpret primarily for deaf adults in situations such as legal or medical interactions.

The role of the *educational interpreter* (sometimes referred to as an *educational transliterator*) has made it possible for many students with hearing loss to enroll in and successfully complete postsecondary programs. There has also been greater use of educational interpreters in elementary and secondary classrooms (Chafin Seal, 2004; Schick, Williams, & Bolster, 1999). Duties of interpreters vary across schools; they are likely to perform tasks such as tutoring, assisting regular and special education teachers, keeping records, and supervising students with hearing loss (Cawthon, 2001).

*Speech-to-Text Translation.*  A fast-developing technology that promises to increase access by deaf students during live presentations, such as public or classroom lectures, is computer-aided speech-to-text translation. A leading example of this technology is the C-Print speech-to-text service developed at the National Technical Institute for the Deaf at the University of Rochester (Stinson, Elliot, McKee, & Francis, 2001). A trained captionist types the teacher's lecture and students' comments into a laptop computer using a shorthand code. Special

*Interpreters*

Council for Exceptional Children — Content Standards for Beginning Teachers—D/HH: Communication modes used by and with individuals who are hearing and those who are D/HH (DH6K5) (also DH4K3, DH6K1).

# Deafness: The Dilemma

*by Bonnie Tucker*

During the last twenty years, technological advances to assist people with hearing loss surpassed the expectation of many. Hearing aids improved tremendously, both with respect to quality and aesthetics. The newer aids block out background noise and emphasize sound in the speech range, which has enabled some severely hearing-impaired people to benefit from aids for the first time.... Cochlear implants have enabled some profoundly deaf people, both children and adults, to understand speech without having to rely on speechreading or interpreters; some cochlear implantees are able to converse on the voice telephone with strangers.

Twenty years ago I, for one, did not foresee these almost Orwellian transformations. Today, however, my vision for the future is unlimited. Given the rapidly advancing state of technology in this area, it is not unrealistic to assume that twenty years hence the technological advances of the past two decades will seem outmoded, even ancient. It is not unrealistic to assume that in twenty years cochlear implants will enable profoundly deaf people to understand speech in most circumstances, including on the telephone. We are not there yet, but we are on our way.

Many members of the Deaf community, including leaders of the National Association of the Deaf (NAD), ... do not want cochlear implants. They do not want to hear. They want their children to be Deaf, and to be a part of the Deaf world. "We like being Deaf," they state. "We are proud of our Deafness...." They claim the right to their own "ethnicity, with our own language and culture, the same way that Native Americans or Italians bond together"; they claim the right to "personal diversity," which is "something to be cherished rather than fixed and erased. And they strongly protest the practice of placing cochlear implants in children.... These same individuals, however, are among the strongest advocates for laws and special programs to protect and assist people with hearing loss. They argue fiercely for the need for interpreters, TTYs, telephone relay services, specially funded educational programs, and close-captioning, at no cost to themselves. On the one hand, therefore, they claim that deafness is not a disability, but a state of being, a "right" that should not be altered. On the other hand, they claim that deafness is a disability that society should compensate for by providing and paying for services to allow deaf people to function in society....

Do Deaf people have the right to refuse to accept new technology, to refuse to "fix" their Deafness if such repair becomes possible? Yes, absolutely. They do have the right, if they wish to exercise that right, to cherish their Deaf culture, their Deaf ethnicity, their "visually oriented" personal diversity. They have every right to choose not to fix their Deafness.... Do Deaf people have the right to demand that society pay for the resulting cost of that choice, however? No, I do not believe they do.

By way of analogy, suppose that blindness and quadriplegia were "curable" due to advanced technology. Blind people could be made to "see" via artificial means such as surgical implantation or three-dimensional eyeglasses; quadriplegic individuals could be made to "walk" and use their arms via artificial means such as surgical nerve implantation or specially built devices. Oh, the blind people might not see as perfectly as sighted people—they might still miss some of the fine print. And the quadriplegic individuals might walk with a limp or move their arms in a jerky fashion. But, for the most part, they would require little special assistance.

Suppose that 10 blind people chose not to make use of available technology for the reason that blindness is not a "disability," not something to be fixed, but that blind people are simply "auditory oriented," and 20 quadriplegic people chose not to make use of available technology for the reason that quadriplegics are simply "out-of-body oriented." How long will society agree to pay for readers, attendants, and other services and devices to assist those blind and quadriplegic individuals who have exercised their right to be diverse? More important, how long should society be asked to pay for such services and devices?

When technology advances to the extent that profoundly deaf people could choose to "hear"—which, eventually, it surely will—Deaf people will have to resolve the dilemma, both for reasons of practicality and morality.... Deaf people will have to decide whether to accept hearing or to remain Deaf. They have every right to choose the latter course. If they do so, however, they must assume responsibility for that choice and bear the resultant cost, rather than thrust that responsibility upon society.... As our grandparents used to say, "You can't have your cake and eat it too."

Bonnie Tucker is a professor of law at Arizona State University. Deaf since infancy, and unable to wear hearing aids, Dr. Tucker had cochlear implant surgery at the age of 52. She is the editor and part author of *Cochlear Implants: A Handbook* (McFarland, 1998).

*Source:* From Tucker, B. (1993). Deafness: 1993–2013—The dilemma. *The Volta Review, 95,* 105–108. Reprinted with permission from the Alexander Graham Bell Association for the Deaf and Hard of Hearing. **www.agbell.org**.

To further your understanding of and answer reflective questions about the issues presented here, go to Chapter 9's Profiles & Perspectives module on the Companion Website, **www.prenhall.com/heward**.

software translates the code (e.g., typing "kfe" produces "coffee"), and the text appears on a screen or a student's personal laptop computer monitor about 3 seconds after the words are spoken. The text display remains on the screen for approximately 1 minute, which provides students with much more time to consider the words than using an interpreter or speechreading would.

The system does not provide a verbatim translation of the lecture, which would be impossible at speech rates of 150 words per minute. Captionists are trained to eliminate redundancies, identify key points, and condense information on the fly, keeping as close as possible to the original (see Figure 9.5). Text files can be saved, edited, and printed after class. Students find the condensed C-Print notes easier to study than stenographer's transcripts (Elliot, Foster, & Stinson, 2002).

*Television Captioning.*   Today most regular programming on commercial and public network television, as well as many live newscasts and sporting events, is captioned (printed

*Speech-to-text translation and TV captioning*

Council for Exceptional Children   Content Standards for Beginning Teachers—D/HH: Communication modes used by and with individuals who are hearing and those who are D/HH (DH6K5) (also DH4K3, DH6K1).

---

## FIGURE 9.5   Sample from a lecture and corresponding C-Print notes

### Original Lecture

If you want to sell me the car, you are going to have to understand that process. You are out there with a car, and I am sitting here with some dollar amount that I am quite prepared to swap for the right car, but if you do not understand what my desires and concerns are, you don't have much chance of selling me the car. That is true whether you are a car dealer or car manufacturer or somebody trying to sell a car. We are looking at the process. The way the process worked in my case, I'll be completely open with you, I picked up the telephone and called an individual who was selling cars.

### C-Print Text

If you want to sell me the car, you are going to have to understand that process. If you do not understand what my desires and concerns are, you don't have much chance of selling me the car. That is true whether you are a car dealer or car manufacturer or an individual selling a car. We are looking at the process. The way it worked in my case is I telephoned an individual selling cars.

*Source:* From "C-Print: A Computerized Speech-to-Print Transcription System" by B. G. McKee, P. G. Giles, V. S. Everhart, M. S. Stinson, & J. B. Henderson, 1998, *Captionist Training Manual,* p. 43. Copyright 1998 by Rochester Institute of Technology. Reprinted with permission.

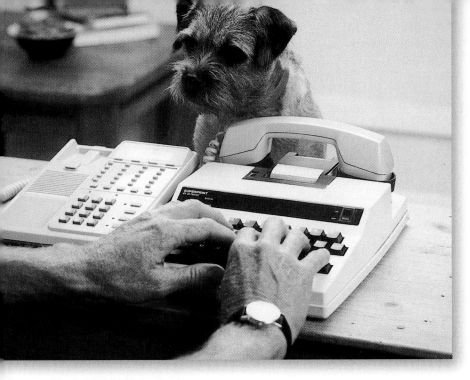

"Hearing dogs" are trained to alert a deaf person to important sounds such as a ringing telephone.

text appears at the bottom of the screen, similar to watching a film with subtitles), providing access to televised news and entertainment for deaf people. Since 1993, a federal law has required that all new television sets sold in the United States be equipped with an internal device that allows the user to position captions anywhere on the screen.

Lewis and Jackson (2001) found that deaf students comprehended more from scripts that were accompanied by video than they did by reading the scripts alone. This finding suggests that visual stimuli provide essential information deaf viewers can use to improve their comprehension. Lewis and Jackson suggest that acquiring "television literacy" (through the use of captioned videos in the classroom) might advance the reading skills of deaf students by exposing them to English vocabulary and syntax.

*Text Telephones.* The telephone served as a barrier to deaf people in employment and social interaction for many years, but acoustic couplers now make it possible to send immediate messages over conventional telephone lines in typed or digital form. Text telephones (TT) (originally called TTY or TDD systems) enable the user to send a typed message over telephone lines to anyone else who has a TT. As a result of the Americans with Disabilities Act, TTs are now available in most public places such as airports and libraries, and every state has a relay service that enables TT users to communicate with a person on a conventional telephone via an operator who relays the messages. Relay numbers are published in every phone directory.

*Alerting Devices.* Some individuals who are deaf or hard of hearing use special devices to alert them to certain sounds or events. For example, to signal the doorbell, a fire alarm, or an alarm clock, a sound- or vibration-sensitive switch can be connected to a flashing light or to a vibrator. Hearing-ear dogs are trained to alert a deaf person to important sounds in the environment.

## EDUCATIONAL APPROACHES

Over the years, many philosophies, theories, and specialized methods and materials have been developed for teaching children who are deaf and hard of hearing. Most of these approaches have been enthusiastically promoted by their advocates and critically denounced by others. Indeed, for more than 100 years people have waged an impassioned debate over how best to teach children who do not hear. Table 9.1 (pp. 366–367) highlights some key historical events and implications for the education of students with hearing loss.

The three major approaches to teaching deaf and hard of hearing students today are the oral/aural approach, total communication, and bilingual-bicultural approach. Regardless of instructional approach or the academic subject area at hand, the primary objective of all teachers of students with hearing loss is the development and use of language and communication skills.

*History of education of students who are D/HH*

Council for Exceptional Children — Content Standards for Beginning Teachers—VI: Major contributors to the field of education of individuals who are D/HH (DH1K5) (also DH7K1).

For the teacher of deaf and hard-of-hearing students, language is the curricular foundation on which the school day is built. The child's acquisition of language in face-to-face communication, reading, and writing is the focal point of instruction. The opportunity that content area instruction provides deaf and hard-of-hearing students to use language expressively and receptively is at least as important, and often considerably more important, than the specific concepts taught within individual subject areas. (Schirmer, 1997, p. 53)

## Oral/Aural Approaches

Educational programs with an oral/aural emphasis view speech as essential if students who are deaf are to function in the hearing world. Training in producing and understanding speech and language is incorporated into virtually all aspects of the child's education. A purely oral approach without any manual communication was used widely in the United States prior to the 1970s. Today, only about one-fourth of educational programs for students with hearing loss identify themselves as solely oral/aural programs (Meadow-Orlans et al., 1997).

A child who attends a program with an oral emphasis typically uses several means to develop residual hearing and the ability to speak as intelligibly as possible (P. Stone, 1997). Auditory, visual, and tactile methods of input are frequently used. Much attention is given to amplification, auditory training, speechreading, the use of technological aids, and, above all, talking. A few schools and classes maintain a purely oral environment and may even prohibit children from pointing, using gestures, or spelling out words to communicate. Children in these programs must express themselves and learn to understand others through speech alone. Other oral/aural programs also emphasize speech and listening skills but are more flexible and may use and encourage a variety of approaches to help students produce and understand spoken language.

Educators who use an oral approach acknowledge that teaching speech to children who are deaf is difficult, demanding, and time-consuming for the teacher, the parents, and—most of all—the student. Speech comes hard to the deaf child. The rewards of successful oral communication, however, are thought to be worth the effort. And indeed, most students with hearing losses no worse than severe can learn speech well enough to communicate effectively with hearing people. The best results are obtained with students who are enrolled in indisputably comprehensive oral programs or who are integrated most of the school day into regular education programs (Paul & Quigley, 1990).

*Auditory Learning.* Listening comprises 45% of daily communication for adults, and children spend up to 60% of the school day in situations where they are expected to be listening effectively (Crandell & Smaldino, 2001b). Many children with hearing loss have much more auditory potential than they actually use, and their residual hearing can be improved in the context of actual communication and daily experiences. All children with hearing loss, regardless of whether their preferred method of communication is oral (speech) or manual (signs), should receive training and practice with improving their listening skills.

*Auditory training* for young children with hearing loss begins by teaching awareness of sound. Parents might direct their child's attention to sounds such as a doorbell ringing or water running. They might then focus on localization of sound—for example, by hiding a radio somewhere in the room and encouraging the child to look for it. Discrimination of sounds is another important part of auditory training; a child might learn to notice the differences between a man's voice and a woman's voice, between a fast song and a slow song, or between the words "rack" and "rug." Identification of sounds comes when a child is able to recognize a sound, word, or sentence through listening.

**Oral/aural approach**

Council for Exceptional Children — Content Standards for Beginning Teachers—D/HH: Models, theories, and philosophies that provide the basis for education practice for individuals who are D/HH (DH1K2) (also DH4K2, DH4K3, DH6K5).

**Auditory training/learning**

Council for Exceptional Children — Content Standards for Beginning Teachers—D/HH: Strategies to facilitate cognitive and communicative development in individuals who are D/HH (DH6K7) (also DH4K3).

A combination of amplification and auditory training can help a child make the most of his residual hearing.

| TABLE 9.1 | A history of the education of students who are deaf or hard of hearing: Key events and implications | |
|---|---|---|
| **Date** | **Historical Event** | **Educational Implications** |
| **Late 16th century** | Pedro Ponce de Leon (1520–1584), an Augustinian monk and scholar, established in Spain a school for the deaf children of noble families. | This was the first educational program for exceptional children of any kind. |
| **18th century** | Schools for children who were deaf were set up in England, France, Germany, Holland, and Scotland. | Both oral and manual methods of instruction were used. |
| **1817** | The American Asylum for the Education of the Deaf and Dumb (renamed the American School for the Deaf) opened in Hartford, CT, under the leadership of Thomas Gallaudet and Laurent Clerc, a deaf French educator. | Children with hearing loss were among the first in the United States to receive special education. Gallaudet and Clerc used sign language as their method of instruction at the school. Some consider Clerc to be the father of deaf education in the United States. |
| **Early 19th century** | Students who were deaf were considered to be most appropriately served in asylums or special sanctuaries and removed from normal society. | The prevailing philosophy of the early 19th century was that persons who were deaf were incapable of benefiting from oral instruction. |
| **1864** | Gallaudet University (then called the National Deaf-Mute College) was founded. | Deaf students now had opportunity to pursue a postsecondary education in a setting that held high expectations for achievement. |
| **Mid- to late 19th century** | Instruction in speech and speechreading became widely available to students who were deaf throughout the United States. Several day schools were established for deaf children. Alexander Graham Bell criticized residential schools and the use of sign language, which he believed contributed to the segregation of deaf people. | Oral approaches dominated to such a great degree that the use of sign language in schools was officially prohibited at an international conference in 1880. It was not until many years later that schools relaxed their restrictions against the use of sign language. This era marked the beginning of what some have called "the Hundred Years War" over what methods of communication are best for deaf children. |
| **Mid- to late 20th century** | The majority of students whose deafness was caused by the rubella epidemics of the mid-1960s departed from the school-age population. | Enrollments in public residential schools for children with hearing impairments in the United States declined sharply as public school programs became more widely available. |

The focus today is on *auditory learning*—that is, teaching the child to learn to listen and to learn by listening instead of simply learning to hear (Ling, 1986). Advocates of auditory learning contend that the first three levels of auditory training—detecting, discriminating, and identifying sounds—are important but insufficient for developing the student's residual hearing. Auditory learning emphasizes a fourth and highest level of listening skills—the comprehension of meaningful sounds.

Some teachers find it helpful to conduct formal auditory training/learning sessions in which a child is required to use only hearing: he would have to recognize sounds and words without looking at the speaker. In actual practice, however, the student gains useful information from vision and the other senses to supplement the information received from hearing. Consequently, all senses should be effectively developed and constantly used.

*Speechreading.*   *Speechreading* is the process of understanding a spoken message by observing the speaker's face. Children with hearing loss, whether they have much or little residual hearing and whether they communicate primarily through oral or manual means,

**TABLE 9.1** *continued*

| Date | Historical Event | Educational Implications |
|------|------------------|--------------------------|
| 1960s | Reserach by linguist William Stokoe at Gallaudet showed that sign language used by the deaf community was a legitimate language in its own right. | What had been called "the Sign Language" was given a new name, American Sign Language (ASL). |
| 1968 | Congress funded the National Technical Institute for the Deaf (NTID) at the Rochester Institute for Technology. | NTID offers technical and vocational degree programs for deaf students. |
| 1970s | Total communication (TC) was adopted as the method of communication and instruction by the majority of deaf education programs. | TC attempts to present instructional content via simultaneous use of speech and sign language. While TC is still used frequently today, it has not raised the academic achievement of deaf students. |
| 1986 | In response to concerns about the academic and employment outcomes of deaf students, Congress established the Commission on Education of the Deaf (CED) with the Education of the Deaf Act of 1986. | CED began its 1988 report to Congress: "The present state of education for persons who are deaf in the United States is unsatisfactory. Unacceptably so" (p. viii). The report included 52 recommendations for improving the education of students with hearing loss. |
| 1988 | Students at Gallaudet University protested the hiring of a hearing president at their college in the Deaf President Now movement. | The movement led to the hiring of I. King Jordan as the first deaf president of Gallaudet, galvanized the deaf community, and increased the awareness of many in hearing society of the concerns and issues facing the Deaf culture. |
| 1989 | FDA approves use of cochlear implant surgery as means of bypassing the inner ear and providing a sense of sound directly through the auditory nerve for those with sensorineural hearing loss. | Educators have to find the most effective methods for helping deaf children receive maximum benefit from cochlear implants. There has been much controversy; many in the Deaf community view cochlear implants as a threat to the existence of their language and culture. |
| 1990s | The Deaf community increased its activism and self-advocacy, especially with regard to ASL as a Deaf child's first language. | There is increased interest in and use of a bilingual/bicultural (bi-bi) approach, in which ASL is the language of instruction and English is taught as a second language. |

use their vision to help them understand speech. Some sounds are readily distinguished by watching the speaker's lips. For example, the word "pail" begins with the lips in a shut position, whereas the lips are somewhat drawn together and puckered at the corners for the word "rail." Paying careful attention to a speaker's lips may help an individual with hearing loss derive important clues—particularly if she is also able to gain additional information through residual hearing, signs or gestures, facial expressions, and the context or situation.

Speechreading, however, is extremely difficult and has many limitations. About half of all English words have some other word(s) that appear the same in pronunciation; that is, although they sound quite different, they look alike on the lips. Words such as "bat," "mat," and "pat," for example, look exactly alike and simply cannot be discriminated by watching the speaker's lips. To complicate matters, visual clues may be blocked by a hand or a pencil, chewing gum, or a mustache. Many speakers are virtually unintelligible through speechreading; they may seem not to move their lips at all. In addition, it is extremely tiring to watch lips for a long time, and it may be impossible to do so at a distance, such as during a lecture.

Walker (1986) estimates that even the best speechreaders detect only about 25% of what is said through visual clues alone; "the rest is contextual piecing together of ideas and

*Speechreading*

Council for Exceptional Children — Content Standards for Beginning Teachers—D/HH: Strategies to facilitate cognitive and communicative development in individuals who are D/HH (DH6K7) (also DH4K2).

expected constructions" (p. 19). Shanny Mow (1973), a teacher who is deaf, graphically describes the frustrations of speechreading:

> Like the whorls on his fingertips, each person's lips are different and move in a peculiar way of their own. When young, you build confidence as you guess correctly "ball," "fish," and "shoe" on your teacher's lips. This confidence doesn't last. As soon as you discover there are more than four words in the dictionary, it evaporates. Seventy percent of the words when appearing on the lips are no more than blurs. Lipreading is a precarious and cruel art which rewards a few who have mastered it and tortures the many that have tried and failed. (pp. 21–22)

Despite the problems inherent in speechreading, it can be a valuable tool in a deaf or hard of hearing person's communication repertoire. Research shows that speechreading skills can be improved when deaf persons practice speechreading their own speech and others via computer-assisted video instruction (DeFilippo, Sims, & Gottermeier, 1995; Sims & Gottermeier, 1995). Initial evaluations of a computer-based, interactive videodisc program developed at Bloomsburg (Pennsylvania) University show promise in helping people with hearing loss make better use of their vision to decode speech (Slike, Thornton, Hobbis, Kokoska, & Job, 1995; Slike & Hobbis, 1998).

Figure 9.6 includes some tips for making your speech more accessible to an individual who is speechreading.

### Cued speech

*Council for Exceptional Children* Content Standards for Beginning Teachers—D/HH: Strategies to facilitate cognitive and communicative development in individuals who are D/HH (DH6K7) (also DH4K2).

*Cued Speech.*   Cued speech is a method of supplementing oral communication. It supplies a visual representation of spoken language by adding cues, in the form of hand signals near the chin, to assist in identifying syllabic and phonetic features of speech that cannot be distinguished through speechreading (Caldwell, 1997). The hand signals must be used in conjunction with speech; they are neither signs nor manual alphabet letters and cannot be read alone. Eight hand shapes are used to identify consonant sounds, and four locations identify vowel sounds. A hand shape coupled with a location gives a visual indication of a syllable. According to Cornett (1974), who developed the system, cued speech can give intensive language input to young children because it clarifies the patterns of spoken English and does not disrupt the natural rhythm of speech.

## Total Communication

### Total communication

*Council for Exceptional Children* Content Standards for Beginning Teachers—D/HH: Models, theories, and philosophies that provide the basis for education practice for individuals who are D/HH (DH1K2) (also DH4K2, DH4K3, DH6K5).

Educational programs with an emphasis on **total communication** (also called *simultaneous communication*, or *simcom*) advocate the use of a variety of forms of communication to teach English to students with hearing loss. Practitioners of total communication maintain that the simultaneous presentation of English language by speech and manual communication (signing and fingerspelling) makes it possible for children to use either one or both types of communication (Hawkins & Brawner, 1997). Since its introduction as a teaching philosophy in the 1960s, total communication has become the most widely used method of instruction in schools for the deaf. A survey of 137 early intervention programs for deaf and hard of hearing students in 39 states found that 66% of the programs used total communication (Meadow-Orlans et al., 1997).

### Manually coded English and fingerspelling

*Council for Exceptional Children* Content Standards for Beginning Teachers—D/HH: Strategies to facilitate cognitive and communicative development in individuals who are D/HH (DH6K7) (also DH4K2).

*Manually Coded English.*   Teachers who practice total communication generally speak as they sign and make a special effort to follow the form and structure of spoken English as closely as possible. Several English-based sign systems have been designed for educational purposes, with the intention of facilitating the development of reading, writing, and other language skills in students with hearing loss. Manually coded English refers to several educationally oriented sign systems, such as Signing Essential English (commonly known as SEE I) (Anthony, 1971), Signing Exact English (SEE II) (Gustason, Pfetzing, & Zawolkow, 1980), and Signed English (Bornstein, 1974). While manually coded English borrows many signs and incorporates some of the features of American Sign Language (to be discussed), it also seeks to follow correct English usage and word order. Unfortunately, deaf

**FIGURE 9.6** **Tips for communicating with someone who is deaf**

When presented with an opportunity to communicate with a person who is deaf, many people with normal hearing are unsure of themselves. As a result, they may avoid deaf people altogether or use ineffective and frustrating strategies when they do attempt to communicate. The following tips for facilitating communication were suggested by the Community Services for the Deaf program in Akron, Ohio. These tips provide basic information about three common ways that deaf persons communicate: through speechreading, with sign language or the assistance of an interpreter, and by written communication. Usually, the person will indicate the approach with which he is most comfortable.

If the person relies mainly on speechreading, here are things you can do to help:

- Face the person and stand or sit no more than four feet away.
- The room should have adequate illumination, but don't seat yourself in front of a strong or glaring light.
- Try to keep your whole face visible.
- Speak clearly and naturally and not too fast.
- Don't exaggerate your mouth movements.
- Don't raise the level of your voice.
- Some words are more easily read on the lips than others are. If you are having a problem being understood, try substituting different words.
- It may take a while to become used to the deaf person's speech. If at first you can't understand what she is saying, don't give up.
- Don't hesitate to write down any important words that are missed.

If the deaf person communicates best through sign language (and you do not), it will probably be necessary to use an interpreter. Here are some considerations to keep in mind:

- The role of the interpreter is to facilitate communication between you and the person who is deaf. The interpreter should not be asked to give opinions, advice, or personal feelings.
- Maintain eye contact with the deaf person and speak directly to him. The deaf person should not be made to take a back seat in the conversation. For example, say, "How are you today?" instead of "Ask him how he is today."
- Remain face-to-face with the deaf person. The best place for the interpreter is behind you and a little to your side. Again, avoid strong or glaring light.
- Remember, it is the interpreter's job to communicate everything that you and the deaf person say. Don't say anything that you don't want to be interpreted.

Written messages can be helpful in exchanging information. Consider the following:

- Avoid the temptation to abbreviate your communication.
- Write in simple, direct language.
- The deaf person's written English may not be grammatically correct, but you will probably be able to understand it. One deaf person, for example, wrote, "Pay off yesterday, finish me," to convey the message, "I paid that loan off yesterday."
- Use visual aids, such as pictures, diagrams, and business cards.
- Don't be afraid to supplement your written messages with gestures and facial expressions.
- Written communication has limitations, but it is often more effective than no communication at all.

students must often learn and use two or more sign language systems, depending on the person with whom they are communicating.

*Fingerspelling.*    *Fingerspelling,* or the manual alphabet, is used to spell out proper names for which no signs exist and to clarify meanings. It consists of 26 distinct hand positions, one for each English letter. A one-hand manual alphabet is used in the United States and Canada (see Figure 9.7). Some manual letters—such as "C," "L," and "W"—resemble the shape of

**FIGURE 9.7** The manual alphabet used to fingerspell English in North America

printed English letters, whereas others—such as "A," "E," and "S"—have no apparent similarity. As in typewriting, each word is spelled out letter by letter.

Some educators have expressed concern about the quality of signing in many total communication classrooms, noting the linguistic inconsistency in the signing behavior of teachers. Although English is promoted as the primary language base in total communication programs, Pidgin Sign English (PSE)—a mixture of English, ASL, and invented signs that represents no standard language—best describes the way in which most teachers tend to sign (Stewart, 1992).

Schirmer (2004) gives two reasons why she believes total communication is going out of favor in deaf education:

> One reason is that using every communication technique and mode available is unrealistic. Teachers typically emphasize speech and audition at the expense of sign language, or vice versa. And students attend more to one mode than to the other.
>
> A second reason is that total communication uses speech and sign language simultaneously; and,... it is not possible to speak and use ASL at the same time. (pp. 441–442)

*ASL*

Council for Exceptional Children — Content Standards for Beginning Teachers—D/HH: Communication modes used by and with individuals who are hearing and those who are D/HH (DH6K5) (also DH4K3, DH6K1).

## American Sign Language and the Bilingual-Bicultural Approach

**American Sign Language (ASL)** is the language of the Deaf culture in the United States and Canada. Although the sign languages used by native deaf speakers were once thought to be nonlanguages (alinguistic), work by the linguist William Stokoe (Stokoe, 1960; Stokoe, Armstrong, & Wilcox, 1995) showed that ASL is a legitimate language in its own right rather than an imperfect variation of spoken English. ASL is a visual-spatial language in which the shape, location, and movement pattern of the hands; the intensity of motions;

and the signer's facial expressions all communicate meaning and content. Because ASL has its own rules of phonology, morphology, syntax, semantics, and pragmatics, it does not correspond to spoken or written English (Drasgow, 1998). Articles, prepositions, tenses, plurals, and word order are expressed differently from English. It is as difficult to make precise word-for-word translations between ASL and English as it is to translate many foreign languages into English word for word.

Some ASL signs are *iconic*; that is, they convey meaning through hand shapes or motions that look like or appear to imitate or act out their message. In making the sign for "cat," for example, the signer seems to be stroking feline whiskers on her face; in the sign for "eat," the hand moves back and forth into an open mouth. Most signs, however, have little or no iconicity; they do not resemble the objects or actions they represent. If sign language were simply a form of pantomime, then most nonsigners would be able to understand it with relative ease. But the vast majority of signs cannot be guessed by people who are unfamiliar with sign language.

Several researchers have found that children as young as 5 months of age are able to produce and understand signs effectively (e.g., Maestas y Moores & Moores, 1980; Orlansky & Bonvillian, 1985). "When deaf children have full visual access to a natural signed language, they acquire it in the same effortless manner as hearing children acquire a spoken language" (Drasgow, 1998, p. 334).

During the 1990s the Deaf community as well as a growing number of both hearing and deaf special educators, began calling for the use of ASL as the language of instruction (Baker & Baker, 1997; Drasgow, 1998; Mahshie, 1995; Pittman & Huefner, 2001; Strong, 1995). They believe that ASL provides a natural pathway to linguistic competence and that English is better learned in the context of a **bilingual-bicultural (bi-bi) approach** after the child has mastered his native or first language (ASL). Proponents of this model view deafness as a cultural and linguistic difference, not a disability, and recognize ASL as the deaf child's natural language. The goal of the bilingual-bicultural education approach is to help deaf students become bilingual adults who are competent in their first language, ASL, and can read and write with competence in their second language, English.

The basic theoretical argument for bilingual education is that students who have a solid foundation in their native language (L1) will be able to use their literacy-related L1 skills as a springboard for learning the majority second language (L2) (Cummins, 1989). Ewolt

*Although some signs, such as "cat" and "eat" are iconic—they look like the objects or actions they represent—most are not.*

*Bilingual-bicultural approach*

Council for Exceptional Children

Content Standards for Beginning Teachers—D/HH: Models, theories, and philosophies that provide the basis for education practice for individuals who are D/HH (DH1K2) (also DH4K2, DH4K3, DH6K5).

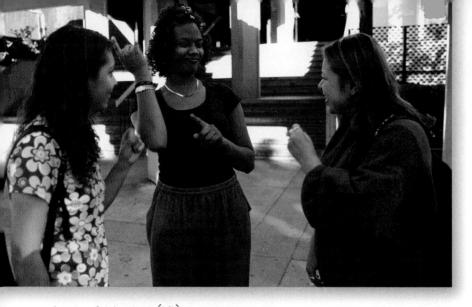

American Sign Language (ASL) is a legitimate language with its own vocabulary, syntax, and grammatical rules. It does not correspond to spoken or written English.

(1996) suggests that a top-down bilingual-bicultural approach that encourages deaf students to pursue "the construction of meaning through relevant, enjoyable, natural communication" (p. 294) will overcome their lack of knowledge of sentence form and print characteristics.

Some related support for the bi-bi approach can be found in research finding a correlation between early exposure to and development of fluency in ASL and increased competence and English literacy (Prinz et al., 1996; Strong & Prinz, 1997). However, Mayer and Akamatsu (1999) question the extent of L1-L2 interdependence when the two languages under consideration are a native sign language and the written form of an oral language. They also point out the logical inconsistency and danger of not providing deaf students with direct instruction and practice in the bottom-up literacy skills such as English language principles and phonics just because those are the skills with which they have the most difficulty. To date, although the rhetoric advocating for bi-bi is high and many programs have been implemented, there are few objective data reporting outcomes and evaluating what features of such programs are and are not effective (Schirmer, 2001).

One important task for IEP teams for students who are deaf or hard of hearing is careful consideration and documentation of the individual communications needs of each student. To learn about one systematic way of doing so, see "Considering the Communication Needs of Students Who Are Deaf or Hard of Hearing," in Chapter 9's Teaching & Learning module on the Companion Website, **www.prenhall.com/heward**.

## EDUCATIONAL PLACEMENT ALTERNATIVES

*Placement options*

Council for Exceptional Children    Content Standards for Beginning Teachers—Common Core: Demands of learning environments (CC5K1) (also DH1K4, DH5K2).

In most areas of the United States, parents and students now have the option of choosing between local public school programs and residential school placement. Today, approximately 82% of children who are deaf or hard of hearing attend local public schools: 45% receive most of their education in regular classrooms, 19% attend resource rooms for part of the school day, 22% are served in separate classrooms, and 7% attend special schools (U.S. Department of Education, 2004). Most students with hearing loss who are included in regular classrooms are hard of hearing and have hearing losses of less than 90 dB.

Of the 6.6% of students with hearing loss who attend residential schools, about one-third live at home with their families and commute to the school. More than 90% of the students currently enrolled in residential schools have severe and profound prelingual hearing loss. Nearly one-third of the students with hearing loss served in residential schools have additional disabilities.

Examining the question of where students who are deaf should be educated yields some research evidence—and much strong opinion—to support both inclusive and segregated settings. With the increased emphasis on inclusion, some question the effectiveness and appropriateness of residential placements for any student. Research, however, has not found that residential schools for the deaf contribute to academic or social deficits in students. On the contrary, some studies suggest that residential schooling may be the most effective placement for certain students. For example, Braden, Maller, and Paquin (1993) report that the performance IQs of children with hearing loss who were educated in residential schools increased over a 3- to 4-year period but that the scores of similar students in regular school day programs did not.

> The results of this study clearly disprove the belief that placement in residential, segregated programs invariably inhibits cognitive abilities. The assumption that children with hearing loss are best served in mainstream settings should be suspended until additional information is available regarding placement effects on such children's cognitive, social and academic development. (p. 432)

As Bat-Chava (2000) notes, where a child who is deaf is educated also influences the likelihood of his or her cultural identity. In schools in which oral English is the language of instruction, supplemented by fingerspelling and English-based sign systems, students are more likely to view hearing loss as a disability. Schools in which ASL is the language of instruction foster the perspective of deafness as a culture.

In a study of the effects of inclusion on the academic achievement of high school students who are deaf, Kluwin (1993) reported that although those students who were included in regular classrooms for academic content fared better on achievement measures than did students who spent all or most of the day in a separate class, the difference may have been the result of curriculum programming and class selection, not the actual place where instruction took place. After assessing the self-concepts of 90 deaf secondary students across different educational placements, Van Gurp (2001) concluded there were academic advantages to more integrated, resource room–type placements and social advantages in attending segregated schools.

Cawthon (2001) found that elementary teachers in inclusive classrooms directed about half as many utterances to deaf students than they did to hearing students and that educational interpreters were critical factors in how well the deaf students understood and participated in classroom discourse and learning activities. The skill level of an educational interpreter plays a major role in the success and appropriateness of a regular classroom placement for students who are deaf (Schick et al., 1999). An educational interpreter must provide the deaf or hard of hearing student with all speech and other auditory information in the classroom, a formidable task for the most highly skilled interpreter. In one study, only 15% of 221 educational interpreters had earned an associate's degree in interpreting (Jones, Clark, & Soltz, 1997); another study found that only 4 of 30 interpreters had attended an interpreter training program (Schick & Williams, 1994). After examining videotaped performances of 59 educational interpreters, Schick et al. (1999) reported that fewer than half performed at a level considered minimally acceptable. The authors concluded that "many deaf children receive an interpretation of classroom discourse that may distort and inadequately represent the information being communicated" (p. 144).

A skilled interpreter in the classroom is no guarantee that students with hearing loss will receive and participate in accurate communication. Garay (2003) recommends that deaf students be taught how to effectively use interpreters: for example, how to let interpreters know when they do not understand something, and how to appropriately and effectively indicate that they have something to ask the teacher or contribute to the class discussion.

In an effort to identify strategies to overcome barriers to meaningful participation by students with hearing loss in general education classrooms, Stinson and Liu (1999) conducted observations and focus groups with elementary general education teachers, teachers of the deaf, interpreters, notetakers, deaf and hard of hearing students, and their hearing classmates. The authors organized their findings into a list of 16 specific strategies to make placement in the regular classroom educationally beneficial. They suggested several strategies for each type of individual in the classroom (e.g., teacher, interpreter, hearing peers). Stinson and Liu made the following recommendations for students with hearing loss:

- Be responsible for taking the initiative in the classroom and believe the outcome will be at least somewhat successful.
- Have and use communication skills for participating in the regular classroom (e.g., repairing miscommunications, taking turns).

*Inclusion*

Council for Exceptional Children Content Standards for Beginning Teachers—D/HH: Impact of educational placement options with regard to cultural identity and linguistic, academic, and social-emotional development (DH3K1) (also DH1K4, DH5K1).

- When participating in small-group learning activities, carry out a specific task and share the information with the group.

While full inclusion in regular classrooms has benefited some deaf students, all of the professional and parent organizations involved with educating students who are deaf have issued position statements strongly in favor of maintaining a continuum of placement options (e.g., Commission on Education of the Deaf, 1988; National Association of the Deaf, 2002). Moores (1993), a respected leader in the field of deaf education, voiced the perspective of many deaf educators and parents:

> For many deaf children the concept of total inclusion, as currently promulgated, could in reality be exclusionary in practice. Placing a deaf child in a classroom in physical contiguity to hearing children does not automatically provide equal access to information. In fact, it can be isolating, both academically and socially. (p. 251)

As with all learners, we should never overlook the most fundamental factor in determining how successful a student will be in the regular classroom (or any other placement): quality of instruction. After studying the math achievement of 215 secondary students with hearing loss who were either in self-contained classrooms or mainstreamed into regular classes with or without an interpreter, Kluwin and Moores (1989) concluded, "Quality of instruction is the prime determinant of achievement, regardless of placement" (p. 327).

## Postsecondary Education

A growing number of educational opportunities are available to students with hearing loss after completion of high school. The oldest and best known is Gallaudet University in Washington, DC, which offers a wide range of undergraduate and graduate programs in the liberal arts, sciences, education, business, and other fields. The National Technical Institute for the Deaf (NTID), located at the Rochester Institute of Technology, provides wide-ranging programs in technical, vocational, and business-related fields such as computer science, hotel management, photography, and medical technology. Both Gallaudet and NTID are supported by the federal government, and each enrolls approximately 1,500 students who are deaf or hard of hearing.

More than 150 other institutions of higher education have developed accredited programs specifically for students with hearing loss (Rawlings, Karchmer, Allen, & DeCaro, 1999). Among these are four regional postsecondary programs that enroll substantial numbers of students with hearing loss: St. Paul (Minnesota) Technical-Vocational Institute, Seattle (Washington) Central Community College, the Postsecondary Education Consortium at the University of Tennessee, and California State University at Northridge.

The percentage of students with hearing loss who attend postsecondary educational programs has risen dramatically in the past 20 years. About 40% of all students with hearing loss go on to receive higher education (Connor, 1986). It is hoped that the increase in postsecondary programs will expand vocational and professional opportunities for deaf adults.

## CURRENT ISSUES AND FUTURE TRENDS

Given the large percentage of children with hearing loss who are educated in regular classrooms for most of the day, it is likely that oral/aural and total communication methods of instruction will continue to be used. Speech, after all, is the most widely used form of communication among teachers and students in regular classes. At the same time, an increasing percentage of the deaf children served in special schools and self-contained classrooms will be taught with the bilingual-bicultural approach, where ASL is the language of instruction.

Educators, scientists, philosophers, and parents—both hearing and deaf—have for many years debated the most appropriate instructional methods for children who are deaf. The controversy continues today. In the past, however, fundamental disagreement focused on the extent to which deaf children should express language through speech and perceive

Council for Exceptional Children Content Standards for Beginning Teachers—D/HH: Model programs, including career/vocational and transition, for individuals who are D/HH (DH7K1) (also DH10K2).

the communication of others through speechreading and residual hearing. Today, the focal point has switched to which language modality—auditory or visual—best suits a child's acquisition of an initial language. Research has yet to provide (and perhaps never will provide) a definitive answer to the question of which communication method is best. There is general agreement, however, that educational programs for students who are deaf leave much room for improvement.

Different children communicate in different ways. Some children with hearing loss, unfortunately, have experienced deep frustration and failure because of rigid adherence to an oral-only program. They have left oral programs without having developed a usable avenue of communication. Equally unfortunate is the fact that other children with hearing loss have not been given an adequate opportunity to develop their auditory and oral skills because they were placed in educational programs that did not provide good oral instruction. In both cases, children have been unfairly penalized. Every child who is deaf should have access to an educational program that uses a communication method best suited to her unique abilities and needs. Mahshie (1995) recommends letting the child choose her first language:

> In environments where the Deaf child encounters both spoken and signed language separately—as whole languages—during the course of natural interactions, it has become apparent to both parents and professionals that the child will be the guide regarding his or her predisposition toward a more oral or more visual language. In this win-win situation, the choice of a first language is clearly the child's. (p. 73).

Early and continued access to language and the communication modality best suited to their individual needs and preferences, effective instruction with meaningful curriculum, and self-determination are the keys to increasing the number of deaf or hard of hearing people who are able to access and enjoy the full spectrum of educational, social, vocational, and recreational opportunities society has to offer.

*Choosing auditory or visual language modality*

Council for Exceptional Children — Content Standards for Beginning Teachers—D/HH: Issues and trends in the field of education of individuals who are D/HH (DH1K4) (also DH6K1, DH6K5).

# Tips for Beginning Teachers

*by Douglas Jackson*

## VISUALIZE, INTERNALIZE, REFLECT

As teachers, we are responsible for covering a variety of academic courses using spoken and/or signed language; for addressing the auditory, speech, and other needs of our students; and for documenting our efforts on IEPs thicker than some metropolitan phone books. With all of this in mind, our task becomes how to do all of this effectively and successfully.

- Visualize what you want to accomplish and how you want to accomplish it. Imagine the obstacles in your way (time and resource limitations, red tape, etc.) and how you can overcome them (collaboration, grants, activities).
- When you learn new skills or information, whether they are new signs or Visual Phonics or making PowerPoint presentations, internalize the new skills and information so that they are entwined with your personality, sensibilities, and particular gifts as an educator.
- Take time to reflect. Think about what worked, what didn't, what you could do differently in the future, and what's next.

## KNOCK DOWN THE CLASSROOM WALLS

We are never more powerful than when we realize not only our strengths but also our weaknesses.

- Use your resources. There are dozens of people in your school who can do things that you can't do and who know things that you don't know. Their skills and knowledge can benefit both you and your students.

- Communicate and collaborate with your peers. You can begin to foster this communication and collaboration by sharing your ideas and materials. Everyone has a different perspective that can be helpful in difficult situations in the classroom with students or outside the classroom with parents.

## KNOCK DOWN THE SCHOOL'S WALLS

Beyond your school walls are doctors, lawyers, artists, business owners, police officers, and civic and government leaders. These professionals can teach your students things they cannot always learn in a classroom.

- Create partnerships. Identify professionals who are willing to become potential partners with your class by sharing their time, skills, and knowledge—or those who are interested in mentoring specific students. In this way you can become an educational bridge between your students and these professionals.
- Design activities (simulations, presentations, art, drama, etc.) to maximize the impact of these work-world opportunities. Try asking your professional partners if they have any feedback or input for you.

## PICK YOUR BATTLES

As educators we are surrounded by situations crying out for change, challenges we feel compelled to take on but battles we can't always fight simultaneously. Pick the battles that are most important and devote your energy, creativity, and passion to them.

- Choose initiatives that make your school a better place for your students. Hold off (for now) on those that don't seem to have a clear outcome or impact.
- Create opportunities in your class to infuse the curriculum with hands-on, meaningful lessons that connect with your students.
- Develop a list of the goals, behaviors, and values that are important to you as an educator. This will ultimately help you decide which battles to pick when they all seem worth fighting.

## IMAGINE YOURSELF SITTING IN THOSE DESKS

Imagine that you are lost in the middle of the night in a broken-down car on a stretch of deserted highway. As students, we have all felt that way—confused, lost, and hopeless. That's not what we want for our students.

Use your skills, experience and tools. We have specific knowledge that can help struggling students. Do not be afraid to use any and all tools available to you—exhausting all possibilities—to enable your students to navigate their particular problem areas with success.

## ENJOY THE RIDE

Sometimes I find myself walking down the hall of my school, obsessing about this meeting or that bit of paperwork or whatever the slings and arrows of outrageous bureaucracy happen to be that day. I will look up and see a small child walking down the hall, wide-eyed with the many possibilities of educational discovery in front of her. And when I look up and see this, I realize that we have the coolest job in the world. We get to be eyewitnesses for so many amazing voyages of discovery.

# KEY TERMS AND CONCEPTS

 To print your own set of SAFMED flash cards for studying and mastering these terms, go to the Companion Website, **www.prenhall.com/heward**.

American sign language (ASL), p. 370
audiogram, p. 354
audiometer, p. 354
auditory training, p. 365
bilingual-bicultural approach, p. 371
cochlear implant, p. 360
conductive hearing loss, p. 351
cued speech, p. 368
Deaf culture, p. 342
deaf, p. 342
decibel (dB), p. 345
fingerspelling, p. 369

hard of hearing, p. 342
hearing aid, p. 357
hertz (Hz), p. 346
oral/aural approach, p. 365
otitis media, p. 353
postlingual hearing loss, p. 351
prelingual hearing loss, p. 351
residual hearing, p. 342
sensorineural hearing loss, p. 351
speech reception threshold, p. 356
speechreading, p. 366
total communication, p. 368

# SUMMARY

## Definitions

- Hearing loss exists on a continuum from mild to profound, and most special educators distinguish between children who are deaf and those who are hard of hearing. A deaf child is not able to understand speech through the ears alone. A hard of hearing child is able to use hearing to understand speech, generally with the help of a hearing aid.
- Many Deaf persons do not view hearing loss as a disability. Like other cultural groups, members of the Deaf community share a common language (ASL) and social practices.
- Sound is measured by its intensity (decibels [dB]) and frequency (Hertz [Hz]); both dimensions are important in considering the special education needs of a child with a hearing loss. The frequencies most important for understanding speech are 500 to 2,000 Hz.

## Characteristics

- Deaf children—especially those with a prelinguistic loss of 90 dB or greater—are at a great disadvantage in acquiring English literacy skills, especially reading and writing.
- The speech of children with hearing loss may be difficult to understand because they omit speech sounds they cannot hear, speak too loudly or softly, speak in an abnormally high pitch, speak with poor inflection, and/or speak at an improper rate.
- Deaf and hard of hearing students lag far behind their hearing peers in academic achievement, and the achievement gap usually widens as they get older.
- Children with severe to profound hearing losses often report feeling isolated and unhappy in school, particularly when their socialization with other children with hearing loss is limited.
- Many deaf individuals choose membership in the Deaf community and culture.

## Prevalence

- Students with hearing loss represent about 1.2% of all school-age students receiving special education.

## Types and Causes of Hearing Loss

- Hearing loss is described as conductive (outer or middle ear) or sensorineural (inner ear) and unilateral (in one ear) or bilateral (in both ears).
- A prelingual hearing loss occurs before the child has developed speech and language; a postlingual hearing loss occurs after that time.
- Causes of congenital hearing loss include genetic factors, maternal rubella, heredity, congenital cytomegalovirus (CMV), and prematurity.
- Causes of acquired hearing loss include otitis media, meningitis, Ménière's disease, and noise exposure.

## Identification and Assessment

- Auditory brain-stem response and otoacoustic emission are two methods of screening for hearing loss in infants.
- A formal hearing test generates an audiogram, which graphically shows the intensity of the faintest sound an individual can hear 50% of the time at various frequencies.
- Hearing loss is classified as slight, mild, moderate, severe, or profound, depending on the degree of hearing loss.

## Technologies and Supports

- Technologies that amplify or provide sound include hearing aids, assistive listening devices, and cochlear implants.
- Technologies and supports that supplement or replace sound include educational interpreters, speech-to-text translation, television captioning, text telephones, and alerting devices.

## Educational Approaches

- The oral/aural approach views speech as essential if students are to function in the hearing world; much emphasis is given to amplification, auditory training, speech-reading, the use of technological aids, and, above all, talking.
- Total communication uses speech and simultaneous manual communication via signs and fingerspelling in English word order.
- In the bilingual-bicultural approach, deafness is viewed as a cultural and linguistic difference, not a disability; and ASL is used as the language of instruction.

## Educational Placement Alternatives

- Forty-five percent of children with hearing impairments attend regular classrooms, 19% attend resource rooms for part of the school day, 22% are served in separate classrooms, and 6.6% go to residential schools.
- All of the professional and parent organizations involved in deaf education have issued position statements strongly in favor of maintaining a continuum of placement options.

## Current Issues and Future Trends

- Given the large percentage of children with hearing loss who are educated in regular classrooms for most of the day, it is likely that oral/aural and total communication methods of instruction will continue to be used.
- The bilingual-bicultural approach will probably be used with a growing percentage of the deaf children served in special schools and self-contained classrooms.
- Although technology holds much promise for addressing the communication problems faced by deaf and hard of hearing people, many leaders of the deaf culture do not view deafness as a disability and oppose efforts to "cure" it or make them more like the mainstream hearing culture.
- Access to the language and communication modality best suited to their individual needs and preferences, effective instruction with meaningful curriculum, and self-advocacy are the keys to improving the future for people who are deaf or hard of hearing.

To check your comprehension of chapter contents, go to the Guided Review and Quiz modules in Chapter 9 of the Companion Website, **www.prenhall.com/heward**.

# BLINDNESS AND
# LOW VISION

# Featured Teacher ──────────

### JEANNA MORA DOWSE

PINON AND GANADO UNIFIED
SCHOOL DISTRICTS
APACHE COUNTY, ARIZONA

*Education—Teaching Credentials—Experience*
- A.A., nursing, New Mexico State University, 1986
- B.S., elementary education, Texas Tech University, 1991
- M.A., visual impairment, University of Arizona, 1997
- Arizona standard elementary education, K–8; Arizona English as a second language, K–12; Arizona standard visually impaired, K–12
- 7 years as a teacher of students with visual impairments

*Current Teaching Position and Students*     I am an itinerant teacher of children with visual impairments (VI) in two rural school districts in Apache County. I have a caseload of nine students in the Pinon Unified School District and eight students in Ganado. My students range in age from 4 to 17 years old and are in preschool through ninth grade. All of my students are members of the Navajo tribe. Many are from families that receive welfare. Some of my students speak both Navajo and English, some have been identified as limited English proficient, and some are not fluent in either language.

*IEP Goals*     The Arizona State Department of Education requires that 75% of a student's IEP goals be based on the Arizona State Curriculum Standards. Most of my students are able to access the general curriculum with adaptations or modifications. It is very important for me to consult with the classroom teachers in order to identify IEP goals and objectives that will accomplish this. Most of my students need help with literacy skills, understanding their visual impairment, and learning how to self-advocate for needed accommodations. Here are some examples of IEP goals and objectives for several of my students this year:

*Annual goal.*   The student will complete the braille program "Patterns: Reading-Readiness Level" (red) with 90% accuracy as documented by program guidelines and recorded by a certified VI teacher.

*Short-term objective 1.*   The student will tactually identify and then verbalize the letters *a–m* in braille as documented by mastery tests.

*Short-term objective 2.*   The student will tactually identify and then verbalize the letters *n–z* in braille as documented by mastery tests.

*Annual goal.*   The student will identify characters in a story and retell the story in sequence with 90% accuracy when five different stories are read aloud on five different occasions.

*Short-term objective 1.*   The student will listen to a variety of story boxes and verbally and tactually identify the main characters in the story with 90% accuracy.

## Focus Questions

- In what ways does loss of vision affect learning?

- How does the age at which vision is lost affect the student?

- Normally sighted children enter school with a great deal of knowledge about trees. How can a teacher help a student who is congenitally blind learn about trees?

- What compensatory skills do students with visual impairments need most?

- How do the educational goals and instructional methods for children with low vision differ from those for children who are blind?

*Short-term objective 2.*   The student will listen to a variety of story boxes and will verbally retell a story in sequence with 90% accuracy.

*Annual goal.*   The student will use interpersonal skills to express to teachers and coaches the need for adaptations or modifications for his visual impairment.

*Short-term objective 1.*   The student will research his visual impairment on the Internet and document in writing four details regarding his visual impairment.

*Short-term objective 2.*   The student will interview at least two individuals with the same type of visual impairment and write a short essay documenting information obtained from the interviews.

To learn about Mrs. Dowse's teaching methods and what it's like to teach students in schools hundreds of miles apart, go to Chapter 10's Teacher Feature module on the Companion Website, **www.prenhall.com/heward**.

***Curriculum Materials and Teaching Strategies***   My students need hands-on activities. I have found that students enjoy story boxes with objects from the stories inside a box. They are able to feel the objects and act out the story. My students need many opportunities to listen to language and books. I encourage parents and teachers to expose my students to as many real-life experiences as possible. They learn the importance of writing when they are able to write or dictate their own books and letters to family and friends. My students who are emergent readers/writers make books from objects they have collected on a walk or from things they bring from home.

***Collaboration and Teaming***   We are required by the state of Arizona to write multidisciplinary team reports. That is, service providers no longer write individual reports but must collaborate to write one assessment report. We also consult with each other when we are providing services to the same student. I am lucky to work with some very good school psychologists, physical therapists (PTs), occupational therapists (OTs), and speech-language pathologists (SLPs). We often work with the same student at one time and explain what each person can do to enhance the student's success. For example, the PT and the OT have given me ideas about positioning, and the SLP has suggested how I can elicit spontaneous speech. When a student is having difficulty in a particular area, we brainstorm about how we can help. For example, the PT was working to help a student use her walker to travel independently from one classroom to another. The student had the ability to move faster, but she seemed to purposely take more time than was necessary. We created a special "telephone book" for her with pictures of her teachers and their 4-digit phone numbers. Each time she reached a classroom, she was to use her book to call her teacher to let that person know she had made it. There were no more problems with her arriving late to class. She loved using the phone, and her teachers would praise her for walking so independently and promptly.

***Advice for Someone Considering a Career in Special Education***   Special education is a very challenging and worthwhile endeavor. Treat every student as an individual and search for a key to unlock his unique way of learning and interpreting the world. Parents and administrators are not the enemy, and every effort should be made to include them in meeting the special needs of your students. Remember that you are part of a team; you should not feel as though you are alone. A positive attitude takes less energy than a negative one.

***The Most Difficult Thing about Being a Special Educator***   The most difficult thing for me is ensuring that classroom teachers and special education teachers follow through with my recommendations. I frequently have to remind the teachers to adhere to the modifications and adaptations needed for my students. I also have to ensure that teaching assistants understand why they are doing certain things that I have recommended. It takes a lot of patience and instruction to make sure that school personnel follow through.

***Meaningful Accomplishments***   During my first year, I worked with a 3-year-old boy who was congenitally blind. His parents were extremely protective of him, and it took a lot of instruction to educate the parents about their child's capabilities and that it was okay to let him explore and discover the world. This student is now in the first grade and flourishing.

I am a certified Irlen screener for scotopic sensitivity syndrome, which is a visual perceptual problem that causes words on a page to become distorted and creates physical symptoms while an individual is reading. Recently, I screened a student who was receiving special education services because of an identified learning disability. I discovered that she had severe scotopic sensitivity syndrome, and I referred her for a lens evaluation. She was fitted for Irlen lenses and immediately began reading everything she could get her hands on. After just 3 months, her scores on a standardized reading test went from the third-grade to the seventh-grade level.

Sixteen-year-old Maria is a bright, college-bound student who has been totally blind since birth. She recently took a series of intellectual and psychological tests and performed well, scoring at about her expected age and grade level. Something unusual happened, however, on one of the test items. The examiner handed Maria an unpeeled banana and asked, "What is this?" Maria held the banana and took several guesses but could not answer correctly. The examiner was astonished, as were Maria's teachers and parents. After all, this section of the test was intended for young children. Even though Maria had eaten bananas many times, she had missed out on one important aspect of the banana experience: she had never held and peeled a banana by herself.

This true story (adapted from Swallow, 1978) illustrates the tremendous importance of vision in obtaining information about the world in which we live. Many concepts that children with normal vision seem to acquire effortlessly may not be learned at all by children with visual impairments—or may be learned incorrectly—unless someone deliberately teaches them. Teachers who work with children with visual impairments find it necessary to plan and present a great many firsthand experiences, enabling children with visual impairments to learn by doing things for themselves. Good teachers understand, however, that even when a concept is deliberately presented to children with visual impairments, they may not learn it in exactly the same way that children with normal vision would.

This is true because, although students with visual impairments may learn to make good use of their other senses (hearing, touch, smell, and taste) as channels for contacting the environment, they do not totally compensate for loss of vision. Touch and taste cannot tell a child much about things that are far away or even just beyond her arms' reach. And while hearing can tell her a good deal about the near and distant environment, it seldom provides information that is as complete, continuous, or exact as the information people obtain from seeing their surroundings.

Vision plays a critical role in learning in the classroom. For example, normally sighted students are routinely expected to exercise several important visual skills. They must be able to focus on different objects and shift their vision from near to far as needed. They must have good hand-to-eye coordination, maintain visual concentration, discriminate among colors and letters, see and interpret many things simultaneously, and remember what they have seen. Children with visual impairments, however, have deficits in one or more of these abilities. As a result, they need special equipment and/or adaptations in instructional materials or procedures to function effectively in school.

To better understand the topics that will be covered in this chapter, go to the Essential Concepts and Chapter at a Glance modules in Chapter 10 of the Companion Website, **www.prenhall.com/heward.**

*Importance of visual experience*

Content Standards for Beginning Teachers—VI: Impact of visual impairment on learning and experience (VI3K1).

## DEFINITIONS

Unlike other disabilities covered by IDEA, visual impairment has both legal and educational definitions.

*Visual acuity, field of vision, tunnel vision*

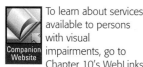

Council for Exceptional Children Content Standards for Beginning Teachers—VI: Specialized terminology used in assessing individuals with VI (VI8K1) (also VI1K5).

To learn about services available to persons with visual impairments, go to Chapter 10's WebLinks on the Companion Website (**www.prenhall.com/heward**) and click on the American Printing House for the Blind and American Federation of the Blind.

# Legal Definition of Blindness

The legal definition of blindness is based on visual acuity and field of vision. **Visual acuity**—the ability to clearly distinguish forms or discriminate among details—is most often measured by reading letters, numbers, or other symbols from the Snellen chart. A person with normal vision can read a ⅜-inch letter at 20 feet. The familiar phrase "20/20 vision" does not, as some people think, mean perfect vision; it simply indicates that at a distance of 20 feet, the eye can see what a normally seeing eye sees at that distance. As the bottom number increases, visual acuity decreases.

A person whose visual acuity is 20/200 or less in the better eye after the best possible correction with glasses or contact lenses is considered **legally blind** by the federal government (Social Security Administration, 2000). If Jane has 20/200 vision while wearing her glasses, she needs to stand at a distance of 20 feet to see what a normally sighted person can see from 200 feet. In other words, Jane must get much closer than normal to see things clearly. Her legal blindness means that she will likely find it difficult to use her vision in many everyday situations. But many children with 20/200, or even 20/400, visual acuity succeed in the regular classroom with special help. Some students' visual acuity is so poor they are unable to perceive fine details at any distance, even while wearing glasses or contact lenses. An individual with visual acuity of no better than 20/70 in the better eye after correction is considered **partially sighted** for legal and governmental purposes.

A person may also be considered legally blind if his **field of vision** is extremely restricted. When gazing straight ahead, a normal eye is able to see objects within a range of approximately 160 to 170 degrees. A person whose vision is restricted to an area of 20 degrees or less is considered legally blind. Some people with **tunnel vision** describe their perception as viewing the world through a narrow tube; they may have good central vision but poor peripheral vision at the outer ranges of the visual field. Conversely, some

**FIGURE 10.1** **A street scene as it might be viewed by persons with 20/20 or 20/200 visual acuity or restricted fields of vision**

eye conditions make it impossible for people to see things clearly in the center of the visual field but allow relatively good peripheral vision. Because a person's visual field often deteriorates gradually over a period of years without notice, a thorough visual examination should always include measurement of the visual field as well as visual acuity. Figure 10.1 shows what a person might see with normal or poor visual acuity or a limited field of vision.

Children who are legally blind are eligible to receive a wide variety of educational services, materials, and benefits from governmental agencies. They may, for example, obtain Talking Books and playback devices from the Library of Congress. Their schools may be able to buy books and educational materials from the American Printing House for the Blind because the federal government allots states and local school districts a certain financial allowance for each legally blind student. A person who is legally blind is also entitled to vocational training, free U.S. mail service, and an income-tax exemption.

Even though these services and benefits are important to know about, the legal definition of blindness is not especially useful for teachers. Some children who do not meet the criteria for legal blindness have visual impairments severe enough to require special education. Other students whose visual impairments qualify them as legally blind have little or no need for special education services.

*Federal entitlements for children who are legally blind*

Council for Exceptional Children — Content Standards for Beginning Teachers—VI: Federal entitlements that provide specialized equipment and materials for individuals with VI (VI1K1).

*Definitions of visual impairment*

Council for Exceptional Children — Content Standards for Beginning Teachers—VI: Educational definitions, identification criteria, labeling issues, and incidence and prevalence figures for individuals with VI (VI1K3).

## Educational Definitions of Visual Impairments

The definition of *visual disability including blindness* in IDEA emphasizes the relationship between vision and learning: "an impairment in vision that, even with correction, adversely affects a child's educational performance." Students with visual impairments display a wide range of visual abilities—from total blindness to relatively good vision. The precise clinical measurements of visual acuity and visual field used to determine legal blindness have limited relevance for educators. Instead, educators classify students with visual impairments based on the extent to which they use vision and/or auditory/tactile means for learning (Bishop, 1996).

- A student who is totally blind receives no useful information through the sense of vision and must use tactile and auditory senses for all learning.
- A child who is functionally blind has so little vision that she learns primarily through the auditory and tactile senses; however, she may be able to use her limited vision to supplement the information received from the other senses and to assist with certain tasks (e.g., moving about the classroom).
- A child with **low vision** uses vision as a primary means of learning but may supplement visual information with tactile and auditory input.

## Age at Onset

Like other disabilities, visual impairment can be congenital (present at birth) or adventitious (acquired). Most visual impairments of school-age children are congenital. It is useful for a teacher to know the age at which a student acquired a visual impairment. A child who has been blind since birth naturally has quite a different perception of the world than does a child who lost his vision at age 12. The first child has a background of learning through hearing, touch, and the other nonvisual senses, whereas the second child has a large background of visual experiences on which to draw. Most people who are adventitiously blind retain a visual memory of things they formerly saw. This memory can be

A child who has been blind since birth has a background of learning through hearing, touch, and the other nonvisual senses.

helpful in a child's education; an adventitiously blind child may, for instance, remember the appearance of colors, maps, and printed letters. At the same time, however, the need for emotional support and acceptance may be greater than it might be for a congenitally blind child, who does not have to make a sudden adjustment to the loss of vision.

# CHARACTERISTICS

## Cognition and Language

This chapter began with a story about a bright teenage girl without sight who could not identify the object she was holding as a banana. Maria had eaten bananas many times, she could spell and read the word *banana*, and she could explain the best climate for growing bananas. But because she'd never held an unpeeled banana, Maria was not able to identify it.

Consider what two children, one with normal vision and one with limited or absent vision, might learn from everyday experiences with a family pet.

> Children with normal vision see a cat's mouth open when it meows or spits, so they can connect the sound to the cat. When they pet the kitty, they feel the soft fur and see the cat's entire body simultaneously. When Dad tells the cat to stop scratching the couch, they look at Dad, see that he is looking at the cat, and follow his gaze over to where the cat is pawing at the couch.
>
> The experience is different for children with visual impairments. They have no way of knowing what the meow, growl, or purr is. They can pinpoint where the sound is coming from, but they cannot see what it is coming from. When the cat remains still long enough, they can feel its soft fur, but they can feel only part of the cat at a time. They can't see that the cat has a head with ears, a body, four legs, four paws with claws, and a tail. . . . And if they get scratched, the paw comes out of and returns to nowhere. Children with visual impairments can still learn the concept of cat, but if they rely on incidental learning, it will take quite a while to put this jumble of isolated experiences together. (Ferrell, 1996, pp. 79–80)

Sighted children without other disabilities are constantly learning from their experiences and interactions with their environment. As they move about, the sense of sight provides a steady stream of detailed information about their environment and about relationships between things in that environment. Without any effort on their part or on the part of others, children with normal sight produce great stores of useful knowledge from everyday experiences. Visual impairments, however, preclude most such incidental learning.

The sense of vision gives children the ability to organize and make connections between different experiences, connections that help the child make the most of those experiences. Children who are blind perform more poorly than sighted children do on cognitive tasks requiring comprehension or relating different items of information. Impaired or absent vision makes it difficult to see (literally, of course, but also cognitively) the connections between experiences. "It is as though all the educational experiences of the blind child are kept in separate compartments" (Kingsley, 1997, p. 27).

This makes learning even simple language concepts such as "cats have tails" and "bananas are smooth" difficult. Abstract concepts, analogies, and idiomatic expressions can be particularly difficult for children who cannot see. Jeanna Mora Dowse shared this experience:

> One morning, the OT was working with a 4-year-old student who was blind. This student was taking his time walking to the therapy room, so the OT told him to "Shake a leg!" The student stopped, shook his right leg, and then continued walking as slowly as before. The OT had to explain to him that "Shake a leg!" was just an expression for "Hurry up."

There is no evidence that these challenges to learning restrict the potential of children with visual impairments. They do, however, magnify the importance of repeated, direct contact with concepts through nonvisual senses.

## Motor Development and Mobility

Blindness or severe visual impairment often leads to delays or deficits in motor development. Stone (1997) explains two reasons for this. First, a significant portion of the purposeful movements of fully sighted babies involves reaching for things they see. The child's efforts to grasp objects, especially those that are just out of reach, strengthen muscles and improve coordination, which in turn enable more effective movement. The absence of sight or clear vision, however, reduces the baby's motivation to move. For the child who is blind, the world is no more interesting when sitting up and turning her head from side to side than it is when she is lying on the floor. Second, a child without clear vision may move less often because movements in the past have resulted in painful contact with the environment.

In addition to limiting a child's opportunities to learn through contact and experience with the physical environment, decreased motor development and movement can lead to physical and social detachment. Children who are blind "may put their natural energy, which would otherwise have found purposeful outlets, into rocking, poking or flapping, all of which can affect their learning and social acceptability" (Stone, 1997, p. 89).

Even limited vision can have negative effects on motor development. Children with low vision have poorer motor skills than do children who are sighted. Their gross motor skills, especially balance, are weak. They frequently are unable to perform motor activities through imitation, and they are usually more careful of space (Bouchard & Tétreault, 2000).

*Motor development*

🕴 Council for Exceptional Children    Content Standards for Beginning Teachers—VI: Effects of visual impairment on development (VI2K3) (also CC2K2).

## Social Adjustment and Interaction

Compared with normally sighted children, children with visual impairments interact less during free time and are often delayed in the development of social skills (Erin, Dignan, & Brown, 1991; Skellenger, Hill, & Hill, 1992). Some young children with sensory impairments experience difficulty in receiving and expressing affection, behaviors that have been shown to facilitate future development in other areas of social competence (Compton & Niemeyer, 1994). Although many adolescents with visual impairments have best friends, many also struggle with social isolation and must work harder than their sighted peers to make and maintain friendships (Leigh & Barclay, 2000; Rosenblum, 1998, 2000; Sacks, Wolffe, & Tierney, 1998).

*Social and emotional development*

🕴 Council for Exceptional Children    Content Standards for Beginning Teachers—VI: Effects of visual impairment on development (VI2K3) (also CC2K2).

Students with visual impairments are often not invited to participate in group activities such as going to a ball game or a movie because sighted peers just assume they are not interested. Over time students with visual impairments and their sighted age mates have fewer and fewer shared experiences and common interests as bases for conversation, social interactions, and friendships.

Rosenblum (2000) identifies several issues influencing the limited social involvement of many adolescents with visual impairments. Because of the low incidence of the disability, many children with visual impairments are unable to benefit from peers or adult role models who are experiencing the same challenges because of visual impairments. Social isolation becomes particularly pronounced for many teenagers with visual impairments when sighted peers obtain drivers' licenses.

Another factor contributing to social difficulties is that the inability to see and respond to the social signals of others reduces opportunities for reciprocal interactions (Frame, 2000; Kirkwood, 1997). During a conversation, for example, a student who is blind cannot see the gestures, facial expressions, and changes in body posture used by his conversation partner. This inability to see important components of communication hampers the blind

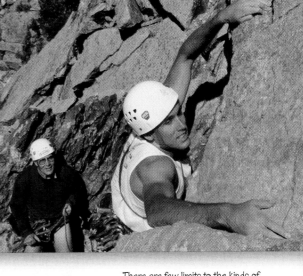

There are few limits to the kinds of activities in which students with visual impairments can participate. This rock climber is totally blind.

*Stereotypic behavior*

Council for
Exceptional
Children   Content
Standards for
Beginning Teachers—VI: Effects
of visual impairment on
development (VI2K3) (also
CC2K2).

student's understanding of the conversation partner's message. And his failure to respond with socially appropriate eye contact, facial expressions, and gestures suggests lack of interest in his partner's communicative efforts and makes it less likely that the individual will seek out his company in the future.

Some individuals with visual impairments engage in repetitive body movements or other behaviors such as body rocking, eye rubbing, hand flapping, and head weaving. These behaviors were traditionally referred to in the visual impairment literature as "blindisms" or "blind mannerisms" (Kingsley, 1997). *Stereotypic behavior* (stereotypy) is a more clearly defined term that subsumes blindisms and mannerisms. It is also a more appropriate term: some sighted children exhibit such behaviors, and they do not occur among all children who are blind (Gense & Gense, 1994).

Although not usually harmful, stereotypic behavior can place a person with visual impairments at a great social disadvantage because these actions are conspicuous and may call negative attention to the person. It is not known why many children with visual impairments engage in stereotypic behaviors (Bak, 1999). However, various behavioral interventions such as reinforcement of incompatible behaviors and self-monitoring have been used to help individuals with visual impairments reduce stereotypic behaviors such as repetitive body rocking (McAdam, O' Cleirigh, & Cuvo, 1993) or head drooping during conversation (Raver, 1984).

Many persons who have lost their sight report that the biggest difficulty socially is dealing with the attitudes and behavior of those around them. The beliefs, superstitions, and mythology that form "the folklore of blindness" no doubt influence some of those attitudes and behaviors.

> The influence of the folklore of blindness generally is expressed in attitudes towards (and by) blind people that sound absurd but are genuinely felt. . . . One finds that folk beliefs are divided into two groups. On the negative side of this dichotomy are the beliefs that blind people are either helpless and pathetic or evil and contagious and probably deserve their fate. On the more positive side are the beliefs that blind people have special or even magical abilities, special powers of perception, and deserve special attention. (Wagner-Lampl & Oliver, 1994, pp. 267–268)

# PREVALENCE

*Prevalence of visual
impairments*

Council for
Exceptional
Children   Content
Standards for
Beginning Teachers—VI:
Educational definitions,
identification criteria, labeling
issues, and incidence and
prevalence figures for individuals
with VI (VI1K3).

Children with visual impairments constitute a very small percentage of the school-age population—fewer than 2 children in 1,000. During the 2003–2004 school year, 25,294 children ages 6 to 21 received special education services under IDEA within the category of visual impairments (U.S. Office of Special Education, 2004). According to Sacks and Silberman (1998), almost one-half of the school-age population of students with visual impairments has at least one additional disability. Thus, the total number of students with visual impairments is somewhat higher than the data reported for IDEA because some students with visual impairments are served and counted under other disability categories such as deaf-blindness and multiple disabilities. Still, visual impairment is a low-incidence disability.

Even when viewed as a percentage of the population of students who receive special education services, the prevalence of visual impairments is very small: only about 0.4%, or 1 in 200, of all school-age children with IEPs are served under the disability category of visual impairments. Educators and parents of children with visual impairments frequently express concern about this low prevalence because they fear that when financial resources are limited, students with visual impairments may not receive adequate services from specially trained teachers. It can be particularly difficult for a local public school to provide comprehensive services for a child with visual impairment who resides in a rural area. Small school districts often cooperate with each other in employing special teachers for students with visual impairments.

## How We See

Effective vision requires proper functioning of three anatomical systems of the eye: the optical system, the muscular system, and the nervous system. A simplified diagram of the eye appears in Figure 10.2. The eye's optical system collects and focuses light energy reflected from objects in the visual field. As light passes through the eye, several structures bend, or refract, the light to produce a clear image. The light first hits the **cornea,** the curved transparent membrane that protects the eye (much as an outer crystal protects a watch face). It then passes through the **aqueous humor,** a watery liquid that fills the front chamber of the eye. Next the light passes through the **pupil,** a circular hole in the center of the colored **iris;** the pupil contracts or expands to regulate the amount of light entering the eye. The light then passes through the **lens,** a transparent, elastic structure. After the light passes through the **vitreous humor,** a jellylike substance that fills most of the eye's interior, it reaches the innermost layer of the eye, the **retina.** This multilayered sheet of nerve tissue at the back of the eye has been likened to the film in a camera: for a clear image to be seen, the light rays must come to a precise focus on the retina.

The eye's muscular system enables **ocular motility,** the eye's ability to move. Six muscles attached to the outside of each eye enable it to search, track, converge, and fixate on images. These muscles also play a significant part in depth perception (**binocular vision**), the ability to fuse the separate images from each eye into a single, three-dimensional image. Inside the eye, tiny muscles adjust the shape of the lens, making it thicker or thinner, so the eye can bring objects at different distances into sharp focus (**accommodation**).

The eye's nervous system converts light energy into electrical impulses and transmits that information to the brain, where it is processed into visual images. The retina consists of millions of light receptors called cones and rods. The **cones** enable detection of color and detail necessary for tasks such as reading and are located in the center of the retina and function best in good light. The **rods,** which are responsible for peripheral vision, detection of movement, and vision in dim light, are distributed around the periphery of the retina. The **optic nerve** carries the electrical messages from the cones and rods directly to the **visual cortex** at the base of the brain.

*Anatomy and function of the eye*

Council for Exceptional Children Content Standards for Beginning Teachers—VI: Basic terminology related to the structure and function of the human eye (VI1K4).

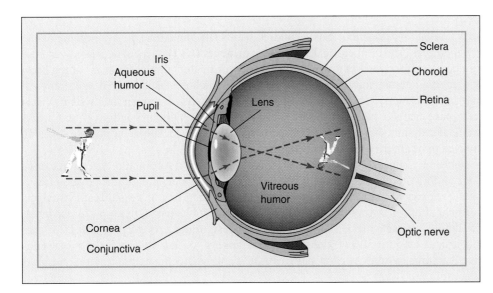

**FIGURE 10.2**
**Basic anatomy of the human eye**

# Causes of Visual Impairments

Damage or disturbances to any part of the eye's optical, muscular, or nervous systems can result in impaired vision. Causes of visual impairments are grouped into three broad categories: refractive errors, structural impairments, and cortical visual impairments (Stiles & Knox, 1996).

*Types and causes of visual
impairment*

Council for
Exceptional
Children
Content
Standards for
Beginning Teachers—VI: Basic
terminology related to diseases
and disorders of the human
visual system (VI1K5).

*Refractive Errors.*   **Refraction** is the process of bending light rays when they pass from one transparent structure into another. As just described, the normal eye refracts, or bends, light rays so that a clear image falls directly on the retina. However, for many people—perhaps half the general population—the size and shape of the eye prevent the light rays from focusing clearly on the retina. In **myopia,** or *nearsightedness*, the eye is longer than normal from front to back, causing the image to fall in front of the retina instead of exactly on it. A child with myopia can see near objects clearly; but more distant objects, such as a chalkboard or a movie, are blurred or not seen at all. The opposite of myopia is **hyperopia,** commonly called *farsightedness*. The hyperopic eye is shorter than normal, preventing the light rays from converging on the retina. A child with hyperopia has difficulty seeing near objects clearly but is able to focus well on more distant objects. Glasses or contact lenses can compensate for many refractive errors by changing the course of light rays to produce as clear a focus as possible.

*Structural Impairments.*   Visual impairments can be caused by poor development of, damage to, or malfunction of one or more parts of the eye's optical or muscular systems. Cataracts and glaucoma are two of the numerous causes of visual impairment due to damage or disintegration of the eye itself. A **cataract** is a cloudiness in the lens of the eye that blocks the light necessary for seeing clearly. **Glaucoma** is abnormally high pressure within the eye caused by disturbances or blockages of the fluids that normally circulate within the eye. Central and peripheral vision are impaired or lost entirely when the increased pressure damages the optic nerve.

Dysfunction of the muscles that control and move the eyes can make it difficult or impossible for a child to see effectively. **Nystagmus,** a rapid, involuntary, back-and-forth movement of the eyes in a lateral, vertical, or rotary direction, can cause problems in focusing and reading. **Strabismus** is an inability to focus on the same object with both eyes because imbalance of the eye muscles creates an inward or outward deviation of one or both eyes. If left untreated, strabismus and other disorders of ocular motility can lead to permanent loss of vision.

*Cortical Visual Impairments.*   Some children with visual impairments have nothing wrong with their eyes. The term **cortical visual impairments (CVI)** refers to decreased vision or blindness due to known or suspected damage to or malfunction of the parts of the brain that interpret visual information. Causes of CVI include insufficient oxygen at birth (anoxia), head injury, hydrocephalus, and infections of the central nervous system. Visual functioning may fluctuate depending upon environment, lighting conditions, and activities. Some children with CVI use their peripheral vision, some are photophobic, some are attracted to bright light, and some will gaze at the sun.

Table 10.1 (pp. 392–393) summarizes some of the most common types and causes of visual impairments. Although a teacher seldom needs detailed knowledge concerning the etiology of a child's visual impairment, understanding how a student's visual impairment affects classroom performance is important. It is useful to know, for example, that Linda's cataracts make it difficult for her to read under strong lights, that Derek has only a small amount of central vision in his right eye, or that Yoko will need to administer eye drops to relieve the pressure caused by her glaucoma before leaving on a class field trip.

# EDUCATIONAL APPROACHES

Numerous specialized teaching methods and curriculum materials have been developed in an effort to overcome the obstacles to learning presented by blindness and low vision. Advances in instructional methodology and, in particular, technology have greatly increased access to the general education curriculum and academic success among students with visual impairments. As one high school student who is blind remarked, "By taking advantage of technology around me, I am able to have an education equal to my sighted peers" (Leigh & Barclay, 2000, p. 129). However, the education of students with visual impairments is a field with a history of more than 150 years, and today's developments were made possible by the contributions of many teachers and researchers who came before (Koenig & Hollbrook, 2000). Table 10.2 (pp. 394–395) highlights some key historical events and their implications for the education of students with visual impairments.

*History of education of students with VI*

Council for Exceptional Children — Content Standards for Beginning Teachers—VI: Historical foundations of education of individuals with VI (VI1K2).

## Special Adaptations for Students Who Are Blind

Because they must frequently teach skills and concepts that most children acquire through vision, teachers of students who are blind must plan and carry out activities that will help their students gain as much information as possible through the nonvisual senses and by participation in active, practical experiences. For example, a blind child may hear a bird singing but get no concrete idea of the bird itself from the sound alone. A teacher interested in teaching such a student about birds might plan a series of activities that has the student touch birds of various species and manipulate related objects such as eggs, nests, and feathers. The student might assume the responsibility for feeding a pet bird at home or in the classroom. Through such experiences, the child with visual impairments can gradually obtain a more thorough and accurate knowledge of birds than she could if her education were limited to reading books about birds, memorizing vocabulary, or feeling plastic models.

*Braille.* Braille is the primary means of literacy for people who are blind. **Braille** is a tactile system of reading and writing in which letters, words, numbers, and other systems are made from arrangements of raised dots (see Figure 10.3 on page 395).

In some ways, braille is like the shorthand that secretaries use. A set of 189 abbreviations, called *contractions*, helps save space and permits faster reading and writing. For example, when the letter *r* stands by itself, it means "rather." The word "myself" in braille is written "myf." Frequently used words, such as "the," "and," "with," and "for," have their own special contractions. For example, the "and" symbol ⠯ appears four times in the following sentence:

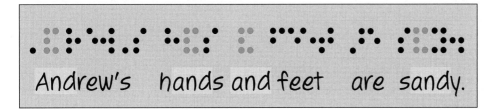

Students who are blind can read braille much more rapidly than they can read the raised letters of the standard alphabet. The speed of braille reading varies a great deal from student to student; however, it is almost always much slower (about 100 words per minute for good braille readers) than the speed of print reading. Most children who are blind are introduced to braille in the first grade. Rex, Koenig, Wormsley, and Baker (1994) recommend that children receive 1½ to 2 hours of instruction in reading and writing braille each day since this is the same amount of time typically devoted to literacy skills for sighted children

*Braille, brailler, slate and stylus*

Council for Exceptional Children — Content Standards for Beginning Teachers—VI: Strategies for teaching braille reading and writing (VI4K1).

## TABLE 10.1  Types and causes of visual impairments

| Condition | Definition/Cause | Remarks/Educational Implications |
|---|---|---|
| Albinism | Lack of pigmentation in the eyes, skin, and hair; results in moderate to severe visual impairment by reducing visual acuity and causing nystagmus; heredity | Children with albinism almost always have photophobia, a condition in which the eyes are extremely sensitive to light; eye fatigue may occur during close work |
| Amblyopia | Reduction in or loss of vision in the weaker eye from lack of use; caused by strabismus, unequal refractive errors, or opacities of the lens or cornea | Close work may result in eye fatigue, loss of place, poor concentration; seating should favor functional eye |
| Astigmatism | Distorted or blurred vision caused by irregularities in the cornea or other surfaces of the eye that produce images on retina not in equal focus (refractive error) | Loss of accommodation when object brought close to face; avoid long periods of reading or close tasks that cause discomfort; child may complain of headaches and fluctuating vision |
| Cataract | Blurred, distorted, or incomplete vision caused by cloudiness in the lens; caused by injury, malnutrition or rubella during pregnancy, glaucoma, retinitis pigmentosa, heredity, aging | Avoid glare of any kind; light source behind child; good contrast between print and paper; variation in near and distant tasks can prevent tiring |
| Color deficiency or color blindness | Difficulty distinguishing certain colors; red-green confusion is most common; caused by cone malformation or absence, macular deficiency, heredity | Usually not an educationally significant visual impairment; teach alternative ways to discriminate objects usually identified by color (e.g., tags for clothing colors, position of red and green on traffic lights) |
| Cortical visual impairment (CVI) | Impaired vision due to damage to or malfunction of the visual cortex and/or optic nerve; causes include anoxia, head injury, and infections of the central nervous system; many children with CVI have additional disabilities, such as cerebral palsy, seizure disorders, mental retardation | Visual functioning may fluctuate depending upon lighting conditions and attention; vision usually does not deteriorate, improvement sometimes occurs over a period of time; some children with CVI use their peripheral vision; some are photophobic; some are attracted to bright light and will gaze at the sun; visual images should be simple and presented singly |
| Diabetic retinopathy | Impaired vision as a result of hemorrhages and the growth of new blood vessels in the area of the retina due to diabetes; leading cause of blindness for people ages 20 to 64 | Provide good lighting and contrast; magnification; pressure to perform can affect blood glucose |
| Glaucoma | Abnormally high pressure within the eye due to disturbances or blockages of the fluids that normally circulate within the eye; vision is impaired or lost entirely when the increased pressure damages the retina and optic nerve | Fluctuations in visual performance may frustrate child; be alert to symptoms of pain; eye drops administered on schedule; child may be subjected to teasing because of bulging eyes |
| Hyperopia (farsightedness) | Difficulty seeing near objects clearly but able to focus well on distant objects; caused by a shorter-than-normal eye that prevents light rays from converging on the retina (refractive error) | Loss of accommodation when object brought close to face; avoid long periods of reading or close tasks that cause discomfort |

in the primary grades. Rather than have the child learn to write out every word, letter by letter, and later unlearn this approach, teachers introduce contractions early in the program (Wormsley, 2004). Of course, it is important for the child to eventually know the full and correct spelling of words, even if every letter does not appear separately in braille.

Although it usually takes several years for children to become thoroughly familiar with braille, it is no more difficult than learning to read print for sighted children.

True, some people claim that the braille code is more *complex* than the print code because more symbols are used. But if a child receives good reading instruction and has a rich variety of

**TABLE 10.1** *continued*

| Condition | Definition/Cause | Remarks/Educational Implications |
|---|---|---|
| Macular degeneration | Central area of the retina gradually deteriorates, causing loss of clear vision in the center of the visual field; common in older adults but fairly rare in children | Tasks such as reading and writing difficult; prescribed low-vision aid or closed-circuit TV; good illumination; avoid glare |
| Myopia (nearsightedness) | Distant objects are blurred or not seen at all but can see near objects clearly; caused by an elongated eye that focuses images in front of the retina (refractive error) | Encourage child to wear prescribed glasses or contact lens; for near tasks child may be more comfortable working without glasses and bringing work close to face |
| Nystagmus | Rapid, involuntary, back-and-forth movement of the eyes, which makes it difficult to focus on objects; when the two eyes cannot focus simultaneously, the brain avoids a double image by suppressing the visual input from one eye; the weaker eye (usually the one that turns inward or outward) can actually lose its ability to see; can occur on its own but is usually associated with other visual impairments | Close tasks for extended period can lead to fatigue; some children turn or tilt head to obtain the best focus; do not criticize this |
| Retinitis pigmentosa (RP) | The most common genetic disease of the eye; causes gradual degeneration of the retina; first symptom is usually difficulty seeing at night, followed by loss of peripheral vision; heredity | High illumination with no glare; contracting visual field causes difficulties with scanning and tracking skills necessary for tasks such as reading; teach student to locate visual objects with systematic search grid; as RP is progressive, curriculum should include mobility training, especially at night, and braille training if prognosis is loss of sight |
| Retinopathy of prematurity (ROP) | Caused by administering high levels of oxygen to at-risk infants; when the infants are later removed from the oxygen-rich incubators, the change in oxygen levels can produce an abnormally dense growth of blood vessels and scar tissue in the eyes, leading to visual impairment and often total blindness | High illumination, magnifiers for close work; telescopes for distance viewing; students may have brain damage resulting in mental retardation and/or behavior problems |
| Strabismus | Inability to focus on the same object with both eyes due to an inward or outward deviation of one or both eyes; caused by muscle imbalance; secondary to other visual impairments | Classroom seating should favor student's stronger eye; some students may use one eye for distance tasks, the other eye for near tasks; frequent rest periods may be needed during close work; may need more time to adjust to unfamiliar visual tasks |

*Sources:* From Levack, Stone, and Bishop (1994); Mason (1997); Sacks and Silberman (1998).

background experiences, learning to read braille should not be "difficult." If a child says that braille is difficult to read, it is probably because she has heard an adult say so. (Koenig, 1996, pp. 233–234)

Young children generally learn to write braille by using a *brailler*, a six-keyed, mechanical device that somewhat resembles a typewriter. Older students are usually introduced to the *slate and stylus*, in which the braille dots are punched out one at a time by hand, from right to left. The slate-and-stylus method has certain advantages in note taking; for example, it is much smaller and quieter than the brailler.

*Braille Technological Aids.* Most braille books are large, expensive, and cumbersome. It can be difficult for students to retrieve information quickly when they must tactually review many pages of braille books or notes. Technological developments have made braille more

**TABLE 10.2    A history of the education of children with visual impairments: Key events and implications**

| Date | Historical Event | Educational Implications |
|---|---|---|
| 1784 | Shocked at seeing people who were blind performing as jesters or begging on the streets of Paris, Victor Hauy resolved to teach them more dignified ways of earning a living. He started the first school for children who were blind. Hauy's curriculum included reading and writing (using embossed print), music, and vocational skills. | The competence of Hauy's students influenced the establishment of other residential schools in Europe and Russia in the early 19th century. |
| 1821 | Samuel Gridley Howe founded the Perkins School for the Blind, the oldest and best-known residential school for students who are blind. | Many methods and materials for teaching students with visual impairments were first developed at Perkins. Anne Sullivan and her famous pupil, Helen Keller, spent several years at Perkins. |
| 1829 | The first draft of a tactile method of reading created by Louis Braille was published. He was a student at a Paris school for children who were blind. | Braille's system of embossed six-dot cells proved the most efficient of several methods of reading by touch and is the primary means of literacy for the blind today. |
| 1862 | The Snellen chart was developed by a Dutch ophthalmologist. | The chart provided a fast, standardized test of visual acuity; it is still used today as a visual screening tool for schoolchildren. |
| 1900; 1909/1913 | The first public school class for children who were blind opened in Chicago; the first classes for children with low vision began in Cleveland and Boston. | Students with visual impairments were educated in public schools; children with low vision were educated in special "sight-saving classes" in which all instruction was conducted orally. |
| 1932 | The Library of Congress made Talking Books available to any person who is legally blind. | Availability of recorded books and other print materials enhanced the range of curriculum content accessible to students with visual impairments. |
| 1938 | The first itinerant teaching program for children with visual impairments attending regular classrooms began in Oakland, California. | This marked the beginning of the long and relatively successful history of including children with visual impairments in regular classrooms. |

efficient, thus enabling many students who are blind to function more independently in regular classrooms, universities, and employment settings.

Braille'n Speak is a battery-powered, pocket-sized device for note taking with a keyboard for braille entry and voice output. It can translate braille into synthesized speech or print.

The Mountbatten Brailler is an electronic brailler that is easier to use than the manual, mechanical brailler. Braille embossers print braille from digital text; and some printers produce pages with both braille and print formats, enabling blind and sighted readers to use the same copy.

*Declining Braille Literacy.*    The vast majority of employed adults who are blind use braille at work; and congenitally blind adults who learn to read braille have higher employment rates, attain greater educational levels, earn more income, and spend more time reading than do those who learn to read print (Ryles, 1996). Nevertheless, there has been a decline in braille literacy over the years (Wittenstein, 1994). In comparison to the early 1960s, when it was estimated that nearly half of blind students could read and write braille, a national census in 1992 found that only 10% of legally blind K–12 students were braille readers (American Printing House for the Blind, 1992). Visual readers—students who primarily

*Braille technological aids*

Council for Exceptional Children    Content Standards for Beginning Teachers—VI: Strategies for teaching braille reading and writing (VI4K1).

TABLE 10.2 *continued*

| Date | Historical Event | Educational Implications |
|------|------------------|--------------------------|
| 1940s–1950s | Thousands of children became blind or severely visually impaired by retinopathy of prematurity (ROP) caused by the increased use of oxygen with premature infants. | Residential schools were not able to accommodate the large influx of visually impaired children; thus, special education programs and services for students with visual impairments became much more widely available in the public schools in the 1950s and 1960s. |
| 1944 | Richard Hoover developed a system for teaching orientation and mobility (O&M) skills to persons with visual impairments. It featured a long white cane. | This system of O&M and the "Hoover cane" become standard parts of the curriculum for students with visual impairments. |
| 1951 | The Perkins brailler was invented. | The first fast and easy method for writing braille improved access to and participation in education. |
| Mid-1960s | Natalie Barraga published research showing that children with low vision do not lose their remaining sight by using it and that visual functioning can be improved by use. | Barraga's (1964, 1970) work was instrumental in ending the sight-saving classes attended by children with low vision for more than 50 years. |
| 1970s | Development of the Kurzweil Reading Machine, the world's first text-to-speech optical scanning machine, provided access to print materials not available in braille, large-print, or recorded formats. | Though large, slow, and very expensive compared to the lightweight, portable technologies available today, the Kurzweil set the stage for a continuing explosion of technological advancements that have benefited the lives of many people with visual impairments. |
| 1997 | The Individuals with Disabilities Education Act (IDEA '97) mandated that orientation and mobility (O&M) services be provided to any student with a disability who needs them. | This expanded the role of O&M specialists in schools to include training in the use of wheelchairs, electronic travel devices, and public transportation for students with disabilities other than visual impairments. |

**FIGURE 10.3**
**The braille system for representing numbers and letters**
*Source:* From the Division for the Blind and Physically Handicapped, Library of Congress, Washington, DC.

use regular or large-print materials—made up the largest group (27%), with 10% being auditory readers, who use recorded materials or are read to aloud. Nonreaders (31%)—students with visual impairments with additional severe disabilities—and prereaders (22%) made up the rest of the student population.

In response to the concern about declining braille literacy, the 1997 amendments to IDEA specified for the first time that IEP teams for students with visual impairments make

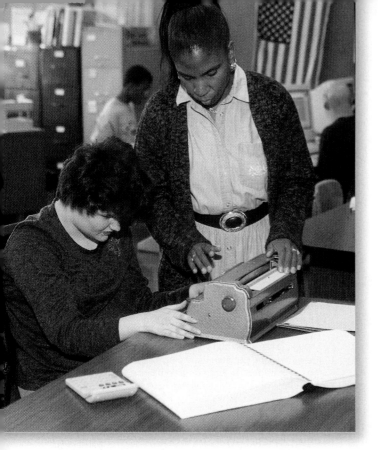

The brailler is a six-keyed device that punches the raised braille dots in special paper.

a determination of the student's preferred reading medium and that instruction in braille must be considered. In addition, at least 27 states have passed legislation, called "braille bills," making braille equipment and instruction available for students if the parents or any other member of the IEP team indicate it is needed and requiring teachers of students with visual impairments to be proficient in braille. IEP teams can use the Learning Media Assessment to help determine the most appropriate reading medium for students with visual impairments (Koenig & Holbrook, 1993).

*Tactile Aids and Manipulatives.* Manipulatives are generally recognized as effective tools in teaching beginning mathematics skills to elementary students. When using most manipulatives, such as Cuisenaire rods, however, sighted students use length and color to distinguish the various numerical values of the rods. Belcastro (1989) has developed a set of rods that enables students who are blind to quickly identify different values by feeling the lengths and tactile markings associated with each number.

Tactile experience books created by gluing, stapling, or otherwise attaching artifacts from actual events experienced by the child to the pages of a simple and sturdy book can help young children who are blind or have severe visual impairments acquire book concepts and early literacy skills (Lewis & Tolla, 2003). Each page of a tactile experience book includes braille or print related to the artifacts on the page.

Another mathematical aid for students who are blind is the Cranmer abacus. Long used in Japan, the abacus has been adapted to assist students who are blind in learning number concepts and making calculations. Manipulation of the abacus beads is particularly useful in counting, adding, and subtracting.

For more advanced mathematical functions, the student is likely to use the Speech-Plus talking calculator, a small electronic instrument that performs most of the operations of any standard calculator. It "talks" by voicing entries and results aloud and also presents them visually in digital form. This is only one of many instances in which the development of synthetic speech technology has helped people who are blind. Talking clocks and spelling aids are also available.

In the sciences and social studies, several adaptations encourage students who are blind to use their tactile and auditory senses for firsthand manipulation and discovery. Examples are embossed relief maps and diagrams, three-dimensional models, and electronic probes that give an audible signal in response to light. Curriculum modification projects, such as MAVIS (Materials Adaptation for Students with Visual Impairments in the Social Studies) and SAVI (Science Activities for the Visually Impaired), emphasize how students with visual impairments can, with some modifications, participate in learning activities along with normally sighted students.

*Technological Aids for Reading Print.* The Optacon (optical-to-tactile converter) is a small, handheld electronic device that converts regular print into a readable vibrating form. The Optacon does not convert print into braille but into a configuration of raised pins representing the letter the camera is viewing. When the tiny camera of the Optacon is held over a printed *E*, for example, the user feels on the tip of one finger a vertical line and three horizontal lines. Although extensive training and practice are required, many children and

*Tactile aids and manipulatives*

Council for Exceptional Children — Content Standards for Beginning Teachers—VI: Strategies for teaching use of the abacus, talking calculator, tactile graphics, and adapted science equipment (VI4K7).

adults who are blind are able to read regular print effectively with the aid of the Optacon. The Optacon II enables the user to scan print on computer screens.

The L&H Kurzweil 1000 is a sophisticated computer-based reading system that uses an optical character recognition system to scan and read printed text with synthetic speech. The user can regulate the speed, have the machine spell out words letter by letter if desired, and even choose from 14 different voices. The "intelligence" of the Kurzweil reading machines is constantly being improved; and the machines are currently in use at most residential schools and also in many public school programs, public libraries, rehabilitation centers, and colleges and universities. The first Kurzweil Reading Machine weighed more than 300 pounds and cost $50,000. But the costs of reading machines have decreased greatly, and machines manufactured by L&H Kurzweil, IBM, and Arenstone with computer accessories can be purchased for about $1,000.

*Computer Access.* Assistive technology that provides access to personal computers offers tremendous opportunities for the education, employment, communication, and leisure enjoyment of individuals with visual impairments. These technologies include (1) hardware and software that magnify screen images, (2) speech recognition software that enables the user to tell the computer what to do, and (3) software that converts text files to synthesized speech.

Keyboarding is an important means of communication between children who are blind and their sighted classmates and teachers and is also a useful skill for further education and employment. Instruction in keyboarding should begin as early as feasible in the child's school program. Today, handwriting is seldom taught to students who are totally blind, with the noteworthy exception of learning to sign one's name in order to assume responsibilities such as maintaining a bank account, registering to vote, and applying for a job.

## Special Adaptations for Students with Low Vision

Between 75% and 80% of school-age children enrolled in educational programs for visually impaired students have some potentially useful vision. Learning by students with low vision need not be restricted to the nonvisual senses, and they generally learn to read print (Corn & Koenig, 1996).

*Functional Vision.* *Visual efficiency* and *functional vision* are related terms denoting how well a person uses whatever vision he has (Barraga & Erin, 2001; Corn, 1989). A child's functional vision cannot be determined or predicted by measurements of visual acuity or visual field. Some children with severe visual impairments use the limited vision they have very capably. Other children with relatively minor visual impairments are unable to function as visual learners; they may even behave as though they were blind.

Utley, Roman, and Nelson (1998) suggest that vision is functional when one or more visual-motor skills (e.g., fixation or localization, scanning, tracking, gaze shift; see Table 10.3) (1) are essential steps in the accurate and efficient performance of a task; (2) promote more independent performance in home, school, vocational, or community environments; or (3) enhance the degree of choice and autonomy of an individual, thereby enhancing her quality of life. The fundamental premises underlying the development of functional vision is that children learn to see, that functional vision is teachable behavior, and that children must be actively involved in using their own vision (Utley et al., 1998).

Merely furnishing a classroom with attractive things for children to see is not sufficient. A child with low vision may, without training, be unable to derive much meaningful information through vision. Forms may be perceived as vague masses and shapeless, indistinct blobs. Systematic training in visual recognition and discrimination is needed to help children learn to use their visual impressions intelligently and effectively, to make sense out of what they see (Li, 2004; Lueck, 2004). Instruction in use of vision skills should not be limited to isolated "visual stimulation sessions" but should be incorporated throughout the

*Computer access and keyboarding*

Council for Exceptional Children Content Standards for Beginning Teachers—VI: Strategies for teaching technology skills to individuals with VI (VI4K6) (also VI4K5).

*Visual efficiency/visual functioning*

Council for Exceptional Children Content Standards for Beginning Teachers—VI: Strategies for teaching visual efficiency skills and use of print adaptations, optical devices, and non-optical devices (VI4K9).

**TABLE 10.3** **Definitions and examples of four visual and visual-motor skills**

| Visual and Visual-Motor Skills | Definitions and Examples |
| --- | --- |
| Fixation | *Definition:*<br>Active alignment of the line of sight (i.e., visual axis) in one or both eyes on a stationary object or person.<br><br>*Example:*<br>Looking at a tube of toothpaste while reaching to pick it up and apply it to the toothbrush. |
| Scanning | *Definition:*<br>Visually searching for an object or person among a display of visual stimuli.<br><br>*Example:*<br>Visually locating the appropriate bus or van at dismissal time. |
| Tracking | *Definition:*<br>Visually following a moving stimulus.<br><br>*Example:*<br>Watching the trajectory of coins as they are sorted into the appropriate locations in the cash drawer. |
| Gaze shift | *Definition:*<br>Shifting fixation in space from one location to another.<br><br>*Example:*<br>Fixating on one type of cutlery and then others (i.e., first soup spoons; then forks, knives, and teaspoons) as the appropriate silverware for a particular meal is selected. |

*Source:* From Utley, B. L., Roman, C., & Nelson, G. L. (1998). Functional vision. In S. Z. Sacks & R. K. Silberman (Eds.), *Educating students who have visual impairments with other disabilities* (p. 399). Baltimore: Paul H. Brookes Publishing Co., adapted with permission.

student's daily schedule (Ferrell & Muir, 1996; Li, 2003) and taught within the context of meaningful activities (see Figure 10.4).

*Optical devices*

Council for Exceptional Children Content Standards for Beginning Teachers—VI: Strategies for teaching visual efficiency skills and use of print adaptations, optical devices, and non-optical devices (VI4K9).

*Optical Devices.* Many ophthalmologists and optometrists specialize in the assessment and treatment of low vision. A professional examination can help determine which types of optical aids, if any, can benefit a particular child with low vision. These special devices might include glasses and contact lenses, small handheld telescopes, and magnifiers placed on top of printed pages. Such aids cannot give normal vision to children with visual impairments but may help them perform better at certain tasks, such as reading small print or seeing distant objects.

Optical aids are usually specialized rather than all-purpose, and children whose vision is extremely limited are more likely to use monocular (one-eye) than binocular (two-eye) aids, especially for seeing things at a distance. Juanita might, for example, use her glasses for reading large print, a magnifier stand for reading smaller print, and a monocular (one-eye) telescope for viewing the chalkboard. A usual disadvantage of corrective lenses and magnifiers is that the more powerful they are, the more they tend to distort or restrict the peripheral field of vision. Some field-widening lenses and devices are now available for students with limited visual fields. These include prisms and fish-eye lenses designed to make objects appear smaller so that a greater area can be perceived on the unimpaired portions of a student's visual field. It is usually a good idea to furnish optical aids on a trial or loan basis so that the student can gradually learn to use and evaluate them in natural settings. A follow-up session should then be scheduled.

**FIGURE 10.4**  Example of embedding opportunities to use and develop functional visual skills throughout the daily schedule for Paula, a 15-year-old girl with cerebral palsy who demonstrates visual skills about 50% of the time.

| Place and time | Activity and visual skills needed |
| --- | --- |
| At home 7:30–8:30 A.M. Getting ready for school | Have Paula choose what she wants to wear. Her mother puts 2 sets of clothes in front of her but does not describe them. She asks Paula what she wants to wear either by naming the color or pointing to the clothing. *Visual skills needed to choose:* Localization and shift attention. |
| At school, First period class: Daily living skills—Grooming | After brushing and arranging Paula's hair have her look in a magnifying mirror and  ask her how she likes her hair. Once in a while change her hairstyle to see if she notices the difference. *Visual skills needed to examine hair:* Visual attending, localization, and scanning. |
| At school, Second period class: Home economics—Laundry | While sorting clothes into a light and a dark pile, ask Paula to decide into which pile each piece of clothing should go. *Visual skills involved:* Visual attending, localization, shifting attention, and scanning. |
| At school, lunch | Present Paula with 2 types of food with which she is familiar without telling her what they are. Have her choose what she wants to eat. If she has difficulty identifying the food, allow her to smell it. *Visual skills she will need:* Visual attending, localization, and shift attention. |
| Afternoon community outing | While grocery shopping, encourage Paula to identify items that are easily recognizable or that she frequently uses. Encourage her to say what the item is and where it is. For example, place her between the bananas and the apples or near just one item. *Visual skills involved:* Visual attending, localization, and scanning.<br><br>While outdoors, encourage Paula to tell you what she sees or ask her to point to specific items (e.g., cars, flowers, green grass, fire hydrants). *Visual skills involved:* Visual attending, localization, tracking, and scanning. |

*Source*: From Li, A. (2003). A model for developing programs to improve the use of vision in students who are visually impaired with multiple disabilities. *RE:view, 35*(1), p. 38. Used by permission.

Closed-circuit television systems are used in some classrooms to enable students with low vision to read regular-sized printed materials. These systems usually include a sliding table on which a book is placed, a television camera with a zoom lens mounted above the book, and a television monitor nearby. The student is able to adjust the size, brightness, and contrast of the material and can select either an ordinary black-on-white image or a negative white-on-black image, which many students prefer. The teacher may also have a television monitor that lets him see the student's work without making repeated trips to the

These students with low vision are using a closed-circuit television system to read regular-sized print materials.

student's desk. A disadvantage of closed-circuit television systems is that they are usually not portable, so the student who uses television as a primary reading medium is largely restricted to the specially equipped classroom or library.

Recent advances in computer and optical technologies have led to the development of a number of low vision devices called *augmented reality systems*. These lightweight, head-mounted devices track the position of the user's head and project the desired images onto beam-splitting optics that allow the user to see an overlay or superimposed image on the environment (Feiner, 2002). One augmented-reality system for people with low vision, called Nomad, uses a high-resolution laser to project an image directly onto the user's retina. Studies have shown that Nomad can function as a substitute computer monitor (Kleweno, Seibel, Viirre, Kelly, & Furness, 2001) and that users can read print with the device (Goodrich, Kirby, Wagstaff, Oros, & McDevitt, 2004).

*Reading print*

 Council for Exceptional Children   Content Standards for Beginning Teachers—VI: Strategies for teaching visual efficiency skills and use of print adaptations, optical devices, and non-optical devices (VI4K9).

*Reading Print.* Students with low vision use three basic approaches for reading print: (1) *approach magnification* (reducing the distance between the eye and the page of print from 40 centimeters to 5 centimeters results in 8x magnification) (Jose, 1983), (2) *lenses* (optical devices), and (3) *large print* (Corn & Ryser, 1989). Many books and other materials are available in large print for children with low vision. The American Printing House for the Blind produces books in 18-point type. Some states and other organizations produce large-type materials; but the size and style of the print fonts, spacing, paper, and quality of production vary widely. The sentence you are reading now is set in 10-point type. Here are four examples of different large-print type sizes:

This is 14-point type.

This is 18-point type.

This is 20-point type.

This is 24-point type.

Although print size is an important variable, other equally important factors to consider are the quality of the printed material, the contrast between print and page, the spacing between lines, and the illumination of the setting in which the child reads (Griffin, Williams, Davis, & Engelman, 2002). It is generally agreed that a child with visual impairments should use the smallest print size that she can read comfortably. A child may be able to transfer from large print to smaller print as reading efficiency increases, just as most normally sighted children do. Table 10.4 compares the advantages and disadvantages of large-print materials and optical devices.

Most children with low vision are able to learn to read regular-sized print with or without the use of optical aids. This makes a much wider variety of materials available to the students and eliminates the added cost of obtaining large-print books or enlarging texts with special duplicating machines. Additionally, regular-size print books are easier to store and carry around than large-print books (Barraga & Erin, 2001).

**TABLE 10.4** Advantages and disadvantages of large-print materials and optical devices for readers with low vision

| Large-Print Materials | Optical Devices |
|---|---|
| **Advantages** | **Advantages** |
| • Little or no instruction is needed to use a large-print book or other materials. | • Users have access to materials of various sizes, such as regular texts, newspapers, menus, and maps. |
| • A low vision clinical evaluation is not needed. | • Optical devices have a lower cost per child than large-print materials do. |
| • Students carry large-print books like other students carry books in their classes. | • Devices are lighter weight and more portable than large-print materials are. |
| • Funds for large-print books come from school districts that may require parental or other funding for optical devices. | • There is no ordering or waiting time for production or availability. |
| | • Users have access to distant print and objects, such as chalkboards, signs, and people. |
| **Disadvantages** | **Disadvantages** |
| • Fewer words can be seen at once; large-print materials are more difficult to read smoothly with a natural sweep of eye movements. | • A low vision clinical evaluation must be obtained for the prescription of optical devices. |
| • Enlarging print by photocopy emphasizes imperfect letters. | • Funding for clinical evaluation and optical devices must be obtained. |
| • Pictures are in black, white, and shades of gray. | • Instruction in the use of the optical devices is needed. |
| • Fractions, labels on diagrams, maps, and so forth are enlarged to a print size smaller than 18-point type. | • The cosmetics of optical devices may cause self-consciousness. |
| • The size and weight of large-print texts make them difficult to handle. | • Optical problems associated with the optics of devices need to be tolerated. |
| • Large-print materials are not readily available after the school years, and students may be nonfunctional readers with regular-size type. | |

*Source:* A. Corn & G. Ryser, "Access to Print for Students with Low Vision." *Journal of Visual Impairment & Blindness, 83,* 340–349. Reprinted with permission from American Foundation for the Blind, 15 West 16th St., New York, NY 10011.

Based on their research on reading by children with low vision, Gompel, van Bon, and Schreuder (2004) recommend that teachers accommodate the slower reading rates of most children with low vision by doing the following:

- Provide 1 1/2 to 2 times as much time as sighted children for reading.
- Ensure sufficient time to study, and use auditory reading aids such as talking books or text-to-speech computer software if time is not available.
- Allow extra time on tests.

*Classroom Adaptations.* A number of minor classroom adaptations can be very important for students with low vision. As Bennett (1997) points out, the most effective low vision device is proper light. Most regular classrooms have adequate lighting, but adjustable lamps may still be helpful for some children. Rosenthal and Williams (2000) recommend that additional lighting should come from the side of the eye with the greatest usable vision. Many students benefit from desks with adjustable or tilting tops so that they can read and write at close range without constantly bending over and casting a shadow. Writing paper should have a dull finish to reduce glare; an off-white color such as buff or ivory is generally

For suggestions on helping students with low vision in the classroom, see "Helping the Student with Low Vision," in the Teaching & Learning module of Chapter 10 on the Companion Website, **www.prenhall.com/heward**.

better than white. Worksheets photocopied on colored paper can be difficult for students with low vision to use; if needed, an aide or a classmate can first go over the worksheet with a dark pen or marker. Some teachers have found it helpful to give students with low vision chairs with wheels so that they can easily move around the chalkboard area or other places in the classroom where instruction is taking place without constantly getting up and down. A teacher can make many other modifications using common sense and considering the needs of the individual student with low vision.

## Expanded Curriculum Priorities

In addition to learning to use braille, functional vision skills, and low vision aids, the "expanded core curriculum" (Hatlen, 1996) for students with visual impairments includes orientation and mobility, listening skills, and functional life skills.

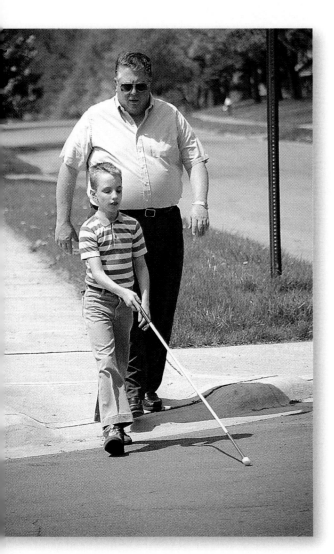

Under the watchful eyes of an orientation and mobility specialist, Eric is learning how to gain information about the path ahead by sweeping his cane in an arc.

*Orientation and Mobility.* **Orientation** is knowing where you are, where you are going, and how to get there by interpreting information from the environment. **Mobility** involves moving safely and efficiently from one point to another. Although the two sets of skills are complementary, orientation and mobility are not the same thing (Hill & Snook-Hill, 1996). A person can know where he is but not be able to move safely in that environment, and a person may be mobile but get disoriented or lost.

Orientation and mobility (O&M) instruction is considered a related service by IDEA and is included in the IEP of virtually all children with significant visual impairments. O&M specialists have developed many specific techniques (e.g., trailing, squaring off, using arms as bumpers) and mobility devices (e.g., a shopping cart, a suitcase on wheels) to teach students with visual impairments to understand their environment and maneuver through it safely and effectively (Perla & Ducret, 1999; Tellefson, 2000; Tolla, 2000).

For most students, more time and effort are spent on orientation training than on learning specific mobility techniques. It is extremely important that, from an early age, children with visual impairments be taught basic concepts that will familiarize them with their own bodies and their surroundings. For example, they must be taught that the place where the leg bends is called a "knee" and that rooms have walls, doors, windows, corners, and ceilings. Perla and O'Donnell (2004) stress the importance of systematically teaching students to respond to orientation and mobility obstacles and puzzles as problem-solving opportunities so that they will not have to depend upon others each time they find themselves in a novel environment.

**Cane Skills.** The long cane is the most widely used device for adults with severe visual impairments who travel independently (Jacobson, 1993). The traveler does not tap the cane but sweeps it lightly in an arc while walking to gain information about the path ahead. Properly used, the cane serves as both a bumper and a probe. It acts as a bumper by protecting the body from obstacles such as parking meters and doors; it is also a probe to detect in advance things such as drop-offs or changes in travel surface (e.g., from grass to concrete or from a rug to a wooden floor).

Even though mastery of cane skills can do much to increase a person's independence and self-esteem, cane use exacts physical effort and poses certain disadvantages (Gitlin, Mount, Lucas, Weirich, & Gramberg, 1997). The cane cannot detect overhanging obstacles such as tree branches and provides only fragmentary information about the environment, particularly if the person who is blind is in new or unfamiliar surroundings. Unfortunately, many adventitiously blinded persons do not begin learning cane travel skills until 1 to 2 years after losing their sight; they mention concern about acceptance by others and the negative stigmas they believe are associated with the cane (Wainapel, 1989).

Until recently, formal O&M instruction, especially for cane use, was seldom given to children younger than about 12 years of age. However, the importance of early development of travel skills and related concepts is now generally recognized. Today, it is not at all unusual for preschool children to benefit from the services of an O&M specialist; but there is disagreement over which, if any, mobility device is most suitable for initial use by very young children (Dykes, 1992). Professionals recognize the long cane's benefits of increased protection and confidence while traveling but question whether preschoolers can handle the motor and conceptual demands of long cane use. These concerns have led to the development of a variety of alternative mobility devices, including modified and smaller canes such as the Connecticut precane (Foy, Von Scheden, & Waiculonis, 1992) and the kiddy cane (Pogrund, Fazzi, & Schreier, 1993).

**Guide Dogs.** Fewer than 2% of people with visual impairments travel with the aid of guide dogs (Hill & Snook-Hill, 1996). Like the cane traveler, the guide dog user must have good O&M skills to select a route and to be aware of the environment. The dog wears a special harness and has been trained to follow several basic verbal commands, to provide protection against obstacles, and to ensure the traveler's safety. Guide dogs are especially helpful when a person must travel over complicated or unpredictable routes, as in large cities. Several weeks of intensive training at special guide dog agencies are required before the person and the dog can work together effectively. Guide dogs are not usually available to children under 16 years of age or to people with multiple disabilities. Young children, however, should have exposure to and positive experiences with dogs so they are comfortable with them and can make informed choices later about the possibilities of working with a guide dog (Young, 1997).

Although owning a guide dog is a major responsibility and sometimes inconvenient, many owners report increased confidence and independence in traveling and say that their dogs often serve as icebreakers for interactions with sighted people (Hill & Snook-Hill, 1996; Minor, 2001). However, guide dogs are not pets but working companions for their owners, and sighted people should abide by the following guidelines (Ulrey, 1994):

- Do not pet a guide dog without first seeking the owner's permission.
- Do not take hold of the dog's harness, as this might confuse the dog and the owner.
- If a person with a guide dog appears to need assistance, approach on his or her right side (guide dogs are usually on the left side) and ask if he or she needs help.

**Sighted Guides.** Most people who are blind find it necessary to rely occasionally on the assistance of others. The *sighted guide technique* is a simple method of helping a person with visual impairments to travel:

- When offering assistance to a person who is blind, speak in a normal tone of voice and ask directly, "May I help you?" This helps the person locate you.
- Do not grab the arm or body of the person who is blind. Permit him to take your arm.
- The person with visual impairment should lightly grasp the sighted person's arm just above the elbow and walk half a step behind in a natural manner. Young children might hold on to the index finger or pinky of an adult sighted guide.

• The sighted person should walk at a normal pace, describing curbs or other obstacles and hesitating slightly before going up or down. Never pull or push a person who is blind when you are serving as a sighted guide.

• Do not try to push a person who is blind into a chair. Simply place his hand on the back of the chair, and the person will seat himself.

When students with visual impairments attend regular classes, it may be a good idea for one of the students and the O&M specialist to demonstrate the sighted guide technique to classmates. To promote independent travel, however, overreliance on the sighted guide technique should be discouraged once the student has learned to get around the classroom and the school.

**Electronic Travel Aids.** Several electronic travel aids have been developed to facilitate the orientation and mobility of individuals with visual impairments. The laser beam cane converts infrared light into sound as the light beam strikes objects in the traveler's path. Different levels of vibration in the cane signal relative proximity to an obstacle. Other electronic travel aids are designed for use in conjunction with a standard cane or guide dog. The Mowat Sensor is a flashlight-sized device that bounces ultrasound off objects and gives the traveler information about the distance and location of obstacles through changes in vibration. The SonicGuide, which is worn on the head, converts reflections of ultrasound into sounds of varied pitch, amplitude, and tone that enable the traveler to determine distance, direction, and characteristics of objects in the environment.

Whatever the preferred method of travel, most students with visual impairments can generally learn to negotiate familiar places, such as school and home, on their own. Many students with visual impairments can benefit from learning to use a systematic method for obtaining travel information and assistance with street crossing. Good orientation and mobility skills have many positive effects. A child with visual impairments who can travel independently is likely to develop more physical and social skills and more self-confidence than will a child who must continually depend on other people to get around. Good travel skills also expand a student's opportunities for employment and independent living.

*Listening skills*

Council for Exceptional Children — Content Standards for Beginning Teachers—VI: Strategies for teaching listening and compensatory auditory skills (VI4K4).

*Listening Skills.* Children with visual impairments, especially those who are blind, must obtain an enormous amount of information by listening. Vision is thought to be the coordinating sense, and it has been estimated that 80% of information received by a normally sighted person comes through the visual channel (Arter, 1997; Best, 1992). Children who are blind must use other senses, predominately touch and hearing, to contact and comprehend their environment. A widely held misconception is that persons who are blind automatically develop a better sense of hearing to compensate for their loss of sight. Children with visual impairments do not have a super sense of hearing, nor do they necessarily listen better than their normally sighted peers do. It is more accurate to say that, through proper instruction and experiences, children with visual impairments learn to use their hearing more efficiently (Koenig, 1996).

The systematic development of listening skills is an important component of the educational program of every child with visual impairments. Listening is not the same thing as hearing; it is possible to hear a sound without understanding it. Listening involves being aware of sounds, discriminating differences in sounds, identifying the source of sounds, and attaching meaning to sounds (Heinze, 1986).

Learning-to-listen activities can take an almost unlimited variety of forms. Young children, for example, might learn to discriminate between sounds that are near and far, loud and soft, high-pitched and low-pitched. A teacher might introduce a new word into a sentence and ask the child to identify it or ask children to clap each time a key word is repeated. In the "shopping game," a child begins by saying, "I went to the store and I bought _____." Each player repeats the whole list of items purchased by previous students and then adds his or her own item to the list (Arter, 1997). It is important to arrange the rules of such games so that children who fail to remember the list are not eliminated, which would result in fewer opportunities to practice for the children with the weakest listening and auditory memory skills (Mangold, 1982). Older students might practice higher-order listening skills such as identifying important details with distracting background noises, differentiating between fact and opinion, or responding to verbal analogies.

Students with visual impairments, particularly in high school, make frequent use of recorded materials. In addition to using recordings of texts, lectures, and class discussions, students with visual impairments and their teachers can obtain on a free-loan basis thousands of recorded books and magazines and playback equipment through the Library of Congress, the American Printing House for the Blind (APH), the Canadian National Institute for the Blind, Recordings for the Blind, and various other organizations. But a listener can process auditory information at more than twice the speed of the average oral reading rate of about 120 words per minute (Aldrich & Parkin, 1989). Variable-speed cassette tape recorders available from the American Printing House for the Blind accelerate the playback rate of recorded text without significantly distorting the quality of the speech. In addition to tactile markings on the controls and a window that allows users to feel with their fingertip if the tape is playing, the APH Handicassette has built-in pitch control and a speech compression feature that electronically shortens the length of selected words. With practice, students can listen to accelerated and compressed speech at speeds of up to 275 words per minute without affecting comprehension (Arter, 1997).

*Functional Life Skills.* Some special educators have expressed concern that efforts to help students with visual impairments match the academic achievement of sighted age mates have too often come at the expense of sufficient opportunities to learn daily living and career skills (Miller, 1993; Sacks et al., 1998). Specific instruction and ongoing supports should be provided to ensure that students with visual impairments learn skills such as cooking, personal hygiene and grooming, shopping, financial management, transportation, and recreational activities that are requisites for an independent and enjoyable adulthood (Corn, 2000; Kaufman, 2000; Rosenblum, 2000). (To find out how three secondary students who are blind were taught to prepare some of their favorite snack foods, see Teaching & Learning, "I Made It Myself, and It's Good!" later in this chapter.)

Some students with visual impairments will also benefit from direct instruction on how to deal with strangers, how to interpret and explain their visual impairments to other people, and how to make socially acceptable gestures in conversation.

*Functional life skills*

Council for Exceptional Children Content Standards for Beginning Teachers—VI: Strategies for teaching social, daily living, and functional life skills to individuals with VI (VI4K15).

# EDUCATIONAL PLACEMENT ALTERNATIVES

In the past, most children with severe visual impairments were educated in residential schools. Today, however, 88% of children with visual impairments are educated in public schools, and two out of three receive at least some of their education in regular school classrooms: 55% of all school-age students with visual impairments are members of regular classes, and 17% attend resource rooms for part of each day (U.S. Department of Education, 2004). Separate classrooms in public schools serve another 16% of the school-age population of children with visual impairments.

## Itinerant Teacher Model

Most students with visual impairments who are included in general education classrooms receive support from itinerant teacher-consultants, sometimes called vision specialists. These specially trained teachers may be employed by the school district; a nearby residential school; or a regional, state, or provincial education agency. Although their roles and caseloads vary widely from program to program, most itinerant teacher-consultants are

*Placement alternatives*

Council for Exceptional Children Content Standards for Beginning Teachers—Common Core: Issues, assurances, and due process right related to assessment, eligibility, and placement with a continuum of services (CC1K6).

# I Made It Myself, and It's Good!

For special education to contribute to meaningful lifestyle changes for students, it must help them gain functional skills for postschool environments. Being able to prepare one's own food is a critical skill for independent living. Steve, Lisa, and Carl were 17 to 21 years old and enrolled in a class for students with multiple disabilities at a residential school for the blind. They were living in an on-campus apartment used to teach daily living skills. Several unsuccessful attempts had been made to teach basic cooking skills to the three. None possessed any functional vision or braille skills, and their IQ scores ranged from 64 to 72 on the Perkins Binet Test of Intelligence for the Blind.

To learn new skills, especially those involving long chains of responses such as following the steps of a recipe, students like Steve, Lisa, and Carl require intensive instruction over many trials. And once they have learned a new skill, it may not generalize to other settings and situations or be maintained over time. The challenge was to discover a method for teaching cooking skills that would be effective initially but also would enable the students to prepare recipes for which they had not received instruction and that resulted in long-term maintenance of their new skills.

## A "WALKMAN COOKBOOK"

Because Steve, Lisa, and Carl were blind, it was not possible to use picture cookbooks or color-coded recipes, which have been used successfully with learners with mental retardation and other disabilities (Book, Paul, Gwalla-Ogisi, & Test, 1990; Johnson & Cuvo, 1981). Instead, tape-recorded recipes were used. Each student wore a cooking apron on which two pockets had been sewn. One pocket at the waist held a small tape recorder; the second pocket, located at the chest, held a switch that the students pushed to turn the tape player on and off. Each

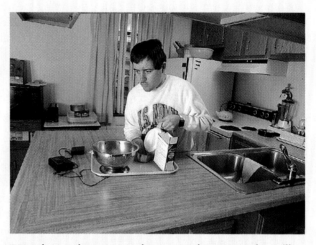

Steve learned to accurately pour and measure the milk for his cake by placing his fingers in the bowl.

step from the task-analyzed recipes was prerecorded in sequence on a cassette tape (e.g., "Open the bag of cake mix by tearing it at the tab."). A beep signaled the end of each direction.

## PERFORMANCE MEASURES

The number of recipe steps each student independently completed was measured during preinstruction (baseline), instruction, and maintenance phases. To assess generalization, probes were conducted on two classes of recipes on which the students received no training. Simple generalization recipes could be prepared with the same set of cooking skills learned in a related trained item. Complex generalization recipes required a combination of skills learned in two different trained recipes. Figure A shows the relationship between the trained recipes and the two types of recipes used to assess generalization. As a measure of social validity, each trial was also scored as to whether the food prepared was edible.

**FIGURE A** Relationships between trained recipes and two classes of untrained recipes used to assess generalization of learning

Relationship between trained recipes and two classes of untrained recipes used to assess generalization

| Simple Generalization | Trained Recipes | Complex Generalization |

French fries (11)[a] ← Pizza (13) [Lisa & Carl]
Pizza (13) ← French fries (11) [Steve]

Popcorn (10) [Lisa & Steve] ←

Tea (10) ← Coffee (10)

Pudding (13) ← Cheesecake(21)

→ Brownies
Cake (27)

*Trained Recipes* - These recipes were taught directly.

*Simple Generalization* - Preparation of these recipes required the same preparation skills as trained recipes.

*Complex Generalization* - Preparation of these recipes required a combination of the food preparation skills learned in two of the three trained recipes.

[a] = Numbers in parentheses indicate number of steps in task analysis.

## BASELINE

To objectively assess whether learning has occurred, student performance must be measured before instruction begins. The first baseline trial was conducted without the tape-recorded recipes to determine which food preparation steps, if any, each student could already perform without any assistance or adaptive equipment. It was then necessary to find out whether the students could successfully prepare any of the recipes if they were simply given the tape-recorded instructions. After being shown how to operate the tape recorder to play back the instructions, each student was asked to prepare each recipe but was given no other prompts, assistance, or feedback.

## INSTRUCTION

Students were told that the taped recipes explained exactly what to do and where to find the food items and utensils. They practiced using the remote switch to control the rate of instructions by stopping the tape each time they heard a beep. Training for each step of the task analysis consisted of a three-component least-to-most prompt hierarchy (verbal, physical, and hand-over-hand guidance) following errors and verbal praise for correct responses. Training on a recipe continued until a student correctly performed all steps on two consecutive trials over two sessions.

## RESULTS

Lisa, Carl, and Steve needed a total of 12, 19, and 35 instructional trials, respectively, to learn the three different recipes. (Steve required a greater number of trials to master the coffee and cheesecake recipes due to repeated spills when pouring liquids. Ms. Trask-Tyler solved this problem by teaching Steve to use his fingers to feel where and how much liquid he was pouring.) Additionally, after mastering the trained recipes, each student was able to prepare both the simple and the complex generalization recipes with the tape recorder, even though they had not received any instruction on those recipes.

The ultimate evaluation of cooking skills instruction is whether or not the food can be eaten; does it taste good. A mistake on any one of several crucial steps in the 27-step task analysis for making microwave cake (e.g., not stirring the egg into the batter) would result in a cake no one would want to eat. Before training, none of Steve's 13 attempts to make any of the trained recipes could be eaten, whereas all 6 of his posttraining attempts were edible. Before training, Steve was unsuccessful in all 20 of his attempts to make the simple generalization recipes and on each of 4 attempts to prepare the complex generalization recipes. After learning how to make the related recipes, he was able to follow tape-recorded recipes to successfully prepare the recipes for which he had received no direct training: on 82% of the trials (9 out of 11) with the simple generalization recipes and on all 3 trials with the complex generality recipes. In two follow-up probes conducted 6 weeks and 4 months after the study ended, Steve was still able to prepare all of the recipes successfully. Lisa and Carl showed similar gains in their ability to prepare food for themselves.

## INDIVIDUALIZED, NORMALIZED, AND SELF-DETERMINED

Self-operated audio prompting systems (SOAPS), such as the one used by Steve, Lisa, and Carl, offer several advantages (also see Briggs et al., 1990; Davis, Brady, Williams, & Burta, 1992; Grossi, 1998; Mechling & Gast, 1997; Post, Storey, & Karabin, 2002). First, the prerecorded instructions or prompts can be individualized. For example:

- Tape-recorded instructions can be as precise or general as necessary, depending on known or probable tasks and environments.
- Vocabulary can be modified, pacing of instructions speeded up or slowed down, and instructions for particularly difficult steps repeated or given in more detail.
- Students might use their own voice to record special prompts or reminders relevant to certain steps of the task (e.g., "Have I checked for spills?").
- Verbal praise and encouragement from teachers, parents, friends, or the student himself could also be included in the instructions.

Second, individuals with disabilities are currently using a variety of assistive devices to increase their independence in domestic, community, and employment settings. The learner in natural settings, however, may not use some assistive devices. A student in a crowded restaurant, for example, may hesitate to remove a laminated ordering card from her pocket or purse because it marks her as different. By contrast, the popularity of Walkman-like personal stereos and iPods enables the wearer of audio headphones to listen to a series of self-delivered prompts in a private, unobtrusive, and normalized manner that does not impose on or bother others.

Third, the self-operated feature of the system puts the student in control of the environment, thereby increasing the probability of independent functioning and level of self-determination. As Carl remarked when sharing with his girlfriend the microwave cake he had just made, "I made it myself, and it's good!"

## HOW TO GET STARTED

*If the SOAPS will be used to help a student complete multi-step activities (e.g., making macaroni and cheese):*

1. Create a task analysis of the activity.

2. Write a script of instructions for each step of the task analysis using language understood by the student.
3. Record the script, embedding a standard phrase or distinct tone between instructions to cue the student when to stop and start the playback device.

*If the SOAPS will be used to help a student stay on task and be productive during an ongoing activity (e.g., washing dishes):*

1. Write a variety of simple statements that are likely to function for the student as prompts to keep working, encouragement and praise, and/or cues to self-evaluate her performance.
2. Record the prompts, praise statement, and/or cues to self-evaluate in a random sequence at irregular intervals.
3. If listening to music would be appropriate for the student while doing the activity, consider embedding the instructions or prompts within a recording of the student's favorite singer or band.

*For all SOAPS:*

1. If necessary, teach the student how to operate the portable audio device before introducing the prerecorded instructions or prompts.
2. Observe and monitor the student's initial use of the SOAPS to determine if the length and complexity of the steps/instructions are appropriate and efficient.
3. Ask the student if any changes in the instructions or prompts would make the system more effective or enjoyable to use.

---

*Source*: Description of the teaching program conducted with Steve, Lisa, and Carl is adapted from Trask-Tyler, S. A., Grossi, T. A., & Heward, W. L. (1994). Teaching young adults with developmental disabilities and visual impairments to use tape-recorded recipes: Acquisition, generalization, and maintenance of cooking skills. *Journal of Behavioral Education, 4,* 283–311. Used by permission.

 To learn more about this strategy and answer questions about what you have learned, go to the Teaching & Learning module in Chapter 10 of the Companion Website, **www.prenhall.com/heward.**

expected to assume some or all of the following responsibilities (Flener, 1993; Willoughby & Duffy, 1989):

- Collaboratively develop with the regular classroom teacher curricular and instructional modifications according to the child's individual needs
- Provide direct instruction on compensatory skills to the student with visual impairments (e.g., listening, typing skills)
- Obtain or prepare specialized learning materials
- Adapt reading assignments and other materials into braille, large-print, or tape-recorded form or arrange for readers
- Make referrals for low-vision aids services; train students in the use and care of low-vision aids
- Interpret information about the child's visual impairment and visual functioning for other educators and parents
- Help plan the child's educational goals, initiate and maintain contact with various agencies, and keep records of services provided
- Consult with the child's parents and other teachers

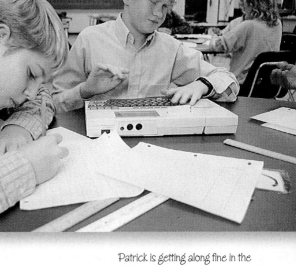

Patrick is getting along fine in the regular classroom—thanks to the instructional adaptations jointly planned by his itinerant vision specialist and his classroom teacher.

The itinerant teacher-consultant may or may not provide instruction in orientation and mobility. Some schools, particularly in rural areas, employ dually certified teachers who are also O&M specialists. Other schools employ one teacher for educational support and another for O&M training. Students on an itinerant teacher's caseload may range from infants to young adults and may include children who are blind, those with low vision, and students with multiple disabilities.

Some public school programs have special resource rooms for students with visual impairments. In contrast with the itinerant teacher-consultant who travels from school to school, the resource room teacher remains in one specially equipped location and serves students with visual impairments for part of the school day. Usually, only large school districts have resource rooms for students with visual impairments.

The amount of time the itinerant teacher-consultant or resource room teacher spends with a visually impaired student who attends regular classes varies considerably. Some students may be seen every day because they require a great deal of specialized assistance. Others may be seen weekly, monthly, or even less frequently because they are able to function well in the regular class with less support.

Inclusive education for students with visual impairments has had advocates for many years. Cruickshank (1986), for example, suggested that "the blind child is perhaps the easiest exceptional child to integrate into a regular grade in the public schools" (p. 104). To make inclusion successful, however, a full program of appropriate educational and related services must be provided (Erin, 2004; Pugh & Erin, 1999).

The key person in the program for a child with visual impairments is the regular classroom teacher. An extensive study of the elements of successful inclusion of children with visual impairments in public school classes found that the single most important factor was the regular classroom teacher's flexibility (Bishop, 1986). Other aspects of the school situation found to be highly important were peer acceptance and interaction, availability of support personnel, and adequate access to special supplies and equipment. (To find out how teachers and sighted classmates supported the inclusion of a young child with visual impairment in a community-based preschool, see Profiles & Perspectives, "Including Ryan," on the next page.)

*Importance of regular classroom teacher*

Council for Exceptional Children Content Standards for Beginning Teachers—VI: Attitudes and actions of teachers that affect the behaviors of individuals with VI (VI3K3).

409

# Including Ryan: Using Natural Supports to Make Inclusion Natural

*Including young children with disabilities in preschool classrooms with their nondisabled peers is widely recognized as a critical component of early childhood special education services. Although efforts have been made to establish more natural preschool settings to accommodate children with disabilities throughout the country, parents of children with visual impairments often have few choices of general early childhood programs that will provide the necessary supports and services for their children. In practice, however, the kinds of inclusive supports of most value are those that are commonsense, casual, and unobtrusive. Elizabeth Erwin describes how classroom staff and sighted peers made effective use of natural supports with Ryan, a 3-year-old boy with visual impairments, to facilitate his membership and meaningful participation in a community-based preschool.*

The preschool teacher, teacher aides, and Ryan's sighted classmates supported his membership and active participation in the most natural ways possible. We defined natural supports as assistance intended to create connections, competence, or teamwork in unobtrusive and individualized ways that lead to the achievement of a task or the provision of important contextual input about the environment. Equally important was acceptance by adults and classmates of the unique adaptive strategies that Ryan used to accomplish tasks and negotiate the classroom environment.

## ADULT INTERVENTIONS

All three adults in the classroom (the classroom teacher; Kima, the full-time assistant; and Dan, a part-time assistant) provided supports for Ryan in several ways.

**Contextual cues.** They provided him with frequent and consistent information about the environment and ongoing activities. For example, during snack time, Dan told Ryan, "I put your cup in front of you but not on the place mat. The other kids have it that way, so if the mat moves, the cup won't

fall over." When Ryan and four classmates were at the sand table, Kima sat behind Ryan providing verbal information: "you have to put more in your cup; it is still empty." Or "Keep your hand inside the table; otherwise, the sand will fall on the floor. Feel the difference?"

Although Kima's responsibilities were to provide assistance to all of the children in the class, she frequently furnished Ryan with information about her physical location. For example, she would alert Ryan that she was returning to or leaving the room or the immediate area and give him contextual information about others in the vicinity (e.g., "Ryan, Sue and Melissa are sitting here").

**Spontaneous events.** The staff took advantage of naturally occurring spontaneous events to promote learning and help Ryan make connections between pieces of information that other children acquired visually. For example, during show-and-tell, Ryan stood in front of the circle with the teacher and answered her questions about the Barney doll he had brought in that day. Toward the end of Ryan's turn, the teacher asked Laurie to come up and stand close to Ryan. She then asked Ryan to look at Laurie's shirt and tell the group what was on it. Ryan bent down and touched Laurie's shirt with his nose because he was so close to her. Then he exclaimed, "It's Barney!" The teacher made a big deal about the fact that the same Barney that Ryan had brought in was also on Laurie's shirt. Ryan and the other children got a big kick out of the coincidence.

**Detailed verbal directions and explanations.** The adults supported Ryan's independence by providing detailed explanations on how he could accomplish tasks. For example, when Ryan finished painting, the teacher told him, "Walk over to the rug, and when you feel the rug you'll see a bright yellow toy in front of you." Ryan followed the instruction and walked cautiously to the rug. He was a little bent over as if he was looking at the ground for cues. When he found the rug, he sat down to play with the yellow toy.

**Simple verbal cues and prompts.** Ryan usually needed explicit instructions or a demonstration only when learning a new behavior. After that, the adults used simple verbal cues to help him anticipate what might be happening next. For example, when another song began, Kima provided prompts like "Don't forget: elbows next," or "Now comes the tricky part." Ryan independently carried out the approximate body movements that corresponded to the song.

**Physical cues.** Physical cues were a natural means to give Ryan specific input about how to carry out a task or activity. He really seemed to like music time. He had a big smile on his face as he moved his body to the music. Kima used physical prompts like positioning his hands straight out in front of him as the song indicated. Once she showed him, he was able to perform the movement correctly and independently the next time the song was played.

## PEER SUPPORTS

Ryan's peers were another viable and natural source of information about and assistance in the environment. At the beginning of the school year, the children did not offer support frequently or spontaneously. Kima said: "At the beginning, they wouldn't come close to Ryan. His movements were a little different at times, and they would just watch him. Eventually, they understood that Ryan was putting his face right into theirs, and I would say this is this person or that person. Now, most of them will say, 'It's me, Ken,' or 'I'm Ronnie.'"

The children did not usually identify themselves to other classmates, but they seemed to recognize that this way of sharing information was useful to Ryan. They also realized that Ryan gained access to certain types of information or needed assistance in ways that might be different from theirs. For example, during show-and-tell it was Sue's turn to show a toy to the group. She first gave the toy to Ryan. Hillary, who was seated next to Ryan, leaned closer to him and guided his hands over the toy, purposely showing him the knobs and buttons.

At other times, the adults orchestrated encounters between Ryan and his classmates to promote positive social and communicative interactions and to reduce the amount of adult intervention. For example, during transitions Kima often enlisted the help of classmates: "I will often say, 'Cathy, can you take Ryan's hand and bring him to the rug?' The children know right away that they need to bring him through a clear path. I have noticed that they don't run him into a chair. They seem to love to do this. He loves it,

too. Ryan will take someone's hand and say, 'Well, hi there,' and start a conversation."

## RYAN'S ADAPTIVE STRATEGIES

To compensate for his visual impairment, Ryan used a variety of adaptive strategies that enabled him to move freely within the classroom and gain access to information. His father described one such strategy: "Ryan becomes physically close to people because that is his means of really figuring out what they are doing. He doesn't know how to regard other people's physical space, and he will have to learn that. Right now, he comes very close to other children, and I think that scares them a little bit." Ryan also maintained close physical proximity when he explored objects in his immediate environment. The classroom staff was cognizant of his need to use this distinctive strategy that his sighted peers did not use, and they never discouraged him from bringing objects close to his face or reprimanded him for standing close to others.

Traveling independently and making choices were age-appropriate and meaningful preschool tasks that Ryan, like his preschool classmates, needed to learn. The difference was in the way the children accomplished those goals. Ryan used familiar landmarks and signals in the classroom to orient himself, which fostered his independent mobility within the environment. Kima said: "He leads himself by touching everything. Lonie [Ryan's vision specialist] told us that he can find the light in the window, so we fostered that right from the beginning. Ryan uses the light from the window to know where the rug is. Also, he can feel the difference when he is on the floor and when he is on the rug. So he can go over and find his toys on the shelf by using the window and rug as guides."

Ryan also used verbal skills to gain information available to his classmates by vision. Kima said: "He will walk over to a group of children, and he always uses his words. If he asks a question, he will not always get an answer. But he will go over and, rather than just join in, say, 'What are you doing?' 'Who are you?' or 'What have you guys got?'"

---

*Source:* Adapted from Erwin, E. J. (1996). Meaningful participation in early childhood general education using natural supports. *Journal of Visual Impairment and Blindness, 90,* 400–411. Used by permission.

 To further your understanding of and answer reflective questions about the concepts and issues presented here, go to the Profiles & Perspectives module in Chapter 10 of the Companion Website, **www.prenhall.com/heward**.

For inclusion to be successful, a child with visual impairments needs a skilled and supportive regular classroom teacher. This was underscored by a study that asked adolescents to assess the impact of visual impairments on their lives (Rosenblum, 2000). All 10 students in the study attended public school general education classrooms for at least 50% of the school day. Several students reported that a general education teacher made it difficult for them to use disability-specific skills such as braille or computerized speech output in the classroom. ("It took him about a quarter to get the stuff [tests and worksheets] to the braillist in the first place" [p. 439].) Other participants reported that insensitive teachers caused them to feel humiliation and frustration about having a visual impairment. ("The science teacher wanted me to identify rocks by a visual method and I told her I can't. She goes, 'Well, you're going to have to if you want to get a good grade'" [p. 439].) Several other participants reported that general education teachers treated them like younger children. ("The teachers talk to me differently like I'm more of a 6 year old rather than a 13 year old" [p. 43].)

## Residential Schools

*Residential schools*

Council for Exceptional Children — Content Standards for Beginning Teachers—VI: Historical foundations of education of individuals with VI (VI1K2) (also VI1K6).

About 6.3% of school-age children with visual impairments attend residential schools (U.S. Department of Education, 2004). Residential schools continue to meet the needs of a sizable number of children with visual impairments. The current population of residential schools consists largely of children with visual impairments with additional disabilities, such as mental retardation, hearing impairment, behavioral disorders, and cerebral palsy. (See Chapter 12 for information on children with multiple disabilities, including those who are deaf-blind.) Some parents are not able to care for their children adequately at home; others prefer the greater concentration of specialized personnel, facilities, and services that a residential school usually offers.

Parents and educators who support residential schools for children with visual impairments frequently point to the leadership that such schools have provided over a long period, with their "wealth and broad range of expertise" (Miller, 1985, p. 160). These supporters argue that a residential school can be the least restrictive environment for some students with visual impairments and multiple disabilities. A follow-up study of students with visual impairments at a state school for the blind found that parents, local education agencies, and the students themselves generally considered the residential school placement to have been appropriate and beneficial (Livingston-White, Utter, & Woodard, 1985). Among the advantages cited were specialized curriculum and equipment, participation in extracurricular activities, individualized instruction, small classes, and improved self-esteem.

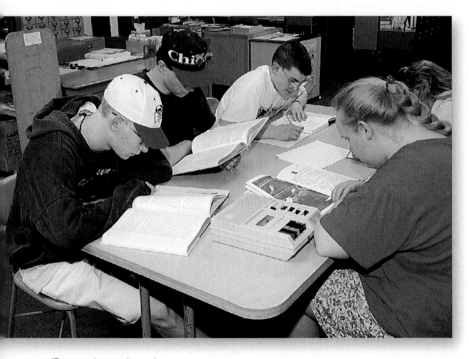

These students with visual impairments at a residential school are reading print materials in various large-size type.

Like placement at any other point in the continuum of educational settings, placement in a residential school should not be regarded as permanent. Many children with visual impairments move from residential schools into public schools (or vice versa) as their needs change. Some students in residential schools attend nearby public schools for part of the school day. Most residential schools encourage parent involvement and have recreational programs that bring students with visual impairments into contact with sighted peers. Independent living skills and vocational training are important parts of the program at virtually all residential schools.

In several states, there is close cooperation between public school and residential school programs that serve children with visual impairments. A residential school for students who are blind has an opportunity to work closely with consumers, parents, professionals, and funding agencies in developing a wide array of community-based services. Cooperative working relationships and creative short- and long-term planning efforts have the potential to generate positive and reality-based services that respond to present-day needs within the context of community integration. Residential schools—primarily because of the expertise of their staff but also because of their location, centralization of resources, and availability of facilities—have the potential to become responsive resource centers on regional and state levels.

Residential schools have long played an important role in training teachers of children with visual impairments on both a preservice and in-service basis. The residential school is usually well equipped to serve as a resource center for instructional materials and as a place where students with visual impairments can receive specialized evaluation services. An increasing number of residential schools now offer short-term training to students with visual impairments who attend regular public schools. One example is a summer workshop emphasizing braille, mobility, and vocational training.

# CURRENT ISSUES AND FUTURE TRENDS

Children with visual impairments constitute a very small portion of the school-age population, but they have many unique needs. Although the current trend toward inclusion of children with visual impairments into regular public school classrooms is generally welcomed, some educators caution against wholesale placement of children with visual impairments in regular schools without adequate support. Many vision professionals resist noncategorical special education programs for students with visual impairments. It is unrealistic, they argue, to expect regular teachers or teachers trained in other areas of special education to be competent in specialized techniques such as braille, orientation and mobility, and visual efficiency. (See Profiles & Perspectives, "A Paper on the Inclusion of Students with Visual Impairments," later in this chapter.)

*Inclusion*

Council for Exceptional Children — Content Standards for Beginning Teachers—VI: Issues and trends in special education and the field of VI (VI1K6).

## Specialization of Services

Although financial restrictions may require some public school and residential school programs for children with visual impairments to close down or consolidate with programs for children with other disabilities, strong support exists for the continuation of highly specialized services. It is likely that both public school and state-run residential programs for children with visual impairments will continue to operate well into the future, occasionally challenging each other for the privilege of serving the relatively small number of available students. The results of this competition may well prove favorable if both types of programs are encouraged to improve the quality of their educational services.

## Emerging Technology and Research

New and emerging electronic and biomedical technologies will continue to aid children and adults with visual impairments, particularly in the areas of mobility, communication, and use of low vision. The U.S. Department of Education and the National Institute on Disability, Rehabilitation, and Research have jointly funded a research and development project to develop accessible and affordable talking global positioning system (GPS) technologies for people with visual impairments. The goal of the 5-year collaborative project involving engineers, designers, O&M specialists, special educators, and rehabilitation

# A Paper on the Inclusion of Students with Visual Impairments

*American Foundation for the Blind*

"Inclusion," "full inclusion" and "inclusive education" are terms which recently have been narrowly defined by some (primarily educators of students with severe disabilities) to espouse the philosophy that ALL students with disabilities, regardless of the nature or the severity of their disability, receive their TOTAL education within the regular education environment. This philosophy is based on the relatively recent placement of a limited number of students with severe disabilities in regular classrooms. Research conducted by proponents of this philosophy lacks empirical evidence that this practice results in programs which are better able to prepare ALL students with visual impairments to be more fully included in society than the current practice, required by federal law, of providing a full range of program options.

Educators and parents of students with visual impairments have pioneered special education and inclusive program options for over 164 years. It is significant that the field of education of visually impaired students was the first to develop a range of special education program options, beginning with specialized schools in 1829 and extending to inclusive (including "full inclusion") public school program options since 1900.

Experience and research clearly support the following three position statements outlining the essential elements which must be in place in order to provide an appropriate education in the least restrictive environment for students with visual impairments.

*I. Students with visual impairments have unique educational needs which are most effectively met using a team approach of professionals, parents and students.* In order to meet their unique needs, students must have specialized services, books and materials in appropriate media (including braille), as well as specialized equipment and technology to assure equal access to the core and specialized curricula, and to enable them to most effectively compete with their peers in school and ultimately in society.

The unique educational needs of all students with visual impairments cannot be met in a single environment, even with unlimited funding. It is critical that a team approach be used in identifying and meeting these needs and that the team must include staff who have specific expertise in educating students with visual impairments. The proposal that ALL of the needs of ALL students can be met in one environment, the regular classroom, violates the spirit as well as the letter of the law—IDEA.

*II. There must be a full range of program options and support services so that the Individualized Education Program (IEP) team can select the most appropriate placement in the least restrictive environment for each individual student with a visual impairment.* The right of every student with a visual impairment to an appropriate placement in the least restrictive environment, selected by the IEP team from a full range of program options and based upon each student's needs, is nothing more or less than is mandated by federal law.

*III. There must be adequate personnel preparation programs to train staff to provide specialized services that address the unique academic and non-academic curriculum needs of students with visual impairments.* There must also be ongoing specialized personnel development opportunities for all staff working with these students as well as specialized parent education.

Students with visual impairments have the right to an appropriate education that is guided by knowledgeable specialists who work collaboratively with parents, the student and other education team members. Access to training on an ongoing basis is essential for all team members, especially parents who provide the necessary continuity and support in their child's education.

## PLACEMENT DOES NOT NECESSARILY PROVIDE ACCESS

Providing equal access to all individuals with disabilities is the key element of the Rehabilitation Act of 1973 and the Americans with Disabilities Act of 1992. Access involves much more than providing ramps. Access is also the key element of inclusion, which involves much more than placement in a particular setting. The relationship of access and inclusion may not be obvious to individuals who are not familiar with the educational and social impact of a vision loss. Placing a student with a visual impairment in a regular classroom does not, necessarily, provide access and the student is not, necessarily, included. A student with a visual impairment, who does not have access to social and physical information because of the visual impairment, is not included, regardless of the physical setting. Students with visual impairments will not be included unless their unique educational needs for access are addressed by specially trained personnel in appropriate environments and unless these students are provided with equal access to core and specialized curricula through appropriate specialized books, materials and equipment.

**Conclusion:** Students with visual impairments need an educational system that meets the individual needs of ALL students, fosters independence, and is measured by the success of each individual in the school and community.

Vision is fundamental to the learning process and is the primary basis upon which most traditional education strategies are based. Students who are visually impaired are most likely to succeed in educational systems where appropriate instruction and services are provided in a full array of program options by qualified staff to address each student's unique educational needs, as required by Public Law 101-476, The Individuals with Disabilities Education Act (IDEA).

*Source*: Executive summary from "A Paper on the Inclusion of Students with Visual Impairments," from the American Foundation for the Blind's Joseph L. Taylor Leadership Institute, Education Work Group. Copyright 2004 by the American Foundation for the Blind. The full text of this paper is available online at **http://www.afb.org/info_document_view. asp?documentid51344**.

To further your understanding of and answer reflective questions about the concepts and issues presented here, go to the Profiles & Perspectives module in Chapter 10 of the Companion Website, **www.prenhall.com/heward**.

professionals is to develop GPS and other way-finding products that can announce present location, provide audible cues for the location of pay phones and restrooms, interpret traffic signals, read street signs, give distance and direction information, and so on.

Although research in artificial sight is in the early experimental stages, it holds much promise. In the future, it may even be possible to provide a form of artificial sight to people who are totally blind by implanting electrodes into the brain and connecting them to a miniature television camera built into an artificial eye.

A number of research teams are exploring a process called *tactile vision sensory substitution*, in which tactile images are projected onto an area of the body that enable the person who is blind to perceive a visionlike sensation. An example of this line of research is work by Kathi Kamm, a professor of occupational therapy at the University of Wisconsin—Milwaukee (Griffin, 2001). Kamm's device sends images from a digital camera to a 144-pixel array of electrodes that are activated according to how bright the image is in that location of the array. In early tactile vision sensory substitution research, the electrode array was placed on a person's back, abdomen, fingers, or toes. But those locations were uncomfortable and impractical and required too much voltage to be felt. Kamm places the electrode array on the tongue because it is more sensitive and requires less voltage. And because the tongue has no sweat glands, there is no pain.

Kamm has begun using the system to teach congenitally blind children to recognize lines, letters, and faces. After 10 to 25 hours of training, the children usually begin to perceive objects in space, not on their tongues, and will begin to reach out for them.

## Fighting against Discrimination and for Self-Determination

Like other groups of individuals with disabilities, people with visual impairments are becoming increasingly aware of their rights as citizens and consumers and are fighting discrimination based on their disabilities (Koestler, 2004). Many people—even some who work with students with visual impairments—tend to underestimate their students' capacities and deny them a full range of occupational and personal choices. The future should bring a shift away from some of the vocations and settings in which people with visual impairments have traditionally worked (e.g., piano tuning, rehabilitation counseling) in favor of a more varied and rewarding range of employment opportunities.

> Some years ago, a reporter asked a prominent blind woman, "What is it that blind people would want from society?" The woman replied, "The opportunity to be equal and the right to be different."
>
> What did this woman mean by two remarks that seem diametrically opposite? Perhaps she meant that print and braille are equal, but very different; that the need for independent travel is similar for sighted and blind persons, but the skills are learned very differently by blind people; and that concepts and learning that occur for sighted people in a natural, spontaneous manner require different learning experiences for blind persons. Perhaps she was emphasizing that blind persons should have the opportunity to learn the same knowledge and skills as sighted people, but that their manner of learning will be different. (Hatlen, 1996)

# Tips for Beginning Teachers

## Supporting Students with Visual Impairments in the Regular Classroom
### by Jeanna Mora Dowse

Although each student with a visual impairment is unique and requires a specially designed set of accommodations and modifications to meet her own academic and social goals, teachers should follow some fundamental guidelines when working with any student who relies on nonvisual senses for communication and learning. Using the following tips and techniques will increase the effectiveness of your communication with students who have visual impairments and encourage and promote their confidence and independence.

### COMMUNICATE WITH CLARITY AND RESPECT

- Always state the name of the student you are speaking to in the classroom. The student with a visual impairment will not notice eye contact.
- Indefinite pronouns such as "this," "that," and "there" can be confusing to students with visual impairments. It is better to name specific items, events, or people.
- Individuals with visual impairments frequently make idiomatic references to sight, and it is okay for their teachers and peers to do so also: e.g., "Do you see what I mean?" or "Let's take a look at this next sentence."

- Always give a verbal warning when you are about to hand something to a student with visual impairments. This avoids unnecessary surprises and helps the student respond efficiently.
- Include specific spatial references when giving your student directions. For example, telling the student, "The book is on your left," or "The desk is 10 feet in front of you," is better than saying, "It's over there," or "It's near the table."
- When writing or drawing on the board, describe your actions verbally in a manner useful for all students in the class. Be sure not to talk down to the student with a visual impairment.
- Introduce yourself by name when meeting your student outside the classroom. Do not assume that he will recognize your voice, and do not ask, "Guess who this is?"
- When you are about to leave the student's vicinity, tell him that you are going.
- When you need to physically show your student how to do something, use the *hand-under-hand* technique. Have the student place her hands on top of yours so she can feel the movement of your hands. This is usually more effective than placing your hands over the student's hands.

## EXPECT AND ENABLE INDEPENDENCE

- If students are expected to perform jobs or responsibilities in your classroom, be sure also to assign a meaningful job to your students with visual impairments.
- Allow students with visual impairments time to obtain and put away materials. If a student had to use glue and scissors for an activity, make sure he returns those items to their proper places. Although it is often much easier to get and put away materials for students with visual impairments, it is critical that they learn to become self-sufficient and pick up after themselves.

- Peers are often the most effective and efficient teachers of social skills. Cooperative groups are a great way for students with visual impairments to learn important social skills.
- Always make safety a priority, but do not overprotect students with visual impairments. Hands-on experiences are the best way for a student to learn new concepts.
- Provide real-life experiences whenever possible. When on a school field trip, give the student with a visual impairment sufficient time to explore her environment.

# KEY TERMS AND CONCEPTS

accommodation, p. 389
binocular vision, p. 389
cataract, p. 390
cortical visual impairment (CVI), p. 390
field of vision, p. 384
functional vision, p. 397
glaucoma, p. 390
legally blind, p. 384

low vision, p. 385
ocular motility, p. 389
orientation and mobility, p. 402
partially sighted, p. 384
refraction, p. 390
sighted-guide technique, p. 403
tunnel vision, p. 384
visual acuity, p. 384

 To print your own set of SAFMED flash cards for studying and mastering these terms, go to the Companion Website, **www.prenhall.com/heward**.

# SUMMARY

## Definitions

- Legal blindness is defined as visual acuity of 20/200 or less in the better eye after correction with glasses or contact lenses or a restricted field of vision of 20% or less.
- An educational definition classifies students with visual impairments based on the extent to which they use vision and/or auditory/tactile means for learning.
- A student who is totally blind receives no useful information through the sense of vision and must use tactile, auditory, and other nonvisual senses for all learning.
- A child who is functionally blind has so little vision that she learns primarily through the auditory and tactile senses; however, she may be able to use her limited vision to supplement the information received from the other senses.
- A child with low vision uses vision as a primary means of learning.
- The age at onset of a visual impairment affects a child's educational and emotional needs.

## Characteristics

- Children with severe visual impairments do not benefit from incidental learning that normally sighted children obtain in everyday experiences and interactions with the environment.

- Visual impairment often leads to delays or deficits in motor development.
- Some students with visual impairments experience social isolation and difficulties in social interactions due to limited common experiences with sighted peers; inability to see and use eye contact, facial expressions, and gestures during conversations; and/or stereotypic behaviors.
- The behavior and attitudes of sighted persons can be unnecessary barriers to the social participation of individuals with visual impairments.

## Prevalence

- Visual impairment is a low-incidence disability affecting approximately 2 of every 1,000 children in the school-age population. About one-half of all students with visual impairments have additional disabilities.

## Types and Causes of Visual Impairment

- The eye collects light reflected from objects and focuses the objects' image on the retina. The optic nerve transmits the image to the visual cortex of the brain. Difficulty with any part of this process can cause vision problems.
- Refractive errors mean that the size and shape of the eye prevent the light rays from focusing clearly on the retina.
- Structural impairments are visual impairments caused by poor development of, damage to, or malfunction of one or more parts of the eye's optical or muscular systems.
- Cortical visual impairment (CVI) refers to decreased vision or blindness due to damage to or malfunction of the parts of the brain that interpret visual information.

## Educational Approaches

- Braille—a tactile system of reading and writing in which letters, words, numbers, and other systems are made from arrangements of embossed six-dot cells—is the primary means of literacy for students who are blind.
- Students who are blind may also use special equipment to access standard print through touch, reading machines, and prerecorded materials.
- Children with low vision should be taught to use visual efficiency or functioning.
- Students with low vision use three basic methods for reading print: approach magnification, optical devices, and large print.
- Students who are blind or have severe visual impairments need instruction in orientation (knowing where they are, where they are going, and how to get there) and mobility (moving safely and efficiently from one point to another).
- Systematic development of listening skills is an important component of the educational program of every child with visual impairments.
- The curriculum for students with visual impairments should also include systematic instruction in functional living skills such as cooking, personal hygiene and grooming, shopping, financial management, transportation, and recreational activities.

## Educational Placement Alternatives

- Two out of three children with visual impairments spend at least part of each school day in regular classes with sighted peers.
- In many districts, a specially trained itinerant vision specialist provides support for students with visual impairments and their regular classroom teachers.
- Some programs also have separate orientation and mobility instructors or separate resource rooms for students with visual impairments.

- About 6% of children with visual impairments, especially those with other disabilities, attend residential schools.
- Most parents can choose between public day and residential schools for their children with visual impairments.

## Current Issues and Future Trends

- Children with visual impairments are likely to receive specialized services in the future in both regular and residential schools. Greater emphasis will be placed on intervention with visually impaired infants and young children and on training older students for independence.
- In the future, increasing numbers of people with visual impairments will benefit from new technological and biomedical developments, and artificial sight may be possible.
- Career opportunities will likely expand as individuals with visual impairments become more aware of their legal and human rights.

 To check your comprehension of chapter contents, go to the Guided Review and Quiz modules in Chapter 10 of the Companion Website, **www.prenhall.com/heward**.

# PHYSICAL DISABILITIES, HEALTH IMPAIRMENTS, AND ADHD

## Featured Teacher

### Mary Kate Ryan-Griffith

Judith A. Resnik Elementary School
Montgomery County Public Schools
Gaithersburg, Maryland

*Education—Teaching Credentials—Experience*
- B.S., special education/elementary education, Peabody College for Teachers, Vanderbilt University, 1980
- M.A., education of the hearing impaired, Gallaudet University, 1984
- Maryland professional certificates: special education, K–12; hearing impaired, K–12; and elementary education, K–6
- 4 years as a fourth-grade teacher; 13 years as a special educator

*Current Teaching Position and Students*    For the first six years of my special education career, I was the resource teacher for the entire elementary school, with a caseload of up to 50 students. Our model for service delivery of special education has changed dramatically in the past several years. We have moved from the traditional model of separate programs with pull-out resource services to a departmentalized approach, assigning each special educator in the building to a grade level. The special educator serves all children with special needs on her grade level in an inclusion model, with minimal pull-out for specialized groups or differentiation. I am currently assigned to the fourth grade. I co-teach in three classrooms and have two pull-out reading groups. I currently work with 16 students with a wide range of disabilities: physical challenges caused by cerebral palsy and bone defects, learning disabilities, attention-deficit/hyperactivity disorder (ADHD), emotionally disabled, and one child who is hard of hearing. The children come from low- to middle-income families. They are white, African American, Hispanic, American Indian, and Native African. Several speak Spanish or Ghanaian as their first language.

*Adaptations and Teaching Strategies*    These children can function within the regular classroom, but they require support. These supports range from academic to physical. Some children in wheelchairs require desks with a cut-out that they can get in and under. Tables and desks may need to be raised, and special seats in bathrooms are sometimes necessary. Walkers, standards, and leg braces are everyday pieces of equipment. If children's hands are not fully functional, special pencil grips and eating utensils are a great help.

The computer has been the greatest advance for improving academic abilities. Bridget's cerebral palsy causes spasticity in her hands, which makes writing or standard keyboarding very difficult. For her I work with the occupational therapist to create *overlays*—pages fitted to a special type of keyboard that run on a special software program. Each overlay is created with specific types of information about a subject, such as different kinds of maps, or generic sentence parts relating to a book we are reading. By touching the keyboard, Bridget can create sentences

## Focus Questions

- In what ways might the visibility of physical or health impairments affect a child's self-perception, social development, and level of independence across different environments?

- How do the nature and severity of a child's physical disability affect IEP goals and objectives?

- What are some of the problems that members of transdisciplinary teams for students with severe physical disabilities and multiple health needs must guard against?

- How might an assistive technology device be a hindrance as well as a help?

- Of the many ways in which the classroom environment and instruction can be modified to support the inclusion of students with physical disabilities, health impairments, and ADHD, which are most important?

related to the subject. She can do this independently and really enjoys her schoolwork since she is relieved of the drudgery of writing or typing and creates it herself. My students use a variety of typing/voice programs. Tim has learning disabilities and severe motoric impact in his hands. His writing is basically illegible; so he types on a program that gives him choices for words, then voices his paragraph back to him. In this way he can work independently and monitor his own spelling and grammar. We also use programs that create graphic organizers for children. This helps to improve comprehension, especially when students are writing a report. I also use low-tech devices and strategies to aid reading and writing such as raised-line paper and multicolored paper; a ruler, index cards, or paper to maintain students' place; or, for the extremely distracted, a cut-out window in a long page so they only see one line at a time.

In the classroom I may read to children from books and tests and have them dictate their responses. Some children use this as a crutch, so I create transitions: first, I write everything, then the student writes a line, then a paragraph, and then she writes it all herself with support for spelling and mechanics. Sometimes children need me to write for them because they lack confidence, so building a positive attitude is paramount to success.

***Advice to Someone Considering a Career in Special Education***     Attitude is everything. I broke my neck in a car accident one week after completing student teaching for my master's degree from Gallaudet University. Clinically, I am an *incomplete quadriplegic* since I only traumatized my spinal cord, not severed it. I am paralyzed from the chest down and have some slight impairment of the arms and hands. I am very independent. I drive myself to work using hand controls, and my van has a special seat and a lift. My husband and I adapted our house with a ramp, a larger bathroom, and a tub seat for showers. I frequently use a reacher (a long metal rod with a clamp at the end) to get things that are out of my reach; but otherwise, I don't require much special equipment. I tend to use things in the environment to help me. Anything that can extend my reach is subject to use, whether it be a spatula in the kitchen or a ruler in school. I am relatively healthy, though I do take daily medication for spasticity. I can punch out any bully when my legs go into spasm.

I have been in a wheelchair for 20 years. For years after my accident I went through all the stages of grief, from denial to acceptance. Much like the death of a loved one, I grieved over the loss of my abilities to dance, run, and do other ambulatory activities; and that loss still pains me occasionally, even now. However, I have always believed that where a door closes, someone opens a window and that human beings are the most adaptable creatures on earth. I have learned to perform cherished activities from my chair. I get a kick out of surprised looks when I take to the dance floor.

I have always taught from a chair. In my job I work with both parents and children who are dealing with challenges. Some parents have children who were born with challenges and medically diagnosed at birth. Others have children who qualified for special education after encountering academic difficulties. At some point, all of these parents must go through the grief process. They need to grieve the loss of the "perfect child," get through the guilt that they did something that made their child that way, and in some cases get past denying that there is a problem. It is a process in which I can relate with parents and help them understand their child on another level. For example, even though I'm in a wheelchair and their child is learning disabled, the need to do things differently and the understanding that it is a lifelong process are the same. It is something that special education teachers need to be sensitive to. This is an enormous realization for the parents, who have to deal with not only the disability but also the meetings, the paperwork, the everyday needs of the child, and the question "where do we go from here?"

Children experience the same grief process, but more on a level of "I can't do what others are doing," whether it be running or reading. I try to relate my experience of having to do things differently to whatever they are concerned with at the time. I explain that having to do things differently doesn't mean they are stupid. Everyone has his own special way of learning, and my job is to find out how children learn so I can teach them better. For older kids I explain their test scores and what an IEP means. I bring them into their challenges so that they own them. Getting vested in and feeling positive about their progress is extremely important. Another important way I get through to kids is by talking about myself. When I encounter a new group of students, I always begin by telling about myself, bringing them into my challenges, explaining why I'm in a wheelchair, and letting them ask questions. This way they also start to talk about themselves, and we can relate our experiences with doing things differently and feelings about our challenges. I also talk to the general education classes so they can become more sensitive to the challenges of others. In this way they can start to see people, not chairs. Then we all go out and take a ride on my lift.

Children with physical disabilities and health impairments are an extremely varied population. Describing them with a single set of characteristics would be impossible, even if we used very general terms. Their physical disabilities may be mild, moderate, or severe. Some children with special health care needs are extremely restricted in their activities and intellectual functioning; others have no major limitations on what they can do and learn. Some appear entirely normal; others have highly visible disabilities. Children may have a single impairment or a combination of disabilities. They may have lived with the physical disability or health impairment since birth or have acquired it recently. Some children must use special assistive devices that call attention to their disability; others display behaviors they cannot control. Some disabilities are always present; others occur only from time to time. Over an extended period, the degree of disability may increase, decrease, or remain about the same.

As you can see, the students whose special education needs we consider in this chapter have a great many individual differences. Linda, for example, has undergone long periods of hospitalization and finds it difficult to keep up with her academic work. Gary takes medication that controls his seizures most of the time, but it also tends to make him drowsy in class. Brian, who uses a wheelchair for mobility, is disappointed that he is unable to compete with his classmates in football, baseball, and track. Yet he participates fully in all other aspects of his high school program with no special modifications other than the addition of a few ramps in the building and a newly accessible washroom. Most of Brian's teachers and friends, in fact, do not think of him as needing special education at all. Janice becomes tired easily and attends school for only 3 hours per day. Kencel does his schoolwork in a specially designed chair that helps him sit more comfortably in the classroom.

An appropriate education for children with physical and health impairments may require modifications in the classroom environment, use of specialized teaching techniques, assistive devices for communication or mobility, and/or provision of related health services in the classroom. It is important for teachers (and often for other students as well) to understand how a particular condition may affect a child's learning, development, and behavior. Because some physical and health impairments may cause possible complications or emergencies to arise in the classroom, it is equally important for the teacher to know how to manage such situations effectively and when and how to seek help. Although we can make general statements about some physical disabilities, health impairments, and ADHD, numerous variations occur in the degree and severity of the conditions and how they may affect a child and his educational needs. Thus, basic information and suggested guidelines shape our basic approach to this chapter.

 To better understand the topics that will be covered in this chapter, go to the Essential Concepts and Chapter at a Glance modules in Chapter 11 of the Companion Website, **www.prenhall.com/heward**.

*Definitions of orthopedic
impairments and other health
impairments*

Council for
Exceptional   Content
Children        Standards for
Beginning Teachers—P&HD:
Issues and educational
definitions of individuals with
P&HD (PH1K1).

# PHYSICAL DISABILITIES AND HEALTH IMPAIRMENTS

## Definitions

Children with physical disabilities and health conditions who require special education are served under two IDEA disability categories: orthopedic impairments and other health impairments. According to IDEA, a severe orthopedic impairment

> adversely affects a child's educational performance. The term includes impairments caused by congenital anomaly (e.g., clubfoot, absence of some member, etc.), impairments caused by disease (e.g., poliomyelitis, bone tuberculosis, etc.), and impairments from other causes (e.g., cerebral palsy, amputations, and fractures or burns that cause contractures). (C.F.R. Sec. 300.7 [b] [7])

Although IDEA uses the term *orthopedic impairments,* children with physical disabilities may have orthopedic impairments or neuromotor impairments. An **orthopedic impairment** involves the skeletal system—bones, joints, limbs, and associated muscles. A **neuromotor impairment** involves the central nervous system, affecting the ability to move, use, feel, or control certain parts of the body. Although orthopedic and neurological impairments are two distinct and separate types of disabilities, they may cause similar limitations in movement. Many of the same educational, therapeutic, and recreational activities are likely to be appropriate for students with orthopedic and neurological impairments (Best, Heller, & Bigge, 2005). And there is a close relationship between the two types: for example, a child who is unable to move his legs because of damage to the central nervous system (neuromotor impairment) may also develop disorders in the bones and muscles of the legs (orthopedic impairment), especially if he does not receive proper therapy and equipment.

Children served under the IDEA category of **other health impairments** have

> limited strength, vitality, or alertness due to chronic or acute health problems such as a heart condition, tuberculosis, rheumatic fever, nephritis, asthma, sickle cell anemia, hemophilia, epilepsy, lead poisoning, leukemia, or diabetes that adversely affects a child's educational performance. (20 U.S.C., 1400 et seq.)

Health impairments include diseases and special health conditions that affect a child's educational activities and performance such as cancer, diabetes, and cystic fibrosis. Some children with attention-deficit/hyperactivity disorder (ADHD) are served under the other health impairments category of IDEA, with the reasoning that their condition results in a heightened alertness that adversely affects their educational performance. However, many children with ADHD who meet eligibility requirements for special education are served under other disability categories, most often specific learning disabilities or emotional disturbance. ADHD is discussed in later in this chapter.

Note the common clause in each definition: *that adversely affects a child's educational performance.* According to IDEA, a child is entitled to special education services if her educational performance is adversely affected by a physical disability or a health-related condition. Physical disabilities and health conditions may be congenital (a child is born with a missing limb) or acquired (a child without disabilities sustains a spinal cord injury at age 15). Not all students with physical disabilities and health conditions need special education. Most physical disabilities and health conditions that result in special education are *chronic conditions*—that is, they are long-lasting, most often permanent conditions (e.g., cerebral palsy is a permanent disability that will affect a child throughout his life). By contrast, an *acute condition,* while it may produce severe and debilitating symptoms, is of limited duration (e.g., a child who acquires pneumonia will experience symptoms, but the disease itself is not permanent). Some chronic physical disabilities and health conditions have flare-ups or episodes of acute symptoms (e.g., a child with cystic fibrosis may experience periods of acute respiratory difficulties).

*Chronic and acute conditions*

Council for
Exceptional   Content
Children        Standards for
Beginning Teachers—P&HD:
Medical terminology related to
P&HD (PH2K1).

# PREVALENCE

It is estimated that chronic medical conditions affect up to 20%—approximately 12 million—school-age children in the United States (Sexson & Dingle, 2001). However, during the 2003–2004 school year, just 67,772 children with between the ages of 6 and 21 received special education services under the disability category of orthopedic impairments and 449,093 children with other health impairments (U.S. Department of Education, 2004). Together, these two disability categories represent 8.6% of all school-age children receiving special education services.

Two factors make the actual number of children with physical disabilities much higher than the number of children receiving special education services under these two IDEA categories. First, because physical and health impairments often occur in combination with other disabilities, children may be counted under other categories, such as learning disabilities, speech impairment, or mental retardation. For example, for the purpose of special education eligibility, a diagnosis of mental retardation usually takes precedence over a diagnosis of physical impairment. Second, there are numerous children whose physical impairments and chronic health conditions do not adversely affect their educational performance sufficiently to warrant special education (Hill, 1999).

*Types and causes of physical disabilities and health impairments*

Council for Exceptional Children — Content Standards for Beginning Teachers—P&HD: Etiology and characteristics of P&HD across the life span (PH2K2) (also PH2K1).

# TYPES AND CAUSES

Literally hundreds of physical impairments and health conditions can adversely affect children's educational performance. Here we address only those that are encountered most frequently in school-age children. For a more extensive discussion of the many physical impairments and chronic health conditions that may result in special education, see Batshaw (2002), Best, Heller, and Bigge (2005), or Hill (1999).

## Cerebral Palsy

**Cerebral palsy**—a disorder of voluntary movement and posture—is the most prevalent physical disability in school-age children. In some programs, half or more of the students considered to have physical or health impairments have cerebral palsy. Cerebral palsy is a permanent condition resulting from a lesion to the brain or an abnormality of brain growth. Many diseases can affect the developing brain and lead to cerebral palsy (Batshaw, 2002). Children with cerebral palsy experience disturbances of voluntary motor functions that may include paralysis, extreme weakness, lack of coordination, involuntary convulsions, and other motor disorders. They may have little or no control over their arms, legs, or speech, depending on the type and degree of impairment. The more severe forms of cerebral palsy are often diagnosed in the first few months of life. In many other cases, however, cerebral palsy is not detected until the child is 2 to 3 years old, when parents notice that their child is having difficulty crawling, balancing, or standing. The motor dysfunction usually does not get progressively worse as a child ages. Cerebral palsy can be treated but not cured; it is not a disease, not fatal, not contagious, and, in the great majority of cases, not inherited.

With a little help from a classmate, another musician joins the marching band.

About one-third of children with cerebral palsy have intelligence within or above the normal range, one-third have mild cognitive impairment, and one-third have moderate to severe mental retardation (e.g., Whaley & Wong, 1995). Sensory impairments are also common in children with cerebral palsy; 5% to 15% have hearing loss (Nechring & Steele, 1996), and up to 50% have impaired vision (Dzienkowski, Smith, Dillow, & Yucha, 1996). It is important to note that no clear relationship exists between the degree of motor impairment and the degree of intellectual impairment (if any) in children with cerebral palsy (or other physical disabilities). A student with only mild motor impairment may experience severe developmental delays, whereas a student with severe motor impairments may be intellectually gifted (Willard-Holt, 1998).

The causes of cerebral palsy are varied and not clearly known (Pellegrino, 2002). It has most often been attributed to the occurrence of injuries, accidents, or illnesses that are *prenatal* (before birth), *perinatal* (at or near the time of birth), or *postnatal* (soon after birth) and that result in decreased oxygen to low-birth-weight newborns. Recent improvements in obstetrical delivery and neonatal care, however, have not decreased the incidence of cerebral palsy, which has remained steady during the past 20 years or so at about 1.5 in every 1,000 live births (Evans & Smith, 1993). An additional 1,200 to 1,500 children acquire cerebral palsy through post-birth trauma or accidents (Heller, Alberto, Forney, & Schwartzman, 1996). Factors most often associated with cerebral palsy are mental retardation of the mother, premature birth (gestational age of 32 weeks or less), low birth weight, and a delay of 5 minutes or more before the baby's first cry.

Because the location and extent of brain damage is so variable in individuals with cerebral palsy, a diagnosis of the condition is not descriptive of its effects. Cerebral palsy is classified in terms of the affected parts of the body and by its effects on movement (Best & Bigge, 2005). The term *plegia* (from the Greek "to strike") is often used in combination with a prefix indicating the location of limb involvement:

*Limbs affected by cerebral palsy*

Council for
Exceptional
Children     Content
Standards for
Beginning Teachers—P&HD:
Medical terminology related to
P&HD (PH2K1).

- *Monoplegia.* Only one limb (upper or lower) is affected.
- *Hemiplegia.* Two limbs on same side of the body are involved.
- *Triplegia.* Three limbs are affected.
- *Quadriplegia.* All four limbs (both arms and legs) are involved; movement of the trunk and face may also be impaired.
- *Paraplegia.* Only legs are impaired.
- *Diplegia.* Impairment primarily involves the legs, with less severe involvement of the arms.
- *Double hemiplegia.* Impairment primarily involves the arms, with less severe involvement of the legs.

*Hypertonia, athetosis, ataxia, and hypotonia*

Council for
Exceptional
Children     Content
Standards for
Beginning Teachers—P&HD:
Medical terminology related to
P&HD (PH2K1) (also PH2K2,
PH3K1, CC2K1).

Cerebral palsy is defined according to its effects on muscle tone (hypertonia or hypotonia) and quality of movement (athetosis or ataxia) (Pellegrino, 2002). Approximately 50% to 60% of all individuals with cerebral palsy have *spastic cerebral palsy,* which is characterized by tense, contracted muscles (**hypertonia**). Their movements may be jerky, exaggerated, and poorly coordinated. They may be unable to grasp objects with their fingers. When they try to control their movements, they may become even jerkier. If they are able to walk, they may use a scissors gait, standing on the toes with knees bent and pointed inward. Deformities of the spine, hip dislocation, and contractures of the hand, elbow, foot, and knee are common.

**Athetosis** occurs in about 20% of all cases of cerebral palsy. Children with *athetoid cerebral palsy* make large, irregular, twisting movements they cannot control. When they are at rest or asleep, there is little or no abnormal motion. An effort to pick up a pencil, however, may result in wildly waving arms, facial grimaces, and extension of the tongue. These children may not be able to control the muscles of their lips, tongue, and throat and may drool. They may also seem to stumble and lurch awkwardly as they walk. At times their muscles may be tense and rigid; at other times, they may be loose and flaccid. Extreme difficulty in expressive oral language, mobility, and activities of daily living often accompanies this form of cerebral palsy.

**Ataxia** is noted as the primary type of involvement in only 1% to 10% of cases of cerebral palsy (Hill, 1999). Children with *ataxic cerebral palsy* have a poor sense of balance and hand use. They may appear to be dizzy while walking and may fall easily if not supported. Their movements tend to be jumpy and unsteady, with exaggerated motion patterns that often overshoot the intended objects. They seem to be constantly attempting to overcome the effect of gravity and stabilize their bodies.

*Rigidity* and *tremor* are additional but much less common types of cerebral palsy. Children with the rare rigidity type of cerebral palsy display extreme stiffness in the affected limbs; they may be fixed and immobile for long periods. Rhythmic, uncontrollable movements mark tremor cerebral palsy; the tremors may actually increase when the children attempt to control their actions.

Most infants born with cerebral palsy have **hypotonia,** or weak, floppy muscles, particularly in the neck and trunk. When hypotonia persists throughout the child's first year without being replaced with spasticity or athetoid involvement, the condition is called generalized hypotonia. Hypotonic children typically have low levels of motor activity, are slow to make balancing responses, and may not walk until 30 months of age (Bleck, 1987). Severely hypotonic children must use external support to achieve and maintain an upright position.

Because most children with cerebral palsy have diffuse brain damage, pure types of cerebral palsy are rare. Children may also be described as having *mixed cerebral palsy,* consisting of more than one of these types, particularly if their impairments are severe. The motor impairment of children with cerebral palsy often makes it frustrating, if not impossible, for them to play with toys. (See Teaching & Learning, "Adapting Toys for Children with Cerebral Palsy," later in this chapter.)

Because cerebral palsy is such a complex condition, it is most effectively managed through the cooperative involvement of physicians, teachers, physical therapists, occupational therapists, communication specialists, counselors, and others who work directly with children and families. Dormans and Pellegrino (1998) have compiled a detailed handbook to guide the education of children with cerebral palsy by interdisciplinary teams. Regular exercise and careful positioning in school settings help the child with cerebral palsy move as fully and comfortably as possible and prevent or minimize progressive damage to muscles and limbs. Most children with cerebral palsy are capable of learning to walk, although many need to use wheelchairs, braces, and other assistive devices, particularly for moving around outside the home. Orthopedic surgery may increase a child's range of motion or obviate complications such as hip dislocations and permanent muscle contractions.

The *Mobility Opportunities Via Education (MOVE) Curriculum* is a systematic program for teaching walking and functional mobility skills to students with cerebral palsy and other severe physical disabilities. There is some research evidence of its effectiveness (Barnes & Whinnery, 2002; Bidabe, Barnes, & Whinnery, 2001). The *MOVE* curriculum is a top-down, activity-based program in which a transdisciplinary team consisting of therapists, teachers, and parents assesses the child's current skills and designs and individualized program of systematic practice of mobility skills within the natural context of the child's typical daily activities. Physical supports are gradually faded: children move from the Rifton Gait Trainer (Community Playthings, 1999), which provides total support for individuals just beginning to bear their weight and learning to take reciprocal steps, to adult assistance, to independent movement as their accomplishments increase.

## Spina Bifida

Congenital malformations of the brain, spinal cord, or vertebrae are known as *neural tube defects*. The most common neural tube defect is **spina bifida,** a condition in which the vertebrae do not enclose the spinal cord. As a result, a portion of the spinal cord and the nerves that normally control muscles and feeling in the lower part of the body fail to develop

# Adapting Toys for Children with Cerebral Palsy

Spontaneous and independent use of commercially available toys is not possible for many children with cerebral palsy. The toys often require more coordination or strength than these youngsters have. Continuous inability to engage in physical activity and gain mastery over the environment may cause the child to lose motivation and become passive. Because playing is an integral part of intellectual, social, perceptual, and physical development, growth in these areas may be limited when the child cannot actively play.

## HOW TO GET STARTED

Fortunately, toys can be adapted to make them more accessible to children with physical disabilities. Six types of modifications are most effective in promoting active, independent use of play materials.

**Stabilize the toy.** Stabilizing a toy enhances its function in two ways. First, it prevents the child's uncontrolled movements and difficulty directing the hand to desired locations from moving objects out of reach or knocking them over. Second, many children with cerebral palsy have difficulty performing tasks that require holding an object with one hand while manipulating it in some way with the other hand. Toys with a base can be clamped to a table. Masking tape is an inexpensive and effective way to secure many toys. Velcro is another. The hook side of Velcro can be placed on the toy, while the loop side is mounted on a clean surface. Suction cups can also stabilize a toy for a short time on a clean, nonwood surface.

**Create boundaries.** Restricting the movement of toys such as cars or trains makes it easier for some children to use and retrieve them if pushed out of reach. Boundaries can be created in various ways depending upon how the object is to be moved. For example, push toys can be placed in the top of a cardboard box or on a tray with edges to create a restricted area. Pull toys can be placed on

a track, and items that require a banging motion, such as a tambourine, can be held in a wooden frame with springs.

**Add a grasping aid.** The ability to hold objects independently can be facilitated in a variety of ways. A Velcro strap can be placed around the child's hand, with Velcro also placed on the materials to be held, thus creating a bond between the hand and the object. A universal cuff can be used for holding sticklike objects such as

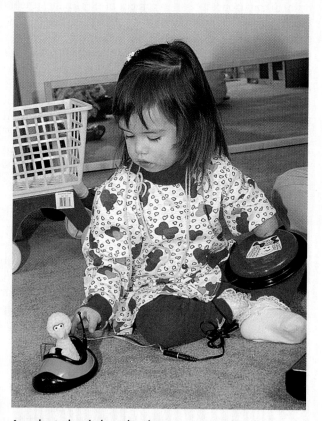

An adapted switch makes battery-operated toys accessible and fun for Madelyn.

crayons or pointers. Simply enlarging an item by wrapping foam or tape around it may make it easier to hold.

**Make the toy easier to manipulate.** Some toys require isolated finger movements, use of a pincer grasp, and controlled movements of the wrist, which are too difficult for a child with physical disabilities. Various adaptations can help compensate for deficits in these movements. Extending and widening pieces of the toy will make swiping and pushing easier. Flat extensions, knobs, or dowels can be used to increase the surface area. A crossbar or a dowel, placed appropriately, can compensate for an inability to rotate the wrist.

**Add a special activation switch.** Some children have such limited hand function that they can only operate toys that are activated by a switch. Commercially available, battery-operated toys can be modified to operate by adapted switches. Teachers can make and adapt their own switches and toys (Burkhardt, 1981; Wright & Momari, 1985) or purchase them from a number of firms that serve persons with disabilities. After determining some physical action (such as moving a knee laterally, lifting a shoulder, or making a sound) that the child can perform consistently and with minimum effort, select the type of switch best suited to that movement. The switch is always positioned in the same place, which facilitates automatic switch activation and allows the child to give full attention to the play activity rather than concentrating on using the switch.

**Consider the child's positioning needs.** An occupational or physical therapist should determine the special positioning needs of each child. Good positioning will maximize freedom of movement, improve the ability to look at a toy, and facilitate controlled, relaxed movement. Placement of the toy is crucial. It should be within easy reach and require a minimum of effort to manipulate. The child should not become easily fatigued or have to struggle. The child must be able to look at the toy while playing.

**Other considerations.** Activities should be interesting and facilitate cognitive growth yet not be beyond the child's conceptual capabilities. Toys should be sturdy and durable. Avoid toys with sharp edges or small pieces that can be swallowed.

These principles for adapting toys can be applied to other devices, such as communication aids, computers, environmental controls, and household items, to make them easier to use. Making an educational environment more accessible gives children with physical disabilities greater control of their surroundings and the opportunity to expand the scope of their learning experiences.

*Source:* Adapted from Schaeffler, C. (1988, Spring). Making toys accessible for children with cerebral palsy. *Teaching Exceptional Children, 20,* 26–28. Used by permission.

 To learn more about these strategies and answer questions about what you have learned, go to the Teaching & Learning module in Chapter 11 of the Companion Website, **www.prenhall.com/heward**.

normally. Of the three types of spina bifida, the mildest form is **spina bifida occulta,** in which only a few vertebrae are malformed, usually in the lower spine. The defect is usually not visible externally. It is estimated that up to 10% of the general population may have spina bifida occulta (Liptak, 2002). If the flexible casing (meninges) that surrounds the spinal cord bulges through an opening in the infant's back at birth, the condition is called **meningocele.** These two forms do not usually cause any loss of function for the child.

In **myelomeningocele**—the most common and most serious form of spina bifida—the spinal lining, spinal cord, and nerve roots all protrude. The protruding spinal cord and nerves are usually tucked back into the spinal column shortly after birth. This condition carries a high risk of paralysis and infection. In general, the higher the location of the lesion on the spine, the greater the effect on the body and its functioning. About 6 in 10,000 live births in the United States result in myelomeningocele; and it affects girls at a much higher rate than boys (Liptak, 2002).

About 80% to 90% of children born with myelomeningocele develop **hydrocephalus,** the accumulation of cerebrospinal fluid in tissues surrounding the brain (Hill, 1999). Left untreated, this condition can lead to head enlargement and severe brain damage. Hydrocephalus is treated by the surgical insertion of a **shunt,** a one-way valve that diverts the cerebrospinal fluid away from the brain and into the bloodstream. Replacements of the shunt are usually necessary as a child grows older. Teachers who work with children who have shunts should be aware that blockage, disconnection, or infection of the shunt may result in increased intracranial pressure. Warning signs such as drowsiness, vomiting, headache,

*Spina bifida and related terms*

Council for Exceptional Children Content Standards for Beginning Teachers—P&HD: Medical terminology related to P&HD (PH2K1) (also PH2K2, PH3K1).

irritability, and squinting should be heeded because a blocked shunt can be life-threatening (Charney, 1992). Shunts can be removed in many school-age children when the production and absorption of cerebrospinal fluid are brought into balance.

Usually children with spina bifida have some degree of paralysis of the lower limbs and lack full control of bladder and bowel functions. In most cases, these children have good use of their arms and upper body (although some children experience fine-motor problems). Children with spina bifida usually walk with braces, crutches, or walkers; they may use wheelchairs for longer distances. Some children need special help in dressing and toileting; others are able to manage these tasks on their own.

Because the spinal defect usually occurs above where nerves that control the bladder emerge from the spinal cord, most children with spina bifida have urinary incontinence and need to use a *catheter* (tube) or bag to collect their urine. **Clean intermittent catheterization (CIC)** is taught to children with urinary complications so that they can empty their bladders at convenient times (Ault, Rues, Graff, & Holvoet, 2006). This technique is effective with both boys and girls, works best if used every 2 to 4 hours, and does not require an absolutely sterile environment (McLone & Ito, 1998).

*Clean intermittent catherization (CIC)*

Council for Exceptional Children — Content Standards for Beginning Teachers—P&HD: Specialized health care interventions for individuals with P&HD (PH5K2).

## Muscular Dystrophy

**Muscular dystrophy** refers to a group of inherited diseases marked by progressive *atrophy* (wasting away) of the body's muscles. **Duchenne muscular dystrophy (DMD)** is the most common and most severe of the 40 some types. DMD affects only boys (1 in 3,500 male births), but about one-third of cases are the result of genetic mutation in families with no history of the disease (Best, 2005a). The child appears normal at birth, but muscle weakness is usually evident between the ages of 2 and 6, when the child begins to experience difficulty in running or climbing stairs. The child may walk with an unusual gait, showing a protruding stomach and hollow back. The calf muscles of a child with muscular dystrophy may appear unusually large because the degenerated muscle has been replaced by fatty tissue.

Children with muscular dystrophy often have difficulty getting to their feet after lying down or playing on the floor. They may fall easily. By age 10 to 14, the child loses the ability to walk; the small muscles of the hands and fingers are usually the last to be affected. Some doctors and therapists recommend the early use of electrically powered wheelchairs; others suggest employing special braces and other devices to prolong walking as long as possible.

At this time, there is no known cure for muscular dystrophy, and in most cases this progressive disease is fatal in adolescence or young adulthood. Death is often caused by heart failure or respiratory failure due to atrophied chest muscles. Treatment focuses on maintaining function of unaffected muscles for as long as possible, facilitating ambulation, helping the child and the family cope with limitations imposed by the disease, and providing emotional support and counseling to the child and the family (Hill, 1999). Regular physical therapy, exercise, and the use of appropriate aids and appliances can maintain a good deal of independence. The child should be encouraged to be as active as possible. However, a teacher should be careful not to lift a child with muscular dystrophy by the arms: even a gentle pull may dislocate the child's limbs.

"I think the best part of the story was when...." Learning self-catheterization has given Kristine more control over her classroom schedule and increased her participation.

## Spinal Cord Injuries

Spinal cord injuries are usually the result of a lesion to the spinal cord caused by a penetrating injury (e.g., a gunshot wound), stretching of the vertebral column (e.g., whiplash during an auto accident), fracture of the vertebrae, or compression of the spinal cord (e.g., a diving accident). Vehicular accidents, sports injuries, and violence are the most common causes of spinal cord injuries in school-age children (Apple, Anson, Hunter, & Bell, 1995). Injury to the spinal column is generally described by letters and numbers indicating the site of the damage; for example, a C5-6 injury means the damage has occurred at the level of the fifth and sixth cervical vertebrae, a flexible area of the neck susceptible to injury from whiplash and diving or trampoline accidents. A T12 injury refers to the 12th thoracic (chest) vertebra and an L3 to the 3rd lumbar (lower back) area. In general, paralysis and loss of sensation occur below the level of the injury. The higher the injury on the spine and the more the injury (lesion) cuts through the entire cord, the greater the paralysis (Hill, 1999).

Males represent 80% of the approximately 7,000 to 10,000 persons in the United States who are victims of traumatic spinal cord injuries each year, and most are 15 to 30 years old (National Spinal Cord Injury Association, 2001). Students who have sustained spinal cord injuries usually use wheelchairs for mobility. Motorized wheelchairs, though expensive, are recommended for those with quadriplegia, whereas children with paraplegia can use self-propelled wheelchairs. Children with quadriplegia may have severe breathing problems because the muscles of the chest, which normally govern respiration, are affected. In most cases, children with spinal cord injuries lack bladder and bowel control and need to follow a careful management program to maintain personal hygiene and avoid infection and skin irritation.

Rehabilitation programs for children and adolescents who have sustained spinal cord injuries usually involve physical therapy, the use of adaptive devices for mobility and independent living, and psychological support to help them adjust to a sudden disability. Personal care attendants (PCAs) assist many individuals with spinal cord injury, particularly those with quadriplegia, with activities of daily living. Adolescents and adults are often particularly concerned about sexual function. Even though most spinal cord injuries do affect sexuality, with understanding partners and positive attitudes toward themselves, many people with spinal cord injuries are able to enjoy satisfying sexual relationships.

## Epilepsy

Whether we are awake or asleep, there is always electrical activity occurring in the brain. A *seizure* is a disturbance of movement, sensation, behavior, and/or consciousness caused by abnormal electrical discharges in the brain. "Some have likened the event, known as a seizure, to an engine misfiring or to a power surge in a computer" (Hill, 1999, p. 231). Anyone can have a seizure. It is common for a seizure to occur when someone has a high fever, drinks excessive alcohol, or experiences a blow to the head.

When seizures occur chronically and repeatedly, however, the condition is known as a *seizure disorder* or, more commonly, **epilepsy.** Epilepsy is not a disease, and it constitutes a disorder only while a seizure is actually in progress. It is estimated that 1% of the general population has epilepsy (Brumback, Mathews, & Shenoy, 2001).

The cause of epilepsy for approximately 30% of cases is identified from among at least 50 different conditions known to result in seizure activitiy, such as cerebral palsy; infections of the brain or central nervous system, metabolic disorders such as hypoglycemia, alcohol or lead poisoning, an underlying lesion caused by scar tissue from a head injury, high fever, an interruption in blood supply to the brain, or rough handling of a baby (shaken-baby syndrome) (Evans & Smith, 1993; Lowenthal, 2001). Epilepsy can occur at any stage of life but most frequently begins in childhood. A wide variety of psychological, physical, and sensory factors are thought to trigger seizures in susceptible persons—for example, fatigue, excitement, anger, surprise, hyperventilation, hormonal changes (as in menstruation or pregnancy), withdrawal from drugs or alcohol, and exposure to certain patterns of light, sound, or touch.

Many unfortunate misconceptions about epilepsy have circulated in the past and are still prevalent even today. Negative public attitudes, in fact, have probably been more

*Location and effects of spinal cord injuries*

Council for Exceptional Children Content Standards for Beginning Teachers—P&HD: Medical terminology related to P&HD (PH2K1).

*Epilepsy and types of seizures*

Council for Exceptional Children Content Standards for Beginning Teachers—P&HD: Medical terminology related to P&HD (PH2K1) (also PH2K2, PH3K1).

harmful to people with epilepsy than has the condition itself. During a seizure, a dysfunction in the electrochemical activity of the brain causes a person to lose control of the muscles temporarily. Between seizures (that is, most of the time), the brain functions normally. Teachers, school health care personnel, and perhaps classmates need to be aware that a child is affected by a seizure disorder so that they can be prepared to deal with a seizure if one should occur in school. There are several types of seizures.

The **generalized tonic-clonic seizure** (formerly called *grand mal*) is the most conspicuous and serious type of seizure. A generalized tonic-clonic seizure can be disturbing and frightening to someone who has never seen one. The affected child has little or no warning that a seizure is about to occur; the muscles become stiff, and the child loses consciousness and falls to the floor. Then the entire body shakes violently as the muscles alternately contract and relax. Saliva may be forced from the mouth, legs and arms may jerk, and the bladder and bowels may be emptied. In most cases, the contractions diminish in 2 to 3 minutes, and the child either goes to sleep or regains consciousness in a confused or drowsy state. Generalized tonic-clonic seizures may occur as often as several times a day or as seldom as once a year. They are more likely to occur during the day than at night. A tonic-clonic seizure, although very frightening to someone who has not witnessed such an episode, is not a medical emergency (Hill, 1999). Figure 11.1 describes procedures for handling seizures in the classroom.

*Procedures for handling seizures*

Council for Exceptional Children — Content Standards for Beginning Teachers—P&HD: Specialized health care interventions for individuals with P&HD (PH5K2).

### FIGURE 11.1  Procedures for handling tonic-clonic seizures

The typical seizure is not a medical emergency, but knowledgeable handling of the situation is important. When a child experiences a generalized tonic-clonic seizure in the classroom, the teacher should follow these procedures:

- Keep calm. Reassure the other students that the child will be fine in a minute.
- Ease the child to the floor and clear the area around him of anything that could hurt him.
- Put something flat and soft (like a folded coat) under his head so it will not bang on the floor as his body jerks.
- You cannot stop the seizure. Let it run its course. Do not try to revive the child and do not interfere with his movements.
- Turn him gently onto his side. This keeps his airway clear and allows saliva to drain away.

  DON'T try to force his mouth open.

  DON'T try to hold on to his tongue.

  DON'T put anything in his mouth.

- When the jerking movements stop, let the child rest until he regains consciousness.
- Breathing may be shallow during the seizure, and may even stop briefly. In the unlikely event that breathing does not begin again, check the child's airway for obstruction and give artificial respiration.

Some students recover quickly after this type of seizure; others need more time. A short period of rest is usually advised. If the student is able to remain in the classroom afterwards, however, he should be encouraged to do so. Staying in the classroom (or returning to it as soon as possible) allows for continued participation in classroom activity and is psychologically less difficult for the student. If a student has frequent seizures, handling them can become routine once teacher and classmates learn what to expect. If a seizure of this type continues for longer than five minutes, call for emergency assistance.

*Source:* Adapted from the Epilepsy Foundation of America. (1994). *Epilepsy school alert.* Washington, DC: Author.

The **absence seizure** (previously called *petit mal*) is far less severe than the generalized tonic-clonic seizure but may occur much more frequently—as often as 100 times per day in some children. Usually there is a brief loss of consciousness, lasting anywhere from a few seconds to half a minute or so. The child may stare blankly, flutter or blink her eyes, grow pale, or drop whatever she is holding. She may be mistakenly viewed as daydreaming or not listening. The child may or may not be aware that she has had a seizure, and no special first aid is necessary. The teacher should keep the child's parents advised of seizure activity and may also find it helpful to explain it to the child's classmates.

A **complex partial seizure** (also called *psychomotor*) may appear as a brief period of inappropriate or purposeless activity. The child may smack her lips, walk around aimlessly, or shout. She may appear to be conscious but is not actually aware of her unusual behavior. Complex partial seizures usually last from 2 to 5 minutes, after which the child has amnesia about the entire episode. Some children may respond to spoken directions during a complex partial seizure.

Sudden jerking motions with no loss of consciousness characterize a **simple partial seizure.** Partial seizures may occur weekly, monthly, or only once or twice a year. The teacher should keep dangerous objects out of the child's way and, except in emergencies, should not try to physically restrain him.

Many children experience a warning sensation, known as an *aura,* a short time before a seizure. The aura takes different forms in different people; distinctive feelings, sights, sounds, tastes, and even smells have been described. The aura can be a useful safety valve enabling the child to leave the class or the group before the seizure actually occurs. Some children report that the warning provided by the aura helps them feel more secure and comfortable about themselves.

In some children, absence and partial seizures can go undetected for long periods. An observant teacher can be instrumental in detecting the presence of a seizure disorder and in referring the child for appropriate medical help. The teacher can also assist parents and physicians by noting both the effectiveness and the side effects of any medication the child takes. With proper medical treatment and the support of parents, teachers, and peers, most students with seizure disorders lead full and normal lives. Antiepileptic drugs may largely or wholly control epileptic seizures in 60% to 70% of children (Pedley, Scheuer, & Walczak, 1995). Some children require such heavy doses of medication, however, that their learning and behavior are adversely affected; and some medications have undesirable side effects, such as drowsiness, nausea, weight gain, and thickening of the gums. All children with seizure disorders benefit from a realistic understanding of their condition and accepting attitudes on the part of teachers and classmates. Although the student with seizure disorders may be uncomfortable about letting friends know about the condition, classmates should be aware so that they will know how to, and how not to, respond in the event of a seizure (Hill, 1999).

## Diabetes

**Diabetes**—a chronic disorder of metabolism—is a common childhood disease, affecting about 1 in 600 school-age children, so it is likely that most teachers will encounter students with diabetes at one time or another (Sexson & Dingle, 2001). Without proper medical management, the diabetic child's system is not able to obtain and retain adequate energy from food. Not only does the child lack energy, but also many important parts of the body—particularly the eyes and the kidneys—can be affected by untreated diabetes. Early symptoms of diabetes include thirst, headaches, weight loss (despite a good appetite), frequent urination, and cuts that are slow to heal.

Children with **Type I diabetes** (formerly called *juvenile diabetes* or *early-onset diabetes*) have insufficient insulin, a hormone normally produced by the pancreas and necessary for the metabolism of glucose, a form of sugar produced when food is digested. To regulate the condition, insulin must be injected daily under the skin. Most children with diabetes learn

*Diabetes and related terms*

Council for Exceptional Children    Content Standards for Beginning Teachers—P&HD: Medical terminology related to P&HD (PH2K1) (also PH2K2, PH3K1).

to inject their own insulin—in some cases as frequently as four times per day—and to determine the amount of insulin they need by testing the level of sugar and other substances in their urine. Children with diabetes must follow a specific and regular diet prescribed by a physician or a nutrition specialist. A regular exercise program is also usually suggested.

Teachers who have a child with diabetes in their classrooms should learn how to recognize the symptoms of both too little sugar and too much sugar in the child's bloodstream and the kind of treatment indicated by each condition (Yousef, 1995). *Hypoglycemia* (low blood sugar), also called *insulin reaction* or *diabetic shock*, can result from taking too much insulin, unusually strenuous exercise, or a missed or delayed meal (the blood sugar level is lowered by insulin and exercise and raised by food). Symptoms of hypoglycemia include faintness, dizziness, blurred vision, drowsiness, and nausea. The child may appear irritable or have a marked personality change. In most cases, giving the child some form of concentrated sugar (e.g., a sugar cube, a glass of fruit juice, a candy bar) ends the insulin reaction within a few minutes. The child's doctor or parents should inform the teacher and school health personnel of the appropriate foods to give in case of insulin reaction.

*Hyperglycemia* (high blood sugar) is more serious; it indicates that too little insulin is present and the diabetes is not under control. Its onset is gradual rather than sudden. The symptoms of hyperglycemia, sometimes called *diabetic coma,* include fatigue; thirst; dry, hot skin; deep, labored breathing; excessive urination; and fruity-smelling breath. A doctor or nurse should be contacted immediately if a child displays such symptoms.

*Causes, characteristics, and effects of asthma*

Council for Exceptional Children   Content Standards for Beginning Teachers—P&HD: Impact of P&HD on individuals, families, society (PH3K1) (also PH2K2, PH3K1, CC2K2).

## Asthma

**Asthma** is a chronic lung disease characterized by episodic bouts of wheezing, coughing, and difficulty breathing. An asthmatic attack is usually triggered by allergens (e.g., pollen, certain foods, pets), irritants (e.g., cigarette smoke, smog), exercise, or emotional stress, which results in a narrowing of the airways in the lungs. This reaction increases the resistance to the airflow in and out of the lungs, making it harder for the individual to breathe. The severity of asthma varies greatly: the child may experience only a period of mild coughing or extreme difficulty in breathing that requires emergency treatment. Many asthmatic children experience normal lung functioning between episodes.

Asthma is the most common lung disease of children; estimates of its prevalence range from 6% to as high as 12% of school-age children (Sexson & Dingle, 2001). The causes of asthma are not completely known, though most consider it the result of an interaction of heredity and environment. Symptoms generally begin in early childhood, but sometimes do not develop until late childhood or adolescence. Asthma tends to run in families, which suggests that an allergic intolerance to some stimulus may be inherited. Symptoms of asthma might also first appear following a viral infection of the respiratory system.

Primary treatment for asthma begins with a systematic effort to identify the stimuli and environmental situations that provoke attacks. The number of potential allergens and irritants is virtually limitless, and in some cases it can be extremely difficult to determine the combination of factors that results in an asthmatic episode. Changes in temperature, humidity, and season (attacks are especially common in autumn) are also related to the frequency of asthmatic symptoms. Rigorous physical exercise produces asthmatic episodes in some children. Asthma can be controlled effectively in most children with a combination of medications and limiting exposure to known allergens. Most children whose breathing attacks are induced by physical

This special educator does not allow Jamika's chronic illness to prevent her from participating in developmentally appropriate play activities.

exercise can still enjoy physical exercise and sports through careful selection of activities (e.g., swimming generally provokes less exercise-induced asthma than running) and/or taking certain medications before rigorous exercise. Although asthma is biochemical in origin, an interrelationship exists between emotional stress and asthma. Periods of psychological stress or higher emotional responses increase the likelihood of asthmatic attacks, and asthmatic episodes produce more stress. Treatment often involves counseling or an asthma teaching program (Hill, 1999) in which children and their families are taught ways to reduce and cope with emotional stress.

Asthma is the leading cause of absenteeism in school. It is estimated that 10 million school days are lost each year because of asthma (Asthma and Allergy Foundation of America, 2001). Chronic absenteeism makes it difficult for the child with asthma to maintain performance at grade level, and homebound instructional services may be necessary. The majority of children with asthma who receive medical and psychological support, however, successfully complete school and lead normal lives. By working cooperatively with parents and medical personnel to minimize the child's contact with provoking factors and constructing a plan to assist the child during attacks, the classroom teacher can play an important role in reducing the impact of asthma (Getch & Neuharth-Pritchett, 1999).

## Cystic Fibrosis

**Cystic fibrosis** is a genetic disorder of children and adolescents in which the body's exocrine glands excrete thick mucus that can block the lungs and parts of the digestive system. It is a hereditary disease found predominantly in Caucasians—affecting approximately 1 in 3,500 Caucasian births, 1 in 11,500 Hispanic births, and 1 in 14,500 African American births (FitzSimmons, 1993). Children with cystic fibrosis often have difficulty breathing and are susceptible to pulmonary disease (lung infections). Malnutrition and poor growth are common characteristics of children with cystic fibrosis because of pancreatic insufficiency that causes inadequate digestion and malabsorption of nutrients, especially fats. They often have large and frequent bowel movements because food passes through the system only partially digested. Getting children with cystic fibrosis to consume enough calories is critical to their health and development. The symptoms may result from a missing chemical or substance in the body. Medical research has not determined exactly how cystic fibrosis functions, and no reliable cure has yet been found. Medications prescribed for children with cystic fibrosis include enzymes to facilitate digestion and solutions to thin and loosen the mucus in the lungs. Children with cystic fibrosis undergo daily physiotherapy in which the chest is vigorously thumped and vibrated to dislodge mucus, followed by positioning the body to drain loosened secretions.

Many children and young adults with cystic fibrosis are able to lead active lives. During vigorous physical exercises, some children may need help from teachers, aides, or classmates to clear their lungs and air passages. Although the life expectancy of people with cystic fibrosis used to be very short—30 years ago the median life expectancy was about 8 years—the long-range outlook for children affected by cystic fibrosis is improving. Today more than 40% of the cystic fibrosis population is age 18 and older; and with current treatment, the median age of survival for people with cystic fibrosis extends into the early 30s (Cystic Fibrosis Foundation, 2003).

## Human Immunodeficiency Virus and Acquired Immunodeficiency Syndrome

Persons with **acquired immunodeficiency syndrome (AIDS)** are not able to resist and fight off infections because of a breakdown in the immune system. Opportunistic infections such as tuberculosis, pneumonia, and cancerous skin lesions attack the person's body and grow in severity and ultimately result in death. At present, there is no known cure or vaccine for AIDS, although there have been recent advances in drugs such as AZT.

*Cystic fibrosis*

Council for Exceptional Children — Content Standards for Beginning Teachers—P&HD: Impact of P&HD on individuals, families, society (PH3K1) (also PH2K2, PH3K1, CC2K2).

*HIV/AIDS*

Council for Exceptional Children — Content Standards for Beginning Teachers—P&HD: Types and transmission routes of infectious and communicable diseases (PH2K4) (also PH2K1, PH3K1).

AIDS is caused by the **human immunodeficiency virus (HIV),** which is found in the bodily fluids of an infected person (blood, semen, vaginal secretions, and breast milk). HIV is transmitted from one person to another through sexual contact and blood-to-blood contact (e.g., intravenous drug use with shared needles, transfusions of unscreened contaminated blood). Pregnant women can also transmit HIV to newborn children. Most people who become infected with HIV show no symptoms of AIDS for 8 to 12 years, and not all persons who have HIV get AIDS (Centers for Disease Control and Prevention [CDC], 2001a).

The number of people worldwide who have contracted HIV/AIDS is staggering. It is estimated that 30 million people worldwide carry the HIV virus, with as many as 3 million new cases per year. Although the incidence rate for new cases of AIDS in the United States has decreased in recent years, the disease is still of epidemic proportions. Of the nearly 800,000 cumulative cases of HIV positive cases reported in the United States through December 2000, approximately 9,000 involved children under the age of 13 (CDC, 2001b).

In addition to health problems and significant weight loss, significant neurological complications and developmental delays have been noted in children with HIV/AIDS, particularly in expressive language, attention, memory, and motor functioning (National Institute of Allergy and Infectious Diseases, 2001; Wolters, Brouwers, & Moss, 1995). The extent to which these complications are caused by the HIV virus's direct effect on the brain, the opportunistic infections that arise because of the weakened immune system, the powerful regiment of medications taken to combat the spread of HIV, or a combination of these factors is unknown (Sexson & Dingle, 2001).

Because of fear generated by misconceptions about the spread of the disease, some school districts have barred children with HIV/AIDS from attending school in defiance of the IDEA principle of zero reject (Turnbull & Turnbull, 2000). However, saliva, nasal secretions, sweat, tears, urine, and vomit do not transmit HIV unless blood is visible; and the presence of a child with HIV/AIDS in the classroom presents no undue health risks to other children (CDC, 1998). Children with HIV/AIDS cannot legally be excluded from attending school unless they are deemed a direct health risk to other children (e.g., exhibit biting behavior, have open lesions).

Because children with HIV/AIDS and their families often face discrimination, prejudice, and isolation, teachers and school personnel should actively facilitate school/peer acceptance and the social adjustment of a child with HIV/AIDS (Hill, 1999). Parents are not required to inform the school that their child has HIV (or any other medical or health condition), and a particular student or staff member may have HIV without knowing it.

*Use universal precautions*

Council for Exceptional Children

Content Standards for Beginning Teachers—Common Core: Learning environments and social interactions (CC5S16).

Additionally, all teachers and school personnel must be trained in **universal precautions,** a set of standard safety techniques that interrupt the chain of infection spread by potential biohazards such as blood and bodily fluids from any child (e.g., how to safely administer first aid for a cut or tend to a child's nose bleed or vomiting). For an excellent overview of the importance of universal precautions, including step-by-step guidelines for proper methods of putting on and removing protective gloves, cleaning up potentially contaminated areas in the classroom, and proper handwashing, see Edens, Murdick, and Gartin (2003).

To prevent the disease from spreading further among the preadolescent and adolescent populations, HIV/AIDS prevention must be included in the curriculum. Students receiving special education services may be more prone to contracting HIV because of a lack of knowledge about the disease. For recommendations on developing and implementing an HIV/AIDS prevention and education curriculum for students with disabilities, see Kelker, Hecimovic, and LeRoy (1994) and Lerro (1994).

# ATTENTION-DEFICIT/HYPERACTIVITY DISORDER

All children have difficulty attending at times (attention deficit) and all children sometimes engage in high rates of purposeless or inappropriate movement (hyperactivity). Children who consistently exhibit this combination of behavioral traits may be diagnosed with *attention-deficit/hyperactivity disorder (ADHD)*. In many respects, ADHD reflects "either too much (e.g., fidgeting) or not enough (e.g., lack of impulse control or attention) of what adults expect in certain settings" (Goldstein & Goldstein, 1998, pp. 4–5). Children with ADHD present a difficult challenge to their families, teachers, and classmates. Their inability to stay on task, impulsive behavior, and fidgeting impair their ability to learn and increase the likelihood of unsatisfactory interactions with others.

Wolraich's (1999) contention that ADHD "has the distinction of being both the most extensively studied mental disorder and the most controversial" (p. 163) suggests that the condition is both well known and little understood (Bicard, 2002). Although the last decade of the 20th century witnessed an explosion of interest in ADHD, historical references to the symptoms that are diagnosed as ADHD today suggest that such children have been with us for centuries (Barkley, 1998; Conners, 2000; Goldstein & Goldstein, 1998). The first published account of the disorder in the medical or scientific literature appeared in 1902 when British physician George Still described Still's disease. Still believed that children who were restless and exhibited problems maintaining attention suffered from a "defect of moral control" that he presumed to be the result of brain injury or dysfunction. Over the years, a variety of terms has been used to refer to this combination of behavioral symptoms: *postencephalitic disorder* in the 1920s, *brain damage syndrome* in the 1940s, *minimal brain dysfunction* in the 1960s, and *hyperkinetic impulse disorder of children* in the 1970s (Mather & Goldstein, 2001). Because medical science has found no clear-cut evidence of brain damage, emphasis in defining and diagnosing the condition has focused and relied on the description and identification of a combination of behavioral symptoms.

## Definition and Diagnosis

The symptoms of ADHD occur in two broad dimensions: those indicative of faulty attention and those related to hyperactivity and impulsivity. Symptoms of hyperactivity and impulsivity tend to occur together with high frequency. With regard to predicting future functioning, however, "the greater the degree of reported impulsive behavior, the more problems in the classroom and later life. Thus, it has been increasingly hypothesized that the core impairment in ADHD represents faulty inhibition or self-control, leading to a constellation of related symptoms" (Mather & Goldstein, 2001, p. 49).

Children are diagnosed as having ADHD according to criteria found in the *Diagnostic and Statistical Manual of Mental Disorders* (DSM-IV-TR) (American Psychiatric Association, 2000a). "The essential feature of attention-deficit/hyperactivity disorder is a persistent pattern of inattention and/or hyperactivity-impulsivity that is more frequent and severe than is typically observed in individuals at a comparable level of development" (p. 85). To diagnose ADHD, a physician must determine that a child has consistently displayed six or more symptoms of either inattention or hyperactivity-impulsivity for a period of at least 6 months (see Figure 11.2).

The diagnosing physician assigns one of three subtypes of ADHD, depending on a child's constellation of symptoms: ADHD, combined type; ADHD, predominantly inattentive type; and ADHD, predominantly hyperactive-impulsive type. Approximately half of the children tested for ADHD are diagnosed with the combined type, 30% the inattentive type, and 20% the hyperactive-impulsive type (Lahey et al., 1994).

The diagnostic criteria for ADHD are diverse and subjective. For example, what is the basis for deciding whether a child is "often 'on the go' "? And how can one determine that a child who avoids or dislikes schoolwork or homework does so because of an attention deficit as opposed to one of many other possible reasons? A child who is diagnosed by one physician as not having ADHD may very well be diagnosed by another as having it. Parents have been known to engage in "physician shopping," taking their child from one doctor to another until a diagnosis of ADHD is made (Reid, Maag, & Vasa, 1994). After their review of 48 articles and books on ADHD written by leading authorities revealed that 69 characteristics and 38 different causes of ADHD were proposed, Goodman and Poillion (1992) concluded that ADD was an acronym for "Any Dysfunction or Difficulty" (p. 37).

*Definition of ADHD*

Council for Exceptional Children — Content Standards for Beginning Teachers—Common Core: Issues in definition and identification of individuals with exceptional learning needs (CC1K5).

**FIGURE 11.2** **Diagnostic criteria for ADHD**

A. Either (1) or (2):
  1. Six (or more) of the following symptoms of *inattention* have persisted for at least 6 months to a degree that is maladaptive and inconsistent with developmental level:
    *Inattention*
    a. Often fails to give close attention to details or makes careless mistakes in schoolwork, work, or other activities.
    b. Often has difficulty sustaining attention in tasks or play activities.
    c. Often does not seem to listen when spoken to directly.
    d. Often does not follow through on instructions and fails to finish schoolwork, chores, or duties in the workplace (not due to oppositional behavior or failure to understand instructions).
    e. Often has difficulty organizing tasks and activities.
    f. Often avoids, dislikes, or is reluctant to engage in tasks that require sustained mental effort (such as schoolwork or homework).
    g. Often loses things necessary for tasks or activities (e.g., toys, school assignments, pencils, books, or tools).
    h. Is often easily distracted by extraneous stimuli.
    i. Is often forgetful in daily activities.
  2. Six (or more) of the following symptoms of *hyperactivity–impulsivity* have persisted for at least 6 months to a degree that is maladaptive and inconsistent with developmental level:
    *Hyperactivity*
    a. Often fidgets with hands or feet or squirms in seat.
    b. Often leaves seat in classroom or in other situations in which remaining seated is expected.
    c. Often runs about or climbs excessively in situations in which it is inappropriate (in adolescents or adults, may be limited to subjective feelings of restlessness).
    d. Often has difficulty playing or engaging in leisure activities quietly.
    e. Is often "on the go" or often acts as if "driven by a motor."
    f. Often talks excessively.
    *Impulsivity*
    g. Often blurts out answers before questions have been completed.
    h. Often has difficulty awaiting turn.
    i. Often interrupts or intrudes on others (e.g., butts into conversations or games).
B. Some hyperactive–impulsive or inattentive symptoms that caused impairment were presented before age 7 years.
C. Some impairment from the symptoms is present in two or more settings (e.g., at school [or work] and at home).
D. There must be clear evidence of clinically significant impairment in social, academic, or occupational functioning.
E. The symptoms do not occur exclusively during the course of pervasive developmental disorder, schizophrenia, or other psychotic disorder and are not better accounted for by another mental disorder (e.g., mood disorder, anxiety disorder, dissociative disorder, or a personality disorder).
  *Code* based on type:
  *Attention-Deficit/Hyperactivity Disorder, Combined Type:* if both Criteria A1 and A2 are met for the past 6 months.
  *Attention-Deficit/Hyperactivity Disorder, Predominantly Inattentive Type:* if Criterion A1 is met but Criterion A2 is not met for the past 6 months.
  *Attention-Deficit/Hyperactivity Disorder, Predominantly Hyperactive–Impulsive Type:* if Criterion A2 is met but Criterion A1 is not met for the past 6 months.
  *Coding note:* For individuals (especially adolescents and adults) who currently have symptoms that no longer meet full criteria, "In Partial Remission" should be specified.

*Source:* Reprinted from American Psychiatric Association. (2000). *Diagnostic and statistical manual of mental disorders* (4th ed., Text Revision, pp. 92–93). Washington, DC: Author.

## Academic Achievement and Comorbidity with Other Disabilities

*Achievement of students with ADHD and comorbidity with other disabling conditions*

Council for Exceptional Children — Content Standards for Beginning Teachers—Common Core: Educational implications of characteristics of various exceptionalities (CC2K2) (also LD3K1).

Most children with ADHD struggle in the classroom. They score lower than do their age mates on IQ and achievement tests, more than half require remedial tutoring for basic skills, and about 30% repeat one or more grades (Barkley, 1998). A considerable percentage of children with ADHD—from 25% to as many as 70%—are also identified as having a learning disability (Kube, Peterson, & Palmer, 2002; Mayes, Calhoun, & Crowell, 2000). Two studies found that 15% and 26% of children with learning disabilities also were diagnosed with ADHD (Gilger, Pennington, & DeFries, 1992; Shaywitz, Fletcher, & Shaywitz, 1995). Students with developmental disabilities, Asperger syndrome, Tourette syndrome, and emotional and behavioral disorders were also identified as having ADHD (Kube et al., 2002; Prestia, 2003).

However, it is important to stress that ADHD is not the same as a learning disability. Although some children with learning disabilities are inattentive, hyperactive, and impulsive, many are calm and work diligently at learning tasks. Many children without learning disabilities also have trouble attending and sitting still. Likewise, some children who display impulsivity, inattention, and/or hyperactivity do well in school.

Many children with ADHD experience serious emotional and behavioral problems. About 60% of adolescents with ADHD develop at least one additional behavioral problem (Barkley, Fischer, Barkley, Edelbrock, & Smallish, 1990). Many students who are identified with emotional and behavioral disorders are also diagnosed with ADHD. A statewide survey in Wisconsin found that 40% of elementary school, 32% of middle school, and 25% of secondary students with emotional and behavioral disorders were taking medications for ADHD (Runnheim, Frankenberger, & Hazelkorn, 1996). In another study, approximately one-fourth of a large sample of juvenile offenders reported they had been diagnosed with and received medication for ADHD (Zabel & Nigro, 1999).

## Eligibility for Special Education

ADHD is not a disability category recognized by IDEA; however, it is estimated that more than one-half of children with ADHD receive special education (Reid & Maag, 1998). A large proportion of students with ADHD are served under the learning disabilities and emotional and behavioral disorders categories. Students with ADHD can be served under the other health impairments category if the outcome of the disorder is a "heightened alertness to environmental stimuli that results in limited alertness with respect to the educational environment" that adversely affects academic performance (U.S. Department of Education, 1999, p. 12422).

Many children with ADHD who are not served under IDEA are eligible for services under Section 504 of the Rehabilitation Act. As discussed in Chapter 1, Section 504 is a civil rights law that provides certain protections for persons with disabilities. Under Section 504, schools may be required to develop and implement accommodation plans designed to help students with ADHD succeed in the general education classroom. Accommodation plans often include such adaptations and adjustments as extended time on tests, preferred seating, additional teacher monitoring, reduced or modified class or homework assignments and worksheets, and monitoring the effects of medication on the child's behavior in school.

*ADHD and eligibility for special education*

Council for Exceptional Children — Content Standards for Beginning Teachers—Common Core: Issues, assurances, and due process rights related to assessment, eligibility, and placement within a continuum of services (CC1K6).

## Prevalence

The most frequently cited estimate of the prevalence of ADHD is 3% to 5% of all school-age children (American Psychiatric Association, 2000a). A random national sample of family pediatricians found that 5.3% of all elementary students screened received a diagnosis of ADHD (Wolraich et al., 1990). These figures suggest that the typical classroom will have one or two children either diagnosed as ADHD or presenting the problems typically associated with ADHD.

Child count data reported by the states reveal a large increase in the numbers of students served under IDEA's other health impairments category since the federal government stipulated that students with ADHD were eligible under that disability category. Some states reported increases of 20% in the number of children served under the other health impairments category between the 1997–1998 and 1998–1999 school years (U.S. Department of Education, 2000). Nationwide, the number of children served in the other health impairments category increased from 63,982 in 1992–1993 to 449,093 in 2003–2004, by far the biggest proportional increase of any disability category (U.S. Department of Education, 2004).

Boys are 3 to 10 times more likely to be diagnosed with ADHD than are girls, with the ratio being higher at younger ages (American Psychiatric Association, 2000a; Barkley, 1998).

# Causes

In most cases, the specific causes of the inattention and hyperactivity-impulsivity that lead to a child's diagnosis of ADHD are not known. Although many consider ADHD to be a neurologically based disorder, there is no clear and consistent causal evidence linking brain damage or dysfunction to the behavioral symptoms of ADHD (National Institute of Health Consensus Statement, 1998). However, there is growing evidence of genetic factors that may place individuals at a greater-than-normal risk of an ADHD diagnosis (Edelbrock, Rende, Plomin, & Thompson, 1995). Genetics may provide certain risk or resilience factors, and environmental influences (i.e., life experiences) then determine whether an individual receives a diagnosis of ADHD (Goldstein & Goldstein, 1998).

ADHD is associated with a wide range of genetic disorders and diseases. For example, individuals with Fragile X syndrome, Turner syndrome, and Williams syndrome (see Chapter 4) frequently have attention and impulsivity problems. Symptoms of ADHD are also associated with conditions such as fetal alcohol syndrome, prenatal exposure to cocaine, and lead poisoning.

Also, a growing body of research using neuroimaging technologies shows that some individuals with ADHD have structural or biochemical differences in their brains (e.g., Berquin et al., 1998; Filipek et al., 1997). But not all individuals diagnosed with ADHD have brains that appear different from those of individuals without ADHD. And some people without ADHD have brain structures similar to those with ADHD. It is possible that biochemical differences in the brains of children with ADHD may play a causal role in their behavioral deficits and excesses (e.g., Ernst, Cohen, Liebenauer, Jons, & Zametkin, 1997).

The causes of ADHD are not well understood. It is likely, if not nearly certain, that similar patterns of behavior leading to the diagnoses of ADHD in two different children will be caused by completely different factors or sets of factors (Goldstein & Goldstein, 1998; Gresham, 2002; Maag & Reid, 1994). It is also possible that different causal factors influence a child's inattention and/or impulsivity in different situations or environments. A full understanding of those causal factors may be necessary for interventions to be optimal and have long-lasting effects.

## Causes of ADHD

Council for Exceptional Children   Content Standards for Beginning Teachers of Students with LD: Etiologies of LD (LD2K1).

# Treatment

Drug therapy and behaviorally based interventions are the two most widely used treatment approaches for children with ADHD.

## Drug treatment for ADHD

Council for Exceptional Children   Content Standards for Beginning Teachers—Common Core: Effects of various medications on individuals with exceptional learning needs (CC2K7).

*Drug Therapy.*   Prescription stimulant medication is the most common intervention for children with ADHD. Methylphenidate, sold under the trade name Ritalin, is the most frequently prescribed medication for ADHD. Other stimulants such as dextroamphetamine (Dexedrine), dextroamphetamine sulfate (Adderall), methamphetamine hydrochloride (Desoxyn), and pemoline (Cylert) are also widely prescribed.

The number of children on stimulant medication has increased tremendously since the early 1990s. An estimated 700,000 children received medication for ADHD in the late 1980s. By 1995 the number had more than doubled to 1.6 million children (Safer, Zito, & Fine, 1996). In 2000 it was estimated that more than 3 million schoolchildren in the United States were receiving drug treatment for ADHD (Jensen, 2000). Diller (1998) reports that sales of Ritalin for children in the United States account for 90% of the worldwide consumption of the drug. According to the U.S. Drug Enforcement Agency (2002), there was a 900% increase in the production of Ritalin from 1990 to 2001, and from 1993 to 2001 the production of amphetatmines (Dexedrine and Adderall) increased 5,767%. The U.S. Drug Enforcement Agency classifies the medications prescribed to treat ADHD as Schedule II drugs (a group that includes barbiturates, codeine, and morphine), meaning they have some therapeutic value but also some potential for abuse.

Why are stimulant medications prescribed so frequently for children with ADHD? Undoubtedly, there are many reasons, but two factors seem certain. First, there are many children whose hyperactivity and impulsivity are troublesome to their parents and teachers. Second, many children with ADHD show marked improvements in behavior when taking stimulant medication.

When prescribed and monitored by a competent physician, Ritalin has proven to be a safe and often effective intervention (Multimodal Treatment Study Group, 1999). Reviews of controlled studies show that 70% to 80% of children diagnosed with ADHD respond positively to Ritalin (Barkley, 1998; Swanson, McBurnett, Christain, & Wigal, 1995), at least in the short term. A positive response typically includes a reduction in hyperactivity, increased attention and time on task, increased academic productivity, and improvements in general conduct. There is no clear evidence that stimulant medications lead to improved academic achievement (e.g., better grades and scores on achievement tests). A longitudinal study that followed children with ADHD who had taken Ritalin for 4 years found the children did not make gains in either specific or general areas of academic achievement from the first through the fifth grade (Frankenberger & Cannon, 1999).

Although teachers and parents generally report favorable outcomes for children who are taking stimulant medication, common side effects include insomnia, decreased appetite, headaches, weight loss, and irritability. These side effects are usually of short duration and can often be controlled with a reduction in dosage (Goldstein & Goldstein, 1998). Additional problems have been reported with children not taking their medication as prescribed, trying to catch up on missed pills by taking too many pills at once, and trading or even selling their medications (Hancock, 1996; Wood & Zabel, 2001).

Mather and Goldstein (2001) believe that "the immediate short-term benefits of stimulant medications far outweigh the liabilities and thus appear to justify the continued use of these medications in the treatment of ADHD" (p. 63). And based on their assessment of two meta-analyses of medication studies, Forness, Kavale, Crenshaw, and Sweeney (2000) suggest that it is unwise and could be considered malpractice not to include drug therapy as part of a comprehensive treatment program for children with ADHD.

Some professionals, however, have voiced concerns that the drugs may have little or no long-term benefits on academic achievement and that educators and parents rely too much on medical interventions (Maag & Reid, 1994; Northup, Galley, Edwards, & Fountain, 2001). They view drug treatment as an inappropriate, easy way out that might produce short-term improvements in behavior but result in long-term harm. "When stimulants work in the short-term, pharmacological intervention may be used as a crutch and may postpone or prevent the use of non-pharmacological interventions, which may be more effective in the long run" (Swanson et al., 1993, p. 158).

It is difficult to predict the effects of stimulant medication on an individual child. Although the majority of children respond positively to stimulants, 20% to 30% show either no response or a negative response (i.e., their symptoms get worse) (Gresham, 2002). A child's response or lack of response to stimulant medication cannot be used as a basis for confirming the ADHD diagnosis (DuPaul & Stoner, 1994). Nor can a child's age, size, or weight be used to determine the optimum dosage in terms of the desired effects on hyperactivity and safety. Direct and daily measurement of a student's performance on academic tasks during alternating drug and placebo conditions is a promising technique for evaluating the effects of the drug and determining appropriate dosage levels (e.g., Northup, Fusilier, Swanson, Roane, & Borrero, 1997; Stoner, Carey, Ikeda, & Shinn, 1994).

Howell, Evans, and Gardiner (1997) provide educators with guidelines for the safe use of stimulant medications in the classroom with optimal benefits. Gadow and Nolan (1993), DuPaul and Stoner (1994), and Goldstein and Goldstein (1998) are excellent sources of information for educators on this important topic.

Because there is no valid, independent test for ADHD, teacher referrals and recommendations play a significant role in whether or not a child is diagnosed. Kwasman,

Tinsley, and Lepper (1995) found that 77% of physicians attempted to get a written report from the school describing the child's behavior in the classroom. Because the diagnosis of ADHD often leads to the prescription of stimulant medication, it is important that teachers have valid knowledge of the condition and its treatment.

Unfortunately, educators hold many misconceptions about ADHD and its treatment by stimulant medication. Snider, Busch, and Arrowood (2003) asked 145 teachers to rate how much they agreed or disagreed with 13 statements about ADHD and its treatment by stimulant medication. Only 5 of the 13 questions, all of which were either true or false on the basis of scientific research, were answered correctly by more than half of the teachers (see Table 11.1). In discussing these results, Snider and colleagues wrote,

> The teachers who responded to this survey had less knowledge about ADHD and the use of stimulant medication that one would expect considering their pivotal role in the recognition and treatment of ADHD. …
>
> A diagnosis of ADHD is thought to explain a cause when in fact it does nothing more than describe a set of symptoms that include inattention, hyperactivity, impulsivity (e.g.,

**TABLE 11.1** **Percentage of classroom teachers who correctly rated statements about ADHD and its treatment by stimulant medication**

| Item | Percentage correct |
|------|--------------------|
| ADHD is the most commonly diagnosed psychiatric disorder of childhood. (True) | 58 |
| There are data to indicate that ADHD is caused by a brain malfunction. (False) | 10 |
| ADHD symptoms (e.g., fidgets, does not follow through on instruction, easily distracted) may be caused by academic deficits. (True) | 63 |
| Stress and conflict in the student's home life can cause ADHD symptoms. (True) | 71 |
| Diagnosis of ADHD can be confirmed if stimulant medication improves the child's attention. (False) | 33 |
| Stimulant medication use may decrease the physical growth rate (i.e., height) of students. (True) | 38 |
| Stimulant medication use may produce tics in students. (True) | 45 |
| Adderall, Ritalin, and Dexedrine have abuse potential similar to Demerol, cocaine, and monphine. (True) | 46 |
| The long-term side effects of stimulant medications are well understood. (False) | 67 |
| Over time, stimulant medication loses its effectiveness. (True) | 46 |
| While on stimulant medication, students exhibit similar amounts of problem behaviors as their normally developing peers. (False) | 27 |
| Short-term studies show that stimulant medication improves the behaviors associated with ADHD. (True) | 86 |
| Studies show that stimulant medication has a positive effect on academic achievement in the long run. (False) | 6 |

*Note.* Statements were rated using a 5-point Likert-type scale (1 = *strongly disagree* to 5 = *strongly agree*). Percentage correct indicates percentage of respondents who answered 4 or 5 to an item that was true and 1 or 2 to an item that was false.

*Source:* From Snider, V. E., Busch, T., & Arrowood, L. (2003). Teacher knowledge of stimulant medication and ADHD. *Remedial and Special Education, 24*, p. 50. Used by permission.

Why is Johnny inattentive? Because he has ADHD. Why does he have ADHD? Because he is inattentive.) When the explanation is circular, the presumed cause is sometimes called an "explanatory fiction" (Michael, 1993, p. 53). This often happens when a cause cannot be observed independent of the effect that it is supposed to explain.

Unnecessary referrals could be avoided if more teachers understood this important concept. ADHD has no known cause or cure, so there is no valid independent way of diagnosing it. Teachers must be especially sensitive to ambiguities in the diagnosis of ADHD because the treatment often involves powerful stimulant drugs. (p. 50, 53–54)

*Behavioral Interventions.* The principles and methods of applied behavior analysis, particularly positive reinforcement for on-task behavior, modifying assignments and instructional activities to promote success, and systematically gradually teaching self-control, provide teachers and parents with practical strategies for teaching and living with children with ADHD (Flick, 2000; Goldstein & Goldstein, 1998). Teacher-administered interventions for children with ADHD include restructuring the environment (e.g., seating the child close to the teacher, breaking assignments into small, manageable chunks), providing frequent opportunities to actively respond within ongoing instruction, and providing differential consequences for child behavior (e.g., positive reinforcement such as praise and tokens for appropriate behavior, ignoring inappropriate behavior, and time out or response cost for inappropriate behavior) (Garrick Duhaney, 2003; Salend, Elhoweris, & van Garderen, 2003). These and related behavioral strategies for helping children learn adaptive behavior are discussed throughout this text.

An important line of research with major implications for treating children with ADHD is exploring how to teach self-control to children whose learning is adversely affected by impulsivity. A deficit of *executive function,* or the ability to verbally think through and control one's actions, has been hypothesized as being a primary characteristic of children diagnosed with ADHD (Barkley, 1998; Sonuga-Bourke, Dalen, Daley, & Remington, 2002). According to this hypothesis, children with ADHD would be unlikely candidates for, and perhaps incapable of, learning self-control (Abikoff, 1991). Recent research has demonstrated, however, that children with ADHD can learn to self-regulate their behavior to reduce impulsiveness.

Neef, Bicard, and Endo (2002) demonstrated that children with ADHD can learn self-control when treatment regimes are directly tied to assessment. Results of a subsequent study demonstrated that children with ADHD can learn to follow rules and describe their own behavior, provided they are given clear instructions and consistent reinforcement (Bicard & Neef, 2002). Results of these studies and research on self-monitoring (e.g., Huff & DuPaul, 1998) and correspondence training, a procedure in which children are reinforced for "do-say" verbal statements about what they had done previously and "say-do" statements describing what they plan to do (e.g., Paniagua, 1992; Shapiro, DuPaul, & Bradley-King, 1998), show promise for treating children who have ADHD.

*Behavioral interventions for ADHD*

Council for Exceptional Children Content Standards for Beginning Teachers—Common Core: Teach individuals to use self-assessment, problem solving, and other cognitive strategies to meet their needs (CC4S2) (also CC5K2).

# CHARACTERISTICS

The characteristics of children with physical disabilities and health impairments are so varied that attempting to describe them is nearly impossible. Knowing the underlying cause of a student's physical impairment or health condition provides limited guidance in planning needed special education and related services. One student with cerebral palsy may require few special modifications in curriculum, instruction, or environment, while the severe limitations in movement and intellectual functioning experienced by another student with cerebral palsy require a wide array of curricular and instructional modifications, adaptive equipment, and related services. Some children with health conditions have chronic but relatively mild health conditions; others have extremely limited endurance and vitality, requiring sophisticated medical technology and around-the-clock support to maintain their very existence. A given physical or health condition may take markedly different *trajectories* in the same child (Best, 2005a). For example, treatment of cancer may have little or no

*Effects of P&HD on academic
achievement and social/
emotional development*

Council for
Exceptional
Children    Content
Standards for
Beginning Teachers—Common
Core: Educational implications of
various exceptionalities (CC2K2)
(also PH3K1).

positive effects on a child's life, prolong and enhance the life of a child, or lead to complete remission of the disease. The treatment itself (e.g., the extent to which hospitalization is required, the immediate effects of chemotherapy on the child's physical and emotional condition) and its outcome will both have significant impact on when and what type of special education and related services are needed.

The combined effects of all of these variables render lists of learning and behavioral characteristics of children with physical disabilities and health impairments highly suspect at best. Nevertheless, two cautiously qualified statements can be made concerning the academic and socioemotional characteristics of children with physical disabilities and health impairments. First, although many individual students with physical disabilities or health impairments achieve well above grade level—indeed, some are intellectually gifted—as a group these children function below grade level academically. In addition to the neurological motor and impairments that hamper their academic performance, the medications and daily health care routines that some children must endure have negative side effects on academic achievement. Educational progress is also hampered by frequent and sometimes prolonged absences from school for medical treatment when flare-ups or relapses require hospitalization (Kline, Silver, & Russell, 2001).

Second, as a group students with physical disabilities perform below average on measures of social-behavioral skills. Coster and Haltiwanger (2004) reported that classroom teachers and other school professionals, such as physical and occupational therapists, rated more than 40% of the 62 elementary students with physical disabilities below mean on six of seven social-behavioral tasks considered necessary for optimal functioning and learning in school (e.g., following social conventions, compliance with adult directives, positive interaction with peers and adults, constructive responses to feedback, personal care awareness).

Coping emotionally with a physical disability or a chronic health impairment presents a major problem for some children (Boekaerts & Roeder, 1999). Maintaining peer relationships and a sense of belonging to the group can be difficult for a child who must frequently leave the instructional activity or the classroom to participate in therapeutic or health care routines. Anxiety about fitting in at school may be created by prolonged absences from school (Olsen & Sutton, 1998). Students with physical disabilities and health impairments frequently identify concerns about physical appearance as reasons for emotional difficulties and feelings of depression (Sexson & Dingle, 2001).

## Variables Affecting the Impact of Physical Disabilities and Health Impairments on Educational Performance

*Factors that affect impact of
P&HD*

Council for
Exceptional
Children    Content
Standards for
Beginning Teachers—P&HD:
Impact of P&HD on individuals,
families, society (PH3K1) (also
PH2K2).

It is both possible and useful to identify the effects of general variables that influence the characteristics of children across various types of physical disabilities and health impairments. Many factors must be taken into consideration in assessing the effects of a physical disability or health impairment on a child's development and behavior. Perrin et al. (1993) have developed a noncategorical system for classifying and understanding children's chronic physical and medical conditions in which the characteristics or effects of 13 dimensions of a child's condition are judged (see Figure 11.3). A physical impairment or medical condition can limit a child's ability to engage in age-appropriate activities, mobility, cognitive functioning, social and emotional development, sensory functioning, and communication across a continuum ranging from normal functioning (no impact) to extremely impaired. A minor or transient physical or health impairment, such as those most children experience while growing up, is not likely to have lasting effects; but a severe, chronic impairment can greatly limit a child's range of experiences. In addition to the severity with which the condition affects different areas of functioning, two particularly important factors are age of onset and visibility.

*Age of Onset.* Some conditions are congenital (present at birth); other conditions are acquired during the child's development as a result of illness, accident, or unknown cause. As with all disabilities, it is important for the teacher to be aware of the child's age at the time

## FIGURE 11.3 Dimensions of a noncategorical system for classifying and describing the effects of a physical disability or a chronic health condition

| Dimension | Effects Continuum | | |
|---|---|---|---|
| Duration | Brief | ◄──────► | Lengthy |
| Age of onset | Congenital | ◄──────► | Acquired |
| Limitation of age-appropriate activities | None | ◄──────► | Unable to conduct |
| Visibility | Not visible | ◄──────► | Highly visible |
| Expected survival | Usual longevity | ◄──────► | Immediate threat to life |
| Mobility | Not impaired | ◄──────► | Extremely impaired |
| Physiologic functioning | Not impaired | ◄──────► | Extremely impaired |
| Cognition | Normal | ◄──────► | Extremely impaired |
| Emotional/social | Normal | ◄──────► | Extremely impaired |
| Sensory functioning | Not impaired | ◄──────► | Extremely impaired |
| Communication | Not impaired | ◄──────► | Extremely impaired |
| Course | Stable | ◄──────► | Progressive |
| Uncertainty | Episodic | ◄──────► | Predictable |

*Source:* Reprinted from Perrin, E. C., Newacheck, P., Piess, B., Drotar, D., Gortmaker, S. L., Leventhal, J., Perrin, J. M., Stein, R. E. K., Walker, D. K., & Weitzman, M. (1993). Issues involved in the definition and classification of chronic health conditions. Reproduced by permission of *Pediatrics,* Vol. 91, pp. 787–793. © 1993.

he acquired the physical or health impairment. A child who has not had the use of his legs since birth may have missed out on some important developmental experiences, particularly if early intervention services were not provided. In contrast, a teenager who suddenly loses the use of her legs in an accident has likely had a normal range of experiences throughout childhood but may need considerable support from parents, teachers, specialists, and peers in adapting to life with this newly acquired disability.

*Visibility.* Physical impairments and health conditions range from highly visible and conspicuous to not visible. How children think about themselves and the degree to which others accept them often are affected by the visibility of a condition. Some children use a variety of special orthopedic appliances, such as wheelchairs, braces, crutches, and adaptive tables. They may ride to school on a specially equipped bus or van. In school they may need assistance using the toilet or may wear helmets. Although such special devices and adaptations help children meet important needs, they often have the unfortunate side effect of making the physical impairment more visible, thus making the child look even more different from nondisabled peers.

The visibility of some physical disabilities may cause other children and adults to underestimate the child's abilities and limit opportunities for participation. By contrast, many health conditions such as asthma or epilepsy are not visible, and others may not perceive that the child needs or deserves accommodations. This misperception is supported by the fact that the child functions normally most of the time (Best, 2005a).

The severity, visibility, and age of acquisition of a physical or health impairment all affect an individual's adaptation and development.

# EDUCATIONAL APPROACHES

Special education of children with physical disabilities and health impairments in the United States has a history of more than 100 years (see Table 11.2). While some students with physical and health impairments can fully access and benefit from education with minimal accommodations or environmental modifications, the intensive health and learning needs of other students require a complex and coordinated array of specialized instruction, therapy, and related services. In addition to progressing in the general education curriculum to the maximum extent possible, many students with physical disabilities or health impairments also need intensive instruction in a "parallel curriculum" on ways of "coping with their disabilities" (Bowe, 2000, p. 75). Similar in function to the "expanded core curriculum" for students with visual impairments, the "parallel curriculum" for students with physical and health impairments includes using adaptive methods and assistive technologies for mobility, communication, and daily-living tasks; increasing independence by self-administering special health care routines; and learning self-determination and self-advocacy skills.

*History of education of students
with P&HD*

Council for Exceptional Children — Content Standards for Beginning Teachers—P&HD: Historical foundations related to knowledge and practices in P&HD (PH1K2).

## Teaming and Related Services

The transdisciplinary team approach has special relevance for students with physical disabilities and health impairments. No other group of exceptional children comes into contact, both in and out of school, with as many different teachers, physicians, therapists, and other specialists. Because the medical, educational, therapeutic, vocational, and social needs of these students are often complex and frequently affect each other, it is especially important that educational and health care personnel openly communicate and cooperate with one another. Two particularly important members of the team for many children with physical disabilities and health impairments are the physical therapist and the occupational therapist. Each is a licensed health professional that must complete a specialized training program and meet rigorous standards.

**Physical therapists (PTs)** are involved in the development and maintenance of motor skills, movement, and posture. They may prescribe specific exercises to help a

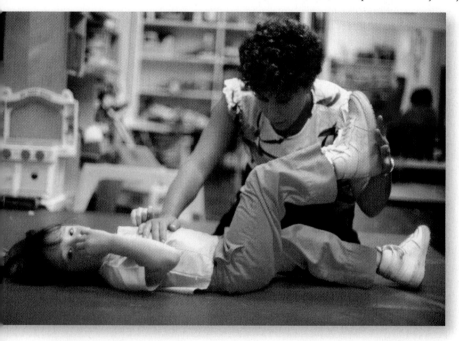

A physical therapist has prescribed specific exercises to increase Tamara's muscular control and range of movement.

child increase control of muscles and use specialized equipment, such as braces, effectively. Massage and prescriptive exercises are perhaps the most frequently applied procedures; but physical therapy can also include swimming, heat treatment, special positioning for feeding and toileting, and other techniques. PTs encourage children to be as motorically independent as possible; help develop muscular function; and reduce pain, discomfort, or long-term physical damage. They may also suggest dos and don'ts for sitting positions and activities in the classroom and may devise exercise or play programs that children with and without disabilities can enjoy together.

**Occupational therapists (OTs)** are concerned with a child's participation in activities, especially those that will be useful in self-help, employment, recreation, communication, and aspects of daily living (e.g., dressing, eating, personal hygiene). They may help a child learn (or relearn) diverse motor behaviors such as drinking from a modified cup, buttoning clothes, tying shoes,

**A history of the education of children with physical disabilities and health impairments: Key events and implications**

| Date | Historical Event | Educational Implications |
|------|------------------|--------------------------|
| 1893 | Industrial School for Crippled and Deformed Children was established in Boston. | This was the first special institution for children with physical disabilities in the United States (Eberle, 1922). |
| Circa 1900 | The first special classes for children with physical impairments began in Chicago. | This was the first time children with physical disabilities were educated in public schools (La Vor, 1976). |
| Early 1900s | There were serious outbreaks of tuberculosis and polio in the United States. | This led to increasing numbers of children with physical impairments being educated by local schools in special classes for the "crippled" or "delicate" (Walker & Jacobs, 1985). |
| Early 20th century | Winthrop Phelps demonstrated that children could be helped through physical therapy and the effective use of braces. Earl Carlson (who himself had cerebral palsy) was a strong advocate of developing the intellectual potential of children with physical disabilities through appropriate education. | The efforts of these two American physicians contributed to increased understanding and acceptance of children with physical disabilities and to recognition that physical impairment did not preclude potential for educational achievement and self-sufficiency. |
| Early 20th century to 1970s | Decisions to "ignore, isolate, and institutionalize these children were often based on mental incompetence presumed because of physical disabilities, especially those involving communication and use of upper extremities" (Conner, Scandary, & Tullock, 1988, p. 6). | Increasing numbers of children with mild physical disabilities and health conditions were educated in public schools. Most children with severe physical disabilities were educated in special schools or community agencies (e.g., the United Cerebral Palsy Association). |
| 1975 | P.L. 94-142 mandated a free, appropriate public education for all children with disabilities and required schools to provide related services (e.g., transportation services, physical therapy, school health services) necessary for students to be educated in the least restrictive environment. | No longer could a child be denied the right to attend the local public school because there was a flight of stairs at the entrance, bathrooms were not accessible, or school buses were not equipped to transport wheelchairs. The related services provision of IDEA transformed schools from "solely scholastic institutions into therapeutic agencies" (Palfrey, 1995, p. 265). |
| 1984 | The Supreme Court ruled in *Independent School District v. Tatro* that schools must provide intermittent catheterization as a supportive or related service if necessary to enable a student with disabilities to receive a public education. | The *Tatro* ruling expanded the range of related services that schools are required to provide and clarified the differences between school health services, which can be performed by a nonphysician, and medical services, which are provided by physicians for diagnostic or eligibility purposes. |
| 1984 | The World Institute on Disability was co-founded by Ed Roberts, an inspirational leader for self-advocacy by persons with disabilities. | This was a major milestone in the civil rights and self-advocacy movement by people with disabilities (Stone, 1995). |
| 1990 | Americans with Disabilities Act (P.L. 101-336) was passed. | ADA provided civil rights protections to all persons with disabilities in private sector employment and mandated access to all public services, accommodations, transportation, and telecommunications. |
| 1990 | Traumatic brain injury was added as a new disability category in the reauthorization of IDEA (P.L. 101-476). | There were increased awareness, services, research, and resources for teachers concerning the educational needs of children with TBI. |
| 1999 | The U.S. Supreme Court ruled in *Cedar Rapids v. Garret F.* that a local school district must pay for the one-on-one nursing care for a medically fragile student who required continuous monitoring of his ventilator and other health-maintenance routines. | The decision reaffirmed and extended the Court's ruling in the 1984 *Tatro* case that schools must provide any and all health services needed for students with disabilities to attend school, as long as performance of those services does not require a licensed physician. |

pouring liquids, cooking, and typing on a computer keyboard. These activities can enhance a child's physical development, independence, vocational potential, and self-concept. OTs conduct specialized assessments and make recommendations to parents and teachers regarding the effective use of appliances, materials, and activities at home and school. Many OTs also work with vocational rehabilitation specialists in helping students find opportunities for work and independent living after completion of an educational program.

Figure 11.4 shows how a PT and an OT worked with a third-grade student with spastic cerebral palsy and other members of the student's IEP team to support five learning outcomes.

Other specialists who frequently provide related services to children with physical disabilities and health impairments include the following (Downing, 2004; Etzel-Wise & Mears, 2004; Neal, Bigby, & Nicholson, 2004):

*PTs, OTs, and other related-services specialists*

Council for Exceptional Children Content Standards for Beginning Teachers—P&HD: Roles and responsibilities of school and community-based medical and related-services personnel (PH10K3).

- *Speech-language pathologists (SLPs),* who provide speech therapy, language interventions, oral motor coordination (e.g., chewing and swallowing), and augmentative and alternative communication (AAC) services
- *Adapted physical educators,* who provide physical education activities designed to meet the individual needs of students with disabilities
- *Recreation therapists,* who provide instruction in leisure activities and therapeutic recreation
- *School nurses,* who provide certain health care services to students, monitor students' health, and inform IEP teams about the effects of medical conditions on students' educational programs
- *Prosthetists,* who make and fit artificial limbs
- *Orthotists,* who design and fit braces and other assistive devices
- *Orientation and mobility specialists,* who teach students to navigate their environment as effectively and independently as possible
- *Biomedical engineers,* who develop or adapt technology to meet a student's specialized needs
- *Health aides,* who carry out medical procedures and health care services in the classroom
- *Counselors and medical social workers,* who help students and families adjust to disabilities

## Environmental Modifications

*Environmental modifications*

Council for Exceptional Children Content Standards for Beginning Teachers—P&HD: Adaptations of educational environments necessary to accommodate individuals with P&HD (PH5K1) (also CC5K1).

Environmental modifications are frequently necessary to enable a student with physical and health impairments to participate more fully and independently in school. Environmental modifications include adaptations to provide increased access to a task or an activity, changing the way in which instruction is delivered, and changing the manner in which the task is done (Best, Heller, & Bigge, 2005; Heller, Dangel, & Sweatman, 1995). Although barrier-free architecture is the most publicly visible type of environmental modification for making community buildings and services more accessible, some of the most functional adaptations require little or no cost. For example:

- Installing paper-cup dispensers near water fountains so they can be used by students in wheelchairs
- Moving a class or an activity to an accessible part of a school building so that a student with a physical impairment can be included
- Providing soft-tip pens that require less pressure for writing
- Providing a head-mounted pointer stick and keyboard guard that enables a student with limited fine-motor control to strike one computer key at a time
- Changing desks and tabletops to appropriate heights for students who are very short or use wheelchairs
- Providing a wooden pointer to enable a student to reach the upper buttons on an elevator control panel
- Modifying response requirements by allowing written responses instead of spoken ones, or vice versa

# FIGURE 11.4 Direct and indirect physical therapy and occupational therapy supports for five IEP goals/learning outcomes for a third-grade student with spastic cerebral palsy.

| One | Two | Three | Four | Five |
|---|---|---|---|---|
| **Learning Outcomes** | | | | |
| Maddie will independently complete her morning routine from exiting school bus to storing her belongings, and preparing for class. | Maddie will use computer at desk to complete 25% of her work independently. | Maddie will attend to educator and focus on task at hand 70% of the time during classroom activities, requiring only minimal assistance 25% of the time to refocus attention despite competing sounds, sights, or actions. | Maddie will participate with classmates in 50% of the physical education activities. | Maddie will participate at least 25% with basic self-care tasks during school. |
| **Physical Therapy Direct Service** | | | | |
| Instruction in maneuvering wheel chair off bus, over school grounds, and into classroom. | Work on postural control and stabilization of upper body to improve use of hands and head control for desktop work. | Work on postural control to improve head, torso, and shoulder stability to allow eyes and hands to move yet still attend to class activity; work on coordination of breathing during activity to maintain focus on task. | Instruct in maneuvering and positioning self during activities; assist in teaching various gross-motor activities. | Work on increasing independence with transfers on/off toilet. |
| **Physical Therapy Indirect Service** | | | | |
| Work with bus driver to assure safe exit from bus. | Instruct aide in techniques to facilitate proper posture at desk. | Consult with educator regarding strengths and limitations during class. | Work with educator to supplement activities with components appropriate for inclusion; train educator and aide to facilitate participation in group activities; work with administrators to ensure accessibility to both indoor and outdoor activity areas. | Teach aide toilet transfers; recommendations made for adaptive toilet and sink to be installed in bathroom. |
| **Occupational Therapy Direct Service** | | | | |
| Work on organizational skills and efficiency during routine. | Introduce computer at desk with adaptations; work on fine motor coordination and equipment use. | Work during class on attention to task—refocusing techniques. | Work on upper extremity coordination to increase participation during group play. | Introduce and instruct in use of adaptive and modified equipment to facilitate independence in hygiene activities of daily living. |
| **Occupational Therapy Indirect Service** | | | | |
| Work with teacher to set up achievable AM schedule; suggest reorganization of materials in classroom to make them more accessible; instruct classroom aide in routine and necessary cues to initially assist with completion of routine. | Instruct educators and aide in computer use, adaptations needed and current limitations; instruct aide and family in techniques to assist with use of device. | Instruct educators and aide in cues to assist with attention to task and identify appropriate reinforcers; make recommendations for environmental changes that will reduce distractions. | Instruct aide to assist with participation in activities. Work with educator to supplement activities with components appropriate for inclusion. | Teach aide use of adaptive equipment and how to assist with the activities of daily living. |

*Source:* From Szabo, J. L. (2000). Maddie's story: Inclusion through physical and occupational therapy. *Teaching Exceptional Children, 33*(2), p. 15. Reprinted by permission.

# Assistive Technology

Although the term *technology* often conjures up images of sophisticated computers and other hardware, technology includes any systematic method based on scientific principles for accomplishing a practical task or purpose. **Assistive technology** is defined in IDEA as

> any item, piece of equipment, or product system, whether acquired commercially off the shelf, modified, or customized, that is used to increase, maintain, or improve functional capabilities of a child with a disability. (20 U.S.C., 1401, Section 602[1])

The types of assistive technology used by persons with disabilities are often the same as those used by individuals without disabilities: "For example, a flexible drinking straw used by persons without disabilities may be viewed as a convenience for drinking purposes. For a student with physical disabilities who cannot grasp and tilt a cup to drink from it, the straw facilitates a functional daily living skill (i.e., drinking from a cup) with little or no assistance from others" (Williams, 1991, p. 206).

Individuals with physical disabilities use both low-tech assistive devices (e.g., adapted eating utensils, picture communication books) and high-tech assistive devices (e.g., computerized synthetic speech devices, electronic switches that can be activated by eye movements) for a wide variety of purposes, including mobility, performance of daily life skills, improved environmental manipulation and control, better communication, access to computers, recreation and leisure, and enhanced learning (Parette, 1998). Education team members should not view a student's acquisition and use of assistive technology as an educational outcome in itself but a means of increasing the student's independence and access to various activities and opportunities (Best, Reed, & Bigge, 2005).

Some students are unable to move freely from place to place without the assistance of a mobility device. Advances in wheelchair design have made manual chairs lighter and stronger, powered chairs have been adapted for use in rural areas, and new environmental controls have put the wheelchair user into contact with both immediate and distant parts of her world. Many children as young as 3 to 5 years old can learn to explore their environment with freedom and independence in "energy efficient, creative, wheeled scooter boards and wheeled go-carts that provide mobility without restricting upper or lower extremity functions" (Evans & Smith, 1993, p. 1418).

Incidentally, a student should not be described as being "confined to a wheelchair." This expression suggests that the person is restrained or even imprisoned. Most students who use wheelchairs leave them from time to time to exercise, travel in an automobile, or lie down. It is preferable to say that a student "has a wheelchair" or "uses a wheelchair to get around."

New technological aids for communication are used increasingly by children whose physical impairments prevent them from speaking clearly. For students who are able to speak but have limited motor function, voice input/output products enable them to access computers (Lahm & Everington, 2002). Such developments allow students with physical impairments to communicate expressively and receptively with others and take part in a wide range of instructional programs. Many individuals with physical disabilities use telecommunications technologies to expand their world, gain access to information and services, and meet new people. Many children and adults with disabilities use e-mail and instant messaging to communicate with others, make new friends, and build and maintain relationships.

Assistive technology includes low-tech devices such as this simple "reacher."

Technology can seldom be pulled off the shelf and serve a student with disabilities with maximum effectiveness. Before purchasing and training a child to use any assistive technology device, the IEP team should carefully consider certain characteristics of the child and the potential technologies that might be selected as well as the impact of using those technologies on the child's family (Bryant & Bryant, 2003; Parette & McMahan, 2002). An assessment of the child's academic skills, social skills, and physical capabilities should help identify the goals and objectives for the technology and narrow down the kinds of devices that may be effective. The child's preferences for certain types of technology should also be determined. At that point, the characteristics of potentially appropriate technologies should be considered, including availability, simplicity of operation, initial and ongoing cost, adaptability to meet the changing needs of the child, and the reliability and repair record of the device. Several excellent handbooks on designing, selecting, and using assistive technology are also available (e.g., Chuch & Glennen, 1992; Cook & Hussey, 1995; Gray, Quartrano, & Liberman, 1998).

## Special Health Care Routines

Many students with physical disabilities have special health care needs that require specialized procedures such as taking prescribed medication or self-administering insulin shots (Harchik, 1994), clean intermittent catheterization (CIC), tracheotomy care, ventilator/respirator care (Lehr & Macurdy, 1994), and managing special nutrition and dietary needs (Heller, Bigge, & Allgood, 2005). These special health-related needs are prescribed in an **individualized health care plan** (IHCP), which is included as part of the student's IEP. According to Poulton (1996), an IHCP is "the written, preplanned and ongoing plan of care for students requiring special health services developed by licensed health personnel and the education team. It includes the nursing process of assessment, nursing diagnosis, planning, intervention, and evaluation. It also includes a plan for emergencies" (p. 1). Figure 11.5 provides examples of possible IHCP objectives that might be included in a student's IEP. Teachers and school personnel must be trained in safely administering health care procedures they are expected to perform (Heller, Fredrick, Best, Dykes, & Cohen, 2000).

Often, well-meaning teachers, classmates, and parents tend to do too much for a child with a physical or health impairment. It may be difficult, frustrating, and/or time-consuming for the child to learn to care for his own needs, but the confidence and skills gained from independent functioning are well worth the effort in the long run (Ault et al., 2006). Students who learn to perform all or part of their daily health care needs increase their ability to function independently in normal environments and lessen their dependence on caregivers (Bosner & Belfiore, 2001; Neef, Parrish, Egel, & Sloan, 1986).

*Importance of Positioning, Seating, and Movement.* Proper positioning, seating, and regular movement are critically important for children with physical disabilities. Proper positioning and movement encourage the development of muscles and bones and help maintain healthy skin (Heller, Forney, Alberto, Schwartzman, & Goeckel, 1999). In addition to these health benefits, positioning can influence how a child with physical disabilities is perceived and accepted by others. Simple adjustments can contribute to improved appearance and greater comfort and increased health for the child with physical disabilities (Best, Reed, & Bigge, 2005; Cantu, 2004):

- Good positioning results in alignment and proximal support of the body.
- Stability positively affects use of the upper body.
- Stability promotes feelings of physical security and safety.
- Good positioning distributes pressure evenly and provides comfort for seating tolerance and long-term use.
- Good positioning can reduce deformity.
- Positions must be changed frequently.

*Assistive technology*

 Council for Exceptional Children Content Standards for Beginning Teachers—P&HD: Communication and social interaction alternatives for individuals who are nonspeaking (PH6K1).

*ICHPs*

Council for Exceptional Children Content Standards for Beginning Teachers—P&HD: Integrate an individual's health care plan into daily programming (PH7S5).

*Positioning, seating, and movement*

Council for Exceptional Children Content Standards for Beginning Teachers—P&HD: Use positioning techniques that decrease inappropriate tone and facilitate appropriate postural reactions to enhance participation (PH5S3) (also PH2K3).

**FIGURE 11.5** Example of IHCP objectives included in an IEP for a student with special health care needs

**Tube feeding:**
- Student will explain (orally, in writing, or through other means) reasons for alternative eating method.
- Student will describe steps necessary in implementing the procedure.
- Student will indicate desire to eat.
- Student will measure feeding liquid to be placed in feeding bag or syringe.
- Student will pour food in feeding bag or syringe.
- Student will direct cleaning of feeding equipment.
- Student will clean equipment.
- Student will feed self.

**Tracheostomy suctioning:**
- Student will indicate need to be suctioned.
- Student will turn on suction machine.
- Student will hold suction tube while procedure is being implemented.
- Student will describe steps necessary to suction.
- Student will explain to others the indicators of need for suctioning.

**Catheterization:**
- Student will indicate time to be catheterized.
- Student will self-catheterize.
- Student will describe steps in implementing the process.
- Student will wash materials necessary.
- Student will assemble materials necessary.
- Student will hold catheter steady during procedure.
- Student will describe indicators of problems related to catheterization.

*Source:* From Lehr, D. H., & Macurdy, S. (1994). Meeting special health care needs of students. In M. Agran, N. E. Marchand-Martella, & R. C. Martella (Eds.), *Promoting health and safety: Skills for independent living* (p. 82). Baltimore, MD: Paul H. Brookes. Reprinted by permission.

Proper seating helps combat poor circulation, muscle tightness, and pressure sores and contributes to proper digestion, respiration, and physical development. Be attentive to the following (Heller et al., 1996):

- Face should be forward, in midline position.
- Shoulders should be in midline position, not hunched over.
- Trunk should be in midline position; maintain normal curvature of spine.
- Seatbelt, pommel or leg separator, and/or shoulder and chest straps may be necessary for shoulder/upper trunk support and upright positions.
- Pelvic position: hips as far back in the chair as possible and weight distributed evenly on both sides of the buttocks.
- Foot support: both feet level and supported on the floor or wheelchair pedals.

Skin care is a major concern for many children with physical disabilities. The skin underneath braces or splints should be checked daily to identify persistent red spots that indicate an improper fit. Someone on the student's team should perform skin checks at least twice daily. Students who are capable of conducting self-checks of their skin should be taught to do so. Use of a long-handled mirror can reduce the student's dependence on others for this self-care task (Ricci-Balich & Behm, 1996). A health care professional should be contacted if any spot does not fade within 20 minutes after the pressure is relieved (Campbell, 2006). Students who are able to use their arms should be taught to perform "chair pushups" in which they lift their buttocks off the seat for 5 to 10 seconds. Doing chair pushups every 30 to 60 minutes may prevent pressure sores. Children who cannot perform pushups can shift their weight by bending forward and sideways.

*Lifting and Transferring Students.*    To prevent the development of pressure sores and help students maintain proper seating and positioning, teachers must know how to move and transfer students with physical disabilities. Routines for lifting and transferring children with physical disabilities should be developed for each child and entail standard procedures for (1) making contact with the child, (2) communicating what is going to happen in a manner the child can understand, (3) preparing the child physically for the transfer, and (4) requiring the child to participate in the routine as much as possible (Stremel et al., 1990). Figure 11.6 shows an example of an individualized routine for lifting and carrying a preschool child with cerebral palsy and spastic quadriplegia. Posting charts and photos of recommended positions for individual students can remind teachers, and other staff to use proper transferring and positioning techniques. Guidelines for shifting the position of students in their wheelchairs and for moving students to and from a wheelchair to toilets and to the classroom floor are provided by Parette and Hourcade (1986).

*Lifting and transferring students*

Council for Exceptional Children    Content Standards for Beginning Teachers—P&HD: Demonstrate appropriate body mechanics to ensure student and teacher safety in transfer, lifting, positioning, and seating (PH5S3).

## Independence and Self-Esteem

All children, whether or not they face the challenges presented by a physical disability or a chronic health condition, need to develop respect for themselves and feel that they have a rightful place in their families, schools, and communities. Effective teachers accept and treat children with physical impairments and special health care needs as worthwhile and whole individuals rather than as disability cases. They encourage the children to develop a positive, realistic view of themselves and their physical conditions. They enable the children to experience success, accomplishment, and, at times, failure. They expect the children to meet reasonable standards of performance and behavior. They help the children cope with disabilities wherever possible and realize that, beyond their physical impairments, these children have many qualities that make them unique individuals.

*Developing independence and self-esteem*

Council for Exceptional Children    Content Standards for Beginning Teachers—P&HD: Barriers to accessibility and acceptance of individuals with P&HD (PH5K3) (also CC5K4).

Students with physical limitations should be encouraged to develop as much independence as possible (Enright, 2000; McGill & Vogle, 2001). Nevertheless, most persons with physical disabilities find it necessary to rely on others for assistance at certain times and in certain situations. Effective teachers can help students cope with their disabilities, set realistic expectations, and accept help gracefully when it is needed.

Many people without disabilities tend to feel uncomfortable in the presence of a person with a visible disability and react with tension and withdrawal. This response is probably attributable to lack of previous contact with individuals with disabilities: people may fear that they will say or do the wrong thing. Belgrave and Mills (1981) found that when people with physical disabilities specifically mentioned their disabilities in connection with a request for help ("Would you mind sharpening my pencil for me? There are just some things a person can't do from a wheelchair"), they were perceived more favorably than they were when no mention was made of the disability.

Many people with disabilities report that their hardware (wheelchairs, artificial limbs, communication devices, etc.) creates a great deal of curiosity and leads to frequent, repetitive questions from strangers. Learning how to explain their physical disabilities or health condition and to respond to questions can be an appropriate component of the educational programs for some children. They may also benefit from discussing concerns such as when to ask for help from others and when to decline offers of assistance.

**Name:** __Tommy___                                    **Date:** ___5/11/06___

**Lifting and Carrying Routine**

Follow these steps each time you up pick Tommy up from the floor or move him from one piece of equipment to another, or move him in the classroom from one location to another.

| Step | Activity | Desired Response |
|------|----------|------------------|
| Contacting | Touch Tommy on his arm or shoulder & tell him you are going to move him from _____ to _____ . | Wait for Tommy to relax. |
| Communicating | Tell Tommy where you are going and show him a picture or object that represents where he is going. For example, show him his coat and say, "we are going outside now to play." | Wait for Tommy to respond with facial expressions and vocalizations. (Try not to get him so hyped that he becomes more spastic.) |
| Preparing | Make sure Tommy's muscle tone is not stiff before you move him. Use deep pressure touch with a flat hand on his chest area to help relax him. | Wait to make sure that Tommy's body is relaxed and in alignment (as much as possible). |
| Lifting | Place Tommy in a sitting position and lift him from sitting unless he is in the stander, where he will need to be lifted from standing. Tell him that you are going to lift him. Put your arms around Tommy's back and under his knees and bend his knees to his chest so that you maintain him in a flexed position. | Wait for Tommy to reach his arms forward toward you and facilitate at his shoulders if he does not initiate reach within 10 sec. |
| Carrying | Turn Tommy away from you so that he is facing away and can see where you are moving. Lean his back against your body to provide support, and hold him with one arm under his hips with his legs in front. If his legs become stiff, use your other arm to hold his legs apart by coming under one leg and between the two legs to hold them gently apart. | Tommy will be able to see where he is going and can use his arms to indicate location (grossly). |
| Repositioning | Put Tommy in the next position he is to use for the activity. Tell him what is happening: "Music is next and you are going to sit on the floor so you can play the instruments with Jilly and Susan." | Tommy is ready to participate in the next activity. |

*Source:* From Campbell, P. H. (2000). Promoting participation in natural environments by accommodating motor disabilities. In M. E. Snell & F. Brown, *Instruction of students with severe disabilities* (5th ed.), (p. 305). Upper Saddle River, NJ: Merrill/Prentice Hall. © 2000 by Merrill/Prentice Hall. Reprinted by permission.

## EDUCATIONAL PLACEMENT ALTERNATIVES

*Placement alternatives*

Council for Exceptional Children — Content Standards for Beginning Teachers—Common Core: Demands of learning environments (CC5K1).

For no group of exceptional children is the continuum of educational services and placement options more relevant than for students with physical impairments and special health needs. Most children with physical and health impairments today spend at least part of the school day in regular classrooms. During the 2003–2004 school year, about 47% of all school-age students who received special education services under the disability category orthopedic impairments and 51% of those with other health impairments were educated in the regular classroom (U.S. Department of Education, 2004). The percentage of students in each disability category served in resource rooms was 21% and 30%. To find out the percentage of school-age students with orthopedic impairments and other health impairments served in six different educational environments during the 2003–2004 school year, see Table 1.7 in Chapter 1.

Many children with physical disabilities are also served in special classes in the public schools. During the 2003–2004 school year, about 26% of all school-age students who received special education services under the disability category orthopedic impairments and 15% of those with other health impairments were educated in separate classrooms (U.S. Department of Education, 2004). Some districts have entire schools designed or adapted especially for students with physical disabilities; in others, special classrooms are housed within regular elementary or secondary school buildings. Special classes usually provide smaller class size, more adapted equipment, and easier access to the services of professionals such as physicians, physical and occupational therapists, adapted physical educators, and specialists in communication disorders and therapeutic recreation.

Some children with the most severe physical and health impairments are served in homebound or hospital education programs. If a child's medical condition necessitates hospitalization or treatment at home for a lengthy period (generally 30 days or more), the local school district is obligated to develop an IEP and provide appropriate educational services to the child through a qualified teacher. Some children need home- or hospital-based instruction because their life-support equipment cannot be made portable. Such *technology-dependent students* are in need of "both a medical device to compensate for the loss of a vital body function and substantial and ongoing nursing care to avoid death or further disability" (Office of Technology Assessment, 1987, p. 3). The term *medically fragile* is also used to refer to students who are dependent on life-support medical technology. As Lehr and McDaid (1993) point out, however, many of these children are "survivors of many adverse conditions, who in fact are not fragile at all, but remarkably strong to be able to rebound from periods of acute illness" (p. 7).

Home or hospital settings are usually regarded as the most restrictive placements because little or no interaction with nondisabled students is possible. Most large hospitals and medical centers employ educational specialists who cooperate with the hospitalized student's home school district in planning and delivering instruction. Homebound children are visited regularly by itinerant teachers or tutors hired by the school district. Some school programs use a closed-circuit TV system to enable children to see, hear, and participate in class discussions and demonstrations from their beds.

One should not assume that a technology-dependent child cannot be educated in the public schools. After examining the experiences of 77 families of children who are ventilator-assisted, the authors of a study on the educational placements of such children concluded that "barriers to the integration of these children into school-based programs are attitudinal more than technological" (Jones, Clatterbuck, Marquis, Turnbull, & Moberly, 1996, p. 47).

## Inclusive Attitudes

After health care objectives are met, acceptance is the most basic need of children with physical disabilities and health impairments. How parents, teachers, classmates, and others react to a child with physical disabilities is at least as important as the disability itself. Many children with physical disabilities suffer from excessive pity, sympathy, and overprotection; others are cruelly rejected, stared at, teased, and excluded from participation in activities with nondisabled children. Turner-Henson, Holaday, Corser, Ogletree, and Swan (1994) conducted interviews with the parents of 365 children with chronic illnesses and reported that one-third (34.5%) of the parents had experienced specific incidences of discrimination concerning their children. Although the study did not focus on the schools, more than half (55%) of the problems cited by the parents occurred at school (e.g., child not allowed to participate in play activities because of a brace or excluded from parties because of food limitations; teacher thinks child is faking low blood sugar). Peers were the second most common source of discrimination (36%).

*Attitudes and practices that hinder or support inclusion of students with P&HD*

Council for Exceptional Children — Content Standards for Beginning Teachers—P&HD: Barriers to accessibility and acceptance of individuals with P&HD (PH5K3) (also CC5K4).

The classroom can be a useful place to discuss disabilities and encourage understanding and acceptance of a child with a physical disability or health impairment. Some teachers find that simulation or role-playing activities are helpful. Classmates might, for example, have the opportunity to use wheelchairs, braces, or crutches to expand their awareness of some barriers a classmate with physical disabilities faces. As Pieper (1983) notes, most children with physical and health impairments are "neither saintly creatures nor pitiable objects" (p. 8). She suggests that teachers emphasize cooperation rather than competition by choosing tasks that require students to work together. It is important to give praise when earned but not to make the child with a physical impairment a teacher's pet who will be resented by other students. Factual information can also help build a general understanding of impairment. Classmates should learn to use accurate terminology and offer the correct kind of assistance when needed.

Some students with chronic illnesses are absent from school for extended periods because of flare-ups or scheduled medical treatment. Successful reentry of a child who has missed extended periods of school because of illness or the contraction of a disease requires preparation of the child, her parents, classmates, and school personnel. The student's classmates should be given information about the child and the disease, encouraged to ask questions, and kept informed of the child's progress (Spinelli, 2004). Figure 11.7 shows questions that peers often ask about a classmate with a health problem and suggests several strategies for preparing the child and her peers for the child's return to the class.

There is a need for improved programs of education and counseling for students with terminal illnesses. These programs should give realistic support to the child and family in dealing with death and in making the best possible use of the time available (Ault et al., 2006). When a child dies, teachers and classmates are seriously affected, and their needs should be considered and talked about. For a discussion of ways in which classroom teachers can help themselves, classmates, and parents deal with the death of a student, see Peckham (1993), Thornton and Krajewski (1993), Spinelli (2004), and Wrenn (1994).

# CURRENT ISSUES AND FUTURE TRENDS

Children with physical disabilities and health impairments are being included in regular educational programs as much as possible today. No longer do professionals believe that the regular classroom is an inappropriate environment for a child with physical limitations or special health care needs. Although architectural and attitudinal barriers still exist in some areas, inclusive public school programs are gradually becoming the norm instead of the exception.

## Related Services in the Classroom

We will likely see a continuation of the trend to serve children with physical and health impairments in regular classrooms as much as possible. Therapists and other support personnel will come into the classroom to assist the teacher, child, and classmates (Szabo, 2000). For example, some school districts in North Carolina employ health aides who carry out medical care plans in the classroom, assist OTs or PTs, help students get lunch trays, or act as teachers' assistants if not needed elsewhere (*CEC Today,* 1998). This appears to be a more effective and economical use of professional time and skill than removing a child with disabilities from the classroom to provide services in an isolated setting. Wherever and by whomever needed health and other related services are carried out, we must heed Orelove and Sobsey's (1991) caution:

> The challenge for the team is to determine how to work with and around the student's medical and physical needs to provide an appropriate education, rather than turning the school day into an extended therapy session. Therapy and specialized health care procedures should facilitate, not replace, instruction. (pp. 3–4)

**FIGURE 11.7** Suggestions for helping peers maintain relationship with and prepare for return of a child who has been absent due to a serious illness or disease

Explain and allow discussion of the child's illness before treatment and before the child's return.

Common questions asked by children include

- What is the child's condition?
- Is it contagious?
- Will the child die?
- Will the child look different?
- Will the child act differently? (e.g., act "funny," bleed, faint, cough, vomit)
- Can the child still do regular activities? (e.g., attend school, play, spend the night with friends, go out)
- Should we talk about the illness, or should we ignore it?
- What will other children think if we stay friends with the child?

Update the class at least weekly on the child's progress.

Encourage and provide opportunities for classmates to maintain contact with the child (e.g., cards, visits, audiotapes, calls).

Encourage and provide opportunities for the child to visit the classroom.

Provide educational materials so that the child feels involved and can keep up with the class.

Have another period of discussion for the class shortly before the child returns to school:

- Consult with child, family, and health care team about what information should be conveyed.
- Consider involving the child and/or a health care team member in the discussion.

Have a welcome-back activity for the child on the day of his or her return.

Monitor peer responses and interactions with the child after the child's return.

*Source:* From Sexson, S. B., & Dingle, A. D. (2001). Medical disorders. In F. M. Kline, L. B. Silver, & S. C. Russell (Eds.), *The educator's guide to medical issues in the classroom* (p. 47). Baltimore: Paul H. Brookes. Reprinted by permission.

Including students with physical impairments and special health care needs in regular classrooms, however, has raised several controversial issues. Many questions center on the extent of responsibility properly assumed by teachers and schools for a child's physical health care needs. Some educators and school administrators believe that services such as catheterization, tracheotomy care, and tube feeding are more medical than educational and should not be the school's responsibility. The expense of such services, the training and supervision of personnel, and the availability of insurance pose potential problems for school districts. Similar questions have been raised with regard to the assistive devices and special therapeutic services that children with physical or health impairments may need to access and benefit from a public education. For example, who should bear the cost of an expensive computerized communication system for a child with cerebral palsy—the parents, the school, both, or some other agency?

Two landmark U.S. Supreme Court cases have made clear the government's position. In *Irving Independent School District v. Tatro* (1984), the Court decided that a school district was

*Tatro and Garret cases*

Council for Exceptional Children    Content Standards for
Beginning Teachers—P&HD:
Laws and policies related to
specialized health care in the
educational setting (PH1K3).

obligated to provide clean intermittent catheterization to a young child with spina bifida. The Court considered catheterization to be a related service, necessary for the child to remain in the least restrictive educational setting and able to be performed by a trained layperson.

*Cedar Rapids Community School District v. Garret F.* (1999) involved nursing care for a middle school student who was paralyzed in a motorcycle accident at the age of 4 and could only breathe with an electric ventilator or by someone pumping an air bag attached to his tracheotomy tube. In addition to having someone monitor and check the settings on his ventilator, Garret required continuous assistance with his tracheotomy, positioning in his wheelchair, observations to determine if he was in respiratory distress, catheterization, assessments of his blood pressure, and assistance with food and drink. Garret's mother had used money from insurance and a settlement with the motorcycle company to hire a nurse to care for his medical needs. When Garret reached middle school, his mother asked the school district to assume the cost of his physical care during the school day. The school district refused, believing it was not responsible under IDEA for providing continuous nursing care. The Supreme Court agreed with lower courts that the nursing services were related services because Garret could not attend school without them and ruled that the school district had to pay for continuous one-on-one nursing care. These two rulings used what is known as a "bright-line test" for making decisions about related services (Katsiyannis & Yell, 2000). A bright-line test is a test that is clearly stated and easy to follow (Thomas & Hawke, 1999). The bright-line test established in the *Tatro* case and upheld by the *Garret* case is that if a licensed physician is required to perform a service, the school district is not responsible for paying for it. If a nurse or a health aide can perform the service, even if it is medical in nature, it is considered a related service that the school district must provide under IDEA to give the child access to a free, appropriate public education.

According to the Court's interpretation of related services, schools are responsible for the very high costs of health-related services for medically fragile students. This places a huge financial burden on schools and may contribute to increased pressure on Congress to relieve their financial burden by raising the level of federal funding for IDEA (Katsiyannis & Yell, 2000). Reviews and discussions of special education law and legal precedents concerning the schools' responsibility for providing assistive technology and special health care services can be found in Heller et al. (2000), Katsiyannis and Yell (2000), Rapport (1996), and Weiss and Dykes (1995).

## New and Emerging Technologies for Persons with Severe Physical Disabilities

Over the past several decades, the use of technology to "minimize disadvantages associated with disabilities has blossomed from a promise that benefited a few individuals to a reality that has improved many people's lives" (Sobsey, 1996, p. 207). New and emerging developments in technology and biomedical engineering hold even more exciting implications for many individuals with physical disabilities. People with paralysis resulting from spinal cord injury and other causes are already benefiting from sophisticated microcomputers that can stimulate paralyzed muscles by bypassing damaged nerves. In 1982 Nan Davis became the first human being to walk with permanently paralyzed muscles; she was able to control a computer with her brain and transmit impulses to sensors placed on her paralyzed muscles. Since that breakthrough event, such systems have become more efficient and widespread, helping many people with various kinds of physi-

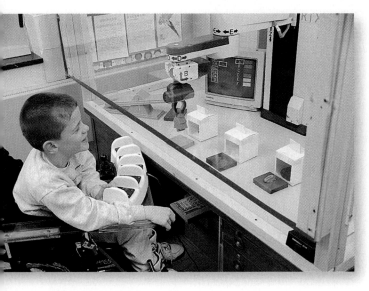

Which object weighs the most? As his skills at controlling the robot increase, Troy comes into contact with ever more complex and exciting learning experiences.

cal impairments. Myoelectric (bionic) limbs are battery-powered artificial limbs that pick up electrical signals from the brain and enable the user to perform certain movements and functions. Robotics also holds promise for increasing the independent functioning of students with physical disabilities. A robot is "any mechanical device operated automatically, especially by remote control, to perform in a seemingly human way" (*Webster's New World Dictionary*, 1986, p. 1231). Robots have great potential as assistive tools for students with disabilities by enabling independent manipulation of the environment and providing increased educational access and opportunities (Howell, 2000).

*Emerging technologies for P&HD*

Council for Exceptional Children Content Standards for Beginning Teachers—P&HD: Barriers to accessibility and acceptance of individuals with P&HD (PH5K3).

## Animal Assistance

Using animals to assist people with physical disabilities has also generated much recent interest. Animals can help children and adults with physical disabilities in many ways. Nearly everyone is familiar with guide dogs, which can help people who are blind travel independently. Some agencies now train hearing dogs to assist people who are deaf by alerting them to sounds. Another recent and promising approach to the use of animals by people with disabilities is the helper or service dog. Depending on a person's needs, dogs can be trained to carry books and other objects (in saddlebags), pick up telephone receivers, turn light switches on or off, and open doors. Dogs can also be used for balance and support—for example, to help a person propel a wheelchair up a steep ramp or stand up from a seated position. And dogs can be trained to contact family members or neighbors in an emergency.

Monkeys have been trained to perform complex tasks such as preparing food, operating record and tape players, and turning the pages of books. Sometimes technological and animal assistance are combined, as when a person uses a laser beam (emitted from a mouth-held device) to show a monkey which light switch to turn on.

In addition to providing practical assistance and enhancing the independence of people with disabilities, animals also have social value as companions. People frequently report that their helper animals serve as icebreakers in opening up conversations and contacts with nondisabled people in the school and community. In addition, the responsibility of caring for an animal is a worthwhile and rewarding experience for many people, with or without disabilities.

"Helper" or "service dogs" can be trained to assist with many daily living and work-related tasks.

## Employment, Life Skills, and Self-Advocacy

A major area of concern is employment, one of the most meaningful aspects of adult life. Many studies show that successful and remunerative work is one of the most important factors enabling people with disabilities to lead satisfying, productive, and independent lives. Yet negative attitudes persist on the part of many employers. Vocational and professional opportunities must be expanded to include individuals with disabilities more equitably. While children are in school, their education should help them investigate practical avenues of future employment, and there should be ongoing contact between educators and vocational rehabilitation specialists.

Traditionally, children and adults with disabilities were viewed as society's responsibility, and it was assumed they should be grateful for the services (i.e., charity) bestowed upon them by a benevolent society (Wolfensberger, 2000). Persons with disabilities neither want nor need charity; rather, they need and deserve equal access to the same educational, employment, housing, and recreational opportunities as persons without disabilities (Giangreco, 1996). Legislation and litigation over the past 20 years have mandated equal access and provided funding for improved opportunities, but many of those advancements have been the direct product of self-advocacy.

Telethons and other fund-raising activities on behalf of persons with disabilities have become controversial in recent years. Some self-advocacy groups and professionals believe they perpetuate negative stereotypes and portray people with disabilities as objects of pity (see the November 1993 issue of the *TASH Newsletter*).

There are many self-help groups for people with disabilities. These groups can help provide information and support to children affected by similar disabilities. It is usually encouraging for a child and parent to meet and observe capable, independent adults who have disabilities; and worthwhile helping relationships can be established. Teachers can help promote self-knowledge and self-confidence in their students with physical disabilities by introducing them to such adults and groups. Some self-advocacy groups operate centers for independent living, which emphasize adaptive devices, financial benefits, access to jobs, and provision of personal care attendants. Other groups are active as advocates for social change, countering instances in which people with disabilities are excluded from meaningful participation in society.

We all must work to improve the quality of education, increase physical access to public buildings, improve public attitudes, and provide greater support for parents and families. As these needs are met, the opportunity to participate fully in all facets of everyday community life will be open to all people with physical disabilities and health impairments.

# Tips for Beginning Teachers

## Promoting the Success of Students with Physical Disabilities and Special Health Care Needs
### by Mary Kate Ryan-Griffith

If you become a teacher, you will have students with physical disabilities or special health care needs in your classroom at different times throughout your career. Here are some basic tips that will make your work with these students more effective and enjoyable for you and your students.

### ENCOURAGE INDEPENDENT MOVEMENT

Sometimes our efforts to assist and be nice to a student with physical and health challenges can contribute to learned helplessness, which becomes increasingly difficult to overcome as the child grows older. Teachers should help children with physical and health challenges learn to be as motorically independent and self-sufficient as possible. Doing things for themselves

develops and maintains children's muscular function and enhances their self-esteem.

- A child's independence can be sabotaged by inefficient room arrangement. Plan the layout of your classroom so that the child can access the water fountain, the blackboard, the reading area, the small-group-activities area, and the computer and enter and exit the classroom for bathroom and emergency situations.
- If one of your students uses a wheelchair, obtain one (ask the school nurse or the PT), get in it, and navigate the classroom layout yourself. Looking at wheelchair access from this level is very sobering.
- Troubleshoot each situation in the classroom and around the school building and grounds that chil-

dren should do themselves if they can: opening doors, turning pages in a book, feeding the class pet, holding up a test tube in science lab, going through the lunch line in the cafeteria. Look for ways to adapt the task and/or provide an assistive device that will enable the student to participate as independently as possible. A student who moves purposively throughout the day develops and maintains muscular function and interacts more naturally with his classmates.

## TEACH STUDENTS TO ASK FOR AND DECLINE HELP

As important as it is to build their independence, students with physical and special health needs must also learn to recognize and accept their limits.

- Teach children that it is okay to politely request assistance with tasks or situations that they cannot do independently. Manners should always be stressed! The pendulum can swing very quickly from a child who does not self-advocate to an imperious leader barking orders at one and all.
- A child who has politely requested and received assistance from others will likely experience an increase in unsolicited offers of help. Teach the student that it is also okay to say, "No thanks, I don't need help now."

## ASK BEFORE YOU PUSH

My school is very large, so I will often enlist the aid of a student to help push me. You'd be surprised how many people start pushing my chair without asking. Why is it important to ask before pushing someone's wheelchair?

- Think of the chair as an extension of the person's body. You wouldn't touch someone, or want someone to touch you, without gaining permission.

- Pushing without the person's knowledge can be dangerous. For example, because my injury was high on the spinal cord, I don't have the balance needed to stay in my chair if I am suddenly pushed.
- Teach the target student's classmates how to ask, "Would you like some help pushing?"
- Ask the PT to co-teach a lesson with you and the target student on how to push the wheelchair in a safe and efficient manner. Too often I've seen children pushing a chair one-handed or racing down the hall with one. Pushers need to know how to take off the brakes and rebrake when they get to where they're going. Wheelchair brakes are very important!

## DON'T BE AFRAID OF THE EQUIPMENT

The special equipment used by some children with physical disabilities and special health needs—braces, wheelchairs, ventilators, and voice boxes—can be intimidating to other children and to adults.

- If one of your students uses special equipment, get to know it. Ask the PT, the OT, the school nurse, or other health professionals on the child's IEP team to demonstrate and explain the equipment to you before the first week of school begins. If appropriate and possible, the student should participate in this demonstration and discussion. Ask what to look for to ensure that the equipment is in good working order and who to contact if you notice any problems.
- Ask the student with physical disabilities or special health care needs to do a show-and-tell of his equipment for the class. This not only helps classmates become comfortable with the equipment but also helps build friendships and quickly puts the equipment in the background where it should be so that children can see their classmate as just another kid.

## KEY TERMS AND CONCEPTS

 To print your own set of SAFMED flash cards for studying and mastering these terms, go to the Companion Website, **www.prenhall.com/heward**.

## SUMMARY

### Definitions of Physical Disabilities and Health Impairments

- Children with physical disabilities and health impairments are eligible for special education under two disability categories of IDEA: orthopedic impairments and other health impairments.
- Orthopedic impairments involve the skeletal system; a neurological impairment involves the nervous system. Both are frequently described in terms of the affected parts of the body.
- Physical disabilities and health impairments may be congenital or acquired, chronic or acute.

### Prevalence of Physical Disabilities and Health Impairments

- In 2003–2004, 8.6% of all school-age students who received special education services were reported under the disability categories of orthopedic impairments and other health impairments. This figure does not include all children with physical or health impairments because some are reported under other disability categories and some do not require special education services.

### Types and Causes of Physical Disabilities and Health Impairments

- Cerebral palsy is a long-term condition arising from impairment to the brain and causing disturbances in voluntary motor functions.
- Spina bifida is a congenital condition that may cause loss of sensation and severe muscle weakness in the lower part of the body. Children with spina bifida can usually participate in most classroom activities but need assistance in toileting.
- Muscular dystrophy is a long-term condition; most children gradually lose the ability to walk independently.
- Spinal cord injuries are caused by a penetrating injury, stretching of the vertebral column, fracture of the vertebrae, or compression of the spinal cord and usually result in some form of paralysis below the site of the injury.
- Epilepsy produces disturbances of movement, sensation, behavior, and/or consciousness.
- Diabetes is a disorder of metabolism that can often be controlled with injections of insulin.

- Children with cystic fibrosis, asthma, HIV/AIDS, and other chronic health conditions may require special education and other related services, such as health care services and counseling.

## Attention-Deficit/Hyperactivity Disorder

- To be diagnosed with attention-deficit/hyperactivity disorder (ADHD), a child must consistently display six or more symptoms listed in the DSM-IV of inattention or hyperactivity-impulsivity for a period of at least 6 months.
- ADHD is not a disability category recognized by IDEA. Many students with ADHD also have learning disabilities and/or emotional and behavioral disorders and receive special education under those categories. Students with ADHD can also be served under the other health impairments category if the disorder results in a "heightened alertness to environmental stimuli" that adversely affects academic performance. Some children with ADHD are eligible for services under Section 504 of the Rehabilitation Act.
- The prevalence of ADHD is estimated to be 3% to 5% of all school-age children.
- Boys are much more likely to be diagnosed with ADHD than are girls.
- Genetic factors may place individuals at a greater-than-normal risk of an ADHD diagnosis. ADHD is associated with a wide range of genetic disorders and diseases such as Fragile X syndrome, Turner syndrome, Williams syndrome, fetal alcohol syndrome, prenatal exposure to cocaine, and lead poisoning.
- Some individuals with ADHD have structural or biochemical differences in their brains that may play a causal role in their behavioral deficits and excesses.
- Ritalin is the most frequently prescribed medication for children with ADHD. Approximately 70% to 80% of children diagnosed with ADHD respond positively to Ritalin. Common but usually manageable side effects of Ritalin and other stimulant medications include insomnia, decreased appetite, headaches, weight loss, and irritability.
- The use of stimulant medications with children is controversial. Some professionals believe the benefits outweigh the liabilities and that drug therapy should be part of a comprehensive treatment program for children with ADHD. Other professionals are concerned that stimulant medications have few long-term benefits for academic achievement and that educators and parents rely too heavily on medical interventions.
- Behaviorally based interventions for students with ADHD included reinforcing on-task behavior, modifying assignments and instructional activities to promote success, and teaching self-control strategies.

## Characteristics of Children with Physical Disabilities and Health Impairments

- Perrin et al., (1993) have proposed a noncategorical system for classifying and understanding children's chronic physical and medical conditions; it includes 13 dimensions that are rated on a continuum from mild to profound.
- Many factors must be taken into consideration when assessing the effects of a physical impairment or health condition on a child's development and behavior. Two particularly important variables are the age of onset and the visibility of the impairment.

## Educational Approaches

- Children with physical disabilities and health impairments typically require services from an interdisciplinary team of professionals.
- Physical therapists (PTs) use specialized knowledge to plan and oversee a child's program for making correct and useful movements. Occupational therapists (OTs) are

concerned with a child's participation in activities, especially those that will be useful in self-help, employment, recreation, communication, and other aspects of daily living.

- Modifications to the physical environment and to classroom activities can enable students with physical and health impairments to participate more fully in the school program.
- Assistive technology is any piece of equipment or device used to increase, maintain, or improve the functional capabilities of individuals with disabilities.
- Students can increase their independence by learning to take care of their personal health care routines such as clean intermittent catheterization and self-administration of medication.
- Proper positioning and seating is important for children with physical disabilities. All teachers and other staff should follow a standard routine for lifting and moving a child with physical disabilities.
- How parents, teachers, classmates, and others react to a child with physical disabilities is at least as important as the disability itself.
- Students with physical limitations should be encouraged to develop as much independence as possible. Effective teachers help students cope with their disabilities, set realistic expectations, and accept help gracefully when needed.

## Educational Placement Alternatives

- About 50% of students with physical impairments and chronic health conditions are served in regular classrooms.
- The amount of supportive help that may be required to enable a student with physical disabilities to function effectively in a regular class varies greatly according to each child's condition, needs, and level of functioning.
- Special classes usually provide smaller class size, more adapted equipment, and easier access to the services of professionals such as physicians, physical and occupational therapists, and specialists in communication disorders and therapeutic recreation.
- Some technology-dependent children require home- or hospital-based instruction because their life-support equipment cannot be made portable.
- Successful reentry of children who have missed extended periods of school because of illness or the contraction of a disease requires preparation of the child, parents, classmates, and school personnel.

## Current Issues and Future Trends

- The education of students with physical and health impairments in regular classrooms has raised several controversial issues, especially with regard to the provision of medically related procedures in the classroom.
- New and emerging technologies such as bionic body parts and robotic assistants offer exciting possibilities for the future.
- Animals, particularly dogs and monkeys, can assist people with physical disabilities in various ways.
- Children with physical disabilities and health impairments can gain self-knowledge and self-confidence by meeting capable adults with disabilities and joining self-advocacy groups.

To check your comprehension of chapter contents, go to the Guided Review and Quiz modules in Chapter 11 of the Companion Website, **www.prenhall.com/heward**.

# Low Incidence Disabilities: Severe/Multiple Disabilities, Deaf-Blindness, and Traumatic Brain Injury

# Featured Teacher

## DIANE K. ELLIS

### BELLEVUE PUBLIC SCHOOL DISTRICT
### BELLEVUE, NEBRASKA

*Education—Certification—Experience*
- B.S., special education and elementary education, University of South Dakota, 1982; M.A., early childhood special education, University of South Dakota, 1988
- Nebraska teacher certification: severe/multiple disabilities, K–12; preschool handicapped; visually impaired, K–12; mild/moderate handicapped, K–12; assistive technology practitioner certification from the Rehabilitation Engineering and Assistive Technology Society of North America
- 23 years of teaching children, adolescents, and adults with a variety of disabilities in educational, vocational, and residential settings.

**Teaching Position and Students**    I am employed by the Bellevue Public School District as an assistive technology and augmentative communication consultant (AAC) and an early childhood special education consultant. I began teaching in the Bellevue schools 16 years ago as the lead teacher for CHAP School (serving students with multiple or severe/profound disabilities) and as an early childhood special education teacher. Currently, I have 68 students on my AAC caseload. They have a variety of disabilities, including multiple disabilities, autism, and other severe disabilities such as traumatic brain injuries and deaf-blindness. My students range in age from 18 months to 14 years old and are educated in a wide variety of placements, including home-based settings.

I'll introduce you to several of my students with the caution that each is unique. These descriptions and labels do not begin to identify their individual strengths, challenges, needs, or potential. First, we'll meet Bobby, a 5-year-old with deaf-blindness. He is ambulatory with inconsistent hearing acuity and has limited vision in one eye. Bobby requires modified materials and instruction for access to and assistance in large groups, unfamiliar environments, and the outdoors. Gary is a fourth grader with traumatic brain injury who exhibits significant communicative, cognitive, and behavioral challenges but has excellent gross-motor skills. This results in some serious safety issues as he runs from staff and does not recognize common dangers. Mary is a kindergartener with significant physical disabilities due to cerebral palsy. She uses a motorized wheelchair and has a voice output communication device. Mary requires adult assistance with adaptive materials and computer access to participate in her educational curriculum. Renae is a 2-year-old with multiple disabilities including visual impairments, mental retardation, and physical disabilities. She has numerous medical and health concerns that affect her development. Renae requires adult assistance to participate in all activities, with some emerging use of switches to activate toys and get another person's attention.

**IEP Goals and Objectives**    The IEP goals and objectives for these students focus on developing functional life skills as well as using assistive technology to access their educational program. This may mean the use of alternate

## Focus Questions

- Why is a curriculum based on typical developmental stages inappropriate for students with severe and multiple disabilities?

- Why is it so critical to select functional and age-appropriate curriculum objectives for students with severe and multiple disabilities?

- Can a teacher increase the learning potential of students with severe and multiple disabilities? How?

- What are the most important skills for a teacher of students with severe and multiple disabilities? Why?

- How much time should students with severe and multiple disabilities spend in the general education classroom with their nondisabled peers?

keyboards with customized overlays so that they can use adaptive software on the computer. Some students need a switch to activate a toy, an appliance, or the computer. Here are some examples of IEP goals designed to influence the functional communication and classroom independence of students with significant disabilities.

> *Annual goal:* Given tactile cues, Bobby will walk to designated areas avoiding obstacles with one or fewer prompts for 4–5 sessions by May 2006.

> *Annual goal:* Using sign language, verbalizations, and/or a picture communication system, Gary will initiate interactions with others at least 10 times during a 30-minute observation for 4–5 sessions by May 2006.

> *Annual goal:* Given a voice output communication device, Mary will request a desired item from another person at least 5 times during group activities for 4–5 sessions by May 2006.

> *Annual goal:* When given switch access, Renae will activate a switch toy at least 5 times in a 10-minute session for 4–5 sessions by May 2006.

Each goal has specific objectives or benchmarks to indicate progress toward the final goal. For students with severe disabilities, this may mean a gradual change in performance criteria and/or fading of the level of prompting—a way to show progress for students who need lots of practice to learn a new skill.

***Services/Instructional Strategies***     Assistive technology or augmentative communication supports should be considered whenever a child is having difficulty participating in her educational program or demonstrates significant frustration with communication. My intervention efforts focus on developing functional communication skills and independence skills for life. It is important to integrate these skills into activities throughout the school day. Although I do provide direct instruction on using assistive technology and augmentative communication supports, my focus is on training classroom staff to use these supports and practice functional skills throughout the day. As a team, we develop specific plans for integrating the use of supports into students' daily activities at home and school. Augmentative communication systems include voice output communication devices, communication boards and overlays, and sign language and other picture communication systems. Teachers always pair spoken language with the augmentative communication system.

One of our strategies has been to focus on literacy during small-group activities. The group reads a short book using visual supports and other modifications, and students use picture symbols and communication devices to participate in reading the repetitive lines of books. For example, Renae hits her switch to ask, "What do you see?" when reading *Brown Bear, Brown Bear.* For older students we have used more age-appropriate reading material such as "News-2-You," an online weekly reader with picture symbol support. It provides activities related to the subject highlighted in the reader. For example, Gary requests items with his picture symbols to make "Bear Paw" cookies after reading about polar bears.

As a member of the IEP team, I help conduct functional behavioral assessments to determine if a child's challenging behavior has a communicative function. It is common for students who have significant difficulties in communication to engage in challenging behaviors such as tantrums, aggression, and running away. When students learn alternate ways to communicate with others, the frequency and/or duration of their behavioral incidents usually decrease.

***What I Like Most about Being a Special Educator***     Since starting college as a special education major, I have never wanted to do anything other than teach children with spe-

To see examples of assistive technologies and instructional materials used by Ms. Ellis, go the Teacher Feature module of the Companion Website, **www.prenhall.com/heward.**

cial needs. The challenges of teaching students with severe and multiple disabilities can be daunting, but the rewards are tremendous with each step a student takes. For instance:

- The joy in Renae's eyes when she discovered that she could control the actions on the computer
- The relief of Gary's parents when he could finally ask them for what he wanted
- Mary's success in counting *all* of the kindergarteners as her friends
- Bobby's change from head banging to communicating with others

A teacher of children with severe and multiple disabilities must learn to accept that progress is measured in tiny steps. However, the impact of those tiny steps can be more than the impact of getting an *A* on a test. The children who challenge us the most are the ones who give us the most joy when we finally develop a successful intervention plan.

My students' most important accomplishments are not always seen on a test but are evident in the quality of their own lives and their families' lives. Seeing a student become more independent can sustain a teacher during challenging times. Knowing that I am part of a team that can positively influence a student's life provides the incentive I need to hang in there.

Preschooler Zack shows a card with a symbol and picture that says, "I want toy," to a classmate, who responds, "Here's the toy, Zack." First-grader Emily is learning to feed herself with a spoon. A teacher shows 13-year-old Terrence that it is more appropriate to shake hands than to hug a person when first introduced. Manuela, who is 20, is learning to ride a city bus to her afternoon job at the cafeteria, where she clears tables and sorts silverware. Zack, Emily, Terrence, and Manuela have severe disabilities or multiple disabilities. Except for their general need for ongoing support from others and for instruction in skills that children without disabilities usually acquire at a younger age, these students have little in common with each other.

Special educators sometimes use the term *low-incidence disabilities* to refer to disabilities that do not occur very often. Together, multiple disabilities, traumatic brain injury and deaf-blindness (the three IDEA disability categories described in this chapter) represent less than 3% of all children who receive special education.

Students with severe disabilities are a highly diverse population. Each student often has a combination of obvious and not-so-obvious disabilities. Because of differences in their intellectual, physical, and behavioral limitations, each student requires different additions or adaptations in their education. Without direct and systematic instruction, however, many individuals with severe and multiple disabilities are not able to perform the most basic, everyday tasks we take for granted, such as eating, toileting, and communicating our needs and feelings to others.

Having a severe disability does not preclude meaningful achievements. Despite the severity and multiplicity of their disabilities, these students can and do learn. An ever-growing body of evidence demonstrates that individuals with severe disabilities can learn and function effectively in integrated school, work, and community settings.

To better understand the topics that will be covered in this chapter, go to the Essential Concepts and Chapter at a Glance modules in Chapter 12 of the Companion Website, **www.prenhall.com/heward.**

# Severe and Multiple Disabilities

## Severe Disabilities

As used by most special educators, the term **severe disabilities** generally encompasses students with significant disabilities in intellectual, physical, and/or social functioning. Students with multiple disabilities and deaf-blindness—two of the three IDEA disability categories described in this chapter—as well as those with severe mental retardation, severe emotional disturbance, and severe disabilities or health impairments are included in the term.

There is no single, widely accepted definition of severe disabilities. Most definitions are based on tests of intellectual functioning, developmental progress, or the extent of educational need. According to the system of classifying levels of mental retardation previously used by the American Association on Mental Retardation, persons receiving IQ scores of 35 to 40 and below were considered to have severe mental retardation; scores of 20 to 25 and below resulted in a classification of profound mental retardation. In practice, however, the term *severe disabilities* often includes many individuals who score in the moderate level of mental retardation (IQ scores of 40 to 55) (Wolery & Haring, 1994).

Traditional methods of intelligence testing are virtually useless with children whose disabilities are profound. Imagine the difficulty, as well as the inappropriateness, of giving an IQ test to a student who cannot hold up his head or point, let alone talk. If tested, such students tend to be assigned IQ scores at the extreme lower end of the continuum. Knowing that a particular student has an IQ of 25, however, is of no value in designing an appropriate educational program. Educators of students with severe and profound disabilities tend to focus on the specific skills a child needs to learn rather than on intellectual level.

It was once common to take a developmental approach to the definition of severe disabilities. For example, Justen (1976) proposed that individuals with severe disabilities are "those individuals age 21 and younger who are functioning at a general developmental level of half or less than the level which would be expected on the basis of chronological age" (p. 5). Most educators now maintain that developmental levels have little relevance to this population and instead emphasize that a student with severe disabilities, regardless of age, is one who needs instruction in basic skills, such as getting from place to place independently, communicating with others, controlling bowel and bladder functions, and self-feeding. Most children without disabilities are able to acquire these basic skills in the first 5 years of life, but the student with severe disabilities needs special instruction to do so. The basic-skills definition makes it clear that special education for students with severe disabilities must not focus on traditional academic instruction.

Although severe disabilities is not recognized as a separate disability category in IDEA, the law's regulations governing programs and services for students who need "highly specialized" services and who experience "intense" problems states:

> The term "children with severe disabilities" refers to children with disabilities who, because of the intensity of their physical, mental, or emotional problems, need highly specialized education, social, psychological, and medical services in order to maximize their full potential for useful and meaningful participation in society and for self-fulfillment. The term includes those children with disabilities with severe emotional disturbance (including schizophrenia), autism, severe and profound mental retardation, and those who have two or more serious disabilities such as deaf-blindness, mental retardation and blindness, and cerebral palsy and

Special education for students with severe disabilities includes systematic instruction in basic skills.

deafness. Children with severe disabilities may experience severe speech, language, and/or perceptual-cognitive deprivations, and evidence abnormal behavior such as failure to respond to pronounced social stimuli, self-mutilation, self-stimulation; manifestation of intense and prolonged temper tantrums, and the absence of rudimentary forms of verbal control; and may also have extremely fragile physiological conditions. (34 C.F.R., Sec. 315.4[d])

The inclusion of extremely challenging behavioral problems in the federal definition, such as self-stimulation and self-injurious behavior, is not intended to imply that all children with severe disabilities exhibit such characteristics; most do not. Rather, their inclusion makes it clear that *all* children are entitled to a free public education in the least restrictive environment no matter how complicated or challenging their learning, behavioral, or medical problems may be—"even those students who, in the judgment of some people, seem to be 'ineducable'" (Turnbull & Cilley, 1999, p. 9).

The Association for Persons with Severe Handicaps (TASH) defines people with severe disabilities as

> individuals of all ages who require extensive ongoing support in more than one major life activity in order to participate in integrated community settings and to enjoy a quality of life that is available to citizens with fewer or no disabilities. Support may be required for life activities such as mobility, communication, self-care, and learning, as necessary for independent living, employment and self-sufficiency. (Lindley, 1990, p. 1)

Compared with other areas of special education (mental retardation, learning disabilities, and behavioral disorders, in particular), there has been much less concern and debate over the definition of severe disabilities. This does not indicate that professionals are uninterested in defining the population of students they serve but reflects two inherent features of severe disabilities. First, there is little need for a definition that precisely describes who is and is not to be identified by the term *severe disabilities*. Although the specific criteria a school district uses to define learning disabilities have a major impact on who will be eligible for special education services, whether or not special education is needed by any student who might be considered severely disabled is never an issue. Second, because of the tremendous diversity of learning and physical challenges experienced by such students, any single set of descriptors is inadequate. Statements that specify the particular educational goals and support needs of individual students are more meaningful.

## Profound Disabilities

Some professionals make a distinction between children with profound disabilities and those with severe disabilities. Sternberg (1994) believes that a distinction between severe and profound disabilities is necessary because the "expectations and implications for each are different. These differences are related not only to one's capability for independent functioning but also to the utility of specific educational or training models and methods" (p. 7). According to Sternberg, an individual with *profound disabilities* is one who

> exhibits profound developmental disabilities in all five of the following behavioral-content areas: cognition, communication, social skills development, motor-mobility, and activities of daily living (self-help skills); and requires a service structure with continuous monitoring and observation.... This definition also posits a ceiling of 2 years of age for each area of functioning (6 years of age for those classified as severely disabled). If the individual functions above that level, the individual cannot be classified as profoundly disabled. (p. 6)

Thus, an individual with profound disabilities, according to Sternberg, functions at a level no higher than that of a typically developing 2-year-old in all five areas (whereas the functioning of a student with severe disabilities in one or more of these areas may be less delayed, up to the level of a typical 6-year-old). (Some educators question whether children with profound disabilities can benefit from education. See Profiles & Perspectives, "Are All Children Educable?," later in this chapter.)

*Definitions of profound disabilities, multiple disabilities, and deaf-blindness*

Council for Exceptional Children — Content Standards for Beginning Teachers—INDEP CURR: Definitions and issues related to the identification of individuals with disabilities (IC1K1) (also CC1K5).

# Are All Children Educable?

Some educators, other professionals, and citizens question the wisdom of spending large amounts of money, time, and human resources attempting to educate children who have such serious and profound disabilities that they may never be able to function independently. Some would prefer to see resources spent on children with higher apparent potential—especially when economic conditions limit the quality of educational services for all children in the public schools. "Why bother with children who fail to make meaningful progress?" they ask.

> Accelerating a response rate may indeed be a worthy first goal in an educational program if there is reasonable hope of shaping the response into a meaningful skill. Nevertheless, after concerted and appropriate effort by highly trained behavior therapists, for a reasonable period of time, a child's failure to make significant progress toward acquisition of a meaningful skill could reasonably be taken as an indication that the child is ineducable.... Granted, all children probably are educable if education is defined as acceleration of any operant response. But such a definition trivializes the meaning of the term education and, even without consideration of benefit, moots the question of educability.... We suggest that public response to the questions "What is education?" "What skills are meaningful?" "What rate of progress is significant?" and "What cost/benefit ratios are acceptable?" sampled with sufficient care, could be invaluable in deciding who is educable and who is not. (Kauffman & Krouse, 1981, pp. 55–56)

A parent of a daughter with severe disabilities disagrees:

> If anyone were to be the judge of whether a particular behavior change is "meaningful," it should certainly not be only the general taxpayer, who has no idea how rewarding it is to see your 19-year-old acquire the skill of toilet flushing on command or pointing to food when she wants a second helping. I suspect that the average taxpayer would not

consider it "meaningful" to him or her for Karrie to acquire such skills. But in truth, it is "meaningful" to that taxpayer whether he recognizes it or not, in the sense that it is saving him or her the cost of Karrie's being institutionalized, which she certainly would have been by now if she never showed any progress.

> The complexity, cost, and hopelessness of evaluating fairly the "meaningfulness" of various types and degrees of learning leads me to conclude that no one should be denied an education.... I would be very resistant to the idea that we should now, at this infant stage of the science and technology of education for severely retarded students, give up intensive skill training for anyone. (R. P. Hawkins, 1984, p. 285)

In many ways, our knowledge of the learning and developmental processes of individuals with severe and profound disabilities is still primitive and incomplete. We do know, however, that children with severe disabilities are capable of benefiting significantly from appropriate and carefully implemented educational programs. Even in cases in which little or no progress has been observed, it would be wrong to conclude that the student is incapable of learning. It may instead be that our teaching methods are imperfect and that the future will bring improved methods and materials to enable that student to learn useful skills. All children, no matter how severe their disabilities, have the right to the best possible public education and training society can offer them.

There are still many unanswered questions about the education of children whose disabilities are complex and pervasive. Even though their opportunities for education and training are expanding rapidly, nobody really knows their true learning potential. What we do know is that students with the most severe disabilities will go no farther than we let them; it is up to us to open doors and to raise our sights, not to create additional barriers.

The late Don Baer, a pioneer in the development of effective teaching methods for persons with severe disabilities, offered this perspective on educability:

Some of us have ignored both the thesis that all persons are educable and the thesis that some persons are ineducable, and instead have experimented with ways to teach some previously unteachable people. Over a few centuries, those experiments have steadily reduced the size of the apparently ineducable group relative to the obviously educable group. Clearly, we have not finished that adventure. Why predict its outcome, when we could simply pursue it, and just as well without a prediction? Why not pursue it to see if there comes a day when there is such a small class of apparently ineducable persons left that it consists of one elderly person who is put forward as ineducable. If that day comes, it will be a very nice day. And the next day will be even better. (D. M. Baer, February 15, 2002, personal communication)

 To further your understanding of and answer reflective questions about the concepts and issues presented here, go to the Profiles & Perspectives module in Chapter 12 of the Companion Website, **www.prenhall.com/heward.**

## Multiple Disabilities

IDEA defines **multiple disabilities** as

> concomitant impairments (such as mental retardation–blindness, mental retardation–orthopedic impairment, etc.), the combination of which causes such severe educational problems that they cannot be accommodated in special education programs solely for one of the impairments. The term does not include deaf-blindness. (34 C.F.R., Sec. 300[b][6])

## DEAF-BLINDNESS

IDEA defines **deaf-blindness** as a combination of both auditory and visual disabilities that causes

> such severe communication and other developmental and learning needs that the persons cannot be appropriately educated in special education programs solely for children and youth with hearing impairments, visual impairments, or severe disabilities, without supplementary assistance to address their educational needs due to these dual, concurrent disabilities. (IDEA, 1990, Sec. 1422)

"There is perhaps no condition as disabling as deaf-blindness, the loss of part or all of one's vision and hearing" (Bullis & Otos, 1988, p. 110). The majority of children who have both visual and hearing impairments at birth experience major difficulties in acquiring communication skills, motor and mobility skills, and appropriate social behavior.

> Because these individuals do not receive clear and consistent information from either sensory modality, a tendency exists to turn inward to obtain the desired level of stimulation. The individual therefore may appear passive, nonresponsive, and/or noncompliant. Students with dual sensory impairments may not respond to or initiate appropriate interactions with others and often exhibit behavior that is considered socially inappropriate (e.g., hand flapping, finger flicking, head rocking). (Downing & Eichinger, 1990, pp. 98–99)

Pease (2000) describes how a deaf-blind child's unresponsiveness can lead parents and caregivers to unwittingly contribute to his communication difficulties.

> Parents are likely to find their deafblind baby's "signals" difficult to read and may become discouraged, especially if the child seems to reject them or show little interest. Parents and carers may find it easier to do things for the children without waiting for his responses so that activities which for the typical child are full of fun and communication become a quiet routine for the deafblind infant. With little encouragement to interact or to exert control with activities, the child may become a passive recipient of care as "learned helplessness" develops. (p. 39)

Although 94% of individuals who are deaf-blind have some functional hearing and/or vision (Baldwin, 1995), the combined effects of the dual impairments severely impede the

✎ *Helpful Hint*

A wealth of information about deaf-blindness can be found at the National Information Clearinghouse on Children Who Are Deaf-Blind, the only federally funded clearinghouse dedicated to a specific disability (**www.tr.wou.edu/dblink**; phone: (800) 438–9376).

development of communication and social skills. An educational program for children who are deaf is often inappropriate for a child who also has limited vision because many methods of instruction and communication rely heavily on the use of sight. On the other hand, programs for visually impaired students usually require good hearing because much instruction is auditory.

Therefore, educational programs for students with dual sensory impairments who require instruction in basic skills are generally similar to those for other students with severe disabilities. Although most students with dual sensory impairments can make use of information presented in visual and auditory modalities, when used in instruction, these stimuli must be enhanced and the students' attention directed toward them. Tactile teaching techniques involving the sense of touch are used to supplement the information obtained through visual and auditory modes (Downing & Chen, 2003; Engelman, Griffin, Griffin, & Maddox, 1999).

A man who is deaf-blind vividly describes the importance of supplementing information about the world with other sensory modes:

> The senses of sight and hearing are unquestionably the two primary avenues by which information and knowledge are absorbed by an individual, providing a direct access to the world in which he lives.... When these senses are lost or severely limited, the individual is drastically limited to a very small area of concepts, most of which must come to him through his secondary senses or through indirect information supplied by others. The world literally shrinks; it is only as large as he can reach with his fingertips or by using his severely limited sight and hearing, and it is only when he learns to use his remaining secondary senses of touch, taste, smell, and kinesthetic awareness that he can broaden his field of information and gain additional knowledge. (Smithdas, 1981, p. 38)

Teaching techniques involving the sense of touch are used to provide and supplement instructional stimuli for students with dual sensory impairments.

*Impact of deaf-blindness*

Council for Exceptional Children
Content Standards for Beginning Teachers—INDEP CURR: Impact of sensory impairments, physical and health disabilities on individuals, families, and society (IC2K2) (also CC2K2, CC2K6).

## CHARACTERISTICS OF STUDENTS WITH SEVERE AND MULTIPLE DISABILITIES

Throughout this book, we have seen how definitions and lists of characteristics used to describe a disability category have limited meaning at the level of the individual student. And, of course, it is at the level of the individual student where decisions about what and how to teach should be made. As various physical, behavioral, and learning characteristics associated with severe disabilities are described, keep in mind that students with severe disabilities constitute the most heterogeneous group of all exceptional children. As Westling and Fox (2004) point out, the differences among students with severe disabilities are greater than their similarities.

Most students with severe disabilities exhibit extreme deficits in intellectual functioning. Many need special services and supports because of motor impediments; communication, visual, and auditory impairments; and medical conditions such as seizure disorders. Many have medical and physical problems that require frequent attention (Rues, Ault, Graff, & Holvoet, 2006). Many students with severe disabilities have more than one disability. Even with the best available methods of diagnosis and assessment, it is often difficult to identify the nature and intensity of a child's multiple disabilities or to determine how combinations of disabilities affect a child's behavior. Some children, for example, do not respond in any observable way to visual stimuli, such as bright lights or moving objects. Is this because the child is blind as a result of eye damage, or is the child unresponsive because of profound mental retardation due to brain damage? Such questions arise frequently in planning educational programs for students with severe disabilities.

*Characteristics of severe disabilities*

Council for Exceptional Children
Content Standards for Beginning Teachers—INDEP CURR: Psychological and social-emotional characteristics of individuals with disabilities (IC2K4) (also CC2K2).

The one defining characteristic of students with severe disabilities is that they exhibit significant and obvious deficits in multiple life-skill or developmental areas. No specific set of behaviors is common to all individuals with severe disabilities. Although each student presents a unique combination of physical, intellectual, and social characteristics, the following behaviors and skill deficits are frequently observed in students with severe disabilities (Brown et al., 1991; Kim & Arnold, 2006; Westling & Fox, 2004; Wolery & Haring, 1994):

- *Slow acquisition rates for learning new skills.* Compared to other students with disabilities, students with severe disabilities learn at a slower rate, require more instructional trials to learn a given skill, learn fewer skills in total, and have difficulty learning abstract skills or relationships.

- *Poor generalization and maintenance of newly learned skills.* Generalization refers to the performance of skills under conditions different from those in which they initially were learned. Maintenance refers to the continued use of a new skill after instruction is terminated. For many students with severe disabilities, generalization and maintenance seldom occur without instruction that is meticulously planned to facilitate it.

- *Limited communication skills.* Almost all students with severe and multiple disabilities are limited in their abilities to express themselves and to understand others. Some cannot talk or gesture meaningfully and might not respond when communication is attempted; some are not able to follow even the simplest requests.

- *Impaired physical and motor development.* Many children with severe disabilities have limited physical mobility. Many cannot walk; some cannot stand or sit up without support. They are slow to perform such basic tasks as rolling over, grasping objects, and holding up their heads. Physical impairments are common and may worsen without consistent physical therapy.

- *Deficits in self-help skills.* Some children with severe disabilities are unable to independently care for their most basic needs, such as dressing, eating, exercising bowel and bladder control, and maintaining personal hygiene. They usually require special training involving prosthetic devices and/or adapted skill sequences to learn these basic skills.

- *Infrequent constructive behavior and interaction.* Nondisabled children and those whose disabilities are less severe typically play with other children, interact with adults, and seek out information about their surroundings. Some children with severe disabilities do not. They may appear to be completely out of touch with reality and may not show normal human emotions. It may be difficult to capture the attention of or evoke any observable response from a child with profound disabilities.

- *Stereotypic and challenging behavior.* Some children with severe disabilities engage in behaviors that are ritualistic (e.g., rocking back and forth, waving fingers in front of the face, twirling the body), self-stimulatory (e.g., grinding the teeth, patting the body), self-injurious (e.g., head banging, hair pulling, eye poking, hitting or scratching or biting oneself), and/or aggressive (e.g., hitting or biting others). The high frequency with which some children emit these challenging behaviors is a serious concern because they interfere with learning more adaptive behaviors and with acceptance and functioning in integrated settings.

Joey's enthusiasm and determination are evident each time his teacher uses music in a lesson.

Descriptions of behavioral characteristics, such as those just mentioned, can easily give an overly negative impression. Despite the intense challenges their disabilities impose on them, many students with severe disabilities also exhibit warmth, persistence, determination, a sense of humor, sociability, and various other desirable traits (Forest & Lusthaus, 1990; Stainback & Stainback, 1991). Many teachers find great satisfaction in working with students who have severe disabilities and in observing their progress in school, home, and community settings.

# PREVALENCE OF SEVERE AND MULTIPLE DISABILITIES

Because there is no universally accepted definition of severe disabilities, there are no accurate and uniform figures on prevalence. Estimates of the prevalence of severe disabilities range from 0.1% to 1% of the population (Kim & Arnold, 2006). Brown (1990) considers students with severe disabilities to be those who function intellectually in the lowest functioning 1% of the school-age population.

Because severe disabilities is not one of the disability categories under which the states make their annual report to the federal government, the number of students with severe disabilities who receive special education services under IDEA cannot be determined from data supplied by the U.S. Department of Education. Students who have severe disabilities are served and reported under other disability categories, including mental retardation, multiple disabilities, other health impairments, autism, traumatic brain injury, and deaf-blindness.

In the 2003–2004 school year, 131,225 school-age students received special education and related services under the IDEA disability category of multiple disabilities. Deaf-blindness is a very low incidence disability. Before the passage of IDEA in 1975, fewer than 100 children with dual sensory impairments were receiving specialized education services, virtually all of which were located at residential schools for children who are blind. In the 2003–2004 school year, 1,603 school-age students with deaf-blindness were served (U.S. Department of Education, 2004).

# CAUSES OF SEVERE AND MULTIPLE DISABILITIES

*Causes of severe disabilities*

Council for Exceptional Children

Content Standards for Beginning Teachers—INDEP CURR: Etiologies and medical aspects of conditions affecting individuals with disabilities (IC2K3).

Severe intellectual disabilities can be caused by a wide variety of conditions, largely biological, that may occur before (prenatal), during (perinatal), or after birth (postnatal). In almost every case, a brain disorder is involved. Brain disorders are the result of either *brain dysgenesis* (abnormal brain development) or *brain damage* (caused by influences that alter the structure or function of a brain that had been developing normally up to that point). From a review of 10 epidemiological studies, Coulter (1994) estimated that prenatal brain dysgenesis accounts for most cases of severe cognitive limitations and that perinatal and postnatal brain damage account for a minority of cases. Coulter states that a brain disorder is "the only condition that will account for the existence of profound disabilities" (p. 41).

A significant percentage of children with severe disabilities are born with chromosomal abnormalities, such as Down syndrome, or with genetic or metabolic disorders that can cause serious problems in physical or intellectual development. Complications of pregnancy—including prematurity, Rh incompatibility, and infectious diseases contracted by the mother—can cause or contribute to severe disabilities. A pregnant woman who uses drugs, drinks alcohol excessively, or is poorly nourished has a greater risk of giving birth to a child with severe disabilities. Because their disabilities tend to be more extreme and more readily observable, children with severe disabilities are more frequently identified at or shortly after birth than are children with mild disabilities.

Severe disabilities also may develop later in life from head trauma caused by automobile and bicycle accidents, falls, assaults, or abuse. Malnutrition, neglect, ingestion of poisonous substances, and certain diseases that affect the brain (e.g., meningitis, encephalitis) also can cause severe disabilities. Although hundreds of medically related causes of severe disabilities have been identified, in about one-sixth of all cases, the cause cannot be clearly determined (Coulter, 1994).

# TRAUMATIC BRAIN INJURY

## Definition

When it was originally passed, IDEA did not specifically mention the needs of children who have experienced head trauma and/or coma. However, when the law was amended in 1990 (P.L. 101–476), traumatic brain injury was added as a new disability category under which children could be eligible for special education services. IDEA defines **traumatic brain injury** as

*Definition of TBI*

 Council for Exceptional Children Content Standards for Beginning Teachers—P&HD: Issues and educational definitions of individuals with P&HD (PH1K1).

> an acquired injury to the brain caused by an external physical force, resulting in total or partial functional disability or psychosocial impairments, or both, that adversely affects a child's educational performance. The term applies to open or closed head injuries resulting in impairments in one or more areas, such as cognition; language; memory; attention; reasoning; abstract thinking; judgment; problem-solving; sensory, perceptual, and motor abilities; psychosocial behavior; physical functions; information processing; and speech. The term does not apply to brain injuries that are congenital or generative, or brain injuries induced by birth trauma. (34 C.F.R., Sec. 300.7[6][12])

As with the IDEA definitions of other disabilities, the key phrase in the definition of traumatic brain injury is *that adversely affects a child's educational performance*. It is also important to note that traumatic brain injury is an *acquired* condition. Although the effects of some types of traumatic brain injury on learning and behavior are similar to the effects of other disabilities, children whose learning or behavioral problems are caused by disease or congenital malformation to the brain (e.g., cerebral palsy, some causes of mental retardation) are not considered to have traumatic brain injury.

## Prevalence of Traumatic Brain Injury

Injuries to the head are common in children and adolescents. Head injuries occur in the pediatric population (1 month to 15 years) at a rate of about 1 million per year (Heller, Alberto, Forney, & Schwartzman, 1996). It is estimated that each year 1 in 500 school-age children will be hospitalized with traumatic head injuries, 1 in 30 children will sustain a significant head injury by the age of 15, and 1 in 10,000 children will die as the result of head trauma (Hill, 1999; Whaley & Wong, 1995). Traumatic brain injury is the leading cause of death in children, accounting for approximately one-third of all accidental deaths in children (Centers for Disease Control, 2001b), and it is the most common acquired disability in childhood (Brain Injury Association, 2001).

In spite of the sobering statistics on head injuries, the number of children receiving special education under the category of traumatic brain injury is very small. In 1991–1992, the first school year after traumatic brain injury was added to IDEA as a separate disability category, only 330 school-age students were served nationally. By 2003–2004 school year, the number had increased to 22,459 (U.S. Department of Education, 2004).

While it is likely that greater numbers of children with traumatic brain injury will be identified and served in the future as educators increase their understanding and recognition of head injuries, the gap between incidence and the number of children served is huge. What accounts for this significant difference? First, recovery is good following most brain injuries. The skull is very good at protecting the brain, and the human brain has a remarkable capacity to naturally compensate for injury. Second, the vast majority of head injuries sustained by children are mild and do not result in obvious adverse effects on educational performance. Third, many students with mild brain injuries are identified and served under another disability category, most likely learning disabilities or emotional or behavioral disorders. Fourth, students with severe head injuries are often served under other disability categories.

*Types and causes of TBI*

 **Council for Exceptional Children** Content Standards for Beginning Teachers—P&HD: Etiology and characteristics of P&HD across the life span (PH2K2) (also PH2K1).

See "Abuse and Neglect of Children with Disabilities" in the Chapter 12 Profiles & Perspectives module on the Companion Website, **www.prenhall.com/heward.**

# Types and Causes of Traumatic Brain Injury

Head injuries are classified by the type of injury (open or closed), by the kind of the damage sustained by the brain, and by the location of the injury. An **open head injury** is the result of penetration of the skull, such as that caused by a bullet or a forceful blow to the head with a hard or sharp object. Open head injuries that are not fatal often result in specific deficits or problems with particular behavioral or sensory functions controlled by the part of the brain where the injury occurred (see Figure 12.1).

The most common type of head injury does not involve penetration of the skull. A **closed head injury** occurs when the head hits a stationary object with such force that the brain slams against the inside of the cranium. The stress of this rapid movement and impact pulls apart and tears nerve fibers or axons, breaking connections between different parts of the brain. Car and bicycle accidents are the primary causes of closed head injuries. *Shaken baby syndrome* is another unfortunate but common cause of traumatic brain injury in children. The rough handling and violent shaking of the baby cause rapid acceleration and deceleration of the head, which in turn causes the brain to be whipped back and forth, bouncing off the inside of the skull.

The effects of traumatic brain injury on learning and behavior are determined by the severity of the injury and the part of the brain that sustained damage. A mild brain injury

**FIGURE 12.1 Parts of the brain and some of their functions**

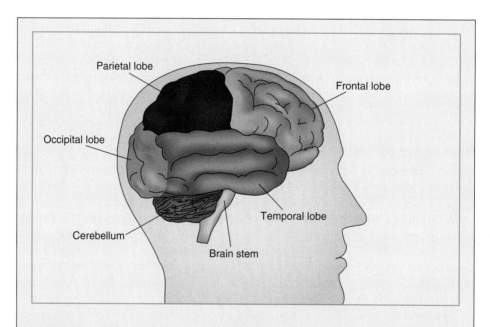

**Frontal lobe**

- Emotions
- Expressive language
- Word associations
- Memory for habits and motor activities
- Problem solving
- Reasoning

**Parietal lobe**

- Integration of different senses
- Location for visual attention
- Location for touch perception
- Manipulation of objects

**Occipital lobe**

- Vision

**Cerebellum**

- Balance and equilibrium
- Some memory for reflex motor acts

**Brain stem**

- Regulates body functions (e.g., breathing, heart rate, swallowing)
- Reflexes to seeing and hearing (e.g., startle response)
- Controls autonomic nervous system (e.g., sweating, blood pressure, digestion, internal temperature)
- Affects level of alertness

**Temporal lobe**

- Hearing
- Speech
- Memory acquisition
- Categorization of objects

results in a *concussion*, a brief or momentary loss of consciousness (from seconds or minutes, up to 30 minutes) without any subsequent complications or damage. Even a mild concussion, however, is often followed by post-concussion syndrome, which can include temporary headaches, dizziness spells, and fatigue.

*Contusions* (bruising, swelling, and bleeding) usually accompany a moderate brain injury. Blood vessels in the brain may also rupture, causing a *hematoma* (aggregation or clotting of blood) that may grow and put pressure on vital brain structures. A moderate brain injury usually results in a loss of consciousness lasting more than 30 minutes up to 24 hours followed by a few days or weeks of confusion. Individuals who sustain a moderate brain injury will experience significant cognitive and behavioral impairments for many months. Most, however, will make a complete or nearly complete recovery.

Severe head trauma almost always results in a *coma*, a state of prolonged unconsciousness lasting days, weeks, or even longer. Persons in coma cannot be awakened and make no meaningful response to external stimulation. In addition to brain contusions and hematomas or damage to the nerve fibers or axons, a person with severe brain injury may have suffered from **anoxia** (loss of oxygen to the brain for a period of time). Although many individuals with severe brain injuries make significant improvements during the first year after their injury and continue to improve at a more gradual pace for many years, most will have permanent physical, behavioral, and/or cognitive impairments.

## Characteristics of Traumatic Brain Injury

Though not always visible and sometimes seemingly minor or inconsequential, traumatic brain injury is complex. The symptoms vary widely depending on the severity of the injury, its extent and site, the age of the child at the time of the injury, and time passed since the injury (von Hahn, 2004). Impairments caused by brain injuries may be temporary or lasting and fall into three main categories: (1) physical and sensory changes (e.g., lack of coordination, spasticity of muscles); (2) cognitive impairments (e.g., short- and long-term memory deficits, difficulty maintaining attention and concentration); and (3) social, behavioral, and emotional problems (e.g., mood swings [emotional lability], self-centeredness, lack of motivation). Figure 12.2 provides additional examples of characteristics that may be signs of traumatic brain injury.

The educational and lifelong needs of students with head injuries are likely to require comprehensive programs of academic, psychological, and family support (Savage & Wolcott, 1994). Recovery from a brain injury is often inconsistent. A student might make excellent progress, then regress to an earlier stage, and then make a rapid series of gains. Individuals with brain injuries sometimes reach plateaus in their recovery during which no improvements occur for some time. A plateau does not signal the end to functional improvement.

Students who have been hospitalized with head injuries reenter school with deficits from their injuries compounded by an extended absence from school. Ylvisaker (1986) recommends that the child return to school when she is physically capable, can respond to instructions, and can sustain attention for 10 to 15 minutes. School programs can assist reentry of the student with traumatic brain injury in several ways (Tyler & Mira, 1993; von Hahn, 2004):

- A shortened school day, concentrating academic instruction during peak performance periods; frequent breaks; and a reduced class load may be necessitated by the chronic fatigue that some students with head injury experience for a year or more.
- Rehearse social situations in advance and provide explicit instructions and prompts about social interactions such as maintaining socially accepted body space and tone of voice.
- Provide clear, uncomplicated instructions; break multistep instructions into simplified steps.
- Pair auditory instructions with visual cues.

*Signs and effects of TBI*

Council for Exceptional Children — Content Standards for Beginning Teachers—Common Core: Educational implications of various exceptionalities (CC2K2) (also PH3K1).

*Accommodations for students with TBI*

Council for Exceptional Children — Content Standards for Beginning Teachers—P&HD: Adaptations of educational environments necessary to accommodate individuals with P&HD (PH5K1) (also CC5K1).

## FIGURE 12.2 Possible signs and effects of traumatic brain injury

### Physical and sensory changes

- Chronic headaches, dizziness, light-headedness, nausea
- Vision impairments (e.g., double vision, visual field defects, blurring, sensitivity to light)
- Hearing impairment (e.g., increased sensitivity to sound)
- Alterations in sense of taste, touch, and smell
- Sleep problems (e.g., insomnia, day/night confusion)
- Stress-related disorders (e.g., depression)
- Poor body temperature regulation
- Recurrent seizure activity
- Poor coordination and balance
- Reduced speed of motor performance and precision of movement

### Cognitive changes and academic problems

- Difficulty keeping up with discussions, instructional presentations, note taking
- Difficulty concentrating or attending to task at hand (e.g., distractible, confused)
- Difficulty making transitions (e.g., home to school, class to class, switching from fractions to decimal problems on same math worksheet)
- Inability to organize work and environment (e.g., difficulty keeping track of books, assignments, lunch box)
- Problems in planning, organizing, pacing tasks and activities
- Extremely sensitive to distraction (e.g., unable to take a test in a room with other students)
- Tendency to perseverate; inflexible in thinking
- Impairments in receptive oral language (e.g., difficulty following directions; misunderstanding what is said by others)
- Inability to perceive voice inflections or nonverbal cues
- Impairments in reading comprehension
- Impairments in expressive oral or written language (e.g., aphasia, difficulty retrieving words, poor articulation, slow speech, difficulty in spelling or punctuation)

### Social, emotional, and behavioral problems

- Chronically agitated, irritable, restless, or anxious
- Increased aggressiveness
- Impaired ability to self-manage; lowered impulse control; poor anger control
- Difficulty dealing with change (i.e., rigid); poor coping strategies
- May overestimate own ability (often evidenced as "bragging")
- Decreased insight into self and others; reduced judgment
- Decreased frustration tolerance; frequent temper outbursts and overreactions to events
- May talk compulsively and excessively
- Inability to take cues from the environment (often leading to socially inappropriate behavior)

*Source*: Adapted from Hill, J. L. (1999). *Meeting the needs of children with special physical and health care needs* (pp. 259–260). Upper Saddle River, NJ: Merrill/Prentice Hall. © 1999 by Merrill/Prentice Hall. Used by permission.

- A special resource period at the beginning and end of each school day when a teacher, counselor, or aide helps the student plan or review the day's schedule, keep track of assignments, and monitor progress may be required because of problems with loss of memory and organization.
- Modifications such as an extra set of textbooks at home, a peer to help the student move efficiently from class to class, and early dismissal from class to allow time to get

to the next room can help the student who has difficulties with mobility, balance, or coordination. (Adaptive physical education is often indicated.)

- Behavior management and/or counseling interventions may be needed to help with problems such as poor judgment, impulsiveness, overactivity, aggression, destructiveness, and socially uninhibited behavior often experienced by students with head injury.
- Modifications of instruction and testing procedures such as tape-recording lectures, assigning a note taker, and allowing extra time to take tests may be needed.
- IEP goals and objectives may need to be reviewed and modified as often as every 30 days because of the dramatic changes in behavior and performance by some children during the early stages of recovery.

# EDUCATIONAL APPROACHES

How does one go about teaching students with severe and multiple disabilities? To begin to answer this question, three fundamental and interrelated questions must be considered:

1. What skills should be taught?
2. What methods of instruction should be employed?
3. Where should instruction take place?

Of course, each of these questions must be asked for all students; but when a student is challenged by severe disabilities, the answers take on enormous importance. During the past 20 years, major changes and advancements in the education of students with severe disabilities have led to new answers.

## Curriculum: What Should Be Taught?

Not long ago, a student's "mental age" as determined by norm-referenced tests of development played a significant role in the selection of curriculum content and teaching activities. This practice led to an emphasis on activities thought to be essential prerequisites for higher-level skills because typically developing children of a given age did such skills. As a result, students with severe disabilities spent many hundreds of hours working on artificially contrived activities that had no immediate value and, because they were not age-appropriate (e.g., teenage students sorting blocks by color or clapping their hands to the rhythm of a song for preschoolers), may have contributed to the perception that students with severe disabilities are eternal children (Bellamy & Wilcox, 1982).

Today, most educators recognize that students with severe disabilities do not acquire skills in the same sequence that nondisabled students do and that developmental "ages" should not serve as the basis for determining curriculum activities. For example, a 16-year-old student who is learning to feed and toilet herself should not be taught in the same way or with the same materials as a nondisabled 2-year-old who is learning to feed and toilet herself. Even though both individuals need to learn the same skill, their past experiences, present environments, and future prospects are significantly different and demand different instructional activities and materials.

Contemporary curriculum content for students with severe disabilities is characterized by its focus on functional skills that can be used in immediate and future domestic, vocational, community, and recreational/leisure environments. Educational programs are future-oriented in their efforts to teach skills that will enable students with severe disabilities to participate in integrated settings as meaningfully and independently as possible after they leave school.

*Functional and age-appropriate skills*

Council for Exceptional Children   Content Standards for Beginning Teachers—Common Core: Theories and research that form the basis of curriculum developments and instructional practice (CC7K1) (also CC4S4, CC7K2, IC5S2, IC5S12).

*Functionality.*   Functional skills are immediately useful to a student, frequently required in school and nonschool environments, result in less dependence on others, and allow the student to participate in less restrictive environments (Slaton, Schuster, Collins, & Carnine,

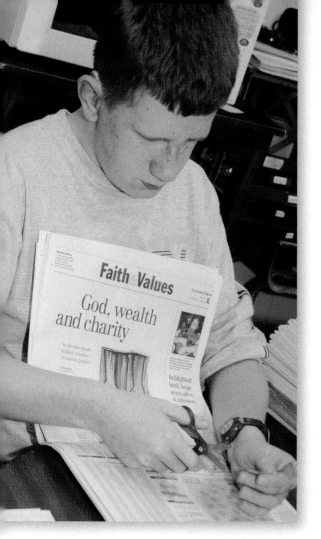

1994). Placing pegs into a pegboard or sorting wooden blocks by color do not meet any of these criteria. Examples of functional skills for many students with severe disabilities include activities such as learning to dress oneself, prepare a snack, ride a public bus, purchase items from coin-operated vending machines, and recognize common sight words in community settings. Whenever possible, functional instructional activities should employ authentic materials (Westling & Fox, 2004). For example, students learning to use money to make purchases should practice with real bills and coins instead of simulated money. (See Profiles & Perspectives, "My Brother Darryl," later in this chapter.)

*Age-Appropriateness.* Students with severe disabilities should participate in activities that are appropriate for same-age peers without disabilities. Adolescents with severe disabilities should not use the same materials as young, nondisabled children; in fact, having teenagers sit on the floor and play clap-your-hands games or cutting and pasting cardboard snowmen highlights their differences and discourages integration. It is more appropriate to teach recreation and leisure skills, such as bowling and CD player operation, or to engage the students in holiday projects, such as printing greeting cards. Teachers of secondary students with severe disabilities should avoid decorating classroom walls with child-oriented cartoon characters and should not refer to their students as "boys," "girls," or "kids" when "young men," "young women," or "students" are more age-appropriate.

It is critically important to build an IEP for a student with severe disabilities around functional and age-appropriate skills. Because nonschool settings demand such skills and nondisabled peers exhibit them, functional and age-appropriate behaviors are more likely to be reinforced in the natural environment and, as a result, maintained in the student's repertoire.

Functional instructional activities employ authentic materials with meaningful outcomes. Each school day, Kevin sorts, labels, and delivers the newspaper to "customers" in his school.

*Making Choices.* Imagine going through an entire day without being able to make a choice, any choice at all. Someone else—a teacher, a staff person, a parent—will decide what you will wear, what you will do next, what you will eat for lunch, whom you will sit next to, and so on throughout the day, every day. In the past, students with severe disabilities had few opportunities to express preferences and make choices; the emphasis was on establishing instructional control over students. Traditionally, persons with severe disabilities were simply cared for and taught to be compliant.

> Some caregivers might feel that to complete tasks for persons with disabilities is easier and faster than allowing them to do it for themselves; while others may have the attitude that the person already has enough problems coping with his or her disability. Regardless of the underlying intention, the result can be to overprotect, to encourage learned helplessness, and to deprive the individual of potentially valuable life experiences. (Guess, Benson, & Siegel-Causey, 1985, p. 83)

Special educators are recognizing the importance of choice as a way of making activities meaningful and as an indicator of quality of life for students with severe disabilities. Increasing efforts are being made to help these students express their preferences and make decisions about matters that will affect them. For example, a child might be presented with pictures of two activities and asked to point to the one she would rather engage in. Another might be asked, "Whom would you like for your partner?" Or the teacher might say, "Should we do this again?" Of course, in presenting such choices, the teacher must be prepared to accept whichever alternative the student selects and to follow through

*Teaching choice making*

Council for Exceptional Children Content Standards for Beginning Teachers—INDEP CURR: Teach individuals to give and receive meaningful feedback from peers and adults (IC5S5) (also IC4K3, CC4S5).

# My Brother Darryl: A Case for Teaching Functional Skills

*by Preston Lewis*

Eighteen years old, moderately/severely handicapped. Been in school for 12 years. Never been served in any setting other than an elementary school. He has had a number of years of "individualized instruction." Darryl can now do lots of things he couldn't do before.

He can put 100 pegs in a board in less than 10 minutes with 95% accuracy, but he can't put quarters into a vending machine.

Upon command he can touch his nose, shoulder, leg, hair, ear. He is still working on wrist, ankle, hips, but he can't blow his nose when needed.

He can do a 12-piece Big Bird puzzle with 100% accuracy and color an Easter bunny and stay in the lines. He prefers music, but has never been taught to use a radio or record player.

He can now fold primary paper in half and even quarters, but he can't sort clothes, white from colors, for washing.

He can roll Play-Doh and make wonderful clay snakes, but he can't roll bread dough and cut out biscuits.

He can string beads in alternating colors and match it to a pattern on a DLM card, but he can't lace his shoes.

He can sing his ABCs and tell me the names of all the letters in the alphabet with 80% accuracy when they are presented on a card in upper case, but he can't tell "Men's" room from "Ladies'" when we go to McDonald's.

He can be told it's cloudy/rainy and take a black felt cloud and put it on the day of the week on an enlarged calendar (with assistance), but he still goes out in the rain without a raincoat or hat.

He can identify with 100% accuracy 100 different Peabody Picture Cards by pointing, but he can't order a hamburger by pointing to a picture or gesturing.

He can walk on a balance beam forward, sideways, and backward, but he can't walk up the steps of the bleachers unassisted in the gym or go to basketball games.

He can count to 100 by rote memory, but he doesn't know how many dollars to pay the waitress for a $2.59 McDonald coupon special.

He can put a cube in the box, under the box, beside the box, and behind the box, but he can't find the trash bin in McDonald's and empty his trash into it.

He can sit in a circle with appropriate behavior and sing songs and play "Duck Duck Goose," but nobody else in his neighborhood his age seems to want to do that.

I guess he's just not ready yet.

---

Preston Lewis is a curriculum specialist in the Kentucky Department of Education.

To further your understanding of and answer reflective questions about the concepts and issues presented here, go to the Profiles & Perspectives module in Chapter 12 of the Companion Website, **www.prenhall.com/heward.**

Since she has learned to make choices and express her preferences, Kimberly's quality of life has improved greatly.

accordingly. Bambara and Koger (1996) describe procedures for providing increased opportunities for choice making throughout the day.

Several studies have found that nonverbal students with severe disabilities can learn to use picture activity schedules to indicate their preferences for learning and leisure-time activities (e.g., Bryan & Gast, 2000; Morrison, Sainato, BenChaaban, & Endo, 2002). Mithaug (2002) describes procedures for teaching students with multiple disabilities to choose and self-regulate their schedules and academic activities in the classroom. Other researchers have discovered ways to help individuals with severe disabilities express preferences for where they will live (Faw, Davis, & Peck, 1996), what foods they will purchase and eat (Cooper & Browder, 1998; Parsons, McCarn, & Reid, 1993), leisure activities (Browder, Cooper, & Lim, 1998), and whether or not they want to participate in daily routines and activities (Bambara & Ager, 1992; Bannerman, Sheldon, Sherman, & Harchik, 1990).

*Communication Skills.*    Effective communication is essential to our quality of life, enabling us to express our desires and choices, obtain and give information, and, most important, form and maintain relationships with others. Concern that communication services and supports may be withheld or removed from persons with severe disabilities led to the formation of the National Joint Committee for the Communicative Needs of Persons with Severe Disabilities, which consists of representatives from professional organizations serving individuals with disabilities such as the American Association on Mental Retardation (AAMR), the American Speech and Hearing Association (ASHA), the Council for Exceptional Children (CEC), and The Association for Persons with Severe Handicaps (TASH) (Snell, 2004). This group created a communication bill of rights for persons with severe disabilities (see Figure 12.3).

Early research and training in communication for persons with severe disabilities focused on remediation of specific forms of communication, such as the production of speech sounds, words, and descriptive phrases (Kaiser & Goetz, 1993). However, the focus of and methods used to teach communication skills to these students have undergone significant changes during the past 20 years. Two changes in perspective regarding the nature of communication are shaping contemporary research and instructional practices (Ferguson, 1994; Kaiser & Goetz, 1993; Kaiser & Grim, 2006):

1. Communication is independent of the specific mode that is used as a channel for communication.
2. Communication occurs when communication partners establish shared meanings.

To be functional, communication must "work"; that is, it must influence the behavior of others to "bring about effects that are appropriate and natural in a given social context" (Calculator & Jorgensen, 1991, p. 204). The responsibility for successful communication rests with both partners. However, shared meaning is more likely when the partner who is relatively more skilled uses the principles of responsive interaction, such as following the lead of the less skilled speaker, balancing turns between conversation partners, and responding with interest and affect.

Many students with severe disabilities are able to learn to understand and produce spoken language. Speech is always a desirable goal, of course, for those who can attain it. A student who can communicate verbally is likely to have a wider range of educational, employment, residential, and recreational opportunities than a student who is unable to speak. But because of sensory, motor, cognitive, or behavioral limitations, some students with severe disabilities may not learn to speak intelligibly even after extensive instruction. Many systems of augmentative and alternative communication (AAC) have proven useful—

**FIGURE 12.3  A communication bill of rights for persons with severe disabilities.**

All people with a disability of any extent or severity have a basic right to affect, through communication, the conditions of their existence. All people have the following specific communication rights in their daily interactions. Each person has the right to:

- request desired objects, actions, events and people
- refuse undesired objects, actions, or events
- express personal preferences and feelings
- be offered choices and alternatives
- reject offered choices
- request and receive another person's attention and interaction
- ask for and receive information about changes in routine and environment
- receive intervention to improve communication skills
- receive a response to any communication, whether or not the responder can fulfill the request
- have access to AAC (augmentative and alternative communication) and other AT (assistive technology) services and devices at all times
- have alternative and augmentative (AAC) and other assistive technology (AT) devices that function properly at all times
- be in environments that promote one's communication as a full partner with other people, including peers
- be spoken to with respect and courtesy
- be spoken to directly and not be spoken for or talked about in the third person while present
- have clear, meaningful and culturally and linguistically appropriate communications

*Source*: Summarized from the National Joint Committee for the Communicative Needs of Persons with Severe Disabilities. (1992). Guidelines for meeting the communication needs of persons with severe disabilities. *ASHA, 34*(Suppl. 7), 2–3.

including gestures, various sign language systems, pictorial communication boards, symbol systems, and electronic communication aids. AAC is described in detail in Chapter 8.

The Picture Exchange Communication System (PECS) (Bondy & Frost, 1994; Frost & Bondy, 2002) is a widely used form of AAC among children with autism and severe developmental disabilities. With PECS, children learn to communicate with others by selecting and showing cards with pictures and symbols representing their wishes. For example, a children who wants more orange juice during snack time puts the picture for juice next to the "I want" symbol on his Velcro talking strip and shows it to his teacher. Teachers, peers, and family members always use spoken language during the exchange. Schwartz, Garfinkle, and Bauer (1998) reported on the use of PECS with 31 children with autism and found that 56% of the children began to spontaneously use speech during their communicative interactions with peers and teachers.

Communication is achieved only with great difficulty by persons who are deaf-blind and requires greater effort on the part of communication partners. The use of dual communication boards can help students who are deaf-blind discriminate the receptive or expressive functions of responses from a partner (Heller & Bigge, 2005). When a communication partner points to pictures or symbols on her board, a receptive message is provided to the student, requiring a response from the student on his board. The partner can point

*AAC and PECS*

Council for Exceptional Children
Content Standards for Beginning Teachers—Common Core: Augmentative and assistive communication strategies (CC6K4) (also IC6K2).

to the student's board and provide imitative prompts or corrective feedback to help the student make expressive messages.

The specialized forms of communication used by some individuals with severe disabilities limit the number of people with whom they can communicate because the contrived and idiosyncratic nature of their systems requires specialized knowledge from the communication partner (Heller & Bigge, 2005). However, they do enable many students with severe disabilities to receive and express basic information, feelings, needs, and wants (Peck, 2004). Sign language and other communication systems also can be learned by a student's teachers, peers, parents, and employers, thus encouraging use outside the classroom. After learning to communicate through PECS, sign language, communication boards, or other strategies, some students are able to acquire speech skills. Researchers are working to develop partner-friendly forms of communication.

*Recreational and Leisure Skills.*   Most children develop the ability to play and later to occupy themselves constructively and pleasurably during their free time. But children with severe disabilities may not learn appropriate and satisfying recreational skills unless they are specifically taught. Teaching appropriate leisure and recreational skills helps individuals with severe disabilities interact socially, maintain their physical skills, and become more involved in community activities. Many persons with severe disabilities do not use their unstructured time appropriately; rather than participate in enjoyable pursuits, they may spend excessive time sitting, wandering, or looking at television. A variety of programs to teach recreational and leisure skills have recently been developed; this area is now generally acknowledged as an important part of the curriculum for students with severe disabilities.

In one study, task analysis, picture prompts, and modified game materials were used to help young elementary children with moderate and severe disabilities learn to independently play the board game Candyland (Raschke, Dedrick, Heston, & Farris, 1996). Sometimes modifying the rules by which team games are played can provide enough supports to enable an individual with severe disabilities to participate (Krebs & Coultier, 1992). For example, Figure 12.4 shows how the rules of a girls' softball league were modified to accommodate the skill limitations of a player with severe disabilities. For information and guidelines for selecting and teaching community-based recreational and leisure activities, see Best, Bigge, Musante, and Macias (2005); Browder and Cooper (2001); Moon (1994); Schlein, Meyer, Heyne, and Brandt (1995); and Schlein and Ray (1998).

*Prioritization of instructional targets*

Council for Exceptional Children   Content Standards for Beginning Teachers—Common Core: Identify and prioritize areas of the general curriculum and accommodations for individuals with exceptional learning needs (CC7S1) (also CC7S2, CC7S3).

*Prioritizing and Selecting Instructional Targets.*   Teachers must learn good choice-making skills too. Students with severe disabilities present numerous skill deficits often compounded by the presence of challenging behaviors, and each of those deficits could (but not necessarily should) be targeted as an IEP goal or instructional objective. It is seldom, if ever, possible, however, to design and implement a teaching program to deal simultaneously with all of the learning needs and challenging behaviors presented by a student with severe disabilities. (In the rare instance in which the resources to do so might be available, such an all-at-once approach would not be recommended anyway.) One of the greatest responsibilities a special educator undertakes in his role as a member of an IEP team is the selection of instructional objectives.

Judgments about how much a particular skill ultimately will contribute to a student's overall quality of life are difficult to make. In many cases, we simply do not know how useful or functional a behavioral change will prove to be. Whichever skills are chosen for instruction, they ultimately must be meaningful for the learner and her family. A variety of person-centered planning methods have been devised to help IEP teams work with the individual and family members to identify and prioritize the relative significance of skills or learning activities (e.g., Browder, 2001; Giangreco, Cloninger, & Iverson, 1998; Keyes & Owens-Johnson, 2003). For example, Figure 12.5 shows a form on which an IEP team summarized the outcomes of various assessment and recommendations for a student's IEP goals within an inclusive classroom setting.

**FIGURE 12.4   Modifications that enabled Katie, a player with severe disabilities, to participate in a girls' softball league**

1. Defensively, it was decided to *play Katie in center field.* This was more of a safety decision than a modification because Katie could not field a hit ball. Children at this age have a tendency to make contact with the ball either too early or too late, resulting in more balls being hit toward the left and right fields and fewer to center field. Also, there would be three other outfielders (natural supports) who could back-up and overshadow Katie's position in front, to her left and right (in softball there are four outfield positions: left field, center field, right field, and short center). Thus, the chances of Katie's being hit by the ball would be minimized if she were put into a position where balls are less likely to be hit.

2. Katie is slow and deliberate when she fields the ball, and she rarely stops balls even when they are hit directly to her. Therefore, out of fairness to Katie and her team, *the offense could only advance two bases if the ball were hit directly to her.* It should be noted that this particular modification was suggested by the coaches and approved by 87% of the players without disabilities.

3. Offensively, it was decided to *allow Katie to hit a ball off a tee* because she could not hit a pitched ball. Katie was allowed three attempts to hit the ball from the tee. The possibility, therefore, for a base on balls and being hit by a pitch did not exist for her. If she did not hit the ball in three attempts she was called "out." When Katie hit the ball, she ran unassisted to first base.

4. For baserunning, *the distance to first base was shortened* to account for Katie's running ability. Prior to the beginning of the season, some of Katie's teammates were timed on how fast they could run to first base, and an average time was computed. Using this average time as a standard, Katie was asked to run toward first base. While her teammates could make it all the way to first base in the given time, Katie only made it about halfway. Thus, the distance to first base for Katie was approximately half the distance to regular first base.

5. In consideration of Katie's safety and out of fairness to Katie's hitting and running ability, *the defense had to play at normal depths.* If Katie made contact with the ball and the ball was in fair territory, the fielder had to throw the ball to the first baseman positioned at regulation first base. If the fielder threw the ball to regulation first base before Katie stepped on her modified first base, Katie was called out. Otherwise, she was called "safe." As a result of a safe call, a pinch runner took Katie's place at regulation first base. At this point, Katie was taken back to the dugout.

*Source*: Reprinted from Bernabe, E. A., & Block, M. E. (1994). Modifying rules of a regular girls softball league to facilitate the inclusion of a child with severe disabilities. *Journal of The Association for Persons with Severe Handicaps, 19*, 26. Used by permission.

## Instructional Methods: How Should Students with Severe and Multiple Disabilities Be Taught?

Care and concern for the well-being of students with severe disabilities and assurance that they have access to educational programs are important. By themselves, however, care and access are not enough. To learn effectively, students need more than love, care, and a supportive classroom environment. They seldom acquire complex skills through imitation and observation alone; they are not likely to blossom on their own.

The learning and behavioral problems of students with severe disabilities are so extreme and significant that instruction must be carefully planned, systematically executed, and continuously monitored for effectiveness. The teacher must know what skill to teach, why it is important, how to teach it, and how to recognize that the student has achieved or performed the skill. Collectively, the authors of leading texts on teaching students with severe

### Summary of Ecological Assessment
### for an Individualized Education Plan (IEP)

**Student's Name:**  Sean Walker                                                    **Date:**  May 23, 2006

**Planning Team:**  Sean, Ms. Walker (Sean's mother), Ms. Harper (current special education teacher), Mr. McBride (current physical therapist); Mr. Atkinson (special education teacher at Northern), Ms. Baker (principal of Northern), Ms. Shey (third-grade teacher at Northern), Ms. Newhart (math and computer teacher at Northern), Mr. Lopez (language arts specialist at Northern)

#### 1. Background on Student

Sean Walker is an 8-year-old boy who has traumatic brain injury as the result of an accident at age 5. Sean made a remarkable recovery from the accident and has continued to show important progress over the last 3 years. He can now walk with a walker and speak in short phrases. Last year Sean mastered writing a cursive signature and putting on his jacket. He made good progress on learning sight words and some math facts, which he often practiced using computer software. Sean did not learn to initiate conversation. Although he talks more this year, his comments are often difficult to comprehend as he searches for the words he wants to use. He also made little progress on reading phrases. A prior evaluation by a neurologist, Dr. Jeffreys, notes that Sean needs continued training in memory strategies and cognitive stimulation.

#### 2. Person-Centered Planning with Student and Family

Sean's mother's priorities are that he (1) be treated well by other students (social inclusion); (2) continue to learn life skills, given his excellent progress this year in learning to put on his jacket; and (3) be taught reading. Sean has expressed an interest in trying out the cafeteria. Currently he eats in his special education classroom with only five other students present.

#### 3. Encouraging Student Self-Determination

Sean has been learning goal setting and decision making this year. He has presented the planning team with a photo album of his preferences, which he placed in rank order. His top five include food (tacos, hamburgers, French fries), working on the computer, playing computer games, swimming at the YMCA, and music. He has also presented the team with his goals, which include being able to walk without his walker and getting his own computer.

#### 4. Development of Personalized Curriculum

Because Sean has emerging functional academic skills, these can be used to create curricular parallels in general education. Expanding his sight word vocabulary, teaching him to read and write short phrases, and helping him build on his knowledge of math facts by learning to add are important priorities. These skills should be embedded in as many academic subjects as possible (e.g., learning sight word vocabulary in math). Sean also has priority needs related to communication, self-direction, social interaction skills, and motor development that can be taught within the typical classroom.

#### 5. Recommendations for the IEP

The team has determined that the priorities for Sean's IEP include (1) functional academics (Sean wants this work to be computer-assisted), (2) continued improvement of his balance and fine-motor skills (Sean's priority is to walk without his walker); (3) initiation of conversations; (4) self-direction (goal setting, self-managed seatwork); and (5) mastery of personal care skills. Sean will spend most of his day with Ms. Shey's third grade and will receive specially designed instruction from Mr. Atkinson and a teaching assistant in the context. He will also receive individual assistance for toileting and individual physical therapy sessions, based on his preference for privacy in these activities.

*Source*: Reprinted from Browder, D. M., & Wilson, B. (2001). Using ecological assessment in planning for inclusion. In D. M. Browder, *Curriculum and assessment for students with moderate and severe disabilities* (pp. 342–343). New York: Guilford. Used by permission.

disabilities recommend that attention should be given to the following components of an instructional program (Browder, 2001; Cipani & Spooner, 1994; Maurice, Green, & Foxx, 2001; Snell & Brown, 2006; Scheuermann & Webber, 2002; Westling & Fox, 2004):

- *The student's current level of performance must be precisely assessed.* Precise assessment of current performance is necessary to determine which skills to teach and at what level instruction should begin. Is Keeshia able to hold her head up without support? For how many seconds? Under what conditions? In response to what verbal or physical signals? Unlike traditional assessment procedures, which may rely heavily on standardized scores and developmental levels, assessment of students with severe disabilities emphasizes each learner's ability to perform specific, observable behaviors. Assessment should not be a one-shot procedure but should take place at different times, in different settings, and with different persons. The fact that a student with severe disabilities does not demonstrate a skill at one particular time or place does not mean that she is incapable of demonstrating that skill.

- *The skill to be taught must be defined clearly.* "Carlos will feed himself" is too broad a goal for many students with severe disabilities. A more appropriate statement might be "When applesauce is applied to Carlos's right index finger, he will put the finger in his mouth within 5 seconds." A clear statement like this enables the teacher and other observers to determine whether Carlos attains this objective. If, after repeated trials, he has not, a different method of instruction should be tried.

- *The skill may need to be broken down into smaller component steps.* An effective teacher of students with severe disabilities knows how to use task analysis (described in Chapter 6) to break down a skill into a series of specific, observable steps. Assessment of student performance on each step of the task analysis helps the teacher determine where to begin instruction. She can gradually teach each required step until the student can accomplish the entire task independently. Without this sort of structure and precision in teaching, a great deal of time is likely to be wasted.

- *The teacher must provide a clear prompt or cue to the child.* It is important for the child to know what action or response is expected. A cue can be verbal; the teacher might say, "Bev, say apple," to indicate what Bev must do before she will receive an apple. Or a cue can be physical; the teacher might point to a light switch to indicate that Bev should turn on the light. It also may be necessary for the teacher to demonstrate an activity many times and to physically guide the child through some or all of the tasks required in the activity. To learn more about delivering and fading instructional prompts to students with severe disabilities, see Doyle, Wolery, Ault, and Gast (1988); Green (2001); and Wolery, Ault, and Doyle (1992).

- *The student must receive feedback and reinforcement.* Students with severe disabilities must receive immediate and clear information about their performance; and like all students, they are more likely to repeat an action if it is followed immediately by a reinforcing consequence. It is critical that effective reinforcers be identified for students with severe disabilities. Unfortunately, it is not always easy to determine what items or events a noncommunicative child finds motivating. Many teachers devote extensive efforts to reinforcer sampling; that is, they attempt to find out which items and activities are reinforcing to a particular child, and they keep careful records of what is

*Elements of systematic instruction*

Council for Exceptional Children

Content Standards for Beginning Teachers—Common Core: Theories and research that form the basis of curriculum developments and instructional practice (CC7K1) (also CC4S4, CC7S5, CC7S13, IC1K7, IC4S6).

As Daniel's teacher systematically faded out response prompts and cues, Daniel learned to select tasks and match items independently.

and is not effective. Methods for assessing stimuli that may serve as reinforcers for individuals with severe and profound disabilities are described in Fisher et al. (1992), Logan and Gast (2001), Logan et al. (2001), and Lohrmann-O'Rouke and Browder (1998).

- *Strategies that promote generalization and maintenance must be used.* Most students with severe disabilities have difficulty generalizing the skills they learn. Thus, an effective teacher has students perform targeted skills in different settings and with different instructors, cues, and materials before concluding with confidence that the student has acquired and generalized a skill. Several strategies for facilitating generalization are discussed in Chapter 4. More detailed information can be found in Baer (1998), Cooper et al. (2006), Snell and Brown (2006), and Westling and Fox (2004). Using naturalistic teaching strategies is one of the best ways to facilitate a student's generalization and maintenance of important skills. (See Teaching & Learning, "Using Naturalistic Teaching Strategies to Build Communication Skills in Students with Severe Disabilities," later in this chapter.)

- *The student's performance must be directly and frequently assessed.* Because the progress of students with severe disabilities most often occurs in very small steps, it is important to measure performance frequently and precisely. Collecting data on a student's performance of each step of a task-analyzed skill or routine gives the teacher precise information. Learning is shown most clearly by student performance data collected every day. Some programs keep videotaped records of students' performance on specific tasks. This record can add an important dimension to documenting behavioral changes over extended periods. Denham and Lahm (2001) describe how students with severe disabilities can use computer and assistive technologies to create alternative portfolios as a means to document their accomplishments.

*Partial Participation.* The principle of **partial participation,** first described by Baumgart et al. (1982), acknowledges that even though some individuals with severe disabilities are not able to independently perform all steps of a given task or activity, they often can be taught to perform selected components or an adapted version of the task. Partial participation can be used to help a learner be more active in a task, make more choices in how the task will be carried out, and provide more control over the activity. Table 12.1 is an example of how partial participation could be used within each step of a task analysis for making a blender drink.

Ferguson and Baumgart (1991) describe and offer suggestions for avoiding four types of errors or common misapplications of partial participation: (1) passive participation—the learner is present but not actively participating; (2) myopic participation—the student's participation is limited to only some parts of the activity, which are chosen for the convenience of others; (3) piecemeal participation—partial participation and the accompanying concepts of functional, activity-based, age-appropriate curriculum activities are only used part of the time; and (4) missed participation—in trying to help students become independent, the point of partial participation is missed altogether.

*Positive Behavioral Support.* Notable changes have occurred in how teachers respond to disruptive, aggressive, or socially unacceptable behaviors by students with disabilities. In the not-too-distant past, a student who engaged in stereotypic head weaving may have had his head restrained or perhaps have had a teacher manipulate his head up and down for several minutes. A student who tantrumed or screamed may have been "treated" with the application of aversive consequences (e.g., being sprayed with water mist) or extended time-out from instruction. These were "modes of intervention which most people would reject as absolutely unacceptable if they were used with a person who does not have disabilities" (Center on Human Policy, 1986, p. 4).

Today, a growing number of special education programs are responding to challenging, excessive, or unacceptable behaviors of students with a nonaversive treatment approach

---

*Naturalistic teaching strategies*

Council for Exceptional Children Content Standards for Beginning Teachers—INDEP CURR: Strategies for integrating student-initiated learning experiences into ongoing instruction (IC4K3) (also CC4S4).

*Partial participation*

Council for Exceptional Children Content Standards for Beginning Teachers—Common Core: Use procedures to increase the individual's self-awareness, self-management, self-control, self-reliance, and self-esteem (CC4S5) (also IC5S6).

*Positive behavioral support*

Council for Exceptional Children Content Standards for Beginning Teachers—Common Core: Laws, policies, and ethical principles regarding behavior management planning and implementation (CC1K2) (also CC5S5).

**TABLE 12.1    Using partial participation within each step of a task analysis for making a blender drink**

| Task: Making a blender drink Teacher's Assistance | Learner: Saundra Learner's Participation | Goal |
|---|---|---|
| 1. Announces activity | Lifts her head to listen | Active |
| 2. Wheels Saundra to the cabinet | — | — |
| 3. Gets out the utensils | Grasps a spoon | Active |
| 4. Wheels Saundra to the table | Releases the spoon on the table | Active |
| 5. Shows fruits | Selects one fruit by grasping it and pushing it to the teacher | Choice |
| 6. Shows beverages | Selects one beverage by grasping it and pushing it to the teacher | Choice |
| 7. Puts the ingredients in the blender | Operates the blender with a switch when the chosen ingredients are in | Control |
| 8. Spoons the blender drink into a glass | Indicates if ready to drink | Control |
| 9. Holds out a straw | Places the straw in the glass and drinks | Active Control |

Key: Partial participation may have the goal of encouraging the learner to be more active in the routine (Active), to make more choices (Choice), or to have more control of the routine (Control). These goals are shown for each step of the task analysis.

Source: Reprinted from Browder, D. M., & Snell, M. E. (1993). Daily living and community skills. In M. E. Snell (Ed.), *Instruction for students with severe disabilities* (4th ed.) (p. 494). Upper Saddle River, NJ: Merrill/Prentice Hall. Used by permission.

called *positive behavioral support*. Elements of positive behavior support include (1) understanding the meaning that a behavior has for a student, (2) teaching the student a positive alternative behavior, (3) using environmental restructuring to make the undesired behaviors less likely, and (4) using strategies that are socially acceptable and intended for use in integrated school and community settings (Carr et al., 2002).

Positive behavioral support begins with a functional assessment of the problem behavior. Although **functional assessment** refers to a variety of behavior assessment methodologies for determining the environmental variables that are setting the occasion for and maintaining challenging behaviors, it usually consists of these three steps (Chandler & Dahlquist, 2006; Conroy & Davis, 2000; Horner & Carr, 1997; Neef & Peterson, 2006):

1. *Structured interviews* are conducted with teachers, family members, and others who know the child well to find out the circumstances that typically surround the occurrence and nonoccurrence of the problem behavior and the reactions the behavior usually evokes from others.

2. *Systematic observations* of the child are conducted to learn (a) the environmental context and events that covary with the problem behavior (e.g., transitions from one classroom or activity to another, task difficulty); (b) the intensity, duration, and form of the problem behavior; and (c) the events that follow the problem behavior and may function to maintain it (e.g., teacher attention, withdrawal of task demands).

3. *Functional analysis* (i.e., experimental manipulation) of the variables identified in steps 1 and 2 is carried out to verify their function in either triggering or maintaining the problem behavior.

Results of functional assessments are used to guide the development of positive behavior support plans. For example, functional assessments conducted by Lalli and colleagues (1993) revealed that self-injury and aggressive outbursts by three nonvocal students with severe disabilities during instructional activities were maintained by teacher attention (in

*Functional assessment, functional analysis*

Council for Exceptional Children    Content Standards for Beginning Teachers—Common Core: Use functional assessments to develop intervention plans (CC7S4) (also CC8K1, IC7S1, IC8S1).

# Using Naturalistic Teaching Strategies to Build Communication Skills in Students with Severe Disabilities

*by Jo Webber and Brenda Scheuermann*

Mark is an 11-year-old student with severe disabilities. Although he is able to talk, he generally shuns social interaction. When someone tries to talk to Mark, he closes one eye, turns to the side, and flaps his hands repeatedly. When he wants something, he usually points or whines. His communication primarily consists of one-word replies to others' questions. Mark attends a special class for most of the school day. However, he goes to lunch and art with general education students from Ms. Jacobs's class. Mark's teachers and parents have identified spontaneous communication as his highest-priority IEP goal: they want him to initiate verbal requests and begin conversations with his peers. Following the recommendations of the speech-language pathologist, Ms. Jacobs is using naturalistic teaching techniques to teach Mark to use spontaneous language.

Students like Mark have extensive communication and social deficits requiring systematic and intensive instructional intervention. Unfortunately, these students are usually not motivated to learn these skills. Even if they do master some skills during class instruction, they often fail to use them in their daily lives, rendering the skills nonfunctional.

Naturalistic teaching directly addresses the problems of low motivation and generalization. As you read in Chapter 8, naturalistic teaching is based on the notion of a "teachable moment," which means that when students demonstrate interest in something, that's a great time to teach them related skills. For example, if Mark gets up from his desk and heads for the water fountain, Ms. Jacobs should use this opportunity to prompt him to ask for a drink of water. This notion of the teachable moment applies to all students, but it is particularly pertinent for students with severe disabilities who learn slowly, do not participate readily in learning activities, and frequently fail to generalize what they have learned. For these students, every teachable moment is a precious learning opportunity.

Naturalistic teaching includes several components. First, it requires environmental conditions that capture student attention and interest. These can be naturally occurring conditions or situations contrived by the teacher (e.g., putting a desired object out of reach). Second, the teacher must be able to control those conditions: blocking access, for example, to the water fountain. Finally, it is important to provide natural reinforcement after desired student responses. Mark was motivated by the presence of the water fountain and his own thirst. In a naturalistic teaching situation, Ms. Jacobs will block his access to the water, prompt him to communicate what he wants, and, when he complies, allow him to get a drink of water (natural reinforcement). Spontaneously asking for water should occur more often in the future, which is the goal.

## WHAT ARE NATURALISTIC TEACHING STRATEGIES?

Several teaching strategies are associated with naturalistic teaching and can be used alone or in combination. Each teaching session should be short and positive (Kaiser & Grim, 2006). Teachers should (1) observe students and note attempts to obtain desired outcomes (e.g., get a toy or food), (2) obtain student attention, and (3) use a responsive interactive style. Specific strategies include the following.

**Mand.** A *mand* is a verbal instruction that cues students to perform a behavior that they may know how to perform but do not do. For example, after blocking Mark's access to the water, Ms. Jacobs obtains his attention and says (mand), "Tell me what you want." After telling Mark what to do, she waits for him to say, "Water." If he complies, she praises him and expands his response (e.g., "Good, Mark. You want a drink of water"), and allows him to get a drink.

Mark enters Ms. Jacobs's general education classroom just as her students are lining up for lunch. Ms. Jacobs quickly steps in front of Mark who is heading for a favorite spot in the corner. "Hi, Mark. Tell me what you need to do"(mand). Mark responds, "Lunch." "Good, Mark. Yes, it's time for lunch" (praise and expanded language). She continues: "Line up so we can go" (mand). Mark lines up. "Good lining up," says Ms. Jacobs and allows the students to walk to the cafeteria (natural reinforcement).

**Mand-Prompt.** Often, even with a mand, students do not perform a desired behavior. In this case teachers need to add prompts. For example, if Mark does not comply with the mand, Ms. Jacobs provides a prompt by saying, "Water," or "I want water." Then she waits for Mark to talk. Once again, teachers first need to gain the student's attention and then repeat the mand-prompt-wait sequence no more than three times. At this point, access to the water (reinforcement) should follow, regardless of Mark's response so as not to discourage him from trying to obtain a drink of water in the future (another teachable moment).

As he goes through the cafeteria line, Mark's peer buddy tells him, "Tell the lady what you want, Mark," (mand) at each food-selection site and prompts by saying, "I want…." As Mark requests food (e.g., "I want Jell-O"), the peer buddy says, "Good, you want the Jell-O" (praise and expanded language). Mark receives the designated food item (natural reinforcement) and moves down the line.

**Model.** When students are able to perform the behavior but hesitate to do so, teachers may dispense with mands and just model the correct behavior for students to imitate.

The peer buddy notices that Mark cannot reach the chocolate-milk carton in the lunch line. He gains Mark's attention and says, "Please help me," or "I want the milk, please" (model), then waits for a response. When Mark imitates the model, his buddy praises him, repeats the correct response, and helps him retrieve the milk. If two models result in incorrect responses, teachers should add a mand and/or a prompt or end the teaching interaction and use a mand and/or prompt procedure at the next opportunity. At the end of the line, the peer buddy again

provides a model for Mark by handing the cashier his money and saying, "You're welcome," when the cashier says, "Thank you." When Mark imitates these responses, the peer praises him and leads him to his seat (natural reinforcement).

## HOW TO GET STARTED

For naturalistic teaching to be effective, teachers must regularly take advantage of natural teaching opportunities. Following are some pointers for successful implementation:

- *Attend to the students.* Teachers should be good observers of student preferences, anticipating student needs and searching for communicative intent in all student behavior.
- *Teach functional skills at opportune moments.* Teach during lunchtime, free time, transition time, before and after class time, and on the bus if possible.
- *Establish a stimulating environment.* Provide many situations in which students will be motivated to produce communicative and social behaviors.
- *Refrain from providing too much assistance.* Require students to use functional behaviors to make requests or to protest. Provide only as much assistance as is necessary for successful responding.
- *Reinforce appropriate communicative and social behaviors.* Begin with frequent reinforcement and fade to less frequent reinforcement and natural consequences.
- *Assess results.* As with all teaching, collect data to determine if the student has learned spontaneous communication and social skills.

Jo Webber and Brenda Scheuermann are professors of special education at Southwest Texas State University in San Marcos, Texas. They are the authors of *Autism: Teaching DOES Make a Difference* (Wadsworth, 2002).

 To learn more about these strategies and answer questions about what you have learned, go to the Teaching & Learning module in Chapter 12 of the Companion Website, **www.prenhall.com/heward.**

the form of reprimands) and/or escape (misbehavior often resulted in termination of the academic task). This information led to the design of successful interventions that included frequent positive comments for appropriate behaviors, withholding attention for problem behavior, and teaching the students a socially acceptable behavior for communicating their wishes (e.g., choosing the next activity by pointing to a picture schedule, tapping the teacher on the shoulder).

When functional analyses are conducted, reinforcement-based interventions are more likely to be implemented than are those that include a punishment component (Pelios, Morren, Tesch, & Axelrod, 1999). In addition, the effects of interventions based on functional

 To read firsthand applications of functional assessment and positive behavioral support, see the feature boxes "Functional Assessment-Based Intervention in a School Setting" (Chapter 13) and "A Parent-Professional Partnership in Positive Behavioral Support" (Chapter 3) on the Companion Website, **www.prenhall.com/heward.**

analyses are likely to be more durable than those that do not take the function of problem behavior into account (Neef & Peterson, 2006). Several books provide guidelines for developing positive behavioral support plans (e.g., Carr, Levin, McConnachie, Carlson, Kemp, & Smith, 1994; Koegel, Koegel, & Dunlap, 1996; O'Neill, et al., 1997).

Problem behaviors such as noncompliance, aggression, acting out, and self-injury can sometimes be reduced in frequency or prevented altogether through relatively simple modifications of curriculum or the way in which learning activities are presented (Ferro, Foster-Johnson, & Dunlap, 1996; Smith & Iwata, 1997; Sprague & Horner, 1990). For example:

- Provide students with a choice of tasks or a task sequence (Kern, Mantegna, Vorndran, Bailin, & Hilt, 2001; Peterson, Neef, Van Norman, & Ferreri, 2005).
- Intersperse easy or high-probability tasks or requests with more difficult items or low-probability requests (Ardoin, Martens, & Wolfe, 1999; Killu, Sainato, Davis, Ospelt, & Paul, 1998).
- Maintain a rapid pace of instruction (Dunlap, Dyer, & Koegel, 1983; Tincani, Ernsbarger, Harrison, & Heward, in press).
- Use a response-prompting procedure that results in fewer errors (Ebanks & Fisher, 2003; Heckaman, Alber, Hooper, & Heward, 1998).
- Reduce task difficulty (Carr & Durand, 1985).
- Deliver reinforcement noncontingently on a fixed time schedule (Carr, Kellum, & Chong, 2001; Kodak, Miltenberger, & Romaniuk, 2003).

Research-based methods of positive behavioral support should not be confused with relationship-based approaches that do not provide systematic environmental arrangements and differential consequences for behavior. For example, gentle teaching is a philosophy and approach for treating problem behaviors by individuals with disabilities that relies on "valuing" the person and "giving warm assistance and protection when necessary" (McGee & Gonzalez, 1990, p. 244). McGee (1992), the major proponent of gentle teaching, claims, "Behavior problems will evaporate like the morning dew if we express unconditional valuing" (McGee & Menolascino, 1992, p. 109). Although gentle teaching and other relationship-based approaches such as holding therapy (Tinbergen & Tinbergen, 1983) may sound wonderful, there is little scientific evidence of their effectiveness (Bailey, 1992; Heflin & Simpson, 2002; Cullen & Mudford, 2005; Romanczyk, Weinter, Lockshin, & Ekdahl, 1999).

*Small-group instruction*

Council for
Exceptional
Children    Content
Standards for
Beginning Teachers—INDEP
CURR: Methods for ensuring
individual academic success in
one-to-one, small-group, and
large-group settings (IC5K4)
(also CC5K3).

*Small-Group Instruction.*    For many years, most professionals believed that one-to-one instruction was the only effective teaching arrangement for students with severe disabilities. The rationale was that one-to-one teaching minimized distractions and increased the likelihood that the student would respond only to the teacher. Although a one-to-one teaching format allows for the intensive, systematic instruction known to be effective with students who have severe disabilities, small-group instruction also has potential advantages (Kamps, Dugan, Leonard, & Daoust, 1994; Keel & Gast, 1992; Munk, Laarhoven, Goodman, & Repp, 1998; Snell & Brown, 2006):

- Skills learned in small-group instruction may be more likely to generalize to group situations and settings.
- Small-group instruction provides opportunities for social interaction and reinforcement from peers that are missed when a student is taught alone and isolated from other students.
- Small-group instruction provides opportunities for incidental or observation learning from other students.
- In some instances, small-group instruction may be a more cost-effective use of the teacher's time.

The effectiveness of group instruction for all students is enhanced when teachers do the following (Kamps et al., 1994; Munk et al., 1998; Snell & Brown, 2006):

- Ensure that students possess basic prerequisite skills such as (1) sitting quietly for a period of time, (2) maintaining eye contact, and (3) following simple instructions or imitating simple responses.
- Encourage students to listen and watch other group members and then praise them for doing so.
- Keep instruction interesting by keeping individual turns short, giving all members turns, giving turns contingent on attending, and using demonstrations and a variety of materials that can be handled.
- Use methods that produce high rates of active student response, such as choral responding and response cards (see Chapter 6), which enable every student in the group to respond to each instructional trial.
- Teach at a lively pace with very brief intertrial intervals.
- Involve all members by using multilevel instruction individualized to each student's targeted skills and mode of response.
- Use partial participation and material adaptation to enable all students to respond.
- Keep waiting time to a minimum by controlling the group size and limiting the amount of teacher talk and the amount/length of student response in a single turn.
- Promote cooperation among group members.

## Where Should Students with Severe Disabilities Be Taught?

*Benefits of the Neighborhood School.*    What is the least restrictive and most appropriate educational setting for a student with severe disabilities? This important question continues to be the subject of much debate and discussion. Lou Brown (who has long championed the inclusion of persons with severe disabilities in integrated school, vocational, and community settings) and his colleagues at the University of Wisconsin make a strong case for why students with severe disabilities should attend the same school they would attend if they were not disabled:

> The environments in which students with severe intellectual disabilities receive instructional services have critical effects on where and how they spend their postschool lives. Segregation begets segregation. We believe that when children with intellectual disabilities attend separate schools, they are denied opportunities to demonstrate to the rest of the community that they can function in integrated environments and activities; their nondisabled peers do not know or understand them and too often think negatively of them; their parents become afraid to risk allowing them opportunities to learn to function in integrated environments later in life; and taxpayers assume they need to be sequestered in segregated group homes, enclaves, work crews, activity centers, sheltered workshops, institutions, and nursing homes. (Brown et al., 1989a, p. 1)

Brown and his colleagues offer four reasons why they believe neighborhood schools should replace segregated and clustered schools. They define a clustered school as "a regular school attended by an unnaturally large proportion of students with intellectual disabilities, but it is not the one any or most would attend if they were not labeled disabled" (p. 1). First, when students without disabilities go to an integrated school with peers who are disabled, they are more likely to function responsibly as adults in a pluralistic society. Second, various sources of information support integrated schools as more meaningful instructional environments. Hunt, Goetz, and Anderson (1986), for example, compared the IEP objectives for students with severe disabilities who were taught at integrated versus segregated schools. They found that the quality of IEP objectives—in terms of age-appropriateness, functionality, and the potential for generalization of what was being taught to other environments—was higher for the students educated in integrated schools. Third, parents and families have greater access to school activities when children are attending their home schools. Fourth, attending one's home school provides greater opportunities to develop a wide range of social relationships with nondisabled peers. Table 12.2 presents examples of 11 kinds of social relationships that might develop between students with severe disabilities and their nondisabled peers when they attend the same school.

*Benefits of neighborhood schools*

Council for Exceptional Children   Content Standards for Beginning Teachers—INDEP CURR: Advantages and disadvantages of placement options and programs on the continuum of services for individuals with disabilities (IC5K5) (also IC1K6, CC5K1).

**TABLE 12.2**  **Social relationships that can develop between students with severe disabilities and their nondisabled peers when they attend the same school**

| Social Relationship | Example |
|---|---|
| Peer tutor | Leigh role-plays social introductions with Margo, providing feedback and praise for Margo's performance. |
| Eating companion | Jennifer and Rick eat lunch with Linda in the cafeteria and talk about their favorite music groups. |
| Art, home economics, industrial arts, music, physical education companion | In art class, students were instructed to paint a sunset. Tom sat next to Dan and offered suggestions and guidance about the best colors to use and how to complete the task. |
| Regular class companion | A fifth-grade class is doing a "Know Your Town" lesson in social studies. Ben helps Karen plan a trip through their neighborhood. |
| During-school companion | "Hangs out" and interacts on social level: after lunch and before the bell for class rang, Molly and Phyllis went to the student lounge for a soda. |
| Friend | David, a member of the varsity basketball team, invites Ralph, a student with severe disabilities, to his house to watch a game on TV. |
| Extracurricular companion | Sarah and Winona prepare their articles for the school newspaper together and then work on the layout in the journalism lab. |
| After-school-project companion | The sophomore class decided to build a float for the homecoming parade. Joan worked on it with Maria, a nondisabled companion, after school and on weekends in Joan's garage. |
| After-school companion | On Saturday afternoon, Mike, who is not disabled, and Bill go to the shopping mall. |
| Travel companion | David walks with Ralph when he wheels from last-period class to the gym, where Ralph helps the basketball team as a student manager. |
| Neighbor | Interacts with student in everyday environments and activities. Parents of nondisabled students in the neighborhood regularly exchange greetings with Mary when they are at school, around the neighborhood, at local stores, at the mall, at the grocery. |

*Source:* Adapted from Brown, L., Long, E., Udvari-Solner, A., Davis, L., VanDeventer, P., Ahlgren, C., Johnson, F., Gruenewald, L., & Jorgensen, J. (1989). The home school: Why students with severe disabilities must attend the schools of their brothers, sisters, friends, and neighbors. *Journal of The Association for Persons with Severe Handicaps, 14,* 4. Used by permission.

*Inclusion and social relationships*

Council for Exceptional Children Content Standards for Beginning Teachers—INDEP CURR: Advantages and disadvantages of placement options and programs on the continuum of services for individuals with disabilities (IC5K5) (also IC5K2, CC5K1).

*Social Relationships.*   Establishing and maintaining a network of social relationships is one of the desired outcomes of inclusive educational practices for students with severe disabilities (Schwartz, 2000; Schwartz, Staub, Peck, & Gallucci, 2006). Although research has shown that simply placing students with disabilities into regular schools and classrooms does not necessarily lead to increased positive social interactions, regular class participation can provide additional opportunities for positive social contacts and the development of friendships (e.g., Hanline, 1993; Staub, Spaulding, Peck, Gallucci, & Schwartz, 1996).

For example, Kennedy and Itkonen (1994) studied the effects of regular class participation on social contacts with peers without disabilities for three high school students with severe and multiple disabilities. Don was 18 years old and classified as having severe intellectual retardation, along with paraplegia, cerebral palsy, and visual impairments. He used a wheelchair to move himself for short distances and lived in a 50-person facility for people with multiple disabilities and intensive health care needs. Manny was also 18 years old and classified as having severe retardation. He communicated with two- or three-word sentences and had a 10-year history of hitting and pinching others. Ann was 19 years old with moderate mental retardation. Her communications ranged from a few words to elaborate sentences. She was receiving instruction regarding appropriate topics of conversation and maintaining physical distance when interacting with others. Ann received medication for generalized tonic-clonic seizures and would often yell, run away, and hit others during transitions from one class or activity to another. Contingency contracts were in effect for both Manny and Ann as a preventive behavior management procedure; they could earn privileges for not engaging in problem behaviors.

A social contact was defined as the interaction of a student with disabilities with a peer(s) in the context of a meaningful activity (e.g., eating lunch, conducting a science project) for a minimum of 15 minutes. Each of the three students participated in a different regular classroom (average size: 25 students) for one period each school day, five days per week. Several aspects of this study deserve special comment. First, regular class participation increased the number of social contacts for each student even though ongoing opportunities to contact nondisabled peers were provided through "friendship" and peer tutoring programs during those weeks when the students were not in the regular classroom. Second, the increases in social contacts were the result of participation for only one class period per day. It might be presumed that additional participation (e.g., two or three periods per day) would result in even more frequent contacts. Third, increased social contacts were obtained without an elaborate training program or intensive intervention. Each student simply began participating in the regular classroom after a "circle of friends" introduction by the special education teacher to the regular class peers that stressed the similarities among all students, the need for students to support one another, and the importance of social relationships.

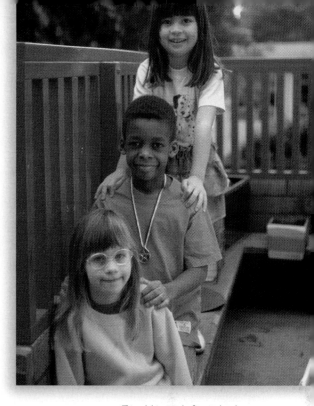

A wide variety of strategies for promoting desired social relationships has been developed. One strategy is to give the student with disabilities a skill for initiating and maintaining interaction (Hughes et al., 2000). For example, Jolly, Test, and Spooner (1993) taught two nonverbal boys with severe and profound mental retardation and multiple physical disabilities to initiate play activities with nondisabled peers by showing badges with photographs of activities. Other strategies focus on teaching classmates without disabilities to initiate social contacts during free time, cooperative learning, or peer tutoring and peer buddy activities (Copeland et al., 2002; Hughes et al., 2001; Putnam, 1998; Romer, White, & Haring, 1996). Still other approaches involve changes in the roles and responsibilities of instructional faculty, such as collaborative teaching teams (Dettmer, Thurston, & Dyck, 2005; Giangreco, Cloninger, Dennis, & Edelman, 2000; Hunt, Soto, Maier, & Doering, 2003; Kochar, West, & Taymans, 2000; Snell & Janney, 2005).

Many of these strategies for facilitating the regular classroom inclusion of students with severe disabilities are compatible with one another; and it is typical for a program to incorporate multiple, concurrent methods for identifying and providing supports for students, their teachers, and their peers. (To learn about a collaborative method for building social supports for students with disabilities in regular classrooms, see Teaching & Learning, "Planning for Inclusion with MAPS," later in this chapter.)

*Experiences and Transformations of General Education Teachers.* To find out how regular education teachers reacted to having a student with severe disabilities placed in their classrooms, Giangreco, Dennis, Cloninger, Edelman, and Shattman (1993) interviewed 19 K–9 general education teachers. They found that regardless of how the child with severe disabilities was placed in the general education classroom, most teachers initially described the placement in cautious or negative terms (e.g., "reluctant," "nervous," "unqualified," "angry"). Despite their initial negative reactions, 17 of the teachers experienced "increased ownership and involvement" with the child with severe disabilities as the school year progressed. Giangreco et al. refer to this process of changing attitude and perspective as *transformation.*

> Transformations were gradual and progressive, rather than discrete and abrupt.... A number of teachers who had these experiences reportedly came to the realization they could be successful and that including the student was not as difficult as they had originally imagined....

Friendships and after-school relationships between students with disabilities and their nondisabled peers are more likely to develop when all students attend their home school.

See the feature box, "The Metropolitan Nashville Peer Buddy Program", on Chapter 12 of the Companion Website, **www.prenhall.com/heward.**

*Planning inclusion with person-centered strategies such as MAPS*

Council for Exceptional Children Content Standards for Beginning Teachers—Common Core: Use strategies to facilitate integration into various settings (CC4S1) (also CC5S1, CC5S3).

The following quotes typify the comments of teachers who underwent significant transformation.

"I started seeing him as a little boy. I started feeling that he's a person too. He's a student. Why should I not teach him? He's in my class. That's my responsibility. I'm a teacher!"

"I made the full swing of fighting against having Bobbi Sue placed in my room to fighting for her to be in a mainstream classroom working with kids in the way that she had worked with them all year long. I'm a perfect example of how you have to have an open mind."

"I started watching my own regular classroom students. They didn't treat him any differently. They went about their business like everything was normal. So I said, 'If they can do it, I can do it.' He's not getting in their way. They're treating him like everybody else.'"

"They were always letting me know when I forgot something. 'You didn't remember to include Sarah.' So they were very good at letting me know."

"The kids help you figure it out." (Giangreco et al., 1993, pp. 359–372)

In the end, the best inclusion facilitators are the students themselves.

*Changing attitudes of general education teachers*

Council for Exceptional Children — Content Standards for Beginning Teachers—Common Core: Teacher attitudes and behaviors that influence behavior of individuals with exceptional learning needs (CC5K4) (also IC5K2).

Detailed information about administrative, curricular, and instructional strategies designed to support the education of students with severe disabilities in regular schools and inclusive classrooms can be found in Bauer and Brown (2001), Browder and Wilson (2001), Downing and Eichinger (2003), Fisher and Ryndak (2001), Giangreco and Doyle (2000), Kennedy and Horn (2004), Snell and Janney (2000b), and Wolfe and Hall (2003).

*How Much Time in the Regular Classroom?*  Although the social benefits of regular class participation for students with disabilities—as well as for their peers without disabilities—have been clearly shown, the effects of full inclusion on the attainment of IEP goals and objectives is not yet known. The functional IEP goals and objectives for students with severe disabilities are seldom reflected in the academic curriculum of the regular classroom (especially at the secondary level). Available instruction time is especially valuable to students who by definition require direct, intensive, and ongoing instruction to acquire basic skills that students without disabilities learn without instruction. A major challenge for both special and general educators is to develop models and strategies for including students with severe disabilities in regular classroom activities without sacrificing their opportunities to acquire, practice, and generalize the functional skills they need most.

The question of how much time students with severe disabilities should spend in the regular classroom is an important one. Although a few full-inclusion advocates might argue that every student with disabilities should have a full-time, regular-class placement regardless of the nature of her educational needs, most special educators probably would agree with Brown et al. (1991), whose position is that students with severe disabilities should be based in the same schools and classrooms they would attend if they were not disabled but that they should also spend some time elsewhere.

> There are substantial differences between being based in and confined to regular education classrooms. "Based in" refers to being a member of a real class, where and with whom you start the school day, you may not spend all your time with your class, but it is still your group and everyone knows it. . . . It is our position that it is unacceptable for students with severe disabilities to spend either 0% or 100% of their time in regular education classrooms.... How much time should be spent in regular classes? Enough to ensure that the student is a member, not a visitor. A lot, if the student is engaged in meaningful activities. Quite a bit if she is young, but less as she approaches 21. There is still a lot we do not know. (pp. 40, 46)

# Planning for Inclusion with MAPS

*by Marsha Forest and Jack Pearpoint*

The movement to integrate children with disabilities into ordinary classrooms is founded on a simple yet profound philosophy: everyone belongs. The McGill Action Planning System (MAPS) is a systems approach to problem solving that has helped many schools welcome and support children with disabilities in regular classrooms (Forest & Lusthaus, 1990; Vandercook, York, & Forest, 1989).

## WHO GOES TO A MAP? FRIENDS!

The size of the group that gathers for a MAP session can vary from two to two dozen. The key ingredients for participants are intimate and personal contact with the individual who is being mapped. A grandmother or neighbor, a friend—all are on equal footing with professionals, who are welcomed and needed, but as individuals, not as therapists. Parents and family members usually have the most to offer. Their perspectives are welcome in a MAP.

Peer participation is critical. Classmates have enormous untapped energy and creative capacity. Their straight talk often offers teachers new ideas. Adults must be careful not to constrain or downgrade the participation of children: they are critical and equal partners in the MAPS process.

Should the individual who is being mapped be present? This is a judgment call; it works both ways. We lean toward full participation. People understand an enormous amount, more than we think. Also, a MAP is a real boost for an individual who previously has been excluded. Full participation also saves time in trying to explain the process later.

## WHAT HAPPENS AT A MAP?

Mapping is a collaborative problem-solving process aided by a facilitator and a recorder. The facilitator, positioned at the open end of a half-circle formed by the participants, pre-

sents eight key questions to the group. The facilitator must be skilled in group process and have a problem-solving orientation. Most important, the facilitator must be committed to building an integrated school community. The information and ideas generated during the session are marked by the recorder on a large piece of chart paper. Public charting is vital to the MAPS process: it generates images that help participants visualize the relationships among people and actions, thus promoting the creation of additional problem-solving strategies. It also serves as a permanent record of the plans and commitments made by the group. The recorder need not be an artist, but it is vital that the MAP be printed or written clearly, using the participants' words. The chart should include contributions from everyone in the group.

## HOW TO GET STARTED

MAPS planning typically occurs in one or two sessions, and approximately three hours are required to fully address these questions:

1.  *What's a MAP?*   The facilitator begins the MAPS process by asking participants, "What is a map?" A recent group gave these answers:

    -   Something that gives direction
    -   A thing that helps you get somewhere
    -   Routes to different places
    -   A way to find a new way

2.  *What is the individual's history?*   The participants most intimate with the child being mapped (e.g., parents and family members) are asked to give a 10- to 15-minute history focusing on key milestones and events in the individual's life.

3.  *What is your dream for the individual?*   This question is intended to get people, especially parents, to imagine their vision for the child's future. Many parents of children with disabilities have lost their

ability to dream about what they really want for their child. This question helps the group focus on the direction in which the individual is now heading and encourages concrete action plans for realizing the vision.

4. *What is your nightmare?* This question is the hardest to ask but is very important to get on the table. We must understand the nightmare to prevent it. No parent has ever said, "I'm worried that my child won't attend a university, won't get an *A* on the next test, or won't learn to spell." Instead, the question brings out what is in the heart of virtually every parent of a child with a severe disability: "We're afraid our child will end up in an institution, work in a sheltered workshop, and have no one to care for her when we die."

5. *Who is the individual?* With this question, the MAPS process shifts into a no-holds-barred brainstorming mode. Participants are asked to give words or phrases that describe the person being mapped. The rule is no jargon, no labels; just describe how you see the person. The image of a unique and distinct personality should emerge. Here are examples from a recent MAP for Miller, a 14-year-old who, to some, is "severely handicapped and mentally retarded."

- She has a brother.
- She gets around in a wheelchair.
- She's lots of fun.
- She's active like crazy.
- She's radical/bad (really means good).
- She's temperamental.
- She likes to touch.
- She wants to be involved.
- She looks at you.
- She can talk some.

6. *What are the individual's strengths, abilities, gifts, and talents?* It is vital to build upon strengths and abilities. Yet all too often, we focus on the things a child with a disability cannot do. This can be a difficult question for parents, who have been struggling with negatives for so long. This question also is intended to produce a brainstormed list from the entire group. Here is part of the list generated for Miller:

- She can make us laugh.
- She moves her arms, can throw a ball.
- She likes to listen to music.
- She's persistent, tries real hard.
- She can count and remember numbers.
- She enjoys stories and movies.

7. *What are the individual's needs?* This, too, is a brainstorm. Don't let people stop each other, but don't get bogged down either. Keep it short and record people's words and perceptions. Parents, teachers, and peers often have different perceptions about needs. For Miller, it was decided that what she needed most of all was

- A communication system that lets her express her wants and feelings
- More independence with dressing and other self-care skills
- To be with her own age group
- Places to go and things to do after school
- Teenage clothes

8. *What is the plan of action?* This is the final and most important question of all. The MAPS planning group imagines what the individual's ideal day at school would look like and what must be done to make it a reality. Step by step, the MAPS group goes through an entire day, envisioning the various environments and activities the individual will experience and what kinds of resources, supports, and adaptations can be created to make the day successful. For example, a peer volunteers to meet the taxi that brings Miller to school each morning and walk with her to the classroom. During language arts period, a classmate will help Miller practice with her communication board. The principle of partial participation will be used

A portion of Miller's MAP.

500

on the playground when Miller bats in the softball game and a teammate runs the bases for her.

## A MAP IS NOT ...

- A trick, a gimmick, or a quick-fix solution to complex human problems. It is not a one-shot session that blasts a vulnerable person into the everyday life and fabric of school and community. MAPS is a problem-solving process; the plans for action are not set in stone but must be reviewed and changed as often as needed.
- A replacement for an IEP. A MAP session may provide useful information for an IEP, but it is not a substitute for the IEP process and must not be treated as such.
- A tool to make any segregated setting better. MAPS was designed to liberate people from segregated settings; it is for people and organizations who are committed to figuring out together how to get a person fully included in life.

- An academic exercise. It is a genuine, personal approach to problem solving with and on behalf of real individuals who are vulnerable. A MAP produces outcomes that have real implications for how the person will live his life.
- Just talk. MAPS is talk and action. A MAP gives clear directions and action steps for inclusion.

The metaphor for MAPS is a kaleidoscope, a beautiful instrument whose design changes constantly. We see the kaleidoscope as the outcome of each MAP. It is a medley of people working together to make something unique and better happen. It is more than anyone can do alone.

To learn more about this strategy and answer questions about what you have learned, go to the Teaching & Learning module in Chapter 12 of the Companion Website, **www.prenhall.com/heward.**

# THE CHALLENGE AND REWARDS OF TEACHING STUDENTS WITH SEVERE AND MULTIPLE DISABILITIES

Virtually every parent of a child with severe disabilities has heard a host of negative predictions from educators, doctors, and concerned friends and family. Parents often are offered such discouraging forecasts as "Your child will never talk" or "Your child will never be toilet-trained." Yet in many instances those children make gains that far exceed the professionals' original predictions: they have learned to walk, talk, toilet themselves, and perform other "impossible" tasks.

Teachers, both special and general educators, who are providing instruction to students with severe and multiple disabilities can rightfully be called pioneers on an exciting new frontier of education. More than 20 years ago, Orelove (1984) stated that professionals who were involved in educating students with severe disabilities could "look back with pride, and even awe, at the advances they have made. In a relatively brief period, educators, psychologists, and other professionals have advocated vigorously for additional legislation and funds, extended the service delivery model into the public schools and community, and developed a training technology" (p. 271).

Although significant progress has been made in the two decades since Orelove's positive assessment, a great deal more must be accomplished. Future research must increase our understanding of how students with severe disabilities acquire, maintain, and generalize functional skills. As more effective techniques for changing behavior are developed, they must be balanced with concern for the personal rights and dignity of individuals with severe disabilities. Current and future teachers of students with severe disabilities have the opportunity to be at the forefront of those developments.

Teaching students with severe disabilities is difficult and demanding. The teacher must be well organized, firm, and consistent. He must be able to manage a complex educational operation, which usually involves supervising paraprofessional aides, student teachers, peer tutors, and volunteers. The teacher must be knowledgeable about one-to-one and small-group instruction formats and be able to work cooperatively with other teachers and related-services professionals. He must maintain accurate records and constant planning for the future needs of his students. Effective communication with parents and families, school administrators, vocational rehabilitation personnel, and community agencies is also vital.

Students with the most severe disabilities sometimes give little or no apparent response, so their teachers must be sensitive to small changes in behavior. The effective teacher is consistent and persistent in designing and implementing strategies to improve learning and behavior (even if some of the students' previous teachers were not). The effective teacher should not be too quick to remove difficult tasks or requests that result in noncompliance or misbehavior. It is better to teach students to request assistance and to intersperse tasks that are easy for the student to perform.

There is a difference between either expecting miracles or being passively patient and simply working each day at the job of designing, implementing, and evaluating systematic instruction and supports. It can be a mistake to expect a miracle:

> In the beginning, we were expecting a sudden step forward, that we might somehow turn a cognitive, emotional, or social key inside the child's mind that would produce a giant leap ahead.… Such a leap would have been so gratifying, and it would have made our work so much easier. But it never happened. Instead, progress followed a slow, step-by-step progression, with only a few and minor spurts ahead from time to time. We learned to settle in for hard work. (Lovaas, 1994, n.p.)

Some might consider it undesirable to work with students with severe and multiple disabilities because of the extent of their behavioral challenges and learning problems. Yet working with students who require instruction at its very best can offer many highly rewarding teaching experiences. Much satisfaction can be felt in teaching a child to feed and dress herself independently; helping a student make friends with nondisabled peers; and supporting a young adult's efforts to live, travel, and work as independently as possible in the community. Both the challenge and the potential rewards of teaching students with severe disabilities are great.

# Tips for Beginning Teachers

## How to Make a Difference in the Lives of Children with Severe Disabilities
### by Diane K. Ellis

Effectively teaching children with severe disabilities demands focus and skill. Here are some tips that will help all teachers who work with these students—novice teachers or 20-year veterans—be more effective and obtain more enjoyment from their work.

### MAKE GOALS FUNCTIONAL AND MEANINGFUL

No matter how intensive and technically proficient, instruction will have little benefit for students with significant disabilities if it is not focused on personalized curriculum goals.

- Focus goals on teaching functional and meaningful life skills that will support the student's participation in activities at school, at home, and in the community.
- Goals should incorporate the student's strengths and interests in order to develop participation and independence within everyday activities. Too often goals are written to meet a failed test item and lack any meaning to the functional needs of the student. By the same token, stringing beads does not have much life-long significance, but being able to dress oneself does.

## BE A TEAM PLAYER; BETTER YET, BE A TEAM LEADER

In no other area is the saying "Special education is a team game" more true. Meeting the extensive and often complicated educational and related-service needs of students with severe disabilities requires the expertise of many disciplines. In addition to myself as special educator, a regular classroom teacher, and the parents, the teams for many of the children I serve include a speech therapist, an OT, a PT, a vision consultant, a hearing consultant, a school psychologist, and an assistive technology specialist. I believe the special education teacher should not only be a good team player but also leader for much of the team's work.

- Meet regularly as a team to serve the needs of students with severe disabilities.
- Use e-mail, phone calls, and notes to team members.
- Collaborate on all areas of student development. The team should collaborate on not only the development of IEP goals and intervention plans but also the ongoing evaluation of the plan.
- Be a good team member by always contributing ideas and asking questions.

## ALWAYS INCLUDE THE FAMILY

Families of children with severe disabilities are often overwhelmed by the needs of their child and intimidated by the team process. You can support and facilitate the involvement of each child's family.

- Coach family members on how to become advocates for their children early on. This skill will become even more vital as their child grows and they need to access adult service providers. Provide parents and families with resources from trusted sites on the Internet and from books.
- Listen to and respect what families tell you. Remember that the family is the only real constant on the student's team; the professionals on the team tend to come and go. Family members know their children better than anyone else.
- Invite parents to your classroom.

## FOCUS ON THE POSITIVE

Use positive behavioral supports in your quest to change challenging behavior in the classroom. Not only are positive approaches more effective than constantly nagging and reprimanding students for their misbehavior, rewarding desirable behavior also teaches students what to do, not just what *not* to do. When teachers rely on punitive consequences to control behavior, the classroom environment acquires a negative and unpleasant tone. Students will model the behavior of the adults in interacting with others and will reinforce this negativity. I have observed classrooms where other students will "punish" a student as they have seen a teacher do.

- Be proactive and use frequent praise and positive consequences for desirable behavior.
- Teach students alternative, acceptable ways to communicate their wants and needs.
- Get students involved in self-regulating their own behavior by providing visual cues, photo activity schedules, and simple ways to record their performance.

## WATCH FOR AND REVEL IN SMALL MEASURES OF PROGRESS

Students with severe disabilities do not make giant steps from one week or month to the next. Their progress needs to be measured based on tiny steps, which demonstrate their improved participation and independence within their daily lives. Although they may not get an *A* on a test, the progress they make is more significant because it is so much harder to achieve. The children who have challenged me the most are the ones who have helped me to become a better teacher!

- Break down learning tasks into small increments and determine a meaningful measure of progress, such as the number of steps in a task analysis of putting on a shirt that the student can do with reduced levels of assistance.
- Take direct and frequent measures—at least once a day for the most important objectives—of a student's performance and share each new level of independence and accomplishment with family and team members.

## BE A STUDENT OF LEARNING

Become a life-long learner in order to become the best teacher you can be. As a professional, you are ethically required to base your instruction on empirically derived best practices. As research continues to expand our knowledge of best practices, quality teachers must become students in order to grow as teachers.

- Maintain membership in CEC and other professional organizations.
- Keep abreast of current literature and best-practice research.
- Take every opportunity to attend seminars, trainings, and conferences offered in your area of expertise.

# KEY TERMS AND CONCEPTS

To print your own set of SAFMED flash cards for studying and mastering these terms, go to the Companion Website, **www.prenhall.com/heward.**

closed head injury, p. 478
deaf-blindness, p. 473
functional assessment, p. 491
multiple disabilities, p. 473
open head injury, p. 478

partial participation, p. 490
profound disabilities, p. 471
severe disabilities, p. 469
traumatic brain injury, p. 477

# SUMMARY

## Definitions and Prevalence of Severe and Multiple Disabilities

- Students with severe disabilities need instruction in many basic skills that most children without disabilities acquire without instruction in the first 5 years of life.
- Students with profound disabilities have pervasive delays in all domains of functioning at a developmental level no higher than 2 years.
- TASH defines persons with severe disabilities as "individuals of all ages who require extensive ongoing support in more than one major life activity in order to participate in integrated community settings and to enjoy a quality of life that is available to citizens with fewer or no disabilities."
- Students with dual sensory impairments cannot be accommodated in special education programs designed solely for students with hearing or visual impairments. Although the vast majority of children labeled deaf-blind have some functional hearing and/or vision, the dual impairments severely impede learning of communication and social skills.
- Students with severe disabilities frequently have multiple disabilities, including physical problems, and usually look and act markedly different from children without disabilities.
- Students with severe and multiple disabilities are served and counted under several disability categories, making prevalence figures hard to determine.
- Estimates of the prevalence of severe disabilities range from 0.1% to 1% of the population.

## Characteristics of Students with Severe and Multiple Disabilities

- Students with severe disabilities need instruction in many basic skills that most children without disabilities learn without help. Children with severe disabilities may show some or all of the following behaviors or skill deficits: slow acquisition rates for learning new skills, difficulty in generalizing and maintaining newly learned skills, severe deficits in communication skills, impaired physical and motor development, deficits in self-help skills, infrequent constructive behavior and interaction, and frequent inappropriate behavior.
- Despite their intense challenges, students with severe disabilities often exhibit many positive characteristics, such as warmth, humor, sociability, and persistence.
- Despite their limitations, children with severe disabilities can and do learn.

## Causes of Severe Disabilities

- Brain disorders, which are involved in most cases of severe intellectual disabilities, are the result of either brain dysgenesis (abnormal brain development) or brain damage (caused by influences that alter the structure or function of a brain that had been developing normally up to that point).

- Severe and profound disabilities most often have biological causes, including chromosomal abnormalities, genetic and metabolic disorders, complications of pregnancy and prenatal care, birth trauma, and later brain damage.
- In about one-sixth of all cases of severe disabilities, the cause cannot be clearly determined.

## Definition of of Traumatic Brain Injury

- Traumatic brain injury is an acquired injury to the brain caused by an external physical force, resulting in total or partial functional disability or psychosocial impairments, or both, that adversely affects a child's educational performance.
- Each year, 1 in 500 school-age children will be hospitalized with traumatic head injuries.
- Traumatic brain injury is the leading cause of death in children and the most common acquired disability in childhood.

## Types and Causes of Traumatic Brain Injury

- Open head injuries are the result of penetration of the skull. Closed head injuries are more common and result from the head hitting a stationary object with such force that the brain slams against the inside of the cranium.
- Major causes of traumatic brain injury in children are car and bicycle accidents, gunshot wounds, shaken baby syndrome, falls, and accidents during contact sports.
- A mild brain injury results in a concussion (a brief or momentary loss of consciousness), usually without any subsequent complications.
- A moderate brain injury usually results in contusions (bruising, swelling, and bleeding), hematomas (aggregation or clotting of blood), loss of consciousness, and significant cognitive and behavioral impairments for many months.
- In addition to brain contusions, hematomas, and damage to the nerve fibers or axons, a severe brain injury results in a coma and often permanant impairments in functioning.

## Characteristics of Children with Traumatic Brain Injury

- Impairments caused by brain injuries fall into three main categories: (1) physical and sensory changes (e.g., lack of coordination, spasticity of muscles); (2) cognitive impairments (e.g., short- and long-term memory deficits, difficulty maintaining attention and concentration); and (3) social, behavioral, and emotional problems (e.g., mood swings [emotional lability], self-centeredness, lack of motivation).

## Educational Approaches

- A curriculum based on typical developmental milestones is inappropriate for most students with severe disabilities.
- Students with severe disabilities must be taught skills that are functional, age-appropriate, and directed toward the community. Interaction with typically developing students should occur regularly.
- Students with severe disabilities should be taught choice-making skills.
- The emphasis of research and training in communication for persons with severe disabilities has shifted from the remediation of specific forms of communication to a focus on functional communication in any mode that enables communication partners to establish shared meanings.
- Some students with severe disabilities use augmentative and alternative systems of communication (AAC), such as gestures, various sign language systems, pictorial communication boards, PECS, and electronic communication aids.

- Students with severe disabilities should also be taught age-appropriate recreation and leisure skills.
- Because each student with severe disabilities has many learning needs, teachers must carefully prioritize and choose IEP objectives and learning activities that will be of most benefit to the student and his family.
- Effective instruction of students with severe disabilities is characterized by these elements:
  - The student's current level of performance is precisely assessed.
  - The skill to be taught is defined clearly.
  - The skills are ordered in an appropriate sequence.
  - The teacher provides clear prompts or cues to the student.
  - The student receives immediate feedback and reinforcement from the teacher.
  - Strategies that promote generalization of learning are used.
  - The student's performance is directly and frequently assessed.
- Partial participation is both a philosophy for selecting activities and a method for adapting activities and supports to enable students with severe disabilities to actively participate in meaningful tasks they are not able to perform independently.
- The teacher of students with severe disabilities must be skilled in positive, instructionally relevant strategies for assessing and dealing with challenging and problem behaviors.
- Research and practice are providing increasing support for the use of integrated small-group instruction arrangements with students with severe disabilities.
- Students with severe disabilities are more likely to develop social relationships with students without disabilities if they attend their home school and are included at least part of the time in the regular classroom.
- Although the initial reactions of many general education teachers who have a student with severe disabilities placed in their classrooms are negative, those apprehensions and concerns often transform into positive experiences as the student becomes a regular member of their classroom.

## The Challenge and Rewards of Teaching Students with Severe and Multiple Disabilities

- Teachers must be sensitive to small changes in behavior. The effective teacher is consistent and persistent in evaluating and changing instruction to improve learning and behavior.
- Working with students who require instruction at its very best can be highly rewarding to teachers.

**Companion Website** To check your comprehension of chapter contents, go to the Guided Review and Quiz modules in Chapter 12 of the Companion Website, **www.prenhall.com/heward.**

# GIFTEDNESS AND TALENT

by Jane Piirto
and William L. Heward

# Featured Teacher

### PATRICIA CONCEPCION LAMBERT

HUNTER COLLEGE ELEMENTARY SCHOOL
NEW YORK, NEW YORK

#### Education—Teaching Credentials—Experience
- B.A., psychology, Hunter College, 1974; M.S., elementary education, Hunter College, 1981; postgraduate degree in administration and supervision, Hunter College, 1996
- New York State teaching certificate, nursery–grade 6
- 22 years of experience as educator of gifted and talented children

I was walking in Central Park one day when a very tall man came up to me and said, "Ms. Lambert?" I looked up at him, a little perplexed, and he said, "I'm sure you don't recognize me because the last time you saw me I was up to your knee. You were my first-grade teacher, and my family moved to Virginia the next year."

As he smiled, I instantly remembered his little face in my classroom more than 15 years ago. "How are you, Ali?" I asked. "And how are your parents? I remember your mom worked at a university, and your dad was an artist."

"I can't believe you remember my name, let alone the occupation of my parents! We are all fine. I've graduated from college with a degree in computer science and now work for Bill Gates. I never forgot you and how much you made me feel I could do whatever it was that I set my mind to do. I remember how you got me interested in many things, especially ancient Egypt."

Ali and I stood there for about 30 minutes reminiscing about his time at Hunter Elementary and catching up on life. Finally we said our good-byes, promising to keep in touch. He took a couple of steps away and then turned around and said, "Oh yeah, I still have the canopic jar that I made in your class, and I keep it right next to my diploma! Thanks for everything." It was a day that I will never forget.

I was a teacher of the gifted for 22 years. All that time was spent in various positions at the Hunter College Elementary School in New York City. This school is unique. The average IQ of our students is about 150, and they come from all racial and ethnic groups in the borough of Manhattan.

Here in New York City, and, I'm sure, elsewhere, there seems to be a public assumption that teaching gifted children is an elitist position and that they are members of an elitist population. I beg to differ. All children deserve an education that is developmentally appropriate and differentiated in a manner that meets their needs. Gifted children are entitled to the same services that one would provide to any category of child in need. Each year we welcome bright little children to an elementary school experience that focuses on fast-paced, in-depth learning not available in most elementary schools. The school is tuition-free, and we help train many student teachers not only from Hunter College but also from Teachers College at Columbia University and other city colleges.

## Focus Questions

- Why do students who are very bright need special education?

- How has the evolving definition of giftedness changed the ways in which students are identified and served?

  - What provisions should be made to accurately identify students with outstanding talents who are from diverse cultural groups or have disabilities?

  - How can the regular classroom teacher provide instruction at the pace and depth needed by gifted and talented students while meeting the needs of other students in the classroom?

  - Should gifted students be educated with their same-age peers or with older students who share the same intellectual and academic talents and interests?

After teaching in kindergarten, first grade, second grade, and several mixed-age early childhood classes, and after a stint as the after-school program coordinator, I became principal of Hunter. The students are taught in self-contained classrooms of 24 students each with a head teacher (and an assistant teacher in the primary grades). We have specialists in science, mathematics, the arts, music, chess, learning disabilities (yes, some gifted children have learning disabilities), foreign languages, and physical education.

We have several objectives for our students. These encompass not only academic intelligence but emotional intelligence as well. Students are guided to become independent thinkers who can work both critically and creatively. We plan interdisciplinary instruction so that the depth and breadth of educational experiences will afford students opportunities to see and make connections across and within curricula areas. For example, among other mathematics goals in kindergarten, the child should understand the meaning of numbers in the real world. The concept of symmetry should be introduced. Whole numbers through 20, sorting by attributes, tallying and organizing information, graphing, picture graphs, bar graphs, estimation, comparison of sets, number patterns, introduction of addition and subtraction algorithms, addition facts to 10, and counting by numbers other than l should be part of the kindergarten mathematics curriculum for academically talented children. As the reader can see, these are advanced academic objectives because gifted children are precocious—that is, they have academic abilities similar to children who are several years older than they are.

Based on the work of Daniel Goleman (1995), we have created a parallel curriculum in emotional intelligence that determines how well one uses the raw intellect that he or she possesses. The following goals are important in educating the young gifted child for emotional intelligence:

1. Children will be able to see things from another's point of view (empathy). When reading books, children are asked to find alternative endings based on another character's point of view. Reading the book *The True Story of the Three Little Pigs* by Jon Scieszka is a wonderful way to introduce children to this concept.
2. Children will be able to control impulsive behavior (self-awareness). Using a traffic light as a metaphor, children are asked to take a signal from themselves whenever they are feeling upset. The upset feeling is like the red light: they should stop and take a moment to note what they are feeling. Next comes the yellow light, a time to use a few moments to think about several ways in which they might respond to that feeling. Finally, they are encouraged to choose the best response from the ones that they've thought of; and like the green light, they go with the best decision.
3. Children will be able to communicate clearly and effectively (communication and cooperation). Students are given many opportunities each day to respond to one another's questions during reading, social studies, and math lessons.

We also collaborate with families. I have always had an open-door policy and encourage parents to be contributors to the educational process. Each year I send out a parent survey. I try to ensure that all families participate in a classroom activity every year. Parents may accompany the class on a field trip, bind student books, make costumes for a class play, give a lecture on a specific area of study (e.g., one parent doctor came in to discuss the human heart), etc.

What I like most about being a special educator is that it allows me to specialize in an area and become an expert in a field. I can focus on securing information and resources. My most meaningful accomplishment right now is being able to give back to the community by speaking at gifted education conferences. On a personal teacher/child level, the love that one receives from the children in the class is incomparable. What I like least is common to most teachers. The remuneration for the countless hours that one puts into activities such as developing lessons, individualizing instruction, attending work-related functions, and continuing education is not commensurate with the position.

However, having been an educator for such a long time, I have difficulty imagining doing anything else with my life. Being not only a teacher but a counselor, a nurturer, a role model, a nurse, an arbitrator, a politician, and all the other roles that one must assume when teaching a special population of children is physically demanding, but I have developed stamina over time. Teachers of the gifted and talented also need humility, for there is always a child who's smarter than you in some area. Teaching the gifted and talented is an intense experience that takes much more time than a day holds.

Our study of exceptional children thus far has focused on students with intellectual, behavioral, or physical disabilities—children who require specially tailored programs to benefit from education. Gifted and talented students lie on the other end of the continuum of cognitive, academic, artistic, and social abilities. Gifted and talented children may find that a traditional curriculum is inappropriate; it may not provide the advanced and unique challenges they require to learn most effectively. They, too, need special education to reach their potential.

Janie has just completed her report on the solar system and is word-processing it for class tomorrow. She looks out her bedroom window and wonders what might be happening on the countless planets that circle all of those stars. And she thinks about the circumstances that made life possible on the third planet from the star called Sol. What Janie is doing may not seem special; after all, most students type school reports and wonder about extraterrestrial life—until we learn that she is just 6 years old. Janie is functioning years ahead of her peers. She writes in complete sentences, expresses herself exceptionally well, and has a powerful urge to know the answers to many and varied problems.

Toney Jojola saunters down a dusty back road near his home in the southwest. Toney is excited because today his mentor and great-aunt has promised to teach him the process of applying the rich charcoal slip to the pottery he is making. His people have been making pottery for hundreds of years, but somehow it seems to take on multiple meanings in his hands. He notices and uses small variations in color and texture to embed symbolism into his pieces. Perhaps this one will have the winged serpent that he favors so much, reminding everyone that an immense trade network existed in prehistoric America that reached from present-day Canada to South America. Toney sees much in his pottery, in his ancestors who have inspired him, in the beauty that is the earth made functional, and in a desire for continuity in his life. Toney does not say much in school or express himself very well in writing, but he understands everything that is being said and talked about. He is very patient and seems tentative in his behavior, not wanting to create a disturbance that would draw attention to himself. During class he dreams of the pottery designs he will someday create in the studio that he will inherit from his great-aunt.

Malcolm, a ninth grader, runs from school to the bus stop for the bus that will take him to the local university, where he is taking his second course in creative writing. He is excited about showing his latest short story to the professor. Malcolm's prose brings into focus all of the pain he sees around him, critically analyzing the leadership of his community and nation. He believes he has a message that must be heard; he is powerfully moved to reach out to the disaffected, the disenfranchised, as well as the ambivalent of all races. He has many ideas for changing what he believes is wrong with his government. He believes deeply in his vision and knows he can make a difference once he learns how to communicate his message as effectively as possible. Bursting with energy and desire, Malcolm struggles to sit still while the bus moves him ever closer to his training ground for the future.

Janie, Toney, and Malcolm need special education—in the form of curriculum modifications and specialized instructional activities—to enhance and develop their individual talents. These precocious youngsters, and others like them, will become the outstanding

To better understand the topics that will be covered in this chapter, go to the Essential Concepts and Chapter at a Glance modules in Chapter 13 of the Companion Website, **www.prenhall.com/heward**.

scientists, artists, writers, inventors, and leaders of the future. Understanding and working to develop the talents of these exceptional children is an important undertaking of special educators who work in the area of gifted and talented education.

# DEFINITIONS

*Early definitions of G&T and Marland Report*

Council for Exceptional Children — Content Standards for Beginning Teachers—G&T: Historical foundations of gifted and talented education (GT1K1) (also CC1K5).

Intelligence, creativity, and talent have been central to the various definitions of giftedness that have been proposed over the years. Lewis Terman (1925), one of the pioneers of the field, defined the gifted as those who score in the top 2% on standardized tests of intelligence. Guilford (1967) called for the identification of people with creative potential. Witty (1951), recognizing the value of including special skills and talents, described gifted and talented children as those "whose performance is consistently remarkable in any potentially valuable area" (p. 62). These three concepts continue to be reflected in the current and still-evolving definitions of gifted and talented children.

## Federal Definitions

The first federal definition of the gifted and talented came with the 1972 Marland Report. This definition said that gifted and talented children were found in six areas:

> Children capable of high performance include those with demonstrated and/or potential ability in any of the following areas, singly or in combination:
>
> - General intellectual ability
> - Specific Academic Aptitude
> - Creative or productive thinking
> - Leadership ability
> - Ability in the visual or performing arts
> - Psychomotor ability (Marland, 1972, p. 5)

The Marland definition had the earliest and most influence on state definitions. Since its beginnings, the field of the education of the gifted and talented has sought to include multiple kinds of giftedness in its definitions, not just the high IQ or superior cognitive type of giftedness. In 1978, the federal definition was revised to eliminate psychomotor ability and include preschool children and adolescents.

*Current federal definition of G&T*

Council for Exceptional Children — Content Standards for Beginning Teachers—G&T: Issues in definition and identification of individuals with gifts and talents, including those from culturally and linguistically diverse backgrounds (GT1K5).

In 1992, a federal report titled *National Excellence: A Case for Developing America's Talent* featured a revised definition of gifted and talented children that was motivated by new cognitive research and concerns about inequity in participation in programs for the intellectually gifted. The word *gifted* was eliminated, and the terms *outstanding talent* and *exceptional talent* were embraced. The definition proposed that giftedness—or talent—occurs in all groups, across all cultures, and is not necessarily apparent in test scores but in a person's "high performance capability" in intellectual, creative, and artistic realms. Giftedness is said to connote "a mature power rather than a developing ability." Talent is identified by "observing students at work in rich and varied educational settings." The best way to find talented children is by "providing opportunities and observing performance" (pp. 54, 55). The new federal definition states:

> Children and youth with outstanding talent perform or show the potential for performing at remarkably high levels of accomplishment when compared with others of their age, experience, or environment.
>
> These children and youth exhibit high performance capability in intellectual, creative, and/or artistic areas, possess an unusual leadership capacity, or excel in specific academic fields. They require services or activities not ordinarily provided by the schools.
>
> Outstanding talents are present in children and youth from all cultural groups, across all economic strata, and in all areas of human endeavor. (*National Excellence*, 1993, pp. 54–57)

A recent survey (Stephens & Karnes, 2000) of state definitions of the gifted and talented showed that many states have now incorporated aspects of the *National Excellence* definition into their definitions of giftedness and talent. Although the general intelligence test element of the definition prevails (39 states consider superior cognitive ability as giftedness), 33 states include specific academic ability, 30 include creative thinking, 20 include the visual and performing arts, and 18 include leadership in their definitions of giftedness and talent. States with no definition of any type of outstanding talent are Massachusetts, Minnesota, Montana, New Hampshire, New Jersey, North Dakota, South Dakota, and Wyoming.

## Other Key Contemporary and Complementary Definitions

This new conception of giftedness represents a growing recognition of the importance of balancing theoretical with practical definitions of giftedness that emphasize situated problem solving (Sternberg, 1988; Sternberg & Grigorenko, 2000); talents that are context- and domain-related (Gagné, 2000, 2003; Gardner, 1983/1994, 1999; Piirto, 2004a, 2004b); and the influence of sustained, deliberate practice on the realization of a person's talent (Ericsson, 2001; Ericsson & Charness, 1994). The following definitions of gifted and talented students, offered by Joseph Renzulli, Jane Piirto, and June Maker, are examples of this contemporary view.

Many gifted and talented students display learning characteristics such as superior memory, observational powers, curiosity, creativity, and the ability to learn school-related subject matters with a minimum of drill and repetition.

*Renzulli's Three-Trait Definition.*   Renzulli's (1978, 2003) definition of giftedness is based on an interaction among three basic clusters of human traits: (1) above-average general intellectual abilities, (2) a high level of task commitment, and (3) creativity. Gifted and talented children are those

> possessing or capable of developing this composite set of traits and applying them to any potentially valuable area of human performance. Children who manifest or are capable of developing an interaction among the three clusters require a wide variety of educational opportunities and services that are not ordinarily provided through regular instructional programs. (p. 184)

Figure 13.1 illustrates how the three components of ability (actual or potential), task commitment, and creative expression are jointly applied to a valuable area of human endeavor. Like the federal definition, Renzulli's definition provides a great deal of freedom in determining who is considered gifted and talented, depending on the interpretation of "valuable area of human performance."

*Piirto's Concept of Talent Development.*   Piirto (1999b) defines the gifted as those individuals who, by way of having certain learning characteristics such as superior memory, observational powers, curiosity, creativity, and the ability to learn school-related subject matters rapidly and accurately with a minimum of drill and repetition, have a right to an education that is differentiated according to those characteristics (p. 28)

Such children become apparent early and should be served throughout their educational lives, from preschool through college. While they may or may not become producers of knowledge or makers of novelty, their education should give them the background to become adults who do produce knowledge or make new artistic and social products. Piirto's pyramid model emphasizes (1) a foundation of genetic endowment; (2) personality

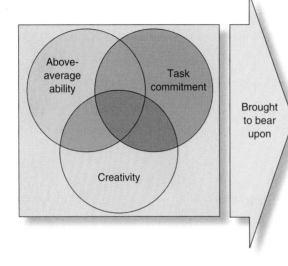

General Performance Areas

Mathematics • Visual Arts • Physical Sciences • Philosophy • Social Sciences • Law • Religion • Language Arts • Music • Life Sciences • Movement Arts

Specific Performance Areas

Cartooning • Astronomy • Public Opinion Polling • Jewelry Design • Map Making • Choreography • Biography • Film Making • Statistics • Local History • Electronics • Musical Composition • Landscape Architecture • Chemistry • Demography • Microphotography • City Planning • Pollution Control • Poetry • Fashion Design • Weaving • Play Writing • Advertising • Costume Design • Meteorology • Puppetry • Marketing • Game Design • Journalism • Electronic Music • Child Care • Consumer Protection • Cooking • Ornithology • Furniture Design • Navigation • Genealogy • Sculpture • Wildlife Management • Set Design • Agricultural Research • Animal Learning • Film Criticism • etc.

**FIGURE 13.1** **Renzulli's three-component definition of giftedness**

*Source:* From Renzulli, J. S. (2003). Conception of giftedness and its relationship to the development of social capital. In N. Colangelo & G. A. Davis (Eds.), *Handbook of gifted education* (3rd ed.), (p. 76). Needham Heights, MA: Allyn & Bacon. Used by permission.

attributes such as drive, resilience, intuition, perception, intensity, and the like; (3) the minimum intelligence level necessary to function in the domain in which the talent is demonstrated; (4) talent in a specific domain such as mathematics, writing, visual arts, music, science, or athletics; (5) and the environmental influences of five "suns": (a) the sun of home; (b) the sun of community and culture; (c) the sun of school; (d) the sun of chance; and (e) the sun of gender (see Figure 13.2). Which talent is developed depends on the "thorn" of passion, calling, or sense of vocation.

*Maker's Problem-Solving Perspective.*    Maker's dynamic perspective incorporates the three elements that appear most often within contemporary definitions of the gifted and talented: high intelligence, high creativity, and excellent problem-solving skills. She characterizes a gifted person as

> a problem solver—one who enjoys the challenge of complexity and persists until the problem is solved in a satisfying way. Such an individual is capable of: a) creating a new or more clear definition of an existing problem, b) devising new and more efficient or effective methods, and c) reaching solutions that may be different from the usual, but are recognized as being effective, perhaps more effective, than previous solutions. (Maker, 1993, p. 71)

There are numerous other conceptions of giftedness and talent, such as Robert Sternberg's (1995, 2003) triarchic theory of successful intelligence, Francoys Gagné's (2000, 2003) differentiated model of giftedness and talent, and Howard Gardner's (1983/1994, 1995) theory of multiple intelligences. To summarize, all these definitions present the new conception of intelligence and giftedness that radically departs from previous definitions by broadening the understanding of talents, reducing the focus on IQ, and emphasizing certain environmental and personality areas as well as on specific talents. In 1998, the two major associations for the gifted and talented, the Council for Exceptional Children's The Association for the Gifted (CEC-TAG), and the National Association for Gifted Children (NAGC), adopted a joint statement of core beliefs and goals incorporating the recent thinking (see Figure 13.3).

*Renzulli's, Piirto's, and Maker's conceptions of G&T*

Council for Exceptional Children   Content Standards for Beginning Teachers—G&T: Issues in definition and identification of individuals with gifts and talents, including those from culturally and linguistically diverse backgrounds (GT1K5).

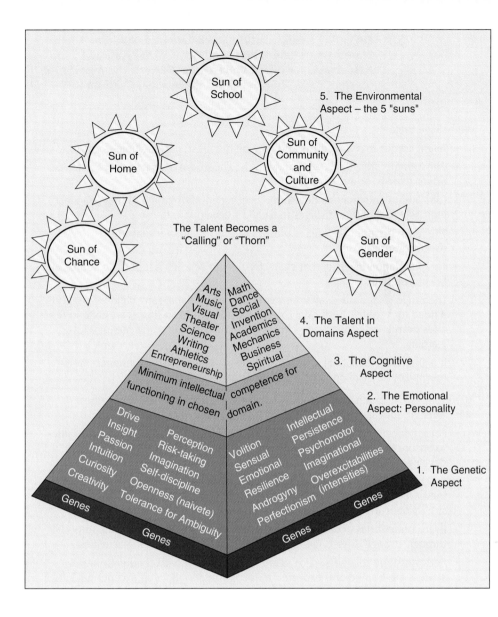

**FIGURE 13.2  Piirto pyramid of talent development**

*Source:* From Piirto, J. (2004). *Understanding creativity.* Scottsdale, AZ: Great Potential. Also in *"My teeming brain": Understanding creative writers.* Cresskill, NJ: Hampton. Original version in Piirto, J. (1994). *Talented children and adults: Their development and education.* Upper Saddle River, NJ: Merrill/Prentice Hall. Revised in Piirto, J. (1999). *Talented children and adults: Their development and education,* 2nd ed. Used with permission.

# CHARACTERISTICS

Giftedness is a complex human condition covering a wide range of abilities and traits. While the definitions of giftedness are social constructions—that is, they are not absolute but vary according to situation—there is no doubt that advanced students have special educational needs. Some students have special talents, but rarely do these match the stereotypes that many people have of giftedness. These students may not be outstanding in academics, but they may have special abilities in areas such as music, dance, art, or leadership. Gifted and highly talented individuals are found across gender, cultural, linguistic, and even disability groups. Learning and intellectual characteristics in those persons who are considered to be gifted and talented include the following (Clark, 2002; Gallagher & Gallagher, 1994; Maker, 1993; Piirto, 1999b):

- The ability to rapidly acquire, retain, and use large amounts of information
- The ability to relate one idea to another
- The ability to make sound judgments

*Cognitive and learning characteristics of G&T*

Council for Exceptional Children — Content Standards for Beginning Teachers—G&T: Cognitive characteristics of individuals with gifts and talents in intellectual, academic, creative, leadership, and artistic domains (GT2K7).

**FIGURE 13.3** Educating America's Gifted and Talented Children: A Joint Statement of Core Beliefs and Goals of the National Association for Gifted Children (NAGC) and The Association for the Gifted, The Council for Exceptional Children (CEC-TAG), 1998

We believe that:

- Talent comes in many forms and may be manifested in multiple domains.
- Children are individuals who bring to the classroom a diverse set of aptitudes, achievements, and potential.
- Gifts and talents may be developed over a period of time and may manifest themselves at different stages in a child's development.
- The full spectrum of talents is present in every cultural, racial, and socioeconomic group.
- The population diversity that characterizes our schools is a positive source of talent potential.
- The range of aptitudes, achievements, and potential among children suggests a need for varied educational experiences designed so that every child in the classroom is actively engaged in respectful, challenging, and meaningful learning.
- It is the responsibility of educators to design educational experiences to maximize the development of talents in all children.

Therefore, we as organizations join in a common commitment to the highest standards for educational practices in an effort to ensure that:

- Local educational agencies provide a continuum of educational opportunities to ensure that a sufficient variety of options is available to assist each child's development in one or more apparent or emergent area of strength.
- Teachers have the opportunity to learn and are encouraged to implement methods necessary to develop the strength areas within every child, from the struggling learner to those who learn more quickly.
- Every student has access to opportunities to develop his or her full potential through strength-based learning and highly engaging learning activities.
- Educators and related-service personnel who work with children in our schools are trained and expected to recognize and develop exceptional gifts and talents in any domain such as the traditional academic areas, the arts, or leadership.
- Curriculum reflects a high level of challenge and is adapted in classrooms to the educational needs of students in that classroom.

To achieve these goals, we envision a partnership based on cooperation, collaboration, and commitment that will result in a common understanding that talent development and enhancement contribute positively to the goal of providing maximum learning for each and every child.

- The ability to perceive the operation of larger systems of knowledge that may not be recognized by the typical person
- The ability to acquire and manipulate abstract symbol systems
- The ability to solve problems by reframing the question and creating novel solutions

Figure 13.4 presents 18 characteristics that can be used to identify gifted children under age 4. Some children may have intellectual abilities found only in 1 child in 1,000 or 1 child in 10,000. Silverman (1995) identifies the following characteristics for the highly gifted—children with IQ scores three standard deviations or greater above the mean (IQ > 145):

## FIGURE 13.4   Identifiers of young talent from the EAEP Project

1. *Exceptional learner* (acquisition and retention of knowledge)
   a. Exceptional memory
   b. Learns quickly and easily
   c. Advanced understanding/meaning of area

2. *Exceptional user of knowledge* (application and comprehension of knowledge)
   a. Exceptional use of knowledge
   b. Advanced use of symbol systems: expressive and complex
   c. Demands a reason for unexplained events
   d. Reasons well in problem-solving: draws from previous knowledge and transfers it to other areas

3. *Exceptional generator of knowledge* (individual creative attributes)
   a. Highly creative behavior in areas of interest or talent
   b. Does not conform to typical ways of thinking, perceiving
   c. Enjoys self-expression of ideas, feelings or beliefs
   d. Keen sense of humor that reflects advanced, unusual comprehension of relationships and meaning
   e. Highly developed curiosity about causes, future, the unknown

4. *Exceptional motivation* (individual motivational attributes)
   a. Perfectionism: striving to achieve high standards, especially in areas of talent and interest
   b. Shows initiative; self-directed
   c. High level of inquiry and reflection
   d. Long attention span, when motivated
   e. Leadership: desire and ability to lead
   f. Intense desire to know

From Shaklee, B., Whitmore, J., Barton, L., Barbour, N., Ambrose, R., & Viechnicki, K. (1989). *Early assessment for educational potential and/or economically disadvantaged students.* (Grant No. R206A00160). Washington, DC: U.S. Department of Education, Office of Educational Research and Improvement.

- Intense intellectual curiosity
- Fascination with words and ideas
- Perfectionism
- Need for precision
- Learning in great intuitive leaps
- Intense need for mental stimulation
- Difficulty conforming to the thinking of others
- Early moral and existential concern
- Tendency toward introversion (pp. 220–221)

We must also realize that many lists of gifted characteristics portray gifted children as having only virtues and no flaws. The very attributes by which we identify gifted children, however, can cause problems. High verbal ability, for example, may prompt gifted students to talk themselves out of troublesome situations or allow them to dominate class discussions. High curiosity may give them the appearance of being aggressive or snoopy as they pursue anything that comes to their attention. Nevertheless, these children are born every day, and teachers and parents who are alert to such cues can notice their characteristics.

## Individual Differences among Gifted and Talented Students

Awareness of individual differences is also important in understanding gifted students. Like other children, gifted children show both inter- and intraindividual differences. For example,

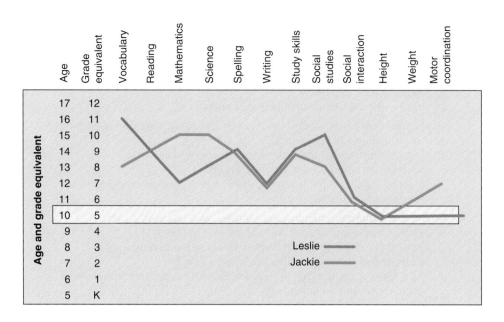

**FIGURE 13.5**
**Profiles of two gifted and talented students, both age 10 and in fifth grade**

Legend: Leslie ——— Jackie ———

Y-axis: Age and grade equivalent

| Age | Grade equivalent |
|---|---|
| 17 | 12 |
| 16 | 11 |
| 15 | 10 |
| 14 | 9 |
| 13 | 8 |
| 12 | 7 |
| 11 | 6 |
| 10 | 5 |
| 9 | 4 |
| 8 | 3 |
| 7 | 2 |
| 6 | 1 |
| 5 | K |

Columns: Vocabulary, Reading, Mathematics, Science, Spelling, Writing, Study skills, Social studies, Social interaction, Height, Weight, Motor coordination

*Inter- and intraindividual differences*

Council for Exceptional Children — Content Standards for Beginning Teachers—G&T: Similarities and differences of individuals with and without gifts and talents and the general population of learners (GT2K2). Similarities and differences among individuals with and without gifts and talents (GT2K3).

if two students are given the same reading achievement test and each obtains a different score, we can speak of *interindividual* differences in reading achievement. If a student who obtains a high reading achievement score obtains a much lower score on an arithmetic achievement test, we say the student has an *intraindividual* difference across the two areas of performance. A graph of any student's abilities would reveal some high points and some lower points; scores would not be the same across all dimensions. The gifted student's overall pattern of performance, however, may be well above the average for that grade and/or age, as we see in Figure 13.5. Leslie performs higher in vocabulary and social studies than Jackie does, however, and Jackie shows higher performance in science and mathematics than Leslie does. These are interindividual differences. Each student also has intraindividual differences in scores. For example, Leslie has the vocabulary of an 11th grader but scores only at a 7th-grade equivalent in mathematics; Jackie earned grade equivalents of 10th grade in science and mathematics and 7th grade in writing.

## Creativity

Many writers and teachers believe that creative ability is central to the definition of giftedness. Clark (1997) calls creativity "the highest form of giftedness" (p. 64), and Sternberg (1988) suggests that "gifted individuals who make the greatest long-range contributions to society are probably those whose gifts involve coping with novelty—specifically, in the area of insight. Creative and insightful individuals make discoveries and devise the inventions that ultimately change society" (p. 74).

Although we all profess to know creativity when we see it, there is no universally accepted definition of creativity. Guilford (1959, 1967, 1987), who studied the emergence of creativity as one aspect of his overall theory concerning human intelligence, describes these dimensions of cognitive creative behavior, which he called *divergent production*, in his Structure of Intellect model:

*Guilford's elements of creativity*

Council for Exceptional Children — Content Standards for Beginning Teachers—G&T: Cognitive characteristics of individuals with gifts and talents in intellectual, academic, creative, leadership, and artistic domains (GT2K7) (also GT2K2, GT7K3).

- *Fluency.* The creative person is capable of producing many ideas per unit of time.
- *Flexibility.* A wide variety of ideas, unusual ideas, and alternative solutions are offered.
- *Novelty/originality.* Unique, low-probability words and responses are used; the creative person has novel ideas.
- *Elaboration.* The ability to provide details is evidenced.
- *Synthesizing ability.* The person has the ability to link unlikely ideas together.

- *Analyzing ability.* The person has the ability to organize ideas into larger, inclusive patterns. Symbolic structures must often be broken down before they can be re-formed into new ones.
- *Ability to reorganize or redefine existing ideas.* The ability to transform an existing object into one of different design, function, or use is evident.
- *Complexity.* The ability to manipulate many interrelated ideas at the same time is shown.

Piirto (1998, 2001, 2004a, 2004b) studied creative individuals in a variety of areas and summarized the characteristics of highly creative individuals within their fields of creativity, thus linking their high abilities to particular areas of expertise. She reports that (1) each of these fields has specific predictive behaviors in childhood, (2) there is a developmental process in the emergence of talents in various domains, and (3) IQ scores should be minimized in importance and subsumed into a more contextual view of children who are performing tasks within specific domains. Piirto maintains that all people are creative and that creativity is more an aspect of personality than a type of giftedness. Testing for creative potential is often invalid and not reliable (Piirto, 1998, 2004b; Gagné, 2003).

Although many gifted and talented students do become scientists, physicians, inventors, and great artists and performers, they have no obligation to do so. Providing them with the differentiated education they need should not be predicated on an expectation that they "owe society," any more than all children do.

It is often difficult to differentiate between the concepts of talent and creativity, perhaps because they may exist on a continuum rather than as separate entities. If we examine the life of a highly talented individual, such as the famous dancer Martha Graham, we can see the relationship between creativity and talent. Her creativity was evident in her pioneering modern dance techniques and her innovative methods of expression in the choreography of the dance. However, her great talent as a dancer, seen in her elegant movements, was equally impressive and deserves notice. Creativity, talent, and/or extreme intellectual ability that is atypical for their age most often identify gifted and talented children. (See Profiles & Perspectives, "Precocity As a Hallmark of Giftedness," later in this chapter.)

Gifted and talented children can often be identified by their precociousness. Although just 13 years old, Sho Yano is a medical student at the University of Chicago.

## PREVALENCE

Using the normal curve, one would predict that 3% to 5% of students would be gifted and talented in the category of superior cognitive ability, scoring two standard deviations above the mean on a standardized intelligence test. If we include those students regarded as highly talented, estimates for the prevalence of giftedness can range as high as 10% to 15% of the total school-age population (Gagné, 2003; Renzulli & Reis, 2003).

During the 1998–1999 school year, 43 states reported serving more than 2 million students in K–12 gifted programs (Council of State Directors of Programs for the Gifted, 2000). This number ranks gifted and talented students as the second-largest group of exceptional children receiving special education services. The number and percentage of students identified as gifted and talented vary widely from state to state; for instance, six states identified more than 10% of the student population as gifted and talented, and six states identified 3% or less.

On the basis of an estimate that gifted and talented children comprise 5% of the school-age population, approximately 2.5 million additional gifted and talented children may need

*Prevalence of G&T*

**Council for Exceptional Children** Content Standards for Beginning Teachers—G&T: Prevalence of individuals with gifts and talents (GT1K6).

# Precocity As a Hallmark of Giftedness

## by Jane Piirto

Four-year-old Maria has been waiting and waiting to go to school. She plays school all the time. She is the teacher, and her dolls are the students. At her day-care center, she is the one who always leads the other kids in games because she is the only one who can read. The other kids look up to her, except when she tries to make them do things they really don't want to do, such as count by twos. The day-care center teacher told Maria's mother that Maria was very bright. When Maria went for her preschool screening, the district recommended that the school psychologist test her. The school psychologist told Maria's mother that Maria had an IQ of 145 on the Stanford-Binet Intelligence Scale, a score that put her in the 99th percentile. This score would qualify her for the district's program for the academically talented, which started at the third grade, although they did have enrichment lessons in first and second grade.

Finally, it is the first day of school; Maria turned 5 in August. She has her new dress and new shoes on. Her mother braids her hair and fastens it with new barrettes. When she gets to school, she is anxious for her mother to leave, yet still she feels shy, with all of these children here. Half of them are crying as their parents leave them. Maria looks around the room and sees a shelf of books. She always reads when she doesn't know what else to do, so she goes over to the shelf and waits for things to calm down. After all of the parents have gone, the teacher tells the children to sit on a line painted on the floor. As the children have come into the room, they have been given large name tags. The teacher sits on a small chair with the children in a semicircle around her and says, "My name is Mrs. Miller, boys and girls. Welcome to kindergarten. In kindergarten, we will learn our letters and our numbers so that we can learn to read in first grade."

"I can read already," Maria says, jumping up.

"That's nice," says Mrs. Miller. "Maria, when we want to talk, first we must stand, and then we must wait until Mrs. Miller calls on us."

"But I can read already!" Maria's voice gets petulant, and tears form in the corners of her eyes.

"Maria, that's nice," said Mrs. Miller. "But in kindergarten, we will learn how to read right. Please sit down now."

Maria is chagrined. Feeling shame and embarrassment, she sits down. She has taken the first step to underachievement.

Underachievement is the prevailing situation in the education of academically talented young children in most schools today. By the time she has been socialized into the kindergarten milieu, Maria will have learned to keep quiet about her abilities and even to suppress that she can read. In first grade, she will comply with the reading tasks in order to fit in. By second grade, even though she will be getting all of her work right, she will have learned that she doesn't have to put forth any effort in school in order to be the best student. By third grade, she will have learned that boredom (as long as she's quietly bored) and waiting (as long as she's not disruptive while she's waiting) are what the school seems to expect of her. By fourth grade, when she gets into a pullout program for academically talented students, she will resent it when the teacher of the academically talented tries to challenge her and, in challenging her, stretches her capabilities. Maria's story, unfortunately, is typical of many young academically talented children who enter the public school system.

Maria's scenario indicates the types of precocious behavior talented students might display when their abilities are great. Like other young gifted and talented children, Maria can easily do things typically seen only in older children. Even without special testing, their talents can be spotted by teachers who are sensitive to the concept of precocity. In fact, I believe the main way to recognize talented students is by their precocity: achievements resembling those of older children. I call these behaviors *predictive behaviors*. These children are often difficult to locate because they might wish to fit in and not to create disturbances; but teachers, parents, and educators who look closely can find their talents.

To further your understanding of and answer reflective questions about the concepts and issues presented here, go to the Profiles & Perspective module in Chapter 13 of the Companion Website, **www.prenhall.com/heward**.

special education (Clark, 2002). The National Association for Gifted Children (2004) estimated that there are 3 million students who could be called gifted. This discrepancy between need and the level of service may make gifted and talented children the most underserved group of exceptional children.

In fact, the No Child Left Behind Act (P.L. 107-110; Elementary and Secondary Education Amendments of 2001), which emphasizes the measurement of educational progress for all students, especially those who may risk lack of academic success, may not serve the gifted and talented students adequately (Gallagher, 2004; Kaplan, 2004). DeLacy (2004) asked these questions: (1) "What group of students makes the lowest achievement gains in school?" (2) "What group of students has been harmed most by the No Child Left Behind Act?" The answer was, "The brightest students" (p. 40). She explained that studies by various states had shown that the emphasis on bringing up the lowest-achieving students mean that the highest-achieving students are neglected and ignored while teachers concentrate on the lowest-achieving students.

Gifted students are truly our forgotten children. Neglected in our schools and ignored by our policymakers, they spend their days dozing through classes in which they aren't learning. Many suffer from depression. It is time to take them out of their holding pens and give them a chance to stretch and to grow.

# IDENTIFICATION AND ASSESSMENT

A multifactored assessment approach that uses information from a variety of sources is considered to be more accurate and equitable in identification of the gifted and talented. This approach includes data from a variety of sources, including the following:

- Group and individual intelligence tests
- Achievement tests
- Portfolios of student work
- Teacher nomination based on reports of student behavior in the classroom
- Parent nomination
- Self-nomination
- Peer nomination
- Extracurricular or leisure activities

*Multidimensional screening for G&T students*

Council for Exceptional Children — Content Standards for Beginning Teachers—G&T: Screening, pre-referral, and identification procedures for individuals with gifts and talents (GT8K4).

Thinkers in the field of education of the gifted and talented describe a comprehensive approach for identifying students who require specialized services for their talents (Clark, 2002; Johnsen, 2004). Each state has its own identification procedures. Figure 13.6 illustrates one comprehensive approach for identifying students who require specialized services for their talents. Based on an identification model first developed by the California Association for Gifted Children, this model features a progressive filtering process that refines a large pool of potentially gifted students down to a smaller, formally identified group. The process is time-consuming and thorough, beginning with the development of a large pool of potentially gifted students in the initial stage (screening); testing, consulting, and analyzing data (development of profile and case study); identification decisions

**FIGURE 13.6**
**A model for identifying gifted and talented students**

*Source:* From Clark, B. A. (2002). *Growing up gifted* (6th ed.), (p. 333). Upper Saddle River, NJ: Merrill/Prentice Hall. Reprinted by permission.

**Multidimensional Screen**

Includes:
1. Nominations–teacher, principal, psychologist, parent, peers, self
2. Teacher report on student functioning
3. Family history and student background
4. Peer identification
5. Student inventory of interests, etc.
6. Student work and achievements
7. Variety of tests, e.g., group achievement, group intelligence, etc.

**Development of Profile (Coordinator)**

*Coordinator decision to refer to committee*

*Parent consent to refer*

**Development of Case Study (Coordinator)**

Includes:
1. Screening data tests    a. Individual intelligence
2. Parent interviews        b. Specific content areas
3. Test protocols           c. Creativity tests

**Committee Meeting for Consideration**

*Committee decision to identify and place in appropriate program*

*Parent decision to place*

**Placement in Gifted Program**

**Assessment for Individual Educational Plan**

Includes:
1. Case study material
2. Functional assessment

**Appropriate Educational Program**

and placement (committee meeting for consideration; placement in gifted program); and finally the development of an appropriate educational program for the child.

Quantitative and qualitative approaches to assessment should be part of the identification process (Ryser, 2004). Types of qualitative assessment include portfolios, interviews, and observations. Observations can be made to find students who are demonstrating characteristics that indicate giftedness. Observations may be done with checklists or rating scales as well as with simple "jot down" procedures (p. 29). Interviews of peers and parents can also indicate potential talent. We can demonstrate how this process would work with a student thought to have great potential—say, the little girl Janie described at the beginning of this chapter. First, Janie's highly refined intellectual behaviors would have to be noticed by a teacher, a parent, her peers, or another person, who would then forward a nomination for additional screening. Figure 13.7 shows questions that Janie's teacher might ask. The teacher's report would contribute to the multidimensional, or multifactored, screening approach that is gaining in popularity among educators of the gifted and talented.

## FIGURE 13.7 Questions about classroom behavior that can guide a teacher's efforts to identify students who may be gifted and talented

### In the classroom does the child

- Ask a lot of questions?
- Show a lot of interest in progress?
- Have lots of information on many things?
- Want to know why or how something is so?
- Become unusually upset at injustices?
- Seem interested and concerned about social or political problems?
- Often have a better reason than you do for not doing what you want done?
- Refuse to drill on spelling, math facts, flash cards, or handwriting?
- Criticize others for dumb ideas?
- Become impatient if work is not "perfect"?
- Seem to be a loner?
- Seem bored and often have nothing to do?
- Complete only part of an assignment or project and then take off in a new direction?
- Stick to a subject long after the class has gone on to other things?
- Seem restless, out of seat often?
- Daydream?
- Seem to understand easily?
- Like solving puzzles and problems?
- Have his or her own idea about how something should be done? And stay with it?
- Talk a lot?
- Love metaphors and abstract ideas?
- Love debating issues?

*This child may be showing giftedness cognitively.*

### Does the child

- Show unusual ability in some area? Maybe reading or math?
- Show fascination with one field of interest? And manage to include this interest in all discussion topics?
- Enjoy meeting or talking with experts in this field?
- Get math answers correct, but find it difficult to tell you how?
- Enjoy graphing everything? Seem obsessed with probabilities?
- Invent new obscure systems and codes?

*This child may be showing giftedness academically.*

### Does the child

- Try to do things in different, unusual, imaginative ways?
- Have a really zany sense of humor?
- Enjoy new routines or spontaneous activities?
- Love variety and novelty?
- Create problems with no apparent solutions? And enjoy asking you to solve them?
- Love controversial and unusual questions?
- Have a vivid imagination?
- Seem never to proceed sequentially?

*This child may be showing giftedness creatively.*

### Does the child

- Organize and lead group activities? Sometimes take over?
- Enjoy taking risks?
- Seem cocky, self-assured?
- Enjoy decision making? Stay with that decision?
- Synthesize ideas and information from a lot of different sources?

*This child may be showing giftedness through leadership ability.*

### Does the child

- Seem to pick up skills in the arts—music, dance, drama, painting, etc.—without instruction?
- Invent new techniques? Experiment?
- See minute detail in products or performances?
- Have high sensory sensitivity?

*This child may be showing giftedness through visual or performing arts ability.*

*Source:* From Clark, B. A. (2002). *Growing up gifted* (6th ed.), (p. 332). Upper Saddle River, NJ: Merrill/Prentice Hall. Reprinted by permission.

Multidimensional screening also involves a rigorous examination of teacher reports, family history, student inventories, and work samples and perhaps the administration of group achievement or group or individual intelligence tests. However, if individual tests can be given by trained psychologists, they should be: individually administered tests are always more reliable than group tests. In many states, the coordinator of gifted services at the school, district, or regional level reviews this information and determines whether the

Assessment of young children's abilities to solve mathematical-spatial problems might include the time used to complete puzzles, the number of puzzles completed, and the particular problem-solving strategies used by the child.

results indicate a potential for giftedness and justify the referral of the case to a placement committee. If the coordinator believes there is sufficient evidence to continue, the parents are asked if they would like to refer Janie for more extensive testing to determine whether she qualifies for gifted services. The coordinator then manages the development of a case study that includes screening data, parent interviews, test protocols, an individual intelligence test, tests in specific content areas, and creativity tests. These data are compiled, organized, and presented to the placement committee for consideration. The committee determines whether Janie qualifies for services and what type of program would be best suited for her particular pattern of giftedness. The parents are an integral part of this meeting and have to agree with the results and placement decisions that are developed in committee. Janie is then placed in a gifted program and the special education teacher or person in charge of the program initiates special services. This level of assessment is more focused and uses all of the previous case study materials and other assessment data to determine where Janie should start in the program and the overall focus of the special education services she will receive.

## Multicultural Assessment and Identification

*Issues and procedures for identifying G&T children from diverse cultural groups*

Council for Exceptional Children

Content Standards for Beginning Teachers—G&T: Issues in definition and identification of individuals with gifts and talents, including those from culturally and linguistically diverse backgrounds (GT1K5) (also GT3K7, GT8K5).

Biases inherent in the identification process are primarily to blame for the underrepresentation of students from non-Asian minority groups such as African Americans, Latinos, and Native Americans in gifted programs nationally (Castellano, 2004; Ford, 1998; Grantham, 2003; Klug, 2004; Montgomery, 2001; Plummer, 1995; Van Tassel-Baska, Patton, & Prillaman, 1991). According to the U.S. Office of Education, demographic studies predict an increase in the minority-group population in the United States. The white college-age population will expand slowly until 2010 and then decline, whereas the college-age population of racial and ethnic minorities will continue to rise. In addition, minorities are not entering many important fields requiring mathematics and science skills. For example, although African Americans make up 12% of the population, they earned just 5% of the bachelor's degrees awarded in 2001 in mathematics and science, received 3% of the doctoral degrees in 2001 (National Science Foundation, 2004), and make up just 2% of all employed scientists and engineers in this country. Hispanics comprise 9% of the population but represent just 3% of the bachelor's degrees in science and mathematics, 2% of the doctoral degrees, and 2% of all employed scientists in this country (U.S. Office of the Census, 2004). Fewer students plan to major in engineering, which is a typical bastion for the gifted and talented. There has been a 35% drop in interest in engineering in the past 10 years (Field, 2004). However, there is room for optimism because, by the year 2000, 4.3 million African American, Hispanic, Asian American, and American Indian students had attended college, up from just under 2 million in 1980 (Gomstyn, 2003).

Frasier and her colleagues (1995) showed 10 core attributes of giftedness across socioeconomic, ethnic, and racial groups. Gifted and talented people across ethnic groups demonstrate (1) communication skills, (2) imagination/creativity, (3) humor, (4) inquiry, (5) insight, (6) interests, (7) memory, (8) motivation, (9) problem solving, and (10) reasoning. Many youth from special populations have not had the extensive opportunities to develop such a broad pattern of giftedness, but they have often developed special talent within a particular domain. The identification process should be designed to find the special talent. Subsequent educational service should focus on facilitating growth in this talent area. Current best practices for identifying gifted and talented students from diverse cultural groups involve a multifactored, or multidimensional, assessment process that meets these criteria (Castellano, 2003; Ford, 1998; Frasier, Garcia, & Passow, 1995; Frasier et al., 1995; Montgomery, 2001; Ortiz & Gonzales, 1991; Plummer, 1995; Tonemah, 1987; Woliver & Woliver, 1991). All sources agree on these goals for the identification of nonwhite and poor students:

- Identification should have a goal of inclusion rather than exclusion.
- Data should be gathered from multiple sources providing both objective and subjective data (e.g., parent interviews, individual intelligence testing, performance on group problem-solving tasks, motivational and behavioral factors, individual conferences with candidates).
- A combination of formal and informal testing techniques, including teacher referrals, the results of intelligence tests, and individual achievement tests, should be used.
- A generally greater sensitivity to aspects of acculturation and assimilation that allows for multiple perspectives to be identified and honored should be demonstrated.
- Identification procedures should begin as early as possible—before children are exposed to prejudice and stereotyping—and be continuous.
- Unconventional measures involving arts and aesthetic expression such as dance, music, creative writing, and crafts should be used.
- Information gathered during the identification process should be used to help determine the curriculum.

Maker (1997, 2001) developed a procedure called DISCOVER, which has been used to assess children from diverse cultural groups and females in an equitable fashion. Based on Gardner's theoretical framework of multiple intelligences, the DISCOVER assessment process involves a series of five progressively more complex problems that provide children with various ways to demonstrate their problem-solving competence by interacting with the content and with one another.

> Problem Types I and II require convergent thinking and are most similar to the types of question found on standardized intelligence and achievement tests. Type I problems are highly structured. The solver knows the solution method and must recall or derive the correct answer and involve convergent thinking. Type II problems also are highly structured, but the solver must decide on the correct method to use. Type III problems are clearly structured, but a range of methods can be used to solve them and they have a range of acceptable answers. Type IV and V problems are more open ended, less structured, and require much more divergent thinking. …Type IV problems are commonly found in tests of creativity. Type V problems are extremely ill structured. The solver must explore the possibilities, identify the questions to be answered, and determine the criteria by which an effective solution will be recognized. (Maker, Nielson, & Rogers, 1994, p. 7)

Figure 13.8 shows an example of DISCOVER problem-solving activities for four types of intelligences for children in grades K–2. Children use a Pablo kit, a 21-piece set of tangrams (geometric shapes), to demonstrate their problem-solving abilities with mathematical-spatial problems. Observers record the time used to complete the puzzles, the number of puzzles completed, and particular problem-solving strategies used by the child. A bag of toys provides the materials for assessing the child's linguistic (storytelling) skills.

Maker et al. (1994, 2001; Sarouphim, 2001) report positive results from using the DISCOVER model to assess the problem-solving abilities of students from African American, Navajo, Tohono O'Odham, and Mexican American cultural groups: (1) the children identified by the process closely resemble the cultural characteristics of the communities from which they come; (2) equitable percentages of children from various ethnic, cultural, linguistic, and economic groups are identified; (3) the process is equally effective with boys

*DISCOVER problem-solving activities*

Council for Exceptional Children · Content Standards for Beginning Teachers—G&T: Differing learning styles of individuals with gifts and talents, including those from culturally diverse backgrounds, and strategies for addressing these styles (GT3K7) (also GT8K4, GT8K5).

## FIGURE 13.8 Examples of activities for assessing K–2 children's problem-solving competence across four different types of intelligence

| Activities and Intelligences | Problem Type | | | | |
|---|---|---|---|---|---|
| | Type I | Type II | Type III | Type IV | Type V |
| Spatial | Find a piece shaped like a ____. (Teacher shows a shape.) | Find pieces that look like a rainbow. (Observer shows pictures.) | Find pieces and make mountains. (Observer shows pictures.) | Make any animal with as many pieces as you need. Tell about your animal if you want. (Observer provides connectors.) | Make anything you want to make. Tell about it if you wish. |
| Mathematical-Spatial | Complete simple tangram puzzles with a one-to-one correspondence between the tangram pieces and the puzzles. | Complete simple tangram puzzles with more than one solution that works. | Complete complex tangram puzzles with multiple solutions. | Make a square with as many tangram pieces as you can. | Make a design or a pattern with the pieces. |
| Mathematical | Complete one- and two-digit addition and subtraction problems. | Complete magic squares using addition and subtraction. | Write correct number sentences using numbers given (in any order). | Write as many correct number problems as you can with an answer of 10. | None |
| Linguistic | Provide a label for toys given. | Make groups of toys and tell how items in the group are alike. (Some are obvious.) | Make different groups of toys and tell how items in each group are alike. (Encourage going beyond the obvious.) | Tell a story that includes all your toys. | Write a story about a personal experience, something you made up, or anything you wish. |

Source: From "Giftedness, Diversity, and Problem-Solving" by C. J. Maker, A. B. Nielson, & J. A. Rogers. *Teaching Exceptional Children, 27*(1), 1994, p. 9. © 1994 by the Council for Exceptional Children. Reprinted with permission.

and girls; and (4) students identified through the process make gains equal to or greater than those of students who were identified by traditional standardized tests when placed in special enrichment programs.

Identifying gifted and talented children from diverse and underrepresented groups is, of course, just the beginning. In the absence of high-quality curriculum and instruction that is sensitive and responsive to their cultural heritage, gifted students from diverse backgrounds will not benefit. (See Diversity & Exceptionality, "Working with Gifted and Talented Native American Students," later in this chapter.)

## Gifted and Talented Girls

Cultural barriers; test and social biases; organizational reward systems; sex-role stereotyping; and conflicts among career, marriage, and family all act as external impediments to the advancement of gifted and talented women (Kerr, 1985). In reviewing the topic of gifted women, Silverman (1986) points out that the history of genius and women's roles has been contradictory (eminent contributions cannot be made from a subservient status) and that identification procedures reflect masculine (product-oriented) versus feminine (development-oriented) concepts of giftedness.

Thus, some of the key issues that appear in the literature concerning the identification and education of females who are gifted and talented involve conflicts concerning role definitions (McCormick & Wolf, 1993; Piirto, 1991; Rimm, 2000, 2002), extreme stress related to a lack of self-esteem (Genshaft, Greenbaum, & Borovosky, 1995), poor course selection based on academic choices made in middle school and high school (Clark, 2002; Boothe, 2004), and a lack of parental and general community support for female achievements (Hollinger, 1995).

## Gifted and Talented Boys

Recently, the problems and situations of gifted and talented boys have been highlighted as well (Kerr & Cohen, 2001). Among these are negative stereotyping for boys who have talent in and want to enter the arts, a boy code (Pollack, 1998) that operates against the expression of feelings and emotions, and a reluctance on the part of parents and teachers to permit boys' creative behavior. However, despite the stereotyping and name calling (nerds, geeks, etc.) that is present in U.S. schools, boys continue to outscore girls at the highest levels on tests such as the Scholastic Aptitude Test, the American College Test, the Differential Aptitude Test, and most achievement tests (Boothe, 2004).

## Gifted and Talented Students with Disabilities

It may be surprising to learn that the incidence of giftedness and talent among a large proportion of students with disabilities mirrors that of the larger general education population. So we would expect to have almost as many gifted students within the subpopulation of all students with disabilities. However, the combination of a disability and giftedness brings with it an even more complicated set of behaviors and attitudes to challenge educators and parents (Reis, Neu, & McGuire, 1995).

Whitmore and Maker (1985) conducted in-depth case studies of the needs and accomplishments of five gifted and talented students with visual, hearing, physical, and learning disabilities. They concluded that teachers and parents can foster the intellectual and talent development of children with disabilities by conveying positive, realistic expectations; encouraging independence; guiding constructive coping strategies; providing daily opportunities to build abilities and enjoy success; and pursuing positive social experiences for the child. Similar implications for practice were drawn by Willard-Holt (1998), who reported case study analyses of the academic and personality characteristics of gifted students with cerebral palsy and no speech.

An appropriate education for gifted students with disabilities requires the creation of what Neu (2003) terms a *dually differentiated* curriculum that recognizes and "meets the needs of students who exhibit two contradictory sets of learning characteristics by creating a balance between nurturing the students' strengths and compensating for their learning deficits" (p. 158).

Affective concerns for twice-exceptional and second-language learners prevail (Rance-Roney, 2004). These include issues of acculturation, including culture shock, loss of first language and second-language acquisition, and delayed identity formation.

*Identification of G&T girls and boys*

Council for Exceptional Children

Content Standards for Beginning Teachers—G&T: Issues in definition and identification of individuals with gifts and talents, including those from culturally and linguistically diverse backgrounds (GT1K5).

See "I Was Thinking About Black Holes" in the Profiles & Perspectives module of Chapter 13 of the Companion Website, **www.prenhall.com/heward**.

The intellectual abilities and talents of children with disabilities are fostered by daily opportunities to practice superior abilities and enjoy the feelings of success.

# Working with Gifted and Talented Native American Students

Because of many Native American cultures' high valuation of group effort and the esteem accorded to an individual who works toward a group goal with little motivation for personal glory, teachers of gifted Native American students should design group activities as often as possible and be keenly aware of the contributions of the group goal of all participants, even those who are not demonstrably leadership-oriented. The Native American group member may seem quiet and uninvolved but will contribute where possible in a meaningful way, perhaps unobtrusively. Teachers should also look for knowledge that is demonstrated in ways other than verbally, perhaps in activities or visually.

Furthermore, teachers should be as aware as possible of the cultural heritage of all children in the classroom, Native Americans included. Sensitivity to Native American cultures can result in lessons that the gifted Native Americans may be able to relate to wholeheartedly, and assessments that take into consideration these cultural differences. Teachers should consider the do's and don'ts shown in Table A when working with gifted Native American students.

**TABLE A**  **Do's and don'ts for teachers of gifted and talented Native American students**

| Do | Don't |
|---|---|
| Present native peoples as appropriate role models with whom a native child can identify | Single out native children, asking them to describe their family's traditions |
| Avoid arts and crafts activities that trivialize native dress, dance, or ceremony | Assume that you have no native children in your class |
| Accurately know the history of native peoples, past and present, before attempting to teach it | Do or say anything that would embarrass a native child |
| Present native people as separate from each other, with unique cultures, languages, spiritual beliefs, and dress | Use ABC books that have an I for Indian or an E for Eskimo |
| Teach native history as a regular part of U.S. history | Use counting resources that count Native Americans |
| Use materials that put history in an objective perspective | Use stories that show non-native children "playing Indian" |
| Use materials that present native heroes who fought to defend their people | Use picture books that show animals dressed as Native Americans |
| Discuss the relationship between native people and the colonists and what went wrong with it | Use books that show native people as savages, primitive craftspeople, or simple tribal people, now extinct |
| Use materials that show respect for and understanding of the sophistication and complexities of native societies | Have children dress up as Native Americans, with paper bag costumes or paper feather headdresses |

*continues*

| Do | Don't |
|---|---|
| Use respectful language when teaching about native peoples | Let children play with Native American artifacts borrowed from a museum or library |
| Use primary source materials—speeches, songs, poetry, writings—that show the linguistic skills of people who come from oral traditions | Teach about Native Americans only at Thanksgiving |
| Use materials that show native women, elders, and children as integral parts of native societies | Use insulting terms, such as squaw, papoose, brave, Indian giver, wild Indians, Indian blankets, or wagon burners |
| Talk about lives of native peoples in the present | Use books that portray native women and elders as subservient to warriors |
| Read and discuss good poetry, suitable for young people, by contemporary native writers | Assume that any native person knows details of other native nations |

*Source:* Foley, K., & Seknandore, O. (2003). Gifted education for the Native American student. In J. A. Castellano (Ed.), *Special populations in gifted education: Working with diverse gifted learners* (pp. 117–118). Boston: Allyn & Bacon. Reprinted by permission.

To further your understanding of and answer questions about what you have learned, go to the Diversity & Exceptionality module in Chapter 13 of the Companion Website, **www.prenhall.com/heward**.

# Educational Approaches

## Curricular Goals

The overall goal of educational programs for gifted and talented students should be the fullest possible development of every child's actual and potential abilities. In the broadest terms, the educational goals for these youngsters are no different from those for all children. Feelings of self-worth, self-sufficiency, civic responsibility, and vocational and avocational competence are important for everyone. However, some additional specific educational outcomes are especially desirable for gifted and talented students.

Gifted students need both content knowledge and the abilities to develop and use that knowledge effectively. Most educators of gifted and talented students agree that the most important concern in developing appropriate curriculum is to match the students' specific needs with a qualitatively different curricular intervention. According to Kaplan (1988), a *differentiated curriculum* should do the following:

1. be responsive to the needs of the gifted student as both a member of the gifted population and as a member of the general population.
2. include or subsume aspects of the regular curriculum.
3. provide gifted students with opportunities to exhibit those characteristics that were instrumental in their identification as gifted individuals.
4. not academically or socially isolate these students from their peers.
5. not be used as either a reward or a punishment for gifted students. (p. 170)

Piirto (1999a) recommends that curriculum and instruction for gifted and talented students should have the following characteristics:

- *Be based on learning characteristics of academically talented students in their area of strength.* These characteristics include "their ability to learn at a faster rate; their ability to think abstractly about content that is challenging; their ability to think productively, critically, creatively, and analytically; and their ability to constantly and rapidly

*Functions and characteristics of differentiated curriculum*

 Council for Exceptional Children — Content Standards for Beginning Teachers—G&T: Differential curriculum needs of individuals with gifts and talents (GT7K6) (also GT7K2, GT7K5).

529

increase their store of knowledge, both knowledge of facts and knowledge of processes and procedures" (p. 365).

- *Possess academic rigor.*    The widespread abuse of grading practices, the dumbing down of the curriculum, and the lowered expectations of teachers have all sapped curriculum of its strength and rigor. Research skills, keyboarding and computer use, speed reading, at least one foreign language, and interpersonal and affective development should be systematically taught as part of the curriculum. There is a distinct need to increase the relevance, discipline, and depth of current curriculum, primarily within the regular education setting, where most gifted students are for most of the day.

- *Be thematic and interdisciplinary.*    Academically talented students should be exposed to the structures, terminologies, and methodologies of various disciplines. The skills of systematic investigation are fundamental abilities that gifted students use throughout a lifetime of learning. These skills include the use of references, the use of the library, the gathering of information (data), and the reporting of findings in a variety of ways. These skills may ultimately be used in diverse settings, such as law and medical libraries, museums, chemical and electrical laboratories, theatrical archives, and national parks.

Feldhusen and Moon (1995) advocate the development of an individualized growth plan designed to develop a broad program of services for gifted and talented students. In some states (for example, Florida and Ohio), an individualized curriculum plan designed to develop a broad program of services for gifted students is required. These plans differ from an IEP along several important dimensions: (1) it is not a requirement for services to be provided; (2) it is more flexible, having no time restrictions, reporting requirements, or physical boundaries; and (3) it is primarily collaboratively planned but essentially student-directed. The growth plan should include assessment information, student-generated goals (in consultation with others), and the recommended activities for accomplishing these goals. A key feature of this approach is that the student is guided toward the establishment of her own goals and is an active participant in all instructional and evaluative activities.

## Differentiating Curriculum: Acceleration and Enrichment

Differentiation is an educational strategy. *Differentiation* is a broad term referring to the need to tailor teaching environments, curricula, and instructional practices to create appropriately different learning experiences for different students. The special education premise—that learners differ in important ways—is the guiding premise of differentiation. The point is to engage learners in instruction through different learning modalities, appeal to differing interests, use varied rates of instruction, and provide varied degrees of complexity within and across a challenging and conceptually rich curriculum.

Because gifted students learn at a faster rate than most students and can absorb and reconfigure more concepts, they benefit from a differentiated curriculum that is modified in both its pace and depth (Piirto, 1999a). **Acceleration** is the general term for modifying the pace at which the student moves through the curriculum; **enrichment** means probing or studying a subject at a greater depth than would occur in the regular curriculum.

*Acceleration*

Council for Exceptional Children

Content Standards for Beginning Teachers—G&T: Acceleration, enrichment, and counseling within a continuum of service options for individuals with gifts and talents (GT5K4) (also GT7K2).

*Acceleration.*    Acceleration is permitting the student to move as swiftly as possible through the required material. What the classroom teacher decides to do to differentiate for the academically talented student depends on the subject matter. There are essentially two types of curriculum material: (1) that which readily lends itself to enrichment, such as reading or social studies; and (2) that which readily lends itself to acceleration, such as mathematics or foreign languages. Subjects that are sequential are candidates for accelerative treatment. In mathematics, a child must learn to add before subtracting, must learn to multiply before dividing. By the time an academically talented child is in the fourth grade, he or she will probably have mastered the skills of reading; enrichment with more difficult reading matter is a way of differentiation. However, in mathematics, the child must be taught; and the sequence of mathematics proceeds from arithmetic to algebra to calculus, etc. Often, one of the most difficult tasks for the teacher of the academically talented is to persuade the administration and fellow teachers that acceleration in mathematics is necessary for the academically talented student and that this acceleration must take place in the structure of more advanced course taking.

Academically talented students often need less explanation; they just need to know the next step. A young academically talented student interested in fractal geometry and attending the Johns Hopkins University summer program told how he had sat, bored, during a plane geometry class that was required at his school for intellectually academically talented students but where testing out of a course was not permitted. To this student, plane geometry consisted of nothing but "two points on a line, two points on a line." Even though the plane geometry class was being offered to eighth graders, whereas in most schools it is offered to sophomores, this student had already mastered the material and was interested in fractal geometry. The high point in his day was being able to ask the teacher one or two questions about fractal geometry at the end of the period when the students began their homework. Although the teacher kept him pointed in the right direction, and he experimented with fractal geometry on his home computer, an accelerated curriculum would have prevented this student from having to sit through plane geometry day after day.

Silverman (1995) believes that acceleration is a "necessary response to a highly gifted student's faster pace of learning" (p. 229). Southern and Jones (1991) listed 15 types of options that they call acceleration options:

1. Early entrance
2. Grade skipping
3. Continuous progress
4. Self-paced instruction
5. Subject-matter acceleration
6. Combined classes
7. Curriculum compacting
8. Telescoping curriculum
9. Mentorships
10. Extracurricular programs
11. Concurrent enrollment
12. Advanced placement
13. Credit by examination
14. Correspondence courses
15. Early entrance into junior high, high school, or college

Of these methods for acceleration, the regular classroom teacher should consider continuous progress, self-paced instruction, and curriculum compacting.

One commonly heard concern is that early admission and grade skipping will lead to social or emotional problems because the child will be in a classroom with older students who are more advanced physically and emotionally. School personnel and parents are usually concerned that talented students will suffer from the pressure to achieve at higher levels and will burn out or become social misfits. Although this concern is understandable, some research shows that if acceleration is done properly, few, if any, socioemotional problems result (Colangelo, Assouline, & Gross, 2004; Southern & Jones, 1991). After reviewing a decade of longitudinal research on the academic acceleration of mathematically precocious youths, Swiatek (1993) found no evidence that acceleration harms willing students either academically or socially. In a meta-analysis of 23 studies of acceleration, Kulik (1992a, 1992b) found that students whose classes were accelerated generally outperformed those who were not accelerated but were of the same ability levels. More recent studies (Colangelo, Assouline, & Gross, 2004) have confirmed these findings; and a nationwide push for accelerative solutions for gifted students has, at this writing, begun in many states.

*Enrichment.*    Enriching the content of instruction to include more innovation, novelty, and sophistication is the most common method of differentiating curriculum for academically talented students. The use of new teaching techniques is also advocated, including new technologies for the organization, manipulation, and presentation of student products. Enriching the curriculum generally involves adding new and different information from a variety of disciplines outside the traditional curriculum. This is the strategy of choice among most regular education teachers who are attempting to provide additional opportunities for gifted and talented students in their classrooms. It is important to remember that enrichment is meant to be thoughtfully and systematically applied to the educational program of targeted students.

Enrichment experiences let students investigate topics of interest in greater detail than is ordinarily possible with the standard school curriculum. Topics of investigation may be based on the ongoing activities of the classroom but may permit students to go beyond the limits of the day-to-day instructional offerings. However, by allowing the students to help define the area of interest and independently access a variety of information and materials, the teacher can learn to facilitate the development of gifted and talented students' competencies and skills.

Enrichment is not a "do-your-own-thing" approach with no structure or guidance. Children involved in enrichment experiences should not be released to do a random, haphazard project. A basic framework that defines limits and sets outcomes is necessary. Projects should have purpose, direction, and specified outcomes. A teacher should provide guidance where necessary—and to the degree that is necessary—to keep students working efficiently.

Although acceleration and enrichment are often viewed as separate options for talented students, as Southern and Jones (1991) point out, the two strategies are intertwined: "advanced study in any discipline may entail the kind of activities normally associated with enrichment" (p. 22). Enrichment is supposed to broaden the curriculum and include material that is not in the regular course of study. However, acceleration often involves advanced material not contained in the regular course of study.

## Lesson Differentiation in the Regular Classroom

In a well-differentiated curriculum the student competes against him or herself more than against other students. The teacher modifies content, activities (or processes), and products by student readiness, interest, and learning profile. Methods for differentiation within the regular classroom include curriculum compacting, tiered lessons, and using Bloom's taxonomy as a guideline for phrasing questions and creating lesson activities.

*Curriculum Compacting.*    Many gifted and talented students have already mastered much of the content of the regular curriculum when the school year begins. **Curriculum compacting** involves compressing the instructional content and materials so that academically able students have more time to work on more challenging materials. One study found that when teachers used curriculum compacting to eliminate 36% to 54% of content in mathematics or language arts curricula for 336 students in grades two through six with demonstrated advanced content knowledge and superior academic ability, there were no perceivable differences in achievement test scores between gifted students whose curriculum had been compacted and those who had received the regular curriculum (Reis, Westberg, Kulikowich, & Purcell, 1998). Another study showed that when teachers compacted the curriculum, gifted and talented students scored significantly higher on tests of mathematics and science concepts after the content was altered (Reis, 1995).

Three steps are involved in curriculum compacting: (1) assess the target content areas, (2) determine the content to be eliminated, and (3) substitute more appropriate content. Step 3 is the most difficult for teachers (Renzulli and Reis, 2004), as many teachers have "a lack of expertise in knowing what to substitute for high-ability students" (p. 98). When

*Enrichment*

Council for Exceptional Children   Content Standards for Beginning Teachers—G&T: Acceleration, enrichment, and counseling within a continuum of service options for individuals with gifts and talents (GT5K4) (also GT7K2).

*Curriculum compacting*

Council for Exceptional Children   Content Standards for Beginning Teachers—G&T: Acceleration, enrichment, and counseling within a continuum of service options for individuals with gifts and talents (GT5K4) (also GT7K2).

pretesting academically talented students to find out what they already know, the most difficult problems or content should be presented first. Students who can solve the most difficult problems do not need to do the other, easier problems (Winebrenner, 2001).

For curriculum compacting to be effective, teachers must have a substantial understanding of the curricular content and not only condense the material but also modify its presentation, create more meaningful instruction, and evaluate that instruction for individual students. For example, Juan's teacher, Mr. Dominguez, suspects that Juan has already mastered substantial amounts of the mathematics that students are doing in the fourth grade, perhaps by as much as two grade levels. To discover if Juan is a good candidate for curricular compacting, Mr. Dominguez first determines the scope and sequence of the mathematics problems that Juan should be able to do in the fifth and sixth grades. Then he constructs an evaluation process that will accurately determine at what level Juan is able to perform the mathematics problems. If Juan is found to have mastered the content and strategies of the higher-level math, then Mr. Dominguez must design and provide replacement activities that are a more challenging and productive use of Juan's time.

*Tiered Lessons.* A **tiered lesson** provides different extensions of the same basic lesson for groups of students of differing abilities. For example, after the whole class is exposed to a basic lesson on a poem, three groups of students might work on follow-up activities or assignments of basic, middle, and high difficulty. Figure 13.9 shows an example of a tiered lesson on riddles.

*Using Bloom's Taxonomy for Phrasing Questions and Assigning Student Products.* Bloom and his colleagues (Bloom, Englehart, Furst, Hill, & Krathwohl, 1956) formulated a useful taxonomy for differentiating curriculum. **Bloom's Taxonomy** includes six different levels or types of cognitive understanding. At the *knowledge* and *comprehension* levels, the student can identify, define, explain, and summarize a concept or fact but is not required to relate the information to other concepts or material. Teachers most often ask knowledge and comprehension questions.

At the *application level*, the student uses general principles or abstract concepts in new concrete situations without being told which principle or rule is the proper one. At the *analysis level*, the student can break a concept or communication into its elements or parts, making hierarchical and other types of relationships between the parts explicit and clear. Analysis requires students to recognize unstated assumptions, check the consistency of hypotheses, and recognize the use of propaganda techniques to demonstrate an understanding of the underlying structure, effect, or theoretical basis of the content.

*Synthesis* involves putting together parts to form a whole so that the student can produce a unique communication either through writing or speaking, produce a plan or set of operations—e.g., a proposal, a unit of instruction, or a blueprint—and show an understanding of abstract relations, classification schemes, hypotheses, and an inductive discovery of principles or generalizations. At the *evaluation* level, the student is able to make judgments about the value of something (e.g., a theory, an idea, or a method) for a given purpose based not only on internal evidence by use of criteria but also on external evidence produced by comparing the work with other works of high quality.

Figure 13.10 illustrates how Bloom's taxonomy could guide the types of questions asked and possible student products in a unit based on the Cinderella story. Although both average and high-ability students should have learning opportunities at all levels of Bloom's taxonomy, opportunities and expectations to work at the advanced levels of the taxonomy are especially important for academically talented students. However, as Clark (2002) points out, it is a mistake to think that gifted learners do not need instructional activities at the lower levels of the taxonomy. To analyze, synthesize, and evaluate information, students must possess basic knowledge and comprehension of that information. (Thomas Krathwohl, one of Bloom's colleagues, published a revised version of the taxonomy in 2002. However, its changes have not yet been widely adopted, and perhaps won't be, as the education community has enthusiastically endorsed the original.)

*Bloom's taxonomy*

Council for Exceptional Children  Content Standards for Beginning Teachers—G&T: Theories and research that form the basis of curriculum development and instructional practice (GT7K3).

## FIGURE 13.9  A tiered lesson using riddles to promote thinking and problem-solving skills

| **Author:** Ms. Erin Morris Miller (National Research Center/Gifted and Talented) | **Author's e-mail:** HOTLINX@virginia.edu |
|---|---|
| Curriculum area(s): math, science, social studies | Grade Level: 3 |
| Time required: 30 minutes | Instructional grouping: heterogeneous |

### Overview
This is a thinking skills lesson to help students practice thinking openly and flexibly. Use this lesson as a mental warm-up session before beginning a challenging lesson that requires the students to think flexibly or counterintuitively. Use this lesson to prepare the students for times when making assumptions would be bad. Examples: solving word problems in math, finding patterns in math, drawing conclusions from reading selections, and making decisions during a unit on economy. (Idea inspired by a high school advanced placement calculus teacher, Fred Pence, who began class with a puzzle to get students in the mood to problem-solve. The concept was adapted for younger students.) In this lesson students first solve a riddle as a whole class and then divide into small groups to solve additional riddles. Groups are formed according to the students' readiness to read and understand difficult vocabulary. Each group works independently as the teacher moves from group to group, facilitating discussions.

### Standards
This lesson helps students develop the skills necessary to achieve any standard that involves problem solving. Examples include math and science problems as well as dilemmas in social studies and analysis of literature.

### Materials
There are three levels of riddles. Level 1 consists of three simple riddles, level 2 consists of one medium-hard riddle, and level 3 consists of one difficult riddle.

### As a result of this lesson, students should
**know . . .**
Riddles are written puzzles.
**understand . . .**
Riddles require people to think creatively.
Riddles require people to not make assumptions.
**be able to do . . .**
Students should be able to solve riddles.

### Preassessment
One main difference between the riddles is the difference in the vocabulary involved. Groups should be formed based on the students' verbal proficiency.

### Basic riddles
What can go up a chimney down but can't go down a chimney up? (an umbrella)

If a rooster laid a brown egg and a white egg, what kind of chicks would hatch? (None. Roosters don't lay eggs!)

What needs an answer, but doesn't ask a question? (the phone)

| **Medium-hard riddle** | **Challenging riddle** |
|---|---|
| I can sizzle like bacon, | This thing devours all, |
| I am made with an egg, | Birds, beasts, trees, flowers, |
| I have plenty of backbone but lack a good leg, | Gnaws iron, bites steel, |
| I peel layers like onions but still remain whole, | Grinds hard stones to meal, |
| I can be long like a flagpole yet fit in a hole. | Slays kings, ruins towns, |
| What am I? | And beats high mountains down. |
| (a snake) | (time) (by J. R. R. Tolkien) |

**FIGURE 13.10** Using Bloom's taxonomy as a guide for differentiating instruction based on the Cinderella story

| Level | Common verbs to use in questions | Examples from Cinderella story | Possible student products |
|---|---|---|---|
| Knowledge | know, collect, cite, repeat, recall, define, enumerate, list, name, label, tell, recount, relate, specify, identify | • How many stepsisters did Cinderella have?<br>• What was the slipper made of? | list, definition, fact, reproduction |
| Comprehension | restate, recognize, locate, summarize, explain, report, convert, discuss, express, retell, describe, identify, translate, estimate | • Discuss the events on the night of the ball.<br>• Describe what happened to the pumpkin. | Same as for knowledge level |
| Application | exhibit, apply, dramatize, solve, employ, practice, compute | • Make an exhibit of the ball gowns that Cinderella's two sisters and stepmother wore.<br>• Dramatize what happened when the prince came to Cinderella's house with the glass slipper. | illustration, diagram, map, diary, model, collection, diorama, puzzle |
| Analysis | interpret, categorize, dissect, analyze, classify, diagram, outline, compare, group, arrange, contrast, examine, inventory, subdivide | • Compare and contrast Cinderella's treatment by her stepmother and by the prince.<br>• Why was the stepmother so cruel to Cinderella? | questionnaire, survey, report, graph, chart, outline |
| Synthesis | compose, propose, produce, invent, imagine, formulate, create, design, predict, construct, create, improve, develop, rearrange | • Compose a song that Cinderella would sing while she did her work in the cinders.<br>• Design Cinderella's ball gown, chariot, or slipper. | formula, invention, film, new game, story, poem, art product, machine, advertisement |
| Evaluation | judge, criticize, prove, decide, assess, revise, appraise, estimate, rate, evaluate, determine, conclude | • Prove that Cinderella deserved to go to the ball.<br>• Determine what would have happened if Cinderella had run away but had not lost her slipper. | panel discussion, evaluation scale, report, survey, editorial, verdict, recommendation |

*Source:* Jane Piirto, © 2001. Used with permission.

Why modify questioning as a means of differentiation? Student-centered instruction requires teachers to ask stimulating questions according to the ability of the student, and proper questioning is a sophisticated facet of teaching. Techniques such as increasing wait time are part of modifying questioning, as is making sure that the discussion "zigzags"—that is, the students get a chance to talk with each other, not just with the teacher. With practice, the regular classroom teacher can "think on her feet" during questioning; thus, all students, both slow and fast, precocious and delayed, can experience challenge and success during classroom activities.

## Curriculum Differentiation Outside the Classroom

For some students with outstanding talents, the things that take place outside the classroom may be more important and rewarding than many of the activities within it. The teacher should always attempt to connect classwork with human and physical resources available in the community. Much more flexibility is offered by outside learning environments because of their relaxed scheduling and lack of physical barriers.

**Internships and Mentor Programs.**   The value and power of a viable mentor to the realization of talent or creativity have been recognized since the Middle Ages. The importance of mentors cannot be underestimated in certain artistic and scientific fields, where the development of both conceptual and performance skills is critical to success. These opportunities allow students with exceptional talents to be exposed to one of the most powerful and proven educational strategies—modeling, practice, and direct feedback and reinforcement of important behaviors—within a real-world setting.

**Special Courses.**   Specialized courses and workshops are offered in many communities, arts and cultural venues, museums, and recreation centers. These courses, which may or may not award high school or college continuing education credits, form a rich variety of opportunities for students to encounter mentors, new friends, and expansive concepts that may not be available in the confines of the school curriculum.

**Junior Great Books.**   This is a highly structured educational program in which students read selections from a number of areas, including classics, philosophy, fiction, and poetry, and then discuss their meaning with teachers. The teachers must undergo special training and use specific questioning techniques designed to evoke high-quality responses from the students.

**Summer Programs.**   Many summer programs are available to gifted and talented students that offer educational experiences as diverse as environmental studies and space and aeronautical studies. A number of new program offerings have been aimed at gifted minority students at the state and local levels. Summer programs are usually relatively brief but intense learning experiences that concentrate on specific areas of intellectual, artistic, or cultural affairs.

*A good mentor provides students with exceptional talents opportunities to develop their conceptual and performance skills in a real-world setting.*

*Differentiating curriculum outside the classroom*

Council for Exceptional Children    Content Standards for Beginning Teachers—G&T: Community-based and service learning opportunities for individuals with gifts and talents (GT7K7).

**International Experiences.**   New Zealanders have a cultural rite of passage they refer to as "the trek," wherein they pack their bags and travel in modest fashion to the far reaches of the planet. It is an eye-opening experience for people from a tiny Pacific island and one that gives them an exceptional opportunity to see and touch the world in an intimate fashion. An international curricular experience can merge this act of exploration with the demands of a structured learning experience—for example, the International Baccalaureate Program. Numerous international programs offer academic credits for study at participating educational agencies around the world. They are excellent opportunities for students to develop global interactional skills with academically rigorous studies. (See Profiles & Perspectives, "What's the Point?," for a gifted student's view of learning.)

## Instructional Models and Methods

Each of the four instructional models described in this section engages students in similar ways, focusing on independent exploration and inquiry, substantial modifications to the individual student's learning environment, and tangible products as an outcome of the learning activities. These models were selected because they offer the best examples of how special education for gifted and talented students can truly be differentiated from the regular curriculum. Although the Schoolwide Enrichment Model (Renzulli & Reis, 2003) is the only model to attempt to provide activities for both typically developing and gifted students, each of the other models includes components that can be modified and applied to a broad range of student abilities and talents within inclusive classrooms.

*The Schoolwide Enrichment Model.*    The Schoolwide Enrichment Model (SEM) not only attempts to meet the needs of gifted and talented students within the regular classroom setting but also is meant to be used with the other students in the class (Renzulli & Reis, 2003).

Schoolwide Enrichment Model

 Council for Exceptional Children    Content Standards for Beginning Teachers—G&T: Models, theories, and philosophies that form the basis of gifted education (GT1K2) (also GT7K3).

> The Schoolwide Enrichment Model (SEM) focuses on applying the know-how of gifted education to a systematic plan for total school improvement. This plan is not intended to replace existing services to students who are identified as gifted according to various state or local criteria. Rather, the model should be viewed as an umbrella under which many different types of enrichment and acceleration services are made available to targeted groups of students, as well as all students within a given school or grade level. (Renzulli, 1998, p. 1)

The first step of the SEM is identifying a talent pool of high-ability students (usually 15% to 25% of the school's enrollment) by using a multifactored assessment approach, including achievement tests, teacher and peer nominations, and creativity assessments. Once the students are identified, they are able to take part in specialized services, many of which are also available and appropriate for other learners in the same classroom. Reis (1995) discusses some of the relevant features of this instructional approach:

- Interest and learning styles assessments are used with talent pool students. Informal and formal methods are used to create and/or identify individual students' interests and to encourage students to further develop and pursue their interests in various ways.
- Curriculum compacting is offered to all eligible students. The regular curriculum of the classroom is modified by eliminating redundant or repetitious information and materials.
- Three types of enrichment activities are offered to students: Type I, general exploratory experiences; Type II, purposefully designed instructional methods and materials; and Type III, advanced-level studies with greater depth and complexity.

Reis and Cellerino (1983) recommend using a "revolving door" identification model that allows all children in the talent pool to participate in Type I and Type II enrichment activities. Only students who show serious interest in a specific topic evolve into Type III investigators. Students are never compelled to begin Type III projects; the level remains an open option for them.

*Maker's Active Problem Solver Model.*    Maker (2001; Maker & Nielson, 1996) proposes a process by which the key elements of content, process, products, and the environment of a child's learning situation can be modified. Extensive research on reliability and validity of the DISCOVER assessment and curriculum model has been conducted, showing that teachers whose beliefs parallel the theory behind the model can help students raise their test scores. Arts infusion with this model has also been successful. The teachers use four kinds of modifications:

Maker's Problem-Solving Model

Council for Exceptional Children    Content Standards for Beginning Teachers—G&T: Models, theories, and philosophies that form the basis of gifted education (GT1K2) (also GT7K3).

- *Content modifications.*    The content of a curriculum is the type of subject matter being taught. In general, the goal is to develop content that is more advanced, complex, innovative, and original than what is usually encountered in the classroom.
- *Process modifications.*    The strategies and methods used in delivering the content to learners are key features of instruction. The goal is to provide students with many opportunities to actively respond to the content, including independent research, cooperative learning, peer coaching, simulations, and apprenticeships.
- *Product modifications.*    The products of learning are the outcomes associated with instruction. The goal is to encourage a variety of ways that students can present their thoughts, ideas, and results.
- *Environment modifications.*    The learning environment includes both the physical characteristics of the setting(s) and the ambiance created by the teachers or facilitators. The goal is first to establish a positive working environment and then to rearrange the layout. Ideas such as peer tutoring, learning centers, management sheets, and learning packets can help students take more active control over and interest in their learning.

# What's the Point?

*by A. Chen*

The most insulting thing a teacher ever said to me was "Our job is to teach you how to learn." I know that is what many teachers believe they are charged with doing; but believe me, we are designed to learn from the minute we are born. All of us are learning machines. For gifted children especially, learning is like eating candy; they learn every waking minute, regardless of what's going on. Becoming educated, then, that is not the most pressing problem. What makes growing up gifted difficult is surviving the environment of childhood—remaining emotionally intact so your intellect can do what it's been prepared for.

## THE PERFECT WAY TO LEARN

During my freshman year in high school, I took a geometry class in an extracurricular program for "talented youth" offered by the local community college. Instead of assigning endless problem sets, Mr. Samide gave us five very difficult problems to do each week. He either came up with the problems himself or chose ones he had encountered while teaching. I spent hours at home working on those problems until they were solved, though I wouldn't spend 5 minutes on the easy problem sets assigned at my regular school. Mr. Samide gave us geometry problems that forced us to use everything we had ever learned about mathematics to solve them, and one great aspect of the class was that there was never a "right" way to solve a problem. After working on them on our own, we would openly discuss our approaches. Mr. Samide even gave us group problems in which we had to work together and feed off each other's ideas to come up with solution strategies. If anyone thought of an original problem or conjecture, it became part of our weekly problem set.

For me, this was the perfect way to learn. It inspired me to work on the mechanics of proofs, geometry, algebra, and arithmetic because I had to master those basic skills to solve the problems. Instead of teaching disjointed blocks of math

skills, Mr. Samide gave us coherent guidance in breaking down problems, applying specific skills, and then recombining problems to find solutions. It was a brilliant way of teaching.

## ALIENATION IN JUNIOR AND SENIOR HIGH SCHOOL

Later I came to realize that a good educational experience is a double-edged sword. Any child's education mixes good and bad teachers, classes, and programs. But the better an experience is, the worse it can make the mediocre or bad ones seem. I'm not saying educators should stop trying to give students a good education, but they need to help them cope with bad experiences.

Most of my junior high and high school experiences were a marked contrast to Mr. Samide's class. Despite my occasional straight-A performance, I had a horrible time! I was depressed a lot; and I hated the kids, the teachers, and the administrators. I often stayed home, and at least once a year I switched schools, repeating my freshman year of high school in hopes of wiping my record clean.

If I had no interest in a class, I put no effort into it. This meant I did no homework, which typically resulted in an F. By that point, I was disenchanted with the notion of school as a learning institution and rejected grades as a motivational factor or fair measure of learning. Even if I received an F in a class, I often learned more from it than did students who got good grades. Everyone who tried to help me said that school was just a game, and I should learn to play it. But I was stubborn: I accepted Fs and continued to crusade against the hypocrisy of the schools I was stuck in.

## GEEKS, NERDS, AND BRAINS

The most difficult thing about being gifted is not having many people like yourself around. Unlike jocks or cool kids, you have no positive identity to associate yourself with, only geeks, nerds, and brains. In my schools, a geek had a lot of applied technical knowledge. A nerd had esoteric interests such as bug collecting or trivia. The brain was the smartest kid in school, usually an academic performer with straight A's. If you chose to play any of those roles, you were ostracized.

Childhood is fraught with rites of passage, and it's important to have someone who can guide you through them. What saved me were programs in which I interacted with kids like myself and adult role models who understood me and weren't condescending. If you have enough exposure to others similar to yourself, you have a chance of finding people you can identify with. Once that occurs, you can begin to develop emotional stability and become who you want to be.

## PROGRAMS THAT WORKED

In retrospect, I've been very lucky. My mother always strove to provide my sister and me with an extraordinary education. Every year she researched local and national programs and sent us to them all year round. They ranged from extracurricular activities such as Suzuki programs for music; St. Louis area SAGE/FOG gifted workshops; an advanced math program called MEGSSS; classes for talented youth at local colleges; and summer programs such as Northwestern University's Center for Talent Development program, Purdue University's Gifted Education Research Institute, and Johns Hopkins University's Center for Talented Youth program. In all of them I was with kids similar to myself so I didn't have to worry about being me. Everyone, both teachers and students, was there because he or she wanted to be. The summer boarding programs and Simon's Rock College, a college for high-school-aged kids, were especially great because I had an additional sense of community and independence.

## REFLECTIONS

Today when I look at the friends I've met over the years, I know they are all intelligent. Probably most of them were or could have been considered gifted when they were in school. But I have come to realize that the label no longer has any meaning for us. All of us have become well-educated adults who work hard, have fun, and try to be socially responsible. We strive to be good people and decent citizens. So no matter how we were educated, we've ended up in the same place; what continues is our social bond.

Gifted kids are no different from any other in terms of what they need during their emotional development. While I was growing up, adults always seemed to be caught up in my potential, never in my current state of being. All the parents and educators out there should pay more attention to how gifted kids are growing up instead of how much or how quickly they are learning. Make sure they know that there are others like themselves, that they're not alone. They will learn for the rest of their lives, but they can only be children once. Families have numerous options for educating kids: public schools, private schools, magnet schools, home schooling, and boarding schools. If the "perfect" school is not a practical solution, consider clubs, extracurricular programs, or supplemental summer programs for gifted and talented youth. No matter how you educate a gifted child, it is important to remember that the true goal is to nurture a healthy, fully functioning member of society. I mean, you may end up with the smartest kids in the world, but if they aren't happy and can't fit into society and apply that intelligence, what's the point, right?

*Source*: Used and adapted with permission of the author and the publisher. Originally published in the *Communicator*, Vol. 31, No. 4, Fall 2000. California Association for the Gifted. The full-text article is provided as a service of the Davidson Institute for Talent Development through its GT-CyberSource (**www.gtcybersource.org**).

To further your understanding of and answer reflective questions about the concepts and issues presented here, go to the Profiles & Perspectives module in Chapter 13 of the Companion Website, **www.prenhall.com/heward**.

*Problem-Based Learning.*    Problem-based learning (PBL) challenges students to "learn to learn" while working cooperatively in groups to seek solutions to real-world problems. The problems are used to engage students' curiosity and initiate learning of subject matter. Since the mid-1990s, Joyce Van Tassel-Baska at the College of William and Mary has served as overall project director for a series of federally funded grants to develop thematic, interdisciplinary, problem-based curriculum for gifted students. Gifted educators throughout the country created and field-tested units in science, language arts, and the social sciences. (Figure 13.11 describes several examples.)

*Problem-Based Learning Units*

Council for Exceptional Children    Content Standards for Beginning Teachers—G&T: Models, theories, and philosophies that form the basis of gifted education (GT1K2) (also GT4K1).

**FIGURE 13.11** **Examples of College of William and Mary problem-based learning units in science, language arts, and social studies**

### SCIENCE

*Acid, Acid Everywhere*

This unit poses an ill-structured problem that leads the students into an interdisciplinary inquiry about the structures of and interaction between several systems, centering around the study of an acid spill on a local highway.

*The Chesapeake Bay*

This unit focuses on the various systems involved in the pollution of the Chesapeake Bay. The systems included in this unit are ecosystems, chemical reaction systems, government systems, and economic systems.

*What a Find!*

An exploration of the field of archaeology. Students are put in the role of junior archaeologists at a research museum and discover that construction work has been halted on a new school because of the discovery of historic artifacts.

*For more information on problem-based units in scence, go to www.wm.edu/education/gifted-ed/Curriculum/Science_materials.htm*

### LANGUAGE ARTS

*Literary Reflections on Personal and Social Change*
(Grades 4–6)

This unit involves students' interacting with literature while enhancing reading comprehension and textual analysis skills. The literature selections, including Burnett's *The Secret Garden* and world-class short stories by such authors as Tolstoy and Singer, serve as a basis for discussion.

*Literature of the 1940's: A Decade of Change*
(Grades 7–9)

This unit looks at the historical events and social issues of the 1940s through the literature of the decade. The unit is rich in materials that highlight the concept of change, including works such as Hersey's *Hiroshima, The Diary of Anne Frank,* and McCuller's *The Member of the Wedding.*

*Change Through Choices:
A Literature Unit for High School Students*
(Grades 10–12)

This unit focuses on catalytic choices that determine change in a variety of situations. This unit attempts to give the student a chance to question real-world choices and problems and decide what valuable lessons can be learned through careful individual examination of options.

*For more information on problem-based units in language arts, go to www.wm.edu/education/gifted-ed/Curriculum/Language_Arts_materials.htm*

### SOCIAL STUDIES

*Ancient China: The Middle Kingdom*
(Grades 2–3)

Human civilizations develop and sustain themselves as a collection of interdependent systems. The unit provides opportunities for students to broaden their understanding by comparing ancient Chinese civilization with aspects of their own lives and communities.

*A House Divided? The Civil War, Its Causes and Effects*
(Grades 5–6)

The concept of cause and effect serves as a central organizing theme of this unit, which explores the events and perspectives leading to the American Civil War and the chronology and context of the war itself, using primary-source documents.

*The 1930s in America: Facing Depression*
(Grades 6–7)

The unit explores Depression-era America from the perspective of many different groups of people, using a variety of primary sources to illustrate events and the social-political context.

*For more information on problem-based units in social studies, go to www.wm.edu/education/gifted-ed/Curriculum/Social_Studies_materials.htm*

An ill-formed, real-world problem serves as the basis for each of the science units, and understanding and applying the concept of systems is the overarching theme. These units give students experience in collecting, organizing, analyzing, and evaluating scientific data and learning to communicate their understanding to others. The PBL language arts units feature change as the overarching theme; the social studies units focus on the concept of interdependence.

The PBL units have won many major curriculum awards from discipline-based subject matter groups as well as the National Association for Gifted Children's "red apple" award for excellence. In addition to wide use in the United States, PBL units are used by teachers in 18 countries and have been adopted by the American Embassy Schools and the Department of Defense schools. Although the PBL units were developed initially for gifted and talented students, they can be used with students of all ability levels by modifying the activities up or down depending on student ability.

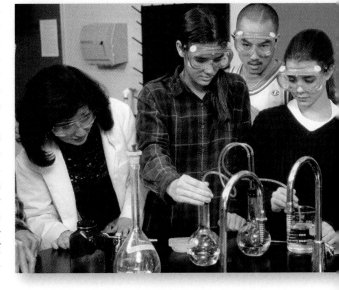

Letting students choose the kinds of problems they wish to study and how they will go about their investigations is one method for differentiating curriculum for students with outstanding academic abilities.

# EDUCATIONAL PLACEMENT ALTERNATIVES AND ABILITY GROUPING

## Special Schools

Special schools for gifted and talented students have a long history. Special high schools for students of both genders began in the early 20th century with the establishment of Stuyvesant High School in New York City. The establishment of the Hunter College High School for Gifted Girls came even earlier. The Hunter College Elementary School for gifted students opened in 1941. Children are selected for admission to these schools on the basis of competitive examinations and scores on individual IQ tests. These arrangements for academically talented children became popular in the 1980s as mandates for desegregation caused urban school systems to change the concept of the neighborhood school to the concept of the magnet school. Even on the elementary school level in many urban areas, special magnet schools emphasize various themes: for example, Columbus, Ohio, has a French language school; most large cities have a special high school for the visual and performing arts and special schools for mathematics and science. Recently, many states have permitted special charter schools for gifted and talented students.

*Placement alternatives*

Council for Exceptional Children — Content Standards for Beginning Teachers—G&T: Issues, assurances, and due process rights related to assessment, eligibility, and placement within a continuum of services (GT1K7).

## Self-Contained Classrooms

There is always the option of creating a self-contained room for talented and gifted students. The primary advantage of the self-contained classroom is that all curriculum and instruction can be focused on needs of high-ability students. Other advantages of self-contained classrooms are that students are more likely to work at a pace commensurate with their abilities, and membership in a class of intellectual equals may challenge some gifted students to excel even further. The self-contained classroom model may also be more efficient because gifted education teachers do not have to move from classroom to classroom or school to school to serve students.

In addition to sharing many of the disadvantages of self-contained classrooms for students with disabilities (e.g., limited opportunity to develop friendships with peers in general education), self-contained classroom programs for gifted and talented students must often deal with the stigma of being viewed as elitist. Some districts may be too small to support the self-contained classroom option, even multi-age or across-grade-level classes.

## Resource Room or Pull-Out Programs

Some educators of the gifted and talented believe that the resource room or pull-out model is the best option for serving these students. While resource room programs offer many of the advantages of a self-contained classroom without the disadvantages of complete segregation from the regular classroom, they pose a number of challenges and disadvantages as well (see Figure 13.12). Administrators and teachers in schools that provide resource room/pull-out services for gifted and talented students should recognize that these children do not stop being gifted when they leave the resource room and return to the regular classroom. Although the learning opportunities and instruction provided to talented students in the resource room may be of the highest quality, they do not eliminate the need to differentiate curriculum for these students when they are in the regular classroom during the rest of the school day.

## Regular Classroom

For gifted and talented students, inclusion in the regular classroom has not been an issue as it is with other exceptional children. Most academically or otherwise talented students

---

**FIGURE 13.12**  **Advantages and disadvantages of resource room and pull-out models for gifted and talented students**

| Advantages | Disadvantages |
|---|---|
| 1. Pullout programs are quite easy to set in motion. | 1. Costs more as extra teachers have to be hired and special facilities provided. |
| 2. The teacher in the regular classroom has more time to work with the other students. | 2. The regular classroom teachers get frustrated and often feel that students leaving disrupts their instructional plan. |
| 3. Students who are left in the classroom have a chance to shine. | 3. Students in the regular classroom might feel resentful. |
| 4. The teacher in the pullout program can focus on critical and creative thinking since the teacher in the regular classroom focuses on the standard curriculum. | 4. The academically talented students might have to make up work in the regular classroom while having more work in the pullout classroom. |
| 5. The differentiation of curriculum is separated from the classroom flow. | 5. Curriculum may have no relationship to curriculum in the regular classroom. |
| 6. Students receive special help in areas of strength. | 6. Students are treated differently according to ability. |
| 7. Teachers can feel as if they have "their" kids. | 7. Teachers are isolated from the other teachers. |
| 8. Students can have time with other students to discuss intellectual interests that may not be shared by students in the regular classroom. | 8. Students may feel different from the rest of the students in their regular classroom. |
| 9. Collaboration with other teachers is encouraged. | 9. Students are academically talented all the time, and not just during pullout time. |
| 10. Small groups of students can do special projects that would not be possible in the regular classroom. | 10. Small groups of students may receive special privileges other students don't receive (e.g., access to computers, field trips). |
| 11. Teachers of the talented can provide intensive instruction in areas of expertise (e.g., the arts, foreign language). | 11. Turf issues with regular classroom teacher may arise (e.g., homework, lessons and assemblies missed). |

*Source:* From Piirto, J. (1999). *Talented children and adults: Their development and education* (2nd ed.), (p. 73). Upper Saddle River, NJ: Merrill/Prentice Hall. Used by permission.

are served in regular classrooms. If the school district has a program for gifted and talented students, a teacher with special training in gifted education provides direct and indirect support for the regular classroom teacher. Working in consultation with the regular classroom teacher this special educator—sometimes called a facilitator, a consulting teacher, or an intervention specialist for the gifted—might provide specialized instruction in science, math, the humanities, or other subjects to flexible groups of students. She may work with a high-ability reading or math group while the rest of class is working in these domains. She may mentor projects and displays, design special learning centers, and help plan special field trips.

An advantage of this model is that the gifted education teacher is no longer isolated and alone, working in her resource room or pull-out classroom without knowledge of what the students are doing in their home classrooms. She is in partnership with regular classroom teachers, collaborating on curriculum planning teams as they plan multi-level lessons. Another important advantage of the consultant teacher model is that students of all ability levels in the regular classroom can benefit from smaller student-teacher ratios, participating in multi-tiered lessons and learning activities on creativity, critical thinking, or study strategies that the gifted specialist may teach to the whole classroom.

Landrum (2002) has written extensively about the consultation/collaboration model. Possible activities can consist of (1) team or grade-level co-planning sessions, where the talent development specialist joins in the planning sessions with the regular education team; (2) communicating about organizational needs such as grouping and scheduling; (3) identifying and placing students in groups; (4) gathering materials to supplement regular classroom activities; (5) facilitating differentiation activities; (6) administering and managing independent studies and student learning contracts; (7) monitoring the progress of student learning through rubrics and pre-assessment.

However, many schools do not have a specialist in the education of the gifted and talented, and the regular classroom teacher is responsible for differentiating curriculum for students with advanced educational needs.

*Consulting teacher model*

*Council for Exceptional Children* Content Standards for Beginning Teachers—G&T: Models and strategies for consultation and collaboration (GT10K4).

## Ability Grouping

An issue involving considerable debate and strong opinions over the years is the extent to which academically talented students should be taught in groups composed of their intellectual equals or in heterogeneous groups of students of all abilities. Social injustices and upheavals have resulted in increased calls for equity in all of society's institutions. For some, equity in education includes the idea that all students should be taught in heterogeneous groups so that no one group can progress faster than any other. But most educators and researchers in the field of gifted education believe that heterogeneous group instruction means that talented students will not be able to reach their potential. (See the National Association for Gifted Children's policy on ability grouping in Figure 13.13.)

**Ability grouping** has been used in schools, both formally and informally, for more than 100 years. As soon as the number of students in any classroom or school became so large that the differences in their abilities to learn stood out, teachers automatically put students into groups for subject matter instruction. These groups were often informal, consisting of two or more students who could keep pace with each other. When students started to be grouped according to chronological age and when developmental experts cautioned that students should remain in classes only with their age mates, ability grouping began to be the norm rather than the exception.

*Ability grouping issues and concerns*

*Council for Exceptional Children* Content Standards for Beginning Teachers—G&T: Relationship of gifted education to the organization and function of educational agencies (GT1K4).

*XYZ Grouping or Tracking.*   *XYZ grouping* places students into different levels of curriculum requirements or offerings according to high, middle, and low ability based on test scores or other indicators or predictors of performance. Detroit had such a plan as early as 1919. Students had the same curricula and the same textbooks; the only differences were in pace of instruction and depth of enrichment. Students in the top 20% in achievement were placed

**FIGURE 13.13** **National Association for Gifted Children's policy on ability grouping**

### Ability Grouping

The National Association for Gifted Children (NAGC) is fully committed to national goals that advocate both excellence and equity for all students, and we believe that the best way to achieve these goals is through *differentiated* educational opportunities, resources, and encouragement for all students.

The practice of grouping, enabling students with advanced abilities and/or performance to be grouped together to receive appropriately challenging instruction, has recently come under attack. NAGC wishes to reaffirm the importance of grouping for instruction of gifted students. Grouping allows for more appropriate, rapid, and advanced instruction, which matches the rapidly developing skills and capabilities of gifted students.

Special attention should be given to the identification of gifted and talented students who may not be identified through traditional assessment methods (including economically disadvantaged individuals, individuals of limited English proficiency, and individuals with handicaps), to help them participate effectively in special grouping programs.

Strong research evidence supports the effectiveness of ability grouping for gifted students in accelerated classes, enrichment programs, advanced placement programs, etc. Ability and performance grouping has been used extensively in programs for musically and artistically gifted students, and for athletically talented students with little argument. Grouping is a necessary component of every graduate and professional preparation program, such as law, medicine, and the sciences. It is an accepted practice that is used extensively in the education programs in almost every country in the western world.

NAGC does not endorse a tracking system that sorts all children into fixed layers in the school system with little attention to particular content, student motivation, past accomplishment, or present potential.

To abandon the proven instructional strategy of grouping students for instruction at a time of educational crisis in the U.S. will further damage our already poor competitive position with the rest of the world, and will renege on our promise to provide an appropriate education for all children. (Approved 11/91)

*Source:* National Association for Gifted Children, Washington, DC. Reprinted by permission.

in the "X" classes, students in the next 60% were placed in the "Y" classes, and the lowest 20% were placed in the "Z" classes. Another name for XYZ grouping is *tracking*. Well-founded concern over the potential dangers (e.g., reduced expectations and limited learning opportunities for children in lower tracks, permanent placement in lower tracks at an early age) and abuses of tracking (e.g., as a procedure for de facto segregation of students by race, culture, and/or socioeconomic status) have caused some critics to call for an elimination of all forms of ability grouping for instruction (e.g., Oaks, 1985).

*Within-class ability groupings*

Council for Exceptional Children Content Standards for Beginning Teachers—G&T: Grouping practices that support differentiated learning environments (GT5K5).

*Within-Class Grouping.*    In contrast to tracking, a second type of ability grouping is *within-class grouping*, in which students within the same heterogeneous class are grouped for instruction according to their achievement. The most common form of within-class grouping is regrouping by subject; students are generally grouped into three or more levels, and they study material from different textbooks at different levels. Meta-analysis studies from the University of Michigan (Kulik, 1992a, 1992b, 2003; Kulik & Kulik, 1984a, 1984b, 1987, 1992) and from Johns Hopkins University (Slavin, 1987, 1991) found that this type of ability grouping had positive results, with gains for low-, middle-, and high-ability students averaging 1.2 years in a school year. Students should be grouped by ability for reading and mathematics. Kulik (2004) said, "Well-designed and well-controlled studies unequivocally show that homogeneous grouping helps children when it is used as a means of providing appropriate curricular material to them" (abstract).

Another form of within-class grouping is *cluster grouping,* in which several talented students receive specialized instruction from a teacher who treats them as talented. Four to six talented students should make up a cluster. Cluster grouping can be used effectively at all grade levels and in all subject areas. It can be especially effective when there are not enough students to form an advanced placement section for a particular subject. Cluster grouping is also a welcome option in rural settings or wherever small numbers of gifted students make appropriate accommodations difficult. The advantage of this type of grouping is that it fits philosophically with the special educational practice of inclusion yet still provides talented students with a peer group. Teachers have found that cluster grouping helps for achievement of the other students as well.

*Cross-Grade Grouping.* **Cross-grade grouping** was first tried in the Joplin Plan in Missouri in the 1950s. In this model, students in the fourth, fifth, and sixth grades were broken into nine reading groups, ranging from the second-grade to the ninth-grade levels. Students went to reading class at the same hour but to the level of instruction at which they were achieving. Other types of cross-grade grouping are (1) ability-grouped class assignments, (2) ability grouping for selected subjects, (3) nongraded plans, and (4) special classes. Cross-grade grouping is an effective means of delivering differentiated instruction, and achievement gains similar to those of within-grade grouping have been found (Lloyd, 1999). Still other types of grouping are peer tutoring dyads, cooperative grouping for like-ability students, and mixed-ability cooperative grouping using the "default" option (Rogers, 2002). It is important to note that using a brighter student to tutor a child of lower ability "does not increase the bright child's achievement. Peer tutoring using mixed-ability dyads will only enhance the achievement and behavior of the lower ability student" (Rogers, 2002, p. 245). Webb, Nemer, and Zuniga (2002), studying heterogeneous and homogeneous grouping of high-ability eighth-grade science students, said that high-ability students could learn in heterogeneous groups if the group dynamics were suitable.

Grouping is not going to go away, but it should always be flexible. That is, students should be able to move into and out of groups depending on task and subject and even on whim. The days of a child's being put into the "redbird" reading group in first grade and remaining with the same students until high school graduation are over. Ability grouping, when used properly, produces academic gains for academically talented students when challenging materials are also used. If students are grouped across grades for high-level instruction, there are no lasting social or emotional effects (Rogers, 2002).

Languages and mathematics seem most amenable for ability grouping. And if there is to be grouping, the curriculum should be adapted as well. While this may seem obvious, some teachers think that just putting children into different ability groups is enough, and they do not provide differentiated curriculum.

The National Research Center on the Gifted and Talented recommends the following guidelines for ability grouping:

*Guideline 1:* Although some school programs that group children by ability have only small effects, other grouping programs help children a great deal. Schools should therefore resist calls for the wholesale elimination of ability grouping.

*Guideline 2:* Highly talented youngsters profit greatly from work in accelerated classes. Schools should therefore try to maintain programs of accelerated work.

*Guideline 3:* Highly talented youngsters also profit greatly from an enriched curriculum designed to broaden and deepen their learning. Schools should therefore try to maintain programs of enrichment.

*Cross-grade ability grouping*

Council for Exceptional Children Content Standards for Beginning Teachers—G&T: Grouping practices that support differentiated learning environments (GT5K5).

*Guidelines for ability grouping*

Council for Exceptional Children Content Standards for Beginning Teachers—G&T: Grouping practices that support differentiated learning environments (GT5K5) (also GT1K4).

*Guideline 4:*    Bright, average, and slow youngsters profit from grouping programs that adjust the curriculum to the aptitude levels of the groups. Schools should try to use ability grouping in this way.

*Guideline 5:*    Benefits are slight from programs that group children by ability but prescribe common curricular experiences for all ability groups. Schools should not expect student achievement to change dramatically with either establishment or elimination of such programs.

## CURRENT ISSUES AND FUTURE TRENDS

The current ethos surrounding the development and provision of special education services to gifted and talented students involves movement on several fronts:

- The conceptual and definitional nature of giftedness is being more intensively questioned.
- There is a possibility that almost all services for gifted and talented students may originate with the regular teacher from within the regular classroom.
- There is increased pressure to identify and serve students from several underserved populations, including different cultural groups, females, students with disabilities, and children from disadvantaged environments.

*Use of the term "gifted"*

**Council for Exceptional Children** Content Standards for Beginning Teachers—G&T: Impact of labeling individuals with gifts and talents (GT1K8) (also GT1K12).

Advocates and writers in the field are growing increasingly wary of the term *gifted*, realizing that in some ways it perpetuates the myth that talent is predetermined and not the result of extensive effort on the part of students, teachers, parents, and communities. It simply makes it too easy for society as a whole to ignore these students' needs and to ascribe their growth and development (or lack thereof) to uncontrollable, unseen forces beyond the reach of our instructional interventions. An unintended result is that both individuals and societal institutions can assert that because these students can easily make it on their own, they need no extra help from society. If only the misconception that all of these students make it were true! The available data indicate that large numbers of students who would qualify for gifted and talented services drop out of school and that many more students who are culturally different, disabled, or economically disadvantaged are never even identified. Estimates of this group of underachieving gifted students range from 10% to 20% of all high school dropouts (Davis & Rimm, 2004).

*Evolving models of G&T education*

**Council for Exceptional Children** Content Standards for Beginning Teachers—G&T: Relationship of gifted education to the organization and function of educational agencies (GT1K4) (also GT1K12).

There is a growing awareness that gifted advocates will need to reconceptualize special services to gifted and talented students in a manner that differs from the traditional model of a gifted teacher in a segregated gifted classroom (Hertzog, 1998). Most of the newer instructional models (e.g., Renzulli's Schoolwide Enrichment Model, Maker's Active Problem Solver Model, problem-based learning) occur in the regular classroom and depend heavily on interactions within the community; few require a special teacher or classroom. There will be obvious and important impacts on teacher training, classroom management, and curriculum if the regular classroom becomes the dominant educational service setting in U.S. schools. It is likely there will be an increased emphasis on collaboration rather than independent instruction. This emphasis implies that teachers of the gifted will have to work closely with regular classroom educators to provide services to gifted and talented students. Finally, the increasingly sophisticated use of technological tools and related methods will provide gifted students with greater connections and independence in the future. In some cases, this ability to communicate with persons from distant and differing cultures and languages will provide new avenues of expression for gifted and talented students. In addition, the ability to explore topics in greater depth through the use of global data bases and to create interactive presentations about their discoveries will allow gifted and talented students to become more independent and exert greater self-determination over their own learning.

Increasing numbers of persons are advocating more accurate and inclusive identification procedures that provide access to special educational services for gifted students who are members of several underserved populations. Persons who have high ability or talent comprise a very different group of exceptional learners; but it is important to remember that all talent, including exceptional talent, can suffer from a lack of quality educational experiences, informative feedback, and emotional support. Students who exhibit high ability and talent are susceptible to the same fears and frustrations that come with a lack of interest or understanding of their needs and abilities, regardless of race, gender, socioeconomic status, and disability status.

In addition, there is a pressing need to provide counseling services to gifted and talented students (Neihart, Robinson, & Moon, 2002). Our track record of understanding and then facilitating the emotional growth of gifted and talented students is weak to nonexistent. As with all children and adults, a number of predictable and unpredictable crises will occur throughout their lives. With their heightened sense of social justice and greater awareness of the needs of others, students who are gifted and talented often experience confusion and estrangement more deeply than their peers. Teachers are not counselors, but they often become aware of issues specific to their individual students' needs.

Gifted and talented students need special education; they need differentiated curriculum, instructional strategies, materials, and experiences that allow them to realize their potential. There are new approaches and perspectives concerning the manner in which students are identified and services are delivered that reflect insights into the way humans learn and create. These innovations promise students with high ability and talents a brighter learning future that benefits both the country and the world in which they live.

*Need for increased identification and services for G&T children from underserved populations*

Council for Exceptional Children Content Standards for Beginning Teachers—G&T: Issues in definition and identification of individuals with gifts and talents, including those from culturally and linguistically diverse backgrounds (GT1K5) (also GT1K12).

# Tips for Beginning Teachers

## Teaching Gifted and Talented Children
### by Anne Efremoff, Lori Pavlik, and Karen Westfall

If you become a general education teacher, you may never have a student who is blind, a student who is deaf, a student with autism, or a student with severe and multiple disabilities. You will, however, have students who are gifted and talented in your classroom. The regular classroom is where gifted and talented students spend most of their time in school.

Young, inexperienced teachers—sometimes armed only with the knowledge gained from the small portion of an introduction to special education course devoted to gifted education—are expected to teach gifted and talented students. This can be daunting, even frightening, at first. Here are some tips that may help.

### LOOK FOR PRECOCIOUSNESS AND RESPECT IT

Gifted children have academic behaviors similar to children who are two, three, or more years older. To provide learning experiences appropriate to their advanced abilities, you should be prepared to do the following:

- *Pretest before you teach.* You may find that a gifted and talented student already knows most or all of the material planned for a unit of study.
- *Compact the curriculum.* Even after you have placed gifted and talented students ahead in the curriculum based on their pretest performances, you will probably find that those students can move through the advanced material faster than most students. You might give them an independent project, a more advanced lesson, or an assignment in the same area but based on their interests.
- *Recommend acceleration.* Accelerating a gifted student one, two, or even three grade levels in certain subject areas is often easier and less costly

than developing your own materials within the classroom.

- *Look for precociousness and recommend students who display it for screening and assessment.* Learn the procedures for screening and identifying students for gifted education services used by your district and state.

## DON'T BE AFRAID TO CREATE YOUR OWN CURRICULUM

Many schools do not have established curricular plans or preexisting menus of enriched learning opportunities for the education of gifted and talented students. This leaves classroom teachers with the responsibility, and the opportunity, to develop differentiated curriculum.

- *Administer an interest survey.* Find out what the students are studying and learning on their own. Young science students may have elaborate collections. Young math students might be interested in elaborate and complicated number games. Young writers may be reading several grade levels above what the other students are reading. Tailor your assignments to these interests.
- *Build a library of curriculum materials spanning several years above grade level and keep those materials in your classroom.* These materials will provide ideas and content for developing tiered lessons.
- *Take advantage of curriculum guides and materials for gifted students.* Explore the William and Mary curriculum units. If you want to develop interdisciplinary units, consider the Core, Connections, Practice, and Identity parallel curriculum strands as explained by Tomlinson and colleagues (2002). For example, when using the Practice strand, the students learn what real scientists do when they are performing an experiment.
- *Provide learning opportunities outside the classroom.* Gifted and talented students often thrive on events such as the Math Olympiad, the Science Olympiad, History Day, Young Writers contests, and the Power of the Pen. Show your support by accompanying your students when they participate in these events. Attending and observing these activities will give you additional ideas for curriculum content and instructional activities to bring back to the classroom.

## TAILOR YOUR INSTRUCTIONAL ARRANGEMENTS AND TEACHING METHODS

Gifted and talented children do not need specialized methods of instruction as much as they need opportunities to explore challenging curriculum in a supportive environment. Differentiate lessons as much as possible according to students' abilities and interests. Tier, or layer, lessons so that the top students are always challenged.

- *Provide regular opportunities for gifted and talented students to share their ideas and talk about what they have learned.*
- *Challenge them to think, not just pass tests.* Many gifted students are already able to pass grade-level tests. Encourage and require them to explore the deeper meaning, extensions, and implications of concepts.
- *Use cooperative or collaborative groups that encourage pair sharing.* It is a mistake to make gifted and talented students responsible for the learning of the whole group.
- *Don't assume that because a gifted and talented student is advanced in some subject area that he has mastered the entire curriculum.* However, when you notice gaps in a student's learning, you will often find that she can quickly catch up with direct instruction in the skills that are missing and that a lot of drill and practice is not necessary.

## DON'T FORGET THE SOCIAL AND EMOTIONAL NEEDS OF GIFTED STUDENTS

Gifted and talented population students are not little brains or miniature professors. They have individual social and emotional needs and academic needs.

- *Remember that gifted and talented students are gifted and talented all the time, not just in their pull-out or special class.* Appreciate them for who they are and encourage self-acceptance.
- *Debunk stereotypes.* For example, all gifted and talented students do not get all As. Emphasize that it is okay to be different. Many terms exist in the popular culture that stereotype bright students: e.g., "nerd," "dweeb," "geek." Do not permit such terms to be used to categorize gifted students.
- *Encourage gifted students to take risks.* Some gifted students may freak out if they get a B. Their sense of perfectionism kicks in, and they feel inadequate. Let students know that it is okay to make a mistake. Create situations in which a person is not expected to be perfect—for example, in learning a new subject or a word list—and emphasize that it is not necessary to always be perfect.
- *Listen when students are talking about something you might not understand or about a book that they have read that is not of interest to you.* The teachers who accept students are often as important as the teachers who challenge them.

## IDENTIFY A SUPPORT NETWORK AND BUILD YOUR PROFESSIONAL KNOWLEDGE

Don't try to go it alone. There may not be a teacher trained in gifted education in your school building, but you can always find experts to call upon. Get to know the gifted education consultant for your district or in your area.

- *Educate yourself on the laws and regulations in your state regarding the education of gifted and talented students.* This will help you learn what a student's rights are in your state and help you be a better advocate.
- *Attend workshops, conferences, and in-service opportunities on teaching gifted students.* Take courses for licensure or, if you teach in a state that does not require licensure, upgrade your knowledge about these students.

- *Finally, enjoy the students.* It's easy for a beginning teacher to feel overwhelmed. Today's teachers are expected to do more than ever before. But teaching should not be only a duty. Teaching gifted and talented students, like teaching all students, should not be an onerous duty but a pleasure and a privilege.

Anne Efremoff teaches gifted and talented middle school students in Canton, Ohio. Lori Pavlik is the coordinator for gifted programs in Fairlawn, Ohio. Karen Westfall teaches gifted and talented children in an elementary pull-out program in the Jackson School District in Ohio. All three are graduate students in the talent development education program at Ashland University in Ohio.

## KEY TERMS AND CONCEPTS

ability grouping, p. 543
acceleration, p. 530
Bloom's taxonomy, p. 533
cross-grade grouping, p. 545

curriculum compacting, p. 532
enrichment, p. 530
tiered lesson, p. 533

 To print your own set of SAFMED flash cards for studying and mastering these terms, go to the Companion Website, **www.prenhall.com/heward**.

## SUMMARY

### Defining Giftedness and Talent

- The federal government defines gifted and talented children as those exhibiting high-performance capability in intellectual, creative, and/or artistic areas; possessing an unusual leadership capacity; or excelling in specific academic fields.
- Renzulli's definition of giftedness is based on the traits of above-average general abilities, high level of task commitment, and creativity.
- Piirto defines the gifted as having superior memory, observational powers, curiosity, creativity, and ability to learn.
- Maker defines the gifted and talented student as a problem solver who is capable of (1) creating a new or clearer definition of an existing problem, (2) devising new and more efficient or effective methods, and (3) reaching solutions that may be different from the usual.

### Characteristics of Students Who Are Gifted and Talented

- Learning and intellectual characteristics of gifted and talented students include the ability to do the following:
  - Rapidly acquire, retain, and use large amounts of information
  - Relate one idea to another
  - Make sound judgments
  - Perceive the operation of larger systems of knowledge that may not be recognized by the ordinary citizen

- Acquire and manipulate abstract symbol systems
- Solve problems by reframing the question and creating novel solutions
- Gifted children are by no means perfect, and their unusual talents and abilities may make them either withdrawn or difficult to manage in the classroom.
- Gifted students need both basic and advanced content knowledge and the abilities to use and develop that knowledge effectively.
- Many gifted children are creative. Although there is no universally accepted definition of creativity, we know that creative children have knowledge, examine it in a variety of ways, critically analyze the outcomes, and communicate their ideas.
- Guilford includes dimensions of fluency, flexibility, originality, and elaboration in his definition of creativity.

## Prevalence

- The most commonly cited prevalence estimate is that high-IQ gifted students make up 3% to 5% of the school-age population and that there are many forms of talents that do not require a high IQ. Perhaps 10% to 15% of students possess such talents.

## Identification and Assessment

- IQ tests are one, but not necessarily the best, means for identifying students with high intellectual ability. The usual means of identification include a combination of IQ scores; achievement measures; checklists; teacher, parent, community, and peer nominations; self-nomination; and leisure interests.
- Maker's DISCOVER procedure can be used to equitably identify gifted and talented females as well as students from diverse cultural groups.
- Teachers and parents can foster the intellectual and talent development of children with disabilities by conveying positive, realistic expectations; encouraging independence; guiding constructive coping strategies; providing daily opportunities to build abilities and enjoy success; and pursuing positive social experiences for the child.

## Educational Approaches

- Curriculum should consider the learning characteristics of gifted and talented students, preserve academic rigor, be thematic and interdisciplinary, consider various curriculum orientations, and be balanced and articulate.
- *Differentiation* is a broad term referring to a variety of strategies for providing gifted and talented students with a challenging and conceptually rich curriculum.
- *Acceleration* is the general term for modifying the pace at which the student moves through the curriculum.
- *Enrichment* means probing or studying a subject at a greater depth than would occur in the regular curriculum.
- Curriculum compacting involves compressing instructional content so students have time to work on more challenging materials.
- Tiered lessons provide extensions of the same basic lesson for groups of students of differing abilities.
- Bloom's taxonomy of educational objectives provides a framework for differentiating curriculum by asking questions and assigning activities that require students to demonstrate different types of knowledge.
- Options for learning outside of school include internships and mentorships, special courses and workshops in the community, Junior Great Books, summer programs, and international experiences.
- Three models for differentiating curriculum for gifted students are Renzulli's School-wide Enrichment Model, Maker's Active Problem Solver Model, and the Problem-Based Learning units.

## Educational Placement Alternatives and Ability Grouping

- Special schools for gifted and talented students have a long history. Students are selected for admission based on competitive exams and IQ scores. Magnet schools emphasize themes such as foreign language, performing arts, or math and science.
- Curriculum and instruction in self-contained classrooms can focus on the needs of high-ability students. In addition to sharing many of the disadvantages of self-contained classrooms for students with disabilities, self-contained classroom programs for gifted and talented students may be viewed by some as elitist.
- Some schools use a resource room or pull-out model for serving gifted and talented students. While resource room programs offer many advantages, they pose a number of challenges and disadvantages as well.
- Most gifted and talented students are served in regular classrooms. A consultant teacher trained in gifted education often helps the regular classroom teacher plan and deliver specialized instruction.
- Most educators and researchers in the field of gifted education believe that ability grouping is necessary if gifted and talented students are to reach their potential. Within-class grouping and cross-age grouping are two forms of ability grouping that offer effective means of delivering differentiated instruction to students according to their achievement and interests.

## Current Issues and Future Trends

- The conceptual and definitional nature of giftedness is being more intensively questioned.
- Most services for gifted and talented students will probably originate from the regular teacher within the regular classroom.
- The importance of realizing the needs of gifted and talented girls and boys, individuals with disabilities, and diverse cultural groups is now recognized. We need better procedures for identifying, assessing, teaching, and encouraging these children.
- As we have seen with other exceptional children, we must improve society's attitudes toward gifted and talented children if we are to improve their futures.

# SPECIAL EDUCATION ACROSS THE LIFE SPAN

part 3

# chapter 14

# EARLY CHILDHOOD SPECIAL EDUCATION

# *Featured Teacher*

### KIM LUNDY

**SPIRITRIDGE ELEMENTARY SCHOOL
BELLEVUE, WASHINGTON**

*Education—Teaching Credentials—Experience*
- B.A., major in English, minor in elementary education, Whitman College, 1994
- M.Ed., early childhood special education, University of Washington, 1996
- Certificate, early childhood special education, birth–grade 3, and general education elementary, K–8, Washington
- 9 years of teaching preschoolers with and without disabilities

*Current Teaching Position and Students*　　I have the greatest job! I teach two half-day sessions of integrated preschool each day. Of my 20 total preschoolers (9 in the morning and 11 in the afternoon), 15 qualify for special education services because of developmental delays in one or more of the following areas: cognitive, adaptive (self-help), social, gross and/or fine motor, and communication. A few of my students qualify for special education services under the IDEA categories of health-impaired or autism. Four of my students are nonverbal or just learning to talk, and four come from families that speak English as a second language.

*Meet Some of My Students*　　I wish I could introduce all of my students to you, but here's a picture of four of them. Abby is a delightful 3-year-old girl who loves bubbles, the color purple, and being around her friends. She has several significant disabilities that make her nonverbal, nonmobile, and medically fragile. Abby has a really cool special chair and a prone stander, and she takes great pride in being able to activate toys that have a switch. Four-year-old Ben enjoys the sensory table and cars. He is eager to learn how to talk but gets overwhelmed by sudden noises, changes in routine, and large groups of children. Grace is a 3-year-old with a beautiful smile and a diagnosis of autism. She is mostly nonverbal and requires a high level of assistance to participate appropriately and safely in most classroom activities. Grace receives a full day of special education services from the school district: she participates in intensive one-on-one instruction in the morning and attends my integrated preschool in the afternoon. Four-year-old Sam is a typically developing child. He enjoys art, music, blocks, and the house area and is a great friend to all of the children.
　　There is no way I could teach all of my terrific students by myself: I am fortunate to have wonderful classroom aides (three in the morning and two in the afternoon) and a team of excellent speech, physical, and occupational therapists.

*IEP Goals*　　I teach skills that increase children's independence and give them a base for future learning. Children's learning goals include following directions, transitioning from one activity to another, playing appropriately, attending, taking turns, communicating, participating in group activities, pre-academic skills (such as counting and identifying colors, shapes, and letters), and functional skills such as toileting, washing hands, and coat skills. Because all preschoolers need to learn

## Focus Questions

- Why is it so difficult to measure the impact of early intervention?

- How can we provide early intervention for a child whose disability is not yet present?

- Which do you think are most important goals of early childhood special education?

- How does early childhood special education differ from special education for school-age children with disabilities?

- How can a play activity or an everyday routine become a specially designed learning opportunity for a preschooler with disabilities?

these skills, they are incorporated into thoughtfully planned classroom activities. When necessary, these skills are addressed by children's IEP goals and objectives. For example:

- **Cognitive skills IEP goal.** Abby will improve her cognitive skills so she can participate in developmentally appropriate activities.

  *Short-term objective 1.* With adult assistance to arrange opportunities, Abby will use eye gaze to correctly identify (a) 5 pictures of familiar objects and/or people by (date) and (b) 10 pictures of familiar objects and/or people by (date) on 3 separate days, as measured by monthly classroom data collection.
  *Short-term objective 2.* With adult assistance to arrange opportunities and assistive technology, Abby will follow adult directions to "turn it on/make it go" and "turn it off/make it stop" (a) 2 times daily by (date) and (b) 4 times daily by (date) on 3 separate occasions, as measured by monthly classroom data collection.

- **Adaptive skills IEP goal.** Ben will improve his adaptive skills so he is better able to care for his own needs.

  *Short-term objective 1.* Ben will complete all steps of the handwashing process (a) 2 times daily with visual/gestural prompts as needed by (date) and (b) 2 times daily independently by (date) on 3 separate days, as measured by monthly classroom data collection.
  *Short-term objective 2.* Ben will unfasten his coat, take his coat and backpack off, and put them in his cubby (a) 1 time daily with verbal/gestural prompts by (date) and (b) 1 time daily independently by (date) on 3 separate days, as measured by monthly classroom data collection.

I think that the present levels of educational performance (PLEP) section of the IEP is just as important, if not more so, than the goals and objectives. PLEPs communicate how you think about a child. If you think about a child in terms of strengths and challenges, instead of deficits, and describe what she can do well, parents are much more willing to listen and work with you on identifying some objectives for areas of improvement. For example, here is the PLEP I wrote to address Abby's cognitive and adaptive skills:

Abby really enjoys preschool! One of her favorite parts of the day is circle.... She loves music and beams her famous smile at everyone when we start singing. She is able to direct her eye gaze to choose a picture of the song she wants to sing. She is also able to visually track objects horizontally, vertically, and in a circular motion when they are moved slowly. Abby is beginning to demonstrate discrimination of objects and colors placed in or near her hands and has been observed pushing the correct item/color when given a direction such as "Give me the red bird/car/person/." She is unable to independently access classroom materials and toys; hence, we've done many trials with different switch styles and positions and have found that a small switch mounted near her right fist is very successful. With this, she can activate toys and communication devices by herself. Abby's limited mobility and communication skills impair her ability to access and play in her school environment and impact her independent participation in developmentally appropriate activities. Objectives in this area should focus on building her emerging cognitive skills.

**Teaching Strategies** I tell anyone who asks that my classroom isn't that different from the tuition-based preschool next door. I begin with general education preschool activities and add structure and accommodations as necessary. One of the most important things I do takes place before the children even arrive. During the summer, I give a lot of thought to arranging the physical classroom environment, designing boundaries, minimizing distractions, allowing for adequate play space, arranging the room so it is accessible to all students, and making sure that all the areas and materials in my room are fun so that children and teachers will want to play.

I place a lot of emphasis on structure and routine. I have an overall classroom schedule and individual schedules as needed to ease transitions and teach independence. I try to make learning *meaningful* for my students: I purposely plan opportunities for communication, I embed learning trials into naturally occurring (but thoughtfully designed) activities, and I use natural reinforcers whenever possible. And I have tons of

To see examples of activity schedules and data collection forms used by Ms. Lundy, go to Chapter 14 on the Companion Website, **www.prenhall.com/heward**.

fun with my kids! I love to play with them. In doing so, I build friendships and connections with them that make my teaching all the more effective.

How do I know that all of this stuff works? Every year, I get better at collecting data on the children's learning. The data tell me if what I am doing is working. Equally important, the data tell me when something is not working and it's time to try a different strategy.

***Communicating with Parents and Families***    As the older sister of a young woman with Down syndrome, I have a very personal view about the role and significance of families. You just can't take a child out of the context of his or her family. I have an open classroom policy, which means that families can come and visit any time—no advance warning needed. When writing and presenting IEPs to families new to special education, I write out acronyms and try to avoid using any jargon or technical terms. I send home a weekly newsletter called "The Adventures of Room 45." I do home visits and help plan birthday parties. I love to have siblings come and visit for a day. I telephone and e-mail families often.

***A Memorable Lesson***    Last year, I had a 3-year-old who missed a lot of school. When Joey did come to school, he wore dirty, stinky clothes; sometimes he came to school sick. Joey's mom *never* came to any scheduled meetings or events, even when she told me she would come. I started thinking some pretty negative things about her. One evening, I took Joey home after another student's birthday party. Since his mom hadn't attended Joey's IEP meeting, I decided to talk with her right then and there. I discovered she was a single parent who loved her two children very much and that after providing food, shelter, and child care for them, her financial and personal resources were totally exhausted. I gained a lot of respect for Joey's mom that night and lost some for myself for not discovering and understanding her situation sooner.

***What I Like Most about Being a Special Educator***    I believe that we can all make significant contributions to society. I count my blessings every day that I am in the position to teach children the skills they will need to do this. I spend my days with a very precious future; I embark on a different adventure every day and strive to make a difference in each adventure. Being a special education teacher is not easy. The field is full of paperwork and miles of red tape. But it's even more full of wonderful children who need your help. If you want to make a difference, want a challenge, and want to learn a lot along the way, then this is the job for you!

**M**ost children learn a phenomenal amount from the time they are born until they enter school. They grow and develop in orderly, predictable ways, learning to move about their world, communicate, and play. As their ability to manipulate their environment increases, so does their level of independence. Normal rates and patterns of child development contrast sharply with the progress experienced by most children with disabilities. If they are to master the basic skills that most children acquire naturally, many preschoolers with disabilities need carefully planned and implemented early childhood special education services.

Early childhood experts agree that the earlier intervention begins, the better. Child development expert Burton White, who has conducted years of research with typically developing infants and preschoolers at Harvard University's Preschool Project, believes that the period between 8 months and 3 years is critical to cognitive and social development: "to begin to look at a child's educational development when he is 2 years of age is already much

To better understand the topics that will be covered in this chapter, go to the Essential Concepts and Chapter at a Glance modules in Chapter 14 of the Companion Website, **www.prenhall.com/heward**.

The first years of life are critical for children with disabilities, who, with each passing month, risk falling even further behind their typically developing age mates.

too late" (White, 1975, p. 4). If the first years of life are the most important for children without disabilities, they are even more critical for the child with disabilities, who, with each passing month, risks falling even further behind her typically developing age mates. Yet parents concerned about deficits in their child's development used to be told, "Don't worry. Wait and see. She'll probably grow out of it."

It is clear that developmental delays do not just go away with time and that young children who are behind don't simply "catch up." In summarizing the findings of their 20-year follow-up of children with developmental delays who had been identified at age 3 years, Keogh, Bernheimer, and Guthrie (2004) noted:

> The majority of the children did not "outgrow" their delays. As young adults they continued to have problems. Most lived with their families or in group homes, were unemployed or underemployed, and had few friends. . . .
>
> In sum, our findings confirm that signs of developmental delay in the preschool years signal the probability of continuing problems in the early adult years (pp. 227, 229).

Over the past 25 years, the "extraordinary vulnerability of young children at risk for developmental problems . . . as well as those with established disabilities has been recognized" (Guralnick, 1998, p. 319). Today, early childhood special education has become one of the most prominent and growing components in education, and the creation of an effective system of early intervention services has become a national priority.

## THE IMPORTANCE OF EARLY INTERVENTION

### Defining Early Intervention

In the early childhood and special education literature, the term *early intervention* sometimes refers only to services provided to infants and toddlers from birth through age 2. *Early childhood special education* refers to educational and related services provided to preschoolers ages 3 to 5. In this book, the two terms generally are used interchangeably to describe special education services provided to children from birth to age 5 and their families. **Early intervention** consists of a wide variety of educational, nutritional, child care, and family supports, all designed to reduce the effects of disabilities or prevent the occurrence of learning and developmental problems later in life for children presumed to be at risk for such problems. McConnell (1994) provides an excellent definition of early intervention as

> home- and classroom-based efforts that provide (1) compensatory or preventative services for children who are assumed to be at risk for learning and behavior problems later in life, particularly during the elementary school years, and (2) remedial services for problems or deficits already encountered. . . . Simply put, early intervention must provide early identification and provision of services to reduce or eliminate the effects of disabilities or to prevent the development of other problems, so that the need for subsequent special services is reduced. (pp. 75, 78)

### Examining the Effectiveness of Early Intervention

Does early intervention work? If so, what kinds of interventions work best? Hundreds of studies have been conducted in an effort to answer these questions. We'll look at a few of those studies here. First, we'll consider two widely cited examples of what Guralnick (1997) calls first-generation research: studies that try to answer the question "Does early intervention make a difference for children and their families?" Then we'll look at three examples of second-generation research studies designed to find what factors make early intervention more or less effective for particular groups of children.

*Skeels and Dye.*   The earliest and one of the most dramatic demonstrations of the critical importance and potential impact of early intervention was conducted by Skeels and Dye (1939). They found that intensive stimulation, one-to-one attention, and a half-morning kindergarten program with 1- to 2-year-old children who were classified as mentally retarded resulted in IQ gains and eventual independence and success as adults when compared to similar children in the institution who received adequate medical and health services but no individual attention. Although the Skeels and Dye study can be justly criticized for its lack of tight experimental methodology, it challenged the widespread belief that intelligence was fixed and that little could be expected from intervention efforts. This study served as the catalyst for many subsequent investigations into the effects of early intervention.

*The Milwaukee Project.*   The goal of the Milwaukee Project was to reduce the incidence of mental retardation through a program of parent education and infant stimulation for children considered at risk for retarded development because of their mothers' levels of intelligence (IQs below 70) and conditions of poverty (Garber & Heber, 1973; Heber & Garber, 1971; Strickland, 1971). The mothers received training in child care and were taught how to interact with and stimulate their children through play. Beginning before the age of 6 months, the children also participated in an infant stimulation program conducted by trained teachers. By the age of 3½, the experimental children tested an average of 33 IQ points higher than did a control group of children who did not participate in the program. (Play is critically important to children's learning and development. See Teaching & Learning, "Selecting Toys for Young Children with Disabilities," later in this chapter.)

Although the Milwaukee Project was criticized for its research methods (e.g., Page, 1972), this study is sometimes offered as proof that a program of maternal education and early infant stimulation can reduce the incidence of mental retardation caused by psychosocial disadvantage. (**Psychosocial disadvantage,** a combination of social and environmental deprivation early in a child's life, is generally believed to be a major cause of mild mental retardation.)

*The Abecedarian Project.*   The Abecedarian Project was designed as an experiment to test whether mental retardation caused by psychosocial disadvantage could be prevented by intensive, early education preschool programs (in conjunction with medical and nutritional supports) beginning shortly after birth and continuing until children enter kindergarten (Martin, Ramey, & Ramey, 1990). Children in the Abecedarian Project received early intervention that was both intensive and long: a full-day preschool program, 5 days per week, 50 weeks per year. Compared with children in a control group who received supplemental medical, nutritional, and social services but no daily early educational intervention services, children in the early intervention group made positive gains in IQ scores by age 3, were 50% less likely to fail a grade, and scored higher on IQ and reading and mathematics achievement tests at age 12.

A related finding was that children of low-IQ mothers benefited most from early intervention. For the mothers with IQs below 70 who were in the control condition, all but one of their children had IQs in the mentally retarded or borderline intelligence range at age 3. In contrast, all of the children in the early intervention group tested in the normal range of intelligence (above 85) by age 3.

> This finding supports the concept of *targeted intervention*, which indicates that primary prevention of childhood disorders is more likely for certain subgroups than for others (Landesman & Ramey, 1989). Because the majority of children with mild and moderate mental retardation come from families with extremely low resources and with parents who have limited intellectual resources themselves, these families are the ones that are most in need of early intervention and are those that benefit the most in terms of outcomes valued by society. (Ramey & Ramey, 1992, p. 338)

For a more complete description of the Skeels and Dye study, see "A Powerful Demonstration of the Potential Impact of Early Intervention," in Chapter 14's Profiles and Perspectives Module on the Companion Website, **www.prenhall.com/heward**.

*Skeels & Dye study and Milwaukee Project*

Council for Exceptional Children   Content Standards for Beginning Teachers of Early Childhood Students: Historical and philosophical foundations of services for young children both with and without exceptional learning needs (EC1K1).

# Selecting Toys for Young Children with Disabilities

In 1916, John Dewey said, "Children learn by doing." He might just have well have said, "Children learn by playing." Play provides children with natural, repeated opportunities for critical learning. It is the way they explore the world and discover their own capabilities. An infant bats a mobile with her hand, repeats the action, and begins learning about her surroundings. As a toddler, her interactions with play materials teach her to discriminate and compare shapes and sizes and learn concepts such as cause and effect and fast and slow (Hughes, Elicker, & Veen, 1995). A preschooler's increasingly complex play develops gross- and fine-motor skills, requires her to communicate and negotiate plans with others, and exposes her to pre-academic math and literacy skills (DiCarlo & Reid, 2004; Morrison, Sainato, BenChaaban, & Endo, 2002; Weber, Behl, & Summers, 1994).

If play is the work of childhood, then toys are the child's tools. Ideally, play materials, whether store-bought toys or everyday household items such as pots and pans, should provide meaningful, motivating activities that serve as a precursor to more complex learning (Brewer & Kieff, 1996; Mann, 1996; Perlmutter & Burrell, 1995). Not all toys, however, are accessible to children with disabilities.

The National Lekotek Center is a nationwide, nonprofit network of play centers, toy lending libraries, and computer loan programs dedicated to making play accessible for children with disabilities and to those living in poverty. Diana Nielander, planning and information officer at Lekotek, recommends keeping the following 10 tips in mind when selecting toys for young children with disabilities:

1. *Multisensory appeal.* Does the toy respond with lights, sounds, or movements? Are there contrasting colors? Does it have scent? Texture?
2. *Method of activation.* Will the toy provide a challenge without frustration? What force is required to activate it? What are the number and complexity of steps required?
3. *Adjustability.* Does the toy have adjustable height, sound, volume, speed, and level of difficulty?
4. *Opportunities for success.* Can play be open-ended with no definite right or wrong way?
5. *Child's individual characteristics.* Does the toy provide activities that reflect both developmental and chronological ages? Does it reflect the child's interests?
6. *Self-expression.* Does the toy allow for creativity and choice making? Will it give the child experience with a variety of media?
7. *Potential for interaction.* Will the child be an active participant during use? Will the toy encourage social and language engagement with others?
8. *Safety and durability.* Are the toy and its parts sized appropriately given the child's size and strength? Can it be washed and cleaned? Is it moisture resistant?
9. *Where the toy will be used.* Will the toy be easy to store? Is there space in the home? Can the toy be used in a variety of positions (e.g., by a child lying on his side) or on a wheelchair tray?
10. *Current popularity.* Is it a toy almost any child would like? Does it tie in with popular books, TV programs, or movies?

Information on specific toys can be found in Lekotek's Toy Guide for Differently-Abled Kids!, a free resource published in conjunction with Toys "R" Us and endorsed by the National Parent Network on Disabilities. The catalog includes pictures and descriptions of more than 100 toys that have been tested with preschoolers with disabilities. Each toy is identified according to its likelihood of promoting growth in 10 developmental or skill areas: auditory, language, visual, tactile, gross motor, fine motor, social skills, self-esteem, creativity, and thinking.

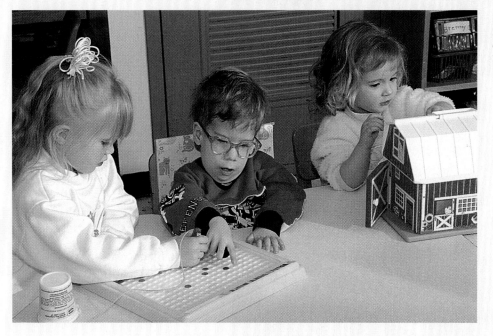

Play provides children with natural, repeated opportunities for critical learning

Information about Lekotek and its services to families can be obtained at its website (http://www.lekotek.org). Lekotek also operates a toy resource helpline at (800) 366-PLAY, a toll-free service that anyone can use to talk directly to trained play experts who will recommend appropriate toys and play activities for a particular child as well as make referrals to other disability-related resources for families.

 To learn more about these strategies and answer questions about what you have learned, go to the Teaching & Learning module in Chapter 14 of the Companion Website, **www.prenhall.com/heward.**

*Project CARE.*    Project CARE compared the effectiveness of home-based early intervention in which mothers learned how to provide developmental stimulation for their infants and toddlers with center-based early intervention like that provided in the Abecedarian Project (Wasik, Ramey, Bryant, & Sparling, 1990). Children who received the full-day, center-based preschool program 5 days per week, supplemented by home visits, showed gains in intellectual functioning almost identical to those found in the Abecedarian Project. A disappointment was that the intellectual functioning of children in the home-based–only treatment group did not improve. Ramey and Ramey (1992) suggest, "One plausible interpretation of these results is that the home-based treatment was not sufficiently intensive, on a day-to-day basis, to produce the same benefits that occur when a more formally organized and monitored center-based program is provided year round" (p. 339).

*The Infant Health and Development Program.*    The Infant Health and Development Program (IHDP) provided early intervention services to infants who were born prematurely and at low birth weight (less than 2,500 grams, or about 5½ pounds), two conditions that place children at risk for developmental delays (Ramey et al., 1992). This large-scale study involved nearly 1,000 children and their families in eight locations throughout the United States. Home visits were conducted from shortly after birth through age 3. Because of health problems associated with prematurity and low birth weight, the children did not begin attending the center-based early education program until 12 months of age and continued until age 3. Improvements in intellectual functioning were noted, with babies of comparatively higher birth weight showing increases similar in magnitude to those found in the Abecedarian Project and Project CARE.

The IHDP study found a positive correlation between how much children and their families participated in early intervention and the intellectual development of the children. The percentages of children whose IQ scores fell into the mental retardation range based on tests administered at age 3 for each of the groups were 17% for the control group, 13% for those with low participation, 4% for medium participation, and less than 2% for high participation. The most active participants had an almost ninefold reduction in the incidence of mental retardation compared to the control group.

Together, these three second-generation studies provide strong evidence that children at risk for developmental delays and poor school outcomes respond favorably to systematic early intervention. They also point to two factors that appear

In addition to enhancing the development of infants and toddlers with disabilities and those who are at risk for developmental delays, early intervention can help reduce the need for special education and related services after those children reach school age.

highly related to the outcome effectiveness of early intervention: the *intensity of the intervention* and the *level of participation* by the children and their families (Ramey & Ramey, 1992).

*Summarizing the Research Base.*   Numerous methodological problems make it difficult to conduct early intervention research in a scientifically sound manner. Among the problems are difficulties in selecting meaningful and reliable outcome measures; the wide disparity among children in the developmental effects of their disabilities; the tremendous variation across early intervention programs in curriculum focus, teaching strategies, length, and intensity; and the ethical concerns of withholding early intervention from some children so that they may form a control group for comparison purposes (Bricker, 1986; Guralnick, 1998; Strain & Smith, 1986).

Despite these problems, most educators agree with Guralnick (1998), who concluded that, when taken as whole, comprehensive early intervention programs reveal a "consistent pattern of effectiveness as these programs are able to reduce the decline in intellectual development that occurs in the absence of intervention" (p. 323). Our national policymakers also believe that early intervention produces positive results for young children with disabilities, those who are at risk for developmental delays, and their families. Citing research and testimony from families, Congress identified the following outcomes for early intervention in the Individuals with Disabilities Education Improvement Act of 2004:

1. to enhance the development of infants and toddlers with disabilities, to minimize their potential for developmental delay, and to recognize the significant brain development that occurs during a child's first 3 years of life;
2. to reduce the educational costs to our society, including our Nation's schools, by minimizing the need for special education and related services after infants and toddlers with disabilities reach school age;

3. to maximize the potential for individuals with disabilities to live independently in society;

4. to enhance the capacity of families to meet the special needs of their infants and toddlers with disabilities; and

5. to enhance the capacity of state and local agencies and service providers to identify, evaluate, and meet the needs of all children, particularly minority, low-income, inner city, and rural children, and infants and toddlers in foster care. (H.R. 1350, Sec 631[A]).

# IDEA AND EARLY CHILDHOOD SPECIAL EDUCATION

When Congress passed P.L. 94–142 in 1975 (the original IDEA), it mandated a free, appropriate public education for all school-age children with disabilities, ages 6 through 21. The law also required a state to provide special education services to all preschool children ages 3 to 5 with disabilities if that state already provided general public education for children in that age group. To encourage states to begin programs for preschoolers with disabilities, P.L. 94–142 included an incentive grant program that provided funds for establishing or improving preschool programs for children with disabilities.

Since 1975, Congress has enacted five bills reauthorizing and amending the original IDEA. The second of those bills, P.L. 99–457, has been called the most important legislation ever enacted for children with developmental delays (Shonkoff & Meisels, 2000). Before passage of this law, Congress estimated that states were serving at most about 70% of preschool children with disabilities, and systematic early intervention services for infants and toddlers with disabilities from birth through age 2 were scarce or nonexistent in many states. P.L. 99–457 included a mandatory preschool component for children with disabilities ages 3 to 5 and a voluntary incentive grant program for early intervention services to infants and toddlers and their families. With the passage of the Individuals with Disabilities Education Improvement Act of 2004, Congress has reaffirmed the nation's commitment to a system of early intervention services.

## Early Intervention for Infants and Toddlers

If a state chooses to provide comprehensive early intervention services to infants and toddlers and their families, it can receive federal funds under IDEA's early intervention provisions. Currently, all states are participating; each state receives federal funds under this program based on the number of children birth through age 2 in the state's general population. In 2003–2004, approximately 39,312 infants and toddlers were served nationally.

The law covers any child under age 3 who meets the following criteria:

a. Needs early intervention services because of developmental delays (as measured by appropriate diagnostic instruments or procedures) in one or more of areas of cognitive development, physical development, social or emotional development, or adaptive development.

b. Has a diagnosed physical or medical condition that has a high probability of resulting in developmental delay.

c. Each State may also, at its discretion, serve infants and toddlers who are at risk of experiencing a substantial developmental delay if early intervention services are not provided.

Thus, states that receive IDEA funds for early intervention services must serve all infants and toddlers with developmental delays or established risk conditions. Although not required to do so, states may also use IDEA early intervention funds to serve infants and toddlers who fall under two types of *documented risk*, biological and environmental.

• *Developmental delays* are significant delays or atypical patterns of development that make children eligible for early intervention. Each state's definition of developmental

*IDEA and early intervention*

**Council for Exceptional Children**  Content Standards for Beginning Teachers of Early Childhood Students: Laws and policies that affect young children, families, and programs for young children (EC1K3).

*Definitions of developmental delays risk conditions*

**Council for Exceptional Children**  Content Standards for Beginning Teachers of Early Childhood Students: Laws and policies that affect young children, families, and programs for young children (EC1K3).

delay must be broad enough to include all disability categories covered by IDEA, but children do not need to be classified or labeled according to those categories to receive early intervention services.

- *Established risk conditions* include diagnosed physical or medical conditions that almost always result in developmental delay or disability. Examples of established risk conditions are Down syndrome, fragile-X syndrome, fetal alcohol syndrome (FAS), and other conditions associated with mental retardation, brain or spinal cord damage, sensory impairments, and maternal acquired immune deficiency syndrome (AIDS). (Down syndrome, fragile-X syndrome, and FAS are discussed in Chapter 4.)
- *Biological risk conditions* include pediatric histories or current biological conditions (e.g., significantly premature birth, low birth weight) that result in a greater-than-usual probability of developmental delay or disability.
- *Environmental risk conditions* include factors such as extreme poverty, parental substance abuse, homelessness, abuse or neglect, and parental intellectual impairment, which are associated with higher-than-normal probability of developmental delay. (See Profiles & Perspectives, "Educating Young Children Prenatally Exposed to Illegal Drugs," later in this chapter.)

*IFSP*

Council for Exceptional Children — Content Standards for Beginning Teachers of Early Childhood Students: Laws and policies that affect young children, families, and programs for young children (EC1K3).

*Individualized Family Services Plan.* IDEA requires that early intervention services for infants and toddlers be delivered according to an **individualized family services plan (IFSP).** The IFSP is developed by a multidisciplinary team that includes the child's parents and other family members and must include each of the following eight elements:

1. a statement of the child's present levels of physical development, cognitive development, communication development, social or emotional development, or adaptive development, based on objective criteria;
2. a statement of the family's resources, priorities, and concerns relating to enhancing the development of the family's infant or toddler with a disability;
3. a statement of the major outcomes expected to be achieved for the infant or toddler and family, and the criteria, procedures, and timelines used to determine the degree to which progress toward achieving the outcomes is being made and whether modifications or revision of the outcomes or services are necessary;
4. a statement of the specific early intervention services necessary to meet the unique needs of the infant or toddler and family, including frequency, intensity, and method of delivering the services;
5. a statement of the natural environments in which early intervention services shall appropriately be provided, including a justification of the extent, if any, to which the services will not be provided in a natural environment;
6. the projected dates for initiation of services and anticipated duration of services;
7. the identification of the service coordinator from the profession most immediately relevant to the infant's or toddler's or family's needs who will be responsible for implementation of the plan and coordination with other agencies and persons; and
8. the steps to be taken to support a successful transition of the toddler with a disability to preschool or other appropriate services. (P.L. 105–17, Sec. 1436)

IFSPs differ from IEPs in several important ways (Bruder, 2000). Unlike the IEP, an IFSP does the following:

- Revolves around the family system as the constant and most important factor in the child's life
- Defines the family as being the recipient of early intervention services rather than the child alone
- Focuses on the natural environments in which the child and family live, extending the settings in which services can be provided beyond formal, contrived settings such as preschools to everyday routines in home and community
- Includes interventions and services provided by a variety of health and human service agencies in addition to education

# Educating Young Children Prenatally Exposed to Illegal Drugs

*by Judith J. Carta*

About 15 years ago, several of my colleagues and I became aware that children who had been identified as being prenatally exposed to drugs, especially cocaine, were entering our local preschool and child care settings. At that time, the media were publishing reports describing a new population of children like no other previously seen. These children were described as out of control, with no ability to focus attention; lacking in affect; and unable to tell the difference between right and wrong. Understandably, teachers felt afraid and ill-equipped to handle such children, and potential foster and adoptive parents were hesitant to open their homes and families to them.

These fears were based on several myths and misconceptions that are conveyed in questions people most frequently asked about children prenatally exposed to drugs.

*Do they all have behavior problems or learning difficulties?* Children whose prenatal histories include their mothers' use of drugs represent a wide range of abilities. Some have physical and mental disabilities; others appear unaffected. Some are passive and socially withdrawn; others are aggressive. Some are unattached; others constantly seek attention and affection. No profile or set of characteristics defines this group of children. Some studies have reported that approximately 30% of these children perform lower academically than typically developing children. But this average figure masks the considerable variation in the way individual children may be affected (from a lot to not at all). It also fails to convey the many other factors in children's lives that may account for their developmental outcomes.

*What accounts for the growing number of inner-city children's sudden episodes of violence, difficulties in attention, or lack of social skills, which appear more often in our classrooms? Aren't these problems caused by mothers' drug use?* It is interesting that only behavior problems in inner-city schools are linked to prenatal drug use. Such a conclusion suggests that only mothers in the urban areas use drugs. In reality, the problem of illegal drug use by pregnant women is not unique to the inner city or to any particular racial or ethnic group. No one group "owns" the problem of prenatal substance exposure. It is as likely to occur in rural areas as in urban areas or the suburbs.

Although prenatal substance exposure may be a factor in explaining the wide-ranging types of problems occurring with greater frequency in our schools, many risk factors associated with living in poverty and less-than-adequate caregiving may also be responsible (Carta et al., 2001). For example, two other factors are associated with a drug-using lifestyle in poverty: violence and drug trafficking. Violence is a fact of life in communities where trafficking occurs. A large percentage of children witness violence in neighborhoods as well as in their homes. Mothers are often victims of abuse, as are the children themselves. A growing body of research on the effects of exposure to violence or maltreatment of children points to many of the same behavioral symptoms attributed to prenatal drug exposure.

Another factor associated with behavioral and learning difficulties is the quality of caregiving that children receive in a substance-using lifestyle. Substance abusers are often inconsistent caregivers, behaving one way toward their children when they are straight, another when they are high or coming down. Attempting to get straight often requires a period of separation from children because many residential treatment centers do not allow them. Drug-using parents are often socially isolated and lack a network of friends or family. They have difficulty getting the things they need for themselves and their children, such as child care, jobs, and education. The lack of support, resources, and sometimes bare necessities challenges any parent's caregiving.

These risk factors and many others can act in combination with prenatal exposure to drugs, as well as with each other, to produce behavior and learning problems. Such factors can threaten a child's developmental and educational outcomes and challenge teachers, caregivers, and parents, who affect a child's development and educational success.

*Will children prenatally exposed to drugs require specialized interventions that have not yet been developed?* There is no current evidence to suggest that these children exhibit a unique set of problems requiring a unique curriculum or set of educational or caregiving procedures. All children prenatally exposed to drugs do not have problems; and when they do, their difficulties are ones that are also exhibited by other children. Some children who are prenatally exposed may have language or social problems; others may have cognitive, motor, or adaptive deficits. Effective interventions are available for improving skills in each of these areas. There is no evidence that these interventions are not effective for children with a history of prenatal exposure to illegal drugs as they have been for other children. We do not need a curriculum or an intervention aimed at the population of children who have been drug-exposed; what we do need is a set of instructional procedures to address the problem behaviors and skill deficiencies exhibited by these children. Therefore, our suggested approach to determining interventions for children who are prenatally exposed to illegal drugs is identical to the approach we use for all children:

- Identify specific behaviors that require remediation.
- Determine specific interventions that address those behaviors.
- Systematically implement those interventions.
- Monitor the effects of the interventions on the specified behaviors.

What do require special attention, however, are the risks these children face growing up in drug-using lifestyles. Until we begin to comprehensively address the risks associated with living in concentrated poverty, our efforts to provide interventions for children will have little chance of producing lasting effects.

---

Judith J. Carta is a senior scientist and director of early childhood research at the Juniper Gardens Children's Project of the University of Kansas.

To further your understanding of and answer reflective questions about the concepts and issues presented here, go to the Profiles & Perspectives module in Chapter 14 of the Companion Website, **www.prenhall.com/heward**.

The IFSP must be evaluated once a year and reviewed with the family at 6-month intervals. Recognizing the critical importance of time for the infant with disabilities, IDEA allows for initiation of early intervention services before the IFSP is completed if the parents give their consent. Figure 14.1 (pp. 568–569) shows portions of an IFSP developed with and for the family of a 26-month-old child with disabilities.

## Special Education for Preschoolers

IDEA requires states to provide special education services to all children with disabilities ages 3 to 5. The regulations governing these programs are similar to those for school-age children, with the following exceptions:

- Preschool children do not have to be identified and reported under existing disability categories (e.g., mental retardation, orthopedic impairments) to receive services. This provision of IDEA also allows, but does not require, states to serve at-risk students from ages 3 through 9 (Turnbull & Cilley, 1999).

IDEA requires states to provide special education to all children with disabilities ages 3 to 5.

- Each state, at its discretion, may also serve children (from ages 3 through 9) who are

a. experiencing developmental delays as defined by the State and as measured by appropriate diagnostic instrument and procedures in one or more of the following areas: physical development, cognitive development, communication development, social or emotional development, or adaptive development; and

b. who, by reason thereof, need special education and related services. (Sec. 1401)

- IEPs must include a section with suggestions and information for parents.
- Local education agencies may elect to use a variety of service delivery options (home-based, center-based, or combination programs), and the length of the school day and year may vary.
- Although preschool special education programs must be administered by the state education agency, services from other agencies may be contracted to meet the requirement of a full range of services. For example, many preschoolers with disabilities are served in community-based Head Start programs (Odom et al., 2000).

# Screening, Identification, and Assessment

Assessment and evaluation in early childhood education are conducted for at least four different purposes, with specific evaluation tools for each (Bondurant-Utz, 2002; Bricker, 2002; Greenwood, Carta, & Walker, 2005; McLean, Wolery, & Bailey, 2004; Neisworth & Bagnato, 2000):

*Screening*: quick, easy-to-administer tests to identify children who may have a disability and who should receive further testing

*Diagnosis*: in-depth, comprehensive assessment of all major areas of development to determine a child's eligibility for early intervention or special education services

*Program planning*: curriculum-based, criterion-referenced assessments to determine a child's current skill level, identify IFSP/IEP objectives, and plan intervention activities

*Evaluation*: curriculum-based, criterion-referenced measures to determine progress on IFSP/IEP objectives and evaluate the program's effectiveness

## Screening Tools

Before young children and their families can be served, they must be identified. Some children's disabilities are so significant that no test is needed. As a general rule, the more severe a disability, the earlier it is detected. In the delivery room, medical staff can identify certain disabilities, such as microcephaly, cleft palate, and other physical conditions, as well as most instances of Down syndrome. Within the first few weeks, other physical characteristics such as paralysis, seizures, or rapidly increasing head size can signal possible disabilities. But most children who experience developmental delays are not identifiable by obvious physical characteristics or behavioral patterns, especially at very young ages. That is where screening tools come into play.

*The Apgar Scale.* The **Apgar scale,** which measures the degree of prenatal *asphyxia* (oxygen deprivation) an infant experiences during birth, is administered to virtually all babies born in U.S. hospitals. The test administrator—nurse, nurse anesthesiologist, or pediatrician—evaluates the newborn twice on five physiological measures: heart rate, respiratory effort, response to stimulation, muscle tone, and skin color. The child is given a score of 0, 1, or 2 on each measure according to the criteria described on the scoring form (see Figure 14.2 on page 570).

The first administration of the test, which is conducted 60 seconds after birth, measures how the baby fared during the birth process. If the newborn receives a low score on the first test, the delivery room staff takes immediate resuscitation action. The scale is given again 5 minutes after birth. At that point a total score of 0 to 3 (out of a possible 10) indicates severe asphyxia, 4 to 6 moderate asphyxia, and 7 to 10 mild asphyxia. Some stress is assumed

*IDEA and preschoolers*

Council for Exceptional Children Content Standards for Beginning Teachers of Early Childhood Students: Laws and policies that affect young children, families, and programs for young children (EC1K3).

*Purposes of assessment and evaluation*

Council for Exceptional Children Content Standards for Beginning Teachers—Common Core: Basic terminology used in assessment (CC8K1).

## FIGURE 14.1    Portion of an IFSP written with the family of a 26-month-old child with disabilities

INDIVIDUALIZED FAMILY SERVICE PLAN (IFSP) for Children Birth to Three Years        SANTA CLARA COUNTY

Child's name: _____Cathy Rae Wright_____    Birth Date: __11-15-01__    Age: __26__ months    Sex: __F__

Parent(s)/Guardian(s): __Martha and Gary Wright__    Address: __1414 Coolidge Drive Cupertino__    Zip: __95014__

Home phone: 408 398-2461  Work phone: 408 554-2490  Primary language of the home: __English__  Other languages _____

Date of this IFSP 1/15/04 Projected periodic review 7/15/04 Projected annual review 1/15/05 Tentative IFSP exit 11/15/04
            (at 6 months or before)

| Service Coordinator Name | Agency | Phone | Date Appointed | Date Ended |
|---|---|---|---|---|
| Sandy Drohman | Regional Center | 408-461-2192 | 12/10/03 | / / |

**Family's strengths and preferred resources** (With the family, identify the family strengths and the resources they might find helpful in addressing family concerns and priorities.)   Mr. and Mrs. Wright are well-educated and constantly seek additional information about Cathy's condition. They are anxious to help Cathy in any way possible. Mrs. Wright's family is very supportive. They provide child care for Cathy's older brother.
Because of Cathy's tendency to be medically fragile, Mr. and Mrs. Wright prefer a home based early intervention program. They appreciate receiving written materials to help them understand how to work with Cathy. Mrs. Wright wants to be home when the home visitor comes so she can learn from her.

**Family's concerns and priorities**   (With the family, identify major areas of concerns for the child with special needs and the family as a whole.)   Mr. and Mrs. Wright are very concerned about Cathy's delays in walking, using her fingers to pick up things, and in talking with other children. They also worry about her small size. Cathy is their second child and was born at 24 weeks gestation. Mr. and Mrs. Wright would like to have more information on the issues of prematurity and they would like to find an appropriate support group for themselves.

### CHILD'S STRENGTHS AND PRESENT LEVELS OF DEVELOPMENT

With the family, identify what the child can do and what the child is learning to do. Include family and professional observations in each of the following areas:

**PHYSICAL** *Based on parent report and HELP Strands

Health   Cathy is said by her parents to be healthy but is very petite. Her parents are working with a nutritionist to help Cathy gain weight.

Vision   Cathy has had corrective surgery for strabismus.

Hearing   She has had numerous ear infections and currently has tubes in her ears.

Gross Motor (large movement)  Cathy stands on tiptoes, runs on toes, makes sharp turns around corners when running, walks upstairs with one hand held

Fine Motor (small movement)  Cathy grasps crayon adaptively and points with index finger; imitates horizontal strokes, builds 6 block tower, turns pages one at a time; has trouble picking up small objects.

**COGNITIVE** (responsiveness to environments, problem-solving)  Cathy finds hidden object; attempts and succeeds in activating mechanical toy; demonstrates use of objects appropriate for age

**COMMUNICATION** (language and speech)

**RECEPTIVE** (understanding)   Cathy points to body parts when asked; obeys two part commands.

**EXPRESSIVE** (making sounds, talking)   Cathy names 8 pictures, interacts with peers using only gestures; attempts to sing songs with words

**SOCIAL/EMOTIONAL** (how relates to others)  Cathy expresses affection, is beginning to obey and respect simple rules, tends to be physically aggressive

**ADAPTIVE/SELF-HELP** (sleeping, eating, dressing, toileting, etc.)   Cathy can put on socks and shoes, verbalizes need to use the toilet, but is not potty trained, feeds self

**DIAGNOSIS** (if known) _____

**FIGURE 14.1** *continued*

INDIVIDUALIZED FAMILY SERVICE PLAN (IFSP) for Children Birth to Three Years     SANTA CLARA COUNTY

Child's name: ___Cathy Rae Wright___

---

**IFSP OUTCOMES**
With the family, identify the goals they would like to work on in the next six months.
These should be directly related to the family's priorities and concerns as stated on page one.

---

OUTCOME:   _Cathy will increase her attempts to vocally communicate in order to make her needs known and to_
_positively interact with others._

| | Service Type (Individual = I Group = G) Location | Frequency of sessions / Length of each session | Start Date | End Date (anticipated) | Responsible Agency/ Group Including payment arrangements (if any) |
|---|---|---|---|---|---|
| **Strategy or activity to achieve the outcome** (Who will do what and when will they do it?) AIM Infant Educator will model for Mr. and Mrs. Wright techniques to solicit Cathy's vocalization efforts. **Criteria** (How will we know if we are making progress?) Increased vocalization will be observed by parents and infant educator. | I – Home-based infant program | 1 hour each week | 1-23-04 | 11-10-04 | AIM (funded by SARC) Family |
| **Strategy or activity to achieve the outcome** (Who will do what and when will they do it?) Mrs. Wright will take Cathy to play with neighborhood children and will invite children to her home. She will encourage play and vocalization. **Criteria** (How will we know if we are making progress?) Mrs. Wright will observe and note extent of interaction | G – Home and in the neighborhood | once each week for at least 30 minutes | 2-1-04 | ongoing | Mrs. Wright |
| **Strategy or activity to achieve the outcome** (Who will do what and when will they do it?) Cathy will be assessed by a speech pathologist by 2-15-03 and followed on an as needed basis. **Criteria** (How will we know if we are making progress?) A follow-up report will be submitted. | I – Regional Center Speech and Language Clinic | 1 hour play based assessment | 2-1-04 | as needed | Sandy Drohman will make arrange-ments (funded by SARC) |

OUTCOME:   _Mr. and Mrs. Wright will join Parents Helping Parents in order to receive peer parent support and_
_learn more about Cathy's condition._

| | Service Type | Frequency / Length | Start Date | End Date | Responsible Agency/ Group |
|---|---|---|---|---|---|
| **Strategy or activity to achieve the outcome** (Who will do what and when will they do it?) Sandy Drohman will provide all referral information to Mr. and Mrs. Wright and will accompany them to their first meeting if they desire. **Criteria** (How will we know if we are making progress?) Mr. and Mrs. Wright will find satisfaction in increased support and knowledge. | G – Parents Helping Parents | ( up to parent's discretion ) | | | Sandy Drohman Mr. and Mrs. Wright Parents Helping Parents |
| **Strategy or activity to achieve the outcome** (Who will do what and when will they do it?) AIM Infant Educator will assist Mr. and Mrs. Wright in obtaining additional information about Cathy's condition. **Criteria** (How will we know if we are making progress?) Mr. and Mrs. Wright will express satisfaction over the assistance received in becoming more informed. | I – Home | ongoing | 2-1-04 | 11-10-04 | AIM Infant Educator |

*Source*: Adapted from Cook, R. E., Klein, M. D., & Tessier, A. (2004). *Adapting early childhood curricula for children in inclusive settings* (6th ed.), (pp. 125–130). Upper Saddle River, NJ: Merrill/Prentice Hall. Used by permission.

## FIGURE 14.2 The Apgar evaluation scale

| | | | 60 sec. | 5 min. |
|---|---|---|---|---|
| Heart rate | Absent<br>Less than 100<br>100 to 140 | (0)<br>(1)<br>(2) | 1 | 2 |
| Respiratory effort | Apneic<br>Shallow, irregular<br>Lusty cry and breathing | (0)<br>(1)<br>(2) | 1 | 1 |
| Response to catheter stimulation | No response<br>Grimace<br>Cough or sneeze | (0)<br>(1)<br>(2) | 1 | 2 |
| Muscle tone | Flaccid<br>Some flexion of extremities<br>Flexion resisting extension | (0)<br>(1)<br>(2) | 1 | 2 |
| Color | Pale, blue<br>Body pink, extremities blue<br>Pink all over | (0)<br>(1)<br>(2) | 0 | 1 |
| | | Total | 4 | 8 |

on all births, and the 5-minute score measures how successful any resuscitation efforts were. A 5-minute score of 6 or less indicates follow-up assessment to determine what is causing the problem and what interventions may be needed.

The Apgar has been shown to identify high-risk infants—those with a greater-than-normal chance of developing later problems. Research has shown that oxygen deprivation at birth contributes to neurological impairment, and the 5-minute Apgar score correlates well with eventual neurological outcomes.

*Newborn Blood Test Screening.* Some form of newborn screening is mandated in all states, but the components of the newborn screen vary from state to state. Phenylketonuria (PKU) is screened in all states. It causes severe mental retardation, which can be easily prevented if the condition is detected before symptoms develop and the child is treated with a special diet. Testing is also done for *hypothyroidism*, which can likewise lead to mental retardation if not detected early. Affected individuals are treated with supplemental thyroid hormone.

Every state and U.S. territory mandates the number of newborn screening tests, which varies from 3 to 30. Screening tests require a few small drops of blood collected from each newborn, usually on the second day of life. This is done by a heel stick and spotting a few small drops of blood on a paper card, which is then sent for laboratory analysis that can test for as many as 30 congenital conditions or diseases that can lead to physical and health problems, sensory impairments, and/or developmental delays. Other common testing includes (but is not limited to) biotinidase deficiency, congenital adrenal hyperplasia, congenital hypothyroidism, cystic fibrosis, sickle cell diseases, maple syrup urine disease, and galactosemia and hemoglobinopathy (diseases of the red blood cells). More information is available from the National Newborn Screening and Genetics Resource Center (**http://genes-r-us.uthscsa.edu/**).

*Developmental Screening Tests.* One of the most widely used screening tools for developmental delays is the Denver II (Frankenburg & Dodds, 1990). It can be used with children from 2 weeks to 6 years of age, using both testing-observation and a parent report format. The Denver II assesses 125 skills arranged in four developmental areas: gross motor, fine motor–adaptive, language, and personal-social. Each test item is represented on the scor-

*Screening tests*

Council for Exceptional Children
Content Standards for Beginning Teachers—Common Core: Screening, pre-referral, referral, and classification procedures (CC8K3).

ing form by a bar showing at what ages 25%, 50%, 75%, and 90% of normally developing children can perform that skill. The child is allowed up to three trials per item. A child's performance on each item is scored as "pass" or "fail" and then interpreted as representing "advanced," "OK," "caution," or "delayed" performance by comparing the child's performance with those of the same age in the standardized population. Physicians most often administer the Denver II, and the test form was designed to fit the schedule of well-baby visits recommended by the American Academy of Pediatrics.

No one observes a child more often, more closely, and with more interest than his parents. Mothers' estimates of their preschool children's levels of development often correlate highly with those that professionals produce by using standardized scales, and parental involvement in screening has been found to reduce the number of misclassifications (Henderson & Meisels, 1994). Recognizing this fact, early childhood specialists have developed a number of screening tools for parent use. One such tool is the Ages and Stages Questionnaire (ASQ) (Bricker & Squires, 1999; see also Squires, Bricker, & Twombly, 2002). The ASQ includes 11 questionnaires to be completed by the parents when the child is 4, 6, 8, 12, 16, 18, 20, 24, 30, 36, and 48 months old. Each questionnaire consists of 30 items covering 5 areas of development: gross motor, fine motor, communication, personal-social, and adaptive. Many of the items include illustrations to help the parents evaluate their child's behavior.

## Diagnostic Tools

When the results of a screening test raise suspicion that a disability or a developmental delay may be present, the child is referred for diagnostic testing. The specific diagnostic tests to be used depend upon the suspected delay or disability (Bondurant-Utz, 2002; McLean et al., 2004). Tests that seek to determine if a child is experiencing a developmental delay usually measure performance in five major developmental areas or domains:

- *Motor development.* The ability to move one's body and manipulate objects within the environment provides a critical foundation for all types of learning. Motor development involves improvements in general strength, flexibility, endurance, and eye-hand coordination and includes gross- or large-muscle movement and mobility (such as walking, running, throwing) and small-muscle, fine-motor control (like that needed to pick up a toy, write, tie a shoe).
- *Cognitive development.* Children use cognitive skills when they attend to stimuli, perform pre-academic skills such as sorting or counting, remember things they have done in the past, plan and make decisions about what they will do in the future, integrate newly learned information with previously learned knowledge and skills, solve problems, and generate novel ideas.
- *Communication and language development.* Communication involves the transmission of messages; information about needs, feelings, knowledge, desires; and so forth. Children use communication and language skills when they receive information from others, share information with other individuals, and use language to mediate their actions and effectively control the environment. This domain encompasses all forms of communication development, including a child's ability to respond nonverbally with gestures, smiles, or actions and the acquisition of spoken language—sounds, words, phrases, sentences, and so on.
- *Social and emotional development.* Children who have developed competence in social skills share toys and take turns, cooperate with others, and resolve conflicts. Children should feel good about themselves and know how to express their emotions and feelings.
- *Adaptive development.* As young children develop self-care and adaptive skills such as dressing/undressing, eating, toileting, tooth brushing, and hand washing, their ability to function independently across multiple environments increases, which provides and enhances opportunities for additional kinds of learning.

*Assessment of developmental domains*

Council for
Exceptional
Children    Content Standards for Beginning Teachers—Common Core: Use and limitations of assessment instruments (CC8K4).

The Bayley Scales can be used to diagnose developmental delays in children from 2 months to 30 months

Generally, these five areas are broken down into specific, observable tasks and sequenced developmentally—that is, in the order in which most children learn them. Sometimes each task is tied to a specific age at which a child should normally be able to perform it. This arrangement allows the examiner to note significant delays or gaps as well as other unusual patterns in a high-risk child's development. These developmental domains are not mutually exclusive. There is considerable overlap between domains as well as across skills within a specific domain. Most activities of children in everyday settings involve skills from multiple domains. For example, playing marbles typically requires a child to use skills from the motor, cognitive, communication, and social domains.

Two widely used tests for diagnosing developmental delays are the Battelle Developmental Inventory (Newborg, Stock, Wnek, Guidubaldi, & Suinicki, 1988) and the Bayley Scales of Infant Development—II (Bayley, 1993). The Battelle can be administered to children with and without disabilities, from birth through age 8; and it has adapted testing procedures for use with children with different disabilities. The Bayley II evaluates development in motor, adaptive, language, and personal-social in infants from 2 to 30 months.

## Program Planning and Evaluation Tools

A growing number of early intervention programs are moving away from assessments based entirely on developmental milestones to curriculum-based assessment (CBA). CBA tools enable early childhood teams to (1) identify a child's current levels of functioning, (2) select IFSP/IEP goals and objectives, (3) determine the most appropriate interventions, and (4) evaluate the child's progress. Each item in a CBA relates directly to a skill in the program's curriculum, thereby providing a direct link among testing, teaching, and progress evaluation (Bagnato, Neisworth, & Munson, 1997).

One thoroughly developed and empirically tested CBA tool is the *Assessment, Evaluation, and Programming System: For Infants and Young Children (AEPS)* (Bricker, 2002). The AEPS is divided into two levels: one for infants and toddlers from birth to 3 years, one for children from 3 to 6 years. The AEPS is divided into six domains: fine motor, gross motor, adaptive, cognitive, social-communication, and social. Each domain is divided into strands that group related behaviors and skills considered essential for infants and young children to function independently. The AEPS tests can be used in conjunction with the associated AEPS curricula (Bricker & Waddell, 2002a, 2002b) or with other similar early childhood curricula such as the Carolina Curriculum for Preschoolers with Special Needs (Johnson-Martin, Attermeier, & Hacker, 2004a, 2004b).

*Curriculum-based assessment in ECSE*

Council for Exceptional Children   Content Standards for Beginning Teachers of Early Childhood Students: Select, adapt and use specialized formal and informal assessment for infants, young children, and their families (EC8S2).

# CURRICULUM AND INSTRUCTION IN EARLY CHILDHOOD SPECIAL EDUCATION

## Curriculum and Program Goals

Most professionals in early childhood special education agree that programs should be designed and evaluated with respect to the following outcomes or goals (Bailey & Wolery, 1992; Pretti-Frontczak & Bricker, 2004; Sandall, McLean, & Smith, 2000; Wolery & Sainato, 1993, 1996):

1. *Support families in achieving their own goals.* Although the child with special needs is undoubtedly the focal point, a major function of early intervention is helping families achieve the goals most important to them. Professionals realize that fami-

*Goals for ECSE*

Council for Exceptional Children   Content Standards for Beginning Teachers of Early Childhood Students: Historical and philosophical foundations of services for young children both with and without exceptional learning needs (EC1K1).

lies function as a system and that separating the child from the system results in limited and fragmented outcomes (Turnbull & Turnbull, 2006).

2. *Promote child engagement, independence, and mastery.* Early childhood special education seeks to minimize the extent to which children are dependent on others and different from their age mates. Intervention strategies should "promote active engagement (participation), initiative (choice making, self-directed behavior), autonomy (individuality and self-sufficiency) and age-appropriate abilities in many normalized contexts and situations" (Wolery & Sainato, 1993, p. 53). In situations in which independence is not safe, possible, or practical, support and assistance should be provided to enable the child to participate as much as she can. "For example, in getting ready for a bath, a 3-year-old child should not be expected to adjust the water to the appropriate temperature, but could be expected to help get ready for the bath (e.g., getting bath toys, assisting in taking off clothing)" (p. 53).

3. *Promote development in all important domains.* Successful early intervention programs help children make progress in each of the key areas of development already described. Because young children with disabilities are already behind their typically developing age mates, early childhood special educators should only use instructional strategies that lead to rapid learning (Wolery & Sainato, 1993, 1996). Strategies that produce rapid learning help the child with disabilities by saving time for other goals and moving closer to normal developmental levels.

4. *Build and support social competence.* Social skills, such as learning to get along with others and making friends, are among the most important skills anyone can learn. Most children learn such skills naturally, but many children with disabilities do not learn to interact effectively and properly simply by playing with others (Goldstein, Kaczmarek, & English, 2001; McEvoy & Yoder, 1993).

5. *Facilitate the generalized use of skills.* Most typically developing children effortlessly generalize what they learn in one situation to another place and time. But many children with disabilities have extreme difficulty remembering and using previously learned skills in other situations. "Early interventionists should not be satisfied if children learn new skills; they should only be satisfied if children use those skills when and wherever they are appropriate" (Wolery & Sainato, 1993, p. 54).

6. *Prepare and assist children for normalized life experiences with their families, in school, and in their communities.* Early intervention should be characterized by the principle of normalization; that is, services should be provided in settings that are as much like the typical settings in which young children without disabilities play and learn as is possible (Cook, Klein, & Tessier, 2004). A large and growing body of published research literature demonstrates the benefits of integrated early intervention to children with disabilities and their families and suggests strategies for effective inclusion programs (Guralnick, 2001; Sainato & Strain, 1993; Sandall & Schwartz, 2002; Wolery & Wilbers, 1994).

7. *Help children and their families make smooth transitions.* A transition occurs when a child and his family move from one early intervention program or service delivery mode to another. For example, program transitions typically occur at age 3 when a child with disabilities moves from a home-based program to an early childhood special education classroom and again at age 5 when the child moves from a preschool classroom to a regular kindergarten classroom. Preparing and assisting children and their families for smooth transitions ensures continuity of services, minimizes disruptions to the family system, and is another important way for promoting the success of young children with disabilities as they move into more normalized environments (Fowler, Schwartz, & Atwater, 1991; Hanson et al., 2000; La Paro, Pianta, & Cox, 2000). Cooperative planning and supports for transitions must come from professionals in both the sending and the receiving programs (Chandler, 1993; Fowler, Donegan, Lueke, Hadden, & Phillips, 2000; Hadden & Fowler, 1997).

To see a strategy for helping preschoolers with disabilities develop independence, go to Oakstone Academy on the *Exceptional Teachers* CD-ROM and click on "Picture Schedules."

# Using Puppets in the Early Childhood Classroom

*by Mary D. Salmon, Stacie McConnell, Diane M. Sainato, and Rebecca Morrison*

Early childhood education promotes active engagement, independence, and mastery across developmental domains for all children by providing a rich variety of experiences, materials, and ideas. Puppets can be useful and developmentally appropriate tools for presenting activities that are engaging, interesting, and appropriate for the wide range of abilities of young children in early childhood settings.

Most young children are delighted by puppets. Their vivid colors, interesting textures, and larger-than-life expressions may encourage curiosity and heighten attention levels among typically developing children as well as children with a range of developmental disabilities. A puppet's physical characteristics, overstated smiles or frowns, and motivational value make it a valuable prop for use with many young children. With this knowledge, we can put puppets to instructional use in inclusive early childhood classrooms.

Every day Ms. Stacie gathers all the children in her inclusive preschool classroom for morning circle time. Seated in a semi circle of colorful, miniature chairs, many of the youngsters are eager to begin their school day, while a few others must be coaxed to join the group. The teacher singles out those children who are participating in circle time activities and asks them to help with the calendar, chart the day's weather, hand out classroom jobs for the day, and select a favorite song to sing or story to read.

Although Ms. Stacie and her teaching assistants provide frequent verbal praise for on-task behavior, sometimes that is not enough to maintain the attention of the entire group. Several of the younger children and a few of those with special needs require numerous verbal, physical, and visual prompts to redirect their attention and encourage their participation in familiar activities. Even when the teacher is able to grab the attention of the entire group, on-task behavior is difficult to sustain. As a result, several children spend a large percentage of each circle time wiggling in their seats, engaging in inappropriate behavior, attempting to escape, or just gazing around the room.

## USING PUPPETS DURING CIRCLE TIME

Circle time is important in the preschool day because it introduces activities and provides a time for review. Introducing new concepts and skills, while reinforcing previously learned material, requires upbeat, appropriately paced, and highly interactive instructional strategies. One way to incorporate these strategies and add dimension and excitement to circle time is by embedding the actions of a variety of puppets into songs, stories, or games.

## USING PUPPETS DURING TRANSITION TIMES

Like circle time, transition times in the preschool classroom can be chaotic, noisy, disruptive, or difficult for some young children. A puppet may help the teacher signal transitions between classroom activities, making them smoother and less stressful for students and teacher alike.

## USING PUPPETS TO ENHANCE SOCIAL AND EMOTIONAL SKILLS

Young children frequently have difficulty expressing their emotions and interpreting the feelings of others. When paired with social stories and role-play activities, the exaggerated facial features of many character puppets make them especially well suited to modeling appropriate emotions. The actions of the puppets' large hands and feet may encourage an unwilling youngster to imitate their movement. Puppets can also help children match their own experiences with language, teach them to be an attentive audience, as well as help them develop more elaborate sociodramatic and symbolic play.

## FINDING RESOURCES

A wide variety of puppets are available from many sources to stimulate the interest and active engagement of young students. Entertaining, engaging puppets such as glove or stick puppets, finger puppets, and sock puppets are quickly adapted for uncomplicated use by younger students or students with special needs.

## HOW TO GET STARTED

### Circle Time

- *Calendar helper.* The teacher or a child can be the puppeteer, leading the class during calendar time.
- *Weather helper.* Dress a large, full-bodied puppet in child-sized clothing to reinforce weather concepts. Spice up his wardrobe with a variety of hats, sunglasses, and mittens as well as attire appropriate for all types of weather.
- *Rule bunny.* Teaching classroom rules is an important and ongoing process. To increase impact, designate a puppet to teach these common procedures: "Rule Bunny says, 'Play nicely with your friends,' or 'Put materials away neatly.'"
- *Other activities.* Puppets can read stories, sing songs, play "Simon Says," and model a variety of motor skills.

### Transition Time

- *Transition prompter.* To signal transition times, a puppet can shake a bell or ring a chime to indicate when it is time to clean up or move to the next activity.
- *Attention getter.* Capture the attention of a busy (and noisy) group of youngsters, using a puppet to lead the way to the next activity.
- *Transition helper.* Classroom helpers can take turns using a puppet to ready the class for special activities. Line leaders can guide the class to the library, gym, music, or art class, using a puppet to improve group attention.
- *Clean-up time.* Puppets can model appropriate clean-up behaviors such as placing blocks in a bin or putting away art materials.

### Sociodramatic Play and Social Skills

- Assume different roles, such as police officer or firefighter, with simple hand puppets and a few accessories (e.g., hats, badges).
- Puppets representing familiar adults can be made by printing photos of faces onto transfer paper using a computer and an inkjet printer. Iron the pictures onto simple hand puppets made from durable fabric and embellish the body with fabric markers or paint.
- Many characters from favorite books are available as puppets. Children can act out their favorite story and become any character they wish.
- Combine favorite stories with representative puppets to teach appropriate social behaviors. For example, *Rainbow Fish* by Marcus Pfister can be used to teach sharing.

**Puppets can help children express their feelings and learn to empathize with others.**

### Dealing with Emotions

- Puppets can make emotions "larger than life." Use them to demonstrate appropriate emotional responses while watching or acting out short skits.
- A child may be more inclined to express her feelings through a puppet. Teachers can also talk through a puppet to discuss appropriate classroom expectations and behavior.
- Help children solve simple problems by using puppets in role-play activities.

To see Stacie McConnell and Mary Salmon use puppets during circle time and with scripted stories to increase language skills, go to the *Exceptional Children* CD-ROM.

To learn more about using puppets in the classroom and reflect on their instructional use, go to Chapter 14's Teaching & Learning module on the Companion Website, **www.prenhall.com/heward**.

Mary D. Salmon is a doctoral student at The Ohio State University, an early childhood special education teacher with more than 15 years experience, and an avid puppet collector. Stacie McConnell teaches in an inclusive preschool classroom at Oakstone Academy in Westerville, Ohio. Diane Sainato is a member of the special education faculty at The Ohio State University, where she coordinates the master's degree program in early childhood special education and conducts research on young children's independent engagement, social, and communicative behavior. Rebecca Morrison, an early childhood special education teacher for 15 years, is the founder and director of Oakstone Academy.

8. *Prevent or minimize the development of future problems or disabilities*. Early intervention programs that serve at-risk infants and toddlers are designed with prevention as their primary goal.

## Developmentally Appropriate Practice

*Developmentally appropriate practice*

Council for Exceptional Children Content Standards for Beginning Teachers of Early Childhood Students: Plan and implement developmentally and individually appropriate curriculum (EC7S2) (also CC7K2).

Virtually all early childhood educators—whether they work with typically developing children or those with disabilities—believe that learning environments, teaching practices, and other components of programs that serve young children should be based on what is typically expected of and experienced by children of different ages and developmental stages. This philosophy and the guidelines for practice based on it are called **developmentally appropriate practice** (DAP) and are described in widely disseminated materials published by the National Association for the Education of Young Children (NAEYC) (Bredekamp & Copple, 1997). The DAP guidelines were created partially in response to concerns that too many early childhood programs were focusing on academic preparedness and not providing young children with enough opportunities to engage in the less structured play and other activities that typify early childhood. "For example, some people considered it developmentally appropriate for 4- and 5-year-olds to do an hour of seatwork, toddlers to sit in high chairs with dittos, or babies in infant seats to 'do' the calendar" (Bredekamp, 1993, p. 261). (To learn how puppets can help preschoolers with disabilities learn language skills, see Teaching & Learning, "Puppets As Teachers in the Early Childhood Classroom," later in this chapter.)

DAP recommends the following guidelines for early childhood education programs:

- Activities should be integrated across developmental domains.
- Children's interests and progress should be identified through teacher observation.
- Teachers should arrange the environment to facilitate children's active exploration and interaction.
- Learning activities and materials should be real, concrete, and relevant to the young child's life.
- A wide range of interesting activities should be provided.
- The complexity and challenges of activities should increase as the children understand the skills involved.

Most early childhood special educators view the DAP guidelines as a foundation from which to provide early intervention for children with special needs, but the guidelines alone may be inadequate to ensure the individualized, specially designed instruction that such children need (Wolery, Ault, & Doyle, 1992):

1. Many children with special needs have delays or disabilities that make them dependent upon others.
2. Many children with special needs have delays or disabilities that keep them from learning well on their own.
3. Many children with special needs develop more slowly than their typically developing peers do.
4. Many children with special needs have disabilities that interfere with how they interact; as a result, they often acquire additional disabilities.

Although Bricker, Pretti-Frontczak, and McComas (1998) find "a basic congruence and compatibility" (p. 213) between DAP and the focused activity-based intervention used by many early childhood special educators, they note two significant differences. First, special educators must target specific goals and objectives to meet the unique developmental needs of individual children, while DAP is concerned with more general developmental goals (e.g., improve language skills or self-esteem) that apply to a broad range of children. Second, early childhood special educators use comprehensive and repeated assessments to determine learning objectives and monitor progress according to stated performance criteria. DAP, by contrast, does not require the use of assessment or evaluation tools.

## Selecting IFSP/IEP Goals and Objectives

The breadth of developmental domains and the activities that young children typically engage in provide an almost unlimited number of possibilities for instructional objectives. Consensus among many early childhood special educators is that potential IFSP/IEP goals and objectives for infants and young children should be evaluated according to five quality indicators (e.g., Notari-Syverson & Shuster, 1995; Pretti-Frontczak & Bricker, 2000):

1. *Functionality.* A functional skill (a) increases the child's ability to interact with people and objects in her daily environment and (b) may have to be performed by someone else if the child cannot do it.
2. *Generality.* In this context, a skill has generality if it (a) represents a general concept as opposed to a particular task; (b) can be adapted and modified to meet the child's disability; and (c) can be used across different settings, with various materials, and with different people.
3. *Instructional context.* The skill should be easily integrated into the child's daily routines and taught in a meaningful way that represents naturalistic use of the skill.
4. *Measurability.* A skill is measurable if its performance or a product produced by its performance can be seen and/or heard. Measurable skills can be counted or timed and enable objective determination of learning progress.
5. *Relation between long-range goals and short-term objectives.* Short-term objectives should be hierarchically related; the achievement of short-term objectives should contribute directly to the attainment of long-term goals.

Figure 14.3 shows 11 questions that can be used to assess potential IFSP/IEP objectives according to those five criteria.

## Instructional Adaptations and Modifications

Providing specialized instruction in an attempt to "remediate delays caused by the child's disabilities and prevent any secondary disabilities from developing" is the cornerstone of what early childhood special educators do (Sandall, Schwartz, & Joesph, 2000, p. 3). Like their colleagues who work with elementary and secondary students with disabilities, teachers who work with young children with disabilities must be skilled in using a wide range of instructional strategies and tactics.

Modifications and adaptations to the physical environment, materials, and activities themselves are often sufficient to support successful participation and learning. Such modifications range from subtle, virtually invisible supports (e.g., changing the duration or sequence of activities, using a child's preferences as a conversation topic while playing) to more obvious interventions and support (e.g., providing the child with an adaptive device, teaching peers to prompt and reward participation) (Sandall, Joseph, et al., 2000). The challenge is determining how much support a child needs for a given skill in a specific context.

> Too much support may result in children becoming over reliant on adult support. Too little support will result in children being unsuccessful, and may lead to decreasing rates of participation and increasing rates of challenging behaviors. (Sandall et al., 2000, p. 4)

*Embedded Learning Opportunities.* One effective method for incorporating specialized instruction into typical preschool activities for children with disabilities is called embedded learning opportunities. The concept of *embedded learning opportunities* is based on the premise that although quality early childhood programs offer opportunities for learning

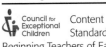

*IFSP/IEP goals and objectives*

Council for Exceptional Children    Content Standards for Beginning Teachers of Early Childhood Students: Plan and implement developmentally and individually appropriate curriculum (EC7S2) (also CC7K1).

*Modifying and adapting physical environment*

Council for Exceptional Children    Content Standards for Beginning Teachers of Early Childhood Students: Design, implement, and evaluate environments to assure developmental and functional appropriateness (EC5S3) (also CC5K1).

Effective early childhood special educators are experts at embedding learning opportunities—brief instructional interactions that focus on a child's IEP objectives—in the context of naturally occurring classroom activities.

**FIGURE 14.3** Five criteria for evaluating IEP/IFSP objectives for infants, toddlers, and preschoolers with disabilities

| FUNCTIONALITY | GENERALITY | INSTRUCTIONAL CONTEXT | MEASURABILITY | HIERARCHICAL RELATION BETWEEN LONG-RANGE GOAL AND SHORT-TERM OBJECTIVE |
|---|---|---|---|---|
| **1. Will the skill increase the child's ability to interact with people and objects within the daily environment?**<br><br>The child needs to perform the skill in all or most of the environments in which he or she interacts.<br><br>*Skill:* Places object into container.<br><br>*Opportunities:* Home—Places sweater in drawer, cookie in paper bag. School—Places lunch box in cubbyhole, trash in trash bin. Community—Places milk carton in grocery cart, rocks and soil in flower pot.<br><br>**2. Will the skill have to be performed by someone else if the child cannot do it?**<br><br>The skill is a behavior or event that is critical for completion of daily routines.<br><br>*Skill:* Looks for object in usual location.<br><br>*Opportunities:* Finds coat on coat rack, gets food from cupboard. | **3. Does the skill represent a general concept or class of responses?**<br><br>The skill emphasizes a generic process, rather than a particular instance.<br><br>*Skill:* Fits objects into defined spaces.<br><br>*Opportunities:* Puts mail in mailbox, places crayon in box, puts cutlery into sorter.<br><br>**4. Can the skill be adapted or modified for a variety of disabling conditions?**<br><br>The child's sensory impairment should interfere as little as possible with the performance.<br><br>*Skill:* Correctly activates simple toy.<br><br>*Opportunities:* Motor impairments—Activates light, easy-to-move toys (e.g., balls, rocking horse, toys on wheels, roly-poly toys).<br>*Visual impairments:* Activates large, bright, noise-making toys (e.g., bells, drums, large rattles).<br><br>**5. Can the skill be generalized across a variety of settings, materials, and/or people?**<br><br>The child can perform the skill with interesting materials and in meaningful situations.<br><br>*Skill:* Manipulates two small objects simultaneously.<br><br>*Opportunities:* Home—Builds with small interlocking blocks, threads laces on shoes. School—Sharpens pencil with pencil sharpener. Community—Takes coin out of small wallet. | **6. Can the skill be taught in a way that reflects the manner in which the skill will be used in daily environments?**<br><br>The skill can occur in a naturalistic manner.<br><br>*Skill:* Uses object to obtain another object.<br><br>*Opportunities:* Uses fork to obtain food, broom to rake toy; steps on stool to reach toy on shelf.<br><br>**7. Can the skill be elicited easily by the teacher/parent within classroom/home activities?**<br><br>The skill can be initiated easily by the child as part of daily routines.<br><br>*Skill:* Stacks objects.<br><br>*Opportunities:* Stacks books, cups/plates, wooden logs. | **8. Can the skill be seen and/or heard?**<br><br>Different observers must be able to identify the same behavior.<br><br>*Measurable skill:* Gains attention and refers to object, person, and/or event.<br><br>*Nonmeasurable skill:* Experiences a sense of self-importance<br><br>**9. Can the skill be directly counted (e.g., by frequency, duration, distance measures)?**<br><br>The skill represents a well-defined behavior or activity.<br><br>*Measurable skill:* Grasps pea-sized object.<br><br>*Nonmeasurable skill:* Has mobility in all fingers.<br><br>**10. Does the skill contain or lend itself to determination of performance criteria?**<br><br>The extent and/or degree of accuracy of the skill can be evaluated.<br><br>*Measurable skill:* Follows one-step directions with contextual cues.<br><br>*Nonmeasurable skill:* Will increase receptive language skills. | **11. Is the short-term objective a developmental subskill or step thought to be critical to the achievement of the long-range goal?**<br><br>*Appropriate:* Short-Term Objective—Releases object with each hand. Long-Range Goal—Places object and releases object balanced on top of another object.<br><br>*Inappropriate:*<br>1. The Short-Term Objective is a restatement of the same skill as the Long-Range Goal, with the addition of an instructional prompt (e.g., Short-Term Objective—Activates mechanical toy with physical prompt. Long-Range Goal—Independently activates mechanical toy) or a quantitative limitation to the extent of the skill (e.g., Short-Term Objective—Stacks 5 1-inch blocks; Long-Range Goal—Stacks 10 1-inch blocks).<br><br>2. The Short-Term Objective is not conceptually or functionally related to the Long-Range Goal (e.g., Short-Term Objective—Releases object voluntarily; Long-Range Goal—Pokes with index finger). |

*Source:* Adapted from Notari-Syverson, A. R., & Shuster, S. L. (1995). Putting real-life skills into IEP/IFSPs for infants and young children. *Teaching Exceptional Children, 272*(2), 31. Used by permission of the Council for Exceptional Children, Reston, VA.

across the day, children with disabilities often need guidance and support to learn from those opportunities (Horn, Lieber, Li, Sandall, & Schwartz, 2000; McBride & Schwartz, 2003). Therefore, teachers should look and plan for ways to embed brief, systematic instructional interactions that focus on a child's IEP objectives in the content of naturally occuring classroom activities. Figure 14.4 shows a teacher's plan for embedding learning opportunities into four different activity centers to support an IEP objective in the fine-motor domain for a 4-year-old boy with cerebral palsy. For an annotated bibliography of research and teacher resources on naturalistic teaching methods featuring embedded learning opportunities and activities-based interventions for young children with and without disabilities, see Pretti-Frontczak, Barr, Macy, and Carter (2003).

*Embedded learning opportunities*

Council for Exceptional Children — Content Standards for Beginning Teachers—Common Core: Effective management of teaching and learning (CC5K3) (also EC7S2).

---

**FIGURE 14.4** **Example of a plan for embedding learning opportunities into four different activity centers to support a child's IEP objective in the fine-motor domain**

Embedded Learning Opportunities at a Glance for: ___Alex___

Objective: ___Will pour liquid or other fluid material (e.g., sand, beans) from one container to another with no spillage.___

Date: __8/14__ Activity: __Center Time__
Material: __All centers available__

| Modifications Needed: | What are you going to do? |
|---|---|
| —Water table: add a variety of containers with spouts (e.g., plastic measuring cups, teapot, play pitcher) | Move through center modeling use of these new activities/materials. Provide physical guidance for Alex |
| | **What are you going to say?** |
| —Snack Center: Add to Alex's workjob pouring juice for other children | Use natural cues— Let's see you do it. Can you do it and get all the beans in the pot? |
| —Art Center: Place tempera paint in small pitcher, have children pour into individual bowls | **How will you respond?** Praise, acknowledgment, feedback on accuracy Engagement in activity created |
| —Housekeeping: Add beans to kitchen cabinet in a small pitcher for pouring into pots, cups or plates | **What materials do you need?** Need to be prepared with clean-up supplies for spills—(see under modifications) |

*Source:* "Supporting Young Children's IEP Goals in Inclusive Settings Through Embedded Learning Opportunities" by E. Horn, J. Lieber, S. Sandall, I. Schwartz, & S. Li, 2000, *Topics in Early Childhood Education, 20,* 208–223. Copyright 2000 by PRO-Ed, Inc. Reprinted with permission.

Embedding learning opportunities to support young children's development of communication and language skills is an especially important teaching responsibility for an early childhood special educator. Most children learn to speak and communicate effectively with little or no formal teaching. But children with disabilities often do not acquire language in the spontaneous manner of their peers without disabilities. And as children with disabilities slip further and further behind their peers, their language deficits make social and academic development even more difficult. Preschoolers with disabilities need repeated opportunities for language use and development (Goldstein, 2002; Goldstein et al., 1994; Justice, 2004). In addition to providing systematic, explicit instruction of language skills to children in individual and small-group learning activities, teachers should embed meaningful opportunities for children to communicate throughout the day. Even transitions between activities can provide opportunities for learning (Wolery, Anthony, & Heckathorn, 1998).

A creative and effective example of embedding language learning opportunities into mealtimes was reported by Robinson Spohn, Timko, and Sainato (1999). Each child was seated at the table in front of a placemat showing a picture of a food item, a cartoon character, an animal, and something silly (e.g., a cat wearing glasses and reading a book) (see Figure 14.5). There were 12 different placemats, and each child sat before a different one each day. At first, the teacher played "The Talking Game" with the children while they ate breakfast in the school lunchroom. The children took turns picking an index card from a shuffled set of cards. Each card had a photo of one of the children in the group. After a child selected a card, the teacher prompted him to say something to the child pictured on the card. If the children could not think of anything to say, they were prompted to talk about one of the pictures on their placemat. After several weeks, the teacher no longer used the index cards and stopped prompting the children's interactions. The children continued talking with one another during mealtimes at rates higher than they had before, often using the pictures on their placemats as conversation starters.

## Preschool Activity Schedules

Teachers in preschool programs for children with disabilities face the challenge of organizing the program day into a schedule that meets each child's individual learning needs and provides children with many opportunities to explore the environment and communicate

*Preschool activity schedules*

Council for Exceptional Children Content Standards for Beginning Teachers–Common Core: Demands of learning environments (CC5K1) (also EC5S3).

**FIGURE 14.5** **A placemat used to encourage preschoolers with developmental disabilities to communicate with one another during mealtime**

*Source:* Courtesy of Diane M. Sainato, The Ohio State University.

with others throughout the day. The schedule should include a balance of child-initiated and planned activities, large- and small-group activities, active and quiet times, and indoor and outdoor activities; it should allow easy transition from activity to activity (Cook et al., 2004). In short, the schedule should provide a framework for maximizing children's opportunities to develop new skills and practice what they have learned while remaining manageable and flexible. In addition, how activities are scheduled and organized has considerable effect on the frequency and type of interaction that occurs between children with and without disabilities (Harris & Handleman, 2000) and on the extent to which children with disabilities benefit from instructional activities.

Pretti-Frontczak and Bricker (2004) describe an activity-planning and scheduling process that combines children's individual IFSP/IEP objectives with group activity plans. Figure 14.6 shows how children's targeted learning goals can be integrated into daily classroom activities.

## A Supportive Physical Environment

The physical arrangement of the classroom must support the planned activities. As Kim Lundy notes at the beginning of this chapter, designing an effective preschool classroom requires thoughtful planning to ensure that play areas and needed materials are accessible to and safe for all students, boundaries between areas minimize distractions, and, most important, the environment makes children want to explore and play. Suggestions for setting up a preschool classroom include the following (Pretti-Frontczak & Bricker, 2004; Cook et al., 2004; Johnson-Martin et al., 2004b; Morrison, 2004):

*Physical arrangement of preschool classroom*

Council for Exceptional Children Content Standards for Beginning Teachers of Early Childhood Students: Design, implement, and evaluate environments to assure developmental and functional appropriateness (EC5S3).

- Organize the classroom into a number of different well-defined areas to accommodate different kinds of activities (e.g., quiet play, messy play, dramatic play, constructive play, active play).
- Locate quiet activities together, away from avenues of traffic, and loud activities together.
- Equip each area with abundant, appropriate materials that are desirable to children.
- Locate materials where children can easily retrieve them and are not dependent on adults.
- Have an open area, perhaps a large rug, where large-group activities such as circle time and story reading can be conducted.
- Label or color-code all storage areas so that aides and volunteers can easily find needed materials.
- Arrange equipment and group areas so that students can move easily from one activity to another. Pictures or color codes can be applied to various work areas.
- Provide lockers or cubbies for students so they know where to find their belongings. Again, add picture cues to help students identify their lockers.

For a guided tour of a well-designed preschool classroom, go to Oakstone Academy on the *Exceptional Teachers* CD-ROM and click on "Preschool Tour."

# SERVICE DELIVERY ALTERNATIVES FOR EARLY INTERVENTION

IDEA requires that early intervention services be provided in natural environments to the greatest extent possible. Natural environments are the same home, school, and community settings that typically developing children inhabit (Sandall & Ostrosky, 2000). Where early intervention takes place varies, depending on the age of the child and the special supports she and her family need.

Early intervention services for infants and newborns with significant disabilities are often provided in hospital settings. Most early childhood special education services, however, are provided in the child's home, in a center- or school-based facility, or in a combination of both settings. Increasingly, young children with mild developmental delays are being served by itinerant special education teachers in regular preschool settings (Dinnebeil & McInerney, 2000; Sadler, 2003).

## FIGURE 14.6 Example of embedding learning opportunities related to children's targeted goals and objectives into a schedule of daily classroom activities

Children's names: Serina, Tianna, and Patrice   Date schedule will be used: First quarter (Sept. to Nov.)

Team members: Classroom staff and therapists

**Daily classroom activities**

| Children and target goals | Arrival | Free play | Circle activities | Snack | Centers |
|---|---|---|---|---|---|
| **Serina** 1. Manipulates objects | Ask Serina to unzip her coat. | Encourage Serina to play with blocks, puzzles, and art materials. | | Provide a spoon or a fork to eat with, foods to prepare, and a knife for spreading or cutting. | Place objects to manipulate in writing center (pencils, scissors) and science center (tweezers, microscope with slides). |
| 2. Uses one and two words to request, inform, and greet. | Model saying "Good morning." Ask Serina to greet peers. | | Sing the Good Morning song. Ask Serina to request a song. Ask Serina to tell the class what color shoes she has on (including black, pink, gray as targets). | Ask Serina what she is having for lunch. Label words related to snack/eating that end with target consonants (milk, nut, fruit, last). | Model greeting peers as they enter the different centers. Ask Serina what she is doing. Ask Serina where she wants to play or what toys she wants. |
| 3. Uses one object to represent another | | Model how to use different size blocks as food or a shoe for a doll's car. | | | Use a small dust pan or a ladle as a shovel in the discovery table. Use sticks as paintbrushes in the art area. |
| **Tianna** 1. Expresses likes and dislikes | | | Present song options for Tianna to choose. | | Ask Tianna which activities she likes and does not like. |
| 2. Sorts like objects | | Ask Tianna to put all of the books together and all of the puppets together. | | Encourage Tianna to put all cups on one table and all snack food on another. | |
| 3. Uses spoon to feed self | | | | Provide food requiring spoon use. | |
| **Patrice** 1. Uses toilet | Ask Patrice if she has to use the bathroom. | | | Ask Patrice if she has to use the bathroom. | |
| 2. Follows routine directions | Remind Patrice to hang up her coat and put away her lunch. | Ask Patrice to put the blocks away. | | Prompt Patrice to take one and pass to her friends. | |

*Source:* Reprinted from Pretti-Frontczak, K., & Bricker, D. (2004). *An activity-based approach to early intervention* (3rd ed.), (p. 134). Baltimore: Brookes. Used by permission.

# Hospital-Based Programs

Increasingly, early intervention services are being provided to hospitalized newborns and their families. Low-birth-weight and other high-risk newborns who require specialized health care are placed in neonatal intensive care units (NICUs). Many NICUs include a variety of professionals, such as neonatologists who provide medical care for infants with special needs, nurses who provide ongoing medical assistance, social workers or psychologists who help parents and families with emotional and financial concerns, and infant education specialists who promote interactions between parents and infants (Brown, Thurman, & Pearl, 1993).

# Home-Based Programs

As the name suggests, a home-based program depends heavily on support of and by families. The parents typically assume primary responsibility as caregivers and teachers for their child with disabilities. They are usually supported by an early intervention specialist who visits the home regularly to model teaching procedures or other interventions, act as a consultant, evaluate the success of intervention, and regularly assess the child's progress. Home visitors (or home teachers or home advisors, as they are often called) in some programs are specially trained paraprofessionals. They may visit as frequently as several times a week but probably no less than a few times a month. They sometimes carry the results of their in-home evaluations back to other professionals, who may recommend changes in the program.

*Differences between home-based, center-based, and combined programs*

Council for Exceptional Children — Content Standards for Beginning Teachers–Common Core: Family systems and the role of families in supporting development (CC2K4) (also CC5K1).

The Portage Project, one of the best known and most widely replicated home-based programs, was begun more than 30 years ago by a consortium of 23 school districts in south-central Wisconsin (Shearer & Shearer, 1979). A project teacher typically visits the home one day each week to review the child's progress during the previous week, describe activities for the upcoming week, demonstrate to the parents how to carry out activities with the child, observe parents and child interacting, offer suggestions and advice as needed, summarize where the program stands, and indicate what records parents should keep during the next week. The Portage Project has produced its own assessment materials and teaching activities: The *Portage Guide to Early Education*, based on 450 behaviors sequenced developmentally and classified into self-help, cognition, socialization, language, and motor skills.

Home-based early intervention programs have several advantages:

- The home is the child's natural environment, and a parent can often give more time and attention to the child than even the most adequately staffed center or school.
- Other family members, such as siblings and grandparents, have more opportunity to interact with the child during instruction and socially. These significant others can play an important role in the child's growth and development.
- Home learning activities and materials are more likely to be natural and appropriate.
- Parents who are actively involved in helping their child learn and develop clearly have an advantage over parents who feel guilt, frustration, or defeat at their seeming inability to help their child.
- Home-based programs can be less costly to operate.

Home-based programs, however, can have disadvantages:

- Because home-based programs place so much responsibility on parents, they are not effective with all families. Not all parents are able or willing to spend the time required to teach their children, and some who try are not effective teachers.
- A large and growing number of young children do not reside in the traditional two-parent family—especially the many thousands of children with teenage mothers who are single, uneducated, and poor. Many of these infants and preschoolers are at risk for developmental delays because of the impoverished conditions in which they live.

It is unlikely that a parent struggling with the realities of day-to-day survival will be able to meet the added demands of involvement in a home-based early intervention program (Turnbull & Turnbull, 2006).

- Because the parent—usually the mother—is the primary service provider, children in home-based programs may not receive as wide a range of services as they would in a center-based program, where they can be seen by a variety of professionals. (Note, however, that the services of professionals such as physical therapists, occupational therapists, and speech therapists are sometimes provided in the home.)
- The child may not receive sufficient opportunity for social interaction with peers.

## Center-Based Programs

Center-based programs provide early intervention services in a special educational setting outside the home. The setting may be part of a hospital complex, a special day care center, or a preschool. Some children may attend a specially designed developmental center or training center that offers a wide range of services for children with varying types and degrees of disabilities. Wherever they are, these centers offer the combined services of many professionals and paraprofessionals, often from several different fields.

Most center-based programs encourage social interaction, and some try to integrate children with disabilities and typically developing children in day care or preschool classes. Some children attend a center each weekday for all or most of the day; others may come less frequently, although most centers expect to see each child at least once a week. Parents are sometimes given roles as classroom aides or encouraged to act as their child's primary teacher. A few programs allow parents to spend time with other professionals or take training while their child is somewhere else in the center. Virtually all effective programs for young children with disabilities recognize the critical need to involve parents, and they welcome parents in every aspect of the program.

A good example of a center-based program is the Precise Early Education of Children with Handicaps (PEECH) project originally developed at the University of Illinois. Designed for children ages 3 to 5 with mild to moderate disabilities, PEECH combines classroom instruction for up to 10 children with disabilities and 5 nondisabled children. A team approach to intervention and parental involvement includes a classroom teacher and a paraprofessional aide, a psychologist, a speech-language pathologist, and a social worker. Children spend 2 or 3 hours in class each day, with some time in large and small groups and individualized activities. Parents are included in all stages of the intervention, including policymaking. The project offers a lending library and a toy library for parents to use as well as a parent newsletter. The project's ultimate goal is to successfully integrate youngsters with disabilities into regular kindergarten classes whenever possible. Early childhood special educators at 200 replication sites in 36 states have received training in various components of the PEECH program (Karnes, Beauchamp, & Pfaus, 1993).

Center-based programs generally offer three advantages that are difficult to build into home-based efforts:

- There is increased opportunity for a team of specialists from different fields—education, physical and occupational therapy, speech and language pathology, medicine, and others—to observe each child and cooperate in intervention and continued assessment. Some special educators feel that the intensive instruction and related services that can be provided in a center-based program are especially important for children with severe disabilities (Rose & Calhoun, 1990).
- The opportunity for interaction with typically developing peers makes center programs especially effective for some children.
- Most parents involved in center programs feel some relief at the support they get from the professionals who work with their child and from other parents with children at the same center.

To watch an early childhood special educator effectively promote language skills and social interaction among preschoolers with and without disabilities, click on "Oakstone Academy: Circle Time" on the *Exceptional Teachers* CD-ROM.

Disadvantages of a center-based program include the expense of transportation, the cost and maintenance of the center itself, and the possibility of less parent involvement than in home-based programs.

## Combined Home-Center Programs

Many early intervention programs combine center-based activities and home visitation. Few center programs take children for more than a few hours a day or more than 5 days per week. But because young children with disabilities require more intervention than a few hours a day, many programs combine the intensive help of a variety of professionals in a center with the continuous attention and sensitive care of parents at home. Intervention that carries over from center to home clearly offers many of the advantages of the two types of programs and negates some of their disadvantages.

St. Mark's Circle School in Charlotte, North Carolina, offers a combination home- and center-based early intervention program for infants and toddlers with severe/profound disabilities. The program is based on the social reciprocity model, which views the child's behavior as affecting the parent, whose behavior in turn affects the behavior of the child—hence the "circle" in the program's name. Nonresponsiveness, nonvocal behavior, irritability, lack of imitation responses, and the need for special health care routines (e.g., tube feeding, suctioning) all present special challenges to normal infant-parent interactions; behaviors associated with these problems are often viewed negatively. The program attempts to identify and increase the frequency of alternative positive behaviors that will cause parents to want to continue their interactions with their child (Calhoun & Kuczera, 1996; Calhoun, Rose, Hanft, & Sturkey, 1991; Rose & Calhoun, 1990). The center-based component of classroom instruction occurs from 9:00 A.M. to 1:00 P.M. throughout the year. The home-based/family-services component entails monthly home visits; the visits include family-focused assessment and planning, demonstrations of instructional techniques, and provision of information and other support. Between regularly scheduled home visits, ongoing individualized consultation and collaboration with parents and families are available as needed.

The St. Mark's Circle Project in North Carolina teaches parents to identify and increase the frequency of positive behaviors by their infants such as smiling or imitating.

# CURRENT ISSUES AND FUTURE TRENDS

Early childhood special education has made tremendous progress over the past 25 years. The number of high-quality inclusive early childhood programs for preschoolers with disabilities increases each year, and family-centered early intervention services are more widely available for infants and toddlers with or at risk for developmental disabilities. Like any young and growing field, however, early childhood special education faces numerous problems, challenges, and opportunities for improvement.

Perhaps no other area of special education presents researchers with a more important array of issues and questions in need of scientific investigation. One fundamental question with enormous implications, and from which literally hundreds of specific research questions and studies can be derived, is "What type of early childhood programs and settings are most effective for which groups of children and their families?" (Holahan & Costenbader, 2000; Odom et al., 2000). Guralnick (2001) has called for a national agenda to focus research and resources on increasing the availability and the quality of inclusive preschool programs for children with special needs.

To ensure that quality early childhood care is available for all children and their families and that specialized early intervention is provided to all children who have or are at risk for developmental delay will require increased recognition of the importance of early intervention by the public and elected policy makers (Kagan & Neuman, 1997; Howard, Williams, & Lepper, 2005). Early intervention, especially for children with significant disabilities, is expensive. More carefully controlled research on the costs and benefits of early intervention is needed, and the results of these studies should be considered in policy and funding decisions (Jacobson, Mulick, & Green, 1998; Odom et al., 2001).

## Families: Most Important of All

The success of efforts to prevent disabilities in children and to identify, assess, and intervene with children who have special needs as early as possible requires the training, experience, and cooperation of a wide range of professionals. Current best-practice guidelines for early childhood services call for a transdisciplinary approach to the delivery of related services in which parents and professionals work together in assessing needs, developing the IFSP or IEP, providing services, and evaluating outcomes (Sandall et al., 2000).

Of all the people needed to make early intervention work, parents and families are the most important. Given enough information and support, parents can help prevent many risks and causes of disabilities—before pregnancy, before birth, and certainly before a child has gone months or years without help. Given the chance, parents can take an active role in determining their children's educational needs and goals. And given some guidance, training, and support, many parents can teach their children at home and even at school.

Of all the people needed to make early intervention effective, parents are the most important.

It is no wonder, then, that all successful intervention programs for young children with disabilities take great care to involve parents (Harris & Handleman, 2000; Howard et al., 2005). Parents are the most frequent and constant observers of their children's behavior. They usually know better than anyone else what their children need, and they can help educators set realistic goals. They can report on events in the home that outsiders might never see—for instance, how a child responds to other family members. They can monitor and report on their children's progress at home, beyond the more controlled environment of the early intervention center or preschool. In short, parents can contribute to their children's programs at every stage—assessment, planning, classroom activities, and evaluation. Many parents even work in preschool classrooms as teacher aides, volunteers, or other staff members.

But in our efforts to involve parents, we must recognize that while professionals come and go, parents and families are in it for the long haul. In their focus to help young children attain critical developmental gains, it is easy for early childhood professionals to overlook that parents are just beginning a lifetime of commitment and responsibility.

As Hutinger, Marshall, and McCarten (1983) aptly reminded us more than 20 years ago, we must not forget that early childhood is supposed to be a fun, happy time for children and for the adults who are fortunate enough to work with them.

> Part of our mission as professionals in the field of early childhood special education is to possess an art of enjoyment ourselves and to help instill it in the young children and families with whom we work.
>
> Early childhood comes but once in a lifetime.... Let's make it count!

# Tips for Beginning Teachers

## Early Childhood Special Education

### by Kim Lundy

### FAMILIES ARE YOUR FRIENDS AND ALLIES IN THE EDUCATION OF THEIR CHILDREN

I'm sure that you have already heard plenty of tales about difficult families. However, families can be the greatest allies you will ever have … *if* you make the effort to understand and form a rapport with them. Families with young children who have special needs are often grieving, and you may be their only outlet. Sometimes their grief appears as general anxiety about their child's classroom and education; other times, it may appear as open and unwarranted hostility toward you. But there are ways to convey that you care and will go out of your way to form a solid and friendly partnership.

- *Engage parents in an open dialogue.* I have found nothing more effective than letting parents and families know that you hear them and understand where they are coming from.
- *Ongoing communication is key.* Start slowly by sending frequent newsletters and invitations to parents and siblings to visit the classroom, or communicate by a phone call or an e-mail to praise something that their child has done that day. Plan fun open houses, attend birthday parties, or even offer to come over for a home visit if it is convenient for the family.

### ALWAYS REMEMBER THAT ALL OF YOUR STUDENTS ARE KIDS FIRST

When you are new at teaching young children with special needs, it's very easy to become overwhelmed by evaluation reports, IEPs, and anxious parents before the school year even begins. "That kid has autism, this one has Down syndrome, she has cerebral palsy, and he doesn't have a diagnosis yet.… " When you feel yourself becoming overwhelmed:

- Stop for a moment and relax.
- Have confidence in yourself and your abilities.
- Remember that your students-to-be are just kids who deserve to have the same school experiences as their typically developing peers and that they will teach *you* a lot in the coming year.

### THE ORGANIZATION OF YOUR CLASSROOM CAN MAKE OR BREAK YOU

Arrange and decorate your classroom thoughtfully before students arrive for the school year. Young children with special needs use their classroom for many more tasks than a typical grade schooler does: they are learning how to play with toys, share, communicate, move, eat, color and cut, attend, and much more. Your classroom must be arranged to accommodate all of this. Ask yourself:

- Can kids who use wheelchairs and walkers access everything?
- Have I created separate, well-defined work and play areas?
- Are shelves and bookcases low enough so I can see all of my students from anywhere in the room?
- Are classroom materials and toys clean, developmentally appropriate, and well organized?
- Are the materials I'll need throughout the day accessible?
- Are my bulletin boards and other decorations too distracting?
- Does the room look cool? Is it a place where young children will want to spend a few hours each day?

### REMEMBER THAT BEHAVIOR HAS A COMMUNICATIVE INTENT

As a teacher of young children (especially preschoolers), you will be the recipient of many interesting behaviors. Inappropriate behaviors can be frustrating for families and teachers alike, but each has a purpose. Your challenge is to pinpoint what the student is trying to communicate and then help him meet his needs.

- *Record the specific offending behavior, what happens to trigger it, and what happens after it.* For example, one of my nonverbal students was seemingly randomly hitting his classmates during choice time. Recording some data on this behavior indicated that he was hitting his classmates when he wanted a turn with the toy they had.
- *Teach the student a new behavior to take the place of the offending behavior.* The speech therapist and I

quickly taught the student who was hitting to sign "me" and also taught him to exchange a picture symbol saying "my turn" with his classmates. As a result, the hitting rapidly decreased.

### PROVIDE A PREDICTABLE DAILY ROUTINE

Young children—regardless of disability—long for routine and consistency. So many things in their worlds change from day to day that routine is very comforting and can actually enhance their learning.

- Plan a sequence of events and activities in your classroom that stay the same from day to day—for example: arrival, circle, small-group activity, choice time, outside, snack, circle, and dismissal.
- Post your daily schedule on the wall at child level so your students can independently check it.
- Create routines within each event or activity. For example, when it's time for snack, my students know to wash their hands, sit down at their place-

mats, wait for the rest of their friends to arrive at the table before eating, and put their placemats and dishes in the appropriate bins when they are finished.

If you can spend extra time during the first weeks of school teaching your schedule and routines to your students, you will quickly stop having to manage them as a group and be able to focus on individual students who need a little extra help. To enhance the likelihood of a decrease in inappropriate behaviors, accompany these strategies with clear expectations and consistent consequences.

### HAVE FUN!

This is the most important thing you can do for yourself and your students each day. I feel so fortunate to have a job that pays me to play and have fun. No day is the same; each is full of new adventures, challenges, and triumphs.

## KEY TERMS AND CONCEPTS

 To print your own set of SAFMED flash cards for studying and mastering these terms, go to the Companion Website, **www.prenhall.com/heward**.

Apgar scale, p. 567
developmentally appropriate practice (DAP), p. 576
early intervention, p. 558

individualized family services plan (IFSP), p. 564
psychosocial disadvantage, p. 559

## SUMMARY

### The Importance of Early Intervention

- Early intervention consists of educational, nutritional, child care, and family supports designed to reduce the effects of disabilities or prevent the occurrence of developmental problems later in life for children at risk for such problems.
- Research has documented that early intervention can provide both intermediate and long-term benefits for young children with disabilities and those at risk for developmental delay. Benefits of early intervention include
  - Gains in physical development, cognitive development, language and speech development, social competence, and self-help skills
  - Prevention of secondary disabilities
  - Reduction of family stress
  - Reduced need for special education services or placement during the school year
  - Savings to society of the costs of additional educational and social services that would be needed later without early intervention
  - Reduced likelihood of social dependence in adulthood
- The effectiveness of early intervention is increased when it begins early in life, is intensive, and lasts for a long time.

# IDEA and Early Childhood Special Education

- States that receive IDEA funds for early intervention services must serve all infants and toddlers birth to age 3 with developmental delays or established risk conditions. At their discretion, states may serve infants and toddlers who are at risk for acquiring disabilities because of certain biological or environmental risk conditions.
- Early intervention services for infants and toddlers are family-centered, transdisciplinary, and described by IFSPs.
- IDEA requires states to provide special education services (via IEPs) to all preschool children with disabilities, ages 3 through 5.
- Preschool children do not have to be identified and reported under disability categories to receive services.

# Screening, Identification, and Assessment

- Four major types of assessment purposes/tools are used in early childhood special education:
  - Screening involves quick, easy-to-administer tests to identify children who may have a disability and who should receive further testing.
  - Diagnosis requires in-depth, comprehensive assessment of all major areas of development to determine a child's eligibility for early intervention or special education services.
  - Program planning uses curriculum-based, criterion-referenced assessments to determine a child's current skill level, identify IFSP/IEP objectives, and plan intervention activities.
  - Evaluation uses curriculum-based, criterion-referenced measures to determine progress on IFSP/IEP objectives and evaluate a program's effects.
- Many early intervention programs are moving away from assessments based entirely on developmental milestones and are incorporating curriculum-based assessment, in which each item relates directly to a skill included in the program's curriculum. This provides a direct link among testing, teaching, and program evaluation.

# Curriculum and Instruction in Early Childhood Special Education

- Early intervention and education programs for children with special needs should be designed and evaluated according to these outcomes or goals:
  - Support families in achieving their own goals
  - Promote child engagement, independence, and mastery
  - Promote development in all important domains
  - Build and support social competence
  - Facilitate the generalized use of skills
  - Prepare for and assist children with normalized life experiences in their families, schools, and communities
  - Help children and their families make smooth transitions
  - Prevent or minimize the development of future problems or disabilities
- Developmentally appropriate practices provide a foundation or context from which to build individualized programs of support and instruction for children with special needs.
- IEP/IFSP objectives for infants and young children should be evaluated according to their functionality, generality, instructional context, measurability, and relation between short- and long-range goals.
- Embedded learning opportunities are brief, systematic instructional interactions that focus on a child's IEP objectives in the context of naturally occuring classroom activities. They are an effective method for incorporating specialized instruction into typical preschool activities.

- A preschool activity schedule should maximize children's opportunities to develop new skills and practice what they have learned previously while remaining manageable and flexible.
- How activities are scheduled and organized affects the interaction between children with and without disabilities.
- Suggestions for setting up a preschool classroom include
  - Organizing the classroom into different, well-defined areas to accommodate different kinds of activities
  - Locating quiet activities together, away from avenues of traffic, and loud activities together
  - Equipping each area with appropriate and desirable materials
  - Locating materials where children can retrieve them without help from adults
  - Having an open area where large-group activities can be conducted
  - Labeling or color-coding all storage areas
  - Arranging equipment and group areas so that students can move easily from one activity to another
  - Providing lockers or cubbies for students

## Service Delivery Alternatives for Early Intervention

- In home-based programs, a child's parents act as the primary teachers, with regular training and guidance from a teacher or specially trained paraprofessional who visits the home.
- In center-based programs, a child comes to the center for direct instruction, although the parents are usually involved. Center programs allow a team of specialists to work with the child and enable the child to meet and interact with other children.
- Many programs offer the advantages of both models by combining home visits with center-based programming.

## Current Issues and Future Trends

- The field of early childhood special education will be advanced by research investigating which combinations of program characteristics are most effective for target groups of children and their families and from studies analyzing the cost-benefit of early intervention.
- Parents are the most important people in an early intervention program. They can act as advocates, participate in educational planning, observe their children's behavior, help set realistic goals, work in the classroom, and teach their children at home.

To check your comprehension of chapter contents, go to the Guided Review and Quiz modules in Chapter 14 of the Companion Website, **www.prenhall.com/heward**.

# TRANSITIONING TO ADULTHOOD

# Featured Teacher

### GAIL GANTT BETTIS

SHELBY HIGH SCHOOL AND
NORTH SHELBY SCHOOL
CLEVELAND COUNTY PUBLIC SCHOOLS
SHELBY, NORTH CAROLINA

***Education—Teaching Credentials—Experience***
- B.A., human services, Gardner-Webb University, 1989; M.Ed., special education, University of North Carolina at Charlotte, 1993
- North Carolina teaching certificates: mentally handicapped, K–12; handicapped disadvantaged, ages 16–21
- 25 years in the field: 8 years as a preschool teacher for students with developmental delays; 14 years as a transition teacher for secondary students with disabilities; 3 years as a transition coordinator

***Current Teaching Position and Students***   I serve in dual roles of transition teacher and transition coordinator. This position affords me the opportunity to serve one high school (Shelby High School) and one special purpose school (North Shelby School) within our school system. The students display a variety of disabilities including, but not limited to, learning disabilities, mental retardation, autism, traumatic brain injury, physical disabilities, hearing impairment, visual impairment, and other health impairments. I am responsible for case management, implementing functional academics, and school- and work-based training. Each student has a different set of special needs that require early transition planning and consistent follow-up to prepare him to move toward independence and become a productive citizen.

Much of my time is spent helping teachers implement our district's occupational course of study (OCS) program at both schools. Students enrolled in the OCS have a postschool outcome goal of employment after graduation. These are students whose postschool needs cannot be met by the North Carolina standard course of study and who wish to pursue one that provides functional academics and hands-on vocational training. OCS students attend self-contained special classes for English, math, science, and social studies. They attend physical education, electives, and career technical education classes in the regular curriculum.

At Shelby High School, I help students ages 14–21 develop and implement transition plans, schedule transition meetings, develop job plans, develop and maintain vocational records and career portfolios, and coordinate job placement and follow-up of all students enrolled. Exit follow-up continues for 3 years after the student graduates. I also serve students in the other courses of study who are receiving exceptional children services. These students are enrolled in college/university prep, tech prep, or career prep courses of study at the high school. I help them plan postsecondary goals to attend a 4-year university, a 2-year technical school, or a special trade school. I work with the guidance counselors and help students move from school to their chosen settings. A small population of these students also chooses to transition directly into a job after graduation.

## Focus Questions

- What can teachers of elementary children with disabilities do to help prepare them for successful lives as adults?

- Why should postschool outcomes drive educational programming for secondary students with disabilities?

- What are the most important factors in determining the success of an individualized transition plan?

- How can programs that are intended to help adults with disabilities limit their participation and enjoyment of adulthood?

- Should quality of life for adults with disabilities be the ultimate outcome measure for special education?

At North Shelby, I serve students ages 19–21 in a classroom setting. These students are self-contained during their 11th and 12th grade years. They spend most of their time working on campus or in the community as well as practicing daily living skills in a variety of settings. I split my responsibilities between transition planning activities and implementing functional academics according to students' individual needs. Much time is spent planning transition activities and meetings to link students to postschool services to ensure a smooth transition from the educational setting to the community.

Let me introduce you to some of my students. Sammy is a senior and functions within the mild range of mental retardation. He is an excellent student with good attendance and a high grade-point average who is well liked by the staff and students at Shelby High and his co-workers. During the past 2 years, a heart ailment has restricted Sammy's physical activities. He is under the care of a specialist but has been able to overcome barriers that prevented him from participating in employment. Sammy has been enrolled in career technical education classes for the past 4 years, and he has participated in school- and work-based training in preparation for competitive employment. Early in high school, he worked briefly at a local hardware store, where he obtained a forklift operator's license. This year, he has a job at a local industry that assembles truck cabs. He is currently employed as a forklift operator working both inside and outside the plant surrounding the loading dock area. He also works as a ticket collector and a custodian at a local movie theater. With two jobs, Sammy works 35–40 hours each week. He holds a driver's license, owns a car, and provides his own transportation to and from work each day. He presently lives at home but plans to live independently in the future. Sammy is involved in sports activities at work and in the community.

Susan, a senior with developmental disabilities, is employed at a local day care as a kitchen planner and also assists with other daily routines. For the past 4 years, she has worked in a variety of school- and work-based settings preparing her for competitive employment. During the past 2 years she was employed as a cafeteria assistant and plans to continue to work there part time after graduation. She also plans to continue working at the day care part time and attend the local community college to take some special trade classes related to her employment. She attends the YMCA, participates in community activities, and plans to continue to live at home.

Roger is a senior with Down syndrome. He lacks good communication skills and uses a picture symbol system to assist with his speech deficits. He participates in a therapeutic horseback-riding program at North Shelby School and other equestrian events as well. Roger requires close supervision but enjoys working as an animal attendant in the stables. He has lived at home with his grandmother for most of his life. However, at the beginning of his senior year he decided to move out. The school-level transition team reconvened to discuss this change in residential placement and the process of moving. Roger requested community-based services (CBS) to provide support for the change. Shortly thereafter, he obtained a placement with a local family who provided CBS. He also plans to participate in compensatory education classes provided by the local community college. He is an avid bowler, a country music fan, and participates in Special Olympics.

**Teaching Strategies**     A variety of classroom instructional strategies are used with students enrolled in the OCS. Functional materials and supplementary curricula, role playing, ongoing simulated case scenarios, integration of skills, and homework assignments are implemented in small groups and one-on-one with students.

Each student enrolled in career technical education classes, grades 9–12, has a career development plan (CDP) on file, which includes academic, vocational, and technical education courses appropriate for her career goal. Incentives, modifications, and accommodations that are necessary for that student to carry out her CDP are listed accordingly. A modified plan is designed for each special-population student according to her needs and achievement capabilities.

Students achieve increased independence the closer they move to graduation and are encouraged to develop a postschool action plan. School level planning meetings on transition are conducted regularly and provide students with the opportunity to become self-advocates. A variety of instructional strategies are used to teach self-determination, assertiveness, anger management, effective communication, negotiation and compromise, effective listening, and navigation of the system to obtain needed services. All OCS students are also required to complete a career placement portfolio that includes their education and employment history, a résumé, references, a list of extracurricular activities, school- and work-based information, worksite evaluations, and financial and medical information. Related-services staff such as the speech pathologist, the physical and occupational therapists, the school nurse, the psychologist, and counselors help implement instructional strategies. Other services include

- Career awareness and exploration lessons
- Learning-style inventories and a variety of vocational assessments
- Work experience, both paid and nonpaid through the school-based enterprise, on-campus jobs, job shadowing, internships, job training, work mentoring, instruction in workplace competencies, and instruction in all aspects of industry

All students attend career fairs, visit the employment security commission, and participate in other job searches using the newspaper, the telephone book, and the Internet. Students also participate in situational assessments to obtain the appropriate job match.

Transition is a team effort that ensures the success of each individual who comes into our program. Teacher assistants provide clerical, instructional, and payroll assistance; serve as bus drivers; and function as job coaches. The school-level transition team coordinates services that help students obtain the best-possible transition into meaningful work and living environments after high school. The team is comprised of the student, parents, administrators, and the transition coordinator and transition teacher. Other members include representatives from vocational rehabilitation services, the Social Security Administration, mental health services, the Department of Social Services, postsecondary educational institutions, community rehabilitation services, state services for the blind, private adult service providers, and advocacy groups. Other school staff such as the speech pathologist, the occupational therapist, a psychologist, guidance counselors, one-on-one workers, employers, or other agency providers are also represented. A community-level transition team (comprised of administrators from various agencies) oversees the development and maintenance of quality transition services and also represents the students.

*Some Personal Reflections*     Every individual deserves to be able to live, work, and play in his community and be successful in doing so as he moves through life. By the time they reach high school, too many students with disabilities have been told that they may never be able to live independently or be gainfully employed. However, with good-quality transition planning and the appropriate supports in place, the student may be able to accomplish independent living and employment with natural stability and ease. If I have been successful in achieving this goal as students leave school, I have done a great job. I make every attempt to remain focused on my goals and follow our school mission statement to "never give up on student success." I attribute my success in the field of transition to belief in this mission and to the principal I am currently working with at North Shelby School. I continue to encourage students to set high expectations and work toward achieving their desired goals, which ultimately will result in successful and productive independent living.

To better understand the topics that will be covered in this chapter, go to the Essential Concepts and Chapter at a Glance modules in Chapter 15 of the Companion Website, **www.prenhall.com/heward**.

What does it mean to become an adult? Ferguson and Ferguson (2006) suggest that adulthood is expressed through autonomy, membership, and change. Adults express autonomy by self-sufficiency (e.g., having the financial and emotional resources to take care of themselves), self-determination, and completeness (a sense of having "arrived"). Adults experience and enjoy membership in the form of connectedness with the community, citizenship activities, and affiliations. Adulthood is characterized by change rather than stasis (e.g., moving to a new community, going back to school, taking a new job, watching old friends move away, and making new friends). Becoming an adult can be tough work for anyone.

However it is conceptualized, transition from high school to adulthood, with its increased privileges and responsibilities, is especially challenging for youth with disabilities. Skill deficits, limited opportunities created by low expectations or discrimination, and the absence of needed supports are just some of the obstacles to successful transition for many youth with disabilities.

We begin our discussion of transition by looking at the results of several studies that focus on what is perhaps the most important question of all regarding the ultimate effectiveness of special education: what do students with disabilities do after they leave school?

## HOW DO FORMER SPECIAL EDUCATION STUDENTS FARE AS ADULTS?

What happens to students with disabilities when they leave high school and enter the adult world? Do graduates of special education programs find work? Where do they live? How do the lives of adults with disabilities compare with the expectations and experiences of most citizens? How do adults with disabilities rate their quality of life? Are they happy?

Obtaining answers to such questions has become one of the highest priorities in special education today. More than 50 studies of graduates and leavers of secondary special education programs provide enlightening information on their experiences as young adults. Before we look at some of the results of these studies on employment, postsecondary education, and overall success of young adults with disabilities, let's examine the percentage of special education students who complete high school.

### Completing High School

Students who do not complete high school are likely to face more difficulties in adult adjustment than are those who do. Special education students who do not complete school are more likely to have lower levels of employment and wages and higher rates of problems with the criminal justice system (Malian & Love, 1998; Wagner, Blackorby, Cameto, & Newman, 1994; Yelin & Katz, 1994). The percentage of students with disabilities who graduate with a standard high school diploma has remained at about 25% for more than a decade (U.S. Department of Education, 2000). The percentage of students with disabilities varies greatly by state, ranging from a low of 6.8% (Mississippi) to a high of 45.4% (New Jersey). A "staggering number" of special education students drop out of school (Patton, Cronin, & Jairrels, 1997, p. 295). According to one study, although many high school dropouts resume their secondary education or obtain a general education development (GED) diploma, only 3% of youth with disabilities complete a program to earn a high school diploma within 3 to 5 years after they have dropped out (Wagner et al., 1994).

As Test, Aspel, and Everson (2006) point out, although completing high school is important to future success, even more critical is that students obtain not just a diploma but also the skills vital to adult living. Too many students with disabilities are focusing solely on achieving academic success at the expense of careful transition planning (Hasazi, Furney, & DeStefano, 1999).

## Employment

The largest and most comprehensive study of the adult adjustment of youth with disabilities after they leave secondary special education programs is the National Longitudinal Transition Study (NLTS). The NLTS is an ongoing effort to assess and monitor changes in the lives of 8,000 youths with disabilities who left U.S. secondary special education programs between 1985 and 1987 (Blackorby & Wagner, 1996).

Data from the NLTS show an unemployment rate of 46% for all youth with disabilities who have been out of school for less than 2 years. The unemployment rate for young adults with disabilities drops to 36.5% when they have been out of school for 3 to 5 years, but nearly one in five persons (19.6%) states she has given up looking for work (NLTS).

The employment outlook is much worse for students with physical, sensory, severe, and multiple disabilities. The NLTS found extremely low employment rates 3 to 5 years after secondary school for young adults with orthopedic impairments (22%), visual impairments (29%), and multiple disabilities (17%) (NLTS).

Between one-half and two-thirds of young adults with disabilities who are employed work in part-time jobs (Frank & Sitlington, 2000; Sitlington, Frank, & Carson, 1993). The incomes of many individuals with disabilities hover near the poverty level (Scuccimarra & Speece, 1990); and relatively few receive health insurance, sick leave, or vacation benefits (Frank & Sitlington, 2000). On average, youth with disabilities in the NLTS earned a median hourly wage of $5.72, less than $12,000 per year for full-time, year-round employment. Only 40% of the young adults with disabilities who had jobs 3 to 5 years after school earned more than $6.00 per hour.

Although the employment earnings of high school graduates with learning disabilities are slightly higher than those of peers without disabilities for the first 4 years after leaving school (because most of their peers are attending college), by the 5th year the earnings of graduates without disabilities "increasingly outpaced those of their peers with LD" (Goldstein, Murray, & Edgar, 1998, p. 60).

A nationwide survey of Americans with disabilities ages 16 to 64 by Louis Harris and Associates (2000) reported even more discouraging findings: approximately two-thirds are unemployed, only 20% have full-time jobs, and 11% are working part time. These results reaffirm a conclusion of a similar Harris poll in 1986 that "not working is perhaps the truest definition of what it means to be disabled" (p. 81). Like other minority groups, persons with disabilities are often in the position of being the last hired and the first fired (Trupin, Sebesta, Yelin, & LaPlante, 1997).

*Results of the NLTS*

Knowledge and Skill Base for Beginning Special Education Transition Specialists: Research on relationships between individual outcomes and transition practices (TS1K4).

*Brian's job gives him a sense of autonomy and connectedness with the community.*

## Postsecondary Education

Attending college and postsecondary vocational programs greatly increases the likelihood of obtaining employment and generally experiencing success as an adult. Compared with their peers without disabilities, fewer former special education students pursue postsecondary education. A follow-up of 1,242 youths with disabilities who had been out of school for 1 year found that 15% had taken at least one postsecondary course compared with 56% of youth without disabilities (Fairweather & Shaver, 1991). NLTS found that 27% of young adults who had left high school had enrolled in some type of postsecondary education program within 3 to 5 years compared with 68% of the general same-age population (Blackorby & Wagner, 1996).

# Overall Adjustment and Success

Being a successful adult involves much more than holding a job; it means achieving status as an independent and active member of society. Independence for an adult includes the ability to participate in society, work, have a home, raise a family, and share the joys and responsibilities of community life (Ferguson & Ferguson, 2006). Adults with disabilities face numerous obstacles in day-to-day living that affect where and how they live, how well they can use community resources, and what opportunities they have for social interaction. After being out of high school for 3 to 5 years, only 37% of youth with disabilities were living independently (alone, with a spouse or a roommate, in a college dormitory or military housing; that is, not as a dependent) compared with 60% of the general population (NLTS).

The NLTS includes a measure of adult adjustment that assesses independent functioning in three domains: (1) employment (competitively employed in a full-time job or engaged in job training or postsecondary education), (2) residential arrangements (living alone or with a spouse or a roommate), and (3) social activities (having friends, belonging to social groups). When assessed at a period less than 2 years out of school, only 6.4% of all youth with disabilities met these three criteria. When the same measures are assessed after individuals have been out of school for 3 to 5 years, 20% were judged to be independent in all three domains (Wagner et al., 1994). Even with this significant improvement after several years, four out of every five former special education students had still not achieved the status of independent adulthood after being out of high school for up to 5 years.

It is important to note that the very small percentage of young adults who met the criteria for successful transition to adult life in this study had graduated from secondary special education programs. Young adults who leave secondary programs by routes other than graduation do not fare as well as those who do complete school with a diploma or a certificate (Blackorby & Wagner, 1996; Malian & Love, 1998).

A follow-up study of graduates of secondary special education programs in Iowa evaluated whether or not transition to adulthood was successful as defined by four criteria: (1) employed (full or part time) in a competitive job, working as a homemaker, enrolled as a full-time student, or enrolled in a job-training program; (2) buying a home, living independently, or living with a friend or a spouse; (3) paying at least a portion of one's living expenses; and (4) being involved in more than three different leisure activities (Sitlington et al., 1993). This study found that only 5.8% of 737 students with learning disabilities, 5 of 142 students with mental retardation (3.5%), and just 1 of 59 students with behavioral disorders could be judged as having made a successful adult adjustment 1 year after they had completed high school.

There is some evidence that outcomes are improving slightly for graduates of secondary special education programs. A study of postschool outcomes for high school graduates with mental retardation in Iowa found that the class of 1993 was slightly better off than the class of 1985 (Frank & Sitlington, 2000). For example, 74% of the 1993 graduates were employed compared to 66% of the 1985 graduates; 28% of the 1993 graduates lived independently compared to 21% of the 1985 graduates; and 39% of the 1993 graduates were enrolled in some type of postsecondary education or training program compared to 21% of the 1985 graduates.

Such findings have focused attention on what has become a dominant issue in special education today—the transition from school to adult life in the community. Many youth who leave secondary special education programs discover to their dismay and discouragement that "the fiscal and logistical demands of daily life [are] far more complex than what they learned in functional math, home-economics, or life skills classes … [and that the] protective nature of their experiences in special education had left them ill-prepared for the real world" (Knoll & Wheeler, 2001, pp. 502–503). And it is not just students with major cognitive limitations or severe physical, sensory, or behavioral disabilities who have trouble adjusting to life after high school. Former special education students with mild disabilities face significant challenges in every aspect of adult life (Tymchuk, Lakin, & Luckasson, 2001).

No longer can special educators be satisfied with students' improved performance on classroom-related tasks. We must work equally hard to ensure that the education students receive during their school years plays a direct and positive role in helping them deal successfully with the multifaceted demands of adulthood.

# TRANSITION SERVICES AND MODELS

## Will's Bridges Model of School-to-Work Transition

In response to growing concern over the failure of so many young adults with disabilities in the job market and community living, Congress authorized funding for secondary education and transitional services for youth with disabilities when it amended IDEA in 1983 (P.L. 98–199). In 1984, Madeline Will, director of the U.S. Office of Special Education and Rehabilitation Services, proposed a model of transition services that encompassed three levels of service, each conceptualized as a bridge between the secondary special education curriculum and adult employment (Will, 1986). Each level differs in terms of the nature and extent of the services an individual with disabilities needs to make a successful transition from school to work. At the first level are students who require no special transition services. On graduation from an appropriate secondary special education curriculum, these young adults, presumably those with mild disabilities, would make use of the generic employment services already available to people without disabilities in the community (e.g., job placement agencies). At the second level are persons with disabilities who require the time-limited transitional services offered by vocational rehabilitation or adult service agencies that are specially designed to help individuals with disabilities gain competitive, independent employment. The third level of transitional services consists of ongoing employment services that are necessary to enable persons with severe disabilities to enjoy the benefits of meaningful paid work.

*Will's Bridges model*

Council for Exceptional Children Knowledge and Skill Base for Beginning Special Education Transition Specialists: Theoretical and applied models of transition (TS1K1) (also TS1K3).

## Halpern's Three-Dimensional Model

Because it showed the federal government's recognition of the need to improve the employment outcomes for special education students, Will's bridges model for school-to-work transition was viewed as a move in the right direction. Many special educators, however, thought that its perspective on transition was too limited. Halpern (1985) wrote that it is a mistake to focus on adult employment as the sole purpose and outcome of transition services: "Living successfully in one's community should be the primary target of transitional services" (p. 480). Halpern proposed a transition model that directed Will's generic, time-limited, and ongoing support services toward helping students with disabilities adjust to adult life in the community in three domains: (1) quality of residential environment, (2) adequacy of social and interpersonal network, and (3) meaningful employment (see Figure 15.1).

Halpern's model influenced subsequent definitions of transition services in the 1990 and 1997 amendments to IDEA. The view that transition must focus on all domains of adult functioning characterizes the field today.

*Halpern's transition model*

Council for Exceptional Children Knowledge and Skill Base for Beginning Special Education Transition Specialists: Theoretical and applied models of transition (TS1K1) (also TS1K3).

## Definition of Transition Services in IDEA

**Transition services** are defined in IDEA as a coordinated set of activities for a student with a disability that:

*IDEA definition of transition services*

Council for Exceptional Children Knowledge and Skill Base for Beginning Special Education Transition Specialists: Transition-related laws and policies (TS1K2).

   a. is designed within an outcome-oriented process, which promotes movement from school to post-school activities, including postsecondary education, vocational training, integrated employment (including supported employment), continuing and adult education, adult services, independent living, or community participation;
   b. is based upon the individual student's needs, taking into account the student's preferences and interests; and

**FIGURE 15.1** Halpern's three-dimensional conceptualization of transition

*Source*: From "Transition: A Look at the Foundation" by A. S. Halpern. *Exceptional Children, 51*, 1985, p. 481. © 1985 by the Council for Exceptional Children. Reprinted with permission.

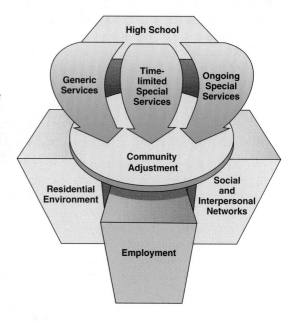

c. includes instruction, related services, community experiences, the development of employment and other post-school adult living objectives, and, when appropriate, acquisition of daily living skills and functional vocational evaluation. (H.R. 1350, Sec. 602[34])

## Individualized Transition Plan

IDEA requires that IEPs for older students include information on how the child's transition from school to adult life will be supported:

Beginning not later than the first IEP to be in effect when the child is 16, and updated annually thereafter—

a. appropriate measurable postsecondary goals based upon age appropriate transition assessments related to training, education, employment, and, where appropriate, independent living skills;

b. the transition services (including courses of study) needed to assist the child in reaching those goals; and

c. beginning not later than 1 year before the child reaches the age of majority under State law, a statement that the child has been informed of the child's rights under this title, if any, that will transfer to the child on reaching the age of majority under section 615(m). (The Individuals with Disabilities Education Improvement Act of 2004, Sec 614 [d] [1] [A] [II])

The intent of this provision is to focus the IEP team's attention on secondary curriculum and course planning related to postschool success. This portion of the student's IEP is called an **individualized transition plan (ITP).** The ITP may be written at an earlier age if the IEP team determines it is appropriate for an individual student. It is important to begin coordinated transition planning early. (See Profiles & Perspectives, "Helping Students Step Into Adult Life with Confidence," later in this chapter.)

In contrast to IEP goals and objectives, which address one year at a time, transition planning requires the IEP team to think and plan several years ahead (deFur, 2000). Developed and included as part of the IEP process, a student's ITP outlines actions, events, and resources that will affect and support her move from school to adulthood. A well-written ITP details the types of curricular programming and supports that will prepare the student for a smooth and successful transition to adult life.

Transition plans are designed within an outcome-oriented process based on the student's and family's vision of the future. The student's IEP/ITP team specifies postschool

*Individualized transition plan (ITP)*

Council for Exceptional Children

Knowledge and Skill Base for Beginning Special Education Transition Specialists: Transition-related laws and policies (TS1K2) (also CC1K4).

outcomes and goals in four major areas—employment, postsecondary education/training, residential, and recreation/leisure—and then develops an individualized program of instruction and activities designed to reach those outcomes. Decisions about needed transition services should be guided by answers to questions such as the following (Brolin & Loyd, 2004; Flexer, Simmons, Luft, & Baer, 2005; Kohler, 1996; Martin & Marshall, 1995; Sitlington & Clark, 2006; Test et al., 2006; Wehman, 2002):

- What are the student's dreams and vision of his life as a young adult?
- What are his strengths? How will he build on them to facilitate a successful transition?
- What skills does the student need to develop or improve to make progress toward her postschool goals?
- Will the student seek a regular high school diploma? If so, what course of study and proficiency tests will be required?
- Will she work toward a vocational certificate of completion instead of a regular diploma?
- Does he have an expressed career interest now? If not, what can the team do to help him explore career possibilities and discover his preferences?
- Is the student likely to remain in high school through the maximum age of eligibility for special education services? If so, what curriculum and work experiences will be needed after age 18?
- In what school and community activities will the student participate?

A well-written transition plan ensures that parents are aware of available adult services and employment options in the community, improves the chances that adult services will be available with few disruptions to the graduating student, and provides school and adult-service personnel with a set of procedures and timelines to follow. After graduation, the ITP can be incorporated into an individual rehabilitation plan if the young adult is served by vocational rehabilitation or made part of an individualized habilitation plan if the young adult is served by a community adult services agency (e.g., a county program for people with developmental disabilities).

Like IEPs, transition plans can take many formats as long as they contain the necessary information. Figure 15.2 shows the ITP developed for Jeff, a 10th grader with learning disabilities. Jeff and his parents share a vision for the future in which Jeff has a good job and lives as independently as possible. He is very interested in obtaining his driver's license; and based on some of his community-work experiences, he thinks he might like to work in the heating and air conditioning field. Jeff also sees himself getting married someday, but first he wants to live on his own for a while, probably in an apartment with a roommate or two. He has also expressed the desire to continue his education after high school; therefore, one of the activities on his ITP is to obtain information about community and technical colleges.

The goals and objectives numbers on the ITP refer to the goals and objectives on Jeff's IEP that support the transition plan (IEP objectives are at the bottom of the figure). Academic goals for Jeff, such as reading comprehension, use the content area from the transition plan—e.g., a heating and air conditioning textbook and the driver's education manual. Jeff frequently relies on adults to assist him in decision making and to request information about days off at work, and he needs to better understand his disability. His self-advocacy goal relates to more self-reliance. Although specific skills will be taught, Jeff will practice his self-advocacy skills at his part-time job.

*Relating transition services to IEP goals and objectives*

Council for Exceptional Children — Knowledge and Skill Base for Beginning Special Education Transition Specialists: Methods for linking academic content to transition goals (TS4K2) (also CC4S6).

## Transition Teaming

Transition planning requires a team—special education teachers, general education teachers, vocational education teachers, school counselors, related-services personnel, personnel from community and adult services agencies such as vocational rehabilitation, higher education, and/or developmental disabilities adult services agencies—that can help the student identify and reach her postschool goals. All people involved must build and maintain communication links and supports among the team members.

# Helping Students Step into Adult Life with Confidence

## by Barbara Horvath

As the school year draws to an end, a group of school and adult agency staff members gather to discuss students' transitions from school to adult life. As transition coordinator for the school district, I begin by suggesting we review the accomplishments of some of our exiting students. Kris, a vocational rehabilitation (VR) counselor, asks about Tom. A great kid, he has worked hard during the past 2 years. Tom realizes that his learning disability will continue to be an issue for him in college, but Kris has worked with him to obtain needed services through the college's disability office. Tom's special education teacher, Gary, has helped Tom learn to advocate for the accommodations he will need in his courses. During school time, Gary and Tom worked on college applications; and Tom's family helped him meet deadlines for applications and federal financial assistance. Gary and I have worked with Tom and his parents to make a list of the skills he needs to hone over the summer: doing laundry, budgeting, maintaining a checkbook, and scheduling and using his time well. I have also given Tom information about organizations and activities on campus since he is shy and may find it difficult to make friends. Tom and his parents think they are ready for this huge step to independent living at college. But Tom has Gary's e-mail address and knows he can count on Gary, Kris, and me for help.

Susan, another VR counselor, suggests we talk about Char. During her sophomore year, Char's case conference committee (which included Char and her father) determined that she would leave school with a certificate of achievement rather than a diploma. Char struggles with reading and clearly would not be able to meet graduation requirements. Karen, our work-study coordinator, has arranged a variety of unpaid work experiences for Char over the past 3 years. Real-work experience in a variety of job settings has helped her determine the type of work she most enjoys and is skilled in, the social and physical environments that are most comfortable for her, and the speed at which she is most successful. Even though Char

thought she wanted to work in a burger joint, she quickly learned that its rushed pace wasn't for her. Clerking at a small grocery store was better, but dealing with so many people was stressful. Toward the end of a 2-hour shift, Char found it difficult to keep being polite to the customers. Now she is enjoying her job stocking shelves and taking inventory in a small shop. She hopes to work more than 4 hours a day and is glad that she is leaving school with a job.

Char's father was concerned about his daughter's safety traveling to and from work, but with Karen's help Char has learned the bus routes without difficulty. If she does miss a connection, she calls her father on her new cell phone so she won't have to wait for the next bus.

Char will benefit from follow-along services provided by an adult service agency. Brenda, the school district's primary contact with the agency, is at our meeting today. As we review Char's transition timeline, Brenda talks about Char's relationship with Tammy, the agency's job coach. Tammy has been getting to know Char during the past 4 weeks, dropping in to see her at work and school. As we fade support from the school district job coach, the adult service job coach provides more and more services. At first Tammy will spend an hour a day on the job with Char. As Char gains independence in job tasks, Tammy will fade her visits to once a week.

Char wants to move to a place of her own within 2 years, and Susan and I are gathering information on low-cost housing since she is not eligible for residential services through the Medicaid waiver program. She wants an apartment on a bus line because she knows that it will be several years before she can afford a car. She would like to have a roommate—preferably her best friend, Beth. The transition team has worked with them on how to proceed after high school.

Now our group turns to Steve, a young man with a traumatic brain injury. At age 15, Steve was in a car accident. He was hospitalized for several months and then underwent several more months of intensive physical therapy. Although he can walk, his gait is uneven, he falls easily, and his stamina is limited. Steve did not receive special education services before the accident. He continues to struggle with the changes in his life, loss of friends, and anger control. His dreams for his future are radically different from what they were 3 years ago. Due to his intense mental health and emotional needs, our team has made connections with a variety of residential, mental health, and employment agencies.

Like many other 18-year-olds, Steve is interested in women, cars, shooting pool, and getting married someday. Although he can carry on a conversation, his short-term memory is poor. He forgets to take his medicine, gets confused about his schedule, often misses his bus, and forgets to set his alarm. He has angry outbursts at his parents, teachers, and peers. Steve has lost several work-study jobs because of trouble taking criticism. He is now working at a job that gives him some freedom to choose which tasks to do first. However, he needs to take a midday break because he tires easily.

Steve has had difficulty, especially during the summer, in making good choices about his free time. Although we hope he will someday take advantage of adult education classes, he is not presently interested in more school. He wants to take guitar lessons and perhaps an art class, so his special education teacher is helping him explore those options.

The group turns to a discussion of Mike. Because his family had not participated in his case conferences for the past 3 years, they had missed a great deal of information about planning for life after high school. Although Mike had attended all of his conferences and will be graduating with a diploma and a decent grade-point average, he had no real plan for his future. According to his special education teacher, Mike had not shown any interest in postsecondary opportunities. He has never had a job and seems content to let his parents take care of him.

Then Mike's father showed up at a case conference. He called me the next day to ask if I could meet with him, his wife, and Mike to talk about the future. It is not unusual for families to put off planning until the last minute. The comfort and routine of school can lull families into a false sense of security. When I met with the family at their home one evening, it was clear that planning for the future was a frightening new topic. I thought we needed to focus on Mike's strengths, his hopes and potential barriers to them, and the beginning of a plan. I asked who might be able to help with the planning: friends, other family members, teachers? The family compiled a list and agreed on a time for our next planning meeting.

Participants at that meeting included Mike's parents, his grandfather, his older sister, two friends of his, one family friend, his landscaping teacher, and his special education teacher. Everyone contributed to the list of his strengths, a very empowering time for him. He talked about his dreams: traveling, working with his hands, being outdoors, staying with his girlfriend, playing golf, and so on. Then we talked about careers. Mike was uncertain until the talk turned to his love of driving and his desire to travel. When one of his friends joked, "Drive semis!" Mike immediately agreed. Someone else mentioned his tendency to fix things. Being an electrician became an option.

When we discovered that Mike was not eligible for vocational rehabilitation services, Kris, the VR counselor, offered information about technical schools for electricians and schools that offered truck-driver training. His high school counselor began helping him apply to those schools. Mike is now excited about the future and is becoming proactive in making contacts and following them up.

Next the group moved to a review of our work on the community transition council (CTC), which meets 4 times per year. Participants include high school work-study coordinators, parents, VR counselors, and representatives from adult service providers and the mental health center. The CTC reviews its task forces and plans for future activities. The task forces meet as needed to prepare the quarterly family newsletter, offer information or professional development opportunities to teachers and counselors, and develop materials and activities about planning transitions to adult life.

After 12 years of CTC activities, we still have unfinished work. Mike is a good example. Students should not be at the end of their school careers before planning begins. Each year a few of our 60 exiting students see their plans crumble after graduation. So while we recognize that we cannot control everything, our long-term plan is to ensure that all of our students step into the adult life they desire. This doesn't mean locking a student into a life plan. It means that each student will leave high school recognizing her personal strengths, knowing where to turn for support, and looking toward adult life with confidence.

Barbara Horvath is transition coordinator of the Monroe County Community School Corporation, Bloomington, Indiana. She has spent 10 years as a classroom teacher and 15 years as a coordinator of special education.

 To further your understanding of and answer reflective questions about the concepts and issues presented here, go to the Profiles & Perspectives module in Chapter 15 of the Companion Website, **www.prenhall.com/heward**.

**FIGURE 15.2**
**Example of an individualized transition plan (ITP)**

*Source*: ITP form from Ohio Department of Education. (1998). *Model policies and procedures for the education of children with disabilities* (p. 608b). Columbus, OH: Author.

## STATEMENT OF NEEDED TRANSITION SERVICES

Name of Student __Jeff Grace__     Date __1-14-06__

Person Responsible for Coordinating Transition Services __Nancy Long__

Title __Work Study Coordinator__

---

**INSTRUCTION:** Goals and objectives for transition should be indicated below in the following areas and be incorporated into the body of the IEP (pages 2 and 3).

*See IEP goals and objectives for curriculum modifications and adaptations*

---

**EMPLOYMENT & POSTSECONDARY OUTCOME(S):** _Full-time job in heating/air conditioning_

| ACTIVITIES AND SERVICES | Goal Number for Transition Goals and Objectives | Responsible Person/Provider | Initiation/Duration |
|---|---|---|---|
| Heating/air cond. voc. class | 1.a, 1.b, 1.C | Voc Educ. Teacher | 1/05 to 1/06 |
| Explore Technical colleges | NA | Jeff, guidance coun. | 1/05 to 6/05 |
| Part-time job | 2.a, 2.b, 2.C | Jeff, work study coord. | 1/05 to 2/06 |

---

**POSTSCHOOL/ADULT LIVING OUTCOME(S):** _Live independently in apartment with roommate_

| ACTIVITIES AND SERVICES | Goal Number for Transition Goals and Objectives | Responsible Person/Provider | Initiation/Duration |
|---|---|---|---|
| Family Planning Class | 1.a, 1.b, 1.C | SPED Teacher/Reg. Teacher | 1/05 to 6/05 |
| Money management | 3.a 3.b | SPED Teacher | 1/05 to 1/06 |
| Self-advocacy skills trn. | 2.a, 2.b, 2.C | Jeff, SPED Teacher | 1/05 to 2/06 |

---

**COMMUNITY PARTICIPATION OUTCOME(S):** _To participate in the community through social relationships and transportation._

| ACTIVITIES AND SERVICES | Goal Number for Transition Goals and Objectives | Responsible Person/Provider | Initiation/Duration |
|---|---|---|---|
| Drivers Ed. | 1.a 1.b 1.C | Driver Ed Teacher / SPED Teacher | 1/05 to 6/06 |
| Register to vote | NA | Jeff and parents | 1/05 to 6/06 |
| Interact Club | NA | Jeff | 1/05 to 6/06 |

---

**Jeff's Transition-Related IEP Objectives**

1. **Reading comprehension.** Goal: Jeff will increase his reading skills.
   a. When given a reading passage from the driver's education manual or heating and air conditioning textbook, Jeff will increase his reading comprehension skills by using the SQ3R study skills method.
   b. Given 10 functional vocabulary words from the course text, Jeff will identify and define each word.
   c. Given an unfamiliar/unknown word in the heating and air conditioning text (or other course texts), Jeff will decode the word using word attack skills.
2. **Self-advocacy.** Goal: Jeff will increase his self-advocacy skills.
   a. Jeff will increase his understanding of his disability by identifying and stating his strengths and areas of difficulty.
   b. When given various community and work situations, Jeff will identify and demonstrate appropriate decision-making skills.
   c. When given various community and work problem situations, Jeff will identify people who can assist him with difficult or unfamiliar situations.
3. **Money management.** Goal: Jeff will manage his personal finances.
   a. Jeff will construct and use a monthly personal budget for his present income.
   b. Jeff will record personal major income and expenses for three months.

Transition involves the coordination, delivery, and transfer of services from the secondary school program to receiving agencies (e.g., employers, postsecondary education and vocational training programs, residential service providers). Although work-study and vocational training programs for special education students and vocational rehabilitation services for adults with disabilities have long existed in every state, systematic coordination of and communication between schools and community-based adult services have not typically occurred. Although interagency cooperation is critical to the success of transition, the amendments to IDEA "made it clear that the initial and ultimately most significant transition responsibilities lie with schools" (Moon & Inge, 1993, p. 583).

Nowhere in special education are teaming and collaboration more important than when planning and delivering transition services for secondary students. The validity and likely effectiveness of the transition services described on a student's ITP depend on the student's involvement, family involvement, and the collaboration of professionals who are helping the student and family plan and implement transition services. Cooperation and communication between and among professionals and families are keys to effective transition planning.

## Beginning Transition Activities and Career Education Early

Numerous models for conceptualizing and guiding the delivery of transition services have been developed (e.g., Kohler, 1998; Sitlington et al., 2006). All stress the importance of providing career education at an early age, the student's choosing goals, a functional secondary school curriculum that offers work experience in integrated community job sites, systematic coordination between the school and adult service providers, and parental involvement and support.

The Council for Exceptional Children's Division on Career Development and Transition (DCDT) believes that career development and transition services should begin in the elementary grades for all children with disabilities (Blalock et al., 2003). According to DCDT, three basic principles underlie the provision of career education and transition services:

1. *Education for career development and transition is for individuals with disabilities of all ages.*
2. *Career development is a process begun at birth and continues throughout life.*
3. *Early career development is essential for making satisfactory choices later.* A frequent criticism of secondary employment training programs is that there are too few choices and that professionals too often end up making those choices for students. . . . The best way to prepare individuals for self-knowledge (interests, abilities, limiting barriers) and decision-making is to begin the process of self-awareness and choice-making as early as possible. (Clark, Carlson, Fisher, Cook, & D'Alonzo, 1991, pp. 115–116)

Developing career awareness and vocational skills during the elementary years does not mean, of course, that 6-year-old children should be placed on job sites for training. Appropriate transition-related objectives should be selected at each age level (Brolin, 1997; Cronin, Patton, & Wood, 2005, Johnson & Wehman, 2001). For example, elementary students might sample different types of jobs through classroom responsibilities such as watering plants, cleaning chalkboards, or taking messages to the office. Young children with disabilities might also visit community worksites where adults with disabilities are employed. Middle school students should begin to spend time at actual community job sites, with an increasing amount of in-school instruction devoted to the development of associated work skills, such as being on time, staying on task, and using interpersonal skills (Beakley & Yoder, 1998).

Developing and operating a school-based business enterprise can help high school students learn functional academic, work, problem-solving, and social skills. For example, Lindstrom, Benz, and Johnson (1997) describe four school-based businesses—an espresso and baked-goods bar, a take-out meals operation, a mail-order seed business, and a winter produce garden—that students with disabilities in several high schools in Oregon have helped develop and operate. Secondary students with moderate and severe disabilities should also spend an increasing amount of time receiving instruction at actual

To read firsthand examples of communication breakdowns that can occur during transition planning meetings and how to avoid them, see "Removing Transition Hurdles with Effective Communication" on Chapter 15's Profiles & Perspectives Module of the Companion Website, **www.prenhall.com/heward**.

*CEC-DCDT*

**Council for Exceptional Children** Knowledge and Skill Base for Beginning Special Education Transition Specialists: Organizations and publications relevant to the field of transition (TS9K3).

Giving secondary students regular opportunities to participate in integrated work settings in the community builds career awareness and teaches valuable vocational skills.

**TABLE 15.1** Examples of transition-related curriculum activities in four domains that might be included in a student's IEP

| | Domestic | Community | Leisure | Vocational |
|---|---|---|---|---|
| **Elementary** | Picking up toys<br>Washing dishes<br>Making bed<br>Dressing<br>Grooming<br>Eating skills<br>Toileting skills<br>Sorting clothes<br>Vacuuming<br>Setting the table at mealtime | Eating meals in a restaurant<br>Using restroom in a local restaurant<br>Putting trash into container<br>Choosing correct change to ride city bus<br>Giving the clerk money to purchase an item<br>Responding appropriately to pedestrian safety signs<br>Going to neighbor's house for lunch | Climbing on swing set<br>Playing board games<br>Playing tag with neighbors<br>Coloring<br>Playing kickball<br>Croquet<br>Riding bicycles<br>Playing with age-appropriate toys<br>Community soccer league | Returning toys to appropriate storage spaces<br>Cleaning the room at the end of the day<br>Working on a task for a designated period<br>Wiping tables after meals<br>Following 2– to 4–step instructions<br>Answering the telephone<br>Emptying trash<br>Taking messages to people |
| **Middle School** | Washing clothes<br>Preparing simple meals (soup, salad, and sandwich)<br>Keeping bedroom clean<br>Making snacks<br>Mowing lawn<br>Raking leaves<br>Making grocery lists<br>Purchasing items from a list<br>Vacuuming and dusting<br>Setting an alarm clock at night and turning it off when waking | Crossing streets safely<br>Purchasing an item from a department store<br>Purchasing a meal at a restaurant<br>Using local transportation system to get to and from recreational facilities<br>Participating in local scout troop<br>Going to a neighbor's house for lunch on Saturday | Playing volleyball<br>Taking aerobics classes<br>Playing checkers with a friend<br>Playing miniature golf<br>Cycling<br>Attending high school or local college basketball games<br>Hanging out at local mall<br>Swimming<br>Attending crafts class at city recreation center | Mopping/waxing floors<br>Cleaning windows<br>Hanging and bagging clothes<br>Busing tables<br>Working for 1–2 hours<br>Operating machinery (e.g., dishwasher, buffer)<br>Cleaning sinks, bathtubs, and fixtures<br>Internship with school janitor or office staff<br>Following a job sequence |
| **High School** | Cleaning all rooms in place of residence<br>Developing a weekly budget<br>Cooking meals<br>Operating thermostat to regulate heat or air<br>Doing yard maintenance<br>Maintaining personal needs<br>Caring for and maintaining clothing | Using bus system to move about the community<br>Depositing checks into bank account<br>Using community department stores<br>Using community grocery stores<br>Using community health facilities (e.g., physician, pharmacist) | Jogging<br>Boating<br>Watching college basketball game<br>Video games<br>Card games<br>YMCA swim class<br>Gardening<br>Going on a vacation<br>Collecting tapes or CDs<br>Reading magazines or comics<br>Hanging out/sleeping over with friends | Janitorial duties (at J. C. Penney)<br>Housekeeping duties (at Days Inn)<br>Grounds keeping duties at local college campus<br>Food service at mall cafeteria<br>Laundry duties at local laundromat<br>Performing job duties to company standards |

*Source*: Adapted from Johnson, S., & Wehman, P. (2001). Teaching for transition. In P. Wehman, *Life beyond the classroom: Transition strategies for young people with disabilities* (3rd ed.), (pp. 156–157). Baltimore: Brookes. Used by permission.

*Career awareness and transition-related curriculum activities*

Council for Exceptional Children Knowledge and Skill Base for Beginning Special Education Transition Specialists: Methods for linking academic content to transition goals (TS4K2) (also TS4K1, CC4S6).

community job sites (Moon & Inge, 2000). The remaining hours of in-school instruction should focus on acquisition of functional skills needed in the adult work, domestic, community, and recreational/leisure environments toward which the student is headed (Benz & Lindstrom, 1997; Patton et al., 1997). Table 15.1 shows examples of transition-related curriculum activities in the domestic, community, leisure, and vocational domains that might be incorporated into a student's IEP. (Self-determination is important. See Teaching & Learning, "Two for One: Teaching Self-Determination and Writing Together," on the next page.)

# Two for One: Teaching Self-Determination and Writing Together

*by Moira Konrad and David W. Test*

Research indicates that educators believe it is important to teach self-determination skills to students with disabilities. However, secondary special education teachers are already overwhelmed with a broad range of roles and responsibilities. Federal requirements have added to the burdens special educators carry. Teachers are now not only held accountable for documenting their students' progress in the general curriculum but also for preparing them to participate in standards-based, high-stakes assessments. In response, both the IEP Template and the GO 4 IT ... NOW! strategies have been developed and can be used to teach a self-determination skill (student involvement in the IEP process) and an academic skill (written expression) simultaneously.

## THE IEP TEMPLATE

The IEP Template is essentially a "fill-in-the-blank" IEP that students can use to write a draft of a first-person IEP. The template serves as an organizer to help students understand the content and format of an IEP. It also helps students draft components of their IEPs in complete sentences.

## GO 4 IT ... NOW!

Once students have successfully used the IEP Template, they can move seamlessly to the GO 4 IT ... NOW! learning strategy and apply their knowledge and skills. GO 4 IT ... NOW! is a strategy that teaches students how to write paragraphs about their IEP goals. Specifically, students learn that each paragraph is about one particular goal. The goal itself serves as the topic sentence of the paragraph. The objectives are the supporting details in the paragraph, and a restatement of the goal with an indication of how long it will take to complete (a timeline) serves as a concluding sentence. The mnemonic GO 4 IT ... NOW! helps students remember the structure of the paragraph, and, more specifically, what to include:

G—Goals
O—Objectives
4—4 objectives
IT—Identify timeline
N—Did I NAME my topic?
O—Did I ORDER my steps?
W—Did I WRAP it up and restate my topic?

## HOW TO GET STARTED

*Help students identify their visions for the future.*

- Use online interest, career inventories, and school guidance counselors to help students develop vision statements about what they want to do when they finish high school.
- Work with students to help them identify their strengths and academic, functional, social, and behavioral needs.
- Explicitly teach students how to turn a need into a goal.
- Provide explicit instruction in how to complete the IEP template, using modeling and guided and independent practice.

*Teach students how to turn visions into goals and objectives.*

- Help students identify their academic, functional, social, and behavioral needs and teach them how to turn a need into a goal using an "I will" statement.
- Provide explicit instruction in how to write a goal paragraph, using modeling and guided and independent practice.
- Emphasize the use of transition words to teach students how to put objectives into logical order.

*Build in writing and communication skills.*

- Use the sentences students develop in their IEP Templates to teach capitalization, punctuation, and parts of speech.

<table>
<tr><td>

**Example of a vision statement <u>before</u> template instruction:**

After high school I plan to . . .
Live _____ in New York _____
Learn _____
Work _____ as a lawyer _____
Play _____

**Example of an academic strength <u>before</u> template instruction:**

I can _____ math _____

**Example of a goal <u>before</u> template instruction:**

I will _____ writing _____

</td><td>

**Example of a vision statement <u>after</u> template instruction:**

After high school I plan to . . .
Live _____ in an apartment _____
Learn _____ how to be a lawyer _____
Work _____ in a restaurant _____
Play _____ basketball at the YMCA with my friends

**Example of an academic strength <u>after</u> template instruction:**

I can _____ say my multiplication facts quickly

**Example of a goal <u>after</u> template instruction:**

I will _____ write and edit paragraphs _____

</td></tr>
</table>

- Teach students how to use transition words and phrases to string sentences into paragraphs. For example, have students write sentences about a specific topic such as "My Strengths" or "My Services and Accommodations" and then use transition words to turn them into paragraphs.
- Weave letter-writing skills into the curriculum by having students write letters to invite the IEP team members to attend annual review meetings.
- Suggest that students prepare to participate in their IEP meetings by (1) bringing their completed templates and/or paragraphs to the meetings or (2) developing presentations about their templates.

*Take it a step further.*

- Emphasize, teach, and model how GO 4 IT . . . NOW! can be used to write all kinds of paragraphs.

- Encourage students to create essays (once they are able to write effective paragraphs) by combining paragraphs.
- Suggest that students bring their paragraphs/essays to their IEP team meetings and share them with the team, or send out the essays with the IEP invitation letters as preparation for the meeting.

---

Moira Konrad is a doctoral student studying transition from high school to adult life in the special education program at the University of North Carolina at Charlotte (UNCC). David W. Test is a professor in the special education program at UNCC and coauthor of the text *Transition Methods for Youth with Disabilities*.

 To learn more about these strategies and answer questions about what you have learned, go to the Teaching & Learning module in Chapter 15 of the Companion Website, **www.prenhall.com/heward**.

# EMPLOYMENT

Work can be defined as using one's physical and/or mental energies to accomplish something productive. Our society is based on a work ethic; we place a high value on work and on people who contribute. Besides providing economic support, work offers opportunities for social interaction and a chance to use and enhance skills in a chosen area. Work generates the respect of others and provides a sense of pride and self-satisfaction. Individuals with disabilities who are employed report a higher-quality life (Kraemer, McIntryre, & Blacher, 2003).

All young adults face important questions about what to do with their lives—attend college or technical school, work as a bricklayer or an accountant—but for the person without disabilities, answering those questions involves choosing from a number of options. By contrast, the young adult with disabilities often has fewer options from which to choose.

Occupational choices decrease if the person with disabilities has limited skills; they may decrease even more due to the nature of the disability and still further because of employers' (needless) prejudices and misconceptions about people with disabilities. For most adults with disabilities, obtaining and holding a job is a major life challenge and goal.

## Competitive Employment

A person who is competitively employed performs work valued by an employer, functions in an integrated setting with nondisabled co-workers, earns at or above the federal minimum wage, and is working without support from an outside human service agency. Virtually all special educators who have studied the transition of students with disabilities from school to adult life believe that only through significant revision of the public school curriculum and improved coordination of school and adult vocational habilitation services can the prospects of competitive employment be enhanced for young adults with disabilities (e.g., Flexer et al., 2005; Johnson & Wehman, 2001; Patton et al., 1997; Sitlington et al., 2006).

Three characteristics are critical to good secondary school programs. First, the curriculum must stress functional skills; that is, students must learn vocational skills that they will actually need and use in local employment situations. Second, school-based instruction must be carried out in integrated settings as much as possible. Students with disabilities must be given ample opportunities to learn the interpersonal skills necessary to work effectively with colleagues in integrated worksites. Third, community-based instruction should ideally begin as early as ages 10–13 for students with severe disabilities and must be used for progressively extended periods as students near graduation. While on worksites in the community, students should receive direct instruction in areas such as specific job skills, ways to increase production rates, and transportation to and from employment sites. Students should train and work in the community whenever possible so they learn "the communication, behavior, dress and other codes critical for success in integrated environments ... [and] to get to and from important places on time or to produce consistently" (Brown, Farrington, Suomi, & Zeigler, 1999, p. 6).

Research found a positive correlation between paid work experiences during the last 2 years of high school and postschool employment and total earnings (e.g., Baer et al., 2003; Benz, Lindstrom, & Yavanoff, 2000; Benz, Lindstrom, Unruh, & Waintrup, 2004; D'Amico, 1991; Kohler, 1994; Scuccimarra & Speece, 1990). Unpaid and volunteer work experience is also valuable for students with disabilities (Brown et al., 1999). Unfortunately, the NLTS found that only 39% of young adults with disabilities had been enrolled in work-experience programs during high school.

## Supported Employment

A new type of vocational opportunity has emerged that helps adults with severe disabilities, who have historically been unemployed or restricted to sheltered settings, earn real wages for real work. The supported employment movement recognizes that many adults with severe disabilities require ongoing, often intensive support to obtain, learn, and hold a job.

**Supported employment** is defined in the Rehabilitation Act Amendments of 1986 (P.L. 99–506) as

- competitive work in integrated work settings;
- for persons with the most severe disabilities;
- for whom competitive employment has not traditionally occurred;
- or for whom competitive employment has been interrupted or intermittent as a result of a severe disability; and
- who, because of the severity of their disability, need intensive support services; or
- extended services in order to perform such work. (P.L. 102-569, Sec. 635[b][6][c][iii])

Supported employment has grown rapidly since its inception. In 1986, fewer than 10,000 individuals were working in federally assisted supported employment demonstration projects

*Characteristics of secondary school programs and competitive employment outcomes*

Council for Exceptional Children — Knowledge and Skill Base for Beginning Special Education Transition Specialists: Research on relationships between individual outcomes and transition practices (TS1K4).

*Definition of supported employment*

Council for Exceptional Children — Knowledge and Skill Base for Beginning Special Education Transition Specialists: Transition-related laws and policies (TS1K2).

The supported employment movement is enabling tens of thousands of individuals like Barry to experience, for the first time in their lives, the benefits of real work for real wages.

*Supported employment models*

Council for Exceptional Children — Knowledge and Skill Base for Beginning Special Education Transition Specialists: Theoretical and applied models of transition (TS1K1).

in 20 states. Just 2 years later, the supported employment movement had grown to a total of 32,342 participants nationally; and the cumulative wages these workers earned grew from $1.4 million to $12.4 million in the 15 states that reported earnings data (Wehman, Kregel, Shafer, & West, 1989). By 1995, it was estimated that almost 140,000 persons with disabilities were working through supported employment with an average hourly wage of $4.70 (Wehman, Revell, & Kregel, 1998). These employees earned more than $750 million in annual wages in 1995, many becoming taxpayers for the first time in their lives. Since 1995 the number of supported employees has grown nearly 30% (Braddock, Hemp, Rizzolo, Parish, & Pomeranz, 2002). A statewide study in Maryland found that average weekly earnings of individuals placed in supported employment was 3.5 times greater than the earnings of individuals in sheltered work environments ($134.33 compared to weekly wages of $40.69) (Conley, 2003).

The success of supported employment depends in large part on job development—the identification and creation of community-based employment opportunities for individuals with disabilities. Four distinct models of supported employment have evolved: small business enterprise, mobile work crew, work enclave, and the individual placement model. A national survey of supported employment programs found that 80% of supported employees were working in the individual placement model (Revell, Wehman, Kregel, West, & Rayfield, 1994).

*Small Business Enterprise.* This model provides supported employment for persons with disabilities by establishing a business that takes advantage of existing commercial opportunities within a community. The business hires a small number of individuals with disabilities as well as several employees without disabilities.

*Mobile Work Crew.* A mobile work crew involves a small group of supported employees organized around a small, single-purpose business, such as building or grounds maintenance, working in an integrated community employment setting. A general manager may be responsible for finding and coordinating the work of several small crews of three to eight individuals, with each crew supervised by a supported employment specialist. Mobile work crews are organized as not-for-profit corporations; the extra costs the organizations incur because their employees do not work at full productivity levels are covered by public funds. Such costs are usually less than would be needed to support the work crew employees in activity centers, which provide little or no real work or reimbursement.

*Enclave (or Workstation).* In this model of supported employment, a small group of no more than eight persons with disabilities performs work with special training or job supports within a normal business or industry. Work enclave employees typically receive wages commensurate with their productivity rates. The work enclave provides a useful alternative to traditional segregated sheltered employment, offering many of the benefits of community-based integrated employment as well as the ongoing supports necessary for long-term job success.

With respect to interaction with nondisabled co-workers, program developers and industrial managers contemplating the enclave model must ensure that

> employees not become segregated from the rest of the working community (much like the "handicapped wing" of a public school). A balance must be attained in providing the structure to support training interventions, to address low productivity, and ensure adaptability to changing work demands, without sacrificing the advantages of a normal industrial environment. (Rhodes & Valenta, 1985, p. 18)

*Individual Placement.*    The individual placement model of supported employment consists of developing jobs with employers in the community, systematically assessing clients' job preferences, carefully placing employees in jobs they want, implementing intensive job-site training and advocacy, building systems of natural supports on the job site, monitoring client performance, and taking a systematic approach to long-term job retention (Wehman, Brooke, & Inge, 2001; Wehman & Kregel, 1998).

The supported employment specialist is the key to making a supported work program effective. The supported employment specialist, sometimes called a job coach, is a community-based professional who works in a nonprofit job placement program, a public vocational or adult services program, or a secondary special education program. The employment specialist is "the most integral aspect in making supported employment work" (Wehman & Revell, 1997, p. 630). Figure 15.3 identifies the major activities and responsibilities of a supported employment specialist in each component of the supported work model. To perform all of these functions, the employment specialist "must move comfortably in and out of a variety of roles associated with a consumer-driven approach to supported employment: planner, consultant, headhunter, technician, and community resource" (Wehman et al., 2001).

*Roles of employment specialist/job coach*

Council for Exceptional Children  Knowledge and Skill Base for Beginning Special Education Transition Specialists: Scope and role of agency personnel related to transition services (TS9K2) (also TS9K1).

In a typical supported employment program, the employment specialist provides direct, on-site job training to the employee with disabilities and serves as her primary source of support and assistance. Although the job coach gradually reduces the time spent in direct, on-site training and support, this model of outside assistance has several inherent drawbacks (Chadsey, Linneman, Rusch, & Cimera, 1997; Mank, Cioffi, & Yovanoff, 2000; Unger & Simmons, 2005):

- The arrival and presence of the job coach can disrupt the natural work setting.
- The supported employee may perform differently in the presence of her job coach.
- The job coach's presence can reduce the frequency of interaction between the supported employee and co-workers without disabilities.
- It is difficult for the employment specialist to be sensitive to the changing demands of the job over time and provide continued support and training consistent with those changes.
- The cost for an employment specialist who must travel to the job site is higher and the efficiency of the approach is lower than one that takes advantage of the natural interactions of co-workers.
- The always-on-call job coach may prevent the employer and co-workers from figuring out and implementing natural solutions to problems.
- This approach may foster too much dependence on the job coach, working against the supported employee's success in learning how to solve problems and assuming responsibility for her own management.

*Natural Supports.*    The role of the employment specialist/job coach is evolving from one of primary supporter for the employee with disabilities to one of working with the employer and co-workers to help identify, develop, and facilitate the typical or indigenous supports of the workplace (Mank, Cioffi, & Yovanoff, 1999). Rogan, Hagner, and Murphy (1993) define natural supports as "any assistance, relationships or interactions that allow a person to secure or maintain a community job … in a way that corresponds to the typical work routines and social interactions of other employees" (p. 275).

*Co-worker support and influence*

Council for Exceptional Children  Knowledge and Skill Base for Beginning Special Education Transition Specialists: Identify and facilitate modifications within work and community environments (TS5S1) (also CC5K1).

*Importance of Co-Workers.*    Social interaction is a natural feature of a typical workplace. It provides an important source of support for any employee, with or without disabilities, and is associated with job performance and job satisfaction. Because of their consistent presence in the work environment, co-workers can be a potentially powerful source of natural support for workers with disabilities (Rusch & Minch, 1988). Rusch, Hughes, McNair, and Wilson (1990) define a co-worker as an employee who works in the proximity of the supported employee, performs the same or similar duties, and/or takes breaks or eats meals in

## FIGURE 15.3   Sample description of a job coach's responsibilities

### Job Description: Employment Specialist

#### General Description

The employment specialist is involved in all aspects of community-based vocational training, placement, and follow-along for persons with an array of severe disabilities as part of the Excel Rehabilitation Program. The successful candidate will meet the employers to secure placements, provide one-on-one training for job and other related skills, and maintain systematic and regular contact with employers after job training has been completed. The employment specialist will work as part of a team and will interact frequently with other professionals related to specific cases.

#### Specific Duties/Responsibilities

1. *Job Development.* The employment specialist will complete job market screening activities and regularly present the employment program to prospective employers until adequate numbers of appropriate open positions have been identified. The specialist will analyze job duties and requirements of potential jobs.
2. *Consumer Assessment.* The employment specialist will complete and/or secure assessment and evaluation information as necessary to assist the consumer with informed decision making. This may include referral to other professionals/agencies and subsequent interpretation of reports, observations, and interviewing persons knowledgeable about the consumer.
3. *Job Placement.* The employment specialist will complete activities to secure placement of individuals with disabilities that include vocational guidance, assistance with application procedures, support during interview processes, advice regarding job offers and negotiation, and initial planning for work.
4. *Job Site Training.* The employment specialist will work with the consumer on and off the job site until the consumer can maintain employment without regular or frequent assistance from the specialist. These duties may include development and implementation of instructional and/or behavioral programming strategies, conferences with the employer, co-workers, and/or consumer, and collection of performance information such as measures of quality and rate of work.
5. *Follow-Along.* The employment specialist will establish and maintain periodic contact with consumers, employers, and others as necessary to facilitate continued successful placement of the employee with disabilities. The employment specialist will be on call to assist in the resolution of obstacles to continued employment.
6. *Other.* The employment specialist will perform other related duties including but not limited to participating in agency meetings, attending training and professional development meetings, developing materials, coordinating consumer services as necessary for continued placement, and maintaining accurate consumer case files.

*Source*: Reprinted from Wehman, P., & Revell, W. G., Jr. (1997). Transition from school to adulthood: Looking ahead. In P. Wehman (Ed.), *Exceptional individuals in school, community, and work* (p. 631). Austin, TX: PRO-ED. Used by permission.

the same area. Six types of co-worker involvement beneficial to supported employees are described in Figure 15.4.

A skilled and friendly co-worker can provide information, answer questions, demonstrate job tasks, provide assistance and repeat instructions as needed, give social praise and feedback for performance, and serve as an important contact point for the supported employee's entry into the social fabric of the workplace (Curl, Hall, Chisholm, & Rule, 1992; Lee, Storey, Anderson, Goetz, & Zivolich, 1997). Although some co-workers provide sup-

## FIGURE 15.4 Six types of co-worker involvement

1. **Advocating.** A co-worker advocates for a supported employee by optimizing, backing, and supporting a supported employee's employment status. *Optimizing* refers to encouraging a supervisor to assign high-status and relevant tasks to a supported employee; *backing* refers to supporting a supported employee's rights, for example, by attempting to prevent practical jokes aimed at her. It also includes speaking up for a supported employee or offering explanations during differences of opinion. *Supporting* relates to providing emotional support to a supported employee in the form of friendship, association, etc.

2. **Associating.** A co-worker interacts socially with a supported employee at the workplace.

3. **Befriending.** A co-worker interacts socially with a supported employee outside the workplace.

4. **Collecting data.** A co-worker collects data by observing and recording social and/or work performance.

5. **Evaluating.** A co-worker appraises a supported employee's work performance and provides (written/oral) feedback to him.

6. **Training.** A co-worker supports a supported employee by providing on-the-job skill training.

*Source*: Adapted from Rusch, F. R., Hughes, C., McNair, J., & Wilson, P. G. (1990). *Co-worker involvement scoring manual and index*. Champaign: University of Illinois Press. Used by permission.

port naturally, observations in the workplace indicate that formal training is usually necessary to make co-workers' "help" effective in maintaining successful employment. For example, Curl, Lignugaris/Kraft, Pawley, and Salzberg (1988) found that co-workers typically presented more than 100 instructions in the first 2 hours of employment training—a frequency likely to overwhelm a newly hired employee with disabilities. Several approaches for co-worker training have been developed. For example, co-workers can be taught how to provide support during brief, 15- to 20-minute sessions during breaks or before or after work. Curl (1990) has developed a program in which co-workers learn to use a simple 4-step procedure in which they (1) provide instructions, (2) demonstrate the job task, (3) observe the supported employee performing the same task, and (4) deliver praise and feedback about the trainee's performance.

*Natural Cues and Self-Management.* The belief that employees with disabilities should be taught independence in the workplace has gained widespread acceptance among supported employment professionals and has spawned exciting and promising research in the use of natural cues and self-management. Natural cues are features already existing in the work environment that the employee can see, hear, touch, or smell and use as a signal for what to do next (Moon & Inge, 2000). For example, clocks or whistles may signal that it is time to go to a job station, the sight of co-workers' stopping work and leaving the job station might be the prompt for break time, and a growing pile of dirty dishes should be the cue to increase the rate of dishwashing. The employment specialist's role expands from training the employee how to perform various vocational and social skills to teaching him how to respond independently to the cues that occur naturally in the workplace. When those cues are insufficient to prompt the desired behavior, the supported employee can be taught to respond to contrived cues, such as picture prompts depicting individual steps in a multistep task (Wilson, Schepis, & Mason-Main, 1987) or prerecorded verbal prompts interspersed within favorite music that the employee might listen to on a Walkman-type cassette player (Barfels, Al-Attrash, & Heward, 1999; Grossi, 1998; West, Rayfield, Clements, Unger, & Thornton, 1994).

*Natural and contrived cues, self-monitoring, and self-instruction in the workplace*

Council for Exceptional Children — Content Standards for Beginning Teachers—Common Core: Use procedures to increase the individual's self-awareness, self-management, self-control, self-reliance, and self-esteem (CC4S5) (also CC4S6, TS5S1, TS8S5).

Self-monitoring can also be effectively used in employment training. Research has shown that employees with disabilities can use self-monitoring (observing and recording one's performance) and self-evaluation (comparing self-monitored performance with a goal or production criterion) to increase their job productivity and independence (Grossi & Heward, 1998; Sowers, Verdi, Bourbeau, & Sheehan, 1985; Wheeler, Bates, Marshall, & Miller, 1988). For example, Allen, White, and Test (1992) developed a picture/symbol form that employees with disabilities can use to self-monitor their performance on the job (see Figure 15.5).

Employees with disabilities can also learn to self-manage their work performance by providing their own verbal prompts and self-instructions (Hughes, 1997). For example, Salend, Ellis, and Reynolds (1989) used a self-instructional strategy to teach four adults with severe mental retardation to "talk while you work." Productivity increased dramati-

**FIGURE 15.5 A picture/symbol form that a student or employee with disabilities could use to self-monitor job performance**

*Source*: From "Using a Picture/Symbol Form for Self-Monitoring within a Community-Based Training Program" by C. P. Allen, J. White, & D. W. Test. *Teaching Exceptional Children*, 24(2), 1992, p. 55. © 1992 by the Council for Exceptional Children. Reprinted with permission.

| Task Sheet | | | | | |
|---|---|---|---|---|---|
| Student: _____ Week of: _____ Observer: _____ | | | | | |
| | M | T | W | Th | Comments |
| 1. Job needs (e.g., name tag, lunch). | | | | | |
| 2. Get work assignment. | | | | | |
| 3. Get cart. | | | | | |
| 4. Find and enter room. | | | | | |
| 5. Check drapes. | | | | | |
| 6. Check TV. | | | | | |
| 7. Make bed. | | | | | |
| 8. Dust. | | | | | |
| 9. Stock amenities. | | | | | |
| 10. Empty wastebaskets. | | | | | |
| 11. Clean bathroom. | | | | | |
| 12. Vacuum. | | | | | |
| 13. Fill out hotel checklist | | | | | |

cally and error rates decreased when the women verbalized to themselves, "Comb up, comb down, comb in bag, bag in box" while packaging combs in plastic bags. Hughes and Rusch (1989) taught two supported employees working at a janitorial supply company how to solve problems by using a self-instructional procedure consisting of four statements:

1. Statement of the problem (e.g., "Tape empty")
2. Statement of the response needed to solve the problem (e.g., "Need more tape")
3. Self-report (e.g., "Fixed it")
4. Self-reinforcement (e.g., "Good")

## Sheltered Employment

Sheltered employment and work activities in segregated settings are the most common types of vocational activities for adults with severe disabilities. Sheltered workshops serve individuals with a wide variety of disabilities, although about half are persons with mental retardation. A national survey of employment programs funded by state agencies serving this population found that 365,165 individuals worked in sheltered and segregated employment settings in 2002, roughly 3 times the number of persons working in supported employment (Braddock, Rizzolo, & Hemp, 2004). **Sheltered workshops** provide one or more of three types of programs: (1) evaluation and training for community-based employment (commonly referred to as transitional workshops), (2) extended or long-term employment, and (3) work activities.

A **work activity center** offers programs of activities for individuals whose disabilities are viewed by local decision makers as too severe for productive work. Rehabilitation and training revolve around concentration and persistence at a task. Intervals of work may be short, perhaps only an hour long, interspersed with other activities—such as training in social skills, self-help skills, household skills, community skills, and recreation. There are approximately 5,000 sheltered work and day activity centers in the United States (Butterworth, Gilmore, Kiernan, & Shalock, 1999).

Many sheltered work programs offer both transitional and extended employment within the same building. Transitional workshops try to place their employees in community-based jobs. Extended employment workshops are operated to provide whatever training and support services are necessary to enable individuals with severe disabilities to work productively within the sheltered environment. The Wage and Hour Division of the U.S. Department of Labor requires that persons working in an extended sheltered workshop receive at least 50% of the minimum wage; they may be paid an hourly wage or a piecework rate.

All sheltered workshops have at least two elements in common. First, they offer rehabilitation, training, and (in some instances) full employment. Second, to provide meaningful work for clients, a sheltered workshop must operate as a business. Sheltered workshops generally engage in one of three types of business ventures: contracting, prime manufacturing, or reclamation.

*Contracting* is the major source of work in most workshops. A contract is an agreement that a sheltered workshop will complete a specified job (e.g., assembling and packaging a company's product) within a specified time for a given price. Most sheltered workshops have one or more professional staff members, called contractors or contract procurement persons, whose sole job is to obtain and negotiate contracts with businesses and industries in the community.

*Prime manufacturing* involves the designing, producing, marketing, and shipping of a complete product. The advantage of prime manufacturing over contracting (assuming that a successful product is being manufactured) is that the workshops do not have problems with downtime when they are between contracts. They can plan their training and labor requirements more directly. Most sheltered workshops, however, are neither staffed nor equipped to handle the more sophisticated business venture of prime manufacturing.

*Sheltered employment*

Council for Exceptional Children — Knowledge and Skill Base for Beginning Special Education Transition Specialists: Range of postschool options within specific outcome areas (TS7K3).

*Poor prospects for sheltered
employees*

Council for
Exceptional
Children    Knowledge and
Skill Base for
Beginning Special Education
Transition Specialists: Research
on relationships between
individual outcomes and
transition practices (TS1K4).

In a *reclamation*, or salvage, operation, a workshop purchases or collects salvageable material, performs the salvage or reclamation operation, and then sells the reclaimed product. Salvage and reclamation operations have proven successful for many sheltered workshops because they require a lot of labor, are low in overhead, and can usually continue indefinitely.

But there are problems with sheltered employment, and most people no longer consider such sites to be appropriate transition outcomes for young people with disabilities (Block, 1997). The theoretical purpose of sheltered workshops is to train individuals in specific job-related skills that will enable them to obtain competitive employment; however, few employees of sheltered workshops are ever placed in jobs in the community. Only about 10% of sheltered workshop employees were placed in community jobs from 1977 to 1987 (U.S. Congress, 1987; U.S. Department of Labor, 1979), and many who are placed do not keep their jobs for long (Brickey, Campbell, & Browning, 1985). By contrast, approximately 50% of all supported employees are still earning wages and paying taxes 1 year after placement alongside nondisabled co-workers (Rusch, 1990).

Many professionals believe that the poor competitive employment record of sheltered workshop graduates may indicate the limitations inherent in these sites rather than in the employment potential of persons with disabilities (Mank, Cioffi, & Yovanoff, 1998; Wehman et al., 2001). Because sheltered workshop employment is conducted in segregated settings, affords limited opportunities for job placement in the community, and provides extremely low pay, it has been called a dead-end street for individuals with mental retardation (Frank & Sitlington, 1993). West, Revell, and Wehman (1998) discuss the challenges faced by agencies that operate sheltered work programs when converting their programs to supported employment.

# POSTSECONDARY EDUCATION

Postsecondary education is no longer a fantasy for individuals with disabilities; it is a reality occurring with greater frequency (Black, Smith, Chang, Harding, & Stodden, 2002). As evidence of this increase in enrollment, in 1996 6%–9% of all undergraduate students reported having a disability (National Center for Education Statistics, 1998), with learning disabilities the most prevalent type reported (29% to 35% of those reporting a disability). In 2000, the National Council on Disability reported that 17% of all students attending higher education programs in the United States had a disability. In that same year, 40% of freshmen with disabilities reported having a learning disability (Henderson, 2001).

*Relationship between
postsecondary education and
employment*

Council for
Exceptional
Children    Knowledge and
Skill Base for
Beginning Special Education
Transition Specialists: Research
on relationships between
individual outcomes and
transition practices (TS1K4).

Many high school students look ahead to college. However, access to postsecondary education may be even more important for persons with disabilities than it is for individuals without them. Postsecondary education significantly improves chances of meaningful employment. Among adults with disabilities, only 15.6% of those who leave high school without a diploma are employed; participation in the labor force doubles to 30.2% for those who have completed high school and triples to 45.1% for those with some postsecondary education (Yelin & Katz, 1994). For individuals with disabilities who are able to obtain a 4-year degree the employment rate rises to 50.3%

Individuals with disabilities who are graduates of postsecondary education programs—technical training; a community college's 2-year associate's degree; or a 4-year bachelor's degree—enjoy increased vocational options and greater lifetime earnings (Gajar, Goodman, & McAfee, 1995). A college degree does not guarantee full-time employment: fewer individuals with disabilities who hold bachelor's degrees work full time as compared to their counterparts without disabilities (National Center for the Study of Postsecondary Educational Supports, 2002). Nevertheless, a college degree is a factor in the salary that can be commanded once students are in the labor market. For example, Witte, Phillips, and Kakela (1998) reported that the annual salaries of a sample of 72 college graduates with learning disabilities (1987–1994) ranged from $20,000 to $40,000 for 49% of the group, while 19% earned $40,000+ annually. Blackorby and Wagner (1997) reported that 40% of students with learning disabilities who did not attend college earned an annual salary of approximately $12,000. Overall, all college graduates can expect to have better health, greater self-confidence, increased career options, higher-level problem-solving skills, improved interpersonal relationships, and a higher level of open-mindedness as well as more involvement in politics, community affairs, recreation, and leadership activities. They will also be less dependent on parents and governmental benefits than will individuals who do not pursue postsecondary education (Pascarella & Terenzini, 1991; Turnbull, Turnbull, Wehmeyer, & Park, 2003).

Increasingly, jobs require technical training, problem solving, and interpersonal skills that can be attained through postsecondary education (Webster, Clary, & Griffith, 2005). In 1950, 60% of jobs were classified as unskilled, but it is estimated that only 12% to 15% of jobs did not require specific skills or training in the year 2000 (Hoye, 1998).

Postsecondary education is increasingly becoming an option for students with significant disabilities such as mental retardation, autism, or multiple disabilities. Some school districts allow students who require special education services past the age of 18 to graduate with their nondisabled peers and continue educational programming on the campuses of community colleges, universities, or vocational-technical schools (Test et al., 2006). These programs enable youth with moderate and severe disabilities to continue their education in a more age-appropriate learning environment and to participate in some aspects of traditional college life, including auditing academic classes and enjoying recreation and physical education activities in an integrated setting with same-age peers (Goldrich Eskow & Fisher, 2004; Hall, Kleinert, & Kerns, 2000; Hamill, 2003). Most programs offer a combination of college classes, basic or functional skills classes, and job experiences (Grigal, Neubert, & Moon, 2002).

Although the range and availability of services offered by colleges and universities for students with disabilities have increased greatly in recent years, the success of students with disabilities as measured by graduation is well below that of students without disabilities. One study found that 80% of students with learning disabilities who had attended postsecondary education programs had not graduated 5 years after high school compared to 56% of students without disabilities (Murray, Goldstein, Nourse, & Edgar, 2000). Ten years after they had left high school, 56% of the students with learning disabilities had not graduated from postsecondary education compared to 32% of those without disabilities.

Several studies have reported that preparation for postsecondary education was frequently lacking in students' transition plans (Grigal, Test, Beattie, & Wood, 1997; Hitchings, Luzzo, Retish, Horvath, & Ristow, 1998). In one study, only 8 out of 97 college students with learning disabilities could remember meeting annually with their high school counselors to discuss courses for the following year and the steps for selecting a college (Hitchings et al., 2001). These results reveal the need for increased emphasis on postsecondary education goals and outcomes during transition planning.

Mull, Sitlington, and Alper (2001) concluded their review of 26 published articles describing or reporting on services for postsecondary students with learning disabilities with the following suggestions:

- High school students need to be prepared to determine which of the accommodations and supports used at the secondary level they will need at the postsecondary level and how to access these supports as needed.
- Students need to be trained how to use assistive technology devices that will increase their access to and ability to manipulate curriculum content.
- Secondary teachers need to be aware of the demands of postsecondary education environments so they can help students acquire the skills, supports, and accommodations to be successful in those environments.
- As a field, special education needs to deal with the issue of documentation of disabilities, which is required for postsecondary students to access the accommodations and support services they need. This is a concern because many secondary special education programs are no longer using specific disability labels and formal psychological testing to diagnose disabilities. (p. 106)

*Needs of postsecondary students with LD*

Council for Exceptional Children Knowledge and Skill Base for Beginning Special Education Transition Specialists: Implications of individual characteristics with respect to postschool outcomes and support needs (TS2K1).

For additional information on promoting the success of postsecondary education for students with learning disabilities, see Brinkerhoff, Shaw, and McGuire (1993); Garten, Rumrill, and Serebreni (1996); Sitlington and Payne (2004); and Skinner (1998).

# RESIDENTIAL ALTERNATIVES

*Where* one lives determines a great deal about *how* one lives. It influences where a person can work, what community services and resources will be available, who her friends will be, what the opportunities for recreation and leisure will be, and, to a great extent, what feelings of self and place in the community will develop. Not long ago, the only place someone with severe disabilities could live, if she did not live with family, was a large, state-operated institution. Although she had done no wrong to society, an institution was considered the best place for the person. There were no other options—no such thing as residential alternatives (Howe, Horner, & Newton, 1998).

Today, however, most communities provide a variety of residential options for adults with disabilities. Increased community-based residential services have meant a greater opportunity for adults with severe disabilities to live in more normalized settings.

## Group Homes

*Residential options*

Council for Exceptional Children — Knowledge and Skill Base for Beginning Special Education Transition Specialists: Range of postschool options within specific outcome areas (TS7K3).

Group homes provide family-style living for a small group of individuals, usually three to six persons. Most group homes serve adults with mental retardation, although some have residents with other disabilities. A national census found 263,415 persons with intellectual and developmental disabilities living in group homes in 2002, a 12-fold increase over the number of persons living there in 1977 (Lakin, Prouty, Polister, & Coucouvanis, 2003).

Some group homes are principally a permanent place to live for their residents. Staff persons in this type of home help the people who live there develop self-care and daily living skills, form interpersonal relationships, and participate in recreation and leisure skills. During the day, most residents work in the community or in a sheltered workshop.

Other group homes operate more as halfway houses. Their primary function is to prepare individuals with disabilities for a more independent living situation, such as a supervised apartment. These transitional group homes typically serve residents who have recently left institutions, bridging the gap between institutional and community living.

Compared to institutions, two aspects of group homes make them a much more normalized place to live: their size and their location. Most people grow up in a typical family-sized group where there is opportunity for personal attention, care, and privacy. The congregate-living arrangement of an institution cannot offer a typical, normalized lifestyle, no matter how much effort a hardworking, caring staff makes. Because the number of people in a group home is small, there is a greater chance for a family-like atmosphere to develop. Size is also directly related to the neighborhood's ability to assimilate the members of the group home into typical activities within the community. Large groups tend to become self-sufficient, orienting inward and thereby resisting movement outward into the community. In groups of more than six or eight people, care providers can no longer relate properly to individuals. Large group homes tend to acquire the characteristics of a place of work for direct-care staff rather than a home where people live (Ferguson & Ferguson, 2000). Indeed, some evidence suggests that quality of life is better for persons residing in smaller rather than larger group homes (Burchard, Hasazi, Gordon, & Yoe, 1991; Conroy, 1996).

The location and physical characteristics of the group home itself are also vital determinants of its ability to provide a normalized lifestyle. A group home must be located within the community in a residential area, not a commercially zoned district. It must be in an area where the people who live there can conveniently access shopping, schools, churches, public transportation, and recreational facilities. In other words, a group home must be located in a normal residential area where any one of us might live. And it must look like a home not conspicuously different from the other family dwellings on the same street.

Research has shown not only that the architectural features of the home influence the degree to which residents and others give it a high rating of homelikeness but also that some interior design features of a home correlate with the frequency of certain adaptive and maladaptive behaviors by residents (Thompson, Robinson, Dietrich, Farris, & Sinclair, 1996a, 1996b). For example, a laundry room located in the basement may present challenges for residents that create behavioral problems, and a cafeteria-style dining room table is not conducive to conversations during meals.

## Foster Homes

When a family opens its home to an unrelated person for an extended period, the term *foster home* applies. Although foster homes have provided temporary residential services and family care for children (usually wards of the court) for many years, more and more families have begun to share their homes with adults with disabilities. In return for providing room and board for their new family member, foster families receive a modest financial reimbursement.

Life in a foster family home can have numerous advantages for an adult with disabilities. Instead of interacting with paid group-home staff who may or may not actually live at the same address, the person with disabilities lives in a residence that is owned or rented by individuals or families as their primary domicile. The person can participate and share in day-to-day family activities, receive individual attention from people vitally interested in his continued growth and development, and develop close interpersonal relationships. As part of a family unit, the adult with disabilities also has more opportunities to interact with and be accepted by the community at large. In their survey of small group homes and foster homes, Hill et al. (1989) found that 80% of foster-home caregivers perceived residents with disabilities primarily as family members. In contrast, group-home staff were more likely to view persons with disabilities as trainees or friends.

## Apartment Living

A rented apartment is one of the most common living arrangements for people without disabilities in our society. Today, an increasing number of adults with disabilities are enjoying the freedom and independence that apartment living offers. Apartment living offers them an even greater opportunity for integration into the community than do group homes. Whereas the resident of a group home interacts primarily with other persons with disabilities, in an apartment-living arrangement (assuming the apartment is in a regular apartment complex), the likelihood of interacting with persons without disabilities is greater. Burchard et al. (1991) found that people who lived in supervised apartments had about twice as many social and leisure activities in the community as did individuals who lived in small group homes or with their natural parents. They also found that persons living in supervised apartments were more likely to be accompanied in the community by peers who were not disabled than those living in group homes were. Another study followed seven young adults with mental retardation who had moved from a campus-type residential setting to community-based apartments (Rose, White, Conroy, & Smith, 1993). Assessments of the young adults' social/communication skills, community-living skills, and general independence conducted at 6 and 12 months after the move found significant and continued gains over pre-move measures.

Three types of apartment living for adults with disabilities are common: the apartment cluster, the co-residence apartment, and the maximum-independence apartment. An *apartment cluster* consists of a small number of apartments housing persons with disabilities and another nearby apartment for a support person or staff member. An apartment cluster allows for a great deal of flexibility in the amount and degree of support needed by residents in the various apartments. Whereas some people might require direct help with such things as shopping, cooking, or even getting dressed, others need only limited assistance or suggestions and prompts. To facilitate social integration, persons without disabilities may also occupy some apartments in an apartment cluster.

A *co-residence apartment* is shared by an individual with disabilities and a roommate without disabilities. Although this arrangement is sometimes permanent, most co-residence apartments are used as a step toward independent living. The live-in roommates are often unpaid volunteers.

Two to four adults with disabilities usually cohabit *maximum-independence apartments*. These adults have all of the self-care and daily living skills required to take care of themselves and their apartment on a day-to-day basis. A supervisory visit is made once or twice a week to help them deal with any special problems they may be having.

## Supported Living

Several innovative models for residential services for adults with disabilities have been developed based on the belief that residential placements must be adapted to the needs of the person with disabilities, not vice versa (Klein, 1994; Knoll & Wheeler, 2005). **Supported living** is the term used to describe a growing movement toward helping people with disabilities live in the community as independently and normally as possible. Similar to the way in which supported employment provides ongoing, individualized supports to help a person with disabilities perform meaningful work in a community-based employment setting, supported living involves a personalized network of various kinds and levels of natural supports. Supported living is neither a place nor a single set of procedures to be provided for a person with disabilities.

Klein (1994) explains what supported living is by describing what it is not. Supported living does not revolve around a professional program. People should not live in a place referred to by an agency or provider name (e.g., UCP Group Home, New Life Center). There are no criteria for participation (e.g., persons in this program must be able to cook for themselves, have a physical disability, need more or less than 3 hours per day of attendant care, have visual impairments). Supported living is not based on readiness and movement through a continuum. Participation in traditional residential services is based on a professional's assessment of the person's readiness or ability to live in a particular program, and a person must perform well (learn new skills on her individual habilitation plan) in order to move ("earn" the right) to the next, less restrictive rung on the continuum.

Rather than a single approach or model, supported living is a philosophy about the kind of living experiences appropriate for citizens with disabilities and about commitment to figuring out how to best approximate the ideal for each individual. Supported living, according to Klein (1994), is guided by these nine principles:

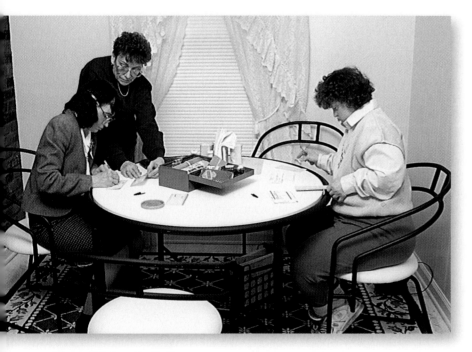

Supported living provides flexible supports when and as they are needed. Twice per month, Judy and Kathy pay their bills and review their budget with the help of a support person.

1. *Individualization.* Supported living must focus on one person without exception. This does not mean that everyone has to live alone. It does mean that if people want

to live with someone else, they choose with whom they live. The magic number becomes one.

2. *Everybody is ready.* There are no criteria for receiving support because what occurs is individually designed. We must give up trying to make people ready by simulating life in a home and begin supporting people to have that home.

3. *Future planning.* People who are assisting others must get to know the individuals they are supporting. What are their desires and preferences? What would an ideal living situation look like for each person? After answers to these questions are determined, the people who care about the person get together regularly to develop a plan for creating, as closely as possible, that ideal living situation.

4. *Use of connections.* Traditional residential services rely on system solutions to problems, referring to the procedures and policy manual to find out what rules and regulations suggest. Supported living relies on the assistance of all who want to and can help. This means that professional care providers and staff are replaced by friends, family members, and neighbors whenever possible. "Who do we know who can help?" becomes a key question for planning and arranging needed supports.

5. *Flexible supports.* Supports are based and provided on the individual's schedule and needs, not on a program's schedule. Persons receive support where, when, how, and with whom it is needed. Supports must be flexible enough to be adjusted to the individual's changing needs, preferences, and desires.

6. *Combining natural supports, learning, and technology.* As much as possible, supports are natural to the time, place, and person. Individuals are given opportunities to learn to provide their own support and use technology to gain control over their environment as much as possible.

7. *Focusing on what people can do.* Traditional residential programs often focus on what people cannot do and design treatment programs to remediate those skill deficiencies. Supportive living focuses on what people can do, provides support for things they cannot do, and provides opportunities for them to learn how to do the things they want to do.

8. *Using language that is natural to the setting. The* language of supported living is natural and promotes inclusion in the community. The places where people live are described as Joe's home or Mary's home. People clean their homes and do their laundry rather than learn programs; people live with roommates, not with staff or care providers; friends, not volunteers, come over to visit; and people with disabilities are referred to as neighbors, friends, and citizens rather than clients, consumers, and residents.

9. *Ownership and control.* Last and most important, the home is the person's, and that person controls the support that is received. Home ownership does not mean that individuals with disabilities who do not have many financial resources must hold the mortgage to a home. It does mean, however, that they sign the lease, that things in the home belong to them, and that the place is their home. Roommates sublet from the person; support people are hired by the person; and support people respond to the need for assistance when, where, and how it is needed as determined by the person. (adapted from Klein, 1994, pp. 17–18)

## Institutions

Most of the large, state-operated institutions in this country were founded in the 19th or early 20th century, when it was generally believed that people with mental retardation could not be educated or trained. Large custodial institutions (many institutions once housed hundreds or even 1,000 or more people with mental retardation and other disabilities) kept people with disabilities segregated from the rest of society; they were never designed to help people learn to live in the community. In the 1960s and 1970s, these institutions came under intense criticism for their inability to provide individualized residential services in a comfortable, humane, and normalized environment (Blatt, 1976; Blatt & Kaplan, 1966; Kugel & Wolfensberger, 1969; Wolfensberger, 1969). The complaints were not leveled against the concept of residential programs; there will probably always be persons whose disabilities are so severe that they require the kind of 24-hour support that residential facilities can offer. The problem lies with the inherent inability of an institutional environment to allow a person to experience a normal lifestyle.

Tremendous improvements have been made in the abysmal living conditions in institutions that Blatt and Kaplan (1966) exposed 40 years ago in their book *Christmas in Purgatory*. During the 1970s, the U.S. Department of Health, Education, and Welfare and the Joint Commission on the Accreditation of Hospitals developed extensive standards for residential facilities for individuals with mental retardation. A facility must meet these standards—which cover topics as diverse as building construction, staffing, and habilitative and educational programming—to qualify for federal and state Medicaid funding. Residential units that meet the standards are referred to as ICF-MR Medicaid facilities. Today, an ICF-MR facility serving 16 or more residents is considered an institution. Although the ICF-MR Medicaid system of rules and regulations has eliminated the inhumane and filthy conditions and the overcrowding that had been defining features of institutional life, the system has become the target of increasing criticism because of residents' quality of life and the high cost (e.g., Stancliffe & Hayden, 1998; Stancliffe & Lakin, 1998).

**Deinstitutionalization**—the movement of people with mental retardation out of large institutions and into smaller, community-based living environments such as group homes or apartments—has been an active reality during the past 35 years. The number of persons with mental retardation living in large state institutions has decreased steadily from a high of 194,650 in 1967 to 43,249 persons in 2002 (Lakin et al., 2003; Lakin, Smith, Prouty, & Polister, 2001).

*Deinstitutionalization*

Council for Exceptional Children   Knowledge and Skill Base for Beginning Special Education Transition Specialists: Range of postschool options within specific outcome areas (TS7K3).

Several studies indicate generally positive outcomes for residents transferred from institutions to group homes to smaller, community-based living arrangements (Conroy & Bradley, 1985; Conroy, Spreat, Yuskauskas, & Elks, 2003; Larson & Lakin, 1989). For example, Conroy (1996) compared 35 quality-of-life measures over a 5-year period for individuals living in small institutions serving an average of eight people with outcomes for persons living in community-based living apartments or group homes of three people. Higher quality was found in the community living arrangements on 10 of the indicators (e.g., choice making, normalization, individualized treatment, family satisfaction). Higher quality was not found in the ICF-MR facilities on any of the indicators.

## RECREATION AND LEISURE

Recreation and the enjoyable use of leisure time are important components of a self-satisfying lifestyle. Most of us take for granted our ability to pursue leisure and recreational activities. We benefit from a lifetime of learning how to play and how to enjoy personal hobbies or crafts.

But recreation and leisure activities do not come easily for many adults with disabilities. To use community recreational resources, one must have transportation, the physical ability or skills to play the game, and, usually, other willing and able friends to play with. These three variables, alone or in com-

Joe loves to fish. Choice is crucial to the enjoyment of leisure activities.

bination, often work to limit the recreation and leisure activities available to the adult with disabilities. Transportation is not available; the person's disability does not allow him to swim, bowl, or play tennis; and he has no friends with similar skills and interests. Because of these problems, the majority of recreation and leisure experiences for many adults with disabilities have consisted of segregated, disabled-only outings.

Too often, the so-called leisure activities for adults with disabilities consist of watching great amounts of television, listening to music in the solitude of their rooms, and spending discretionary time socially isolated (Strand & Kreiner, 2005). Choice is a crucial element for meaningful leisure activities (Browder et al., 1998).

> Without choice, activities become simply tasks rather than providing elements of control that lead to leisure satisfaction. If television is the only offering, choice is neglected. ...Leisure education programs should focus on development of all of the knowledge, skills, and attitudes necessary to facilitate choice—not only traditional group activity skills, but also those individual skills that will have lifetime applications. (Best, Bigge, Musante, & Macias, 2005, p. 349)

Special educators must realize the importance of including training for recreation and leisure in curricula for school-age children with disabilities. Best et al. (2005) describe how numerous games, hobbies, crafts, and projects can be adapted to become enjoyable, worthwhile, leisure-time pursuits for persons with disabilities. Areas they suggest include raising guinea pigs, music appreciation and study, photography, card games, and nature study. Suggestions are also available for adapting leisure activities for young adults who are deaf-blind, such as using permanent tactile prompts (e.g., attaching fabric to the flipper buttons of a pinball machine), adequately stabilizing materials, enhancing the visual or auditory input provided by the materials (e.g., using large-print, low-vision playing cards), and simplifying the requirements of the task (e.g., raising the front legs on a pinball machine, thereby reducing the speed with which the ball approaches the flippers).

Learning appropriate leisure skills is particularly important for adults with severe disabilities (Bambara, Browder, & Koger, 2006). Most persons with severe disabilities have ample free time, but many do not use it constructively and may instead engage in inappropriate behaviors such as body rocking, hand flapping, or bizarre vocalizations. A number of studies have been reported in which age-appropriate leisure skills have been taught to secondary students and adults with moderate and severe mental retardation (Collins, Hall, & Branson, 1997; Nietupski & Svoboda, 1982; Schleien, Kiernan, & Wehman, 1981). Schleien, Wehman, and Kiernan (1981) successfully taught three adults with severe and multiple disabilities to throw darts. Vandercook (1991) taught five high school students with severe mental retardation and physical disabilities to play pinball and bowl with nondisabled peer partners. In another study, four adults with moderate mental retardation learned to order drinks in an Irish pub (O'Reilly, Lancioni, & Kiernans, 2000).

Participating in community recreation and leisure activities with an adult with disabilities can be an excellent way to appreciate the importance of a functional curriculum for school-age students. (See Profiles & Perspectives, "A Friendship Program for Future Special Education Teachers," later in this chapter.)

*Teaching recreation and leisure activities*

Council for Exceptional Children — Knowledge and Skill Base for Beginning Special Education Transition Specialists: Arrange and evaluate instructional activities in relation to postschool goals (TS7S2) (also TS4S1).

Mike does not let anything get in the way of his quality of life. He enjoys an active lifestyle that includes softball and other fitness activities.

# A Friendship Program for Future Special Education Teachers

*by Jill C. Dardig*

Scott and Ted, both big sports fans, attended several local basketball and baseball games together. They cheered for the Pickerington High School Lady Tigers in the state tournament and scarfed frank after frank on Dime-a-Dog Night at a Columbus Clippers game. Kelly and Kami went out to dinner at several of their favorite restaurants. They also spent some quiet nights at home baking brownies, looking at family pictures, and just talking. Paula and Todd attended a concert, went to the mall, and spent an evening with popcorn and a video at Todd's apartment.

Scott, Kelly, and Paula, all college students learning to become special education teachers, were doing their fieldwork for a required course called "Focus on Adults with Disabilities." Each student in this class is paired with an adult with developmental disabilities living in a group home, a family home, or a supported living apartment in the community. Each student gets to know her new friend on an informal and personal basis by planning some at-home and community-based activities they can enjoy together during the semester. Students function as friends or companions. In this way, they are able to look at their special friends in a different light—not as a school-age child but as a similar-aged peer who is learning to be an independent adult.

After meeting with his friend (and sometimes group home or supported living staff) to determine what the friend might enjoy doing, each college student designs a calendar or schedule of planned activities. The schedule may be written; but if the friend cannot read, the scheduled activities are illustrated by photos, pictures, symbols, or objects (e.g., a menu, a K-Mart ad, a puzzle piece, or a page from *TV Guide*). This schedule allows the friend to anticipate and prepare for each activity and provides cues for friends, family, and caregivers to ask questions and discuss the person's weekly activities.

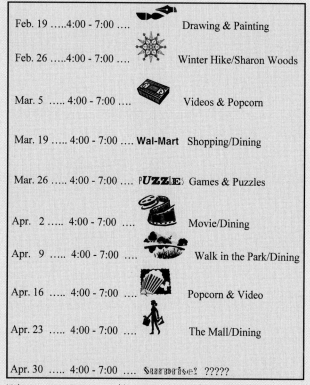

| | | |
|---|---|---|
| Feb. 19 .....4:00 - 7:00 .... | | Drawing & Painting |
| Feb. 26 .....4:00 - 7:00 .... | | Winter Hike/Sharon Woods |
| Mar. 5 ..... 4:00 - 7:00 .... | | Videos & Popcorn |
| Mar. 19 ..... 4:00 - 7:00 .... | **Wal-Mart** | Shopping/Dining |
| Mar. 26 ..... 4:00 - 7:00 .... | **PUZZLE** | Games & Puzzles |
| Apr. 2 ..... 4:00 - 7:00 .... | | Movie/Dining |
| Apr. 9 ..... 4:00 - 7:00 .... | | Walk in the Park/Dining |
| Apr. 16 ..... 4:00 - 7:00 .... | | Popcorn & Video |
| Apr. 23 ..... 4:00 - 7:00 .... | | The Mall/Dining |
| Apr. 30 ..... 4:00 - 7:00 .... | Surprise? ????? | |

Using computer-generated icons, Susan Snyder prepared this schedule of activities for her friend Terry.

## WE BOTH HAD A GOOD TIME

Students also keep a journal. They record and reflect on their activities and pay special attention to identifying which skills their friend is lacking that she could have learned in school to enable her to become more independent as an adult. Here are some journal entries from a recent class:

> We visited the Northland Mall, where we wandered in and out of stores. Mary and I tried on a pair of high heels, and we both had a good time laughing as we attempted to walk. (Norma Bernstein)

Upon returning to his apartment, Ted was very happy, almost ecstatic. He acted out dribbling and shooting a basketball, to let everyone know that he and his "Special Friend" had gone to a game. This made me feel fantastic, and I could sense that we were starting to bond. (Scott Martin)

I did not know what to expect on my first "date" with Jack. Nothing had been planned, and I expected to stay around the home so that we could get acquainted. Jack must have seen me pull in because he was waiting outside with his hat and jacket on. He wanted to see my truck; I don't just mean looking at my truck; I mean getting in, listening to the radio, and examining everything. It was a good icebreaker, and we sat outside for some time. (Dean Scheiderer)

After dinner, Kami and I went shopping at the Target department store. Kami picked out a card for her brother's birthday and helped me choose a present for my newborn nephew. After Target, we went to a pet store, since she loves animals. (Kelly Byers)

## IF EDNA COULD REDO HER EDUCATION

Aside from having a good time, students gain many valuable insights from this experience. Their most frequent observation and strongest recommendation had to do with many of their friends' lack of social skills. Several students noticed that basic social skills—such as saying, "Please," when requesting items; greeting the student when she arrived; and shaking hands and saying, "Thank you," at the end of the evening—were lacking. Students thought that many of these important skills could have been acquired easily and naturally if their friends had experienced early inclusion with their nondisabled peers while participating in informal school and community activities.

Edna and I spent a lot of our time at the City Center Mall—an activity she had expressed an interest in. Edna had a difficult time navigating her way around people; she would just "bulldoze" ahead without going around people. We browsed in many stores and had pizza there, too, and had a great time. As soon as we got back to her home, however, Edna vanished without a word. . . . Later, during a trip to the movies and out to dinner, Edna spoke very loudly and annoyed other customers. Edna can be such a pleasant and nice young woman, but she seems oblivious to others around her. . . . If Edna could redo her education, I think she would have benefited from spending time, both in and outside school, with her nondisabled peers. (Barbara Miller)

Another critical skill that many of the friends lacked was the ability to make choices.

Today, Kami and I went to dinner at Pizza Hut. We continued to talk about our families and our work. I noticed

Kami waits for me to do everything. Open the door, serve the food, anything that requires a decision. (Kelly Byers)

A really big difference was that [in spending time with Ted] I always took the lead with decision making. I had to be sure to wait and prompt responses from him, or else I would not have known which store he wanted to visit or what flavor of ice cream he preferred. (Scott Martin)

Future teachers can keep this in mind and give students repeated opportunities to choose snacks, books, and leisure-time activities.

Appropriate affect and expression of feelings were other areas in which many adults had some difficulty.

Todd lacks a sense of humor. I usually associate with people who like to have fun and laugh. It was very hard for me to relate to Todd, who hardly ever laughed or seemed to want to have a good time. (Paula Kruer)

Many students observed that their adult friends, even if they were quite verbal, did not have adequate conversation skills. Some adults could answer questions but did not ask questions of the students or initiate conversation.

Edna apparently has little or no concept of friendship. Her life experiences have provided her with the model that adults are "providers." Our conversation was usually one-sided, with me asking her a lot of questions, but rarely was the reverse true. She never asked me when she would see me again. (Barbara Miller)

Money-handling skills were also identified as critically important in making a person more adept in the community, and many of the adults experienced difficulty paying for items independently.

Ben could have been taught basic skills that would have been helpful in integrating him into society. Handling money transactions and telling time could have prevented the need for someone to keep track of Ben's every move in stores and restaurants. (Beth Wahl)

Self-care skills were another area in which some of the adults were weak.

I believe that Mary could have been taught basic hygiene, housekeeping, and social skills during her school years so that she could enjoy more independence and less frustration as she deals with these issues now. (Norma Bernstein)

This placement helped me realize the need for an emphasis in schools to be placed on daily living skills, skills that students will need when they become adults living in the community. It will be helpful to remember this when I become a teacher. (Beth Wahl)

# THE ULTIMATE GOAL: A BETTER LIFE

## Quality of Life

Without question, significant strides have been made in the lives of many people with disabilities. Tens of thousands of people who previously were relegated to life in an institution now live in real homes in regular neighborhoods. Many thousands who never had an opportunity to learn meaningful job skills go to work each day and bring home a paycheck each week. But living in a community-based residence and having a job in an integrated setting do not translate automatically into a better life.

Most advocates and professionals now realize that the physical presence of individuals with disabilities in integrated residential, work, and community settings is an important first step but that the only truly meaningful outcome of human service programs must be an improved quality of life. How highly would we rate the quality of life for a woman who always sits alone during lunch and breaks at work because she has not developed a social relationship with her co-workers? Recent research on social interaction patterns in integrated work settings suggests that this is an all-too-common scenario. Several studies have found that most contact between employees with disabilities and their nondisabled co-workers involves task performance; disabled workers are less involved in good-natured teasing and joking, and few workers with disabilities are befriended by their co-workers (e.g., Lignugaris/Kraft, Rule, Salzberg, & Stowitscheck, 1988; Rusch, Johnson, & Hughes, 1990).

And what is the quality of life for a young man who lives in a group home in a residential neighborhood but seldom or never gets to choose what will be served for dinner or when he will go to bed and whose only "friends" are the paid staff responsible for supervising him on his weekly trip to the shopping mall? One measure of the quality of a person's life is the extent to which he can make choices. The choices we make play a significant role in defining our individual identities—from everyday matters, such as what to eat or wear, to the choices we make on larger matters, such as where to live or what kind of work to do (Ferguson & Ferguson, 2006).

There are numerous conceptions and definitions of quality of life, debates over how or whether it can be measured, and recommendations about what should or must be done to improve it (e.g., Dennis, Williams, Giangreco, & Cloninger, 1993; Halpern, 1993; Hatton,

1998; Sands & Kozleski, 1994; Schalock, Bonham, & Marchand, 2000; Syzmanski, 2000; Wehmeyer, 1994).

Schalock, Keith, Hoffman, and Karan (1989) have proposed an objective measure of quality of life. They present 28 criterion-referenced questions that comprise the Quality of Life Index. The questions are organized under three aspects: control of one's environment, involvement in the community, and social relationships. They note that the Quality of Life Index is more appropriate for living rather than work environments and that generalizations across all types of living environments are not possible. A sample of the 28 questions follows:

- How many people sleep in your bedroom?
- How much control do you have when you go to bed and when you get up?
- Who plans your meals?
- Can you do what you want to do?
- Who decides how you spend your money?
- When can friends visit your home?
- Does your job make you feel good?
- How often do you use public transportation?
- How frequently do you spend time in recreational activities in town? (from Schalock et al., 1989, p. 27)

## Misguided and Limiting Presumptions

A continuing problem for many adults with disabilities is lack of acceptance as full members of our society, with all the rights, privileges, and services granted to any citizen (Taylor, Bogdan, & Lutfiyya, 1995). Progress has been made in this regard (witness the litigation and legislation on behalf of persons with disabilities that have been discussed throughout this book), but we still have a long way to go. Courts can decree and laws can require, but neither can alter the way in which individuals treat people with disabilities. People with disabilities often seem "in the community but not of it" (Ferguson & Ferguson, 2000, p. 645).

Most adults with disabilities believe the biggest barriers to full integration into society are not inaccessible buildings or the actual restrictions imposed by their disabilities but the differential treatment afforded them by nondisabled people. Just as the terms *racism* and *sexism* indicate prejudiced, discriminatory treatment of racial groups and women, the term **handicapism** has been coined to describe biased reactions toward a person with a disability. Those reactions are not based on an individual's qualities or performance but on a presumption of what the person with a disability must feel or be like because of the disability (Bogdan & Taylor, 1994).

Only when a man or a woman with a disability is allowed to be simply an ordinary person—given the opportunity to strive and perhaps succeed but also allowed the freedom and dignity to strive and sometimes fail—can full membership and participation in society become a reality. Only then can people with disabilities enjoy a quality of life that citizens without disabilities take for granted.

> The truth is that every human being has some ordinary ways of being and some unusual ways. Everyone suffers sometimes and has burdens and sometimes burdens others. Everyone also has times of joy, sometimes gives something to someone else, and has the possibility of creating opportunity for others in the world. Paradoxically the most common thing about people is that everyone has unique ways of being himself or herself. (Snow, 2001, p. 8)

## Self-Advocacy and Self-Determination

Advocacy on behalf of children and adults with disabilities has had a tremendous impact, especially during the past 30 years. Indeed, most of the pervasive changes in education, employment opportunities, and residential services have occurred because of the efforts of advocates. Family members, friends, professionals, and attorneys have traditionally

*Handicapism*

 Content Standards for Beginning Teachers—Common Core: Teacher attitudes and behaviors that influence behavior of individuals with exceptional learning needs (CC5K4).

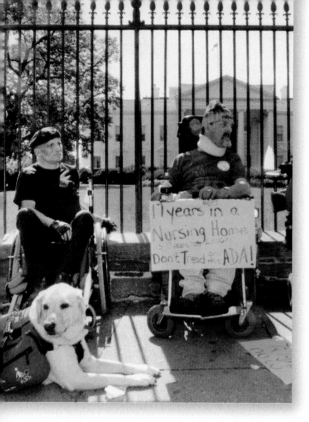

Self-advocacy: responsibility for the utilization and protection of one's rights.

*Self-advocacy and self-determination*

Council for Exceptional Children Knowledge and Skill Base for Beginning Special Education Transition Specialists: Use support systems to facilitate self-advocacy in transition planning (TS5S2) (also CC4S5).

undertaken advocacy for persons with disabilities. Like a growing number of professionals and most individuals with disabilities, Bigge (1991) believes that

the age of "doing for" a person with a disability is rapidly diminishing. Increasingly, our society is viewing individuals with disabilities as integral and contributing members of the community in which they are a part. Federal and state legislation have provided and supported equal access of individuals with disabilities into all walks of life. . . . Along with the acquisition of these equal rights has come the responsibility for the utilization and protection of these rights. It is now necessary for those with disabilities, as individuals and as groups, to assert themselves as self-advocates. (p. 493)

Persons with disabilities have begun to assert their legal rights, challenging the view that they are incapable of speaking for themselves. Perhaps most conspicuous has been the self-advocacy of individuals with physical disabilities, who have been highly effective in their lobbying as part of the independent living movement. Individuals with sensory impairments have also engaged in self-advocacy. A striking and successful example is students' refusal at Gallaudet University to accept the appointment of a hearing president who did not know American Sign Language. Persons with mental retardation, however, have engaged in little self-advocacy, perhaps because many have not learned to recognize when their rights are being violated and because they lack the verbal skills to advocate on their behalf.

Self-advocacy requires self-determination (see Chapter 4).

Self-determined people know how to choose. They know what they want and how to get it. From an awareness of personal needs, self-determined individuals choose goals, then doggedly pursue them. This involves asserting an individual's presence, making his or her needs known, evaluating progress toward meeting goals, adjusting performance, and creating unique approaches to solve problems. (Martin & Marshall, 1995, p. 147)

This is a tall order for anyone with or without disabilities. But along with these skills comes freedom.

Freedom to choose, what kind of job to have, where to live, to have relationships, to make all of the everyday decisions (big and small), and the freedom to make mistakes. Dignity of failure.

Tony Coehlo, chair of the President's Committee on Employment of People with Disabilities, opened the 1994 National Self-Advocacy Conference, "Voices for Choices'" with these remarks:

We want everything we are entitled to as citizens, nothing more, but nothing less. We want the privileges of full citizenship, but we also welcome its responsibilities. We want the respect we deserve, and we demand the rights we have been denied. We now recognize that empowerment is not a gift to be given, but a right to be demanded. (Cone, 1994, p. 445)

## Still a Long Way to Go

In general, the quality of life for most adults with disabilities is better today than it has ever been. Not only do more adults with disabilities live, work, and play in community-based, integrated environments, but more adults with disabilities have acquired or are acquiring the personal, social, work, and leisure skills that enable them to enjoy the benefits of those settings. But *more* persons with disabilities does not mean *all* persons with disabilities. And individuals don't live life "in general"; they experience specific instances of joy and sadness, success and failure. There is still a long way to go.

True, the quality of life for someone who now has his own bedroom in a group home and works for wages in a sheltered workshop may be appreciably better than it was before he left the institution where he ate and slept communally and his "work" consisted of an endless series of arts-and-crafts projects. But do the unacceptable standards of the past mean that a relatively better quality of life today is therefore good? Would it be good enough for you?

# Tips for Beginning Teachers

## Attributes for Success
### by Gail Gantt Bettis

As a new teacher, you will begin and end each day with many different challenges. The following tips might be helpful as you put your ideas, methods of teaching, behavior management techniques, character traits, and other job skills into practice.

### ACCEPT CHALLENGES

When you teach students with disabilities, every day will present a new challenge. Some days will bring challenges that you can resolve immediately, while others will require brainstorming sessions with colleagues or special team meetings. For instance, you may need to design a jig that will help a student meet production criteria on a particular job, arrange alternate transportation when a student's schedule changes and she is no longer able to ride the local transit system, or locate a job for a student with multiple disabilities when the local unemployment rate is 13%.

### BE A GOOD LISTENER

Every child has something to say. Students will relay messages in many different ways—through their words, body language, gestures, etc. Stay attuned to what is happening in your classroom. You will be amazed at what you can learn when you are willing not only to listen but also to pay attention to students' actions.

### BE A STRONG ADVOCATE

As students prepare to leave high school and enter the adult world, they will encounter many challenges that may become obstacles to success:

- A student may need case management services but lack family support to obtain it.
- A student may want to move into a group home or a supervised apartment but not know how to navigate the system.
- A student may perform the essential functions of a job but not understand how his work affects his employment under the ADA.

Students may not always advocate for themselves. Therefore, it becomes your responsibility as an educator to carry out this task. Teachers with the courage to speak up and reach out can greatly impact the lives of many students with disabilities. If you are willing to take on this role, you can help your students achieve their full potential and, in the process, help them learn to be effective self-advocates.

### BE FLEXIBLE

You may have the best lesson ever planned, but one little issue can ruin your entire day if you allow it to. Be willing to accept change, keep moving through your day, and adjust as necessary. When a child has a toothache and the school nurse is out sick, you might have to stop in the middle of the lesson to schedule a dental appointment. When only three students show up for a job that requires at least six to complete it in the hour you have available during school-based enterprise, you might find yourself working alongside them.

### REMEMBER TO SAY "THANK YOU"

It takes a community to raise a child; therefore, a lot of people will reach out to offer assistance from time to time. No matter how little the gesture, be sure to say thank you and always ensure that the students do too. This may help you receive additional assistance from others in the future. Always make it part of the regular day to say thank you in many different kinds of ways and let volunteers and other supporters know how much they are appreciated.

## EXHIBIT AND TEACH GOOD CHARACTER

Teachers have a tremendous influence on their students. Teach your students good character skills; practice good habits, and students will too. To do this, choose a character trait (e.g., be polite and respectful to others, take

responsibility for your actions) each month to integrate into all curricular and extracurricular goals. Then conduct your lessons and community-based instruction keeping this character trait in mind.

## PERSISTENCE PAYS OFF

The next time you present a learning opportunity may just be the moment when a student finally demonstrates an understanding of the task at hand. Going through the routine of day-to-day teaching can become frustrating at times, but you must act on the belief that every child can, and will, learn. It's active persistence, not passive patience, that pays off.

# KEY TERMS AND CONCEPTS

To print your own set of SAFMED flash cards for studying and mastering these terms, go to the Companion Website, **www.prenhall.com/heward**.

deinstitutionalization, p. 622
handicapism, p. 627
individualized transition plan (ITP), p. 600
sheltered workshop, p. 615

supported employment, p. 609
supported living, p. 620
transition services, p. 599
work activity center, p. 615

# SUMMARY

### How Do Former Special Education Students Fare As Adults?

- The percentage of students with disabilities who graduate with a standard school diploma has remained at about 25% for more than a decade.
- Data from the National Longitudinal Transition Study (NLTS) show an unemployment rate of 46% for all youth with disabilities who have been out of school for less than 2 years; most of the young adults who had found competitive employment were working in part-time, low-paying jobs.
- The unemployment rate for young adults with disabilities drops to 36.5% when they have been out of school for 3 to 5 years, but nearly one in five (19.6%) states she has given up looking for work (NLTS).
- NTLS found that 27% of young adults who had left high school had enrolled in post-secondary education programs within 3 to 5 years compared with 68% of the general same-age population.
- Although the percentage of college students who indicate they have a disability has increased in recent years, compared to their peers without disabilities, fewer former special education students pursue postsecondary education.
- NLTS reported that four out of every five former special education students had still not achieved the status of independent adulthood after being out of high school for up to 5 years.

### Transition Models and Services

- Transition from school to life in the community has become perhaps the most challenging issue in special education today. Models for school-to-adult-life transition stress the importance of a functional secondary school curriculum that provides work experience in integrated community job sites, systematic coordination between school and adult service agencies, parental involvement and support, and a written individualized transition plan (ITP) to guide the entire process.

- Development of career awareness and vocational skills should begin in the elementary grades for children with severe disabilities.
- Middle school students should begin to spend time on actual community job sites.
- Secondary students should spend more time on actual community job sites, with in-school instruction focusing on the functional skills needed in the adult work, domestic, community, and recreational/leisure environments.

## Employment

- Secondary school programs can enhance the competitive employment prospects for young adults with disabilities by (1) stressing functional, vocational skills; (2) conducting school-based instruction in integrated settings as much as possible; and (3) beginning community-based instruction as early as age 12 for students with severe disabilities and for progressively extended periods as the student nears graduation.
- Supported employment is a relatively new concept that recognizes that many adults with severe disabilities require ongoing support to obtain and hold a job. Supported employment is characterized by performance of real paid work in regular, integrated worksites; it requires ongoing support from a supported work specialist.
- The role of the employment specialist/job coach is evolving from one of primary supporter for the employee with disabilities to one who works with the employer and co-workers to create innovative and natural support networks.
- Self-monitoring, self-evaluation, learning how to respond independently to naturally occurring cues in the workplace, and self-instructions are four ways that employees with disabilities can increase their independence and job productivity in the workplace.
- Many adults with severe disabilities work in sheltered workshops that provide one or a combination of three kinds of programs: training for competitive employment in the community, extended or long-term employment, and work activities.

## Postsecondary Education

- Participation in postsecondary education significantly improves chances of meaningful employment for persons with disabilities.
- Although the percentage of postsecondary students who indicate they have a disability has tripled in the past 25 years, graduation rates of college students with disabilities is far below that of students without disabilities.
- The difficulties reported by many college students with disabilities reveal the need for greater emphasis on postsecondary education goals and outcomes during high school transition planning.

## Residential Alternatives

- Group homes provide family-style living for three to six persons. Most group homes serve adults with mental retardation, although some have residents with other disabilities. Staff persons in this type of home help the people who live there develop self-care and daily living skills, form interpersonal relationships, and participate in recreation and leisure skills.
- Foster home placement allows the adult with disabilities to participate in day-to-day activities of family life, receive attention from people interested in his development, and experience close personal relationships.
- Apartment living offers the greatest opportunities for integration into the community and interaction with people without disabilities. Three common forms of apartment

living for adults with disabilities are the apartment cluster, the co-residence apartment, and the maximum-independence apartment.

- Supported living is an approach toward helping people with disabilities live in the community as independently and normally as they can by providing a network of various kinds and levels of natural supports.
- Despite deinstitutionalization—the movement of persons with mental retardation out of large public institutions and into smaller, community-based residences such as group homes—in 2000, approximately 47,580 persons, mostly adults with severe or profound mental retardation, still lived in large institutions.

## Recreation and Leisure

- Learning to participate in age-appropriate recreation and leisure activities is necessary for a self-satisfying lifestyle.

## The Ultimate Goal: A Better Life

- Adults with disabilities continue to face lack of acceptance as full members of society.
- Handicapism—discriminatory treatment and biased reactions toward someone with a disability—occurs on personal, professional, and societal levels. It must be eliminated before normalization can become a reality for every man and woman with a disability.
- Persons with disabilities have begun to assert their legal rights, challenging the view that they are incapable of speaking for themselves.

To check your comprehension of chapter contents, go to the Guided Review and Quiz modules in Chapter 15 of the Companion Website, **www.prenhall.com/heward**.

# Postscript

# Developing Your Own Personal View of Special Education

All introductory textbooks contain a great deal of information. In that respect, this book is no different from any other. I hope, however, that you have gained more than just basic facts and information about learners with exceptional educational needs and special education, the profession dedicated to meeting those needs. I hope you have examined your own attitudes toward and relationships with children and adults with disabilities. At the beginning of the book, I shared 10 fundamental beliefs that underlie my personal, but by no means unique, view of special education. I would like to repeat those beliefs.

- People with disabilities have a fundamental right to live and participate in the same settings and programs—in school, at home, in the workplace, and in the community—as do people without disabilities. People with and without disabilities have a great deal to contribute to and learn from one another. We cannot do that without regular, meaningful interaction.

- Individuals with disabilities have the right to as much self-determination as we can help them achieve. Special educators have no more important teaching task than helping children and adults with disabilities learn how to increase the level of control over their own lives.

- Special education must expand and improve the effectiveness of its early identification and prevention efforts.

- Special education must do a better job of helping students with disabilities transition from school to adult life.

- Special education must improve its cultural competence.

- School and family partnerships enhance both the meaningfulness and the effectiveness of special education.

- The efforts of special educators are most effective when they incorporate the input and services of all of the disciplines in the helping professions.

- All students have the right to an effective education. As special educators, our primary responsibilities are to design, implement, and evaluate instruction that helps students with disabilities acquire, generalize, and maintain knowledge and skills that improve the quality of their lives in school, at home, in the community, and in the workplace—now and in the future. To put it another way, the proof of the process is in the product. Therefore …

- Teachers must demand effectiveness from the curriculum materials and instructional tools they use. Although students with disabilities often need more instructional trials than their nondisabled peers need to master a skill, requiring perseverance and energy on the part of the teacher, the belief that special educators require unending patience is a disservice to students with special needs and to the educators—both special and general education teachers—who teach them. Teachers should not wait patiently for exceptional children to learn but should modify the instructional program to improve its effectiveness.

- Finally, the future for individuals with disabilities holds great promise. We have only begun to discover ways to improve teaching, increase learning, prevent or

Council for Exceptional Children

Content Standards for Beginning Teachers—Common Core: Articulate personal philosophy of of special education (CC1S1).

minimize the effects of some of the conditions that lead to disabilities, and use technology to compensate for the handicapping effects of disabilities. We have not come as far as we can in learning how to help exceptional individuals build and enjoy fuller, more independent lives.

# AS A MEMBER OF THE PROFESSION

If you consider yourself a prospective special educator, view special education as a profession and yourself as a professional. You should see yourself as someone with special skills and knowledge; you are different from people without your special training. This has nothing to do with arrogance but everything to do with recognizing that each of us must develop and use responsibly as much professional competence as we can muster.

Obtaining an objective understanding of the nature and scope of the job's responsibilities is the first step toward professional competence. Special education is serious business. The learning and adjustment problems faced by students with disabilities are real, and they require intensive and systematic intervention. Professional competence begins with an objective sense of the job to be done. Be wary of the conception of disabilities as merely socially constructed phenomena: that all children who are identified as disabled would achieve success and behave well if others simply viewed them more positively. This romantic ideology is seldom, if ever, promoted by individuals with disabilities themselves or by their parents and families. Children with disabilities have skill deficits and difficulties in acquiring and generalizing new knowledge and skills—real disabilities that won't be deconstructed away. Don't let the needs of exceptional children and their families get lost in such postmodern ideologies. They need and deserve systematic, effective special education.

It is commendable that you have the commitment and the desire to help children with exceptional educational needs. You will probably hear often that you are "wonderful" or "patient" because of this. Good intentions are fine, but desire and commitment are only a beginning. What learners with disabilities need more than anything are teachers who are in some ways *impatient*—impatient with instructional methods, materials, and policies that do not help their students acquire and subsequently use new knowledge and skills required for successful functioning in the home, school, workplace, and community. So don't be patient; be effective.

You will increase your effectiveness as a teacher by using only instructional methods and materials backed by sound, empirical research evidence. Special education research has produced a significant and reliable knowledge base about effective teaching practices. While no reasonable person believes research has discovered everything important that can be known about teaching exceptional students—many important questions remain to be answered—today's special educator can turn to a research base that includes many instructional strategies that did not exist when the Education of All Handicapped Children Act was signed into law in 1975. For example, research has developed a substantial body of knowledge about strategic approaches (e.g., functional assessment) and tactical procedures (e.g., progressively fading response prompts) that special education teachers must learn how to select and apply with professional expertise.

When considering a new curriculum, program, or instructional method, teachers must ask questions such as the following:

Council for Exceptional Children

Content Standards for Beginning Teachers—Common Core: Methods to remain current regarding reserach-validated practice (CC9K4).

Has this program been tested in the classroom?

What evidence shows that this program works?

What measures of student performance were used to evaluate this program?

Has any research on this program been published in peer-reviewed journals?

Is there any evidence to suggest the program will be successful if modified to meet the skill levels and ages of my students?

Educating students with disabilities has always posed a complex and difficult challenge. And today's special education teacher is expected to do more than ever before. For example, special educators must ensure students' access to the general education curriculum while teaching them the functional skills needed for daily living and successful transition from school to life in the community and workplace. Prepare yourself for meeting this challenge the best way you can. Demand relevant, up-to-date information and hands-on practical experiences from your teacher-education program. Continue your education and training throughout your career. Stay abreast of the continuing developments in special education by reading professional journals, participating in in-service training opportunities, and attending conferences. Even better, experiment with instructional methods and share the results of your research with colleagues through presentations and publications.

Special education is not a grim, thankless business. Quite the opposite: special education is an exciting, dynamic field that offers personal satisfaction and feelings of accomplishment unequaled in most areas of endeavor. Welcome aboard!

*Professional development*

 Council for Exceptional Children — Content Standards for Beginning Teachers—Common Core: Continuum of lifelong professional development (CC9K3).

## As a Member of the Community

The degree of success and happiness a person with disabilities enjoys in the normal routines of everyday life does not depend solely on his skills and abilities. In large measure, the integration of people with disabilities into contemporary society depends on the attitudes and actions of citizens with little knowledge of or experience with exceptional learners. How can people come to accept and support a group they do not know?

Society controls who enters and who is kept out, much as a gatekeeper lets some visitors pass but refuses others. For a particular individual, society's gatekeeper may have been a doctor who urged parents to institutionalize their child or a teacher who resisted having any difficult-to-teach kids in her classroom. It may have been an employer who refused to hire workers with disabilities. It may have been a social worker, a school board member, a voter. Saddest of all, it may have been a parent whose low expectations kept the gate closed.

How society views people with disabilities influences how individual members of the community respond. Society's views are changing gradually for the better—they are being changed by people who believe that our past practices of exclusion and denial of opportunities were primitive, unfair, and ultimately detrimental to everyone. But to have maximum impact, the movement toward integration and opportunities described in this book must ultimately translate into personal terms for those of you who will not choose careers in special education. People with disabilities and people without disabilities do experience certain aspects of life differently, but they are more like one another than they are different. And the conclusion I hope you have reached is this: every child and adult with disabilities must be treated as an individual, not as a member of a category or a labeled group.

## In Sum

Viewing every individual with disabilities first as a person and second as a person with a disability may be the most important step in integrating the individual into the mainstream of school and community life. But changing our attitudes will not diminish the disability. What it will do is give us a new outlook—a more objective and positive one—and allow us to see a disability as a set of special needs. Viewing exceptional people as individuals with special needs tells us much about how to respond to them—and how we respond is the essence of special education.

# Appendix

# Coverage of Content Areas for PRAXIS II Test Special Education Core Principles: Content Knowledge (0353)

Many states require a passing score on one or more of the PRAXIS II™ tests for licensure or certification as a special education teacher. The PRAXIS II tests—the Subject Assessment/Specialty Area Tests of the PRAXIS Series of Professional Assessments for Beginning Teachers™—assess students' knowledge of critical content standards.

One of the most frequently required PRAXIS II tests in special education is Special Education Core Principles: Content Knowledge (0353). This Appendix enables you to locate the page numbers where each of the Content Areas covered by this test is explained in the text. A complete outline of the Content Areas covered by test 0353 is printed inside the back cover of this text.

The organization and format of this Appendix, when used in conjunction with the CEC Margin Notes throughout the text and Subject Index at the end of the book, will also aide you in determining Content Areas covered by other PRAXIS II tests in special education.

A great deal of the basic content knowledge that a beginning special education teacher should possess is presented in this text, and learning this content will contribute to your obtaining a passing score on any of the PRAXIS II tests in special education. However, two important qualifiers must be recognized. First, each of the PRAXIS II tests in special education requires some knowledge beyond that included in an introductory text. That is why you will see a few of the PRAXIS Content Areas without very much text coverage. Second, no matter how extensive and current the textbook, how well the instructor teaches the course, and how thoroughly you master the text content and course objectives, you will not be prepared to teach students with exceptional learning needs as the result of this course. Successful completion of an introductory course in special education is but one step in a teacher preparation program.

## I. Understanding Exceptionalities

| PRAXIS Content Area | Relevant Textbook Content | |
|---|---|---|
| *Human development and behavior as related to students with disabilities, including*<br>• Social and emotional development and behavior | • Mental retardation, 147–148<br>• Learning disabilities, 190<br>• Emotional and behavioral disorders, 224–225<br>• Autism spectrum disorders, 268, 271<br>• Communication disorders, 309<br>• Hearing impairments, 355<br>• Visual impairments, 387–388 | • Physical disabilities and health impairments, 443–444<br>• ADHD, 438–439<br>• Severe/multiple disabilities, 474–476<br>• Deaf-blindness, 473–474<br>• Traumatic brain injury, 479–481<br>• Infants and preschoolers with disabilities, 557–559 |
| • Language development and behavior | • Learning disabilities, 188–189<br>• Autism spectrum disorders, 268–269<br>• Communication disorders, 305–307, 313–314 | • Hearing impairments, 341–342, 346–347<br>• Visual impairments, 383, 386<br>• Severe/multiple disabilities, 474–476<br>• Deaf-blindness, 473–474 |

| PRAXIS Content Area | Relevant Textbook Content | |
|---|---|---|
| • Cognition | • Mental retardation, 146–147<br>• Learning disabilities, 183–185<br>• Emotional and behavioral disorders, 225–228<br>• Autism spectrum disorders, 269–270<br>• Hearing impairments, 346–347<br>• Visual impairments, 386 | • Physical disabilities and health impairments, 443–444<br>• Severe/multiple disabilities, 474–476<br>• Deaf-blindness, 474–476<br>• Traumatic brain injury, 479–481 |
| • Physical development, including motor and sensory | • Mental retardation, 148<br>• Autism spectrum disorders, 270<br>• Visual impairments, 387 | • Physical disabilities and health impairments, 425–433<br>• Severe/multiple disabilities, 474–476<br>• Deaf-blindness, 473–474<br>• Traumatic brain injury, 479–481 |
| *Characteristics of students with disabilities, including influence of*<br>• Cognitive factors: Cognitive development and academic achievement of students with | • Mental retardation, 146–147<br>• Learning disabilities, 183–185, 188–190<br>• Emotional and behavioral disorders, 225, 228<br>• Autism spectrum disorders, 269–270<br>• Hearing impairments, 347, 350 | • Physical disabilities and health impairments, 443–445<br>• ADHD, 438–439<br>• Severe/multiple disabilities, 474–476<br>• Traumatic brain injury, 479–481 |
| • Affective and social-adaptive factors, including cultural, linguistic, gender, and socioeconomic factors | • Mental retardation, 148<br>• Learning disabilities, 190–191<br>• Emotional and behavioral disorders, 223–228, 229<br>• Autism spectrum disorders, 268<br>• Communication disorders, 310–314<br>• Hearing impairments, 350<br>• Visual impairments, 387–388 | • Physical disabilities and health impairments, 443–444<br>• ADHD, 439<br>• Severe/multiple disabilities, 474–476<br>• Traumatic brain injury, 479–481 |
| • Genetic, medical, motor, sensory, and chronological-age factors | • Mental retardation, 148<br>• Learning disabilities, 192–193<br>• Autism spectrum disorders, 270<br>• Communication disorders, 310–314<br>• Hearing impairments, 346–347, 351<br>• Visual impairments, 383–385 | • Physical disabilities and health impairments, 424<br>• ADHD, 440–441, 444–445<br>• Severe/multiple disabilities, 474–476<br>• Traumatic brain injury, 478–479 |
| *Basic concepts in special education, including*<br>• Definitions of all major categories and specific disabilities | • Exceptional children, impairment, disability, handicap, at risk, 10–11<br>• Mental retardation, 140–142, 169–170<br>• Learning disabilities, 182–184, 209–210<br>• Emotional and behavioral disorders, 221–223<br>• Autism spectrum disorders, 264–267, 270–273<br>• Communication disorders, 308–310<br>• Hearing impairments, 342–346, 351–352<br>• Visual impairments, 383–385 | • Physical disabilities and health impairments, 424<br>• ADHD, 436–438<br>• Severe/multiple disabilities, 469–471, 473<br>• Deaf-blindness, 473–474<br>• Traumatic brain injury, 477<br>• Developmental delay, 563–564<br>• Dyslexia, 185<br>• Anxiety, mood, and other emotional disorders, 226–227 |
| • Incidence and prevalence of various types of disabilities | • All disabilities, 10–13<br>• Mental retardation, 149<br>• Learning disabilities, 191–192<br>• Emotional and behavioral disorders, 228–229, 232<br>• Autism spectrum disorders, 273–274<br>• Communication disorders, 314<br>• Hearing impairments, 350–351<br>• Visual impairments, 388 | • Physical disabilities and health impairments, 425<br>• ADHD, 439–440<br>• Severe/multiple disabilities, 476<br>• Deaf-blindness, 476<br>• Traumatic brain injury, 477 |

| PRAXIS Content Area | Relevant Textbook Content | |
|---|---|---|
| • The causation and prevention of disability | • Preventive intervention, 38<br>• Mental retardation, 149–154<br>• Learning disabilities, 192–194<br>• Emotional and behavioral disorders, 232–236, 252–253<br>• Autism spectrum disorders, 274–275<br>• Communication disorders, 314–315<br>• Hearing impairments, 351–353<br>• Visual impairments, 389–390, 392–393 | • Physical disabilities and health impairments, 425–427, 429–436<br>• ADHD, 440<br>• Severe/multiple disabilities, 476<br>• Traumatic brain injury, 478<br>• Early intervention as prevention, 559, 561–562 |
| • The nature of behaviors, including frequency, duration, intensity, and degrees of severity | • Measurable dimensions of behavior, 238–239 | |
| • Classification of students with disabilities within IDEA | • Disability categories within IDEA, 12<br>• Emotional and behavioral disorders, 224–225<br>• Mental retardation, 141–143, 146<br>• Hearing impairments, 356, 358–359<br>• Visual impairments, 384–385 | • ILEP classification system, 142–143 |
| • Implications of classification and labeling for persons classified | • Pros and cons of labeling and classification, 13–16, LD-211, EBD-222<br>• Alternatives to labeling, 16 | • Disproportional representation of culturally diverse children in special education, 60–63 |
| • The influence of (an) exceptional condition throughout an individual's life span | • Family life-cycle stages, 106–108 | • Early pattern of antisocial behavior for children with EBD, 235–236 |

## II. Legal and Societal Issues

| PRAXIS Content Area | Relevant Textbook Content | |
|---|---|---|
| *Federal laws and legal issues related to special education, including*<br>• Individuals with Disabilities Education Act (IDEA) | • Six major principles IDEA, 19–21<br>• IDEA and early intervention for infants and toddlers, 21–22, 563–564<br>• IDEA and preschoolers, 21–22, 566–567<br>• Individuals with Disabilities Education Improvement Act of 2004, 24, 27–28, 90–91 | • Definition of transition services, 599–600<br>• Individualized transition plan (ITP), 600–601, 604<br>• Definition of supported employment, 609–611 |
| • Section 504 | • Basic provisions, 32–33<br>• ADHD and eligibility for special education services under IDEA or Section 504, 447 | |
| • Americans with Disabilities Act (ADA) | • Implications for educational agencies, 33 | |
| • No Child Left Behind (NCLB) | • Key provisions of NCLB, 33, 36–37, 90–91 | |
| • Important legal issues, such as those raised in following cases: Rowley re: program appropriateness, Taro re: related services, Honig re: discipline, Oberti re: inclusion | • PARC case and equal protection, 18–19<br>• Rowley case, 28–29, 30<br>• Tatro case, 29, 31, 457–458 | • Honig case, 29, 31<br>• Garret case, 29, 31<br>• Legal aspects of disciplining students with disabilities, 29, 253–254 |

| PRAXIS Content Area | Relevant Textbook Content | |
|---|---|---|
| *The school's connections with the families, prospective and actual employers, and communities of students with disabilities, for example* <br> • Teacher advocacy for students and families, developing student self-advocacy | • Respite care, 103–104 <br> • Developing independence and self-esteem, 173 | • Promoting self-advocacy and self-determination, 157, 159, 173, 627–628 <br> • Teaching choice-making, 623, 626–627 |
| • Parent partnerships and roles | • IDEA and parent participation, 58–60, 69–76, 101 <br> • Roles & responsibilities of exceptional parents, 99–100, 102–107 <br> • Effects of child's disability on family system, 102–107 <br> • Barriers to effective communication and partnership with parents, 112–113 | • Developing cultural reciprocity with parents & families from diverse backgrounds, 114–119 <br> • Communicating with parents, 108–111 <br> • Parent participation in transition planning, 601–603, 605 (margin note) |
| • Public attitudes toward individuals with disabilities | • Society's and education's past and changing attitudes toward individuals with disabilities, 16–19, 626–628 <br> • Handicapism, 627 | • Normalization, 170, 173 <br> • Social role valorization, 173 |
| • Cultural and community influences on public attitudes toward individuals with disabilities | • Deaf culture and community, 343–345 | |
| • Interagency agreements | • Coordinating transition services with community agencies, 604 | |
| • Cooperative nature of the transition planning process | • Relationship between postsecondary education and employment, 597 <br> • Transition team collaboration, 601–603 | |
| *Historical movements/trends affecting the connections between special education and the larger society, for example* <br> • Deinstitutionalization and community-based placements | • Residential options for adults with disabilities, 618–621 | • Supported living, 620–621 <br> • Deinstitutionalization, 621–622 |
| • Inclusion | • Individuals with disabilities access to and placement in public education, 16–19 | • Components of inclusive education, 79–81, 85 <br> • Perspectives on inclusion, 81, 85–89, MR–166–169, LD–212, 213, HI–372–374, VI–414, 415, PD–455–458, Severe/multiple, 495–501 |
| • Application of technology | • Cochlear implants, 360–363 | • Choosing auditory or visual language modality, 365–366 |
| • Transition | • Will's Bridges model, 599 <br> • Halpren's transition model, 599–600 | • Competitive, supported, and sheltered employment, 609–616 <br> • Postsecondary education, 374, 616–618 |

| PRAXIS Content Area | Relevant Textbook Content | |
|---|---|---|
| • Advocacy | • History of education of children with MR–154–155, 170–173, LD–199, ASD–276, HI–366–367, VI–394–395, PD–447 <br> • Normalization and social role valorization, 170, 173 | |
| • Accountability and meeting educational standards | • IDEA, 19–28 | • No Child Left Behind Act, 33, 36–37 |

# III. Delivery of Services to Students with Disabilities

| PRAXIS Content Area | Relevant Textbook Content | |
|---|---|---|
| *Background knowledge, including* <br> • Conceptual approaches underlying service delivery to students with disabilities, including cognitive, constructivist, psychodynamic, behavioral, sociological, ecological, therapeutic (speech/language, physical, and occupational and medical approaches) | • Applied behavior analysis, 277–280 <br> • Early intensive behavioral intervention, 275, 277 <br> • Oral/aural approach, 365–368 <br> • Speechreading, 366–367 <br> • Cued speech, 368 <br> • Drug therapy for children with ADHD, 440–442 | • Total communication, 368–370 <br> • Fingerspelling, 369–370 <br> • ASL, 370–371 <br> • Bicultural-bilingual approach, 371–372 <br> • Goals for ECSE, 558, 562–563 <br> • Developmentally appropriate practice, 576 |
| • Placement and program issues such as early intervention; LRE; inclusion, role of IEP team; due process guidelines, continuum of services; related services; accommodations, access to assistive technology; community-based training; post-school transitions | • Definitions of educational placements, 40–41, 78 <br> • Placement alternatives for students with <br>    • Mental retardation, 165–166 <br>    • Learning disabilities, 206–209 <br>    • Emotional and behavioral disorders, 251–252 <br>    • Autism spectrum disorders, 275–277, 284 <br>    • Communication disorders, 328, 330–331 <br>    • Hearing impairments, 372–374 <br>    • Visual impairments, 405, 409, 412–413 <br>    • Physical disabilities, health impairments, 454–455 <br>    • Severe/multiple disabilities, 495–499 | • Infants and preschoolers with disabilities, 581, 583–585 <br> • Least restrictive environment, 76–79, HL–373, VI–413, PD–455 <br> • Components of inclusive education, 79–81, 85 <br> • Benefits of neighborhood schools, 495 <br> • Inclusion and social relationships, 167–169 <br> • Role of IEP team, 70–71, 77–79 <br> • Due process safeguards, 20 <br> • Continuum of services, 76–78, VI-413 <br> • Related services, 22–23, 28–29, 456–458 <br> • Planning inclusion with MAPS, 499–501 <br> • Social relationships, 496, 497 |
| • Integrating best practices from multidisciplinary research and professional literature into the education setting | • Asking for research evidence of effectiveness, 91–92, 285, 289–293, 635–636 | • Closing research-to-practice gap, 44–45 |
| *Curriculum and instruction and their implementation across the continuum of educational placements, including* <br> • IFSP/IEP process | • IEP process, 68–76 <br> • IEP team membership, 69 <br> • IEP components, 69–70, 72–74 <br> • IEP goals and objectives, 74–75, 486, 488, 577–578 <br> • IFSP definition, purpose, and content, 564, 566, 568–569 <br> • IHCP, 451–452 | • Considering communication needs of students who are deaf or hard of hearing, 372 <br> • IEP teams for students with VI must determine the student's preferred reading medium and considered instruction in braille, 395–396 |

| PRAXIS Content Area | Relevant Textbook Content | |
|---|---|---|
| • Instructional development and implementation, for example: instructional activities, curricular materials and resources, working with classroom and support personnel, tutoring options | • Programming and delivering instruction in inclusive settings for students with<br>  • Mental retardation, 156–157<br>  • Learning disabilities, 186–188<br>  • Emotional and behavioral disorders, 240–241<br>  • Autism spectrum disorders, 280–284, 286–288<br>  • Communication disorders, 320–325 | • Visual impairments, 409–412<br>• Physical disabilities, health impairments, and ADHD, 443<br>• Severe/multiple disabilities, 481–487, 496–497, 499–501<br>• Traumatic brain injury, 479–481<br>• Preschoolers with special needs, 572–576 |
| • Teaching strategies and methods, for example: modification of materials and equipments, learning centers, facilitated groups, study skills groups, self-management, cooperative learning, diagnostic-prescriptive methods, modeling skill drill, guided practice, concept generalization, learning strategy instruction, and Direct Instruction | • Self-determination, MR–157, 159, 173<br>• Task analysis, MR–159<br>• Providing systematic feedback, MR–162<br>• Promoting generalization and maintenance, MR–164<br>• Content enhancements: guided notes, graphic organizers, and mnemonic strategies, 203–206<br>• Active student response, 159–162<br>• Direct instruction, 199 (margin note)<br>• Explicit or direct instruction, 198–202 | • Learning strategies, 206<br>• Discrete trial training, 272, 279<br>• Picture activity schedules, 280–283<br>• Naturalistic teaching strategies, 492–493<br>• Elements of systematic instruction, 159, 197, 487, 489–490<br>• Structure of learning environment, 235–236 |
| • Instructional format and components, for example: small and large-group instruction, facilitated group strategies, functional academics, general academics with focus on special education, ESL and limited English proficiency, language and literacy acquisition, self-care and daily living skills, pre-vocational skills | • Functional curriculum goals, MR–156, Severe/multiple, 481–482<br>• Classwide peer tutoring, 82–84<br>• Integrating life skills into curriculum, MR–157<br>• Phonemic awareness and alphabetic principle, 185–188 | • Comprehension and beginning reading instruction, 185–188<br>• Response cards, 230–232<br>• Functional life skills for students, MR–157–158, VI–405<br>• Small-group instruction, 494–495<br>• Orientation and mobility for students with VI, 404<br>• Functional vision, 397–399<br>• Functional life skills, VI–405–408 |
| • Career development and transition issues as related to curriculum design and implementation according to the criteria of ultimate functioning | • Teaching functional and age-appropriate skills, 481–482<br>• Partial participation, 490–491<br>• Relating transition services to IEP goals and objectives, 601–604<br>• Career awareness and transition related curriculum activities, 605–609 | • Characteristics of secondary school programs and competitive employment outcomes, 609<br>• Teaching recreation and leisure activities, 486–487, 622–623 |

| PRAXIS Content Area | Relevant Textbook Content | |
| --- | --- | --- |
| • Technology for teaching and learning in special education settings, for example: integrating assistive technology, computer-assisted instruction, augmentative and alternative communication (AAC), adaptive access for microcomputers; position and power mobility for students with physical disabilities; accessing and using information technology; technology for sensory disabilities; and voice-activated, speech-synthesis, speech recognition and word-prediction software | • Assistive technology defined, 23<br>• Augmentative and alternative communication, 324–330, 484–486<br>• Hearing aids, 357<br>• Group listening devices, 360<br>• Speech-to-text translation and TV captioning, 361, 363<br>• Auditory training/learning, 365<br>• Braille, brailler, slate and stylus, 391–396<br>• Tactile aids and manipulatives for students with VI, 396<br>• PDAs in classroom, 25–27<br>• Adapting toys for children with physical impairment, 428–429 | • Optional devices and technological aids for students with VI, 396–400<br>• Reading print, 400–401<br>• Listening skills for students with VI, 404–405<br>• Self-operated audio prompting systems, 406–408<br>• Assistive technology for students with physical disabilities, 450–451, 458–459 |
| *Assessment, including*<br>• Use of assessment for screening, diagnosis, placement, and the making of instructional decisions, for example: how to select and conduct nondiscriminatory assessments; how to interpret standardized and specialized assessment results; how to use evaluation results in IFSP/IEP development; how to prepare written reports and communicate findings | • Definitions of standardized tests, norm-referenced tests, the normal curve, and standard deviation, 143–145, 194<br>• IQ scores and diagnosis of MR, 142–144<br>• Projective tests, 238<br>• Issues to consider with IQ tests/scores, LD–183<br>• Criterion-referenced tests, LD–194–195<br>• Informal reading inventories, LD–195<br>• Purposes of screening assessment, and evaluation, 354<br>• Standardized achievement tests, 194<br>• Response to instruction for diagnosis of LD, 209–211 | • Screening tools for emotional and behavioral disorders, 236–238<br>• Screening and diagnostic tools for autism spectrum disorders, 271–273<br>• Screening, assessment and diagnosis of communication disorders, 315–320<br>• Audiometry and audiograms, 354–356<br>• Screening and assessment tools for early intervention, 567, 570–572<br>• Functional behavior assessment, 238–239, 491, 493–494<br>• Screening and assessment for hearing impairment, 354–356 |
| • Procedures and test materials, both formal and informal, typically used for pre-referral, screening, referral, classification, placement, and ongoing program monitoring | • Prereferral intervention, 56–58<br>• Multifactored evaluation, 57–60<br>• Monitoring student progress, 65<br>• Precision teaching, 196<br>• Curriculum-based measurement, 195–196, 572 | • Assessing adaptive behavior, 145<br>• Direct and frequent measurement, 164, 196, 238–239<br>• Manifestation determination, 29, 253–254 |

| PRAXIS Content Area | Relevant Textbook Content | |
|---|---|---|
| • How to select, construct, and modify nondiscriminatory, developmentally and chronologically age-appropriate informal assessments, including teacher-made tests, curriculum-based assessment, and alternative to norm-referenced testing (including observations, anecdotal records, error analysis miscue analysis, self-evaluation questionnaire and interviews, journals and learning logs, portfolio assessment) | • See text content under, "Use of assessment for screening, diagnosis, placement, and the making of instructional decisions"<br>• Assessing the communicative competence of culturally and linguistically diverse students, 318–319<br>• Nondiscriminatory assessment, 61–63 | |
| *Structuring and managing the learning environment, including*<br>• Structuring the learning environment, for example: the physical-social environment for learning (e.g., expectations, rules, consequences, consistency, attitudes, lighting, acoustics, seating, access, safety provisions, strategies for positive interactions) | • Effects of teacher's reactions to noncompliance, 234–235, 241–242<br>• Schoolwide positive behavior support, 241–243<br>• Proactive classroom management strategies, 243, 246–247<br>• Helping the student with low vision, 402 (margin note)<br>• Modifying and adapting physical environment for students with physical disabilities, 427, 448 | • Positioning, seating, and movement, 451–453<br>• Lifting and transferring students, 453<br>• Positive behavioral support, 247–248, 250, 490–491<br>• Embedding learning opportunities for preschool children, 577, 579–580, 582<br>• Preschool activity schedules, 580–581<br>• Physical arrangement of preschool classroom, 581 |
| • Classroom management techniques, e.g., behavior analysis (identification and definitions of antecedents, target behavior, and consequent events); behavioral interventions; functional analysis; data gathering procedures (e.g., anecdotal data, frequency methods, and interval methods); self-management strategies and reinforcement; cognitive-behavioral interventions; social skills training | • Social stories, 280<br>• Social skills curricula and instruction, 240–241<br>• Contingent teacher praise and positive reinforcement, 244–245<br>• Signaling and recruiting teacher attention, 42–43, 160–161 | • Self-management, including self-monitoring and self-evaluation, 246, 248–250, 613–615<br>• Peer-mediated support and interventions, 246–247<br>• Behavioral interventions for ADHD, 443 |
| • Ethical considerations inherent in behavior management | • Positive behavioral support, 247–248, 250, 490–491 | • Teaching choice-making, 482, 484, 623, 626–627<br>• Manifestation determination, 253–254 |

| PRAXIS Content Area | Relevant Textbook Content |
|---|---|
| *Professional roles, including*<br>• Specific roles and responsibilities of teachers, for example: teacher as collaborator with other teachers, teacher educators, parents, community groups, and outside agencies; teacher as multidisciplinary team member; maintaining effective and efficient documentation, selecting appropriate environments and service for students; critical evaluation and use of professional literature and organizations; reflecting on one's own teaching; teacher's role in a variety of teaching settings (e.g., self-contained classroom, resource room, itinerant, co-teacher in inclusion setting, etc.); and maintaining student confidentiality | • Using research-based practices, 44–45, 91–92<br>• Types of collaboration, 65–66<br>• Teaming models, 66–67<br>• Co-teaching models, 67–68<br>• Wraparound services for students with EBD, 254–255<br>• Interpreters, 361<br>• Professional organizations<br>AAMR, 141<br>ACALD, 181<br>ASAT, 293<br>CCBD, 223<br>CEC, 86<br>CEC-TAG, 514<br>NAGC, 514<br>NJCLD, 182<br>TASH, 99<br>• Itinerant teachers for students with VI, 405, 409<br><br>• Collaborating with PTs, OTs, SLPs, and other related-services specialists, 333–334, 446, 448–449, 456–458<br>• Effective communication among transition team members, 601, 603, 605 (margin note)<br>• Job coach/employment specialist, 611–612 |
| • Influence of teacher attitudes, values, and behaviors on the learning of exceptional students | • Differential acceptance and empathetic relationship, 247–248<br>• Focusing on alterable variables, 250–251<br><br>• Promoting self-advocacy, 459–460, 627–628<br>• Interacting with a child who stutters, 321–323<br>• Changing attitudes of general education teachers toward students with severe disabilities, 497–498<br>• Expectation that all students can learn, 472–473, 634–636 |
| • Communicating with parents, guardians, and community collaborators, for example: directing parents and guardians to parent-educators or to other groups and resources; writing reports directly to parents; meeting with parents to discuss student concerns, progress, and IEPs; encouraging parent participation; reciprocal communication and training with other service providers | • Principles of effective communication, 108–111<br>• Active listening, 110–111<br>• Roadblocks to communication, 112–113<br>• Dialoguing to resolve conflicts, 113–114<br>• Planning and conducting parent-teacher conferences, 117, 119–121<br><br>• Home-school written communications, 121–123<br>• Guidelines for communicating with parents, 125<br>• Parents as tutors, 126–127<br>• Parent education and parent support groups, 127–128<br>• Mirror model for parent involvement, 129–130 |

# Glossary

**absence seizure**   A type of epileptic seizure in which the individual loses consciousness, usually for less than half a minute; can occur very frequently in some children.

**acceleration**   An educational approach that provides a child with learning experiences usually given to older children; most often used with gifted and talented children.

**accommodation**   The adjustment of the eye for seeing at different distances; accomplished by muscles that change the shape of the lens to bring an image into clear focus on the retina.

**acquired immune deficiency syndrome (AIDS)**   A fatal illness in which the body's immune system breaks down. At present there is no known cure for AIDS or a vaccine for the virus that causes it (see *human immunodeficiency virus*).

**acquisition stage of learning**   The initial phase of learning when the student is learning how to perform a new skill or use new knowledge; feedback should focus on the accuracy and topography of the student's response.

**active student response (ASR)**   A frequency-based measure of a student's active participation during instruction; measured by counting the number of observable responses made to an ongoing lesson or to curriculum materials.

**adaptive device**   Any piece of equipment designed to improve the function of a body part. Examples include standing tables and special spoons that can be used by people with weak hands or poor muscle control.

**adventitious**   A disability that develops at any time after birth, from disease, trauma, or any other cause; most frequently used with sensory or physical impairments (contrasts with *congenital*).

**advocate**   Someone who pleads the cause of a person with disabilities or group of people with disabilities, especially in legal or administrative proceedings or public forums.

**albinism**   A congenital condition marked by deficiency in, or total lack of, pigmentation. People with albinism have pale skin; white hair, eyebrows, and eyelashes; and eyes with pink or pale blue irises.

**amblyopia**   Dimness of sight without apparent change in the eye's structures; can lead to blindness in the affected eye if not corrected.

**American sign language (ASL)**   A visual-gestural language with its own rules of syntax, semantics, and pragmatics; does not correspond to written or spoken English. ASL is the language of the Deaf culture in the United States and Canada.

**amniocentesis**   The insertion of a hollow needle through the abdomen into the uterus of a pregnant woman. Used to obtain amniotic fluid in order to determine the presence of genetic and chromosomal abnormalities. The sex of the fetus can also be determined.

**anencephaly**   Congenital malformation of the skull with absence of all or part of the brain.

**anorexia nervosa**   Refusal to maintain body weight at or above a minimally normal weight for age and height; obsessive concern with body weight or shape and intense anxiety about gaining weight, even though severely underweight. Two subtypes: restricting food intake by starving oneself down to an abnormal weight and binge-eating/purging (see *bulimia nervosa*).

**anoxia**   A lack of oxygen severe enough to cause tissue damage; can cause permanent brain damage and mental retardation.

**aphasia**   Loss of speech functions; often, but not always, refers to inability to speak because of brain lesions.

**applied behavior analysis**   "The science in which procedures derived from the principles of behavior are systematically applied to improve socially significant behavior to a meaningful degree and to demonstrate experimentally that the procedures employed were responsible for the improvement in behavior" (Cooper, Heron, & Heward, 1987, p. 14).

**aqueous humor**   Fluid that occupies the space between the lens and the cornea of the eye.

**arena assessment**   A group assessment procedure sometimes used with infants and preschoolers; professionals from different disciplines (e.g., early childhood specialist, speech-language pathologist, psychologist, physical therapist) seat themselves in a circle around the child and conduct simultaneous evaluations while the child interacts with parent or play materials.

**articulation**   The production of distinct language sounds by the vocal organs.

**Asperger syndrome**   Developmental disorder characterized by normal cognitive and language development with impairments in all social areas, repetitive and stereotyped behaviors, preoccupation with atypical activities or items, pedantic speech patterns, and motor clumsiness; included in autism spectrum disorder.

**assistive technology**   Any item, piece of equipment, or product system, whether acquired commercially off the shelf, modified, or customized, that is used to increase, maintain, or improve the functional capabilities of children with disabilities. (IDEA regulations, 34 C.F.R. § 300.5)

**asthma**   A chronic respiratory condition characterized by repeated episodes of wheezing, coughing, and difficulty breathing.

**astigmatism**   A defect of vision usually caused by irregularities in the cornea; results in blurred vision and difficulties in focusing. Can usually be corrected by lenses.

**ataxia** Poor sense of balance and body position and lack of co-ordination of the voluntary muscles; characteristic of one type of cerebral palsy.

**at risk** A term used to refer to children who are not currently identified as disabled but are considered to have a greater-than-usual chance of developing a disability. Physicians use the terms *at risk* or *high risk* to refer to pregnancies with a greater-than-normal probability of producing a baby with disabilities.

**athetosis** A type of cerebral palsy characterized by large, irregular, uncontrollable twisting motions. The muscles may be tense and rigid or loose and flaccid. Often accompanied by difficulty with oral language.

**attention deficit disorder (ADD)** See *attention deficit/hyperactivity disorder (ADHD)*.

**attention deficit/hyperactivity disorder (ADHD)** Diagnostic category of the American Psychiatric Association for a condition in which a child exhibits developmentally inappropriate inattention, impulsivity, and hyperactivity.

**audiogram** A graph of the faintest level of sound a person can hear in each ear at least 50% of the time at each of several frequencies, including the entire frequency range of normal speech.

**audiologist** A professional who specializes in the evaluation of hearing ability and the treatment of impaired hearing.

**audiology** The science of hearing.

**audiometer** A device that generates sounds at specific frequencies and intensities; used to examine hearing.

**audiometric zero** The smallest sound a person with normal hearing can perceive; also called the zero hearing-threshold level (HTL).

**audition** The act or sense of hearing.

**auditory canal (external acoustic meatus)** Slightly amplifies and transports sound waves from the external ear to the middle ear.

**auditory training** A program that works on listening skills by teaching individuals with hearing impairments to make as much use as possible of their residual hearing.

**augmentative and alternative communication (AAC)** A diverse set of nonspeech communication strategies and methods to assist individuals who are unable to meet their communication needs through speech; includes sign language, symbol systems, communication boards, and synthetic speech devices.

**auricle** External part of the ear; collects sound waves into the auditory canal.

**autism** See *autistic disorder; autism spectrum disorders* (ASD)

**autism spectrum disorders** Group of five related developmental disorders that share common core deficits or difficulties in social relationships, communication, and ritualistic behaviors; differentiated from one another primarily by the age of onset and severity of various systems; includes autistic disorder, Asperger syndrome, Rett syndrome, childhood disintegrative disorder, and pervasive developmental disorder not otherwise specified (PDD-NOS).

**autistic disorder** A pervasive developmental disorder marked by three defining features with onset prior to age 3: (1) impairment of social interaction; (2) impairment of communication; and (3) restricted, repetitive, and stereotyped patterns of behavior, interests, and activities.

**autistic savant** Individual who exhibits extraordinary ability in a specific area such as memorization, mathematical calculations, or musical ability while functioning at the mental retardation level in all other areas; very rare.

**baseline** A measure of the level or amount of a specific target behavior prior to implementation of an intervention designed to change the behavior. Baseline data are used as an objective measure against which to compare and evaluate the results obtained during intervention.

**behavior observation audiometry** A method of hearing assessment in which an infant's reactions to sounds are observed; a sound is presented at an increasing level of intensity until a response, such as head turning, eye blinking, or cessation of play, is reliably observed.

**behavioral contract** A written agreement between two parties in which one agrees to complete a specified task (e.g., a child agrees to complete a homework assignment by the next morning) and in return the other party agrees to provide a specific reward (e.g., the teacher allows the child to have 10 minutes of free time) upon completion of the task.

**behavioral disorder** A disability characterized by behavior that differs markedly and chronically from current social or cultural norms and adversely affects educational performance.

**bilingual special education** Using the child's home language and home culture along with English in an individually designed program of special education.

**binocular vision** Vision using both eyes working together to perceive a single image.

**bipolar disorder** (formerly called *manic-depressive disorder*) Alternative episodes of depressive and manic states; during manic episodes person is in an elevated mood of euphoria and exhibits three or more of the following symptoms: excessive egotism; very little sleep needed; incessant talkativeness; rapidly changing thoughts and ideas in uncontrolled order; easily distracted; agitated, "driven" activities, and participation in personally risky activities.

**blind** Having either no vision or only light perception; learning occurs through other senses.

**blindness, legal** See *legally blind*.

**braille** A system of writing letters, numbers, and other language symbols with a combination of six raised dots. A person who is blind reads the dots with his fingertips.

**bulimia nervosa** Recurrent episodes of binge eating and inappropriate compensatory behavior to prevent weight gain (e.g., self-induced vomiting, misuse of laxatives or other medications, fasting, excessive exercise).

**cataract** A reduction or loss of vision that occurs when the crystalline lens of the eye becomes cloudy or opaque.

**catheter** A tube inserted into the body to permit injections or withdrawal of fluids or to keep a passageway open; often refers to a tube inserted into the bladder to remove urine from a person who does not have effective bladder control.

**cerebral palsy** Motor impairment caused by brain damage, which is usually acquired during the prenatal period or during the birth process. Can involve a wide variety of symptoms (see *ataxia, athetosis, rigidity, spasticity,* and *tremor*) and range from mild to severe. Neither curable nor progressive.

**childhood disintegrative disorder**   Shares behavioral characteristics with autistic disorder, but does not begin until after age two and sometimes not until age 10; medical complications are common; included in the autism spectrum disorders.

**choral responding**   Each student in the class or group responding orally in unison to a question, problem, or item presented by the teacher.

**chorion villus sampling (CVS)**   A procedure for prenatal diagnosis of chromosomal abnormalities that can be conducted during the first 8 to 10 weeks of pregnancy; fetal cells are removed from the chorionic tissue, which surrounds the fetus, and directly analyzed.

**clean intermittent catheterization (CIC)**   A clean (not sterile) catheter (tube) is inserted into the urethra and advanced into the bladder; catheter remains in place until urine is released into a bag.

**cleft palate**   A congenital split in the palate that results in an excessive nasal quality of the voice. Can often be repaired by surgery or a dental appliance.

**closed head injury**   Caused by the head hitting a stationary object with such force that the brain slams against the inside of the cranium; stress of this rapid movement and impact pulls apart and tears nerve fibers or axons of the brain.

**cluttering**   A type of fluency disorder in which speech is very rapid, with extra sounds or mispronounced sounds; speech may be garbled to the point of unintelligibility.

**cochlea**   Main receptor organ for hearing located in the inner ear; tiny hairs within the cochlea transform mechanical energy into neural impulses that then travel through the auditory nerve to the brain.

**communication**   An interactive process requiring at least two parties in which messages are encoded, transmitted, and decoded by any means, including sounds, symbols, and gestures.

**communication disorder**   "An impairment in the ability to receive, send, process, and comprehend concepts or verbal, nonverbal and graphic symbols systems … disorder may be evident in the processes of hearing, language, and/or speech" (ASHA, 1993, p. 40).

**complex partial seizure**   A type of seizure in which an individual goes through a brief period of inappropriate or purposeless activity (also called psychomotor seizure). Usually lasts from two to five minutes, after which the person has amnesia about the entire episode.

**conduct disorder**   A group of behavior disorders including disobedience, disruptiveness, fighting, and tantrums, as identified by Quay (1975).

**conductive hearing loss**   Hearing loss caused by obstructions in the outer or middle ear or malformations that interfere with the conduction of sound waves to the inner ear. Can often be corrected surgically or medically.

**cones**   Light receptors that enable detection of color and detail; located in the center of the retina and function best in good light.

**congenital**   Any condition that is present at birth (contrasts with *adventitious*).

**constant time delay**   A procedure for transferring stimulus control from teacher-provided response prompts to the instructional item itself. The teacher begins by simultaneously presenting the stimulus being taught and a controlling response prompt (e.g., as the teacher holds up a flashcard with the word "ball" printed on it, she says, "Ball"). After a number of zero-second-delay trials the teacher waits for a fixed amount of time (e.g., four seconds) between presentation of the instructional stimulus and the response prompt. Practice trials are repeated with the constant delay until the student begins to respond correctly prior to the teacher's prompt.

**contingency contract**   A document that specifies an if-then relationship between performance of a specified behavior(s) and access to or delivery of a specified reward.

**continuum of services**   The range of different placement and instructional options that a school district can use to serve children with disabilities. Typically depicted as a pyramid, ranging from the least restrictive placement (regular classroom) at the bottom to the most restrictive placement (residential school or hospital) at the top.

**convulsive disorder**   See *epilepsy.*

**cornea**   The transparent part of the eyeball that admits light to the interior.

**cortical visual impairments (CVI)**   Decreased vision or blindness due to known or suspected damage or malfunction of the parts of the brain that interpret visual information.

**cri-du-chat syndrome**   A chromosomal abnormality resulting from deletion of material from the fifth pair of chromosomes. It usually results in severe retardation. Its name is French for "cat cry," named for the high-pitched crying of the child due to a related larynx dysfunction.

**cued speech**   A method of supplementing oral communication by adding cues in the form of eight different hand signals in four different locations near the chin.

**cultural-familial mental retardation**   See *psychosocial disadvantage.*

**cultural interpreter**   An individual who helps school personnel and family members from a diverse culture communicate effectively; may or may not speak the family's home language, but has sufficient understanding of both the home culture and school culture, policies, and practices to help the family and school understand one another.

**cultural pluralism**   The value and practice of respecting, fostering, and encouraging the cultural and ethnic differences that make up society.

**culture**   The established knowledge, ideas, values, and skills shared by a society; its program of survival and adaptation to its environment.

**curriculum-based measurement**   Evaluation of a student's progress in terms of her performance on the skills that comprise the curriculum of the local school.

**curriculum compacting**   Strategy for differentiating curriculum for gifted and talented students by replacing content that students have already mastered with more challenging material.

**cystic fibrosis**   An inherited disorder that causes a dysfunction of the pancreas, mucus, salivary, and sweat glands. Cystic fibrosis causes severe, long-term respiratory difficulties. No cure is currently available.

**cytomegalovirus (CMV)**   A common virus that infects most people worldwide; can remain alive but dormant in the body for life; usually harmless, but in a very small percentage of children infected at birth, CMV may later develop and lead to various conditions including mental retardation, visual impairment, and, most often, hearing impairment.

**deaf**   The result of a hearing loss severe enough so that speech cannot be understood through the ears alone, even with a hearing aid; some sounds may still be perceived.

**deaf-blindness**   Any combination of hearing and visual impairments that causes such severe communication, developmental, and educational needs such that the individual cannot be accommodated in a special education program designed solely for children with hearing impairments or visual impairments.

**decibel (dB)**   The unit of measure for the relative intensity of sound on a scale beginning at zero. Zero dB refers to the faintest sound a person with normal hearing can detect.

**deinstitutionalization**   The social movement to transfer individuals with disabilities, especially persons with mental retardation, from large institutions to smaller, community-based residences and work settings.

**diabetes**   Chronic disease in which the body does not produce or properly use insulin, a hormone needed to convert sugar, starches, and other food into energy (see Type I diabetes).

**diabetic retinopathy**   Visual impairment caused by hemorrhages on the retina and other disorders of blood circulation in people with diabetes.

**dialect**   A variety within a specific language; can involve variation in pronunciation, word choice, word order, and inflected forms.

**differential reinforcement of other behavior (DRO)**   A procedure in which any behavior except the targeted inappropriate response is reinforced; results in a reduction of the inappropriate behavior.

**diplegia**   Paralysis that affects the legs more often than the arms.

**direct instruction**   Any systematic approach to teaching characterized by clear specification of learning objectives, explicit presentation of curriculum content, active engagement by students, systematic feedback for student performance, and evaluation by direct and frequent measures of student learning (a.k.a. little "d," little "i").

**Direct Instruction (DI)**   Published curricula authored by Engelmann and colleagues for teaching reading, math, spelling, language, and thinking skills; DI programs are thoroughly field-tested to ensure effectiveness and feature high rates of student engagement, immediate feedback and error correction, and scripted lessons to ensure consistent instruction.

**disability**   Condition characterized by functional limitations that impede typical development as the result of a physical or sensory impairment or difficulty in learning or social adjustment.

**discrete trial training (DTT)**   Instructional format involving a series of three-part trials: (1) an antecedent stimulus (e.g., flashcard with "2 + 2 = ?"), (2) student response (e.g., "four"), and (3) feedback (reinforcement for a correct response; ignoring or correcting an incorrect response; and providing a response prompt or ignoring nonresponses).

**double-blind, placebo-controlled study**   Procedure used to control for expectancy effects by subjects and bias by researchers in studies evaluating the effects of a treatment or intervention; some subjects receive the actual treatment being tested; others receive a placebo (fake) designed to appear like the actual treatment; subjects do not know whether they are getting the real treatment or a placebo (they are "blind"); the researchers do not know which subjects received the treatment (making it a "double-blind" experiment).

**double hemiplegia**   Paralysis of the arms, with less severe involvement of the legs.

**Down syndrome**   A chromosomal anomaly that often causes moderate to severe mental retardation, along with certain physical characteristics such as a large tongue, heart problems, poor muscle tone, and a broad, flat bridge of the nose.

**dual sensory impairments**   See *deaf-blindness.*

**Duchenne muscular dystrophy**   The most common form of muscular dystrophy, a group of long-term diseases that progressively weaken and waste away the body's muscles.

**due process**   Set of legal steps and proceedings carried out according to established rules and principles; designed to protect an individual's constitutional and legal rights.

**duration (of behavior)**   Measure of how long a person engages in a given activity.

**dysarthia**   A group of speech disorders caused by neuromuscular impairments in respiration, phonation, resonation, and articulation.

**dyslexia**   A specific language-based disorder of constitutional origin characterized by difficulties in single word decoding, usually reflecting insufficient phonological processing. These difficulties, which are not the result of generalized developmental disability or sensory impairment, are often unexpected in relation to age and other cognitive and academic abilities and severely impair the individual's ability to read (Orton Dyslexia Society Research Committee, 1994).

**echolalia**   The repetition of what other people say as if echoing them; characteristic of some children with delayed development, autism, and communication disorders.

**electroencephalograph (EEG)**   Device that detects and records brain wave patterns.

**encephalitis**   Inflammation of the brain; can cause permanent damage to the central nervous system and mental retardation.

**endogenous**   Refers to an inherited cause of a disability or impairment.

**enrichment**   Educational approach that provides a child with extra learning experiences that the standard curriculum would not normally include. Most often used with gifted and talented children.

**epilepsy**   A condition marked by chronic and repeated seizures, disturbances of movement, sensation, behavior, and/or consciousness caused by abnormal electrical activity in the brain (see *generalized tonic-clonic seizure, complex partial seizure, simple partial seizure,* and *absence seizure*). Can usually be controlled with medication, although the drugs may have undesirable side effects. May be temporary or lifelong.

**equal protection**   Legal concept included in the 14th Amendment to the Constitution of the United States, stipulating that no state may deny any person equality or liberty because of that person's classification according to race, nationality, or religion. Several major court cases leading to the passage of P.L. 94–142 (IDEA) found that children with disabilities were not provided with equal protection if they were denied access to an appropriate education solely because of their disabilities.

**ethnocentrism**   The view that the practices of one's own culture are natural and correct, while perceiving the practices of other cultures as odd, amusing, inferior, and/or immoral.

**etiology**   The cause(s) of a disability, impairment, or disease. Includes genetic, physiological, and environmental or psychological factors.

**evoked-response audiometry**   A method of testing hearing by measuring the electrical activity generated by the auditory nerve in response to auditory stimulation. Often used to measure the hearing of infants and children considered difficult to test.

**exceptional children**   Children whose performance deviates from the norm, either below or above, to the extent that special educational programming is needed.

**exogenous**   Refers to a cause of a disability or impairment that stems from factors outside the body such as disease, toxicity, or injury.

**extinction**   A procedure in which reinforcement for a previously reinforced behavior is withheld. If the actual reinforcers that are maintaining the behavior are identified and withheld, the behavior will gradually decrease in frequency until it no longer, or seldom, occurs.

**facilitated communication (FC)**   A type of augmentative communication in which a "facilitator" provides assistance to someone in typing or pointing to vocabulary symbols; typically involves an alphanumeric keyboard on which the user types out his message one letter at a time. To date, research designed to validate FC has repeatedly demonstrated either facilitator influence (correct or meaningful language is produced only when the facilitator "knows" what should be communicated) or no unexpected language competence compared to the participants' measured IQ or a standard language assessment.

**fetal alcohol effects (FAE)**   Term used to identify the suspected etiology of developmental problems experienced by infants and toddlers who have some but not all of the diagnostic criteria for fetal alcohol syndrome (FAS) and have a history of prenatal alcohol exposure.

**fetal alcohol syndrome (FAS)**   A condition sometimes found in the infants of alcoholic mothers; can involve low birth weight, developmental delay, and cardiac, limb, and other physical defects. Caused by excessive alcohol use during pregnancy; often produces serious physical defects and developmental delays; diagnosed when the child has two or more craniofacial malformations and growth is below the 10th percentile for height and weight. FAS is one of the leading known causes of mental retardation. In addition to physical problems, many children with FAS have neurological damage that contributes to cognitive and language delays.

**field of vision**   The expanse of space visible with both eyes looking straight ahead, measured in degrees; 180 degrees is considered normal.

**fluency**   A performance measure that includes both the accuracy and the rate with which a skill is performed; a fluent performer is both accurate and fast. In communication, the term refers to the rate and smoothness of speech; stuttering is the most common fluency disorder in speech.

**foster home**   A living arrangement in which a family shares its home with a person who is not a relative. Long used with children who for some reason cannot live with their parents temporarily, foster homes are now being used with adults with disabilities as well.

**fragile-X syndrome**   A chromosomal abnormality associated with mild to severe mental retardation. Thought to be the most common known cause of inherited mental retardation. Affects males more often and more severely than females; behavioral characteristics are sometimes similar to individuals with autism. Diagnosis can be confirmed by studies of the X chromosome.

**functional analysis**   Experimental manipulation of antecedent or consequent events representing those observed in the child's natural environment to verify their function in either triggering or maintaining problem behavior.

**functional behavior assessment (FBA)**   Systematic process of gathering information about the purposes (functions) a problem behavior serves for an individual; that information then guides the design of three basic types of interventions: indirect assessment (structured interviews with significant others), direct descriptive assessment (systematic observations), and functional analysis (see *functional analysis*).

**generalization**   Extent to which a previously learned knowledge or skill either occurs under conditions different from those under which it was originally learned or is performed in a different but functionally equivalent manner. Situation or setting generalization occurs when a student performs a behavior in the presence of relevant stimuli (e.g., people, settings, instructional materials) other than those that were present originally (e.g., a child who has learned to label baseballs and beach balls as "ball" identifies a basketball as "ball"). Response generalization occurs when a person performs relevant behaviors that were never directly trained but have the same effect on the environment as the original trained behavior (e.g., a child who was taught to say, "Hello, how are you?" and "Hi, nice to see you," as greetings says, "Hi, how are you?").

**generalized anxiety disorder**   Excessive, unrealistic worries, fears, tension that lasts six months or more; in addition to chronic anxiety, symptoms include restlessness, fatigue, difficulty concentrating, muscular aches, insomnia, nausea, excessive heart rate, dizziness, and irritability.

**generalized tonic-clonic seizure**   The most severe type of seizure, in which the individual has violent convulsions, loses consciousness, and becomes rigid. Formerly called grand mal seizure.

**genetic counseling**   A discussion between a specially trained medical counselor and persons who are considering having a baby about the chances of having a baby with a disability, based on the prospective parents' genetic backgrounds.

**glaucoma**  An eye disease characterized by abnormally high pressure inside the eyeball. If left untreated, it can cause total blindness, but if detected early most cases can be arrested.

**grand mal seizure**  See *generalized tonic-clonic seizure.*

**graphic organizers**  Visual-spatial arrangements of information containing words or concepts connected graphically that help students see meaningful hierarchical, comparative, and sequential relationships.

**group home**  A community-based residential alternative for adults with disabilities, most often persons with mental retardation, in which a small group of people live together in a house with one or more support staff.

**group contingencies**  A type of behavior management and motivation procedure in which consequences (rewards and/or penalties) are applied to the entire group or class of students and are contingent upon the behavior of selected students or the entire group.

**guided notes**  Teacher-prepared handouts that provide background information and standard cues with specific spaces where students can write key facts, concepts, and/or relationships during a lecture.

**handicap**  Refers to the problems a person with a disability or impairment encounters in interacting with the environment. A disability may pose a handicap in one environment but not in another.

**handicapism**  Prejudice or discrimination based solely on a person's disability, without regard for individual characteristics.

**hard of hearing**  Level of hearing loss that makes it difficult, although not impossible, to comprehend speech through the sense of hearing alone.

**hearing impairment**  A hearing loss significant enough to require special education, training, and/or adaptations; includes deafness as well as hard-of-hearing conditions.

**hemiplegia**  Paralysis of both the arm and the leg on the same side of the body.

**hemophilia**  An inherited deficiency in blood-clotting ability, which can cause serious internal bleeding.

**hertz (Hz)**  A unit of sound frequency equal to one cycle per second; used to measure pitch.

**human immunodeficiency virus (HIV)**  The virus that causes acquired immune deficiency syndrome (AIDS).

**hydrocephalus**  An enlarged head caused by cerebral spinal fluid accumulating in the cranial cavity; often causes brain damage and severe retardation. A condition present at birth or developing soon afterward. Can sometimes be treated successfully with a shunt.

**hyperactive**  Excessive motor activity or restlessness.

**hyperopia**  Farsightedness; condition in which the image comes to a focus behind the retina instead of on it, causing difficulty in seeing near objects.

**hypertonia**  Muscle tone that is too high; tense, contracted muscles.

**hypotonia**  Muscle tone that is too low; weak, floppy muscles.

**immaturity**  Group of behavior disorders, including short attention span, extreme passivity, daydreaming, preference for younger playmates, and clumsiness, as identified by Quay (1975).

**impedance audiometry**  Procedure for testing middle ear function by inserting a small probe and pump to detect sound reflected by the eardrum.

**incidence**  The percentage of people who, at some time in their lives, will be identified as having a specific condition. Often reported as the number of cases of a given condition per 1,000 people.

**individualized education program (IEP)**  Written document required by the Individuals with Disabilities Education Act (P.L. 94-142) for every child with a disability; includes statements of present performance, annual goals, short-term instructional objectives, specific educational services needed, relevant dates, regular education program participation, and evaluation procedures; must be signed by parents as well as educational personnel.

**individualized family services plan (IFSP)**  A requirement of P.L. 99-457, Education of the Handicapped Act Amendments of 1986, for the coordination of early intervention services for infants and toddlers with disabilities from birth to age 3. Similar to the IEP, which is required for all school-age children with disabilities.

**individualized health care plan (IHCP)**  IEP component for students with special health care needs; specifies health care procedures and services administered by school personnel and a plan for emergencies.

**individualized transition plan (ITP)**  Specifies desired post-school outcomes in four areas (employment, postsecondary education, residential, and recreation/leisure) and instructional programming and supports to help student attain those outcomes; required part of student's IEP by age 16.

**inflection**  Change in pitch or loudness of the voice to indicate mood or emphasis.

**in-service training**  Any educational program designed to provide practicing professionals (e.g., teachers, administrators, physical therapists) with additional knowledge and skills.

**interdisciplinary team**  Group of professionals from different disciplines (e.g., education, psychology, speech and language, medicine) who work together to plan and implement an individualized education program (IEP) for a child with disabilities.

**interindividual differences**  Differences between two or more people in one skill or set of skills.

**interobserver agreement**  The degree to which two or more independent observers record the same results when observing and measuring the same target behavior(s); typically reported as a percentage of agreement.

**interrater agreement**  See *interobserver agreement.*

**intervention**  Any effort made on behalf of children and adults with disabilities; may be preventive (keeping possible problems from becoming a serious disability), remedial (overcoming disability through training or education), or compensatory (giving the individual new ways to deal with the disability).

**intraindividual differences**  Differences within one individual on two or more measures of performance.

**iris**  The opaque, colored portion of the eye that contracts and expands to change the size of the pupil.

**kinesics**  The study of bodily movement, particularly as it relates to and affects communication.

**Klinefelter syndrome**  A chromosomal anomaly in which males receive an extra X chromosome; associated with frequent social retardation, sterility, underdevelopment of male sex organs, development of secondary female sex characteristics, and borderline or mild levels of mental retardation.

**language**   A system used by a group of people for giving meaning to sounds, words, gestures, and other symbols to enable communication with one another. Languages can use vocal (speech sounds) or nonvocal symbols, such as American Sign Language, or use movements and physical symbols instead of sounds.

**language disorder**   Impaired comprehension and/or use of spoken, written, and/or other symbol systems.

**learning channel**   A description of the modes with which a learner receives and sends information in performing a given learning task. Orally reading sight words, for example, uses the "see/say" learning channel; the "hear/write" learning channel is involved in taking a spelling test.

**learning trial**   Consists of three major elements: (1) antecedent (i.e., curricular) stimuli, (2) the student's response to those stimuli, and (3) consequent stimuli (i.e., instructional feedback) following the response; serves as a basic unit of analysis for examining teaching and learning from both the teacher's perspective, as an opportunity to teach, and the student's perspective, as an opportunity to learn (Heward, 1994). Also called a *learn unit* or *practice trial.*

**least restrictive environment (LRE)**   The educational setting that most closely resembles a regular school program and also meets the child's special educational needs. For many students with disabilities, the regular classroom is the LRE; however, the LRE is a relative concept and must be determined for each individual student with disabilities.

**legally blind**   Visual acuity of 20/200 or less in the better eye after the best possible correction with glasses or contact lenses, or vision restricted to a field of 20 degrees or less. Acuity of 20/200 means the eye can see clearly at 20 feet what the normal eye can see at 200 feet.

**lens**   The clear part of the eye that focuses rays of light on the retina.

**longitudinal study**   A research study that follows one subject or group of subjects over an extended period of time, usually several years.

**low-incidence disability**   A disability that occurs relatively infrequently in the general population; often used in reference to sensory impairments, severe and profound mental retardation, autism, and multiple disabilities.

**low vision**   Visual impairment severe enough so that special educational services are required. A child with low vision is able to learn through the visual channel and generally learns to read print.

**macular degeneration**   A deterioration of the central part of the retina, which causes difficulty in seeing details clearly.

**magnitude (of behavior)**   The force with which a response is emitted.

**mainstreaming**   The process of integrating children with disabilities into regular schools and classes.

**maintenance**   Extent to which a learner continues to exhibit a previously learned behavior after a portion or all of the instructional intervention originally used to teach the skill has been terminated.

**manifestation determination**   A review of the relationship between a student's misconduct and his disability conducted by the IEP team and other qualified personnel. Required by the IDEA amendments of 1997 when school officials seek to discipline a student with disabilities in a manner that would result in a change of placement, suspension, or expulsion in excess of 10 days.

**mediated scaffolding**   Refers to a variety of instructional procedures that entail providing the learner with response prompts, cues, and other contrived supports and then gradually withdrawing those supports so student can respond independently to naturally occurring stimuli.

**meningitis**   An inflammation of the membranes covering the brain and spinal cord; can cause problems with sight and hearing and/or mental retardation.

**meningocele**   Type of spina bifida in which the covering of the spinal cord protrudes through an opening in the vertebrae but the cord itself and the nerve roots are enclosed.

**mental retardation**   A disability characterized by significant limitations in both intellectual functioning and conceptual, social, and practical adaptive skills. This disability originates before age 18 (AAMR, 2002).

**microcephalus**   A condition characterized by an abnormally small skull with resulting brain damage and mental retardation.

**milieu teaching strategies**   A variety of strategies used to teach speech and language that naturally occur during real or simulated activities in the home, school, or community environments in which a child normally functions; characterized by dispersed learning trials, following the child's attentional lead within the context of normal conversational interchanges, and teaching the form and content of language in the context of normal use.

**minimal brain dysfunction**   A once-popular term used to describe the learning disabilities of children with no clinical (organic) evidence of brain damage.

**mnemonic strategies**   Memory-enhancing strategies such as acronyms, acrostics, keywords, and pegwords.

**mobility**   The ability to move safely and efficiently from one point to another.

**model program**   A program that implements and evaluates new procedures or techniques in order to serve as a basis for development of other similar programs.

**monoplegia**   Paralysis affecting one limb.

**morpheme**   The smallest element of a language that carries meaning.

**morphology**   Concerned with the basic units of meaning in a language and how those units are combined into words.

**multicultural education**   An educational approach in which a school's curriculum and instructional methods are designed and implemented so that all children acquire an awareness, acceptance, and appreciation of cultural diversity and recognize the contributions of many cultures.

**multifactored assessment**   Assessment and evaluation of a child with a variety of test instruments and observation procedures. Required by IDEA when assessment is for educational placement of a child who is to receive special education services. Prevents the misdiagnosis and misplacement of a student as the result of considering only one test score.

**multiple-gating screening**  A multistep process for screening children who may have disabilities. The initial step casts the broadest net (e.g., a multiple-gated screening for children who may have emotional and behavior problems might begin with teacher nominations); children identified in the first step are assessed more closely in a second step (e.g., a behavior checklist); children who have passed through the first two "gates" are screened further (e.g., direct observations in the classroom).

**muscular dystrophy**  A group of diseases that gradually weakens muscle tissue; usually becomes evident by the age of 4 or 5.

**myelomeningocele**  A protrusion on the back of a child with spina bifida, consisting of a sac of nerve tissue bulging through a cleft in the spine.

**myopia**  Nearsightedness; results when light is focused on a point in front of the retina, resulting in a blurred image for distant objects.

**neurologic impairment**  Any physical disability caused by damage to the central nervous system (brain, spinal cord, ganglia, and nerves).

**neuromotor impairment**  Involves the central nervous system, affecting the ability to move, use, feel, or control certain parts of the body.

**normal curve**  A mathematically derived curve depicting the theoretical probability or distribution of a given variable (such as a physical trait or test score) in the general population. Indicates that approximately 68% of the population will fall within one standard deviation above and below the mean; approximately 27% will fall between one and two standard deviations either above or below the mean; and less than 3% will achieve more extreme scores of more than two standard deviations in either direction.

**normalization**  As a philosophy and principle, the belief that individuals with disabilities should, to the maximum extent possible, be physically and socially integrated into the mainstream of society regardless of the degree or type of disability. As an approach to intervention, the use of progressively more normal settings and procedures "to establish and/or maintain personal behaviors which are as culturally normal as possible" (Wolfensberger, 1972, p. 28).

**nystagmus**  A rapid, involuntary, rhythmic movement of the eyes that may cause difficulty in reading or fixating on an object.

**obsessive/compulsive disorder (OCD)**  Persistent, recurring thoughts (obsessions) that reflect exaggerated anxiety or fears; typical obsessions include worry about being contaminated, behaving improperly, or acting violently. Obsessions may lead an individual to perform compulsive rituals or routines—such as washing hands, repeating phrases or hoarding—to relieve the anxiety caused by the obsession.

**occupational therapist (OT)**  A professional who programs and/or delivers instructional activities and materials to help children and adults with disabilities learn to participate in useful activities.

**ocular motility**  The eye's ability to move.

**open head injury**  Result of penetration of the skull, such as caused by a bullet or a forceful blow to the head with a hard or sharp object.

**operant conditioning audiometry**  Method of measuring hearing by teaching the individual to make an observable response to sound. For example, a child may be taught to drop a block into a box each time a light and a loud tone are presented. Once this response is learned, the light is no longer presented and the volume and pitch of the tone are gradually decreased. When the child no longer drops the block into the box, the audiologist knows the child cannot hear the tone. Sometimes used to test the hearing of nonverbal children and adults.

**ophthalmologist**  A physician who specializes in the diagnosis and treatment of diseases of the eye.

**optic nerve**  The nerve that carries impulses from the eye to the brain.

**optometrist**  A vision professional who specializes in the evaluation and optical correction of refractive errors.

**oral approach**  A philosophy and approach to educating deaf children that stresses learning to speak as the essential element for integration into the hearing world.

**orientation**  The ability to establish one's position in relation to the environment.

**orthopedic impairment**  Impairment of the skeletal system—bones, joints, limbs, and associated muscles.

**ossicles**  Three small bones (hammer, anvil, and stirrup) that transmit sound energy from the middle ear to the inner ear.

**osteogenesis imperfecta**  A hereditary condition in which the bones do not grow normally and break easily; sometimes called brittle bones.

**otitis media**  An infection or inflammation of the middle ear that can cause a conductive hearing loss.

**otologist**  A physician who specializes in the diagnosis and treatment of diseases of the ear.

**overcorrection**  A procedure in which the learner must make restitution for, or repair, the effects of his undesirable behavior and then put the environment in even better shape than it was prior to the misbehavior. Used to decrease the rate of undesirable behaviors.

**paraplegia**  Paralysis of the lower part of the body, including both legs; usually results from injury to or disease of the spinal cord.

**paraprofessionals (in education)**  Trained classroom aides who assist teachers; may include parents.

**partial participation**  Teaching approach that acknowledges that even though an individual with severe disabilities may not be able to independently perform all the steps of a given task or activity, she can often be taught to do selected components or an adapted version of the task.

**perceptual handicap**  A term formerly used to describe some conditions now included under the term *learning disabilities;* usually referred to problems with no known physical cause.

**perinatal**  Occurring at or immediately after birth.

**peripheral vision**  Vision at the outer limits of the field of vision.

**personality disorder**  A group of behavior disorders, including social withdrawal, anxiety, depression, feelings of inferiority, guilt, shyness, and unhappiness, as identified by Quay (1975).

**pervasive developmental disorders–not otherwise specified (PDD-NOS)**   Children who meet some but not all of the criteria for autistic disorder are often diagnosed as having PDD-NOS; included in the autism spectrum disorders.

**petit mal seizure**   See *absence seizure.*

**phenylketonuria (PKU)**   An inherited metabolic disease that can cause severe retardation; can now be detected at birth and the detrimental effects prevented with a special diet.

**phoneme**   The smallest unit of sound that can be identified in a spoken language. There are 45 phonemes, or sound families, in the English language.

**phonological disorder**   A language disorder in which the child produces a given sound correctly in some instances but does not produce the sound correctly at other times.

**phonology**   Refers to the linguistic rules governing a language's sound system.

**photophobia**   Extreme sensitivity of the eyes to light; occurs most notably in albino children.

**physical therapist (PT)**   A professional trained to help people with disabilities develop and maintain muscular and orthopedic capability and make correct and useful movement.

**play audiometry**   A method for assessing a child's hearing ability by teaching the child to perform simple but distinct activities, such as picking up a toy or putting a ball into a cup whenever he hears the signal, either pure tones or speech.

**positive reinforcement**   Presentation of a stimulus or event immediately after a behavior has been emitted, which has the effect of increasing the occurrence of that behavior in the future.

**postlingual**   Occurring after the development of language; usually used to classify hearing losses that begin after a person has learned to speak.

**postnatal**   Occurring after birth.

**post-traumatic stress disorder**   Prolonged and recurrent emotional reactions after exposure to a traumatic event (e.g., sexual or physical assault; unexpected death of a loved one; witnessing or being a victim of a natural disaster, acts of war, or terrorism). Symptoms: flashbacks and nightmares of the traumatic event; avoiding places or things related to the trauma; emotional detachment from others; difficulty sleeping, irritability, or poor concentration.

**practice stage of learning**   After the student has learned how to perform a new skill, she should work to develop fluency with the target skill. Feedback during the practice stage of learning should emphasize the rate or speed with which the student correctly performs the skill.

**Prader-Willi syndrome**   A condition linked to chromosomal abnormality that is characterized by delays in motor development, mild to moderate mental retardation, hypogenital development, an insatiable appetite that often results in obesity, and small features and stature.

**pragmatics**   Study of the rules that govern how language is used in a communication context.

**precision teaching**   An instructional approach that involves (1) pinpointing the skills to be learned; (2) measuring the initial frequency or rate per minute with which the student can perform those behaviors; (3) setting an aim, or goal, for the child's improvement; (4) using direct, daily measurement to monitor progress made under an instructional program; (5) charting the results of those measurements on a *standard celeration chart;* and (6) changing the program if progress is not adequate.

**prelingual**   Describes a hearing impairment acquired before the development of speech and language.

**prenatal**   Occurring before birth.

**prenatal asphyxia**   A lack of oxygen during the birth process usually caused by interruption of respiration; can cause unconsciousness and/or brain damage.

**prevalence**   The number of people who have a certain condition at any given time.

**primary prevention**   Intervention designed to eliminate or counteract risk factors so that a disability is never acquired; aimed at all relevant persons.

**projective tests**   Psychological tests that require a person to respond to a standardized task or set of stimuli (e.g., draw a picture or interpret an ink blot). Responses are thought to be a projection of the test taker's personality and are scored according to the given test's scoring manual to produce a personality profile.

**prosthesis**   Any device used to replace a missing or impaired body part.

**psychomotor seizure**   See *complex partial seizure.*

**psychosocial disadvantage**   Category of causation for mental retardation that requires evidence of subaverage intellectual functioning in at least one parent and one or more siblings (when there are siblings). Typically associated with impoverished environments involving poor housing, inadequate diets, and inadequate medical care. Often used synonymously with cultural-familial retardation; suggests that mental retardation can be caused by a poor social and cultural environment.

**pupil**   The circular hole in the center of the iris of the eye, which contracts and expands to let light pass through.

**quadriplegia**   Paralysis of all four limbs.

**rate (or frequency of behavior)**   A measure of how often a particular action is performed; usually reported as the number of responses per standard unit of time (e.g., 5 per minute).

**refraction**   The bending or deflection of light rays from a straight path as they pass from one medium (e.g., air) into another (e.g., the eye). Used by eye specialists in assessing and correcting vision.

**regular education initiative (REI)**   A position advocated by some special educators that students with disabilities can and should be educated in regular classrooms under the primary responsibility of the general education program.

**rehabilitation**   A social service program designed to teach a newly disabled person basic skills needed for independence.

**reinforcement**   See *positive reinforcement.*

**related services**   Developmental, corrective, and other supportive services required for a child with disabilities to benefit from special education. Includes special transportation services, speech and language pathology, audiology, psychological services, physical and occupational therapy, school health services, counseling and medical services for diagnostic and evaluation purposes, rehabilitation counseling, social work services, and parent counseling and training.

**remediation** An educational program designed to teach a person to overcome a disability through training and education.

**residual hearing** The remaining hearing, however slight, of a person who is deaf.

**resource room** Classroom in which special education students spend part of the school day and receive individualized special education services.

**respite care** The temporary care of an individual with disabilities by nonfamily members; provides much-needed support for many families of children with severe disabilities.

**response cards** Cards, signs, or items that are simultaneously held up by all students to display their response to a question or problem presented by the teacher; response cards enable every student in the class to respond to each question or item.

**response cost** A procedure for reducing the frequency of inappropriate behavior by withdrawing a specific amount of reinforcement contingent upon occurrence of the behavior.

**response to instruction** An approach for identifying learning disabilities. The at-risk child receives intensive supplemental tutoring using a research-validated program for fixed-duration trial; failure to respond to the intensive instruction confirms the presence of a learning disability.

**retina** A sheet of nerve tissue at the back of the eye on which an image is focused.

**retinitis pigmentosa (RP)** An eye disease in which the retina gradually degenerates and atrophies, causing the field of vision to become progressively more narrow.

**retinopathy of prematurity (ROP)** A condition characterized by an abnormally dense growth of blood vessels and scar tissue in the eye, often causing visual field loss and retinal detachment. Usually caused by high levels of oxygen administered to premature infants in incubators. Also called retrolental fibroplasia (RLF).

**retrolental fibroplasia (RLF)** See *retinopathy of prematurity*.

**Rett syndrome** Neurodevelopmental disorder of childhood characterized by normal early development followed by loss of purposeful use of the hands, distinctive hand movements, slowed brain and head growth, gait abnormalities, seizures, and mental retardation; affects females almost exclusively; included in autism spectrum disorders.

**Reye's syndrome** A relatively rare disease that appears to be related to a variety of viral infections; most common in children over the age of 6. About 30% of children who contract it die; survivors sometimes show signs of neurological damage and mental retardation. The cause is unknown, although some studies have found an increased risk after the use of aspirin during a viral illness.

**rigidity** A type of cerebral palsy characterized by increased muscle tone, minimal muscle elasticity, and little or no stretch reflex.

**rods** Light receptors for peripheral vision, detection of movement, and vision in dim light; located around the periphery of the retina.

**rubella** German measles; when contracted by a woman during the first trimester of pregnancy, may cause visual impairments, hearing impairments, mental retardation, and/or other congenital impairments in the child.

**schizophrenia** A severe psychotic disorder characterized by delusions, hallucinations (hearing voices), unfounded fears of persecution, disorganized speech, catatonic behavior (stupor and muscular rigidity), restricted range and intensity of emotional expression (affective flattening), reduced thought and speech productivity and decreased initiation of goal-directed behavior. Most persons with schizophrenia alternate between acute psychotic episodes and stable phases with few or no symptoms.

**screening** A procedure in which groups of children are examined and/or tested in an effort to identify children who are most likely to have a disability; identified children are then referred for more intensive examination and assessment.

**secondary prevention** Intervention directed at reducing or eliminating the effects of existing risk factors; aimed at individuals exposed to or displaying specific risk factors.

**selective mutism** Speaking normally in some settings or situations and not speaking in others.

**self-contained class** A special classroom, usually located within a regular public school building, that includes only exceptional children.

**self-determination** A combination of skills, knowledge, and beliefs that enable a person to engage in goal-directed, self-regulated, autonomous behavior; includes skills such as choice/decision making, goal setting, problem solving, self-evaluation, self-management, self-advocacy, and self-awareness.

**self-evaluation** Comparing the results of a self-assessment of one's performance with a standard or goal, which may or may not be self-determined.

**self-monitoring** A behavior change procedure in which an individual observes and records the frequency and/or quality of his own behavior.

**semantics** The study of meaning in language.

**sensorineural hearing loss** A hearing loss caused by damage to the auditory nerve or the inner ear.

**severe disabilities** Term used to refer to challenges faced by individuals with severe and profound mental retardation, autism, and/or physical/sensory impairments combined with marked developmental delay. Persons with severe disabilities exhibit extreme deficits in intellectual functioning and need systematic instruction for basic skills such as self-care and communicating with others.

**shaping** A process for teaching new behavior through differential reinforcement of successive approximations of targeted performance.

**sheltered workshop** A structured work environment where persons with disabilities receive employment training and perform work for pay. May provide transitional services for some individuals (e.g., short-term training for competitive employment in the community) and permanent work settings for others.

**shunt** Tube that diverts fluid from one part of the body to another; often implanted in people with hydrocephalus to remove extra cerebrospinal fluid from the head and send it directly into the heart or intestines.

**simple partial seizure** A type of seizure characterized by sudden jerking motions with no loss of consciousness. Partial seizures may occur weekly, monthly, or only once or twice a year.

**Snellen chart** A chart used to test visual acuity; developed by a Dutch ophthalmologist in 1862 and still used today. Consists of rows of letters, or Es facing up, down, left, or right; each row corresponds to the distance that a normally sighted person can discriminate the letters.

**social validity** A desirable characteristic of the objectives, procedures, and results of intervention, indicating their appropriateness for the learner. For example, the goal of riding a bus independently would have social validity for students residing in most cities but not for those in small towns or rural areas.

**socialized aggression** A group of behavior disorders, including truancy, gang membership, theft, and delinquency, as identified by Quay (1975).

**spasticity** A type of cerebral palsy characterized by tense, contracted muscles.

**special education** Individually planned, specialized, intensive, outcome-directed instruction. When practiced most effectively and ethically, special education is also characterized by the systematic use of research-based instructional methods, the application of which is guided by frequent measures of student performance.

**speech** A system of using breath and muscles to create specific sounds for communicating.

**speech audiometry** Tests a person's detection and understanding of speech by presenting a list of two-syllable words at different decibel (sound volume) levels.

**speech impairment** Speech that "deviates so far from the speech of other people that it (1) calls attention to itself, (2) interferes with communication, or (3) provokes distress in the speaker or the listener" (Van Riper & Erickson, 1996, p. 110). The three basic types of speech disorders are articulation, fluency, and voice.

**speechreading** Process of understanding a spoken message by observing the speaker's lips in combination with information gained from facial expressions, gestures, and the context or situation.

**speech reception threshold (SRT)** The decibel (sound volume) level at which an individual can understand half of the words during a speech audiometry test; the SRT is measured and recorded for each ear.

**spina bifida** A congenital malformation of the spine in which the vertebrae that normally protect the spine do not develop fully; may involve loss of sensation and severe muscle weakness in the lower part of the body.

**spina bifida occulta** A type of spina bifida that usually does not cause serious disability. Although the vertebrae do not close, there is no protrusion of the spinal cord and membranes.

**standard celeration chart** Chart for graphically displaying a student's learning progress from day to day in terms of changes in the frequency of correct and incorrect responses per minute.

**standard deviation** A descriptive statistic that shows the average amount of variability among a set of scores. A small standard deviation indicates that the scores in the sample are distributed close to the mean; a larger standard deviation indicates that more scores in the sample fall farther from the mean.

**stereotype** An overgeneralized or inaccurate attitude held toward all members of a particular group, on the basis of a common characteristic such as age, sex, race, or disability.

**stereotypic behavior (stereotypy)** Repetitive, nonfunctional movements (e.g., hand flapping, rocking).

**stimulus control** Occurs when a behavior is emitted more often in the presence of a particular stimulus than it is in the absence of that stimulus.

**strabismus** A condition in which one eye cannot attain binocular vision with the other eye because of imbalanced muscles.

**stuttering** Fluency disorder of speaking marked by rapid-fire repetitions of consonant or vowel sounds, especially at the beginning of words, prolongations; hesitations; interjections; and complete verbal blocks.

**supported employment** Providing ongoing, individualized supports to persons with disabilities to help them find, learn, and maintain paid employment at regular work sites in the community.

**supported living** Personalized networks of natural supports to help people with disabilities live successfully in homes of their own in the community.

**syntax** The system of rules governing the meaningful arrangement of words in a language.

**systematic replication** A strategy for extending and determining the generality of research findings by changing one or more variables from a previous study to see if similar results can be obtained. For example, testing a particular instructional method with elementary students that a previous study found effective with secondary students.

**task analysis** Breaking a complex skill or chain of behaviors into smaller, teachable units.

**Tay-Sachs disease** A progressive nervous system disorder causing profound mental retardation, deafness, blindness, paralysis, and seizures. Usually fatal by age 5. Caused by a recessive gene; blood test can identify carrier; analysis of enzymes in fetal cells provides prenatal diagnosis.

**tertiary prevention** Intervention designed to minimize the impact of a specific condition or disability; aimed at individuals with a disability.

**time out** A behavior management technique that involves removing the opportunity for reinforcement for a specific period of time following an inappropriate behavior; results in a reduction of the inappropriate behavior.

**time trials** A fluency-building procedure in which a student performs a new skill as many times as she can during a short period of time; one-minute time trials are effective for most academic skills.

**token economy (token reinforcement system)** An instructional and behavior management system in which students earn tokens (e.g., stars, points, poker chips) for performing specified behaviors. Students accumulate their tokens and exchange them at prearranged times for their choice of activities or items from a menu of backup rewards (e.g., stickers, hall monitor for a day).

**topography (of behavior)**   The physical shape or form of a response.

**total communication**   An approach to educating deaf students that combines oral speech, sign language, and fingerspelling.

**Tourette syndrome**   An inherited neurological disorder characterized by motor and vocal tics (repeated, involuntary movements) such as eye blinking, facial grimacing, throat clearing, arm thrusting, or kicking. About 15% of cases include *coprolalia* (repeated cursing, obscene language and ethnic slurs). Symptoms typically appear before age 18; males affected 3 to 4 times more often than females.

**traumatic brain injury**   An acquired injury to the brain caused by an external physical force, resulting in total or partial functional disability, psychosocial impairments, or both that adversely affects a child's educational performance.

**tremor**   A type of cerebral palsy characterized by regular, strong, uncontrolled movements. May cause less overall difficulty in movement than other types of cerebral palsy.

**triplegia**   Paralysis of any three limbs; relatively rare.

**tunnel vision**   Visual impairment in which a person has good central vision but poor peripheral vision.

**Turner's syndrome**   A sex chromosomal disorder in females, resulting from an absence of one of the X chromosomes; lack of secondary sex characteristics, sterility, and short stature are common. Although not usually a cause of mental retardation, it is often associated with learning problems.

**tympanic membrane (eardrum)**   Located in the middle ear, the eardrum moves in and out to variations in sound pressure, changing acoustical energy to sound energy.

**Type I diabetes (formerly called *juvenile diabetes* or *early-onset diabetes*)**   A disease characterized by inadequate secretion or use of insulin and the resulting excessive sugar in the blood and urine. Managed with diet and/or medication but can be difficult to control. Can cause coma and eventually death if left untreated or treated improperly. Can also lead to visual impairments and limb amputation. Not curable at the present time.

**universal precautions**   A set of safety guidelines (e.g., wearing protective gloves) that interrupt the chain of infection spread by potential biohazards such as blood and bodily fluids.

**Usher's syndrome**   An inherited combination of visual and hearing impairments. Usually, the person is born with a profound hearing loss and loses vision gradually in adulthood because of retinitis pigmentosa, which affects the visual field.

**visual acuity**   The ability to clearly distinguish forms or discriminate details at a specified distance.

**visual cortex**   Interprets electrical signals from the optic nerve into visual images; located in the occipital lobe at the back of the brain.

**visual efficiency**   A term used to describe how effectively a person uses his vision. Includes such factors as control of eye movements, near and distant visual acuity, and speed and quality of visual processing.

**vitreous humor**   The jellylike fluid that fills most of the interior of the eyeball.

**vocational rehabilitation**   A program designed to help adults with disabilities obtain and hold employment.

**voice disorder**   "Abnormal production and/or absences of vocal quality, pitch, loudness, resonance, and/or duration, which is inappropriate for an individual's age and/or sex" (ASHA, 1993, p. 40).

**work activity center**   A sheltered work and activity program for adults with severe disabilities; teaches concentration and persistence, along with basic life skills, for little or no pay.

# References

Aaroe, L., & Nelson, J. R. (2000). A comparative analysis of teachers', Caucasian parents', and Hispanic parents' view of problematic school survival behaviors. *Education and Treatment of Children, 23,* 314–324.

Abikoff, H. (1991). Cognitive training in ADHD children: Less to it than meets the eye. *Journal of Learning Disabilities, 24,* 205–209.

Achenbach, T. M., & Edelbrock, C. S. (1991). *Manual for the child behavior checklist.* Burlington: University of Vermont, Department of Psychiatry.

Ad Hoc Committee on Terminology and Classification. (2001). Request for comment on proposed new edition of *Mental Retardation: Definition, classification, and systems of supports. AAMR News and Notes, 14*(5), 1, 9–12.

Adams, G., & Carnine, D. (2003). Direct Instruction. In H. L. Swanson, K. R. Harris, & S. Graham (Eds.), *Handbook of learning disabilities* (pp. 403–416). New York: Guilford.

Adelman, H. S. (1994). Intervening to enhance home involvement in schooling. *Intervention in School and Clinic, 29*(5), 276–284.

Agran, M., Blanchard, C., Wehmeyer, M., & Hughes, C. (2002). Increasing problem-solving skills of students with developmental disabilities participating in general education. *Remedial and Special Education, 23,* 279–288.

Agran, M., Snow, K., & Swaner, J. (1999). Teacher percpetions of self-determination: Benefits, characteristics, and strategies. *Education and Training in Mental Retardation and Developmental Disabilities, 34,* 293–301.

Aiello, B. (1976, April 25). Up from the basement: A teacher's story. *New York Times,* p. 14.

Akshoomoff, N. (2000). *Neurological underpinnings of autism* (Vol. 9). Baltimore: Brookes.

Al Otaiba, S. (2001). IRA outstanding dissertation award for 2001: Children who do not respond to early literacy instruction: A longitudinal study across kindergarten and first grade [Abstract]. *Reading Research Quarterly, 36,* 344–345.

Al Otaiba, S., & Hosp, M. K. (2004). Providing effective literacy instruction to students with Down syndrome. *Teaching Exceptional Children, 36*(4), 28–35.

Al Otaiba, S., & Smartt, S. M. (2003). Summer sound camp: Involving parents in early literacy intervention for children with speech and language delays. *Teaching Exceptional Children, 35*(3), 30–34.

Alber, S. R., & Heward, W. L. (2000). Teaching students to recruit positive attention: A review and recommendations. *Journal of Behavioral Education, 10,* 177–204.

Alber, S. R., & Walshe, S. E. (2004). When to self-correct spelling words: A systematic replication. *Journal of Behavioral Education, 13,* 51–66.

Alber, S. R., Heward, W. L., & Hippler, B. J. (1999). Training middle school students with learning disabilities to recruit positive teacher attention. *Exceptional Children, 65,* 253–270.

Alber, S. R., Nelson, J. S., & Brennan, K. B. (2002). A comparative analysis of two homework study methods on elementary and secondary school students' acquisition and maintenance of social studies content. *Education and Treatment of Children, 26,* 172–196.

Alberto, P. A., & Fredrick, L. D. (2000). Teaching picture reading as an enabling skill. *Teaching Exceptional Children, 33*(6), 60–64.

Alberto, P. A., & Troutman, A. C. (2006). *Applied behavior analysis for teachers* (7th ed.). Upper Saddle River, NJ: Merrill/Prentice Hall.

Aldrich, F. K., & Parkin, A. J. (1989). Listening at speed. *British Journal of Visual Impairment, 7*(1), 16–18.

Algozzine, B., Audette, B., Ellis, E., Marr, M. B., & White, R. (2000). Supporting teacher, principals, and students, through unified discipline. *Teaching Exceptional Children, 33*(2), 42–47.

Algozzine, B., Browder, D., Karvonen, M., Test, D. W., & Wood, W. M. (2001). Effects of interventions to promote self-determination for individuals with disabilities. *Review of Educational Research, 71,* 219–277.

Algozzine, B., & Kay, P. (Eds.). (2002). *Preventing problem behaviors: A handbook of successful prevention strategies.* Thousand Oaks, CA: Corwin.

Allen, C. P., White, J., & Test, D. W. (1992). Using a picture/symbol form for self-monitoring within a community-based training program. *Teaching Exceptional Children, 24*(2), 54–56.

Allen, D. A., & Affleck, G. (1985). Are we stereotyping parents? A postscript to Blacher. *Mental Retardation, 23,* 200–202.

Allen, T. (1986). Patterns of academic achievement among hearing impaired students: 1974 and 1983. In A. Schildroth & M. Karchmer (Eds.), *Deaf children in America* (pp. 161–206). San Diego: Little, Brown.

Allen, T. E. (1994). *Who are the deaf and hard-of-hearing students leaving high school and entering postsecondary education?* Unpublished manuscript, Gallaudet University, Center for Assessment and Demographic Studies, Washington, DC.

Al-Hassan, S., & Gardner, III, R. (2002). Involving immigrant parents of students with disabilities in the educational process. *Teaching Exceptional Children, 35*(2), 52–58.

American Association on Mental Retardation. (2002). *Mental retardation: Definition, classification, and systems of supports* (10th ed.). Washington, DC: Author.

American Council on Science and Health. (1979, May). *Diet and hyperactivity: Is there a relationship?* New York: Author.

American Printing House for the Blind. (1992). *Annual report.* Louisville, KY: Author.

American Psychiatric Association. (1999). *Obsessive-compulsive disorder.* Washington, DC: Author. http://www.psych.org.

American Psychiatric Association. (2000a). *Diagnostic and statistical manual of mental disorders, text revision: DSM-IV-TR* (4th ed.). Washington, DC: Author.

American Psychiatric Association. (2000b). *Practice guideline for the treatment of patients with schizophrenia.* Washington, DC: Author. http://www. psych.org/clin_res/pg_schizo.cfm.

American Psychiatric Association. (2000c). *Practice guideline for the treatment of patients with bipolar disorder.* Washington, DC: Author. http://www. psych.org/clin_res/pg_bipolar.cfm.

American Psychological Association. (1994, August). *Resolution on facilitated communication by the American Psychological Association.* Washington, DC: Author.

American Speech-Language-Hearing Association. (1983). Position paper on social dialects. *ASHA, 25*(9), 23–27.

American Speech-Language-Hearing Association. (1995). Position paper and guidelines for acoustics in educational settings. *ASHA, 37*(Suppl. 14), 15–19.

American Speech-Language-Hearing Association. (1996, Spring). Inclusive practices for children and youths with communication disorders: Position statement and technical report). *ASHA, 38* (Suppl. 16), 33–44.

American Speech-Language-Hearing Association. (2000). *Healthy people 2010—Health objectives for the nation and roles for speech-language pathologists and speech-language-hearing scientists.* Rockville, MD: Author.

American Speech-Language-Hearing Association. (2001a). *Effects of hearing loss.* http://www.asha.org.

American Speech-Language-Hearing Association. (2001b). *Language and literacy development.* Washington, DC: U.S. Department of Education and American Speech-Language-Hearing Association. http://www.asha.org/speech/development/languagedevelopment.cfm.

American Speech-Language-Hearing Association. (ASHA). (2001c). *Pragmatics, socially speaking.* www.asha.org.

American Speech-Language-Hearing Association. (ASHA). (2001d). Roles and responsibilities of speech-language pathologists with respect to reading and writing in children and adolescents. (Position statement, executive summary of guidelines, technical report). *ASHA Supplement 21,* 17–27. Rockville, MD: Author.

American Speech-Language-Hearing Association. (ASHA). (2001e). *Schools survey.* www.asha.org.

American Speech-Language-Hearing Association. (2004). *Pragmatics, socially speaking.* www.asha.org. Retrieved July 16, 2004.

Anderegg, M. L., Vergason, G. A., & Smith, M. C. (1992). A visual representation of the grief cycle for use by teachers with families of children with disabilities. *Remedial and Special Education, 13*(2), 17–23.

Anderson, C., & Katsiyannis, A. (1997). By what token economy: A classroom learning tool for inclusive settings. *Teaching Exceptional Children, 29*(4), 65–67.

Anderson, J. A., & Matthews, B. (2001). We CARE for students with emotional and behavioral disabilities and their families. *Teaching Exceptional Children, 33*(5), 34–39.

Anderson, S. R., & Romancyzk, R. G. (1999). Early intervention for young children with autism: Continuum-based models. *Journal of The Association for Persons with Severe Handicaps, 24,* 162–173.

Andrews, J. F., Leigh, I. W., & Weiner, M. T. (2004). *Deaf people: Evolving perspectives from psychology, education, and sociology.* Boston: Allyn & Bacon.

Anthony, D. (1971). *Signing essential English.* Anaheim, CA: Anaheim School District.

Antunez, B. (2000). *When everyone is involved: Parents and communities in school reform.* National Council for Bilingual Education. http://www.ncbe.gwu.edu/ncbepubs/tasynthesis/framing/6parents.htm.

Anxiety Disorders Association of America. (2001). *Brief overview of anxiety disorders.* Rockville, MD: Author. [On-line].

Available: http://www.adaa.org/AnxietyDisorderInfor/OverviewAnxDis.cfm.

Apple, D. F., Anson, C. A., Hunter, J. D., & Bell, R. B. (1995). Spinal cord injury in youth. *Clinical Pediatrics, 34,* 90–95.

Ardoin, S. P., Martens, B. K., & Wolfe, L. A. (1999). Using high-probability instruction sequences with fading to increase student compliance during transitions. *Journal of Applied Behavior Analysis, 32,* 339–351.

Armbruster, B. B., Lehr, F., & Osborn, J. (2003). *Put reading first: The research building blocks for teaching children to read, kindergarten through grade 3.* Jessup, MD: National Institute for Literacy.

Armendariz, F., & Umbreit, J. (1999). Using active responding to reduce disruptive behavior in a general education classroom. *Journal of Positive Behavior Interventions, 1,* 152–158.

Armstrong v. Kline, 476 F. Supp. 583 (E.D. Pa. 1979), *modified and remanded sub nom.,* Battle vs. Commonwealth of Pennsylvania, 629 F.2d 259 (3rd Cr. 1980), on remand, 513 F. Supp. 425 (E.D. Ps. 1980), *cert. denied sub nom.,* Scanlon v. Battle 101 S.Ct. 3123 (1981).

Arnold, L. E., Christopher, J., Huestis, R. D., & Smeltzer, D. J. (1978). Megavitamins for minimal brain dysfunction: A placebo controlled study. *Journal of the American Medical Association, 240,* 2642–2643.

Arrasmith, D. (2003). *Definition of explicit instruction and systematic curriculum.* Retrieved April 19, 2004, from http://www.studydog.com/.

Arter, C. (1997). Listening skills. In H. Mason & S. McCall (Eds.), *Visual impairment: Access to education for children and young people* (pp. 143–148). London: Fulton.

Artiles, A. J., Aguirre-Munoz, Z., & Abedi, J. (1998). Predicting placement in learning disabilities programs: Do predictors vary by ethnic group? *Exceptional Children, 64,* 543–559.

Artiles, A., & Zamora-Durán, G. (1997). *Reducing disproportionate representation of culturally diverse students in special and gifted education.* Reston, VA: Council for Exceptional Children.

Asthma and Allergy Foundation of America. (2001). *Facts and figures.* Washington, DC: Author. www.aafa.org.

Ault, M. M., Rues, J. P., Graff, J. C., & Holvoet, J. F. (2006). Special health care procedures. In M. E. Snell & F. Brown (Eds.), *Instruction of students with severe disabilities* (6th ed.). Upper Saddle River, NJ: Merrill/Prentice Hall.

Austin, J. L., Lee, M. G., Thibeault, M. D., Carr, J. E., & Bailey, J. S. (2002). Effects of guided notes on university students' responding and recall of information. *Journal of Behavioral Education, 11,* 243–254.

Autism Research Institute. (1998). Another genetic defect linked to autistic behavior, retardation. *Autism Research Review International, 12*(1), 4.

Autism Society of America. (2000). *Advocate, 33*(1), 3.

Award-winning researchers raise questions about "inclusion." (2001). *DLD Times, 18*(2), 4.

Baer, D. M. (1998). *How to plan for generalization* (2nd ed.). Austin, TX: PRO-ED.

Baer, D. M. (1999). *How to plan for generalization* (2nd ed.). Austin, TX: PRO-ED.

Baer, D. M. (2005). Letters to a lawyer. In W. L. Heward, T. E. Heron, N. A. Neef, S. M. Peterson, D. M. Sainato, G. Cartledge, R. Gardner III, L. D. Peterson, S. B. Hersh, & J. C. Dardig (Eds.), *Focus on behavior analysis in education: Achievements, challenges, and opportunities* (pp. 3–30). Upper Saddle River, NJ: Merrill/Prentice Hall.

Baer, R. M., Flexer, R. W., Beck, S., Amstutz, N., Hoffman, L., Brothers, J., Stelzer, D., & Zechman, C. (2003). A collaborative follow-up study on transition service utilization and postschool outcomes. *Career Development for Exceptional Individuals, 26,* 7–25.

Bagnato, S. J., Neisworth, J. T., & Munson, S. M. (1997). *LINKing assessment and early intervention: An authentic curriculum-based approach.* Baltimore: Brookes.

Bailey, D., Skinner, D., Correa, V., Arcia, E., Reyes-Blanes, M., Rodriguez, P., Vazquez, E., & Skinner, M. (1999). Needs and supports reported by Latino families of young children with developmental disabilities. *American Journal on Mental Retardation, 104,* 437–451.

Bailey, D., Skinner, D., Correa, V., Blanes, M., Vasquez, E., & Rodriguez, P. (1999). Awareness, use, and satisfaction with services for Latino parents of young children with disabilities. *Exceptional Children, 65,* 367–381.

Bailey, D. B., & Simeonsson, R. J. (1988). *Family assessment in early intervention.* Upper Saddle River, NJ: Merrill/Prentice Hall.

Bailey, D. B., & Wolery, M. (1992). *Teaching infants and preschoolers with disabilities* (2nd ed.). Upper Saddle River, NJ: Merrill/Prentice Hall.

Bailey, J. S. (1992). Gentle teaching: Trying to win friends and influence people with euphemism, metaphor, smoke, and mirrors. *Journal of Applied Behavior Analysis, 25,* 879–883.

Bak, S. (1999). Relationships between inappropriate behaviors and other factors in young children with visual impairments. *RE:view, 31,* 84–91.

Baker, B. L. (1989). *Parent training and developmental disabilities.* Washington, DC: American Association on Mental Retardation.

Baker, E., Wang, M., & Walberg, H. (1995). The effects of inclusion in learning. *Educational Leadership, 52*(4), 33–34.

Baker, J. M., & Zigmond, N. (1995). The meaning and practice of inclusions for students with learning disabilities: Themes and implications for the five cases. *Journal of Special Education, 29,* 163–180.

Baker, S., & Baker, K. (1997). Educating children who are deaf or hard of hearing: Bilingual-bicultural education. *ERIC Digest #553*. (ERIC Document Reproduction Service No. ED 416 671).

Baker, S., Gersten, R., & Scanlon, D. (2002). Procedural facilitators and cognitive strategies: Tools for unraveling the mysteries of comprehension and the writing process, and for providing meaningful access to the general curriculum. *Learning Disabilities Research & Practice, 17,* 65–77.

Bambara, L. M., & Ager, C. (1992). Using self-scheduling to promote self-directed leisure activity in home and community settings. *Journal of The Association for Persons with Severe Handicaps, 17,* 67–76.

Bambara, L., & Koger, F. (1996). *Innovations: Providing opportunities for choice throughout the day.* Washington, DC: American Association on Mental Retardation.

Bambara, L. M., Browder, D. M., & Koger, F. (2006). Home and community. In M. E. Snell & F. Brown (Eds.), *Instruction of students with severe disabilities* (6th ed.). Upper Saddle River, NJ: Merrill/Prentice Hall.

Banks, J. A., & Banks, C. A. M. (Eds.). (2004). *Multicultural education: Issues and perspectives* (5th ed.). Boston: Allyn & Bacon.

Bannerman, D. J., Sheldon, J. B., Sherman, J. A., & Harchik, A. E. (1990). Balancing the right to habilitation with the right to personal liberties: The rights of people with developmental disabilities to eat too many doughnuts and take a nap. *Journal of Applied Behavior Analysis, 23,* 79–89.

Barbetta, P. M. (1990a). GOALS: A group-oriented adapted levels system for children with behavior disorders. *Academic Therapy, 25,* 645–656.

Barbetta, P. M. (1990b). Red light—green light: A classwide management system for students with behavior disorders in the primary grades. *Preventing School Failure, 34*(4), 14–19.

Barbetta, P. M. (2002, January). Personal communication.

Barbetta, P. M., & Heron, T. E. (1991). Project SHINE: Summer home instruction and evaluation. *Intervention in School and Clinic, 26,* 276–281.

Barfels, M., Heward, W. L., & Al-Attrash, M. (1999). Using audio prompts to improve work performance by adults with developmental disabilities in an enclave supported employment setting. Manuscript submitted for publication.

Barkley, R. A. (1998). *Attention-deficit/ hyperactivity disorder: A handbook for diagnosis and treatment* (2nd ed.). New York: Guilford.

Barkley, R. A., Fischer, M., Edelbrock, C. S., & Smallish, L. (1990). The adolescent outcome of hyperactive children diagnosed by research criteria: I. An eight-year prospective follow-up study. *Journal of the American Academy of Children and Adolescent Psychiatry, 29,* 546–557.

Barlow, J. A. (2001). Prologue: Recent advances in phonological theory and treatment. *Language, Speech, and Hearing Services in Schools, 32,* 225–228.

Barnes, S. B., & Whinnery, K. W. (2002). Effects of functional mobility skills training for young students with physical disabilities. *Exceptional Children, 68,* 313–324.

Barnett, S. W., & Boyce, G. C. (1994). Effects of children with Down syndrome on parents' activities. *American Journal of Mental Retardation, 100,* 115–127.

Barnhill, G. P., Hagiwara, T., Myles, B. S., Simpson, R. L., Brick, M. L., & Griswold, D. E. (2000). Parent, teacher, and self–report of problems and adaptive behaviors in children and adolescents with Asperger syndrome. *Diagnostique, 25*(2), 147–167.

Baron-Cohen, S., Allen, J., & Gillberg, C. (1992). Can autism be detected at 18 months? The needle, the haystack, and the CHAT. *British Journal of Psychiatry, 161,* 839–843.

Barraga, N. C., & Erin, J. N. (2001). *Visual impairments and learning* (4th ed.). Austin, TX: Exceptional Resources.

Barrera, I. (1995). To refer or not to refer: Untangling the web of diversity, "deficit," and disability. *New York State Association for Bilingual Education Journal, 10,* 54–66.

Bat-Chava, Y. (2000). Diversity of deaf identities. *American Annals of the Deaf, 145,* 420–428.

Bateman, B. D., & Linden, M. L. (1998). *Better IEPs: How to develop legally correct and educationally useful programs* (3rd ed.). Longmont, CO: Sopris West.

Batshaw, M. L. (Ed.). (2002). *Children with disabilities* (5th ed.). Baltimore: Brookes.

Battle, D. E. (Ed.). (1998). *Communication disorders in multicultural populations* (2nd ed.). Boston: Butterworth-Heinemann.

Bauer, A. M., & Brown, G. M. (2001). *Adolescents and inclusions: Transforming secondary schools.* Baltimore: Brookes.

Bauer, A. M., & Ulrich, M. E. (2002). "I've got a Palm in my pocket": Using handheld computers in an inclusive classroom. *Teaching Exceptional Children, 35*(2), 18–22.

Baumgart, D., & Giangreco, M. F. (1996). Key lessons learned about inclusion. In D. H. Lehr & F. Brown (Eds.), *People with disabilities who challenge the system* (pp. 79–97). Baltimore: Brookes.

Baumgart, D., Brown, L., Pumpian, I., Nisbet, J., Ford, A., Sweet, M., Messina, R., & Schroeder, J. (1982). Principle of partial participation and individualized adaptations in educational programs for severely handicapped students. *Journal of The Association for Persons with Severe Handicaps, 7,* 17–27.

Bayley, N. (1993). *Bayley Scales of Infant Development manual—Second edition manual.* San Antonio, TX: Psychological Corporation.

Beakley, B. A., & Yoder, S. L. (1998). Middle schoolers learn community skills. *Teaching Exceptional Children, 30*(3), 16–21.

Beatty, L. S., Madden, R., Gardner, E. F., Karlsen, B. (1995). *Stanford Diagnostic Mathematics Test—Fourth edition.* San Antonio, TX: Harcourt Brace Educational Measurement.

Bebko, J. M., & Luhaorg, H. (1998). The development of strategy use and metcognitive processing in mental retardation: Some source of difficulty. In J. A. Burack, R. M. Hodapp, & E. Zigler (Eds.), *Handbook of mental retardation and development* (pp. 382–407). Cambridge, UK: Cambridge University Press.

Beck, J., Broers, J., Hogue, E., Shipstead, J., & Knowlton, E. (1994). Strategies for functional community-based instruction and inclusion for children with mental retardation. *Teaching Exceptional Children, 26*(2), 44–48.

Beck, R., Conrad, D., & Anderson, P. (1995). *Skill builders handbook.* Longmont, CO: Sopris West.

Becker, W. C., Engelmann, S., & Thomas, D. R. (1971). *Teaching: A course in applied psychology.* Chicago: Science Research Associates.

Beckley, C. G., Al-Attrash, M., Heward, W. L., & Morrison, H. (1999). Using guided notes in an eighth-grade social studies class: Effects on next-day quiz scores and notetaking accuracy. Manuscript submitted for publication.

Behr, S. K., Murphy, D. L., & Summers, J. A. (1992). *User's manual: Kansas inventory of parental perceptions (KIPP).* Lawrence: University of Kansas, Beach Center on Families and Disability.

Beirne-Smith, M., Patton, J. R., & Kim, S. H. (2006). *Mental retardation* (7th ed.). Upper Saddle River, NJ: Merrill/Prentice Hall.

Belcastro, F. P .(1989). Use of Belcastro Rods to teach mathematical concepts to blind students. *RE:view, 21,* 71–79.

Belgrave, F. Z., & Mills, J. (1981). Effect upon desire for social interaction with a physically disabled person of mentioning the disability in different contexts. *Journal of Applied Social Psychology, 11,* 44–57.

Bellamy, G. T., & Wilcox, B. (1982). Secondary education for severely handicapped students: Guidelines for quality services. In K. P. Lynch, W. E. Kiernan, & J. A. Stark (Eds.), *Prevocational and vocational education for special needs youth: A blueprint for the 1980s.* Baltimore, Brookes.

Belmont, J. M. (1966). Long term memory in mental retardation. *International Review of Research in Mental Retardation, 1,* 219–255.

Belser, R. C., & Sudhalter, V. (2001). Conversational characteristics of children with Fragile X syndrome: Repetitive speech. *American Journal of Mental Retardation, 106,* 28–38.

Beninghof, A. M. (1998). *Ideas for inclusion: The classroom teacher's guide to integrating students with severe disabilities.* Longmont, CO: Sopris West.

Bennett, D. (1997). Low vision devices for children and young people with a visual impairment. In H. Mason & S. McCall

(Eds.), *Visual impairment: Access to education for children and young people* (pp. 64–75). London: Fulton.

Benson, V., & Marano, M. A. (1998, October). Current estimates from the National Health Interview Survey, 1995. National Center for Health Statistics. *Vital Health Stat 10, 199.*

Benz, M. R., & Lindstrom, L. E. (1997). *Building school-to-work programs: Strategies for youth with special needs.* Austin, TX: PRO-ED.

Benz, M. R., Lindstrom, L., & Yavanoff, P. (2000). Improving graduation and employment outcomes of students with disabilities: Predictive factors and student perspectives. *Exceptional Children, 66,* 509–529.

Benz, M. R., Lindstrom, L., Unruh, B., & Waintrup, M. (2004). Sustaining secondary transition programs in local schools. *Remedial and Special Education, 25,* 39–50.

Berkson, G. (2004). Intellectual and physical disabilities in prehistory and early civilization. *Mental Retardation, 42,* 195–208.

Berney, T. P. (2000). Autism: An evolving concept. *British Journal of Psychiatry, 176,* 20–25.

Berquin, P. C., Giedd, J. N., Jacobson, L. K., Hamburger, S. D., Krain, A. L., Rappaport, J. L., & Castellanos, E. X. (1998). Cerebellum in attention-deficit/hyperactivity disorder: A Morphometric MRI study. *Neurology, 50,* 1087–1093.

Bess, F. (1999). School-aged children with minimal sensorineural hearing loss. *Hearing Journal, 52,* 10–16.

Best, A. B. (1992). *Teaching children with visual impairments.* Milton Keynes, England: Open University Press.

Best, S. J. (2005a). Physical disabilities. In S. J. Best, K. W. Heller, & J. L. Bigge, *Teaching individuals with physical or multiple disabilities* (5th ed.), (pp. 31–58). Upper Saddle River, NJ: Merrill/Prentice Hall.

Best, S. J. (2005b). Health impairments and infectious diseases. In S. J. Best, K. W. Heller, & J. L. Bigge, *Teaching individuals with physical or multiple disabilities* (5th ed.), (pp. 59–85). Upper Saddle River, NJ: Merrill/Prentice Hall.

Best, S. J., & Bigge, J. L. (2005). Cerebral palsy. In S. J. Best, K. W. Heller, & J. L. Bigge, *Teaching individuals with physical or multiple disabilities* (5th ed.), (pp. 87–109). Upper Saddle River, NJ: Merrill/Prentice Hall.

Best, S. J., Bigge, J. L., Musante, C. M., & Macias, C. M. (2005). Adaptations in physical education, leisure education, and recreation. In S. J. Best, K. W. Heller, & J. L. Bigge, (Eds.), *Teaching individuals with physical or multiple disabilities* (5th ed.), (pp. 337–366). Upper Saddle River, NJ: Merrill/Prentice Hall.

Best, S. J., Heller, K. W., & Bigge, J. L. (2005). *Teaching individuals with physical or multiple disabilities* (5th ed.). Upper Saddle River, NJ: Merrill/Prentice Hall.

Best, S. J., Reed, P., & Bigge, J. L. (2005). Assistive technology. In S. J. Best, K. W.

Heller, & J. L. Bigge, *Teaching individuals with physical or multiple disabilities* (5th ed.), (pp. 179–226). Upper Saddle River, NJ: Merrill/Prentice Hall.

Bettelheim, B. (1967). *The empty fortress: Infantile autism and the birth of the self.* London: Collier-Macmillan.

Beukelman, D. R., & Miranda, P. (1998) *Augmentative and alternative communication: Management of severe communication disorder in children and adults* (2nd ed.). Baltimore: Brookes.

Bevill, A. R., Gast, D. L., MaGuire, A. M., & Vail, C. O. (2001). Increasing engagement of preschoolers with disabilities through correspondence training and picture cues. *Journal of Early Intervention, 24,* 129–145.

Bicard, D. F. (2000). Using classroom rules to construct behavior. *Middle School Journal, 31*(5), 37–45.

Bicard, D. F. (2002, September). *Behavior analysis in education: Research on attention deficit disorder.* Paper presented at The Ohio State University's Third Focus on Behavior Analysis in Education Conference, Columbus.

Bicard, D. F., & Neef, N. A. (2002). Effects of strategic versus tactical instructions on adaptation to changing contingencies in children with ADHD. *Journal of Applied Behavior Analysis, 35,* 375–389.

Bidabe, D. L., Barnes, S. B., & Whinnery, K. W. (2001). M.O.V.E: Raising expectations for individuals with severe disabilities. *Physical Disabilities: Education and Related Services, 19*(2), 31–48.

Bigge, J. L. (1991). *Teaching individuals with physical and multiple disabilities* (3rd ed.). Upper Saddle River, NJ: Merrill/Prentice Hall.

Bigge, J. L., Stump, C. S., Spagna, M. E., & Silberman, R. K. (1999). *Curriculum, assessment, and instruction for students with disabilities.* Belmont, CA: Wadsworth.

Biglan, A. (1995). Translating what we know about the context of antisocial behavior into a lower prevalence of such behavior. *Journal of Applied Behavior Analysis, 28,* 479–492.

Biklen, D. (1990). Communication unbound: Autism and praxis. *Harvard Educational Review, 60,* 291–314.

Biklen, D. (1992). Typing to talk: Facilitated communication. *American Journal of Speech Language Pathology, 1*(2), 15–17.

Billingsley, F. F., Liberty, K. A., & White, O. R. (1994). The technology of instruction. In E. C. Cipani & F. Spooner (Eds.), *Curricular and instructional approaches for persons with severe disabilities* (pp. 81–116). Boston: Allyn & Bacon.

Bishop, V. E. (1986). Identifying the components of successful mainstreaming. *Journal of Visual Impairment and Blindness, 80,* 939–946.

Blacher, J. (1984). A dynamic perspective on the impact of a severely handicapped child on the family. In J. Blacher (Ed.), *Severely handicapped children and their families* (pp. 3–50). Orlando, FL: Academic Press.

Blacher, J. (2001). Transition to adulthood: Mental retardation, families, and culture.

*American Journal of Mental Retardation, 106,* 173–188.

Black, R., Smith, G., Chang, C., Harding, T., & Stodden, R. A. (2002). Provision of educational supports to students with disabilities in two-year postsecondary programs. *Journal for Vocational Special Needs Education, 24*(2/3), 3–17.

Blackorby, J., & Wagner, M. (1996). Longitudinal postschool outcomes of youth with disabilities: Findings from the National Longitudinal Transition Study. *Exceptional Children, 62,* 399–413.

Blackorby, J., & Wagner, M. (1997). The employment outcomes of youth with learning disabilities: A review of findings from the National Longitudinal Study of Special Education Students. In P. J. Gerber & D. S. Bowen (Eds.), *Learning disabilities and employment* (pp. 57–74). Austin, TX: PRO-ED.

Blake, C., Wang, W., Cartledge, G., & Gardner, R. (2000). Middle school students with serious emotional disturbances serve as social skills trainers and reinforcers for peers with SED. *Behavioral Disorders, 25,* 280–298.

Blalock, G., Kochhar-Bryant, C., Test, D. W., Kohler, P., White, W., Lehmann, J., Bassett, D., & Patton, J. (2003). The need for comprehensive personnel preparation in transition and career development: DCDT position statement. *Career Development for Exceptional Individuals, 26,* 207–226.

Blatt, B. (1976). *Revolt of the idiots: A story.* Glen Ridge, NJ: Exceptional Press.

Blatt, B. (1987). *The conquest of mental retardation.* Austin, TX: PRO-ED.

Blatt, B. (1999). *In search of the promised land: The collected papers of Burton Blatt.* Washington, DC: American Association on Mental Retardation.

Blatt, B., & Kaplan, F. (1966). *Christmas in purgatory: A photographic essay on mental retardation.* Boston: Allyn & Bacon.

Bleck, E. E. (1987). *Orthopedic management of cerebral palsy—Clinics in developmental medicine No. 99/100.* Philadelphia: Lippincott.

Block, S. R. (1997). Closing the sheltered workshop: Toward competitive employment opportunities for persons with developmental disabilities. *Journal of Vocational Rehabilitation, 9,* 267–275.

Bloodstein, O. (1995). *A handbook on stuttering* (5th ed.). San Diego: Singular.

Bloom, B. S. (1980). The new direction in educational research: Alterable variables. *Phi Delta Kappan, 61,* 382–385.

Bloom, B. S., Englehart, M., Furst, E., Hill, W., & Krathwohl, D. (1956). *Taxonomy of educational objectives: The classification of educational goals. Handbook I: Cognitive domain.* New York: Longman's Green.

Blosser, J. L., & Kratcoski, A. (1997). PACs: A framework for determining appropriate service delivery options. *ASHA, 28,* 99–107.

Blue-Banning, M., Summers, J. A., Frankland, H. C., Nelson, L. L., & Beegle, G. (2004). Dimensions of family and professional partnerships: Constructive guidelines for collaboration. *Exceptional Children, 70,* 167–184.

Bluestone, C. D., & Klein, J. O. (2001). *Otitis media in infants and children* (3rd ed.). Philadelphia: Saunders.

Board of Education of the Hendrick Hudson Central School District v. Rowley, 102 S. Ct. 3034 (1982).

Boekaerts, M. R., & Roeder, I. (1999). Stress, coping, and adjustment in children with a chronic disease: A review of the literature. *Disability and Rehabilitation, 21,* 311–327.

Bogdan, R., & Taylor, S. J. (1994). *The social meaning of mental retardation.* New York: Teachers College Press.

Bolt, S. E., & Thurlow, M. L. (2004). Five of the most frequently allowed testing accommodations in state policy. *Remedial and Special Education, 25,* 141–152.

Bondurant-Utz, J. (2002). *Practical guide to assessing infants and preschoolers with special needs.* Upper Saddle River, NJ: Merrill/Prentice Hall.

Bondy, A., & Frost, L. (1994). PECS: The picture exchange communication system. *Focus on Autistic Behavior, 9,* 1–9.

Bondy, A., & Frost, L. (2002). *A picture's worth: PECS and other visual communication strategies in autism.* Bethesda, MD: Woodbine, House.

Book, D., Paul, T. L., Gwalla-Ogisi, N., & Test, D. W. (1990). No more bologna sandwiches. *Teaching Exceptional Children, 22*(2), 62–64.

Boothe, D. (2004). Gender differences in achievement and aptitude test results: Perspectives from the recent literature. In D. Boothe & J. Stanley (Eds.), *In the eyes of the beholder: Critical issues for diversity in gifted education* (pp. 179–189). Waco, TX: Prufrock.

Bornstein, H. (1974). Signed English: A manual approach to English language development. *Journal of Speech and Hearing Disorders, 3,* 330–343.

Borsch, J., & Oaks, R. (1993). *The collaboration companion: Strategies and activities in and out of the classroom.* East Moline, IL: LinguiSystems.

Borthwick-Duffy, S. (1994). Review of mental retardation: Definition, causes, and systems of supports. *American Journal on Mental Retardation, 98,* 541–544.

Borthwick-Duffy, S. A., & Eyman, R. K. (1990). Who are the dually diagnosed? *American Journal on Mental Retardation, 94,* 586–595.

Bosner, S. M., & Belfiore, P. J. (2001). Strategies and considerations for teaching an adolescent with Down syndrome and type I diabetes to self-administer insulin. *Education and Treatment in Mental Retardation and Developmental Disabilities, 36,* 94–102.

Bouchard, D., & Tétreault, S. (2000). The motor development of sighted children and children with moderate low vision aged 8–13. *Journal of Visual Impairments and Blindness, 94,* 564–573.

Boudah, D. J., Schumaker, J. B., & Deshler, D. D. (1997). Collaborative instruction: Is it an effective option for inclusion in secondary classrooms? *Learning Disability Quarterly, 4,* 293–316.

Boulware, G. L., Schwartz, I. S., & McBride, B. M. (1999). Addressing challenging behavior at home: Working with families to find solutions. In S. R. Sandall & M. Ostrosky (Eds.), *Practical ideas for addressing challenging behaviors.* Monograph of *Young Exceptional Children* (pp. 29–40). Denver: Sopris West.

Bowe, F. (2000). *Teaching individuals with physical and multiple disabilities* (4th ed.). Upper Saddle River, NJ: Merrill/Prentice Hall.

Bowen, J., Olympia, D., & Jensen, W. (1996). *Study buddies: Parent tutoring tactics.* Longmont, CO: Sopris West.

Bower, E. M. (1960). *Early identification of emotionally handicapped children in the schools.* Springfield, IL: Thomas.

Bower, E. M. (1982). Defining emotional disturbance: Public policy and research. *Psychology in the Schools, 19,* 55–60.

Bowers, F. E., McGinnis, J. C., Ervin, R. A., & Friman, P. C. (1999). Merging research and practice: The example of positive peer reporting applied to social rejection. *Education and Treatment of Children, 22,* 218–226.

Boykin, A. W. (1983). The academic performance of Afro-American children. In J. Spence (Ed.), *Achievement and achievement motives* (pp. 324–371). San Francisco: Freeman.

Boyle, J. R. (2001). Enhancing the note-taking skills of students with mild disabilities. *Intervention in School and Clinic, 36,* 221–224.

Braddock, D., Rizzolo, M. C., & Hemp, R. (2004). Most employment services growth in developmental disabilities during 1988–2002 was in segregated settings. *Mental Retardation, 42,* 317–320.

Braden, J. P., Maller, S. J., & Paquin, M. M. (1993). The effects of residential versus day placement on the performance IQs of children with hearing impairment. *Journal of Special Education, 26,* 423–433.

Bradley, R., Danielson, L., & Hallahan, D. P. (Eds.). (2002). *Identification of learning disabilities: Research to practice.* Mahwah, NJ: Erlbaum.

Bradley, V. J., Knoll, J., & Agosta, J. M. (Eds.). (1992). *Emerging issues in family support.* Washington, DC: American Association on Mental Retardation.

Brain Injury Association. (2001). *Brain injury and you.* Alexandria, VA: Author. http://www.bia.org.

Brame, P. (2000). Using picture storybooks to enhance the social skills training of special needs students. *Middle School Journal, 32*(1), 41.

Bray, N. W., Fletcher, K. L., & Turner, L. A. (1997). Cognitive competencies and strategy use in individuals with mental retardation. In W. W. MacLean, Jr. (Ed.), *Ellis' handbook of mental deficiency, psychological theory, and research* (3rd ed.), (pp. 197–217). Mahwah, NJ: Erlbaum.

Bredekamp, S. (1993). The relationship between early childhood education and early childhood special education: Healthy marriage or family feud? *Topics in Early Childhood Special Education, 13,* 258–273.

Bredekamp, S., & Copple, C. (Eds.). (1997). *Developmentally appropriate practice in early childhood programs.* Washington, DC: National Association for the Education of Young Children.

Brewer, J., & Kieff, J. (1996). Fostering mutual respect for play at home and school. *Childhood Education, 7,* 92–96.

Bricker, D. (1986). An analysis of early intervention programs: Attendant issues and future directions. In R. J. Morris & B. Blatt (Eds.), *Special education: Research and trends* (pp. 28–65). New York: Pergamon.

Bricker, D. (Ed.). (2002). *Assessment, evaluation, and programming system (AEP) for infants and children* (2nd ed.). Baltimore: Brookes.

Bricker, D., Pretti-Frontczak, K., & McComas, N. (1998). *An activity-based approach to early intervention* (2nd ed.). Baltimore: Brookes.

Bricker, D., & Squires, J. (1999). *Ages & Stages Questionnaires: A parent-completed, child-monitoring system* (2nd ed.). Baltimore: Brookes.

Bricker, D., & Waddell, M. (2002a). *AEPS curriculum for birth to three years* (2nd ed.). Baltimore: Brookes.

Bricker, D., & Waddell, M. (2002b). *AEPS curriculum for three to six years* (2nd ed.). Baltimore: Brookes.

Brickey, M. P., Campbell, K. M., & Browning, L. J. (1985). A five-year follow-up of sheltered workshop employees placed in competitive jobs. *Mental Retardation, 23,* 67–73.

Brigance, A. H. (1999). *Brigance Diagnostic Comprehensive Inventory of Basic Skills—Revised.* N. Billerica, MA: Curriculum Associates.

Briggs, A., Alberto, P., Sharpton, W., Berlin, K., McKinley, C., & Ritts, C. (1990). Generalized use of a self-operated audio prompt system. *Education and Training in Mental Retardation, 25,* 381–389.

Brigham, F. J., & Cole, J. E. (1999). Selective mutism: Developments in definition, etiology, assessment and treatment. In T. Scruggs & M. Mastropieri (Eds.), *Advances in learning and behavioral disabilities* (Vol.13, pp. 183–216). Greenwich, CT: JAI.

Brigham, F. J., & Kauffman, J. M. (1998). Creating supportive environments for students with emotional or behavioral disorders. *Effective School Practices, 17*(2), 25–35.

Brigham, R., & Brigham, M. (2001). *Current practice alerts: Mnemonic instruction.* Reston, VA: Division for Learning Disabilities and Division for Research of the Council for Exceptional Children.

Brinkerhoff, L. C., Shaw, S. F., & McGuire, J. M. (1993). *Promoting postsecondary education for students with learning disabilities.* Austin, TX: PRO-ED.

Bristol, M., Cohen, D., Costello, J., Denckla, M., Eckberg, T., Kallen, R., Kraemer, H., Lord, C. Maurer, R., McIlvane, W., Minshew, N. Sigman, M., & Spence, M. (1996). State of the science in autism:

Report to the National Institute of Health. *Journal of Autism and Developmental Disorders, 26,* 121–154.

Brolin, D. E. (1991). *Life-centered career education: A competency-based approach* (3rd ed.). Reston, VA: Council for Exceptional Children.

Brolin, D. E., & Loyd, R. J. (2004). *Career development and transition services* (4th ed.). Upper Saddle River, NJ: Merrill/Prentice Hall.

Bronicki, G. J., & Turnbull, A. P. (1987). Family-professional interactions. In M. E. Snell (Ed.), *Systematic instruction of persons with severe handicaps* (3rd ed.), (pp. 9–35). Upper Saddle River, NJ: Merrill/Prentice Hall.

Brookes, J., & Brookes, M. (1993). In search of understanding: The case for constructivist classrooms. Alexandria, VA: Association for Supervision and Curriculum Development.

Browder, D. M. (2000). *Comments made as guest faculty for OSU teleconference seminar: Contemporary issues in special education.* Columbus, OH: The Ohio State University.

Browder, D. M. (2001). *Curriculum and assessment for students with moderate and severe disabilities.* New York: Guilford.

Browder, D. M., & Cooper, K. J. (2001). Community and leisure skills. In D. M. Browder, *Curriculum and assessment for students with moderate and severe disabilities* (pp. 244–278). New York: Guilford.

Browder, D. M., Cooper, K. J., & Lim, L. (1998). Teaching adults with severe disabilities to express their choice of settings for leisure activities. *Education and Training in Mental Retardation and Developmental Disabilities, 33,* 228–238.

Browder, D. M., & Cooper-Duffy, K. (2003). Evidence-based practices for students with severe disabilities and the requirements for accountability in "No Child Left Behind." *Journal of Special Education, 37,* 157–163.

Browder, D. M., & Snell, M. E. (2000). Functional academics. In M. E. Snell & F. Brown, *Instruction of students with severe disabilities* (5th ed.), (pp. 493–542). Upper Saddle River, NJ: Merrill/Prentice Hall.

Browder, D. M., & Wilson, B. (2001). Using ecological assessment in planning for inclusion. In D. M. Browder, *Curriculum and assessment for students with moderate and severe disabilities* (pp. 337–360). New York: Guilford.

Brown v. Board of Education of Topeka, 347 U.S. 483 (1954).

Brown, L. (1990). Who are they and what do they want? An essay on TASH. *TASH Newsletter, 16*(9), 1.

Brown, L., Farrington, K., Suomi, J., & Zeigler, M. (1999). Work-wage relationships and individuals with disabilities. *Journal of Vocational Rehabilitation, 13*(1), 5–13.

Brown, L., Ford, A., Nisbet, J., Sweet, M., Donnellan, A., & Gruenewald, L. (1983). Opportunities available when severely handicapped students attend chronological age appropriate regular schools. *Journal of the Association for Persons with Severe Handicaps, 8,* 16–24.

Brown, L., Long, E., Udvari-Solner, A., Davis, L., VanDeventer, P., Ahlgren, C., Johnson, F., Gruenewald, L., & Jorgensen, J. (1989a). The home school: Why students with severe disabilities must attend the schools of their brothers, sisters, friends, and neighbors. *Journal of The Association for Persons with Severe Handicaps, 14,* 1–7.

Brown, L., Long, E., Udvari-Solner, A., Davis, L., VanDeventer, P., Ahlgren, C., Johnson, F., Gruenewald, L., & Jorgensen, J. (1989b). Should students with severe intellectual disabilities be based in regular or in special education classrooms in home schools? *Journal of The Association for Persons with Severe Handicaps, 14,* 8-12.

Brown, L., Schwartz, P., Udvari-Solner, A., Kampschroer, E. F., Johnson, F., Jorgensen, J., & Gruenewald, L. (1991). How much time should students with severe intellectual disabilities spend in regular education classrooms and elsewhere? *Journal of The Association for Persons with Severe Handicaps, 16,* 39–47.

Brown, L. L., & Hammill, D. D. (1990). *Behavior rating profile: An ecological approach to behavioral assessment* (2nd ed.). Austin, TX: PRO-ED.

Brown, V. L., Cronin, M. E., & McEntire, E. (1994). *Test of Mathematical Abilities—2.* Austin, TX: PRO-ED.

Brown, V. L., Hammill, D. D., & Wiederholt, J. L. (1995). *Test of reading comprehension* (3rd ed.). Austin, TX: PRO-ED.

Brown, W., Thurman, S. K., & Pearl, L. W. (1993). *Family-centered intervention with infants and toddlers: Innovative cross-disciplinary approaches.* Baltimore: Brookes.

Brownell, W. E. (1999). How the ear works: Nature's solutions for listening. *Volta Review, 99*(5), 9–28.

Bruder, M. B. (2000, December). *The Individual Family Service Plan (IFSP).* Reston, VA: ERIC Clearinghouse on Disabilities and Gifted Education. (EDO-EC-00-14).

Brumback, R. A., Mathews, S., & Shenoy, S. R. (2001). Neurological disorders. In F. M. Kline, L. B. Silver, & S. C. Russell, (Eds.), *The educator's guide to medical issues in the classroom* (pp. 49–64). Baltimore: Brookes.

Bruninks, R. H., Woodcock, R. W., Weatherman, R. F., & Hill, B. K. (1996). *Scales of Independent Behavior—Revised.* Itasca, IL: Riverside.

Bryan, L. C., & Gast, D. L. (2000). Teaching on-task and on-schedule behaviors to high-functioning children with autism via picture activity schedules. *Journal of Autism and Developmental Disorders, 30,* 553–567.

Bryan, T. (1997). Assessing the personal and social status of students with learning disabilities. *Learning Disabilities Research and Practice, 12,* 63–76.

Bryan, T., & Ryan, A. (2001). Jacob's story: Amazing discoveries. In A. K. Ryan, *Strengthening the safety net: How school can help youth with emotional and behavioral needs complete their high school education and prepare for life after school* (p. 10).

Burlington, VT: School Research Office, University of Vermont.

Bryant, D. P., & Bryant, B. R. (2003). *Assistive technology for people with disabilities.* Boston: Allyn & Bacon.

Buck, G. H., Polloway, E. A., Smith-Thomas, A., & Cook, K. W. (2003). Prereferral intervention processes: A survey of state practices. *Exceptional Children, 69,* 349–360.

Bulgren, J. A., Deshler, D. D., Schumaker, J. B., & Lenz, B. K. (2000). The use and effectiveness of analogical instruction in diverse secondary content classrooms. *Journal of Educational Psychology, 16,* 426–441.

Bull, G. L., & Rushakoff, G. E. (1987). Computers and speech and language disordered individuals. In J. D. Lindsey (Ed.), *Computers and exceptional individuals* (pp. 83–104). Upper Saddle River, NJ: Merrill/Prentice Hall.

Bullis, M., & Otos, M. (1988). Characteristics of programs for children with deaf-blindness: Results of a national survey. *Journal of The Association for Persons with Severe Handicaps, 13,* 110–115.

Burchard, S. N., Hasazi, J. S., Gordon, L. R., & Yoe, J. (1991). An examination of lifestyle and adjustment in three community residential alternatives. *Research in Developmental Disabilities, 12,* 127–142.

Bureau of Labor Statistics. (1999). *National industry—occupation employment matrix: Occupation report-teachers, special education.* Retrieved August 23, 2001, from http://www.bls.gov/opub/ooq/2000/spring/contents.htm.

Burkhardt, L. J. (1981). *Homemade battery powered toys and educational devices for severely disabled children.* Millville, PA: Burkhardt.

Bursuck, W., Polloway, E. A., Plante, L., Epstein, D. H., Jayanthi, M., & McConeghy, J. I. (1996). Report card grading and adaptations: A national survey of classroom practices. *Exceptional Children, 62,* 301–318.

Bushell, D., Jr., & Baer, D. M. (1994). Measurably superior instruction means close, continual contact with the relevant outcome data. Revolutionary! In R. Gardner III, D. M. Sainato, J. O. Cooper, T. E. Heron, W. L. Heward, J. Eshleman, & T. A. Grossi (Eds.), *Behavior analysis in education: Focus on measurably superior instruction* (pp. 3–10). Pacific Grove, CA: Brooks/Cole.

Butterworth, J., Gilmore, D., Kiernan, W. E., & Shalock, R. (1999). *Day and employment service in developmental disabilities: State and national trends.* Washington, DC: American Association on Mental Retardation.

Bybee, J., & Zigler, E. (1998). Outerdirectedness in individuals with and without mental retardation: A review. In J. A. Burack, R. M. Hodapp, & E. Zigler (Eds.), *Handbook of mental retardation* (pp. 434–460). Cambridge: Cambridge University Press.

Calculator, S. N., & Jorgensen, C. M. (1991). Integrating augmentative and alternative communication instruction into regular education settings: Expounding on best practices. *Augmentative and Alternative Communication, 7,* 204–214.

Calderon, R., & Naidu, S. (2000). Further support for the benefits of early identification and intervention for children with hearing loss. *Volta Review, 100*(5), 53–84.

Caldwell, B. (1997). Educating children who are deaf or hard of hearing: Cued speech. *ERIC Digest #555.* (ERIC Document Reproduction Service No. ED 414 673).

Calhoun, M. L., & Kuczera, M. (1996). Increasing social smiles of young children with disabilities. *Perceptual and Motor Skills, 82,* 1265–1266.

Calhoun, M. L., Rose, T. L., Hanft, B. & Sturkey, C. (1991). Social reciprocity interventions: Implications for developmental therapists. *Physical and Occupational Therapy in Pediatrics, 11,* 45–46.

California Department of Developmental Services (1999). *A report to the legislature: Changes in the populations of persons with autism and pervasive developmental disorders in California's Department of Developmental Services system: 1987 through 1998.* Sacramento, CA: California Health and Human Service Agency.

Callahan, K., Rademacher, J. A., & Hildreth, B. L. (1998). The effect of parent participation in strategies to improve the homework performance of students who are at risk. *Remedial and Special Education, 19*(3), 131–141.

Callister, J. P., Mitchell, L., & Talley, G. (1986). Profiling family preservation efforts in Utah. *Children Today, 15,* 23–25, 36–37.

Cameron, J. (2005). The detrimental effects of reward hypothesis: Persistence of a view in the face of disconfirming evidence. In W. L. Heward, T. E. Heron, N. A. Neef, S. M. Peterson, D. M. Sainato, G. Cartledge, R. Gardner, III, L. D. Peterson, S. B. Hersh, & J. C. Dardig (Eds.), *Focus on behavior analysis in education: Achievements, challenges, and opportunities* (pp. 304–315). Upper Saddle River, NJ: Merrill/Prentice Hall.

Cameron, J., Banko, K. M., & Pierce, W. D. (2001). Pervasive negative effects of rewards on intrinsic motivation: The myth continues. *Behavior Analyst, 24,* 1–44.

Campbell, C., Campbell, S., Collicott, J., Perner, D., & Stone, J. (1988). Individualized instruction. *Education New Brunswick, 3,* 17–20.

Campbell, P. H. (2006). Promoting participation in natural environments by accommodating motor disabilities. In M. E. Snell & F. Brown (Eds.), *Instruction of students with severe disabilities* (6th ed.), (pp. 291–329). Upper Saddle River, NJ: Merrill/Prentice Hall.

Campbell Miller, M., Cooke, N. L. Test, D. W., & White, R. (2003). Effects of friendship circles on the social interactions of elementary age student with mild disabilities. *Journal of Behavioral Education, 12,* 167–184.

Cantu, C. O. (2004). Wheelchair positioning: Foundation in wheelchair selection. *Exceptional Parent, 34*(5), 33–35.

Cardon, L. R., Smith, S. D., Fulker, D. W., Kimberling, B. F., Pennington, B. F., & DeFries, J. C. (1994). Quantitative trait locus for reading disability on chromosome 6. *Science, 226,* 276–279.

Carey, W. B. (1998). Temperament and behavior problems in the classroom. *School Psychology Review, 27,* 522–533.

Carnine, D. (1997). Bridging the research to practice gap. *Exceptional Children, 63,* 513–521.

Carnine, D., Jones, E., & Dixon, R. (1994). Mathematics: Educational tools for diverse learners. *School Psychology Review, 23,* 406–427.

Carnine, D. W., Silbert, J., Kame' enui, E. J., & Tarver, S. (2004). *Direct instruction reading* (4th ed.). Upper Saddle River, NJ: Merrill/Prentice Hall.

Caro, P., & Derevensky, J. L. (1997). An exploratory study using the sibling interaction scale: Observing interactions between siblings with and without disabilities. *Education and Treatment of Children, 20*(4), 383–403.

Carr, E. G., & Durand, V. M. (1985). Reducing behavior problems through functional communication training. *Journal of Applied Behavior Analysis, 18,* 111–126.

Carr, E. G., Dunlap, G., Horner, R. H., Koegel, R. L., Turnbull, A. P., Sailor, W., Anderson, J., Albin, R. W., Koegel, L. K., & Fox, L. (2002). Positive behavioral support: Evolution of an applied science. *Journal of Positive Behavior Interventions, 4,* 4–16.

Carr, E. G., Levin, L., McConnachie, G., Carlson, J. I., Kemp, D. C., & Smith, C. E. (1994). *Communication-based intervention for problem behavior: A user's guide for producing positive change.* Baltimore: Brookes.

Carr, J. (1988). Six-weeks to twenty-one years old: A longitudinal study of children with Down syndrome and their families. *Journal of Child Psychology and Psychiatry, 29*(4), 407–431.

Carr, J. E., Kellum, K. K., & Chong, I. M. (2001). The reductive effects of noncontingent reinforcement: Fixed-time versus variable-time schedules. *Journal of Applied Behavior Analysis, 34,* 505–509.

Carr, S. C., & Punzo, R. P. (1993). The effects of self-monitoring of academic accuracy and productivity on the performance of students with behavioral disorders. *Behavioral Disorders, 18,* 241–250.

Carta, J. J., Atwater, J. B., Greenwood, C. R., McConnell, S. R., McEvoy, M. A., & Williams, R. (2001). Effects of cumulative prenatal substance exposure and environmental risks on children's developmental trajectories. *Journal of Clinical Child Psychology, 30*(3), 327–337.

Cartledge, G., Kea, C. D., & Ida, D. J. (2000). Anticipating differences—celebrating strengths: Providing culturally competent services for students with serious emotional disturbance. *Teaching Exceptional Children, 32*(3), 6–12.

Cartledge, G., & Milburn, J. F. (1995). *Teaching social skills to children and youth: Innovative approaches* (3rd ed.). Boston: Allyn & Bacon.

Caspi, A., Henry, B., McGee, R. O., Moffitt, T. W., & Silva, P. A. (1995). Temperamental origins of child and adolescent behavior problems: From age three to age fifteen. *Child Development, 66,* 55–68.

Castellano, J. (2004). Empowering and serving Hispanic students in gifted education. In D. Boothe & J. Stanley (Eds.), *In the eyes of the beholder: Critical issues for diversity in gifted education* (pp. 1–14). Waco, TX: Prufrock.

Castellano, J. A. (2003). *Special populations in gifted education: Working with diverse gifted learners.* Boston: Allyn & Bacon.

Catts, H. W. (1993). The relationship between speech-language impairments and reading disabilities. *Journal of Speech and Hearing Research, 36,* 948–958.

Cavanaugh, R. A., Heward, W. L., & Donelson, F. (1996). Effects of response cards during lesson closure on the academic performance of secondary students in an earth science course. *Journal of Applied Behavior Analysis, 29,* 403–406.

Cawley, J. F., Parmar, R. S., Foley, T. E., Salmon S., & Roy, S. (2001). Arithmetic performance of students: Implications for standards and programming. *Exceptional Children, 67,* 311–328.

Cawley, J. F., Parmar, R. S., Yan, W., & Miller, J. H. (1998). Arithmetic computation performance of students with learning disabilities: Implications for curriculum. *Learning Disabilities Research and Practice, 13,* 68–74.

Cawthon, S. W. (2001). Teaching strategies in inclusive classrooms with deaf students. *Journal of Deaf Studies and Deaf Education, 6,* 212–225.

Cazden, C. B. (1992). *Whole language plus: Essays on literacy in the United States and New Zealand.* New York: Teachers College Press.

*CEC Today.* (1998). Growing challenge for teachers—Providing medical procedures for students. 5(3), 1, 5, 15.

Cedar Rapids Community School District v. Garret F., 67 U.S. L. W. 4165 (1999).

Center for Positive Behavioral Interventions & Supports. (2001). *School-wide behavioral support.* http://www.pbis.org/.

Center on Human Policy. (1986, December). Positive interventions for challenging behavior. *The Association for Persons with Severe Handicaps Newsletter, 12*(12), 4.

Centers for Disease Control and Prevention. (1998). HIV/AIDS prevention: Frequently asked questions. *CDC Update.* http://www.cdc.gov.hiv/pubs/facts/hivre/pfs/htm.

Centers for Disease Control and Prevention. (2001a). Divisions of HIV/AIDS prevention. *Surveillance Report, 12*(2). http://www.cdc.gov.hiv/stats/hasr1202.

Centers for Disease Control and Prevention. (2001b). *National health statistics.* Atlanta: Author.

Chadsey, J. G., Linneman, D., Rusch, F. R., & Cimera, R. E. (1997). The impact of social integration interventions and job coaches in work settings. *Education and Training in Mental Retardation and Developmental Disabilities, 32,* 281–292.

Chafin Seal, B. (2004). *Best practices in educational interpreting* (2nd ed.). Boston: Allyn & Bacon.

Chaikind, S., Danielson, L. C., & Brauen, M. L. (1993). What do we know about the costs of special education? A selected review. *Journal of Special Education, 26,* 344–370.

Chambers, J. G., Parrish, T. B., & Harr, J. J. (2002, March). *What are we spending on special education in the United States, 1999–2000? Advance report #1,* Washington, DC: American Institutes for Research: Special Education Expenditure Project.

Chandler, L. K. (1993). Steps in preparing for transition: Preschool to kindergarten. *Teaching Exceptional Children, 25*(4), 52–55.

Chandler, L. K., & Dahlquist, C. M. (2006). *Functional assessment: Strategies to prevent and remediate challenging behavior in school settings* (2nd ed.). Upper Saddle River, NJ: Merrill/Prentice Hall.

Chard, D. J., & Kame'enui, E. J. (2000). Struggling first-grade readers: The frequency and progress of their reading. *Journal of Special Education, 34,* 28–38.

Charney, E. B. (1992). Neural tube defects: Spina bifida and myelomeningocele. In M. L. Batshaw & Y. M. Perret, *Children with disabilities: A medical primer* (3rd ed.) (pp. 471–488). Baltimore: Brookes.

Chesapeake Institute. (1994, September). *National agenda for achieving better results for children and youth with serious emotional disturbance.* Washington, DC: U.S. Department of Education.

Chesley, G. M., & Calaluce, P. D. (1997). The deception of inclusion. *Mental Retardation, 35,* 488–490.

Christle, C. A., & Schuster, J. W. (2003). The effects of using response cards on student participation, academic achievement, and on-task behavior during whole-class, math instruction. *Journal of Behavioral Education, 12,* 147–165.

Chuch, G., & Glennen, S. (1992). *The handbook of assistive technology.* San Diego: Singular.

Cipani, E. (2004). *Classroom management for all teachers: 12 plans for evidence-based practice* (2nd ed.) Upper Saddle River, NJ: Merrill/Prentice Hall.

Cipani, E. C., & Spooner, F. (Eds.). (1994). *Curricular and instructional approaches for persons with severe disabilities.* Boston: Allyn & Bacon.

Clark, B. (1997). *Growing up gifted: Developing the potential of children at home and at school* (5th ed.). Upper Saddle River, NJ: Merrill/Prentice Hall.

Clark, B. A. (2002). *Growing up gifted* (6th ed.). Upper Saddle River, NJ: Merrill/Prentice Hall.

Clark, G. M. (1994). Is a functional curriculum approach compatible with an inclusive education model? *Teaching Exceptional Children, 26*(2), 36–39.

Clark, G. M., Carlson, B. C., Fisher, S., Cook, I. D., & D'Alonzo, B. J. (1991). Career development for students with disabilities in elementary schools: A position statement of the division on career development. *Career Development for Exceptional Individuals, 14,* 109–120.

Clark, S. G. (2000). The IEP process as a tool for collaboration. *Teaching Exceptional Children, 33*(2), 56–66.

Clarke-Klein, S., & Hodson, B. W. (1995). A phonologically based analysis of misspellings by third graders with disordered-phonology histories. *Journal of Speech and Hearing Research, 38,* 839–849.

Cleeland, L. K. (1984). The function of the auditory system in speech and language development. In R. K. Hull & K. I. Dilka (Eds.), *The hearing-impaired child in school* (pp. 15–16). Orlando, FL: Grune & Stratton.

Clements, S. D. (1966). *Minimal brain dysfunction in children* (NINDS Monograph No. 3, Public Health Service Bulletin No. 1415). Washington, DC: U.S. Department of Health, Education, and Welfare.

Cline, D. H. (1990). Interpretations of emotional disturbance and social maladjustment as policy problems: A legal analysis of initiatives to exclude handicapped/disruptive students from special education. *Behavioral Disorders, 15,* 159–173.

*Clinical Practice Guideline: Report of the Recommendations.* (1999). Publication No. 4215. Albany: New York State Department of Health.

Cochran, L., Feng, H., Cartledge, G., & Hamilton, S. (1993). The effects of cross-age tutoring on the academic achievement, social behaviors, and self-perceptions of low-achieving African-American males with behavioral disorders. *Behavioral Disorders, 18,* 292–302.

Cohen, S., Agosta, J., Cohen, J., & Warren, R. (1989). Supporting families of children with severe disabilities. *Journal of The Association for Persons with Severe Handicaps, 14,* 155–162.

Colangelo, N., Assouline, S. G., & Gross, M. U. M. (2004). *A nation deceived: How schools hold back America's brightest students.* Iowa City: University of Iowa Press.

Cole, C. M., Waldron, N., & Majd, M. (2004). Academic progress of students across inclusive and traditional settings. *Mental Retardation, 42,* 136–144.

Coleman, M., & Vaughn, S. R. (2000). Reading interventions with students with emotional/behavioral disorders. *Behavioral Disorders, 25,* 93–104.

Coleman, M., & Webber, J. (1988). Behavior problems? Try groups! *Academic Therapy, 23,* 265–274.

Collicott, J. (1991). Implementing multi-level instruction: Strategies for classroom teachers. In G. Porter & D. Richler (Eds.), *Changing Canadian Schools: Perspectives on disability and inclusion* (pp. 191–218). Ottawa, Ontario, Canada: Roeher Institute.

Collins, B. C., Hall, M., & Branson, T. A. (1997). Teaching leisure skills to adolescents with moderate disabilities. *Exceptional Children, 63,* 499–512.

Colvin, G., Kame'enui, E., & Sugai, G. (1993). Reconceptualizing behavior management and school-wide discipline in general education. *Education and Treatment of Children, 16,* 361–381.

Commission on Education of the Deaf. (1988). *Toward equality: Education of the deaf.* Washington, DC: U.S. Government Printing Office.

Community Playthings. (1999). *Rifton equipment* [Catalog]. Rifton, NY: Community Products.

Compton, M. V., & Niemeyer, J. A. (1994). Expressions of affection in young children with sensory impairments: A research agenda. *Education and Treatment of Children, 17,* 68–85.

Cone, A. A. (1994). Reflections on "Self-advocacy: Voices for choices." *Mental Retardation, 32,* 444–445.

Coniglio, S. J., Lewis, J. D., Lang, C., Burns, T. G., Subhani-Siddique, R., Weintraub A., et al. (2001). A randomized, double-blind, placebo-controlled trial of a single-dose intravenous secretin as treatment for children with autism. *Journal of Pediatrics, 138*(5), 649–655.

Conley, R. W. (2003). Supported employment in Maryland: Successes and issues. *Mental Retardation, 41,* 237–249.

Connell, M. C., Carta, J. J., & Baer, D. M. (1993). Programming generalization of in-class transition skills: Teaching preschoolers with developmental delays to self-assess and recruit contingent teacher praise. *Journal of Applied Behavior Analysis, 26,* 3.

Connell, M. C., Randall, C., Wilson, J., Lutz, S., & Lamb, D. R. (1993). Building independence during in-class transitions: Teaching in-class transition skills to preschoolers with developmental delays through choral-response-based self-assessment and contingent praise. *Education and Treatment of Children, 16,* 160–174.

Conners, C. K. (2000). Attention-deficit/hyperactivity disorder: Historical development and overview. *Journal of Attention Disorders, 3,* 173–191.

Connolly, A. J. (1998). *KeyMath—Revised: A Diagnostic Inventory of Essential Skills.* Circle Pines, MN: American Guidance Services.

Connor, L. E. (1986). Oralism in perspective. In D. M. Luterman (Ed.), *Deafness in perspective* (pp. 116–129). San Diego: College-Hill.

Conroy, J., Spreat, S., Yuskauskas, A., & Elks, M. (2003). The Hissom closure outcomes study: A report on six years of movement to supported living. *Mental Retardation, 41,* 263–275.

Conroy, J. W. (1996). The small ICF/MR program: Dimensions of quality and cost. *Mental Retardation, 34,* 13–26.

Conroy, J. W., & Bradley, V. J. (1985). *The Pennhurst longitudinal study: A report on five years of research and analysis.* Philadelphia: Temple University Developmental Disabilities Center.

Conroy, M. A., & Davis, C. A. (2000). Early elementary-aged children with challenging behaviors: Legal and educational issues related to IDEA and assessment. *Preventing School Failure, 44,* 163–168.

Conte, R., & Andrews, J. (1993). Social skills in the context of learning disability definitions: A reply to Gresham and Elliott and directions for the future. *Journal of Learning Disabilities, 26,* 146–153.

Cook, A. M., & Hussey, S. M. (1995). *Assistive technologies: Principles and practice.* St. Louis: Mosby.

Cook, B. G. (2001). A comparison of teachers' attitudes toward their included students with mild and severe disabilities. *Journal of Special Education, 34,* 203–213.

Cook, B. G., & Semmel, M. I. (1999). Peer acceptance of included students with disabilities as a function of severity of disability and classroom composition. *Journal of Special Education, 33,* 50–61.

Cook, B. G., Tankersley, M., Cook, L., & Landrum, T. J. (2000). Teachers' attitudes toward their included students with disabilities. *Exceptional Children, 67,* 115–135.

Cook, R. E., Klein, M. D., & Tessier, A. (2004). *Adapting early childhood curricula for children in inclusive settings* (6th ed.). Upper Saddle River, NJ: Merrill/Prentice Hall.

Cooke, N. L., Heron, T. E., & Heward, W. L. (1983). *Peer tutoring: Implementing classwide programs in the primary grades.* Columbus, OH: Special Press.

Cooke, N. L., Heward, W. L., Test, D. W., Spooner, F., & Courson, F. H. (1991). Student performance data in the special education classroom: Measurement and evaluation of student progress. *Teacher Education and Special Education, 13,* 155–161.

Cooper, J. O., Heron, T. E., & Heward, W. L. (2006). *Applied behavior analysis* (2nd ed.) Upper Saddle River, NJ: Merrill/Prentice Hall.

Cooper, J. O., Kubina, R., & Malanga, P. (1998). Six procedures for showing standard celebration charts. *Journal of Precision Teaching & Celebration, 15*(2), 58–76.

Cooper, K. J., & Browder, D. M. (1998). Enhancing choice and participation for adults with severe disabilities in community-based instruction. *Journal of The Association for Persons with Severe Handicaps, 23,* 252–260.

Copeland, S. R., McCall, J., Williams, C. R., Guth, C., Carter, E. W., Fowler, S. E., Presely, J. A., & Hughes, C. (2002). High school peer buddies: A win-win situation. *Teaching Exceptional Children, 35*(1), 16–21.

Corn, A. L. (1989). Instruction in the use of vision for children and adults with low vision: A proposed program model. *RE:view, 21,* 26–38.

Corn, A. L. (2000). *Finding wheels: A curriculum for non-drivers with visual impairments for gaining control of transportation needs.* Austin: PRO–ED.

Corn, A. L., & Koenig, A. J. (1996). *Foundations of low vision: Clinical and functional perspectives.* New York: AFB Press.

Corn, A., & Ryser, G. (1989). Access to print for students with low vision. *Journal of Visual Impairment and Blindness, 83,* 340–349.

Cornett, R. O. (1974). What is cued speech? *Gallaudet Today, 5*(2), 3–5.

Correa, V. I., & Heward, W. L. (2003). Special education in a culturally diverse society. In W. L. Heward, *Exceptional children: An introduction to special education* (7th ed.), (pp. 86–119). Upper Saddle River, NJ: Merrill/Prentice Hall.

Correa, V. I., Blanes-Reyes, M., & Rapport, M. J. (1995). Minority issues. In H. R. Turnbull & A. P. Turnbull (Eds.), *A compendium report to Congress.* Lawrence, KS: Beach Center.

Correa, V. I., Gollery, T., & Fradd, S. (1988). The handicapped undocumented alien student dilemma: Do we advocate or abdicate? *Journal of Educational Issues of Language Minority Students, 3,* 41–47.

Correa, V., & Jones, H. (2000). Multicultural issues related to families of children with disabilities. In M. J. Fine (Ed.), *Collaboration with parents of exceptional children* (2nd ed.), (pp. 133–154). Austin, TX: PRO-ED.

Coster, W. J., & Haltiwanger, J. T. (2004). Social-behavioral skills of elementary students with physical disabilities included in general education classrooms. *Remedial and Special Education, 25,* 95–103.

Cott, A. (1972). Megavitamins: The orthomolecular approach to behavioral disorders and learning disabilities. *Academic Therapy, 7,* 245–258.

Coulter, D. L. (1994). Biomedical conditions: Types, causes, and results. In L. Sternberg (Ed.), *Individuals with profound disabilities: Instructional and assistive strategies* (3rd ed.), (pp. 41–58). Austin, TX: PRO-ED.

Council for Children with Behavioral Disorders. (1989). Best assessment practices for students with behavioral disorders: Accommodation to cultural diversity and individual differences. *Behavioral Disorders, 14,* 263–278.

Council for Children with Behavioral Disorders. (1993, June). Staff position statement: Inclusion. CCBD *Newsletter,* p. 1.

Council for Exceptional Children. (2003). *What every special educator must know: The standards for the preparation and licensure of special educators* (5th ed.). Arlington, VA: Author.

Council for Exceptional Children (2004). *The new IDEA: CEC's summary of significant issues.* Arlington, VA: Author.

Council for Exceptional Children. (2004, May 14). *CEC disappointed in lack of full funding in Senate IDEA bill: Once again, students with disabilities are let down* (Press release). Arlington, VA: Author.

Council for Learning Disabilities. (1993). Concerns about the full inclusion of students with learning disabilities in regular education classrooms. *Journal of Learning Disabilities, 26,* 595.

Council of State Directors of Programs for the Gifted. (2000). *1998–99 state of the states gifted and talented education report.* Longmont, CO: Author.

Council of State Directors of Programs for the Gifted. (2003). *2001–2002 state of the states gifted and talented education report.* Longmont, CO: Author.

Courson, F. H., & Hay, G. H. (1996). Parents as partners. *Beyond Behavior, 7*(3), 19–23.

Court, D., & Givon, S. (2003). Group intervention: Improving social skills of adolescents with learning disabilities. *Teaching Exceptional Children, 36*(2), 46–51.

Craft, M. A., Alber, S. R., & Heward, W. L. (1998). Teaching elementary students with developmental disabilities to recruit teacher attention in a general education classroom: Effects on teacher praise and academic productivity. *Journal of Applied Behavior Analysis, 31,* 399–415.

Craig, S., Hall, K., Haggart, A. G., & Perez-Selles, M. (2000). Promoting cultural competence through teacher assistance teams. *Teaching Exceptional Children, 32*(3), 6–12.

Crandall, J., Jacobson, J., & Sloane, H. (Eds.). (1997). *What works in education.* Cambridge, MA: Cambridge Center for Behavioral Studies.

Crandell, C. C., & Smaldino, J. J. (2001a). Improving classroom acoustics: Utilizing hearing-assistive technology and communication strategies in the educational setting. *Volta Review, 101*(5), 47–64.

Crandell, C. C., & Smaldino, J. J. (2001b). Rehabilitative technologies for individuals with hearing loss and normal hearing. In J. Katz (Ed.), *Handbook of clinical audiology* (5th ed.), (pp. 607–630). New York: Lippincott, Williams, & Wilkins.

Cronin, M. E., Patton, J. R., & Wood, S. J. (2005). *Life skills instruction: A practical guide for integrating real-life content into the curriculum at the elementary and secondary levels for students with special needs or who are placed at risk.* Austin: PRO-ED.

Cronin, M. E., Slade, D. L., Bechtel, C., & Anderson, P. (1992). Home-school partnerships: A cooperative approach to intervention. *Intervention in School and Clinic, 27,* 286–292.

Cronin, M. S., & Patton, J. R. (1993). *Life skills instruction for all students with special needs: A practical guide for integrating real-life content into the curriculum.* Austin, TX: PRO-ED.

Crossley, R. (1988). *Unexpected communication attainments by persons diagnosed as autistic and intellectually impaired.* Caulfield, Victoria: Deal Communication Centre.

Crossley, R., & Remington-Guerney, J. (1992). Getting the words out: Facilitated communication training. *Topics in Language Disorders, 12*(4), 29–45.

Cruickshank, W. M. (1986). *Disputable decisions in special education.* Ann Arbor: University of Michigan Press.

Crutchfield, M. D. (2003). What do CEC standards mean to me? Using the CEC standards to improve my practice. *Teaching Exceptional Children, 35*(6), 40–45.

Cruz, L. & Cullinan, D. (2001). Awarding points, using levels to help children improve behavior. *Teaching Exceptional Children, 33*(3), 16–23.

Cullen, C., & Mudford, O. (2005). Gentle teaching. In J. W. Jacobson, J. A. Mulick, & R. M. Foxx, (Eds.). *Controversial therapies in developmental disabilities: Fads, fashion, and science in professional practice* (pp. 423–432). Hillsdale, NJ: Lawrence Erlbaum Associates.

Cullinan, D. (2002). *Students with emotional and behavioral disorders: An introduction for teachers and other helping professionals.* Upper Saddle River, NJ: Merrill/Prentice Hall.

Cullinan, D., & Epstein, M. H. (1995). Behavior disorders. In N. G. Haring & L. McCormick (Eds.), *Exceptional children and youth* (6th ed.). Upper Saddle River, NJ: Merrill/Prentice Hall.

Cullinan, D., Epstein, M. H., & Sabornie, E. J. (1992). Selected characteristics of a national sample of seriously emotionally disturbed adolescents. *Behavioral Disorders, 17,* 273–280.

Cummins, J. (1989). A theoretical framework for bilingual special education. *Exceptional Children, 56,* 111–119.

Curl, R. M. (1990). A demonstration project for teaching entry-level job skills: The Co-Worker Transition Model for Youths with Disabilities. *Exceptional News, 13*(3), 3–7.

Curl, R. M., Hall, S. M., Chisholm, L. A., & Rule, S. (1992). Co-workers as trainers for entry-level workers: A competitive employment model for individuals with developmental disabilities. *Rural Special Education Quarterly, 11,* 31–35.

Curl, R. M., Lignugaris/Kraft, B., Pawley, J. M., & Salzberg, C. L. (1988). "What's next?" A quantitative and qualitative analysis of the transition for trainee to valued worker. Unpublished manuscript.

Cushing, L. S., & Kennedy, C. H. (1997). Academic effects of providing peer support in general education classrooms on students without disabilities. *Journal of Applied Behavior Analysis, 30,* 139–152.

Cystic Fibrosis Foundation. (2001). *Facts about cystic fibrosis.* Bethesda, MD: Author. www.cff.org.

Cystic Fibrosis Foundation. (2003). *Facts about CF.* Bethesda, MD: Author. www.cff.org.

Daly. P. M., & Ranalli, P. (2003). Using countoons to teach self-monitoring skills. *Teaching Exceptional Children, 35*(5), 30–35.

D'Amico, R. (1991). The working world awaits. In M. Wagner, L. Newman, R. D'Amico, E. D. Jay, P. Butler-Nalin, C. Marder, & R. Cox (Eds.), *Youth with disabilities: How are they doing? A comprehensive report from Wave 1 of the National Longitudinal Transition Study of special education students.* Menlo Park, CA: SRI International.

Danforth, S., & Navarro, V. (1998). Speech acts: Sampling the social construction of mental retardation in everyday life. *Mental Retardation, 36,* 31–43.

Danforth, S., & Rhodes, W. C. (1997). On what basis hope? Modern progress and postmodern possibilities. *Remedial and Special Education, 18,* 357–366.

Daugherty, D. (2001). *IDEA '97 and disproportionate placement.* http://www.naspcenter.org/teachers/ IDEA_disp.html.

Davis, C. A., Brady, M. P., Williams, R. E., & Burta, M. (1992). The effects of self-operated auditory prompting tapes on the performance fluency of persons with severe mental retardation. *Education and Training in Mental Retardation, 27,* 39–50.

Davis, G. A., & Rimm, S. B. (2004). *Education of the gifted and talented* (5th ed.). Boston: Allyn & Bacon.

Davis, J. M., Elfenbein, J., Schum, R., & Bentler, R. A. (1986). Effects of mild and moderate hearing impairments on language, educational, and psychological behavior of children. *Journal of Speech and Hearing Disorders, 51,* 53–62.

Davis, L. L., & O'Neill, R. E. (2004). Use of response cards with a group of students with learning disabilities including those for whom English is a second language. *Journal of Applied Behavior Analysis, 37,* 219–222.

Dawson, G., & Osterling, J. (1997). Early intervention in autism. In M. J. Guralnick (Ed.), *The effectiveness of early intervention* (pp. 307–326). Baltimore: Brookes.

DeAvila, E. (1976). Mainstreaming ethnically and linguistically different children: An exercise in paradox or a new approach? In R. I. Jones (Ed.), *Mainstreaming and the minority child* (pp. 93–108). Reston, VA: Council for Exceptional Children.

Deci, E. L., Koestner, R., & Ryan, R. M. (1999). A meta-analytic review of experiments examining the effects of extrinsic rewards on intrinsic motivation. *Psychological Bulletin, 125,* 627–668.

DeFilippo, C. L., Sims, D. G., & Gottermeier, L. (1995). Linking visual and kinesthetic imagery in lipreading instruction. *Journal of Speech and Hearing Research, 38,* 244–256.

deFur, S. (2000). Designing Individualized Education (IEP) Transition Plans. *ERIC Digest* (EDO-EC-00-7). Reston, VA: Council for Exceptional Children/ERIC Clearinghouse on Disabilities and Gifted Education.

DeLacy, M. (2004, June 23). The "No Child" Law's biggest victims? An answer that may surprise. *Education Week, 23*(40), 1.

Delaney, E. M., & Kaiser, A. P. (2001). The effects of teaching parents blended communication and behavior support strategies. *Behavior Disorders, 26,* 93–116.

De La Paz, S., & Graham, S. (1997). Strategy instruction in planning: Effects on the writing performance and behavior of students with learning difficulties. *Exceptional Children, 63,* 167–181.

Denham, A., & Lahm, E. A. (2001). Using technology to construct alternate portfolios of students with moderate and severe disabilities. *Teaching Exceptional Children, 33*(5), 10–17.

Denning, C. B., Chamberlain, J. A., & Polloway, E. A. (2000). An evaluation of state guidelines for mental retardation: Focus on definition and classification practices. *Education and Training in Mental Retardation and Developmental Disabilities, 35,* 226–232.

Dennis, R. E., & Giangreco, M. F. (1996). Creating conversation: Reflections on cultural sensitivity in family interviewing. *Exceptional Children, 53,* 103–116.

Dennis, R. E., Williams, W., Giangreco, M. F., & Cloninger, C. J. (1993). Quality of life as context for planning and evaluation of services for people with disabilities. *Exceptional Children, 53,* 499–512.

Deno, S. L. (1985). Curriculum-based measurement: The emerging alternative. *Exceptional Children, 52,* 219–232.

Deno, S. L. (1997). Whether thou goest ... perspectives on progress monitoring. In J. W. Lloyd, E. J. Kame'enui, & D. Chard (Eds.), *Issues in educating students with disabilities* (pp. 77–99). Mahwah, NJ: Erlbaum.

Deno, S., Maruyama, G., Espin, C., & Cohen, C. (1990). Educating students with mild disabilities in general education classrooms: Minnesota alternatives. *Exceptional Children, 57,* 150–161.

Deshler, D. D., & Lenz, B. K. (1989). The strategies instructional approach. *International Journal of Disability, Development, and Education, 6*(3), 203–244.

Deshler, D. D., & Schumaker, J. B. (1993). Strategy mastery by at-risk students: Not a simple matter. *Elementary School Journal, 94,* 153–157.

Deshler, D. D., Schumaker, J. B., Bulgren, J. A., Lenz, B. K., Jantzen, J., Adams, G., Carnine, D., Grossen, B., Davis, B., & Marquis, J. (2001). Making things easier: Connecting new knowledge to things students already know. *Teaching Exceptional Children, 33*(4), 82–85.

Deshler, D. D., Schumaker, J. B., Lenz, B. K., Bulgren, J. A., Hock, M. F., Knight, J., & Ehren, B. J. (2001). Ensuring content-area learning by secondary students with learning disabilities. *Learning Disabilities Research and Practice, 16,* 96–108.

Dettmer, P., Thurston, L. P., & Dyck, N. J. (2005). *Consultation, collaboration, and teamwork for students with special needs* (5th ed.). Boston: Allyn and Bacon.

Dever, R. B. (1988). *Community living skills: A taxonomy.* Washington, DC: American Association on Mental Retardation.

Dewey, J. (1916). *Democracy and education*. New York: Macmillan.

Díaz–Rico, L. T., & Weed, K. Z. (2002). *The cross-cultural, language, and academic development handbook: A complete K–12 reference guide* (2nd ed.). Boston: Allyn & Bacon.

DiCarlo, C. F., & Reid, D. H. (2004). Increasing pretend toy play of toddlers with disabilities in an inclusive setting. *Journal of Applied Behavior Analysis, 37,* 197–207.

Diefendorf, A. O. (1999). Screening for hearing loss in infants. *Volta Review, 99*(5), 43–61.

Dieker, L. A. (2002). *Co-teaching lesson plan book: Academic year version*. Arlington, VA: Council for Exceptional Children.

Diller, L. H. (1998). *Running on Ritalin*. New York: Bantam.

Dimitropoulos, A., Feurer, I. D., Butler, M. G., & Thompson, T. (2001). Emergence of compulsive behavior and tantrums in children with Prader-Willi syndrome. *American Journal of Mental Retardation, 106,* 39–51.

Dinnebeil, L., & McInerney, W. (2000). Supporting inclusion in community-based settings: The role of the "Tuesday morning teacher." *Young Exceptional Children, 4*(1), 19–26.

Division for Learning Disabilities. (1993). *Inclusion: What does it mean for students with learning disabilities?* Reston, VA: Author.

Division for Learning Disabilities. (2001). Award-winning researchers raise questions about "inclusion." *DLD Times, 18*(2), 4.

Dodd, A. W. (1996). Involving parents, avoiding gridlock. *Educational Leadership, 53*(7), 50–54.

Dodge, K. (1993). The future of research on conduct disorder. *Development and Psychopathology, 5*(1/2), 311–320.

Dohan, M., & Schulz, H. (1998). The speech-language pathologist's changing role: Collaboration with the classroom. *Journal of Children's Communication Development, 20,* 9–18.

Donley, C. R., & Williams, G. (1997). Parents exhibit children's progress at a poster session. *Teaching Exceptional Children, 29*(4), 46–51.

Doren, B., Bullis, M., & Benz, M. R. (1996a). Predicting the arrest status of adolescents with disabilities in transition. *Journal of Special Education, 29,* 363–380.

Doren, B., Bullis, M., & Benz, M. R. (1996b). Predictors of victimization experiences of adolescents with disabilities in transition. *Exceptional Children, 63,* 7–18.

Dormans, J. P., & Pellegrino, L. (Ed.). (1998). *Caring for children with cerebral palsy: A team approach*. Baltimore: Brookes.

Downing, J. (1999). *Teaching communication skills to students with severe disabilities*. Baltimore: Brookes.

Downing, J. (2000). Augmentative communication services: A critical aspect of assistive technology. *Journal of Special Education Technology, 15*(3), 35–38.

Downing, J., & Eichinger, J. (1990). Instructional strategies for learners with dual sensory impairments in integrated settings. *Journal of The Association for Persons with Severe Handicaps, 15,* 98–105.

Downing, J. A. (2004). Related services for student with disabilities: Introcution to the special issue. *Invertantion in School and Clinic, 39,* 195–208.

Downing, J. E., & Chen, D. (2003). Using tactile strategies with students who are blind and have severe disabilities. *Teaching Exceptional Children, 36*(2), 56–60.

Downing, J. E., & Eichinger, J. (2003). Creating learning opportunities for students with severe disabilities in inclusive classrooms. *Teaching Exceptional Children, 36*(1), 26–31.

Doyle, P. M., Wolery, M., Ault, M. J., & Gast, D. L. (1988). System of least prompts: A literature review of procedural parameters. *Journal of The Association for Persons with Severe Handicaps, 13,* 28–40.

Drasgow, E. (1998). American Sign Language as a pathway to linguistic competence. *Exceptional Children, 64,* 329–342.

Duckworth, S., Smith-Rex, S., Okey, S., Brookshire, M. A., Rawlinson, D., Rawlinson, R., Castillo, S., & Little, J. (2001). Wraparound services for young school children with emotional and behavior disorders. *Teaching Exceptional Children, 33*(4), 54–60.

Dugan, E., Kamps, D., Leonard, B., Watkins, N., Rheinberger, A., & Stackhaus, J. (1995). Effects of cooperative learning groups during social studies for students with autism and fourth-grade peers. *Journal of Applied Behavior Analysis, 28,* 175–188.

Dunlap, G., Clarke, S., Jackson, M., Wright, S., Ramos, E., & Brinson, S. (1995). Self-monitoring of classroom behaviors with students exhibiting emotional and behavioral challenges. *School Psychology Quarterly, 10,* 165–177.

Dunlap, G., Dyer, K., & Koegel, R. L. (1983). Autistic self-stimulation and intertrial interval duration. *American Journal of Mental Deficiency, 88,*194–204.

Dunlap, G., & Fox, L. (1996). Early intervention and serious problem behavior: A comprehensive approach. In L. K. Koegel, R. L. Koegel, & G. Dunlap (Eds.), *Positive behavioral support: Including people with difficult behavior in the community* (pp. 31–50). Baltimore: Brookes.

Dunn, L. M., & Dunn, L. M. (1997). *Peabody Picture Vocabulary Test—III*. Circle Pines, MN: American Guidance Services.

Dunn-Geier, J., Ho, H. H., Auersberg, E., Doyle, D., Eaves, L., Matsuba, C., et al. (2000). Effects of secretin on children with autism: A randomized controlled trial. *Developmental Medicine and Child Neurology, 42*(12), 796–802.

Dunst, C. (2001). Participation of young children with disabilities in community learning activities. In M. Guralnick (Ed.), *Early childhood inclusion: Focus on change* (pp. 307–333). Baltimore: Brookes.

Dunst, C. J., Trivette, C. M., & Deal, A. G. (1988). *Enabling and empowering families: Principles and guidelines for practice*. Cambridge, MA: Brookline.

DuPaul, G. J., & Stoner, G. (1994). *ADHD in the schools: Assessment and intervention strategies*. New York: Guilford.

Dwyer, K. P., Osher, D., & Hoffman, C. C. (2000). Creating responsive schools: Contextualizing early warning, timely response. *Exceptional Children, 66,* 347–365.

Dye, G. A. (2000). Graphic organizers to the rescue! Helping student link—and remember—information. *Teaching Exceptional Children, 32*(3), 72–76.

Dykens, E. M. (2000). Contaminated and unusual food combinations: What do people with Prader-Willi syndrome choose? *Mental Retardation, 38,* 163–171.

Dykens, E. M., Hodapp, R. M., & Finucane, B. M. (2000). *Genetics and mental retardation syndromes: A new look at behavior and interventions*. Baltimore: Brookes.

Dykens, E. M., & Rosner, B. A. (1999). Refining behavioral phenotypes: Personality-motivation in Williams and Prader-Willi syndromes. *American Journal of Mental Retardation, 104,* 158–169.

Dykes, J. (1992). Opinions of orientation and mobility instructors about using the long cane with preschool-age children. *RE:view, 24,* 85–92.

Dyson, L. (1996). The experiences of families of children with learning disabilities: Parental stress, family functioning, and sibling self-concept. *Journal of Learning Disabilities, 29*(3), 280–286.

Dyson, L., Edgar, E., & Crnic, K. (1989). Psychological predictors of adjustment by siblings of developmentally disabled children. *American Journal of Mental Retardation, 94,* 292–302.

Dzienkowski, R. C., Smith, K. K., Dillow, K. A., & Yucha, C. B. (1996). Cerebral palsy: A comprehensive review. *Nurse Practitioner, 21*(2), 45–59.

Easterbrooks, S. (1999). Improving practices for students with hearing impairments. *Exceptional Children, 65,* 537–554.

Ebanks, M. E., & Fisher, W. W. (2003). Altering the timing of academic prompts to treat destructive behavior maintained by escape. *Journal of Applied Behavior Analysis, 36,* 355–359.

Eber, L., Nelson, C. M., & Miles, P. (1997). School-based wraparound for students with emotional and behavioral challenges. *Exceptional Children, 63,* 539–555.

Edelbrock, C., Rende, R., Plomin, R., & Thompson, L. A. (1995). A twin study of competence and problem behavior in childhood and early adolescence. *Journal of Child Psychology and Psychiatry, 36,* 775–785.

Eden-Piercy, G. V. S., Blacher, J. B., & Eyman, R. K. (1986). Exploring parents' reactions to their young child with severe handicaps. *Mental Retardation, 24,* 285–291.

Edens, J. F. (1997). Home visitation programs with ethnic minority families: Cultural issues in parent consultation. *Journal of Educational and Psychological Consultation, 8*(4), 373–383.

Edens, R. M., Murdick, N. L., & Gartin, B. C. (2003). Preventing infection in the classroom: The use of universal precautions. *Teaching Exceptional Children, 35*(4), 62–66.

Ehren, B. J. (2000). Maintaining a therapeutic focus and sharing responsibility for student success: Keys to in-classroom speech-language services. *Language, Speech, and Hearing Services in Schools, 31,* 219–229.

Eikeseth, S., & Lovaas, O. I. (1992). The autistic label and its potentially detrimental effect on the child's treatment. *Journal of Behavioral Therapy and Experimental Psychiatry, 23*(3), 151–157.

Elbaum, B. (2002). The self-concept of students with learning disabilities: A meta-analysis of comparison across different placements. *Learning Disabilities Research and Practice, 17,* 216–226.

Elliot, L., Foster, S., & Stinson, M. (2002). Student study habits using notes from a speech-to-text support service. *Exceptional Children, 69,* 25–40.

Ellis, E. S., Deshler, D. D., Lenz, B. K., Schumaker, J. B., & Clark, F. L. (1991). An instructional model for teaching learning strategies. *Focus on Exceptional Children, 24*(1), 1–14.

Ellis, N. R. (1963). The stimulus trace and behavior inadequacy. In N. R. Ellis (Ed.), *Handbook of mental deficiency* (pp. 134–158). New York: McGraw-Hill.

Emlen, A. C. (1998). *AFS consumer survey: From parents receiving child care assistance.* Portland, OR: Portland State University, Regional Research Institute for Human Services.

Engelman, M. D., Griffin, H. C., Griffin, L. W., & Maddox, J. I. (1999). A teacher's guide to communicating with students with deaf-blindness. *Teaching Exceptional Children, 31*(5), 64–70.

Engelmann, S. (1977). Sequencing cognitive and academic tasks. In R. D. Kneedler & S. G. Tarver (Eds.), *Changing perspectives in special education* (pp. 46–61). Upper Saddle River, NJ: Merrill/Prentice Hall.

Engelmann, S. (1997). Theory of mastery and acceleration. In J. W. Lloyd, E. J. Kame'enui, & D. Chard (Eds.), *Issues in educating students with disabilities* (pp. 177–195). Mahwah, NJ: Erlbaum.

Engelmann, S., Osborn, J., Bruner, E. C., Engelmann, O., & Davis, K. L. (2002). *Reading mastery plus, level K.* Columbus, OH: SRA/McGraw-Hill.

Englert, C., Raphael, T., Anderson, L., Anthony, H., Stevens, D., & Fear, K. L. (1991). Making writing strategies and self-talk visible: Cognitive strategy instruction in writing in regular and special education classrooms. *American Educational Research Journal, 28,* 337–373.

Englert, C., Tarrant, K. L., Mariage, T. V., & Oxer, T. (1994). Lesson talk as the work of reading groups: The effectiveness of two interventions. *Journal of Learning Disabilities, 27,* 165–186.

Enright, R. (2000). If life is a journey, make it a joyride: Some tips for young people. *Exceptional Parent, 31*(7), 50–51.

Epstein, M. H., Hertzog, M. A., & Reid, R. (2001). The Behavioral and Emotional Rating Scale: Long term test-retest reliability. *Behavioral Disorders, 26,* 314–320.

Epstein, M. H., Kutash, K., & Duchnowski, A. (1998). *Outcomes for children and youth with emotional and behavioral disorders and their families: Programs and evaluation of best practices.* Austin, TX: PRO-ED.

Epstein, M. H., & Sharma, J. (1998). *Behavioral and Emotional Rating Scale.* Austin, TX: PRO-ED.

Erickson, K. A., & Koppenhaver, D. A. (1998). Using the "write talk-nology" with Patrick. *Teaching Exceptional Children, 31*(1), 58–64.

Ericsson, A. (2001). The acquired nature of expert performance: Implications for conceptions of giftedness and innate talent? In N. Colangelo & S. Assouline (Eds.), *Talent development IV: Proceedings from the 1998 Henry B. and Jocelyn Wallace National Research Symposium on Talent Development* (pp. 1–26). Scottsdale, AZ: Great Potential Press.

Ericsson, K. A., & Charness, N. (1994). Expert performance. Its structure and acquisition. *American Psychologist, 49*(8), 725–747.

Erin, J. N. (2004). *When you have a visually impaired student in your classroom: A guide for teachers.* New York: AFB Press.

Erin, J. N., Dignan, K., & Brown, P. A. (1991). Are social skills teachable? A review of the literature. *Journal of Visual Impairment and Blindness, 85,* 58–61.

Ernst, M., Cohen, R. M., Liebenauer, L. L., Jons, P. H., & Zametkin, A. J. (1997). Cerebral glucose metabolism in adolescent girls with attention-deficit/hyperactivity disorder. *Journal of Child Psychology and Psychiatry, 36,* 1399–1406.

Etzel-Wise, D., & Mears, B. (2004). Adapted physical education and therapeutic recreation in schools. *Intervention in School and Clinic, 39,* 223–232.

Evans, J. C., & Smith, J. (1993). Nursing planning, intervention, and evaluation for altered neurologic function. In D. B. Jackson & R. B. Saunders (Eds.), *Child health nursing: A comprehensive approach to the care of children and their health* (pp. 1353–1430). Philadelphia: Lippincott.

Ewolt, C. (1996). Deaf bilingualism: A holistic perspective. *Australian Journal of the Education of the Deaf, 2,* 5–9.

Fairweather, J. S., & Shaver, D. M. (1991). Making the transition to postsecondary education and training. *Exceptional Children, 57,* 264–270.

Farlow, L. J., & Snell, M. E. (1994). *Making the most of student performance data.* Washington, DC: American Association on Mental Retardation.

Farrington, D. P. (1995). The development of offending and antisocial behavior from childhood: Key findings from the Cambridge Study in Delinquent Development. *Journal of Child Psychology and Psychiatry, 36,* 929–964.

Faw, G. D., Davis, P. K., & Peck, C. (1996). Increasing self-determination: Teaching people with mental retardation to evaluate residential options. *Journal of Applied Behavior Analysis, 29,* 173–188.

Feinberg, E., & Vacca, J. (2000). The drama and trauma of creating public policies on autism: Critical issues to consider in the new millennium. *Focus on Autism and Other Developmental Disabilities, 15*(3), 130–137.

Feiner, S. K. (2002). Augmented reality: A new way of seeing. *Scientific American, 286*(4), 48–55.

Feingold, B. F. (1975). *Why your child is hyperactive.* New York: Random House.

Feingold, B. F. (1976). Hyperkinesis and learning disabilities linked to ingestion of artificial food colors and flavorings. *Journal of Learning Disabilities, 9,* 551–559.

Feldhusen, J. F., & Moon, S. (1995). The educational continuum and delivery of services. In J. L. Genshaft, M. Bireley, & C. L. Hollinger (Eds.), *Serving gifted and talented students: A resource for school personnel* (pp. 103–121). Austin, TX: PRO-ED.

Feldman, D., Kinnison, L., Jay, R., & Harth, R. (1983). The effects of differential labeling on professional concepts and attitudes toward the emotionally disturbed/behaviorally disordered. *Behavioral Disorders, 8,* 191–198.

Ferguson, D. L. (1994). Is communication really the point? Some thoughts on interventions and membership. *Mental Retardation, 1,* 7–18.

Ferguson, D. L., & Baumgart, D. (1991). Partial participation revisited. *Journal of The Association for Persons with Severe Handicaps, 16,* 218–227.

Ferguson, P. M. (2003). A place in the family: An historical interpretation of research on parental reactions to having a child with a disability. *Journal of Special Education, 36,* 124–130.

Ferguson, P. M., & Ferguson, D. L. (2006). The promise of adulthood. In M. E. Snell & F. Brown (Eds.), *Instruction of students with severe disabilities* (6th ed.). Upper Saddle River, NJ: Merrill/Prentice Hall.

Ferrell, K. A. (1996). Your child's development. In M. C. Holbrook (Ed.), *Children with visual impairments: A parents' guide* (pp. 73–96). Bethesda, MD: Woodbine House.

Ferrell, K. A., & Muir, D. W. (1996). A call to end vision stimulation training. *Journal of Visual Impairments and Blindness, 90,* 364–366.

Ferro, J., Foster-Johnson, L., & Dunlap, G. (1996). Relations between curricular activities and problem behaviors of students with mental retardation. *American Journal on Mental Retardation, 101,* 184–194.

Field, K. (2004, July 9). Battling the image of "a nerd's profession": Universities devise programs to lure more students to engineering. *Chronicle of Higher Education, 50*(44), A15.

Field, S., Martin, J., Miller, R., Ward, M., & Wehmeyer, M. L. (1998). *A practical guide for teaching self-determination.* Reston, VA: Council for Exceptional Children.

Figueroa, R. A. (1989). Psychological testing of linguistic-minority students: Knowledge gaps and regulations. *Exceptional Children, 56,* 145–152.

Filipek, P. A., et al. (2000). Practice parameter: Screening and diagnosis of autism. *Neurology, 55,* 468–479.

Filipek, P. A., Semrud-Clikmann, M., Steingard, R. J., Renshaw, P. F., Kennedy, D. N., & Biederman, J. (1997). Volumetric MRI analysis comparing subject having attention-deficit/hyperactivity disorder with normal controls. *Neurology, 48,* 589–601.

Finn, C. E., Rotherham, A. J., & Hokanson, C. R., Jr. (Eds.). (2001). *Rethinking special education for a new century.* Washington, DC: Thomas B. Fordham Foundation and the Progressive Policy Institute.

Fisher, C. W., & Berliner, D. C. (Eds.). (1985). *Perspectives on instructional time.* New York: Longman.

Fisher, D., & Ryndak, D. L. (Eds.). (2001). *The foundations of inclusive education: A compendium of articles on effective strategies to achieve inclusive education.* Baltimore: The Association for Persons with Severe Handicaps.

Fisher, W., Piazza, C. C., Bowman, L. G., Hagopian, L. P., Owens, J. C., & Slevin, I. (1992). A comparison of two approaches for identifying reinforcers for persons with severe and profound disabilities. *Journal of Applied Behavior Analysis, 25,* 491–498.

FitzSimmons, S. C. (1993). The changing epidemiology of cystic fibrosis. *Journal of Pediatrics, 122,* 1–9.

Flener, B. S. (1993). The consultative-collaborative teacher for students with visual handicaps. *RE:view, 25,* 173–182.

Fletcher, J. M., Lyon, G. R., Barnes, M., Stuebing, K. K., Francis, D. J., Olson, R. K., Shaywitz, S. E., & Shaywitz, B. A. (2002). Classification of learning disabilities: An evidence-based evaluation. In R. Bradley, L. Danielson, & D. P. Hallahan (Eds.), *Identification of learning disabilities: Research to practice* (pp. 185–250). Mahwah, NJ: Erlbaum.

Fletcher, J. M., Shaywitz, S. E., Shankweiler, D. P., Katz, L., Liberman, I. Y., Fowler, A., Francis, D. J., Stuebing, K. K., & Shaywitz, B. A. (1994). Cognitive profiles of reading disability: Comparisons of discrepancy and low achievement definitions. *Journal of Educational Psychology, 86,* 1–18.

Flexer, R. W., Simmons, T. J., Luft, P., & Baer, R. M. (2005). *Transition planning for secondary students with disabilities* (2nd ed.). Upper Saddle River, NJ: Merrill/Prentice Hall.

Flick, G. L. (2000). *How to reach & teach teenagers with ADHD.* West Nyack, NY: Center for Applied Research in Education.

Flora, S. R. (2004). *The power of reinforcement.* Albany: State University of New York Press.

Fombonne, E. (1999). The epidemiology of autism: A review. *Psychological Medicine, 29,* 769–786.

Fombonne, E. (2003). The prevalence of autism. *Journal of the American Medical Association, 289*(1), 87–89.

Foorman, B., Francis, D., Fletcher, J., Schatschneider, C., & Mehta, p. (1998). Early interventions for children with reading problems: Study designs and preliminary findings. *Journal of Educational Psychology, 90*(1), 1–12.

Ford, B. A. (2000). *Multiple voices for ethnically diverse exceptional learners, 2000.* Reston, VA: Council for Exceptional Children.

Ford, D. Y. (1998). The underrepresentation of minority students in gifted education. *Journal of Special Education, 32*(1), 4–14.

Forest, M., & Lusthaus, E. (1990). Everyone belongs with the MAPS Action Planning System. *Teaching Exceptional Children, 22*(2), 32–35.

Forgatch, M. S., & Paterson, G. R. (1998). Behavioral family therapy. In F. M. Dattilo (Ed.), *Case studies in couple and family therapy: Systematic and cognitive perspectives* (pp. 85–107). New York: Guilford.

Forness, S. R., & Kavale, K. A. (2000). Emotional or behavior disorders: Background and current status of the E/BD terminology and definition. *Behavioral Disorders, 25,* 264–269.

Forness, S. R., & Kavale, K. A. (in press). Impact of ADHD on school systems. In P. S. Jensen & J. R. Cooper (Eds.). Bethesda, MD: National Institutes of Health.

Forness, S. R., Kavale, K. A., Crenshaw, T. M., & Sweeney, D. P. (2000). Best practice in treating children with ADHD: Does not using medication in a comprehensive intervention program verge on malpractice? *Beyond Behavior, 10*(2), 4–7.

Forness, S., & Knitzer, J. (1992). A new proposed definition and terminology to replace "serious emotional disturbance" in the Individuals with Disabilities Education Act. *School Psychology Review, 21,* 12–20.

Fowler, S. A., Donegan, M., Lueke, B., Hadden, D. S., & Phillips, B. (2000). Evaluating community collaboration in writing interagency agreements on the age 3 transition. *Exceptional Children, 67,* 35–50.

Fowler, S. A., Dougherty, S. B., Kirby, K. C., & Kohler, F. W. (1986). Role reversals: An analysis of therapeutic effects achieved with disruptive boys during their appointments as peer monitors. *Journal of Applied Behavior Analysis, 19,* 437–444.

Fowler, S. A., Schwartz, I., & Atwater, J. (1991). Perspectives on the transition from preschool to kindergarten for children with disabilities and their families. *Exceptional Children, 58,* 136–145.

Fox, J., Shores, R., Lindeman, D., & Strain, P. (1986). Maintaining social initiations of withdrawn handicapped and nonhandicapped preschoolers through a

response-dependent fading tactic. *Journal of Abnormal Child Psychology, 14,* 387–396.

Fox, L., Vaughn, B. J., Wyatte, M. L., & Dunlap, G. (2002). "We can't expect other people to understand": Family perspectives on problem behavior. *Exceptional Children, 68,* 437–450.

Fox, W., & Gay, G. (1995). Integrating multicultural and curriculum principles in teacher education. *Principles in Teacher Education, 70*(3), 64–82.

Foy, C. J., Von Scheden, M., & Waiculonis, J. (1992). The Connecticut pre-cane: Case study and curriculum. *Journal of Visual Impairment and Blindness, 86,* 178–181.

Frame, M. J. (2000). The relationship between visual impairment and gestures. *Journal of Visual Impairments and Blindness, 94,* 155–171.

Frank, A. R., & Sitlington, P. L. (2000). Young adults with mental disabilities—Does transition planning make a difference? *Education and Training in Mental Retardation and Developmental Disabilities, 35,* 119–134.

Frankenberger, W., & Cannon, C. (1999). Effects of Ritalin on academic achievement from first to fifth grade. *International Journal of Disability, Development, and Education, 46,* 199–221.

Frankenburg, W. K., & Dodds, J. B. (1990). *The Denver II training manual.* Denver: Denver Developmental Materials.

Frasier, M., Garcia, J., & Passow, A. (1995). *A review of assessment issues in gifted education and their implications for identifying gifted minority students.* Storrs: University of Connecticut, National Research Center on the Gifted and Talented. (Research Monopoly RM95204).

Frasier, M., Hunsaker, S., Lee, J., Mitchell, S., Cramond, B., Krisel, S., Garcia, J., Martin, D., Frank, E., & Finley, S. (1995). *Core attributes of giftedness: A foundation for recognizing the gifted potential of minority and economically disadvantaged students.* Storrs: University of Connecticut, National Research Center on the Gifted and Talented.

Freeman, F., & Alkin, M. (2000). Academic and social attainments of children with mental retardation in general education and special education settings. *Remedial and Special Education, 21,* 3–18.

Frey, K. S., Fewell, R. R., & Vadasy, P. F. (1989). Parental adjustment and changes in child outcomes among families of young handicapped children. *Topics in Early Childhood Special Education, 8*(4), 38–57.

Friend, M., & Bursuck, W. D. (1999). *Including students with special needs: A practical guide for classroom teachers* (2nd ed.). Needham Heights, MA: Allyn & Bacon.

Frost, L., & Bondy, A. (2002). *The Picture Exchange Communication System (PECS) training manual* (2nd ed.). Newark, DE: Pyramid Products.

Fryxell, D., & Kennedy, C. H. (1995). Placement along the continuum of services and its impact on students' social relationships. *Journal of The Association for*

*Persons with Severe Handicaps, 20,* 259–269.

Fuchs, D., & Fuchs, L. S. (1994). Inclusive schools movement and the radicalization of special education reform. *Exceptional Children, 60,* 294–309.

Fuchs, D., & Fuchs, L. S. (1998). Researchers and teachers working together to adapt instruction for diverse learners. *Learning Disabilities Research and Practice, 13,* 126–137.

Fuchs, D., Fuchs, L. S., Bahr, M. W., Fernstrom, P., & Stecker, P. (1990). Prereferral intervention: A prescriptive approach. *Exceptional Children, 56,* 493–513.

Fuchs, D., Fuchs, L. S., Fernstrom, P., & Hohn, M. (1991). Toward a responsible reintegration of behaviorally disordered students. *Behavioral Disorders, 16,* 133–147.

Fuchs, D., Fuchs, L. S., Mathes, P. G., & Simmons, D. C. (1996). *Peer-assisted learning strategies in reading: A manual.* (Available from Box 328 Peabody, Vanderbilt University, Nashville, TN 37203).

Fuchs, D., Fuchs, L. S., Mathes, P. G., Lipsey, M. W., & Roberts, P. H. (2002). Is "learning disabilities" just a fancy term for low achievement?: A meta-analysis of reading differences between low achievers with and without the label. In R. Bradley, L. Danielson, & D. P. Hallahan (Eds.), *Identification of learning disabilities: Research to practice* (pp. 737–762). Mahwah, NJ: Erlbaum.

Fuchs, D., Fuchs, L. S., McMaster, K. N., & Al Otaiba, S. (2003). Identifying children at risk for reading failure: Curriculum-based measurement and the deal-discrepancy approach. In H. L. Swanson, K. R. Harris, & S. Graham (Eds.), *Handbook of learning disabilities* (pp. 431–449). New York: Guilford.

Fuchs, D., Fuchs, L. S., Thompson, A., Svenson, E., Yen, L., Al Otaiba, S., Yang, N., McMaster, K. N., Prentice, K., Kazdan, S., & Saenz, L. (2001). Peer-assisted learning strategies in reading: Extension for kindergarten, first grade, and high school. *Remedial and Special Education, 22,* 15–21.

Fuchs, L. S., & Fuchs, D. (1996). Combining performance assessment and curriculum-based measurement to strengthen instructional planning. *Learning Disabilities Research and Practice, 11*(3), 183–192.

Fuchs, L. S., & Fuchs, D. (2001). Principles for the prevention and intervention of mathematics disabilities. *Learning Disabilities Research and Practice, 16,* 85–95.

Fuchs, L. S., & Fuchs, D. (2003). Enhancing the mathematical problem solving of students with mathematics disabilities. In H. L. Swanson, K. R. Harris, & S. Graham (Eds.), *Handbook of learning disabilities* (pp. 306–322). New York: Guilford.

Fuchs, L. S., Fuchs, D., Hamlett, C. L., & Steecker, P. M. (1991). Effects of curriculum-based measurement and consultation on teacher planning and student achievement in mathematics operations. *American Educational Research Journal, 28,* 617–641.

Fuchs, L. S., Fuchs, D., & Kazdan, S. (1999). Effects of peer-assisted learning strategies on high school students with serious reading problems. *Remedial and Special Education, 20,* 309–318.

Fujiura, G. T. (2003). Continuum of intellectual disabilities: Demographic evidence for the "forgotten generation." *Mental Retardation, 41,* 420–429.

Fujiura, G. T., & Yamaki, K. (2000). Trends in demography of childhood poverty and disability. *Exceptional Children, 66,* 187–199.

Fujiura, J. E., & Yamaki, K. (1997). Analysis of ethnic variations in developmental disability prevalence and household economic status. *Mental Retardation, 35,* 286–294.

Furth, H. G. (1973). *Deafness and learning: A psychosocial approach.* Belmont, CA: Wadsworth.

Gabel, S. (2004). South Asian Indian cultural orientations toward mental retardation. *Mental Retardation, 42,* 12–25.

Gadow, K. D., & Nolan, E. E. (1993). Practical considerations in conducting school-based medication evaluations for children with hyperactivity. *Journal of Emotional and Behavioral Disorders, 1,* 118–126.

Gagné, F. (2000). Understanding the complex choreography of talent development through DMGT-based analysis. In K. A. Heller, F. J. Monks, R. J. Sternberg, & R. Subotnik (Eds.), *International handbook for research on giftedness and talent* (2nd ed.), (pp. 67–79). Oxford: Paragon.

Gagné, F. (2003). Transforming gifts into talents: The DMGT as a developmental theory. In N. Colangelo & G. A. Davis (Eds.), *Handbook of gifted education* (3rd ed.), (pp. 60–74). Needham Heights, MA: Allyn & Bacon.

Gagnon, J. C., & Maccini, P. (2001). Preparing students with disabilities for algebra. *Teaching Exceptional Children, 34*(1), 8–15.

Gajar, A., Goodman, L., & McAfee, J. (1993). *Secondary schools and beyond: Transition of individuals with mild disabilities.* Upper Saddle River, NJ: Merrill/Prentice Hall.

Gallagher, J. J. (1984). The evolution of special education concepts. In B. Blatt & R. J. Morris (Eds.), *Perspectives in special education: Personal orientations* (pp. 210–232). Glenview, IL: Scott, Foresman.

Gallagher, J. J., (2004). No Child Left Behind and gifted education. *Roeper Review, 26*(3), 121–123.

Gallaudet University. (1998). *1996–1997 annual survey of deaf and hard-of-hearing children and youth.* Washington, DC: Gallaudet University, Center for Assessment and Demographic Studies.

Gallivan-Fenlon, A. (1994). Integrated transdisciplinary teams. *Teaching Exceptional Children, 26*(3), 16–20.

Garay, S. V. (2003). Listening to the voices of deaf students: Essential transition issues.

*Teaching Exceptional Children, 35*(4), 44–48.

Garber, H., & Heber, R. (1973). *The Milwaukee Project: Early intervention as a technique to prevent mental retardation* [Technical paper]. Storrs: University of Connecticut.

Gardner, H. (1983/1994). *Frames of mind: The theory of multiple intelligences.* New York: Basic Books.

Gardner, H. (1999). *Intelligence reframed: Multiple intelligences for the 21st century.* New York: Basic Books.

Gardner, R., III, Cartledge, G., Seidl, B., Woolsey, M. L., Schley, G. S., & Utley, C. A. (2001). Mt. Olivet after-school program. *Remedial and Special Education, 22,* 22–33.

Gardner, R., III, Heward, W. L., & Grossi, T. A. (1994). Effects of response cards on student participation and academic achievement: A systematic replication with inner-city students during whole-class science instruction. *Journal of Applied Behavior Analysis, 27,* 63–71.

Garrick Duhaney, L. M. (2003). A practical approach to managing the behaviors of students with ADD. *Intervention in School and Clinic, 38,* 267–279.

Garten, B. C., Rumrill, P., & Serebreni, R. (1996). The higher education transition model: Guidelines for facilitating college transition among college-bound students with disabilities. *Teaching Exceptional Children, 29*(3), 30–33.

Gartland, D. (1993). Elementary teacher-parent partnerships: Effective communication strategies. *LD Forum, 18*(3), 40–42.

Garton, A., & Pratt, C. (1998). *Learning to be literate: The development of spoken and written language.* Oxford: Blackwell.

Gelb, S. A. (1997). The problem of typological thinking in mental retardation. *Mental Retardation, 35,* 448–457.

Gense, M. H., & Gense, D. J. (1994). Identifying autism in children with blindness and visual impairments. *RE:view, 26,* 55–62.

Genshaft, J. L., Greenbaum, S., & Borovsky, S. (1995). Stress and the gifted. In J. L. Genshaft, M. Bireley, & C. L. Hollinger (Eds.), *Serving gifted and talented students: A resource for school personnel* (pp. 257–268). Austin, TX: PRO-ED.

German, S. L., Martin, J. E., Huber Marshall, L., & Sale, R. P. (2000). Promoting self-determination: Using Take Action to teach goal attainment. *Career Development for Exceptional Individuals, 23,* 27–38.

Gersten, R. (1998). Recent advances in instructional research for students with learning disabilities: An overview. *Learning Disabilities Research and Practice, 13,* 162–170.

Gersten, R. (2001). Sorting out the roles of research in the improvement of practice. *Learning Disabilities Research and Practice, 16,* 45–50.

Getch, Y. Q., & Heuharth-Pritchett, S. (1999). Children with asthma: Strategies for educators. *Teaching Exceptional Children, 31*(3), 30–36.

Getty, L. A., & Summey, S. E. (2004). The course of due process. *Teaching Exceptional Children, 36*(3), 40–44.

Giangreco, M. F. (1992). Curriculum in inclusion–oriented schools: Trends, issues, challenges, and potential solutions. In S. Stainback & W. Stainback (Eds.), *Curriculum considerations in inclusive classrooms: Facilitating learning for all students* (pp. 239–263). Baltimore: Brookes.

Giangreco, M. F. (1996). "The stairs don't go anywhere!" A self-advocate's reflections on specialized services and their impact on people with disabilities [Invited interview]. *Physical Disabilities and Related Services, 14*(2), 1–12.

Giangreco, M. F., Cloninger, C. J., Dennis, R. E., & Edelman, S. W. (2000). Problem-solving methods to facilitate inclusive education. In R. A. Villa & J. S. Thousand (Eds.), *Restructuring for caring and effective education: Piecing the puzzle together* (2nd ed.), (pp. 293–327). Baltimore: Brookes.

Giangreco, M. F., Cloninger, C. J., & Iverson, V. S. (1998). *Choosing options and accommodations for children: A guide to educational planning for students with disabilities* (2nd ed.). Baltimore: Brookes.

Giangreco, M. F., Dennis, R., Cloninger, C., Edelman, S., & Schattman, R. (1993). "I've counted Jon": Transformational experiences of teachers educating students with disabilities. *Exceptional Children, 59,* 359–372.

Giangreco, M. F., & Doyle, M. B. (2000). Curricular and instructional considerations for teaching students with disabilities in general education classrooms. In S. Wade (Ed.), *Inclusive education: A casebook of readings for prospective and practicing teachers* (Vol. 1), (pp. 51–69). Hillsdale, NJ: Erlbaum.

Giangreco, M. F., & Doyle, M. B. (2002). Students with disabilities and paraprofessional support: Benefits, balance, and Band-Aids. *Focus on Exceptional Children, 34*(7), 1–12.

Giangreco, M. F., Edelman, S., & Dennis, R. (1991). Common professional practices that interfere with the integrated delivery of related services. *Remedial and Special Education, 12*(2), 16–24.

Giangreco, M. F., & Meyer, L. H. (1988). Expanding service delivery options in regular schools and classrooms for students with severe disabilities. In J. L. Graden, J. E. Zins, & M. J. Curtis (Eds.), *Alternative educational delivery systems: Enhancing instructional options for all students* (pp. 241–267). Washington, DC: National Association of School Psychologists.

Giangreco, M. F., & Putnam, J. W. (1991). Supporting the education of students with severe disabilities in regular education environments. In L. H. Meyer, C. A. Peck, & L. Brown (Eds.), *Critical issues in the lives of people with severe disabilities* (pp. 245–270). Baltimore: Brookes.

Gibb, G. S., & Dyches, T. T. (2000). *Guide to writing quality individualized education programs.* Boston: Allyn & Bacon.

Giek, K. A. (1992). Monitoring student progress through efficient record keeping. *Teaching Exceptional Children, 24*(3), 22–26.

Gilchrist, E. (1916). The extent to which praise and reproof affect a pupil's work. *School and Society, 4,* 872–874.

Gilger, J. W., Pennington, B. F., & DeFries, J. C. (1992). A twin study of the etiology of comorbidity: Attention deficit-hyperactivity disorder and dyslexia. *Journal of the American Academy of Children and Adolescent Psychiatry, 31,* 343–348.

Gillberg, C., & Wing, L. (1999). Autism: Not an extremely rare disorder. *Acta Psychiatric Scand, 99*(6), 399–406.

Gilliam, J. E. (1995). *The Gilliam autism rating scale.* Austin: PRO-ED.

Gitlin, L. N., Mount, J., Lucas, W., Weirich, L. C., & Gramberg, L. (1997). The physical costs and psychosocial benefits of travel aids for persons who are visually impaired or blind. *Journal of Visual Impairment and Blindness, 91,* 347–359.

Glassberg, L. A., Hooper, S. R., & Mattison, R. E. (1999). Prevalence of learning disabilities at enrollment in special education students with behavioral disorders. *Behavioral Disorders, 26,* 164–172.

Gleason, J. B. (1999). *The development of language* (4th ed.). Boston: Allyn & Bacon.

Goddard, Y. I., & Heron, T. E. (1998). Please teacher: Help me learn to spell better, teach me self-correction. *Teaching Exceptional Children, 30*(6), 38–43.

Godfrey, S. A., Grisham-Brown, J., Schuster, J. W., & Hemmeter, M. L. (2003). The effects of three techniques on student participation with preschool children with attending problems. *Education and Treatment of Children, 26,* 255–272.

Goldberg, D. (1997). *Educating children who are deaf/hard of hearing: Auditory/verbal option.* Reston, VA: ERIC Clearinghouse on Disabilities and Gifted Education. (ERIC Document Reproduction Service No. ED 414 670).

Goldman, R., Fristoe, M., & Woodcock, R. W. (1990). *Goldman-Fristoe-Woodcock Test of Auditory Discrimination.* Austin, TX: PRO-ED.

Goldman, R. M., & Fristoe, M. (2000). *Goldman-Fristoe Test of Articulation* (2nd ed.). Circle Pines, MN: American Guidance Service.

Goldrich Eskow, K., & Fisher, S. (2004). Getting together in college: An inclusion program for young adults with disabilities. *Teaching Exceptional Children, 36*(3), 26–32.

Goldstein, D. E., Murray, C., & Edgar, E. (1998). Employment earnings and hours of high school graduates with learning disabilities through the first decade after graduation. *Learning Disabilities Research and Practice, 13,* 53–64.

Goldstein, H. (2002). Communication intervention for children with autism: A review of treatment efficacy. *Journal of Autism and Developmental Disabilities, 32,* 373–396.

Goldstein, H., Kaczmarek, L. A., & English, K. M. (2001). *Promoting social communication: Children with developmental disabilities from birth to adolescence.* Baltimore: Brookes.

Goldstein, H., Kaczmarek, L., & Hepting, N. (1994). Communication interventions: The challenges of across-the-day implementation. In R. Gardner, III, D. M. Sainato, J. O. Cooper, T. E. Heron, W. L. Heward, J. Eshleman, & T. A. Grossi (Eds.), *Behavior analysis in education: Focus on measurably superior instruction* (pp. 101–113). Pacific Grove, CA: Brooks/Cole.

Goldstein, S., & Goldstein, M. (1998). *Managing attention-deficit hyperactivity disorder in children: A guide for practitioners* (2nd ed.). New York: Wiley.

Goleman, D. (1995). *Emotional intelligence: Why it can matter more that IQ.* New York: Bantam.

Gollnick, D. M., & Chinn, P. G. (2002). *Multicultural education in a pluralistic society* (6th ed.). Upper Saddle River, NJ: Merrill/Prentice Hall.

Gompel, M., van Bon, W. J. J., & Schreuder, R. (2004). Reading by children with low vision. *Journal of Visual Impairments and Blindness, 98,* 77–89.

Gomstyn, A. (2003, October 17). Minority enrollment in colleges more than doubled in past 20 years, study finds. *Chronicle of Higher Education, 50*(8), A25.

Gonzalez-Mena, J. (2002). *The child in the family and the community.* Upper Saddle River, NJ: Merrill/Prentice Hall.

Good, R. H., & Kaminski, R. A. (2003). *DIBELS: Dynamic indicators of basic early literacy skills* (6th ed.). Longmont, CO: Sopris West.

Good, R. H., Simmons, D. C., & Kame' enui, E. J. (2001). The importance and decision-making utility of a continuum of fluency-based indicators of foundational reading skills for third-grade high-stakes outcomes. *Scientific Studies of Reading, 5*(3), 257–288.

Goodman, G., & Poillion, M. J. (1992). ADD: Acronym for any dysfunction or difficulty. *Journal of Special Education, 26,* 37–56.

Goodman, L. V. (1976). A bill of rights for the handicapped. *American Education, 12*(6), 6–8.

Goodrich, G. L., Kirby, J., Wagstaff, P., Oros, T., & McDevitt, B. (2004). A comparative study of reading performance with a head-mounted laser display and conventional low vision devices. *Journal of Visual Impairments and Blindness, 98,* 148–159.

Gottesman, I. I. (1991). *Schizophrenia genesis: The origins of madness.* New York: Freeman.

Graham, S., & Harris, K. R. (1993). Self-regulated strategy development: Helping students with learning problems develop as writers. *Elementary School Journal, 94,* 169–181.

Graham, S., & Harris, K. R. (2003). Students with learning disabilities and the process of writing. In H. L. Swanson, K. R. Harris,

& S. Graham (Eds.), *Handbook of learning disabilities* (pp. 323–344). New York: Guilford.

Grandin, T. (1995). *Thinking in pictures and other reports of my life with autism*. New York: Vintage Books.

Grant, G., & McGrath, M. (1990). Need for respite-care services for caregivers of persons with mental retardation. *American Journal on Mental Retardation, 94*, 638–648.

Grantham, T. (2003). Increasing black student enrollment in gifted programs: An exploration of the Pulaski County Special School District's advocacy efforts. *Gifted Child Quarterly, 47*, 46–65.

Gray, C., & Garand, J. (1993). Social stories: Improving responses of student with autism with accurate social information. *Focus on Autistic Behavior, 8*, 1–10.

Gray, C. A. (1994). The social story kit. In C. A. Gray (Ed.), *The new social story book* (pp. 215–224). Arlington, TX: Future Horizons.

Gray, C. A. (2000). *Writing social stories with Carol Gray*. Arlington, TX: Future Horizons.

Gray, D. B., Quartrano, L. A., & Liberman, M. L. (1998). *Designing and using assistive technology*. Baltimore: Brookes.

Green, G. (1992, October). *Facilitated communication: Scientific and ethical issues: Research symposium for the E. K. Shriver Center University Affiliated Program*. Waltham, MA.

Green, G. (2001). Behavior analytic instruction for learners with autism: Advances in stimulus control technology. *Focus on Autism and Other Developmental Disabilities, 16*, 72–85.

Green, S. K., & Shinn, M. R. (1995). Parent attitudes about special education and reintegration: What is the role of student outcomes? *Exceptional Children, 61*, 269–281.

Greenbaum, P. E., Dedrick, R. F., Friedman, R. M., Kutash, K., Brown, E. C., Lardieri, S. P., & Pugh, A. M. (1996). National adolescent and children treatment study (NACTS): Outcomes for children with serious emotional and behavior disturbance. *Journal of Emotional and Behavioral Disorders, 4*, 130–146.

Greenen, S., Powers, L. E., & Lopez-Vasquez, A. (2001). Multicultural aspects of parent involvement in transition planning. *Exceptional Children, 67*, 265–282.

Greenspan, S. (1992). Reconsidering the diagnosis and treatment of very young children with autistic spectrum or pervasive developmental disorder. *Zero to Three, 13*(2), 1–9.

Greenspan, S. (1997). Dead manual walking? Why the 1992 AAMR definition needs redoing. *Education and Training in Mental Retardation and Developmental Disabilities, 32*, 179–190.

Greenspan, S., & Weider, S. W. (1997). Developmental patterns and outcomes in infants and children with disorders in relating and communicating: A chart review of 200 cases of children with autistic spectrum diagnoses. *Journal of Developmental and Learning Disorders, 1*, 87–141.

Greenwood, C. R., Carta, J. J., Hart, B., Kamps, D., Terry, D., Delquadri, J. C., Walker, D., & Risley, T. (1992). Out of the laboratory and into the community: Twenty-six years of applied behavior analysis at the Juniper Gardens Children's Center. *American Psychologist, 47*, 1464–1474.

Greenwood, C. R., Carta, J. J., & Walker, D. (2005). Individual growth and development indicators: Tools for assessing intervention results for infants and toddlers. In W. L. Heward, T. E. Heron, N. A. Neef, S. M. Peterson, D. M. Sainato, G. Cartledge, R. Gardner, III, L. D. Peterson, S. B. Hersh, & J. C. Dardig (Eds.), *Focus on behavior analysis in education: Achievements, challenges, and opportunities* (pp. 103–136). Upper Saddle River, NJ: Prentice Hall/Merrill.

Greenwood, C. R., & Delquadri, J. (1995). Classwide peer tutoring and the prevention of school failure. *Preventing School Failure, 39*(4), 21–25.

Greenwood, C. R., Delquadri, J., & Carta, J. J. (1997). *Together we can: Classwide peer tutoring to improve basic academic skills*. Longmont, CO: Sopris West.

Greenwood, C. R., Delquadri, J., & Hall, R. V. (1984). Opportunity to respond and student academic achievement. In W. L. Heward, T. E. Heron, D. S. Hill, & J. Trap-Porter (Eds.), *Focus on behavior analysis in education* (pp. 58–88). Upper Saddle River, NJ: Merrill/Prentice Hall.

Greenwood, C. R., Hart, B., Walker, D., & Risley, T. (1994). The opportunity to respond and academic performance revisited: A behavioral theory of developmental retardation and its prevention. In R. Gardner, III, D. M. Sainato, J. O. Cooper, T. E. Heron, W. L. Heward, J. Eshleman, & T. A. Grossi (Eds.), *Behavior analysis in education: Focus on measurably superior instruction* (pp. 213–223). Pacific Grove, CA: Brooks/Cole.

Greenwood, C. R., & Maheady, L. (1997). Measurable change in student performance: Forgotten standard in teacher preparation? *Teacher Education and Special Education, 20*, 265–275.

Greenwood, C. R., Maheady, L., & Delquadri, J. C. (2002). Classwide peer tutoring. In G. Stoner, M. R. Shinn, & H. Walker (Eds.), *Interventions for achievement and behavior problems* (2nd ed.), (pp. 611–649). Washington, DC: National Association of School Psychologists.

Grenot-Scheyer, M., Fisher, M., & Staub, D. (2001). *Lessons learned in inclusive education at the end of the day*. Baltimore: Brookes.

Gresham, F. (2002). Responsiveness to intervention: An alternative approach to the identification of learning disabilities. In R. Bradley, L. Danielson, & D. P. Hallahan (Eds.), *Identification of learning disabilities: Research to practice* (pp. 467–519). Mahwah, NJ: Erlbaum.

Gresham, F. M., Lane, K. L., MacMillan, D.L., & Bocian, K. M. (1999). Social and academic profiles of externalizing and internalizing groups; Risk factors for emotional and behavioral disorders. *Behavioral Disorders, 24*, 231–245.

Gresham, F. M., & MacMillan, D. L. (1997a). Autistic recovery? An analysis and critique of the empirical evidence on the Early Intervention Project. *Behavioral Disorders, 22*, 185–201.

Gresham, F. M., & MacMillan, D. L. (1997b). Denial and defensiveness in the place of fact and reason: Rejoinder to Smith and Lovaas. *Behavioral Disorders, 22*, 219–230.

Griffin, H. C., Williams, S. C., Davis. M. L., & Engelman, M. (2002). Using technology to enhance cues for children with low vision. *Teaching Exceptional Children, 35*(2), 36–42.

Griffin, K. L. (2001, October 7). Blind "see" via camera that tickles tongue. *Columbus Dispatch*, p. C6.

Grigal, M., Neubert, D. A., & Moon, M. S. (2002). Postsecondary options for students with significant disabilities. *Teaching Exceptional Children, 35*(2), 68–73.

Grigal, M., Test, D. W., Beattie, J., & Wood, W. (1997). An evaluation of transition components of individualized education programs. *Exceptional Children, 63*, 357–372.

Grossi, T. A. (1998). Using a self-operated auditory prompting system to improve the work performance of two employees with severe disabilities. *Journal of The Association for Persons with Severe Handicaps, 23*, 149–154.

Grossi, T. A., & Heward, W. L. (1998). Using self-evaluation to improve the work productivity of trainees in a community-based restaurant training program. *Education and Training in Mental Retardation and Developmental Disabilities, 33*, 248–263.

Grossman, H. (Ed.). (1983). *Classification in mental retardation*. Washington, DC: American Association on Mental Deficiency.

Guess, D., Benson, H. A., & Siegel-Causey, E. (1985). Concepts and issues related to choice-making and autonomy among persons with severe disabilities. *Journal of The Association for Persons with Severe Handicaps, 10*, 79–86.

Guilford, J. P. (1959). Traits of creativity. In H. H. Anderson (Ed.), *Creativity and its cultivation* (pp. 142–161). New York: Harper.

Guilford, J. P. (1967). *The nature of human intelligence*. New York: McGraw-Hill.

Guilford, J. P. (1987). Creativity research: Past, present and future. In S. Isaksen (Ed.), *Frontiers of creativity research* (pp. 33–66). Buffalo, NY: Bearly.

Gumpel, T. P., & Shlomit, D. (2000). Exploring the efficiency of self-regulation as a possible alternative to social skills training *Behavioral Disorders, 25*, 131–141.

Gunter, P. L., Denny, R. K., Jack, S. L., Shores, R. E., & Nelson, C. M. (1993). Aversive stimuli in academic interactions between students with serious emotional disturbance and their teachers. *Behavioral Disorders, 18,* 265–274.

Gunter, P. L., Miller, K. A., Venn, M. L., Thomas, K., & House, S. (2002). Self-graphing to success: Computerized data management. *Teaching Exceptional Children, 35*(2), 30–34.

Gupta, V. B. (2003). The history, definition and classification of pervasive developmental disorders. *Exceptional Parent, 33*(2), 58–62.

Gunter, P. L., Hummel, J. H., & Conroy, M. A. (1998). Increasing correct academic responding: An effective intervention strategy to decrease behavior problems. *Effective School Practices, 17*(2), 55–62.

Guralnick, M. J. (1997). *The effectiveness of early intervention.* Baltimore: Brookes.

Guralnick, M. J. (1998). Effectiveness of early intervention for vulnerable children: A developmental perspective. *American Journal of Mental Retardation, 102*(4), 319–345.

Guralnick, M. J. (2001). *Early childhood inclusion: Focus on change.* Baltimore: Brookes.

Gustason, G. (1997). Educating children who are deaf or hard of hearing: English-based sign systems. *ERIC Digest #556.* (ERIC Document Reproduction Service No. ED 414 674).

Gustason, G., Pfetzing, D., & Zawolkow, E. (1980). *Signing exact English.* Los Alamitos, CA: Modern Signs.

Haager, D., & Vaughn, S. (1995). Parent, teacher, peer, and self-reports of the social competence of students with learning disabilities. *Journal of Learning Disabilities, 28,* 205–231.

Hadden, S., & Fowler, S. A. (1997). Preschool: A new beginning for children and parents. *Teaching Exceptional Children, 30*(1), 36–39.

Hadley, P. A. (1998). Language sampling protocols for eliciting text-level discourse. *Language, Speech, and Hearing Services in the Schools, 29,* 132–147.

Hadley, P. A., Simmerman, A., Long, M., & Luna, M. (2000). Facilitating language development for inner-city children: Experimental evaluation of a collaborative classroom-based intervention. *Language, Speech, and Hearing Services in Schools, 31,* 280–295.

Hagerman, R. J., & Cronsiter, A. (Eds.). (1996). *Fragile X syndrome: Diagnosis, treatment, and research* (2nd ed.). Baltimore: Johns Hopkins University Press.

Hagiwara, T., & Myles, B. (1999). A multi-media social story intervention: Teacher skills to children with autism. *Focus on Autism and Other Developmental Disabilities, 14,* 82–95.

Hale, J. E. (2001). *Learning while black: Creating educational excellence for African American children.* Baltimore: Johns Hopkins University Press.

Hall, B. J., Oyer, H. J., & Haas, W. H. (2001). *Speech, language, and hearing disorders: A guide for the teacher* (3rd ed.). Boston: Allyn & Bacon.

Hall, M., Kleinert, H. L., & Kerns, J. F. (2000). Going to college! Postsecondary programs for students with moderate and severe disabilities. *Teaching Exceptional Children, 32*(2), 58–65.

Hall, R. V., Lund, D., & Jackson, D. (1968). Effects of teacher attention on study behavior. *Journal of Applied Behavior Analysis, 1,* 1–12.

Hall, T. E., Wolfe, P. S., & Bollig, A. A. (2003). The home-to-school notebook: An effective communication strategy for students with severe disabilities. *Teaching Exceptional Children, 36*(2), 68–73.

Hallahan, D. P. (1992). Some thoughts on why the prevalence of learning disabilities has increased. *Journal of Learning Disabilities, 25,* 523–528.

Hallahan, D. P. (1998). Teach. Don't flinch. *DLD Times, 16*(1), 1, 4.

Hallahan, D. P., & Mock, D. R. (2003). A brief history of the field of learning disabilities. In H. L. Swanson, K. R. Harris, & S. Graham (Eds.), *Handbook of learning disabilities* (pp. 16–29). New York: Guilford.

Hallenbeck, B. A., & Kauffman, J. M. (1995). How does observational learning affect the behavior of students with emotional or behavioral disorders? A review of research. *Journal of Special Education, 29,* 43–71.

Haller, A. K., & Montgomery, J. K. (2004). Noise-induced hearing loss in children: What educators need to know. *Teaching Exceptional Children, 36*(4), 22–27.

Halpern, A. S. (1985). Transition: A look at the foundations. *Exceptional Children, 51,* 479–486.

Halpern, A. S. (1993). Quality of life as a conceptual framework for evaluating transition outcomes. *Exceptional Children, 59,* 486–498.

Ham, R. (1986). *Techniques of stuttering therapy.* Upper Saddle River, NJ: Prentice Hall.

Hamill, L. B. (2003). Going to college: The experiences of a young woman with Down syndrome. *Mental Retardation, 41,* 340–353.

Hamilton, S. L., Seibert, M. A., Gardner, R., III, & Talbert-Johnson, C. (2000). Using guided notes to improve the academic achievement of incarcerated adolescents with learning and behavior problems. *Remedial and Special Education, 21,* 133–140.

Hammer, M. R. (2004). Using the self-advocacy strategy to increase student participation in IEP conferences. *Intervention in School and Clinic, 39,* 295–300.

Hammill, D., & Larsen, S. (1978). The effectiveness of psycholinguistic training: A reaffirmation of position. *Exceptional Children, 44,* 402–417.

Hammill, D., & Newcomer, P. L. (1997). *Test of Language Development—3.* Austin, TX: PRO–ED.

Hancock, L. (1996, March 18). Mother's little helper. *Newsweek, 137*(12), 50–56.

Hanline, M. F. (1993). Inclusion of preschoolers with profound disabilities: An analysis of children's interactions. *Journal of The Association for Persons with Severe Handicaps, 18,* 28–35.

Hanson, M. J., Beckman, P. J., Horn, E., Marquart, J., Sandall, S., Greig, D., & Breenan, E. (2000). Entering preschool: Family and professional experiences in this transition process. *Journal of Early Intervention, 23,* 279–293.

Hanson, M. J., Horn, E., Sandall, S., Beckman, P., Morgan, M., Marquart, J., Barnwell, D. K., & Chou, H. (2001). After preschool inclusion: Children's educational pathways over the early school years. *Exceptional Children, 68,* 65–83.

Harchik, A. E. (1994). Self-medication skills. In M. Agran, N. E. Marchand-Martella, & R. C. Martella (Eds.), *Promoting health and safety: Skills for independent living* (pp. 55–69). Pacific Grove, CA: Brooks/Cole.

Hardin, D. M., & Littlejohn, W. (1995). Family-school collaboration: Elements of effectiveness and program models. *Preventing School Failure, 39*(1), 4–8.

Hardman, M. L., McDonnell, J., & Welch, M. (1997). Perspectives on the future of IDEA. *Journal of The Association for Persons with Severe Handicaps, 22,* 61–77.

Harland, V. T. (1997). *Youth street gangs: Breaking the gangs cycles in urban America.* San Francisco: Austin & Winfield.

Harmston, K. A., Strong, C. J., & Evans, D. D. (2001). International pen-pal correspondence for students with language-learning disabilities. *Teaching Exceptional Children, 33*(3), 46–51.

Harn, W., Bradshaw, M., & Ogletree, B. (1999). The speech-language pathologist in the schools: Changing roles. *Intervention in School and Clinic, 34,* 7.

Harris, H., & Harris, S. (1997). *The voice clinic handbook.* London: Whurr.

Harris, K. R., & Graham, S. (1996). Memo to constructivists: Skills count, too. *Educational Leadership, 53*(5), 26–29.

Harris, L., & Associates. (1986). *The ICD survey of disabled Americans: Bringing disabled Americans into the mainstream.* New York: Author.

Harris, S. L., & Handleman, J. S. (Eds.). (2000). *Preschool programs for children with autism* (2nd ed.). Austin, TX: PRO-ED.

Harrop, A., & Swinson, J. (2000). Natural rates of approval and disapproval in British infant, junior, and secondary classrooms. *British Journal of Educational Psychology, 70,* 473–483.

Harry, B. (1992a). *Cultural diversity, families, and the special education system: Communication and empowerment.* New York: Teachers College Press.

Harry, B. (1992b). Making sense of disability: Low-income, Puerto Rican parents' theories of the problem. *Exceptional Children, 59,* 27–40.

Harry, B. (1994). *The disproportionate representation of minority students in special education: Theories and recommendations.* Alexandria, VA: National Association of State Directors of Special Education.

Harry, B. (2003). Trends and issues in serving culturally diverse families of children with disabilities. *Journal of Special Education, 36,* 131–138.

Harry, B., Kalyanpur, M., & Day, M. (1999). *Building cultural reciprocity with families: Case studies in special education.* Baltimore: Brookes.

Harry, B., Rueda, R., & Kalyanpur, M. (1999). Cultural reciprocity in sociocultural perspective: Adapting the normalization principle for family collaboration. *Exceptional Children, 66,* 123–136.

Hart, B., & Risley, T. R. (1995). *Meaningful differences in the everyday experience of young American children.* Baltimore: Brookes.

Hart, B., & Risley, T. R. (1999). *The social world of children learning to talk.* Baltimore: Brookes.

Hasazi, S. B., Furney, K. S., & DeStefano, L. (1999). Implementing the IDEA transition mandates. *Exceptional Children, 65*(4), 555–566.

Haseltine, B., & Mittenburger, R. G. (1990). Teaching self-protection skills to persons with disabilities. *American Journal of Mental Retardation, 95,* 188–197.

Hatlen, P. (1996). *The core curriculum for blind and visually impaired students, including those with additional disabilities.* New York: American Foundation for the Blind.

Havey, J. M. (1999). School psychologists' involvement in special education due process hearings. *Psychology in the Schools, 36*(2), 117–121.

Hawkins, B. A., Eklund, S. J., James, D. R., & Foose, A. K. (2003). Adaptive behavior and cognitive function of adults with Down syndrome: Modeling change with age. *Mental Retardation, 41,* 7–28.

Hawkins, L., & Brawner, J. (1997). *Educating children who are deaf/hard of hearing: Total communication.* Reston, VA: ERIC Clearinghouse on Disabilities and Gifted Education. (ERIC Document Reproduction Service No. ED 414 677).

Haynes, W., & Pindzola, R. (2004). *Diagnosis and evaluation in speech pathology* (6th ed.). Needham Heights, MA: Allyn & Bacon.

Heber, R. F., & Garber, H. (1971). An experiment in prevention of cultural-familial mental retardation. In D. A. Primrose (Ed.), *Proceedings of the Second Congress of the International Association for the Scientific Study of Mental Deficiency.* Warsaw: Polish Medical Publishers.

Heckaman, K. A., Alber, S. R., Hooper, S., & Heward, W. L. (1998). A comparison of least-to-most prompts and progressive time delay on the disruptive behavior of students with autism. *Journal of Behavior Education, 8,* 171–201.

Heckaman, K., Conroy, M., Fox, J., & Chait, A. (2000). Functional assessment-based interventions research on students with or at risk for emotional and behavioral disorders in school settings. *Behavioral Disorders, 25,* 196–210.

Heflin, L. J., & Simpson, R. L. (2002). Understanding intervention controversies. In B. Scheuermann & J. Webber, *Autism: Teaching does make a difference* (pp. 248–277). Belmont, CA: Wadsworth.

Heinze, T. (1986). Communication skills. In G. T. Scholl (Ed.), *Foundations of education for blind and visually handicapped children and youth: Theory and practice* (pp. 301–314). New York: American Foundation for the Blind.

Heller, K. W., Alberto, P. A., Forney, P. E., & Schwartzman, M. N. (1996). *Understanding physical, sensory and health impairments.* Pacific Grove, CA: Brooks/Cole.

Heller, K. W., & Bigge, J. (2005). Augmentative and alternative communication. In S. J. Best, K. W. Heller, & J. L. Bigge, (Eds.), *Teaching individuals with physical or multiple disabilities* (5th ed.), (pp. 227–274). Upper Saddle River, NJ: Merrill/Prentice Hall.

Heller, K. W., Bigge, J. L., & Allgood, P. (2005). Adaptations for personal independence. In S. J. Best, K. W. Heller, & J. L. Bigge, (Eds.), *Teaching individuals with physical or multiple disabilities* (5th ed.), (pp. 309–335). Upper Saddle River, NJ: Merrill/Prentice Hall..

Heller, K. W., Dangel, H., & Sweatman, L. (1995). Systematic selection of adaptations for students with muscular dystrophy. *Journal of Developmental and Physical Disabilities, 7,* 253–265.

Heller, K. W., Forney, P. E., Alberto, P. A., Schwartzman, M. N., & Goeckel, T. M. (1999). *Meeting physical and health needs of children with disabilities.* Belmont, CA: Wadsworth.

Heller, K. W., Fredrick, L. D., Best, S., Dykes, M. K., & Cohen, E. T. (2000). Specialized health care procedures in the schools: Training and service delivery. *Exceptional Children, 66,* 173–186.

Henderson, C. (2001). *College freshman with disabilities: A triennial statistical profile.* Washington, DC: American Council on Education/HEATH Resource Center.

Henderson, L. W., & Meisels, S. J. (1994). Parental involvement in the developmental screening of their young children: A multiple-source perspective. *Journal of Early Intervention, 18,* 141–154.

Henggler, S. (1989). *Delinquency in adolescence.* Beverly Hills, CA: Sage.

Herer, G. R., Knightly, C. A., & Steinberg, A. G. (2002). Hearing: Sounds and silences. In M. L. Batshaw (Ed.), *Children with disabilities* (5th ed.), (pp. 193–228). Baltimore: Brookes.

Hernandez, H. (2001). *Multicultural education: A teacher's guide to linking context, process, and content* (2nd ed.). Upper Saddle River, NJ: Merrill/Prentice Hall.

Heron, T. E., & Harris, K. C. (2001). *The educational consultant: Helping professionals, parents, and students in inclusive classrooms* (4th ed.). Austin, TX: PRO-ED.

Heron, T. E., Heward, W. L., Cooke, N. L., & Hill, D. S. (1983). Evaluation of a classwide peer tutoring system: First graders teach each other sight words. *Education & Treatment of Children, 6,* 137–152.

Heron, T. E., Welsch, R. G., & Goddard, Y. L. (2003). Applications of tutoring systems in specialized subject areas. *Remedial and Special Education, 24,* 288–300.

Hertzog, N. B. (1998). The changing role of the gifted education specialist. *Teaching Exceptional Children, 30*(3), 39–43.

Heward, W. L. (1994). Three "low-tech" strategies for increasing the frequency of active student response during group instruction. In R. Gardner, III, D. M. Sainato, J. O. Cooper, T. E. Heron, W. L. Heward, J. Eshleman, & T. A. Grossi (Eds.), *Behavior analysis in education: Focus on measurably superior instruction* (pp. 283–320). Pacific Grove, CA: Brooks/Cole.

Heward, W. L. (2001). *Guided notes: Improving the effectiveness of your lectures.* Columbus, OH: The Ohio State University Partnership Grant for Improving the Quality of Education for Students with Disabilities.

Heward, W. L. (2003). Ten faulty notions about teaching and learning that hinder the effectiveness of special education. *Journal of Special Education, 36*(4), 186–205.

Heward, W. L. (2005). Reasons applied behavior analysis is good for education and why those reasons have been insufficient. In W. L. Heward, T. E. Heron, N. A. Neef, S. M. Peterson, D. M. Sainato, G. Cartledge, R. Gardner, III, L. D. Peterson, S. B. Hersh, & J. C. Dardig (Eds.), *Focus on behavior analysis in education: Achievements, challenges, and opportunities* (pp. 316–348). Upper Saddle River, NJ: Merrill/Prentice Hall.

Heward, W. L., & Dardig, J. C. (2001, Spring). What matters most in special education. *Education Connection, 41*–44.

Heward, W. L., Gardner, R., III, Cavanaugh, R. A., Courson, F. H., Grossi, T. A., & Barbetta, P. M. (1996). Everyone participates in this class: Using response cards to increase active student response. *Teaching Exceptional Children, 28*(2), 4–10.

Heward, W. L., Heron, T. E., & Cooke, N. L. (1982). Tutor huddle: Key element in a classwide peer tutoring system. *Elementary School Journal, 83,* 115–123.

Heward, W. L., Heron, T. E., Gardner, R., III, & Prayzer, R. (1991). Two strategies for improving students' writing skills. In G. Stoner, M. R. Shinn, & H. M. Walker (Eds.), *A school psychologist's interventions for regular education* (pp. 379–398). Washington, DC: National Association of School Psychologists.

Heward, W. L., & Silvestri, S. M. (2005). The neutralization of special education. In J. W. Jacobson, J. A. Mulick, & R. M. Foxx, (Eds.). *Controversial therapies in developmental disabilities: Fads, fashion, and science in professional practice* (pp. 193–214). Hillsdale, NJ: Lawrence Erlbaum Associates.

Hill, B. K., Lakin, K. C., Bruininks, R. H., Amado, A. N., Anderson, D. J., & Copher, J. I. (1989). *Living in the community: A comparative study of foster homes and small group homes for people with mental retardation* (Report No. 28). Minneapolis: University of Minnesota, Center for Residential and Community Services.

Hill, E. W., & Snook-Hill, M. (1996). Orientation and mobility. In M. C. Holbrook (Ed.), *Children with visual impairments: A parents' guide* (pp. 259–286). Bethesda, MD: Woodbine House.

Hill, J. L. (1999). *Meeting the needs of students with special physical and health care needs.* Upper Saddle River, NJ: Merrill/Prentice Hall.

Hintz, R., & Driscoll, A. (1988). Praise or encouragement? New insights into praise: Implications for early childhood teachers. *Young Children, 16,* 6–13.

Hitchings, W. E., Luzzo, D. A., Retish, P., Horvath, M., & Ristow, R. (1998). Identifying the needs of college students with disabilities. *Journal of College Student Development, 39*(1), 23–32.

Hock, M. F., Schumaker, J. B., & Deshler, D. D. (1999). Closing the gap to success in secondary schools: A model for cognitive apprenticeship. In S. Graham, K. R. Harris, & M. Pressley (Series Eds.) & D. D. Deshler, K. R. Harris, & S. Graham (Vol. Eds.), *Advances in teaching and learning, teaching every child every day: Learning in diverse schools and classrooms* (pp. 1–52). Cambridge, MA: Brookline.

Hodapp, R. M., & Dykens, E. M. (2001). Strengthening behavioral research on genetic mental retardation syndromes. *American Journal of Mental Retardation, 106,* 4–15.

Hodson, B. W. (1994). Helping individuals become intelligible, literate, and articulate: The role of phonology. *Topics in Language Disorders, 14*(2), 1–16

Holahan, A., & Costenbader, V. (2000). A comparison of developmental gain for preschool children with disabilities in inclusive and self-contained classrooms. *Topics in Early Childhood Special Education, 20,* 224–235.

Holden-Pitt, L., & Diaz, J. (1998). Thirty years of the annual survey of deaf and hard-of-hearing children and youth: A glance over the decades. *American Annals of the Deaf, 142*(2), 72–76.

Hollinger, C. L. (1995). Counseling gifted young women about educational and career choices. In J. L. Genshaft, M. Bireley, & C. L. Hollinger (Eds.), *Serving gifted and talented students: A resource for school personnel* (pp. 269–283). Austin, TX: PRO-ED.

Holt, J. (1993). Stanford Achievement Test—8th edition: Reading comprehension subgroup results. *American Annals of the Deaf, 138,* 172–175.

Honig v. Doe, 485 U.S. 305, 108 S.Ct. 592, 98 L.Ed. 2d 686 (1988).

Hoover, H. D., Hieronymus, A. N., Frisbie, D. A., & Dunbar, S. B. (1996). *Iowa Tests of Basic Skills.* Chicago: Riverside.

Horn, E., Lieber, J., Li, S., Sandall, S., & Schwartz, I. (2000). Supporting young children's IEP goals in inclusive settings through embedded learning opportunities. *Topics in Early Childhood Special Education, 20,* 208–223.

Horner, R. H., & Carr, E. G. (1997). Behavioral support for students with severe disabilities: Functional assessment and comprehensive intervention. *Journal of Special Education, 31,* 84–104.

Horner, R. H., Carr, E. G., Strain, P. S., Todd, A. W., & Reed, H. K. (2002). Problem behavior interventions for young children with autism: A research synthesis. *Journal of Autism and Developmental Disabilities, 32,* 423–441.

Horner, R. H., Dunlap, G., & Koegel, R. L. (1988). *Generalization and maintenance: Life-style changes in applied settings.* Baltimore: Brookes.

Horstmeier, D. (2004). *Teaching math to people with Down syndrome and other hands-on learners.* Bethesda, MD: Woodbine House.

Horton, S. V., Lovitt, T. C., & Bergerud, D. (1990). The effectiveness of graphic organizers for three classifications of secondary students in content area classes. *Journal of Learning Disabilities, 23,* 12–22.

Horvath, K., Stefanatos, G., Sokolski, K. N., Wachtel, R., Nabors, L., & Tildon, J. T. (1998). Improved social and language skills after secretin administration in patients with autistic spectrum disorders. *Journal of the Association for Academic Minority Physicians, 9*(1), 9–15.

Hosp, J. L., & Reschly, D. J. (2003). Referral rates for intervention or assessment: A meta-analysis of racial differences. *Journal of Special Education, 37,* 67–80.

House, J. W. (1999). Hearing loss in adults. *Volta Review, 99*(5), 161–166.

Howard, V. F., Williams, B. F., & McLaughlin, T. F. (1994). Children prenatally exposed to alcohol and cocaine: Behavioral solutions. In R. Gardner, III, D. M. Sainato, J. O. Cooper, T. E. Heron, W. L. Heward, J. Eshleman, & T. A. Grossi (Eds.), *Behavior analysis in education: Focus on measurably superior instruction* (pp. 131–146). Pacific Grove, CA: Brooks/Cole.

Howard, V. F., Williams, B. F., & Lepper, C. (2005). *Very young children with special needs: A formative approach for today's children* (3rd ed.). Upper Saddle River, NJ: Merrill/Prentice Hall.

Howe, J., Horner, R. H., & Newton, J. S. (1998). Comparison of supported living and traditional residential services in the state of Oregon. *Mental Retardation, 36,* 1–11.

Howell, K. W., Evans, D., & Gardiner, J. (1997). Medications in the classroom: A hard pill to swallow. *Teaching Exceptional Children, 29*(6), 58–61.

Howell, K. W., & Nolet, V. (2000). *Curriculum-based evaluation: Teaching and decision making* (3rd ed.). Belmont, CA: Wadsworth/Thompson Learning.

Howell, R. D. (2000). Grasping the future with robotic aids. In W. L. Heward, *Exceptional children: An introduction to special education* (6th ed.), (pp. 478–480). Upper Saddle River, NJ: Merrill/Prentice Hall.

Hoye, J. D. (1998, July). *Integrating school-to-work into preservice teacher education.* Paper presented at Conference for Professors of Education in Ohio, Kent, OH.

Hudson, P., Lignugaris/Kraft, B., & Miller, T. (1993). Using content enhancements to improve the performance of adolescents with learning disabilities in content classes. *Learning Disabilities Research and Practice, 8,* 106–126.

Hudson, P., & Miller, S. P. (1993). Home and school partnerships: Parent as teacher. *LD Forum, 18*(2), 31–33.

Huefner, D. S. (2000). The risks and opportunities of the IEP requirements under IDEA '97. *Exceptional Children, 63,* 195–204.

Huff, K. E., & DuPaul, G. J. (1998). Reducing disruptive behavior in general education classrooms: The use of self-management strategies. *School Psychology Review, 27,* 290–303.

Hughes, C. (1997). Self-instruction. In M. Agran (Ed.), *Student directed learning: Teaching self-determination skills* (pp. 144–170). Pacific Grove, CA: Brooks/Cole.

Hughes, C., Copeland, S. R., Guth, C., Rung, L. L., Hwang, B., Kleeb, G., & Strong, M. (2001). General education students' perspective on their involvement in a high school peer buddy program. *Education and Training in Mental Retardation and Developmental Disabilities, 36,* 343–356.

Hughes, C., Rung, L. L., Wehmeyer, M. L., Agran, M., Copland, S. R., & Hwang, B. (2000). Self-prompted communication book to increase social interaction among high school students. *Journal of The Association for Persons with Severe Handicaps, 25,* 153–166.

Hughes, C., & Rusch, F. R. (1989). Teaching supported employees with severe mental retardation to solve problems. *Journal of Applied Behavior Analysis, 22,* 365–372.

Hughes, F., Elicker, J., & Veen, L. (1995, January). A program of play for infants and their caregivers. *Young Children,* 52–58.

Hulit, L. M., & Howard, M. R. (2002). *Born to talk: An introduction to speech and language development* (3rd ed.), Boston: Allyn & Bacon.

Hunt, P., Goetz, L., & Anderson, J. (1986). The quality of IEP objectives associated with placement on integrated versus segregated school sites. *Journal of The Association for Persons with Severe Handicaps, 11,* 125–130.

Hunt, P., Soto, G., Maier, J., & Doering, K. (2003). Collaborative teaming to support students at risk and students with severe disabilities in general education classrooms. *Exceptional Children, 69,* 315–332.

Hunt, P., Staub, D., Alwell, M., & Goetz, L. (1994). Achievement by all students within the context of cooperative learning groups. *Journal of The Association for Persons with Severe Handicaps, 19,* 290–301.

Huntze, S. L. (1985). A position paper of the Council for Children with Behavioral Disorders. *Behavioral Disorders, 10,* 167–174.

Hutinger, P. L., Marshall, S., & McCarten, K. (1983). *Core curriculum: Macomb 0–3 regional project* (3rd ed.). Macomb: Western Illinois University.

Inghram, J. (2003). Evidence-based treatment of stuttering: I. Definition and application. *Journal of Fluency Disorders, 28,* 197–206.

Ingram, A. L., Hathorn, L. G., and Evans, A. D. (2000). Beyond chat on the Internet. *Computers and Education, 35*(1), 21–35.

Ireland, J. C., Wray, D., & Flexer, C. (1988). Hearing for success in the classroom. *Teaching Exceptional Children, 20*(2), 15–17.

Irving Independent School District v. Tatro, 104 S. Ct. 3371, 82 L.Ed. 2d 664 (1984).

Iscoe, I., & Payne, S. (1972). Development of a revised scale for the functional classification of exceptional children. In E. P. Trapp & P. Himelstein (Eds.), *Readings on the exceptional child* (pp. 7–29). New York: Appleton-Century-Crofts.

Ita, C. M., & Friedman, H. A. (1999). The psychological development of children who are deaf or hard of hearing: A critical review. *Volta Review, 101,* 165–181.

Itard, J. M. G. (1806/1962). *The wild boy of Aveyron* (G. Humphrey & M. Humphrey, Eds. and Trans.). Englewood Cliffs, NJ: Prentice Hall. (Original work published in Paris by Guoyon).

Ives, B., & Hoy, C. (2003). Graphic organizers applied to higher-level secondary mathematics. *Learning Disabilities Research & Practice, 18,* 36–51.

Ivey, M. L., Heflin, L. J., & Alberto, P. (2004). The use of social stories to promote independent behaviors in novel events for children with PDD-NOS. *Focus on Autism and Other Developmental Disabilities, 19,* 164–176.

Iwata, B. A., Dorsey, M., Slifer, K., Bauman, K., & Richman, G. (1994). Toward a functional analysis of self-injury. *Journal of Applied Behavior Analysis, 27,* 197–209.

Jacobson, J. J., & Mulick, J. (1996). *Manual on diagnosis and professional practice in mental retardation.* Washington, DC: American Psychological Association.

Jacobson, J. W., Mulick, J. A., & Foxx, R. M. (Eds.). (2005). *Fads: Dubious and improbable treatments for developmental disabilities.* Hillsdale, NJ: Erlbaum.

Jacobson, J. W., Mulick, J. A., & Green, G. (1998). Cost-benefit estimates for early intensive behavioral intervention for young children with autism: General model and single state case. *Behavioral Interventions, 13,* 201–226.

Jacobson, W. H. (1993). *The art and science of teaching orientation and mobility to persons with visual impairments.* New York: American Federation for the Blind.

Janney, R. E., & Snell, M. E. (1996). Using peer interactions to include students with extensive disabilities in elementary general education classes. *Journal of The Association for Persons with Severe Handicaps, 21,* 72–80.

Janney, R. E., & Snell, M. E. (1997). How teachers include students with moderate and severe disabilities in elementary classes: The means and meaning of inclusion. *Journal of The Association for Persons with Severe Handicaps, 42*(3), 159–169.

Janney, R., & Snell, M. E. (2000). *Modifying schoolwork.* Baltimore: Brookes.

Janney, R., & Snell, M. E. (2000). *Teacher's guides to inclusive practices: Behavioral support.* Baltimore: Brookes.

Jenkins, J. R., & O'Conner, R. E. (2002). Early identification and intervention for young children with reading/learning disabilities. In R. Bradley, L. Danielson, & D. P. Hallahan (Eds.), *Identification of learning disabilities: Research to practice* (pp. 99–149). Mahwah, NJ: Erlbaum.

Jensen, P. S. (2000). Pediatric psychopharmacology in the United States: Issues and challenges in the diagnosis and treatment of attention-deficit/hyperactivity disorder. In L. L. Greenhill & B. B. Osman (Eds.), *Ritalin: Theory and practice* (2nd ed.) Larchmont, NY: Mary Ann Liebert, Inc.

Jensen, W. R., Sheridan, S. M., Olympia, D., & Andrews, D. (1994). Homework and students with learning disabilities and behavior disorders: A practical, parent-based approach. *Journal of Learning Disabilities, 27*(9), 538–548.

Jimenez, R. T. (2002). Fostering the literacy development of Latino students. *Focus on Exceptional Children, 34*(6), 1–10.

Johnsen, S. K. (Ed.). (2004). *Identifying gifted students: A practical guide.* Waco, TX: Prufrock.

Johnson, B., & Cuvo, A. (1981). Teaching mentally retarded adults to cook. *Behavior Modification, 12,* 69–73.

Johnson, D. R., Stodden, R. A., Emanuel, E. J., Luecking, R., & Mack, M. (2002). Current challenges facing secondary education and transition services: What research tells us. *Exceptional Children, 68,* 519–531.

Johnson, D. W., & Johnson, R. T. (1987). *Learning together and alone: Cooperative, competitive, and individualistic learning* (2nd ed.). Englewood Cliffs, NJ: Prentice Hall.

Johnson, H. A. (1997, June). *Internet use within deaf education: Current status, trends and applications.* Paper presented at the CAID/CEASD Conference, Hartford, CT.

Johnson, H. L. (1993). Stressful family experiences and young children: How the classroom teacher can help. *Intervention in School and Clinic, 28*(3), 165–171.

Johnson, R. (1985). *The picture communication symbols—Book II.* Solana Beach, CA: Mayer-Johnson.

Johnson, S., & Wehman, P. (2001). Teaching for transition. In P. Wehman (Ed.), *Life beyond the classroom: Transition strategies for young people with disabilities* (3rd ed.). Baltimore: Brookes.

Johnson, T. P. (1986). *The principal's guide to the educational rights of handicapped students.* Reston, VA: National Association of Secondary School Principals.

Johnson-Martin, N. M., Attermeier, S. M., & Hacker, B. (2004a). *The Carolina Curriculum for infants and toddlers with special needs* (3rd ed.). Baltimore: Brookes.

Johnson-Martin, N. M., Attermeier, S. M., & Hacker, B. (2004b). *The Carolina Curriculum for preschoolers with special needs* (2nd ed.). Baltimore: Brookes.

Johnston, D. (1994a). *Co:Writer* (Version 2.0) [Computer software]. Wauconda, IL: Don Johnston, Inc.

Johnston, D. (1994b). *Write:OutLoud* (Version 2.0) [Computer software]. Wauconda, IL: Don Johnston, Inc.

Johnston, R., & Umberger, R. (1996). *The voice companion.* East Moline, IL: LinguiSystems.

Jolly, A. C., Test, D. W., & Spooner, F. (1993). Using badges to increase initiations of children with severe disabilities in a play setting. *Journal of The Association for Persons with Severe Handicaps, 18,* 46–51.

Jones, B. E., Clark, G. M., & Soltz, D. F. (1997). Characteristics and practices of sign language interpreters in inclusive education programs. *Exceptional Children, 63,* 257–268.

Jones, C. J. (2001). Teacher-friendly curriculum-based assessment in spelling. *Teaching Exceptional Children, 34*(3), 32–38.

Jones, D. E., Clatterbuck, C. C., Marquis, J., Turnbull, H. R., & Moberly, R. L. (1996). Educational placements for children who are ventilator assisted. *Exceptional Children, 63,* 47–57.

Jones, T. M., Garlow, J. A., Turnbull, H. R., & Barber, P. A. (1996). Family empowerment in a family support program. In G. H. S. Singer, L. E. Powers, & A. L. Olson (Eds.), *Redefining family support: Innovations in public-private partnerships* (p. 91). Baltimore: Brookes.

Jordan, L., Reyes-Blane, M. E., Peel, B. B., Peel, H. A., & Lane, H. B. (1998). Developing teacher–parent partnerships: Effective parent conferences. *Intervention in School and Clinic, 33,* 141–147.

Jordan, N. C., & Hanich, L. B. (2000). Mathematical thinking in second-grade children with different forms of LD. *Journal of Learning Disabilities, 33,* 567–578.

Jose, R. (1983). *Understanding low vision.* New York: American Foundation for the Blind.

Joseph, L., & Seery, M. E. (2004). Where is the phonics? A review of the literature on the use of phonetic analysis with students with mental retardation. *Remedial and Special Education, 25,* 88–94.

Justen, J. E. (1976). Who are the severely handicapped? A problem in definition. *AAESPH Review, 1*(2), 1–12.

Justice, L. M. (2004). Creating language-rich preschool classroom environments. *Teaching Exceptional Children, 37*(2), 36–44.

Kadesjo, B., Gillberg, C., & Hagberg, B. (1999). The prevalence of autism and autism spectrum disorders. In F. C. Verhult & H. N. Koot (Eds.), *The epidemiology of child and adolescent psychopathology* (pp. 227–257). Oxford: Oxford University Press.

Kagan, S. L., & Neuman, M. J. (1997, September). Highlights of the Quality 2000 Initiative: Not by chance. *Young Children,* pp. 54–62.

Kaiser, A. P., & Goetz, L. (1993). Enhancing communication with persons labeled severely disabled. *Journal of The Association for Persons with Severe Handicaps, 18,* 137–142.

Kaiser, A. P., & Grim, J. C. (2006). Teaching functional communication skills. In M. E. Snell & F. Brown (Eds.), *Instruction of students with severe disabilities* (6th ed.). Upper Saddle River, NJ: Merrill/Prentice Hall.

Kaiser, A. P., Hancock, T. B., Cai, X., Foster, E. M., & Hester, P. P. (2000). Parent-reported behavioral problems and language delays in boys and girls enrolled in head start classrooms. *Behavioral Disorders, 26,* 26–41.

Kame'enui, E. J., Carnine, D. W., Dixon, R. C., Simmons, D. C., & Coyne, M. D. (Eds.), (2002). *Effective teaching strategies that accommodate diverse learners* (2nd ed.). Upper Saddle River, NJ: Merrill/Prentice Hall.

Kame'enui, E. J., Good R., III, & Harn, B. A. (2005). Beginning reading failure and the quantification of risk: Reading behavior as the supreme index. In W. L. Heward, T. E. Heron, N. A. Neef, S. M. Peterson, D. M. Sainato, G. Cartledge, R. Gardner, III, L. D. Peterson, S. B. Hersh, & J. C. Dardig (Eds.), *Focus on behavior analysis in education: Achievements, challenges, and opportunities* (pp. 69–89). Upper Saddle River, NJ: Merrill/Prentice Hall.

Kame'enui, E. J., & Simmons, D. C. (1990). *Designing instructional strategies: The prevention of academic learning problems.* Upper Saddle River, NJ: Merrill/Prentice Hall.

Kamps, D. M., Dugan, E. P., Leonard, B. R., & Daoust, P. M. (1994). Enhanced small group instruction using choral responding and student interactions for children with autism and developmental disabilities. *American Journal on Mental Retardation, 99,* 60–73.

Kangas, K. A., & Lloyd, L. L. (2002). Augmentative and alternative communication. In G. H. Shames & N. B. Anderson (Eds.), *Human communication disorders: An introduction* (6th ed.), (pp. 545–593). Boston: Allyn & Bacon.

Kanner, L. (1943/1985). Autistic disturbance of affective contract. In A. M. Donnellan (Ed.), *Classic readings in autism* (pp. 11–53). New York: Teachers College Press.

Kaplan, D. E., Gayan, J., Ahn, J., Won, T. W., Pails, D. L., Olson, R. K., DeFries, C., Wood, F. B., Pennington, B. F., Page, G. P., Smith, S. D., & Gruen, J. R. (2002). Evidence for linkage and association with reading disability. *American Journal of Human Genetics, 70,* 1287–1298.

Kaplan, S. (1988). Maintaining a gifted program. *Roeper Review, 11*(1), 35–37.

Kaplan, S. (2004). Where we stand determines the answers to the question: Can the No Child Left Behind legislation be beneficial to gifted students? *Roeper Review, 26*(3), 124–125.

Karnes, K. B., Beauchamp, K. D. F., & Pfaus, D. B. (1993). PEECH: A nationally validated early childhood special education model. *Topics in Early Childhood Special Education, 13,* 120–135.

Katsiyannis, A., & Maag, J. W. (2001). Manifestation determination as a golden fleece. *Exceptional Children, 68,* 85–96.

Katsiyannis, A., & Yell, M. L. (2000). The Supreme Court and school health services: Cedar Rapids v. Garret F. *Exceptional Children, 66,* 317–326.

Katsiyannis, A., & Yell, M. L. (2004). Critical issues and trends in the education of students with emotional or behavioral disorders [Introduction to special issue]. *Behavioral Disorders, 29,* 209–210.

Kauffman, J. M. (1999). How we prevent the prevention of emotional and behavioral disorders. *Exceptional Children, 65,* 448–468.

Kauffman, J. M. (2003). Appearance, stigma, and prevention. *Remedial and Special Education, 24,* 195–198.

Kauffman, J. M. (2005). *Characteristics of emotional and behavioral disorders of children and youth* (8th ed.). Upper Saddle River, NJ: Merrill/Prentice Hall.

Kauffman, J. M., & Hallahan, D. K. (1994). *The illusion of full inclusion: A comprehensive critique of a current special education bandwagon.* Austin, TX: PRO-ED.

Kauffman, J. M., & Krouse, J. (1981). The cult of educability: Searching for the substance of things hoped for; the evidence of things not seen. *Analysis and Intervention in Developmental Disabilities, 1*(1), 53–61.

Kaufman, A. (2000). Clothing-selection habits of teenage girls who are sighted and blind. *Journal of Visual Impairments and Blindness, 94,* 527–531.

Kavale, K. A. (2002). Discrepancy models in the identification of learning disability. In R. Bradley, L. Danielson, & D. P. Hallahan (Eds.), *Identification of learning disabilities: Research to practice* (pp. 369–426). Mahwah, NJ: Erlbaum.

Kavale, K. A., & Forness, S. R. (1996). Social skills deficits and learning disabilities: A meta-analysis. *Journal of Learning Disabilities, 29,* 226–237.

Kavale, K. A., & Forness, S. R. (2000). History, rhetoric and reality: Analysis of the inclusion debate. *Remedial and Special Education, 21,* 279–296.

Kavale, K. A., & Reese, J. H. (1992). The character of learning disabilities: An Iowa profile. *Learning Disability Quarterly, 15,* 74–94.

Kay, P. J., & Fitzgerald, M. (1997). Parents + teachers + action research = Real parent involvement. *Teaching Exceptional Children, 30*(1), 8–11.

Kazdin, A. (1987). *Conduct disorders in childhood.* Newbury Park, CA: Sage.

Kearsley, G. (2000). *Online education: Learning and teaching in cyberspace.* Belmont, CA: Wadsworth.

Keel, M. C., & Gast, D. L. (1992). Small-group instruction for students with learning disabilities: Observational and incidental learning. *Exceptional Children, 58,* 357–368.

Keith, T., Keith, P., Quirk, K., Sperduto, J., Santillo, S., & Killings, S. (1998). Longitudinal effects of parent involvement on high school grades: Similarities and differences across gender and ethnic groups. *Journal of School Psychology, 36,* 335–363.

Kelker, K., Hecimovic, A., & LeRoy, C. H. (1994). Designing a classroom and school environment for students with AIDS: A checklist for teachers. *Teaching Exceptional Children, 26*(4), 52–55.

Kelly, D. J. (1998). A clinical synthesis of the "late talker" literature: Implications for service delivery. *Language, Speech and Hearing Services in the School, 29,* 76–84.

Kelly, M. L. (1990). *School-home notes.* New York: Guilford.

Kelly, S. J., Macaruso, P., & Sokol, S. M. (1997). Mental calculations in an autistic savant: A case study. *Journal of Clinical and Experimental Neuropsychology, 19*(2), 172–184.

Kennedy, C. H., & Fisher, D. (2001). *Inclusive middle schools.* Baltimore: Brookes.

Kennedy, C. H., & Horn, E. H. (2004). *Including students with severe disabilities.* Boston: Allyn and Bacon.

Kennedy, C. H., & Itkonen, T. (1994). Some effects of regular class participation on the social contacts and social network of high school students with disabilities. *Journal of The Association for Persons with Severe Handicaps, 19,* 1–10.

Kennedy, C. H., Shukla, S., & Fryxell, D. (1997). Comparing the effects of educational placement on the social relationships of intermediate school students with severe disabilities. *Exceptional Children, 64,* 31–47.

Keogh, B. K., Bernheimer, L. P., & Guthrie, D. (2004). Children with developmental delays twenty years later: Where are they? How are they? *American Journal of Mental Retardation, 109,* 219–230.

Kern, J. K., Miller, V. S., Evans, P. A., & Trivedi, M. H. (2002). Efficacy of porcine secretin in children with autism and pervasive development disorder. *Journal of Autism and Developmental Disorders, 32,* 153–160.

Kern, L., Mantegna, M. E., Vorndran, C. M., Bailin, D., & Hilt, A. (2001). Choice of task sequence to reduce problem behaviors. *Journal of Positive Behavior Interventions, 3,* 3–10.

Kerr, B. (1985). Smart girls, gifted women: Special guidance concerns. *Roeper Review, 8*(1), 30–33.

Kerr, B., & Cohen, S. (2001). *Smart boys.* Tempe, AZ: Great Potential Press.

Kerr, M. M., & Nelson, C. M. (2002). *Strategies for addressing behavior problems in the classroom* (4th ed.). Upper Saddle River, NJ: Merrill/Prentice Hall.

Kerr, M. M., & Nelson, C. M. (2006). *Strategies for managing behavior problems in the classroom* (5th ed.). Upper Saddle River, NJ: Merrill/Prentice Hall.

Kershner, J., Hawks, W., & Grekin, R. (1977). Megavitamins and learning disorders: A controlled double-blind experiment. Unpublished manuscript, Ontario Institute for Studies in Education.

Keyes, M. W., & Owens-Johnson, L. (2003). Developing person-centered IEPs. *Intervention in School and Clinic, 38,* 145–152.

Kiewra, K. A. (2002). How classroom teachers can help students learn and teach them how to learn. *Theory and Practice, 41,* 71–80.

Killu, K., Sainato, D. M., Davis, C. A., Ospelt, H., & Paul, J. N. (1998). Effects of high-probability request sequences on preschoolers' compliance and disruptive behavior. *Journal of Behavioral Education, 8,* 347–368.

Kim, S. H., & Arnold, M. B. (2006). Characteristics of persons with severe mental retardation. In M. Beirne-Smith, J. R. Patton, & S. H. Kim, (Eds.), *Mental retardation* (7th ed.). Upper Saddle River, NJ: Merrill/Prentice Hall.

Kingsley, M. (1997). The effects of a visual loss. In H. Mason & S. McCall (Eds.), *Visual impairment: Access to education for children and young people* (pp. 23–29). London: Fulton.

Kirkwood, R. (1997). The adolescent. In H. Mason & S. McCall (Eds.), *Visual impairment: Access to education for children and young people* (pp. 110–123). London, Fulton.

Kirsten, I. (1981). *The Oakland picture dictionary.* Wauconda, IL: Johnston.

Kishi, G. S., & Meyer, L. H. (1994). What children report and remember: A six-year follow-up of the effects of social contact between peers with and without severe disabilities. *Journal of The Association for Persons with Severe Handicaps, 19,* 277–289.

Klein, J. (1994). Supported living: Not just another "rung" on the continuum. *TASH Newsletter, 20*(7), 16–18.

Kleinheksel, K. A., & Summy, S. E. (2003). Enhancing student learning and social behavior through mnemonic strategies. *Teaching Exceptional Children, 36*(2), 30–35.

Kleweno, C. P., Seibel, E. J., Viirre, E. S., Kelly, J. P., & Furness, T. A. (2001). The virtual-retinal display as a low-vision computer interface: Pilot study. *Journal of Rehabilitation Research and Development, 38,* 431–441.

Kliewer, C., & Biklen, D. (1996). Labeling: Who wants to be retarded? In W. Stainback & S. Stainback (Eds.), *Controversial issues confronting special education: Divergent perspectives* (pp. 83–95). Boston: Allyn & Bacon.

Kline, F. M., Silver, L. B., & Russell, S. C. (Eds.). (2001). *The educator's guide to medical issues in the classroom.* Baltimore: Brookes.

Klingner, J. K., & Vaughn, S. (1999). Students' perceptions of instruction in inclusion classrooms: Implications for students with learning disabilities. *Exceptional Children, 66,* 23–37.

Klingner, J. K., Vaughn, S., Hughes, M. T., Schumm, J. S., & Elbaum, B. (1998). Outcomes for students with and without learning disabilities in inclusive classrooms. *Learning Disabilities Research and Practice, 13,* 153–161.

Klug, B. J. (2004). Children of the starry cope: Gifted and talented Native American students. In D. Boothe & J. Stanley (Eds.), *In the eyes of the beholder: Critical issues for diversity in gifted education* (pp. 49–72). Waco, TX: Prufrock.

Kluth, P. (2004). Autism, autobiography, and adaptations. *Teaching Exceptional Children, 36*(4), 42–47.

Kluwin, T. N. (1985). Profiling the deaf student who is a problem in the classroom. *Adolescence, 20,* 863–875.

Kluwin, T. N. (1993). Cumulative effects of mainstreaming on the achievement of deaf adolescents. *Exceptional Children, 60,* 73–81.

Kluwin, T. N., & Moores, D. F. (1989). Mathematics achievement of hearing impaired adolescents in different placements. *Exceptional Children, 55,* 327–335.

Knecht, H. A., Whitelaw, G. M., & Nelson, P. B. (2000). *Structural variables and their relationship to background noise levels and reverberation times in unoccupied classrooms.* Unpublished manuscript.

Knoll, J. A., & Wheeler, C. B. (2005). My home and community: Developing supports for adult living. In R. W. Flexer, T. J. Simmons, P. Luft, & R. M. Baer (Eds.), *Transition planning for secondary students with disabilities* (2nd ed.), (pp. 499–539). Upper Saddle River, NJ: Merrill/Prentice Hall.

Knotek, S. (2003). Bias in problem solving and the social process of student study teams. *Journal of Special Education, 37,* 2–14.

Knowlton, E. (1998). Considerations in the design of personalized curricula supports for students with developmental disabilities. *Education and Training in Mental Retardation and Developmental Disabilities, 33,* 95–107.

Kochar, C. A., West, L. L., & Taymans, J. M. (2000). *Successful inclusion: Practical strategies for a shared responsibility.* Upper Saddle River, NJ: Merrill/Prentice Hall.

Kodak, T., Miltenberger, R. G., & Romaniuk, C. (2003). The effects of differential negative reinforcement of other behavior and noncontingent escape on compliance. *Journal of Applied Behavior Analysis, 36,* 379–382.

Koegel, L. K., Koegel, R. L., & Dunlap, G. (1996). *Positive behavioral support: Including people with difficult behavior in the community.* Baltimore: Brookes.

Koegel, L. K., Koegel, R. L., Harrower, J. K., & Carter, C. M. (1999). Pivotal response intervention I: Overview of approach. *Journal of The Association for Persons with Severe Handicaps, 24,* 174–185.

Koegel, R. L., & Koegel, L. (1995). *Teaching children with autism.* Baltimore: Brookes.

Koenig, A. J. (1996). Growing into literacy. In M. C. Holbrook (Ed.), *Children with visual impairments: A parents' guide* (pp. 227–257). Bethesda, MD: Woodbine House.

Koenig, A. J., & Holbrook, M. C. (2000a). Ensuring high-quality instruction for students in braille literacy programs. *Journal of Visual Impairments and Blindness, 94,* 677–694.

Koenig, A. J., & Holbrook, M. C. (Eds.). (2000b). *Foundations of education: Vol. 1: History and theory of teaching children and youths with visual impairments* (2nd ed.). New York: AFB Press.

Koestler, F. A. (2004). *The unseen minority: A social history of blindness in the United States.* New York: AFB Press.

Kohler, P. (1996). *A taxonomy for transition programming: Linking research and practice.* Champaign: University of Illinois, Transition Research Institute.

Kohler, P. D. (1994). On-the-job training: A curricular approach to employment. *Career Development for Exceptional Individuals, 17,* 29–40.

Kohler, P. D. (1998). Implementing a transition perspective of education: A comprehensive approach to planning and delivering secondary education and transition service. In F. R. Rusch & J. G. Chadsey (Eds.), *Beyond high school: Transition from school to work* (pp. 179–205). New York: Wadsworth.

Kohler, P. D., & Field, S. (2003). Transition-focused education: Foundation for the future. *Journal of Special Education, 37,* 174–183.

Kohn, A. (1993a). *Punished by rewards.* Boston: Houghton Mifflin.

Kohn, A. (1993b). Why incentive plans cannot work. *Harvard Business Review, 71*(5), 54–63.

Kohn, A. (2001). Five reasons to stop saying "Good job!" *Young Children, 56*(5), 24–28.

Konold, K. E., Miller, S. P., & Konold, K. B. (2004). Using teaching feedback to enhance student learning. *Teaching Exceptional Children, 36*(6), 64–69.

Koyanagi, C., & Gaines, S. (1993). *All systems failure: An examination of the results of neglecting the needs of children with serious emotional disturbance.* Alexandria, VA: National Mental Health Association.

Kozloff, M. A., & Rice, J. (2000). Parent and family issues: Stress and knowledge. In P. Accardo (Ed.), *Autism: Clinical and research issues* (pp. 303–325). Timonium, MD: York.

Krajewski, J. J., & Flaherty, T. (2000). Attitudes of high school students toward individuals with mental retardation. *Mental Retardation, 38,* 154–162.

Kratochwill, T. R., & Stoiber, K. C. (2000). Empirically supported interventions and school psychology. *School Psychology Quarterly, 15,* 233–253.

Krebs, P., & Coultier, G. (1992). Unified sports: I've seen the light. *Palaestra, 8*(2), 42–45.

Kroth, R. L., & Edge, D. (1997). *Strategies for communicating with parents of exceptional children* (3rd ed.). Denver: Love.

Kube, D. A., Peterson, M. C., & Palmer, F. B. (2002). Attention deficit hyperactivity disorder: Comorbidity and medication use. *Clinical Pediatrics, 41,* 461–469.

Kubina, R., & Cooper, J. O. (2001). Changing learning channels: An efficient strategy to facilitate instruction and learning. *Intervention in School and Clinic, 35,* 161–166.

Kugel, R. B., & Wolfensberger, W. (Eds.). (1969). *Changing patterns in residential services for the mentally retarded.* Washington, DC: Superintendent of Documents.

Kuhn, T. (1962). *The structure of scientific revolutions.* Chicago: University of Chicago Press.

Kulik, J. A. (1992a). Ability grouping and gifted students. In N. Colangelo, S. G. Assouline, & D. L. Ambroson (Eds.), *Talent development: Proceedings from the 1991 Henry B. and Jocelyn Wallace National Research Symposium on Talent Development* (pp. 261–266). Unionville, NY: Trillium.

Kulik, J. A. (1992b). An analysis of the research on ability grouping: Historical and contemporary perspectives. *Research-Based Decision Making Series.* Storrs: University of Connecticut, National Research Center on the Gifted and Talented.

Kulik, J. A. (2003). Grouping and tracking. In N. Colangelo & G. A. Davis (Eds.), *Handbook of gifted education* (3rd ed.), (pp. 268–281). Needham Heights, MA: Allyn & Bacon.

Kulik, J. A., & Kulik, C. L. C. (1984a). Effects of accelerated instruction on students. *Review of Educational Research, 54,* 409–425.

Kulik, J. A., & Kulik, C. L. C. (1984b). Synthesis of research of effects of accelerated instruction. *Educational Leadership, 42,* 84–89.

Kulik, J. A., & Kulik, C. L. C. (1987). Effects of ability grouping on student achievement. *Equity and Excellence, 23,* 22–30.

Kulik, J. A., & Kulik, C. L. C. (1990). Ability grouping and gifted students. In N. Colangelo & G. A. Davis (Eds.), *Handbook of gifted education* (pp. 178–196). Boston, MA: Allyn & Bacon.

Kulik, J. A., & Kulik, C. L. C. (1992). Meta-analytic findings on grouping programs. *Gifted Child Quarterly, 36,* 73–77.

Kulman, L. (1999, April 26). What'd you say? *U.S. News & World Report, 66–68,* 71–74.

Kuna, J. (2001). The Human Genome Project and eugenics: Identifying the impact on individuals with mental retardation. *Mental Retardation, 39,* 158–160.

Kuntze, M. (1998). Literacy and deaf children: The language question. *Topics in Language Disorders, 18*(4), 1–15.

Kuoch, H., & Mirenda, P. (2003). Social story interventions for young children with autism spectrum disorders. *Focus on Autism and Other Developmental Disabilities, 18,* 219–227.

Kwasman, A., Tinsley, B. J., & Lepper, H. S. (1995). Pediatricians' knowledge and attitudes concerning diagnosis and treatment of attention deficit hyperactivity disorder. *Archives of Pediatric Adolescent Medicine, 149,* 1211–1216.

Laborit, E. (1998). *The cry of the gull.* Washington, DC: Gallaudet University Press.

Lago-Delello, E. (1998). Classroom dynamics and the development of serious emotional disturbance. *Exceptional Children, 64,* 479–492.

Lahey, B. B., Applegate, B., McBurnett, K., Biederman, J., Greenhill, L., Hynd, G. W., Barkley, R. A., Newcorn, J., Jensen, P., Richters, J., Garfinkel, B., Kerdyk, L., Frick, P. J., Ollendick, T., Perez, D., Hart, E. L., Waldman, I., & Shaffer, D. (1994). DSM-IV field trials for attention deficit hyperactivity disorder in children and adolescents. *American Journal of Psychiatry, 151,* 1673–1685.

Lahm, E. A., & Everington, C. (2002). Communication and technology supports. In L. Hamill & C. Everington, *Teaching students with moderate to severe disabilities: An applied approach for inclusive environments* (pp. 51–79). Upper Saddle River, NJ: Merrill/Prentice Hall.

Lake, J. F., & Billingsley, B. S. (2000). An analysis of factors that contribute to parent-school conflict in special education. *Remedial and Special Education, 21,* 240–251.

Lakin, K. C., Prouty, R., Polister, B., & Coucouvanis, K. (2003). Selected changes in residential service systems over a quarter century, 1977–2002. *Mental Retardation, 41,* 303–306.

Lakin, K. C., Smith, J., Prouty, R., & Polister, B. (2001). State institutions during the 1990s: Changes in the number of facilities, average, daily populations, and expenditures between fiscal years 1991 and 2000. *Mental Retardation, 39,* 72–75.

Lalli, J. S., Browder, D. M., Mace, F. C., & Brown, D. K. (1993). Teacher use of descriptive analysis data to implement interventions to decrease students' problem behaviors. *Journal of Applied Behavior Analysis, 26,* 227–238.

Lambert, M. C., Cartledge, G., Lo, Y.-Y. & Heward, W. L. (2004). *Effects of response cards on disruptive behavior and participation by fourth-grade students during math lessons in an urban school.* Unpublished manuscript.

Lambert, N., Nihira, K., & Leland, H. (1993). *Adaptive Behavior Scale—School* (2nd ed.). Austin, TX: PRO-ED.

Lambie, R. (2000). *Family systems within educational contexts: Understanding at-risk special needs students.* Denver: Love.

Lancaster, J. (1806). *Improvement in education.* London: Collins & Perkins.

Landa, R. (2003). Early identification of autism spectrum disorders. *Exceptional Parent, 33*(7), 60–63.

Landesman, S., & Ramey, C. T. (1989). Developmental psychology and mental retardation: Integrating scientific principles with treatment practices. *American Psychologist, 44,* 409–415.

Landrum, M. (2002). *Consultation in gifted education: Teachers working together to serve students.* Mansfield, CT: Creative Learning.

Landy, S. (2002). *Pathways to competence: Encouraging healthy social and emotional development in young children.* Baltimore: Brookes.

Lane, H. L. (1988). Is there a "psychology of the deaf"? *Exceptional Children, 55,* 7–19.

Lane, H. L., & Bahan, B. (1998). Ethics of cochlear implantation in young children: A review and reply from a Deaf-World perspective. *Otolaryngology Head and Neck Surgery, 119,* 297–308.

Lane, K. L., Gresham, F. M., & O'Shaughnessy, T. E (2002). *Interventions for children with or at risk for emotional and behavioral disorders.* Boston: Allyn & Bacon.

Lane, K. L., Pierson, M. R., & Givner, C. C. (2003). Teacher expectations of student behaviors: Which skills do elementary and secondary teachers deem necessary for success in the classroom? *Education and Treatment of Children, 26,* 413–430.

Langdon, H. W., Novak, J. M., Quintanar, R. S. (2000). Setting the teaching-learning wheel in motion in assessing language minority students. *Multicultural Perspectives, 2*(2), 3–9.

Lanigan, K. J., Audette, R. M. L., Dreier, A. E., & Kobersy, M. R. (2001). Nasty, brutish … and often not very short: The attorney perspective in due process. In C. E. Finn, A. J. Rotherham, & C. R. Hokanson, Jr. (Eds.), *Rethinking special education for a new century* (pp. 213–232). Washington, DC: Thomas B. Fordham Foundation and the Progressive Policy Institute.

La Paro, K. M., Pianta, R. C., & Cox, M. J. (2000). Teachers' reported transition practices for children transitioning into kindergarten and first grade. *Exceptional Children, 67,* 7–20.

Larrivee, L. S., & Catts, H. W. (1999). Early reading achievement in children with expressive phonological disorders. *American Journal of Speech-Language Pathology, 8*(2), 118–128.

Larson, S. A., & Lakin, K. C. (1989). Deinstitutionalization of persons with mental retardation. *Journal of The Association for Persons with Severe Handicaps, 14,* 324–332.

Larson, S. A., Lakin, K. C., Anderson, L., Kwak, N., Hak Lee, J., & Anderson, D. (2001). Prevalence of mental retardation and developmental disabilities: Estimates from the 1994/1995 National Health Interview Survey Disability Supplements. *American Journal of Mental Retardation, 105,* 231–252.

Lazarus, B. D. (1993). Guided notes: Effects with secondary and postsecondary students with mild disabilities. *Education and Treatment of Children, 16,* 272–289.

Lazarus, B. D. (1996). Flexible skeletons: Guided notes for adolescents with mild disabilities. *Teaching Exceptional Children, 28*(3), 37–40.

Leach, D. J., & Siddall, S. W. (1992). Parental involvement in the teaching of reading: A comparison of Hearing Reading, Paired Reading, Pause, Prompt, Praise and Direct Instruction methods. *ADI News, 11*(2), 14–19.

Learning Disabilities of America Association. (1993, March/April). Position paper on full inclusion of all students with learning disabilities in the regular classroom. *LDA Newsbrief, 28*(2), 1.

Lee, M., Storey, K., Anderson, J. L., Goetz, L., & Zivolich, S. (1997). The effect of mentoring versus job coach instruction on integration in supported employment settings. *Journal of The Association for Persons with Severe Handicaps, 22,* 151–158.

Lehr, D. H., & Macurdy, S. (1994). Meeting special health care needs of students. In M. Agran, N. E. Marchand-Martella, & R. C. Martella (Eds.), *Promoting health and safety: Skills for independent living* (pp. 71–84). Pacific Grove, CA: Brooks/Cole.

Lehr, D. H., & McDaid, P. (1993). Opening the door further: Integrating students with complex health needs. *Focus on Exceptional Children, 25*(6), 1–7.

Leigh, S. A., & Barclay, L. A. (2000). High school braille readers: Achieving academic success. *RE:view, 32,* 123–131.

Lenz, B. K., & Bulgren, J. A. (1995). Promoting learning in content classes. In P. A. Cegelka & W. H. Berdine (Eds.), *Effective instruction for students with learning problems* (pp. 385–417). Needham Heights, MA: Allyn & Bacon.

Leonard, C. M. (2001). Imaging brain structure in children: Differentiating language disability and reading disability. *Learning Disability Quarterly, 24,* 158–176.

Leone, P. E., & Meisel, S. (1997). Improving education services for students in detention and confinement facilities. *Children's Legal Rights Journal, 17*(1), 2–12.

Leone, P. E., Rutherford, R. B., & Nelson, C. M. (1991). *Special education and juvenile corrections.* Reston, VA: Council for Exceptional Children.

Lepper, M. R., Keavney, M., & Drake, M. (1996). Intrinsic motivation and extrinsic rewards: A commentary on Cameron and Pierce's Meta-Analysis. *Review of Educational Research, 66,* 5–32.

Lerro, M. (1994). Teaching adolescents about AIDS. *Teaching Exceptional Children, 26*(4), 49–51.

Levack, N., Stone, G., & Bishop, V. (1994). *Low vision: A resource guide with adaptations for students with visual impairments* (2nd ed.) Austin, TX: Texas School for the Blind and Visually Impaired.

Levendoski, L. S., & Cartledge, G. (2000). Self-monitoring for elementary school children with serious emotional disturbances: Classroom applications for increased academic responding. *Behavioral Disorders, 25,* 211–224.

Levine, K., & Wharton, R. (2000). Williams syndrome and happiness. *American Journal of Mental Retardation, 105,* 363–371.

Lewis, M. S., & Jackson, D. W. (2001). Television literacy: Comprehension of program content using closed captions for the deaf. *Journal of Deaf Studies and Deaf Education, 5,* 43–53.

Lewis, R. B., & Doorlag, D. H. (2006). *Teaching special education in general education classrooms* (7th ed.). Upper Saddle River, NJ: Merrill/Prentice Hall.

Lewis, S., & Tolla, J. (2003). Creating and using tactile experience books for young children with visual impairments. *Teaching Exceptional Children, 35*(3), 22–28.

Lewis, T., & Sugai, G. (1999). *Safe schools: School-wide discipline practices.* Reston, VA: Council for Exceptional Children.

Li, A. (2003). A model for developing programs to improve the use of vision in students who are visually impaired with multiple disabilities. *RE:view, 35*(1), 31–45.

Li, A. (2004). Classroom strategies for improving and enhancing visual skills in students with disabilities. *Teaching Exceptional Children, 36*(6), 38–46.

Lian, M. G. J., & Fontánez-Phelan, S. M. (2001). Perceptions of Latino parents regarding cultural and linguistic issues and advocacy for children with disabilities. *Journal of The Association for Persons with Severe Handicaps, 26,* 189–194.

Lichtenstein, E. H. (1998). The relationships between reading processes and English skills of deaf college students. *Journal of Deaf Studies and Deaf Education, 3,* 80–134.

Lieberth, A. K. (1991). Use of scaffolded dialogue journals to teach writing to deaf students. *Teaching English to Deaf and Second-Language Students, 9*(1), 10–13.

Lignugaris/Kraft, B., Marchand-Martella, N., & Martella, R. C. (2001). Writing better goals and short-term objectives or benchmarks. *Teaching Exceptional Children, 34*(1), 52–58.

Lignugaris/Kraft, B., Rule, S., Salzberg, C. L., & Stowitschek, J. J. (1988). Social-vocational skills of handicapped and nonhandicapped adults at work. *Journal of Employment Counseling, 23,* 20–31.

Lin, S. (2000). Coping and adaptations in families of children with cerebral palsy. *Exceptional Children, 66,* 201–218.

Lindfors, J. W. (1987). *Children's language and learning* (2nd ed.). Upper Saddle River, NJ: Prentice Hall.

Lindley, L. (1990, August). Defining TASH: A mission statement. *TASH Newsletter, 16*(8), 1.

Lindsley, O. R. (1996). The four free-operant freedoms. *Behavior Analyst, 19,* 199–210.

Lindstrom, L. E., Benz, M. R., & Johnson, M. D. (1997). From school grounds to coffee grounds: An introduction to school-based enterprises. *Teaching Exceptional Children, 29*(4), 20–24.

Ling, D. (1986). Devices and procedures for auditory learning. *Volta Review, 88*(5), 19–28.

Lippke, B. A., Dickey, S. E., Selmar, J. W., & Soder, A. L. (1997). *Photo articulation test* (3rd ed.). Austin, TX: PRO-ED.

Lipsey, M. W., & Derzon, J. H. (1998). Predictors of violent or serious delinquency in adolescence and early adulthood: A synthesis of longitudinal research. In R. Loeber & D. P. Farrington (Eds.), *Serious and violent juvenile offenders: Risk factors and successful interventions* (pp. 6–105). Thousand Oaks, CA: Sage.

Liptak, G. S. (2002). Neural tube defects. In M. L. Batshaw (Ed.), *Children with disabilities* (5th ed.) Baltimore: Brookes.

Livingston-White, D., Utter, C., & Woodard, Q. E. (1985). Follow-up study of visually impaired students of the Michigan School for the Blind. *Journal of Visual Impairment and Blindness, 79,* 150–153.

Llewellyn, G., Gething, L., Kendig, H., & Cant, R. (2004). Older parent caregiver's engagement with the service system. *American Journal of Mental Retardation, 109,* 379–396.

Lloyd, J. W., Kauffman, J. M., & Gansneder, B. (1987). Differential teacher response to descriptions of aberrant behavior. In R. B. Rutherford, C. M. Nelson, & S. R. Forness (Eds.), *Severe behavior disorders of children and youth* (pp. 41–52). Boston: College Hill Press.

Lloyd, L. (1999). Multi-age classes and high ability students. *Review of Educational Research, 69*(2), 187–212.

Lockshin, S. B., Gillis, J. M., & Romanczyk, R. G. (in press). *Defying autism: Keep your sanity and take control.* New York: DRL.

Logan, K. R., & Gast, D. L. (2001). Conducting preference assessments and reinforcer testing for individuals with profound multiple disabilities: Issues and procedures. *Exceptionality, 9*(3), 123–134.

Logan, K. R., Hansen, C. D., Nieminen, P. K., & Wright, E. H. (2001). Student support teams: Helping students succeed in general education classrooms or working to place students in special education? *Education and Training in Mental Retardation and Developmental Disabilities, 36,* 280–292.

Logan, K. R., Jacobs, H. A., Gast, D. L., Smith, P. D., Daniel, J., & Rawls, J. (2001). Preferences and reinforcers for students with profound multiple disabilities: Can we identify them? *Journal of Developmental and Physical Disabilities, 13,* 97–122.

Lohrmann-O'Rouke, S., & Browder, D. M. (1998). Empirically based methods to assess the preferences of individuals with severe disabilities. *American Journal on Mental Retardation, 103,* 146–161.

Lord, C., Rutter, M., & Le Couteur, A. (1994). Autism diagnostic interview—revised: A revised version of a diagnostic interview for caregivers of individuals with possible pervasive developmental disabilities. *Journal of Autism and Developmental Disorders, 24,* 659–685.

Lovaas, O. I. (1987). Behavioral treatment and normal educational and intellectual functioning in young autistic children. *Journal of Consulting and Clinical Psychology, 55,* 3–9.

Lovaas, O. I. (1994, October). Comments made during Ohio State University teleconference on applied behavior analysis, The Ohio State University, Columbus.

Lovaas, O. I., & Newsom, C. D. (1976). Behavior modification with psychotic children. In H. Leitenberg (Ed.), *Handbook of behavior modification and behavior therapy* (pp. 303–360). Englewood Cliffs, NJ: Prentice-Hall.

Lovett, M. W., Steinbach, K. A., & Frijters, J. C. (2000). Remediating the core deficits of developmental reading disability: A double-deficit perspective. *Journal of Learning Disabilities, 33,* 334–358.

Lovitt, T. C. (1977). *In spite of my resistance ... I've learned from children.* Upper Saddle River, NJ: Merrill/Prentice Hall.

Lovitt, T. C. (2000). *Preventing school failure: Tactics for teaching adolescents* (2nd ed.). Austin, TX: PRO-ED.

Lovitt, T. C., & Cushing, S. S. (1994). High school students rate their IEPs: Low opinions and lack of ownership. *Intervention in School and Clinic, 30,* 34–37.

Lowenthal, B. (2001). Abuse and neglect: The educator's guide to the identification and prevention of child maltreatment. Baltimore: Brookes.

Luchshyn, J. M., Dunlap, G., & Albin, R. W. (Eds.). (2002). *Families and positive behavioral support: Addressing the challenge of problem behavior in family contexts.* Baltimore: Brookes.

Luckasson, R., Coulter, D. L., Polloway, E. A., Reiss, S., Schalock, R. L., Snell, M. E., Spitalnik, D. M., & Stark, J. A. (1992). *Mental retardation: Definition, classification, and systems of supports* (9th ed.). Washington, DC: American Association on Mental Retardation.

Luckasson, R., Coulter, D. L., Polloway, E. A., Reiss, S., Schalock, R. L., Snell, M. E., Spitalnik, D. M., & Stark, J. A. (2002). *Mental retardation: Definition, classification, and systems of supports* (10th ed.). Washington, DC: American Association on Mental Retardation.

Luckasson, R., & Reeve, A. (2001). Naming, defining, and classifying in mental retardation. *Mental Retardation, 39,* 47–52.

Luckner, J. (1994). Developing independent and responsible behaviors in students who are deaf or hard of hearing. *Teaching Exceptional Children, 26*(2), 13–17.

Lue, M. S. (2001). *A survey of communication disorders for the classroom teacher.* Boston: Allyn & Bacon.

Lueck, A. H. (2004). *Functional vision: A practitioner's guide to evaluation and intervention.* New York: AFB Press.

Luterman, D. (1999). Emotional aspects of hearing loss. *Volta Review, 99*(5), 75–83.

Lynch, E., & Hanson, M. (1998). *Developing cross-cultural competence* (2nd ed.). Baltimore: Brookes.

Lyon, G. R. (1995). Toward a definition of dyslexia. *Annals of Dyslexia, 45,* 3–27.

Lyon, G. R. (1999, December 12). Special education in state is failing on many fronts. *Los Angeles Times,* p. A1.

Lyon, G. R., Shaywitz, S. E., & Shaywitz, B. A. (2003). Defining dyslexia. *Annals of Dyslexia, 53,* 1–14.

Lytle, R. K., & Bordin, J. (2001). Enhancing the IEP team: Strategies for parents and professionals. *Teaching Exceptional Children, 33*(5), 28–33.

Maag, J. W. (2001). Rewarded by punishment: Reflections on the disuse of positive reinforcement in schools. *Exceptional Children, 67,* 173–186.

Maag, J. W. (2003). A contextually based approach for treating depression in school-age children. *Intervention in School and Clinic, 37,* 149–155.

Maag, J. W., & Reid, R. (1994). Attention-deficit hyperactivity disorder: A functional approach to assessment and treatment. *Behavioral Disorders, 20,* 5–23.

Maccini, P., & Hughes, C. A. (2000). Effects of problem-solving strategy on the algebraic subtraction of integers by secondary students with learning disabilities. *Learning Disabilities Research and Practice, 15,* 10–15.

MacGinitie, W. H., MacGinitie, R. K., Maria, K., & Dreyer, L. G. (2000). *Gates-MacGinitie Reading Tests—Fourth Edition.* Itasca, IL: Riverside.

Macht, J. (1998). *Special education's failed system: A question of eligibility.* Westport, CT: Bergin & Garvey.

MacMillan, D. L., Gresham, F. M., Bocian, K. M., & Lambros, K. M. (1998). Current plight of borderline students: Where do they belong? *Education and Training in Mental Retardation and Developmental Disabilities, 33,* 83–94.

MacMillan, D. L., Gresham, F. M., & Siperstein, G. N. (1993). Conceptual and psychometric concerns about the 1992 AAMR definition of mental retardation. *American Journal on Mental Retardation, 98,* 325–335.

MacMillan, D. L., Gresham, F. M., & Siperstein, G. N. (1996). Heightened concerns about the 1992 AAMR definition of mental retardation: Advocacy versus precision. *American Journal on Mental Retardation, 100,* 87–97.

MacMillan, D. L., Gresham, F. M., Siperstein, G. N., & Bocian, K. M. (1996). The labyrinth of IDEA: School decisions on referred students with subaverage general intelligence. *American Journal on Mental Retardation, 101,* 161–174.

MacMillan, D. L., & Reschly, D. J. (1998). Overrepresentation of minority students: The case for greater specificity or reconsideration of the variables examined. *Journal of Special Education, 32,* 15–24.

MacMillan, D. L., & Siperstein, G. N. (2002). Learning disabilities as operationally defined by schools. In R. Bradley, L. Danielson, & D. P. Hallahan (Eds.), *Identification of learning disabilities: Research to practice* (pp. 287–333). Mahwah, NJ: Erlbaum.

Madsen, C. H., Jr., Becker, W. C., & Thomas, D. R. (1968). Rules, praise, and ignoring: Elements of elementary classroom control. *Journal of Applied Behavior Analysis, 1,* 343–353.

Maestas y Moores, J., & Moores, D. F. (1980). Language training with the young deaf child. In D. Bricker (Ed.), *Early language intervention with handicapped children.* San Francisco: Jossey-Bass.

Maheady, L., Harper, G. F., Sacca, M. K., & Mallette, B. (1991). *Classwide Student Tutoring Teams (CSTT): Instructor's manual and video package.* Fredonia, NY: SUNY College at Fredonia, School of Education.

Maheady, L., Mallette, B., & Harper, G. F. (in press). Four classwide peer tutoring models: Similarities, differences, and implications for research and practice. *Reading and Writing Quarterly.*

Maheady, L., Mallette, B., Harper, G. F., & Saca, K. (1991). Heads together: A peer-mediated option for improving the academic achievement of heterogeneous learning groups. *Remedial and Special Education, 12*(2), 25–33.

Maheady, L., Sacca, M. K., & Harper, G. F. (1987). Classwide peer tutoring teams: Effects on the academic performance of secondary students. *Journal of Special Education, 21*(3), 107–121.

Mahr, G., & Leith, W. (1992). Psychogenic stuttering of adult onset. *Journal of Speech and Hearing Research, 35,* 283–286.

Mahshie, S. N. (1995). *Educating deaf children bilingually.* Washington, DC: Gallaudet University Press.

Maker, C. J. (1993). Creativity, intelligence, and problem solving: A definition and design for cross-cultural research and measurement related to giftedness. *Gifted Education International, 9*(2), 68–77.

Maker, C. J. (1997). DISCOVER problem solving assessment. *Quest, 8*(1), 3, 4, 7.

Maker, C. J. (2001). DISCOVER: Assessing and developing problem solving. *Gifted Education International, 15,* 232–251.

Maker, C. J., & Nielson, A. B. (1996). *Curriculum development and teaching strategies for gifted learners* (2nd ed.). Austin: TX: PRO-ED.

Maker, C. J., Nielson, A. B., & Rogers, J. A. (1994). Giftedness, diversity, and problem-solving. *Teaching Exceptional Children, 27*(1), 4–19.

Malian, I. M., & Love, L. L. (1998). Leaving high school: An ongoing transition study. *Teaching Exceptional Children, 30*(3), 4–10.

Mangold, S. (1982). (Ed.), *A teacher's guide to the special educational needs of blind and visually handicapped children.* New York: American Foundation for the Blind.

Mank, D., Cioffi, A., & Yovanoff, P. (1998). Employment outcomes for people with severe disabilities: Opportunities for improvement. *Mental Retardation, 36,* 205–216.

Mank, D., Cioffi, A., & Yovanoff, P. (1999). The impact of coworker involvement with supported employees on wage and integrated outcomes. *Mental Retardation, 37,* 383–394.

Mank, D., Cioffi, A., & Yovanoff, P. (2000). Direct support in supported employment and its relation to job typicalness, coworker involvement, and employment outcomes. *Mental Retardation, 38,* 506–516.

Mank, D. M., & Horner, R. H. (1987). Self-recruited feedback: A cost-effective procedure for maintaining behavior. *Research in Developmental Disabilities, 8,* 91–112.

Mann, D. (1996). Serious play. *Teachers College Record, 97*(3), 447–469.

Marchand-Martella, N. E., Slocum, T. A., & Martella, R. C. (Eds.). (2004). *Introduction to Direct Instruction.* Boston: Allyn & Bacon.

Marchisan, M. L., & Alber, S. R. (2001). The write way: Tips for teaching the writing process to resistant writers. *Intervention in School and Clinic, 36*(3), 154–162.

Margolis, H., & Brannigan, G. (1990). Calming the storm. *Learning, 18,* 40–42.

Markwardt, F. C., Jr. (1998). *Peabody Individual Achievement Test—Revised.* Circle Pines, MN: American Guidance Services.

Marschark, M., & Clark, M. D. (Eds.). (1998). *Psychological perspectives on deafness* (Vol. 2). Mahwah, NJ: Erlbaum.

Marsh, L. G., & Cooke, N. L. (1996). The effects of using manipulatives in teaching math problem solving to students with learning disabilities. *Learning Disabilities Research and Practice, 11*(1), 58–65.

Martella, R. C., Marchand-Martella, N. E., Young, K. R., & MacFarlane, C. A. (1995). Determining the collateral effects of peer tutoring on a student with severe disabilities. *Education and Treatment of Children, 19,* 170–191.

Martens, B. K., Lochner, D. G., & Kelly, S. Q. (1992). The effects of variable interval reinforcement on academic engagement: A demonstration of matching theory. *Journal of Applied Behavior Analysis, 25,* 143–151.

Martin, J. E., Huber Marshall, L., & Sale, P. (2004). A 3-year study of middle, junior high, and high school IEP meetings. *Exceptional Children, 70,* 285–297.

Martin, J. E., & Marshall, L. H. (1995). ChoiceMaker: A comprehensive self-determined transition program. *Intervention in School and Clinic, 30,* 147–156.

Martin, J. R. (1985). *Reclaiming a conversation: The ideal of the educated woman.* New Haven, CT: Yale University Press.

Martin, S. L., Ramey, C. T., & Ramey, S. L. (1990). The prevention of intellectual impairment in children of impoverished families: Findings of a randomized trial of educational daycare. *American Journal of Public Health, 80,* 844–847.

Masataka, N. (1996). Perception of mothers in a signed language by 6-month-old deaf infants. *Developmental Psychology, 32,* 874–879.

Mason, C., Field, S., & Sawilowsky, S. (2004). Implementation of self-determination activities and student participation in IEPs. *Exceptional Children, 70,* 441–451.

Mason, C. Y., McGahee-Kovac, M., & Johnson, L. (2004). How to help students lead their IEP meetings. *Teaching exceptional children, 36*(3), 18–25.

Mason, H. (1997). Common eye defects and their educational implications. In H. Mason & S. McCall (Eds.), *Visual impairment: Access to education for children and young people* (pp. 38–50). London: Fulton.

Massey, N. G., & Wheeler, J. J. (2000). Acquisition and generalization of activity schedules and their effects on task engagement in a young child with autism in an inclusive preschool classroom. *Education and Training in Mental Retardation and Developmental Disabilities, 35,* 326–335.

Mastropieri, M. A., & Scruggs, T. E. (1993). *A practical guide for teaching science to students with special needs in inclusive settings.* Austin, TX: PRO-ED.

Mastropieri, M. A., & Scruggs, T. E. (2004). *The inclusive classroom: Strategies for effective instruction* (2nd ed.). Upper Saddle River, NJ: Merrill/Prentice Hall.

Mather, N., & Goldstein, S. (2001). *Learning disabilities and challenging behaviors.* Baltimore: Brookes.

Mathes, P. G., Clancy-Menchetti, J., & Torgesen, J. K. (2003). *K-PALS: Kindergarten peer-assisted literacy strategies.* Longmont, CO: Sopris West.

Mathes, P. G., Torgesen, J. K., Allen, S. H., & Howard-Allor, J. (2003). *First grade PALS: Peer-assisted literacy strategies.* Longmont, CO: Sopris West.

Matson, J. L. (Ed.). (1994). *Autism in children and adults: Etiology, assessment, and intervention.* Pacific Grove, CA: Brooks/Cole.

Maughan, B., Pickles, A., Hagell, A., Rutter, M., & Yule, W. (1996). Reading problems and antisocial behavior: Developmental trends in comorbidity. *Journal of Child Psychology and Psychiatry, 37,* 405–418.

Mauk, J. E., Reber, M., & Batshaw, M. L. (1997). Autism. In M. L. Batshaw (Ed.), *Children with disabilities* (pp. 425–448). Baltimore: Brookes.

Maurice, C., Green, G., & Foxx, R. M. (2001). *Making a difference: Behavioral intervention for autism.* Austin, TX: PRO-ED.

Maurice, C., & Taylor, B. A. (2005). Early intensive behavioral intervention for autism. In W. L. Heward, T. E. Heron, N. A. Neef, S. M. Peterson, D. M. Sainato, G. Cartledge, R. Gardner, III, L. D. Peterson, S. B. Hersh, & J. C. Dardig (Eds.), *Focus on behavior analysis in education: Achievements, challenges, and opportunities* (pp. 31–52). Upper Saddle River, NJ: Merrill/Prentice Hall.

Mayer, C., & Akamatsu, C. T. (1999). Bilingual-bicultural models of literacy education for deaf students: Considering the claims. *Journal of Deaf Studies and Deaf Education, 4,* 1–8.

Mayer, G. R. (1995). Preventing antisocial behavior in schools. *Journal of Applied Behavior Analysis, 28,* 467–478.

Mayer-Johnson, R. (1986). *The picture communications symbols—Book 1.* Solana Beach, CA: Mayer-Johnson.

Mayes, S. D., Calhoun, S. L., & Crowell, E. W. (2000). Learning disabilities and ADHD: Overlapping spectrum disorders. *Journal of Learning Disabilities, 33,* 417–424.

McAdam, D. B., O'Cleirigh, C. M., & Cuvo, A. J. (1993). Self-monitoring and verbal feedback to reduce stereotypic body rocking in a congenitally blind adult. *RE:view, 24,* 163–172.

McBride, B. J., & Schwartz, I. (2003). Effects of teaching early interventionists to use discrete trials during ongoing classroom activities. *Topics in Early Childhood Special Education, 23,* 5–17.

McCauley, R. J. (2001). *Assessment of language disorders in children.* Mahwah, NJ: Erlbaum.

McClannahan, L. E., & Krantz, P. J. (1999). *Activity schedules for children with autism: Teaching independent behavior.* Woodbine House.

McConnell, M. E. (1999). Self-monitoring, cueing, recording, and managing: Teaching students to manage their own behavior. *Teaching Exceptional Children, 32*(2), 14–21.

McConnell, S. (2002). Interventions to facilitate social interactions for young children with autism: Review of available research and recommendations for education intervention and future research. *Journal of Autism and Developmental Disabilities, 32,* 351–372.

McConnell, S. R. (1994). Social context, social validity, and program outcome in early intervention. In R. Gardner, III, D. M. Sainato, J. O. Cooper, T. E. Heron, W. L. Heward, J. Eshleman, & T. A. Grossi (Eds.), *Behavior analysis in education: Focus on measurably superior instruction* (pp. 75–85). Pacific Grove, CA: Brooks/Cole.

McCormick, M. E., & Wolf, J. S. (1993). Intervention programs for gifted girls. *Roeper Review, 16,* 85–88.

McDermott, S. (1994). Explanatory model to describe school district prevalence rates for mental retardation and learning disabilities. *American Journal on Mental Retardation, 99,* 175–185.

McDonnell, J., Thorson, N., Disher, S., Mathot-Buckner, C., Mendel, J., & Ray, L. (2003). The achievement of students with developmental disabilities and their peers without disabilities in inclusive settings: An exploratory study. *Education and Treatment of Children, 26,* 224–236.

McDonough, C. S., Covington, T., Endo, S., Meinberg, D., Spencer, T. D., & Bicard, D. F. (2005). The Hawthorne Country Day School: A behavioral approach to schooling. In W. L. Heward, T. E. Heron, N. A. Neef, S. M. Peterson, D. M. Sainato, G. Cartledge, R. Gardner, III, L. D. Peterson, S. B. Hersh, & J. C. Dardig (Eds.), *Focus on behavior analysis in education: Achievements, challenges, and opportunities* (pp. 188–210). Upper Saddle River, NJ: Merrill/Prentice Hall.

McEachin, J. J., Smith, T., & Lovaas, I. O. (1993). Long-term outcome for children with autism who received early intensive behavioral treatment. *American Journal on Mental Retardation, 97,* 359–372.

McEvoy, A., & Welker, R. (2000). Antisocial behavior, academic failure, and school climate: A critical review. *Journal of Emotional and Behavioral Disorders, 8,* 130–140.

McEvoy, M. A., & Yoder, P. (1993). Interventions to promote social skills and emotional development. In *DEC Recommended Practices* (pp. 77–81). Reston, VA: Council for Exceptional Children, Division for Early Childhood.

McGee, G. G., Morrier, M. J., & Daly, T. (1999). An incidental teaching approach to early intervention for toddlers with autism. *Journal of The Association for the Severely Handicapped, 24,* 133–146.

McGee, J. J. (1992). Gentle teaching's assumptions and paradigm. *Journal of Applied Behavior Analysis, 25,* 869–872.

McGee, J. J., & Gonzalez, L. (1990). Gentle teaching and the practice of human interdependence: A preliminary group study of 15 persons with severe behavioral disorders and their caregivers. In A. C. Repp & N. N. Singh (Eds.), *Current perspectives on the use of nonaversive and aversive interventions for persons with developmental disabilities* (pp. 237–254). Sycamore, IL: Sycamore.

McGee, J. J., & Menolascino, F. J. (1991). *Beyond gentle teaching: A nonaversive approach to helping those in need.* New York: Plenum.

McGill, T., & Vogle, L. K. (2001). Driver's education for students with physical disabilities. *Exceptional Children, 67,* 455–466.

McGonigel, M. J., Woodruff, G., & Roszmann-Millican, M. (1994). The transdisciplinary team: A model for family-centered early intervention. In L. J. Johnson, R. J. Gallagher, M. J. LaMontagne, J. B. Jordan, J. J. Gallagher, P. L. Hutinger, & M. B. Karnes (Eds.) *Meeting early intervention challenges: Issues from birth to three* (pp. 95–131). Baltimore: Brookes.

McHale, S. M., & Gamble, W. W. (1989). Sibling relationships of children with disabled and nondisabled brothers and sisters. *Developmental Psychology, 25*(3), 421–429.

McHugh, M. (2003). *Special siblings: Growing up with someone with a disability.* Baltimore: Brookes.

McIntyre, T. (1993a).Behaviorally disordered youth in correctional settings: Prevalence, programming, and teacher training. *Behavioral Disorders, 18,* 167–176.

McIntyre, T. (1993b). Reflections on the new definition for emotional or behavioral disorders: Who still falls through the cracks and why. *Behavioral Disorders, 18,* 148–160.

McIntyre, T., & Forness, S. R. (1996). Is there a new definition yet or are kids still seriously emotionally disturbed? *Beyond Behavior, 7*(3), 4–9.

McKinley, A. M., & Warren, S. F. (2000). The effectiveness of cochlear implants for children with prelingual deafness. *Journal of Early Intervention, 23,* 252–263.

McLaren, J., & Bryson, S. E. (1987). Review of recent epidemiological studies of mental retardation: Prevalence, related disorders and etiology. *American Journal on Mental Retardation, 92,* 243–254.

McLaughlin, S. (1998). *Introduction to language development.* San Diego: Singular.

McLean, M., Wolery, M., & Bailey, D. B. (2004). *Assessing infants and preschoolers with special needs* (3rd ed.) Upper Saddle River, NJ: Merrill/Prentice Hall.

McLeskey, J. (1992). Students with learning disabilities at primary, intermediate, and secondary grade levels: Identification and characteristics. *Learning Disability Quarterly, 15,* 13–19.

McLeskey, J., Tyler, N. C., & Flippin, S. S. (2004). The supply and demand for special education teachers: A review of research regarding the chronic shortage of special education teachers. *Journal of Special Education, 38,* 5–21.

McLone, D. G., & Ito, J. (1998). *An introduction to spina bifida.* Chicago: Children's Memorial Hospital, Spina Bifida Team.

McLoughlin, J. A., & Lewis, R. B. (2005). *Assessing students with special needs* (6th ed.) Upper Saddle River, NJ: Merrill/Prentice Hall.

McNamara, K., & Hollinger, C. (2003). Intervention-based assessment: Evaluation rates and eligibility findings. *Exceptional Children, 69,* 181–193.

McReynolds, L. V. (1990). Articulation and phonological disorders. In G. H. Shames & E. H. Wiig (Eds.), *Human communication disorders* (3rd ed.), (pp. 30–73). Upper Saddle River, NJ: Merrill/Prentice Hall.

Meadow-Orlans, K. P. (1985). Social and psychological effects of hearing loss in adulthood: A literature review. In H. Orlans (Ed.), *Adjustment to adult hearing loss* (pp. 35–57). San Diego: College-Hill.

Meadow-Orlans, K. P., Mertens, D. M., Sass-Lehrer, M. A., & Scott-Olson, K. (1997). Support services for parents and their children who are deaf or hard of hearing. *American Annals of the Deaf, 142,* 278–288.

Meadows, N. B., Neel, R. S., Scott, C. M., & Parker, G. (1994). Academic performance, social competence, and mainstream accommodations: A look at mainstreamed and nonmainstreamed students with serious behavioral disorders. *Behavioral Disorders, 19,* 170–180.

Mechling, L. C., & Gast, D. L. (1997). Combination audio/visual self-prompting system for teaching chained tasks to students with intellectual disabilities. *Education and Training in Mental Retardation and Developmental Disabilities, 32,* 138–153.

Mehler, J., Jusczyk, P. W., Lambertz, G., Halsted, N., Bettoncini, J., & Ameil-Tison, C. (1988). A precursor of language acquisition in young infants. *Cognition, 29,* 143–178.

Menlove, R. R., Hudson, P. J., & Suter, D. (2001). A field of IEP dreams: Increasing general education teacher participation in the IEP development process. *Teaching Exceptional Children, 33*(5), 28–33.

Mercer, C. D., Jordan, L., Allsopp, D. H., & Mercer, A. R. (1995). Learning disabilities definitions and criteria used by state education departments. Unpublished manuscript.

Mercer, C. D., & Mercer, A. (2005). *Teaching students with learning problems* (7th ed.). Upper Saddle River, NJ: Merrill/Prentice Hall.

Mercer, C. D., & Pullen, P. C. (2005). *Students with learning disabilities* (6th ed.). Upper Saddle River, NJ: Merrill/Prentice Hall.

Merrill, E. C. (1990). Attentional resource allocation and mental retardation. In N. W. Bray (Ed.), *International review of research in mental retardation: Vol. 16* (pp. 51–88). San Diego: Academic Press.

Merritt, D. D., & Culatta, B. (1998). *Language intervention in the classroom.* San Diego: Singular.

Mervis, C. B., Klein-Tasman, B. P., & Mastin, M. E. (2001). Adaptive behavior of 4-through 8-year-old children with Williams syndrome. *American Journal of Mental Retardation, 106,* 82–93.

Meyer, D. (1995). *Uncommon fathers: Reflections on raising a child with a disability.* Bethesda, MD: Woodbine House.

Michael, J. (1993). *Principles and concepts of behavior analysis.* Kalamazoo, MI: Association for Behavior Analysis.

Miller, A. D., Barbetta, P. M., & Heron, T. E. (1994). START tutoring: Designing, training, implementing, adapting, and evaluating tutoring programs for school and home settings. In R. Gardner, III, D. M. Sainato, J. O. Cooper, T. E. Heron, W. L. Heward, J. Eshleman, & T. A. Grossi (Eds.), *Behavior analysis in education: Focus on measurably superior instruction* (pp. 75–85). Pacific Grove, CA: Brooks/Cole.

Miller, A. D., Hall, S. W., & Heward, W. L. (1995). Effects of sequential 1-minute time trials with and without intertrial feedback and self-correction on general and special education students' fluency with math facts. *Journal of Behavioral Education, 5,* 319–345.

Miller, C. J., Sanchez, J., & Hynd, G. W. (2003). Neurological correlates of reading disabilities. In H. L. Swanson, K. R. Harris, & S. Graham (Eds.), *Handbook of learning disabilities* (pp. 242–255). New York: Guilford.

Miller, G. (1993). Expanding vocational options. *RE:view, 25*(1), 27–31.

Miller, W. H. (1985). The role of residential schools for the blind in educating visually impaired students. *Journal of Visual Impairment and Blindness, 79,* 160.

Minner, S., Beane, A., & Prater, J. (1986). Try telephone answering machines. *Teaching Exceptional Children, 19*(1), 62–63.

Minor, R. J. (2001). The experience of living with and using a dog guide. *RE:view, 32,* 183–190.

Mitchell, D. (Ed.). (2004a). *Contextualizing inclusive education: Evaluating old and new international paradigms.* London: Routledge Falmer.

Mitchell, D. (Ed.). (2004b). *Special educational needs and inclusive education: Major themes in education.* London: Routledge Falmer.

Mithaug, D. K. (2002). "Yes" means success: Teaching students with multiple disabilities to self-regulate during independent work. *Teaching Exceptional Children, 35*(1), 22–27.

Molloy, C. A., Manning-Courtney, P., Swayne, S., Bean, J., Brown, J. M., Murray, D. S., Kinsman, A. M., Brasington, M., & Ulrich II, C. D. (2002). Lack of benefit of intravenous synthetic human secretin in the treatment of autism. *Journal of Autism and Developmental Disorders, 32,* 545–551.

Monda-Amaya, L. E., Dieker, L., & Reed, F. (1998). Preparing students with learning disabilities to participate in inclusive classrooms. *Learning Disabilities Research and Practice, 13*(3), 171–182.

Montgomery, W. (2001). Creating culturally responsive, inclusive classroooms. *Teaching Exceptional Children, 33*(4), 4–9.

Moody, S. W., Vaughn, S., Hughes, M. T., & Fischer, M. (2000). Reading instruction in the resource room: Set up for failure. *Exceptional Children, 66,* 305–316.

Moon, M. S. (1994). *Making school and community recreation fun for everyone: Places and ways to integrate.* Baltimore: Brookes.

Moon, M. S., & Inge, K. (2000). Vocational preparation and transition. In M. E. Snell & F. Brown (Eds.), *Instruction of students with severe disabilities* (5th ed.), (pp. 591–628). Upper Saddle River, NJ: Merrill/Prentice Hall.

Moores, D. F. (1993). Total inclusion/zero rejection models in general education: Implication for deaf children. *American Annals of the Deaf, 138,* 251.

Moores, D. F. (2001). *Educating the deaf: Psychology, principles, and practices* (5th ed.). Boston: Houghton Mifflin.

Moores, D. F. (2004). No Child Left Behind: The good, the bad, and the ugly. *American Annals of the Deaf, 148,* 347–348.

Morgan, C. D., & Murray, H. A. (1935). A method for investigating fantasies: The Thematic Apperception Test. *Archives of Neurology and Psychiatry, 34,* 289–306.

Morgan, D., Young, K. R., & Goldstein, S. (1983). Teaching behaviorally disordered students to increase teacher attention and praise in mainstreamed classrooms. *Behavioral Disorders, 8,* 265–273.

Morris, R. J., & Kratochwill, T. R. (1998). Childhood fears and phobias. In R. J. Morris & T. R. Kratochwill (Eds.), *The practice of child therapy* (3rd ed.). Boston: Allyn & Bacon.

Morrison, G. S. (2004). *Early childhood education today* (9th ed.). Upper Saddle River, NJ: Merrill/Prentice Hall.

Morrison, R. S., Sainato, D. M., BenChaaban, D., & Endo, S. (2002). Increasing play skills of children with autism using activity schedules and correspondence training. *Journal of Early Intervention, 25,* 58–72.

Morse, T. E., & Schuster, J. W. (2000). Teaching elementary students with moderate intellectual disabilities how to shop for groceries. *Exceptional Children, 66,* 273–288.

Morse, W. C. (1976). Worksheet on life-space interviewing for teachers. In N. Long, W.

Morse, & R. Newman (Eds.), *Conflict in the classroom* (pp. 337–341). Belmont, CA: Wadsworth.

Morse, W. C. (1985). *The education and treatment of socioemotionally impaired children and youth.* Syracuse, NY: Syracuse University Press.

Mortweet, S. L., Utley, C. A., Walker, D., Dawson, H. L., Delquadri, J. C., Reddy, S. S., Greenwood, C. R., Hamilton, S., & Ledford, D. (1999). Classwide peer tutoring: Teaching students with mild mental retardation in inclusive classrooms. *Exceptional Children, 65,* 524–536.

Moser, H. W. (2000). Genetics and gene therapies. In M. L. Wehmeyer & J. R. Patton (Eds.), *Mental Retardation in the 21st century* (pp. 235–250). Austin, TX: PRO-ED.

Most, T., & Greenbank, A. (2000). Auditory, visual, and auditory-visual perception of emotions by adolescents with and without learning disabilities, and their relationship to social skills. *Learning Disabilities Research and Practice, 15,* 171–178.

Mow, S. (1973). How do you dance without music? In D. Watson (Ed.), *Readings on deafness* (pp. 20–30). New York: New York University School of Education, Deafness Research and Training Center.

Moxley, R. A. (1998). Treatment-only designs and student self-recording strategies for public school teachers. *Education and Treatment of Children, 21,* 37–61.

Mudford, O. C. (1995). Review of the gentle teaching data. *American Journal on Mental Retardation, 99,* 345–355.

Mueller, R. A., & Courchesne, E. (2000). Autism's home in the brain: Reply. *Neurology, 54*(1), 270.

Mulick, J. A., & Antonak, R. (Eds.). (1994). *Life styles: Transitions in mental retardation* (Vol. 5). Norwood, NJ: Ablex.

Mull, C., Sitlington, P. L., & Alper, S. (2001). Postsecondary education for students with learning disabilities: A synthesis of the literature. *Exceptional Children, 68,* 97–118.

Multimodal Treatment Study Group. (1999). A 14-month randomized clincial trial of treatment strategies for attention-deficit/hyperactivity disorder. *Archives of General Psychiatry, 56,* 1088–1096.

Munk, D. D., Van Laarhoven, T., Goodman, S., & Repp, A. C. (1998). Small-group Direct Instruction for students with moderate to severe disabilities. In A. Hilton & R. Ringlaben (Eds.), *Best and promising practices in developmental disabilities* (pp. 127–138). Austin, TX: PRO-ED.

Murdick, N., Gartin, B., & Crabtree, T. (2006). *Special education law* (2nd ed.). Upper Saddle River, NJ: Merrill/Prentice Hall.

Murphy, C. M. (2003). *Using functional assessment to determine the maintaining contingencies of non-contextual speech by children with autism.* Unpublished master's thesis, The Ohio State University, Columbus.

Murray, C., Goldstein, D. E., Nourse, S., & Edgar, E. (2000). The postsecondary

school attendance and completion rates of high school graduates with learning disabilities. *Learning Disabilities Research and Practice, 15,* 119–127.

Myers, P. I., & Hammill, D. D. (1990). *Learning disabilities: Basic concepts, assessment practices, and instructional strategies* (3rd ed.). Austin, TX: PRO-ED.

Myles, B. S., & Simpson, R. L. (2001). Effective practices for students with Asperger syndrome. *Focus on Exceptional Children, 34*(3) 1–14.

Myles, B. S., Bock, S. J., & Simpson, R. L. (2001). *Asperger syndrome diagnostic scale.* Austin: PRO-ED.

Narayan, J. S., Heward, W. L., Gardner, R., III, Courson, F. H., & Omness, C. (1990). Using response cards to increase student participation in an elementary classroom. *Journal of Applied Behavior Analysis, 23,* 483–490.

Naseef, R. A. (2001). *Special children, challenged parents: The struggles and rewards of raising a child with a disability* (Rev. ed.). Baltimore: Brookes.

National Association of the Deaf. (2002). *Inclusion: NAD position statement.* [Approved by the NAD Board of Directors on January 26, 2002.] Silver Spring, MD: Author. Available online at http://www.nad.org/site/pp.asp?c=foINKQ MBF&b=180362.

National Center for Educational Statistics. (1998). *Postsecondary education quick information system: Survey of students with disabilities at postsecondary education institutions.* Washington, DC: U.S. Department of Education.

National Center for the Study of Postsecondary Educational Supports. (2002, July). *Preparation for and support of youth with disabilities in postsecondary education and employment: Implications for policy, priorities and practice.* Proceedings and briefing book for the National Summit on Postsecondary Education for People with Disabilities, presented in Washington, DC, on July 8, 2002. Retrieved January 7, 2004, from http://www.ncset.hawaii.edu/ summits/july2002/briefing/default.htm.

National Council on Disability. (2000, May 15). *National disability policy: A progress report: December 2001–December 2002.* http://www.ncd.gov/newsroom/publications/ progressreport2000.html.

*National excellence: A case for developing America's talent.* (1993). Washington, DC: U.S. Department of Education, Office of Educational Research and Improvement.

National Institute of Allergy and Infectious Diseases. (2001). *Fact sheet: HIV infection and adolescents.* http://www.niaid.nih.gov/ factsheets/hivadolescent.htm.

National Institute of Child Health and Human Development. (2000). *Report of the National Reading Panel. Teaching children to read: An evidence-based assessment of the scientific research literature on reading and its implications for reading instruction: Reports of the subgroups* (NIH Publication No. 00-4754). Washington, DC: U.S. Government Printing Office.

National Institute of Health Consensus Statement. (1998). Diagnosis and treatment of attention deficit/hyperactivity disorder. *NIH Consensus Statement, 16*(2), 1–37.

National Institute on Deafness and Other Communication Disorders. (2001). Cochlear implants. In *Health information: Hearing and balance.* http://www.nih.gov/nidcd/health/pubs_hb/coch.htm.

National Joint Committee on Learning Disabilities. (1989, September 18). Letter from NJCLD to member organizations. Topic: Modifications to the NJCLD definition of learning disabilities.

National Joint Committee on Learning Disabilities. (1993, January). *A reaction to full inclusion: A reaffirmation of the right of students with learning disabilities to a continuum of services.* http://www.ldonline.org/njcld/react_inclu.html.

National Reading Panel (2000). *Teaching children to read: An evidence-based assessment of the scientific research literature on reading and its implications for reading instruction. Reports of the subgroups.* http://www.nichd.nih.gov/publications/nrp/smallbook.htm.

National Research Council. (1998). *Preventing reading difficulties in young children.* Washington, DC: National Academy Press.

National Research Council. (2000). *Testing English-language learners in U.S. schools: Report and workshop summary.* http://www.nap.edu.

National Research Council. (2001). *Educating children with autism.* Washington, DC: National Academy Press.

National Science Foundation. (2004). *Women, minorities, and persons with disabilities in science and engineering.* Washington, DC: Author.

National Spinal Cord Injury Association. (2001). *Facts and figures.* Birmingham: University of Alabama.

Neal, J., Bigby, L., & Nicholson, R. (2004). Occupational therapy, physical therapy, and orientation and mobility services in public schools. *Intervention in School and Clinic, 39,* 218–222.

Nechring, W. M., & Steele, S. (1996). Cerebral palsy. In P. L. Jackson & J. A. Vessey (Eds.), *Primary care of the child with a chronic condition* (2nd ed.), (pp. 232–254). St. Louis: Mosby.

Neef, N. A., Bicard, D. F., & Endo, S. (2001). Assessment of impulsivity and the development of self-control in students with attention-deficit hyperactivity disorder. *Journal of Applied Behavior Analysis, 34,* 397–407.

Neef, N. A., Parrish, J. M., Egel, A. L., & Sloan, M. E. (1986). Training respite care providers for families with handicapped children: Experimental analysis and validation of an instructional package. *Journal of Applied Behavior Analysis, 19,* 105–124.

Neef, N. A., & Peterson, S. M. (2006). Functional behavior assessment. In J. O. Cooper, T. E. Heron, & W. L. Heward (Eds.), *Applied behavior analysis* (2nd ed.). Upper Saddle River, NJ: Merrill/Prentice Hall.

Nehring, W. M. (2003). Newborn screening in the 21st century: Current status and considerations. *Exceptional Parent, 33*(4), 53–57.

Neihart, M., Robinson, N., & Moon, S. (2002). *The social and emotional development of gifted children: What do we know?* Waco, TX: Prufock.

Neisworth, J. T., & Bagnato, S. J. (2000). Recommended practices in assessment. In S. Sandall, M. E. McLean, & B. J. Smith (Eds.), *DEC recommended practices in early intervention/early childhood special education* (pp. 29–33). Reston, VA: Council for Exceptional Children, Division for Early Childhood.

Neisworth, J. T., & Wolfe, P. S. (2004). *The autism encyclopedia.* Baltimore: Brookes.

Nelson, C., & Huefner, D. S. (2003). Young children with autism: Judicial responses to the Lovaas and discrete trial training debates. *Journal of Early Intervention, 26,* 1–19.

Nelson, C. M. (2000). Educating students with emotional and behavioral disabilities in the 21st century: Looking through windows, opening doors. *Education and Treatment of Children, 23,* 204–222.

Nelson, L. G. L., Summers, J. A., & Turnbull, A. P. (2004). Boundaries in family-professional relationships: Implications for special education. *Remedial and Special Education, 25,* 153–165.

Nelson, P. (2001). The changing demand for improved acoustics in our schools. *Volta Review, 101*(5), 23–32.

Neu, T. (2003). When the gifts are camouflaged by disability: Identifying and developing the talent in gifted students with disabilities. In J. A. Castellano (Ed.), *Special populations in gifted education: Working with diverse gifted learners* (pp. 151–162). Boston: Allyn & Bacon.

Newbold, S. (2000). *Emergent literacy for young blind children.* Phoenix, AZ: FBC Publications.

Newborg, J., Stock, J., Wnek, J., Guidubaldi, & Suinicki, J. (1988). *Battelle Developmental Inventory.* Chicago: Riverside.

Newcomer, J. R., & Zirkel, P. A. (1999). An analysis of judicial outcomes of special education cases. *Exceptional Children, 65,* 469–480.

Newcomer, P. L., & Barenbaum, E. M. (1991). The written composing ability of children with learning disabilities: A review of the literature from 1980 to 1990. *Journal of Learning Disabilities, 24,* 578–593.

Newman, R. S., & Golding, L. (1990). Children's reluctance to seek help with school work. *Journal of Educational Psychology, 82,* 92–100.

Nieto, S. (2000). *Affirming diversity: The sociopolitical context of multicultural education* (3rd ed.). New York: Addison Wesley Longman.

Nietupski, J., & Svoboda, R. (1982). Teaching a cooperative leisure skill to severely handicapped adults. *Education and Training of the Mentally Retarded, 17,* 38–43.

Nihira, K., Leland, H., & Lambert, N. K. (1993). *Adaptive Behavior Scale—Residential and Community* (2nd ed.). Austin, TX: PRO-ED.

Nirje, B. (1969). The normalization principle and its human management implications. In R. Kugel & W. Wolfensberger (Eds.), *Changing patterns in residential services for the mentally retarded* (pp. 181–195). Washington, DC: President's Committee on Mental Retardation.

Northern, J. L., & Downs, M. P. (1991). *Hearing in children* (4th ed.). Baltimore: Williams & Wilkins.

Northup, J., Fusilier, I., Swanson, V., Roane, H., & Borrero, J. (1997). An evaluation of methylphenidate as a potential establishing operation for some common classroom reinforcers. *Journal of Applied Behavior Analysis, 30,* 615–625.

Northup, J., Galley, V., Edwards, S., & Fountain, L. (2001). The effects of methylphenidate in the classroom: What dosage, for which children, for what problems? *School Psychology Quarterly, 16,* 303–323.

Norton, L. S., & Hartley, J. (1986). What factors contribute to good examination marks? The role of notetaking in subsequent examination performance. *Higher Education, 15,* 355–371.

Notari-Syverson, A. R., & Shuster, S. L. (1995). Putting real-life skills into IEP/IFSPs for infants and young children. *Teaching Exceptional Children, 27*(2), 29–32.

Nowacek, E. J., McKinney, J. D., & Hallahan, D. P. (1990). Instructional behaviors of more and less effective beginning regular and special educators. *Exceptional Children, 57,* 140–149.

Oakes, J. (1985). *Keeping track.* New Haven, CT: Yale University Press.

Ochoa, S. H., & Palmer, D. J. (1995). A meta-analysis of peer rating sociometric studies with learning disabled pupils. *Journal of Special Education, 29,* 1–9.

O'Conner, R. E. (2000). Increasing the intensity of intervention in kindergarten and first grade. *Learning Disabilities Research and Practice, 15,* 44–54.

Odom, S. L., & Brown, W. H. (1993). Social interaction skills interventions for young children with disabilities in integrated settings. In C. A. Peck, S. L. Odom, & D. Bricker (Eds.), *Integrating young children with disabilities into community programs: Ecological perspectives on research and implementation* (pp. 39–64). Baltimore: Brookes.

Odom, S. L., Hanson, M. J., Lieber, J., Marquart, J., Sandall, S., Wolery, R., Horn, E., Wolfberg, P., Schwartz, I., Beckman, P., Hikido, C., & Chambers, J. (2001). The costs of preschool inclusion. *Topics in Early Childhood Special Education, 21,* 146–155.

Office of Technology Assessment. (1987). *Technology-dependent children: Hospital v. home care—A technical memorandum.* OTA-TM-H-38. Washington, DC: Author.

Olsen, R., & Sutton, J. (1998). More hassle, more alone: Adolescents with diabetes and the role of formal and informal support. *Child: Care, Health, and Development, 24*(1), 31–39.

Olympia, D., Andrews, D., Valum, L., & Jenson, W. (1993). *Homework teams: Homework management strategies for the classroom.* Longmont, CO: Sopris West.

O'Neill, R. E., Horner, R. H., Albin, R. W., Sprague, J. R., Storey, K., & Newton, J. S. (1997). *Functional assessment and program development for problem behavior: A practical handbook.* Pacific Grove, CA: Brooks/Cole.

Onslow, M., Packman, A., & Harrison, E. (2003). *The Lidcombe Program of early stuttering intervention: A clinician's guide.* Austin, TX: PRO-ED.

O'Reilly, M. F., Lancioni, G. E., & Kierans, I. (2000). Teaching leisure social skills to adults with moderate mental retardation: An analysis of acquisition, generalization, and maintenance. *Education and Training in Mental Retardation and Developmental Disabilities, 35,* 250–258.

Orelove, F. P. (1984). The educability debate: A review and a look ahead. In W. L. Heward, T. E. Heron, D. S. Hill, & J. Trap-Porter (Eds.), *Focus on behavior analysis in education* (pp. 271–281). Upper Saddle River, NJ: Merrill/Prentice Hall.

Orelove, F. P., & Sobsey, D. (1996). *Educating children with multiple disabilities: A transdisciplinary approach* (3rd ed.). Baltimore: Brookes.

Orlansky, M. D., & Bonvillian, J. D. (1985). Sign language acquisition: Language development in children of deaf parents and implications for other populations. *Merrill-Palmer Quarterly, 31,* 127–143.

Orsillo, S. M., McCaffrey, R. J., & Fisher, J. M. (1993). Siblings of head-injured individuals: A population at risk. *Journal of Head Trauma Rehabilitation, 8*(1), 102–115.

Orsmond, G. I., & Seltzer, M. M. (2000). Brothers and sisters of adults with mental retardation: Gendered nature of the sibling relationship. *American Journal of Mental Retardation, 105,* 486–508.

Ortiz, A. (1997). Learning disabilities occurring concomitantly with linguistic differences. *Journal of Learning Disabilities, 30,* 321–333.

Ortiz, V., & Gonzales, A. (1991). Gifted Hispanic adolescents. In M. Bireley & J. Genshaft (Eds.), *Understanding the gifted adolescent* (pp. 240–247). New York: Teachers College Press.

Ostad, S. A. (1998). Developmental differences in solving simple arithmetic word problems and simple number-fact problems: A comparison of mathematically normal and mathematically disabled children. *Mathematical Cognition, 4,* 1–20.

Oswald, D. P. (1994). Facilitator influence in facilitated communication. *Journal of Behavioral Education, 4,* 191–200.

Oswald, D. P., & Coutinho, M. J. (2001). Trends in disproportionate representation: Implications for multicultural education. In C. Utley & F. Obiakor (Eds.), *Special education, multicultural education, and school reform: Components of quality education for learners with mild disabilities* (pp. 53–73). Springfield: Thomas.

Oswald, D. P., Coutinho, M. J., Best, A. M., & Singh, N. N. (1999). Ethnic representation in special education: The influence of school-related economic and demographic variables. *Journal of Special Education, 32,* 194–206.

Ovando, C. J. (2004). Language diversity and education. In J. A. Banks & C. A. M. Banks (Eds.), *Multicultural education: Issues and perspectives* (5th ed.), (pp. 289–313). New York: Wiley.

Overton, T. (2003). *Assessment in special education: An applied approach* (4th ed.). Upper Saddle River, NJ: Merrill/Prentice Hall.

Owen, R. L., & Fuchs, L. S. (2002). Mathematical problem-solving strategy instruction for third-grade student with learning disabilities. *Remedial and Special Education, 23,* 268–278.

Owens, R. E. (1999). *Language disorders: A functional approach to assessment and intervention.* (4th ed.). Boston: Allyn & Bacon.

Owens, R. E. (2005). *Language development: An introduction* (6th ed.). Boston: Allyn & Bacon.

Owens-Johnson, L., & Hamill, L. B. (2002). Community-based instruction. In L. Hamill & C. Everington, *Teaching students with moderate to severe disabilities: An applied approach for inclusive environments* (pp. 347–378). Upper Saddle River, NJ: Merrill/Prentice Hall.

Owley, T., Steele, M., Corsello, C., Risi, S., McKaig, K., Lord, C., et al. (1999). A double-blind, placebo-controlled trial of secretin for the treatment of autistic disorder. *Medscape General Medicine/journal/1999/v.01.n10.*

Page, E. B. (1972). Miracle in Milwaukee: Raising the IQ. *Educational Researcher, 15,* 8–16.

Pakulski, L. A., & Kaderavek, J. N. (2002). Children with minimal hearing loss: Interventions in the classroom. *Intervention in School and Clinic, 38,* 96–103.

Palincsar, A. S., Collins, K. M., Marano, N. L., & Magnusson, S. J. (2000). Investigating the engagement and learning of students with learning disabilities in guided inquiry science teaching. *Language, Speech, and Hearing Services in Schools, 31.*

Palmer, D. S., Fuller, K., Arora, T., & Nelson, M. (2001). Taking sides: Parents' views on inclusion for their children with severe disabilities. *Exceptional Children, 67,* 467–484.

Panerai, S., Ferrante, L., Caputo, V., & Impellizzeri, C. (1998). Use of structured teaching for the treatment of children with autism and severe and profound mental retardation. *Education and Training in Mental Retardation and Developmental Disabilities, 33,* 367–374.

Paniagua, F. A. (1992). Verbal-nonverbal correspondence training with ADHD children. *Behavior Modification, 16,* 226–252.

Parette, H. P. (1998). Assistive technology effective practices for students with mental retardation and developmental disabilities. In A. Hilton and R. Ringlaben (Eds.), *Best and promising practices in developmental disabilities* (pp. 205–224). Austin, TX: PRO-ED.

Parette, H. P., & Brotherson, M. J. (1996). Family participation in assistive technology assessment for young children with mental retardation and developmental disabilities. *Education and Training in Mental Retardation and Developmental Disabilities, 31,* 29–43.

Parette, H. P., & Petch–Hogan, B. (2000). Approaching families: Facilitating culturally/linguistically diverse family involvement. *Teaching Exceptional Children, 33*(2), 4–10.

Parette, H. P., & Hourcade, J. J. (1986). Management strategies for orthopedically handicapped students. *Teaching Exceptional Children, 18*(4), 282–286.

Parette, P., & McMahan, G. A. (2002). What should we expect of assistive technology? Being sensitive to family goals. *Teaching Exceptional Children, 35*(1), 56–61.

Park, J., Turnbull, A. P., & Park, H. S. (2001). Quality of partnerships in service provision for Korean American parents of children with disabilities: A qualitative inquiry. *Journal of The Association for Persons with Severe Handicaps, 26,* 158–170.

Parrish, T. B. (2001, April). Who's paying the rising cost of special education? *Journal of Special Education Leadership, 14*(1), 4–12.

Parson, L. R., & Heward, W. L. (1979). Training peers to tutor: Evaluation of a tutor training package for primary learning disabled students. *Journal of Applied Behavior Analysis, 12,* 309–312.

Parsons, M. B., McCarn, J. E., & Reid, D. H. (1993). Evaluating and increasing meal-related choices throughout a service setting for people with severe disabilities. *Journal of The Association for Persons with Severe Handicaps, 18,* 253–260.

Pascarella, E., & Terenzini, P. (1991). *How college affects students: Findings and insights from twenty years of research.* San Francisco, CA: Jossey-Bass.

Patterson, G. R. (1982). *Coercive family process.* Eugene, OR: Castilia.

Patterson, G. R., Cipaldi, D., & Bank, L. (1991). An early starter model for predicting delinquency. In D. J. Pepler & K. H. Rubin (Eds.), *The development and treatment of childhood aggression* (pp. 139–168). Hillsdale, NJ: Erlbaum.

Patterson, G. R., Reid, J. B., & Dishion, T. J. (1992). *Antisocial boys.* Vol. 4: *A social interactional approach.* Eugene, OR: Castalia.

Patterson, J. M., & Leonard, B. J. (1994). Caregiving and children. In E. Kahan, D. Biegel, & M. Wykle (Eds.), *Family caregiving across the lifespan* (pp. 133–158). Beverly Hills, CA: Sage.

Patton, J. M. (1998). The disproportionate representation of African Americans in special education: Looking behind the curtain for understanding and solutions. *Journal of Special Education, 32,* 25–31.

Patton, J. R., Cronin, M. E., & Jairrels, V. (1997). Curricular implications of transition: Life-skills instruction as an integral part of transition education. *Remedial and Special Education, 18,* 294–306.

Patton, J. R., Jayanthi, M., & Polloway, E. A. (2001). Home-school collaboration about homework: What do we know and what should we do? *Reading and Writing Quarterly: Overcoming Learning Difficulties, 17,* 227–242.

Paul, P. V., & Jackson, D. (1993). *Towards a psychology of deafness* (2nd ed.). San Diego: Singular.

Paul, P. V., & Quigley, S. P. (1990). *Education and deafness.* New York: Longman.

Pavri, S. (2001). Developmental delay or cultural differences? Developing effective child find practices for young children from culturally and linguistically diverse families. *Young Exceptional Children, 4,* 2–9.

Pavri, S., & Monda-Amaya, L. (2000). Loneliness and students with learning disabilities in inclusive classrooms: Self-perceptions, coping strategies, and preferred interventions. *Learning Disabilities Research and Practice, 15*(2), 22–33.

Peacock Hill Working Group. (1991). Problems and promises in special education and related services for children and youth with emotional or behavioral disorders. *Behavioral Disorders, 16,* 299–313.

Pearson Education. (2000). *Scott Foresman reading: Links to reading first, grade 1, unit 1.* Glenview, IL: Author.

Pease, L. (2000). Creating a communication environment. In S. Aitken, M. Buultjenns, C. Clark, J. T. Eyre, & L. Pease (Eds.), *Teaching children who are deafblind: Contact communication and learning* (pp. 35–82). London: Fulton.

Peck, S. (2004). Communication made easier: Facilitating transitions for students with multiple disabilities. *Teaching Exceptional Children, 36*(5), 60–63.

Peckham, V. C. (1993). Children with cancer in the classroom. *Teaching Exceptional Children, 26*(1), 27–32.

Pedley, T. A., Scheuer, M. L., & Walczak, T. S. (1995). Epilepsy. In L. P. Rowland (Ed.), *Merritt's textbook of neurology* (9th ed.), (pp. 845–868). Baltimore: Williams & Wilkins.

Pelios, L., Morren, J., Tesch, D., & Axelrod, S. (1999). The impact of functional analysis methodology on treatment choice for self-injurious and aggressive behavior. *Journal of Applied Behavior Analysis, 32,* 185–195.

Pellegrino, L. (2002). Cerebral palsy. In M. L. Batshaw (Ed.), *Children with disabilities* (5th ed.). Baltimore: Brookes.

Pennington, B. F. (1995). Genetics of learning disabilities. *Journal of Child Neurology, 10,* 69–77.

Pennsylvania Association for Retarded Children v. Commonwealth of Pennsylvania, 343 F. Supp. 279 (1972).

Perl, J. (1995). Improving relationship skills for parent conferences. *Teaching Exceptional Children 28*(1), 29–31.

Perla, F., & Ducret, W. D. (1999). Guidelines for teaching orientation and mobility to children with multiple disabilities. *RE:view, 31,* 113–119.

Perla, F., & O'Donnell, B. (2004). Encouraging problem solving in orientation and mobility. *Journal of Visual Impairments and Blindness, 98,* 47–52.

Perlmutter, J., & Burrell, L. (1995, January). Learning through play as well as work. *Young Children,* pp. 14–21.

Perrin, E. C., Newacheck, P., Pless, B., Drotar, D., Gortmaker, S. L., Leventhal, J., Perrin, J. M., Stein, R. E. K., Walker, D. K., & Weitzman, M. (1993). Issues involved in the definition and classification of chronic health conditions. *Pediatrics, 91,* 787–793.

Perske, R. (2004). Nirje's eight planks. *Mental Retardation, 42,* 147–150.

Peterson, L. D., & Lacy-Rismiller, L. (2005). Building behaviors versus suppressing behaviors: Perspectives and prescriptions for schoolwide positive behavior change. In W. L. Heward, T. E. Heron, N. A. Neef, S. M. Peterson, D. M. Sainato, G. Cartledge, R. Gardner, III, L. D. Peterson, S. B. Hersh, & J. C. Dardig (Eds.), *Focus on behavior analysis in education: Achievements, challenges, and opportunities* (pp. 252–266). Upper Saddle River, NJ: Prentice Hall/Merrill.

Peterson, L. D., Young, K. R., West, R. P., & Hill Peterson, M. (1999). Effects of student self-management on generalization of student performance on regular classrooms. *Education and Treatment of Children, 19,* 170.

Peterson, S. M., & Neef, N. A. (2006). Functional behavior assessment. In J. O. Cooper, T. E. Heron, & W. L. Heward, *Applied behavior analysis.* Upper Saddle River, NJ: Merrill/Prentice Hall.

Peterson, S. M., Neef, N. A., Van Norman, R., & Ferreri, S. J. (2005). Choice making in educational settings. In W. L. Heward, T. E. Heron, N. A. Neef, S. M. Peterson, D. M. Sainato, G. Cartledge, R. Gardner, III, L. D. Peterson, S. B. Hersh, & J. C. Dardig (Eds.), *Focus on behavior analysis in education: Achievements, challenges, and opportunities* (pp. 125–136). Upper Saddle River, NJ: Merrill/Prentice Hall.

Pieper, E. (1983). *The teacher and the child with spina bifida* (2nd ed.). Rockville, MD: Spina Bifida Association of America.

Piirto, J. (1991). Why are there so few? (Creative women: mathematicians, visual artists, musicians). *Roeper Review, 13*(3), 142–147.

Piirto, J. (1998). *Understanding those who create* (2nd ed.). Scottsdale, AZ: Gifted Psychology Press.

Piirto, J. (1999). Implications of postmodern curriculum theory for the education of the talented. *Journal for the Education of the Gifted, 22*(4), 386–406.

Piirto, J. (2002). *My teeming brain: Understanding creative writers.* Cresskill, NJ: Hampton.

Piirto, J. (2004a). The creative process in poets. In J. Kaufman & J. Baer (Eds.), *Creativity in domains: Faces of the muse* (pp. 1–15). Mahway, NJ: Erlbaum.

Piirto, J. (2004b). *Understanding creativity.* Scottsdale, AZ: Great Potential.

Pittman, P., & Huefner, D. S. (2001). Will the courts go bi-bi? IDEA '97, the courts, and deaf education. *Exceptional Children, 67,* 187–198.

Plomin, R. (1995). Genetics and children's experiences in the family. *Journal of Child Psychology and Psychiatry, 36,* 33–68.

Plummer, D. (1995). Serving the needs of gifted children from a multicultural perspective. In J. L. Genshaft, M. Bireley, & C. L. Hollinger (Eds.), *Serving gifted and talented students: A resource for school personnel* (pp. 285–300). Austin, TX: PRO-ED.

Pogrund, R. L., Fazzi, D. L., & Schreier, E. M. (1993). Development of a preschool "kiddy cane." *Journal of Visual Impairment and Blindness, 87,* 52–54.

Pollack, W. (1998). *Real boys: Rescuing our sons from the myths of boyhood.* New York: Holt.

Polloway, E. A., Smith, J. D., Patton, J. R., & Smith, T. E. C. (1996). Historic changes in mental retardation and developmental disabilities. *Education and Training in Mental Retardation and Developmental Disabilities, 31,* 3–12.

Polsgrove, L., & Ochoa, T. (2004). Trends and issues in behavioral interventions. In A. McCray Sorrells, H. J. Rieth, & P. T. Sindelar (Eds.), *Critical issues in special education: Access, diversity, and accountability* (pp. 16–37). Boston: Allyn & Bacon.

Porter, J. H., & Hodson, B. W. (2001). Collaborating to obtain phonological acquisition data for local schools. *Language, Speech, and Hearing Services in Schools, 32,* 165–171.

Porterfield, K. (1998). British researchers identify genetic area affecting speech. *ASHA Leader, 3*(4), 1, 4.

Post, M., & Storey, K. (2000). Review of using auditory prompting systems with persons who have moderate to severe disabilities. *Education and Training in Mental Retardation and Developmental Disabilities, 37,* 317–327.

Post, M., Storey, K., & Karabin, M. (2002). Cool headphones for effective prompts: Supporting students and adults in work and community environments. *Teaching Exceptional Children, 34,* 60–65.

Poulson, C. L., & Kymissis, E. (1988). Generalized imitation in infants. *Journal of Experimental Child Psychology, 46,* 324–336.

Poulton, S. (1996). *Guidelines to writing individualized healthcare plans.* http://www.nursing.uiowa.edu/www/ nursing/courses/96-22/students/sp1996/ 96-222WEguideline/htm.

Powell, D. S., Batsche, C. J., Ferro, J., Fox, L., & Dunlap, G. (1997). A strength-based approach in support of multi-risk families: Principles and issues. *Topics in Early Childhood Special Education, 17*(1), 1–26.

Powell, L., Houghton, S., & Douglas, J. (1997). Comparison of etiology-specific cognitive functioning profiles for individuals with fragile X and individuals with Down syndrome. *Journal of Special Education, 34,* 362–376.

Poyadue, F. S. (1993). Cognitive coping at Parents Helping Parents. In A. P. Turnbull, J. M. Paterson, S. K. Behr, D. L. Murphy, J. G. Marquis, & M. J. Blue-Banning (Eds.), *Cognitive coping, families, and disability* (pp. 95–110). Baltimore: Brookes.

Prelock, P. A. (2000a). Prologue: Multiple perspectives for determining the roles of speech-language pathologists in inclusionary classrooms. *Language, Speech, and Hearing Services in Schools, 31,* 213–218.

Prelock, P. A. (2000b). Epilogue: An intervention focus for inclusionary practice. *Language, Speech, and Hearing Services in Schools, 31,* 296–298.

Pretti-Frontczak, K., & Bricker, D. (2004). *An activity-based approach to early intervention* (3rd ed.). Baltimore: Brookes.

Pretti-Frontczak, K., Barr, D. M., Macy, M., & Carter, C. (2003). Research and resources related to activity-based intervention, embedded learning opportunities, and routines-based instruction. *Topics in Early Childhood Special Education, 23*(1), 29–39.

Pretti-Frontczak, K. L., & Bricker, D. (2000). Enhancing the quality of Individualized Education Plan (IEP) goals and objectives. *Journal of Early Intervention, 23,* 92–105.

Price, L., Field, S., & Patton, J. R. (Guest Eds.). (2003). Adults with learning disabilities (Special Issue). *Remedial and Special Education, 24,* 322–382.

Prinz, P. M., Strong, M., Kuntze, M., Vincent, J., Friedman, J., Moyers, P. P., & Helman, E. (1996). A path to literacy through ASL and English for deaf children. In C. E. Johnson & J. H. V. Gilbert (Eds.), *Children's language* (Vol. 9), (pp. 235–251). Mahwah, NJ: Erlbaum.

Prizant, B. M., & Rubin, E. (1999). Contemporary issues in interventions for autism spectrum disorders: A commentary. *Journal of the Association for Persons with Severe Handicaps, 24,* 199–208.

Professional Development in Autism Center, Personnel Development in Autism. (2004). Available at http://depts.washington.edu/pdacent/sites/uw.html.

Public Law 95–561. Gifted and Talented Children's Education Act. *Congressional Record* (1978, October 10). H–12179.

Pugh, G. S., & Erin, J. (1999). (Eds.). *Blind and visually impaired students: Education service guidelines.* Watertown, MA: Perkins School for the Blind.

Putnam, J. W. (1998). *Cooperative learning and strategies for inclusion: Celebrating diversity in the classroom* (2nd ed.). Baltimore: Brookes.

Ramey, C. T., Bryant, D. M., Wasik, B. H., Sparling, J. J., Fendt, K. H., & LaVange, L. M. (1992). The Infant Health and Development Program for low birthweight, premature infants: Program elements, family participation, and child intelligence. *Pediatrics, 89,* 454–465.

Ramey, C. T., & Ramey, S. L. (1992). Effective early intervention. *Mental Retardation, 30,* 337–345.

Ramig, P. R., & Shames, G. H. (2002). Stuttering and other disorders of fluency. In G. H. Shames & N. B. Anderson (Eds.), *Human communication disorders: An introduction* (6th ed.), (pp. 258–302). Boston: Allyn & Bacon.

Rance-Roney, J. A. (2004). The affective dimension of second culture/second language acquisition in gifted adolescents. In D. Boothe & J. Stanley (Eds.), *In the eyes of the beholder: Critical issues for diversity in gifted education* (pp. 73–85). Waco, TX: Prufrock Press.

Rao, S. S. (2000). Perspectives of an African American mother on parent-professional relationships in special education. *Mental Retardation, 38,* 475–488.

Rapport, M. J. K. (1996). Legal guidelines for the delivery of health care services in schools. *Exceptional Children, 62,* 537–549.

Raschke, D. B., Dedrick, C. V. L., Heston, M. L., & Farris, M. (1996). Everyone can play! Adapting the Candy Land board game. *Teaching Exceptional Children, 28*(4), 28–33.

Raskind, W. H. (2001). Current understanding of the genetic basis of reading and spelling disability. *Learning Disability Quarterly, 24,* 141–157.

Ratner, N. B. (2004). Caregiver-child interactions and their impact on children's fluency: Implications for treatment. *Language, Speech, and Hearing Services in Schools, 35,* 46–56.

Raver, S. (1984). Modification of head droop during conversation in a 3-year-old visually impaired child: A case study. *Journal of Visual Impairment and Blindness, 78,* 307–310.

Rawlings, B. W., Karchmer, M. A., Allen, T. E., & DeCaro, J. J. (1999). *College and career programs for deaf students* (10th ed.). Washington, DC, and Rochester, NY: Gallaudet University and National Technical Institute for the Deaf.

Rea, P. J., McLaughlin, V. L., & Walther-Thomas, C. (2002). Outcomes for students with learning disabilities in inclusive and pullout programs. *Exceptional Children, 68,* 203–222.

Reed, V. A. (2005). *An introduction to children with language disorders* (3rd ed.). Needham Heights, MA: Allyn & Bacon.

Rehfeldt, R. A., Kinney, E. M., Root, S., & Stromer, R. (2004). Creating activity schedules using Microsoft PowerPoint. *Journal of Applied Behavior Analysis, 37,* 115–128.

Reid, R., & Maag, J. W. (1998). Functional assessment: A method for developing classroom-based accommodations and interventions. *Reading & Writing Quarterly, 14,* 7–15.

Reid, R., Maag, J. W., & Vasa, S. F. (1994). Attention deficit hyperactivity disorder as a disability category: A critique. *Exceptional Children, 60,* 198–214.

Reilly, J. S., & Bellugi, U. (1996). Competition on the face: Affect and language in ASL mothers. *Journal of Child Language, 23,* 219–239.

Reis, S. (1995). What gifted education can offer the reform movement: Talent development. In J. L. Genshaft, M. Bireley, & C. L. Hollinger (Eds.), *Serving gifted and talented students: A resource for school personnel* (pp. 371–387). Austin, TX: PRO-ED.

Reis, S., & Cellerino, M. (1983). Guiding gifted students through independent study. *Teaching Exceptional Children, 15,* 136–139.

Reis, S., Neu, T. W., & McGuire, J. M. (1995). *Talents in two places: Case studies of high ability students with learning disabilities who have achieved* (Research monograph 95114). Storrs: University of Connecticut, National Research Center on the Gifted and Talented.

Reis, S. M., Westberg, K. L., Kulikowich, J. M., & Purcell, J. H. (1998). Curriculum compacting and achievement test scores: What does the research say? *Gifted Child Quarterly, 42,* 123–129.

Reiss, S., & Reiss, M. M. (2004). Curiosity and mental retardation: Beyond IQ. *Mental Retardation, 42,* 77–81.

Renzulli, J. (1978). What makes giftedness? Reexamining a definition. *Phi Delta Kappan, 61,* 180–184.

Renzulli, J. (1998). *Relationship between gifted programs and total school improvement using the schoolwide enrichment model.* Storrs: University of Connecticut, National Resource Center on the Gifted and Talented.

Renzulli, J. S. (2003). Conception of giftedness and its relationship to the development of social capital. In N. Colangelo & G. A. Davis (Eds.), *Handbook of gifted education* (3rd ed.), (pp. 75–87). Needham Heights, MA: Allyn & Bacon.

Renzulli, J. S., & Reis, S. M. (2003). The schoolwide enrichment model: Developing creative and productive giftedness. In N. Colangelo & G. A. Davis (Eds.), *Handbook of gifted education* (3rd ed.), (pp. 184–203). Needham Heights, MA: Allyn & Bacon.

Renzulli, J., & Reis, S. (2004). Curriculum compacting. In D. Boothe & J. Stanley (Eds.), *In the eyes of the beholder: Critical issues for diversity in gifted education* (pp. 87–100). Waco, TX: Prufrock.

*Report of the autism task force.* (1999). Augusta: Maine Administrators of Services for Children with Disabilities. Available at http://www.madsec.org.

Reschly, D. J. (1996). Identification and assessment of students with disabilities. *Future of Children, 6*(1), 40–53.

Revell, W. G., Wehman, P., Kregel, J., West, M., & Rayfield, R. (1994). Supported employment for persons with severe disabilities: Positive trends in wages, models, and funding. *Education and Training in Mental Retardation, 29,* 256–264.

Rex, E. J., Koenig, A. J., Wormsley, D. P., & Baker, R. L. (1994). *Foundations of braille literacy.* New York: American Foundation for the Blind.

Reyes-Blanes, M., Rodriguez, P., Vázquez, E., & Skinner, M. (1999). Needs and supports reported by Latino families of young children with developmental disabilities. *American Journal on Mental Retardation, 104*, 437–451.

Reynolds, M. C., & Heistad, D. (1997). 20/20 analysis: Estimating school effectiveness in serving students at the margins. *Exceptional Children, 63*, 439–449.

Reynolds, M. C., Zetlin, A. G., & Heistad, D. (1996). *A manual for 20/20 analysis.* Philadelphia: Temple University, Center for Research in Human Development and Education. (ERIC Document Reproduction Service No. ED 358 183).

Rhode, G., Jenson, W. R., & Morgan, D. P. (2003). *Tough kid new teacher kit.* Longmont, CO: Sopris West.

Rhode, G., Jenson, W. R., & Reavis, H. K. (1998). *The tough kid book: Practical classroom management strategies.* Longmont, CO: Sopris West.

Rhode, G., Morgan, D. P., & Young, K. R. (1983). Generalization and maintenance of treatment gains of behaviorally handicapped students from resource rooms to regular classrooms using self-evaluation procedures. *Journal of Applied Behavior Analysis, 16*, 171–188.

Ricci-Balich, J., & Behm, J. A. (1996). Pediatric rehabilitation nursing. In S. P. Hoeman (Ed.), *Rehabilitation nursing: Process and application* (pp. 660–682). St. Louis: Mosby.

Richards, T. L. (2001). Functional magnetic resonance imaging and spectroscopic imaging of the brain: Application of fMRI and fMRS to reading disabilities and education. *Learning Disability Quarterly, 24*, 189–203.

Richardson, B. G., & Shupe, M. J. (2003). The importance of teacher self-awareness in working with students with emotional and behavior disorders. *Teaching Exceptional Children, 36*(2), 8–13.

Rigby. (2004). *Rigby literacy teacher's guide, grade 1.* Barrington, IL: Author.

Riggs, C. G. (2001). Working effectively with paraeducators in inclusive settings. *Intervention in School and Clinic, 35*, 54–70.

Rimland, B. (1993). Beware the advozealots: Mindless good intentions injure the handicapped. *Autism Research Review International, 7*(4), 1.

Rimland, B. (1994). The modern history of autism: A personal perspective. In J. L. Matson (Ed.), *Autism in children and adults: Etiology, assessment, and intervention.* Pacific Grove, CA: Brooks/Cole.

Rimm, S. (2000). *See Jane win.* New York: Crown.

Rimm, S. (2002). *How Jane won.* New York: Crown.

Roberts, C. D., Stough, L. M., & Parrish, L. H. (2002). The role of genetic counseling in the elective termination of pregnancies involving fetuses with disabilities. *Journal of Special Education, 36*, 48–55.

Roberts, J. E., Wallace, I. F., & Henderson, F. W. (1997). *Otitis media in young children:*

*Medical, developmental, and education considerations.* Baltimore: Brookes.

Robins, D., Fein, D., Barton, M., & Green, J. (2001). The modified checklist for autism in toddlers: An initial study investigating the early detection of autism and pervasive developmental disorders. *Journal of Autism and Developmental Disorders, 31*, 131–144.

Robinson Spohn, J. R., Timko, T. C., & Sainato, D. M. (1999). Increasing the social interactions of preschool children with disabilities during mealtimes: The effects of an interactive placemat game. *Education and Treatment of Children, 22*, 1–18.

Rock, M. L. (2000). Parents as equal partners: Balancing the scales in IEP development. *Teaching Exceptional Children, 32*(6), 30–37.

Rockwell, S., & Guetzloe, E. (1996). Group development for students with emotional/behavioral disorders. *Teaching Exceptional Children, 29*(1), 38–43.

Roeser, R., & Yellin, W. (1987). Pure-tone tests with preschool children. In F. Martin (Ed.), *Hearing disorders in children: Pediatric audiology* (pp. 217–264). Austin, TX: PRO-ED.

Rogan, P., Hagner, D., & Murphy, S. (1993). Natural supports: Reconceptualizing job coach roles. *Journal of The Association for Persons with Severe Handicaps, 18*, 275–281.

Rogers, K. (2002). *Re-forming gifted education.* Scottsdale, AZ: Great Potential.

Romanczyk, R. G., Weinter, T., Lockshin, S., & Ekdahl, M. (1999). Research in autism: Myths, controversies, and perspectives. In D. B. Zager (Ed.), *Autism: Identification, education, and treatment* (2nd ed.), (pp. 23–61). Mahwah, NJ: Erlbaum.

Romer, L. T., White, J., & Haring, N. G. (1996). The effect of peer mediated social competency training on the type and frequency of social contacts with students with deaf-blindness. *Education and Training in Mental Retardation and Developmental Disabilities, 31*, 324–338.

Rorschach, H. (1942). *Rorschach psychodiagnostic plates.* New York: Psychological Corporation.

Rose, K. C., White, J. A., Conroy, J., & Smith, D. M. (1993). Following the course of change: A study of adaptive and maladaptive behaviors in young adults living in the community. *Education and Training in Mental Retardation, 28*, 149–154.

Rose, T. L., & Calhoun, M. L. (1990). The Charlotte Circle Project: A program for infants and toddlers with severe/profound disabilities. *Journal of Early Intervention, 14*, 175–185.

Rosenblum, L. P. (1998). Best friendships of adolescents with visual impairments: A descriptive study. *Journal of Visual Impairments and Blindness, 92*, 593–608.

Rosenblum, L. P. (2000). Perceptions of the impact of visual impairments on the lives of adolescents. *Journal of Visual Impairments and Blindness, 94*, 434–445.

Rosenshine, B. V. (1986). Synthesis of research on explicit teaching. *Educational Leadership, 43*(7), 60–69.

Rosenshine, B. V. (1987). Explicit teaching and teacher training. *Journal of Teacher Education, 38*(3), 34–36.

Rosenthal, B., & Williams, D. (2000). Devices primarily for people with low vision. In B. Silverstone, M. Lang, B. Rosenthal, & E. Faye (Eds.), *The lighthouse handbook on vision impairment and vision rehabilitation* (pp. 951–982). New York: Oxford University Press.

Ross, M., & Levitt, H. (2000). Developments in research and technology: Otoacoustic emissions. *Volta Voices, 7*, 30–31.

Rousch, W. (1995). Arguing over why Johnny can't read. *Science, 267*, 1896–1898.

Rues, J. P., Ault, M. M., Graff, J. C., & Holvoet, J. F. (2006). Special health care procedures. In M. E. Snell & F. Brown (Eds.), *Instruction of students with severe disabilities* (6th ed.). Upper Saddle River, NJ: Merrill/Prentice Hall.

Runnheim, V., Frankenberger, W. R., & Hazelkorn, M. N. (1996). Medicating students with emotional and behavioral disorders and ADHD: A state survey. *Behavioral Disorders, 21*, 306–314.

Rusch, F. R., (1990). *Supported employment: Models, methods, and issues.* Sycamore, IL: Sycamore.

Rusch, F. R., Hughes, C., McNair, J., & Wilson, P. G. (1990). *Co-worker involvement scoring manual and instrument.* Champaign: University of Illinois, Board of Trustees.

Rusch, F. R., Johnson, J. R., & Hughes, C. (1990). Analysis of co-worker involvement in relations to level of disability versus placement approach among supported employees. *Journal of The Association for Persons with Severe Handicaps, 15*, 32–39.

Rusch, F. R., & Minch, K. E. (1988). Identification of co-worker involvement in supported employment: A review and analysis. *Research in Developmental Disabilities, 9*, 247–254.

Rush, A. J., & Francis, A. (Eds.). (2000). Expert consensus guideline series: Treatment of psychiatric and behavioral problems in mental retardation. *American Journal of Mental Retardation, 105*, 159–228.

Rutter, M. (1976). *Helping troubled children.* New York: Plenum.

Ryan, B. P. (2004). Contingency management and stuttering in children. *Behavior Analyst Today, 5*, 144–150.

Ryan, R. M., & Deci, E. L. (1996). When paradigms clash: Comments on Cameron and Pierce's claim that rewards do not undermine intrinsic motivation. *Review of Educational Research, 66*, 33–38.

Ryles, R. (1996). The impact of braille reading skills on employment, income, education, and reading habits. *Journal of Visual Impairment and Blindness, 90*, 219–226.

Ryndak, D. L., & Alper, S. (1996). *Curriculum content for students with moderate and severe disabilities in inclusive settings.* Boston: Allyn & Bacon.

Ryser, G. (2004). Qualitative and quantitative approaches to assessment. In S. Johnsen (Ed.), *Identifying gifted students: A practical guide* (pp. 23–40). Waco, TX: Prufrock.

Sabornie, E. J., & Kauffman, J. M. (1986). Social acceptance of learning disabled adolescents. *Learning Disabilities Quarterly, 9,* 55–60.

Sacks, S. Z., & Silberman, R. K. (Eds.). (1998). *Educating students who have visual impairments with other disabilities.* Baltimore: Brookes.

Sacks, S. Z., Wolffe, K. E., & Tierney, D. (1998). Lifestyles of students with visual impairments—adolescents. Preliminary studies of social networks. *Exceptional Children, 64,* 463–478.

Sadler, F. H. (2003). The itinerant special education teacher in the early childhood classroom. *Teaching Exceptional Children, 35*(3), 8–15.

Safer, D. J., Zito, J. M., & Fine, E. M. (1996). Increased methylphenidate usage for attention-deficit disorder in the 1990s. *Pediatrics, 98,* 1084–1088.

Safford, P. L., & Safford, E. J. (1996). *A history of childhood disability.* New York: Teachers College Press.

Safran, J. S. (2002). A practitioner's guide to resources on Asperger syndrome. *Intervention in School and Clinic, 37,* 283–291.

Safran, S. P. (2001). Asperger syndrome: The emerging challenge to special education. *Exceptional Children, 67,* 151–160.

Sainato, D. M., & Strain, P. S. (1993). Increasing integration success for preschoolers with disabilities. *Teaching Exceptional Children, 25*(2), 36.

Salend, S. J. (2005). *Creating inclusive classrooms: Effective and reflective practices for all students* (5th ed.). Upper Saddle River, NJ: Merrill/Prentice Hall.

Salend, S. J., Elhoweris, H., & van Garderen, D. (2003). Educational interventions for students with ADD. *Intervention in School and Clinic, 38,* 280–288.

Salend, S. J., Ellis, L. L., & Reynolds, C. J. (1989). Using self-instruction to teach vocational skills to individuals who are severely retarded. *Education and Training of the Mentally Retarded, 24,* 248–254.

Salend, S. J., Jantzen, N. R., & Giek, K. (1992). Using a peer confrontation system in a group setting. *Behavioral Disorders, 17,* 211–218.

Salend, S. J., & Salinas, A. (2003). Language differences of learning difficulties: The work of the multidisciplinary team. *Teaching Exceptional Children, 35*(4), 36–43.

Salvia, J., & Ysseldyke, J. E. (2001). *Assessment in special and remedial education* (8th ed.). Boston: Houghton Mifflin.

Sameroff, A. (2001). *Rick and resilience from infancy to adolescence: Is it better to change the child or the context?* Keynote address at Research Project Directors' Conference, U.S. Office of Special Education Programs, Washington, DC. (July 11).

Sandall, S., Joseph, G., Chou, H. Y., Schwartz, I. S., Horn, E., Lieber, J., Odom, S. L., &

Wolery, R. (2000). *Talking to practitioners: Focus group report on curriculum modifications in inclusive preschool classrooms.* Unpublished manuscript.

Sandall, S., McLean, M. E., & Smith, B. J. (Eds.). (2000). *DEC recommended practices in early intervention/early childhood special education.* Reston, VA: Council for Exceptional Children, Division for Early Childhood.

Sandall, S., & Ostrosky, M. (2000). *Natural environments and inclusion: Young exceptional children.* (Monograph series no. 2). Reston, VA: Council for Exceptional Children, Division for Early Childhood.

Sandall, S., & Schwartz, I. (2002). *Building blocks for teaching preschoolers with special needs.* Baltimore: Brookes.

Sandall, S., Schwartz, I., & Joseph, G. (2000). A building blocks model for effective instruction in inclusive early childhood settings. *Young Exceptional Children, 4*(3), 3–9.

Sandler, A. D, Sutton, K. A., DeWeese, J., Giradi, M. A., Sheppard, V., & Bodfish, J. W. (1999). Lack of benefit of a single-dose of synthetic human secretin in the treatment of autism and pervasive developmental disorders. *New England Journal of Medicine, 341*(24). 1801–1806.

Sandler, A. G., Arnold, L. B., Gable, R. A., & Strain, P. S. (1987). Effects of peer pressure on disruptive behavior of behaviorally disordered students. *Behavioral Disorders, 16,* 9–22.

Sandler, A. G., & Mistretta, L. A. (1998). Positive adaptation in parents of adults with disabilities. *Education and Training in Mental Retardation and Developmental Disabilities, 33,* 123–130.

Sands, D. J., & Kozleski, E. B. (1994). Quality of life differences between adults with and without disabilities. *Education and Training in Mental Retardation, 29,* 90–101.

Santelli, B., Poyadue, F. S., & Young, J. L. (2001). *The Parent to Parent handbook: Connecting families of children with special needs.* Baltimore: Brookes.

Sapienza, C., & Hicks, D. M. (2002). Voice disorders. In G. H. Shames & N. B. Anderson (Eds.), *Human communication disorders: An introduction* (6th ed.), (pp. 349–393). Boston: Allyn & Bacon.

Sarouphim, K. M. (2001). DISCOVER: Concurrent validity, gender differences, and identification of minority students. *Gifted Child Quarterly, 45*(2), 130–139.

Sasso, G. (2001). The retreat from inquiry and knowledge in special education. *Journal of Special Education, 34,* 178–193.

Savage, R. C., & Wolcott, G. F. (Eds.). (1994). *Educational dimensions of acquired brain injury.* Austin, TX: PRO-ED.

Schalock, R., Coutler, D., Polloway, E., Reiss, S., Snell, M., Spitalnik, D., & Stark, J. (1994). The changing conception of mental retardation: Implications for the field. *Mental Retardation, 32,* 181–193.

Schalock, R. L. (Ed.). (1999). *Adaptive behavior and its measurement: Implications for the field of mental retardation.* Washington, DC:

American Association on Mental Retardation.

Schalock, R. L., Bonham, G. S., & Marchand, C. B. (2000). Consumer based quality of life assessment: A path model of perceived satisfaction. *Evaluator and Program Planning, 23,* 75–85.

Schalock, R. L., Keith, K. D., Hoffman, K., & Karan, O. C. (1989). Quality of life: Its measurement and use. *Mental Retardation, 27,* 25–31.

Scheetz, N. A. (2004). *Psychosocial aspects of deafness.* Boston: Allyn & Bacon.

Schessel, D. A. (1999). Ménière's disease. *Volta Review, 99*(5), 177–183.

Scheuermann, B., & Webber, J. (2002). *Autism: Teaching does make a difference.* Belmont, CA: Wadsworth.

Schick, B., & Williams, K. (1994). The evaluation of educational interpreters. In B. Schick & M. P. Moeller (Eds.), *Sign language in the schools: Current issues and controversies.* Omaha, NE: Boys Town Press.

Schick, B., Williams, K., & Bolster, L. (1999). Skill levels of educational interpreters working in public schools. *Journal of Deaf Studies and Deaf Education, 4,* 144–155.

Schirmer, B. R. (1997). Boosting reading success: Language, literacy, and content area instruction for deaf and hard-of-hearing students. *Teaching Exceptional Children, 30*(1), 52–55.

Schirmer, B. R. (2000). *Language and literacy development in children who are deaf* (2nd ed.). Boston: Allyn & Bacon.

Schirmer, B. R. (2001). *Psychological, social, and educational dimensions of deafness.* Boston: Allyn & Bacon.

Schirmer, B. R. (2004). Hearing loss. In R. Turnbull, A. Turnbull, M. Shank, & S. J. Smith, *Exceptional lives: Special education in today's schools* (4th ed.), (pp. 424–454). Upper Saddle River, NJ: Merrill/Prentice Hall.

Schleien, S. J., Kiernan, J., & Wehman, P. (1981). Evaluation of an age-appropriate leisure skills program for moderately retarded adults. *Education and Training of the Mentally Retarded, 16,* 13–19.

Schleien, S. J., Meyer, L. H., Heyne, L. A., & Brandt, B. B. (1995). *Lifelong leisure skills and lifestyles for persons with developmental disabilities.* Baltimore: Brookes.

Schleien, S. J., & Ray, M. T. (1998). *Community recreation and persons with disabilities: Strategies for integration* (2nd ed.). Baltimore: Brookes.

Schleien, S. J., Wehman, P., & Kiernan, J. (1981). Teaching leisure skills to severely handicapped adults: An age-appropriate darts game. *Journal of Applied Behavior Analysis, 14,* 513–519.

Schneider, B. H., & Leroux, J. (1994). Educational environments for the pupil with behavioral disorders: A "best evidence" synthesis. *Behavioral Disorders, 19,* 192–204.

Schonert-Reichl, K. A. (1993). Empathy and social relationships in adolescents with behavioral disorders. *Behavioral Disorders, 18,* 189–204.

Schopler, E., Reichler, R. J., & Renner, B. R. (1988). *The childhood autism rating scale.* Los Angeles: Western Psychological Services.

Schroeder, S. (Ed.). (1987). *Toxic substances and mental retardation: Neurobiological toxicology and teratology.* Washington, DC: American Association on Mental Retardation.

Schulz, J. B. (1985). The parent-professional conflict. In H. R. Turnbull & A. P. Turnbull (Eds.), *Parents speak out: Then and now* (pp. 3–11). Upper Saddle River, NJ: Merrill/Prentice Hall.

Schumaker, J. B., & Deshler, D. D. (1992). Validation of learning strategy interventions for students with learning disabilities: Results of a programmatic research effort. In B. Y. L. Wong (Ed.), *Contemporary intervention research in learning disabilities* (pp. 22–46). New York: Springer-Verlag.

Schumm, J. S., Moody, S. W., & Vaughn, S. (2000). Grouping for reading instruction: Does one size fit all? *Journal of Learning Disabilities, 33,* 477–488.

Schumm, J. S., Vaughn, D., Haager, D., McDowell, J., Rothlein, L., & Saumell, L. (1995). General education teacher planning: What can students with learning disabilities expect? *Exceptional Children, 61,* 335–352.

Schwartz, I. (2000). Standing on the shoulders of giants: Looking ahead to facilitating membership and relationships for children with disabilities. *Topics in Early Childhood Special Education, 20,* 123–128.

Schwartz, I. S., & Baer, D. M. (1991). Social validity assessments: Is current practice state of the art? *Journal of Applied Behavior Analysis, 24,* 189–204.

Schwartz, I., Garfinkle, A. N., & Bauer, J. (1998). The Picture Exchange Communication System: Communicative outcomes for young children with disabilities. *Topics in Early Childhood Special Education, 18,* 144–159.

Schwartz, I., Sandall, S. R., Garfinkle, A. N., & Bauer, J. (1998). Outcomes for children with autism: Three case studies. *Topics in Early Childhood Special Education, 18,* 132–143.

Schwartz, I. S. (2005). Inclusion and applied behavior analysis: Mending fences and building bridges. In W. L. Heward, T. E. Heron, N. A. Neef, S. M. Peterson, D. M. Sainato, G. Cartledge, R. Gardner, III, L. D. Peterson, S. B. Hersh, & J. C. Dardig (Eds.), *Focus on behavior analysis in education: Achievements, challenges, and opportunities* (pp. 239–251). Upper Saddle River, NJ: Merrill/Prentice Hall.

Schwartz, I. S., Staub, D., Peck, C. A., & Gallucci, C. (2006). Peer relationships. In M. E. Snell & F. Brown (Eds.), *Instruction of students with severe disabilities* (6th ed.). Upper Saddle River, NJ: Merrill/Prentice Hall.

Schwartz, N. H., Wolf, J. N., & Cassar, R. (1997). Predicting teacher referrals of emotionally disturbed children. *Exceptionality, 3,* 81–98.

Scorgie, K., & Sobsey, D. (2000). Transformational outcomes associated with parenting children who have disabilities. *Mental Retardation, 38,* 195–206.

Scott, B. J., & Vitale, M. R. (2003). Teaching writing process to students with LD. *Intervention in School and Clinic, 38,* 220–224.

Scuccimarra, D. J., & Speece, D. L. (1990). Employment outcomes and social integration of students with mild handicaps: The quality of life two years after high school. *Journal of Learning Disabilities, 23,* 213–219.

Semel, E., Wiig, E. H., & Secord, W. (1995). *Clinical evaluation of language fundamentals* (3rd ed.). San Antonio, TX: Psychological Corporation.

Serna, L. A., Forness, S. R., & Nielson, M. E. (1998). Intervention versus affirmation: Proposed solutions to the problem of disproportionate minority representation in special education. *Journal of Special Education, 32,* 48–51.

Sexson, S. B., & Dingle, A. D. (2001). Medical disorders. In F. M. Kline, L. B. Silver, & S. C. Russell, (Eds.), *The educator's guide to medical issues in the classroom* (pp. 29–48). Baltimore: Brookes.

Sexton, M., Harris, K. R., & Graham, S. (1998). Self-regulated strategy development and the writing process: Effects on essay writing and attributions. *Exceptional Children, 64,* 295–311.

Seymour, H. N., Bland-Stewart, L., & Green, L. J. (1998). Difference versus deficit in child African American English. *Language, Speech, and Hearing Services in the Schools, 29,* 96–108.

Shaklee, B., Whitmore, J., Barton, L., Barbour, N., Ambrose, R., & Viechnicki, K. (1989). *Early assessment for exceptional potential for young and/or economically disadvantaged students.* (Grant No. R206A00160). Washington, DC: U.S. Department of Education, Office of Educational Research and Improvement.

Shames, G. H., & Anderson, N. B. (2002). *Human communication disorders: An introduction* (6th ed.). Boston: Allyn & Bacon.

Shapiro, D. R., & Sayers, L. K. (2003). Who does what on the interdisciplinary team regarding physical education for students with disabilities? *Teaching Exceptional Children, 35*(6), 32–38.

Shapiro, E. S., DuPaul, G. J., & Bradley-King, K. L. (1998). Self-management as a strategy to improve the classroom behavior of adolescents with ADHD. *Journal of Learning Disabilities, 31,* 545–555.

Shapiro, E. S., Miller, D. N., Swaka, K., Gardill, M. C., & Handler, M. W. (1999). Facilitating the inclusion of students with EBD into general education classrooms. *Journal of Emotional and Behavioral Disorders, 7,* 83–93.

Shaywitz, B. A., Fletcher, J. M., & Shaywitz, S. E. (1995). Defining and classifying learning disabilities and attention-deficit/hyperactivity disorder. *Journal of Child Neurology, 10,* 50–57.

Shaywitz, B. A., Shaywitz, S. E., Blachman, B. A., Pugh, K. R., Fulbright, R. K., Skudlarski, P., Menci, W. E., Constable, R. T., Holahan, J. M., Marchione, K. E., Fletcher, J. M., Lyon, G. R., & Gore, J. C. (2004). Development of left occipitotemporal systems for skilled reading in children after a phonologically-based intervention. *Biological Psychiatry, 55,* 926–933.

Shearer, M. S., & Shearer, D. E. (1979). *The Portage Project: A model for early childhood education.* Portage, WI: Portage Project.

Shildroth, A. N., & Hotto, S. A. (1994). Inclusion or exclusion? Deaf students and the inclusion movement. *American Annals of the Deaf, 139,* 239–242.

Shinn, M. R., Tindal, G. A., & Spira, D. A. (1987). Special education referrals as an index of teacher tolerance: Are teachers imperfect tests? *Exceptional Children, 54,* 32–40.

Shonkoff, J. P., & Meisels, S. J. (Eds.). (2000). *Handbook of early childhood intervention* (2nd ed.). New York: Cambridge University Press.

Shores, R. E., Gunter, P. L., & Jack, S. L. (1993). Classroom management strategies: Are they setting events for coercion? *Behavioral Disorders, 18,* 92–102.

Shores, R. E., Jack, S. L., Gunter, P. L., Ellis, D. N., DeBriere, T. J., & Wehby, J. H. (1993). Classroom interactions of children with disorders. *Journal of Emotional and Behavioral Disorders, 1,* 27–39.

Shukla, S., Kennedy, C. H., & Cushing, L. S. (1998). Adult influence on the participation of peers without disabilities in peer support programs. *Journal of Behavioral Education, 8,* 397–413.

Sicley, D. (1993). Effective methods of communication: Practical interventions for classroom teachers. *Intervention in School and Clinic, 29,* 105–108.

Sidman, M. (1989). *Coercion and its fallout.* Boston: Authors Group.

Sidman, M. (1994). *Equivalence relations and behavior: A research story.* Boston: Authors Cooperative.

Siegel, I. J., & Senna, J. J. (1994). *Juvenile delinquency: Theory, practice, and law* (5th ed.). St. Paul, MN: West.

Silliman, E. R., Bahr, R., Beasman, J., & Wilkinson, L. C. (2000). Scaffolds for learning to read in an inclusion classroom. *Language, Speech, and Hearing Services in Schools, 31,* 265–269.

Silliman, E. R., & Diehl, S. F. (2002). Assessing children with language learning disabilities. In D. K. Berstein & E. Tiegerman-Farber (Eds.), *Language and communication disorders in children* (5th ed.). Needham Heights, MA: Allyn & Bacon.

Silliman, E. R., Ford, C. S., Beasman, J., & Evans, D. (1999). An inclusion model for children with language learning disabilities: Building classroom partnerships. *Topics in Language Disorders, 19*(3), 1–18.

Silliman, E. R., Mills, L. R., & Murphy, M. M. (1997). How to start? One story of change in a middle school. In N. W. Nelson & B. Hoskins (Eds.), *Strategies for supporting classroom success* (pp. 1–22). San Diego: Singular.

Silverman, L. K. (1986). Parenting young gifted children. *Journal of Children in Contemporary Society, 18,* 73–87.

Silverman, L. K. (1995). Highly gifted children. In J. L. Genshaft, M. Bireley, & C. L. Hollinger (Eds.), *Serving gifted and talented students: A resource for school personnel* (pp. 124–160). Austin, TX: PRO-ED.

Silvestri, S. M., Wood, C. L., Allen, N. J., Anderson, M. A., Murphy, C. M., & Heward, W. L. (in press). What is ABA? In E. A. Boutot & M. Tincani (Eds.), *Autism articles: What parents need to know.* Austin, TX: PRO-ED.

Simeonsson, R. J. (1994). Promoting children's health, education, and well-being. In R. J. Simeonsson (Ed.), *Risk, resilience, and prevention* (pp. 3–11). Baltimore: Brookes.

Simmons, D. C., Kame'enui, E. J., & Chard, D. J. (1998). General education teachers' assumptions about learning and students with learning disabilities: Design-of-instruction analysis. *Learning Disability Quarterly, 21,* 6–21.

Simmons, D. C., Kame'enui, E. J., Coyne, M. D., & Chard, D. J. (2002). Effective strategies for teaching beginning reading. In E. J. Kame'enui, D. W. Carnine, R. C. Dixon, D. C. Simmons, & M. D. Coyne (Eds.), *Effective teaching strategies that accommodate diverse learners* (2nd ed.), (pp. 53–92). Upper Saddle River, NJ: Merrill/Prentice Hall.

Simon, R. (1987). *After the tears: Parents talk about raising a child with a disability.* San Diego: Harcourt Brace Jovanovich.

Simos, P. G., Breier, J. I., Fletcher, J. M., Bergman, E., & Papanicolaou, A. C. (2000). Cerebral mechanisms involved in word reading in dyslexic children: A magnetic source imaging approach. *Cerebral Cortex, 10,* 809–816.

Simpson, R. L. (1996). *Working with families and parents of exceptional children and youth: Techniques for successful conferencing and collaboration* (3rd ed.). Austin, TX: PRO-ED.

Simpson, R. L. (2001). ABA and students with autism spectrum disorders: Issues and considerations for effective practice. *Focus on Autism and Other Developmental Disabilities, 16,* 68–71.

Simpson, R. L. (2004). Finding effective intervention and personnel preparation practices for students with autism spectrum disorders. *Exceptional Children, 70,* 135–144.

Simpson, R. L., & Myles, B. S. (1995). Effectiveness of facilitated communication with children and youth with autism. *Journal of Special Education, 28,* 424–439.

Sims, D. G., & Gottermeier, L. (1995). Computer-assisted, interactive video methods for speechreading instruction: A review. In K. Erik-Spens & G. Plant (Eds.), *Speech, communication and profound deafness* (pp. 220–241). London: Whurr.

Singer, G. H. S., Powers, L. E., & Olson, A. (1996). *Redefining family support: Innovations in public/private partnerships.* Baltimore: Brookes.

Sitlington, P. L., & Clark, G. M. (2006). *Comprehensive transition education and services for students with disabilities* (4th ed.). Needham Heights, MA: Allyn & Bacon.

Sitlington, P. L., Clark, G. M., & Kolstoe, O. P. (2000). *Comprehensive transition education and services for adolescents with disabilities* (3rd ed.). Needham Heights, MA: Allyn & Bacon.

Sitlington, P. L., Frank, A. R., & Carson, R. (1993). Adult adjustment among high school graduates with mild disabilities. *Exceptional Children, 59,* 221–233.

Sitlington, P. L., & Payne, E. M. (2004). Information needed by postsecondary education: Can we provide it as part of the transition assessment process? *Learning Disabilities, 2*(2), 1–14.

Skeels, H. M., & Dye, H. B. (1939). A study of the effects of differential stimulation on mentally retarded children. *Convention Proceedings, American Association on Mental Deficiency, 44,* 114–136.

Skellenger, A., Hill, E., & Hill, M. (1992). The social functioning of children with visual impairments. In S. L. Odom, S. R. McConnell, & M. A. McEvoy (Eds.), *Social competence of young children with disabilities: Issues and strategies for intervention* (pp. 165–188). Baltimore: Brookes.

Skinner, B. F. (1989). *Recent issues in the analysis of behavior.* Columbus, OH: Merrill.

Skinner, D., Bailey, D. D., Jr., Correa, V. I., & Rodriguez, P. (1999). Narrating self and disabilities: Latino mothers' construction of identities vis-à-vis their children with special needs. *Exceptional Children, 65,* 481–495.

Skinner, D., Correa, V., Skinner, M., & Bailey, D. (2001). Role of religion in the lives of Latino families of young children with developmental delays. *American Journal on Mental Retardation, 106,* 297–313.

Skinner, M. (1998). Promoting self-advocacy among college students with learning disabilities. *Intervention in School and Clinic, 33*(5), 278–283.

Slaton, D. E., Schuster, J., Collins, B., & Carnine, D. (1994). A functional approach to academic instruction. In E. Cipani & F. Spooner (Eds.), *Curricular and instructional approaches for persons with severe disabilities* (pp. 149–183). Boston: Allyn & Bacon.

Slavin, R. (1987). Ability grouping and student achievement in elementary schools: A best-evidence synthesis. *Review of Educational Research, 57,* 293–336.

Slavin, R. (1991). Synthesis of research on cooperative learning. *Educational Leadership, 47*(4), 3.

Slavin, R. E. (1986). *Using student team learning* (3rd ed.). Baltimore: Johns Hopkins University, Center for Research on Elementary and Middle Schools.

Slavin, R. E. (1990). Research on cooperative learning. *Educational Leadership, 47*(4), 52–54.

Slike, S. B., & Hobbis, D. H. (1998, March). *The development of a CD-ROM to teach speechreading skills.* Paper presented at the Association of College Educators of the Deaf and Hard of Hearing, Lexington, KY.

Slike, S. B., Thornton, N. E., Hobbis, D. H., Kokoska, S. M., & Job, K. A. (1995). The development and analysis of interactive videodisc technology to teach speechreading. *American Annals of the Deaf, 140*(4), 346–351.

Smith, C. R. (1997). Advocacy for students with emotional and behavior disorders: One call for redefined efforts. *Behavioral Disorders, 22,* 96–105.

Smith, C. R. (2000). Behavioral and discipline provisions of IDEA '97: Implicit competencies yet to be confirmed. *Exceptional Children, 66,* 403–412.

Smith, J. D. (1994). The revised AAMR definition of mental retardation: The MRDD position. *Education and Training in Mental Retardation, 29,* 179–183.

Smith, J. D. (2000). The power of mental retardation: Reflections on the value of people with disabilities. *Mental Retardation, 38,* 70–72.

Smith, J. D. (2004). In A. McCray Sorrells, H. J. Rieth, & P. T. Sindelar (Eds.), *Critical issues in special education: Access, diversity, and accountability* (pp. 1–15). Boston: Allyn & Bacon.

Smith, J. D., & Hilton, A. (1997). The preparation and training of the educational community for the inclusion of students with developmental disabilities: The MRDD position. *Education and Training of Mental Retardation and Developmental Disabilities, 32,* 3–10.

Smith, J. D., & Mitchell, A. L. (2001a). Disney's Tarzan, Edgar Rice Burroughs' eugenics, and visions of utopian perfection. *Mental Retardation, 39,* 221–225.

Smith, J. D., & Mitchell, A. L. (2001b). "Me? I'm not a drooler. I'm the assistant": Is it time to abandon mental retardation as a classification? *Mental Retardation, 39,* 144–146.

Smith, J. D., & Prior, M. (1995). Temperament and stress resilience in school-age children: A within-families study. *Journal of the American Academy of Children and Adolescent Psychiatry, 34,* 168–179.

Smith, L., & Fowler, S. A. (1984). Positive peer pressure: The effects of peer monitoring on children's disruptive behavior. *Journal of Applied Behavior Analysis, 17,* 213–227.

Smith, R. G., & Iwata, B. A. (1997). Antecedent influences of behavior disorders. *Journal of Applied Behavior Analysis, 30,* 343–375.

Smith, S. B., Baker, S., & Oudeans, M. K., Sr. (2001). Making a difference in the classroom with early literacy instruction. *Teaching Exceptional Children, 33*(6), 8–14.

Smith, S. W. (1990a). Comparison of Individualized Education Programs (IEPs) of students with behavioral disorders and learning disabilities. *Journal of Special Education, 24*(1), 85–100.

Smith, S. W. (1990b). Individualized Education Programs (IEPs) in special education—From intent to acquiescence. *Exceptional Children, 57,* 6–14.

Smith, S. W., & Brownell, M. T. (1995). Individualized education programs: From intent to acquiescence. *Focus on Exceptional Children, 28*(1), 1–12.

Smith, S. W., & Simpson, R. L. (1989). An analysis of individualized education programs (IEPs) for students with behavioral disorders. *Behavioral Disorders, 14,* 107–116.

Smith, T., Eikeseth, S., Klevstrand, M., & Lovaas, O. I. (1997). Intensive behavioral treatment for preschoolers with severe mental retardation and pervasive developmental disorders. *American Journal on Mental Retardation, 102,* 238–249.

Smith, T., & Lovaas, O. I. (1998). Intensive and early behavioral intervention with autism: The UCLA young autism project. *Infants and Young Children, 10*(3), 67–78.

Smith, T. B., Oliver, M. N. I., & Innocenti, M. S. (2001). Parenting stress in families of children with disabilities. *American Journal of Orthopsychiatry, 71,* 257–261.

Smith, T. E. C. (2002). Section 504: What teachers need to know. *Intervention in School and Clinic, 37,* 259–266.

Smithdas, R. (1981). Psychological aspects of deaf-blindness. In S. R. Walsh & R. Holzberg (Eds.), *Understanding and educating the deaf-blind/severely and profoundly handicapped: An international perspective.* Springfield, IL: Thomas.

Snell, M. E. (2004). What if your child lacks needed communication services and supports? *Exceptional Parent, 34*(2), 41–44.

Snell, M. E., & Beckman-Brindley, S. (1984). Family involvement in intervention with children having severe handicaps. *Journal of The Association for Persons with Severe Handicaps, 9,* 213–230.

Snell, M. E., & Brown, F. (Eds.). (2006). *Instruction of students with severe disabilities* (6th ed.). Upper Saddle River, NJ: Merrill/Prentice Hall.

Snell, M. E., & Janney, R. E. (2000). Teachers' problem-solving about children with moderate and severe disabilities in elementary classrooms. *Exceptional Children, 66,* 472–490.

Snell, M. E., & Janney, R. E. (2005). *Practices for inclusive schools: Collaborative teaming* (2nd ed.). Baltimore: Brookes.

Snider, V. E., Busch, T., & Arrowood, L. (2003). Teacher knowledge of stimulant medication and ADHD. *Remedial and Special Education, 24,* 46–56.

Snow, K. (2001). *Disability is natural.* Woodland Park, CO: Braveheart.

Snyder, H. N. (2000). *Juvenile arrests 1999.* Washington, DC: Office of Juvenile Justice and Delinquency Prevention.

Sobsey, D. (1996). Review of assistive technologies: Principles and practice by A. M. Cook & S. M. Hussey. *Journal of The Association for Persons with Severe Handicaps, 21,* 207–209.

Social Security Administration. (2000). *Titles II and XVI: Basic disability.* www.ssa.gov/disability.

Sonnenschein, S. (1981). Parents and professionals: An uneasy relationship. *Teaching Exceptional Children, 14,* 62–65.

Sontag, E., Sailor, W., & Smith, J. (1977). The severely/profoundly handicapped: Who are they? Where are we? *Journal of Special Education, 11*(1), 5–11.

Sonuga-Bourke, E. J. S., Dalen, L., Daley, D., & Remington, B. (2002). Are planning, working, memory, and inhibition associated with individual differences in preschool ADHD symptoms? *Developmental Neuropsychology, 21,* 255–272.

Southern, W. T., & Jones, E. (1991). *The academic acceleration of gifted children.* New York: Teachers College Press.

Sowers, J., Verdi, M., Bourbeau, P., & Sheehan, M. (1985). Teaching job independence to mentally retarded students through the use of a self-control package. *Journal of Applied Behavior Analysis, 18,* 81–85.

Sparrow, S. S., Balla, D. A., & Cicchetti, D. V. (1984a). *Vineland Adaptive Behavior Scales: Interview edition, expanded form.* Circle Pines, MN: American Guidance Service.

Sparrow, S. S., Balla, D. A., & Cicchetti, D. V. (1984b). *Vineland Adaptive Behavior Scales: Interview edition, survey form.* Circle Pines, MN: American Guidance Service.

Sparrow, S. S., Balla, D. A., & Cicchetti, D. V. (1985). *Vineland Adaptive Behavior Scales: Classroom edition form.* Circle Pines, MN: American Guidance Service.

Spear-Swerling, L., & Sternberg, R. J. (2001). What science offers teachers of reading. *Learning Disabilities Research and Practice, 16,* 51–57.

Spencer, P. E. (2001, July). *Cochlear implants for children: Language, culture, and education.* Paper presented at Office of Special Education Program Project Director's Conference, Washington, DC.

Spinelli, C. G. (2004). Dealing with cancer in the classroom: The teacher's role and responsibilities. *Teaching Exceptional Children, 36*(4), 14–21.

Sprague, J., & Walker, H. (2000). Early identification and intervention for youth with antisocial and violent behavior. *Exceptional Children, 66,* 367–379.

Sprague, J. R., & Horner, R. H. (1990). Preventing challenging behaviors. *Teaching Exceptional Children, 23*(1), 13–15.

Spring, C., & Sandoval, J. (1976). Food additives and hyperkinesis: A critical evaluation of the evidence. *Journal of Learning Disabilities, 9,* 560–569.

Squires, J., Bricker, D., & Twombly, E. (2002). *Ages and Stages Questionnaires: Social-Emotional (ASQ:SE).* Baltimore: Brookes.

Sridhar, D., & Vaughn, S. (2000). Bibliotherapy for all: Enhancing reading comprehension, self-concept, and behavior. *Teaching Exceptional Children, 33*(2), 74–82.

Ssasz, T. (1961). *The myth of mental illness: Foundations of a theory of personal conduct.* New York: Harper.

Stahl, L., & Pry, R. (2002). Joint attention and set-shifting in young children with autism. *Autism, 6,* 383–396.

Stainback, S., & Stainback, W. (Eds.). (1991). *Teaching in the inclusive classroom: Curriculum design, adaptation and delivery.* Baltimore: Brookes.

Stainback, S., & Stainback, W. (Eds.). (1996). *Inclusion: A guide for educators* (2nd ed.). Baltimore: Brookes.

Stainton, T., & Besser, H. (1998). The positive impact of children with an intellectual disability on the family. *Journal of Intellectual and Developmental Disability, 23,* 57–70.

Stancliffe, R. J., & Hayden, C. (1998). Longitudinal study of institutional downsizing: Effects on individuals who remain in the institution. *American Journal on Mental Retardation, 102,* 500–510.

Stancliffe, R. J., & Lakin, K. C. (1998). Analysis of expenditures and outcomes of residential alternatives for persons with developmental disabilities. *American Journal on Mental Retardation, 102,* 552–568.

Stanovich, K. E., & Siegel, L. S. (1994). The phenotypic performance profile of reading-disabled children: A regression-based test of the phonological-core variable-difference model. *Journal of Educational Psychology, 86,* 24–53.

Stark, K. D., Bronik, M. D., Wong, S., Wells, G., & Ostrander, R. (2000). Depressive disorders. In M. Hersen & R. T. Ammerman (Eds.), *Advanced abnormal child psychology* (2nd ed.), (pp. 291–326). Hillsdale, NJ: Erlbaum.

Staub, D., Spaulding, M., Peck, C. A., Gallucci, C., & Schwartz, I. S. (1996). Using nondisabled peers to support the inclusion of students with disabilities at the junior high school level. *Journal of The Association for Persons with Severe Handicaps, 21,* 194–205.

Staub, R. W. (1990). The effects of publicly posted feedback on middle school students' disruptive hallway behavior. *Education and Treatment Children, 13,* 249–257.

Steeker, P. M., & Fuchs, L. S. (2000). Effecting superior achievement using curriculum-based measurement: The importance of individual progress monitoring. *Learning Disabilities Research and Practice, 15,* 128–134.

Stephens, K. R., & Karnes, F. A. (2000). State definitions for the gifted and talented revisited. *Exceptional Children, 66*(2), 219–238.

Stephens, T. M., & Wolf, J. S. (1989). *Effective skills in parent/teacher conferencing* (2nd ed.). Columbus: The Ohio State University, College of Education, School Study Council of Ohio.

Sternberg, L. (Ed.). (1994). *Individuals with profound disabilities: Instructional and assistive strategies.* Austin, TX: PRO-ED.

Sternberg, R. (1988). *The triarchic mind: A new theory of human intelligence.* New York: Viking.

Sternberg, R., & Grigorenko, E. (2000). *Teaching for successful intelligence.* Upper Saddle River, NJ: Prentice Hall.

Sternberg, R. J. (2003). Giftedness according to the theory of successful intelligence. In N. Colangelo & G. A. Davis (Eds.), *Handbook of gifted education* (3rd ed.), (pp. 88–99). Needham Heights, MA: Allyn & Bacon.

Stevens, R., & Rosenshine, B. (1981). Advances in research on teaching. *Exceptional Education Quarterly, 2,* 1–9.

Stewart, D. A. (1992). Initiating reform in total communication programs. *Journal of Special Education, 26,* 68–84.

Stewart, J. L. (1977). Unique problems of handicapped Native Americans. In *The White House Conference on Handicapped Individuals* (vol. 1), (pp. 438–444). Washington, DC: U.S. Government Printing Office.

Stiles, S., & Knox, R. (1996). Medical issues, treatments, and professionals. In M. C. Holbrook (Ed.), *Children with visual impairments: A parents' guide* (pp. 21–48). Bethesda, MD: Woodbine House.

Stinson, M. S., Elliot, L. B., McKee, B. G., & Francis, P. G. (2001). Accessibility in the classroom: The pros and cons of C-Print. *Volta Voices, 8*(3), 16–19.

Stinson, M. S., & Liu, Y. (1999). Participation of deaf and hard-of-hearing students in classes with hearing students. *Journal of Deaf Studies and Deaf Education, 4,* 191–202.

Stokes, T. F., Fowler, S. A., & Baer, D. M. (1978). Training preschool children to recruit natural communities of reinforcement. *Journal of Applied Behavior Analysis, 11,* 285–303.

Stokoe, W. (1960). *The calculus of structure.* Washington, DC: Gallaudet University Press.

Stokoe, W., Armstrong, D. F., & Wilcox, S. (1995). *Gesture and the nature of language.* New York: Cambridge University Press.

Stone, C. A. (2002). Promises and pitfalls of scaffolded instruction for students with language learning disabilities. In K. G. Butler & E. R. Silliman (Eds.), *Speaking, reading, and writing in children with language learning disabilities: New paradigms for research and practice* (pp. 175–198). Mahwah, NJ: Erlbaum.

Stone, J. (1997). The preschool child. In H. Mason & S. McCall (Eds.), *Visual impairment: Access to education for children and young people* (pp. 87–96). London: Fulton.

Stone, P. (1997). Educating children who are deaf or hard of hearing: Auditory-oral option. *ERIC Digest #551.* (ERIC Document Reproduction Service No. ED 414 669).

Stoneman, Z. (1998). Research on siblings of children with mental retardation: Contributions of developmental theory and etiology. In J. A. Burach, R. M. Hodapp, & E. Zigler (Eds.), *Handbook of mental retardation and development* (pp. 669–692). Cambridge: Cambridge University Press.

Stoner, G., Carey, S. P., Ikeda, M. J., & Shinn, M. R. (1994). The utility of curriculum-based measurement for evaluating the effects of methylphenidate on academic performance. *Journal of Applied Behavior Analysis, 27,* 101–113.

Strain, P. S., & Joseph, G. E. (2004). A not so good job with "Good job." *Journal of Positive Behavior Interventions, 6*(1), 55–59.

Strain, P. S., & Schwartz, I. (2001). ABA and the development of meaningful social relations for young children with autism. *Focus on Autism and Other Developmental Disabilities, 16,* 120–128.

Strain, P. S., & Smith, B. J. (1986). A counter-interpretation of early intervention effects: A response to Casto and Mastropieri. *Exceptional Children, 53,* 260–265.

Strain, P. S., & Timm, M. A. (2001). Remediation and prevention of aggression: An evaluation of the Regional Intervention Program over a quarter century. *Behavioral Disorders, 26,* 297–313.

Strand, J., & Kreiner, J. (2005). Recreation and leisure in the community. In R. W. Flexer, T. J. Simmons, P. Luft, & R. M. Baer (Eds.), *Transition planning for secondary students with disabilities* (2nd ed.), (pp. 460–482). Upper Saddle River, NJ: Merrill/Prentice Hall.

Strauss, M. (1999). Hearing loss and cytomegalovirus. *Volta Review, 99*(5), 71–74.

Stremel, K., Molden, V., Leister, C., Matthews, J., Wilson, R., Goodall, D. V., & Hoston, J. (1990). *Communication systems and routines: A decision making process.* Washington, DC: U.S. Office of Special Education.

Strickland, B. B., & Turnbull, A. P. (1993). *Developing and implementing Individualized Education Programs* (3rd ed.). Upper Saddle River, NJ: Merrill/Prentice Hall.

Strickland, S. P. (1971). Can slum children learn? *American Education, 7*(6), 3–7.

Strong, C. J., & North, K. H. (1996). *The magic of stories: Literature–based language intervention.* Eau Claire, WI: Thinking Publications.

Strong, M. (1995). A review of bilingual/bicultural programs for deaf children in North America. *American Annals of the Deaf, 140*(2), 84–94.

Strong, M., & Prinz, P. M. (1997). A study of the relationship between American Sign Language and English literacy. *Journal of Deaf Studies and Deaf Education, 2,* 36–46.

Stroul, B. A., & Friedman, R. M. (1996). *A system of care for children and adolescents with severe emotional disturbance* (Rev. ed.). Washington, DC: Georgetown University Child Development Center, National Technical Assistance Center for Child Mental Health.

Stuart v. Nappi, 443 F. Supp. 1235 (D. Conn. 1978).

Sudhalter, V., & Belser, R. C. (2001). Conversational characteristics of children with fragile X syndrome: Tangential language. *American Journal of Mental Retardation, 106,* 389–400.

Sugai, G., & Horner, R. H. (2005). Schoolwide positive behavior supports: Achieving and sustaining effective learning environments for all students. In W. L. Heward, T. E. Heron, N. A. Neef, S. M. Peterson, D. M. Sainato, G. Cartledge, R. Gardner, III, L. D. Peterson, S. B. Hersh, & J. C. Dardig (Eds.), *Focus on behavior analysis in education: Achievements, challenges, and opportunities* (pp. 90–102). Upper Saddle River, NJ: Merrill/Prentice Hall.

Sugai, G., Sprague, J. R., Horner, R. H., and Walker, H. M. (2000). Preventing school violence: The use of office discipline referrals to assess and monitor school-wide discipline interventions. *Journal of Emotional and Behavioral Disorders, 8,* 94–101.

Sundberg, M. L., & Partington, J. W. (1998). *Teaching language to children with autism or other developmental disabilities.* Pleasant Hill, CA: Behavior Analysts.

Sunderland, L. C. (2004). Speech, language, and audiology services in public schools. *Intervention in School and Clinic, 39,* 209–217.

Sutherland, K. S., & Wehby, J. H. (2001). Exploring the relationship between increased opportunities to respond to academic requests and the academic and behavioral outcomes of students with EBD: A review. *Remedial and Special Education, 22,* 113–121.

Sutherland, K. S., Wehby, J. H., & Copeland, S. R. (2000). Effects of varying rates of behavior specific praise on the on-task behavior of students with emotional and behavioral disorders. *Journal of Emotional and Behavioral Disorders, 8,* 2–8.

Sutherland, K. S., Wehby, J. H., & Yoder, P. J. (2002). An examination of the relation between teacher praise and students with emotional/behavioral disorders' opportunities to respond to academic requests. *Journal of Emotional and Behavioral Disorders, 10,* 5–13.

Swallow, R. M. (1978, May). *Cognitive development.* Paper presented at the North American Conference on Visually Handicapped Infants and Preschool Children, Minneapolis.

Swanson, H. L. (1999). *Interventions for students with learning disabilities: A meta-analysis of treatment outcomes.* New York: Guilford.

Swanson, H. L. (2000). Issues facing the field of learning disabilities. *Learning Disability Quarterly, 23,* 37–50.

Swanson, H. L. (2001). Searching for the best model for instructing students with learning disabilities. *Focus on Exceptional Children, 34*(2), 1–14.

Swanson, J., McBurnett, K., Christain, D., & Wigal, T. (1995). Stimulant medication and treatment of children with ADHD. In T. H. Ollendick & R. J. Prinz (Eds.), *Advances in clinical child psychology,* (Vol. 17), (pp. 265–322). New York: Plenum.

Sweeney, W. J., Ehrhardt, A. M., Gardner, R., Jones, L., Greenfield, R., & Fribley, S. (1999). Using guided notes with academically at-risk high school students during a remedial summer social studies class. *Psychology in the Schools, 36,* 305–318.

Swiatek, M. A. (1993). A decade of longitudinal research on academic acceleration through the study of mathematically precocious youth. *Roeper Review, 15,* 120–123.

Switzky, H. N. (1997). Mental retardation and the neglected construct of motivation. *Education and Training in Mental Retardation and Developmental Disabilities, 32,* 194–196.

Symons, F. J., Butler, M. G., Sanders, Feurer, I. D., & Thompson, T. (1999). Self-injurious behavior in Prader-Willi syndrome: Behavioral forms and body location. *American Journal of Mental Retardation, 104,* 260–269.

Symons, F. J., Clark, R. D., Roberts, J. P., & Bailey, Jr., D. B. (2001). Classroom behavior of elementary school-age boys with fragile X syndrome. *Journal of Special Education, 34,* 194–202.

Syzmanski, L. S. (2000). Happiness as a treatment goal. *American Journal of Mental Retardation, 105,* 352–362.

Szabo, J. L. (2000). Maddie's story: Inclusion through physical and occupational therapy. *Teaching Exceptional Children, 33*(2), 26–32.

Talbott, E., & Thiede, K. (1999). Pathways to antisocial behavior among adolescent girls. *Journal of Emotional and Behavioral Disorders, 7,* 31–39.

Taylor, P. B., Gunter, P. L., & Slate, J. R. (2001). Teachers' perceptions of inappropriate student behaviors as a function of teachers' and students' gender and ethnic background. *Behavioral Disorders, 26,* 146–151.

Taylor, S. J. (1988). Caught in the continuum: A critical analysis of the principle of the least restrictive environment. *Journal of The Association for Persons with Severe Handicaps, 13,* 41–53.

Taylor, S. J., & Blatt, S. D. (Eds.). (1999). *In search of the promised land: The collected papers of Burton Blatt.* Washington, DC: American Association on Mental Retardation.

Taylor, S. J., Bogdan, R., & Lutfiyya, Z. M. (1995). *The variety of community experience: Qualitative studies of family and community life.* Baltimore: Brookes.

Tellefson, M. (2000). Suitcase mobility: A case study packed with opportunities for learning. *RE:view, 32,* 25–33.

Terman, L. (Ed.). (1925). *Genetic studies of genius* (Vol. 1). Stanford, CA: Stanford University Press.

Test, D. W., Aspel, N., & Everson, J. M. (2006). *Transition methods for youth with disabilities.* Upper Saddle River, NJ: Merrill/Prentice Hall.

Test, D. W., Browder, D. M., Karvonen, M., Wood, W. M., & Algozzine, B. (2002). Writing lesson plans for promoting self-determination. *Teaching Exceptional Children, 35*(1), 8–14.

Test, D. W., Cooke, N. L., Weiss, A. B., Heward, W. L., & Heron, T. E. (1986). A home-school communication system for special education. *Pointer, 30,* 4–7.

Test, D. W., Karvonen, M., Wood, W. M., Browder, D. M., & Algozzine, B. (2000). Choosing a self-determination curriculum. *Teaching Exceptional Children, 33*(2), 48–54.

Test, D. W., Mason, C., Hughes, C., Konrad, M., Neale, M., & Wood, W. M. (2004). Student involvement in individualized education program meetings. *Exceptional Children, 70,* 391–412.

Test, D. W., Spooner, F. H., Keul, P. K., & Grossi, T. A. (1990). Teaching adolescents with severe disabilities to use the public telephone. *Behavior Modification, 14,* 157–171.

Thomas, C., Correa, V., & Morsink, C. (2001). *Interactive teaming: Enhancing programs for students with special needs* (3rd ed.). Upper Saddle River, NJ: Merrill/Prentice Hall.

Thomas, L. A. (2001). Living with Prader-Willi: The "starving syndrome." *Exceptional Parent, 31*(11), 66–72.

Thomas, S. B., & Hawke, C. (1999). Health care standards for children with disabilities: Emerging standards and implications. *Journal of Special Education, 32,* 226–237.

Thompson, T., Robinson, J., Dietrich, M., Farris, M., & Sinclair, V. (1996a). Architectural features and perceptions of community residences for people with mental retardation. *American Journal on Mental Retardation, 101,* 292–314.

Thompson, T., Robinson, J., Dietrich, M., Farris, M., & Sinclair, V. (1996b). Interdependence of architectural features and program variables in community residences for people with mental retardation. *American Journal on Mental Retardation, 101,* 315–327.

Thorndike, R. L., Hagen, E. P., & Sattler, J. M. (1986). *Technical manual, the Stanford-Binet Intelligence Scale: Fourth edition.* Chicago: Riverside.

Thornton, C., & Krajewski, J. (1993). Death education for teachers: A refocused concern relative to medically fragile children. *Intervention in School and Clinic, 29,* 31–35.

Thurston, L. P., & Dasta, K. (1990). An analysis of in-home parent tutoring in children's academic behavior at home and in school and on parents' tutoring behaviors. *Remedial and Special Education, 11*(4), 41–52.

Timothy W. v. Rochester, N. H., School District, 875 F.2d 954 (1st Cir. 1989), *cert. Denied* 493 U.S. 983, 110 S.Ct. 519 (1989).

Tinbergen, N., & Tinbergen, E. A. (1983). *"Autistic" children: New hope for a cure.* London: Allen & Unwin.

Tincani, M., Ernsbarger, S., Harrison, T., & Heward, W. L. (in press). Effects of two instructional paces on pre-K students' participation rate, accuracy, and off-task behavior in the *Language for Learning* program. *Journal of Direct Instruction.*

Todis, B., Severson, H. H., & Walker, H. M. (1990). The critical events scale: Behavioral profiles of students with externalizing and internalizing behavior disorders. *Behavioral Disorders, 15,* 75–86.

Tolan, P. H., & Thomas, P. (1995). The implications of age of onset for delinquency risk II: Longitudinal data. *Journal of Abnormal Child Psychology, 23,* 157–181.

Tolla, J. (2000). Follow that bear! Encouraging mobility in a young child with visual impairment and multiple disabilities. *Teaching Exceptional Children, 32*(5), 72–77.

Tomlinson, C. A., Kaplan, S. N., Renzulli, J. S., Purcell, J., Leppien, J., & Burns, D. (2002). *The parallel curriculum: A design to develop high potential and challenge high-ability learners.* Thousand Oaks, CA: Corwin.

Tonemah, S. A. (1987). Assessing American Indian gifted and talented student's abilities. *Journal for the Education of the Gifted, 10,* 181–194.

Torgeson, J. K. (2001). Individual differences in response to early intervention in reading: The lingering problem of treatment resisters. *Learning Disabilities Research & Practice, 15,* 55–644.

Torgesen, J. K., & Bryant, B. (1994). *Test of Phonological Awareness.* Austin, TX: PRO–ED.

Torgesen, J. K., & Wagner, R. K. (1998). Alternative diagnostic approaches for specific developmental reading disabilities. *Learning Disabilities Research and Practice, 13,* 220–232.

Torgesen, J. K., Wagner, R. K., & Rashotte, C. A. (1997). Prevention and remediation of severe reading disabilities: Keeping the end in mind. *Scientific Studies of Reading, 1,* 217–234.

Tourette Syndrome Association. (2000). *What is Tourette syndrome?* Bayside, NY: Author. http://www.tsa-usa.org.

Townsend, B. L. (2000). The disproportionate discipline of African American learners: Reducing school suspensions and expulsions. *Exceptional Children, 66,* 381–391.

Tran, L. P., & Grunfast, K. M. (1999). Hereditary hearing loss. *Volta Review, 99*(5), 63–69.

Treanor, R. B. (1993). *We overcame: The story of civil rights for disabled people.* Falls Church, VA: Regal Direct.

Treffert, D. A. (1989). *Extraordinary people: Understanding "idiots savants."* New York: Harper & Row.

Trembley, R. E. (2000). The development of aggressive behavior during childhood: What have we learned in the past century? *International Journal of Behavioral Development, 24,* 129–141.

Trent, J. W. (1994). *Inventing the feeble-minded: A history of mental retardation in the United States.* Berkeley: University of California Press.

Trupin, L., Sebesta, D., Yelin, E., & LaPlante, M. (1997). T*rends in labor force participation among persons with disabilities, 1983–1994.* San Francisco: University of California, Disabilities Statistics Rehabilitation Research and Training Center, Institute for Health and Aging.

Turnbull, A. P., & Ruef, M. (1996). Family perspectives on problem behavior. *Mental Retardation, 34,* 280–293.

Turnbull, A. P., & Turnbull, H. R. (2001). *Families, professionals, and exceptionality:*

*Collaborating for empowerment* (4th ed.). Upper Saddle River, NJ: Merrill/Prentice Hall.

Turnbull, A. P., & Turnbull, H. R. (2006). *Families and exceptionality* (5th ed.). Upper Saddle River, NJ: Merrill/Prentice Hall.

Turnbull, H., Turnbull, P., Wehmeyer, M., & Park, J. (2003). A quality of life framework for special education outcomes. *Remedial and Special Education, 24,* 67–74.

Turnbull, H. R., & Cilley, M. (1999). *Explanations and implications of the 1997 amendments to IDEA.* Upper Saddle River, NJ: Merrill/Prentice Hall.

Turnbull, H. R., & Turnbull, A. P. (2000). *Free appropriate public education: The law and children with disabilities* (6th ed.). Denver: Love.

Turner-Henson, A., Holaday, B., Corser, N., Ogletree, G., & Swan, J. H. (1994). The experiences of discrimination: Challenges for chronically ill children. *Pediatric Nursing, 20,* 571–577.

Tyler, J. S., & Mira, M. P. (1993). Educational modifications for students with head injuries. *Teaching Exceptional Children, 25*(3), 24–27.

Tymchuk, A. J., Lakin, K. C., & Luckasson, R. (2001). *The forgotten generation: The status and challenges of adults with mild cognitive limitations.* Baltimore: Brookes.

Uffen, E. (1997). Speech and language disorders: Nature or nurture? *ASHA Leader, 2*(14), 8.

Ulrey, P. (1994). When you meet a guide dog. *RE:view, 26,* 143–144.

Ulrich, M. E., & Bauer, A. M. (2003). Levels of awareness: A closer look at communication between parents and professionals. *Teaching Exceptional Children, 35*(6), 20–23.

Umbreit, J., & Blair, K. C. (1996). The effects of preference, choice, and attention on problem behavior at school. *Education and Training in Mental Retardation and Developmental Disabilities, 31,* 151–161.

Unger, D., & Simmons, T. J. (2005). Transition to employment. In R. W. Flexer, T. J. Simmons, P. Luft, & R. M. Baer (Eds.), *Transition planning for secondary students with disabilities* (2nd ed.), (pp. 360–387). Upper Saddle River, NJ: Merrill/Prentice Hall.

U.S. Congress. (1987). *Promotion opportunities for blind and handicapped workers in sheltered workshops under the Javitz-Wagner-O'Day Act.* Washington, DC: U.S. Government Printing Office.

U.S. Department of Education. (1998). *The schools and staffing survey (SASS) and teacher followup survey (TFS) CD-ROM: Electronic codebook and public-use data for three cycles of ASSASS and TFS.* Washington, DC: National Center for Educational Statistics. (NCES 98–312).

U.S. Department of Education. (1998). *Twenty-first annual report to Congress on the implementation of the Individuals with Disabilities Education Act.* Washington, DC: Author.

U.S. Department of Education. (1999). Assistance to states for the education of children with disabilities and the early intervention program for infants and toddlers with disabilities: Final regulations. *Federal Register, 64*(48), CFR Parts 300 and 303.

U.S. Department of Education. (2000a). *Guide to the individualized education program.* Washington, DC: Author.

U.S. Department of Education. (2000b). *Twenty-second annual report to Congress on the implementation of the Individuals with Disabilities Education Act.* Washington, DC: Author.

U.S. Department of Education. (2002). *No Child Left Behind: A desktop reference.* Washington, DC: Author.

U.S. Department of Education. (2002). *Twenty-fourth annual report to Congress on the implementation of the Individuals with Disabilities Education Act.* Washington, DC: Author.

U.S. Department of Education. (2003). *Twenty-fifth annual report to Congress on the implementation of the Individuals with Disabilities Education Act.* Washington, DC: Author.

U.S. Department of Education, National Center for Education Statistics. (2001). *Teacher preparation and professional development: 2000* (NCES 2001-088, by B. Parsad, L. Lewis & E. Farris). Washington, DC: Author. (ERIC Document Reproduction Service No. ED 458 204)

U.S. Department of Education, Office of Civil Rights. (1990). *Elementary and secondary school civil rights compliance report.* Washington, DC: Author.

U.S. Department of Labor. (1979). *Study of handicapped clients in sheltered workshops* (Vol. 2). Washington, DC: Author.

U.S. Drug Enforcement Agency. (2002). *Yearly agggregate production quotas (1990–1999).* Washington, DC: Office of Public Affairs, U.S. Drug Enforcement Agency.

U.S. Office of Education. (1977a). Implementation of Part B of the Education of the Handicapped Act. *Federal Register, 42,* 42474–42518.

U.S. Office of Education. (1977b). Procedures for evaluating specific learning disabilities. *Federal Register, 42,* 65082–65085.

U.S. Office of Special Education. (2004). *Individuals with Disabilities Education Act (IDEA) data.* Washington, DC: Author. http://www.ideadata.org/.

U.S. Office of Special Education Programs. (2004). Individuals with Disabilities Education Act (IDEA) data. Washington, DC: Author. http://www.ideadata.org/PartBdata.asp.

U.S. Office of the Census. (2004, June). *Educational attainment in the U.S.: 2003.* Washington, DC: U.S. Government Printing Office.

U.S. Public Health Service. (1990). *Healthy people 2000.* Washington, DC: U.S. Government Printing Office.

Utley, B. L., Roman, C., & Nelson, G. L. (1998). Functional vision. In S. Z. Sacks & R. K. Silberman (Eds.), *Educating students who have visual impairments with other disabilities* (pp. 371–412). Baltimore: Brookes.

Utley, C. A., & Obiakor, F. E. (2001). Learning problems or learning disabilities of multicultural learners: Contemporary perspectives. In C. Utley & F. Obiakor (Eds.), *Special education, multicultural education, and school reform: Components of quality education for learners with mild disabilities* (pp. 90–117). Springfield, IL: Thomas.

Valdes, K. A., Williamson, C. L., & Wagner, M. (1990). *The national longitudinal transition study of special education students.* Vol. 3: *Youth categorized as emotionally disturbed.* Palo Alto, CA: SRI International.

Van Acker, R., Grant, S. H., & Henry, D. (1996). Teacher and student behavior as a function of risk for aggression. *Education and Treatment of Children, 19,* 316–334.

Vance, J., Fernandez, G., & Biber, M. (1998). Educational progress in a population of youth with aggression and emotional disturbance: the role of risk and protective factors. *Journal of Emotional and Behavioral Disorders, 6,* 214–221.

Vandercook, T. (1991). Leisure instruction outcomes: Criterion performance, positive interactions, and acceptance by typical high school peers. *Journal of Special Education, 25,* 320–339.

Vandercook, T., York, J., & Forest, M. (1989). The McGill Action Planning System (MAPS): A strategy for building the vision. *Journal of The Association for Persons with Severe Handicaps, 14,* 205–215.

Van Gurp, S. (2001). Self-concept of deaf secondary school students in different educational settings. *Journal of Deaf Studies and Deaf Education, 6,* 54–69.

Van Houten, R. (1984). Setting up performance feedback systems in the classroom. In W. L. Heward, T. E. Heron, D. S. Hill, & J. Trap-Porter (Eds.), *Focus on behavior analysis in education* (pp. 114–125). Upper Saddle River, NJ: Merrill/Prentice Hall.

Van Keulen, J. E., Weddington, G. T., & DeBose, C. E. (1998). *Speech, language, learning, and the African American child.* Boston: Allyn & Bacon.

Van Riper, C., & Erickson, R. L. (1996). *Speech correction: An introduction to speech pathology and audiology* (9th ed.). Boston: Allyn & Bacon.

Van Tassel-Baska, J., Patton, J. M., & Prillaman, D. (1991). *Gifted youth at risk: A report of a national study.* Reston, VA: Council for Exceptional Children.

Vaughn, B. J., Clarke, S., & Dunlap, G. (1997). Assessment-based intervention for severe behavior problems in a natural family context. *Journal of Applied Behavior Analysis, 30,* 713–716.

Vaughn, S., Elbaum, B. E., & Schumm, J. S. (1996). The effects of inclusion on the social functioning of students with learning disabilities. *Journal of Learning Disabilities, 29,* 598–608.

Vaughn, S., & Fuchs, L. S. (Guest Eds.) (2003a). Redefining learning disabilities as inadequate response to instruction (Special Issue). *Learning Disabilities Research and Practice, 18,* 137–211.

Vaughn, S., & Fuchs, L. S. (2003b). Redefining learning disabilities as inadequate response to instruction: The promise and potential problems. *Learning Disabilities Research & Practice, 18,* 137–146.

Vaughn, S., Gersten, R. L., & Chard, D. J. (2000). The underlying message in LD intervention research: Findings from research syntheses. *Exceptional Children, 67,* 99–114.

Vaughn, S., Klingner, J., Hughes, M. (2000). Sustainability of research-based practices. *Exceptional Children, 66,* 163–171.

Vaughn, S., Linan-Thompson, S., & Hickman, P. (2003). Response to instruction as a means of identifying students with reading/learning disabilities. *Exceptional Children, 69,* 391–409.

Vaughn, S., McIntosh, R., Schumm, J. S., Haager, D., & Callwood, D. (1993). Social status, peer acceptance, and reciprocal friendships revisited. *Learning Disabilities Research and Practice, 8,* 82–88.

Vaughn, S., Schumm, J. S., & Arguelles, M. E. (1997). The ABCDEs of co-teaching. *Teaching Exceptional Children, 30*(2), 42–45.

Vaughn, S., Schumm, J. S., & Brick, J. B. (1998). Using a rating scale to design and evaluate inclusion programs. *Teaching Exceptional Children, 30*(4), 41–45.

Venn, J. (2004). *Assessment of students with special needs* (3rd ed.). Upper Saddle River, NJ: Merrill/Prentice Hall.

Vig, S., & Jedrysek, E. (1996). Application of the 1992 AAMR definition: Issues for preschool children. *Mental Retardation, 34,* 244–246.

Villa, R. A., Thousand, J. S., & Nevin, A. I. (2004). *A guide to co-teaching: Practical tips for facilitating student learning.* Arlington, VA: Council for Exceptional Children.

Volkmar, F., & Pauls, D. (2003). Autism. *Lancet, 362,* 1133–1144.

Voltz, D. L. (1994). Developing collaborative parent-teacher relationships with culturally diverse parents. *Intervention in School and Clinic, 29*(5), 288–291.

von Hahn, L. (2004). Bipolar disorder: An overview. *Exceptional Parent, 34*(5), 56, 58–61.

von Hahn, L. (2004). Traumatic brain injury: Medical considerations and educational implications. *Exceptional Parent, 33*(11), 40–42.

Wagner, B. W. (2000). Presidential address 2000—Changing visions into reality. *Mental Retardation, 38,* 436–443.

Wagner, L., & Lane, L., (1998). Lane County Department of Youth Services: 1997 report: Juvenile justice services. Eugene, OR Department of Youth Services.

Wagner, M., Blackorby, J., Cameto, R., & Newman, L. (1994). *What makes a difference? Influences on postschool outcomes of youth with disabilities.* Menlo Park, CA: SRI International.

Wagner, R. K., Torgeson, J. K., & Rahsotte, C. A. (1999). *Comprehensive Test of Phonological Processing.* Austin, TX: PRO-ED.

Wagner-Lampl, A., & Oliver, G. W. (1994). Folklore of blindness. *Journal of Visual Impairment and Blindness, 88,* 267–276.

Wahler, R. G., & Dumas, J. E. (1986). "A chip off the old block": Some interpersonal characteristics of coercive children across generations. In P. S. Strain, M. J. Guralnick, & H. M. Walker (Eds.), *Children's social behavior: Development, assessment, and modification* (pp. 49–91). Orlando, FL: Academic Press.

Wainapel, S. F. (1989). Attitudes of visually impaired persons toward cane use. *Journal of Visual Impairment and Blindness, 83,* 446–448.

Walker, H. M. (1997). *The acting out child: Coping with classroom disruption* (2nd ed.). Longmont, CO: Sopris West.

Walker, H. M., Colvin, G., & Ramsey, E. (1995). *Antisocial behavior in schools: Strategies and best practices.* Pacific Grove, CA: Brooks/Cole.

Walker, H. M., & Severson, H. H. (1990). *Systematic screening for behavior disorders.* Longmont, CO: Sopris West.

Walker, H. M., Sprague, J. R., Close, D. W., & Starlin, C. M. (1999–2000). What is right with behavior disorders: Seminal achievements and contributions of the behavior disorders field. *Exceptionality, 8,* 13–28.

Walker, H. M., & Sylvester, R. (1998). Reducing student refusal and resistance. *Teaching Exceptional Children, 30*(6), 52–57.

Walker, L. A. (1986). *A loss for words: The story of deafness in a family.* New York: Harper & Row.

Wallace, G., & Hammill, D. (2002). *Comprehensive Receptive and Expressive Vocabulary Test* (2nd ed.). Austin, TX: PRO-ED.

Walsh, J. M. (2001). Getting the "big picture" of IEP goals and state standards. *Teaching Exceptional Children, 33*(5), 18–26.

Walther-Thomas, C., Korinek, L., McLaughlin, V., & Williams, B. (2000). *Collaboration for inclusive education.* Boston: Allyn & Bacon.

Warfield, M. E., & Hauser-Cram, P. (1996). Child care needs, arrangements, and satisfaction of mothers of children with developmental disabilities. *Mental Retardation, 34,* 294–302.

Wasik, B. H., Ramey, C. T., Bryant, D. M., & Sparling, J. J. (1990). A longitudinal study of two early intervention strategies: Project CARE. *Child Development, 61,* 1682–1692.

Webb, N. M., Nemer, K. M., & Zuniga, S. (2002). Short circuits of superconductors? Effects of group composition on high-achieving students' science assessment performance. *American Educational Research Journal, 39*(4), 943–989.

Webber, J., & Scheuermann, B. (1991). Managing behavior problems: Accentuate the positive ... Eliminate the negative! *Teaching Exceptional Children, 24,* 13–19.

Webber, J., Scheuermann, B., McCall, C., & Coleman, M. (1993). Research on self-monitoring as a behavior management technique in special education classrooms: A descriptive review. *Remedial and Special Education, 14*(2), 38–56.

Webb-Johnson, G. C. (2003). Behaving while black: A hazardous reality for African American learners. *Beyond Behavior, 12*(2), 3–7.

Weber, C., Behl, D., & Summers, M. (1994). Watch them play—watch them learn. *Teaching Exceptional Children, 27*(1), 30–35.

*Webster's New World Dictionary of the American Language* (2nd ed.). (1986). New York: Simon & Schuster.

Webster, D. D., Clary, G., & Griffith, P. L. (2005). Postsecondary education and career paths. In R. W. Flexer, T. J. Simmons, P. Luft, & R. M. Baer. *Transition planning for secondary students with disabilities* (2nd ed.), (pp. 388–423). Upper Saddle River, NJ: Merrill/Prentice Hall.

Wechsler, D. (1991). *Wechsler Intelligence Scale for Children–Revised.* San Antonio, TX: Psychological Corporation.

Wedel, J. W., & Fowler, S. A. (1984). "Read me a story, Mom": A home-tutoring program to teach prereading skills to language-delayed children. *Behavior Modification, 8,* 245–266.

Wehby, J. H., Symons, F. J., Canale, J. A., & Go, F. J. (1998). Teaching practices in classrooms for students with emotional and behavioral disorders: Discrepancies between recommendations and observations. *Behavioral Disorders, 24,* 51–56.

Wehby, J. H., Symons, F. J., & Shores, R., E. (1995). A descriptive analysis of aggressive behaviors in classrooms for children with emotional and behavioral disorders. *Behavioral Disorders, 20,* 87–105.

Wehman, P. (Ed.). (2002). *Individual transition plans: The teacher's curriculum guide for helping youth with special needs* (2nd ed.). Austin, TX: PRO–ED.

Wehman, P., Brooke, V., & Inge, K. J. (2001). Vocational placements and careers. In P. Wehman (Ed.), *Life beyond the classroom: Transition strategies for young people with disabilities* (3rd ed.), (pp. 211–246). Baltimore: Brookes.

Wehman, P., & Kregel, J. (1998). *More than a job: Securing satisfying careers for people with disabilities.* Baltimore: Brookes.

Wehman, P., Kregel, J., Shafer, M., & West, M. (1989). *Emerging trends in supported employment: A preliminary analysis of 27 states.* Richmond: Virginia Commonwealth University, Rehabilitation Research and Training Center.

Wehman, P., & Revell, G. (1997). Transition from school to adulthood: Looking ahead. In P. Wehman (Ed.), *Exceptional individuals in school, community, and work* (pp. 597–648). Austin, TX: PRO-ED,

Wehman, P., Revell, G., & Kregel, J. (1998). Supported employment: A decade of rapid growth and impact. *American Rehabilitation, 24*(1), 31–43.

Wehmeyer, M. L. (1994). Perceptions of self-determination and psychological empowerment of adolescents with mental retardation. *Education and Training in Mental Retardation, 29,* 9–21.

Wehmeyer, M. L., Kelchner, K., & Richards, S. (1996). Essential characteristics of self-determined behavior of individuals with mental retardation. *American Journal on Mental Retardation, 100,* 632–642.

Wehmeyer, M. L., Martin, J. E., & Sands, D. J. (1998). Self-determination for children and youth with developmental disabilities. In A. Hilton & R. Ringlaben (Eds.), *Best and promising practices in developmental disabilities* (pp. 191–203). Austin, TX: PRO-ED.

Wehmeyer, M. L., Palmer, S. B., Agran, M., Mithaug, D. E., & Martin, J. E. (2000). Promoting causal agency: The self-determined learning model of instruction. *Exceptional Children, 66,* 273.

Wehmeyer, M. S., & Schalock, R. L. (2001). Self-determination and quality of life: Implications for special education services and supports. *Focus on Exceptional Children, 33*(8), 1–14.

Weiner, J. (1999). *Time, love, and memory: a great biologist and his quest for the origins of behavior.* New York: Knopf.

Weintraub, F. J., & Abeson, A. (1974). New education policies for the handicapped: The quiet revolution. *Phi Delta Kappan, 55,* 526–529, 569.

Weiserbs, B. (2000). Social and academic integration using e-mail between children with and without hearing impairments. *Computers in the Schools, 16*(2), 29–44.

Weiss, K. W., & Dykes, M. K. (1995). Legal issues in special education: Assistive technology and supportive services. *Physical Disabilities: Education and Related Services, 14*(1), 29–36.

Weisz, J. R., Bromfield, R., Vines, D. L., & Weiss, B. (1985). Cognitive development, helpless behavior, and labeling effects in the lives of the mentally retarded. *Applied Developmental Psychology, 2,* 129–167.

Werker, J. E., & Lalonde, C. E. (1988). Cross language speech perception: Initial capabilities and developmental change. *Developmental Psychology, 24,* 672–683.

Werts, M. G., Caldwell, N. K., & Wolery, M. (2003). Instructive feedback: Effects of a presentation variable. *Journal of Special Education, 37,* 124–133.

Werts, M. G., Wolery, M., Gast, D. L., & Holcomb, A. (1996). Sneak in some extra learning by using instructive feedback. *Teaching Exceptional Children, 28*(3), 70–71.

Wesson, C. (1991). Curriculum-based measurement and two models of follow-up consultation. *Exceptional Children, 77,* 246–256.

Wesson, C., Wilson, R., & Higbee Mandlebaum, L. (1988). Learning games for active student responding. *Teaching Exceptional Children, 20*(2), 12–14.

West, M., Rayfield, R. G., Clements, C., Unger, D., & Thornton, T. (1994). An illustration of positive behavioral support in the workplace for individuals with severe mental retardation. *Journal of Vocational Rehabilitation, 4*(4), 265–271.

West, M., Revell, G., & Wehman, P. (1998). Conversion from segregated services to supported employment: A continuing challenge to the VR service system. *Education and Training in Mental Retardation and Developmental Disabilities, 33,* 239–247.

Westling, D. L., & Fox, L. (2004). *Teaching students with severe disabilities* (3rd ed.). Upper Saddle River, NJ: Merrill/Prentice Hall.

Whaley, L. F., & Wong, D. L. (1995). *Nursing care of infants and children* (5th ed.). St. Louis: Mosby.

Wheeler, D. L., Jacobson, J. W., Paglieri, R. A., & Schwartz, A. A. (1993). An experimental assessment of facilitated communication. *Mental Retardation, 31,* 49–60.

Wheeler, J. J., Bates, P., Marshall, K. J., & Miller, S. R. (1988). Teaching appropriate social behaviors to a young man with moderate mental retardation in a supported competitive employment setting. *Education and Training in Mental Retardation, 23,* 105–116.

White, B. L. (1975). *The first three years of life.* Upper Saddle River, NJ: Prentice Hall.

White, M. A. (1975). Natural rates of teacher approval and disapproval in the classroom. *Journal of Applied Behavior Analysis, 8,* 367–372.

Whitmore, J. R., & Maker, C. J. (1985). *Intellectual giftedness in disabled persons.* Rockville, MD: Aspen.

Wiederholt, J. L., & Bryant, B. R. (2001). Gray oral reading tests (4th ed.). Austin, TX: PRO-ED.

Wiener, J., & Tardif, C. Y. (2004). Social and emotional functioning of children with learning disabilities: Does special education placement make a difference? *Learning Disabilities Research and Practice, 19,* 20–32.

Wilkinson, G. S. (1994). *Wide Range Achievement Test—3.* Austin, TX: PRO-ED.

Will, M. C. (1986). Educating children with learning problems: A shared responsibility. *Exceptional Children, 52,* 411–415.

Willard-Holt, C. (1998). Academic and personality characteristics of gifted students with cerebral palsy: A multiple case study. *Exceptional Children, 65,* 37–50.

Williams, C. B., & Finnegan, M. (2003). From myth to reality: Sound information for teachers about students who are deaf. *Teaching Exceptional Children, 35*(3), 40–45.

Williams, R. R. (1991). Assistive technology and people with disabilities: Separating fact from fiction. *A. T. Quarterly, 2*(3), 6–7.

Williams, S. C. (2002). How speech-feedback and word-prediction software can help students write. *Teaching Exceptional Children, 34*(3), 72–78.

Williams, V. L., & Cartledge, G. (1997). Passing notes to parents. *Teaching Exceptional Children, 30*(1), 30–34.

Williamson, G. G. (1978). The individualized education program: An interdisciplinary endeavor. In B. Sirvis, J. W. Baken, & G. G. Williamson (Eds.), *Unique aspects of the IEP for the physically handicapped, homebound, and hospitalized.* Reston, VA: Council for Exceptional Children.

Willoughby, D. M., & Duffy, S. (1989). *Handbook for itinerant and resource teachers of blind and visually impaired students.* Baltimore: National Federation of the Blind.

Willy, L. H. (2001). *Asperger syndrome in the family: Redefining normal.* Philadelphia: Kingsley.

Wilson, C. L. (1995). Parents and teachers: "Can we talk?" *LD Forum, 20*(2), 31–33.

Wilson, C. L., & Hughes, M. (1994). Involving linguistically diverse parents. *LD Forum, 19*(3), 25–27.

Wilson, P. G., Schepis, M. M., & Mason-Main, M. (1987). In vivo use of picture prompt training to increase independent work at a restaurant. *Journal of The Association for Persons with Severe Handicaps, 12,* 145–150.

Winebrenner, S. (2001). *Teaching gifted kids in the regular classroom* (2nd ed). Minneapolis: Free Spirit.

Winett, R. A., & Winkler, R. C. (1972). Current behavior modification in the classroom: Be still, be quiet, be docile. *Journal of Applied Behavior Analysis, 5,* 499–504.

Witte, R. H., Phillips, L., & Kakela, M. (1998). Job satisfaction of college students with learning disabilities. *Journal of Learning Disabilities, 31,* 259–265.

Wittenstein, S. H. (1994). Braille literacy: Preservice training and teachers' attitudes. *Journal of Visual Impairment and Blindness, 88,* 516–524.

Witty, P. A. (Ed.). (1951). *The gifted child.* Boston: Heath.

Witzel, B. S., Mercer, C. D., & Miller, M. D. (2003). Teaching algebra to students with learning difficulties: An investigation of an explicit instruction model. *Learning Disabilities Research and Practice, 18,* 121–131.

Witzer, B. S., & Mercer, C. D. (2003). Using rewards to teach students with disabilities: Implications for motivation. *Remedial and Special Education, 24,* 88–96.

Wolery, M. (2000). Recommended practices in child-focused interventions. In S. Sandall, M. E. McLean, & B. J. Smith (Eds.), *DEC recommended practices* (pp. 34–38). Longmont, CO: Sopris West.

Wolery, M., Anthony, L., & Heckathorn, J. (1998). Transition-based teaching: Effects on transitions, teachers' behavior, and children's learning. *Journal of Early Intervention, 21,* 117–131.

Wolery, M., Ault, M. J., & Doyle, P. M. (1992). *Teaching students with moderate to severe disabilities.* New York: Longman.

Wolery, M., Cybriwski, C. A., Gast, D. L., & Boyle-Gast, K. (1991). Use of constant time delay and attentional responses with adolescents. *Exceptional Children, 57,* 462–474.

Wolery, M., & Haring, T. G. (1994). Moderate, severe, and profound disabilities. In N. G. Haring, L. McCormick, & T. G. Haring (Eds.), *Exceptional children and youth* (6th ed.) (pp. 258–299). Upper Saddle River, NJ: Merrill/Prentice Hall.

Wolery, M., & Sainato, D. M. (1993). General curriculum and intervention strategies. In *DEC Recommended Practices* (pp. 50–57). Reston, VA: Council for Exceptional Children, Division for Early Childhood.

Wolery, M., & Sainato, D. M. (1996). General curriculum and intervention strategies. In S. L. Odom & M. McClean (Eds.), *Recommended practices in early intervention* (pp. 125–158). Austin, TX: PRO-ED.

Wolery, M., & Wilbers, J. S. (1994). *Including young children with special needs in early childhood programs*. Washington, DC: National Association for the Education of Young Children.

Wolf, M., & Bowers, P. G. (2000). Naming-speed processes and developmental reading disabilities: An introduction to the special issue on the double-deficit hypothesis. *Journal of Learning Disabilities, 33,* 322–324.

Wolf, M., Bowers, P. G., & Biddle, K. (2000). Retrieval, automaticity, vocabulary elaboration, orthography (RAVE-O): A comprehensive, fluency-based reading intervention program. *Journal of Learning Disabilities, 33,* 375–386.

Wolfe, P. S., & Hall, T. E. (2003). Making inclusion a reality for students with severe disabilities. *Teaching Exceptional Children, 35*(4), 56–60.

Wolfensberger, W. (1969). The origin and nature of our institutional models. In R. B. Kugel & W. Wolfensberger (Eds.), *Changing patterns in residential services for the mentally retarded* (pp. 59–71). Washington, DC: President's Committee on Mental Retardation.

Wolfensberger, W. (1972). *Normalization: The principle of normalization in human services*. Toronto: National Institute on Mental Retardation.

Wolfensberger, W. (1983). Social role valorization: A proposed new term for the principle of normalization. *Mental Retardation, 21,* 234–239.

Wolfensberger, W. (2000). A brief overview of social role valorization. *Mental Retardation, 38,* 105–123.

Wolford, T., Alber, S. R., & Heward, W. L. (2001). Teaching middle school students with learning disabilities to recruit peer assistance during cooperative learning group activities. *Learning Disabilities and Research and Practice, 16,* 161–173.

Woliver, R., & Woliver, G. M. (1991). Gifted adolescents in the emerging minorities: Asians and Pacific Islanders. In M. Bireley & J. Genshaft (Eds.), *Understanding the gifted adolescent* (pp. 248–258). New York: Teachers College Press.

Wolraich, M. L., (1999). Attention-deficit hyperactivity disorder: The most studied yet most controversial diagnosis. *Mental*

*Retardation and Development Disabilities Research Reviews, 5,* 163–168.

Wolraich, M. L., Lindgren, S., Stromquist, A., Milich, R., Davis, C., & Watson, D. (1990). Stimulant medications used by primary care physicians in the treatment of attention deficit hyperactivity disorder. *Pediatrics, 86,* 95–101.

Wolters, P., Brouwers, P., & Moss, H. (1995). Pediatric HIV disease: Effect on cognition, learning, and behavior. *School Psychology Quarterly, 10,* 305–328.

Wood, B. A., Frank, A. R., & Hamre-Nietupski, S. M. (1996). How do you work this lock? Adaptations for teaching combination lock use. *Teaching Exceptional Children, 28*(2), 35–39.

Wood, F. H., Cheney, C. O., Cline D. H., Sampson, K., Smith, C. R., & Guetzloe, E. C. (1997). *Conduct disorders and social maladjustments: Policies, politics, and programming*. Reston, VA: Council for Children with Behavioral Disorders.

Wood, J. G. & Zabel, R. H. (2001). Adderall: special education's new (?) fix-it drug. *Beyond Behavior, 11*(1), 39–41.

Wood, J. W. (2006). *Inclusion: Adapting instruction to accommodate students in inclusive settings* (5th ed.). Upper Saddle River, NJ: Merrill/Prentice Hall.

Wood, S. J., Murdock, J. Y., Cronin, M. E., Dawson, N. M., & Kirby, P. C. (1998). Effects of self-monitoring on on-task behaviors of at-risk middle school students. *Journal of Behavioral Education, 8,* 263–279.

Wood, W. M., Karvonen, M., Test, D. W., Browder, D., & Algozzine, B. (2004). Promoting student self-determination skills in IEP planning. *Teaching Exceptional Children, 70,* 391–412.

Woodcock, R. W. (1998). *Woodcock Reading Mastery Tests—Revised*. Circle Pines, MN: American Guidance Services.

Woodcock, R. W., McGrew, K. S., & Mather, N. (2001). *Woodcock-Johnson III tests of achievement*. Itasaca, IL: Riverside.

Woolsey, M. L. (1999, January). Personal communication.

Wormsley, D. P. (2004). *Braille literacy: A functional approach*. New York: AFB Press.

Wrenn, R. L. (1994). A death at school: Issues and interventions. *Counseling and Human Development, 26*(7), 1–7.

Wright, C., & Momari, M. (1985). *From toys to computers: Access for the physically disabled child*. San Jose, CA: Wright.

Wright, J. E., Cavanaugh, R. A., Sainato, D. M., & Heward, W. L. (1995). Somos todos ayudantes y estudiantes: Evaluation of a classwide peer tutoring program in a modified Spanish class for secondary students identified as learning disabled or academically at-risk. *Education and Treatment of Children, 18,* 33–52.

Yairi, E. (1998). Is the basis for stuttering genetic? *American Speech-Language-Hearing Association, 70*(1), 29–32.

Yairi, E., & Ambrose, E. N. (1999). Early childhood stuttering. I: Persistence and recovery rates. *Journal of Speech and Hearing Research, 42,* 1097–1112.

Yelin, E., & Katz, P. (1994). Labor force trends of persons with and without disabilities. *Monthly Labor Review, 72,* 593–620.

Yell, M. L. (1995). Least restrictive environment, inclusion, and students with disabilities: A legal analysis. *Journal of Special Education, 28,* 389–404.

Yell, M. L. (2006). *The law and special education* (2nd ed.). Upper Saddle River, NJ: Merrill/Prentice Hall.

Yell, M. L., & Drasgow, E. (2000). Litigating a free appropriate public education: The Lovaas hearing and cases. *Journal of Special Education, 33,* 205–214.

Yell, M. L., & Drasgow, E. (2005). *No Child Left Behind: A guide for professionals*. Upper Saddle River, NJ: Merrill/Prentice Hall.

Yell, M. L., Rozalski, M. E., & Drasgow, E. (2001). Disciplining students with disabilities. *Focus on Exceptional Children, 30*(1), 1–19.

Yergin-Allsopp, M., Rice, C., Karapurkar, T., Doemberg, N., Boyle, C., & Murphy, C. (2003). Prevalence of autism in a U.S. metropolitan community. *Journal of the American Medical Association, 289,* 49–55.

Ylvisaker, M. (1986). Language and communication disorders following pediatric head injury. *Journal of Head Trauma Rehabilitation, 1,* 48–56.

Yopp, R. H., & Yopp, H. K. (2001). *Literature-based reading activities*. Boston: Allyn & Bacon.

Young, J. L. (1997). Positive experiences with dogs: An important addition to the curriculum for blind and visually impaired children. *RE:view, 29*(2), 55–61.

Young, R. K., West, R. P., Smith, D. J., & Morgan, D. P. (1991). *Teaching self-management strategies to adolescents*. Longmont, CO: Sopris West.

Yousef, J. M. S. (1995). Insulin-dependent diabetes mellitus: Education implications. *Physical Disabilities: Education and Related Services, 13*(2), 43–53.

Ysseldyke, J. (2001). Reflections on a research career: Generalizations from 25 years of research on assessment and instructional decision making. *Exceptional Children, 67,* 295–309.

Zabel, R. H., & Nigro, F. A. (1999). Juvenile offenders with behavioral disorders, learning disabilities, and no disabilities: Self-reports of personal, family, and school characteristics. *Behavioral Disorders, 25,* 22–40.

Zamora-Durán, G., & Reyes, E. (1977). From tests to talking in the classroom: Assessing communicative competence. In A. Artiles & Zamora-Durán (Eds.), *Reducing disproportionate representation of culturally diverse students in special and gifted education* (p. 51). Reston, VA: Council for Exceptional Children.

Zeaman, D., & House, B. J. (1979). A review of attention theory. In N. R. Ellis (Ed.), *Handbook of mental deficiency: Psychological theory and research* (2nd ed.), (pp. 63–120). Hillside, NJ: Erlbaum.

Ziegler, D. (2002). *Reauthorization of the Elementary and Secondary Education Act: No*

*Child Left Behind Act of 2001.* Arlington, VA: Council for Exceptional Children.

Zigmond, N. (2003). Where should students with disabilities receive special education services? Is one place better than another? *Journal of Special Education, 37,* 193–199.

Zigmond, N., & Magiera, K. (2001). *Current practice alerts: Co-teaching.* Reston, VA: Division for Learning Disabilities and Division for Research of the Council for Exceptional Children.

Zimmerman, E. H., & Zimmerman, T. (1962). The alteration of behavior in a special classroom situation. *Journal of the Experimental Analysis of Behavior, 5,* 59–60.

Zionts, P., Simpson, R., & Zionts, L. (2001). *Emotional and behavioral problems: A handbook for understanding and handling students.* Thousand Oaks, CA: Corwin.

# Name Index

# Subject Index

# Photo Credits